Decision Support and Business Intelligence Systems

Decision Support and Business Intelligence Systems

EIGHTH EDITION

Efraim Turban
University of Hawaii

Jay E. Aronson
The University of Georgia

Ting-Peng Liang
National Sun Yat-sen University

Ramesh Sharda
Oklahoma State University

Upper Saddle River, New Jersey 07458

Library of Congress Cataloging-in-Publication Data
Decision support and business intelligence systems/Efraim terban . . . [et al.]. –8th ed.
p. cm.
Rev. ed. of: Turban, Efraim. Decision support and expert systems. 7th ed. c2005.
Includes index
ISBN: 0-13-198660-0
1. Management—Data processing. 2. Decision support systems. 3. Expert systems (Computer science) I. Turban, Efraim. II. Turban, Efraim. Decision support and expert systems.
HD30. 2. D39 2007
658. 4′ 038011—dc22 2006033354

AVP/Executive Editor: Bob Horan
VP/Editorial Director: Jeff Shelstad
Manager, Product Development: Pamela Hersperger
Assistant Editor: Ana Jankowski
Editorial Assistant: Kelly Loftus
Product Development Manager, Media: Nancy Welcher
Assistant Editor, Media: Ashley Lulling
Marketing Assistant: Laura Cirigliano
Associate Director, Production Editorial: Judy Leale
Senior Managing Editor: Cynthia Zonneveld
Senior Production Editor: Carol Samet
Permissions Coordinator: Charles Morris
Associate Director, Manufacturing: Vinnie Scelta
Manufacturing Buyer: Michelle Klein
Design/Composition Manager: Christy Mahon
Cover Design: Bruce Kenselaar
Cover Illustration/Photo: Jim Frazier/Stock Illustration Source/Getty Images, Inc
Manager, Cover Visual Research & Permissions: Karen Sanatar
Composition: GGS Book Services
Full-Service Project Management: GGS Book Services
Printer/Binder: Hamilton Printing Company

Credits and acknowledgments borrowed from other sources and reproduced, with permission, in this textbook appear on appropriate page within text.

Pearson Education LTD.
Pearson Education Singapore, Pte. Ltd
Pearson Education, Canada, Ltd
Pearson Education–Japan
Pearson Education Australia PTY, Limited
Pearson Education North Asia Ltd
Pearson Educación de Mexico, S.A. de C.V.
Pearson Education Malaysia, Pte. Ltd.

10 9 8 7 6 5 4 3 2 1
ISBN 0-13-198660-0

Dedicated to
our spouses and children
with love
—The authors

About the Authors

Efraim Turban (M.B.A., Ph.D., University of California, Berkeley) is a visiting scholar at the Pacific Institute for Information System Management, University of Hawaii. Prior to this, he was on the staff of several universities, including City University of Hong Kong, Lehigh University, Florida International University, California State University, Long Beach, Eastern Illinois University, and the University of Southern California. Dr. Turban is the author of more than 100 refereed papers published in leading journals, such as *Management Science*, *MIS Quarterly*, and *Decision Support Systems*. He is also the author of 20 books, including *Electronic Commerce: A Managerial Perspective* and *Information Technology for Management.* He is also a consultant to major corporations worldwide. Dr. Turban's current areas of interest are Web-based decision support systems, the use of intelligent agents in e-commerce systems, and collaboration issues in global e-commerce.

Jay E. Aronson (M.S., M.S., Ph.D., Carnegie Mellon University) is a professor of management information systems in the Terry College of Business at The University of Georgia. Prior to this, he was on the faculty at Southern Methodist University. Dr. Aronson is the author of more than 50 refereed papers that have appeared in leading journals, including *Management Science*, *Information Systems Research*, *MIS Quarterly*, and *Decision Sciences.* He is the author of three books, and he regularly contributes to several professional encyclopedias. He is also a consultant to major international corporations and organizations. Dr. Aronson's current areas of research include knowledge management, collaborative computing, and parallel computing.

Ting-Peng Liang (M.A., Ph.D., University of Pennsylvania) is a National Chair Professor of Information Systems at National Sun Yat-sen University in Taiwan and a visiting professor at Chinese University of Hong Kong. Prior to this, he was on the faculties of University of Illinois (Urbana–Champaign) and Purdue University. Dr. Liang has published more than 50 refereed research papers in leading journals, such as *Management Science*, *MIS Quarterly*, *Decision Support Systems*, and *Journal of MIS*. He is also the author of three books and a consultant to several major companies in the United States and Taiwan. Dr. Liang's current research and teaching interests include Web-based intelligent systems, e-commerce, knowledge management, and strategic applications of information technologies.

Ramesh Sharda (M.B.A., Ph.D., University of Wisconsin–Madison) is director of the Institute for Research in Information Systems (IRIS), ConocoPhillips Chair of Management of Technology, and a Regents Professor of Management Science and Information Systems in the Spears School of Business Administration at Oklahoma State University (OSU). He started and served as the director of the M.S. in Telecommunications Management Program at OSU. More than 100 papers describing his research have been published in major journals, including *Management Science*, *Information Systems Research*, *Decision Support Systems*, and *Journal of MIS*. Dr. Sharda serves on several editorial boards, including those of *INFORMS Journal on Computing*, *Decision Support Systems*, and *Information Systems Frontiers*. His current research interests are in decision support systems, collaborative applications, and technologies for managing information overload. Dr. Sharda is also a co-founder of iTradeFair.com, a company that produces virtual trade fairs.

Brief Contents

CONTENTS

ONLINE MATERIAL

BI Preview Chapter Online Files

Chapter 6 Online Files

Chapter 7 Online Files

Chapter 8 Online Files

Chapter 9 Online Files

Chapter 10 Online Files

Chapter 11 Online Files

Chapter 12 Online Files

Chapter 13 Online Files

Preface

As we begin the 21st century, we are seeing major changes in how managers use computerized support in making decisions. As more and more decision makers become computer and Web literate, they are using more computerized tools to support their work. The field of decision support systems (DSS)/business intelligence (BI) is evolving from its beginnings as primarily a personal-support tool and is quickly becoming a shared commodity across organizations. Organizations can now easily use intranets and the Internet to deliver high-value performance-analysis applications to decision makers around the world. Corporations regularly develop distributed systems, intranets, and extranets that enable easy access to data stored in multiple locations, collaboration, and communication worldwide. Various information systems applications are integrated with one other and/or with other Web-based systems. Some integration even transcends organizational boundaries. Managers can make better decisions because they have more accurate information at their fingertips.

Today's decision support tools utilize the Web for their analysis, and they use graphical user interfaces that allow decision makers to flexibly, efficiently, and easily view and process data and models by using familiar Web browsers. The easy-to-use and readily available capabilities of enterprise information, knowledge, and other advanced systems have migrated to the PC and personal digital assistants (PDAs). Managers communicate with computers and the Web by using a variety of handheld wireless devices, including mobile phones and PDAs. These devices enable managers to access important information and useful tools, communicate, and collaborate. Data warehouses and their analytical tools (e.g., online analytical processing [OLAP], data mining) dramatically enhance information access and analysis across organizational boundaries.

Decision support for groups continues to improve, with major new developments in groupware for enhancing collaborative work, anytime and anywhere. Artificial intelligence methods are improving the quality of decision support and have become embedded in many applications, ranging from automated pricing optimization to intelligent Web search engines. Intelligent agents perform routine tasks, freeing up time that decision makers can devote to important work. Developments in wireless technologies, organizational learning, and knowledge management deliver an entire organization's expertise on the solution of problems anytime and anywhere.

The purpose of this book is to introduce the reader to these technologies, which we call, collectively, *management support systems (MSS)*. The core technology is BI. This book presents the fundamentals of the techniques and the manner in which these systems are constructed and used.

The theme of this totally revised edition is BI for enterprise decision support. In addition to traditional decision support applications, this edition expands the reader's understanding of the world of the Web by providing examples, products, services, and exercises and by discussing Web-related issues throughout the text. We highlight Web intelligence/Web analytics, which parallel BI/business analytics (BA) for e-commerce and other Web applications. The book is supported by a Web site **(prenhall.com/turban)** providing two complete chapters that supplement the text, as well as many online files for each individual chapter.

Most of the specific improvements made in this eighth edition concentrate on three areas: BI, data mining, and automated decision support (ADS). Despite the many changes, we have preserved the comprehensiveness and user friendliness that have made the text a market leader. We have also reduced the book's size by eliminating generic material and by moving material to the Web site. Finally, we present accurate and updated material that is not available in any other text.

BI, DSS, and expert systems (ES) courses and portions of courses are recommended jointly by the Association for Computing Machinery (ACM), the Association for Information Systems (AIS), and the Association of Information Technology Professionals (AITP, formerly DPMA). This course is designed to cover the decision support and artificial intelligence components of the model curriculum for information systems; it actually covers more than the curriculum recommends. The text also covers the decision support and artificial intelligence components of the Master of Science Information Systems (MSIS) 2000 Model Curriculum draft (see **acm.org/education/curricula.html#MSIS2000**). Another objective is to provide practicing managers with the foundations and applications of BI, group support systems (GSS), knowledge management, ES, data mining, intelligent agents, and other intelligent systems.

WHAT'S NEW IN THE 8TH EDITION?

With the goal of improving the text, this eighth edition makes a major departure from the previous editions. The major changes in the eighth edition are the transformation of the book from the traditional DSS to BI and the tight linking with Teradata University Network (TUN). The following major specific changes have been made:

- *New chapters.* The following chapters have been added:

  Chapter 5, "Data Warehousing"
  Chapter 6, "Business Analytics and Data Visualization"
  Chapter 7, "Data, Text, and Web Mining"
  Chapter 8, "Neural Networks for Data Mining"
  Chapter 9, "Business Performance Management"

- *Significantly modified chapters.* The following chapters have been significantly revised:

  Chapter 1, "Decision Support Systems and Business Intelligence"
  Chapter 15, "System Development and Acquisition"
  Chapter 17 (an online chapter), "Enterprise Systems"

- *Links to TeradataUniversityNetwork (TUN).* Most chapters include links to TUN (**teradatauniversitynetwork.com**). The student side of the Teradata site (Teradata Student Network [TSN]; **teradatastudentnetwork.com**) mainly includes assignments for students. A visit to TSN allows students to read cases, view Web seminars, answer questions, search material, and more.
- *Book's format and size.* The book has been shortened by over 100 pages. Review questions are now in each section rather than at the end of the chapter. The chapter one-commerce has been deleted, and its content has been distributed to other chapters.
- *Fewer boxes, better organized.* We reduced the number of boxes by more than 50 percent. Important material was incorporated in the text or moved to online files. Only two types of boxes now exist: Application Cases and Technology Insights.
- *References and other resources.* We reduced the number of references (students can find more at TUN and at **scholar.google.com**). We added a large number of URLs, so students can conduct research if needed.

- *Book title change.* We changed the title of the book to *Decision Support and Business Intelligence Systems*.
- *Software support.* The TUN Web site provides software support at no charge. It also provides links to free data mining and other software. In addition, the site provides exercises in the use of such software.
- *New topics and updates.* Many new topics were added, such as automated decision systems. Also, new figures, exercises, cases, and tables were added.
- *New author.* Ramesh Sharda (Okalahoma State University), an expert on data mining, was added to the existing team of Turban, Aronson, and Liang.
- *New contributors.* The following people have contributed to this edition:

  Dave King (JDA Systems), a co-author of *The Strategy Gap* (a book on corporate performance management) contributed Chapter 9: Business Performance Management

  Mike Goul (Arizona State University), an expert on BI and a member of the TUN advisory board, contributed to the Special Supplement on Business Intelligence

  Linda Lai (Macau Polytechnic University of China), an expert on systems development revised Chapter 15: System Development and Acquisition

  Christy Cheung (Hong Kong Baptist University), a researcher in the area of business analytics, contributed to Chapter 11: Knowledge Management and to literature searches for several chapters

  Leila A. Halawi (Bethune-Cookman College), a researcher in the area of data warehousing, contributed to Chapter 5: Data Warehousing

THE SUPPLEMENT PACKAGE: PRENHALL.COM/TURBAN

A comprehensive and flexible technology-support package is available to enhance the teaching and learning experience. The following instructor and student supplements are available on the book's Web site, **prenhall.com/turban**:

- *Instructor's Manual.* The Instructor's Manual includes learning objectives for the entire course and for each chapter, answers to the questions and exercises at the end of each chapter, and teaching suggestions (including instructions for projects). The Instructor's Manual is available on the secure faculty section of **prenhall.com/turban**.
- *Test Item File and TestGen Software.* The Test Item File is a comprehensive collection of true/false, multiple-choice, fill-in-the-blank, and essay questions. The questions are rated by difficulty level, and the answers are referenced by book page number. The Test Item File is available in Microsoft Word in the computerized form of Prentice Hall TestGen. TestGen is a comprehensive suite of tools for testing and assessment. It allows instructors to easily create and distribute tests for their courses, either by printing and distributing through traditional methods or by online delivery via a local area network (LAN) server. TestGen features

[1] Note that Web site URLs are dynamic. As this book went to press, we verified that all the cited Web sites were active and valid. Web sites to which we refer in the text sometimes change or are discontinued because companies change names, are bought or sold, merge, or fail. Sometimes Web sites are down for maintenance, repair, or redesign. Most organizations have dropped the initial "www" designation for their sites, but some still use it. If you have a problem connecting to a Web site that we mention, please be patient and simply run a Web search to try to identify the new site. Most times, the new site can be found quickly. We apologize in advance for this inconvenience.

wizards that assist in moving through the program, and the software is backed with full technical support. Both the Test Item File and TestGen software are available on the secure faculty section of **prenhall.com/turban**.

- *PowerPoint slides.* PowerPoint slides are available that illuminate and build on key concepts in the text. Both students and faculty can download the PowerPoint slides from **prenhall.com/turban**.
- *Materials for your online course.* Prentice Hall supports our adopters using online courses by providing files ready for upload into both WebCT and Blackboard course management systems for testing, quizzing, and other supplements. Please contact your local Prentice Hall representative or e-mail *mis_service@prenhall.com* for further information on your particular course.

ACKNOWLEDGEMENTS

Many individuals have provided suggestions and criticisms since the publication of the first edition of this book. Dozens of students participated in class testing of various chapters, software, and problems and assisted in collecting material. It is not possible to name everyone who participated in this project, but our thanks go to all of them. Certain individuals made significant contributions, and they deserve special recognition.

First, we appreciate the efforts of those individuals who provided formal reviews of the first through eighth editions:

Robert Blanning, Vanderbilt University
Ranjit Bose, University of New Mexico
Warren Briggs, Suffolk University
Lee Roy Bronner, Morgan State University
Charles Butler, Colorado State University
Sohail S. Chaudry, University of Wisconsin–La Crosse
Kathy Chudoba, Florida State University
Wingyan Chung, University of Texas
Woo Young Chung, University of Memphis
Paul "Buddy" Clark, South Carolina State University
Pi'Sheng Deng, California State University–Stanislaus
Joyce Elam, Florida International University
Gary Farrar, Jacksonville University
George Federman, Santa Clara City College
Jerry Fjermestad, New Jersey Institute of Technology
Joey George, Florida State University
Paul Gray, Claremont Graduate School
Orv Greynholds, Capital College (Laurel, MD)
Ray Jacobs, Ashland University
Leonard Jessup, Indiana University
Jeffrey Johnson, Utah State University
Saul Kassicieh, University of New Mexico
Anand S. Kunnathur, University of Toledo
Shao-ju Lee, California State University at Northridge
Yair Levy, Nova Southeastern University
Hank Lucas, New York University
Jane Mackay, Texas Christian University
George M. Marakas, University of Maryland

Dick Mason, Southern Methodist University
Nick McGaughey, San Jose State University
Ido Millet, Pennsylvania State University–Erie
Benjamin Mittman, Northwestern University
Larry Moore, Virginia Polytechnic Institute and State University
Simitra Mukherjee, Nova Southeastern University
Marianne Murphy, Northeastern University
Peter Mykytyn, Southern Illinois University
Souren Paul, Southern Illinois University
Joshua Pauli, Dakota State University
Roger Alan Pick, University of Missouri–St. Louis
W. "RP" Raghupaphi, California State University–Chico
Loren Rees, Virginia Polytechnic Institute and State University
David Russell, Western New England College
Steve Ruth, George Mason University
Vartan Safarian, Winona State University
Glenn Shephard, San Jose State University
Jung P. Shim, Mississippi State University
Meenu Singh, Murray State University
Randy Smith, University of Virginia
James T.C. Teng, University of South Carolina
John VanGigch, California State University at Sacramento
David Van Over, University of Idaho
Paul J.A. van Vliet, University of Nebraska at Omaha
B. S. Vijayaraman, University of Akron
Howard Charles Walton, Gettysburg College
Diane B. Walz, University of Texas at San Antonio
Paul R. Watkins, University of Southern California
Randy S. Weinberg, Saint Cloud State University
Jennifer Williams, University of Southern Indiana
Steve Zanakis, Florida International University

Second, several individuals contributed material to the text or the supporting material. For this edition, we acknowledge the contributions of Mike Goul (Arizona State University), Leila A. Halawi (Bethune-Cookman College) Linda Lai (Macau Polytechnic University of China), Christy Cheung (Hong Kong Baptist University), and Dave King (JDA Software Group, Inc.). Major contributors for the previous editions include Lou Frenzel, an independent consultant whose books *Crash Course in Artificial Intelligence and Expert Systems* and *Understanding of Expert Systems* (both published by Howard W. Sams, New York,1987) provided material for the early editions; Larry Medsker (American University), who contributed substantial material on neural networks; and Richard V. McCarthy (Quinnipiac University), who performed major revisions in the seventh edition.

Third, the book benefited greatly from the efforts of many individuals who contributed advice and interesting material (such as problems), gave feedback on material, or helped in class testing. These individuals are Warren Briggs (Suffolk University), Frank DeBalough (University of Southern California), Mei-Ting Cheung (University of Hong Kong), Alan Dennis (Indiana University), George Easton (San Diego State University), Janet Fisher (California State University, Los Angeles), David Friend (Pilot Software, Inc.), Paul Gray (Claremont Graduate School), Dustin Huntington (Exsys, Inc.), Subramanian Rama Iyer (Oklahoma State University), Elena Karahanna (The

University of Georgia), Mike McAulliffe (The University of Georgia), Chad Peterson (The University of Georgia), Neil Rabjohn (York University), Jim Ragusa (University of Central Florida), Elizabeth Rivers, Alan Rowe (University of Southern California), Steve Ruth (George Mason University), Linus Schrage (University of Chicago), Antonie Stam (University of Missouri), Ron Swift (NCR Corp.), Merril Warkentin (Northeastern University), Paul Watkins (The University of Southern California), Ben Mortagy (Claremont Graduate School of Management), Dan Walsh (Bellcore), Richard Watson (The University of Georgia), and the many other instructors and students who have provided feedback.

Fourth, several vendors cooperated by providing development and/or demonstration software: CACI Products Company (LaJolla, CA), California Scientific Software (Nevada City, CA), Cognos, Inc. (Ottawa, ON), DS Group, Inc. (Greenwich, CT), Expert Choice, Inc. (Pittsburgh, PA), Exsys, Inc. (Albuquerque, NM), Palisade Software (Newfield, NY), Promised Land Technologies (New Haven, CT), Ward Systems Group, Inc. (Frederick, MD), Idea Fisher Systems, Inc. (Irving, CA), and Wordtech Systems (Orinda, CA), StatSoft (Tulsa, OK).

Fifth, special thanks to the Teradata University Network and especially to its director, Hugh Watson, senior director, TUN; and to Mary Gros, director, academic relations, Teradata, a division of NCR, and a liaison between Teradata and the academic community, for their encouragement to tie this book with TUN and for providing useful material for the book.

Sixth, many individuals helped us with administrative matters and editing, proofreading, and preparation. The project began with Jack Repcheck (a former Macmillan editor), who initiated this project with the support of Hank Lucas (New York University).

Seventh, the work of so many authors, contributors, and participants was skillfully orchestrated and managed by Judy Lang, who collaborated with all of us, provided editing, and guided us during the entire project. Judy also prepared the PowerPoint slides.

Finally, the Prentice Hall team is to be commended: Executive Editor Bob Horan, who orchestrated this project; Kitty Jarrett, who copyedited the manuscript; the production team, Carol Samet at Prentice Hall and the staff at GGS Book Services, who transformed the manuscript into a book; our editorial project manager, Ana Jankowski; and our media project manager, Peter Snell.

We would like to thank all these individuals and corporations. Without their help, the creation of this book would not have been possible.

E.T.
J.E.A.
T.P.L.
R.S.

PART

I

Decision Support and Business Intelligence

Learning Objectives for Part I

- ◆ Understand the complexity of today's business environment
- ◆ Understand the foundations and key issues of managerial decision making
- ◆ Recognize the difficulties in managerial decision making today
- ◆ Learn the major frameworks of computerized decision support: decision support systems (DSS) and business intelligence

This book deals with a collection of computer technologies that support managerial work—essentially, decision making. These technologies have had a profound impact on corporate strategy, performance, and competitiveness. These techniques are also strongly connected to the Internet, intranets, and Web tools, as shown throughout the book. In Part I, we cover two major topics in one chapter. The first topic is managerial decision making and its computerized support; the second is frameworks for decision support. We also provide brief coverage of the tools used and their implementation, as well as a preview of the entire book.

Decision Support Systems and Business Intelligence

Learning Objectives

- Understand today's turbulent business environment and describe how organizations survive and even excel in such an environment (solving problems and exploiting opportunities)
- Understand the need for computerized support of managerial decision making
- Understand an early framework for managerial decision making
- Learn the conceptual foundations of the decision support systems (DSS[1]) methodology
- Describe the business intelligence (BI) methodology and concepts and relate them to DSS
- Describe the concept of work systems and its relationship to decision support
- List the major tools of computerized decision support
- Understand the major issues in implementing computerized support systems

The business environment (climate) in which organizations operate today is ever changing, and it is becoming more and more complex. Organizations, both private and public, feel increasing pressures that force them to respond quickly to changing conditions and to be innovative in the way they operate. Such activities require organizations to be agile and make frequent and quick strategic, tactical, and operational decisions, some of which are very complex. Making such decisions may require considerable amounts of relevant data, information, and knowledge. Processing these, in the framework of the needed decisions, must be done quickly, frequently in real-time, and usually requires some computerized support.

This book is about using business intelligence as a computerized support for managerial decision making. It concentrates both on the theoretical and conceptual foundations of decision support, as well as on the commercial tools and techniques that are available. This introductory chapter provides more details of these topics as well as an overview of the book. This chapter has the following sections:

1.1 Opening Vignette: Toyota Uses Business Intelligence to Excel

1.2 Changing Business Environments and Computerized Decision Support

1.3 Managerial Decision Making

[1]The acronym *DSS* is treated as both singular and plural throughout this book. Similarly, other acronyms, such as *MIS* and *GSS*, designate both plural and singular forms.

1.1 OPENING VIGNETTE: TOYOTA USES BUSINESS INTELLIGENCE TO EXCEL

PROBLEM

Toyota Motor Sales USA (**toyota.com**) is the U.S. distributor of cars and trucks built by Toyota (i.e., it is a subsidiary of Toyota). The company buys the cars at the Toyota factories in Japan and elsewhere, takes ownership of the vehicles, and then sells them to Toyota dealers across the United States. An average vehicle costs $8/day to keep while in transit. Because it used to take 9 to 10 days in transit, the financial charge was $72 to $80 per car. For 2 million cars per year, the cost to the company was $144 to $160 million per year. This was too much.

In the late 1990s, the company faced increased problems in its supply chain and its operations, and its car-keeping costs mounted. Also, the inability to deliver cars to the dealers resulted in unhappy customers purchasing cars from competitors, such as Honda. This became extremely important in 2003 and 2004, when hybrid cars were introduced and the competition with Honda intensified.

In the past, managers used computers that generated huge numbers of directionless reports and data. Managers were unable to use such data and reports strategically. Furthermore, internal departments regularly failed to share information, or they did it too slowly. Actionable reports were often produced too late. In addition, overlapping reporting systems provided data that were not always accurate. Managers were unable to make timely decisions because they were not certain what portion of the data was accurate. The situation was especially dire in the Toyota Logistic Services (TLS) division, which manages the transport of vehicles.

The managers of TLS require precision tracking and supply-chain management to ensure that the right cars go to the right dealers in a timely manner. Manual scheduling and other related business processes that were conducted with incorrect information caused additional problems. For example, if one individual made a data entry mistake when a ship docked, the mistake would endure throughout the entire supply chain. (For example, some data indicated to managers that ships never made it to a port weeks after the ships had safely docked.) The information technology (IT) organization was unable to respond to the growing needs of the business. Finally, a new chief information officer (CIO) was hired in 1997 in order to fix the problems.

SOLUTION

Barbara Cooper, the new CIO of TMS started by trying to identify the problems. Cooper realized that a data warehouse was needed. A *data warehouse* is a central repository of historical data, organized in such a way that it is easy to access (using a Web browser) and it can be manipulated for decision support. (See the discussion of data warehousing later in this chapter and in Chapter 5.) Cooper also saw that software tools to process, mine, and manipulate the data were needed. A system was therefore set up to provide real-time, accurate data. Unfortunately, the system did not work properly. To begin with, the historical data input into the system included years of human errors that had gone unnoticed, including inconsistent duplicated data as well as missing data. This resulted in erroneous results and analysis. In addition, the new system lacked capabilities to provide what managers needed. By 1999, it had become clear that the solution did not work. It was the right concept but used the wrong technology from the wrong vendors. In 2000, Toyota switched to a better technology. The new TLS system used Oracle's data warehouse and Hyperion's business intelligence platform. The system also included Hyperion's *dashboard* feature (discussed in Chapters 6 and 9), which allows executives to visually see hot spots in their business units and investigate further to identify problems and their causes.

With the new TLS system, which uses colors meaningfully (e.g., red for danger), a business manager can see in real-time, for example, when delivery times are slowing and can immediately find the sources of the problems and even evaluate potential solutions by using "what-if" analysis.

RESULTS

Within a few days, the new TLS system started to provide eye-popping results. For example, the system helped managers discover that Toyota was getting billed twice for a specific rail shipment (an $800,000 error). Overall, Toyota USA managed to increase the volume of cars it handled by 40 percent between 2001 and 2005, while increasing head count by just 3 percent. In addition, in-transit time was reduced by more than 5 percent. Word of the success of TLS's new BI quickly spread throughout Toyota USA and then all over the company, and many other areas of the company started to adopt BI. For example, the former manager of TLS, who now runs the Toyota Customer Services Division, uses dashboards in his office, as do chief financial officers (CFOs) and other top executives throughout Toyota (e.g., to better manage expenses, purchasing, and so on).

It is clear now that the more people who use data analysis tools, the more money Toyota can earn. The TLS system was upgraded in 2003 and 2005, and tools are continuously added as needed. Thanks to the new TLS system and other BI, the parent company, Toyota Motor Corporation, reached the highest profit margins in the automotive industry in 2003. Also, Toyota's market share has increased consistently. (Incidentally, Toyota, which is an agile company, will start to produce consumer-helping robots—that is, service robots for the elderly—in the year 2010.)

Finally, an independent study by IDC, Inc., about the justification of business performance management (see Chapter 9) and BI systems indicates that Toyota achieved a 506 percent return on its BI investment. The median return on investment [ROI] for the 43 other Fortune 500 companies that participated in the study was 112 percent.

Sources: Compiled from D. Briody, "Toyota's Business Intelligence: Oh! What a Feeling!" *CIO Insight*, October 1, 2004, and Hyperion Solution Corporation, "Toyota Motor Sales—A Customer White Paper" **hyperion.com/customers/stories/us_toyota_motor.cfm**[2] (accessed March 2006); and **toyota.com** (accessed March 2006).

---

[2]As this book went to press, we verified that all the cited Web sites were active and valid. However, URLs are dynamic. Web sites to which we refer in the text sometimes change or are discontinued because companies change names, are bought or sold, merge, or fail. Sometimes Web sites are down for maintenance, repair, or redesign. Many organizations have dropped the initial "www" designation for their sites, but some still use it. If you have a problem connecting to a Web site that we mention, please be patient and simply run a Web search to try to identify the possible new site. Most times, you can quickly find the new site through one of the popular search engines. We apologize in advance for this inconvenience.

Questions for the Opening Vignette

1. In what ways did the old information systems create problems for Toyota?
2. What information needs of managers are satisfied by the new BI system? What decisions are satisfied by the BI support?
3. Relate the TLS problem to the supply chain (from factories, to dealers, to consumers).
4. List the decision support tools cited here.
5. What strategic advantage can Toyota derive from this system?
6. Relate Toyota's decision to make consumer-helping robots to the changing business environment.

WHAT WE CAN LEARN FROM THIS VIGNETTE

This vignette illustrates a typical case in which information flow could not meet the needs of managers. Information was late, sometimes inaccurate, and not shared by all. The old system did not meet the needs to make fast decisions, evaluate large amounts of information that was stored in different locations, and collaborate. The solution is a technology called *business intelligence*, which is based on a data warehouse and provides a strategic advantage. The major objective of this book is to show how it is done. In this chapter, we provide a preview of the book.

1.2 CHANGING BUSINESS ENVIRONMENTS AND COMPUTERIZED DECISION SUPPORT

The opening vignette illustrates how a global company excels in the highly competitive automotive market. Toyota, which is known for pioneering manual management techniques, such as just-in-time (JIT) techniques, has moved aggressively to computerized support of its operations. To understand why Toyota and many other companies are embracing computerized support, including business intelligence, we developed a model called the *Business Pressures–Responses–Support Model*, which is shown in Figure 1.1.

THE BUSINESS PRESSURES–RESPONSES–SUPPORT MODEL

The Business Pressures–Responses–Support model, as its name indicates, has three components: business pressures that result from today's business climate, responses (actions taken) by companies to counter the pressures (or to take advantage of the opportunities available in the environment), and computerized support that facilitates the monitoring of the environment and enhances the response actions taken by organizations.

The Business Environment

The environment in which organizations operate today is becoming more and more complex (Huber, 2003). This complexity creates opportunities on one hand and problems on the other. Take globalization as an example. Today, you can easily find suppliers and customers in many countries, which means you can buy cheaper materials

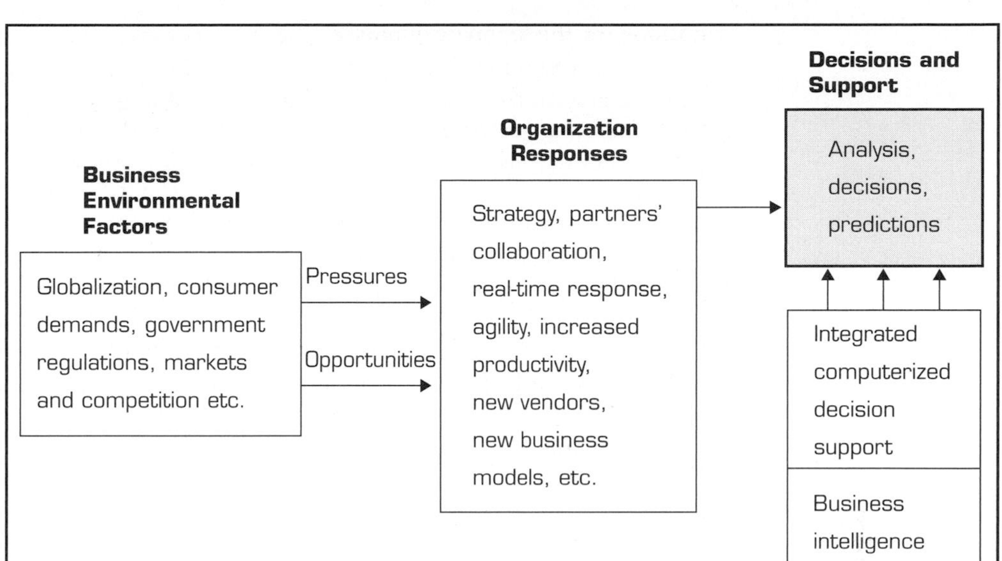

FIGURE 1.1 The Business Pressures–Responses–Support Model

and sell more of your products and services; great opportunities exist. However, globalization also means more and stronger competitors. Business environment factors can be divided into four major categories: *markets*, *consumer demands*, *technology*, and *societal*. These categories are summarized in Table 1.1.

TABLE 1-1 Business Environment Factors That Create Pressures on Organizations

Factor	*Description*
Markets	Strong competition
	Expanding global markets
	Blooming electronic markets on the Internet
	Innovative marketing methods
	Opportunities for outsourcing with IT support
	Need for real-time, on-demand transactions
Consumer demands	Desire for customization
	Desire for quality, diversity of products, and speed of delivery
	Customers getting powerful and less loyal
Technology	More innovations, new products, and new services
	Increasing obsolescence rate
	Increasing information overload
Societal	Growing government regulations and deregulation
	Work force more diversified, older, and composed of more women
	Prime concerns of homeland security and terrorist attacks
	Necessity of Sarbanes-Oxley Act and other reporting-related legislation
	Increasing social responsibility of companies

Note that the *intensity* of most of these factors increases with time, leading to more pressures, more competition, and so on. In addition, organizations and departments within organizations face decreased budgets and amplified pressures from top managers to increase performance and profit. In this kind of environment, managers must respond quickly, innovate, and be agile. Let's see how they do it.

Organizational Responses: Be Reactive, Anticipative, Adaptive, and Proactive

Both private and public organizations are aware of today's business environment and pressures. They use different actions to counter the pressures. Toyota TLS, for example, turned to BI to improve communication and to support executives in their effort to know exactly what is going on in each area of operation, almost in real-time. TLS also uses its BI system to better collaborate with business partners. By doing so, it can cut expenses and increase customer satisfaction. Managers may take other actions, including the following:

- Employ strategic planning
- Use new and innovative business models
- Restructure business processes
- Participate in business alliances
- Improve corporate information systems
- Improve partnership relationships
- Encourage innovation and creativity
- Improve customer service and relationships
- Move to electronic commerce (e-commerce)
- Move to make-to-order production and on-demand manufacturing and services
- Use new IT to improve communication, data access (discovery of information), and collaboration
- Respond quickly to competitors' actions (e.g., in pricing, promotions, new products and services)
- Automate many tasks of white-collar employees
- Automate certain decision processes, especially those dealing with customers
- Improve decision making

Many, if not all, of these actions require some computerized support.

These and other response actions are frequently facilitated by computerized DSS such as the Toyota TLS BI system.

Closing the Strategy Gap

One of the major objectives of computerized decision support is to facilitate closing the gap between the current performance of an organization and its desired performance, as expressed in its mission, objectives, and goals, and the strategy to achieve them. For details, see Coveney et al. (2003) and the discussion in Chapter 9. In order to understand why computerized support is needed and how it is provided, especially for decision-making support, let's look at managerial decision making.

Section 1.2 Review Questions

1. List the components of and explain the Business Pressures–Responses–Support model.
2. What are the major factors in today's business environment?
3. What are some of the major response activities that organizations take?
4. Define the strategy gap.

1.3 MANAGERIAL DECISION MAKING

Management is a process by which organizational goals are achieved using resources. The resources are considered inputs, and attainment of goals is viewed as the output of the process. The degree of success of the organization and the manager are often measured by the ratio of outputs to inputs. This ratio is an indication of the organization's *productivity*, which is a reflection of the *organizational and managerial performance*.

The level of productivity or the success of management depends on the performance of managerial functions, such as planning, organizing, directing, and controlling. To perform their functions, managers are engaged in a continuous process of making decisions. Making a decision means selecting the best alternative from two or more solutions.

THE NATURE OF MANAGERS' WORK

Mintzberg's (1980) classic study of top managers and several replicated studies suggest that managers perform 10 major roles that can be classified into three major categories: *interpersonal*, *informational*, and *decisional* (see Table 1.2).

To perform these roles, managers need information that is delivered efficiently and in a timely manner to personal computers (PCs) on their desktops, to mobile computers, to personal digital assistants (PDAs), and to cell phones. This information is delivered by networks, generally via Web technologies.

In addition to obtaining information necessary to better perform their roles, managers use computers directly to support and improve decision making, which is a key task that is part of most of these roles. Many managerial activities in all roles revolve around decision making. *Managers, especially those at high managerial levels, are primarily decision makers* (see Technology Insights 1.1). Organizations are filled with decision makers at various levels (see Ireland and Miller, 2004).

THE PROCESS OF DECISION MAKING

For years, managers considered decision making purely an art—a talent acquired over a long period through experience (i.e., learning by trial-and-error) and by using intuition. Management was considered an art because a variety of individual styles could be used in approaching and successfully solving the same types of managerial problems. These styles were often based on creativity, judgment, intuition, and experience rather than on systematic quantitative methods grounded in a scientific approach.

Managers usually make decisions by following a four-step process:

1. Define the problem (i.e., a decision situation that may deal with some difficulty or with an opportunity).
2. Construct a model that describes the real-world problem.
3. Identify possible solutions to the modeled problem and evaluate the solutions.
4. Compare, choose, and recommend a potential solution to the problem.

To follow this process, one must make sure that sufficient alternative solutions are being considered, that the consequences of using these alternatives can be reasonably

TABLE 1.2 Mintzberg's 10 Managerial Roles

Role	***Description***
Interpersonal	
Figurehead	Is symbolic head; obliged to perform a number of routine duties of a legal or social nature
Leader	Is responsible for the motivation and activation of subordinates; responsible for staffing, training, and associated duties
Liaison	Maintains self-developed network of outside contacts and informers who provide favors and information
Informational	
Monitor	Seeks and receives a wide variety of special information (much of it current) to develop a thorough understanding of the organization and environment; emerges as the nerve center of the organization's internal and external information
Disseminator	Transmits information received from outsiders or from subordinates to members of the organization; some of this information is factual, and some involves interpretation and integration
Spokesperson	Transmits information to outsiders about the organization's plans, policies, actions, results, and so forth; serves as an expert on the organization's industry
Decisional	
Entrepreneur	Searches the organization and its environment for opportunities and initiates improvement projects to bring about change; supervises design of certain projects
Disturbance handler	Is responsible for corrective action when the organization faces important, unexpected disturbances
Resource allocator	Is responsible for the allocation of organizational resources of all kinds; in effect, is responsible for the making or approval of all significant organizational decisions
Negotiator	Is responsible for representing the organization at major negotiations

Sources: Compiled from H.A. Mintzberg, *The Nature of Managerial Work*. Prentice Hall, Englewood Cliffs, NJ, 1980; and H.A. Mintzberg, *The Rise and Fall of Strategic Planning*. The Free Press, New York, 1993.

predicted, and that comparisons are done properly. However, the environmental factors listed in Table 1.1 make such an evaluation process difficult for the following reasons:

- Technology, information systems, advanced search engines, and globalization result in more and more alternatives from which to choose.
- Government regulations and the need for compliance, political instability and terrorism, competition, and changing consumer demands produce more uncertainty, making it more difficult to predict consequences and the future.

TECHNOLOGY INSIGHTS 1.1

Decision-Making Ability Rated First in Survey

In almost any survey of what constitutes good management, the ability to make clear-cut decisions when needed is prominently mentioned. It is not surprising, therefore, to learn that the ability to make crisp decisions was rated first in importance in a study of 6,500 managers in more than 100 companies, many of them large blue-chip corporations.

Managers starting a training course at Harbridge House, a Boston-based firm, were asked how important it was for managers to follow certain managerial practices. They were also asked how well, in their estimation, managers performed these practices. From a statistical distillation of the answers it received, Harbridge ranked making clear-cut decisions when needed as the most important of 10 managerial practices. Unfortunately, the respondents concluded that only 20 percent of the managers performed well on this.

Ranked second in managerial importance was getting to the heart of problems rather than dealing with less important issues, a finding that shows up in similar studies. Most of the remaining eight management practices were related directly or indirectly to decision making.

This situation is timeless. See any recent survey in *Baseline, CIO Insight, Forbes, Fortune, or InformationWeek.* For a specific survey see CIO Research Report, "State of the CIO 2006," *CIO.com,* December 30, 2005. **cio.com/research/surveyreport.cfm?id=101** (accessed September 2006).

- Other factors are the need to make rapid decisions, the frequent and unpredictable changes that make trial-and-error learning difficult, and the potential costs of making mistakes.
- These environments are growing more complex every day. Therefore, making decisions today is indeed a complex task (Huber, 2003).

Because of these trends and changes, it is nearly impossible to rely on a trial-and-error approach to management, especially for decisions for which the factors shown in Table 1.1 are strong influences. Managers must be more sophisticated; they must use the new tools and techniques of their fields. Most of those tools and techniques are discussed in this book. Using them to support decision making can be extremely rewarding in making effective decisions.

In the following section, we look now at why we need computer support and how it is provided.

Section 1.3 Review Questions

1. Describe the three major managerial roles, and list some of the specific activities in each.
2. Why have some argued that management is the same as decision making?
3. Describe the four steps managers take in making a decision.
4. Explain why intuition and trial-and-error approaches to managerial decision making may not be effective in today's business environment.

1.4 COMPUTERIZED SUPPORT FOR DECISION MAKING

From traditional uses in payroll and bookkeeping functions, computerized systems are now penetrating complex managerial areas ranging from the design and management of automated factories to the application of artificial intelligence methods to the evaluation of proposed mergers and acquisitions. Nearly all executives know that information technology is vital to their business and extensively use information technologies, especially Web-based ones.

Computer applications have moved from transaction processing and monitoring activities to problem analysis and solution applications, and much of the activity is done with Web-based technologies (see Geoffrion and Krishnan, 2001). BI tools such as data warehousing, data mining, online analytical processing (OLAP), dashboards, and the use of the Web for decision support are the cornerstones of today's modern management. Managers must have high-speed, networked information systems (wireline or wireless) to assist them with their most important task: making decisions (see Huber, 2003). Let's look at why and how computerized systems can help.

WHY WE USE COMPUTERIZED DECISION SUPPORT SYSTEMS

Today's computerized systems possess capabilities that can facilitate decision support in a number of ways, including the following:

- *Speedy computations.* A computer enables the decision maker to perform many computations quickly and at a low cost. Timely decisions are critical in many situations, ranging from a physician in an emergency room to a stock trader on the trading floor. With a computer, thousands of alternatives can be evaluated in seconds. Furthermore, the benefits-to-cost ratio of computers and the speed of executions are constantly increasing.
- *Improved communication and collaboration.* Many decisions are made today by groups whose members may be in different locations. Groups can collaborate and communicate readily by using Web-based tools. Collaboration is especially important along the supply chain, where partners—all the way from vendors to customers—must share information (recall the Toyota TLS case discussed earlier in this chapter; also see Chapters 10 and 17).
- *Increased productivity of group members.* Assembling a group of decision makers, especially experts, in one place can be costly. Computerized support can improve the collaboration process of a group and enable its members to be at different locations (saving travel costs). In addition, computerized support can increase the productivity of staff support (e.g., financial and legal analysts). Decision makers can also increase their productivity by using software optimization tools that help determine the best way to run a business (see Chapter 4).
- *Improved data management.* Many decisions involve complex computations. Data for these can be stored in different databases anywhere in the organization and even possibly at Web sites outside the organization. The data may include text, sound, graphics, and video, and they can be in foreign languages. It may be necessary to transmit data quickly from distant locations. Computers can search, store, and transmit needed data quickly, economically, securely, and transparently.
- *Managing giant data warehouses.* Large data warehouses, like the one operated by Wal-Mart, contain terabytes and even petabytes of data. Computers can provide extremely great storage capability for any type of digital information, and this information can be accessed and searched very rapidly. Special

methods, including parallel computing, are available to organize, search, and mine the data. The costs related to data warehousing are declining.

- *Quality support.* Computers can improve the quality of decisions made. For example, more data can be accessed, more alternatives can be evaluated, forecasts can be improved, risk analysis can be performed quickly, and the views of experts (some of whom are in remote locations) can be collected quickly and at a reduced cost. Expertise can even be derived directly from a computer system using artificial intelligence methods (discussed in Chapter 12). With computers, decision makers can perform complex simulations, check many possible scenarios, and assess diverse impacts quickly and economically.
- *Agility support.* Competition today is based not just on price but also on quality, timeliness, customization of products, and customer support. In addition, organizations must be able to frequently and rapidly change their mode of operation, reengineer processes and structures, empower employees, and innovate in order to adapt to their changing environments. Decision support technologies such as intelligent systems can empower people by allowing them to make good decisions quickly, even if they lack some knowledge.
- *Overcoming cognitive limits in processing and storing information.* According to Simon (1977), the human mind has only a limited ability to process and store information. People sometimes find it difficult to recall and use information in an error-free fashion due to their cognitive limits. The term **cognitive limits** indicates that an individual's problem-solving capability is limited when a wide range of diverse information and knowledge is required. Computerized systems enable people to overcome their cognitive limits by quickly accessing and processing vast amounts of stored information (see Chapter 2).
- *Using the Web.* Since the development of the Internet and Web servers and tools, there have been dramatic changes in how decision makers are supported. Most important, the Web provides (1) access to a vast body of data, information, and knowledge available around the world; (2) a common, user-friendly graphical user interface (GUI) that is easy to learn to use and readily available; (3) the ability to effectively collaborate with remote partners; and (4) the availability of intelligent search tools that enable managers to find the information they need quickly and inexpensively.
- *Anywhere, anytime support.* Using wireless technology, managers can access information anytime and from anyplace, analyze and interpret it, and communicate with those involved.

These and other capabilities have been driving the use of computerized decision support since the late 1960s, but especially since the mid-1990s. Next, we present an early framework for decision support.

Section 1.4 Review Questions

1. How have the capabilities of computing evolved over time?
2. List some capabilities of computing that can facilitate managerial decision making.
3. How can a computer help overcome the cognitive limits of humans?
4. Why is the Web considered so important for decision support?

1.5 AN EARLY FRAMEWORK FOR COMPUTERIZED DECISION SUPPORT

An early framework for computerized decision support includes several major concepts that are used in forthcoming sections and chapters of this book. Gorry and Scott-Morton created and used this framework in the early 1970s, and the framework then evolved into a new technology called DSS.

THE GORRY AND SCOTT-MORTON CLASSICAL FRAMEWORK

Gorry and Scott-Morton (1971) proposed a framework that is a 3-by-3 matrix, as shown in Figure 1.2. Its two dimensions are the degree of structuredness and the types of control.

Degree of Structuredness

The left side of Figure 1.2 is based on Simon's (1977) idea that decision-making processes fall along a continuum that ranges from highly structured (sometimes called *programmed*) to highly unstructured (i.e., *nonprogrammed*) decisions. Structured processes are routine and typically repetitive problems for which standard solution methods exist. *Unstructured processes* are fuzzy, complex problems for

FIGURE 1.2 Decision Support Frameworks

	Type of Control		
Type of Decision	**Operational Control**	**Managerial Control**	**Strategic Planning**
Structured	1 Accounts receivable, accounts payable, order entry	2 Budget analysis, short-term forecasting, personnel reports, make-or-buy	3 Financial management (investment), warehouse location, distribution systems
Semistructured	4 Production scheduling, inventory control	5 Credit evaluation, budget preparation, plant layout, project scheduling, reward system design, inventory categorization	6 Building new plant, mergers and acquisitions, new product planning, compensation planning, quality assurance planning, HR policies, inventory planning
Unstructured	7 Selecting a cover for a magazine, buying software, approving loans, help desk	8 Negotiating, recruiting an executive, buying hardware, lobbying	9 R & D planning, new technology development, social responsibility planning

which there are no cut-and-dried solution methods. Simon also described the decision-making process with a three-phase process of *intelligence*, *design*, and *choice*. Later, a fourth phase was added: *implementation* (see Chapter 2). The four phases are defined as follows:

1. *Intelligence.* This phase involves searching for conditions that call for decisions.
2. *Design.* This phase involves inventing, developing, and analyzing possible alternative courses of action (solutions).
3. *Choice.* This phase involves selecting a course of action from among those available.
4. *Implementation.* This phase involves adapting the selected course of action to the decision situation (i.e., problem solving or opportunity exploiting).

The relationships among the four phases are shown in Figure 1.3.

An *unstructured problem* is one in which none of the four phases described in Figure 1.3 is structured.

In a *structured problem*, all phases are structured. The procedures for obtaining the best (or at least a good enough) solution are known. Whether the problem involves finding an appropriate inventory level or choosing an optimal investment strategy, the objectives are clearly defined. Common objectives are cost minimization and profit maximization.

Semistructured problems fall between structured and unstructured problems, having some structured elements and some unstructured elements. Keen and Scott-Morton (1978) mentioned trading bonds, setting marketing budgets for consumer products, and performing capital acquisition analysis as semistructured problems.

FIGURE 1.3 The Steps of Decision Support

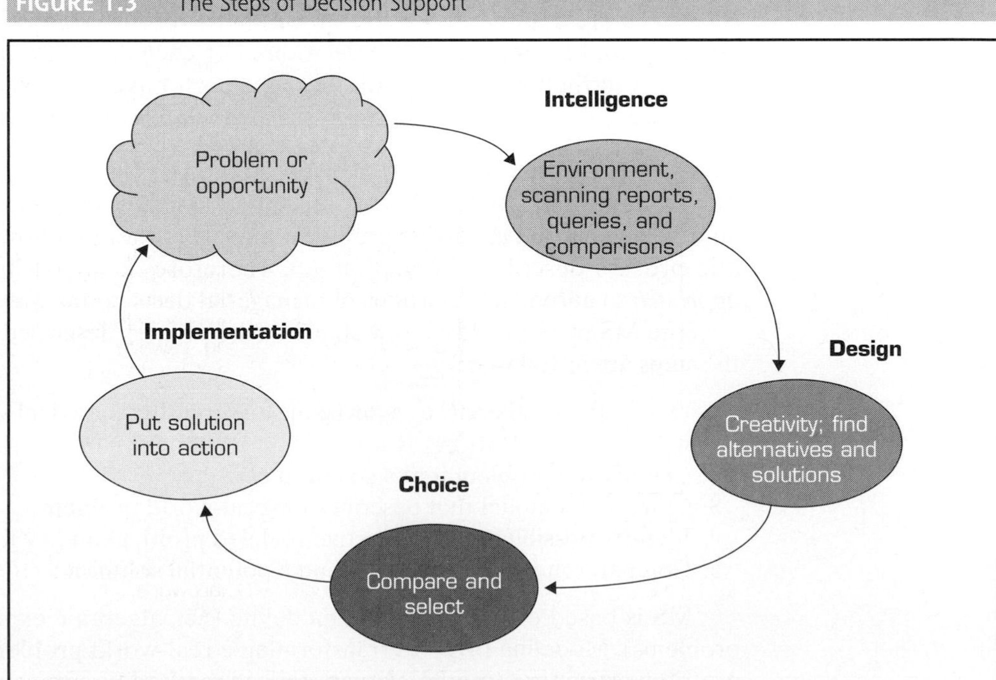

Types of Control

The second half of the Gorry and Scott-Morton framework (refer to Figure 1.2) is based on Anthony's (1965) taxonomy, which defines three broad categories that encompass all managerial activities: *strategic planning*, which involves defining long-range goals and policies for resource allocation; *management control*, the acquisition and efficient use of resources in the accomplishment of organizational goals; and *operational control*, the efficient and effective execution of specific tasks.

The Decision Support Matrix

Anthony's and Simon's taxonomies are combined in the nine-cell decision support matrix shown in Figure 1.2. The initial purpose of this matrix was to suggest different types of computerized support to different cells in the matrix. Gorry and Scott-Morton suggested, for example, that for *semistructured decisions* and *unstructured decisions*, conventional management information systems (MIS) and management science (MS) tools are insufficient. Human intellect and a different approach to computer technologies are necessary. They proposed the use of a supportive information system, which they called a DSS.

Note that the more structured and operational control-oriented tasks (such as those in cells 1, 2, and 4) are performed by low-level managers, whereas the tasks in cells 6, 8, and 9 are the responsibility of top executives or highly trained specialists.

COMPUTER SUPPORT FOR STRUCTURED DECISIONS

Computers have supported structured and some semistructured decisions, especially those that involve operational and managerial control, since the 1960s. Operational and managerial control decisions are made in all functional areas, especially in finance and production (i.e., operations) management.

Structured problems, which are encountered repeatedly, have a high level of structure. It is therefore possible to abstract, analyze, and classify them into specific categories. For example, a make-or-buy decision is one category. Other examples of categories are capital budgeting, allocation of resources, distribution, procurement, planning, and inventory control decisions. For each category of decision, an easy-to-apply prescribed model and solution approach have been developed, generally as quantitative formulas. This approach is called *management science*.

Management Science

The **management science (MS)** approach (also called the **operations research [OR]** approach) says that in solving problems, managers should follow the four-step systematic process described in Section 1.3. Therefore, it is possible to use a *scientific approach* to automating portions of managerial decision making.

The MS process adds a new step 2 to the process described in Section 1.3 so that the steps are as follows:

1. Define the problem (i.e., a decision situation that may deal with some difficulty or with an opportunity).
2. Classify the problem into a standard category.
3. Construct a model that describes the real-world problem.
4. Identify possible solutions to the modeled problem and evaluate the solutions.
5. Compare, choose, and recommend a potential solution to the problem.

MS is based on mathematical modeling (i.e., algebraic expressions that describe problems). Modeling involves transforming a real-world problem into an appropriate prototype structure (model). Computerized methodologies can find solutions to the standard category models quickly and efficiently (see Chapter 4). Some of these, such as linear programming, are deployed directly over the Web.

Automated Decision Making

A relatively new approach to supporting decision making is called **automated decision systems (ADS)**, also known as *decision automation systems* (DAS; see Davenport and Harris, 2005). An ADS is a rule-based system that provides a solution, usually in one functional area (e.g., finance, manufacturing), to a specific repetitive managerial problem, usually in one industry (e.g., to approve or not to approve a request for a loan, to determine the price of an item in a store). Application Case 1.2 shows an example of applying ADS.

Application Case 1.2

Intelligent Price Setting Using an ADS

The pricing of several thousand items at Longs Drug Stores (a U.S. chain of about 400 drug stores; **longs.com**) is a decentralized process. Each store is empowered to price each of the items it carries in the store in order to better compete locally. Pricing was traditionally done manually by modifying the manufacturer's suggested retail price. Similar practices existed in most other retail chains, including supermarkets. Furthermore, when a price war occurred, or when a seasonal sales time arrived, prices were slashed across the board, without regard to demand forecast, profitability, pricing strategy, or price consistency across stores.

Today, price setting is undergoing a radical change, largely as a result of improved IT support systems. Following what airlines and automobile leasing companies have done for years, the retail industry, including Longs Drug Stores and about half of all other U.S. retailers, is introducing *price-optimization* programs. These programs—such as those offered by SAS, Inc. (**sas.com**), and others—combine business rules with some calculating algorithms to form a system that automatically recommends a price for each item in each store. The input data used for these programs are seasonal sales figures, actual sales at each store (in real-time), each product's price–demand curve, competitors' prices, profitability metrics, and more. By using an ADS program, a retailer can identify the most price-sensitive products and can test within seconds what impact a price change would probably have on profit margin (or another desired goal, such as sales volume). Each store can use its own priorities, policies, and constraints to develop and test strategies.

Results of using an ADS at Longs Drugs and at other retail stores that have used similar programs show volume, revenue, and profit increases of between 2 and 10 percent. The software is still fairly expensive, so as of 2006, only large retailers could afford to use it. As more competitors produce similar software, however, it will become less expensive, and more stores will use it. Consumers will be the ultimate beneficiaries because they will pay less for items.

Sources: Compiled from A. Cortese, "The Power of Optimal Pricing," *Business 2.0,* September 2002; and **sas.com** (accessed March 2006).

ADS appeared initially in the airline industry, where they were called *revenue* (or *yield*) *management* (or revenue optimization) systems. Airlines attempted to use these systems to dynamically price their tickets depending on actual demand. Today, many service industries use similar pricing models. In contrast with MS, which provides a model-based solution to generic structured problems (e.g., resource allocation, inventory level determination), ADS provide rule-based solutions. The following are examples of business rules: "If only 70 percent of the seats on a flight from Los Angeles to New York are sold three days prior to departure, offer a discount of x percent to nonbusiness travelers," "If an applicant owns a house and makes over $100,000 a year, offer a $10,000 credit line," and "If an item costs more than $2,000, and if your company buys it only once a year, the purchasing agent does not need special approval." Such rules, which are based on experience or derived through statistical analysis (see Chapter 13), can be combined with mathematical models to form solutions that can be automatically and instantly applied to problems (e.g., "Based on the information provided and subject to verification, you will be admitted to our university"), or they can be provided to a human, who will make the final decision (see Figure 1.4). ADS attempt to automate highly repetitive decisions (in order to justify the computerization cost), based on business rules. ADS are mostly suitable for frontline employees who can see the customer information online and frequently must make quick decisions. For further information on ADS, see Chapters 6 and 16, and also see Davenport and Harris (2005).

COMPUTER SUPPORT FOR UNSTRUCTURED DECISIONS

Unstructured problems can be only partially supported by standard computerized quantitative methods. It is usually necessary to develop customized solutions. However, such solutions may require certain expertise that can sometimes be provided by intelligent systems (see Chapters 12-14). Intuition and judgment may play a large role in this type of decisions, as may computerized communication and collaboration technologies (see Chapter 10), as well as knowledge management (see Chapter 11).

COMPUTER SUPPORT FOR SEMISTRUCTURED PROBLEMS

Solving semistructured problems may involve a combination of standard solution procedures and human judgment. MS can provide models for the portion of a decision-making problem that is structured. For the unstructured portion, a DSS can improve the quality of the information on which the decision is based by providing, for example, not only a single solution but also a range of alternative solutions, along with their potential impacts. These capabilities help managers to better understand the nature of problems and thus to make better decisions.

FIGURE 1.4 Automated Decision-Making Framework

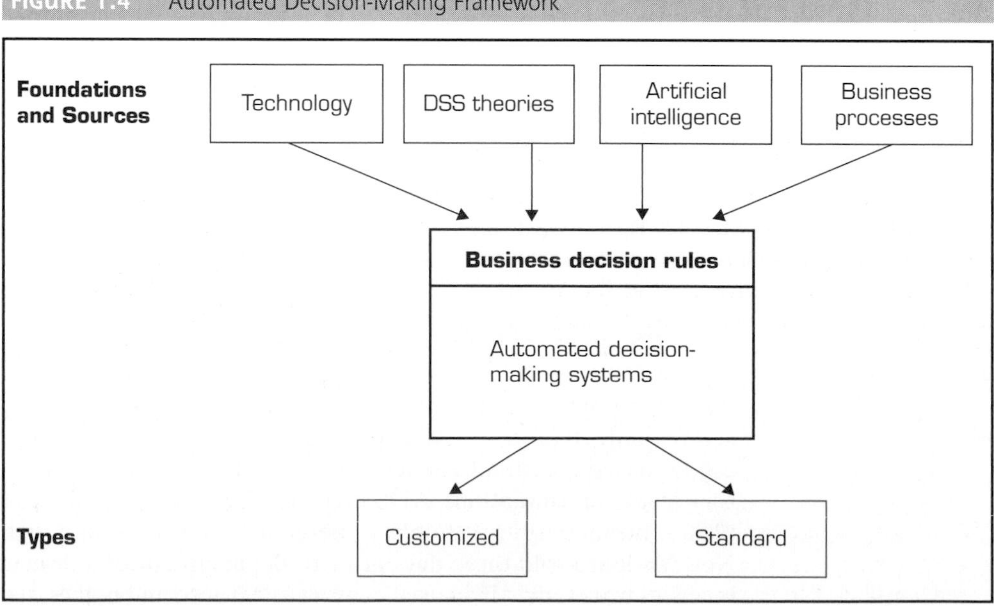

In Chapter 2, we provide a detailed description of how decisions are supported during the major phases of decision making: intelligence, design, choice, and implementation.

THE BENEFITS OF COMPUTERIZED DECISION SUPPORT

The following are some of the main reasons major corporations have developed large-scale computerized decision support:

- Companies work in an unstable or rapidly changing economy.
- The company has difficulty tracking its numerous business operations.
- Competition—especially global competition—has increased.
- E-commerce is changing the ways business is done.
- Existing information systems do not fully support decision making.
- The company's information systems department is too busy to address all of management's inquiries.
- The company needs a special analysis of profitability and efficiency.
- Accurate information is needed.
- Computerized support is viewed as an organizational winner.
- New information is needed.
- Management mandates computerized decision support.
- Higher decision quality is needed.
- The company desires improved communication.
- The company wants improved customer and employee satisfaction.
- Timely information is needed.
- The company wants to reduce costs.
- The company wants to see improved employee productivity.

For an example of how Hallmark Cards is supporting several strategic and operational decisions, see Application Case 1.3.

Application Case 1.3

Decision Support at Hallmark for Better Strategy and Performance

Hallmark Cards exceeds $4 billion a year in sales in more than 42,000 retail outlets across the United States. The company's challenge is to maintain its lead in the competitive greeting card and gift industry. To accomplish this, the company needs to make decisions such as the following:

- Which of more than 40,000 different items to display in each store, when, and how many of each item.
- How to improve item inventory along the supply chain.
- How to reduce production cost.
- How to decide on major new initiatives, such as the launching of the Expressions from Hallmark brand.
- How to design new cards and which design promotes the highest number of sales.
- How to decide on advertising and promotions.
- How to conduct strategic planning.

To make such decisions, Hallmark managers need to have a clear picture of what is going on in the marketplace. They need to analyze sales data by store, by customer segment, by holiday, and so on. The company must be able to understand sales trends and to predict relationships between stores' displays and sales at given locations and times.

To support the decisions, some of which are made by 40,000 store managers, Hallmark Cards is using a computerized decision-making system from MicroStrategy, Inc. (**microstrategy.com**). The system involves BI software, a data warehouse, data mining, and a diversified collection of business analytics tools. In addition to the BI system, some decisions, especially one-time strategic decisions, are supported by MicroStrategy's DSS software.

The Hallmark system allows managers to make more than 1,000 ad hoc queries per week, and it provides faster turnaround of reports on actionable business trends. In addition, product testing time has been reduced through faster analysis of point-of-sale (POS) terminals, helping to eliminate items that are unprofitable or that are less profitable than others. A promotional analysis has been improved, thanks to faster response time (and the resultant improvement recommendations). All this enables more strategically targeted promotion activities.

Sources: Compiled from MicroStrategy, "Success Story: Hallmark Cards, Inc.," **microstrategy.com/Customers/Successes/Hallmark.asp** (accessed March 2006); and TDWI.org, "From Small Pieces to the Big Picture: Hallmark Cards Creates a Flexible IT Infrastructure," *What Works*, Vol. 5, May 1998, **tdwi.org/research/display.aspx?ID=5552** (accessed March 2006).

Another reason for developing managerial computerized decision support is that many managers have low levels of computer and Web literacy. Most managers are not programmers, but they need access to data in an understandable format, and they need to be able to easily manipulate data in meaningful ways. In the following sections, we explore how this is done.

Section 1.5 Review Questions

1. What are structured, unstructured, and semistructured decisions? Provide two examples of each.
2. Define *operational control*, *managerial control*, and *strategic planning*. Provide two examples of each.
3. What are the nine cells of the decision framework? Explain what each is for.
4. How can computers provide support for making structured decisions?
5. Define *automated decision systems (ADS)*.
6. How can computers provide support to semistructured and unstructured decisions?
7. What are some of the drivers and benefits of computerized decision support?

1.6 THE CONCEPT OF DECISION SUPPORT SYSTEMS (DSS)

In the early 1970s, Scott-Morton first articulated the major concepts of DSS. He defined **decision support systems (DSS)** as "interactive computer-based systems, which help decision makers utilize *data* and *models* to solve unstructured problems" (Gorry and Scott-Morton, 1971). The following is another classic DSS definition, provided by Keen and Scott-Morton (1978):

> Decision support systems couple the intellectual resources of individuals with the capabilities of the computer to improve the quality of decisions. It is a computer-based support system for management decision makers who deal with semistructured problems.

Note that the term *decision support system*, like *management information system* (MIS) and other terms in the field of IT, is a content-free expression (i.e., it means different things to different people). Therefore, there is no universally accepted definition of DSS. (We present additional definitions in Chapter 3.) Actually, DSS can be viewed as a *conceptual methodology*—that is, a broad, umbrella term. However, some view DSS as a narrower, specific decision support application.

DSS AS AN UMBRELLA TERM

The term *DSS* can be used as an umbrella term to describe any computerized system that supports decision making in an organization. An organization may have a knowledge management system to guide all its personnel in their problem solving. I may have separate support systems for marketing, finance, and accounting; a supply-chain management (SCM) system for production; and several expert systems for product repair diagnostics and help desks. DSS encompasses them all.

Application Case 1.4 demonstrates some of the major characteristics of the DSS framework. The problem to be solved was unstructured, but the initial analysis was based on the decision maker's structured definition of the situation, using an MS approach. Then the executive vice president, using his experience, judgment, and intuition, felt that the model should be scrutinized. The initial model, although mathematically correct, was incomplete. The DSS provided a quick what-if analysis (see Chapter 4). Furthermore, the DSS was flexible and responsive enough to allow managerial intuition and judgment to be incorporated into the analysis.

Application Case 1.4

The Houston Minerals Case

Houston Minerals Corporation was interested in a proposed joint venture with a petrochemical company to develop a chemical plant. The Houston executive vice president who was responsible for the decision wanted an analysis of the risks involved in the areas of supplies, demands, and prices. Bob Sampson, manager of planning and administration, and his staff built a DSS in a few days, using a specialized planning language. The results strongly suggested that the project should be accepted.

Then came the real test of the DSS. Although the executive vice president accepted the validity and value of the results, he was worried about the project's downside risk: the chance of a catastrophic outcome. As Sampson tells it, he said something like this: "I know how much work you have already done, and I am ninety-nine percent confident with it. However, I would like to see this in a different light. I know we are short of time, but we have to get back to our partners with our yes or no decision quickly."

Sampson replied that the executive could have the risk analysis he needed in less than an hour. He continued, "Within twenty minutes, there in the executive boardroom, we were reviewing the results of executives' 'what-if?' questions. The results led to the eventual dismissal of the project, which we otherwise would probably have accepted."

Source: Based on information provided by Comshare, Inc. (now part of Geac Computer Corporation, Ltd., a Golden Gate Capital Company).

How can a thorough risk analysis, like the one in Application Case 1.4, be performed so quickly? How can the judgment factors be elicited, quantified, and worked into a model? How can the results be presented meaningfully and convincingly to the executive? What are what-if questions? How can the Web be used to access and integrate appropriate data and models? We provide answers to these questions in Chapters 3 and 4. The DSS concepts introduced in Chapter 3 provide considerable insights to software vendors that develop decision support tools, to builders that construct specific decision support applications, and to users.

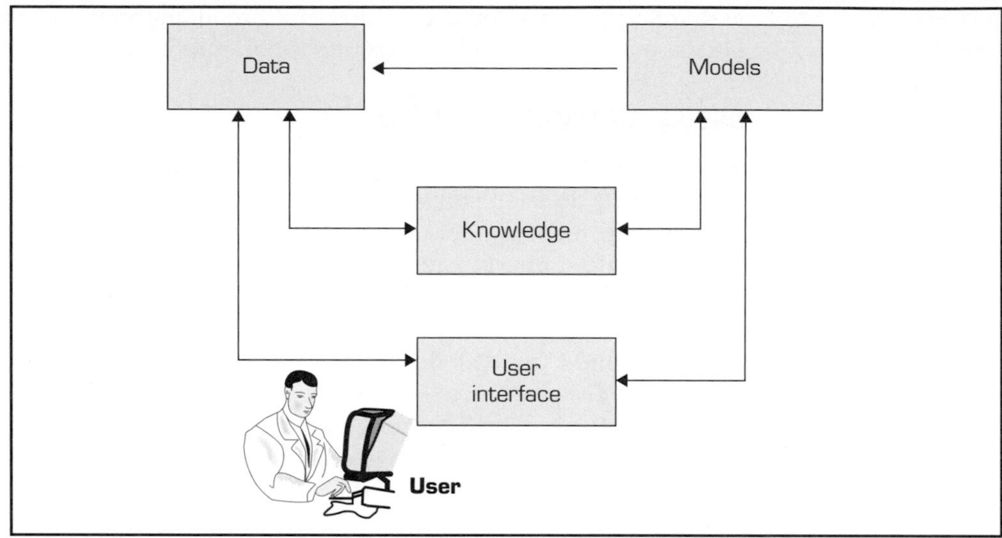

FIGURE 1.5 High-Level Architecture of a DSS

DSS As A Specific Application

While *DSS* usually refers to the umbrella term, some use it in a narrower scope, referring to a process for building customized applications for unstructured or semistructured problems, using the umbrella methodology and concepts. Others use the term *DSS* to refer to the DSS application itself.

The Architecture of DSS

The DSS methodology recognizes the need for data to solve problems. These data can come from many sources, including the Web (see Chapter 5). Every problem that has to be solved and every opportunity or strategy to be analyzed requires some data. Data are the first component of the DSS architecture (see Figure 1.5). Data related to a specific situation are manipulated by using models (see Chapter 2). These models, which are the second component of the DSS architecture, can be standard (e.g., an Excel function) or customized. Some systems have a knowledge (or intelligence) component. This is the third component of the DSS architecture. Users are the vital fourth component of the architecture. Interfacing with the system via a user interface is the fifth component of the DSS architecture.

When creating a DSS, it is important to plan the system and then purchase (or build) the components and "glue" them together. In many DSS, the components are standards and can be purchased. But in other situations, especially unstructured ones, it is necessary to custom build some or all of the components (see Chapter 15). The details of the major components are provided in Chapter 3.

Types Of DSS

There are many types of DSS, with different objectives. The two major types are the *model-oriented DSS*, in which quantitative models are used to generate a recommended solution to a problem, and *data-oriented DSS*, which support ad hoc reporting and queries. For details and other types, see Chapter 3 and the Special Interest Group on Decision Support, Knowledge and Data Management Systems (SIGDSS) Web site, at **sigs.aisnet.org/sigdss**.

CONCLUDING REMARKS

In the early days of DSS, managers let their staff do some supportive analysis by using DSS tools. As PC technology advanced, a new generation of managers evolved—one that was comfortable with computing and knew that technology can directly help them make intelligent business decisions faster. During the 1990s, purchases of commercialized decision support tools grew steadily, with revenues reaching into the low billions of dollars, according to an IDC report from that period (reported in DSStar, 1998). New tools such as OLAP, data warehousing, data mining, and intelligent systems, delivered via Web technology, added promised capabilities and easy access to tools, models, and data for computer-aided decision making. These tools started to appear under the names BI and *business analytics* in the mid-1990s (see Section 1.7). The overall results of using a DSS application can be impressive, as indicated by the Atlantic Electric Company case described in Application Case 1.5.

Application Case 1.5

Helping Atlantic Electric Company Survive in the Deregulated Marketplace

Atlantic Electric Company of New Jersey was losing the monopoly it had once held. Some of its old clients were already buying electricity from a new, unregulated type of competitor: an independent co-generator that generated its own electricity and sold its surplus capacity to electricity-using companies at low prices. The competitor picked up especially the easy-to-serve commercial accounts. Atlantic Electric Company was even in danger of losing its residential customer base because the local regulatory commission was about to rule that those customers would be better served by another utility.

To survive, Atlantic Electric had to become the least expensive provider in its territory. One way to do this was to provide employees with the information they needed to make more up-to-date and accurate business decisions. The old information technology included a mainframe and a corporate network for mainframe access. However, this system was unable to meet the new challenge. It was necessary to develop user applications, in a familiar format, and to do so rapidly and with minimum cost. This required a PC-based DSS, run on the corporate intranet.

The following are some of the DSS applications Atlantic Electric developed:

- A DSS for fuel-purchasing decisions
- A DSS for customized rates, based on a database for customers and their electricity usage patterns
- A DSS for substation design and transmission
- A cash-management DSS for the finance department

The implementation of these and other decision support applications helped the company survive and successfully compete in its field.

Sources: Compiled from 2000–2003 press releases from the Atlantic Electric Company.

Today, the term *DSS* serves mainly as an umbrella for convening groups of researchers interested in studies related to computer support for decision making (e.g., SIGDSS; **sigs.aisnet.org/sigdss**). It is also used as the name of the leading journal in the field, as well as in the title of academic courses. On the other hand, the term *DSS* is not used much today by vendors who develop managerial decision support tools. Vendors seem to prefer buzzwords or new terms that describe the products more precisely than the term *DSS*. The most popular term used in the industry today in *business intelligence*, the topic we present next.

Section 1.6 Review Questions

1. Provide two definitions of *DSS*.
2. Describe *DSS* as an umbrella term.
3. Describe the architecture of DSS.
4. How is the term *DSS* used in the academic world?

1.7 A FRAMEWORK FOR BUSINESS INTELLIGENCE (BI)

The decision support concepts presented in Sections 1.5 and 1.6 have been implemented incrementally, under different names, by many vendors that have created tools and methodologies for decision support. By 2006, the major *commercial* products and services appeared under the umbrella term *BI*, as used in the Toyota TLS opening vignette.

CHARACTERISTICS OF TOYOTA'S SYSTEM

As you may recall from the opening vignette, Toyota TLS's BI system was driven by the following:

- Too much directionless data, full of errors
- Strong competition in the automotive industry, mostly from Honda
- Problems of communication and coordination along the supply chain
- Departments' inability to share data in a timely manner
- Managers' inability to get information they needed for decision making

Toyota's systems included the following:

- A data warehouse with historical data
- Tools for conducting analysis and data manipulation
- A graphical user interface (i.e., a dashboard), mainly for top managers

As the TLS case indicates, the use of BI solved the company's problems and was an overwhelming success. Let's explore BI and see why it is such a successful technology.

DEFINITIONS OF BI

Business intelligence (BI) is an umbrella term that combines architectures, tools, databases, analytical tools, applications, and methodologies (see Raisinghani, 2004). It is, like DSS, a content-free expression, so it means different things to different people. Part of the confusion about BI lies in the flurry of acronyms and buzzwords that are associated with BI (e.g., business performance management [BPM]). BI's major objective is to enable interactive access (sometimes in real-time) to data, to enable manipulation of data, and to give business managers and analysts the ability to conduct appropriate analysis. By analyzing historical and current data, situations, and performances, decision makers get valuable insights that enable them to make more informed and better decisions (see Zaman, 2005). The process of BI is based on the *transformation* of data to information, then to decisions, and finally to actions. (Details are provided in Chapters 5–7.)

A BRIEF HISTORY OF BI

The term *BI* was coined by the Gartner Group in the mid-1990s. However, the concept is much older; it has its roots in the MIS reporting systems of the 1970s. During that period, reporting systems were static, two dimensional, and had no analytical capabilities. In the early 1980s, the concept of *executive information systems (EIS)* emerged. This concept expanded the computerized support to top-level managers and executives. Some of the capabilities introduced were dynamic multidimensional (ad hoc or on-demand) reporting, forecasting and prediction, trend analysis, drill-down to details, status access, and critical success factors (see Chapter 6). These features appeared in dozens of commercial products until the mid-1990s. Then the same capabilities and some new ones appeared under the name BI. Today, a good BI-based enterprise information system contains all the information executives need. So, the original concept of EIS was transformed into BI. By 2005, BI systems started to include *artificial intelligence* capabilities as well as powerful analytical capabilities. Figure 1.6 illustrates the various tools and techniques that may be included in a BI system. It illustrates the evolution of BI as well. The tools shown in Figure 1.6 provide the capabilities of BI. The most sophisticated BI products include most of these capabilities; others specialize in only some of them. For further details, see Zaman (2005) and Raisinghani (2004).

THE ARCHITECTURE OF BI

As discussed in the opening vignette, a BI system has four major components: a *data warehouse*, with its source data; *business analytics*, a collection of tools for manipulating, mining, and analyzing the data in the data warehouse; *business performance management (BPM)* for monitoring and analyzing performance; and a *user interface* (e.g., a dashboard). The relationship among these components is illustrated in Figure 1.7. For details see Chapter 5–8.

FIGURE 1.6 Evolution of BI

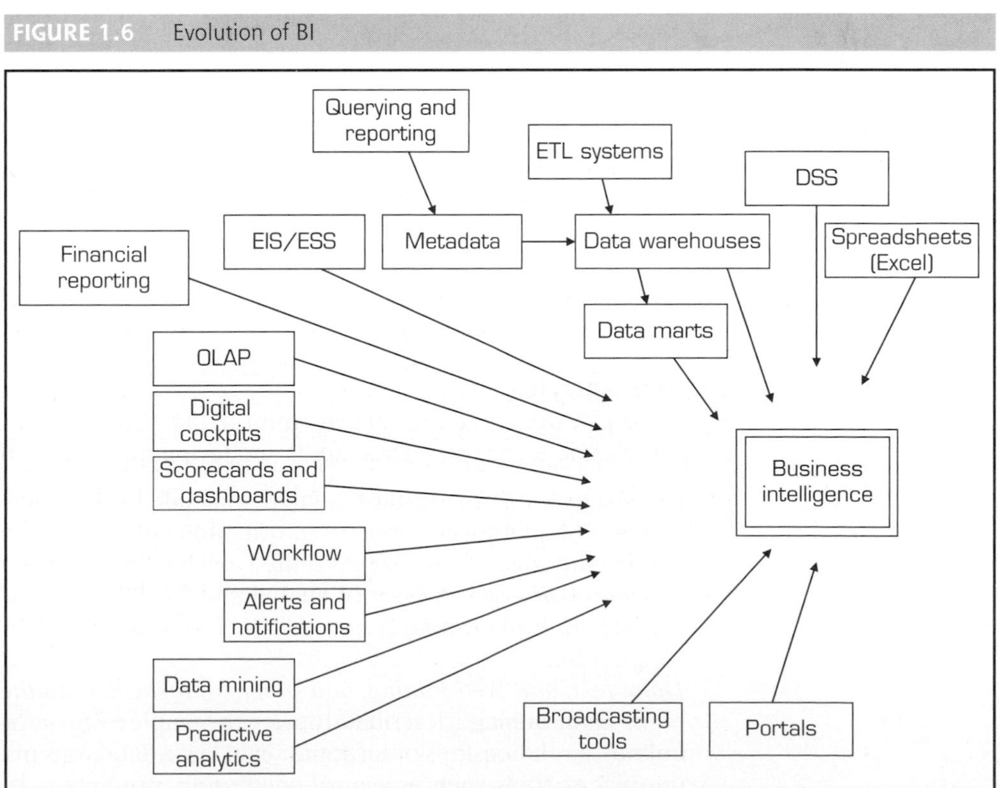

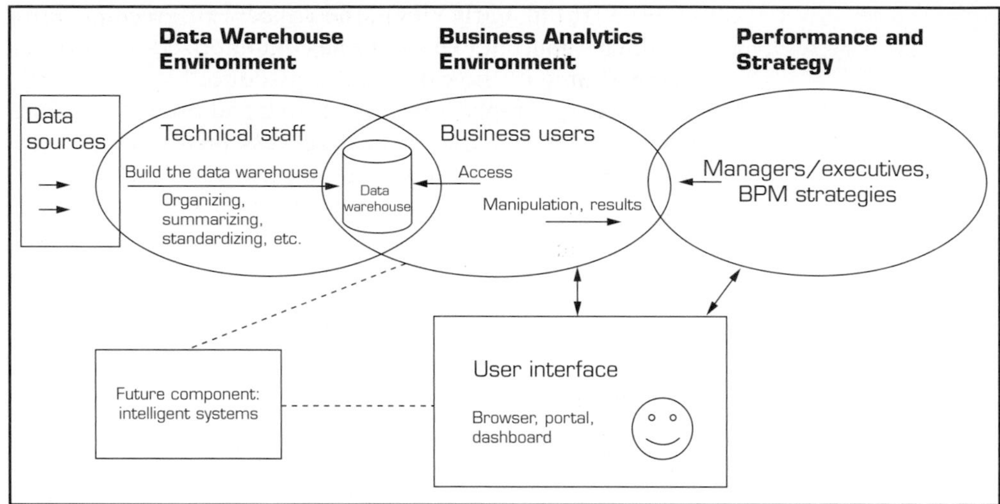

FIGURE 1.7 A High-Level Architecture of BI

Source: Based on W. Eckerson, *Smart Companies in the 21st Century: The Secrets of Creating Successful Business Intelligent Solutions*. The Data Warehousing Institute, Seattle, WA, 2003, p. 32, Illustration 5.

Notice that the data warehousing environment is mainly the responsibility of technical staff, while the analytical environment (also known as *business analytics*) is the realm of business users. Any user can connect to the system via the user interface, such as a browser, and top managers may use the BPM component and also a dashboard.

Some business analytics and user interface tools are introduced briefly in Section 1.9 and in Chapter 6. However, one set of tools, *intelligent systems* (see Chapters 12–14), can be viewed as a futuristic component of BI. According to Zaman (2005), intelligent systems may cause the field's name to be changed to *artificial business intelligence*.

Data Warehousing

The data warehouse and its variants are the cornerstone of any medium-to-large BI system. Originally, the data warehouse included only historical data that were organized and summarized, so end users could easily view or manipulate data and information. Today, some data warehouses include current data as well, so they can provide real-time decision support (see Chapter 5).

Business Analytics

End users can work with the data and information in a data warehouse by using a variety of tools and techniques. These tools and techniques fit into three categories:

1. *Reports and queries.* Business analytics include both static and dynamic reporting, all types of queries, discovery of information, multidimensional view, drill-down to details, and so on. These are presented in Chapter 6.
2. *Advanced analytics.* Advanced analytics include many statistical, financial, mathematical, and other models that are used in analyzing data and information (see Chapter 6).
3. *Data, text, and Web mining, and other sophisticated mathematical and statistical tools.* **Data mining** (described further in Chapter 7) is a process of searching for unknown relationships or information in large databases or data warehouses, using intelligent tools such as *neural computing*, predictive analytics techniques, or

advanced statistical methods (see Chapter 8). For an application in customer relationship management, see Online File W1.1.3. As discussed further in Chapter 7, mining can be done on Web data as well. Two examples of useful applications of data mining follow:

Example 1

National Australia Bank uses data mining to aid its predictive marketing. The tools are used to extract and analyze data stored in the bank's Oracle database. Specific applications focus on assessing how competitors' initiatives are affecting the bank's bottom line. The data mining tools are used to generate market analysis models from historical data. The bank considers initiatives to be crucial to maintaining an edge in the increasingly competitive financial services marketplace.

Example 2

FAI Insurance Group uses its data mining to reassess the relationship between historical risk from insurance policies and the pricing structure used by its underwriters. The data analysis capabilities allow FAI to better serve its customers by more accurately assessing the insurance risk associated with a customer request. Through the use of neural networks and linear statistics, the analysts comb the data for trends and relationships.

Business Performance Management

Business performance management (BPM), which is also referred to as **corporate performance management (CPM),** is an emerging portfolio of applications and methodology that contains evolving BI architecture and tools in its core (see Hyperion Solution Corporation, 2004). BPM extends the monitoring, measuring, and comparing of sales, profit, cost, profitability, and other performance indicators by introducing the concept of management and feedback. It embraces processes such as planning and forecasting as core tenets of a business strategy. In contrast with the traditional DSS, EIS, and BI, which support the bottom-up extraction of information from data, BPM provides a top-down enforcement of corporate-wide strategy. BPM is the topic of Chapter 9 and is usually combined with the *balanced scorecard methodology* and dashboards.

The User Interface: Dashboards and Other Information Broadcasting Tools

Dashboards (which resemble automobile dashboards) provide a comprehensive visual view of corporate performance measures (also known as key performance indicators), trends, and exceptions. They integrate information from multiple business areas. Dashboards present graphs that show actual performance compared to desired metrics; thus, a dashboard presents an at-a-glance view of the health of the organization. In addition to dashboards, other tools that broadcast information are corporate portals (see Chapter 17), digital cockpits, and other visualization tools (see Chapter 6). Many visualization tools, ranging from multidimensional cube presentation to virtual reality, are integral parts of BI systems. Recall that BI emerged from EIS, so many visual aids for executives were transformed to BI software (see Chapter 6). Also, technologies such as geographical information systems (GIS) play an increasing role in decision support.

STYLES OF BI

The architecture of BI depends on its applications. MicroStrategy Corp. distinguishes five styles of BI and offers special tools for each. The five styles are report delivery and alerting; enterprise reporting (using dashboards and scorecards); cube analysis (also

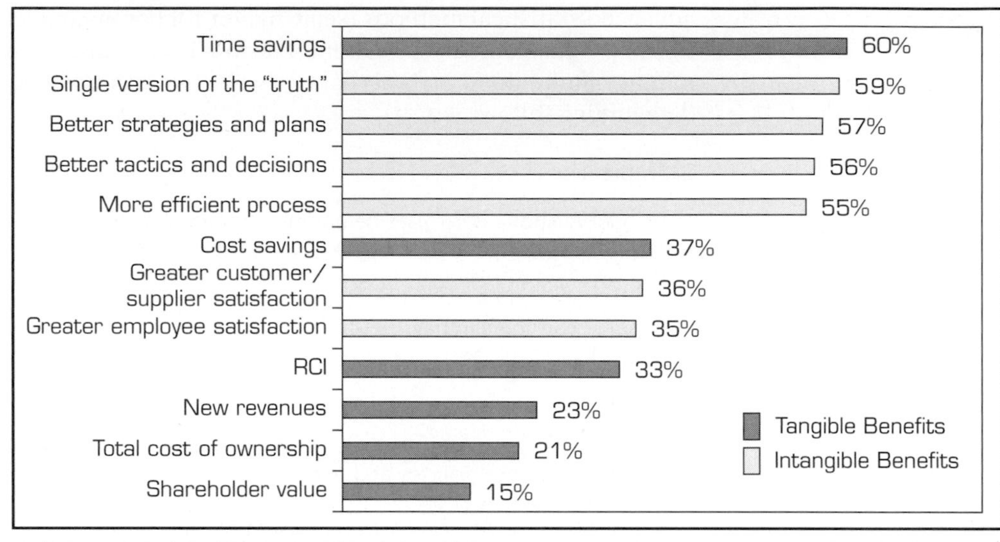

FIGURE 1.8 Benefits of BI

Source: Eckerson (2003)

known as slice-and-dice analysis); ad-hoc queries; and statistics and data mining. For further details, see Chapters 6 and 7, as well as **microstrategy.com**.

THE BENEFITS OF BI

As illustrated by the Toyota TLS case, the major benefit of BI to a company is the ability to provide accurate information when needed, including a real-time view of the corporate performance and its parts. Such information is a must for all types of decisions, for strategic planning, and even for survival (refer to Application Case 1.5). Eckerson (2003) reported the results of a survey of 510 corporations that indicates the benefits as viewed by the participants (see Figure 1.8).

Thompson (2004) reported the following to be the major benefits of BI, based on the results of a survey:

- Faster, more accurate reporting (81 percent)
- Improved decision making (78 percent)
- Improved customer service (56 percent)
- Increased revenue (49 percent)

Notice that many of the benefits of BI are *intangible*. This is why, according to Eckerson (2003), so many executives *do not* insist on a rigorous cost-justification for BI projects (see the detailed discussion in Chapter 15).

Thompson (2004) also noted that the most common application areas of BI are general reporting, sales and marketing analysis, planning and forecasting, financial consolidation, statutory reporting, budgeting, and profitability analysis. An interesting data mining application using *predictive analytics* tools (discussed further in Chapters 6 and 7) is illustrated in Application Case 1.6.

Application Case 1.6

Predictive Analytics Helps Texas Collect Taxes

Tax gaps exist between taxes owed and the amount collected in many public entities. The state of Texas is no exception. To overcome the problems, tax collectors use audits, which are expensive and time-consuming to conduct. Also, many audits are unproductive, resulting in little or no tax recovery. In order to make better decisions on whom to audit (and thus increase the percentage of productive audits), the state of Texas uses predictive analytics.

Millions of records are stored in the state's data warehouse. Using data mining–based software from **spss.com**, Texas can cross-match millions of records to identify promising leads. Specifically, the system has helped identify thousands of businesses that were operating in the state without complying with the tax obligations. Also, it has helped field auditors adopt better audit target selections. When the employees gained confidence in the program, they started to use it extensively, saving over $150 million per year.

Sources: Compiled from L. Gates, "State of Texas Recovers $400 Million Through Predictive Analytics," *ADTmag.com*, May 26, 2005, **adtmag.com/article.asp?id=11214** (accessed March 2006); and "SPSS Predictive Analytics Helps Texas Recover $400 Million in Unpaid Taxes," *Business Intelligence Network*, May 16, 2005. **b-eye-network.com/view/868** (accessed March 2006).

THE DSS–BI CONNECTION

By now, you should be able to see some of the similarities and differences between DSS and BI. First, their architectures are very similar because BI evolved from DSS. However, BI implies the use of a data warehouse, whereas DSS may or may not have such a feature. BI is therefore more appropriate for large organizations (because data warehouses are expensive to build and maintain), but DSS can be appropriate to any type of organization.

Second, most DSS are constructed to *directly* support specific decision making. BI systems, in general, are geared to provide accurate and timely information, and they support decision support *indirectly*. This situation is changing, however, as more and more decision support tools are being added to BI software packages.

Third, BI has an executive and strategy orientation, especially in its BPM and dashboard components. DSS, on the other hand, is oriented toward analysts.

Fourth, most BI systems are constructed with commercially available tools and components that are fitted to the needs of organizations. In building DSS, the interest may be in constructing solutions to very unstructured problems. In such situations, more programming (e.g., using tools such as Excel) may be needed to customize the solutions.

Fifth, DSS methodologies and even some tools were developed mostly in the academic world. BI methodologies and tools were developed mostly by software companies. (See Zaman, 2005, for information on how BI has evolved.)

Sixth, many of the tools that BI uses are also considered DSS tools. For example, data mining and predictive analysis are core tools in both areas.

Although some people equate DSS with BI, these systems are not, at the present, the same. It is interesting to note that some people believe that DSS is a part of BI—one of its analytical tools. Others think that BI is a special case of DSS that deals mostly with reporting, communication, and collaboration (a form of data-oriented DSS). Another explanation (Watson, 2005) is that BI is a result of a continuous revolution and, as such, DSS is one of BI's original elements. In this book, we separate DSS from BI. However, we point to the DSS–BI connection frequently.

Management Support Systems (MSS)

Due to the lack of crisp and universal definitions of DSS and BI, some people refer to DSS and BI, as well as their tools either independently or in combination, as **management support systems (MSS)**. MSS is a broad enough concept to be viewed as a technology that supports managerial tasks in general and decision making in particular. In this book, we use *MSS* when the nature of the technology involved is not clear, and we use it interchangeably with the combined term *DSS/BI*.

In addition to the major frameworks of decision support presented so far, we need to look at a new proposed framework—the *work system*—which we present next.

Section 1.7 Review Questions

1. Define *BI*.
2. List and describe the major components of BI.
3. List and describe the major tangible and intangible benefits of BI.
4. What are the major similarities and differences of DSS and BI?
5. Define *MSS*.

1.8 A WORK SYSTEM VIEW OF DECISION SUPPORT

Claiming that the revolutionary DSS agenda is now "ancient history," Alter (2004), a DSS pioneer, suggested a new approach to managerial decision support. Alter dropped the word *systems* from DSS, focusing on *decision support*, which he defines as the use of any plausible computerized or noncomputerized means for improving decision making in a particular repetitive or nonrepetitive business situation in a particular organization.

By adding noncomputerized means, Alter expanded the landscape of decision support to include nontechnical decision-improvement interventions and strategies. To cope with the possibility of a huge field with many disciplines, Alter postulated that decision support may come from the different aspect of *work systems*. He defined a **work system** as a system in which human participants and/or machines perform a business process, using information, technology, and other resources, to produce products and/or services for internal or external customers. A work system operates within a surrounding environment, often using shared infrastructure, and sometimes within a conscious strategy for the organization or work system. Furthermore, Alter postulated that a work system usually has nine elements. Each of these elements can be varied or modified in order to provide better organizational performance, decision quality, or business process efficiency. The following are the nine elements, along with some possible sources of improvements:

1. *Business process.* Variations in the process rationale, sequence of steps, or methods used for performing particular steps
2. *Participants.* Better training, better skills, higher levels of commitment, or better real-time or delayed feedback
3. *Information.* Better information quality, information availability, or information presentation

4. *Technology.* Better data storage and retrieval, models, algorithms, statistical or graphical capabilities, or computer interaction
5. *Product and services.* Better ways to evaluate potential decisions
6. *Customers.* Better ways to involve customers in the decision process and to obtain greater clarity about their needs
7. *Infrastructure.* More effective use of shared infrastructure, which might lead to improvements
8. *Environment.* Better methods for incorporating concerns from the surrounding environment
9. *Strategy.* A fundamentally different operational strategy for the work system

The work system concept is interesting, and it has considerably expanded the field of managerial decision support. Much more research is needed before this concept can be used as a guide to both the academic and practical worlds.

Now that you are familiar with the major frameworks of the field, we can look at its major tools.

Section 1.8 Review Questions

1. What is Alter's definition of *decision support*?
2. Define *work system*.
3. List the nine elements of a work system.
4. Explain how decision making can be improved by changing an element of a work system.

1.9 THE MAJOR TOOLS AND TECHNIQUES OF MANAGERIAL DECISION SUPPORT

How DSS/BI is implemented depends on which tools are used.

THE TOOLS AND TECHNIQUES

A large number of tools and techniques have been developed over the years to support managerial decision making. Some of them appear under different names and definitions. (For a list of tools and demos, see **dmreview.com/rg/resources/demos.cfm.**) The major computerized tool categories are summarized in Table 1.3. A brief description of each major category is provided in Online File W1.1. Full descriptions are provided in other chapters of this book, as shown in Table 1.3.

THE TOOLS–WEB CONNECTION

All these tools are available today either solely as Web-based versions or in both Web-based and non-Web-based formats. The relationships between these tools and the Web can be viewed as a two-way street. We present the potential impacts of the Web on each of the major categories of tools in Online File W1.3. In that file, we also show the potential impact of each tool on Web technologies. In the following chapters, we provide more details on the tools–Web connection.

TABLE 1.3 Computerized Tools for Decision Support

Tool Category	*Tools and Their Acronyms*	*Chapter in the Book*
Data management	Databases and database management system (DBMS)	3, 5
	Extraction, transformation, and load (ETL) systems	5
	Data warehouses (DW), real-time DW, and data marts	5
Reporting status tracking	Online analytical processing (OLAP)	6
	Executive information systems (EIS)	6
Visualization	Geographical information systems (GIS)	6
	Dashboards	9
	Information portals	17
	Multidimensional presentations	6
Business analytics	Optimization	4
	Data mining, Web mining, and text mining	7, 8
	Web analytics	4, 6
Strategy and performance management	Business performance management (BPM)/Corporate performance management (CPM)	9
	Business activity management (BAM)	9
	Dashboards and scorecards	9
Communication and collaboration	Group decision support systems (GDSS)	10
	Group support systems (GSS)	10
	Collaborative information portals and systems	17
Knowledge management	Knowledge management systems (KMS)	11
	Expert locating systems	11
Intelligent systems	Expert systems (ES)	12
	Artificial neural networks (ANN)	8
	Fuzzy logic	13
	Genetic algorithms	13
	Intelligent agents	13
	Automated decision systems (ADS)	6, 12
Enterprise systems	Enterprise resource planning (ERP), customer relationship management (CRM), and supply-chain management (SCM)	17

HYBRID SUPPORT SYSTEMS

The objective of computerized decision support, regardless of its name or nature, is to assist management in solving managerial or organizational problems (and assess opportunities and strategies) faster and better than possible without computers. To attain this objective, a support system may use several of the tools and techniques mentioned in Table 1.3 in what is known as a **hybrid (integrated) support system**. Every type of tool has certain capabilities and limitations. By integrating several tools, we can improve decision support because one tool can provide advantages where another is weak (see Chapter 16).

Machine repair provides a useful example of a hybrid support system. A repair technician diagnoses a problem and identifies the best tools to make the repair. Although only one tool may be sufficient, it is often necessary to use several tools to improve results. Sometimes there may be no standard tools. In such a case, special tools must be developed, such as a ratchet tip at the end of a screwdriver handle, or a screwdriver blade at the end of a ratchet wrench to reach into hard-to-reach places. The managerial decision-making process described in Application Case 1.7 illustrates the combined use of several decision support technologies in solving a single enterprise-wide problem.

Application Case 1.7

United Sugars Corporation Optimizes Production, Distribution, and Inventory Capacity with Different Decision Support Tools

United Sugars Corporation, headquartered in Bloomington, Minnesota, is a grower-owned cooperative that sells and distributes sugar products for its member companies. United has a 25 percent U.S. market share and sales of more than $1 billion annually. When the United States Sugar Corporation in southern Florida joined the cooperative, United Sugars decided to revise its marketing and distribution plans to gain access to new markets and serve existing ones more efficiently. Improvements in managing the supply chain and in the supply chain's design were in order.

A strategic model was developed to identify the minimum-cost solutions for packaging, inventory, and distribution. The company's enterprise resource planning (ERP) system (see Chapter 17) and a legacy database system provided data for several mathematical models (see Chapter 4). This first model contains about 1 million decision variables and more than 250,000 relationships.

A Web-based GIS (see Chapter 6) graphically displays reports and optimal solutions. A map of the United States indicates the locations of plants, warehouses, and customers. Each one is a hotspot that links to additional information about the solutions.

This model is also used to schedule production and distribution. Results are uploaded into the ERP to support operational decisions. The results of the strategic model drive the generation of subsequent models for inventory analysis. These models simulate a variety of inventory situations, through what-if analyses, and help analysts reduce the overall inventory. Results are displayed in a variety of formats in a Web browser.

This hybrid decision support system consists of several optimization and simulation models, an ERP, and Web interfaces.

Sources: Compiled from M.D. Cohen, C.B. Charles, and A.L. Medaglia, "Decision Support with Web-Enabled Software," *Interfaces*, Vol. 31, No. 2, 2001, and "U.S. Sugar in the News," **unitedsugars.com** (accessed July, 2006).

A hybrid approach is often related to a problem-solving approach that uses several tools in different ways, such as the following:

- Use each tool independently to solve different aspects of the problem.
- Use several loosely integrated tools. This mainly involves transferring data from one tool to another for further processing.
- Use several tightly integrated tools. From the user's standpoint, the tool appears as a unified system.

In addition to performing different tasks in the problem-solving process, tools can support each other. For example, an expert system (ES) can enhance the modeling and data management of a DSS. A neural computing system or a group support system (GSS) can support the knowledge acquisition process in building an ES. ES and artificial neural networks play an increasingly important role in enhancing other decision support technologies by making them "smarter." The components of such systems may also include MS, statistics, and a variety of other computer-based tools. For details, see Chapter 16.

EMERGING TECHNOLOGIES AND TECHNOLOGY TRENDS

A number of emerging technologies directly and indirectly influence DSS. As technology advances, the speed of computation increases, leading to greater computational capability, while the physical size of the computer decreases. Every few years, there is a several-factor change in these parameters. Some specific technologies to watch are presented in Online File W1.3.

Section 1.9 Review Questions

1. List the nine major categories of decision support tools.
2. In what ways can the Web facilitate the use of these tools?
3. What is a hybrid system? What are its benefits?

1.10 IMPLEMENTING COMPUTER-BASED MANAGERIAL DECISION SUPPORT SYSTEMS

Now that you have a basic understanding of the need to support managerial decision making with computers and the available frameworks and tools, let's look at some of its major implementation issues.

DEVELOPING OR ACQUIRING SUPPORT SYSTEMS

The inception of the DSS raises the issue of how to build such systems. Initially, such systems were programmed from scratch at a large cost in both dollars and time. It soon became clear that some tools could help. This led to the creation of special decision support programming languages (e.g., IFPS; see Chapter 4) and DSS development generators (e.g., Lotus 1-2-3, Excel). Also, special tools for report generation, queries, presentation, and summarization were developed. Some of them were later incorporated into Excel.

Today, many vendors offer a great number of tools, some of which are completely preprogrammed (called *shells*); all you have to do is insert your numbers. These tools can be purchased or leased. (For a list of product demos, see **dmreview.com/rg/resources/demos.**) As a matter of fact, almost all BI systems are constructed using shells, frequently by outsourced vendors. The issue that companies face is what alternative to select: purchase, lease, or build? These options are discussed in Chapter 15. One of the major ways to make the decision is to use justification and cost–benefit analysis.

JUSTIFICATION AND COST–BENEFIT ANALYSIS

As the number of potential managerial decision support applications increases, so does the need to justify and prioritize them. This is not an easy task because these applications have a large number of intangible benefits. However, starting in 2003, top managers began insisting on a cost–benefit analysis for any system that cost above a certain level. As you will see in Chapter 15, there are several ways of doing this.

SECURITY AND PROTECTION OF PRIVACY

Security and protection of privacy is an extremely important issue in the development of any computerized system. It is especially important for DSS and BI because these systems contain data that may have strategic value. In addition, the privacy of employees and customers needs to be protected (see Chapter 16).

INTEGRATION OF SYSTEMS AND APPLICATIONS

With the exception of some small applications, all MSS applications must be integrated with other systems, such as databases, legacy systems, enterprise systems (particularly ERP and customer relationship management [CRM]), e-commerce systems (on the sell side and the buy side), and many more. In addition, BI and DSS are usually connected to the Internet and often to information systems of business partners. Furthermore, BI/DSS tools sometimes need to be integrated among themselves to create synergy (see Chapter 16).

The need for integration has pushed software vendors to continuously add capabilities to their products. Customers that buy an all-in-one software package deal with only one vendor and do not have to deal with systems' connectivity. But they may lose the advantage of creating systems composed from the "best-of-breed" components.

THE WEB IN DSS/BI IMPLEMENTATION

As is illustrated throughout this book, many MSS applications involve the use of Web technology such as browsers and search engines. As mentioned earlier in this chapter, the relationship between MSS applications and the Web can be viewed as a two-way street. We provide a detailed discussion about this in every chapter. In addition, in Online File W1.2, we have a table divided into three columns that lists the MSS technologies, the representative potential impacts of the Web on each specific technology, and the potential effect of each specific technology on the Web.

Information Portals and MSS

To ease the implementation of MSS, it is advisable to use visualization aids (see the Toyota TLS case and Chapter 6). Visualization can serve both employees and customers. For an interesting application of an information portal using an interactive dialog, see Online File W1.5.

Section 1.10 Review Questions

1. Describe the issues involved in acquiring or building an MSS application.
2. Why it is difficult to justify decision support applications?
3. What type of integration is needed in implementing MSS?
4. Describe the MSS–Web connection
5. Relate information portals to decision support.

1.11 PLAN OF THE BOOK

The 18 chapters of this book are organized into seven parts, as shown in Figure 1.9.

PART I: DECISION SUPPORT AND BUSINESS INTELLIGENCE

In Chapter 1, we provide an introduction, definitions, and an overview of decision support systems and business intelligence.

PART II: COMPUTERIZED DECISION SUPPORT

Chapter 2 describes the process and methodologies of managerial decision making. Chapter 3 provides an overview of DSS and its major components. Chapter 4 describes the difficult topic of (mathematical) modeling and analysis. It describes

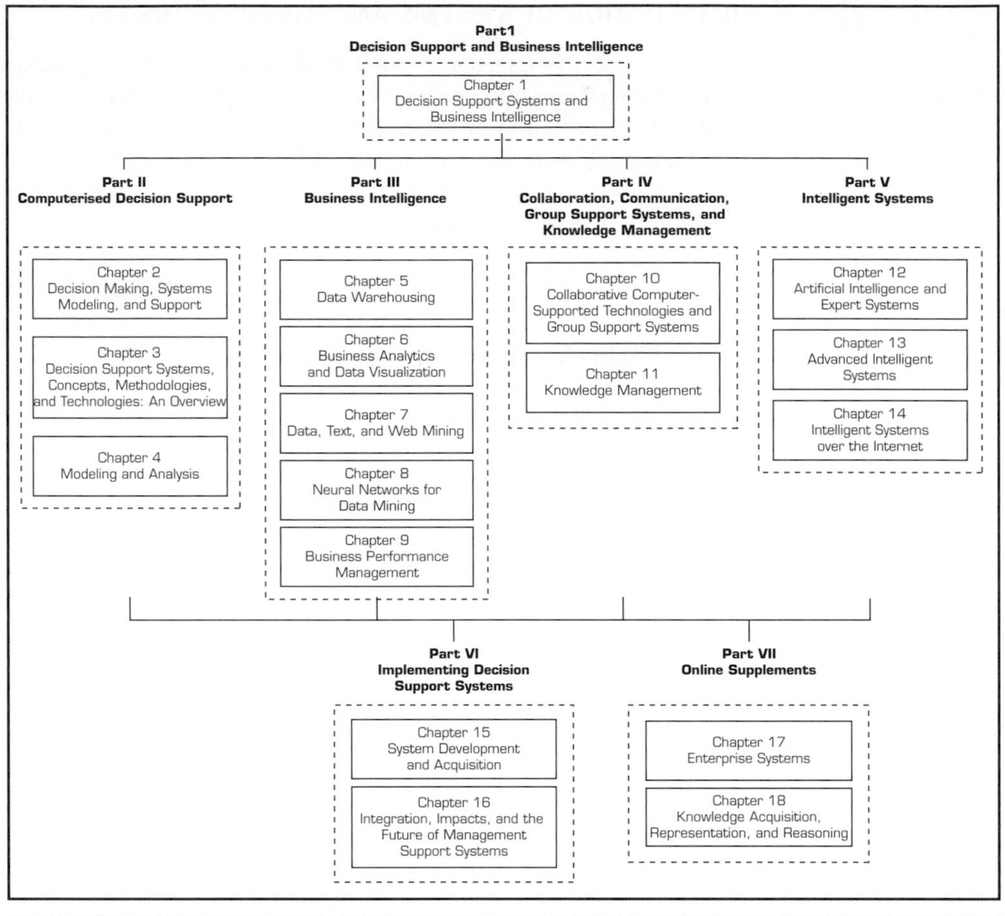

FIGURE 1.9 Plan of the Book

both structured models and modeling tools. It also describes how unstructured problems can be modeled.

PART III: BUSINESS INTELLIGENCE

BI includes several distinct components. First, data warehousing and data marts are the subject of Chapter 5. Then reports and queries, business analytics, and visualization are described in Chapter 6. Chapter 7 presents data, text, and Web mining; Chapter 8 describes neural networks and other data mining techniques; and Chapter 9 covers BPM, dashboards, scorecards, and related topics.

PART IV: COLLABORATION, COMMUNICATION, GROUP SUPPORT SYSTEMS, AND KNOWLEDGE MANAGEMENT

In this part, Chapter 10 deals with the support provided to groups working either in the same room or at different locations, especially via the Web. Chapter 11 is an in-depth discussion of knowledge management (KM) systems, which are enterprise-level support systems that manage the knowledge needed for decision support.

PART V: INTELLIGENT SYSTEMS

The fundamentals of artificial intelligence and ES are the subject of Chapter 12. Advanced intelligent systems, including genetic algorithms, fuzzy logic, and hybrids, are the subjects of Chapter 13. Chapter 14 describes how intelligent systems, including intelligent agents, work over the Internet.

PART VI: IMPLEMENTING DECISION SUPPORT SYSTEMS

Chapter 15 provides a guide to the development or acquisition of various support systems. Finally, Chapter 16 talks about integrating different support tools, the impacts of MSS, and the future of the discipline.

PART VII: ONLINE SUPPLEMENTS

Chapter 17 presents interesting applications of MSS in enterprise systems, such as CRM, ERP, and SCM. Chapter 18 deals with methods of knowledge acquisition and representation, as well as with reasoning approaches.

1.12 RESOURCES, LINKS, AND THE TERADATA UNIVERSITY NETWORK CONNECTION

The use of this chapter and most other chapters in this book can be enhanced by the tools described in the following sections.

RESOURCES AND LINKS

We recommend the following major resources and links:

- The Data Warehousing Institute (**dw-institute.com**)
- *DM Review* (**dmreview.com**)
- The OLAP Report (**olapreport.com**)
- DSS Resources (**dssresources.com**)
- Information Technology Toolbox (**businessintelligence.ittoolbox.com**)
- Business Intelligence Network (**b-eye-network.com**)
- AIS World (**isworld.org**)

CASES

All major MSS vendors (e.g., MicroStrategy, Microsoft, Oracle, IBM, Hyperion, Cognos, Exsys, SAS, Fair Issac, Business Objects, SAP, Information Builders) provide interesting customer success stories. Academic-oriented cases are available at Harvard Business School Case Collection (**hbsp.harvard.edu/b01/en/academic/edu_home.jhtml**), Business Performance Improvement Resource (**bpir.com**), Idea Group Publishing (**idea-group.com**), Ivy League Publishing (**ivylp.com**), ICFAI Center for Management Research (**icmr.icfai.org/casestudies/icmr_case_studies.htm**), KnowledgeStorm (**knowledgestorm.com**), and other sites.

MILLER'S *MIS Cases*

Miller's *MIS Cases* (2005) contains simple cases, using spreadsheet and database exercises that support several of the chapters in this book.

VENDORS, PRODUCTS, AND DEMOS

A comprehensive list of demos is available at **dmreview.com/rg/resources/demos.cfm**.

Information about products, architecture, and software is available at **dsslab.com**.

PERIODICALS

We recommend the following periodicals:

- *Decision Support Systems*
- *CIO Insight* (**cioinsight.com**)
- *Technology Evaluation* (**technologyevaluation.com**)
- *Baseline Magazine* (**baselinemag.com**)
- *Business Intelligence Journal* (**tdwi.org**)
- *Advisor* (**advisor.com**)

ADDITIONAL REFERENCES

Additional selected references are provided in the online files of each chapter. For this chapter, see Online File W1.4.

THE TERADATA UNIVERSITY NETWORK CONNECTION

This book is tightly connected with the free resources provided by Teradata University Network (TUN; see **teradatauniversitynetwork.com** and Online File W1.5 for a description).

The TUN portal is divided into two major parts: one for students and one for faculty. This book is connected to the TUN portal via a special section at the end of each chapter. That section includes appropriate links for the specific chapter, pointing to relevant resources. In addition, we provide hands-on exercises, using software and other material (e.g., cases), at TUN.

THE BOOK'S WEB SITE

This book's Web site, **prenhall.com/turban**, contains supplemental textual material organized as Web chapters that correspond to the printed book's chapters. The topics of these chapters are listed in the online chapter table of contents. The Web site also contains the book's PowerPoint presentations.

Chapter Highlights

- The business environment is becoming complex and is rapidly changing, making decision making more difficult.
- Businesses must respond and adapt to the changing environment rapidly by making faster and better decisions.
- The time frame for making decisions is shrinking, whereas the global nature of decision making is expanding, necessitating the development and use of computerized DSS.
- The rate of computerization is increasing rapidly, and so is its use for managerial decision support.

- Managerial decision making has become complex. Intuition and trial-and-error methods may not be sufficient.
- MSS are technologies designed to support managerial work. They can be used independently or in combination.
- Computerized support for managers is often essential for the survival of an organization.
- An early decision support framework divides decision situations into nine categories, depending on the degree of structuredness and managerial activities. Each category is supported differently.
- Structured repetitive decisions are supported by standard quantitative analysis methods, such as MS, MIS, and rule-based automated decision support.
- DSS use data, models, and sometimes knowledge management to find solutions for semistructured and some unstructured problems.
- Automated decision support is provided today in many industries to find solutions to repetitive decisions (such as item pricing) based on business rules.
- BI methods utilize a central repository called a data warehouse that enables efficient data mining, OLAP, BPM, and data visualization.
- BI architecture includes a data warehouse, business analytics tools used by end users, and a user interface (such as a dashboard).
- Many organizations use BPM systems to monitor performance, compare it to standards and goals, and show it graphically (e.g., using dashboards) to managers and executives.
- Data mining is a tool for discovering information and relationships in a large amount of data.
- All MSS technologies are interactive and can be integrated together and with other computer-based information systems (CBIS) into hybrid support systems.
- Web technology and the Internet, intranets, and extranets play a key role in the development, dissemination, and use of MSS.
- The work system is a new concept in decision support that broadens the field to include noncomputerized methods combined with computerized ones.

Key Terms

- automated decision system (ADS)
- business intelligence (BI)
- business performance management (BPM) (or corporate performance management [CPM])
- cognitive limits
- dashboard
- data mining
- decision support system (DSS)
- hybrid (integrated) support system
- management science (MS) (or operations research [OR])
- management support system (MSS)
- work system

QUESTIONS FOR DISCUSSION

1. Give examples for the content of each cell in Figure 1.2.
2. Survey the literature from the past six months to find one application each for DSS, BI, and intelligent systems. Summarize the applications on one page and submit it with the exact sources.
3. Observe an organization with which you are familiar. List three decisions it makes in each of the following categories: strategic planning, management control (tactical planning), and operational planning and control.
4. Compare and contrast MS with ADS.
5. Describe how hybrid systems might help a manager in decision making.
6. How is e-commerce related to decision support?
7. Why is the role of knowledge management so important for decision support? Discuss an example of how the two can be integrated.
8. Which organizational responses can be considered reactive and which proactive?
9. Discuss how a wireless system can improve decision making.
10. Discuss the importance of ADS.
11. Distinguish BI from DSS.
12. Discuss the difficulties in implementing the concept of work systems in decision support.
13. Discuss the major issues involved in implementing MSS.

Exercises

Teradata Student Network (TSN) and Other Hands-On Exercises

1. Go to **teradatastudentnetwork.com**. Using the registration your instructor provides, log on and learn the content of the site. Prepare a list of all materials available there. You will receive assignments related to this site. Prepare a list of 20 items in the site that you think could be beneficial to you.
2. Enter the TUN site and select "cases, projects and assignments." Then select the case study: "Harrah's High Payoff from Customer Information." Answer the following questions about this case:
   a. What information does the data mining generate?
   b. How is this information helpful to management in decision making? (Be specific.)
   c. List the types of data that are mined.
   d. Is this a DSS or BI application? Why?

   For additional information about Harrah's, see Loveman (2003).
3. Write a 5- to 10-page report describing how your company or a company you are familiar with currently uses computers and information systems, including Web technologies, in decision support. In light of the material in this chapter, describe how a manager could use such support systems if they were readily available. Which ones are available to you and which ones are not?
4. Design a computerized system for a brokerage house that trades securities, conducts research on companies, and provides information and advice to customers (such as "buy," "sell," and "hold"). In your design, clearly distinguish the tools you plan to use. Be sure to discuss input and output information. Assume that the brokerage company is a small one with only 20 branches in four different cities.

Team Assignments and Role-Playing

1. Find information on the proactive use of computers versus transaction processing systems (TPS) to support ad hoc decisions. Each member of the group should choose an application in a different industry (e.g., retail, banking, insurance, food). Be sure to include the impacts of the Web/Internet. Summarize the findings and point out the similarities and differences of the applications. Use as sources companies that employ students, trade magazines, Internet newsgroups, and vendor Web sites. Finally, prepare a class presentation on your findings.
2. Go to **fairisaac.com**, **ilog.com**, and **pega.com**. View the demos at these sites. Prepare a list of ADS by industry and by functional area. Specify what types of decisions are automated.

Internet Exercises

1. Search the Internet for material regarding the work of managers, the need for computerized support, and the role DSS play in providing such support. What kind of references to consulting firms, academic departments, and programs do you find? What major areas are represented? Select five sites that cover one area and report your findings.
2. Explore the public areas of **dssresources.com**. Prepare a list of its major available resources. You might want to refer to this site as you work through the book.
3. Go to **fairisaac.com**, and use the information there to identify five problems in different industries and five problems in different functional areas that can be supported by ADS.
4. Go to **sap.com** and **oracle.com**, and find information on how ERP software helps decision makers. In addition, examine how these software products use Web technology and the Web itself. Write a report about all this.
5. Go to **intelligententerprise.com**. For each topic cited in this chapter, find some interesting developments reported on the site, and prepare a report.
6. Go to **crmondemand.com/**, and review the Siebel's (now an Oracle company) business analytics capabilities. Relate it to improvements in CRM. Write a report about this.
7. Go to **cognos.com** and **businessobjects.com**, and compare the capabilities of the two companies' BI products in a report.
8. Go to **microsoft.com**. Examine its BI offerings.
9. Go to **oracle.com**. Check out its BI offering. How do Oracle's BI offerings relate to the company's ERP software?
10. Go to **microstrategy.com** and find information on the five styles of BI. Prepare a summary table for each style.
11. Go to **hyperion.com** and determine what the company's major products are. Relate these to the support technologies cited in this chapter.

End of Chapter Application Case

Decision Support at a Digital Hospital

Heart disease is the number-one killer in the United States, and in a cardiac crisis, each minute matters. Indiana Heart Hospital (IHH) is a new cardiac hospital that saves life by radically cutting the time it takes to treat a heart attack. In addition, this for-profit hospital is making profits for its investors, using state-of-the-art information and decision support systems.

At IHH, physicians, nurses, administrators, and other employees constantly make decisions. Some decisions must be made very quickly, so the needed data must be in the right time and place in seconds.

IHH is the first wholly digital hospital in the United States. Let's take a look at how decisions are supported there. At the heart of the hospital information system, as of 2005, there were 18 terabytes of data (even more today) stored in a network of IBM Shark storage servers. Note that in contrast with the Toyota TLS data warehouse, which stores only historical data, the Shark server enables the storage of both historical and real-time data. When a patient arrives at the hospital, his or her medical records can be on a screen in 15 seconds, so a quick decision can be made on what treatment or tests the patient needs. The results of any test are immediately added to the patient's medical record. Of the various software used for planning and analysis, especially in the financial area, IHH uses software solutions provided by **mezzia.com**. This software enables improved collaboration, and it provides support for financial and operational decisions. The data and software tools are accessible to all authorized staff. All physicians, for example, carry pocket-size wireless tablet devices for data access, entry, and communication. These digital systems enable physicians to type in and send orders to the pharmacy or to testing departments. All records are digital, including X-ray films. Also, all computer transactions create an audit trail that increases accountability. In addition, having more consistent data to analyze promotes best practices that make the hospital more efficient and patients safer and healthier.

The IHH communications and collaboration system (Centricity, from GE Healthcare) eliminates delays in the supply chain. Doctors and other employees can consult each other, make quicker joint decisions, and locate needed experts (even outside the hospital) quickly. Centricity runs across 60 Compaq servers running Window NT and 600 laptops and other devices. Some data can be accessed by touching screen, to increase speed. In addition, there is a computer next to each patient room. Medications are tracked by more than 100 wireless barcode scanners.

New devices and technologies are added all the time (e.g., sensors for vital sign monitoring). The inputs from such devices go directly to the patient's electronic chart (near the bed) as well as to the medical records. The electronic chart enables nurses to enter patient status and also verifies the output of the automatic vital signs monitoring. Physicians enter data into the system when visiting the patients, so there are no scribbled notes in the hospital. All this enables nurses to stay longer with patients, increasing their safety. The digitization has contributed to a 40 percent reduction in length of stay at the hospital, a 75 percent reduction in medical errors, and a significant increase in the number of patients treated in the hospital.

Sources: Complied from K.M. Nash, "Real-Time E.R.," *Baseline*, May 4, 2005. **baselinemag.com/article2/0,1540,1812777,00.asp** (accessed March 2006); and "Customer Success Story: Indiana Heart Hospital," May 2005, **mezzia.com/tihh_case_study.pdf** (accessed March 2006).

QUESTIONS FOR THE CASE

1. Identify the medical and administrative decisions that the IHH system supports.
2. Explain how the IHH system is able to reduce the time needed to make medical decisions.
3. In your opinion, what administrative decisions that are not cited in the case can the IHH system expedite?
4. Explain why this is a DSS application. Identify its components—the data, models, and user interface cited in the case.
5. What strategic advantage can IHH derive from its digitization?

References

Alter, S. (2004, December). "A Work System View of DSS in Its Fourth Decade." *Decision Support Systems*.

Anthony, R.N. (1965). *Planning and Control Systems: A Framework for Analysis*. Cambridge, MA: Harvard University Graduate School of Business.

Coveney, M., B. Hartlen, D. Ganster, and D. King. (2003). *The Strategy Gap*. Hoboken, NJ: Wiley.

Davenport, T. H., and J. G. Harris. (2005, Summer). "Automated Decision Making Comes of Age." *MIT Sloan Management Review*, Vol. 46, No. 4, pp. 83–89.

DSStar, "Worldwide Analytic Applications Market on Course to Double in Three Years, According to IDC," *Taborcommunications.com*, Vol. 2, No. 48, December 1, 1998.

Eckerson, W. (2003). *Smart Companies in the 21st Century: The Secrets of Creating Successful Business Intelligent Solutions*. Seattle, WA: The Data Warehousing Institute.

Geoffrion, A.M., and R. Krishman. (2001, March/April). "Prospects for Operations Research in the E-business Era." *Interfaces*, Vol. 31, No. 2, pp. 6–36.

Gorry, G.A., and M.S. Scott-Morton. (1971). "A Framework for Management Information Systems." *Sloan Management Review*, Vol. 13, No. 1, pp. 55–70.

Huber, G. (2003). *The Necessary Nature of Future Firms: Attributes of Survivors in a Changing World*. San Francisco: Sage.

Hyperion Solution Corporation. (2004, Summer). "A Strategy for Performance Management." *Business Intelligence Journal*.

Ireland, R.D., and C.C. Miller. (2004, November). "Decision Making and Firm Success." *The Academy of Management Executive*.

Keen, P.G.W., and M.S. Scott-Morton. (1978). *Decision Support Systems: An Organizational Perspective*. Reading, MA: Addison-Wesley.

Loveman, G. (2003, May). "Diamonds in the Data." *Harvard Business Review*.

Miller, M.L. (2005). *MIS Cases*, 3rd ed. Upper Saddle River, NJ: Prentice Hall.

Mintzberg, H.A. (1980). *The Nature of Managerial Work*. Englewood Cliffs, NJ: Prentice Hall.

Mintzberg, H.A. (1993). *The Rise and Fall of Strategic Planning*. New York: The Free Press.

Raisinghani, M. (2004). *Business Intelligence in the Digital Economy*. Hershey, PA: The Idea Group.

Simon, H. (1977). *The New Science of Management Decision*. Englewood Cliffs, NJ: Prentice Hall.

Thompson, O. (2004, October). "Business Intelligence Success, Lessons Learned," **technologyevaluation.com/research/center/BusinessIntelligence/index.asp**.

Watson, H. (2005, Winter). "Sorting Out What's New in Decision Support." *Business Intelligence Journal*.

Zaman M. (2005, January). "Business Intelligence: Its Ins and Outs," **technologyevaluationcenters.com/Search/For/Business%20Intelligence:%20Its%20Ins%20and%20Outs**.

PART

II

Learning Objectives for Part II

- ◆ Understand the conceptual foundations of decision making
- ◆ Understand Simon's four phases of decision making: intelligence, design, choice, and implementation
- ◆ Understand the concept of rationality and its impact on decision making
- ◆ Understand the foundations, definitions, and capabilities of decision support systems (DSS) and business intelligence (BI)
- ◆ Describe DSS components and technology levels
- ◆ Describe the various types of DSS and explain their use
- ◆ Explain the importance of databases and database management
- ◆ Explain the importance of models and model management

In Part II, we concentrate on decision making, the decision support methodology, technology components, and development. Throughout, we highlight the major impacts of the Internet on DSS. Chapter 2 contains an overview of the conceptual foundations of decision making, the reason that all DSS are developed. Chapter 3 provides an overview of DSS: its characteristics, structure, use, and types. Some of the major components of DSS are presented in Chapter 4 (Modeling and Analysis) and Chapter 5 (Data Warehouses and Data Management). Modern DSS and BI systems are presented in Chapters 6 and 7 (Online Analytical Processing [OLAP] and Data Mining).

Decision Making, Systems, Modeling, and Support

Learning Objectives

- Understand the conceptual foundations of decision making
- Understand Simon's four phases of decision making: intelligence, design, choice, and implementation
- Recognize the concepts of rationality and bounded rationality and how they relate to decision making
- Differentiate between the concepts of making a choice and establishing a principle of choice
- Learn how DSS support for decision making can be provided in practice
- Understand the systems approach (described in Online File W2.2)

Our major focus in this book is the support of decision making through computer-based information systems. The purpose of this chapter is to describe the conceptual foundations of decision making and how support is provided. Online, we provide definitions of systems and the systems thinking approach. In addition to the opening vignette, we use the MMS running case (see Online File W2.1) to illustrate the process of decision making in practice. This chapter includes the following sections:

2.1 Opening Vignette: Decision Making at the U.S. Federal Reserve
2.2 Decision Making: Introduction and Definitions
2.3 Models
2.4 Phases of the Decision-Making Process
2.5 Decision Making: The Intelligence Phase
2.6 Decision Making: The Design Phase
2.7 Decision Making: The Choice Phase
2.8 Decision Making: The Implementation Phase
2.9 How Decisions Are Supported
2.10 Resources, Links, and the Teradata University Network Connection

2.1 OPENING VIGNETTE: DECISION MAKING AT THE U.S. FEDERAL RESERVE

How does Alan Greenspan, the U.S. Federal Reserve chairman, decide to raise or lower interest rates? He analyzes statistical indicators and raw data describing the U.S. economy. He gathers and synthesizes the often-conflicting reports of the governors of the Federal Reserve Board and those of the presidents of the 12 Federal Reserve Banks and other major banking institutions. He combines all this with his 25 years of experience and intuition, along with real-time information that includes anecdotal insights from leaders of important sectors of the U.S. economy. Data and other knowledge are provided through this extensive network that comprises a knowledge management system extraordinaire.

Given the reports from the Federal Reserve Bank, Federal Reserve Board, and presidents, Greenspan utilizes the results of economic analyses of some 255 economists dedicated to understanding the U.S. economy and its relationship to economies throughout the rest of the world, plus those at the 12 Federal Reserve Districts (totaling around 500 economists). Before each meeting, the Fed financial experts gather economic data and develop and analyze many important economic indices. As reports on the gross domestic product (GDP), consumer prices, and other economic indicators are available: they are gathered and loaded into the Fed's Forecasting, Analysis, and Modeling Environment (FAME). Most data are gathered electronically. The information system runs on about 100 servers. Greenspan's information system combines raw data and computerized intelligence with personalized tales from the key economic hubs. The system comprises several software tools developed by and for a group of international economists to determine the health of the U.S. economy. These range from a set of economic modeling systems developed in-house for the United States, several countries, and the world, and a number of systems developed in commercial software tools: a cross-sectional analysis system, a historical economic data pattern analysis system, tools for seasonally adjusting data, a mathematical computations engine, a large-scale database, and e-mail. Forecasting at the Fed utilizes scientific principles but also includes personal insights, knowledge, and intuition. Greenspan has a good sense of how much to trust statistics and how much to trust his intuition.

Many corporate executives want such a system, but fewer than 10 percent of U.S. corporations have created systems to gather, analyze, and act on economic data in close to real-time.

Though every one of the six governors vote at meetings and the Federal Reserve Bank presidents provide input, very little dissension occurs at the Fed. Such disagreement could shake the confidence of the economy.

Greenspan's decisions affect the flow of billions of dollars between banks and countries, affect corporate profits in a major way, and affect millions of jobs. His savvy decision-making approach toward adjusting interest rates and the money supply led to the longest modern surge in the U.S. economy, which lasted throughout most of the 1990s.

Sources: Adapted from M. Duvall and K.S. Nash, "Inside the Mind of Alan Greenspan," *Baseline*, April 6, 2005, pp. 32–51; J. B. Taylor, "Lessons Learned from the Greenspan Era," *Symposium Sponsored by the Federal Reserve Bank of Kansas City*, Jackson Hole, WY, August 2005; Laurence Meyer, "A Term at the Fed: An Insider's View," *HarperBusiness*, New York, 2004; and public domain publications.

Questions for the Opening Vignette

1. What is the primary decision that Alan Greenspan makes?
2. Why are Greenspan's decisions so important?

3. How does Greenspan actually make decisions? How does he utilize technology in making decisions? How does he involve others in the decision-making process?
4. What information sources does Greenspan use in his decision making?
5. Why are so many analysts needed to sift through the data and create and run models of the economy for decision making?
6. How can executives and managers at a national or multinational company (e.g., Wal-Mart) utilize a procedure like that used at the U.S. Federal Reserve? Answer this question in the context of the kinds of decisions made by such firms. (If you like, refer to Duvall and Nash, 2005, directly.)

WHAT WE CAN LEARN FROM THIS VIGNETTE

The opening vignette demonstrates some aspects of a typical business or government decision:

- Individuals are generally responsible for making decisions.
- There may be many (hundreds, or even thousands) of alternatives to consider.
- A decision maker needs data and detailed analysis and understanding of the data in order to make a good decision.
- Complicated decisions require computer systems to access data and run analyses.
- Teams of analysts may need to sift through data and run analyses.
- Past results and data may be insufficient to predict future results.
- Human judgment is often necessary to achieve superior results.
- The results of making business or government policy decisions usually materialize in the future. No one is a perfect predictor of the future, especially in the long run.
- Decisions are interrelated. A specific decision may affect many individuals and groups within and even outside the organizational system.
- Decision making involves a process of thinking about the problem leading to the need for data and modeling of the problem (i.e., understanding the relationships among its different aspects). This leads to interpretation and application of knowledge.
- There can be several objectives, and they may conflict with one another.
- Many decisions involve risk. Different people have different attitudes toward risk.
- Feedback is an important aspect of decision making.
- A decision may be the responsibility of a group (although in the case of the Fed, agreement is critical for the health of the economy).
- Group members may have biases.
- Empowering a group leads to better decisions.

2.2 DECISION MAKING: INTRODUCTION AND DEFINITIONS

We are about to examine how decision making is practiced and some of the underlying theories and models of decision making. You will also learn about the various traits of decision makers, including what distinguishes a good decision maker from the rest. Knowing all this will help you clearly understand the types of decision support tools that managers can use to make more effective decisions. In the following sections, we discuss aspects of decision making.

CHARACTERISTICS OF DECISION MAKING

In addition to the characteristics presented in the opening vignette, the following may be involved in decision making:

- Groupthink (buy-in by group members without thinking for themselves) can lead to bad decisions.
- Decision makers are interested in evaluating what-if scenarios.
- Experimentation with a real system (e.g., develop a schedule, try it, and see how well it works)—trial and error—may result in failure.
- Experimentation with a real system is possible only for one set of conditions at a time and can be disastrous.
- Changes in the decision-making environment may occur continuously, leading to invalidating assumptions about a situation (e.g., deliveries around holiday times may increase, requiring a different view of the problem).
- Changes in the decision-making environment may affect decision quality by imposing time pressure on the decision maker.
- Collecting information and analyzing a problem takes time and can be expensive. It is difficult to determine when to stop and make a decision.
- There may not be sufficient information to make an intelligent decision.
- There may be too much information available (i.e., information overload).

Ultimately, we want to help decision makers make better decisions (e.g., see Churchman, 1982). However, making better decisions does not necessarily mean making decisions more quickly. The fast-changing business environment often requires faster decisions, which may be detrimental to decision quality.

Fast decision making can be detrimental to decision quality. Managers were asked which areas suffered most when fast decision making is required. Horgan (2001) found that these areas (with numbers in parentheses indicating the percentage of managers responding) suffered the most: personnel/human resources (27 percent), budgeting/finance (24 percent), organizational structuring (22 percent), quality/productivity (20 percent), information technology (IT) selection and installation (17 percent), and process improvement (17 percent).

To determine how real decision makers make decisions, we must first understand the process and the important issues of decision making. Then we can understand appropriate methodologies for assisting decision makers and the contributions information systems can make. Only then can we develop DSS to help decision makers.

This chapter is organized based on the three key words that form the term DSS: *decision*, *support*, and *systems*. A decision maker should not simply apply IT tools blindly. Rather, the decision maker gets support through a rational approach that simplifies reality and provides a relatively quick and inexpensive means of considering various alternative courses of action to arrive at the best (or at least a very good) solution to the problem.

A WORKING DEFINITION OF DECISION MAKING

Decision making is a process of choosing among two or more alternative courses of action for the purpose of attaining a goal or goals. According to Simon (1977), managerial decision making is synonymous with the whole process of management. Consider the important managerial function of planning. Planning involves a series of decisions: What should be done? When? Where? Why? How? By whom? Managers set goals, or plan; hence, planning implies decision making. Other managerial functions, such as organizing and controlling, also involve decision making.

DECISION MAKING AND PROBLEM SOLVING

A problem occurs when a system does not meet its established goals, does not yield the predicted results, or does not work as planned. Problem solving may also deal with identifying new opportunities. Differentiating the terms **decision making** and **problem solving** can be confusing. One way to distinguish between the two is to examine the phases of the decision process (see Chapter 1): (1) intelligence, (2) design, (3) choice, and (4) implementation. Some consider the entire process (phases 1–4) as problem solving, with the choice phase as the real decision-making process. Others view phases 1–3 as formal decision making, ending with a recommendation, with problem solving additionally including the actual implementation of the recommendation (phase 4). Note that a problem may include situations in which a person must decide which opportunity to exploit.

In this book, we use the terms *decision making* and *problem solving* interchangeably.

DECISION-MAKING DISCIPLINES

Decision making is directly influenced by several major disciplines, some of which are behavioral and some of which are scientific in nature. We must be aware of how their philosophies can affect our ability to make decisions and provide support. Behavioral disciplines include anthropology, law, philosophy, political science, psychology, social psychology, and sociology. Scientific disciplines include computer science, decision analysis, economics, engineering, the hard sciences (e.g., biology, chemistry, physics), management science/operations research, mathematics, and statistics.

Each discipline has its own set of assumptions about reality and methods. Each also contributes a unique, valid view of how people make decisions. Finally, there is a lot of variation in what constitutes a successful decision in practice. For example, Crainer (2002) discussed the "75 greatest management decisions ever made." All of them were successful for a number of reasons, some serendipitous. Other great decisions, such as building the Great Wall of China, made good sense at the time (Crainer considered it a success) but actually failed in practice because of bad managerial practices. Other decisions eventually failed as well.

Online File W2.2 includes an overview of systems, including definitions, structure, and the notions of system **effectiveness** ("doing the right thing") and **efficiency** ("doing the thing right"). An important characteristic of management support systems (MSS) is their emphasis on the effectiveness, or "goodness," of the decision produced rather than on the computational efficiency of obtaining it; this is usually a major concern of a transaction processing system. Most Web-based DSS are focused on improving decision effectiveness. Efficiency may be a byproduct. The systems thinking approach is important for BI/DSS use and development, so we suggest that you review this material in the systems tutorial in Online File W2.2.

DECISION STYLE AND DECISION MAKERS

In the following sections, we examine the notion of decision style and specific aspects about decision makers.

Decision Style

Decision style is the manner in which decision makers think and react to problems. This includes the way they perceive, their cognitive responses, and how values and beliefs vary from individual to individual and from situation to situation. As a result, people make decisions in different ways. Although there is a general process of decision making, it is far from linear. People do not follow the same steps of the process in the same sequence, nor do they use all the steps. Furthermore, the emphasis, time allotment, and priorities given to each step vary significantly, not only from one person to another but also from one situation to the next. The manner in which managers make decisions (and the way they interact with other people) describes their decision style. Because decision styles depend on the factors described earlier, there are many decision styles. Personality temperament tests are often used to determine decision styles. Because there are many such tests, it is important to try to equate them in determining decision style. However, the various tests measure somewhat different aspects of personality, so they cannot be equated.

There are a number of decision-making styles. These include heuristic and analytic styles; one can also distinguish between autocratic versus democratic styles; another style is consultative (with individuals or groups). Of course, there are many combinations and variations of styles. For example, a person can be analytic and autocratic, or consultative (with individuals) and heuristic.

For a computerized system to successfully support a manager, it should fit the decision situation as well as the decision style. Therefore, the system should be flexible and adaptable to different users. The ability to ask what-if and goal-seeking questions provides flexibility in this direction. A Web-based interface using graphics is a desirable feature in supporting certain decision styles. If an MSS is to support varying styles, skills, and knowledge, it should not attempt to enforce a specific process. Rather, it should help decision makers use and develop their own styles, skills, and knowledge.

Different decision styles require different types of support. A major factor that determines the type of support required is whether the decision maker is an individual or a group. Individual decision makers need access to data and to experts who can provide advice, whereas groups additionally need collaboration tools. Web-based MSS can provide support to both.

There is a lot of information on the Web about cognitive style and decision style (e.g., see Birkman International, Inc., **birkman.com**; Keirsey Temperament Sorter and Keirsey Temperament Theory, **keirsey.com**). Many personality/temperament tests are available to help managers identify their own styles and those of their employees. Identifying an individual's style can help establish the most effective communication patterns and ideal tasks for which the person is suited.

Decision Makers

Decisions are often made by individuals, especially at lower managerial levels and in small organizations. There may be conflicting objectives even for a sole decision maker. For example, in an investment decision, an individual investor may consider the rate of return on the investment, liquidity, and safety as objectives. Finally, decisions may be fully automated (but only after a human decision maker decides to do so!).

This discussion of decision making focuses in large part on an individual decision maker. The opening vignette primarily describes an individual decision maker, although formally a board, as a group, is responsible for the decisions. Most major decisions in medium-sized and large organizations are made by groups. Obviously, there are often conflicting objectives in a group decision-making setting. Groups can be of variable size and may include people from different departments or from different organizations. Collaborating individuals may have different cognitive styles, personality types, and decision styles. Some clash, whereas others are mutually enhancing. Consensus can be a difficult political problem. Therefore, the process of decision making by a group can be very complicated. Computerized support (see Chapter 10) can greatly enhance group decision making. Computer support can be provided at a broad level, enabling members of whole departments, divisions, or even entire organizations to collaborate online. Such support has evolved over the past few years into enterprise information systems (EIS) and includes group support systems (GSS), enterprise resource management (ERM)/enterprise resource planning (ERP), supply chain management (SCM), knowledge management systems (KMS), and customer relationship management (CRM) systems.

Section 2.2 Review Questions

1. What are the various aspects of decision making?
2. Why is decision making so complex in today's business environment?
3. Identify similarities and differences between individual and group decision making.
4. Compare decision making and problem solving. Determine whether it makes sense to distinguish the two from one another.
5. Define *decision style* and describe why it is important to consider in the decision-making process.

2.3 MODELS[1]

A major characteristic of a DSS and many BI tools (notably those of business analytics) is the inclusion of at least one model. The basic idea is to perform the DSS analysis on a model of reality rather than on the real system. A *model* is a simplified representation or abstraction of reality. It is usually simplified because reality is too complex to describe exactly and because much of the complexity is actually irrelevant in solving a specific problem. Models can represent systems or problems with various degrees of abstraction. They are classified, based on their degree of abstraction, as either iconic, analog, or mathematical.

ICONIC (SCALE) MODELS

An **iconic model**, also called the *scale model*—the least abstract type of model—is a physical replica of a system, usually on a different scale from the original. An iconic model may be three-dimensional, such as a model of an airplane, a car, a bridge, or a production line. Photographs are two-dimensional iconic models.

ANALOG MODELS

An **analog model** behaves like the real system but does not look like it. It is more abstract than an iconic model and is a symbolic representation of reality. Models of this type are usually two-dimensional charts or diagrams. They can be physical models, but the shape of the model differs from that of the actual system. The following are some examples of analog models:

- Organization charts that depict structure, authority, and responsibility relationships
- Maps on which different colors represent objects, such as bodies of water or mountains

[1]Caution: Many students and professionals view models strictly as those of "data modeling" in the context of systems analysis and design. Here, we consider analytical models such as those of linear programming, simulation, and forecasting.

- Stock market charts that represent the price movements of stocks
- Blueprints of a machine or a house
- Animations, videos, and movies

MENTAL MODELS

Decision makers sometimes develop mental models, especially in time-pressure situations (e.g., when airplane pilots consider whether to fly). **Mental models** are descriptive representations of decision-making situations that people form in their heads and think about. Their thought processes work through scenarios to consider the utility of and risks involved in each potential alternative. Typically, mental models are used when there are mostly qualitative factors in the decision-making problem. Mental models help frame the decision-making situation, a topic of cognition theory (see Shoemaker and Russo, 2004). The methodology provided by cognitive maps can be used in practice to explicate a mental model of an individual or to develop a group consensus.

MATHEMATICAL (QUANTITATIVE) MODELS

The complexity of relationships in many organizational systems cannot be represented by icons or analogically because such representations would soon become cumbersome, and using them would be time-consuming. Therefore, more abstract models are described mathematically. Most DSS analyses are performed numerically with mathematical or other quantitative models.

THE BENEFITS OF MODELS

An MSS uses models for the following reasons:

- Model manipulation (changing decision variables or the environment) is much easier than manipulating a real system. Experimentation is easier and does not interfere with the daily operation of the organization.
- Models enable the compression of time. Years of operations can be simulated in minutes or seconds of computer time.
- The cost of modeling analysis is much lower than the cost of a similar experiment conducted on a real system.
- The cost of making mistakes during a trial-and-error experiment is much lower when models are used than with real systems.
- The business environment involves considerable uncertainty. With modeling, a manager can estimate the risks resulting from specific actions.
- Mathematical models enable the analysis of a very large, sometimes infinite, number of possible solutions. Even in simple problems, managers often have a large number of alternatives from which to choose.
- Models enhance and reinforce learning and training.
- Models and solution methods are readily available on the Web.
- Many Java applets (and other Web programs) are available to readily solve models.

Advances in computer graphics, especially through Web interfaces and their associated object-oriented programming languages, have led to an increased tendency to use iconic and analog models to complement MSS mathematical modeling. For example, visual simulation combines all three types of models. We defer our detailed discussion on models until Chapter 4.

Section 2.3 Review Questions

1. Describe the different categories of models.
2. How can mathematical models provide the benefits listed in this section?
3. How can mental models be utilized in decision making involving many qualitative factors?
4. How can modern IT tools help synthesize qualitative and quantitative factors in decision making? (Hint: See Online File 2.11.)

2.4 PHASES OF THE DECISION-MAKING PROCESS

It is advisable to follow a systematic decision-making process. Simon (1977) said that this involves three major phases: intelligence, design, and choice. He later added a fourth phase, implementation. Monitoring can be considered a fifth phase—a form of feedback. However, we view monitoring as the *intelligence phase* applied to the *implementation phase*. Simon's model is the most concise and yet complete characterization of rational decision making. A conceptual picture of the decision-making process is shown in Figure 2.1.

There is a continuous flow of activity from intelligence to design to choice (see the bold lines in Figure 2.1), but at any phase, there may be a return to a previous phase (feedback). Modeling is an essential part of this process. The seemingly chaotic nature of following a haphazard path from problem discovery to solution via decision making can be explained by these feedback loops.

The decision-making process starts with the **intelligence phase**; in this phase, the decision maker examines reality and identifies and defines the problem. *Problem ownership* is established as well. In the **design phase**, a model that represents the system is constructed. This is done by making assumptions that simplify reality and writing down the relationships among all the variables. The model is then validated, and criteria are determined in a principle of choice for evaluation of the alternative courses of action that are identified. Often, the process of model development identifies alternative solutions and vice versa.

The **choice phase** includes selection of a proposed solution to the model (not necessarily to the problem it represents). This solution is tested to determine its viability. When the proposed solution seems reasonable, we are ready for the last phase: implementation of the decision (not necessarily of a system). Successful implementation results in solving the real problem. Failure leads to a return to an earlier phase of the process. In fact, we can return to an earlier phase during any of the latter three phases. The decision-making situations described in the opening vignette and the MMS running case (in Online File W2.1) follow Simon's four-phase model, as do almost all other decision-making situations. Web impacts on the four phases, and vice versa, are shown in Table 2.1.

Note that there are many other decision-making models. Notable among them is the Kepner-Tregoe (Kepner and Tregoe, 1998) method, which has been adopted by many firms because its tools are readily available from Kepner-Tregoe, Inc. (**kepner-tregoe.com**; also see Bazerman, 2005). We have found that these alternative models, including the Kepner-Tregoe method, readily map into the Simon four-phase model.

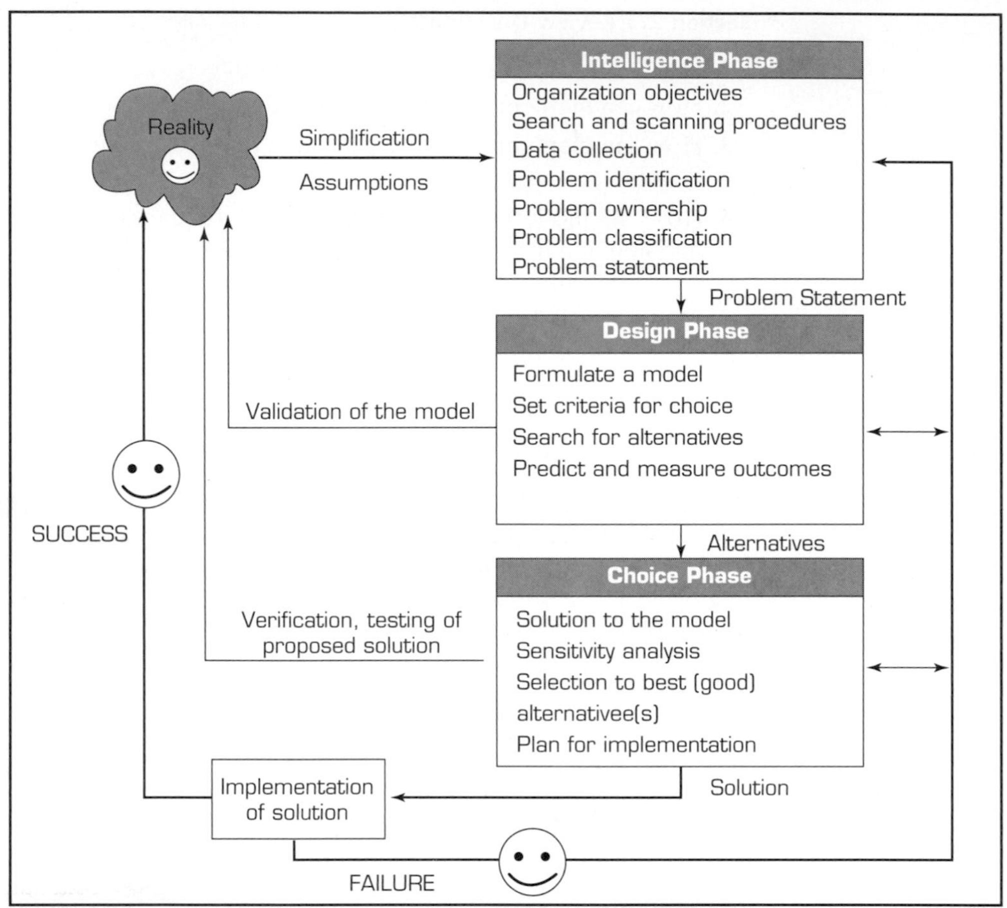

FIGURE 2.1 The Decision Making/Modeling Process

Even though ultimately a human decision maker is responsible for every decision, automated systems have evolved to help businesses make decisions more productively and consistently. A complication in the business environment is that decisions often must be made frequently and rapidly, utilizing online information. Typically, these problems are highly structured. The insurance industry was one of the first to adopt such automated decision-making (ADM) technology. It uses ADM in underwriting, but utilizes rules-base technology. For details on ADM decision making, see Davenport (2004) and Indart (2005).

We next turn to a detailed discussion of the four phases illustrated by the MMS running case described in Online File W2.1. Note that Online File W2.1 has four distinct parts, corresponding to Simon's four phases of decision making.

Section 2.4 Review Questions

1. List and briefly describe Simon's four phases of decision making.
2. Why is a fifth phase, evaluation, not necessary?
3. What can cause a problem to exist in decision making?

TABLE 2.1 Simon's Four Phases of Decision Making and the Web

Phase	*Web Impacts*	*Impacts on the Web*
Intelligence	Access to information to identify problems and opportunities from internal and external data sources	Identification of opportunities for e-commerce, Web infrastructure, hardware and software tools, etc.
	Access to artificial intelligence methods and other data mining methods to identify opportunities	Intelligent agents, which reduce the burden of information overload Smart search engines
	Collaboration through group support systems (GSS) and knowledge management systems (KMS)	
	Distance learning, which can provide knowledge to add structure to problems	
Design	Access to data, models, and solution methods	Brainstorming methods (e.g., GSS) to collaborate in Web infrastructure design
	Use of online analytical processing (OLAP), data mining, and data warehouses	Models and solutions of Web infra-structure issues
	Collaboration through GSS and KMS	
	Similar solutions available from KMS	
Choice	Access to methods to evaluate the impacts of proposed solutions	Decision support system (DSS) tools, which examine and establish criteria from models to determine Web, intranet, and extranet infra structure
		DSS tools, which determine how to route messages
Implementation	Web-based collaboration tools (e.g., GSS) and KMS, which can assist in implementing decisions	Decisions implemented on browser and server design and access, which ultimately determined how to set up the various components that have evolved into the Internet
	Tools, which monitor the performance of e-commerce and other sites, including intranets, extranets, and the Internet	

2.5 DECISION MAKING: THE INTELLIGENCE PHASE

Intelligence in decision making involves scanning the environment, either intermittently or continuously. It includes several activities aimed at identifying problem situations or opportunities. It may also include monitoring the results of the implementation phase of a decision-making process. (See the MMS running case situations in Online File W2.1.1.)

PROBLEM (OR OPPORTUNITY) IDENTIFICATION

The intelligence phase begins with the identification of organizational goals and objectives related to an issue of concern (e.g., inventory management, job selection, lack of or incorrect Web presence) and determination of whether they are being met. Problems occur because of dissatisfaction with the status quo. Dissatisfaction is the result of a difference between what people desire (or expect) and what is occurring. In this first phase, a decision maker attempts to determine whether a problem exists, identify its symptoms, determine its magnitude, and explicitly define it. Often, what is described as a problem (e.g., excessive costs) may be only a symptom (i.e., measure) of a problem (e.g., improper inventory levels). Because real-world problems are usually complicated by many interrelated factors, it is sometimes difficult to distinguish between the symptoms and the real problem, as described in the MMS running case in Online File W2.1.1. New opportunities and problems certainly may be uncovered while investigating the causes of symptoms.

The existence of a problem can be determined by monitoring and analyzing the organization's productivity level. The measurement of productivity and the construction of a model are based on real data. The collection of data and the estimation of future data are among the most difficult steps in the analysis. The following are some issues that may arise during data collection and estimation and thus plague decision makers:

- Data are not available. As a result, the model is made with, and relies on, potentially inaccurate estimates.
- Obtaining data may be expensive.
- Data may not be accurate or precise enough.
- Data estimation is often subjective.
- Data may be insecure.
- Important data that influence the results may be qualitative (soft).
- There may be too many data (i.e., information overload).
- Outcomes (or results) may occur over an extended period. As a result, revenues, expenses, and profits will be recorded at different points in time. To overcome this difficulty, a present-value approach can be used if the results are quantifiable.
- It is assumed that future data will be similar to historical data. If this is not the case, the nature of the change has to be predicted and included in the analysis.

When the preliminary investigation is completed, it is possible to determine whether a problem really exists, where it is located, and how significant it is. A key issue is whether an information system is reporting a problem or only the symptoms of a problem. For example, in the MMS running case (see Online File W2.1), sales are down; there is a problem, but the situation, no doubt, is symptomatic of the problem.

PROBLEM CLASSIFICATION

Problem classification is the conceptualization of a problem in an attempt to place it in a definable category, possibly leading to a standard solution approach. An important approach classifies problems according to the degree of structuredness evident in them. This ranges from totally structured (i.e., programmed) to totally unstructured (i.e., unprogrammed), as described in Chapter 1.

PROBLEM DECOMPOSITION

Many complex problems can be divided into subproblems. Solving the simpler subproblems may help in solving a complex problem. Also, seemingly poorly structured problems sometimes have highly structured subproblems. Just as a semistructured problem results when some phases of decision making are structured while other phases are unstructured, so when some subproblems of a decision making problem are structured with others unstructured, the problem itself is semistructured. As a DSS is developed and the decision maker and development staff learn more about the problem, it gains structure. Decomposition also facilitates communication among decision makers. Decomposition is one of the most important aspects of the Analytical Hierarchy Process (AHP; see Bhushan and Rai, 2004; Forman and Selly, 2001; Saaty, 2001; and **expertchoice.com**), which helps decision makers incorporate both qualitative and quantitative factors into their decision-making models. In the MMS running case (see Online File W2.1), there are several aspects to be investigated: advertising, sales, new car acquisition, and so on. Each of them is a subproblem that interacts with the others.

PROBLEM OWNERSHIP

In the intelligence phase, it is important to establish problem ownership. A problem exists in an organization only if someone or some group takes on the responsibility of attacking it and if the organization has the ability to solve it. The assignment of authority to solve the problem is called **problem ownership**. For example, a manager may feel that he or she has a problem because interest rates are too high. Because interest rate levels are determined at the national and international levels, and most managers can do nothing about them, high interest rates are the problem of the government, not a problem for a specific company to solve. The problem companies actually face is how to operate in a high–interest rate environment. For an individual company, the interest rate level should be handled as an uncontrollable (environmental) factor to be predicted.

When problem ownership is not established, either someone is not doing his or her job or the problem at hand has yet to be identified as belonging to anyone. It is then important for someone to either volunteer to own it or assign it to someone. This was done, very clearly, in the MMS running case (see Online File W2.1.1).

The intelligence phase ends with a formal problem statement.

Section 2.5 Review Questions

1. Explain the differences and similarities between problems and opportunities.
2. What is the difference between a problem and its symptoms?
3. Why is it important to classify a problem?
4. What is meant by *problem decomposition*?
5. Why is establishing problem ownership so important in the decision-making process?

2.6 DECISION MAKING: THE DESIGN PHASE

The design phase involves finding or developing and analyzing possible courses of action. These include understanding the problem and testing solutions for feasibility. A model of the decision-making problem is constructed, tested, and validated. (See the MMS running case in Online File W2.1.2.)

Modeling involves conceptualizing a problem and abstracting it to quantitative and/or qualitative form (see Chapter 4). For a mathematical model, the variables are identified, and their mutual relationships are established. Simplifications are made, whenever necessary, through assumptions. For example, a relationship between two variables may be assumed to be linear even though in reality there may be some nonlinear effects. A proper balance between the level of model simplification and the representation of reality must be obtained because of the cost–benefit trade-off. A simpler model leads to lower development costs, easier manipulation, and a faster solution but is less representative of the real problem and can produce inaccurate results. On the other hand, a simpler model generally requires fewer data, or the data are aggregated and easier to obtain.

The process of modeling is a combination of art and science. As a science, there are many standard model classes available, and with practice, an analyst can determine which one is applicable to a given situation. As an art, creativity and finesse are required when determining what simplifying assumptions can work, how to combine appropriate features of the model classes, and how to integrate models to obtain valid solutions. In the MMS running case (see Online File W2.1.1 through W2.1.4), the problem at hand was very vague: The MMS team investigated the data to develop an understanding that was more of a mental model of the situation, as teams are wont to do in such a situation. Models were indeed used and tested, but they were not described in the MMS running case (Part 2). Data mining, OLAP, and revenue management software have many models embedded in them (see Yeoman and McMahon-Beattie, 2004; Talluri and van Ryzin, 2005; and Chapter 6).

Models have **decision variables** that describe the alternatives among which a manager must choose (e.g., how many cars to deliver to a specific rental agency, how to advertise at specific times, which Web server to buy or lease), a result variable or a set of result variables (e.g., profit, revenue, sales) that describes the objective or goal of the decision-making problem, and uncontrollable variables or parameters (e.g., economic conditions) that describe the environment. The process of modeling involves determining the (usually mathematical, sometimes symbolic) relationships among the variables. These topics are discussed in Chapter 4.

SELECTION OF A PRINCIPLE OF CHOICE

A **principle of choice** is a criterion that describes the acceptability of a solution approach. In a model, it is a result variable. Selecting a principle of choice is not part of the choice phase but involves how a person establishes decision-making objective(s) and incorporates the objective(s) into the model(s). Are we willing to assume high risk, or do we prefer a low-risk approach? Are we attempting to optimize or satisfice? It is also important to recognize the difference between a criterion and a constraint (see Technology Insights 2.1). Among the many principles of choice, normative and descriptive are of prime importance.

NORMATIVE MODELS

Normative models are models in which the chosen alternative is demonstrably the best of all possible alternatives. To find it, the decision maker should examine all the alternatives and prove that the one selected is indeed the best, which is what the person would normally want. This process is basically **optimization**. In operational terms, optimization can be achieved in one of three ways:

1. Get the highest level of goal attainment from a given set of resources. For example, which alternative will yield the maximum profit from an investment of $10 million?

TECHNOLOGY INSIGHTS 2.1

The Difference Between a Criterion and a Constraint

Many people new to the formal study of decision making inadvertently confuse the concepts of criterion and constraint. Often, this is because a criterion may imply a constraint, either implicit or explicit, thereby adding to the confusion. For example, there may be a distance criterion that the decision maker does not want to travel too far from home. However, there is an implicit constraint that the alternatives from which he selects must be within a certain distance from his home. This constraint effectively says that if the distance from home is greater than a certain amount, then the alternative is not feasible—or, rather, the distance to an alternative must be less than or equal to a certain number (this would be a formal relationship in some models; in the model in this case, it reduces the search, considering fewer alternatives). This is similar to what happens in some cases when selecting a university, where schools beyond a single day's driving distance would not be considered by most people, and, in fact, the utility function (criterion value) of distance can start out low close to home, peak at about 70 miles (about 100 km)—say the distance between Atlanta (home) and Athens, Georgia—and sharply drop off thereafter.

2. Find the alternative with the highest ratio of goal attainment to cost (e.g., profit per dollar invested) or maximize productivity.
3. Find the alternative with the lowest cost (or smallest amount of other resources) that will meet an acceptable level of goals. For example, if your task is to select hardware for an intranet with a minimum bandwidth, which alternative will accomplish this goal at the least cost?

Normative decision theory is based on the following assumptions of rational decision makers:

- Humans are economic beings whose objective is to maximize the attainment of goals; that is, the decision maker is rational. (More of a good thing [revenue, fun] is better than less; less of a bad thing [cost, pain] is better than more.)
- For a decision-making situation, all viable alternative courses of action and their consequences, or at least the probability and the values of the consequences, are known.
- Decision makers have an order or preference that enables them to rank the desirability of all consequences of the analysis (best to worst).

Kontoghiorghes et al. (2002) described the rational approach to decision making, especially as it relates to using models and computing.

Are decision makers really rational? See Technology Insights 2.2 and Schwartz (1998, 2004) for anomalies in rational decision making. Though there may be major anomalies in the presumed rationality of financial and economic behavior, we take the view that they could be caused by incompetence, lack of knowledge, multiple goals being framed inadequately, misunderstanding of a decision maker's true expected utility, and time-pressure impacts. For more on rationality, see Gharajedaghi (2006), and Ranganathan and Sethi (2002).

There are other anomalies, often caused by time pressure. For example, Stewart (2002) described a number of researchers working with intuitive decision making. The idea of "thinking with your gut" is obviously a heuristic approach to decision making. It works well for firefighters and military personnel on the battlefield. One critical aspect of decision making in this mode is that many scenarios have been thought through in

TECHNOLOGY INSIGHTS 2.2

Are Decision Makers Really Rational?

Some researchers question the concept of rationality in decision making. There are countless cases of individuals and groups behaving irrationally in real-world and experimental decision-making situations. For example, suppose you need to take a bus to work every morning, and the bus leaves at 7:00 a.m. If it takes you one hour to wake up, prepare for work, and get to the bus stop, you should therefore always awaken at or before 6:00 a.m. However, sometimes (perhaps many times) you may sleep until 6:30, knowing that you will miss breakfast and not perform well at work. Or you may be late and arrive at the bus stop at 7:05, hoping that the bus will be late, too. So, why are you late? Multiple objectives and hoped-for goal levels may lead to this situation. Or your true expected utility for being on time might simply indicate that you should go back to bed most mornings!

advance. Even when a situation is new, it can quickly be matched to an existing one on-the-fly, and a reasonable solution can be obtained (through *pattern recognition*). Luce et al. (2004) described how emotions affect decision making, and Pauly (2004) discussed of inconsistencies in decision making. Bonabeau and Meyer (2001) described a decision-making approach called *swarm intelligence*, which is based on chaos theory and is based on the way an anthill functions successfully. There is a certain rationality underlying its approach. Daniel Kahneman and Amos Tversky received the Nobel Prize in Economics in 2002 for their work on what appears to be irrationality in decision making.

We believe that irrationality is caused by the factors listed previously. For example, Tversky et al. (1990) investigated the causes of preference reversal, which is a known problem in applying the AHP to problems. They conducted experiments to investigate the phenomenon. However, some criterion or preference is generally omitted from the analysis. Ratner et al. (1999) investigated how variety can cause individuals to choose less-preferred options, even though they will enjoy them less. But we maintain that variety clearly has value, is part of a decision maker's utility, and is a criterion and/or constraint that should be considered in decision making.

In the MMS running case in Online File W2.1.2, rationality prevailed. Maximizing profit was clearly the principle of choice. On the other hand, in Application Case 2.1, rationality is present, but it may be preventing the Lafko family from obtaining and implementing a viable decision.

Application Case 2.1

Decision Making Between a Rock and a Hard Place; or What Can You Do When There are No Good or Even Feasible Alternatives?

Fred J. Lafko, an entrepreneur in Poughkeepsie, New York, had a vision in the early 1980s. He bought the *Alexander Hamilton*, a side-wheeler ship used by the Hudson River Day Line from the early 1900s until the latter part of the twentieth century (you can see a photo at **ulster.net/~hrmm/steamboats/dayline/dayline1920.html**). Fred planned to move the ship from the New York City area to Poughkeepsie and make it into a tourist site. He would build a trendy restaurant, shops, and offices into it and moor it along the banks of the Hudson River. As it happens, the *Alexander Hamilton* was one of the few ships listed as a National Historical Monument. This was because of its unique engine design. It was the last ship of its type that could sail. Fred arranged to have it moved to Poughkeepsie, but unfortunately, the ship ran aground on a sandbar in the river. Experts said Fred would have to wait until the next major high tide (when the moon was full) to pull it off. He arranged for tugboats to pull the ship off the sandbar. Unfortunately, the tugboats were late. A month later, he arranged to have them come a day early, and they successfully pulled the *Alexander Hamilton* off the sandbar. Fred arranged to have the ship tied up at the U.S. Navy's Sulko Pier so that he could assess the damage. When the ship was made seaworthy, he arranged again to tow it to Poughkeepsie. Before the ship could be moved, a hurricane sunk it, just below the water line. Shortly after, Fred died, and his brother, Jack, who handled his estate, did nothing about the ship, much to the consternation of Fred's six grown children and the Navy, which wanted its pier back.

In the summer of 2002, Jack died. Fred's children had to make a decision about the ship. After 20 years underwater, there was probably very little left of it worth salvaging. But because the ship is a National Historical Monument, they could not simply cut it up and scrap it. They also could not remove the engine. The conventional way to lift a ship out of the water is to build a watertight fence around it and pump out the silt. The U.S. Environmental Protection Agency would not allow this because the silt would pollute the river (even though that is where the silt is now). Other salvage methods are very dangerous or expensive. The Navy would not take ownership of the ship (because then it would have to deal with the problem directly), and it was not clear if the children could donate the ship to anyone else or to another agency interested in preserving the past. No one would buy the ship because of all the complications. There did not appear to be any good or even feasible decisions. What could Fred's family do?

Sources: Dennis Lafko, one of Fred's sons, as told to Jay Aronson on a flight from Atlanta to Colorado Springs, July 2002; and public domain references.

SUBOPTIMIZATION

By definition, optimization requires a decision maker to consider the impact of each alternative course of action on the entire organization because a decision made in one area may have significant effects (positive or negative) on other areas. Consider, for example, a marketing department that implements an electronic commerce (e-commerce) site. Within hours, orders far exceed production capacity. The production department, which plans its own schedule, cannot meet demand. It may gear up for as high demand as is possible to meet. Ideally and independently, the department should produce only a few products in extremely large quantities to minimize manufacturing costs. However, such a plan might result in large, costly inventories and marketing difficulties caused by the lack of a variety of products, especially if customers start to cancel orders that are not met in a timely way. This situation illustrates the sequential nature of decision making (see Borges et al., 2002; and Sun and Giles, 2001).

A systems point of view assesses the impact of every decision on the entire system. Thus, the marketing department should make its plans in conjunction with other departments. However, such an approach may require a complicated, expensive, time-consuming analysis. In practice, the MSS builder may close the system within narrow boundaries, considering only the part of the organization under study (the marketing and/or production department, in this case). By simplifying, the model then does not incorporate certain complicated relationships that describe interactions with and among the other departments. The other departments can be aggregated into simple model components. Such an approach is called **suboptimization**.

If a suboptimal decision is made in one part of the organization without considering the details of the rest of the organization, then an optimal solution from the point of view of that part may be inferior for the whole. However, suboptimization may still be a very practical approach to decision making, and many problems are first approached from this perspective. It is possible to reach tentative conclusions (and generally usable results) by analyzing only a portion of a system, without getting bogged down in too many details. After a solution is proposed, its potential effects on the remaining departments of the organization can be tested. If no significant negative effects are found, the solution can be implemented.

Suboptimization may also apply when simplifying assumptions are used in modeling a specific problem. There may be too many details or too many data to incorporate into a specific decision-making situation, and so not all of them are used in the model. If the solution to the model seems reasonable, it may be valid for the problem and thus be adopted. For example, in a production department, parts are often partitioned into A/B/C inventory categories. Generally, A items (e.g., large gears, whole assemblies) are expensive (say, $3,000 or more each), built to order in small batches, and inventoried in low quantities; C items (e.g., nuts, bolts, screws) are very inexpensive (say, less than $2) and ordered and used in very large quantities; and B items fall in between. All A items can be handled by a detailed scheduling model and physically monitored closely by management; B items are generally somewhat aggregated, their groupings are scheduled, and management reviews these parts less frequently; and C items are not scheduled but are simply acquired or built based on a policy defined by management with a simple economic order quantity (EOQ) ordering system that assumes constant annual demand. The policy might be reviewed once a year. This situation applies when determining all criteria or modeling the entire problem becomes prohibitively time-consuming or expensive.

Suboptimization may also involve simply bounding the search for an optimum (e.g., by a heuristic) by considering fewer criteria or alternatives or by eliminating large portions of the problem from evaluation. If it takes too long to solve a problem, a good-enough solution found already may be used and the optimization effort terminated.

DESCRIPTIVE MODELS

Descriptive models describe things as they are or as they are believed to be. These models are typically mathematically based. Descriptive models are extremely useful in DSS for investigating the consequences of various alternative courses of action under different configurations of inputs and processes. However, because a descriptive analysis checks the performance of the system for a given set of alternatives (rather than for all alternatives), there is no guarantee that an alternative selected with the aid of descriptive analysis is optimal. In many cases, it is only satisfactory.

Simulation is probably the most common descriptive modeling method. **Simulation** is the imitation of reality and has been applied to many areas of decision making. Computer and video games are a form of simulation: An artificial reality is created, and the game player lives within it. Virtual reality is also a form of simulation because the environment is simulated, not real. A common use of simulation is in manufacturing. Again, consider the production department of a firm with complications caused by the marketing department. The characteristics of each machine in a job shop along the supply chain can be described mathematically. Relationships can be established based on how each machine physically runs and relates to others. Given a trial schedule of batches of parts, it is possible to measure how batches flow through the system and to use the statistics from each machine. Alternative schedules may then be tried and the statistics recorded until a reasonable schedule is found. Marketing can examine access and purchase patterns on its Web site. Simulation can be used to determine how to structure a Web site for improved performance and to estimate future purchases. Both departments can therefore use primarily experimental modeling methods.

Classes of descriptive models include the following:

- Complex inventory decisions
- Environmental-impact analysis
- Financial planning
- Information flow
- Markov analysis (predictions)
- Scenario analysis
- Simulation (alternative types)
- Technological forecasting
- Waiting-line (queuing) management

There are a number of nonmathematical descriptive models for decision making. One is the cognitive map (see Eden and Ackermann, 2002; and Jenkins, 2002). A cognitive map can help a decision maker sketch out the important qualitative factors and their causal relationships in a messy decision-making situation. This helps the decision maker (or decision-making group) focus on what is relevant and what is not, and the map evolves as more is learned about the problem. The map can help the decision maker understand issues better, focus better, and reach closure. One interesting software tool for cognitive mapping is Decision Explorer from Banxia Software Ltd. (**banxia.com**; try the demo).

Another descriptive decision-making model is the use of narratives to describe a decision-making situation. A *narrative* is a story that helps a decision maker uncover the important aspects of the situation and leads to better understanding and framing. This is extremely effective when a group is making a decision, and it can lead to a more common viewpoint, also called a frame. Juries in court trials typically use narrative-based approaches in reaching verdicts (see Allan, Frame and Turney, 2003; Beach, 2005; and Denning, 2000).

GOOD ENOUGH, OR SATISFICING

According to Simon (1977), most human decision making, whether organizational or individual, involves a willingness to settle for a satisfactory solution, "something less than the best." When **satisficing**, the decision maker sets up an aspiration, a goal, or a desired level of performance and then searches the alternatives until one is found that achieves this level. The usual reasons for satisficing are time pressures (e.g., decisions may lose value over time), the ability to achieve optimization (e.g., solving some models could take longer than until when the sun is supposed to become a supernova), and recognition that the marginal benefit of a better solution is not worth the marginal cost to obtain it (e.g., in searching the Internet, you can look at only so many Web sites before you run out of time and energy). In such a situation, the decision maker is behaving rationally, though in reality he or she is satisficing. Essentially, satisficing is a form of suboptimization. There may be a best solution, an optimum, but it would be difficult, if not impossible, to attain. With a normative model, too much computation may be involved; with a descriptive model, it may not be possible to evaluate all the sets of alternatives.

Related to satisficing is Simon's idea of *bounded rationality*. Humans have a limited capacity for rational thinking; they generally construct and analyze a simplified model of a real situation by considering fewer alternatives, criteria, and/or constraints than actually exist. Their behavior with respect to the simplified model may be rational. However, the rational solution for the simplified model may not be rational for the real-world problem. Rationality is bounded not only by limitations on human processing capacities but also by individual differences, such as age, education, knowledge, and attitudes. Bounded rationality is also why many models are descriptive rather than normative. This may also explain why so many good managers rely on intuition, an important aspect of good decision making (see Stewart, 2002; and Pauly, 2004).

Because rationality and the use of normative models lead to good decisions, a natural question to ask is Why are so many bad decisions made in practice? Intuition is a critical factor that decision makers use in solving unstructured and semistructured problems. The best decision makers recognize the trade-off between the marginal cost of obtaining further information and analysis versus the benefit of making a better decision. But sometimes decisions must be made quickly, and ideally, the intuition of a seasoned, excellent decision maker is called for. When adequate planning, funding, or information is not available, or when a decision maker is inexperienced or ill trained, disaster can strike. See Application Case 2.2 for an example. We describe some complications contributing to bad decisions in Technology Insights 2.3.

Application Case 2.2

Decision Making From the Gut: When Intuition Can Fail

In September 2005, President George W. Bush, along with federal, state (Louisiana), and local (New Orleans) officials were ultimately responsible for delaying the evacuation of New Orleans when Hurricane Katrina struck the city. It cannot be denied that poor planning leading to squandering resources meant to shore up the Mississippi River levees and prevent flooding was part of the problem. However, when the levees burst through and water flooded a good portion of the city, officials delayed action and were then incapable of acting to ensure the safety of New Orleans residents. Problem ownership was a major issue.

Bush is known for his decision style of thinking from the gut. In many instances, this implies not developing a clear picture of all the details and implications of the situation. Many analysts and reporters characterize this gut-based decision-making process as the brilliance of a leader who quickly synthesizes situational information from his analysts to make an informed decision, while others attribute this behavior to a lack of understanding of the facts and analysis, possibly based on laziness. Decision making from the gut has become known as "blink"—that is, after two seconds of looking at a problem, the decision maker's glance shows that he or she has an answer. The best decision makers indeed do blink, but they also know when to apply it and when not to. It will likely be some 50 years before we know if Bush's blinking process served him and the United States well.

Sources: Modified and condensed from E. Thomas, "How Bush Blew It," *Newsweek*, September 19, 2005, pp. 30–40; M. Allen and D.S. Broder, "Bush: Decisive, But Not Curious?" *The Washington Post*, September 1, 2004 (available at **seattletimes.nwsource.com/html/nationworld/2002021866_bushstyle01.html**); H. Dalal, "America Unbound: The Bush Revolution in Foreign Policy (review)," *SAIS Review*, Vol. 24, No. 2, Summer–Fall 2004, pp. 198–200; B. Burnett, "Bush's Decision-Making Style Is Full of Gut-Feelings and 'Blinks,' " *Berkeley Daily Planet*, March 8, 2005; and M. Gladwell, *Blink: The Power of Thinking Without Thinking*. Time Warner Book Group, New York, 2005.

DEVELOPING (GENERATING) ALTERNATIVES

A significant part of the process of model building is generating alternatives. In optimization models (such as linear programming), the alternatives may be generated automatically by the model. In most MSS situations, however, it is necessary to

TECHNOLOGY INSIGHTS 2.3

Some Reasons for Bad Decision Making

Bad decisions are made for a variety of reasons by the very people we presume are capable and responsible for quality decision making. One reason is definitely the effect of time pressure. As mentioned earlier, when experts are forced to make decisions quickly, they simply follow patterns that have worked previously. Such pattern recognition may work in simple cases, but it can fail miserably in complex cases (refer to Application Case 2.2). Also, in complex cases, intuition can be flat out wrong! In 2005, *BusinessWeek* ("The Fact Gap: The Disconnect Between Data and Decisions," conducted by *BusinessWeek* Research Services for Business Objects, available at **businessobjects.com/factgap**) surveyed several hundred executives and managers around the world. These managers worked in different industries and for organizations of different sizes. Not surprisingly, most of the decision makers utilize gut-based decision making most of the time. Only about 3 percent did not use it at all, while more than 60 percent said they used it 50 percent of the time or more. Furthermore, 77 percent of those surveyed said that they make bad decisions because of insufficient information. Bad decisions were attributed mainly to the inability to determine whether the information was accurate, the length of time required, and technological limitations.

There is a strong correlation between bad decisions and bad information; decisions based on gut feelings rather than accurate data are typically decisions based on bad information. Irrationality can also play a major role. Essentially, a decision maker may misread or misrepresent the true risk of the wrong conclusion. Sometimes decision makers simply do not know how much to pay for something (i.e., *coherent arbitrariness*) and often confuse value with utility. Even though emotions and intuition can lead to quick decisions or at least influence them dramatically, because they inhibit the gathering and use of accurate data and analysis, they typically lead to bad decisions.

Sources: Compiled and condensed from G.G. Weismantel, "Business Intelligence Tells You 'Why,' " *Business Integration Journal*, July/August 2005, pp. 35–38; M.L. Gonzales, "What's Your BI Environment IQ?" *DM Review*, Vol. 15, No. 8, August 2005, pp. 33–36; D. Ariely, "Why Good CIOs Make Bad Decisions," *CIO*, May 1, 2003, pp. 82–86; J. Martirossian and D.H. Lewin (eds.), *Decision Making in Communities: Why Groups of Smart People Sometimes Make Bad Decisions*. Alexandria, VA: Community Associations Press, 2001; "The Psychology of Investing," *TIAA-CREF Participant*, August 2003, pp. 7–10; R.D. Ireland and C.C. Miller, "Decision Making and Firm Success," *Academy of Management Executives*, Vol. 18, No. 4, November 2004, pp. 8–12; and H.A. Simon, "Making Management Decisions: The Role of Intuition and Emotion," *Academy of Management Executives*, Vol. 1, No. 1, February 1987, pp. 57–64.

generate alternatives manually. This can be a lengthy process that involves searching and creativity, perhaps utilizing electronic brainstorming in a GSS. It takes time and costs money. Issues such as when to stop generating alternatives can be very important. Too many alternatives can be detrimental to the process of decision making. A decision maker may suffer from information overload (see Application Case 2.3). Cross (2001) described a new initiative for administrators in higher-education institutions to handle information overload: The National Learning Infrastructure Initiative (NLII) Institute Readiness Program (READY) provides a way to organize and communicate information about the incorporation of technology into higher education. The Web-based READY portal filters through large amounts of information to select only relevant items for alternative selection. Generating alternatives is heavily dependent on the availability and cost of information and requires expertise in the problem area. This is the least formal aspect of problem solving. Alternatives can be generated and evaluated using heuristics. The generation of alternatives from either individuals or groups can be supported by electronic brainstorming software in a Web-based GSS.

Application Case 2.3

Too Many Alternatives Spoils the Broth

The decision-making situation described here was overheard on a bus ride at a national meeting.

A major university was in the process of moving its distance-learning activities to the Web. A professor was assigned the task of looking into the possible alternatives. He created a list of 23 companies. In his report, he included detailed descriptions of and documentation about the alternatives and what the university needed. He wanted to be thorough, even though not all the alternatives were appropriate for the university (constraints clearly would have cut the list down). He felt it was a good report.

The day before the decision was to be made, a salesman for such products stopped by the president's office. The president picked that company's product. As was overheard on the bus: "Studies on decision making show that when you give someone too many options to choose from, plus a deadline, he or she usually freezes and is likely to choose the last one mentioned."

Three to five alternatives seems to be about right. In this professor's case, an executive summary would have been a good idea. After all, the university was trying to solve a problem, not survey the marketplace. Even using a software tool—such as Expert Choice (**expertchoice.com**)—to compare these few valid alternatives would have been a good idea.

Sources: Modified and condensed from S.M. Johnstone, "Decision Support for Distance Learning Solutions: Help Is Online," *Syllabus*, October 1, 2001; and material from Expert Choice, Inc., at **expertchoice.com** (accessed March 2006).

Note that the search for alternatives usually occurs after the criteria for evaluating the alternatives are determined. This sequence can ease the search for alternatives and reduce the effort involved in evaluating them, but identifying potential alternatives can sometimes aid in identifying criteria. Identifying criteria and alternatives proved difficult in the online MMS running case (see Online File W2.1.2). The analysts first had to identify the many problems. After the problems were identified, years of experience and access to information through the CLAUDIA portal made it easy for the team to develop obvious solutions and establish their value to the bottom line.

The outcome of every proposed alternative must be established. Depending on whether the decision-making problem is classified as one of certainty, risk, or uncertainty, different modeling approaches may be used (see Drummond, 2001; and Koller, 2000). These are discussed in Chapter 4.

MEASURING OUTCOMES

The value of an alternative is evaluated in terms of goal attainment. Sometimes an outcome is expressed directly in terms of a goal. For example, profit is an outcome, profit maximization is a goal, and both are expressed in dollar terms. An outcome such as customer satisfaction may be measured by the number of complaints, by the level of loyalty to a product, or by ratings found through surveys. Ideally, a decision maker would want to deal with a single goal, but in practice, it is not unusual to have multiple goals (see Barba-Romero, 2001; and Koksalan and Zionts, 2001). When groups make decisions, each group participant may have a different agenda. For example, executives might want to maximize profit, marketing might want to maximize market penetration, operations might want to minimize costs, and stockholders might want to maximize the bottom line. Typically, these goals conflict, so special multiple-criteria methodologies have been developed to handle this. One such method is the AHP.

RISK

All decisions are made in an inherently unstable environment. This is due to the many unpredictable events in both the economic and physical environments. Some risk (measured as probability) may be due to internal organizational events, such as a valued employee quitting or becoming ill, while others may be due to natural disasters, such as a hurricane. Aside from the human toll, one economic aspect of Hurricane Katrina was that the price of a gallon of gasoline doubled overnight due to uncertainty in the port capabilities, refining, and pipelines of the southern United States. What can a decision maker do in the face of such instability?

In general, people have a tendency to measure uncertainty and risk badly. Purdy (2005) said that people tend to be overconfident and have an illusion of control in decision making. The results of experiments by Adam Goodie at The University of Georgia indicate that most people are overconfident most of the time (Goodie, 2004; see also Vlahos, 2005). This may explain why people often feel that one more pull of a slot machine will definitely pay off.

However, methodologies for handling extreme uncertainty do exist. For example, Yakov (2001) described a way to make good decisions based on very little information, using an information gap theory and methodology approach. Aside from estimating the potential utility or value of a particular decision's outcome, the best decision makers are capable of accurately estimating the risk associated with the outcomes that results from making each decision. Thus, one important task of a decision maker is to attribute a level of risk to the outcome associated with each potential alternative being considered. Some decisions may lead to unacceptable risks in terms of success and can therefore be discarded or discounted immediately.

In some cases, some decisions are assumed to be made under conditions of certainty simply because the environment is assumed to be stable. Other decisions are made under conditions of uncertainty, where risk is unknown. Still, a good decision maker can make working estimates of risk. Also, the process of developing BI/DSS involves learning more about the situation, which leads to a more accurate assessment of the risks.

SCENARIOS

A **scenario** is a statement of assumptions about the operating environment of a particular system at a given time; that is, it is a narrative description of the decision-situation setting. A scenario describes the decision and uncontrollable variables and parameters for a specific modeling situation. It may also provide the procedures and constraints for the modeling.

Scenarios originated in the theater, and the term was borrowed for war gaming and large-scale simulations. Scenario planning and analysis is a DSS tool that can capture a whole range of possibilities. A manager can construct a series of scenarios (i.e., what-if cases), perform computerized analyses, and learn more about the system and decision-making problem while analyzing it. Ideally, the manager can identify an excellent, possibly optimal, solution to the model of the problem.

Scenarios are especially helpful in simulations and what-if analyses. In both cases, we change scenarios and examine the results. For example, we can change the anticipated demand for hospitalization (an input variable for planning), thus creating a new scenario. Then we can measure the anticipated cash flow of the hospital for each scenario.

Scenarios play an important role in MSS because they:

- Help identify opportunities and problem areas
- Provide flexibility in planning
- Identify the leading edges of changes that management should monitor
- Help validate major modeling assumptions
- Allow the decision maker to explore the behavior of a system through a model
- Help to check the sensitivity of proposed solutions to changes in the environment, as described by the scenario

POSSIBLE SCENARIOS

There may be thousands of possible scenarios for every decision situation. However, the following are especially useful in practice:

- The worst possible scenario
- The best possible scenario
- The most likely scenario
- The average scenario

The scenario determines the context of the analysis to be performed. Scenarios were used in the MMS running case (see Online File W2.1.2) in establishing the value of each alternative.

ERRORS IN DECISION MAKING

The model is a critical component in the decision-making process, but a decision maker may make a number of errors in its development and use. Validating the model before it is used is critical. Gathering the right amount of information, with the right level of precision and accuracy, to incorporate into the decision-making process is also critical. Sawyer (1999) described "the seven deadly sins of decision making," most of which are behavior or information related.

Section 2.6 Review Questions

1. Define *optimization* and contrast it with *suboptimization*.
2. Compare the normative and descriptive approaches to decision making.
3. Define *rational decision making*. What does it really mean to be a rational decision maker?
4. Why do people exhibit bounded rationality when solving problems?
5. Define *scenario*. How is a scenario used in decision making?
6. Some "errors" in decision making can be attributed to the notion of decision making from the gut. Explain what is meant by this and how such errors can happen.

2.7 DECISION MAKING: THE CHOICE PHASE

Choice is the critical act of decision making. The choice phase is the one in which the actual decision is made and the commitment to follow a certain course of action is made. The boundary between the design and choice phases is often unclear because certain activities can be performed during both of them and because the decision maker can return frequently from choice activities to design activities (e.g., generate new alternatives while performing an evaluation of existing ones). The choice phase includes the search for, evaluation of, and recommendation of an appropriate solution to a model. A solution to a model is a specific set of values for the decision variables in a selected alternative. In the MMS running case (see Online File W2.1.2), choices were evaluated as to their viability and profitability. A choice was made to correct data errors and to move a specific number of cars from one set of locations to another. The advertising plan was modified, and new data and features were to be added to the firm's DSS.

Note that solving a model is not the same as solving the problem the model represents. The solution to the model yields a recommended solution to the problem. The problem is considered solved only if the recommended solution is successfully implemented.

Solving a decision-making model involves searching for an appropriate course of action. Search approaches include **analytical techniques** (i.e., solving a formula), **algorithms** (i.e., step-by-step procedures), heuristics (i.e., rules of thumb), and blind searches (i.e., shooting in the dark, ideally in a logical way). These approaches are covered in Chapter 4.

Each alternative must be evaluated. If an alternative has multiple goals, they must all be examined and balanced against each other. **Sensitivity analysis** is used to determine the robustness of any given alternative; slight changes in the parameters should ideally lead to slight or no changes in the alternative chosen. **What-if analysis** is used to explore major changes in the parameters. Goal seeking helps a manager determine values of the decision variables to meet a specific objective. All this is covered in Chapter 4.

Section 2.7 Review Questions

1. Explain the difference between a principle of choice and the actual choice phase of decision making.
2. Why do some people claim that the choice phase is the point in time when a decision is really made?
3. How can sensitivity analysis help in the choice phase?

2.8 DECISION MAKING: THE IMPLEMENTATION PHASE

In *The Prince*, Machiavelli astutely noted some 500 years ago that there was "nothing more difficult to carry out, nor more doubtful of success, nor more dangerous to handle, than to initiate a new order of things." The implementation of a proposed solution to a problem is, in effect, the initiation of a new order of things or the introduction of change. And change must be managed. User expectations must be managed as part of change management.

The definition of *implementation* is somewhat complicated because implementation is a long, involved process with vague boundaries. Simplistically, the **implementation phase** involves putting a recommended solution to work, not necessarily implementing a computer system. Many generic implementation issues, such as resistance to change, degree of support of top management, and user training, are important in dealing with MSS. In the MMS running case (see Online File W2.1.4), implementation was a little fuzzy. Some decisions were pilot tested by the people responsible for those aspects of decision making before the decision was implemented nationally. Essentially for MMS, implementation involved updating computer systems, testing models and scenarios for impacts, and physically moving the cars from some locations to others. The computer system updates ideally should involve some kind of formal information system development approach, while the actual implementation of the decision may not.

Implementation is covered in detail in later chapters. The decision-making process, though conducted by people, can be improved with computer support, which is the subject of the next section.

Section 2.8 Review Questions

1. Define *implementation*.
2. How can a DSS support the implementation of a decision?

2.9 HOW DECISIONS ARE SUPPORTED

In Chapter 1 we discussed the need for computerized decision support and briefly described some decision aids. Here we relate specific MSS technologies to the decision-making process (see Figure 2.2). Databases, data marts, and especially data warehouses are especially important technologies in supporting all phases of decision making, especially when accessed via Web-based interfaces. They provide the data that drive decision making.

SUPPORT FOR THE INTELLIGENCE PHASE

The primary requirement of decision support for the intelligence phase is the ability to scan external and internal information sources for opportunities and problems and to interpret what the scanning discovers. Web tools and sources are extremely useful for environmental scanning. Web browsers provide useful front ends for a variety of tools, from OLAP to data mining and data warehouses. Data sources can be internal or external. Internal sources may be accessible via a corporate intranet. External sources are many and varied. For a list of many Web sites with global macroeconomic and business data, see Hansen (2002).

Decision support/BI technologies can be very helpful. For example, an EIS can support the intelligence phase by continuously monitoring both internal and external information, looking for early signs of problems and opportunities through a Web-based enterprise information portal (also called a dashboard), as in the MMS running case (see Online File W2.1.2). Similarly, (automatic) data (and Web) mining (which may include expert systems [ES], CRM, genetic algorithms, neural networks, and other ADM systems) and (manual) OLAP also support the intelligence phase by identifying relationships among activities and other factors. Geographic information systems (GIS) can be utilized either as standalones or integrated with these systems so that a decision maker can determine opportunities and problems in a spatial sense. These tools are often described as business analytics (BA), or Web analytics, applications. These relationships can be exploited for competitive advantage (e.g., CRM identifies classes of customers to approach with specific products and services; see Sparacino and O'Reilly, 2000). A KMS can be used to identify similar past situations and how they were handled. GSS can be used to share information and for brainstorming.

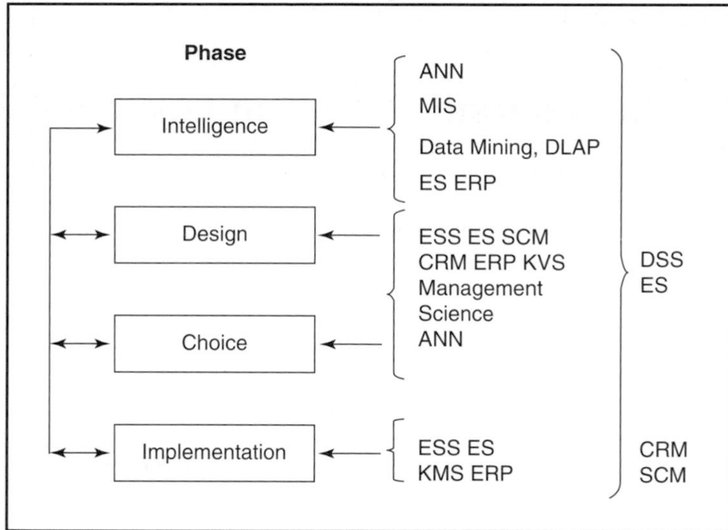

FIGURE 2.2 DSS Support

Source: Based in part on Sprague, R. H., Jr., "A Framework for the Development of DSS." MIS Quarterly, Dec, 1980, Fig. 5. p. 13.

Artificial neural networks (ANN) can be used to identify the best takeover targets, as demonstrated for banks by Shawver and Aronson (2003). The Internet provides consistent, familiar interface tools via portals and access to critical, often fuzzy information necessary to identify problems and opportunities. Finally, visualization systems and tools, typically embedded within many of these packages, can be utilized to present results in formats that assist decision makers in identifying opportunities and problems.

Another aspect of identifying internal problems and capabilities involves monitoring the current status of operations. When something goes wrong, it can be identified quickly and the problem can be solved. Tools such as business activity monitoring (BAM), business process management (BPM), and product life-cycle management (PLM) provide such capability to decision makers.

ES, on the other hand, can render advice regarding the nature of a problem, its classification, its seriousness, and the like. ES can advise on the suitability of a solution approach and the likelihood of successfully solving the problem. One of the primary areas of ES success is interpreting information and diagnosing problems. This capability can be exploited in the intelligence phase. Even intelligent agents can be used to identify opportunities (see Desouza, 2001).

Another area of support is reporting. Both routine and ad hoc reports can aid in the intelligence phase. For example, regular reports can be designed to assist in the problem-finding activity by comparing expectations with current and projected performance. Web-based OLAP tools are excellent at this task. So are visualization tools and electronic document management systems.

Much of the information used in seeking new opportunities is qualitative, or soft. This indicates a high level of unstructuredness in the problems, thus making DSS quite useful in the intelligence phase. For example, see Application Case 2.4, in which Union Pacific seeks out opportunities in the avalanche of data that it must, by law, collect.

Application Case 2.4

Union Pacific Railroad: If You're Collecting Data, Use It Profitably!

Union Pacific is required by law to collect dozens of gigabytes of data every month about rail conditions, but its competitive spirit is why the company leverages those data, stored in several incompatible formats in various relational and mainframe systems, for its BI initiative. Data are collected via Motorola's Canopy wireless broadband platform. Using reporting, analysis, and querying applications, decision makers can find the needed and appropriate information from existing systems and derive answers from composite, incompatible data—without waiting for daily or monthly batch loads into a centralized data warehouse.

Sources: Modified from "Smarter, Faster, More Profitable: 20 Organizations That Get It," *IntelligentEnterprise*, Vol. 4, No. 15, October 4, 2001, pp. 18–19; and Motorola, Inc., *The Largest Railroad in the U.S. Uses Wireless Broadband to Increase Switching Yard Productivity*, 2004, **motorola.com/Enterprise/contentdir/en_US/Enterprise/Files/UnionPacCaseStudy.pdf** (accessed March 2006).

The Internet and advanced database technologies have created a glut of data and information available to decision makers—so much that it can detract from the quality and speed of decision making. Fortunately, intelligent agents and other artificial intelligence tools can lessen the burden. Technology Insights 2.4 describes some of the issues that managers are grappling with in the digital age of decision making.

SUPPORT FOR THE DESIGN PHASE

The **design phase** involves generating alternative courses of action, discussing the criteria for choices and their relative importance, and forecasting the future consequences of using various alternatives. Several of these activities can use standard models provided by a DSS (e.g., financial and forecasting models, available as applets). Alternatives for structured problems can be generated through the use of either standard or special models. However, the generation of alternatives for complex problems requires expertise that can be provided only by a human, brainstorming software, or an ES. OLAP and data mining software are quite useful in identifying relationships that can be used in models (see the MMS running case in Online File W2.1.2). Most DSS have quantitative analysis capabilities, and an internal ES can assist with qualitative methods as well as with the expertise required in selecting quantitative analysis and forecasting models. A KMS should certainly be consulted to determine whether such a problem has been encountered before or whether there are experts on hand who can provide quick understanding and answers. CRM systems, revenue management systems (as in the MMS running case), ERP, and SCM systems software are useful in that they provide models of business processes that can test assumptions and scenarios. If a problem requires brainstorming to help identify important issues and options, a GSS may prove helpful. Tools that provide cognitive mapping can also help. All these tools can be accessed via the Web. Cohen et al. (2001) described several Web-based tools that provide decision support, mainly in the design phase, by providing models and reporting of alternative results. Each of their cases has saved millions of dollars annually by utilizing these tools. Web-based DSS are helping engineers in product design as well as decision makers solving business problems.

TECHNOLOGY INSIGHTS 2.4

Decision Making in the Digital Age

Kepner-Tregoe, Inc. (**kepner-tregoe.com**), surveyed managers and workers across the United States to determine how they cope with the need for faster decision making and how companies are balancing the requirement for speed with the concomitant need for quality.

Decision makers are under pressure to keep up, but in the process, they are too often sacrificing the quality of decision making. Digital-age decision makers are not making the most of what is available. They are often unable to gather sufficient information, they do a poor job of sharing that information, and they fail to involve the right people in the decision process. Here are Kepner-Tregoe's key findings:

- *More decisions are being made in less time.* Both managers and workers must make more decisions in the same or less time. Sixty-five percent of workers and 77 percent of managers said that they must make more decisions every day. At the same time, most also agreed that the amount of time they have to make decisions has either decreased or stayed the same.
- *Respondents are missing opportunities.* Despite the pressure to make speedy decisions, nearly 75 percent of workers and 80 percent of managers said they miss opportunities because they don't make decisions quickly enough. Most agreed that decisions are frequently not implemented in a timely manner.
- *Many feel as if they are losing the race.* When asked to compare the speed of their organization's decision making to that of rivals, only one-quarter of workers and fewer than one-third of managers said they are moving faster than their competition.
- *Many barriers to speed are human.* Workers and managers closely agreed that the need for multiple approvals is the most frequently encountered barrier. Other common roadblocks mentioned are organizational politics, changing priorities, and getting people to agree up front on what they want a decision to accomplish.
- *IT clearly has a widespread influence.* When asked specifically where IT has become the most important source of information for decision making, both workers and managers listed budgeting/finance, purchasing, and customer service, followed closely by daily product management, quality/productivity, personnel/human resources, and process improvement.
- *Sources of information are constantly changing.* When asked where they get the information on which they base their decisions today (compared to three years ago), both workers and managers described a major shift from real to virtual sources. The most dramatic change was in the increased use of e-mail. Most also agreed not only that the quantity of information has increased but that the quality of the information has increased as well.
- *Decision making amnesia is rampant.* Organizations are not very effective at preserving their decision-making experiences. Of those who said that their organizations have a system in place to house decision criteria, 77 percent of workers and 82 percent of managers said they couldn't assess the utility of their databases.

Decision-leading firms have figured out ways to counter these deficiencies. See the source for details.

Sources: Modified from D.K. Wessel, "Decision Making in the Digital Age," *DM Review 2002 Resource Guide*, Vol. 12, No. 12, December 2001; and material from Kepner-Tregoe, Inc., **kepner-tregoe.com** (accessed July 2006).

SUPPORT FOR THE CHOICE PHASE

In addition to providing models that rapidly identify a best or good-enough alternative, a DSS can support the choice phase through what-if and goal-seeking analyses. Different scenarios can be tested for the selected option to reinforce the final decision. Again, a KMS helps identify similar past experiences; CRM, ERP, and SCM systems are used to test the impacts of decisions in establishing their value, leading to an intelligent choice. An ES can be used to assess the desirability of certain solutions as well as to recommend an appropriate solution. If a group makes a decision, a GSS can provide support to lead to consensus.

SUPPORT FOR THE IMPLEMENTATION PHASE

This is where "making the decision happens" occurs. The DSS benefits provided during implementation may be as important as or even more important than those in the earlier phases. DSS can be used in implementation activities such as decision communication, explanation, and justification.

Implementation-phase DSS benefits are partly due to the vividness and detail of analyses and reports. For example, one chief executive officer (CEO) gives employees and external parties not only the aggregate financial goals and cash needs for the near term but also the calculations, intermediate results, and statistics used in determining the aggregate figures. In addition to communicating the financial goals unambiguously, the CEO signals other messages. Employees know that the CEO has thought through the assumptions behind the financial goals and is serious about their importance and attainability. Bankers and directors are shown that the CEO was personally involved in analyzing cash needs and is aware of and responsible for the implications of the financing requests prepared by the finance department. Each of these messages improves decision implementation in some way. In the MMS running case (see Online File W2.1), team members had access to information in order to make decisions, and they also had information about the results of the decisions.

BAM, BPM, PLM, KMS, EIS, ERP, CRM, and SCM are all useful in tracking how well an implementation is working. GSS is useful for a team to collaborate in establishing implementation effectiveness. For example, a decision might be made to get rid of unprofitable customers. An effective CRM can identify classes of customers to get rid of, identify the impact of doing so, and then verify that it really worked that way (see Murphy, 2002; and Swift, 2001).

All phases of the decision-making process can be supported by improved communication through collaborative computing via GSS and KMS. Computerized systems can facilitate communication by helping people explain and justify their suggestions and opinions.

Decision implementation can also be supported by ES. An ES can be used as an advisory system regarding implementation problems (such as handling resistance to change). Finally, an ES can provide training that may smooth the course of implementation.

Impacts along the value chain, though reported by an EIS through a Web-based enterprise information portal, are typically identified by BAM, BPM, SCM, and ERP systems. CRM systems report and update internal records, based on the impacts of the implementation. These inputs are then used to identify new problems and opportunities—a return to the intelligence phase.

NEW TECHNOLOGY SUPPORT FOR DECISION MAKING

Web-based systems have clearly influenced how decision making is supported. With the development of mobile commerce (m-commerce), more and more personal devices (e.g., personal digital assistants [PDAs], cell phones, tablet computers, laptop computers) can access information sources, and users can respond to systems with information updates, collaboration efforts, and decisions. This is especially important for salespeople, who can be more effective if they can access their CRM while on the road and then enter orders. Constant access to corporate data, inventory and otherwise, can only help them in their work. Overall, wireless devices are taking on greater importance in the enterprise, generally by accessing specialized Web servers that provide data and communication directly to m-commerce devices.

East Bay Restaurant Supply (Oakland, CA) reported that although it had not evaluated the effectiveness of providing instantaneous information to all its sales representatives, it had saved $45,000 by providing each of its 15 reps with a PDA instead of a notebook computer. (For details on how East Bay Restaurant Supply and other firms have initiated m-commerce efforts, see McVicker, 2001.) Museums are even utilizing wireless technology to provide better access and service (see Application Case 2.5). Finally, advanced artificial intelligence technologies can be utilized in decision making. Camacho et al. (2001) described how travel planning in e-tourism can be handled by intelligent agents; Desouza (2001) surveyed applications of intelligent agents for competitive intelligence.

Application Case 2.5

Advanced Technology for Museums: RFID Makes Art Come Alive

Museums are not known for utilizing state-of-the-art technology in general. However, some are now using high-tech devices to understand their visitors (customers) to determine what they want to see (demand) and when. Visitors using handheld devices at several of the Smithsonian museums can get maps; find interactive lists of exhibits; get help finding specific items; find schedules of guided tours, see video clips and pictures; including some items not on the floor; instant message (IM) other visitors; and locate information about others in their group. The Smithsonian hopes that this system, called SIguide, will produce a better museum experience for visitors and allow them to spend their time effectively. It can also promote various underutilized exhibits, essentially advertising them to an appropriate audience based on interest detected by the system. Through location-tracking technology, the system can track demand for specific exhibits or types of exhibits, and the Smithsonian can make better decisions about future exhibits.

The Cleveland Museum of Art is taking its tracking technology a step further by using radio frequency identification (RFID) tags. This system collects detailed information about visitors' use of the exhibits and helps determine individual versus group behavior to determine which are high-demand exhibits. It can also track viewing and movement patterns through the museum, ultimately leading to an experience personalized for each visitor.

The Museum of Natural History in Aarhus, Denmark has put RFID tags next to an exhibit of 50 stuffed birds. Visitors carry a PDA to access the text, quizzes, and audio and video clips that are stored in them. Some museums are even tagging their collections with RFID to track them internally.

Source: Modified and abstracted from C. Lindquist, "Magical History Tour," *CIO*, July 15, 2005; "RFID Enhances Visitors' Museum Experience at the Exploratorium," *Communications of the ACM*, Vol. 48, No. 9, September 2005, pp. 60–65; NJE Consulting, *Advantages of RFID in Museum Setting*, **nje.ca/Index_RFID_Museum.htm** (accessed January 2006); Access Control & Security Systems, *RFID Takes Chicago Museum Visitors Inside the Internet*, **securitysolutions.com/mag/security_rfid_takes_chicago**, (accessed January 2006); and F. Khan, "Museum Puts Tags on Stuffed Birds," *RFID Journal*, September 7, 2004.

The Web provides a vehicle to disseminate knowledge and information about decision making and DSS. We list some of the many sources for decision-making support and theory in Online File W2.3.

Section 2.9 Review Questions

1. Describe how DSS/BI technologies and tools can aid in each phase of decision making.
2. Describe how new technologies can provide decision-making support.

2.10 RESOURCES, LINKS, AND THE TERADATA UNIVERSITY NETWORK CONNECTION

The use of this chapter and most other chapters in this book can be enhanced by the tools described in the following sections.

RESOURCES AND LINKS

Along with the references listed in Online File W2.4, we recommend looking at the following resources and links for further reading and explanations:

- The Data Warehousing Institute (**tdwi.org**)
- *DM Review* (**dmreview.com**)
- *CIO* magazine (**cio.com**)
- DSS Resources (**dssresources.com**)

CASES

All major BI/BA vendors (e.g., MicroStrategy, Teradata, Oracle, IBM, Hyperion, Cognos, FairIsaac, SAP, Information Builders, Expert Choice) provide interesting customer success stories on BI/BA technology use. Because these technologies are ultimately utilized in decision making, there are always aspects of the decision-making process described in the story. Look at the vendors' Web sites for cases. Cases are also available at the Teradata University Network (**teradatauniversitynetwork.com**). Specifically, consider "Harrah's High Payoff from Customer Information" and "Whirlpool." Academic-oriented cases are available at the Harvard Business School Case Collection (**www.hbsp.harvard.edu/b01/en/cases/cases_home.jhtml**).

MILLER'S MIS CASES

All the spreadsheet and database cases in Miller's *MIS Cases* (2005) involve decision making and can be utilized.

VENDORS, PRODUCTS, AND DEMOS

There are many online sources for online decision making. Many vendors are listed in Chapter 4. However, to get started, consider the Expert Choice package (**expertchoice.com**). Also see the list at **dmreview.com/resources/demos.cfm**. Finally, go to **terry.uga.edu/people/jaronson/mist5620**, select Course Materials, and then click the BI software link.

PERIODICALS

We recommend the following periodicals:

- *Decision Support Systems* (**elsevier.com**)
- *CIO* (**cio.com**)
- *CIO Insight* (**cioinsight.com**)
- *Baseline Magazine* (**baselinemag.com**)

ADDITIONAL REFERENCES

Additional selected references are provided in the online files of each chapter. For this chapter, see Online File W2.4.

THE TERADATA UNIVERSITY CONNECTION

Teradata University Network.com (TUN) (**teradatastudentnetwork.com**, for students) provides a wealth of material related to decision making, mostly through BI tools that include data warehouses, data marts, visualization, OLAP, data mining, and other forms of business analytics. The site provides cases, articles, exercises, and software.

Chapter Highlights

- Managerial decision making is synonymous with the whole process of management.
- Human decision styles need to be recognized in designing MSS.
- Individual and group decision making can both be supported by MSS.
- Problem solving is also opportunity evaluation.
- A model is a simplified representation or abstraction of reality.
- Models are used extensively in MSS; they can be iconic, analogical, or mathematical.
- Decision making involves four major phases: intelligence, design, choice, and implementation.
- In the intelligence phase, the problem (opportunity) is identified, classified, and decomposed (if needed), and problem ownership is established.
- In the design phase, a model of the system is built, criteria for selection are agreed on, alternatives are generated, results are predicted, and a decision methodology is created.
- There is a trade-off between model accuracy and cost.
- Rationality is an important assumption in decision making. Rational decision makers can establish preferences and order them consistently.
- In the choice phase, alternatives are compared, and a search for the best (or a good-enough) solution is launched. Many search techniques are available.
- In implementing alternatives, a decision maker should consider multiple goals and sensitivity-analysis issues.
- Satisficing is a willingness to settle for a satisfactory solution. In effect, satisficing is suboptimizing. Bounded rationality results in decision makers satisficing.
- Computer systems, especially those that are Web based, can support all phases of decision making by automating many of the required tasks or by applying artificial intelligence.

Key Terms

- algorithm
- analog model
- analytical techniques
- choice phase
- decision making
- decision style
- decision variable
- descriptive model
- design phase
- effectiveness
- efficiency
- iconic model
- implementation phase
- intelligence phase
- mental model
- normative model
- optimization
- principle of choice
- problem ownership
- problem solving
- satisficing
- scenario
- sensitivity analysis
- simulation
- suboptimization
- what-if analysis

Questions For Discussion

1. Why is intuition still an important aspect of decision making?
2. Define *efficiency*, define *effectiveness*, and compare and contrast the two.
3. Why is it important to focus on the effectiveness of a decision, not necessarily the efficiency of making a decision?

4. What are some of the measures of effectiveness in a toy manufacturing plant, a restaurant, an educational institution, and the U.S. Congress?
5. Even though implementation of a decision involves change, and change management is very difficult, explain how change management has *not* changed very much in thousands of years. Use specific examples throughout history.
6. Despite the advances in ADM methods and tools, why should we still insist that a human being still be responsible for every decision?
7. Why should all information system development projects focus on some aspect of decision making in practice?
8. Your company is considering opening a branch in China. List typical activities in each phase of the decision (intelligence, design, choice, implementation) of whether to open or not open.
9. You are about to sell your car. What principles of choice are you most likely to use in deciding whether to offer or reject offers? Why?
10. You are about to buy a car. Using Simon's four-phase model, describe your activities at each step.
11. The use of scenarios is popular in computerized decision making. Why? For what types of decisions is this technique most appropriate?
12. Explain, through an example, the support given to decision makers by computers in each phase of the decision process.
13. Some experts believe that the major contribution of DSS is to the implementation of a decision. Why is this so?
14. Most managers are capable of using the telephone without understanding or even considering the electrical and magnetic theories involved. Why is it necessary for managers to understand MSS tools to use them wisely?

Exercises

Teradata University and Other Hands-On Exercises

1. Choose a case at TSN or use the case that your instructor chooses. Describe in detail what decisions were to be made in the case and what process was actually followed. Be sure to describe how technology assisted or hindered the decision-making process and what the decision's impacts were.
2. Most companies and organizations have downloadable demos or trial versions of their software products on the Web so that you can copy and try them out on your own computer. Others have online demos. Find one that provides decision support, try it out, and write a short report about it. Include details about the intended purpose of the software, how it works, and how it supports decision making.
3. Early in the chapter, we mention the Great Wall of China as a major blunder. Investigate it. Study the history of the Great Wall. Look up why it was constructed, how it was done, how long it took, and similar facts. Why did it fail to meet its primary objective? Identify four other equally major blunders and explain what happened in each case.
4. According to Bennis and Nanus (2003), "Managers are people who do things right and leaders are people who do the right thing. The difference may be summarized as activities of vision and judgment—effectiveness—versus activities of mastering routines—efficiency." (Also see Baron and Padwa, 2000.) Explain how this view relates to decision making, managers, executives, and systems.
5. Comment on Simon's (1977) philosophy that managerial decision making is synonymous with the whole process of management. Does this make sense? Explain. Use a real-world example in your explanation.
6. Consider a situation in which you have a preference about where you go to college: You want to be not too far away from home and not too close. Why might this situation arise? Explain how this situation fits with rational decision-making behavior.
7. When you were looking for a college program, somehow you were able to decide on going where you are now. Examine your decision-making process and describe it in a report. Explain how you eliminated the many thousands of programs around the world and then in your own country or region. What criteria were important? What was your final set of alternatives? How did you decide among them? Compare your results with those of others in the class.
8. You are about to buy a car. What criteria are important? What specific choices do you have, and how will you limit your choices? Go to Expert Choice, Inc. (**expertchoice.com**), to learn about the AHP and structure your problem within its framework. Does this make intuitive sense? Explain why it does or does not.
9. Stories about suboptimization issues abound in some formerly centrally planned national economies in

which the output of factories was measured by seemingly useful measures, with unexpected and disastrous results. Specifically, a ball-bearing factory's output was measured by the total weight of the ball bearings produced, so the plant manager decided to produce one very large ball bearing each month. There was a shoe factory where output was measured by the number of left shoes, so the plant manager decided to make only left shoes to double the factory's official output. Explain in detail how the measure of the result variable (output) of a subsystem can contribute to bad decisions that lead to suboptimized results for the entire system and what the consequences might be. Think in terms of what it means to establish a principle of choice. This is not unique to centrally planned economies but can happen in any organization. Give an example from your personal or professional life in which this happened.

10. According to H.L. Mencken, "There is always an easy solution to every human problem—neat, plausible and wrong" ("The Divine Afflatus," *New York Evening Mail*, Nov. 16, 1917; later published in *Prejudices: Second Series*, 1920; and *A Mencken Chrestomathy*, 1949). Explain this statement in the light of the decision-making material in this chapter and examples with which you are familiar.

Team Assignments and Role-Playing

1. Interview a person who has recently been involved in making a business decision. Try to identify the following:
   a. The scope of the problem solved.
   b. The people involved in the decision. (Explicitly identify the problem owners.)
   c. Simon's phases. (You may have to ask specific questions, such as how the problem was identified.)
   d. The alternatives (choices) and the decision chosen.
   e. How the decision was implemented.
   f. How computers were used to support the decision making or why they were not used.

   Produce a detailed report, describing an analysis of this information, and clearly state how closely this real-world decision-making process compares to Simon's suggested process. Clearly identify how computers were used or why they were not used in this situation.
2. Develop a cognitive map of the decision-making problem of selecting a job or a university program, using Decision Explorer from Banxia Software, Ltd. (**banxia.com**). Describe your thought processes and how you developed the map.
3. Watch the movie *12 Angry Men* (1957), starring Henry Fonda. Comment on the group decision-making process that the jury followed. Explain how this is a demonstration of group decision making. Does it fit into Simon's four-phase model? Explain why or why not, citing examples from the movie.
4. Watch the movie *The Bachelor* (1999), starring Chris O'Donnell. In it, a man must marry by a deadline to inherit $100 million. There are many alternatives, but the criteria are quite fuzzy. Watch the scene toward the end of the movie where about 1,000 brides converge on a church and want to know what the criteria are. Explain how the main character describes his criteria and what they are. Explain why they are quite vague. Explain what his criteria really are. Given enough time, compare your answers to Piver (2000).
5. Sometimes you find yourself between the proverbial rock and a hard place. All the alternatives you have discovered are bad or infeasible. You have a real problem. Examine the decision making situation regarding the *Alexander Hamilton*, described in Application Case 2-3. Explore the situation regarding the ship and suggest some possible alternatives and why they are feasible.
6. Have everyone in your group individually make a list of the factors they considered when selecting a place to live (or alternatively, the program of study in which you are enrolled) and approximately how much weight (percentage) they individually put on each factor. Determine which and how many of the factors were common. Using a common list of factors, have each individual weight them. Discuss within the group why certain factors were important and others were not. Take an average of the factors' weights and see if anyone's factor weights were close. Write up your results in a report, indicating how these factors affect this type of decision making.

Internet Exercises

1. Search the Internet for material on managerial decision making. What general classes of materials can you identify in a sample of 10 sites?
2. Many colleges and universities post their course catalogs, course descriptions, and syllabi on the Web. Examine a sample of 10 courses in at least 4 different disciplines within a business school. Compare their topical material and identify how each course relates to decision making. What is the major focus of these courses? What percentage of them include computerized support? In which departments are they typically found?

3. Search the Internet for companies and organizations that provide computerized support for managerial decision making. (Hint: Search for *business intelligence*.) Take a sample of five software vendors and characterize their products, based on specific functional market area (e.g., marketing, manufacturing, insurance, transportation), level of managerial support (e.g., strategic, tactical, operational, transactional), type of computerized tool (e.g., DSS, data mining, BI, OLAP, EIS, ES, ANN, cluster analysis), and how they utilize Web technologies. Take a sample of 10 nonvendors (e.g., consultants). What kinds of support do they provide?
4. Access a DSS/BI software vendor's Web site (select one or use the one your instructor selects). Select a success story of the software or use the one your instructor selects. Describe in detail what decisions were to be made and what process was actually followed. Be sure to describe how technology assisted (or hindered) the decision-making process and what the decision's impacts were.

End of Chapter Application Case

Strategic Decision Making In the Pharmaceutical Industry: How Bayer Decides Whether or Not to Develop a New Drug

Deciding whether to bring a new product to market is typically a major strategic decision. For a pharmaceutical firm, it is a critical decision in that just a few major successes can mean the difference between great success and abject failure. Drug development is time-consuming, resource intensive, risky, and heavily regulated. On average, it can take some 12 to 15 years of research and development to get a drug to the market, at a cost of between (U.S.) $750 and $850 million (in 2002). An FDA white paper in 2004 ("Innovation or Stagnation: Challenge and Opportunity on the Critical Path to New Medical Products," U.S. Food and Drug Administration, Docket No. 2004N-0181, March 2004, available at **fda.gov/oc/initiatives/criticalpath/whitepaper.pdf**) indicated that the cost could reach as much as $1.7 billion. Boston Consulting Group estimated that the effective use of IT to improve decision making in this process could save between $100 to $200 million dollars per drug (J.A. DiMasi, R.W. Hansen, and H.G. Grabowski, "The Price of Innovation: New Estimates of Drug Development Costs," *Journal of Health Economics*, Vol. 22, No. 2, March 2003, pp. 151–185).

THE DECISION-MAKING PROCESS

Bayer Pharmaceuticals (Pharma) uses a structured process based on the principles of decision analysis to evaluate the technical feasibility and market potential of each of its new drugs. The process, beyond the initial chemistry, is one of many sequential decisions to pursue or not pursue the next phase of testing, from preclinical animal trials to clinical human testing, with many applications to the Food and Drug Administration (FDA) for permission to proceed. There are three phases of human testing to determine whether a drug is safe and effective. Phase 1 is a safety test; phase 2 determines the drug's clinical effectiveness in its proposed use, along with the optimum dosage; and phase 3 expands on the data from the first two phases, ultimately leading to the FDA application for approval. In parallel, the firm develops and determines the feasibility of the production process of the drug, along with a worldwide market analysis. Ultimately, the FDA approves only about one in four applications. About half the drugs move from animal to clinical trials.

The strategic planning department at Bayer Biological Products (BP), a business unit of Pharma, became responsible for the commercial evaluation of drugs in July 1999, starting with the new blood-clot-busting drug BAY 57-9602. The decision to introduce this drug was based on BP's use of a formal decision analysis method to determine its commercial viability every step of the way.

A cross-functional team was responsible for gathering and analyzing data. This team was responsible to the BP leadership committee consisting of senior managers. This was clearly a team decision-making process. The team initially met to establish goals and problem ownership. Brainstorming and role-playing exercises were used for team building and to identify issues not previously known. Essentially, the process involved the team gathering and synthesizing data and meeting with experts every step of the way to estimate costs and risks. For example, following preclinical animal trials, experts estimated the viability of the drug. This included estimates of the costs of continued testing and application, along with those of production, and probability estimates of success. Influence diagrams were used throughout the process due to the complexity of the problem. Each particular drug is viewed as a project. As new data are available, essentially at the end of each phase of testing, knowledge updates are made, and a go/no go decision is made. If the estimate of the drug's profitability, including risk adjustments, is not worth the effort, then the development of the drug is cancelled.

It is important to remember that the input from many experts, ranging from chemists to packaging engineers, to production engineers, to marketing specialists, is utilized both in a financial sense and a risk sense. The likelihood of success is a primary factor in making the final decision. Also, sensitivity analysis was utilized to determine whether the decision would fluctuate based on small and large changes in the estimates.

RESULTS

When the results were presented to the BP leadership committee, several surprises occurred. One important one was that certain factors thought to be key in decision making were not because Bayer, unlike many other firms, actually manufactures its own products. This directly affected the estimates of risk and, consequently, success. Ultimately, BAY 57-9602 was deemed commercially viable and moved through all phases of development, as the results were validated at the end of each phase of testing via adjustments. The project team did a great job in analyzing this situation, leading to a set of new standards for BP in analyzing the commercial viability of new drugs.

Sources: Modified and compiled from J.S. Stonebraker, "How Bayer Makes Decisions to Develop New Drugs," *Interfaces*, Vol. 32, No. 6, November–December 2002, pp. 77–90; "Speedy Cures," *ComputerWorld*, Vol. 36, No. 51, December 23, 2002, p. 38; E. Venere, "Research Universities Join Effort to Reduce Costs of Drug Development, Manufacturing," *Purdue University News*, West Lafayette, IN, November 3, 2005, **news.uns.purdue.edu/html4ever/2005/051103.Basu.pharmacy.html** (accessed March 2006); "Bayer BP Uses Decision Analysis to Manage Drug Development, Says O.R. Study," *Science Blog*, February 2003, **scienceblog.com/community/older/2003/E/20033178.html** (accessed January 2006); and **covance.com** (accessed March 2006).

QUESTIONS FOR THE CASE

1. Describe the different areas that must be considered when bringing a new drug to market.
2. In this case, how was information about risk gathered and then used?
3. Does it make sense to use net present value as a measure of success? Explain why or why not.
4. Why is it important in sequential decision making to reevaluate for a go/no-go decision?
5. It is estimated that IT can have the most impact on phase 3 of human testing. Investigate why this is the case. (Hint: Check the *ComputerWorld* article.)
6. Explain the similarities and differences between the decision that Bayer and other major pharmaceutical firms face in new drug development and those of a major motion picture studio considering developing a film.
7. How could the process that Bayer developed be provided to a smaller firm in the industry?

References

Allan, N., R. Frame, and I. Turney. (2003). "Trust and Narrative: Experiences of Sustainability." *The Corporate Citizen*, Vol. 3, No. 2.

Barba-Romero, S. (2001, July/August). "The Spanish Government Uses a Discrete Multicriteria DSS to Determine Data Processing Acquisitions." *Interfaces*, Vol. 31, No. 4, pp. 123-131.

Baron, D., and L. Padwa. (2000). *Moses on Management*. New York: Pocket Books.

Bazerman, M.H. (2005). *Judgment in Managerial Decision Making*, 6th ed. New York: Wiley.

Beach, L.R. (2005). *The Psychology of Decision Making: People in Organizations*, 2nd ed. Thousand Oaks, CA: Sage.

Bennis, W., and B. Nanus. (2003). *Leaders: Strategies for Taking Charge*. New York: HarperBusiness Essentials.

Bonabeau, E., and C. Meyer. (2001, May 1). "Swarm Intelligence: A Whole New Way to Think About Business." *Harvard Business Review*, Vol. 79, No. 5, pp. 106–114.

Borges, M.R.S., J.A. Pino, and C. Valle. (2002, July 4–7). "On the Implementation and Follow-up of Decisions." *Proceedings of DSIage 2002*, Cork, Ireland.

Bhushan, N. and K. Rai. (2004). *Strategic Decision Making: Applying the Analytic Hierarchy Process*. Heidelberg: Springer-Verlag.

Camacho, D., D. Borrajo, and J.M. Molina. (2001). "Intelligent Travel Planning: A MultiAgent Planning

System to Solve Web Problems in the e-Tourism Domain." *Autonomous Agents and Multi-Agent Systems*, Vol. 4, No. 4, pp. 387–392.

Churchman, C.W. (1982). *Prediction and Optimal Decision*. Westport, CT: Greenwood Publishing Group.

Cohen, M.-D., C.B. Charles, and A.L. Medaglia. (2001, March/April). "Decision Support with Web-Enabled Software." *Interfaces*. Vol. 31, No. 2, pp. 109–129.

Crainer, S. (2002). *The 75 Greatest Management Decisions Ever Made: . . . And 21 of the Worst*, New York: MJF Books.

Cross, V. (2001, May/June). "Ready for Some Decision Making Help?" *EDUCAUSE Review*, Vol. 36, No. 3.

Davenport, T. (2004, October 1). "Decision Evolution." *CIO*.

Denning, S. (2000). *The Springboard: How Storytelling Ignites Action in Knowledge-Era Organizations*. Burlington, MA: Butterworth-Heinemann.

Desouza, H.C. (2001). "Intelligent Agents for Competitive Intelligence: Survey of Applications." *Competitive Intelligence Review*, Vol. 12, No. 4.

Drummond, H. (2001). *The Art of Decision Making: Mirrors of Imagination, Masks of Fate*. New York: Wiley.

Eden, C., and F. Ackermann. (2002). "Emergent Strategizing." In A. Huff and M. Jenkins (eds.). *Mapping Strategic Thinking*. Thousand Oaks, CA: Sage Publications.

Forman, E.H., and M.A. Selly. (2001). *Decision by Objectives*. Singapore: World Scientific Publishing Co.

Gharajedaghi, J. (2006). *Systems Thinking: Managing Chaos and Complexity: A Platform for Designing Business Architecture*, 2nd ed. Woburn, MA: Butterworth-Heinemann.

Goodie, A. (Fall, 2004). "Goodie Studies Pathological Gamblers' Risk-Taking Behavior," *The Independent Variable*. Athens, GA: The University of Georgia, Institute of Behavioral Research. **www.ibr.uga.edu/publications/fall2004.pdf**

Hansen, F. (2002, May). "Global Economic and Business Data for Credit Managers." *Business Credit*, Vol. 104, No. 5.

Horgan, D.J. (2001, November 15). "Management Briefs: Decision Making: Had We but World Enough and Time," *CIO*.

Indart, B. (2005, Summer). "Navigating the Decision Making Process Through Automation." *Business Intelligence Journal*, Vol. 10, No. 3.

Jenkins, M. (2002). "Cognitive Mapping." In D. Partington (ed.). *Essential Skills for Management Research*. Thousand Oaks, CA: Sage Publications.

Kepner, C., and B. Tregoe. (1998). *The New Rational Manager*. Princeton, NJ: Kepner-Tregoe.

Koksalan, M., and S. Zionts (eds.). (2001). *Multiple Criteria Decision Making in the New Millennium*. Heidelberg: Springer-Verlag.

Koller, G.R. (2000). *Risk Modeling for Determining Value and Decision Making*. Boca Raton, FL: CRC Press.

Kontoghiorghes, E.J., B. Rustem, and S. Siokos. (2002). *Computational Methods in Decision Making, Economics and Finance*. Boston: Kluwer.

Luce, M.F., J.W. Payne, and J.R. Bettman. (2004). "The Emotional Nature of Decision Trade-offs." In S.J. Hoch, H.C. Kunreuther, and R.E. Gunther (eds.). *Wharton on Making Decisions*. New York: Wiley.

McVicker, D. (2001, March 12). "Hands-on Decision Making: Logistics and Warehousing Executives Led the Way with PDAs." *InternetWeek*.

Miller, M.L. (2005). *MIS Cases*, 3rd ed. Upper Saddle River, NJ: Prentice Hall.

Murphy, C. (2002, May 20). "Technology Nudges Managers to Do Better." *Information Week*, No. 889.

Pauly, M.V. (2004). "Split Personality: Inconsistencies in Private and Public Decisions." In S.J. Hoch, H.C. Kunreuther, and R. E. Gunther (eds.). *Wharton on Making Decisions*. New York: Wiley.

Piver, S. (2000). *The Hard Questions: 100 Essential Questions to Ask Before You Say "I Do."* New York: J.P. Tarcher.

Purdy, J. (2005, Summer). "Decisions, Delusions, & Debacles." *UGA Research Magazine*.

Ranganathan C., and V. Sethi. (2002, Winter). "Rationality in Strategic Information Technology Decisions: The Impact of Shared Domain Knowledge and IT Unit Structure." *Decision Sciences*, Vol. 33, No. 1.

Ratner, R.K., B.E. Kahn, and D. Kahneman. (1999, June). "Choosing Less-Preferred Experiences for the Sake of Variety." *Journal of Consumer Research*, Vol. 26, No. 1.

Saaty, T.L. (2001). *Decision Making for Leaders: The Analytic Hierarchy Process for Decisions in a Complex World*, new ed. Pittsburgh: RWS Publications.

Sawyer, D.C. (1999). *Getting It Right: Avoiding the High Cost of Wrong Decisions*. Boca Raton, FL: St. Lucie Press.

Schwartz, H. (1998). *Rationality Gone Awry? Decision Making Inconsistent with Economic and Financial Theory*. Westport, CT: Praeger.

Schwartz, H. (2004). *The Paradox of Choice*. New York: HarperCollins.

Shawver, T., and J.E. Aronson. (2003). "A Neural Network Approach to Determine Accurate Bank Merger Premiums." Working paper. Athens, GA: The University of Georgia, Terry College of Business, Department of MIS.

Shoemaker, P.J.H., and J.E. Russo. (2004). "Managing Frames to Make Better Decisions." In S.J. Hoch, H.C. Kunreuther, and R.E. Gunther (eds.). *Wharton on Making Decisions*. New York: Wiley.

Simon, H. (1977). *The New Science of Management Decision*. Englewood Cliffs, NJ: Prentice Hall.

Sparacino, D., and C. O'Reilly. (2000, October). "Leveraging Customer Metrics for Strategic Decision Making." *Call Center CRM Solutions*, Vol. 19, No. 4.

Stewart, T.A. (2002, November). "How to Think with Your Gut." *Business 2.0*.

Sun, R., and C.L. Giles. (2001, July/August). "Sequence Learning: From Recognition and Prediction to Sequential Decision Making." *IEEE Intelligent Systems*.

Swift, R.S. (2001). *Accelerating Customer Relationships: Using CRM and Relationship Technologies*. Upper Saddle River, NJ: Prentice Hall.

Talluri, K.T., and G. J. van Ryzin. (2005). *The Theory and Practice of Revenue Management*. Heidelberg: Springer.

Tversky, A., P. Slovic, and D. Kahneman. (1990, March). "The Causes of Preference Reversal." *American Economic Review*, Vol. 80, No. 1.

Vlahos, J. (2005, July). "AAAAAiiiEEE." *Popular Science*.

Yakov, B.-H. (2001). *Information Gap Decision Theory: Decisions Under Severe Uncertainty*. New York: Academic Press.

Yeoman, I., and U. McMahon-Beattie. (2004). *Revenue Management and Pricing: Case Studies and Applications*. Toronto: International Thomson Business Press.

Decision Support Systems Concepts, Methodologies, and Technologies: An Overview

Learning Objectives

- Understand possible decision support system (DSS) configurations
- Understand the key differences and similarities between DSS and business intelligence (BI) systems
- Describe DSS characteristics and capabilities
- Understand the essential definition of DSS
- Understand DSS components and how they integrate
- Describe the components and structure of each DSS component: the data management subsystem, the model management subsystem, the user interface (dialog) subsystem, the knowledge-based management subsystem, and the user
- Explain Internet impacts on DSS and vice versa
- Explain the unique role of the user in DSS versus management information systems (MIS)
- Describe DSS hardware and software platforms
- Understand important DSS classifications
- Become familiar with some DSS application areas and applications
- Understand important, current DSS issues

In Chapter 1, we introduced DSS and stressed its support in the solution of complex managerial problems. In Chapter 2, we presented the methodology of decision making. In this chapter, we show how DSS superiority is achieved by examining its capabilities, structure, and classifications in the following sections:

3.1 Opening Vignette: Decision Support System Cures for Health Care

3.2 Decision Support System Configurations

3.3 Decision Support System Description
3.4 Decision Support System Characteristics and Capabilities
3.5 Components of Decision Support System
3.6 The Data Management Subsystem
3.7 The Model Management Subsystem
3.8 The User Interface (Dialog) Subsystem
3.9 The Knowledge-Based Management Subsystem
3.10 The User
3.11 Decision Support System Hardware
3.12 Decision Support System Classifications
3.13 Resources, Links, and the Teradata University Network Connection

3.1 OPENING VIGNETTE: DECISION SUPPORT SYSTEM CURES FOR HEALTH CARE

DSS can provide benefits in terms of increased effectiveness and efficiency in health systems. Here are several examples in which hospitals and agencies in the health care industry have implemented successful DSS initiatives.

DSS ASSISTS DIRECTLY IN PROVIDING PATIENT CARE AT RIVERSIDE HEALTH SYSTEM

Riverside Health System (Newport News, VA) developed Soarian, a fully integrated, workflow-driven hospital information system (HIS) from Siemens Medical Solutions Health Services Corp. The enterprise-wide, Web-based system is at the heart of Riverside's information technology (IT) program. All relevant patient information, documentation, and orders are structured so that all health care providers have all the information necessary. Internal rules and models automatically generate alerts when care conflicts occur.

DSS MONITORS AND IMPROVES OKLAHOMA HEART HOSPITAL'S IT PERFORMANCE

When constructing a new facility, Oklahoma Heart Hospital developed a new electronic medical records system and digitized *all* hospital records. This enterprise information management system monitors events and generates alarms (i.e., exceptions). The BMC Patrol Analytics tool (from Netuitive, Inc.) *learns* which alarms are real and which are not. Access and reporting are paperless; they occur via Web interfaces, with a bedside computer in every room. Patient charts and other information are available instantly everywhere.

Patrol Analytics dynamically predicts problems in the information system and alerts IT staff to take corrective measures. It also determines situations such as resource underutilization. By automating trouble detection, the IT staff can focus on helping people, leading ultimately to higher-quality patient care. Patient satisfaction at Oklahoma Heart Hospital is in the top 1 percent in the nation.

DSS IMPROVE HEALTH CARE OPTIONS EFFECTIVELY

DSS that include analytical tools help employers, insurance companies, and health care providers in providing the best care for employees, in the most efficient and effective manner. Large firms saw their health care costs rise by more than 80 percent between

2000 and 2005. One approach to health care is to analyze where expenses go by using analytical tools to analyze data from a database and then recommend effective treatment. For example, detailed analysis revealed that Navistar's International Truck and Engine Corp. employees were nearly twice as likely as the general population to suffer from diabetes. This condition alone accounted for some 24 percent of the firm's health care spending. Artificial intelligence and statistical methods were used to analyze claims to search for combinations of factors that would be likely to lead to large medical claims. At Pitney Bowes, diabetes and asthma occurred frequently. Pitney Bowes managers decided to cut copayments on drugs for diabetics and asthmatics so that workers would follow through with their treatments. This immediately decreased the average annual care cost by 6 and 15 percent for diabetics and asthmatics, respectively. In some cases, employers have increased health care insurance premiums for employees who maintain destructive behaviors such as smoking. The state of Georgia has sharply increased premiums for smokers. Managers at some firms have added wellness care for employee health segments (analogous to customer segments utilized in marketing).

The Humana, Inc., Center for Health Metrics DSS generates clinical profiles that look like geographical information system (GIS) displays that utilize color to indicate different risk segments. Humana is effectively developing advanced analytical models to control costs, improve service, and identify business opportunities. These models include statistical methods, pattern recognition, complexity theory, agent-based modeling, genetic programming, Markov models, and Bayesian learning networks. Simulation models run scenarios combining previous results. By early 2004, 8 to 10 people supported the modeling effort, and $1 million had been invested.

It is possible to effectively segment employees based on health care need characteristics. These *benefit segments* can be determined by using cluster analysis and class analysis, among other methodologies embedded in a DSS. Financial analyses can reveal appropriate types of medical benefits that are beneficial to each segment and to the organization in which they work (identical to customer relationship management [CRM] customer segmentation). The goal is to provide each employee with the right benefits package in the right format at the right time at the right price. Simulation tools are used to determine the impacts of existing and new products/packages for each segment. DSS Research reported that by segmenting employees, market share increased some 35 percent in two years for one health care provider. Government health care providers and social services agencies can utilize DSS tools and methods similarly. GHS LLC has developed a short, accurate survey instrument called Predicted Insurance Expenditures (PIE) to quickly stratify clients with an accurate prediction of future expenses.

DSS GROWTH IN HEALTH CARE

Health care DSS applications are expected to grow dramatically in the coming decade. The general population is aging, and the incidence of chronic diseases is rising, leading to necessary cost containment and market/benefit segmentation. Health care providers, insurance companies, employers, and government agencies can make effective decisions about medical benefits and costs by using the right data and models.

Sources: Modified from R.R. Rogoski, "All Roads Lead to Soarian," *Health Management Technology*, Vol. 26, No. 7, July 2005, pp. 10–14; P. Musich, "Mission Critical," *eWeek*, Vol. 22, No. 28, July 18, 2005, pp. 29–31; DSS Research, *Case Studies in Health Plan Marketing Research*, **dssresearch.com** (accessed March 2006); Wanless, Scott, "Top 10 BI Applications for Clinical Healthcare: Tidal Wave of Demand for Clinical Quality Information," *DM Review*, Vol. 15, No. 5, May 2005, pp. 62–63, 79; B. Rose, "Claims Offer Clues to Worker's Health," *Atlanta Journal-Constitution*, June 12, 2005, pp. R1, R4; and GHS, LLC, **ghsglobal.com** (accessed March 2006).

Questions for the Opening Vignette

1. The key issue in DSS in health care is decision making. What kinds of decisions are being made, and how is DSS helping?
2. Explain why it is so important for a hospital (or a bank, an airline, etc.) to continually monitor and forecast the condition of its information technology platforms.
3. Look up the basic concepts of CRM and describe how they apply in determining benefit segments.
4. Make a list of benefits that DSS can provide to health care systems. Justify each item.
5. Search the Web for additional examples of patient or benefit segmentation in health care. Report on your findings.

WHAT WE CAN LEARN FROM THIS VIGNETTE

The opening vignette illustrates the versatility of a DSS. Specifically, it shows support systems with important characteristics, including the following:

- DSS supports individual members and an entire team, even at the enterprise level.
- DSS is used repeatedly and constantly.
- DSS has three major components: data, models, and a user interface.
- DSS uses subjective, personal, and objective data.
- DSS is used in the private and public sectors.
- DSS is assembled from a variety of tools, including databases, Web servers and clients, and analytical engines, often from several vendors.
- DSS helps the user to make smarter, better decisions more quickly.

Overall, the focus of DSS is more effective (i.e., better) decision-making and, ideally, better decisions. The systems described in this vignette demonstrate some of the potential diversification of DSS.

3.2 DECISION SUPPORT SYSTEM CONFIGURATIONS

Decision support can be provided in many different configurations. These configurations depend on the nature of the management-decision situation and the specific technologies used for support, as described in Chapter 1 (refer to Figure 1.1). These technologies are assembled from four basic components (each with several variations)—data, models, user interface, and (optionally) knowledge—and are typically deployed over the Web. Each of these components is managed by software that is either commercially available or must be programmed for the specific task. The manner in which these components are assembled defines their major capabilities and the nature of the support provided. For example, models are emphasized in a model-oriented DSS. Such models can be customized with a spreadsheet or a programming language or can be provided by standard algorithm-based tools that include linear programming. Similarly, in a data-oriented DSS, a database and its management play the major roles. Both approaches were used in the situations in the opening vignette. In this chapter, we explore all these and related topics, but first we revisit the definitions of a DSS.

Section 3.2 Review Questions

1. List and describe the three major components of DSS.

2. Explain how subjective data can be utilized in a DSS in light of the situations described in the opening vignette examples.

3. Models play a key role in DSS. Why? Explain how models exist in spreadsheet packages such as Excel.

3.3 DECISION SUPPORT SYSTEM DESCRIPTION

The early definitions of a DSS identified it as a system intended to support managerial decision makers in semistructured and unstructured decision situations. DSS were meant to be adjuncts to decision makers to extend their capabilities but not to replace their judgment. They were aimed at decisions in which judgment was required or at decisions that could not be completely supported by algorithms. Not specifically stated but implied in the early definitions was the notion that the system would be computer based, would operate interactively online, and preferably would have graphical output capabilities, now simplified via Web servers and browsers. The early definitions were open to several interpretations. Soon, several other definitions appeared that caused considerable disagreement as to what a DSS really is. For details, see Alter (1980), Bonczek et al. (1980), Keen (1980), Little (1970), and Moore and Chang (1980).

A DSS APPLICATION

A DSS is typically built to support the solution of a certain problem or to evaluate an opportunity. This is a key difference between DSS and BI applications. In a very strict sense, **business intelligence (BI)** systems monitor situations and identify problems and/or opportunities, using analytic methods. Reporting plays a major role in BI; the user generally must identify whether a particular situation warrants attention, and then analytical methods can be applied. Again, although models and data access (generally through a data warehouse) are included in BI, DSS typically have their own databases and are developed to solve a specific problem or set of problems. They are therefore called **DSS applications**.

Formally, a DSS is an approach (or methodology) for supporting decision making. It uses an interactive, flexible, adaptable computer-based information system CBIS especially developed for supporting the solution to a specific nonstructured management problem. It uses data, provides an easy user interface, and can incorporate the decision maker's own insights. In addition, a DSS includes models and is developed (possibly by end users) through an interactive and iterative process. It supports all phases of decision making and may include a knowledge component. Finally, a DSS can be used by a single user on a PC or can be Web based for use by many people at several locations.

Later in this chapter, we explore the various DSS configurations. However, it is beneficial first to deal with the characteristics and capabilities of DSS. We present these next.

Figure 3.1 shows a typical Web-based DSS architecture. This DSS structure utilizes models in BI work. Processing is distributed across several servers in solving large analytical problems. This multitiered architecture uses a Web browser to run programs on an application server. The server accesses data to construct one or more models. Data may also be provided by a data server that optionally extracts data from a data warehouse or a legacy mainframe system. When the user requires that the model be optimized, the model, populated with the data, is transferred to an optimization server. The optimization server accesses additional data from the data server, if needed, solves the problem, and provides the solution directly to the user's Web browser. Generated

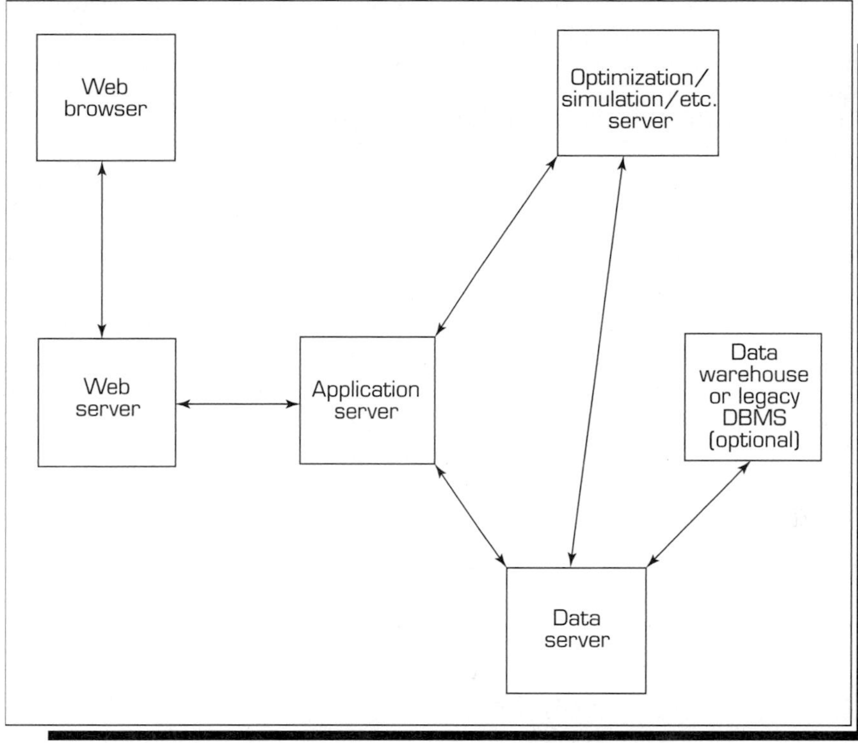

FIGURE 3.1 Multitiered Architecture for Incorporating Optimization, Simulation, and Other Models into Web-Based DSS

Source: Adapted from M.D. Cohen, C.B. Kelly, and A.L Medaglia, "Decision Support with Web-Enabled Software, *Interfaces*, Vol. 31, No. 2, 2001, pp. 109–129.

solution reports, which the application server may massage to make readable by managers, may be sent directly to appropriate parties via e-mail or may be made available through another Web portal as part of this enterprise information system (EIS). The Web-based DSS described in the End of Chapter Application Case is structured along these lines, as is Application Case 3.1.

Application Case 3.1

Web/GIS-Based DSS Aid in Disaster Relief and Identifying Food Stamp Fraud

Training classes on the new Mississippi Department of Human Services food stamp fraud-detection system ended just two weeks before Hurricane Katrina struck the U.S. Gulf Coast in August 2005. This Web/GIS-based system links models with the spatial data of a GIS to ensure that food stamp monies are not wasted or stolen in the coastal counties slated for additional food stamp benefits. Suspicious behavior is highlighted in color directly on the maps.

The location-based system was later deployed to other state agencies for applications ranging from tracking foster children to analyzing spending on Medicaid recipients. The system, developed with Web-Focus reporting tools (from Information Builders, Inc.) and Environmental

Systems Research Institute Inc.'s (ESRI's) GIS, displays key information and analytical results in maps. The state of Louisiana utilizes some of the same software for similar applications.

Such tools can also be utilized in disaster planning and recovery. Mississippi's elderly and special needs populations can be highlighted readily in evacuation planning and execution. The American Red Cross used such tools to prepare for both Hurricane Katrina and Hurricane Wilma (in October 2005). The location-based system was used to decide where to send relief supplies and set up service centers. The American Red Cross system uses Web-based query and reporting tools from Business Objects SA and GIS tools from ESRI.

Sources: Adapted from H. Havenstein, "BI–GIS Systems Support Disaster Relief Efforts," *Computerworld*, Vol. 39, No. 43, October 24, 2005, p. 5; and M. Schwartz, "Louisiana Battles Food Stamp Fraud," *Business Intelligence Journal*, Vol. 10, No. 4, Fall 2005, pp. 20–23.

Section 3.3 Review Questions

1. Provide two definitions of *DSS*. What do they have in common? What features differentiate them?
2. Why do people attempt to narrow the definition of DSS?
3. Give your own definition of *DSS*. Compare it to the definitions in question 1.
4. Explain how the systems described in Application Case 3.1 are DSS. Use the definitions from questions 1 and 3.

3.4 DECISION SUPPORT SYSTEM CHARACTERISTICS AND CAPABILITIES

Because there is no consensus on exactly what a DSS is, there is obviously no agreement on the standard characteristics and capabilities of DSS. The capabilities in Figure 3.2 constitute an ideal set, some members of which are described in the definitions and illustrated in the opening vignette. The term *BI* is not quite synonymous with *DSS*, but the two terms are often used interchangeably in practice. We differentiate the two in that DSS are generally built to solve a specific problem and include their own database(s), whereas BI applications focus on reporting and identifying problems by scanning data extracted from a data warehouse. Both systems generally include analytical tools, although BI systems with such tools are typically called *business analytics systems*. Both DSS and BI applications have become tightly aligned with Web implementations in terms of data and model access from servers and browsers as clients to run the system (refer to Application Case 3.1).

Business analytics (BA) implies the use of models and data to improve an organization's performance or competitive posture. In business analytics, the focus is on the use of models, even if they are deeply buried inside the system. Although extremely effective, advanced models are rarely utilized in BI. (Humana Corp. in the opening vignette does so, though.) This is because few managers and even analysts truly understand how and when to apply appropriate models to describe and analyze a particular situation. Data mining and OLAP systems have models embedded in them, but they are still not well understood in practice. *Web analytics* is an approach to using business analytics tools on real-time Web information to assist in decision making. Most of these applications are related to electronic commerce (e-commerce), especially in CRM, but some have been initiated in product development and supply-chain management (SCM). Finally, the term **predictive analytics** describes the business analytics method of forecasting problems and opportunities rather than simply reporting them as they occur. Predictive analytics utilizes advanced forecasting and simulation models. Humana Corp. and the Oklahoma Heart Hospital, as described in the opening

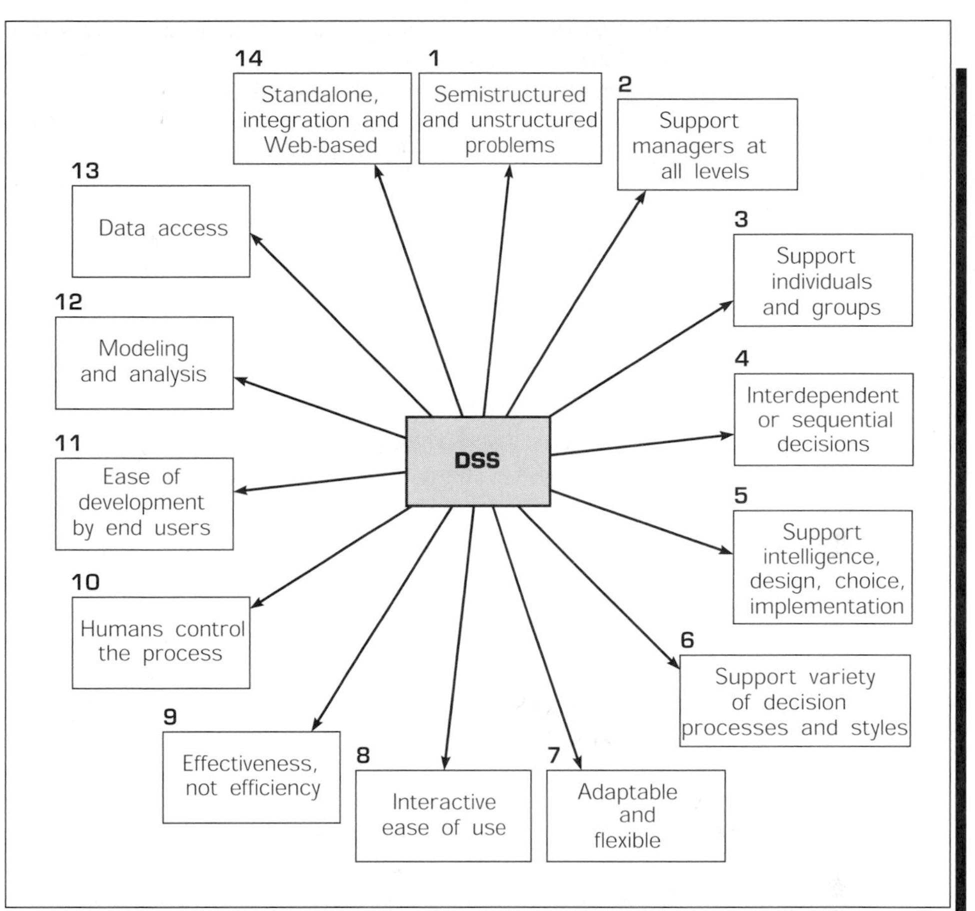

FIGURE 3.2 Key Characteristics and Capabilities of DSS

vignette, have developed some fairly sophisticated analysis tools that are currently described as predictive analytics tools.

The key characteristics and capabilities of DSS (as shown in Figure 3.2) are:

1. Support for decision makers, mainly in semistructured and unstructured situations, by bringing together human judgment and computerized information. Such problems cannot be solved (or cannot be solved conveniently) by other computerized systems or through use of standard quantitative methods or tools. Generally, these problems gain structure as the DSS is developed. Even some structured problems have been solved by DSS.
2. Support for all managerial levels, ranging from top executives to line managers.
3. Support for individuals as well as groups. Less-structured problems often require the involvement of individuals from different departments and organizational levels or even from different organizations. DSS support virtual teams through collaborative Web tools. DSS have been developed to support individual and group work, as well as to support individual decision making and groups of decision makers working somewhat independently.
4. Support for interdependent and/or sequential decisions. The decisions may be made once, several times, or repeatedly.

5. Support in all phases of the decision-making process: intelligence, design, choice, and implementation.
6. Support for a variety of decision-making processes and styles.
7. The decision maker should be reactive, able to confront changing conditions quickly, and able to adapt the DSS to meet these changes. DSS are flexible, so users can add, delete, combine, change, or rearrange basic elements. They are also flexible in that they can be readily modified to solve other, similar problems.
8. User-friendliness, strong graphical capabilities, and a natural language interactive human–machine interface can greatly increase the effectiveness of DSS. Most new DSS applications use Web-based interfaces.
9. Improvement of the effectiveness of decision making (e.g., accuracy, timeliness, quality) rather than its efficiency (e.g., the cost of making decisions). When DSS are deployed, decision making often takes longer, but the decisions are better.
10. The decision maker has complete control over all steps of the decision-making process in solving a problem. A DSS specifically aims to support and not to replace the decision maker.
11. End users are able to develop and modify simple systems by themselves. Larger systems can be built with assistance from information system (IS) specialists. Spreadsheet packages have been utilized in developing simpler systems. Online analytical processing (OLAP) and data mining software, in conjunction with data warehouses, allow users to build fairly large, complex DSS.
12. Models are generally utilized to analyze decision-making situations. The modeling capability enables experimentation with different strategies under different configurations. In fact, the models make a DSS different from most MIS.
13. Access is provided to a variety of data sources, formats, and types, including GIS, multimedia, and object oriented.
14. Can be employed as a standalone tool used by an individual decision maker in one location or distributed throughout an organization and in several organizations along the supply chain. It can be integrated with other DSS and/or applications, and it can be distributed internally and externally, using networking and Web technologies.

These key DSS characteristics and capabilities allow decision makers to make better, more consistent decisions in a timely manner, and they are provided by the major DSS components, which we describe next.

Section 3.4 Review Questions

1. List the key characteristics and capabilities of DSS.
2. Describe how providing support to a workgroup is different from providing support to group work. Explain why it is important to differentiate these concepts.
3. What kinds of DSS can end users develop in spreadsheets?
4. Why is it so important to include a model in a DSS?

3.5 COMPONENTS OF DECISION SUPPORT SYSTEMS

A DSS application can be composed of the data management subsystem, the model management subsystem, the user interface subsystem, and a knowledge-based management subsystem. We show these in Figure 3.3.

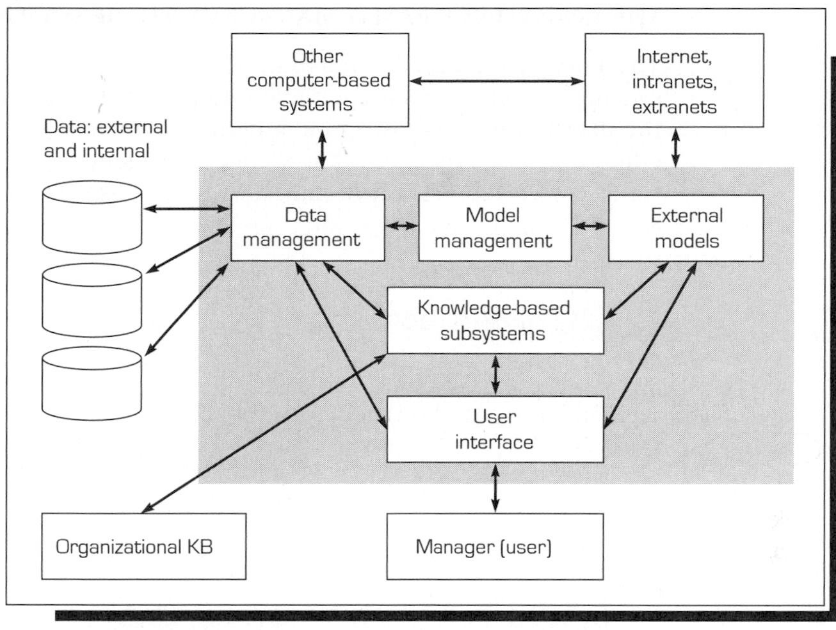

FIGURE 3.3 A Schematic View of DSS

THE DATA MANAGEMENT SUBSYSTEM

The data management subsystem includes a database that contains relevant data for the situation and is managed by software called the **database management system (DBMS)**.[1] The data management subsystem can be interconnected with the corporate **data warehouse**, a repository for corporate relevant decision-making data. Usually, the data are stored or accessed via a database Web server.

THE MODEL MANAGEMENT SUBSYSTEM

The model management subsystem is a software package that includes financial, statistical, management science, or other quantitative models that provide the system's analytical capabilities and appropriate software management. Modeling languages for building custom models are also included. This software is often called a **model base management system (MBMS)**. This component can be connected to corporate or external storage of models. Model solution methods and management systems are implemented in Web development systems (such as Java) to run on application servers.

THE USER INTERFACE SUBSYSTEM

The user communicates with and commands the DSS through the user interface subsystem. The user is considered part of the system. Researchers assert that some of the unique contributions of DSS are derived from the intensive interaction between the computer and the decision maker. The Web browser provides a familiar, consistent graphical user interface (GUI) structure for most DSS.

[1]*DBMS* is used as both singular and plural (*system* and *systems*), as are many other acronyms in this text.

THE KNOWLEDGE-BASED MANAGEMENT SUBSYSTEM

The knowledge-based management subsystem can support any of the other subsystems or act as an independent component. It provides intelligence to augment the decision maker's own. It can be interconnected with the organization's knowledge repository (part of a knowledge management system [KMS]), which is sometimes called the **organizational knowledge base**. Knowledge may be provided via

FIGURE 3.4 Summary of DSS Component Capabilities

Overall Capabilities

Create a variety of DSS applications (specific DSS) quickly and easily
Facilitate iterative design process

General Capabilities

User Interface	*Data*	*Models*	*Knowledge*
Easy to use For routine use and modification and construction of DSS	Access to a variety of data sources, types, and formats for a variety of problems and contexts	Access to a variety of analysis capabilities with some suggestion or guidance available	Access to a variety of artificial intelligence tools to provide intelligence to the other three components and to provide mechanisms for problem solving directly

Component Capabilities

User Interface	*Data*	*Models*	*Knowledge*
1. A consistent GUI, usually via a Web client 2. Variety of user input devices 3. Variety of output formats and devices 4. Variety of flexible dialog styles 5. Support communication among users and with developer 6. Support knowledge of users (documentation) 7. Capture, store, analyze (and track) dialogs 8. Flexible and adaptive dialog support 9. Provides integration of DSS components	1. Variety of data forms and types 2. Extraction, capture, and integration, especially into local, multidimensional data cubes 3. Data access function: a. Retrieval/query b. Report/display c. User/efficient data handling 4. Database management function on both clients and servers 5. Variety of logical data views available 6. Data documentation 7. Tracking of data usage 8. Flexible and adaptive data support	1. Library of models to constitute a model base: a. Many types b. Maintain, catalog, integrate c. Canned (preprogrammed) library 2. Model building facility 3. Model manipulation and use facility 4. Model base management functions 5. Model documentation 6. Tracking of model usage 7. Flexible and adaptive model support	1. Library of artificial intelligence techniques to assist users in: a. The user interface b. The database c. The model base 2. Assistance directly in decision making 3. Enables automated decision making 4. Symbolic reasoning capabilities directly for decision making 5. Improved decision making through more accurate tools, such as expert systems (ES) and artificial neural networks

Source: Based on R. H. Sprague and E. Carlson, *Building Effective Decision Support Systems*, Prentice Hall, Englewood Cliffs, NJ, 1982, p. 313. Reprinted by permission of Prentice Hall.

TABLE 3.1 DSS Components and Web Impacts

DSS Component	*Web Impacts*	*Impacts on the Web*
Database management system (DBMS)	Database servers provide data directly Consistent, friendly graphical user interface (GUI) Provides for a direct mechanism to query databases Provides a consistent communication channel for data, information, and knowledge Connections to data via portable devices (PDA, cell phones, etc.) Connections to data warehouses Connections to internal and external data sources Data access through mobile-commerce (m-commerce) and universal-commerce (u-commerce, also known as ultimate-commerce and ubiquitous-commerce) devices Direct access by customers Intranets and extranets Web-based development tools New programming languages and systems Proliferation of database use throughout organizations, which made enterprise-wide systems feasible Access to information about databases	A means to conduct e-commerce, m-commerce, and u-commerce (transactions must be stored and acted upon) Customer tracking and use implies cross-selling, up-selling, and help system access, which impact Web traffic Database Web servers store data about the Web for analysis, using models to determine effectiveness and efficiency (via Web intelligence and Web analytics)
Model base management system (MBMS)	Access to models and solution methods implemented as Java applets and other Web development systems Use of models by untrained managers (and analysts) because they are so easy to use Access to Web-based artificial intelligence tools to suggest models and solution methods in DSS Access to information about models	Improved infrastructure design and updates Models and solutions of Web infrastructure issues Models of Web message routing improve performance Forecasting models predict viability of hardware and software choices
User interface dialog system	Web browsers provide a flexible, consistent, and familiar DSS GUI Access to information about user interfaces Experimental user interfaces are tested, distributed, and used via the Web New interfaces are readily available Artificial intelligence–based tools communicate directly with users via Web-based interface tools	Initial GUIs and the computer mouse helped define how Web browsers work Users have an expectation of how they will access data, information, models, etc. Speech recognition and generation are deployed over the Web New graphical-oriented display mechanisms are deployed over the Web
Knowledge-based management system (KBMS)	Access to artificial intelligence methods	Artificial intelligence methods readily handle network design

(continued)

TABLE 3.1 (*cont.*)

	Access to information about artificial intelligence methods Access to knowledge Web-based artificial intelligence tools deployed as Java applets or as other Web development system tools Artificial intelligence–based tools readily run and provide access to customers directly (help desks, newscasts, etc.)	issues and message routing ES diagnose problems and workarounds for failures in Internet communication, hardware, and software in servers and clients ES and intelligent agents diagnose hardware problems and recommend specific repairs Intelligent search engines learn user patterns Intelligent agents readily monitor Internet performance and alert IT staff when problems arise or are predicted to arise
User	User attitudes and expectations are strongly influenced by Web tools and access Users expect ready access and 100% reliability of information, other sources, and other users	The proliferation of the Web and access has increased commercial development via and on the Web E-commerce proliferation led to the need for fast servers, clients, and communication channels

Web servers. Many artificial intelligence methods have been implemented in Web development systems such as Java and are easy to integrate into the other DSS components.

By definition, a DSS must include the three major components; DBMS, MBMS, and user interface. The knowledge-based management subsystem is optional, but it can provide many benefits by providing intelligence in and to the three major components. As in any other MIS, the user may be considered a component of DSS.

HOW THE DSS COMPONENTS INTEGRATE

The four components just described form the DSS application system, which can be connected to a corporate intranet, to an extranet, or to the Internet. Typically, the components communicate via Internet technology. Web browsers typically provide the user interface. The schematic view of a DSS and the components shown in Figure 3.3 provide a basic understanding of the general structure of a DSS. In Figure 3.4, we show a summary of DSS capabilities, broken down by components. It will be useful to refer to this figure as you read the rest of the chapter.

In Table 3.1, we provide a sampling of the impacts of the Web on DSS components and vice versa. These impacts have been substantial because improvements in the Internet have had a major effect on how we access, use, and think of DSS. Next, we present a more detailed look at each component; we provide details of them in later chapters.

Section 3.5 Review Questions

1. List the major components of DSS and briefly define each of them.
2. Briefly explain how the Web is utilized in each major component of DSS.
3. How can a knowledge-based component help each of the other DSS components?
4. Explain the basic structure of DSS and its components.

3.6 THE DATA MANAGEMENT SUBSYSTEM

The data management subsystem is composed of the following elements:

- DSS database
- DBMS
- Data directory
- Query facility

These elements are shown schematically in Figure 3.5 (in the shaded area). The figure also shows the interaction of the data management subsystem with the other parts of the DSS, as well as its interaction with several data sources. A brief discussion of these

FIGURE 3.5 The Structure of the Data Management Subsystem

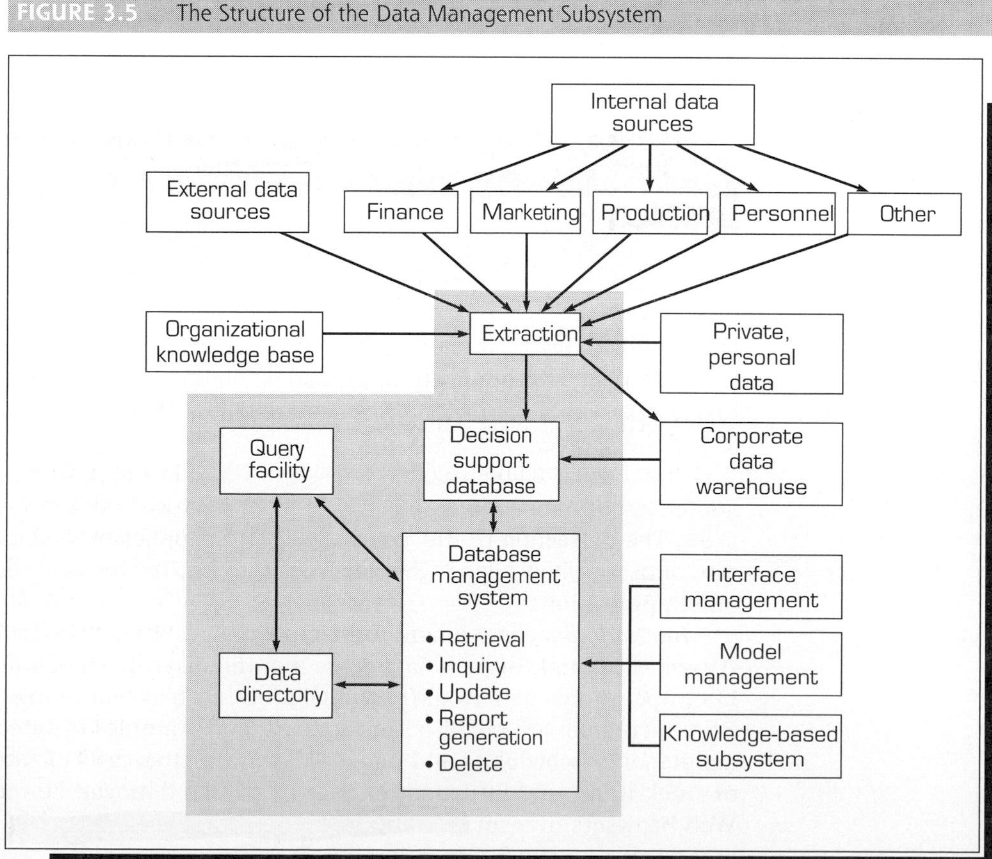

elements and their function follows; extensive further discussion is provided in Online File W3.1 and in Chapter 5. In Application Case 3.2, the primary focus of the DSS is on the database.

Application Case 3.2

Roadway Drives Legacy Applications onto the Web

It was time for Roadway Express, Inc. (Akron, OH), to move from a mainframe green screen to a more popular Web browser interface. The existing system could handle data requests and updates, but it looked old and did not present customers with a good impression of the company. So rather than reinvent the wheel, Roadway polished its surface instead. Roadway's Web design group developed a Web server front end for access to mainframe scheduling and tracking data. The Janus Web Server (Sirius Software Inc.) front ends the mainframe, allowing Roadway to reuse its existing transportation-management and administrative systems. The link between the two systems is so seamless that users don't realize they are using 14-year-old technology. Customers can access the system and generate reports on their own shipments. Roadway's Web site is one of the most sophisticated and capable on the market.

Its Web-based system allowed Roadway to create online billing directly to its customers, thus expediting payments. The system's tracking and tracing capability lets shippers see shipment status in real-time. The online pickup request feature creates scheduled pickups more quickly and efficiently. Front ending the legacy system led to substantial savings. The **my.roadway.com** site cost less than $1 million to develop.

Sources: Adapted from L. Rosencrance, "Roadway Drives Legacy Apps onto the Web," *Computerworld*, Vol. 36, No. 15, April 9, 2002, p. 48; T. Wilson, "Web Technologies Help Trucker Roll," *InternetWeek*, August 20, 2001; and Roadway Express, Inc., **roadway.com**

THE DATABASE

A **database** is a collection of interrelated data, organized to meet the needs and structure of an organization that can be used by more than one person for more than one application. We provide the fundamentals of databases here and extensive details in Online File W3.1. There are several possible configurations for a database. In many DSS instances, data are ported from the data warehouse or a legacy mainframe database system through a database Web server. (Refer to Application Case 3.1.) For other DSS applications, a special database is constructed, as needed. Several databases can be used in one DSS application, depending on the data sources. Generally, users expect to utilize a Web browser for access, and database Web servers deliver the data, regardless of the source.

The data in a DSS database, as shown in Figure 3.5, are extracted from internal and external data sources, as well as from personal data belonging to one or more users. The extraction results go to the specific application's database or to the corporate data warehouse (see Chapter 5), if it exists. In the latter case, it can be used for other applications.

Internal data come mainly from the organization's transaction processing system. A typical example of such data is the monthly payroll. Depending on the needs of the DSS, operational data from functional areas, such as marketing (e.g., Web transactions from e-commerce), might be included. Other examples of internal data are machine maintenance scheduling and budget allocations, forecasts of future sales, costs of out-of-stock items, and future hiring plans. Internal data can be made available through Web browsers over an *intranet*, an internal Web-based system. Currently, data warehouses also contain internal data for the purpose of analysis.

External data include industry data, market research data, census data, regional employment data, government regulations, tax rate schedules, and national economic data. These data can come from government agencies, trade associations, market research firms, econometric forecasting firms, and the organization's own efforts to collect external data. Like internal data, external data can be maintained in the DSS database or accessed directly when the DSS is used. External data are provided, in many cases, over the *Internet* (e.g., from computerized online services or as picked up by search engines). For example, the U.S. National Weather Service and U.S. Census readily provide data, as do many other government, university, and private sources.

Private data can include guidelines used by specific decision makers and assessments of specific data and/or situations.

DATA ORGANIZATION

Should a DSS have a standalone database? It depends. In small, ad hoc DSS, data can be entered directly into models, sometimes extracted directly from larger databases. In large organizations that use extensive amounts of data, such as Wal-Mart, AT&T, and American Airlines, data are organized in a data warehouse and used when needed. Note that a data warehouse is a large store of nonvolatile, cleansed, standard-formatted data. It is not used for transaction processes, but for analysis. Transactions are aggregated and loaded into the data warehouses. Although some DSS access transaction data from a transaction-processing system (TPS), typically those data are offloaded into another source (such as a data warehouse or other type of large DBMS), so that the analysis software will not interfere with the TPS and vice versa. (This aspect will become clear in the discussion on data warehousing in Chapter 5.)

Some large DSS have their own fully integrated, multiple-source DSS databases. A separate DSS database need not be physically separate from the corporate database. They can be stored together physically for economic reasons. Respicio et al. (2002) described a spreadsheet-oriented DSS for production planning and scheduling. This DSS has a separate database, essentially in an Excel spreadsheet, populated with data extracted from a legacy database. Updates to the legacy database based on the DSS solutions are uploaded.

A DSS database can also share a DBMS with other systems. A DSS database can include multimedia objects (e.g., pictures, maps, sounds). Object-oriented databases in Extensible Markup Language (XML) exist and are used in DSS. These are becoming more important as mobile commerce (m-commerce) applications are deployed because XML is becoming the standard, consistent data translation method for m-commerce devices (e.g., PDAs, cell phones, notebook computers, tablet computer). The XML format is also used for standard Web browser access to data.

DATA EXTRACTION

To create or load a DSS database or a data warehouse, it is often necessary to capture data from several sources. This operation is called **extraction**. It basically consists of the importing of files, summarization, standardization filtration, and condensation of data; this process is known also as *extraction, transformation, and load (ETL)*. Integration from disparate sources is a key part of this process. Extraction also occurs when the user produces reports from data in the DSS database. The data for the warehouse are extracted from internal and external sources (see Chapter 5). The extraction process is frequently managed by a DBMS. OLAP and data mining systems have the capability to extract data directly from all these systems, as well as from Web sources stored as HTML and XML documents, and transform them into a format suitable for analysis. To some degree, even spreadsheet systems such as Excel have this capability.

The extraction process is not trivial. MIS professionals generally structure this process so that users need not deal with its complicated details. Much effort is required to structure the extraction process properly. To extract needed data, an exact query must typically be made to several related data tables that may span several independent databases. The pieces to be extracted must be integrated so that a useful DSS database results.

THE DATABASE MANAGEMENT SYSTEM

A database is created, accessed, and updated by a DBMS. Most DSS are built with a standard commercial relational DBMS that provides the capabilities described in Technology Insights 3.3. DBMS are often purchased from major vendors (e.g., IBM, Microsoft, Oracle), but there is a growing trend to utilize low-cost, open-source alternatives, such as MySQL AB (MySQL, **mysql.com**), Berkeley DB Java Edition (Sleepycat Software Inc./Oracle, **sleepycat.com**), IBM Cloudscape / Apache Derby (Apache Software Foundation, **db.apache.org/derby/**), and PostgreSQL (PostgreSQL Global Development Group, **postgresql.org**).

An effective database and its management can support many managerial activities; some typical examples are general navigation among records, support for creating and maintaining a diverse set of data relationships, and report generation. However, the real power of a DSS occurs when data are integrated with the models of the decision-making problem(s). (Refer to the opening vignette and Application Case 3.1.)

THE QUERY FACILITY

In building and using DSS, it is often necessary to access, manipulate, and query data. The **query facility** performs these tasks. It accepts requests for data from other DSS components (refer to Figure 3.5), determines how the requests can be filled (consulting the data directory if necessary), formulates the detailed requests, and returns the results to the issuer of the request. The query facility includes a special query language

TECHNOLOGY INSIGHTS 3.3

The Capabilities of a Relational DBMS in a DSS

- Captures or extracts data for inclusion in a DSS database
- Updates (i.e., adds, deletes, edits, changes) data records and files
- Interrelates data from different sources
- Retrieves data from the database for queries and reports (e.g., using SQL via the Web)
- Provides comprehensive data security (e.g., protection from unauthorized access and recovery capabilities)
- Handles personal and unofficial data so that users can experiment with alternative solutions, based on their own judgment
- Performs complex data manipulation tasks based on queries
- Tracks data use within the DSS
- Manages data through a data dictionary

(e.g., SQL). Programming languages (e.g., .NET Framework languages and Java) and other systems utilize SQL query structures directly as well. Important functions of a DSS query system are selection and manipulation operations (e.g., the ability to follow a computer instruction, such as "Search for all sales in the Southeast Region during June 2006 and summarize sales by salesperson"). Although it is transparent to the user, this is a critical activity. All the user may see is a screen with a simple request for data, and following the click of a button, the user gets the results neatly formatted in a table in a dynamic HTML (or other Web-structured) page displayed on the screen.

THE DIRECTORY

The data **directory** is a catalog of all the data in a database. It contains data definitions, and its main function is to answer questions about the availability of data items, their source, and their exact meaning. The directory is especially appropriate for supporting the intelligence phase of the decision-making process by helping to scan data and identify problem areas or opportunities. The directory, like any other catalog, supports the addition of new entries, deletion of entries, and retrieval of information about specific objects.

All the database elements have been implemented on database Web servers that respond to Web browser screens. The Web has dramatically changed the way we access, use, and store data. Next we touch on some important database and DBMS issues—some of which are general, and some that pertain specifically to DSS.

KEY DATABASE AND DATABASE MANAGEMENT SYSTEM ISSUES

Although many issues affect databases and are caused by databases, here we focus on four important ones that affect DSS dramatically: data quality, data integration, scalability, and security. These are also discussed in part in Online File W3.1.

Data Quality

A key issue in data management is data quality. As we discussed in Chapter 2, decision makers (specifically executives and managers) generally do not feel that they get the data and information they really need to do their work. In a research study, only 54 percent indicated that their employees were extremely satisfied or satisfied with data access; but of those, only 77 percent were happy about the data quality. Overall, only 52.6 percent were extremely satisfied or satisfied with their data quality (see "Data Architecture," 2002). A PricewaterhouseCoopers study indicated that there was no significant gain in confidence in data quality for IT executives from 2001 to 2004. According to a Gartner, Inc., study, at least 25 percent of critical data of Fortune 1000 companies will continue to be inaccurate through 2007 (see Gilhooly, 2005).

Poor quality data, which leads to poor quality information, leads directly to waste. The data cannot be trusted, and therefore neither can any analysis based on them. The old adage garbage in/garbage out (GIGO) applies. With poor data, processes will fail or simply perform badly. For example, given inaccurate data in a CRM system, customers may be contacted many times, clustered into incorrect groupings, and so on, leading to missed sales opportunities and unhappy customers. The main notion underlying poor data quality is that it leads to waste (see English, 2002, 2005; "Getting Clear," 2004; and Gonzales, 2004). Waste in manufacturing leads to scrap and rework. English (2005) indicated that some 10 to 20 percent of operating revenue is used to pay for information scrap and rework (e.g., updates to prevent bad decisions). According to a TDWI report (W. Erickson, *Data Quality and the Bottom Line*, **tdwi.org**), in the

United States alone, firms routinely lose over $600 billion per year due to poor data quality. And its financial impacts are rising exponentially (see Wheatley, 2004). Allstate Insurance devotes significant resources to maintaining high-data quality standards. Customer confidence is critical in Allstate's success (see Marco, 2005; and Marco and Jennings, 2004). Wheatley (2004) described several large-scale efforts in practice, including those of the British Defense Ministry, Carlson Wagonlit Travel, Cendant, and the U.S. Census, all of which rely on critical data accuracy. See Technology Insights 3.4 for details on how to tackle data quality at the enterprise level.

Data quality cleanup (e.g., validation and verification) tools are different from those utilized in data warehousing for data cleansing. Tools for cleansing and matching data are available from Firstlogic Inc., Group 1 Software Inc., Trillium Software, DataFlux Corp., and others. Additional information about data quality and its causes, impacts, examples, and best practices appear in Online File W3.1. Also see Fisher et al. (2003), who determined that higher-quality data generally leads to higher-quality decisions, as well as Gilhooly (2005) and Stahl (2004).

Data Integration

A single version of the truth is ultimately what decision makers want from their information systems. Data and information are all over the place in most organizations. When it comes time to develop any enterprise system, or even a single DSS, data must be gathered from disparate sources and integrated into that single version of the truth so that everyone is on the same page. The U.S. Department of Homeland Security has experienced expensive disasters in terms of its attempt to integrate data from its semi-independent, siloed agencies (see details in Online File W3.1). Initially, enterprise

TECHNOLOGY INSIGHTS 3.4

The 10 Essential Ingredients of Data (Information) Quality Management

Because poor data (and consequently information) quality can lead to disastrous results and significant expense, it is important to understand how to manage data in a quality manner by design. Here are Larry English's top 10 suggestions:

1. Understand that data quality is a business problem, not only a systems problem. Solve it as a business process, not just a systems process. Poor data quality affects the entire business and its operations. Some issues impacting poor quality occur as the result of business processes (e.g., data entry).
2. Focus on information customers and suppliers, not just data. Quality improvement of the data is the key.
3. Focus on all components of information and data, including their definition, content, and presentation.
4. Implement data/information quality management processes, not just software to handle them.
5. Measure data accuracy in addition to validity.
6. Measure real costs, not just the percentage, of poor quality data/information; also measure their results.
7. Emphasize process improvement and preventive maintenance, not just data cleansing.
8. Improve processes (and hence data quality) at the source.
9. Provide quality training to managers and information producers. Educate them as to the impacts of poor data quality and how to improve it.
10. Actively transform the culture to one that values data quality.

Sources: Adapted from L. English, "IQ and Muda," *DM Review*, Vol. 15, No. 9, September 2005, pp. 40–46; and L. English, "The Essentials of Information Quality Management," *DM Review*, Vol. 12, No. 9, September 2002, pp. 36–44.

information portals were utilized to bring data together and present it as a unified whole; however, it is critical to create a true master view of the data. It is possible for one person's portal to access what is believed to be similar data from a different source than that for another person's portal. The two individuals think they have the same data in front of them, but they do not. Just as with data quality issues, a careful analysis of all data, their sources, and precision and accuracy must be mapped into a set of metadata that can be used to create a single version of the truth.

Integration issues generally become critical when implementing an EIS such as a CRM. Information about customers may be scattered throughout several databases, but customers expect to be treated as if there is a single organization reaching them. Also, when migrating to a new system, integration becomes key. Even when attempting to integrate content into a content management system, major problems occur. For example, York International migrated some 8,000 engineering documents from one CMS to the enterprise standard CMS over a weekend, but it took months to deal with access and security problems. Middleware, such as products from ECI Services, can help by scanning documents and identifying problems and applying solutions (see Raden, 2005; and Siluer, 2005). For database integration, enterprise information integration (EII) products, such as DB2 Information Integrator, Oracle XML Data Synthesis, Informatica Integration Competency Center, and even XML standardization can help (see Hayes and Mattos, 2003; Junnarkar et al., 2005; Monash, 2005; and Yang, 2005).

Scalability

Large databases (and data warehouses) present major scalability problems. As the size of the data to be stored and accessed increases, processing times and storage space also grow, sometimes dramatically. For example, between 2001 and 2003, the size of the largest databases increased in size two-fold for TPS (about 11 to 20 terabytes), and three-fold for DSS (about 11 to 30 terabytes). System workloads increase as well. Clearly, new storage technologies and search mechanisms need to be and are continually being developed. For example, part of the storage issue can be solved by carefully splitting data up and having them span multiple disk drives, perhaps each with access by several processors. Multiprocessor clusters, symmetric multiprocessing (SMP) systems, and massively parallel processing (MPP) hardware systems with appropriate parallel processing software can provide effective parallel search and access capabilities. In mid-2005, petabyte-size databases were deployed, necessitating deployment of these types of hardware and software. Teradata Corp. is well known for its parallel systems. (See Winter and Auerbach, 2004).

Leading researchers discussed additional issues about databases in general in 2003, as reported by Abiteboul et al. (2005). Key issues and important new directions discussed include the Internet as the main driving force for applications, especially across the enterprise. The physical sciences, biological sciences, medicine, and engineering are growing in importance in terms of the size of databases and types of analyses being performed. Genetics provides a ready example in terms of the kinds and size of data needed for genome projects. The pharmaceutical industry needs large-scale databases not only for processing forms for approval but also for analysis and prediction of the effectiveness of new compounds. In addition to the two major directions, there will be major changes in traditional DBMS areas, including data models, access methods, query processing algorithms, concurrency control, recovery, query languages, and user interfaces to DBMS. Finally, related technologies (e.g., data mining) are maturing. See Abiteboul et al. (2005) for details.

Data Security

One key issue that DBMS is supposed to handle by its very nature is data security. The consequences of unauthorized access to unsecured data can be extremely detrimental to the financial well-being of an organization. In some cases, data security is required by confidentiality laws (e.g., in medicine, law enforcement). In some situations, unauthorized access extends to modifying data in place or destroying it. Data must be protected from unauthorized access through security measures such as ID and password protection. It is also important to identify exactly who has access to and why they have access to specific sets of data and to what level an individual is allowed to change the data in the system. Finally, data can be encrypted so that even in the case of unauthorized access, the viewed data is scrambled and unintelligible.

New tools have been developed to monitor database activity and provide audit trails. For example, SQL Guard from Guardium, Inc., tracks database access and transactions. When unusual patterns of activities are identified, it generates an alert. This type of tool is critical for safety and safeguarding of airport operations and their sensitive data; for example, McCarron International Airport in Las Vegas uses SQL Guard to protect its data in its 14 database servers. See Hildreth (2005) for more details.

Section 3.6 Review Questions

1. Why does a DSS generally includes its own database?
2. Describe the similarities and differences among internal, external, and private data.
3. Describe the components of a DBMS: the query facility, the directory, and the data.
4. What are the major functions (capabilities) of a DBMS?
5. What is extraction?
6. What is the function of a query facility?
7. What is the function of a directory?

3.7 THE MODEL MANAGEMENT SUBSYSTEM

The model management subsystem of a DSS is composed of the following elements:

- Model base
- MBMS
- Modeling language
- Model directory
- Model execution, integration, and command processor

These elements and their interfaces with other DSS components are shown in Figure 3.6. The following sections define and describe the function of each of these elements.

THE MODEL BASE

A **model base** contains routine and special statistical, financial, forecasting, management science, and other quantitative models that provide the analysis capabilities in a DSS. The ability to invoke, run, change, combine, and inspect models is a key DSS capability that differentiates it from other CBIS. The models in the model base can be divided into four major categories: strategic, tactical, operational, and analytical. In addition, there are model building blocks and routines.

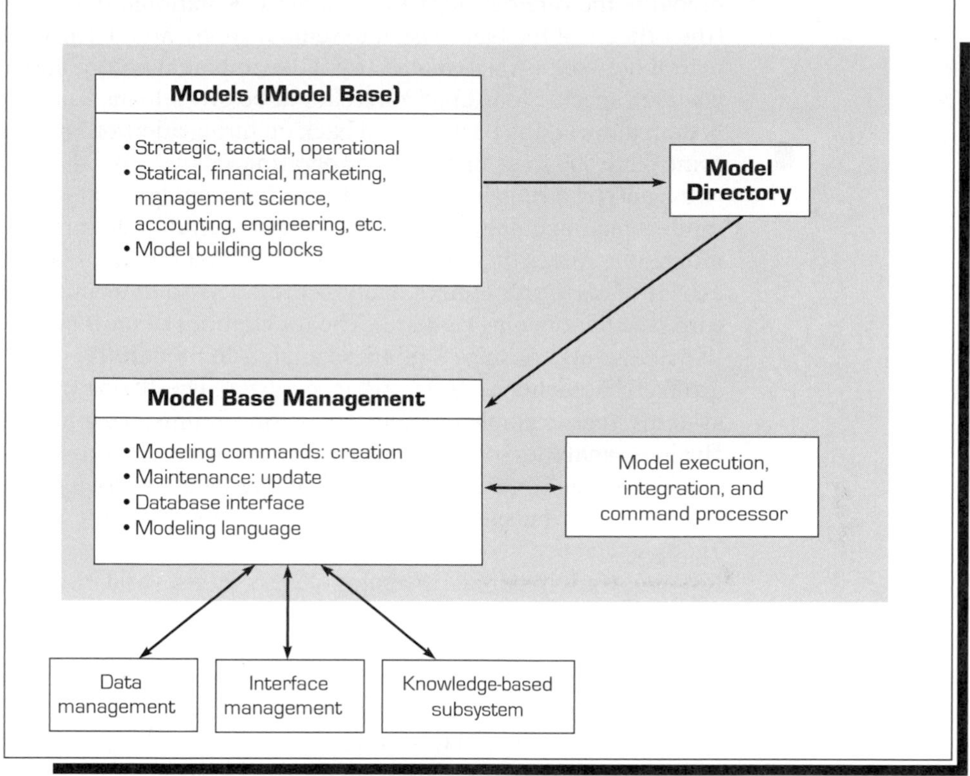

FIGURE 3.6 The Structure of the Model Management Subsystem

Strategic models are used to support top managers' strategic planning responsibilities. Potential applications include devising an e-commerce venture, developing corporate objectives, planning for mergers and acquisitions, selecting a plant location, analyzing environmental impact, and creating a nonroutine capital budget. An example of a DSS strategic model is that of Southwest Airlines (Songini, 2002). Southwest used its system to create accurate financial forecasts so that it could identify strategic opportunities. A large-scale linear programming model is at the heart of Southwest's POP DSS, which allows executives of the company to plan large, expensive equipment needs as many years ahead as needed. FedEx's Web-based ISIS DSS is used in making strategic decisions (see the End of Chapter Application Case).

Tactical models are used mainly by middle managers to assist in allocating and controlling the organization's resources. Examples of tactical models include those for Web server selection, labor requirement planning, sales promotion planning, plant-layout determination, and routine capital budgeting. Tactical models are usually applicable only to an organizational subsystem, such as the accounting department. Their time horizons vary from one month to less than two years. Some external data are needed, but the greatest requirements are for internal data.

Operational models are used to support the day-to-day working activities of the organization. Typical decisions involve e-commerce transaction acceptance (e.g., purchases), approval of personal loans by a bank, production scheduling, inventory control, maintenance planning and scheduling, and quality control. Operational models mainly support first-line managers' decision making with a daily to monthly time horizon. These models normally use only internal data. An excellent example of an operational model is the one developed by a large U.S. national bank with hundreds of branches (the officers of the bank wish it to remain anonymous). The bank developed an artificial neural network (ANN) model (for a development cost of about $300,000) to determine whether specific loan applicants should be given loans. The accurate predictions of the system allowed the bank to hold back on hiring additional loan officers, saving the bank some $200,000 in its first year of operation.

Analytical models are used to perform analysis on data. They include statistical models, management science models, data mining algorithms, financial models, and more. Sometimes they are integrated with other models, such as strategic planning models. Humana Corp. utilizes analytical models to determine benefit classes for health care (see the opening vignette). The foundations of *business analytics* (including predictive analytics) encompass all these analytical models. Typically, business analytics tools are Web based, hence the term *Web analytics*. These tools may readily be applied to Web systems; one example of their use is for administering and monitoring e-commerce. Business analytics software is generally easy to use.

The models in the model base can also be classified by functional areas (e.g., financial models, production control models) or by discipline (e.g., statistical models, management science allocation models). The number of models in a DSS can vary from a few to several hundred. Examples of DSS with several integrated models are described in Application Case 3.1 and Respicio et al. (2002). In addition, Camm et al. (1997) described Procter & Gamble's redesign of its distribution system. Models in DSS are basically mathematical; that is, they are expressed by formulas. These formulas can be preprogrammed using DSS development tools such as Excel. They can be written in a spreadsheet and stored for future use, or they can be programmed for only one use.

MODEL BUILDING BLOCKS AND ROUTINES

In addition to strategic, tactical, and operational models, the model base can contain **model building blocks** and routines. Examples of the software elements used to build computerized models include a random number generator routine, a curve- or line-fitting routine, a present-value computational routine, and regression analysis. Such building blocks can be used in several ways. They can be used on their own for such applications as data analysis. They can also be used as components of larger models. For example, a present-value component can be part of a make-or-buy model. Some of these building blocks are used to determine the values of variables and parameters in a model, as in the use of regression analysis to create trend lines in a forecasting model. Such building blocks are available in DSS commercial development software, such as the functions and add-ins of Excel, and in the general modeling structures of OLAP and data mining software. The implementation of model solution methods directly in Java and other Web development systems has simplified access and integration of models.

MODEL COMPONENTS FOR BUILDING DSS

At a higher level than building blocks, it is important to consider the different types of models and solution methods needed in the DSS. Often at the start of development, there is some sense of the model types to be incorporated, but this may change as more is learned about the decision problem. Some DSS development systems include a wide variety of components (e.g., Analytica from Lumina Decision Systems), while others have a single one (e.g., Lindo). Often, the results of one type of model component (e.g., forecasting) are used as input to another (e.g., production scheduling). In some cases, a modeling language is a component that generates input to a solver, while in other cases, the two are combined.

Typical deterministic modeling components include those for linear programming and its specializations (e.g., network programming, integer programming) and its generalizations (e.g., nonlinear programming), modeling languages (e.g., AMPL, GAMS), PERT and CPM charts (typically embedded in project management software), dynamic programming, and so on. On the probabilistic side, typical modeling components include those for forecasting (i.e., predictive analytics), Markov modeling, queuing, simulation, and so on. Others that can be treated either deterministically or probabilistically include vehicle routing and scheduling and production planning, which each contain a number of modeling components. These components are typically embedded directly into OLAP and data mining software.

MODELING TOOLS

Because DSS deal with semistructured or unstructured problems, it is often necessary to customize models, using programming tools and languages. Some examples of these are .NET Framework languages, C++, and Java. OLAP software may also be used to work with models in data analysis. Even languages for simulation such as SLAM and statistical packages such as those of SPSS offer modeling tools developed through using a proprietary programming language. A Web-based system that uses a cluster analysis model for recommending movies is described in Application Case 3.5. For small and medium-sized DSS or for less complex ones, a spreadsheet (e.g., Excel) is usually used. We will use Excel for many key examples in this book.

Application Case 3.5

Web-Based Cluster Analysis DSS Matches Up Movies and Customers

Netflix.com (Los Gatos, CA) is a mail-order DVD movie rental firm. Netflix provides movie recommendations to its 3.5 million subscribers. The recommendations are provided by the subscribers themselves. But how do you go about identifying which movies are similar, so that you can make recommendations (e.g., "Customers who liked movie X also liked movie Y")? Canned software cannot evaluate the many subjective, on-the-fly reviews provided by tens of thousands of critics. Netflix needed to do this to remain competitive. Enter *cluster analysis*. Mathematicians encoded cluster analysis software to define movie clusters, relate opinions to the clusters, evaluate thousands of ratings per second, and factor in current Web site behavior to deliver a specially configured Web page before a customer can click again. Improved methods increased the average queue length from four to eight titles between 2001 and 2004. The real-time analytics can also tell marketing managers what Web page design is working best for a given promotion. They can then change the Web page design immediately, based on the dynamic feedback. Cluster analysis is a very effective modeling tool that is used in CRM systems when trying to determine what products appeal to which customers.

Sources: Adapted from L. Stevens, "We Try Harder," Case Study No. 5, *CIO Insight*, No. 59, Fall 2005 Special Issue, pp. 45–47; M. Hall, "Web Analytics: Get Real," *Computer World*, Vol. 36, No. 14, April 1, 2002, pp. 42–43; and material from **netflix.com**.

THE MODEL BASE MANAGEMENT SYSTEM

MBMS software has four main functions:

- Model creation, using programming languages, DSS tools and/or subroutines, and other building blocks
- Generation of new routines and reports

- Model updating and changing
- Model data manipulation

The MBMS is capable of interrelating models with the appropriate linkages through a database (see Technology Insights 3.6.)

THE MODEL DIRECTORY

The role of the model directory is similar to that of a database directory. It is a catalog of all the models and other software in the model base. It contains model definitions, and its main function is to answer questions about the availability and capability of the models.

MODEL EXECUTION, INTEGRATION, AND COMMAND

The following activities are usually controlled by model management. *Model execution* is the process of controlling the actual running of the model. *Model integration* involves combining the operations of several models when needed (e.g., directing the output of one model, say forecasting, to be processed by another one, say a linear programming planning model; refer to Application Case 3.2) or integrating the DSS with other applications. Portucel Industrial (a major Portuguese paper producer) uses a DSS that contains six integrated models: three capacity planning and scheduling models, two cutting plan models, and one demand forecasting model (see Respicio et al., 2002).

A *model command processor* is used to accept and interpret modeling instructions from the user interface component and route them to the MBMS, model execution, or integration functions.

An interesting question for a DSS might be Which models should be used for what situations? Such model selection cannot be done by the MBMS because it requires expertise and therefore is done manually. This is a potential automation area for a knowledge component to assist the MBMS.

Another interesting, more subtle, question is What method should be used to solve a particular problem in a specific model class? For example, an assignment problem (say assigning 10 jobs to 10 people) is a type of transportation problem, which is a type of network flow problem, which is a type of linear programming problem, which is a type of mathematical optimization problem. Special solution methods are generally

TECHNOLOGY INSIGHTS 3.6

Major Functions of an MBMS

- Creates models easily and quickly, either from scratch or from existing models or from the building blocks
- Allows users to manipulate models so that they can conduct experiments and sensitivity analyses ranging from what-if to goal-seeking analyses
- Stores, retrieves, and manages a wide variety of different types of models in a logical and integrated manner
- Accesses and integrates the model building blocks
- Catalogs and displays the directory of models for use by several individuals in the organization
- Tracks model data and application use
- Interrelates models with appropriate linkages with the database and integrates them within the DSS
- Manages and maintains the model base with management functions analogous to those in database management: store, access, run, update, link, catalog, and query
- Uses multiple models to support problem solving

more efficient when dealing with more specialized structures. In other words, special methods for solving an assignment problem should work better than applying transportation problem algorithms to it, and so on. But this is not always true. And to complicate matters, there may be many ways to solve a specific problem, depending on its characteristics. Again, there is potential for the knowledge component to assist in selecting an appropriate solution method. In the late 1990s, the elements of the MBMS migrated to Web-based systems, deployed as Java applets or modules of other Web development systems.

Section 3.7 Review Questions

1. Models are classified as strategic, tactical, or operational. What is the purpose of such a classification? Give an example of each type of model.
2. List some of the major functions of an MBMS.
3. Compare the features and structure of an MBMS to those of a DBMS.
4. Why is model selection for DSS difficult?
5. How can a knowledge component assist in model selection?

3.8 THE USER INTERFACE (DIALOG) SUBSYSTEM

The term **user interface** covers all aspects of communication between a user and the DSS or any MSS. It includes not only the hardware and software but also factors that deal with ease of use, accessibility, and human–machine interactions. Some MSS experts feel that the user interface is the most important component because it is the source of many of the power, flexibility, and ease-of-use characteristics of MSS. Others believe that the user interface is the system from the user's standpoint because it is the only part of the system that the user sees. A difficult user interface is one of the major reasons managers do not use computers and quantitative analyses as much as they could, given the availability of these technologies. The Web browser has been recognized as an effective DSS GUI because it is flexible, user friendly, and a gateway to almost all sources of necessary information and data. Essentially, Web browsers have led to the development of portals and dashboards, which front end many DSS.

MANAGEMENT OF THE USER INTERFACE SUBSYSTEM

The user interface subsystem is managed by software called the **user interface management system (UIMS)**. The UIMS is composed of several programs that provide the capabilities listed in Online File W3.2. The UIMS is also known as the *dialog generation and management system*.

THE USER INTERFACE PROCESS

The user interface process for an MSS is shown schematically in Figure 3.7. The user interacts with the computer via an action language processed by the UIMS. It enables the user to interact with the model management and data management subsystems. In advanced systems, the user interface component includes a natural language processor or can use standard **objects** (e.g., pull-down menus, buttons) through a **graphical user interface (GUI)**.

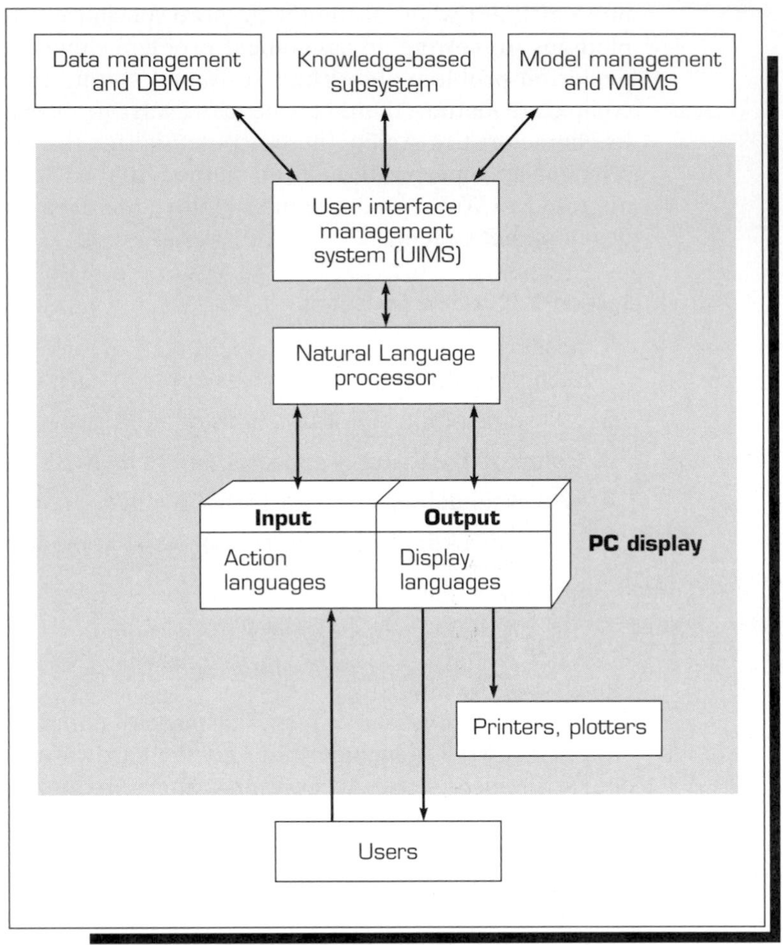

FIGURE 3.7 Schematic View of the User Interface System

DSS USER INTERFACES

Actual DSS (and data, information, and knowledge) access is provided through Web browsers, including voice input and output, portable devices, and direct sensing devices (mainly for input). We discuss these next, along with some speculation as to the future of interfaces.

DSS are typically accessed via Web browser technology (or at least a similar-looking screen). Essentially, the Web browser provides a portal or dashboard to access the system. Even when a customized user interface is developed, it typically is a GUI and appears to the user to behave as if it were a Web browser. For example, a DSS can be developed in the Temtec Executive Viewer OLAP package (**temtec.com**).

Web browser technologies have changed our expectations of how software should look and feel. Many DSS provide drill-down capabilities (to look into data for the source of problems) and a traffic light display (i.e., green = OK, red = problems, yellow = problem brewing; see Temtec's Executive Viewer software and Microsoft's Data Analyzer). A DSS is used on the Web in several ways. First, users can go on the intranet and activate ready-made DSS applications. All they need do is enter some data or specify dates and other information. The DSS is then run, and the users can see the results.

Second, they can get online advice and help on how to use the DSS applications. Third, they can communicate with others regarding the interpretation of the DSS results. Finally, they can collaborate in implementing solutions generated by the DSS model. Web tools provide communication and collaboration capabilities for group support systems (GSS) and KMS, as well as for content management systems, EIS, CRM, and SCM.

Given that Web browsers are the typical user access path for DSS and data, most major software vendors, especially those providing database access, provide portals or dashboards, which allow access to data and methods to solve problems—essentially DSS. IBM's WebSphere portal (**www-306.ibm.com/software/info1/websphere/**; see Ben-Natan et al., 2004, and see Correlate Technologies, at **correlate.com/wps/image.asp**, for an example) lets employees access information and business processes in a comfortable format, leading to collaboration and faster and better decision making. This includes IBM's e-commerce and SCM applications. The WebSphere portal provides capabilities that allow an organization to connect everyone involved in its supply chain (vendors through customers) together so that collaboration is smooth and effective. EIS ranging from SCM to knowledge management can effectively be accessed though the Microsoft Digital Dashboard and IBM WebSphere portal.

A variety of portable devices have been made Web-ready, including notebook and tablet PCs, PDAs, pocket PCs (another type of PDA), and cell phones. Many of these devices include technology to tap directly into the Web. They allow either handwritten input or typed input from internal or external keyboards. Some DSS user interfaces utilize natural language input (i.e., text in a human language) so that the user can easily express himself or herself in a meaningful way. Because of the fuzzy nature of human language, it is fairly difficult to develop software to interpret it. However, these package increase in accuracy every year, and they will ultimately lead to accurate input, output, and language translators (e.g., look into research at Carnegie Mellon University's Language Technologies Institute at **lti.cs.cmu.edu**).

Voice input for these devices and PCs are common and fairly accurate (but not perfect). The IBM WebSphere portal was enhanced in 2003 to accept voice input, and most Microsoft products have been enhanced in this way as well. When voice input with accompanying speech recognition software (and readily available text-to-speech software) is used, verbal instructions with accompanied actions and outputs can be invoked. These are readily available for DSS and are incorporated into the portable devices listed earlier. For example, the National Aeronautics and Space Administration (NASA) has developed a voice input/output (I/O) system for astronauts to use in space (Application Case 3.7).

Application Case 3.7

Clarissa: A Hands-Free Helper for Astronauts

The NASA Ames Research Team developed Clarissa, a hands-free helper for astronauts. A bit like HAL from *2001: A Space Odyssey*, Clarissa is there to assist astronauts in space, where they typically have their hands full and need computer access. An astronaut chats with Clarissa, who guides the astronaut through a complex series of tasks. Clarissa runs on a standard notebook PC. The Clarissa Spoken Dialogue System reads aloud instructions to procedures so that astronauts can give full attention to their work. Clarissa was successfully tested in June 2005 in the International Space Station. Images of Clarissa's use are available at **nasa.gov/centers/ames/multimedia/images/2005/Clarissa.html**

Clarissa is far more advanced than menu-based voice input for telephone use by banks and airlines. Clarissa can distinguish between a command and ongoing conversation among people in a room. Clarissa therefore does not need to be told "computer!" to get her attention, as the computer in *Star Trek* did. Clarissa also learns appropriate responses to her commands. There are applications in industry where hands-free operations are critical, but there are also applications in using Clarissa's natural language capabilities anywhere human–computer interactions are utilized.

Sources: Adapted from D. Daniel, "A Computer at Astronauts' Command," *CIO*, October 15, 2005, p. 26; and NASA, *Clarissa*, February 7, 2005, **nasa.gov/centers/ames/multimedia/images/2005/Clarissa.html** (accessed March 2006).

Finally, as far as DSS and data access devices go, personal music players such as iPods and other MP3 players can display data, pictures, and video (via podcasting), thus making them capable of displaying portal information and effectively giving them access to DSS.

In addition to text to speech capabilities, gestures are important for human understanding. Visit **ananova.com** to see an example of an artificial newscaster and **alicebot.org** for an example of natural language text processing with speech output capabilities. When you activate Alice, she will keep a close watch on the mouse indicator on the screen. The voice-capable Alice Silver Edition won the prestigious Loebner Prize in 2004. It is possible to use speech generation (e.g., text-to-speech) technology with or without an animated character. SitePal (**oddcast.com/sitepal2/**) provides animated characters that include facial gestures for Web sites for a small monthly fee. Other such software is available for free (e.g., from NaturalSoft Ltd. at **naturalreaders.com**; the paid version has more features). And Microsoft's Agent technology provides both voice input and speech generation from text.

Recent efforts in business process management (BPM) have led to inputs directly from physical devices for analysis via DSS. For example, radio frequency identification (RFID) chips can record data from sensors in railcars or in process products in a factory. Data from these sensors (e.g., recording an item's status) can be downloaded at key locations and immediately transmitted to a database or data warehouse, where they can be analyzed and decisions can be made concerning the status of the items being monitored. Wal-Mart and Best Buy are developing this technology in their SCM, and such *sensor networks* are also being used effectively by other firms. For example, BP plc uses sensor networks to track its railcars and to monitor their physical characteristics. Before doing so, it lost track of 900 of its railcars annually and thus lost some 5 percent of its oil and gas inventory. Each lost railcar cost BP between $50,000 and $125,000. See D'Agostino (2004) and AberdeenGroup (2004) for more information on sensor networks.

Several user interface developments are under way in terms of software and hardware. On the software side, scientists are constantly developing improvements in voice recognition, natural language processing in both directions, voice input (speech recognition), voice output (speech-to-text), and language translation. These may or may not include gestures for input and output. In addition, virtual reality technology can be used for data display, allowing a decision maker to "fly" over a landscape that represents the data being analyzed, for example. Artificial intelligence methodologies and technologies directly affect these improvement efforts. For example, scientists at the University of London's Goldsmiths College and at Cornell University are developing systems that attempt to make computers recognize and respond to users' emotions and even help users understand their own emotions better following their interaction with computational devices. Scientists at Cornell are also developing methods for letting computers deal with human ambiguity in a meaningful way. See Anthes (2006) for some initial details.

On the hardware side, the quality and size of visual output displays are physically limited by the size of molecules. Even so, displays are getting better and better, especially in PDAs and mobile phones. Holographic displays that require neither specialized hardware nor glasses have finally left the labs. For videoconferencing, Microsoft has developed RingCam, an omnidirectional video camera that allows offsite meeting attendees to view the entire room as if they were really at the meeting. It utilizes eight microphones and five small cameras. Tactile interfaces present a small problem. However, Immersion Corp.'s Cyberforce System includes a spandex glove that simulates the tactile sense that doctors get when performing surgery. This *haptic* interface allows surgeons to simulate their work before actually performing a real operation. In this way, medical students can experience virtual operations that feel so real that they have essentially performed the real thing. Finally, see Technology Insights 3.8 for a description of a *gesture interface* that utilizes holographic displays.

DSS DEVELOPMENTS

We conclude the sections on the three major DSS components with information on some recent technology and methodology developments that affect DSS and decision making. Many developments in DSS components are the result of new developments in hardware and software computer technology, data warehousing, data mining, OLAP, Web technologies, integration of technologies, and DSS application to various and new functional areas.

There is also a clear link between hardware and software capabilities and improvements in DSS. Hardware continues to shrink in size while increasing in

TECHNOLOGY INSIGHTS 3.8

Human Gestures for Computer Input

Researchers at the Human Computer Interaction Institute at Carnegie Mellon University in Pittsburgh (**hcii.cmu.edu/Research/projects.html**) are developing a human–automobile interface. Hand gestures (e.g., pointing, waving) toward icons projected onto the windshield are captured by cameras in the car and translated directly into instructions for adjusting the radio, putting someone on hold on the cell phone, or programming the on-board navigation system. This gesture interface can assist drivers in getting past the distractions caused by many electronic devices, whether a part of the car or brought on board (e.g., a cell phone). The goal is to increase safety. However, this new interface has implications for computer interfaces in general. General Motors continues to fund this research and is testing the system in prototype cars.

The next generation of PC interfaces could be holographic in nature or simply projected, and it may be programmable. Gestures can be detected, instead of using hardware such as a mouse or keyboard. There are no moving parts, and the user is able to use a set of preprogrammed gestures or can customize the system accordingly. In virtual reality settings, the glove that detects motion will eventually become a relic. In addition to DSS, video games can benefit from gesture interface technology.

Sources: K. Whitfield, "Gesture Interfaces for Automotive CONTROL: (Beyond Digital Expletives)," *Automotive Design & Production*, **autofieldguide.com/articles/070307.html** (accessed January 2006); B. Spice, "CMU Work Aims to Change Relationship Between Vehicle, Driver," *Pittsburgh Post-Gazette* (**post-gazette.com**), November 4, 2002 ; and the HCII at CMU, at **hcii.cmu.edu/Research/projects.html**

speed and other capabilities. The sizes of databases and data warehouses have increased dramatically. Since 2005, data warehouses could provide hundreds of petabytes of sales data for retail organizations and content for major news networks.

As Web tools, both on the browser and server sides, and Java and other development systems improve, so will the interface and data and model access capabilities of DSS. Scalability, as discussed earlier, remains a problem. However, parallel processing hardware and software technologies have made major inroads in solving the scalability issue.

We expect to see more seamless integration of DSS components as they adopt Web technologies, especially XML. These Web-based technologies have become the center of activity in developing DSS. Web-based DSS have reduced technological barriers and made it easier and less costly to make decision-relevant information and model-driven DSS available to managers and staff users in geographically distributed locations, especially through mobile devices.

Artificial intelligence continues to make inroads in improving DSS. Faster, intelligent search engines are an obvious outcome. There are many others, especially in interface use. Intelligent agents promise to improve the interface in areas as diverse as direct natural language processing and creating facial gestures.

The development of ready-made (or near-ready-made) DSS solutions for specific market segments has been increasing. This is happening especially because Web deployment makes it easy to deliver these products. Artificial intelligence solutions can readily be incorporated into or used as a DSS. Exsys Corvid, an expert system (ES) shell, requires Java programming capability to create an application, but it runs directly on a Web server. Consequently, applications can be readily made available directly to anyone, anytime, almost anywhere in the world. International Assignment Profile (IAP) Systems, Inc. (**iapsystems.com**), through its online ES (try the demo) increases the likelihood of international assignment success by identifying positive and negative aspects of the relocation for the individual decision maker in question.

DSS is becoming more embedded in or linked to most EIS. A major area to expect improvements in DSS is in GSS in supporting collaboration at the enterprise level. This is true even in the educational arena (see Technology Insights 3.9). Almost every new area of information systems involves some level of decision-making support. Thus DSS, either directly or indirectly, has impacts on CRM, SCM, ERP, KM, PLM, BAM, BPM, and other EIS. As these systems evolve, the active decision-making component that utilizes mathematical, statistical, or even descriptive models increases in size and capability, although it may be buried deep within the system.

Finally, different types of DSS components are being integrated more frequently. For example, GIS are readily integrated with other, more traditional, DSS components and tools for improved decision making, as described in Application Case 3.1.

Section 3.8 Review Questions

1. What is the major purpose of a user interface system?
2. Describe the user interface process.
3. What are the major functions of a UIMS?
4. Describe why Web tools are typically used for DSS interfaces.

TECHNOLOGY INSIGHTS 3.9

Blackboard: A DSS for E-learning

Blackboard Inc. (Washington, DC; **blackboard.com**) offers a complete Web-based suite of enterprise software products and services that power a total e-education infrastructure for schools, colleges, universities, and other education providers. Blackboard solutions deliver the promise of the Internet for online teaching and learning, campus communities, auxiliary services, and integration of Web-enabled student services and back-office systems. Blackboard provides a means of communication, collaboration, access to course materials (e.g., text, data, software) and course tools (e.g., gradebook/grade reporting, e-mail), and so on. Essentially, Blackboard is a DSS for a course instructor and students. Blackboard is a course *portal* in the same sense as an enterprise information portal. (Note that in October 2005, Blackboard and WebCT announced their forthcoming merger.)

Sources: Blackboard Inc. (**blackboard.com**), "Seven Ways to Blackboard," Education Resources Information Center, **eric.ed.gov**; and J.E. Aronson's personal experience using Blackboard for course management and delivery.

5. List four new developments in user interfaces.

6. List four new developments in DSS, other than user interface developments.

3.9 THE KNOWLEDGE-BASED MANAGEMENT SUBSYSTEM

Many unstructured and even semistructured problems are so complex that their solutions require expertise. This can be provided by an ES or another intelligent system. Therefore, advanced DSS are equipped with a component called a *knowledge-based management subsystem*. This component can supply the required expertise for solving some aspects of the problem and provide knowledge that can enhance the operation of other DSS components. Knowledge components may be provided by ES, neural networks, intelligent agents, fuzzy logic, case-based reasoning systems, and so on.

There are several ways to integrate knowledge-based ES and mathematical modeling. These include knowledge-based aids that support parts of the decision process not handled by mathematics (e.g., selecting a model class or solution methodology); intelligent decision modeling systems to help with developing, applying, and managing model libraries; and decision analytic ES to integrate uncertainty into the decision-making process.

The knowledge component consists of one or more intelligent systems. Like database and model management software, knowledge-based management software provides the necessary execution and integration of the intelligent system. *Caution:* A KMS is typically a text-oriented DSS; not a knowledge-based management system.

A DSS that includes such a component is called an intelligent DSS, a DSS/ES, an expert-support system, an active DSS, or a knowledge-based DSS (see Application Case 3.10 for an example that includes both an ES and an ANN in a Web-based package written in Java). Most data mining applications include intelligent systems, such as ANN and rule induction methods for ES, to search for potentially profitable patterns in data. Many OLAP systems include ANN and data induction tools that extract rules for ES (e.g., KnowledgeSEEKER from Angoss Software Corp., **angoss.com**).

Application Case 3.10

IAP Systems's Intelligent DSS Determines the Success of Overseas Assignments and Learns from the Experience

Overseas assignments for managers and executives can be an exciting adventure for the entire family; or they can be disastrous. If an assignment is a failure, the cost of replacing the manager and the impact on his or her family can cost well over $250,000. Many companies (e.g., Coca-Cola) require employees to have overseas assignments before they can move into high executive positions. The critical issue is to be able to predict whether a specific assignment will be a good or bad experience for the manager and his or her family.

Enter intelligent DSS. The International Assignment Profile (IAP) is a new, state-of-the-art method for use in ex-pat preparation (or selection) that collects important comprehensive information about the family and compares their answers to known conditions in the anticipated international location.

IAP increases the human and business success of international assignments by spotting key issues and pinpointing the weak links or problems that could compromise an international relocation or assignment while there is still time to plan and prevent problems.

IAP's goals include the following:

- Better preparation for transfer
- Faster adjustment to international locations
- Significant reduction in compromised assignments
- No failed assignments

IAP is written in Exsys Corvid, a Web-based ES shell (**exsys.com**). Through feedback from past assignments, ANN learn emerging patterns. IAP uses modern technology and artificial intelligence to assist companies in making more accurate, less stressful foreign placements and international relocations.

The employee and his or her spouse complete the IAP interview process on the Web or on their computers. The system analyzes the information, detects, and isolates critical patterns that might jeopardize the business purpose of the relocation, and it produces a report for planning and problem prevention. IAP produces a detailed list of exactly what issues need to be resolved and what planning needs to be done to ensure success. When the entire family is happy, the assignment succeeds. For a large firm, using IAP can readily save millions of dollars per year.

Sources: Adapted from International Assignment Profile Systems, Inc., **iapsystems.com** (accessed March 2006); and Exsys, Inc., **exsys.com** (accessed March 2006).

Section 3.9 Review Questions

1. List the various knowledge-based tools that can comprise a knowledge-based management system.

2. What capabilities does a knowledge-based management system provide to DSS either in total or to each component?

3.10 THE DECISION SUPPORT SYSTEM USER

The person faced with a decision that an MSS is designed to support is called the *user*, the *manager*, or the *decision maker*. However, these terms fail to reflect the heterogeneity that exists among the users and usage patterns of MSS (see Alter, 1980). There are differences in the positions users occupy, their cognitive preferences and abilities, and their ways of arriving at a decision (i.e., decision styles). The user can be an individual or a group, depending on who is responsible for the decision. The user, although not listed as a major component of DSS, by definition provides the *human intellect*. The user, as the person or people primarily responsible for making the decision, provides expertise in guiding the development and use of a DSS. This intellectual capability is critical to the system's success and proper use. If the main user of a DSS is replaced by another, less knowledgeable, user (in terms of the decision-making problem and environment), the DSS will generally be less effective.

An MSS has two broad classes of users: managers and staff specialists. Staff specialists, such as financial analysts, production planners, and market researchers, outnumber managers by about three to two, and they use computers much more than managers. When designing an MSS, it is important to know who will actually have hands-on use of it. In general, managers expect systems to be more user-friendly than do staff specialists. Staff specialists tend to be more detail oriented, are more willing to use complex systems in their day-to-day work, and are interested in the computational capabilities of the MSS. That is why the first users of OLAP were staff specialists. Often, staff analysts are the intermediaries between managers and the MSS.

An **intermediary** allows a manager to benefit from a DSS without actually having to use the keyboard. Several types of intermediaries reflect different support for the manager:

- **Staff assistants** have specialized knowledge about management problems and some experience with decision support technology.
- **Expert tool users** are skilled in the application of one or more types of specialized problem-solving tools. An expert tool user performs tasks that the problem solver does not have the skill or training to perform.
- **Business (system) analysts** have a general knowledge of the application area, a formal business administration education (not in computer science), and considerable skill in using DSS construction tools.
- **Facilitators (in a GSS)** control and coordinate the use of software to support the work of people working in groups. The facilitator is also responsible for the conduct of workgroup sessions.

Within the categories of managers and staff specialists, there are important subcategories that influence MSS design. For example, managers differ by organizational level, functional area, educational background, and need for analytic support. Staff specialists differ with respect to education, functional area, and relationship to management.

Today's users are typically very hands-on oriented, in both creating and using DSS, although they may need help from analysts in initially setting up access to needed data.

Section 3.10 Review Questions

1. List and describe the two broad classes of DSS users.
2. List and describe the four types of DSS intermediaries.
3. Why are most users typically very hands-on in their DSS usage patterns?

3.11 DECISION SUPPORT SYSTEM HARDWARE

DSS have evolved simultaneously with advances in computer hardware and software technologies. Hardware affects the functionality and usability of the MSS. The choice of hardware can be made before, during, or after the design of the MSS software, but it is often determined by what is already available in the organization. Typically, MSS run on standard hardware. The major hardware options are the organization's servers, mainframe computers with legacy DBMS, workstations, personal computers, or client/server systems. Distributed DSS run on various types of networks, including the

Internet, intranets, and extranets. Access may be provided for mobile devices, including notebook PCs, tablet PCs, PDAs, and cell phones. This portability has become critical for deploying decision-making capability in the field, especially for salespersons and technicians. The de facto DSS hardware standard is a Web server through which the DBMS provides data accessed from existing databases on the server, data warehouses, or legacy databases. Users access the DSS by using client PCs (or mobile devices) on which Web browsers are running. Models are provided directly through packages running either on the server, the mainframe, or some external system, or even on the client PC. See Figure 3.1 for the typical DSS hardware architecture configuration.

The power and capabilities of the World Wide Web have a dramatic impact on DSS. The Web can be used for collecting both external and internal (intranet) data for a DSS database. The Web can be used for communication and collaboration among DSS builders, users, and management. In addition, the Web can be used to download DSS software, use DSS applications provided by the company, or buy online from application service providers (ASPs).

All major database vendors (e.g., IBM, Microsoft, Oracle, Sybase) provide Web capabilities by running directly on Web servers. Data warehouses and even legacy systems running on mainframes or ported to small RISC workstations can be accessed through Web technologies. Typically, models are solved on fast machines, but they are also run on Web servers, either running in the background or accessed from other systems, such as mainframes. Optimization, simulation, statistics systems, and ES currently run in Java. These developments simplify access to data, models, and knowledge, and they simplify their integration. EIS/portals and OLAP systems provide powerful tools with which to develop DSS applications, generally via Web tools.

New software development tools, such as Java, PHP, and the .NET Framework, automatically provide powerful onscreen objects (e.g., buttons, text boxes) for interfacing with databases and models. These readily open up direct access to the Web for the DSS developer. In many ways, this simplifies the developer's tasks, especially by providing common development tools and a common interface structure through Web browser technologies.

Section 3.11 Review Questions

1. Why are DSS hardware and software choices often based on a firm's existing systems?
2. List potential PCs and mobile devices that decision makers could use to connect to a DSS.
3. List the potential hardware options for DSS implementation.
4. List the reasons the Web is utilized for DSS development and deployment.

3.12 DECISION SUPPORT SYSTEM CLASSIFICATIONS

There are several ways to classify DSS applications (see Power, 2002). The design process, as well as the operation and implementation of DSS, depends in many cases on the type of DSS involved. However, remember that not every DSS fits neatly into one category. Most fit into the classification provided by the Association for Information Systems Special Interest Group on Decision Support Systems (AIS SIGDSS). We discuss this classification first, followed by other well-known classifications that more or less fit into the former's classification set.

THE AIS SIGDSS CLASSIFICATION FOR DSS

The AIS SIGDSS (**sigs.aisnet.org/SIGDSS/**) has produced a concise classification scheme for DSS. It includes the following categories:

- Communications-driven and group DSS (GSS)
- Data-driven DSS
- Document-driven DSS
- Knowledge-driven DSS, data mining, and management ES applications
- Model-driven DSS

There may also be hybrids of these categories that combine two or more. These are also called *compound DSS*. We discuss the major categories next.

Communications-Driven and Group DSS (GSS)

Communications-driven and GSS include how computer, collaboration, and communication technologies support groups in tasks that may or may not include decision making. Essentially, all DSS that involve supporting any group work fall into this category. Relevant DSS generators include those that support meetings, design collaboration, and even the best SCM. KMS that are developed around communities that practice collaborative work fall into this category.

Data-Driven DSS

Data-driven DSS primarily rely on data and their processing into information, along with the presentation of this information to a decision maker. Many DSS developed in OLAP and data mining software systems essentially fall into this category. There is minimal emphasis on utilizing mathematical models. In this type of DSS, the database organization, often in a data warehouse, plays a major role in the DSS structure. Early generations of database-oriented DSS mainly used the *relational* database configuration. The information handled by relational databases tends to be voluminous, descriptive, and rigidly structured. A database-oriented DSS features strong report generation and query capabilities. Hendriks (2002) described how the government of The Netherlands provides Web-based property management for intelligent decision making. The system, which is primarily data oriented, assists a government agency through standard and GIS databases in the effective use of its large portfolio of properties. (Also see Government Buildings Agency Property Management, at **vrom.nl/rijksgebouwendienst**.) Application Case 3.11 describes another example.

Application Case 3.11

Database-Oriented DSS: Glaxo Wellcome Accesses Life-Saving Data

When Glaxo Wellcome revealed that a combination of two of its drugs, Epivir and Retrovir, was effective in treating AIDS, doctors began writing prescriptions en masse almost overnight. Such a tidal wave of demand could have resulted in lower inventories to pharmaceutical wholesalers and shortages.

Thanks to a data warehouse application, however, market analysts at Glaxo Wellcome were able to track the size and sources of demand and generate reports within hours—or even minutes. The result: Wholesalers around the world never ran out of Epivir and Retrovir. Because of the two drugs' effectiveness with a third drug, Ziagen, the three drugs were eventually combined into one tablet.

Called GWIS (Glaxo Wellcome Information System), the data warehouse application was built with MicroStrategy's DSS relational online analytical processing (ROLAP) technology. GWIS works directly with data stored in a relational DBMS, integrating internal data with data from external sources.

The application was rolled out in June 1996 to 150 employees in Glaxo Wellcome's marketing analysis department. Users can analyze sales, inventory, and prescription data for drugs on-the-fly, which helps Glaxo Wellcome streamline its distribution process and cut operational costs. An additional IS benefit is that users can access information from various databases and computers. They no longer create local, PC-based databases that ultimately interfere with data integrity or require IT support. GWIS helps the IT organization design and manage the disparate data sources.

Sources: Condensed and modified from AIDSMeds.com, **aidsmeds.com**, November 2005; **microstrategy.com** (accessed March 2006); and B. Fryer, "Fast Data Relief," *Information Week*, No. 608, December 2, 1996, pp. 133–136.

Document-Driven DSS

Document-driven DSS rely on knowledge coding, analysis, search, and retrieval for decision support. They essentially include all DSS that are text based. Most KMS fall into this category. These DSS also have minimal emphasis on utilizing mathematical models.

Knowledge-Driven DSS, Data Mining, and Management Expert Systems Applications

These DSS involve the application of knowledge technologies to address specific decision support needs. Essentially, all artificial intelligence–based DSS fall into this category. When symbolic storage is utilized in a DSS, it is generally in this category. ANN and ES are included here. Because the benefits of these *intelligent DSS* or *knowledge-based DSS* can be large, organizations have invested in them. For example, refer to Application Case 3.10. These DSS are utilized in the creation of *automated decision-making systems*, as described in Chapter 2. The basic idea is that rules are utilized to automate the decision-making process. These rules are basically either an ES, or structured like one. This is important when decisions must be made quickly, as in many e-commerce situations.

Model-Driven DSS

The major emphases of DSS that are primarily developed around one or more (large-scale/complex) optimization or simulation model typically include significant activities in model formulation, model maintenance, model management in distributed computing environments, and what-if analysis. Many large-scale applications fall into this category. Notable examples include DuPont (ProModel, 1999), Fiat (ProModel, 2006), and Procter & Gamble (Camm et al., 1997). The focus is on utilizing the model(s) to optimize one or more objective values (e.g., profit). The most common end user tool for developing DSS is the spreadsheet Microsoft Excel. Excel includes dozens of statistical packages, a linear programming package (Solver), and many financial and management science models (e.g., see Respicio et al., 2002).

Compound DSS

A compound, or hybrid, DSS includes two or more of the major categories described earlier. Often, an ES can benefit by utilizing some optimization, or clearly a data-driven DSS can feed a large-scale optimization model. Sometimes documents are critical in understanding how to interpret the results of visualizing data from a data-driven DSS.

HOLSAPPLE AND WHINSTON'S CLASSIFICATION

Holsapple and Whinston (2000) classified DSS into the following six frameworks: text-oriented DSS, database-oriented DSS, spreadsheet-oriented DSS, solver-oriented DSS, rule-oriented DSS, and compound DSS. Essentially, these frameworks readily map into the AIS SIGDSS categories:

- The *text-oriented DSS* are the same as the document-driven DSS.
- The *database-oriented DSS* are the data-driven DSS of the AIS SIGDSS.
- The *spreadsheet-oriented DSS* are generally another form of model-driven DSS, in which the functions and add-in programs of the spreadsheet are used to create and manage the models. Because packages such as Excel can include a rudimentary DBMS or can readily interface with one, they can handle some properties of a database-oriented DSS, especially the manipulation of descriptive knowledge.
- The *solver-oriented DSS* map directly into the model-driven DSS.
- The *rule-oriented DSS* include most knowledge-driven DSS, data mining, and management ES applications.
- The *compound DSS* integrates two or more of those cited above and is defined the same as by the SIGDSS.

ALTER'S OUTPUT CLASSIFICATION

Alter's (1980) classification is based on the "degree of action implication of system outputs," or the extent to which system outputs can directly support (or determine) the decision. According to this classification, there are seven categories of DSS (see Table 3.2). The first two types are data oriented, performing data retrieval or analysis; the third deals both with data and models. The remaining four are model oriented, providing simulation capabilities, optimization, or computations that suggest an answer. Clearly, these correspond to the AIS SIGDSS data-driven and model-driven categories, along with compound DSS.

OTHER DSS CATEGORIES

There are several other important categories of DSS, including (1) institutional and ad hoc DSS; (2) personal, group, and organizational support; (3) individual support system versus FSS; and (4) custom-made systems versus ready-made systems. We discuss these next.

Institutional and Ad Hoc DSS

Institutional DSS (see Donovan and Madnick, 1977) deal with decisions of a recurring nature. A typical example is a portfolio management system (PMS), which has been used by several large banks for supporting investment decisions. An institutionalized DSS can be developed and refined as it evolves over a number of years because the DSS is used repeatedly to solve identical or similar problems. It is important to remember that an institutional DSS may not be used by everyone in an organization; it is the *recurring nature of the decision-making problem* that determines whether a DSS is institutional versus ad hoc.

Ad hoc DSS deal with specific problems that are usually neither anticipated nor recurring. Ad hoc decisions often involve strategic planning issues and sometimes management control problems. Justifying a DSS that will be used only once or twice is a major issue in DSS development. Countless ad hoc DSS applications have evolved into institutional DSS. Either the problem recurs and the system is reused or others

TABLE 3.2 Characteristics of Different Classes of Decision Support Systems

Orientation	*Category*	*Type of Operation*	*Type of Task*	*User*	*Usage Pattern*	*Time*
Data	File drawer systems	Access data items	Operational	Nonmanagerial line personnel	Simple inquiries	Irregular
	Data analysis systems	Ad hoc analysis of data files	Operational analysis	Staff analyst or managerial line personnel	Manipulation and display of data	Irregular or periodic
Data or Models	Analysis information systems	Ad hoc analysis involving multiple databases and small models	Analysis, planning	Staff analyst	Programming special reports, developing small models	Irregular, on request
Models	Accounting models	Standard calculations that estimate future results on the basis of accounting definitions	Planning, budgeting	Staff analyst or manager	Input estimates of activity; receive estimated monetary results as output	Periodic (e.g., weekly, monthly, yearly)
	Representational models	Estimating consequences of particular actions	Planning, budgeting	Staff analyst	Input possible decision; receive estimated results as output	Periodic or irregular (ad hoc analysis)
	Optimization models	Calculating an optimal solution to a combinatorial problem	Planning, resource allocation	Staff analyst	Input constraints and objectives; receive answer	Periodic or irregular (ad hoc) analysis
	Suggestion models	Performing calculations that generate a suggested decision	Operational	Nonmanagerial line personnel	Input a structured description of the decision situation; receive a suggested decision as output	Daily or periodic

Source: Condensed from Alter (1980), pp. 90–91.

in the organization have similar needs that can be handled by the formerly ad hoc DSS. See Online File W3.3 for a description of an ad hoc DSS that evolved into an institutional DSS.

Personal, Group, and Organizational Support

The support given by DSS can be separated into three distinct, interrelated categories (Hackathorn and Keen, 1981): personal support, group support, and organizational support.

Personal Support Here the focus is on an individual user performing an activity in a discrete task or decision. The task is fairly independent of other tasks. The situation described in Online File W3.3 started with the development of a personal support DSS.

Group Support The focus here is on a group of people, all of whom are engaged in separate but highly interrelated tasks. An example is a typical finance department in which one DSS can serve several employees working on the preparation of a budget. If the use of an ad hoc DSS spreads, it becomes a group support DSS. *Caution:* This is not the same as a GSS that provides collaboration and communication capabilities to a group working together.

Organizational Support Here the focus is on organizational tasks or activities involving a sequence of operations, different functional areas, possibly different locations, and massive resources. This may also be considered enterprise-wide support. The opening vignette contains several examples of this level of support.

Individual DSS Versus a Group Support System

Several DSS researchers and practitioners (e.g., Keen, 1980) have pointed out that the fundamental model of a DSS—the lonely decision maker striding down the hall at high noon—is true only for minor decisions. In most organizations, be they public, private, Japanese, European, American, or other, most major decisions are made collectively and cooperatively. Working in a group can be a complicated process, and it can be supported by computers in what is called a **group support system (GSS)**.

Originally, GSS were designed to operate with all participants in the same room (i.e., a decision room) at the same time (e.g., same time/same place situation). Currently, GSS are deployed over the Web and are designed to operate in anytime/anyplace mode. They include courseware (e.g., course management software), such as the Blackboard distance-learning system (see Technology Insights 3.9; and **blackboard.com**), which provides support to all individuals and groups involved in a course. As a content management system, it provides support to the group of students taking the course: It stores and distributes course materials. It supports the individual instructor through an online grade book and other course management tools. In addition, it functions as a GSS through its discussion lists, e-mail feature, and virtual classroom. *Note:* The term *group support* introduced earlier should not be confused with the concept of a GSS. In group support, the work of individuals is interrelated, but the work may not involve collaboration.

CUSTOM-MADE SYSTEMS VERSUS READY-MADE SYSTEMS

Many DSS are custom made for individual users and organizations (e.g., the system in the opening vignette, the real estate DSS application in Online File W3.3). However, a comparable problem may exist in similar organizations. For example, hospitals, banks, and universities share many similar problems. Similarly, certain nonroutine problems in a functional area (e.g., finance, accounting) can repeat themselves in the same functional area of different areas or organizations. Therefore, it makes sense to build generic DSS that can be used (sometimes with modifications) in several organizations. Such DSS are called *ready made* and are sold by various vendors (e.g., Cognos, MicroStrategy, Temtec, Teradata). Essentially, the database, models, interface, and other support features are built in: Just add an organization's data and logo. The major OLAP and data mining vendors provide DSS templates for a variety of functional areas, including finance, real estate, marketing, and accounting. Essentially, computer-aided software engineering (CASE) tools function as a DSS for MIS systems analysts and implementers. The IAP Systems application described in Application Case 3.10 is a ready-made DSS. The real estate applications described in Online File W3.3 may be viewed as a ready-made DSS, as can Blackboard. The number of ready-made DSS continues to increase because of their flexibility and low cost. They are typically developed using Internet technologies for database access and communications, and Web browsers for interfaces. They also readily incorporate OLAP and other easy-to-use DSS generators (refer to Application Case 3.10).

One complication in terminology results when an organization develops an institutional system but, because of its structure, uses it in an ad hoc manner. An organization can build a large data warehouse but then use OLAP tools to query it and perform ad hoc analysis to solve nonrecurring problems. The DSS exhibits the traits of ad hoc and institutional systems and also of custom and ready-made systems. We describe such a Web-based system in the End of Chapter Application Case. Several ERP, CRM, knowledge management (KM), and SCM companies offer DSS applications online. These kinds of systems can be viewed as ready made, although typically they require modifications (sometimes major) before they can be used effectively.

Section 3.12 Review Questions

1. List the DSS classifications of the AIS SIGDSS.
2. Define *document-driven DSS*.
3. List and compare the Holsapple and Whinston classifications to those of the AIS SIGDSS.
4. List the capabilities of institutional DSS and ad hoc DSS.
5. Define the term *ready-made DSS*.

3.13 RESOURCES, LINKS, AND THE TERADATA UNIVERSITY NETWORK CONNECTION

The use of this chapter and most other chapters in this book can be enhanced by the tools described in the following sections.

RESOURCES AND LINKS

We recommend looking at the following resources and links for further reading and explanations:

- The Data Warehousing Institute (**tdwi.org**)
- *DM Review* (**dmreview.com**)
- The OLAP Report (**olapreport.com**)
- DSS Resources (**dssresources.com**)

CASES

All major MSS vendors (e.g., MicroStrategy, Microsoft, Oracle, IBM, Hyperion, Cognos, Exsys, Fair Issac, SAP, Information Builders) provide interesting customer success stories. Academic-oriented cases are available at the Harvard Business School Case Collection (**hbsp.harvard.edu/products/cases.html**), Business Performance Improvement Resource (**bpir.com**), Idea Group Publishing (**idea-group.com**), Ivy League Publishing (**ivylp.com**), ICFAI Center for Management Research (**icmr.icfai.org/casestudies/icmr_case_studies.htm**), KnowledgeStorm (**knowledgestorm.com**), and other sites. For additional case resources, see Teradata University Network (**teradatauniversitynetwork.com**).

MILLER'S *MIS CASES*

All the cases in Miller's *MIS Cases* (2005) involve decision making and can be utilized. The spreadsheet cases are all essentially model-driven DSS, and the database cases are all data-driven DSS.

VENDORS, PRODUCTS, AND DEMOS

A comprehensive list is available at the *DM Review* Software Demo Lab, **dmreview.com/rg/resources/demos.cfm**.

PERIODICALS

We recommend the following periodicals:

- *Advisor* (**advisor.com**)
- *Baseline Magazine* (**baselinemag.com**)
- *Business Intelligence Journal* (**tdwi.org**)
- *CIO* (**cio.com**)
- *CIO Insight* (**cioinsight.com**)
- *Computerworld* (**computerworld.com**)
- *Decision Support Systems* (**elsevier.com**)
- *DM Review* (**dmreview.com**)
- *eWEEK* (**eweek.com**)
- *InfoWeek* (**infoweek.com**)
- *InfoWorld* (**infoworld.com**)
- *InternetWeek* (**internetweek.com**)
- *Management Information Systems Quarterly (MIS Quarterly)* (**misq.org**)
- *Technology-Evaluation* online magazine (**technologyevaluation.com**)

ADDITIONAL REFERENCES

Additional selected references are provided in the online files of each chapter. For this chapter, see Online File W3.4.

THE TERADATA UNIVERSITY CONNECTION

Teradata University Network (TUN) (**teradatastudentnetwork.com**, for students) provides a wealth of information and cases on DSS; however, it is typically termed as BI. All cases and white papers that involve aspects of decision making are DSS relevant pieces of literature.

Chapter Highlights

- There are several definitions of *DSS*.
- A DSS is designed to support complex managerial problems that other computerized techniques cannot. DSS is user oriented, and it uses data and models.
- DSS are generally developed to solve specific managerial problems, whereas BI systems typically report status, and when a problem is discovered, their analysis tools are utilized by decision makers.
- DSS can provide support in all phases of the decision-making process and to all managerial levels for individuals, groups, and organizations.
- DSS is a user-oriented tool. Many applications can be developed by end users, often in spreadsheets.
- DSS can improve the effectiveness of decision making, decrease the need for training, improve management control, facilitate communication, save effort by

the users, reduce costs, and allow for more objective decision making.

- The major components of a DSS are a database and its management, a model base and its management, and a user-friendly interface. An intelligent (knowledge-based) component can also be included. The user is also considered to be a component of a DSS.
- The components of DSS are typically deployed and integrated via Internet technologies. Web browsers are typically used as user interfaces.
- Data warehouses, data mining, and OLAP have made it possible to develop DSS quickly and easily.
- The data management subsystem usually includes a DSS database, a DBMS, a data directory, and a query facility.
- Data are extracted from several sources, internal and external.
- The DBMS provides many capabilities to the DSS, ranging from storage and retrieval to report generation.
- The model base includes standard models and models specifically written for the DSS.
- Custom-made models can be written in programming languages, in special modeling languages, and in Web-based development systems (e.g., Java, the .NET Framework.).
- The user interface (or dialog) is of utmost importance. It is managed by software that provides the needed capabilities. Web browsers commonly provide a friendly, consistent DSS GUI.
- The user interface capabilities of DSS have moved into small, portable devices, including PDAs, mobile telephones, and even MP3 players.
- The DSS is supplemented by the user's intellectual capabilities. The user is knowledgeable about the problem being solved.
- A DSS can be used directly by managers (and analysts), or it can be used by intermediaries.
- DSS applications are typically developed, delivered, and run on the Web. It is convenient to distribute them to remote locations.
- The AIS SIGDSS classification of DSS include communications-driven and group DSS (GSS), data-driven DSS, document-driven DSS, knowledge-driven DSS, data mining and management ES applications, and model-driven DSS. Several other classifications map into this one.
- Several useful classifications of DSS are based on why they are developed (institutional vs. ad hoc), what level within the organization they support (personal, group, or organizational), whether they support individual work or group work (individual DSS vs. GSS), and how they are developed (custom vs. ready made).

Key Terms

- ad hoc DSS
- analytical model
- business (system) analyst
- business analytics (BA)
- business intelligence (BI)
- data warehouse
- database
- database management system (DBMS)
- directory
- DSS application
- expert tool user
- extraction
- facilitator (in a GSS)
- graphical user interface (GUI)
- group support system (GSS)
- institutional DSS
- intermediary
- model base
- model base management system (MBMS)
- model building blocks
- object
- operational models
- organizational knowledge base
- predictive analytics
- query facility
- staff assistant
- strategic models
- tactical models
- user interface
- user interface management system (UIMS)

Questions for Discussion

1. Review the major characteristics and capabilities of DSS. How do each of them relate to the major components of DSS?
2. List some internal data and external data that could be found in a DSS for a university's admissions office.
3. Explain how poor data quality can lead to bad decisions.
4. Why is it so important for an organization to make data quality a key organizational issue?
5. Why is it so important to have a single version of the truth when it comes to data integration for decision making? Give or find an example of when not having a single version of the truth in believed data integration led to problems for an organization.

6. Why is scalability an important database issue?
7. Why is data security an important database issue?
8. Provide a list of possible strategic, tactical, and operational models for a university, a restaurant, and a chemical plant.
9. Review the models described in the situations described in the opening vignette, the End of Chapter Application Case, and the other Application Cases for this chapter. Compare and contrast what they are and how they are used. Explain how this illustrates the difficulty in model management as compared with that of database management.
10. Show the similarities between DBMS and MBMS. What is common to both and why? What are the differences and why?
11. Why was DSS the first MIS ever defined as requiring a computer?
12. Why does a DSS need a DBMS, a model management system, and a user interface, but not necessarily a knowledge-based management system?
13. Why might the user be considered a component of a DSS?
14. Why do managers use intermediaries? Will they continue to use them in the future? Why or why not? Would you? Why or why not?
15. Why are DSS typically developed on an organization's existing hardware and software?
16. Why are DSS typically developed and deployed with Web-based technology? Discuss the potential benefits that a DSS application can derive from the Web in terms of both developers and users.
17. What are the benefits and the limitations of the AIS SIGDSS classification for DSS?
18. Compare an individual DSS to a group DSS. How are they similar? How are they different?
19. How has the Web affected the components of DSS and vice versa?
20. Compare a custom-made DSS with a ready-made DSS. Describe and discuss the advantages and disadvantages of each.
21. Search for a ready-made DSS. What type of industry is its market? Explain why it is a ready-made DSS.

Exercises

Teradata University and Other Hands-on Exercises

1. Explore **teradatastudentnetwork.com**. In a report, describe at least three interesting DSS applications and three interesting DSS areas (e.g., CRM, SCM) that you have discovered there.
2. Examine Daniel Power's DSS Resources site, at **dssresources.com**. Take the Decision Support Systems Web Tour (**dssresources.com/tour/index.html**). Explore other areas of the Web site.
3. On the Web, locate free speech input software and try speech input. In a report, describe your experience. Try to find someone with a strong accent to use it as well as someone with a fairly neutral accent. What happens? Would you use this package on a regular basis? Why or why not?
4. On the Web, locate a free text-to-speech software package and try it. In a report, describe your experience. Describe several good applications of this software package.
5. On the Web, locate a free language translation software package (text-to-text) and try it. In a report, describe your experience. (Note: Some of these are readily available running on Web servers. Among other tests, try translating something with many idioms into another language and then back to the first language. Compare the initial text to the final version. Is it understandable?)
6. On the Web, find a DSS software vendor with downloadable demo software. Download the software, install it, and test it. Report your findings to the class and demonstrate the software's capabilities.

Team Assignments and Role Playing

1. In groups of no more than five students each, consider how each of you decided into which university or program you wanted to enroll. Each member should write down on a piece of paper two lists: (1) the important factors (criteria) that you considered and (2) the specific universities or programs you considered. As a group, consider what factors you had in common and which ones were different. Do the same for the specific universities or programs. Describe where each of you got your information for this problem. Also, think about what types of software you could have used (a DSS) to help you in the decision-making process. Write up your results in a report.

Internet Exercises

1. Search the Internet for literature and information about DSS and its relationship to BI, business analytics, and predictive analytics. Describe what you find.
2. Identify a DSS software vendor. Obtain information about its products. Write up your findings about its products in a report.
3. On the Internet, identify a course syllabus and materials for a DSS/BI/business analytics course at another college or university. Compare the course description to that of your own course. Repeat this assignment, using a DSS/BI/business analytics course syllabus from a university in another country. Use **isworld.org**.
4. Search the Web for capabilities of mobile devices (e.g., PDAs, cells phones) and describe how decision makers can utilize them effectively.
5. Perform a Web search and report on the current status of data security. What tools exist and what features do they have? Can any of them be called DSS? Why or why not?

End of Chapter Application Case

FedEx Tracks Customers Along with Packages

Federal Express Corp. is well known for keeping track of its ever-moving overnight packages. It's one of the most important things the company does. In fact, there's only one thing that's more important for FedEx to track—its customer base. Until recently, FedEx wasn't doing a great job of quickly getting its business managers the information they needed to keep up with the company's fast-moving customers.

FedEx maintained a network of 46,000 U.S. drop-off points (more than 56,000 worldwide in 220 countries and territories) as of early 2006. But the company was not always sure that those points were in the optimal locations. New customers appear, old customers disappear, and some customers relocate. As businesses move from urban centers to suburban business parks, and as more and more individuals telecommute, FedEx wants its drop-off points, from large service centers to drop boxes, to be conveniently located for customers. But until recently, FedEx managers did not have easy access to traffic information about its drop-off locations.

FedEx has a proprietary, mainframe-based Cosmos tracking and billing application that collects massive amounts of operational data, including information on where packages are picked up. But FedEx analysts could not easily access the data. Analysts submitted requests for custom reports (i.e., ad hoc use) to a staff of eight programmers and then waited for up to two weeks for a report. FedEx was using a mainframe version of the Information Builders FOCUS decision-support database to produce the reports. The old system did not support quick decision making.

SOLUTION

FedEx decided to give analysts direct access to information. The company deployed a Web-based version of the FOCUS database, WebFOCUS (**informationbuilders.com**). The new system runs on the company's intranet and has a self-service data warehouse to help company executives make up-to-the-minute decisions about where it should locate the service centers and drop boxes that customers use every day. Data are downloaded from the Cosmos mainframe system to the WebFOCUS server running Windows NT. Analysts can query the data either by using a set of preconfigured reports (institutional use/ready-made DSS) or by creating their own ad hoc queries (ad hoc use/custom-made DSS).

FedEx evaluated several Web-based DSS. It selected WebFOCUS primarily because the company already had programmers with FOCUS experience from its $250,000 International Strategic Information System (ISIS) project, designed to extend decision-making capabilities via the Internet across the supply chain to 75 delivery agents in 150 countries. Previous experience with FOCUS helped FedEx get an initial release of the intranet-based application deployed in just three weeks.

RESULTS

FedEx's self-service, intranet-based DSS application makes it easier to get a more complete view of population shifts and other customer trends by combining the company's own drop-off point usage data with demographic data purchased from vendors. Programmers who had previously been developing reports from FedEx's mainframe FOCUS database have integrated external data with the WebFOCUS data to allow analysts to anticipate and more accurately track customer trends.

Being able to anticipate customer trends is increasingly critical not only to FedEx but also to other companies in the distribution and logistics business. As companies such as FedEx try to link their distribution services directly into the supply-chain operations of their large corporate customers, they need to make sure they have support centers, trucks, and people in the right place at the right time.

FedEx expanded its system in several ways. First, it extended the WebFOCUS database to store 25 months' worth of data instead of the original 3 months of historical shipment information. That increased the data warehouse's capacity from 21 million records to 260 million records and required a hardware upgrade.

FedEx continuously improves the system's reporting capabilities. The company rolled out the managed reporting features of WebFOCUS to allow analysts to schedule and create more predefined reports. FedEx deployed new applications in the Information Builders Cactus development tool to allow analysts to update and enhance drop-off point data in the WebFOCUS database—not just read it. With the new self-service data warehouse and planned enhancements, FedEx acquired a better handle on tracking its fast-moving customers.

Redeploying the DSS application on the intranet has already paid off in quicker access to information and quicker decisions. Analysts using WebFOCUS can tap directly into up-to-the-minute drop site usage data from any PC running a Web browser and get reports on their screens in seconds instead of weeks. FedEx can more actively manage the location of its service centers and drop-off points as populations shift and customer habits change. The payoff is better customer service and lower operating costs.

In addition to more accurately tracking drop-off point usage, FedEx analysts get fresh information on the profitability of each service center and drop-off box. Doing a better job of placing the boxes will help cut costs and increase revenue. Through these tools, FedEx initially got a 470 percent return on its investment, equal to about $2.3 million in savings. Take a look at the FedEx video at **informationbuilders.com**.

Sources: Modified and condensed from material at Information Builders, Inc., **informationbuilders.com** (accessed November 2005); FedEx, **fedex.com** (accessed November 2005); Mel Duvall, "FedEx Generates Big Returns with Real-Time Information Delivery," *Information Builders Magazine*, Vol. 13, No. 2, Spring/Summer 2002 ; G.D. Cohen, "IT Does Matter," *Information Builders Magazine*, Vol. 14, No. 2, Fall 2003 ; and J. Dash, "FedEx Launches Global Business-Intelligence Application, *Computerworld*, Vol. 35, No. 22, May 28, 2001, pp. 12.

QUESTIONS FOR THE CASE

1. Describe the benefits of the FedEx system. What other benefits might FedEx obtain with other features?
2. Why is it important for a company such as FedEx to manage its drop-off locations effectively?
3. Describe the benefits of switching from FOCUS to WebFOCUS. Do you think this was the right approach? Why or why not?
4. How can the FedEx approach taken in this case be applied to other industries?

References

AberdeenGroup. (2004, December). "Maximizing Service Performance with Machine-to-Machine Solutions." *Next Generation Post-Sales Service Benchmark Report*. Boston: AberdeenGroup.

Abiteboul, S., et al. (2005, May). "The Lowell Database Research Self-Assessment." *Communications of the ACM*, Vol. 48, No. 5, pp. 111–118.

Alter, S.L. (1980). *Decision Support Systems: Current Practices and Continuing Challenges*. Reading, MA: Addison-Wesley.

Anthes, G.H. (2006, January 23). "Computer to User: You Figure It Out." *Computerworld*, Vol. 40, No. 4, p. 24.

Ben-Natan, R., R. Gornitsky, T. Hanis, and O. Sasson. (2004). *Mastering IBM WebSphere Portal: Expert Guidance to Build and Deploy Portal Applications*. Indianapolis: Wiley.

Bonczek, R.H., C.W. Holsapple, and A.B. Whinston. (1980). "The Evolving Roles of Models in Decision Support Systems." *Decision Sciences*, Vol. 11, No. 2, pp. 337–356.

Camm, J.D., T.E. Chorman, F.A. Dill, J.R. Evans, D.J. Sweeney, and G.W. Wegryn. (1997, January/February). "Blending OR/MS, Judgment, and GIS: Restructuring P&G's Supply Chain," *Interfaces*, Vol. 27, No. 1, pp. 128–142.

D'Agostino, D. (2004, December). "Sense and Sensibility." *CIO Insight*, Issue 47, pp. 61–67.

"Data Architecture: The CIO Insight Research Study." (2002, July). *CIO Insight*, Issue 16, pp. 70–75

Donovan, J.J., and S.E. Madnick. (1977). "Institutional and Ad Hoc DSS and Their Effective Use." *Data Base*, Vol. 8, No. 3, pp. 79–88.

English, L. (2002, September). "The Essentials of Information Quality Management." *DM Review*, Vol. 12, No. 9.

English, L. (2005, September). "IQ and Muda." *DM Review*, Vol. 15, No. 9, pp. 40–46.

Fisher, C.W., I. Chengalur-Smith, and D.P. Ballou. (2003, June). "The Impact of Experience and Time on the Use of Data Quality Information in Decision Making." *Information Systems Research*, Vol. 14, No. 2, pp. 170–188.

"Getting Clean: Strategic Technology: Data Management." (2004, August). *CIO Insight*, No. 42, pp. 72–77

Gilhooly, K. (2005, November 7). "Dirty Data Blights the Bottom Line." *Computerworld*, Vol. 39, No. 45, pp. 23–24.

Gonzales, M.L. (2004, June 1). "The Architecture of Enterprise Data Quality." *Intelligent Enterprise*, Vol. 7, No. 9, p. 17.

Hackathorn, R.D., and P.G.W. Keen. (1981, September). "Organizational Strategies for Personal Computing in Decision Support Systems." *MIS Quarterly*, Vol. 5, No. 3, pp. 21–27.

Hayes, H., and N. Mattos. (2003, Quarter 3). "Information on Demand." *DB2 Magazine*, Vol. 8, No. 3.

Hendriks, L. (2002, June). "Customers in Sight: Supporting Corporate Accommodation Decisions with Real Estate Data." *Journal of Corporate Real Estate*, Vol. 4, No. 3, pp. 275–297.

Hildreth, S. (2005, November). "Data Detectives." *Computerworld*, Vol. 39, No. 46, pp. 29–37.

Holsapple, C.W., and A.B. Whinston. (2000). *Decision Support Systems: A Knowledge-Based Approach*. Cambridge, MA: Thomson Learning.

Junnarkar, N., N. Chanchani, and J. Basu. (2005, March/April). "Aggregate Data with XQuery." *Oracle Magazine*.

Keen, P.G.W. (1980, Fall). "Adaptive Design for Decision Support Systems." *Data Base*, Vol. 12, Nos. 1 and 2, pp. 15–25.

Little, J.D.C. (1970, April). "Models and Managers: The Concept of a Decision Calculus." *Management Science*, Vol. 16, No. 8, pp. 466–485.

Marco, D. (2005, February). "Meta Data & Knowledge Management: MME Best Practices Case Study: Allstate Insurance, Part 1." *DM Review*, Vol. 15, No. 2.

Marco, D., and M. Jennings. (2004). *Universal Meta Data Models*. New York: Wiley.

Miller, M.L. (2005). *MIS Cases*, 3rd ed. Upper Saddle River, NJ: Prentice Hall.

Monash, C.A. (2005, August 8). "Time for a New View of Data Management." *Computerworld*, Vol. 39, No. 32, pp. 36.

Moore, J.H., and M.G. Chang. (1980, Fall). "Design of Decision Support Systems." *Data Base*, Vol. 12, Nos. 1 and 2, pp. 8–14.

Power, D.J. (2002). *Decision Making Support Systems: Achievements, Trends and Challenges*. Hershey, PA: Idea Group Publishing.

ProModel. (1999). *ProModel Saves DuPont $480,000*. Orem, UT: ProModel Corporation, (**promodel.com**).

ProModel. (2006, March). *Fiat Case*. Orem, UT: ProModel Corporation (**promodel.com**).

Raden, N. (2005, October). "Start Making Sense." *Intelligent Enterprise*, Vol. 8, No. 10, pp. 25–31.

Respicio, A., M.E. Captivo, and A.J. Rodrigues. (2002, July 4–7). "A DSS for Production Planning and Scheduling in the Paper Industry," *Proceedings of DSIage2002*, Cork, Ireland.

Siluer, B. (2005, October). "Content: The Other Half of the Integration Problem." *Intelligent Enterprise*, Vol. 8, No. 10, pp. 33–37.

Songini, M.L. (2002, July 15). "Southwest Expands Business Tools' Role," *Computerworld*, Vol. 36, No. 29, pp. 6.

Stahl, S. (2004, August 30). "Data Quality Is Everyone's Problem." *InformationWeek*, No. 1003, pp. 8.

Wheatley, M. (2004, July 1). "Operation Clean Data." *CIO*.

Winter, R., and K. Auerbach. (2004, May 1). "Contents Under Pressure," *Intelligent Enterprise*, Vol. 7, No. 7, pp. 18–25.

Yang, S.J. (2005, June). "Master Data Management." *Baseline*, No. 45, pp. 89.

CHAPTER 4

Modeling and Analysis

Learning Objectives

- Understand the basic concepts of management support system (MSS) modeling
- Describe how MSS models interact with data and the user
- Understand some different, well-known model classes
- Understand how to structure decision making with a few alternatives
- Describe how spreadsheets can be used for MSS modeling and solution
- Explain the basic concepts of optimization, simulation, and heuristics, and when to use them
- Describe how to structure a linear programming model
- Understand how search methods are used to solve MSS models
- Explain the differences among algorithms, blind search, and heuristics
- Describe how to handle multiple goals
- Explain what is meant by sensitivity analysis, what-if analysis, and goal seeking
- Describe the key issues of model management

In this chapter, we describe the model base and its management, one of the major components of decision support systems (DSS). We present this material with a note of caution: Modeling can be a very difficult topic and is as much an art as a science. The purpose of this chapter is not necessarily for you to *master the topics* of modeling and analysis. Rather, the material is geared toward *gaining familiarity* with the important concepts as they relate to DSS and their use in decision making. It is important to recognize that the modeling we discuss here is only cursorily related to the concepts of data modeling. You should not confuse the two. We walk through some basic concepts and definitions of modeling before introducing the influence diagram (see Online File W4.1), which can aid a decision maker in sketching a model of a situation and even solving it. We next introduce the idea of modeling directly in spreadsheets. Only then do we describe the structure and application of some successful time-proven models and methodologies: decision analysis, decision trees, optimization, search methods, heuristic programming, and simulation. In several online files, we provide a wealth of detail of how important models are constructed and how they are used in practice.

4.1 OPENING VIGNETTE: WINNING ISN'T EVERYTHING . . . BUT LOSING ISN'T ANYTHING: PROFESSIONAL SPORTS MODELING FOR DECISION MAKING

Professional sports teams are always seeking a performance edge. Some of the more successful teams in the U.S. have learned that overspending your rivals for talent may not necessarily lead to more victories, but the application of analytical models may, and often does. Here are some examples of how professional sports teams have succeeded with analytical models.

THE BOSTON RED SOX AND OAKLAND ATHLETICS BASEBALL TEAMS

Analytical models helped lift the Boston Red Sox baseball team's "Curse of the Bambino" in 2004. The Red Sox had not won a World Series since 1918. When owner Harry Frazee traded Babe Ruth to the New York Yankees in 1920, so began the "Curse of the Bambino." But current Red Sox owners John Henry and Tom Werner hired excellent analytical talent and implemented sophisticated scouting software to analyze statistics, with the goal of identifying the best talent available, acquiring the players first, and determining when to release them. These innovative ways of identifying winning characteristics of human capital can lead a team, or a company, to victory. The Sox tracked the tiniest of performance data to maximize team performance.

Sabermetrics (named for the Society for American Baseball Research, **sabr.org**) is the mathematical analysis of player batting and pitching performance. Theo Epstein, the senior vice president and general manager of the Red Sox, adapted new, accurate metrics well beyond the two standard ones—runs batted in (RBI) and earned run average (ERA)—typically tracked to identify batting and pitching strength. For example, a metric such as "runs created" indicates how often a player contributes to earning a run, whether he walks or gets a hit. Regardless of how he gets on base and scores, he gets credit for contributing to the creation of a run. Other factors can indicate the power of a hit. All in all, the contribution to winning a game is what is important. Analysis of these and other factors, using appropriate models, can indicate whether a current, minor league, or high school player will contribute to the bottom line: won games. The obvious connection to any modern enterprise is obvious. Identifying the right talent at a reasonable price will predictably lead to improved performance for the enterprise.

The Oakland Athletics is one of the best practitioners of using models and the data from Sabermetrics. The team consistently fields one of the best teams on the eighth-lowest payroll in the league ($50 million vs. $150 million for the New York Yankees, which is known to pay a hefty price to buy the best talent available). Since 2000, Oakland has made the playoffs every year.

The Red Sox also use ScoutAdvisor from E Solutions. ScoutAdvisor tracks players' records, pulling and integrating data from multiple sources and analyzing the data in an online analytical processing (OLAP) framework. It also allows the entry and use of qualitative factors from the scouts. From the built-in models, Red Sox decision makers determine players' salaries and when to release players. In 2004, partly through effective prediction models, the Boston Red Sox, after 86 years, put an end to the Curse of the Bambino and won the World Series![1]

THE SAN JOSE SHARKS HOCKEY TEAM

The San Jose (California) Sharks hockey team managed to cut its payroll costs by 29 percent (from $48.5 million to $34.5 million) and boost its overall performance. The team focused on finding players with a wider set of skills rather than hiring a few star players with narrow specialties. The Sharks did not even make the playoffs in 2003; they came in last place and earned a mere 73 points for the season (2 points for a win, 1 for a tie, and 1 for a loss in overtime). In 2004, the team earned 104 points in an 82-game season. The team used models and heavy statistical analysis to determine the right set of players to put on the team, out of hundreds of prospects.

Like the baseball teams mentioned in the preceding section, the Sharks integrated data and determined realistic metrics that led to success. For hockey, a new measure of effectiveness is whether a player creates scoring opportunities, not whether he has scored. Predictive analytical models indicate whether certain younger players could perform as well as veteran players. By using these models, the Sharks created a team that, in 2004, won its division and earned home ice advantage for at least the first two rounds of the playoffs. Using analytical models allowed the Sharks to get the most out of their players.

HOOPMASTERS.COM BASKETBALL

Van Coleman and Bob Gibbons, well-known college basketball scouts, created a Web site called **Hoopmasters.com** as an online decision-making tool for coaches. The subscription site publishes information on top amateur players. It also provides written evaluations of players' skills and attitudes, along with videos of them playing. Hoopmasters also estimates what types of schools would be best for each player. Because there are over 500,000 amateur players, this information is invaluable in allowing coaches to identify prospects quickly. However, it is still up to the coaches to identify appropriate metrics and run predictive statistical analysis to determine a player's potential.

[1] Author Jay Aronson is a lifelong Red Sox fan. Check with Boston Red Sox or Chicago Cubs fans to really get a feel for this part of the vignette.

THE GREEN BAY PACKERS FOOTBALL TEAM

Like the Boston Red Sox and San Jose Sharks, the Green Bay Packers football team uses performance metrics and predictive models to predict how well players will perform. The Packers also use these metrics one-on-one with players to improve their performance. For example, a linebacker such as Nick Barnett wants to have two dominating blocks per game. (With a dominating block, an opposing player is removed from the play and has no hands in a tackle.) The Packers have developed and continue to develop metrics like these that lead to winning games. Tracking these metrics is done primarily through both traditional database mechanisms and digital video.

Business intelligence (BI) mechanisms are used to identify trouble spots. For example, when running back Ahman Green's performance was evaluated in 2003, data were queried by his jersey number, readily identified on video. In minutes, a compilation of all his plays was created for analysis. Coaches noticed that he fumbled the ball whenever his elbow was not horizontal to the ground as he was hit. Green adjusted his playing style and then fumbled the ball (and even recovered it) only once in seven games. The next issue is to determine how predictive models can be used within the system.

Sources: Adapted and modified in part from M. Duvall, "Boston Red Sox: Backstop Your Business," *Baseline*, Case 117, May 2004, pp. 30–47; C. Schultz, *Lucy Must Be Traded, Charlie Brown*. Aired on ABC August 29, 2003; M. Duvall, "Billy Beane: What MBAs Can Learn from MLB," *Baseline Online*, May 20, 2004, **baselinemag.com/may04/** (accessed March 2006); D.F. Carr, "Gotcha! Weigh Your Human-Resources Software Options with Care," *Baseline Online*, May 14, 2004, **baselinemag.com/may04/** (accessed March 2006); M. Duvall, "Roadblock: Getting Old-line Managers to Think in New Ways," *Baseline Online*, May 14, 2004, **baselinemag.com/may04/** (accessed March 2006); E. Cone, "Courting Success," *Baseline*, Case 118, May 2004, pp. 48–51; L. Dignan, "Reel Time," *Baseline*, Case 119, May 2004, pp. 52–60; and L. Barrett, "On Thick Ice," *Baseline*, Case 120, May 2004, pp. 62–66.

Questions for the Opening Vignette

1. Why is it more important to measure a player's ability to create scoring situations than whether he or she scores? How can this concept be transferred to industry?
2. How could college basketball and professional football benefit from analytical models for analyzing potential team members? Refer to the baseball and hockey situations described here.
3. Consider the case of a law firm. How can the concepts illustrated here justify hiring good, multiskilled attorneys instead of superstars in one narrow area?
4. How can the concepts described here be applied to industry? Use specific examples.
5. How can the concepts described here be applied to government services? Use specific examples.

WHAT WE CAN LEARN FROM THIS VIGNETTE

The opening vignette shows how analytical models can be used by organizations that most people would suspect as being not familiar with such techniques. However, the use of predictive analytical models, typically statistics based, by professional and college sports teams (and announcers) is not new. The sophistication of these models and the data tracked, gathered, and integrated has increased dramatically with data gathering capabilities, modeling tool improvements, accessibility of these tools, and the embedding of these tools into other software. Coaches, managers, and scouts have become more computer savvy in terms of developing player metrics that really lead to winning games, and they have developed strategies that involve putting together teams based on forecasts of players' potentials to provide scoring opportunities and work as a team. This is critical in selecting new players for a team when the players have minimal or no professional sports experience. These new metrics and the ability to accurately predict them led the Boston Red Sox to a World Series victory, and they consistently lead the San Jose Sharks and Oakland Athletics to the playoffs. Although the specific models described here are proprietary, their effective use is illustrated in a very high-profile, highly profitable business. The teams that are capable of focusing on winning games as a goal; of gathering appropriate, accurate data; and of using modeling tools typically outperform the others.

We are about to discuss some details about analytical models, how they are solved, and how they can be used in DSS to assist managers in decision making. Before turning to the details, in the next section, we initially describe a few more lessons that other organizations have faced and solved by using models.

4.2 MANAGEMENT SUPPORT SYSTEMS MODELING

Many readily accessible applications describe how the models incorporated in DSS contribute in a major way to organizational success. These include DuPont (see ProModel, 1999), Procter & Gamble (see Camm et al., 1997), Fiat (see ProModel, 2006), and others. Although we do not describe these actual cases, we do discuss some modeling lessons from these organizations next.

LESSONS FROM MODELING AT DUPONT

DuPont Corp. faced a complex decision-making problem for which conventional wisdom dictated an inferior decision alternative (see ProModel, 1999). By accurately *modeling* and *simulating* its rail transportation system, decision makers were able to experiment with different policies and alternatives quickly and inexpensively. The DuPont simulation model was implemented with commercial software, which is typical. The simulation approach saves DuPont a substantial amount of money annually. Instead of investing in expensive railcars and then experimenting with how best to use them (which is also quite expensive), all the work was performed on a computer, initially in two weeks, saving around $500,000 immediately.

Before the first flight to the moon, the National Aeronautics and Space Administration (NASA) performed countless simulations. NASA still simulates space shuttle missions. General Motors now simulates all aspects of new car development and testing (see Gallagher, 2002; Gareiss, 2002; and Witzerman, 2001). And Pratt & Whitney uses a simulated (virtual reality) environment in designing and testing engines for jet fighters (see Marchant, 2002). It is extremely easy to change a model of a physical system's operation by using computer simulation.

The DuPont simulation model was used to learn about the problem at hand, not necessarily to derive new alternative solutions. The alternative solutions were known but had been untested until the simulation model was developed and tested. Some other examples of simulation are given by Van der Heijden et al. (2002) and Rossetti and Selandar (2001). Van der Heijden et al. (2002) used an object-oriented simulation to design an automated underground freight transportation system at Schiphol Airport (Amsterdam). Rossetti and Selandar (2001) developed a simulation model that compared using human couriers to robots in a university hospital. The simulation showed that the hospital could save over $200,000 annually by using the robots.

Simulation models can enhance an organization's decision-making process and enable it to see the impact of its future choices. Fiat (see ProModel, 2006) experienced similarly dramatic results as those of DuPont. For example, Fiat saves $1 million annually in manufacturing costs through simulation. The 2002 Winter Olympics (Salt Lake City, UT) used simulation to design security systems and bus transportation for most of the venues. This predictive technology enabled the Salt Lake Organizing Committee to model and test a variety of scenarios, including security operations, weather, and transportation-system design, in its highly variable and complex vehicle-distribution network. Savings of over $20 million per year have been realized. Benefits include lower costs and improved customer service. (See **promodel.com** for details.) The New South Wales (Australia) Treasury also simulated the economic impact of the 2000 Summer Olympics in Sydney (see **treasury.nsw.gov.au/pubs/trp97_10/chapter3.htm**).

LESSONS FROM MODELING AT PROCTER & GAMBLE

Modeling is a key element in most DSS and a necessity in a model-based DSS. There are many classes of models, and there are often many specialized techniques for solving each one. Simulation is a common modeling approach, but there are several others. For example, consider the optimization approach Procter & Gamble took in redesigning its distribution system (see Camm et al., 1997). Procter & Gamble's DSS for its North America supply-chain redesign includes several models:

- A generating model (based on an algorithm) to make transportation-cost estimates. This model is programmed directly into the DSS.
- A demand-forecasting model (statistics based).
- A distribution center location model. This model uses aggregated data (a special modeling technique) and is solved with a standard linear/integer optimization package.
- A transportation model (i.e., a specialization of a linear programming model) to determine the best shipping option from product sources to distribution centers (fed to it from the previous model) and hence to customers. This model is solved using commercial software and is loosely integrated with the distribution location model. These two problems are solved sequentially. The DSS must interface with commercial software and integrate the models.
- A financial and risk simulation model that takes into consideration some qualitative factors that require important human judgment.
- A geographical information system (GIS; effectively a graphical model of the data) for a user interface.

The Procter & Gamble situation demonstrates that a DSS can be composed of several models—some standard and some custom built—used collectively to support strategic decisions in the company. It further demonstrates that some models are built directly into the DSS software development package, some need to be constructed externally to the DSS software, and others can be accessed by the DSS when needed. Sometimes, a massive effort is necessary to assemble or estimate reasonable model data; in the case of Procter & Gamble, about 500 employees were involved over the course of about a year. In addition, the models must be integrated, models may be decomposed and simplified, sometimes a suboptimization approach is appropriate, and finally, human judgment is an important aspect of using models in decision making.

LESSONS FROM ADDITIONAL MODELING APPLICATIONS

As is evident from the situations described in the preceding section, modeling is not a simple task. For further information, see Stojkovic and Soumis (2001), which describes a model for scheduling airline flights and pilots; Gabriel et al. (2001), which describes a model for the U.S. national energy-economic situation; and Teradata (2003), which describes how Burlington Northern Santa Fe Corporation optimizes railcar performance through **mathematical (quantitative) models** (a system of symbols and expressions representing a real situation) embedded in its OLAP tool. The model developer must balance the model's simplification and representation requirements so that it will capture enough of reality to make it useful for the decision maker.

Applying models to real-world situations can save millions of dollars or generate millions of dollars in revenue. At American Airlines, models were used extensively in SABRE through the American Airlines Decision Technologies (AADT) Corp. AADT pioneered many new techniques and their application, including management. For example, optimizing the altitude ascent and descent profile for its planes saved several million dollars per week in fuel costs. AADT saved hundreds of millions of dollars annually in the early 1980s, and its incremental revenues eventually exceeded $1 billion annually, exceeding the revenue of the airline itself (see Horner, 2000; Mukherjee, 2001; Smith et al., 2001; and the End of Chapter Application Case). Trick (2003) described how Continental Airlines was able to recover from the 9/11 disaster by using a system developed for snowstorm recovery. This system was instrumental in saving millions of dollars. We provide an important example of a model application in Application Case 4.1.

Application Case 4.1

United Airlines Model-Based DSS Flies the Friendly Skies

United Airlines created a new generation of model-based DSS tools for planning, scheduling, and operations. United performed a major integration effort to determine the optimal schedule that can be designed and managed to maximize profitability. The key to integration and collaboration is a Web-based system called 1PLAN that provides a platform for planners, schedulers, and other analysts across the airline to collaborate during the decision support process. It uses a suite of decision support tools:

- SIMON optimally designs a flight network and fleet assignment simultaneously.
- ARM uses neighborhood search techniques for optimal multiple-objective fleet assignment.
- AIRSIM uses advanced statistical tools to predict airline reliability.
- SKYPATH performs optimal flight planning for minimizing fuel burn on flights.
- CHRONOS enables dynamic multiple-objective operations management.

SKYPATH alone has reduced United's average flying time, leading directly to improvements in the airline's on-time performance.

Sources: Adapted from A. Mukherjee, "Advanced Decision Support Tools in Airline Scheduling, Planning and Operations," *Proceedings of the PRISM Symposium*, West Lafayette, IN, August 9–11, 2001; "Customer Service Best Practices: The SKYPATH Program," United Airlines, **united.com/page/article/0,6722,2751,00.html** (accessed March 2006); and United Airlines Argentina, *A Real-Time Airline Operations Prediction and Solution Tool*, **united.com.ar** (no longer available online).

CURRENT MODELING ISSUES

There are still problems in identifying the correct measures that lead to overall goal success; this was touched on in the opening vignette. New, better metrics have been developed for major sports teams. The objective that ultimately indicates a model's objective function or measure(s) of success must be properly and accurately determined. For the situations described in the opening vignette, the number of games won is more important than any single player's success statistics. Data access, gathering, and integration are also critical. Data must be fed into the model properly for it to be solved and have the results be meaningful. These issues are discussed in Chapter 3.

We next discuss some major modeling issues, such as problem identification and environmental analysis, variable identification, forecasting, the use of multiple models, model categories (or appropriate selection), model management, and knowledge-based modeling.

Identification of the Problem and Environmental Analysis

We discussed problem and environmental analysis in depth in Chapter 2. One very important aspect of it is **environmental scanning and analysis**, which is the monitoring, scanning, and interpretation of collected information. No decision is made in a vacuum. It is important to analyze the scope of the domain and the forces and dynamics of the environment. A decision maker needs to identify the organizational culture and the corporate decision-making processes (e.g., who makes decisions, degree of centralization). It is entirely possible that environmental factors have created the current problem. BI/business analytics (BA) tools can help identify problems by scanning for them (see Hall, 2002a; Hall, 2000b; Whiting, 2003; the MSS running case in Online File W2.5; and Application Case 3.6, where we describe how Netflix.com creates usable environmental information for movie watchers). The problem must be understood, and everyone involved should share the same frame of understanding because the problem will ultimately be represented by the model in one form or another (as done at DuPont and in the opening vignette by the sports teams). Otherwise, the model will not help the decision maker.

Variable Identification

Identification of a model's variables (e.g., decision, result, uncontrollable) is critical, as are the relationships of the variables. Influence diagrams, which are graphical models of mathematical models, can facilitate the identification process. A more general form of an influence diagram, a cognitive map, can help a decision maker develop a better understanding of a problem, especially of variables and their interactions.

Forecasting (Predictive Analytics)

Forecasting is predicting the future. This form of predictive analytics is essential for construction and manipulating models because when a decision is implemented, the results usually occur in the future. Whereas DSS are typically designed to determine what will be, traditional MIS report what is or what was. There is no point in running a what-if (sensitivity) analysis on the past because decisions made then have no impact on the future. As mentioned in the opening vignette, a sports team might predict each potential player's performance to determine his effectiveness on the team. Forecasting is getting easier as software vendors automate many of the complications of developing such models. For example, SAS (**sas.com**)has a High Performance Forecasting system that incorporates its predictive analytics technology, ideally for retailers. This software is more automated than most other forecasting packages.

E-commerce has created an immense need for forecasting and an abundance of available information for performing it. E-commerce activities occur quickly, yet information about purchases is gathered and should be analyzed to produce forecasts. Part of the analysis involves simply predicting demand; however, forecasting models can use product life cycle needs and information about the marketplace and consumers to analyze the entire situation, ideally leading to additional sales of products and services (see Gung et al., 2002).

Many organizations have accurately predicted demand for products and services, using a variety of qualitative and quantitative methods. But until recently, most companies viewed their customers and potential customers by categorizing them into only a few, time-tested groupings. Today, it is critical not only to consider customer characteristics, but also to consider how to get the right product(s) to the right customers at the right price at the right time in the right format/packaging. The more accurately a firm does this, the more profitable the firm is. In addition, a firm needs to recognize when not to sell a particular product or bundle of products to a particular set of customers. Part of this effort involves identifying lifelong customer profitability. These customer relationship management (CRM) system and revenue management system (RMS) approaches rely heavily on forecasting techniques, which are typically described as *predictive analytics*. These systems attempt to predict who their best (i.e., most profitable) customers (and worst ones as well) are and focus on identifying products and services at appropriate prices to appeal to them. We describe an effective example of forecasting at Cox Communications in Application Case 4.2. Further details on forecasting can be found in Online Tutorial T2.

Application Case 4.2

Forecasting/Predictive Analytics Boosts Sales for Cox Communications

Seymour Douglas, director of CRM and database marketing at Cox Communications, started out as an economist trying to understand data behavior. Now he develops, uses, and promotes forecasting techniques to understand and predict how consumers behave. Since 2002, Douglas has been developing methods to get the right product in front of the right customer at the right time. Cox Communications was initially a cable TV firm, but it has expanded into computer access via cable modem, networking solutions, and so on.

Typically, certain traditional metrics or variables were used to determine whether a particular customer was likely to buy a particular product. For example, for high-speed broadband and Voice over Internet Protocol (VoIP), income was typically used. But Douglas discovered that lifestyle (a more qualitative variable) was a more accurate predictor. By developing prediction tools in KXEN and its Analytical Framework (a suite of predictive and descriptive modeling engines attached to Cox's Oracle database), connected to SAS data tables, Douglas was able to submerge the complexity of the models and data interfaces deeply into the information system. Employees working with customers do not see the complexity but instead simply see the recommendations of products, bundles, and prices for the particular customer with whom they are interacting.

These models are used in different ways within the organization. For example, the contact center that receives customer calls makes offers based on recommendations. The marketing people develop campaigns on how to approach specific customers with specific products and bundles. Now, direct-mail campaigns are much more accurately targeted to appropriate customers for appropriate products. Part of the touchpoint linking with customers is designed to prevent churning (customers leaving) by making it attractive for them to stay as well. The results are impressive. Direct-mail campaign responses have increased from 1.5 percent to 5.5 percent, growth of almost a factor of four. And the number of relationships per customer has risen from 1.2 to 1.4. These are significant numbers, given that Cox Communications has some 10 million customers.

Sources: Adapted from J. Ericson, "Perfect Pitch: Cox Communications Improves Selling Strategy with Predictive Analytics," *BI Review*, December/January 2006; T. Davenport, "Competing with Analytics," *BI Review*, December/January 2006; G.H. Anthes, "The Forecast Is Clear," *Computerworld*, April 14, 2003; KXEN, Inc., **kxen.com**; and SAS, Inc., **sas.com**.

Multiple Models

A DSS can include several models (sometimes dozens), each of which represents a different part of the decision-making problem. For example, the Procter & Gamble supply-chain DSS includes a location model to locate distribution centers, a product-strategy model, a demand-forecasting model, a cost-generation model, a financial- and risk-simulation model, and even a GIS model. Some of the models are standard and built in to DSS development generators and tools. Others are standard but are not available as built-in functions. Instead, they are available as freestanding software that can interface with a DSS. Nonstandard models must be constructed from scratch. The Procter & Gamble models were integrated by the DSS, and the problem had multiple goals. Even though cost minimization was the stated goal, there were other goals, as is shown by the way the managers took political and other criteria into consideration when examining solutions before making a final decision. Sodhi and Aichlmayr (2001) described how Web-based tools can be readily applied to integrating and accessing supply-chain models for true supply-chain optimization. Also see Application Case 4.1 to see how United Airlines integrated its models into a very effective DSS.

Model Categories

Table 4.1 classifies DSS models into seven groups and lists several representative techniques for each category. Each technique can be applied to either a static or a dynamic model, which can be constructed under assumed environments of certainty, uncertainty, or risk. To expedite model construction, we can use special decision analysis systems that have modeling languages and capabilities embedded in them. These include spreadsheets, data mining systems, OLAP systems, and even fourth-generation languages (formerly financial planning languages) such as the Cognos PowerHouse 4GL, PowerHouse Web, and Axiant 4GL.

Model Management

Models, like data, must be managed to maintain their integrity and thus their applicability. Such management is done with the aid of model base management systems (MBMS), which are analogous to database management systems (DBMS).

TABLE 4.1 Categories of Models

Category	*Process and Objective*	*Representative Techniques*
Optimization of problems with few alternatives	Find the best solution from a small number of alternatives	Decision tables, decision trees
Optimization via algorithm	Find the best solution from a large number of alternatives, using a step-by-step improvement process	Linear and other mathematical programming models, network models
Optimization via an analytic formula	Find the best solution in one step, using a formula	Some inventory models
Simulation	Finding a good enough solution or the best among the alternatives checked, using experimentation	Several types of simulation
Heuristics	Find a good enough solution, using rules	Heuristic programming, expert systems
Predictive models	Predict the future for a given scenario	Forecasting models, Markov analysis
Other models	Solve a what-if case, using a formula	Financial modeling, waiting lines

Knowledge-Based Modeling

DSS uses mostly quantitative models, whereas expert systems use qualitative, knowledge-based models in their applications. Some knowledge is necessary to construct solvable (and therefore usable) models. We defer the description of knowledge-based models until later chapters.

Current Trends in Modeling

One recent trend in modeling involves the development of model libraries and solution technique libraries. Some of these codes can be run directly on the owner's Web server for free, and others can be downloaded and run on an individual's PC, Unix machine, or server. The availability of these codes means that powerful optimization and simulation packages are available to decision makers who may have only experienced these tools from the perspective of classroom problems. For example, the Mathematics and Computer Science Division at Argonne National Laboratory (Argonne, IL) maintains the NEOS Server for Optimization at **neos.mcs.anl.gov/neos/index.html**. You can find links to other sites by clicking the Resources link at **informs.org**, the Web site of the Institute for Operations Research and the Management Sciences (INFORMS). A wealth of modeling and solution information is available from INFORMS.

There is a clear trend toward developing and using Web tools and software to access and even run software to perform modeling, optimization, simulation, and so on. This has, in many ways, simplified the application of many models to real-world problems. However, to use models and solution techniques effectively, it is necessary to truly gain experience through developing and solving simple ones. This aspect is often overlooked. Another trend, unfortunately, involves the lack of understanding of what models and their solutions can do in the real world. Organizations that have key analysts who understand how to apply models indeed apply them very effectively. This is most notably occurring in the revenue management area, which has moved from the province of airlines, hotels, and automobile rental to retail, insurance, entertainment, and many other areas. CRM also uses models, but they are often transparent to the user. With management models, the amount of data and model sizes are quite large, necessitating the use of data warehouses to supply the data and parallel computing hardware to obtain solutions in a reasonable time frame.

There is a continuing trend toward making MSS models completely transparent to the decision maker. For example, **multidimensional analysis (modeling)** involves data analysis in several dimensions. In multidimensional analysis (modeling) and some other cases, data are generally shown in a spreadsheet format, with which most decision makers are familiar. Many decision makers accustomed to slicing and dicing data cubes are now using OLAP systems that access data warehouses. Although these methods may make modeling palatable, they also eliminate many important and applicable model classes from consideration, and they eliminate some important and subtle solution interpretation aspects. Modeling involves much more than just data analysis with trend lines and establishing relationships with statistical methods. This subset of methods does not capture the richness of modeling, some of which we touch on next, in several online files, and in the End of Chapter Application Case.

There is also a trend to model a model to help in its analysis. An **influence diagram** is a graphical representation of a model; that is, it is a model of a model. Some influence diagram software packages are capable of generating and solving the resultant model. We describe influence diagrams in depth in Online File W4.1.

Section 4.2 Review Questions

1. List three lessons learned from modeling.
2. List and describe the major issues in modeling.

3. What are the major types of models used in DSS?
4. Describe why it is important to establish an objective before developing a model.
5. Why are models not used in industry as frequently as they should or could be?

4.3 STATIC AND DYNAMIC MODELS

DSS models can be classified as static or dynamic.

STATIC ANALYSIS

A **static model** takes a single snapshot of a situation. During this snapshot, everything occurs in a single *interval*. For example, a decision about whether to make or buy a product is static in nature. A quarterly or annual income statement is static, and so is the investment decision example in Section 4.6. When a model represents a year's operations, it occurs in a fixed time frame. The time frame can be rolled forward, but it is nonetheless static. This is true for the Procter & Gamble decision-making problem discussed earlier. However, the impacts of these decisions may last several decades. Most static decision-making situations are presumed to repeat with identical conditions (as in the MBI Corporation linear programming model described later in this chapter). The stability of the relevant data is assumed in a static analysis.

DYNAMIC ANALYSIS

There are stories about model builders spending months developing a complex, ultra-large-scale, hard-to-solve static model representing a week's worth of a real-world decision-making for a situation such as sausage production. They deliver the system and present the results to the company president, who responds, "Great! Well, that handles one week. Let's get started on developing the 52-week model."[2]

Dynamic models represent scenarios that change over time. A simple example is a 5-year profit-and-loss projection in which the input data, such as costs, prices, and quantities, change from year to year.

Dynamic models are *time dependent*. For example, in determining how many checkout points should be open in a supermarket, it is important to take into consideration the time of day because different numbers of customers arrive during each hour. Demands must be forecasted over time. Dynamic simulation, in contrast to steady-state simulation, represents what happens when conditions vary from the steady state over time. There might be variations in the raw materials (e.g., clay) or an unforeseen (even random) incident in some of the processes.

Dynamic models are important because they use, represent, or generate trends and patterns over time. They also show averages per period, moving averages, and comparative analyses (e.g., profit this quarter against profit in the same quarter of last year). Furthermore, when a static model is constructed to describe a given situation—say, product distribution—it can be expanded to represent the dynamic nature of the problem. For example, the transportation model (a type of network flow model) describes a static model of product distribution. It can be expanded to a dynamic network flow model to accommodate inventory and back ordering (Aronson, 1989).

[2]Thanks to Dick Barr of Southern Methodist University, Dallas, Texas, for this one.

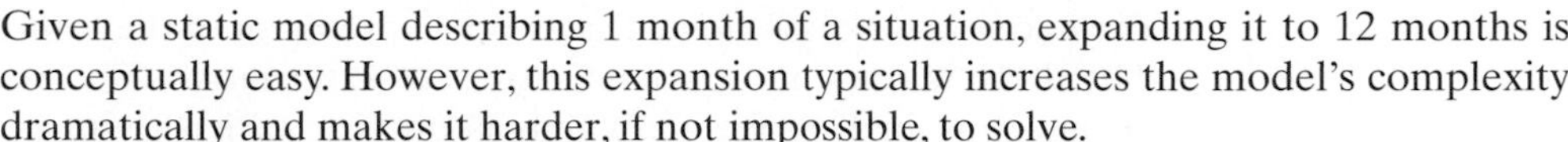

Given a static model describing 1 month of a situation, expanding it to 12 months is conceptually easy. However, this expansion typically increases the model's complexity dramatically and makes it harder, if not impossible, to solve.

Section 4.3 Review Questions

1. Distinguish between a static model and a dynamic model. Give an example of each.
2. Explain how a static model can be modified to create a dynamic model.

4.4 CERTAINTY, UNCERTAINTY, AND RISK[3]

Part of Simon's decision-making process described in Chapter 2 involves evaluating and comparing alternatives; during this process, it is necessary to predict the future outcome of each proposed alternative. Decision situations are often classified on the basis of what the decision maker knows (or believes) about the forecasted results. We customarily classify this knowledge into three categories (see Figure 4.1), ranging from complete knowledge to total ignorance:

- Certainty
- Risk
- Uncertainty

When we develop models, any of these conditions can occur, and different kinds of models are appropriate for each case. Next, we discuss both the basic definitions of these terms and some important modeling issues for each condition.

DECISION MAKING UNDER CERTAINTY

In decision making under **certainty**, it is *assumed* that complete knowledge is available so that the decision maker knows exactly what the outcome of *each course of action* will be (as in a deterministic environment). It may not be true that the outcomes are 100 percent known, nor is it necessary to really evaluate *all* the outcomes, but often this assumption simplifies the model and makes it tractable.

FIGURE 4.1 The Zones of Decision Making

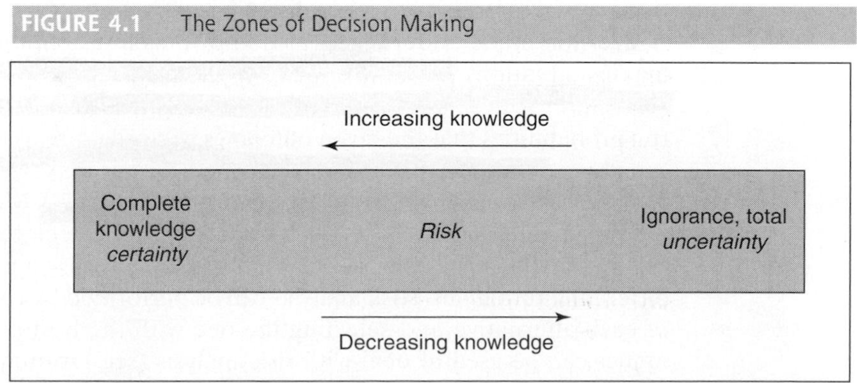

[3]Some parts of the original versions of Sections 4.4, 4.6, 4.8, and 4.11 were adapted from Turban and Meredith (1994).

The decision maker is viewed as a perfect predictor of the future because it is assumed that there is only one outcome for each alternative. For example, the alternative of investing in U.S. Treasury bills is one for which there is complete availability of information about the future return on the investment. A situation involving decision making under certainty occurs most often with structured problems with short time horizons (up to one year). Another example is that every time you park downtown, you get a parking ticket because you exceed the time limit on the parking meter—although once it did not happen. This situation can still be treated as one of decision making under certainty. Some problems under certainty are not structured enough to be approached using analytical methods and models; they require a DSS approach.

Certainty models are relatively easy to develop and solve, and they can yield optimal solutions. Many financial models are constructed under assumed certainty, even though the market is anything but 100 percent certain. Problems that have an infinite (or a very large) number of feasible solutions are extremely important and are discussed in Sections 4.9 and 4.12.

DECISION MAKING UNDER UNCERTAINTY

In decision making under **uncertainty**, the decision maker considers situations in which several outcomes are possible for each course of action. In contrast to the risk situation, in this case, the decision maker does not know, or cannot estimate, the probability of occurrence of the possible outcomes. Decision making under uncertainty is more difficult than decision making under certainty because there is insufficient information. Modeling of such situations involves assessment of the decision maker's (or the organization's) attitude toward risk (see Nielsen, 2003).

Managers attempt to avoid uncertainty as much as possible, even to the point of assuming it away. Instead of dealing with uncertainty, they attempt to obtain more information so that the problem can be treated under certainty (because it can be "almost" certain) or under calculated (i.e., assumed) risk. If more information is not available, the problem must be treated under a condition of uncertainty, which is less definitive than the other categories.

DECISION MAKING UNDER RISK (RISK ANALYSIS)

A decision made under **risk**[4] (also known as a probabilistic, or stochastic, decision-making situation) is one in which the decision maker must consider several possible outcomes for each alternative, each with a given probability of occurrence. The long-run probabilities that the given outcomes will occur are assumed to be known or can be estimated. Under these assumptions, the decision maker can assess the degree of risk associated with each alternative (called *calculated* risk). Most major business decisions are made under assumed risk. **Risk analysis** (i.e., calculated risk) is a decision-making method that analyzes the risk (based on assumed known probabilities) associated with different alternatives. Risk analysis can be performed by calculating the expected value of each alternative and selecting the one with the best expected value. Several techniques can be used to deal with risk analysis (see Drummond, 2001; Koller, 2000; and Laporte et al., 2002).

[4]Our definitions of the terms *risk* and *uncertainty* were formulated by F.H. Knight of the University of Chicago in 1933. There are other, comparable definitions in use.

Section 4.4 Review Questions

1. Define what it means to perform decision making under assumed certainty, risk, and uncertainty.
2. How can decision-making problems under assumed certainty be handled?
3. How can decision-making problems under assumed uncertainty be handled?
4. How can decision-making problems under assumed risk be handled?

4.5 MANAGEMENT SUPPORT SYSTEMS MODELING WITH SPREADSHEETS

Models can be developed and implemented in a variety of programming languages and systems. These range from third-, fourth-, and fifth-generation programming languages to computer-aided software engineering (CASE) systems and other systems that automatically generate usable software. (For example, influence diagram software typically generates and sometimes solves usable models; see Online File W4.1.) We focus primarily on *spreadsheets* (with their add-ins), modeling languages, and transparent data analysis tools.

With their strength and flexibility, spreadsheet packages were quickly recognized as easy-to-use implementation software for the development of a wide range of applications in business, engineering, mathematics, and science. Spreadsheets include extensive statistical, forecasting, and other modeling and database management capabilities, functions, and routines. As spreadsheet packages evolved, add-ins were developed for structuring and solving specific model classes. Among the add-in packages, many were developed for DSS development. These DSS-related add-ins include Solver (Frontline Systems Inc., **solver.com**) and What's*Best!* (a version of Lindo, from Lindo Systems, Inc., **lindo.com**) for performing linear and nonlinear optimization; Braincel (Promised Land Technologies, Inc., **promland.com**) and NeuralTools (Palisade Corp., **palisade.com**) for artificial neural networks; Evolver (Palisade Corp.) for genetic algorithms; and @RISK (Palisade Corp.) for performing simulation studies. Some comparable add-ins are available for free or at a very low cost. (Do a Web search to find them; new ones are added to the marketplace on a regular basis.) Because of fierce market competition, the better add-ins are eventually incorporated directly into spreadsheets (e.g., Solver in Excel is the well-known GRG-2 nonlinear optimization code).

The spreadsheet is clearly the most popular *end-user modeling tool* (see Figure 4.2) because it incorporates many powerful financial, statistical, mathematical, and other functions. Spreadsheets can perform model solution tasks such as linear programming and regression analysis. The spreadsheet has evolved into an important tool for analysis, planning, and modeling (see Denardo, 2001; Hsiang, 2002; Monahan, 2000; Powell and Baker, 2003; Ragsdale, 2004; and Winston and Albright, 2006.)

Other important spreadsheet features include what-if analysis, goal seeking, data management, and programmability (i.e., macros). With a spreadsheet, it is easy to change a cell's value and immediately see the result. Goal seeking is performed by indicating a target cell, its desired value, and a changing cell. Extensive database management can be performed with small data sets, or parts of a database can be imported for analysis (which is essentially how OLAP works with multidimensional data cubes; in fact, most OLAP systems have the look and feel of advanced spreadsheet software after the data are loaded). Templates, macros, and other tools enhance the productivity of building DSS.

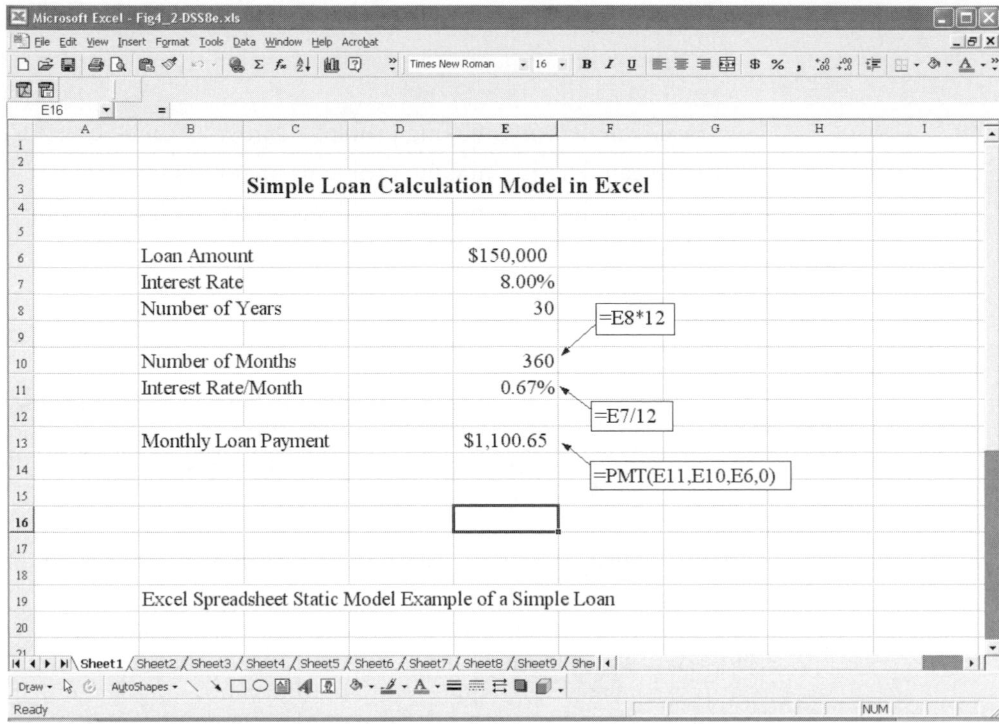

FIGURE 4.2 Excel Spreadsheet Static Model Example of a Simple Loan Calculation of Monthly Payments

Most spreadsheet packages provide fairly seamless integration because they read and write common file structures and easily interface with databases and other tools. Microsoft Excel is the most popular spreadsheet package. We provide access to the Excel files used in this chapter in Online File W4.2. In Figure 4.2, we show a simple loan calculation model in which the boxes on the spreadsheet describe the contents of the cells, which contain formulas. A change in the interest rate in cell E7 is immediately reflected in the monthly payment in cell E13. The results can be observed and analyzed immediately. If we require a specific monthly payment, we can use goal seeking (see Section 4.9) to determine an appropriate interest rate or loan amount.

Static or dynamic models can be built in a spreadsheet. For example, the monthly loan calculation spreadsheet shown in Figure 4.2 is static. Although the problem affects the borrower over time, the model indicates a single month's performance, which is replicated. A dynamic model, on the other hand, represents behavior over time. The loan calculations in the spreadsheet shown in Figure 4.3 indicate the effect of prepayment on the principal over time. Risk analysis can be incorporated into spreadsheets by using built-in random-number generators to develop simulation models (see Section 4.11; Online File W4.3, which describes an economic order-quantity simulation model under assumed risk; and the spreadsheet simulation model of cash flows in Figure 4.3). We describe how to perform waiting-line management (queuing) in a spreadsheet in Online File W4.4.

LeBlanc et al. (2000) described an excellent example of a model-based DSS developed in a spreadsheet. It assigns managers to projects for a major construction firm. By using the system, the company did not have to replace a manager who resigned and thus

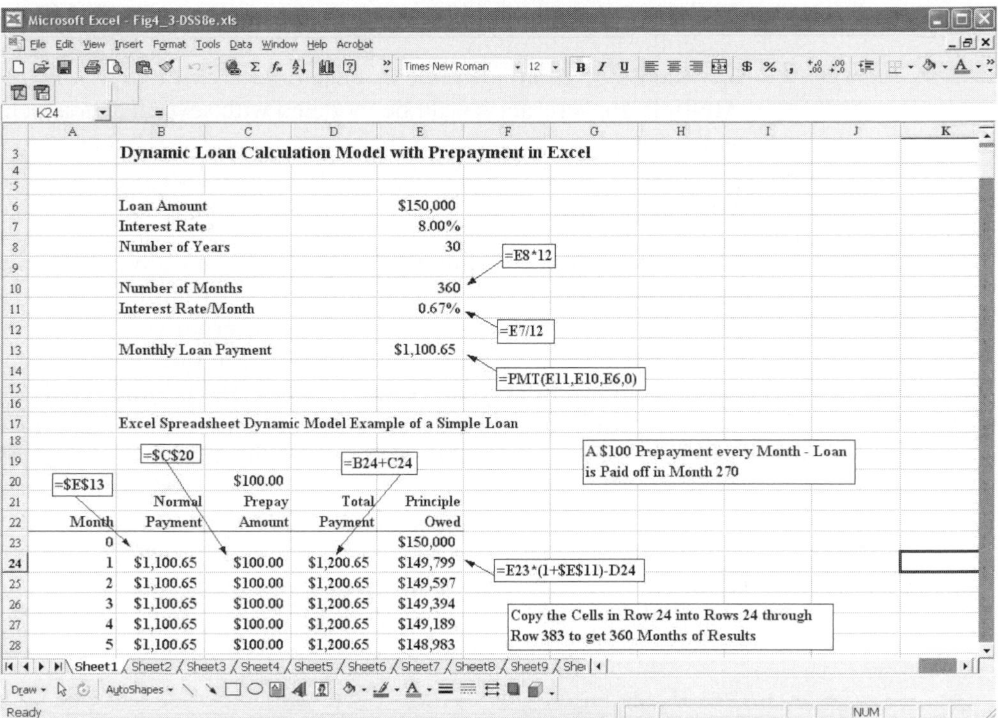

FIGURE 4.3 Excel Spreadsheet Dynamic Model Example of a Simple Loan Calculation of Monthly Payments and the Effects of Prepayment

substantially reduced travel costs. Buehlmann et al. (2000) described a spreadsheet-based DSS for wood panel manufacturing. This system handles many complex real-time decisions in a dynamic shop floor environment. Respicio et al. (2002) described how Portucel Industrial developed a complete spreadsheet-based DSS for planning and scheduling paper production.

Spreadsheets were developed for personal computers, but they also run on larger computers. The spreadsheet framework is the basis for multidimensional spreadsheets and OLAP tools.

Section 4.5 Review Questions

1. What is a spreadsheet?
2. What is a spreadsheet add-in? How can add-ins help in DSS creation and use?
3. Explain why a spreadsheet is so conducive to the development of DSS.

4.6 DECISION ANALYSIS WITH DECISION TABLES AND DECISION TREES

Decision situations that involve a finite and usually not too large number of alternatives are modeled through an approach called **decision analysis** (see Arsham, 2006a, 2006b; and Decision Analysis Society, **faculty.fuqua.duke.edu/daweb/**). Using this approach, the alternatives are listed in a table or a graph, with their forecasted contributions to the goal(s) and the probability of obtaining the contribution. These can be evaluated to select the best alternative.

Single-goal situations can be modeled with *decision tables* or *decision trees*. Multiple goals (criteria) can be modeled with several other techniques, described later in this chapter.

DECISION TABLES

Decision tables conveniently organize information and knowledge in a systematic, tabular manner to prepare it for analysis. For example, say that an investment company is considering investing in one of three alternatives: bonds, stocks, or certificates of deposit (CDs). The company is interested in one goal: maximizing the yield on the investment after one year. If it were interested in other goals, such as safety or liquidity, the problem would be classified as one of *multicriteria decision analysis* (see Koksalan and Zionts, 2001; also see Application Case 3.2; Application Case 4.1; and Dias and Climaco, 2002).

The yield depends on the state of the economy sometime in the future (often called the *state of nature*), which can be in solid growth, stagnation, or inflation. Experts estimated the following annual yields:

- If there is solid growth in the economy, bonds will yield 12 percent, stocks 15 percent, and time deposits 6.5 percent.
- If stagnation prevails, bonds will yield 6 percent, stocks 3 percent, and time deposits 6.5 percent.
- If inflation prevails, bonds will yield 3 percent, stocks will bring a loss of 2 percent, and time deposits will yield 6.5 percent.

The problem is to select the one best investment alternative. These are assumed to be discrete alternatives. Combinations such as investing 50 percent in bonds and 50 percent in stocks must be treated as new alternatives.

The investment decision-making problem can be viewed as a *two-person game* (see Kelly, 2002). The investor makes a choice (i.e., a move), and then a state of nature occurs (i.e., makes a move). Table 4.2 shows the payoff of a mathematical model. The table includes *decision variables* (the alternatives), *uncontrollable variables* (the states of the economy; e.g., the environment), and *result variables* (the projected yield; e.g., outcomes). All the models in this section are structured in a spreadsheet framework.

If this were a decision-making problem under certainty, we would know what the economy will be and could easily choose the best investment. But that is not the case, so we must consider the two situations of uncertainty and risk. For uncertainty, we do not know the probabilities of each state of nature. For risk, we assume that we know the probabilities with which each state of nature will occur.

TABLE 4.2 Investment Problem Decision Table Model

	State of Nature (Uncontrollable Variables)		
Alternative	***Solid Growth (%)***	***Stagnation (%)***	***Inflation (%)***
Bonds	12.0	6.0	3.0
Stocks	15.0	3.0	−2.0
CDs	6.5	6.5	6.5

Treating Uncertainty

There are several methods of handling uncertainty. For example, the *optimistic approach* assumes that the best possible outcome of each alternative will occur and then selects the best of the best (i.e., stocks). The *pessimistic approach* assumes that the worst possible outcome for each alternative will occur and selects the best of these (i.e., CDs). Another approach simply assumes that all states of nature are equally possible. (See Clemen and Reilly, 2000; Goodwin and Wright, 2000; and Kontoghiorghes et al., 2002.) There are serious problems with every approach for handling uncertainty. Whenever possible, the analyst should attempt to gather enough information so that the problem can be treated under assumed certainty or risk.

Treating Risk

The most common method for solving this risk analysis problem is to select the alternative with the greatest expected value. Assume that experts estimate the chance of solid growth at 50 percent, the chance of stagnation at 30 percent, and the chance of inflation at 20 percent. The decision table is then rewritten with the known probabilities (see Table 4.3). An expected value is computed by multiplying the results (i.e., outcomes) by their respective probabilities and adding them. For example, investing in bonds yields an expected return of 12(0.5) + 6(0.3) + 3(0.2) = 8.4 percent.

This approach can sometimes be a dangerous strategy because the utility of each potential outcome may be different from the value. Even if there is an infinitesimal chance of a catastrophic loss, the expected value may seem reasonable, but the investor may not be willing to cover the loss. For example, suppose a financial advisor presents you with an "almost sure" investment of $1,000 that can double your money in one day, and then the advisor says, "Well, there is a .9999 probability that you will double your money, but unfortunately there is a .0001 probability that you will be liable for a $500,000 out-of-pocket loss." The expected value of this investment is as follows:

0.9999 ($2,000 – $1,000) + .0001 (–$500,000 – $1,000) = $999.90 – $50.10 = $949.80

The potential loss could be catastrophic for any investor who is not a billionaire. Depending on the investor's ability to cover the loss, an investment has different expected utilities. Remember that the investor makes the decision only *once*.

DECISION TREES

An alternative representation of the decision table is a decision tree (for examples, see Mind Tools Ltd., **mindtools.com**). A **decision tree** shows the relationships of the problem graphically and can handle complex situations in a compact form. However, a decision tree can be cumbersome if there are many alternatives or states of nature. TreeAge Pro (TreeAge Software Inc., **treeage.com**) and PrecisionTree (Palisade Corp.,

TABLE 4.3 Decision Under Risk and Its Solution

Alternative	*Solid Growth, .50 (%)*	*Stagnation, .30 (%)*	*Inflation, .20 (%)*	*Expected Value (%)*
Bonds	12.0	6.0	3.0	8.4 (maximum)
Stocks	15.0	3.0	–2.0	8.0
CDs	6.5	6.5	6.5	6.5

palisade.com) include powerful, intuitive, and sophisticated decision tree analysis systems. These vendors also provide excellent examples of decision trees used in practice. Russell A. Dewey at Georgia Southern University provides an excellent example of a decision tree at **psychwww.com/mtsite/dectree.html**. Also see Mind Tools Ltd. (**mindtools.com**). We describe how experts at Johnson & Johnson Pharmaceutical evaluate new drugs via decision trees in Application Case 4.3.

Application Case 4.3

Johnson & Johnson Decides About New Pharmaceuticals by Using Trees

Johnson & Johnson Pharmaceutical Services LLC (JJPS), a division of Johnson & Johnson (J&J), conducts research and development and seeks approval for its drugs. The strategic marketing group performs economic evaluation of new drugs as they are developed. In addition to being medically effective, drugs that reach market must be cost-effective. It takes an average of 12 years for a drug in the United States to reach the market. The drug must pass through many phases, including laboratory and animal studies, several phases of human clinical trials, and the new drug application for review by the Food and Drug Administration. During or at the end of any phase, development of a potential drug may be terminated because it is not effective or because there are alternative treatments available, and those treatments are cost-effective or medically more effective. JJPS has developed models in TreeAge's decision analysis software. These include decision trees, Markov (statistical-based) models, and Monte Carlo simulations.

Data are gathered from results of the sequential drug testing phases are and used in decision trees to model the progress of treatment scenarios that use the tree paths to represent all reasonable alternatives and outcomes. Uncertainties are represented as probabilities, estimated using historical data predictions and expert opinion. Even though the total development time for creating a decision tree–based model takes about six months, the payoff is dramatic. The decision tree results are fed into Markov models and Monte Carlo simulations to predict the results of real, long-term studies, perhaps incorporating 10,000 patients, all within TreeAge Pro. Overall, these models produce significant time savings, have simplified the evaluation of new drugs' value, and have simplified the comparison of new drugs to alternative treatments.

Source: Adapted from TreeAge Software, Inc., *Johnson & Johnson Pharmaceutical Group Evaluates New Drugs More Efficiently: Case Study*, **treeage.com/resources/includes/jj_cs.pdf** (accessed March 2006).

A simplified investment case of **multiple goals** (a decision situation in which alternatives are evaluated with several, sometimes conflicting, goals) is shown in Table 4.4. The three goals (criteria) are yield, safety, and liquidity. This situation is under assumed certainty; that is, only one possible consequence is projected for each alternative; the more complex cases of risk or uncertainty could be considered. Some of the results are qualitative (e.g., low, high) rather than numeric.

TABLE 4.4 Multiple Goals

Alternative	*Yield (%)*	*Safety*	*Liquidity*
Bonds	8.4	High	High
Stocks	8.0	Low	High
CDs	6.5	Very high	High

See Clemen and Reilly (2000), Goodwin and Wright (2000), and Decision Analysis Society (**faculty.fuqua.duke.edu/daweb/**) for more on decision analysis. Although doing so is quite complex, it is possible to apply mathematical programming directly to decision-making situations under risk. We discuss several other methods of treating risk later in the book. These include simulation, certainty factors, and fuzzy logic.

Section 4.6 Review Questions

1. What is a decision table?
2. What is a decision tree?
3. How can a decision tree be used in decision making?
4. Describe what it means to have multiple goals.

4.7 THE STRUCTURE OF MATHEMATICAL MODELS FOR DECISION SUPPORT

In the following sections, we present the topics of MSS mathematical models (e.g., mathematical, financial, engineering). These include the components and the structure of models.

THE COMPONENTS OF DECISION SUPPORT MATHEMATICAL MODELS

All models are made up of four basic components (see Figure 4.4): result (or outcome) variables, decision variables, uncontrollable variables (and/or parameters), and intermediate result variables. Mathematical relationships link these components together. In nonquantitative models, the relationships are symbolic or qualitative. The results of decisions are determined based on the decision made (i.e., the values of the decision variables), the factors that cannot be controlled by the decision maker (in the environment), and the relationships among the variables. The modeling process involves identifying the variables and relationships among them. Solving a model determines the values of these and the result variable(s).

Result (Outcome) Variables

Result (outcome) variables reflect the level of effectiveness of a system; that is, they indicate how well the system performs or attains its goal(s). These variables are outputs. Examples of result variables are shown in Table 4.5. Result variables are considered *dependent variables*. Intermediate result variables are sometimes used in modeling to identify intermediate outcomes. In the case of a dependent variable,

FIGURE 4.4 The General Structure of a Quantitative Model

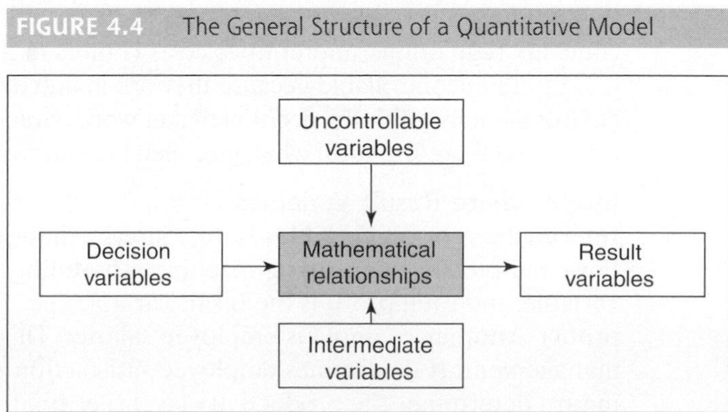

TABLE 4.5 Examples of the Components of Models

Area	*Decision Variables*	*Result Variables*	*Uncontrollable Variables and Parameters*
Financial investment	Investment alternatives and amounts	Total profit, risk Rate of return on investment (ROI) Earnings per share Liquidity level	Inflation rate Prime rate Competition
Marketing	Advertising budget Where to advertise	Market share Customer satisfaction	Customer's income Competitor's actions
Manufacturing	What and how much to produce Inventory levels Compensation programs	Total cost Quality level Employee satisfaction	Machine capacity Technology Materials prices
Accounting	Use of computers Audit schedule	Data processing cost Error rate	Computer technology Tax rates Legal requirements
Transportation	Shipments schedule Use of smart cards	Total transport cost Payment float time	Delivery distance Regulations
Services	Staffing levels	Customer satisfaction	Demand for services

another event must occur first before the event described by the variable can occur. Result variables depend on the occurrence of the decision variables and the uncontrollable variables.

Decision Variables

Decision variables describe alternative courses of action. The decision maker controls the decision variables. For example, for an investment problem, the amount to invest in bonds is a decision variable. In a scheduling problem, the decision variables are people, times, and schedules. Other examples are listed in Table 4.5.

Uncontrollable Variables, or Parameters

In any decision-making situation, there are factors that affect the result variables but are not under the control of the decision maker. Either these factors can be fixed, in which case they are called **uncontrollable variables**, or **parameters**, or they can vary, in which case they are called *variables*. Examples of factors are the prime interest rate, a city's building code, tax regulations, and utilities costs (others are shown in Table 4.5). Most of these factors are uncontrollable because they are in and determined by elements of the system environment in which the decision maker works. Some of these variables limit the decision maker and therefore form what are called the *constraints* of the problem.

Intermediate Result Variables

Intermediate result variables reflect intermediate outcomes in mathematical models. For example, in determining machine scheduling, spoilage is an intermediate result variable, and total profit is the result variable (i.e., spoilage is one determinant of total profit). Another example is employee salaries. This constitutes a decision variable for management: It determines employee satisfaction (i.e., intermediate outcome), which in turn determines the productivity level (i.e., final result).

THE STRUCTURE OF MSS MATHEMATICAL MODELS

The components of a quantitative model are linked together by mathematical (algebraic) expressions—equations or inequalities.

A very simple financial model is

$$P = R - C$$

where P = profit, R = revenue, and C = cost. This equation describes the relationship among the variables.

Another well-known financial model is the simple present-value cash flow model, where P = present value, F = a future single payment in dollars, i = interest rate (percentage), and n = number of years. With this model, it is possible to determine the present value of a payment of $100,000 to be made five years from today, at a 10 percent (0.1) interest rate, as follows:

$$P = 100{,}000 \,/\, (1 + 0.1)^5 = \$62{,}092$$

We present more interesting and complex mathematical models in the following sections.

Section 4.7 Review Questions

1. What is a decision variable?
2. List and briefly discuss the three major components of linear programming.
3. Explain the role of intermediate result variables.

4.8 MATHEMATICAL PROGRAMMING OPTIMIZATION

The basic idea of optimization was introduced in Chapter 2. **Linear programming (LP)** is the best-known technique in a family of optimization tools called *mathematical programming*; in LP, all relationships among the variables are linear. It is used extensively in DSS (see Application Case 4.4). LP models have many important applications in practice. For example, Procter & Gamble has used several LP problems.

MATHEMATICAL PROGRAMMING

Mathematical programming is a family of tools designed to help solve managerial problems in which the decision maker must allocate scarce resources among competing activities to optimize a measurable goal. For example, the distribution of machine time (the resource) among various products (the activities) is a typical allocation problem. LP allocation problems usually display the following characteristics:

- A limited quantity of economic resources is available for allocation.
- The resources are used in the production of products or services.
- There are two or more ways in which the resources can be used. Each is called a solution or a program.
- Each activity (product or service) in which the resources are used yields a return in terms of the stated goal.
- The allocation is usually restricted by several limitations and requirements, called constraints.

Application Case 4.4

Complex Teacher Selection Is a Breeze in Flanders

The Flemish Minister of Education (in Flanders, which is in northern Belgium) asked the VDAB (Flemish Service for Employment and Vocational Training) to determine how to select the best-qualified teaching candidates for the Flemish supply substitute teacher pool. These teachers are on standby for interim jobs. Using an LP model developed in SAS/OR (**sas.com**), the VDAB was able to create an efficient and fair system to fill the pool with the best available candidates and to allocate candidates to the most appropriate public school districts. This complex model considers full-time and part-time needs, work locations, and the candidates' backgrounds, grade levels, and training. The model attempts to fill positions such that the candidates have professional activities to perform, even when they are not teaching, and they are thus paid for a full year. This keeps many teachers in the system, so the VDAB doesn't lose top talent to the private sector. It also maintains teachers on standby to fill expected vacancies due to illness, maternity leave, and so on. Essentially, the model matches supply with demand in the best possible way throughout the 45 Flemish school districts. The model took three months to develop, and it is run every month. Problems with as many as about 6,000 teachers have been successfully solved in this DSS.

Sources: Modified from SAS Inc., "SAS Technology Makes Supply Teacher Pool Both Efficient and Fair," *SAS Success Stories*, **sas.com/success/vdab_or.html** (accessed March 2006); and VDAB (Flemish Service for Employment and Vocational Training), **vdab.be** (accessed March 2006).

The LP allocation model is based on the following rational economic assumptions:

- Returns from different allocations can be compared; that is, they can be measured by a common unit (e.g., dollars, utility).
- The return from any allocation is independent of other allocations.
- The total return is the sum of the returns yielded by the different activities.
- All data are known with certainty.
- The resources are to be used in the most economical manner.

Allocation problems typically have a large number of possible solutions. Depending on the underlying assumptions, the number of solutions can be either infinite or finite. Usually, different solutions yield different rewards. Of the available solutions, at least one is the best, in the sense that the degree of goal attainment associated with it is the highest (i.e., the total reward is maximized). This is called an **optimal solution**, and it can be found by using a special algorithm.

LINEAR PROGRAMMING

Every LP problem is composed of *decision variables* (whose values are unknown and are searched for), an *objective function* (a linear mathematical function that relates the decision variables to the goal, measures goal attainment, and is to be optimized), *objective function coefficients* (unit profit or cost coefficients indicating the contribution to the objective of one unit of a decision variable), *constraints* (expressed in the form of linear inequalities or equalities that limit resources and/or requirements; these relate the variables through linear relationships), *capacities* (which describe the upper and sometimes lower limits on the constraints and variables), and *input/output (technology) coefficients* (which indicate resource utilization for a decision variable). See Technology Insights 4.5.

THE LP PRODUCT-MIX MODEL FORMULATION

MBI Corporation, which manufactures special-purpose computers, needs to make a decision: How many computers should it produce next month at the Boston plant?

TECHNOLOGY INSIGHTS 4.5

Linear Programming

LP is perhaps the best-known optimization model. It deals with the optimal allocation of resources among competing activities. The allocation problem is represented by the model described here.

The problem is to find the values of the decision variables X_1, X_2, and so on, such that the value of the result variable Z is maximized, subject to a set of linear constraints that express the technology, market conditions, and other uncontrollable variables. The mathematical relationships are all linear equations and inequalities. Theoretically, there are an infinite number of possible solutions to any allocation problem of this type. Using special mathematical procedures, the LP approach applies a unique computerized search procedure that finds a best solution(s) in a matter of seconds. Furthermore, the solution approach provides automatic sensitivity analysis.

MBI is considering two types of computers: the CC-7, which requires 300 days of labor and \$10,000 in materials, and the CC-8, which requires 500 days of labor and \$15,000 in materials. The profit contribution of each CC-7 is \$8,000, whereas that of each CC-8 is \$12,000. The plant has a capacity of 200,000 working days per month, and the material budget is \$8 million per month. Marketing requires that at least 100 units of the CC-7 and at least 200 units of the CC-8 be produced each month. The problem is to maximize the company's profits by determining how many units of the CC-7 and how many units of the CC-8 should be produced each month. Note that in a real-world environment, it could possibly take months to obtain the data in the problem statement, and while gathering the data, the decision maker would no doubt uncover facts about how to structure the model to be solved. Web-based tools for gathering data can help.

MODELING IN LP: AN EXAMPLE

A standard LP model can be developed for the MBI Corporation problem just described. As discussed in Technology Insights 4.5, the LP model has three components: decision variables, result variables, and uncontrollable variables (constraints).

The decision variables are as follows:

$$X_1 = \text{units of CC-7 to be produced}$$
$$X_2 = \text{units of CC-8 to be produced}$$

The result variable is as follows:

$$\text{Total profit} = Z$$

The objective is to maximize total profit:

$$Z = 8{,}000X_1 + 12{,}000X_2$$

The uncontrollable variables (constraints) are as follows:

$$\text{Labor constraint: } 300X_1 + 500X_2 \leq 200{,}000 \text{ (in days)}$$
$$\text{Budget constraint: } 10{,}000X_1 + 15{,}000X_2 \leq 8{,}000{,}000 \text{ (in dollars)}$$
$$\text{Marketing requirement for CC-7: } X_1 \geq 100 \text{ (in units)}$$
$$\text{Marketing requirement for CC-8: } X_2 \geq 200 \text{ (in units)}$$

This information is summarized in Figure 4.5.

The model also has a fourth, hidden component. Every LP model has some internal intermediate variables that are not explicitly stated. The labor and budget constraints

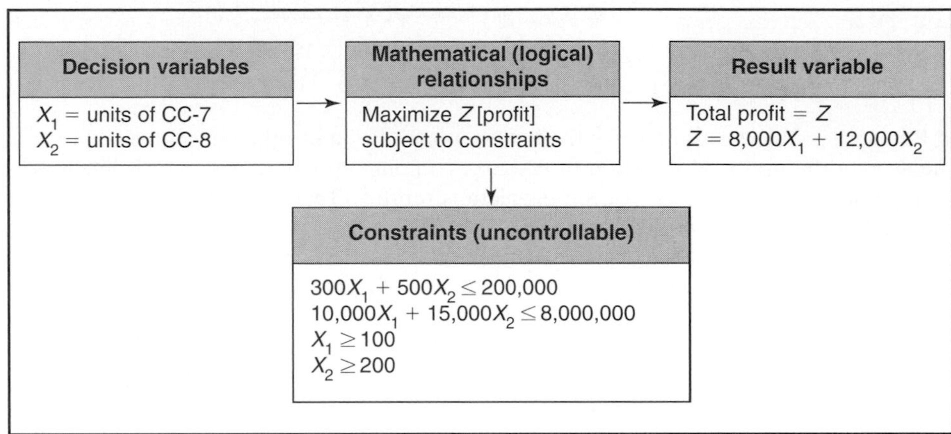

FIGURE 4.5 Mathematical Model of a Product-Mix Example

may each have some slack in them when the left-hand side is strictly less than the right-hand side. This slack is represented internally by slack variables that indicate excess resources available. The marketing requirement constraints may each have some surplus in them when the left-hand side is strictly greater than the right-hand side. This surplus is represented internally by surplus variables indicating that there is some room to adjust the right-hand sides of these constraints. These slack and surplus variables are intermediate. They can be of great value to a decision maker because LP solution methods use them in establishing sensitivity parameters for economic what-if analyses.

The product-mix model has an infinite number of possible solutions. Assuming that a production plan is not restricted to whole numbers—which is a reasonable assumption in a monthly production plan—we want a solution that maximizes total profit: an optimal solution. Fortunately, Excel comes with the add-in Solver, which can readily obtain an optimal (best) solution to this problem. We enter these data directly into an Excel spreadsheet, activate Solver, and identify the goal (by setting Target Cell equal to Max), decision variables (by setting By Changing Cells), and constraints (by ensuring that Total Consumed elements is less than or equal to Limit for the first two rows and is greater than or equal to Limit for the third and fourth rows). Also, in Options, we activate the boxes Assume Linear Model and Assume Non-negative, and then we solve the problem. Next, we select all three reports—Answer, Sensitivity, and Limits—to obtain an optimal solution of $X_1 = 333.33$, $X_2 = 200$, Profit = \$5,066,667, as shown in Figure 4.6. Solver produces three useful reports about the solution. Try it.

The evaluation of the alternatives and the final choice depend on the type of criteria selected. Are we trying to find the best solution? Or will a good-enough result be sufficient? (See Chapter 2.)

LP models (and their specializations and generalizations) can be specified directly in a number of user-friendly modeling systems. Two of the best known are Lindo and Lingo (Lindo Systems, Inc., **lindo.com**; demos are available). Lindo is an LP and integer programming system. Models are specified in essentially the same way that they are defined algebraically. Based on the success of Lindo, the company developed Lingo, a modeling language that includes the powerful Lindo optimizer and extensions for solving nonlinear problems. Lindo and Lingo models and solutions of the product-mix model are provided in Online Files W4.6 and W4.7, respectively.

The uses of mathematical programming, especially of LP, are fairly common in practice. There are standard computer programs available. Optimization functions are

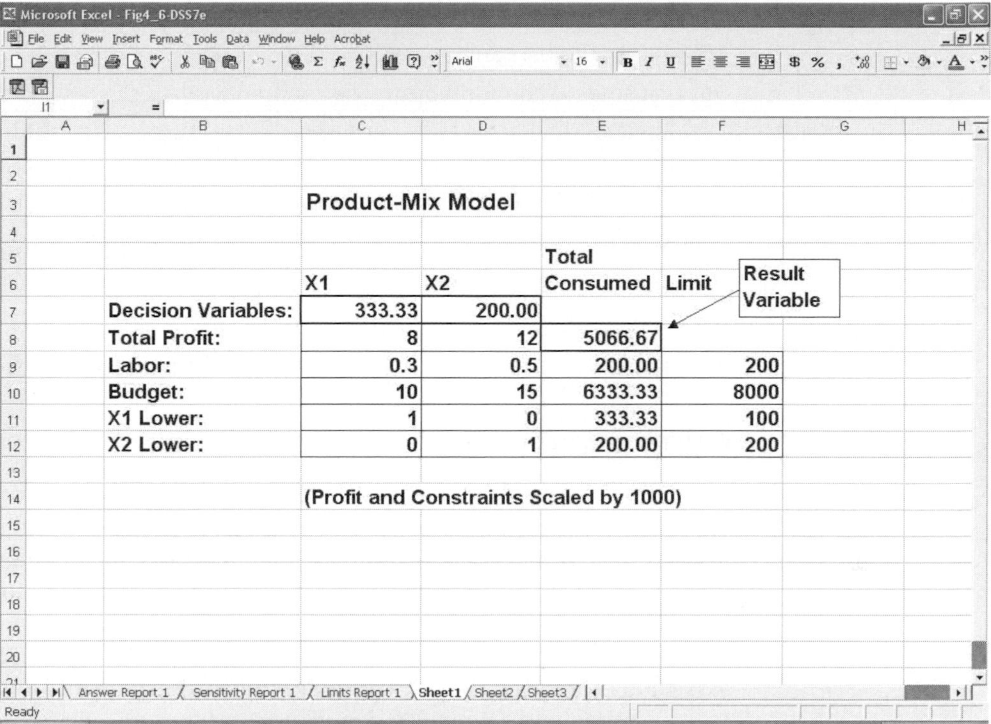

FIGURE 4.6 Excel Solver Solution to the Product-Mix Example

available in many DSS integrated tools, such as Excel. Also, it is easy to interface other optimization software with Excel, DBMS, and similar tools. Optimization models are often included in decision support implementations, as shown in Application Cases 4.2 and 4.3. More details on LP, a description of another classic LP problem called the *blending problem*, and an Excel spreadsheet formulation and solution are described in Online File W4.5.

The most common optimization models can be solved by a variety of mathematical programming methods, including the following:

- Assignment (best matching of objects)
- Dynamic programming
- Goal programming
- Investment (maximizing rate of return)
- Linear and integer programming
- Network models for planning and scheduling
- Nonlinear programming
- Replacement (capital budgeting)
- Simple inventory models (e.g., economic order quantity)
- Transportation (minimize cost of shipments)

Section 4.8 Review Questions

1. List and explain the assumptions involved in LP.
2. List and explain the characteristics of LP.
3. Describe an allocation problem.

4. Define the product-mix problem.
5. Define the blending problem.
6. List several common optimization models.

4.9 MULTIPLE GOALS, SENSITIVITY ANALYSIS, WHAT-IF ANALYSIS, AND GOAL SEEKING

The search process described earlier in this chapter is coupled with evaluation. Evaluation is the final step that leads to a recommended solution.

MULTIPLE GOALS

The analysis of management decisions aims at evaluating, to the greatest possible extent, how far each alternative advances managers toward their goals. Unfortunately, managerial problems are seldom evaluated with a single simple goal, such as profit maximization. Today's management systems are much more complex, and one with a single goal is rare. Instead, managers want to attain *simultaneous goals*, some of which may conflict. Different stakeholders have different goals. Therefore, it is often necessary to analyze each alternative in light of its determination of each of several goals (see Koksalan and Zionts, 2001).

For example, consider a profit-making firm. In addition to earning money, the company wants to grow, develop its products and employees, provide job security to its workers, and serve the community. Managers want to satisfy the shareholders and at the same time enjoy high salaries and expense accounts, and employees want to increase their take-home pay and benefits. When a decision is to be made—say, about an investment project—some of these goals complement each other, whereas others conflict. Kearns (2004) described how the analytic hierarchy process (AHP), combined with integer programming, handled multiple goals in evaluating IT investments.

Many quantitative models of decision theory are based on comparing a single measure of effectiveness, generally some form of utility to the decision maker. Therefore, it is usually necessary to transform a multiple-goal problem into a single-measure-of-effectiveness problem before comparing the effects of the solutions. This is a common method for handling multiple goals in an LP model. For example, in Online File W4.8, we show how to modify the MBI Corporation model into a *goal programming* model.

Certain difficulties may arise when analyzing multiple goals:

- It is usually difficult to obtain an explicit statement of the organization's goals.
- The decision maker may change the importance assigned to specific goals over time or for different decision scenarios.
- Goals and subgoals are viewed differently at various levels of the organization and within different departments.
- Goals change in response to changes in the organization and its environment.
- The relationship between alternatives and their role in determining goals may be difficult to quantify.
- Complex problems are solved by groups of decision makers, each of whom has a personal agenda.
- Participants assess the importance (priorities) of the various goals differently.

Several methods of handling multiple goals can be used when working with MSS. The most common ones are:

- Utility theory
- Goal programming
- Expression of goals as constraints, using LP
- A points system

With some methods, the decision maker needs to search the solution space for an alternative that provides for required attainment of all goals while searching for an efficient solution (e.g., see **expertchoice.com**).

SENSITIVITY ANALYSIS

A model builder makes predictions and assumptions regarding input data, many of which deal with the assessment of uncertain futures. When the model is solved, the results depend on these data. **Sensitivity analysis** attempts to assess the impact of a change in the input data or parameters on the proposed solution (i.e., the result variable).

Sensitivity analysis is extremely important in MSS because it allows flexibility and adaptation to changing conditions and to the requirements of different decision-making situations, provides a better understanding of the model and the decision-making situation it attempts to describe, and permits the manager to input data in order to increase the confidence in the model. Sensitivity analysis tests relationships such as the following:

- The impact of changes in external (uncontrollable) variables and parameters on the outcome variable(s)
- The impact of changes in decision variables on the outcome variable(s)
- The effect of uncertainty in estimating external variables
- The effects of different dependent interactions among variables
- The robustness of decisions under changing conditions

Sensitivity analyses are used for:

- Revising models to eliminate too-large sensitivities
- Adding details about sensitive variables or scenarios
- Obtaining better estimates of sensitive external variables
- Altering a real-world system to reduce actual sensitivities
- Accepting and using the sensitive (and hence vulnerable) real world, leading to the continuous and close monitoring of actual results

The two types of sensitivity analyses are automatic and trial-and-error.

Automatic Sensitivity Analysis

Automatic sensitivity analysis is performed in standard quantitative model implementations such as LP. For example, it reports the range within which a certain input variable or parameter value (e.g., unit cost) can vary without having any significant impact on the proposed solution. Automatic sensitivity analysis is usually limited to one change at a time, and only for certain variables. However, it is very powerful because of its ability to establish ranges and limits very fast (and with little or no additional computational effort). For example, automatic sensitivity analysis is part of the LP solution report for the MBI Corporation product-mix problem described earlier. Sensitivity analysis is provided by both Solver and Lindo. Sensitivity analysis could be used to determine that if the right-hand side of the marketing constraint on CC-8 could be decreased by one unit, then the net profit would increase by $1,333.33. This is valid for the right-hand side decreasing to zero. For details, see Hillier and Lieberman (2005) and Taha (2006).

Trial-and-Error Sensitivity Analysis

The impact of changes in any variable, or in several variables, can be determined through a simple trial-and-error approach: You change some input data and solve the problem again. When the changes are repeated several times, better and better solutions may be discovered. Such experimentation, which is easy to conduct when using appropriate modeling software, such as Excel, has two approaches: what-if analysis and goal seeking.

WHAT-IF ANALYSIS

What-if analysis is structured as *What will happen to the solution if an input variable, an assumption, or a parameter value is changed?* Here are some examples:

- What will happen to the total inventory cost if the cost of carrying inventories increases by 10 percent?
- What will be the market share if the advertising budget increases by 5 percent?

With the appropriate user interface, it is easy for managers to ask a computer model these types of questions and get immediate answers. Furthermore, they can perform multiple cases and thereby change the percentage, or any other data in the question, as desired. The decision maker does all this directly, without a computer programmer.

Figure 4.7 shows a spreadsheet example of a what-if query for a cash flow problem. (You can link to the Excel file for Figure 4.7 from Online File W4.9.) When the user changes the cells containing the initial sales (from 100 to 120) and the sales growth rate (from 3 percent to 4 percent per quarter), the program immediately recomputes the

FIGURE 4.7 Example of a What-If Analysis Done in an Excel Worksheet

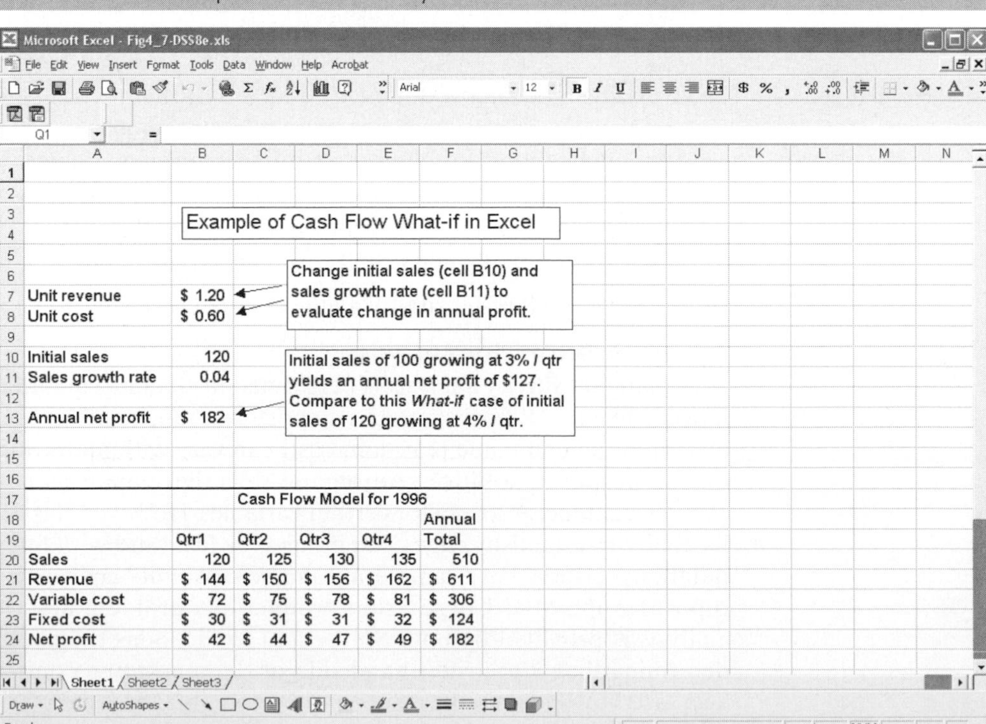

value of the annual net profit cell (from $127 to $182). What-if analysis is common in expert systems. Users are given the opportunity to change their answers to some of the system's questions, and a revised recommendation is found.

GOAL SEEKING

Goal seeking calculates the values of the inputs necessary to achieve a desired level of an output (goal). It represents a backward solution approach. The following are some examples of goal seeking:

- What annual R&D budget is needed for an annual growth rate of 15 percent by 2009?
- How many nurses are needed to reduce the average waiting time of a patient in the emergency room to less than 10 minutes?

An example of goal seeking is shown in Figure 4.8. Initially, initial sales were 100, growing at 3 percent per quarter, yielding an annual net profit of $127. Changing the initial sales cell to 120 and the sales growth rate to 4 percent causes the annual net profit to rise to $182. (You can link to the Excel files and its resultant solution for Figure 4.8 from Online File W4.9.)

Computing a Break-Even Point by Using Goal Seeking

Some modeling software packages can directly compute break-even points, which is an important application of goal seeking. This involves determining the value of the decision variables (e.g., quantity to produce) that generate zero profit. For example, in a financial planning model in Excel, the internal rate of return is the interest rate that produces a net present value (NPV) of zero.

FIGURE 4.8 Goal Seeking Analysis

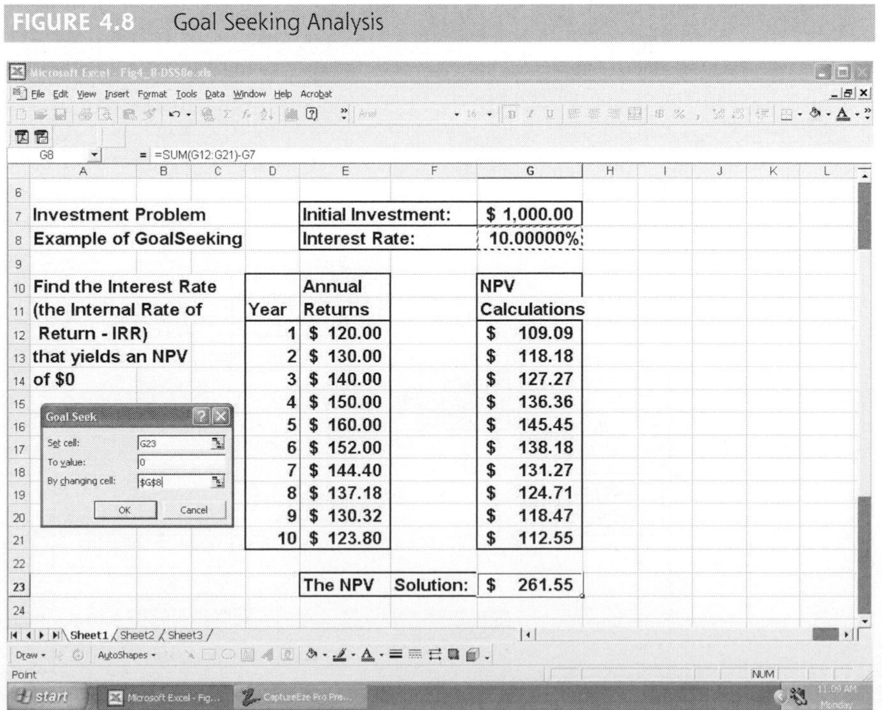

In many DSS, it can be difficult to conduct sensitivity analysis because the prewritten routines usually present only a limited opportunity for asking what-if questions. In a DSS, the what-if and the goal seeking options must be easy to perform.

The goal to be achieved is NPV equal to zero, which determines the internal rate of return (IRR) of this cash flow, including the investment. We set the NPV cell to the value 0 by changing the interest rate cell. The answer is 38.77059 percent.

Section 4.9 Review Questions

1. List some difficulties that may arise when analyzing multiple goals.
2. List the reasons for performing sensitivity analysis.
3. Explain why a manager might perform what-if analysis.
4. Explain why a manager might use goal seeking.

4.10 PROBLEM-SOLVING SEARCH METHODS

We next turn to several well-known search methods used in the choice phase of problem solving. These include analytical techniques, algorithms, blind searching, and heuristic searching.

The choice phase of problem solving involves a search for an appropriate course of action (among those identified during the design phase) that can solve the problem. There are several major search approaches, depending on the criteria (or criterion) of choice and the type of modeling approach used. These search approaches are shown in Figure 4.9. For normative models, such as mathematical programming-based ones, either an analytical approach is used or a complete, exhaustive enumeration (comparing

FIGURE 4.9 Formal Search Approaches

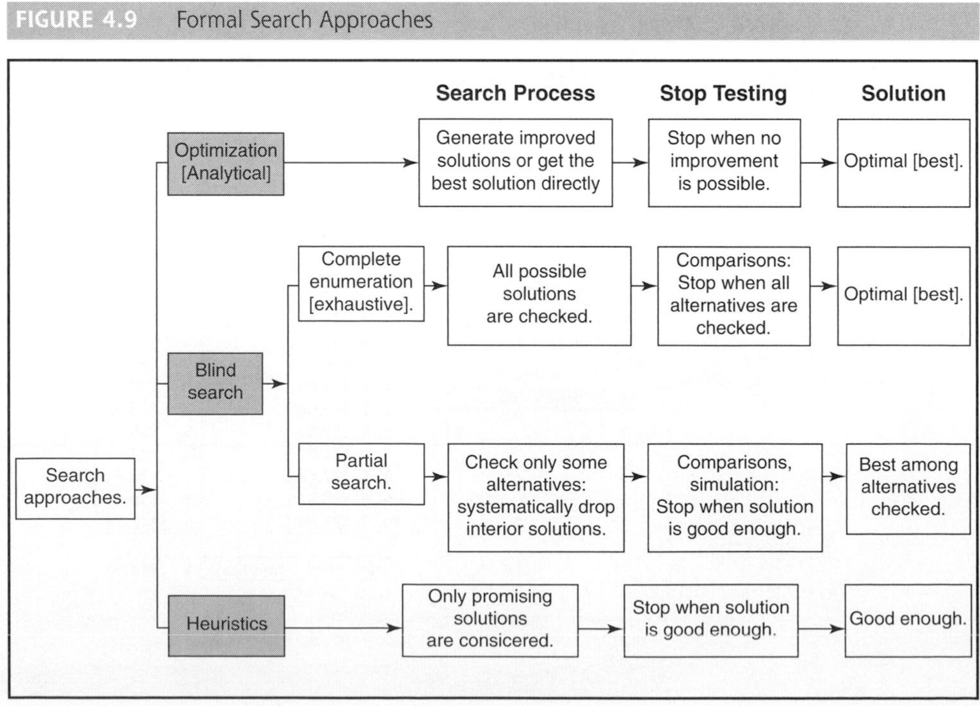

the outcomes of all the alternatives) is applied. For descriptive models, a comparison of a limited number of alternatives is used, either blindly or by employing heuristics. Usually the results guide the decision maker's search.

ANALYTICAL TECHNIQUES

Analytical techniques use mathematical formulas to derive an optimal solution directly or to predict a certain result. Analytical techniques are used mainly for solving structured problems, usually of a tactical or operational nature, in areas such as resource allocation or inventory management. Blind or heuristic search approaches are generally employed to solve more complex problems.

ALGORITHMS

Analytical techniques may use algorithms to increase the efficiency of the search. An algorithm is a step-by-step search process for obtaining an optimal solution (see Figure 4.10). (Note: There may be more than one optimum, so we say *an* optimal solution rather than *the* optimal solution.) Solutions are generated and tested for possible improvements. An improvement is made whenever possible, and the new solution is subjected to an improvement test, based on the principle of choice (i.e., objective value found). The process continues until no further improvement is possible. Most mathematical programming problems are solved by using efficient algorithms. Web search engines use algorithms to speed up searches and produce accurate results. Google's search algorithms are so good that Yahoo pays millions of dollars annually to use them.

BLIND SEARCHING

In conducting a search, a description of a desired solution may be given. This is called a *goal*. A set of possible steps leading from initial conditions to the goal is called the *search steps*. Problem solving is done by searching through the possible solutions. The first of these search methods is blind searching. The second is heuristic searching.

FIGURE 4.10 The Process of Using an Algorithm

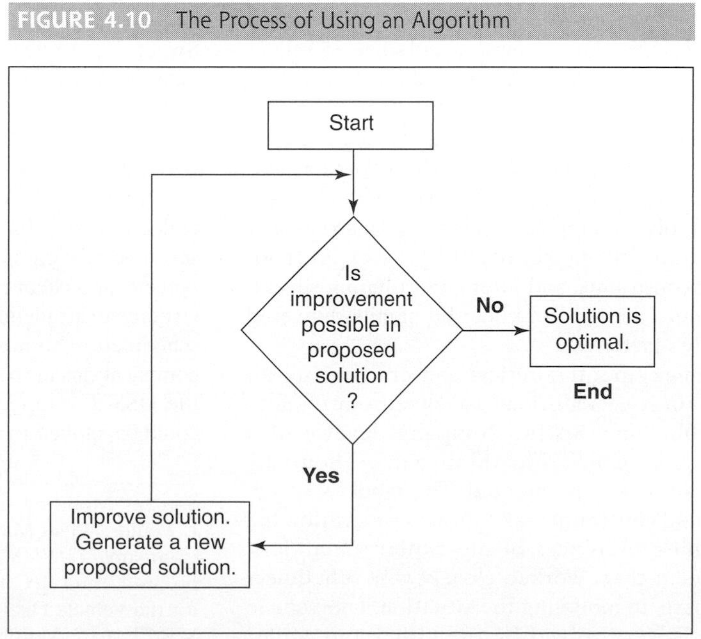

Blind search techniques are arbitrary search approaches that are not guided. There are two types of blind searches: a *complete enumeration*, for which all the alternatives are considered and therefore an optimal solution is discovered; and an *incomplete*, or partial, search, which continues until a good-enough solution is found. The latter is a form of suboptimization.

There are practical limits on the amount of time and computer storage available for blind searches. In principle, blind search methods can eventually find an optional solution in most search situations, and in some situations, the scope of the search can be limited; however, this method is not practical for solving very large problems because too many solutions must be examined before an optimal solution is found.

HEURISTIC SEARCHING

For many applications, it is possible to find rules to guide the search process and reduce the number of necessary computations through heuristics. **Heuristics** are the informal, judgmental knowledge of an application area that constitute the rules of good judgment in the field. Through domain knowledge, they guide the problem-solving process. **Heuristic programming** is the process of using heuristics in problem solving. This is done via heuristic search methods, which often operate as algorithms but limit the solutions examined either by limiting the search space or stopping the method early. Usually, rules that have either demonstrated their success in practice or are theoretically solid are applied in heuristic searching. We provide an example of a DSS in which the models are solved using heuristic searching in Application Case 4.6. A similar system was developed for Waste Management of Delaware (see Dignan, 2004).

Application Case 4.6

Heuristic-Based DSS Moves Milk in New Zealand

A major New Zealand dairy company had some 350 client farmers served by 12 tankers over two shifts. Because of its rising client base and rising milk collection costs, the company decided to improve its milk tanker scheduling by implementing a heuristic-based DSS. The vehicle schedulers, who had previously set up schedules manually, estimated milk supply by supplier (which varied seasonally and daily); operated the tanker fleet within location, budget, and other constraints; and attempted (among several goals) to minimize the cost per kilogram of milk delivered to the company's factories.

This complex (in a theoretical and practical sense) routing problem is very difficult to solve to optimality in a reasonable time. So the company developed a model-based DSS called FleetManager. A heuristic search approach was implemented. The model's objective function and constraints take into consideration the experience and preferences of the expert schedulers. The development team worked closely with schedulers and other experts in modeling the situation. The vehicle routing models were solved by the Gillet and Miller Sweep Heuristic to create trial solutions that schedulers examined via a graphical user interface. The schedulers were then able to adjust solutions based on additional knowledge about their practicality. Output screens of the system can be found at **orms-today.com**.

Since implementing FleetManager, the company's collection costs have decreased by more than 30 percent, schedule development time has decreased by more than 50 percent, and client complaints have decreased by more than 60 percent. Intangible benefits include a morale boost among schedulers, who now have time to deal with unanticipated complications in the schedule. The heuristic methodology of the DSS developed for this New Zealand dairy company could be applied to almost any complex delivery system.

Sources: Modified and condensed from C. Basnet and L. Foulds, "Fleet Manager Milks Efficiency Out of Dairy Company," *OR/MS Today*, Vol. 32, No. 6, December 2005, pp. 36–42; and B. Gillet and L. Miller, "A Heuristic Algorithm for the Vehicle Dispatch Problem," *Operations Research*, Vol. 22, No. 2, March/April 1974, pp. 340–349.

Section 4.10 Review Questions

1. What is a search approach?
2. List the different problem-solving search methods.
3. What are the practical limits to blind searching?
4. How are algorithms and heuristic search methods similar? How are they different?

4.11 SIMULATION

Simulation is the appearance of reality. In MSS, simulation is a technique for conducting experiments (e.g., what-if analyses) with a computer on a model of a management system.

Typically, there is some randomness in a real decision-making situation. Because DSS deals with semistructured or unstructured situations, reality is complex, which may not be easily represented by optimization or other models but can often be handled by simulation. Simulation is one of the most commonly used DSS methods. See Application Case 4.7 and Seila et al. (2003).

Application Case 4.7

Pratt & Whitney Canada Gets Real Savings Through Virtual Manufacturing

It used to take five long years to design and deliver a new aircraft engine to market. In 2002, Pratt & Whitney Canada (P&W) launched its Digital Engine initiative, along with other improvements, and cut that time to three years. Simulation now identifies production flaws and assesses maintenance costs. By designing engines and testing them in a simulation, every new engine program saves $500,000. In addition, some 70 percent of the conflicts between production parts (e.g., not fitting together) are resolved in the early design stage. The simulations also verify whether an engine is cost-effective to maintain, even before a prototype is constructed.

Ford, General Motors, DaimlerChrysler, Boeing, and other firms have begun applying similar tools in design and manufacturing. Results from a 2003 CIMdata survey indicate that companies using these methods achieve one or more of these benefits: 30 percent reduction in time to market, 65 percent reduction in the number of design changes, 40 percent reduction in the manufacturing planning process, and an average 15 percent increase in throughput. In addition, investments in digital manufacturing technologies are expected to grow by more than 25 percent annually through at least 2008.

Sources: Adapted from B. Stackpole, "Virtually Flawless?" *CIO*, May 15, 2005; G. MacSweeney, "Innovation Mastery: Pratt & Whitney Canada," *Managing Automation*, March 2005; COE NewsNet, *CIMdata Survey Confirms That the Digital Manufacturing Technology Is a Key Component in PLM, by Providing OEMs the Tools to Achieve Real Savings*, April 2003, **coe.org/newsnet/apr03/** (accessed March 2006); CIMdata, *The Benefits of Digital Manufacturing* (white paper), March 2003, **delmia.com/gallery/pdf/CIMdata_ROI_Study.pdf** (accessed March 2006); and Silicon Graphics, Inc., *Customer Successes: Pratt & Whitney*, **sgi.com** (accessed March 2006).

MAJOR CHARACTERISTICS OF SIMULATION

Simulation is not strictly a type of model; models generally *represent* reality, whereas simulation typically *imitates* it. In a practical sense, there are fewer simplifications of reality in simulation models than in other models. In addition, simulation is a technique for *conducting experiments*. Therefore, it involves testing specific values of the decision or uncontrollable variables in the model and observing the impact on the output variables. At DuPont, decision makers had initially chosen to purchase more railcars; however, an alternative involving better scheduling of the existing railcars was developed, tested, and found to have excess capacity, and it ended up saving money.

Simulation is a *descriptive* rather than a *normative* method. There is no automatic search for an optimal solution. Instead, a simulation model describes or predicts the characteristics of a given system under different conditions. When the values of the characteristics are computed, the best of several alternatives can be selected. The simulation process usually repeats an experiment many times to obtain an estimate (and a variance) of the overall effect of certain actions. For most situations, a computer simulation is appropriate, but there are some well-known manual simulations (e.g., a city police department simulated its patrol car scheduling with a carnival game wheel).

Finally, simulation is normally used only when a problem is too complex to be treated using numerical optimization techniques. **Complexity** in this situation means either that the problem cannot be formulated for optimization (e.g., because the assumptions do not hold), the formulation is too large, there are too many interactions among the variables, or the problem is stochastic in nature (i.e., exhibits risk or uncertainty). Designing and testing a new model of an automobile is extremely complex. That is one reason why General Motors uses simulation throughout the entire design process (see Stackpole, 2005). The success of General Motors, which saved $75 million in the first year (see Stackpole, 2005), may have prompted Daimler-Chrysler to move in this direction. By 2005, its Digital Factory, which uses simulation and visualization tools, had helped to design, build, and retrofit all its plants. One new German plant was constructed at a savings of 30 percent in total time, and plant floor costs were reduced by 10 percent (see Stackpole, 2005; and **allpar.com/history/digital.html**). Also, see how Pratt & Whitney used simulation in Application Case 4.7.

ADVANTAGES OF SIMULATION

Simulation is used in MSS for the following reasons:

- The theory is fairly straightforward.
- A great amount of *time compression* can be attained, quickly giving a manager some feel as to the long-term (1- to 10-year) effects of many policies.
- Simulation is descriptive rather than normative. This allows the manager to pose what-if questions. Managers can use a trial-and-error approach to problem solving and can do so faster, at less expense, more accurately, and with less risk.
- A manager can experiment to determine which decision variables and which parts of the environment are really important, and with different alternatives.
- An accurate simulation model requires an intimate knowledge of the problem, thus forcing the MSS builder to constantly interact with the manager. This is desirable for DSS development because the developer and manager both gain a better understanding of the problem and the potential decisions available.
- The model is built from the manager's perspective.
- The simulation model is built for one particular problem and typically cannot solve any other problem. Thus, no generalized understanding is required of the manager; every component in the model corresponds to part of the real system.
- Simulation can handle an extremely wide variety of problem types, such as inventory and staffing, as well as higher-level managerial functions, such as long-range planning.

- Simulation generally can include the real complexities of problems; simplifications are not necessary. For example, simulation can use real probability distributions rather than approximate theoretical distributions.
- Simulation automatically produces many important performance measures.
- Simulation is often the only DSS modeling method that can readily handle relatively unstructured problems.
- There are some relatively easy-to-use simulation packages (e.g., Monte Carlo simulation). These include add-in spreadsheet packages (e.g., @RISK), influence diagram software, Java-based (and other Web development) packages, and the visual interactive simulation systems to be discussed shortly.

DISADVANTAGES OF SIMULATION

The primary disadvantages of simulation are as follows:

- An optimal solution cannot be guaranteed, but relatively good ones are generally found.
- Simulation model construction can be a slow and costly process, although newer modeling systems are easier to use than ever.
- Solutions and inferences from a simulation study are usually not transferable to other problems because the model incorporates unique problem factors.
- Simulation is sometimes so easy to explain to managers that analytic methods are often overlooked.
- Simulation software sometimes requires special skills because of the complexity of the formal solution method.

THE METHODOLOGY OF SIMULATION

Simulation involves setting up a model of a real system and conducting repetitive experiments on it. The methodology consists of the following steps, as shown in Figure 4.11:

1. *Define the problem.* We examine and classify the real-world problem. Here we specify why a simulation approach is appropriate. The system's boundaries, environment, and other such aspects of problem clarification are handled here.
2. *Construct the simulation model.* This step involves determination of the variables and their relationships, as well as data gathering. Often the process is described by using a flowchart, and then a computer program is written.

FIGURE 4.11 The Process of Simulation

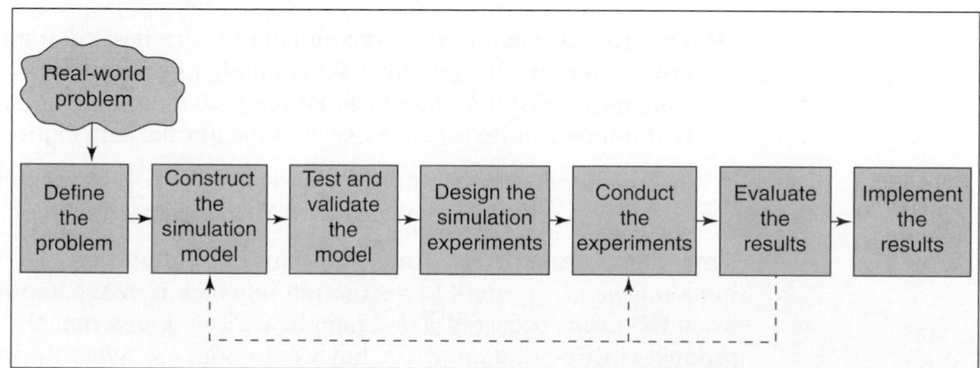

3. *Test and validate the model.* The simulation model must properly represent the system being studied. Testing and validation ensure this.
4. *Design the experiment.* When the model has been proven valid, an experiment is designed. Determining how long to run the simulation is part of this step. There are two important and conflicting objectives: accuracy and cost. It is also prudent to identify typical (e.g., mean and median cases for random variables), best-case (e.g., low-cost, high-revenue), and worst-case (e.g., high-cost, low-revenue) scenarios. These help establish the ranges of the decision variables and environment in which to work and also assist in debugging the simulation model.
5. *Conduct the experiment.* Conducting the experiment involves issues ranging from random-number generation to result presentation.
6. *Evaluate the results.* The results must be interpreted. In addition to standard statistical tools, sensitivity analyses can also be used.
7. *Implement the results.* The implementation of simulation results involves the same issues as any other implementation. However, the chances of success are better because the manager is usually more involved with the simulation process than with other models. Higher levels of managerial involvement generally lead to higher levels of implementation success.

Many simulation packages are Web ready. They are typically developed along the lines of the DSS architecture shown in Figure 3.1, where a user connects to the main server through a Web browser. This server connects to optimization servers and database servers, and the optimization and database servers in turn may connect to data warehouses, which populate the models. For example, see Pooley and Wilcox (2000) and the OR40 Simulation Stream home page at Brunel University, West London (**people.brunel.ac.uk/~csstsjt/ssg/ssghome.html**) for information on Java-based simulation systems. You can find many online demos of Java-based simulations by performing a search on "Java" and "simulation." For example, you can watch the NASA simulation of a rocket engine (**grc.nasa.gov/WWW/K-12/airplane/ngnsim.html**). Also see major vendors' Web sites.

SIMULATION TYPES

In the following sections, we describe the major types of simulation: probabilistic simulation, time-dependent and time-independent simulation, object-oriented simulation, and visual simulation.

Probabilistic Simulation

In probabilistic simulation, one or more of the independent variables (e.g., the demand in an inventory problem) are probabilistic. They follow certain probability distributions, which can be either discrete distributions or continuous distributions:

- *Discrete distributions* involve a situation with a limited number of events (or variables) that can take on only a finite number of values.
- *Continuous distributions* are situations with unlimited numbers of possible events that follow density functions, such as the normal distribution.

The two types of distributions are shown in Table 4.6. Probabilistic simulation is conducted with the aid of a technique called Monte Carlo simulation, which DuPont used.

Time-Dependent Versus Time-Independent Simulation

Time-independent refers to a situation in which it is not important to know exactly when the event occurred. For example, we may know that the demand for a certain product is three units per day, but we do not care *when* during the day the item is

TABLE 4.6 Discrete Versus Continuous Probability Distributions

Daily Demand	*Discrete Probability*	*Continuous Probability*
5	.10	Daily demand is normally distributed with a mean of 7 and a standard deviation of 1.2.
6	.15	
7	.30	
8	.25	
9	.20	

demanded. In some situations, time may not be a factor in the simulation at all, such as in steady-state plant control design. On the other hand, in waiting-line problems applicable to e-commerce, it is important to know the precise time of arrival (to know whether the customer will have to wait). This is a *time-dependent* situation.

Object-Oriented Simulation

There have been some advances in the area of developing simulation models by using the object-oriented approach. SIMPROCESS (CACI Products Company, **caciasl.com**) is an object-oriented process modeling tool that lets the user create a simulation model by using screen-based objects (e.g., metro cars). Unified Modeling Language (UML) is a modeling tool that was designed for object-oriented and object-based systems and applications. Because UML is object oriented, it could be used in practice for modeling complex, real-time systems. UML is particularly well suited for modeling. A real-time system is a software system that maintains an ongoing, timely interaction with its environment; examples include many DSS and information and communication systems (see Selic, 1999). Also, Java-based simulations are essentially object oriented.

Visual Simulation

The graphical display of computerized results, which may include animation, is one of the most successful developments in computer–human interaction and problem solving. We describe this in the next section.

SIMULATION SOFTWARE

There are hundreds of simulation packages for a variety of decision-making situations. Most run as Web-based systems, and newer implementation packages are Java based. There are many online demonstrations of simulations written in Java. PC software packages include Analytica (Lumina Decision Systems, **lumina.com**) and the Excel add-ins Crystal Ball (Decisioneering, **decisioneering.com**) and @RISK (Palisade Corp., **palisade.com**). Web-based systems include WebGPSS (GPSS, **webgpss.com**), and SIMUL8 (SIMUL8 Corp., **SIMUL8.com**).

SIMULATION EXAMPLES

We show an example of a spreadsheet-based economic order quantity simulation model and a spreadsheet simulation model for evaluating a simple cash-flow problem in Online File W4.3. CACI Products Company now provides COMNET III, a simulation system specifically for analyzing these types of IT network design problems.

Saltzman and Mehrotra (2001) used a simulation approach to analyze a call center. Jovanovic (2002) determined how to schedule tasks in distributed systems via simulation. This is important when managing grid computer networks. Dronzek (2001) used simulation to improve critical care in a military hospital. He analyzed proposed changes in a health care system, using simulation modeling to determine the impact of potential changes without disrupting the established process of care or disturbing staff, patients, or the facility. Credit Suisse First Boston uses an ASP simulation system to predict the risk and reward potential of investments (see Dembo et al., 2000). General Motors (see Stackpole, 2005; Gallagher, 2002; Gareiss, 2002; and Witzerman, 2001) delays constructing physical models of automobiles until late in the design process because simulation (e.g., crash tests, wind tunnel tests) is less expensive and produces more accurate results in testing new products. Witzerman (2001) described how GM's paint shop robots are simulated for improved performance.

The simulation tools in use today are very effective and have led to major improvements. It now takes only 18 months to develop a new vehicle, down from 48 months. Engineering productivity is way up, as is quality. In Application Case 4.8, we provide several additional examples of simulation applications, including those for e-learning systems.

Application Case 4.8

Simulation Applications

Applications of simulation vary widely. Some are in scientific disciplines, while others are in business, and yet others are, essentially, video/computer games. Here is a sampler of several simulation applications:

- *E-learning.* Tacit skill training is expensive, and if people can experience walk-throughs, without one-on-one human interaction, savings can be dramatic. For example, the U.S. Department of Agriculture (USDA) developed a Web-based simulation system to provide more than 400 geographically dispersed federal employees training on how to use the PeopleSoft 8.0 human resource management system. The cost of developing e-learning simulations, even with custom video, can be less than $20,000. Humana, Inc., used simulation to train 150 top executives in navigating complex change initiatives. Business simulations have been used for decades at leading colleges of business (e.g., the Carnegie Mellon Tepper School of Business).
- *Production scenarios.* Agilent's California Semiconductor Test division simulates supply-side production scenarios to coordinate sourcing for new product launches, to keep excess and obsolete inventory (caused by engineering changes) low, and to respond quickly to promised orders. One clear benefit has been a reduction of 30 to 40 percent in the inventory of most components, with some as high as 60 percent.
- *IT/software products.* CNA Financial Corp. uses simulation tools from iRise, Inc., to determine how potential software system requirements will work out. The simulations bring products to life and show business users how they will function in practice. In this way, the firm can communicate requirements from business users to software developers more accurately, which in turn shortens the requirements cycle. This is critical when development is offshored (i.e., outsourced to a firm in another country). Serena developed its ProcessView Composer software to simulate, visualize, and prototype business processes and application requirements. This has greatly reduced rework resulting from catching flawed requirements.
- *Web applications.* In a manner similar to CNA, Wachovia Corp. uses iRise simulation tools in a user design laboratory to simulate Web applications before their release to internal users.
- *Military battles.* The U.S. military simulates battles, both urban and field, using simulation software based largely on that developed for the entertainment industry (video and computer games), running on high-powered graphics engines and supercomputers. These systems create a training environment that

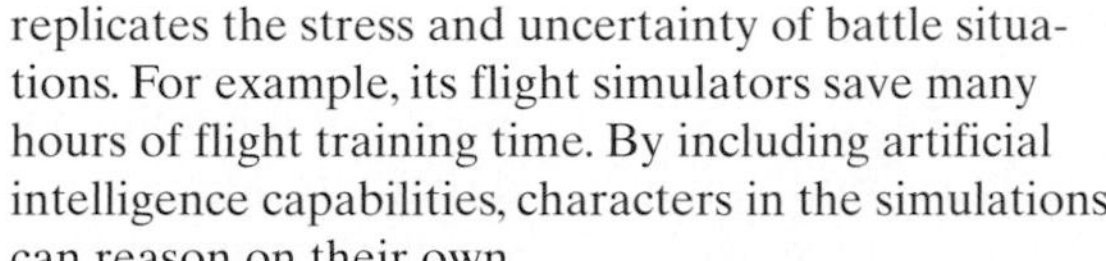

replicates the stress and uncertainty of battle situations. For example, its flight simulators save many hours of flight training time. By including artificial intelligence capabilities, characters in the simulations can reason on their own.

- *Pharmaceutical development*. Pharmaceutical firms simulate how drugs interact with the human body, down to the DNA level, thus accurately predicting impacts; savings are realized in the testing phases if potential compounds prove ineffective in the computer simulation. Pharmaceutical development simulations run on high-powered parallel computers.
- *Public sector applications*. Microsimulation can readily be applied in representing how government agencies function, leading to operational improvements.
- *Product design*. Even simple products can benefit from simulation. Earlier in this section, we described how Pratt & Whitney and General Motors use simulation in new product design and manufacturing. Even the aerodynamics of Pringles chips have been analyzed by using simulation methods to determine how air flows around their unique double-saddle shape. The problem was that the chip created lift that made it unstable, so that it might fly off the manufacturer's conveyer belt if the belt was running too fast. Based on information found through simulation, the shape was redesigned.

Sources: Modified and abstracted from T. Hoffman, "Simulations Revitalize E-Learning," *Computerworld*, August 4, 2003, pp. 26–27; S. Boehle, "The Next Generation of E-Learning," *Training*, January 2005, pp. 23–31; R. Michel, "Decision Support Smoothes Semiconductor Test Division's Outsourced Model," *Manufacturing Business Technology*, June 2005, p. 30; H. Havenstein, "App Simulation in Demand," *Computerworld*, June 27, 2005, pp. 1, 77; D. Verton, "Simulating Fallujah," *Computerworld*, January 31, 2005, p. 28; "Million-Atom Biology Simulation Could Improve Drug Development," *Computerworld*, November 14, 2005, p. 39; P. Arena, S. Rhody, and M. Stavrianos, "The Truth About Facts," *DM Review*, January 2006, pp. 30–34; and D. Briody, "The Flight of the Pringle," *CIO Insight*, August 2005, p. 22.

Section 4.11 Review Questions

1. List the characteristics of simulation.
2. List the advantages and disadvantages of simulation.
3. List and describe the steps in the methodology of simulation.
4. List and describe the types of simulation.

4.12 VISUAL INTERACTIVE SIMULATION

We next examine methods that show a decision maker a representation of the decision-making situation in action as it runs through scenarios of the decision maker's choices of alternatives. These powerful methods overcome some of the inadequacies of conventional methods and help build trust in the solution attained because they can be visualized directly.

CONVENTIONAL SIMULATION INADEQUACIES

Simulation is a well-established, useful, descriptive, mathematics-based method for gaining insight into complex decision-making situations. However, simulation does not usually allow decision makers to see how a solution to a complex problem evolves over (compressed) time, nor can decision makers interact with the simulation (which would be useful for training purposes and teaching). Simulation generally reports statistical results at the end of a set of experiments. Decision makers are thus not an integral part of simulation development and experimentation, and their experience and judgment cannot be used directly. If the simulation results do not match the intuition or judgment of the decision maker, a *confidence gap* in the results can occur.

VISUAL INTERACTIVE SIMULATION

Visual interactive simulation (VIS), also known as **visual interactive modeling (VIM)** and *visual interactive problem solving*, is a simulation method that lets decision makers see what the model is doing and how it interacts with the decisions made, as they are made. The technique has been used with great success in operations management DSS. The user can employ his or her knowledge to determine and try different decision strategies while interacting with the model. Enhanced learning, about both the problem and the impact of the alternatives tested, can and does occur. Decision makers also contribute to model validation. Decision makers who use VIS generally support and trust their results.

VIS uses animated computer graphic displays to present the impact of different managerial decisions. It differs from regular graphics in that the user can adjust the decision-making process and see the results of the intervention. A visual model is a graphic used as an integral part of decision making or problem solving, not just as a communication device. VIS displays the effects of different decisions in graphic form on a computer screen, as was done through the GIS in the Procter & Gamble supply-chain redesign through optimization. Some people respond better than others to graphical displays, and this type of interaction can help managers learn about the decision-making situation. For example, Swisher et al. (2001) applied an object-oriented visual simulation to examining the functioning of a physician clinic environment within a physician network to provide high-quality, cost-effective health care in a family practice. The simulation system identified the most important input factors that significantly affected performance. These inputs, when properly managed, led to lower costs and higher service levels. Many Java-based VIS demonstrations run directly on the Internet.

VIS can represent static or dynamic systems. Static models display a visual image of the result of one decision alternative at a time. Dynamic models display systems that evolve over time, and the evolution is represented by animation. The latest visual simulation technology has been coupled with the concept of virtual reality, where an artificial world is created for a number of purposes, from training to entertainment to viewing data in an artificial landscape. For example, the U.S. military uses VIS systems so that ground troops can gain familiarity with terrain or a city in order to very quickly orient themselves. Pilots also use VIS to gain familiarity with targets by simulating attack runs. The VIS software can also include GIS coordinates.

VISUAL INTERACTIVE MODELS AND DSS

VIM in DSS has been used in several operations management decisions. The method consists of priming (like priming a waterpump) a visual interactive model of a plant (or company) with its current status. The model then runs rapidly on a computer, allowing managers to observe how a plant is likely to operate in the future.

Waiting-line management (queuing) is a good example of VIM. Such a DSS usually computes several measures of performance for the various decision alternatives (e.g., waiting time in the system). Complex waiting-line problems require simulation. VIM can display the size of the waiting line as it changes during the simulation runs and can also graphically present the answers to what-if questions regarding changes in input variables.

The VIM approach can also be used in conjunction with artificial intelligence. Integration of the two techniques adds several capabilities that range from the ability to build systems graphically to learning about the dynamics of the system. High-speed parallel computers such as those made by Silicon Graphics, Inc., and Hewlett-Packard make large-scale, complex, animated simulations feasible in real-time. (For example, the movie *Toy Story* and its sequel were essentially long VIM applications.) The *grid computing paradigm* may help in large-scale simulations. These systems, especially those developed for the military and video gaming industry, have "thinking" characters who can behave with a relatively high level of intelligence in their interactions with users.

General-purpose commercial dynamic VIS software is readily available. For several excellent videos of real VIS applications, examine the results of the Orca Visual Simulation Environment (VSE; Orca Computer Inc., **orcacomputer.com**). The Orca VSE allows for easy implementation and testing of these systems. Other vendors include GPSS/PC (Minuteman Software, **minutemansoftware.com**), and VisSim (Visual Solutions, Inc., **vissim.com**). For information about simulation software, visual and otherwise, see IMAGE Society Inc. (**public.asu.edu/~image//**), the Society for Modeling and Simulation International (**scs.org**), and the annual software surveys at *OR/MS Today* (**orms-today.com**).

Section 4.12 Review Questions

1. Define *visual simulation* and compare it to conventional simulation.
2. Describe the features of VIS (i.e., VIM) that make it attractive for decision makers.
3. How can VIS be used in operations management?
4. How is an animated film like a VIS application?

4.13 QUANTITATIVE SOFTWARE PACKAGES AND MODEL BASE MANAGEMENT

Quantitative software packages are preprogrammed (sometimes called ready-made) models and optimization systems that sometimes serve as building blocks for other quantitative models. A variety of these are readily available for inclusion in DSS as major and minor modeling components; in addition, there are complete packages that can be considered ready-made DSS. The latter tend to be developed and sold for a very specific application, whereas the former may be used as vehicles in which to develop models. We discuss these briefly next.

The Excel spreadsheet system has hundreds of models, ranging from functions to add-in packages (e.g., Solver). For data that can be dropped into a spreadsheet, generally Excel has many of the capabilities needed to produce usable results for many decision-making situations.

OLAP systems are essentially collections of optimization, simulation, statistical, and artificial intelligence packages that access large amounts of data for analysis. Some OLAP packages, such as those from SAS and SPSS, were initially developed for analysis, and data management capabilities were added, while others, such as the Oracle Financials Suite, evolved from DBMS to which modeling capabilities were added. Data mining software, such as that from MicroStrategy (**microstrategy.com**; also available from **teradatauniversitynetwork.com**) and Megaputer PolyAnalyst (**megaputer.com**), contain models and solution methods that can be activated either automatically or directly by the user.

Traditional statistical packages and management science packages are also available for model construction and solution. For a comprehensive resource directory of these types of systems, see *OR/MS Today* (**orms-today.com**). Revenue management systems (RMSs) focus on identifying the right product for the right customer at the right price in the right channel. Similar in idea to CRM, RMS focus mainly on competing based on price and time. Airlines have used such systems (sometimes called *yield management systems*) to determine the right price for each airline seat on each flight. These systems are also available for retail operations, entertainment venues, and many other industries. RMS typically involve determining customer behavior and using sophisticated economics and optimization models to set prices and the quantities of products or services available for that price at every given time. Because the Web has promoted the widespread use of modeling, optimization, simulation, and related techniques, we list a sampling of Web impacts on these areas, and vice versa, in the table in Online File W4.10. Also see J. Aronson's DSS Software Web page (**terry.uga.edu/people/jaronson/dss/DSS-Software.html**) for an extensive list of DSS software links. Many of these software packages are model based.

MODEL BASE MANAGEMENT

Now that you are aware of the different model classes and solution methods, you need to realize that it is important, especially in large-scale DSS for use at the enterprise level, to manage the models and their solutions. This is the job of a **model base management system (MBMS)**, a software package that theoretically has capabilities similar to those of a DBMS—to manage, manipulate, and run the models embedded in the DSS. There are also **relational model base management system (RMBMS)** and **object-oriented model base management system (OOMBMS)** that provide the capabilities of the MBMS, paralleling the concepts of RDBMS and OODBMS, respectively.

Model management is an extremely difficult task because unlike databases—of which there may be three very common databases plus two more deployed in practice—there are hundreds of model classes and often many different solution algorithms that can be used within each class. Plus, models are used in a variety of different ways in different organizations. Consequently, MBMS are generally unique for each type of problem being solved. We cannot manage statistical models in the same way as simulation models or optimization models. For examples of how to manage models in practice, examine how Procter & Gamble handles it. We discuss details of how this is done in practice in Online File W4.11.

Section 4.13 Review Questions

1. Explain how a spreadsheet system such as Excel can be used in DSS modeling.
2. Explain why OLAP is a kind of modeling system.
3. Identify three classes of models and list two kinds of problems each can solve.
4. List the reasons model management is difficult.

4.14 RESOURCES, LINKS, AND THE TERADATA UNIVERSITY NETWORK CONNECTION

The use of this chapter and most other chapters in this book can be enhanced by the tools described in the following sections.

RESOURCES AND LINKS

We recommend looking at the following resources and links for further reading and explanations:

- The INFORMS Web site (**informs.org**) includes Michael Trick's optimization pages. Be sure to look at the Resources link at **informs.org**. A wealth of modeling and solution information is available from INFORMS, including its journals.
- *OR/MS Today* (**orms-today.com**) has many important modeling and analysis software system reviews. They are updated regularly and are available online. It also publishes excellent, model-based DSS applications regularly.
- COIN-OR (**coin-or.org**) is open source software for operations research (and management science) professionals.
- The Mathematics and Computer Science Division at Argonne National Laboratory in Argonne, Illinois, maintains the NEOS Server for Optimization at **neos.mcs.anl.gov/neos/index.html**. The NEOS Guide offers the Java-based Simplex Tool, which demonstrates the workings of the simplex method on small user-entered problems and is especially useful for educational purposes.
- See H. Arsham's Modeling & Simulation Resources page, at **home.ubalt.edu/ntsbarsh/Business-stat/RefSim.htm**, and Decision Science Resources page, **home.ubalt.edu/ntsbarsh/Business-stat/Refop.htm**, for a wealth of information.
- See Jay Aronson's DSS Software Web page, at **terry.uga.edu/people/jaronson/dss/DSS-Software.html**, for an extensive list of DSS software links. Many of these software packages are model based.
- See Decision Analysis Society, **faculty.fuqua.duke.edu/daweb/dasw6.htm**, for resources on decision analysis.
- At Berkeley, the Interactive Linear Programming group provides Web-based tools as a service. These tools appear to be useful for solving small LP models. See **faqs.org/faqs/linear-programming-faq/** for more info.

CASES

Major optimization and simulation vendors provide success stories on their Web sites. See Lindo Systems, Inc. (**lindo.com**), as an example. Academic-oriented cases and sample problems are available from links from the Linear Programming FAQs at **faqs.org/faqs/linear-programming-faq**, Business Performance Improvement Resource (**bpir.com**), Idea Group Publishing (**idea-group.com**), Ivy League Publishing (**ivylp.com**), ICFAI Center for Management Research (**icmr.icfai.org/casestudies/icmr_case_studies.htm**), KnowledgeStorm (**knowledgestorm.com**), and other sites. For additional case resources, see Teradata University Network (**TeradataUniversityNetwork.com**)

MILLER'S *MIS CASES*

All the cases in Miller's *MIS Cases* (2005) involve decision making in some way. The spreadsheet cases are all essentially model-driven DSS, and the database cases are all data-driven DSS.

VENDORS, PRODUCTS, AND DEMOS

The best source for information about modeling and solution method packages and systems is the "OR/MS Today Software Surveys" published in *OR/MS Today*. These include software for LP, statistical analysis, forecasting, decision analysis, vehicle routing, supply-chain management (SCM), spreadsheet add-ins, and nonlinear programming. Complete surveys, including full vendor contact information, are freely accessible from **orms-today.com**. Other information can be readily reached from the INFORMS Resources page at **informs.org**, as well as from the many excellent INFORMS publications, such as

Management Science, *Interfaces*, and *Operations Research*. See **terry.uga.edu/people/jaronson/dss/DSS-Software.html** for an extensive list of DSS software links. Many of these software packages are model based.

Extensive examples and success stories are readily available at vendor Web sites.

PERIODICALS

We recommend the following periodicals:

- *Decision Sciences* **decisionsciences.org**
- *Decision Support Systems* **elsevier.com**
- *Interfaces* **informs.org**
- *Management Science* **informs.org**
- *Operations Research* **informs.org**
- *OR/MS Today* (**orms-today.com**)

ADDITIONAL REFERENCES

Additional selected references are provided in the online files of each chapter. For this chapter, see Online File W4.12.

THE TERADATA UNIVERSITY NETWORK (TUN) CONNECTION

At the Teradata University Network Web site (**teradatauniversitynetwork.com**), we recommend a specific case, report, and software, along with their accompanying questions. These include the Continental Airlines case, the report by Wayne Erickson, "The Rise of Analytic Applications: Build or Buy?" and, the MicroStrategy software with the three questions in "AdVent Technology: Using the MicroStrategy Sales Analytic Model Assignment."

Chapter Highlights

- Models play a major role in DSS because they are used to describe real decision-making situations. There are several types of models.
- Models can be either static (i.e., a single snapshot of a situation) or dynamic (i.e., multiperiod).
- Analysis is conducted under assumed certainty (which is most desirable), risk, or uncertainty (which is least desirable).
- Influence diagrams graphically show the interrelationships of a model. They can be used to enhance the use of spreadsheet technology.
- Influence diagram software can be used to generate and solve a model.
- Spreadsheets have many capabilities, including what-if analysis, goal seeking, programming, database management, optimization, and simulation.
- Decision tables and decision trees can model and solve simple decision-making problems.
- Mathematical programming is an important optimization method.
- LP is the most common mathematical programming method. It attempts to find an optimal allocation of limited resources under organizational constraints.
- The major parts of an LP model are the objective function, the decision variables, and the constraints.
- Multicriteria decision-making problems are difficult but not impossible to solve.
- The AHM (e.g., Expert Choice software) is a leading method for solving multicriteria decision-making problems.
- What-if and goal seeking approaches are the two most common methods of sensitivity analysis.
- Heuristic programming involves problem solving using general rules or intelligent search.

- Simulation is a widely used DSS approach that involves experimentation with a model that represents the real decision-making situation.
- Simulation can deal with more complex situations than optimization, but it does not guarantee an optimal solution.
- VIS/VIM allows a decision maker to interact directly with a model and shows results in an easily understood manner.
- Many DSS development tools include built-in quantitative models (e.g., financial, statistical) or can easily interface with such models.
- MBMS perform tasks analogous to those performed by DBMS.
- Unlike DBMS, there are no standard MBMS because of the many classes of models, their use, and the many techniques for solving them.
- Artificial intelligence techniques can be effectively used in MBMS.
- The Web has had a profound impact on models and model management systems, and vice versa.
- Web application servers provide model management capabilities to DSS.

Key Terms

- certainty
- complexity
- decision analysis
- decision table
- decision tree
- decision variable
- dynamic models
- environmental scanning and analysis
- forecasting
- goal seeking
- heuristic programming
- heuristics
- influence diagram
- intermediate result variable
- linear programming (LP)
- mathematical (quantitative) model
- mathematical programming
- model base management system (MBMS)
- multidimensional analysis (modeling)
- multiple goals
- object-oriented model base management system (OOMBMS)
- optimal solution
- parameter
- quantitative software package
- relational model base management system (RMBMS)
- result (outcome) variable
- risk
- risk analysis
- sensitivity analysis
- simulation
- static models
- uncertainty
- uncontrollable variable
- visual interactive modeling (VIM)
- visual interactive simulation (VIS)
- what-if analysis

Questions for Discussion

1. What is the relationship between environmental analysis and problem identification?
2. Explain the differences between static and dynamic models. How can one evolve into the other?
3. What is the difference between an optimistic approach and a pessimistic approach to decision making under assumed uncertainty?
4. Explain why solving problems under uncertainty sometimes involves assuming that the problem is to be solved under conditions of risk.
5. Excel is probably the most popular spreadsheet software for PCs. Why? What can we do with this package that makes it so attractive for modeling efforts?
6. Explain how OLAP provides access to powerful models in a spreadsheet structure.
7. Explain how decision trees work. How can a complex problem be solved by using a decision tree?
8. Explain how LP can solve allocation problems.
9. What are the advantages of using a spreadsheet package to create and solve LP models? What are the disadvantages?
10. What are the advantages of using an LP package to create and solve LP models? What are the disadvantages?
11. What is the difference between decision analysis with a single goal and decision analysis with multiple goals (i.e., criteria)? Explain in detail the difficulties that may arise when analyzing multiple goals.
12. Explain how multiple goals can arise in practice.
13. Compare and contrast what-if analysis and goal seeking.
14. Describe the general process of simulation.
15. List some of the major advantages of simulation over optimization and vice versa.

16. What are the advantages of using a spreadsheet package to perform simulation studies? What are the disadvantages?
17. Compare the methodology of simulation to Simon's four-phase model of decision making. Does the methodology of simulation map directly into Simon's model? Explain.
18. Many computer games can be considered visual simulation. Explain why.
19. Explain why VIS is particularly helpful in implementing recommendations derived by computers.
20. There are hundreds of DBMS packages on the market. Explain why there are no packages for MBMS.
21. Does Simon's four-phase decision-making model fit into most of the modeling methodologies described? How or how not?

Exercises

Teradata University and Other Hands-on Exercises

1. Explore **teradatastudentnetwork.com** and determine how models are used in the BI cases and papers. Specifically, solve the three problems listed earlier, in the section "The Teradata University Network (TUN) Connection."
2. Each group in the class should access a different online Java-based Web simulation system (especially those systems from visual interactive simulation vendors) and run it. Write up your experience and present it to the class.
3. Each group in the class should access a different online Java-based optimization system and run it. Write up your experience and present it to the class.
4. Go to **orms-today.com** and access the article "The 'Sound' Science of Scheduling," by L. Gordon and E. Erkut from *OR/MS Today*, Vol. 32, No. 2, April 2005. Describe the overall problem, the DSS developed to solve it, and the benefits.
5. Investigate via a Web search how models and their solutions are used by the U.S. Department of Homeland Security in the "War Against Terrorism." Also investigate how other governments or government agencies are using models in their missions.
6. Read M.S. Sodhi, "Breast Cancer and O.R.," *OR/MS Today*, Vol. 32, No. 6, 2005, p. 14. Consider the problem of accurately diagnosing diseases such as breast cancer and how modeling and simulation can help improve accuracy. Investigate this topic and write a detailed report. Include in your report real-world modeling and simulation efforts.
7. Read S. Boehle, "Simulations: The Next Generation of E-Learning," *Training*, Vol. 42, No. 1, January 2005, pp. 22–31. Investigate and write a report about the types of systems that have been deployed for the development of e-learning simulations and what kinds of e-learning systems have been developed in them. Try one out and include your experience in your report.

Team Assignments and Role-Playing

1. People do not like to wait in line. Many models have been developed and solved for waiting-line models to assist organizations such as banks, theme parks, airports (for security, ticket counters, and gate counters), fast food outlets, movie theaters, and post offices. These models are known as queuing models. Look into organizations that have applied these models and their associated solution methodologies in practice and investigate what kinds of goals and specific decision variables these models incorporate. Visit some organizations where queuing occurs and observe the behavior of the customers and servers. If possible, run a demo of some software and/or create and solve a queuing model. Also investigate behavioral issues about these problems. These behavioral issues often lead to information about how people waiting in line interpret their experience and are more important than the actual waiting time. (You may also find information about how theme parks handle this as a revenue management problem.) Write up your results in a report. (This exercise was inspired by Hendrick, B., "Bottom Line: Folks Hate to Wait," *The Atlanta Journal-Constitution*, February 13, 2006, pp. A1, A6.)
2. Create the spreadsheet models shown in Figure 4.2 and Figure 4.3.
   a. What is the effect of a change in the interest rate from 8 percent to 10 percent in the spreadsheet model shown in Figure 4.2?
   b. For the original model in Figure 4.2, what interest rate is required to decrease the monthly payments by 20 percent? What change in the loan amount would have the same effect?

c. In the spreadsheet shown in Figure 4.3, what is the effect of a prepayment of $200 per month? What prepayment would be necessary to pay off the loan in 25 years instead of 30 years?

3. As a class, build a predictive model. Everyone in the class should write his or her weight, height, and gender on a piece of paper (no names please!). If the sample is too small (you need about 20–30 students), add more students from another class.

   a. Create a regression (causal) model for height versus weight for the whole class and one for each gender. If possible, use a statistical package (e.g., SPSS) and a spreadsheet (e.g., Excel) and compare their ease of use. Produce a scatterplot of the three sets of data.

   b. Based on your plots and regressions, do the relationships appear to be linear? How accurate were the models (e.g., how close to 1 is the value of R^2)?

   c. Does weight cause height, does height cause weight, or does neither really cause the other? Explain.

   d. How can a regression model like this be used in building or aircraft design? diet or nutrition selection? a longitudinal study (e.g., over 50 years) to determine whether students are getting heavier and not taller or vice versa?

4. It has been argued in a number of venues that a higher education level indicates a greater average income. The question for a college student might therefore be Should I stay in school?

   a. Using publicly available U.S. Census data for the 50 states and Washington, DC, develop a linear regression model (causal forecasting) to see whether this relationship is true. (Note that some data massaging may be necessary.) How high was the R^2 value (a measure of quality of fit)? Scatterplot the data.

   b. Does the relationship appear to be linear? If not, check a statistics book and try a nonlinear function. How well does the nonlinear function perform?

   c. Which five states have the highest average incomes, and which five states have the highest average education levels? From this study, do you believe that a higher average education level tends to cause a higher average income? Explain.

   d. If you have studied (or will study) neural networks, using the same data, build a neural network prediction model and compare it to your statistical results.

5. Set up spreadsheet models for the decision table models from Section 4.6 and solve them.

6. Solve the MBI product-mix problem described in this chapter, using either Excel's Solver or a student version of an LP solver, such as Lindo or Win QSB. Lindo is available from Lindo Systems, Inc., at **lindo.com**; others are also available—search the Web. Examine the solution (output) reports for the answers and sensitivity report. Did you get the same results as reported in this chapter? Try the sensitivity analysis outlined in the chapter; that is, lower the right-hand side of the CC-8 marketing constraint by 1 unit, from 200 to 199. What happens to the solution when you solve this modified problem? Eliminate the CC-8 lower bound constraint entirely (this can be done easily by either deleting it in Solver or setting the lower limit to zero) and re-solve the problem. What happens? Using the original formulation, try modifying the objective function coefficients and see what happens.

7. *Software demonstration.* Each group should review, examine, and demonstrate in class a different state-of-the-art DSS software product. The specific packages depend on your instructor and the group interests. You may need to download a demo from a vendor's Web site, depending on your instructor's directions. Be sure to get a running demo version, not a slide show. Do a half-hour in-class presentation, which should include an explanation of *why the software is appropriate* for assisting in decision making, a *hands-on demonstration* of selected important capabilities of the software, and your *critical evaluation* of the software. Try to make your presentation interesting and instructive to the whole class. The main purpose of the class presentation is for class members to see as much state-of-the-art software as possible, both in breadth (through the presentations by other groups) and in depth (through the experience you have in exploring the ins and outs of one particular software product). Write a 5- to 10-page report on your findings and comments regarding this software. Include screenshots in your report. Would you recommend this software to anyone? Why or why not?

8. *Expert Choice software familiarity.* Have a group meeting and discuss how you chose a place to live when you relocated to start your college program (or relocated to where you are now). What factors were important for each individual then, and how long ago was it? Have the criteria changed? As a group, identify the five to seven most important criteria used in making the decision. Using the current group members' living arrangements as choices, develop an Expert Choice model that describes this decision-making problem. Do not put your

judgments in yet. You should each solve the Expert Choice model independently. Be careful to keep the inconsistency ratio less than 0.1. How many of the group members selected their current home using the software? For those who did, was it a close decision, or was there a clear winner? If some group members did not choose their current homes, what criteria made the result different? (In this decision-making exercise, you should not consider spouses or parents, even those who cook really well, as part of the home.) Did the availability of better choices that meet their needs become known? How consistent were your judgments? Do you think you would really prefer to live in the winning location? Why or why not? Finally, average the results for all group members (by adding the synthesized weights for each choice and dividing by the number of group members). This is one way Expert Choice works. Is there a clear winner? Whose home is it, and why did it win? Were there any close second choices? Turn in your results in a summary report (up to 2 typed pages), with copies of the individual Expert Choice runs.

Internet Exercises

1. Search the Internet for literature and information about DSS and its relationship to BI, BA, and predictive analytics. Describe what you find.
2. Use TreeAge Pro decision tree software and then describe how it works and what kinds of problems can be solved with it.
3. Explore decision analysis software vendor Web sites. Identify the purpose of the package(s) that the vendor offers and the organizations that have had successes with them.
4. Go to **baselinemag.com** and access the online articles by M. Duvall, "Billy Beane: What MBAs Can Learn From MLB," May 20, 2004; D.F. Carr, "Gotcha! Weigh Your Human-Resources Software Options with Care," May 14, 2004; and M. Duvall, "Roadblock: Getting Old-line Managers to Think in New Ways," May 14, 2004. Describe the concepts of how models can be applied in industry in the same manner that the Boston Red Sox and Oakland Athletics used them.

End of Chapter Application Case

Major League Baseball Scheduling: Computerized Mathematical Models Take Us out to the Ballgame

Scheduling sports tournaments is complex, and scheduling sports seasons for an entire league is even more complex. Many conflicting goals and issues must be considered. For example, in the U.S. NCAA (college sports) Southeast Conference Baseball (SEC) situation, two teams are fairly distant from the rest, which are clustered fairly closely together. One desirable goal is not to have any team travel to both of the distant teams for the away-game series in consecutive weeks. These types of goals (although not quite constraints) apply directly to major league baseball (MLB), where there are many more teams and the distances traveled can be extensive. In MLB scheduling, one desired feature is not to have the same teams play in back-to-back series at home and then away. Avoiding these semi-repeaters is important. Also, projecting the importance of a game (i.e., television and ticket revenue) can help maximize these projections. For example, team rivalries lead to higher television revenue and ticket sales. The Boston Red Sox and New York Yankees are intense rivals (the Sox beat out the Yankees ultimately to win the World Series in October 2004), so it was no accident that the computerized optimization scheduling system selected these teams to play on opening day.

COMPUTERIZED MATHEMATICAL MODELING AND SCHEDULING

Although each team views the schedule from its own perspective, the whole process of scheduling has become more of a science than an art. Computerized modeling systems can take into consideration the types of constraints necessary to limit travel (i.e., keeping costs down) and balance this against creating what is predicted to be an exciting series of games at times when the demand for tickets and televised revenue will be highest. Mike Trick and George Nemhauser of The Sports Scheduling Group (**sports-scheduling.com**) have developed computerized mathematical models for scheduling MLB. Overall, preparing a schedule is very complex because it is difficult to balance the goals of maximizing revenue, maximizing travel efficiencies, maintaining competitive fairness, and accommodating the needs of the many constituent groups, including fans, coaches, players, the media, sponsors, and facility owners and operators. All these diverse stakeholders not only want a say in the schedule but benefit in different ways from it.

The complexity of creating a schedule increases dramatically with the number of teams. Ten teams, as in the SEC, can produce more solutions than are possible for a person to consider in a lifetime. MLB has two leagues and 30 teams; each team plays 162 games per season, for a total of 2,430 games over six months. Complicating the schedule are interleague play and blackout dates when the various venues are unavailable. Road trips have to be limited to 20 consecutive days, back-to-back home and away series between the same two teams have to be avoided, and the schedule has to be balanced between division rivals (i.e., Boston Red Sox vs. the New York Yankees). Some of these are hard constraints that must be met, while others are soft constraints which can be relaxed but not too much.

Standard optimization models and methods could not be used to create a schedule for MLB. Trick and Nemhauser adapted a number of methods and computer codes, and they ultimately produced, refined, and solved a complicated but solvable mathematical model, producing several viable MLB schedules. MLB officials could then choose a schedule from those presented. In the process of refinement, new requests necessitated tweaking the model and method to produce the desired results.

RESULTS

Although it faced an extremely complex problem, The Sports Scheduling Group, through its modeling and implementation skills, produced an MLB schedule that is quite robust in that it takes into consideration the major objectives and constraints in a fair fashion for all stakeholders. Although the exact cost of creating the schedule and the increase in revenue and other benefits are not publicly available, clearly they have all improved quite a bit. MLB officials are very pleased with the results. In addition to producing the MLB schedule, The Sports Scheduling Group has developed viable schedules for several National Collegiate Athletic Association sports conferences.

Sources: Adapted from B. Gerson, "Trick and Colleagues Produce Master Schedule for Major League Baseball's 2005 Season," *Carnegie Mellon Today*, April 4, 2005 "Trick and Colleagues Produce Master Schedule for Major League Baseball's 2005 Season," *Tepper Magazine*, Spring 2005; "Matchmakers vs. the Machine," *Sports Illustrated*, November 1, 2004; "Striking It Big," *Pittsburgh Business Times*, November 12, 2004; "MLB Gets a New Scheduler for '05: Husband–Wife Team Out Bid After 24 Years," *New York Times*, December 1, 2004 (and **espn.com**); M. Knobler, "In This Business, There's a Time, Place for Everything," *The Atlanta Journal-Constitution*, September 26, 2005, pp. D1, D13; The Sports Scheduling Group, **sports-scheduling.com**; and J.E. Aronson, *The Southeastern Conference (SEC) Baseball Scheduling Process for a Decade*, private communication, December 2005.

QUESTIONS FOR THE CASE

1. Describe the conflicting goals of the MLB schedule. Relate them to the stakeholders as you describe them.
2. Explain why the MLB scheduling situation results in such a complex problem and why computerized mathematical models are ideally suited to solving it.
3. Describe the kinds of benefits that can be obtained by using this type of scheduling modeling approach.
4. Describe some non-sports areas in which these kinds of methods and models can be applied.
5. Even though the client managers (i.e., decision makers), really did not understand the methodology used, they were able to use the results effectively. Explain why this is a reasonable thing for them to do.

References

Aronson, J.E. (1989). "A Survey of Dynamic Network Flows." *Annals of Operations Research*, Vol. 20, pp. 1–66.

Arsham, H. (2006a). *Modeling and Simulation Resources.* **home.ubalt.edu/ntsbarsh/Business-stat/RefSim.htm** (accessed March 2006).

Arsham, H. (2006b). *Decision Science Resources.* **home.ubalt.edu/ntsbarsh/Business-stat/Refop.htm** (accessed March 2006).

Buehlmann, U., C.T. Ragsdale, and B. Gfeller. (2000). "A Spreadsheet-Based Decision Support System for Wood Panel Manufacturing." *Decision Support Systems*, Vol. 29, No. 3, pp. 207–227.

Camm, J.D., T.E. Chorman, F.A. Dill, J.R. Evans, D.J. Sweeney, and G.W. Wegryn. (1997, January/February). "Blending OR/MS, Judgment, and GIS: Restructuring P&G's Supply Chain," *Interfaces*, Vol. 27, No. 1, pp. 128–142.

Clemen, R.T., and T. Reilly. (2000). *Making Hard Decisions with Decision Tools Suite*. Belmont, MA: Duxbury Press.

Dembo, R., A. Aziz, D. Rosen, and M. Zerbs. (2000). *Mark-to-Future: A Framework for Measuring Risk and Reward*. Toronto: Algorithmics Publications.

Denardo, E.V. (2001, August). "The Science of Decision Making." *OR/MS Today*, Vol. 28, No. 4.

Dias, L.C., and J.N. Climaco. (2002, July 4–7). "A Multi-Criteria DSS for Group Decisions Using Value Functions with Imprecise Information." *Proceedings of DSIage 2002*, Cork, Ireland.

Dignan, L. (2004, August). "Waste Not." Case 130, *Baseline*.

Dronzek, R. (2001, November). "Improving Critical Care." *IIE Solutions*, Vol. 33, pp. 42–47.

Drummond, H. (2001). *The Art of Decision Making*. New York: Wiley.

Gabriel, S.A., A.S. Kydes, and P. Whitman. (2001, January/February). "The National Energy Modeling System: A Large-Scale Energy-Economic Equilibrium Model." *Operations Research*. Vol. 49, No. 1, pp. 14–25.

Gallagher, S. (2002, November). "Grand Test Auto." *Baseline*. No. 12.

Gareiss, R. (2002, December 2). "Chief of the Year: Ralph Szygenda." *InformationWeek*.

Goodwin, P., and G. Wright. (2000). *Decision Analysis for Management Judgment*, 2nd ed. New York: Wiley.

Gung, R.R., Y.T. Leung, G.Y. Lin, and R.Y. Tsai. (2002, December). "Demand Forecasting Today." *OR/MS Today*, Vol. 29, No. 6.

Hall, M. (2002a, April 1). "Web Analytics: Get Real." *Computerworld*, Vol. 36, No. 14.

Hall, M. (2002b, July 1). "Decision Support Systems." *Computerworld*, Vol. 36, No. 27, p. 11.

Hillier, F.S., and G.J. Lieberman. (2005). *Introduction to Operations Research*, 8th ed. New York: McGraw-Hill.

Horner, P. (2000, June). "The SABRE Story." *OR/MS Today*, Vol. 27, No. 3, pp. 46–47.

Hsiang, T. (2002, June). "How to Conduct Product Mix Analysis." *OR/MS Today*, Vol. 29, pp. 36–39.

Jovanovic, N. (2002, September). "Task Scheduling in Distributed Systems by Work Stealing and Mugging: A Simulation Study." *Journal of Computing and Information Technology*, Vol. 10, No. 3.

Kearns, G.S. (2004, January–March). "A Multi-Objective, Multi-Criteria Approach for Evaluating IT Investments: Results from Two Case Studies." *Information Resources Management Journal*, Vol. 17, No. 1, pp. 37–62.

Kelly, A. (2002). *Decision Making Using Game Theory: An Introduction for Managers*. Cambridge, UK: Cambridge University Press.

Koksalan, M., and S. Zionts (eds.). (2001). *Multiple Criteria Decision Making in the New Millennium*. Berlin: Springer-Verlag.

Koller, G.R. (2000). *Risk Modeling for Determining Value and Decision Making*. Boca Raton, FL: CRC Press.

Kontoghiorghes, E.J., B. Rustem, and S. Siokos. (2002). *Computational Methods in Decision Making, Economics, and Finance*. Boston: Kluwer.

Laporte, G., F.V. Louveeaux, and L. Van Hamme. (2002, May/June). "An Integer L-Shaped Algorithm for the Capacitated Vehicle Routing Problem with Stochastic Demands." *Operations Research*, Vol. 50, No. 3, pp. 415–423.

LeBlanc, L.J., D.R. Randalls, and T.K. Swann. (2000). "Heery International's Spreadsheet Optimization Model for Assigning Managers to Construction Projects." *Interfaces*, Vol. 30, No. 6, pp. 95–106.

Marchant, B. (2002, October). "Virtual Tune-up: Simulated Design and Upkeep for a Fighter-Jet Engine." *AV Video Multimedia Producer*.

Miller, M.L. (2005). *MIS Cases*, 3rd ed. Upper Saddle River, NJ: Prentice Hall.

Monahan, G.E. (2000). *Management Decision Making: Spreadsheet Modeling, Analysis, and Applications*. Cambridge, UK: Cambridge University Press.

Mukherjee, A. (2001, August 9–11). "Advanced Decision Support Tools in Airline Scheduling, Planning and Operations," *Proceedings of the PRISM Symposium*, West Lafayette, IN.

Nielsen, K. (ed.). (2003). *Uncertainty in Economic Decision Making: Ambiguity Mental Models and Institutions.* Northampton, MA: Edward Elgar.

Pooley, R., and P. Wilcox. (2000, April). "Distributing Decision Making Using Java Simulation Across the World Wide Web." *Journal of the Operational Research Society*, Vol. 51, No. 4, pp. 395–404.

Powell, S.G., and K.R. Baker. (2003). *The Art of Modeling with Spreadsheets: Management Science, Spreadsheet Engineering, and Modeling Craft*. New York: Wiley.

ProModel. (1999). *ProModel Saves DuPont $480,000*. **promodel.com**.

ProModel. (2006, March). *Fiat Case*. **promodel.com**.

Ragsdale, C. (2004). *Spreadsheet Modeling and Decision Analysis*, 4th ed., Cambridge, MA: South-Western College Publishing.

Respicio, A., M.E. Captivo, and A.J. Rodrigues (2002, July 4–7). "A DSS for Production Planning and Scheduling in the Paper Industry." *Proceedings of DSIage2002*, Cork, Ireland.

Rossetti, M.D., and F. Selandar. (2001, December). "Multiobjective Analysis of Hospital Delivery Systems." *Computers & Industrial Engineering*, Vol. 41, No. 3, pp. 309–333.

Saltzman, R.M., and V. Mehrotra. (2001, May/June). "A Call Center Uses Simulation to Drive Strategic Change." *Interfaces*, Vol. 31, No. 3, pp. 87–101.

Seila, A., V. Ceric, and P. Tadikamalla. (2003). *Applied Simulation Modeling*. Pacific Grove, CA: Duxbury Press.

Selic, B. (1999, October). "Turning Clockwise: Using UML in the Real-Time Domain." *Communications of the ACM*, Vol. 42, No. 10, pp. 46–54.

Smith, B.C., D.P. Gunther, B.V. Rao, and R.M. Ratliff. (2001, March/April). "E-Commerce and Operations Research in Airline Planning, Marketing, and Distribution." *Interfaces*, Vol. 31, No. 2, pp. 37–55.

Sodhi, M.S., and M. Aichlmayr. (2001, September). "Intelligent Software and the Web: The Brain Behind the Brawn." *Transportation & Distribution*, Vol. 42, No. 9.

Stackpole, B. (2005, May 15). "Virtually Flawless?" *CIO*.

Stojkovic, M., and F. Soumis. (2001, September). "An Optimization Model for the Simultaneous Operational Flight and Pilot Scheduling Problem." *Management Science*, Vol. 47, No. 9, pp. 1290–1305.

Swisher, J.R., S.H. Jacobson, J.B. Jun, and O. Balci. (2001). "Modeling and Analyzing a Physician Clinic Environment Using Discrete-Event (Visual) Simulation." *Computers & Operations Research*. Vol. 28, No. 2, pp. 105–125.

Taha, H. (2006). *Operations Research: An Introduction*, 8th ed. Upper Saddle River, NJ: Prentice Hall.

Teradata. (2003). *Burlington Northern Santa Fe*. **teradatalibrary.com/pdf/eb3082.pdf** (accessed March 2006).

Trick, M. (2003, January). "Best Possible Outcome." *Optimize Magazine*, No. 15, pp. 36–41.

Turban, E., and J. Meredith. (1994). *Fundamentals of Management Science*, 6th ed. Homewood, IL: Irwin.

Van der Heijden, M.C., A. van Harten, and M.J.R. Ebben. (2002, July/August). "Using Simulation to Design an Automated Underground System for Transporting Freight around Schiphol Airport." *Interfaces*, Vol. 32, No. 4, pp. 1–19.

Whiting, R. (2003, May 12). "Business-Intelligence Buy-in." *InformationWeek*.

Winston, W.L., and S.C. Albright. (2006). *Spreadsheet Modeling and Applications Essentials of Practical Management Science*. Cambridge, MA: Thomson South-Western.

Witzerman, J.P. (2001, August 9–11). "Using Robotic Simulation to Support General Motors Paint Shops." *Proceedings of the PRISM Symposium*, West Lafayette, IN.

PART

III

Business Intelligence

Learning Objectives for Part III

- Understand the drivers for business intelligence (BI) initiatives in modern organizations
- Understand the structure, components, and process of BI
- Learn about data warehouses and data marts
- Learn about the different models of business analytics (BA)
- Gain familiarity with data visualization in BI
- Learn advanced analytic applications, including data, text, and Web mining, and their current and potential uses
- Gain familiarity with the techniques that are used in data mining
- Learn about business performance management (BPM)/corporate performance management (CPM)

In this part of the book, we embark on examining an exciting phenomenon in modern organizations: emerging efforts to use BI to improve decision making, enhance strategic position, and sustain competitive advantage. This part includes five chapters (5 through 9), which are described in the special introductory section that follows.

Special Introductory Section: The Essentials of Business Intelligence

Section III includes five chapters about BI. Due to the increased importance of the topic, we elected to present a special introductory that provides an overview of the field and its strategic importance.

The following topics are presented in this special introductory section:

S.1 A PREVIEW OF THE CONTENT OF CHAPTERS 5 THROUGH 9

As discussed in Chapter 1, BI is a broad field, and it is viewed differently by different people. However, most people agree that BI includes the following major components, which constitute the chapters of Part III:

- A centralized repository of data, usually the *data warehouse (DW)*, which is the topic of Chapter 5.
- An end-user set of tools that can be used to create reports and queries from data and information and to analyze the data, information, and reports. This set of tools is referred to as *BA* and also includes data visualization; these tools are described in Chapter 6.

- To find non-obvious relationships among large amounts of data, we can use a statistical-mathematical approach known as *data mining*. For text, we can use *text mining*, and for Web data, we can use *Web mining*; all of these are described in Chapter 7. The statistical tools and the methodology for mining, including neural computing, are covered in Chapters 7 and 8.
- To gain a competitive edge, companies need to be innovative and to excel. In order to find out how well a company is performing today, where it wants to go, and how to get there, we can use a methodology referred to as *BPM*. It includes setting up goals as metrics and standards and monitoring and measuring performance by using the BI methodology. This is the topic of Chapter 9.

In this special introductory section, we describe how these parts are interrelated, to create the field of BI. For details, see Baum (2006), Biere (2003), Loschin (2003), and Thompson and Jakovljevic (2005).

S.2 THE ORIGINS AND DRIVERS OF BUSINESS INTELLIGENCE (BI)

Where did modern approaches to DW and BI come from? What are their roots, and how do those roots affect the way organizations are managing these initiatives today? Today's investments in information technology are under increased scrutiny in terms of their bottom line impact and potential. The same is true of DW and the BI applications that make these initiatives possible.

TABLE S.1 Business Value of BI Analytical Applications

Analytic Application	*Business Question*	*Business Value*
Customer segmentation	What market segments do my customers fall into, and what are their characteristics?	Personalize customer relationships for higher satisfaction and retention.
Propensity to buy	Which customers are most likely to respond to my promotion?	Target customers based on their need to increase their loyalty to your product line. Also, increase campaign profitability by focusing on the most likely to buy.
Customer profitability	What is the lifetime profitability of my customer?	Make individual business interaction decisions based on the overall profitability of customers.
Fraud detection	How can I tell which transactions are likely to be fraudulent?	Quickly determine fraud and take immediate action to minimize cost.
Customer attrition	Which customer is at risk of leaving?	Prevent loss of high-value customers and let go of lower-value customers.
Channel optimization	What is the best channel to reach my customer in each segment?	Interact with customers based on their preference and your need to manage cost.

Source: A. Ziama and J. Kasher, *Data Mining Primer for the Data Warehousing Professional.* Teradata, Dayton, OH, 2004.

Organizations are being compelled to capture, understand, and harness their data to support decision making in order to improve business operations. On the one hand, legislation and regulation (e.g., the Sarbanes-Oxley Act of 2002) has required business leaders to document their business processes and sign off on the legitimacy of the information they rely on and report to stakeholders. Moreover, business cycle times are now extremely compressed; faster, more informed, and better decision making is therefore a competitive imperative. Managers need the *right information* at the *right time* and in the *right place*. This is the mantra for modern approaches to BI. Organizations have to work smart. Paying careful attention to the management of BI initiatives is a necessary aspect of doing business (Baum, 2006). It is no surprise, then, that organizations are increasingly championing BI. The opening vignette in Chapter 1 discusses a BI success story at Toyota Motor Company. You will hear about more BI successes and the fundamentals of those successes in Chapters 5 through 9. Examples of typical applications of BI are provided in Table S.1.

S.3 THE GENERAL PROCESS OF INTELLIGENCE CREATION AND USE

The methodologies for assessing the business value of BI are complex due to the many intangible benefits of BI and the fact that the DW is an infrastructure that serves many applications. (For suggested methodologies, see Gartner, Inc., 2004; and Williams and Williams, 2003.)

Managers and executives need BI solutions to better manage the business. Enterprises that fail to properly implement these solutions put themselves at a competitive disadvantage. To be successful in today's business environment, enterprises must:

- Assess their readiness for meeting the challenges posed by these new business realities
- Take a holistic approach to BI functionality
- Leverage best practices and anticipate hidden costs

Gartner, Inc. (2004), suggested the following key questions as a framework for BI analysis:

- How can enterprises maximize their BI investments?
- What BI functionality do enterprises need, and what are they using today?
- What are some of the hidden costs associated with BI initiatives?

We will deal with these issues in Chapters 5 through 9.

An example of how BI helped a company deal with the Sarbanes-Oxley Act of 2002 is provided next (extracted from Gartner, Inc., 2004).

Example

The Sarbanes-Oxley Act of 2002 mandates drove one firm to implement a new financial performance management system, capable of meeting the new requirements to:

- Perform flawless analysis and compilation of thousands of transactions and journal entries.
- Balance more access to data with the need to control access to sensitive insider information.
- Deliver reports to the SEC in less time.

The company deployed a BI infrastructure and applications that met these challenges. Within the overarching goal of achieving financial-reporting compliance, these objectives included the following:

- Get "more eyes on the data" and key performance indicators and build in strict security controls
- Provide live reports that allow people to drill down to the lowest level of transaction detail
- Put a spotlight on the accounting treatment of material components
- Proactively scour the financial databases for anomalies, using variance triggers
- Gather all financial data into a cohesive database

An implementation tightly linked to these objectives provided the company with a financial performance management system that enables analysis to complement accounting and budgeting applications for flexible reporting, free-form investigation, and automated data analysis.

The BI infrastructure and applications support large numbers and types of users and uses automatic data mining for anomaly detection. It can proactively alert specific individuals whenever an anomaly is detected.

A CYCLICAL PROCESS

DW and BI initiatives typically follow a process similar to that used in military intelligence initiatives. In fact, BI practitioners often follow the national security model depicted in Figure S.1. The process is cyclical with a series of interrelated steps. One of the most important steps, analysis, is the main step for converting raw data to decision

FIGURE S.1 Process of Intelligence Creation and Use

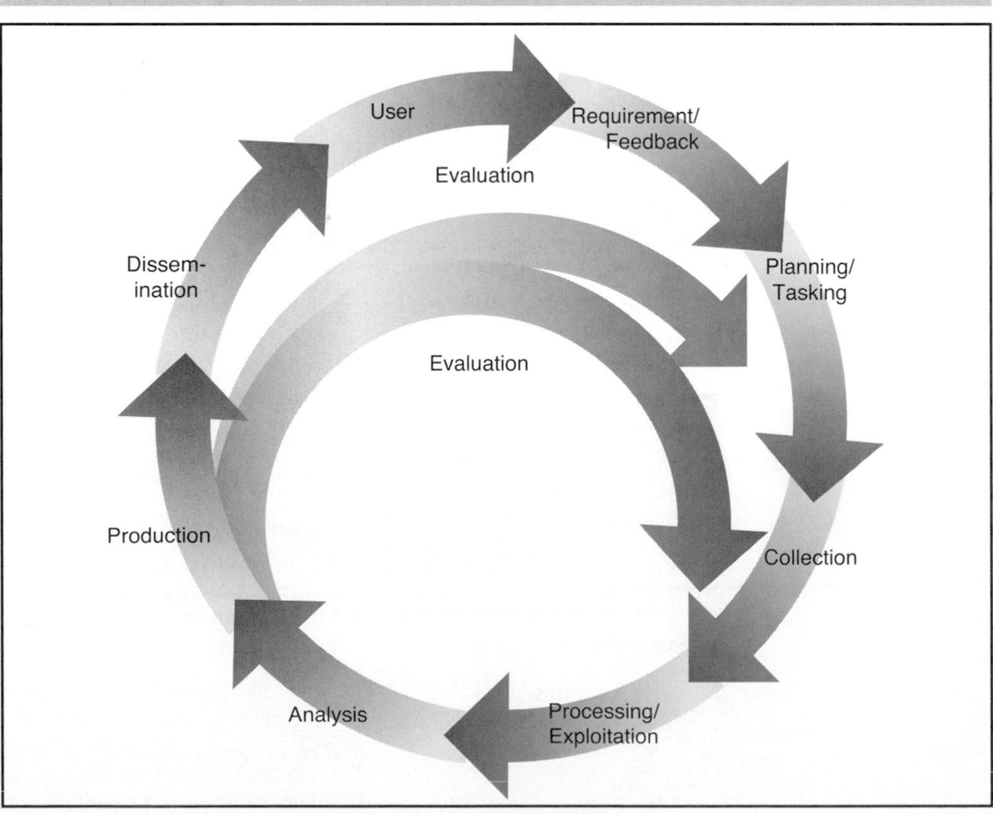

Source: L. Krizan. *Intelligence Essentials for Everyone.* Department of Defense, Joint Military Intelligence College, Washington, DC, June 1999, p. 6.

supporting information. However *analysis* isn't possible, accurate, or reliable unless other steps along the way have been properly addressed. The details of the process and its steps—including the five Ws: who, what, when, where, and why—are provided in Online File WS.1 and in Krizan (1999). More details are discussed next.

INTELLIGENCE CREATION AND USE AND BI GOVERNANCE

When a DW is in place, the general process of *intelligence creation* starts by identifying and prioritizing *specific* BI projects (see Dignan, 2003). For each potential BI project in the portfolio, it is important to use return on investments (ROI) and total cost of ownership (TCO) measures to estimate the cost–benefit ratio. This means that each project must be examined through costing associated with the general process phases as well as costs of maintaining the application for the business user. In addition, the benefits estimations need to involve end-user examinations of decision-making impacts, including measures reflecting benefits such as cash flow acceleration. Some organizations refer to the project prioritization process as a form of **BI governance** (see Matney and Larson, 2004; and Online File WS.2). A major issue is who should serve as decision makers involved in prioritizing BI projects. Some (e.g., Dignan, 2003) suggest that successful prioritization requires "middle integration." For example, we can characterize people by the organizational role they play: tops, middles, bottoms, customers, and providers. The two critical partnerships required for BI governance are a partnership between functional area heads and/or product/service area leaders (i.e., middles), and a partnership between potential customers and providers (i.e., representatives of the business side and representatives from the information technology side). Middles can look across an organization to ensure that project priorities reflect the needs of the entire business; they make sure a project does not just serve to suboptimize one area over others. Customers can offer insight into the potential usefulness of the intelligence generated in a project, and providers are important from the standpoint of reflecting delivery realities. A typical set of issues for the BI governance team is to address the following:

- Creating categories of projects (e.g., investment, business opportunity, strategic, mandatory)
- Defining criteria for project selection
- Determining and setting a framework for managing project risk
- Managing and leveraging project interdependencies
- Continually monitoring and adjusting the composition of the portfolio

Although many believe the very term *intelligence* sounds like a cloak-and-dagger euphemism for clandestine operations dedicated to stealing corporate secrets or the government's CIA, that couldn't be further from the truth. While such *espionage* does, of course, occur, intelligence involves how modern companies ethically and legally organize themselves to glean as much as they can from their customers, their business environment, their stakeholders, their business processes, their competitors, and other such sources of potentially valuable information.

But collecting data is just the beginning of intelligence. Vast amounts of data need to be catalogued, tagged, analyzed, sorted, and filtered, and they must undergo a host of other operations to yield usable information that can affect decision making and improve the bottom line. The importance of these topics increases every day, as companies track and accumulate more and more data. For example, exacerbating the exponential growth in the amount of raw data is the emergence of *radio frequency identification (RFID)*. RFID applications will likely be among the most exciting and fastest-growing application categories for the next generation of BI specialists (see

Heinrich, 2005). RFID coupled with new approaches to synthesizing information from text sources through text mining and from the Web via Web mining (see Chapter 7) suggest that organizations are on the verge of an explosive new era of BI for decision support. Also, the advance of Web use facilitates intelligence gathering (see Giovinazzo, 2002).

BI has adapted nomenclature, systems, and concepts that clearly distinguish it from its espionage-oriented counterpart of national and international intelligence. That said, there are many analogies between the two, including the fact that major effort must be expended to achieve the collection of reputable sources of intelligence, the processing of that intelligence for purity and reliability, the analysis of raw intelligence to produce usable and actionable information, and the mechanisms for the appropriate dissemination of that information to the right users.

S.4 THE MAJOR CHARACTERISTICS OF BUSINESS INTELLIGENCE

To illustrate the major characteristics of BI, first we will discuss what BI is not—namely, transaction processing.

TRANSACTION PROCESSING VERSUS ANALYTIC PROCESSING

Enterprise software systems are designed as transaction processing tools, and today, the main job is to optimize an informed decision-making process for users at all levels of the organizational hierarchy. Recent trends seem to indicate that access to key operational data is no longer the purview of executives alone. Many executives of manufacturing and service companies today are allowing (and even encouraging) low-level managers, supervisors, and analysts on the shop floor and in distribution centers access to operational performance data, to enable better and more timely decision making by those employees.

You're familiar with the information systems that support your transactions, such as ATM withdrawals, bank deposits, and cash register scans at the grocery store. The *transaction processing* systems involved with these transactions constantly handle updates to what we might call *operational databases*. For example, an ATM withdrawal transaction needs to reduce the bank balance accordingly, a bank deposit adds to an account, and a grocery store purchase is likely reflected in the store's calculation of total sales for the day and should reflect an appropriate reduction in the store's inventory for the items we bought. These **online transaction processing (OLTP)** systems handle a company's ongoing business. In contrast, a DW is typically a distinct system that provides storage for data that will be made use of in *analysis*. The intent of that analysis is to give management the ability to scour data for information about the business, and it can be used to provide tactical decision support whereby, for example, line personnel can make quicker and/or more informed decisions. We will provide a more technical definition of DW in Chapter 5; at this point, it suffices to say that DWs are intended to work with informational data used for online analytical processing (OLAP) systems (see Chapter 6).

Most operational data in enterprise resource planning (ERP) systems—and in their complementing siblings, such as *supply-chain management* (SCM) or *customer relationship management* (CRM), are stored in what is referred to as OLTP systems, which are computer-processing systems in which the computer responds immediately to user requests. Each request is considered to be a *transaction*, which is a computerized record of a discrete event, such as the receipt of inventory or a customer order. In other words, a transaction requires a set of two or more database updates that must be completed in an all-or-nothing fashion.

The very design that makes an OLTP system efficient for transaction processing makes it inefficient for end-user ad hoc reports, queries, and analyses. In the 1980s, many business users referred to their mainframes as "the black hole" because information went into it but none ever came back out. All requests for reports had to be programmed by the IT staff, and only canned reports could be generated on a scheduled basis; ad hoc real-time querying was virtually impossible. Although the client/server-based ERP systems of the 1990s were somewhat more report friendly, they were still a far cry from the desired usability by regular, nontechnical, end users for things such as operational reporting and interactive analysis. To resolve these issues, the notions of DW and BI were created.

THE INFORMATION FACTORY VIEW

The term *warehouse* is associated with the concept of a factory. Factories have their own warehouses, receive supplies from warehouses, and deliver finished products to them. Indeed, some use the phrase *enterprise information factory* as a way to describe how companies conduct and organize BI efforts. A cornerstone component of that factory concept is the DW (see Inmon, 2005).

The information factory view sees BI/DW as a central, critical component of any business organization (corporate or government), and today it is moving more and more toward the Web environment (see Inmon, 2005). As with a physical factory, with an information factory, there are *inputs* (e.g., data sources, acquisition), *storage* (e.g., DW, data marts), *processing of inputs* (e.g., analysis, data mining), and *outputs* (e.g., data delivery, BI applications). Details on this as well as details about an information factory for governments are available at **inmoncif.com**.

An information factory is connected to other internal information systems, such as ERP, CRM, and e-commerce, as well as to external information systems, usually via the Internet or an extranet. The information factory concept is illustrated in Figure S.2.

DATA WAREHOUSING AND BUSINESS INTELLIGENCE

A DW is a collection of data, designed to support management decision making. DW*s* contain a wide variety of data that present a coherent picture of business conditions at a single point in time. The theory was to create a database infrastructure that is always online and that contains all the information from the OLTP systems, including historical data, but reorganized and structured in such a way that it is fast and efficient for querying, analysis, and decision support.

TERADATA ADVANCED ANALYTICS METHODOLOGY

Teradata, a division of NCR **(teradata.com)**, created a methodology for BI that is illustrated in Figure S.3. As shown in the figure, BI applications (upper-left side) are supported by advanced analytics techniques and tools (left side). The methodology is shown on the right side as a cyclical process that circles the enterprise DW. The process includes steps such as business understanding and data understanding (right side of figure). Some of the advanced analytical tools are described in Chapters 6 and 7.

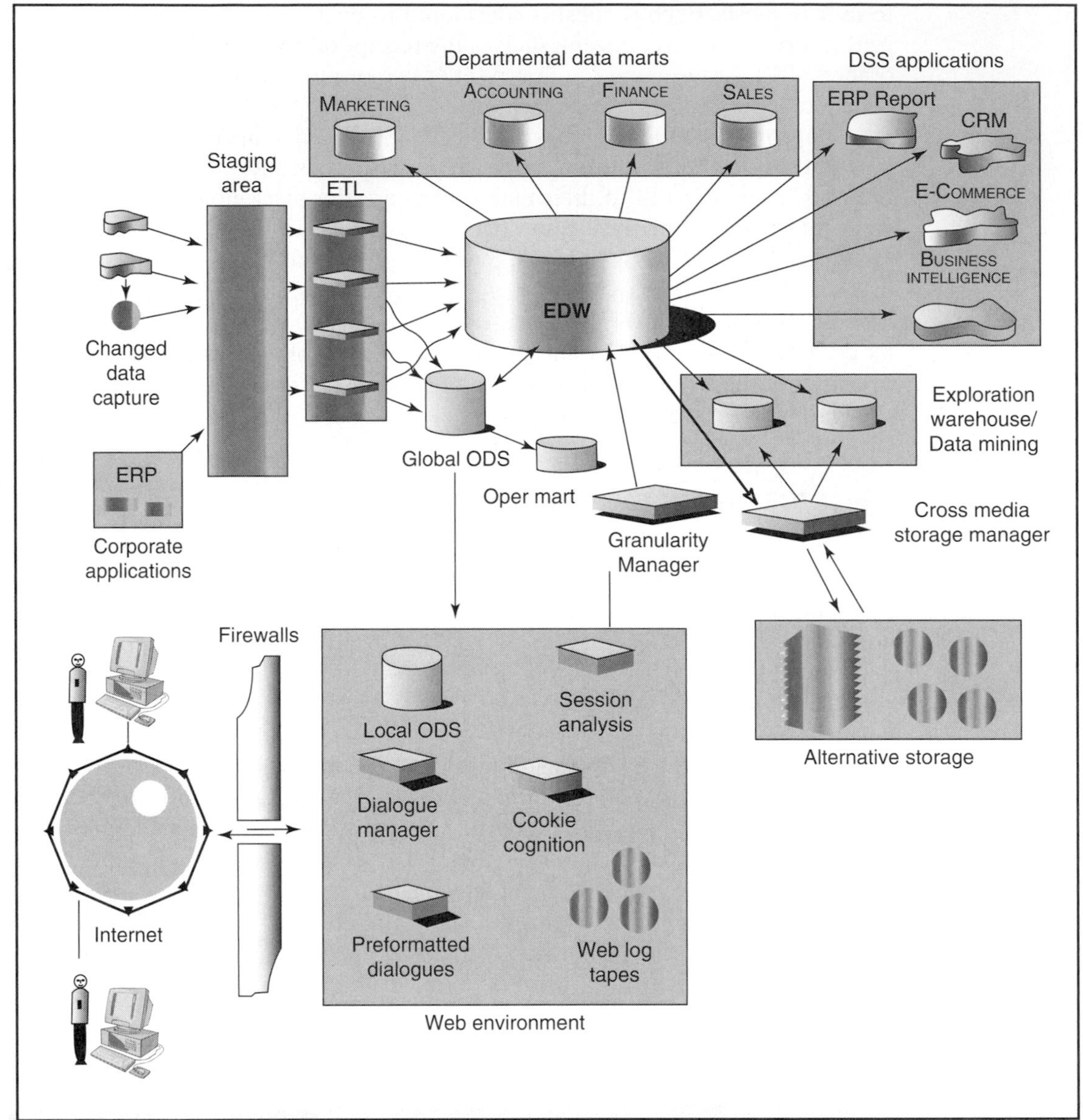

FIGURE S.2 The Corporate Information Factory

Source: Inmon Data Systems, **inmoncif.com/library/cif/**.

The Teradata methodology provides a business-focused approach, comprising all the techniques that help build models, enable new views of data, assist in simulation to create different scenarios, and help understand realities as well as predict future states and results. (Details are available in different issues of the free online magazine *Teradata Magazine*, at **teradatamagazine.com**.)

Separating the OLTP from analysis and decision support enables the benefits of BI that were described in Chapter 1 and that provides for competitive intelligence and advantage, as described next.

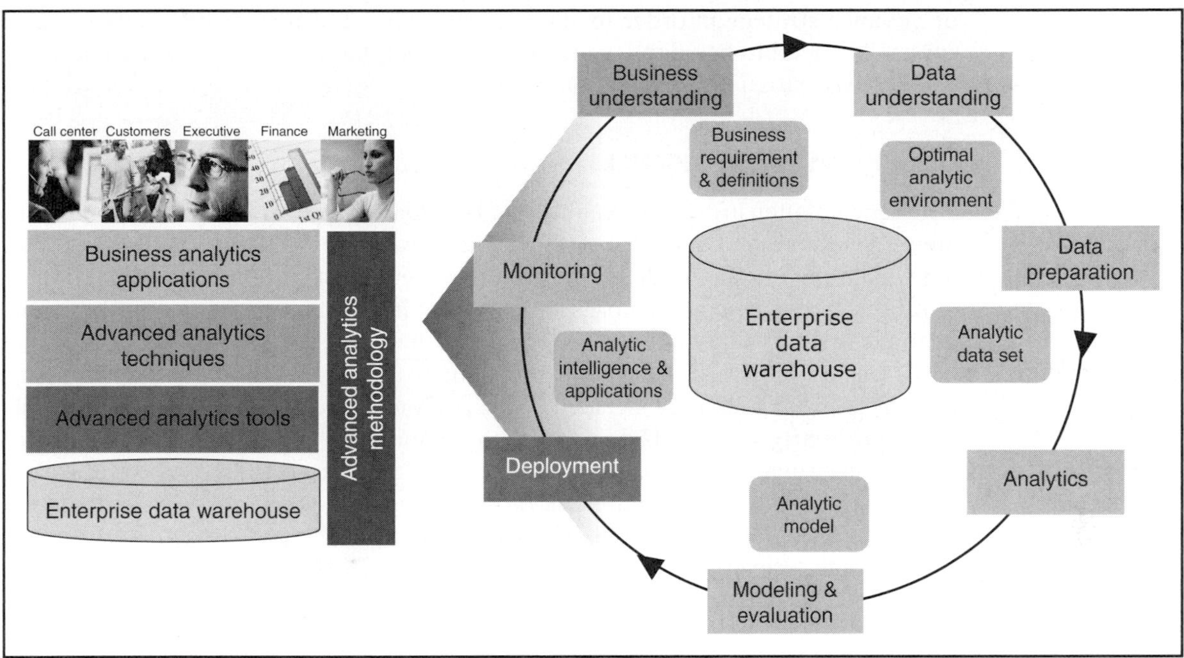

FIGURE S.3 Teradata Advanced Analytics Methodology

Source: Teradata, a division of NCR Corp.

S.5 TOWARD COMPETITIVE INTELLIGENCE AND ADVANTAGE

Many believe that the major contribution of BI is the role it plays in giving companies strategic advantage.

STRATEGIC IMPERATIVE

BI projects have shown significant business value to organizations (see Williams and Williams, 2003). In addition to ROI, TCO, and other tangible cost–benefit analyses, there is increasing evidence that BI initiatives are becoming a *strategic imperative*. Several benefits of BI factors are shaping this emerging belief. First, in many markets, "barriers to entry of a new competitor to an industry" (see Porter, 1985) are being significantly diminished. This means that an organization that has a strong position within its industry could easily face new competitors because the costs and other constraints to becoming a player in the market have decreased. This is due to increasing globalization, as companies from around the world are challenging major players in industries such as automobile manufacturing, electronics, textile manufacturing, and computer software development, just to name a few. Furthermore, the ability to deliver goods throughout the world through readily available supply-chain channels such as FedEx, UPS, and DHL, as well as e-commerce, is making it easier for potential competitors to get products and services to more customers almost anywhere. Similarly, companies are finding better or less expensive suppliers all around the globe.

Organizations today must carefully understand what is happening in every facet of their operation, their industry, and the business environment, and they must nurture the ability to constantly improve processes when necessary. Organizations must change or advance strategy in order to stay one step ahead of increasing competitive pressures; they need to be adaptive and agile. This is related to an emerging field of study called *competitive intelligence (CI)*.

COMPETITIVE INTELLIGENCE

Although CI often involves more than the BI initiatives used in most organizations, there are some important overlaps. One difference between CI and BI is that CI implies tracking what competitors are doing by gathering sources of materials on their recent and in-process activities. For example, it may be that important competitive information can be found in sources such as transcripts of agency hearings, public court documents, and the paper trails of governmental agencies where there are patent filings. In BI initiatives, some outside sources of data are included in the analysis process, but they are often available from third-party vendors. For example, an organization might want to combine demographic information such as population characteristics, weather, and so on with data on customers, and it might purchase those demographic data and integrate them with their customer data for analysis. Members of the Society of Competitive Intelligence Professionals (**scip.org**) view BI as an emerging aspect of their overall charter, which typically includes more generic competitor analysis. For details, see Chapter 6.

COMPETITIVE STRATEGY IN AN INDUSTRY

Competitor analysis is a component of *industry analysis*, which serves as a basis for strategic planning processes. Several generic strategies are commonly based on an industry analysis for strategic planning (see Porter, 1985). For example, an organization may choose to be a low-cost leader in a particular market. If it can maintain its low-cost leadership strategy, then the barriers to entry are high because another organization would find it difficult to compete. Competitive intelligence in this context would imply that companies need to know if some major new means of producing/generating/delivering a service or product would result in significantly lower costs, thereby shifting the competitive landscape. BI applications in this context might include scrutinizing quality metrics associated with specific production processes, analyzing raw materials from various suppliers to assess defect rates, tracking costs of goods sold as a percentage of run volume, and so on. In addition, BI applications can generate business rules that can actually be integrated with business processes. For example, there is a form of BI called *clickstream analysis* that uses information gathered from users who visit a Web site (see Chapter 6).

Another competitive strategy is to focus on a particular *market niche*, perhaps through some form of product or service differentiation. This means that a specific market segment that has a special preference, perhaps for upscale goods and services, would be the target of the strategy. There are many applications of BI in this context (e.g., to make sure customer needs are met and loyalty is built, to track customer preferences and remember those preferences in the next customer encounter). For example, having a hotel room prepared according to a business traveler's common wishes, with the appropriate newspaper delivered in the morning, might be a way to build loyalty to serve a lucrative market niche. Also, a gambling concern, such as the Harrah's case in Exercise 3 at the end of this chapter, might focus on a BI-based approach to building loyalty; in this approach, customers get the same treatment if they are in any of the geographical locations of the company's business, and their information from the associated loyalty program is also available in each location. The rewards they earn from visiting any location accrue with the company, creating a loyal and frequently returning customer, which is the targeted, high-value market niche. In addition, the reward program creates a product and service *differentiation* from the very large and more opulent casinos that may exist in only one location.

SUSTAINING COMPETITIVE ADVANTAGE

As with other IT investments, attempting to achieve a competitive advantage is only one aspect. Another very important aspect is the ability to *sustain* that advantage. Organizations do this through building brand and customer loyalty, for example, through BI applications for product differentiation/market niche strategies. Most strategic analysts agree that low-cost leadership may not yield a sustainable advantage unless the low cost can be sustained. For this reason, BI projects and DW are becoming increasingly important weapons in sustaining competitive advantage across industries; the type of BI projects might vary based on strategy, and, in particular, the BI governance team might prioritize potential projects based on their ability to offer sustained competitive advantage. Thus, even with advantageous TCO and ROI calculations, an intangible aspect such as a strategic imperative is one of the main reasons organizations adopt BI.

S.6 THE TYPICAL DATA WAREHOUSE AND BUSINESS INTELLIGENCE USER COMMUNITY

Which personnel in an organization would be the most likely to make use of BI? One of the most important aspects of a successful DW/BI initiative is that it must be of benefit to the enterprise as a whole. This implies that there are likely to be a host of users in the enterprise, many of whom should be involved from the outset of a DW investment decision. Not surprisingly, there are likely to be users who focus at the strategic level and those who are more oriented to the tactical level. An appropriate framework for describing user communities is to discuss the following categories: farmers, tourists, operators, explorers, and miners (suggested by Imhoff and Pettit, 2004). The details are provided in Online File WS.3.

TABLE S.2 Matching User Types and Functionality to Maximum Value

			Types of Users			
Functionality	***IT***	***Power Users***	***Executives***	***Functional Managers***	***Occasional Information Consumers***	***Extranet: Partners and Customers***
Number of users	Few	Dozens	Dozens	Dozens to hundreds	Hundreds to thousands	Hundreds to thousands
BI tools and functions	Developer, administrator, metadata, security, data management	Ad hoc query, OLAP reports, data mining, advanced analysis	Dashboard, scorecard, reports, CPM	Reports, spreadsheets, OLAP view, business activity monitoring (BAM), corporate performance management (CPM)	Reports, spreadsheets	Reports
Strategic value		High	High	Medium	Low	High
←Extranet→	←……Intranet……					……→

Source: Gartner, Inc., 2004.

Gartner, Inc. (2004), distinguishes six similar types of users. Table S.2 shows these different users, how many there are, what BI tools they use, and the strategic value of their usage.

The various classes of DW and BI users that exist in an organization can help to guide how the DW is structured and the types of BI tools and other supporting software needed. Members of each group are excellent sources of information on assessing the costs and benefits of specific BI projects when a DW is in place.

S.7 SUCCESSFUL BUSINESS INTELLIGENCE IMPLEMENTATION

From the discussion in Section S.6, it is obvious that one important characteristic of a company that excels in its approach to BI is a proper appreciation for different classes of potential users. But what are some of the other important characteristics? First and foremost, the fundamental reasons for investing in BI must be aligned with the company's business strategy. BI cannot simply be a technical exercise for the IS department. It has to serve as a way to change the manner the company conducts business by improving its business processes and transforming decision-making processes to be more data driven.

Many BI consultants and practitioners involved in successful BI initiatives advise that a framework for planning is a necessary precondition. One framework, developed by Gartner, Inc. (2004), decomposes planning and execution into business, organization, functionality, and infrastructure components. At the business and organizational levels, it is important to define strategic and operational objectives while considering the available organizational skills to achieve those objectives. Upper managers need to consider issues of organizational culture surrounding BI initiatives and building enthusiasm for those initiatives and procedures for the intraorganizational sharing of BI best practices. It is also important to have in place plans to prepare the organization for change. One of the first steps in that process is to assess the IS organization, the skill sets of the potential classes of users, and whether the culture is amenable to change. This assessment is required before any significant investments are made. From this assessment, and assuming that there is reason to move ahead, a company can prepare a detailed action plan. (For details, see Online File WS.4.) A critical issue for BI implementation success is the integration of several BI projects (most enterprises use several BI projects) with each other and with the other IT systems in the organization and its business partners.

Gartner, Inc. (2004), prepared a comprehensive report regarding the implementation of BI and its relationships to other enterprise systems, such as ERP and CRM; this report also provides interesting case studies. The report covers the following major topics:

- BI trends and technologies
- Effective BI approaches for today's business world
- Organizing for BI success
- Best practices for defining effective business metrics
- Building an agile infrastructure for strategic BI
- The benefits of effective data quality and metadata management
- Managing costs and enhancing value of DW and BI
- Business trends and best practices in managing corporate performance
- The BPM road map

- Key trends in corporate governance and compliance management
- Using business activity monitoring to gain a real-time edge
- Getting the most out of ERP through BI
- The role of analytics in successful CRM strategies
- Web analytics: From software to service model
- Driving workplace productivity with portals and enterprise suites

If a company's strategy is properly aligned with the reasons for a DW and BI initiatives, if the company's IS organization is or can be made capable of playing its role in such a project, and if the requisite user community is in place and has the proper motivation, it is wise to start BI and establish a BI competency center (BICC) within the company. What can a company's BICC achieve? Following are several potential achievements, as exemplified by France Telecom (see Application Case S.1):

- The center can demonstrate how BI is clearly linked to strategy and execution of strategy.
- The center can serve to encourage interaction between the potential business user communities and the IS organization.
- The center can serve as a repository and disseminator of best BI practices between and among the different lines of business.
- Standards of excellence in BI practices can be advocated and encouraged throughout the company.
- The IS organization can learn a great deal through interaction with the user communities, such as knowledge about the variety of types of analytical tools needed.
- The business user community and IS organization can better understand why the DW platform must be flexible enough to provide for changing business requirements.
- The BICC can help important stakeholders, such as high-level executives, see how BI can play an important role.

For more on BICC, see Gartner, Inc. (2004).

Application Case S.1

France Telecom Business Intelligence

In a short period of time, France Telecom transitioned from being France's only telecom provider to one of several in an industry that was becoming deregulated. With new competitors rapidly entering the telecom market, France Telecom's executives knew they had to use their information systems as a major strategic weapon. They initiated a repositioning under the banner of becoming the "Net Company." This required substantial rethinking to foster information systems standardization throughout the company and its subsidiaries. To this end, they set out to migrate all applications to a technical architecture more suitable for Web-based capabilities. In the past, the company had been organized on a regional basis, with each regional business unit managing its own IT budget. This led to the coexistence of a myriad of dissimilar technologies, applications software versions, and so on.

Standardization was a first step in laying an infrastructure foundation for a major DW and BI initiative. The company established a four-person team to facilitate its BICC. The BICC was charged with overseeing the data warehousing implementation, ensuring that different business units and BI teams share best practices, and maintaining consistency in all BI-related projects. The BICC was responsible for several important tasks. First, the BICC was charged with providing consulting and development services, including offering advice to project managers on deployment strategies with respect to design, auditing, installation, and so on. Second, the BICC provided support for project managers, architects, designers, developers, and operators via a hotline and help desk. Support also included an intranet Web site to provide BI tool advice, tips, methodology advice, and installation documentation. Next, the BICC was the designated negotiator for the company with BI vendors. The BICC centralized the opening of all case files; requests for product upgrades; certification of new software versions; and tracking, distribution, and maintenance of license agreements. Finally, the BICC helped support end users with tools to help them become more autonomous, including an intranet site dedicated to user support, online training, and interactive help. The intranet site was also used to disseminate information on BI success stories (i.e., projects that resulted in superior performance in line with the company's strategy and objectives). To that end, the site was a source of information for executives on the state of the BI initiative in delivering business value.

In summary, France Telecom's BICC was developed to help the organization manage its portfolio of BI projects, standardize analytical approaches across the enterprise, train and educate end users, help power users, provide knowledge management through the sharing of best practices, and handle all associated vendor relations and support. France Telecom's service to more than 91 million customers in 220 countries on 5 continents has been significantly enhanced through its DW and ongoing BI projects. As an example of executive leadership's support for the BICC and its initiatives, the director of operations for Customer Relations Information Systems stated, "To win new customers and develop loyalty, we now base our action on a business intelligence process in which BI plays a key role of retrieving and analyzing data in our corporate resources. Today, the company has 130,000 PCs, nearly half of which run BI software."

Sources: Compiled from the Business Objects case study *France Telecom Business Intelligence in Action*, 2002, **businessobjects.com/pdf/success/France_Telecom.pdf** (accessed April 2006); and Gartner, Inc., *Using Business Intelligence to Gain a Competitive Edge*, 2004.

Another important success factor of BI is to facilitate a real-time, on-demand environment.

ATTAINING REAL-TIME, ON-DEMAND BI

The demand for instant, on-demand access to dispersed information has grown as the need to close the gap between the operational data and strategic objectives has become more pressing. As a result, a category of products called *real-time BI* applications have emerged. The introduction of new data-generating technologies, such as RFID, is accelerating this growth and the subsequent need for real-time BI. Traditional BI systems use a large volume of *static* data that have been extracted, cleansed, and loaded into a *DW* to produce reports and analyses. However, the need is not just reporting because users need business monitoring, performance analysis, and an understanding of why things are happening. These can alert users, virtually in real-time, about changes in data or the availability of relevant reports, alerts, and notifications regarding events and emerging trends in Web, e-mail, or instant messaging (IM) applications. In addition, business applications can be programmed to act on what these real-time BI systems discover. For example, an SCM application might automatically place an order for more "widgets" when real-time inventory falls below a certain threshold, or a CRM application might automatically trigger a customer service representative and credit control clerk to check a customer who has placed an online order larger than $10,000.

The first approach to real-time BI uses the DW model of traditional BI systems. In this case, products from innovative BI platform providers such as Ascential **(ascential.com)** or Informatica **(informatica.com)** provide a service-oriented, near-real-time solution that populates the DW much faster than the typical nightly extraction, transformation, and load (ETL) batch update does (see Chapter 5). The second approach to real-time BI is commonly called *business activity monitoring* (BAM; see Chapter 9). This approach is used by pure-play BAM and hybrid BAM middleware providers such as Savvion **(savvion.com)**, Iteration Software **(itteration.com)**, Vitria **(vitria.com)**, webMethods **(webmethods.com)**, Quantive **(quantive.com)**, and Tibco **(tibco.com)**. It bypasses the DW entirely and uses

Web services or other monitoring means to discover key business events. These software monitors (or *intelligent agents*) can be placed on a separate server in the network or on the transactional application databases themselves, and they can use event- and process-based approaches to proactively and intelligently measure and monitor operational processes. Also, the use of the Web facilitates real-time BI (Giovinazzo, 2002).

For further details on attaining real-time, on-demand BI, see Thompson and Jakovljevic (2005).

S.8 STRUCTURE AND COMPONENTS OF BUSINESS INTELLIGENCE

In Chapter 1, we presented the high-level architecture of BI (refer to Figure 1.7). Here, we present more details. The major components are presented in Figure S.4 and described in the following sections.

THE DATA WAREHOUSE

Starting from the left side of Figure S.4, you see data flow from operational systems (e.g., CRM, ERP) to a DW, which is a special database or repository of data that has been prepared to support decision-making applications ranging from those for

FIGURE S.4 The Major Components of Business Intelligence

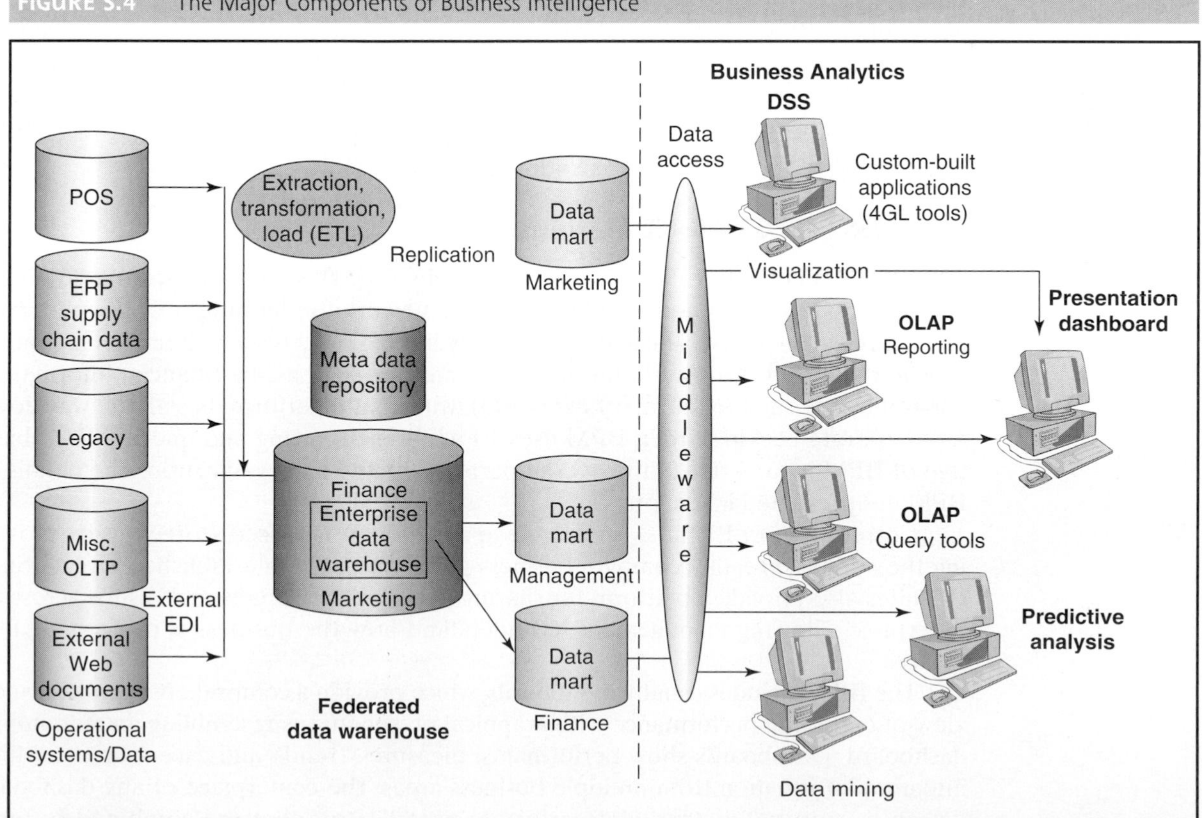

Drawn by E. Turban

simple reporting and querying to complex optimization. The DW is constructed with methodologies, mainly metadata and ETL, as described in Chapter 5. Also described there are *data marts*, which are repositories of a particular subject or department (e.g., marketing).

BUSINESS ANALYTICS

Many software tools allow users to create on-demand reports and queries and to conduct analysis of data. They appear originally under the name **online analytical processing (OLAP).** For example, users can analyze different dimensions of multidimensional data, such as time series and trend analysis views. Hence, business users can quickly and easily identify performance trends by using time-phased information analysis and graphing capabilities of products that support more sophisticated data analysis and have full calculated field capabilities integrated into Chapter 6. To conduct BA, the user needs interactivity software that is called *middleware* to access the DW. It is considered *infrastructure*, and it is a user interface to the system.

DATA MINING

Data mining is a class of database information analysis that looks for hidden patterns in a group of data that can be used to predict future behavior. For example, it can help retail companies find customers who have common interests. However, the term is commonly misused to describe software that presents data in new ways because true data mining software does not just change the presentation but actually *discovers* previously unknown relationships among the data; this knowledge is then applied to achieving specific business goals. These tools are used to replace or enhance human intelligence by scanning through massive storehouses of data to discover meaningful new correlations, patterns, and trends, by using pattern recognition technologies and advanced statistics. Data mining is described in Chapter 7, with its powering technologies, such as neural networks, are described in Chapter 8.

BUSINESS PERFORMANCE MANAGEMENT

The final component of the BI process is BPM/CPM. This component is based on the *balanced scorecard* methodology, which is a framework for defining, implementing, and managing an enterprise's business strategy by linking objectives with factual measures. In other words, it is a way to link top-level metrics, such as the financial information created by the chief financial officer (CFO), with actual performance all the way down the corporate pecking order. BPM uses BI analysis reporting and queries. The objective of BPM is to optimize the overall performance of an organization. The details of BPM are presented in Chapter 9.

Currently, most BI suites enable the application of balanced scorecards by providing the ability to readily compare business performance with established targets. Such BI suites also provide a platform for sharing performance targets and results across an enterprise, allowing management to understand how the business is performing at a glance.

The BPM includes usually **dashboards**, which provide a comprehensive, at-a-glance, view of corporate performance with graphical presentations resembling an automobile dashboard. Dashboards show performance measures, trends, and exceptions, and they integrate information from multiple business areas. The centerpiece of any dashboard design is captured metrics and performance indicators that are combined to form graphs reflecting the health of the business.

S.9 CONCLUSION: BUSINESS INTELLIGENCE TODAY AND TOMORROW

In today's highly competitive business, the quality and timeliness of business information for an organization is not just a choice between profit and loss; it may be a question of survival or bankruptcy. No business organization can deny the inevitable benefits of BI. Recent industry analyst reports show that in the coming years, millions of people will use BI visual tools and analytics every day (see Baum, 2006).

Today's organizations are deriving more value from BI by extending actionable information to many types of employees, maximizing the use of existing data assets. Producers, retailers, governments, special agencies, and others use visualization tools, including dashboards. More and more industry-specific analytical tools will flood the market to do almost any kind of analysis and help to make informed decision making from the top level to the user level.

A potential trend involving BI is its possible merger with artificial intelligence (AI). AI has been used in business applications since the 1980s, and it is widely used for complex problem-solving and decision support techniques in real-time business applications (see Chapters 12–14). It will not be long before AI applications are merged with BI, bringing in a new era in business. To enable this integration, BI vendors are starting to use service-oriented architecture (see Lal, 2005) and enterprise information integration (EII). See Thompson and Jakovljevic (2005).

BI is spreading its wings to cover small, medium, and large companies. Large BI players are for large enterprises, and small, niche players service midsize and small companies. Analytics tools are also penetrating the market for very specialized functions, which will help some companies to go just for BA instead of full DW-based BI implementation.

BI takes advantage of already developed and installed components of IT technologies, helping companies leverage their current IT investments and use valuable data stored in legacy and transactional systems. For many large-size companies that have already spent millions of dollars building DW and data marts, now is the right time to build BI as the next step to get the full benefit of their investment, which will directly affect ROI. However, although some components of BI, such as the DW, may change (e.g., data may be stored online), the need for conducting BI in our rapidly changing business environment will increase, making BI a necessity. For more on the future of BI, see Lal (2005).

S.10 RESOURCES, LINKS, AND THE TERADATA UNIVERSITY NETWORK CONNECTION

The use of this chapter and most other chapters in this book can be enhanced by the tools described in the following sections.

RESOURCES AND LINKS

We recommend looking at the following resources and links for further reading and explanations:

- Bez Systems **(bez.com)**
- IT Toolbox Business Intelligence Knowledge Base **(businessintelligence.ittoolbox.com)**

- datawarehousing.com **(datawarehousing.com)**
- Business Intelligence and Data Warehousing Insight Portal **(datawarehousingonline.com)**
- *DM Review* **(dmreview.com)**
- DSS Resources **(dssresources.com)**
- AISWorld Net **(isworld.org)**
- The Data Administration Newsletter **(tdan.com)**
- The Data Warehousing Institute **(tdwi.org)**
- *Teradata Magazine* **(teradatamagazine.com)**

THE TERADATA UNIVERSITY CONNECTION

Teradata University Network (TUN; **teradatastudentnetwork.com**, for students) provides a wealth of information and cases on BI. All cases and white papers that involve aspects of decision making are DSS relevant pieces of literature.

Key Terms

- BI governance
- dashboard
- online analytic processing (OLAP)
- online transaction processing (OLTP)

QUESTIONS FOR DISCUSSION

1. How does the "when" issue relate to "right time" and to requirements for the DW infrastructure?
2. Why is evaluating tangible benefits of ROI or TCO for a DW investment insufficient? Why is it difficult?
3. What is BI governance?
4. What is a portfolio approach to BI governance?
5. What is competitive intelligence?
6. What upper management issues must be assessed prior to launching a DW/BI initiative?
7. What additional questions—beyond those discussed in this section regarding the assessment of the IS organization—would you want to have answers to before you invest in a DW project?
8. What are the most important roles that a BICC plays in an organization?
9. Why is it necessary to use BPM methodology? Why not just use BI analysis?

Exercises

Teradata University and Other Hands-on Exercises

1. Go to **teradatastudentnetwork.com** and find the paper titled "Data Warehousing Supports Corporate Strategy at First American Corporation" (by Watson, Wixom, and Goodhue). Read the paper and answer the following questions:
   a. What were the drivers for the DW/BI project in the company?
   b. What strategic advantages were realized?
   c. What operational and tactical advantages were achieved?
   d. What were the critical success factors (CSF) for the implementation?
2. Go to **teradatastudentnetwork.com** and find the Web seminar titled *Enterprise Business Intelligence: Strategies and Technologies for Deploying BI on a Large Scale* (by Eckerson and Howson). View the Web seminar and answer the following:
   a. What are the benefits of deploying BI to the many?

b. Who are the potential users of BI? What does each type of user attempt to achieve?
c. What implementation lessons did you learn from the seminar?

3. Go to **teradatastudentnetwork.com** and find the Harrah's case (by Watson and Volonino). Answer the following:
   a. What were the objectives of the project?
   b. What was the role of the DW?
   c. What kind of analyses were used?
   d. What strategic advantages does the BI provide?
   e. What is the importance of an executive innovator?

References

Baum, D. (2006, March/April). "The Face of Intelligence." *ORACLE Magazine*.

Biere, M. (2003). *Business Intelligence for the Enterprise*. Upper Saddle River, NJ: Prentice Hall.

Dignan, K.G. (2003, September). "Project Portfolio Management for BI." *TDWI*.

Gartner Inc. (2004). *Using Business Intelligence to Gain a Competitive Edge. A special report*. Stamford, CT: Gartner, Inc., **gartner.com**.

Giovinazzo, W.A., (2002). *Internet-Enabled Business Intelligence*. Upper Saddle River, NJ: Prentice Hall.

Heinrich, C. (2005). *RFID and Beyond*. Indianapolis: Wiley.

Imhoff, C., and R. Pettit. (2004). *The Critical Shift to Flexible Business Intelligence*. Boulder, CO: Intelligent Solutions, Inc.

Inmon, W.H. (2005). *Building Data Warehouses*, 4th ed. New York: Wiley, C. (2001, June 14). "Calculating Data Warehousing ROI." *Data Warehousing and Business Intelligence*.

Krizan, L. (1999, June). *Intelligence Essentials for Everyone*. Washington, DC: Department of Defense, Joint Military Intelligence College.

Lal, V. (2005). *The Future of Business Intelligence*. Santa Clara, CA: Hyperion.

Loschin, D. (2003). *Business Intelligence: The Savvy Manager's Guide*. San Francisco: Morgan Kaufmann.

Matney, D., and D. Larson. (2004, Summer). "The Four Components of BI Governance." *Business Intelligence Journal*.

Porter, M.E. (1985). *Competitive Strategy: Techniques for Analyzing Industries and Competitors*, 2nd ed. New York: The Free Press.

Thompson, O., and P.J. Jakovljevic. (2005, July 16). *Business Intelligence Status Report*. Montreal: Technology Evaluation Centers Inc, **technologyevaluation.com**.

Williams, S., and N. Williams. (2003, Fall). "The Business Value of Business Intelligence." *Business Intelligence Journal*.

Data Warehousing

Learning Objectives

- ◆ Understand the basic definitions and concepts of data warehouses
- ◆ Understand data warehousing architectures
- ◆ Describe the processes used in developing and managing data warehouses
- ◆ Explain data warehousing operations
- ◆ Explain the role of data warehouses in decision support
- ◆ Explain data integration and the extraction, transformation, and load (ETL) processes
- ◆ Describe real-time (active) data warehousing
- ◆ Understand data warehouse administration and security issues

The concept of data warehousing has been around since the late 1980s. This chapter provides the foundation for an important type of database, called a data warehouse, that is used increasingly for decision support and provides improved analytical capabilities. We discuss data warehousing in the following sections:

5.1 Opening Vignette: Continental Airlines Flies High with Its Real-Time Data Warehouse
5.2 Data Warehousing Definitions and Concepts
5.3 Data Warehousing Process Overview
5.4 Data Warehousing Architectures
5.5 Data Integration and the Extraction, Transformation, and Load (ETL) Processes
5.6 Data Warehouse Development
5.7 Real-Time Data Warehousing
5.8 Data Warehouse Administration and Security Issues
5.9 Resources, Links, and the Teradata University Network Connection

5.1 OPENING VIGNETTE: CONTINENTAL AIRLINES FLIES HIGH WITH ITS REAL-TIME DATA WAREHOUSE

As business intelligence (BI) becomes a critical component of daily operations, real-time data warehouses that provide end users with rapid updates and alerts generated from transactional systems are increasingly being deployed. Real-time data warehousing and BI, supporting its aggressive Go Forward business plan, have helped Continental

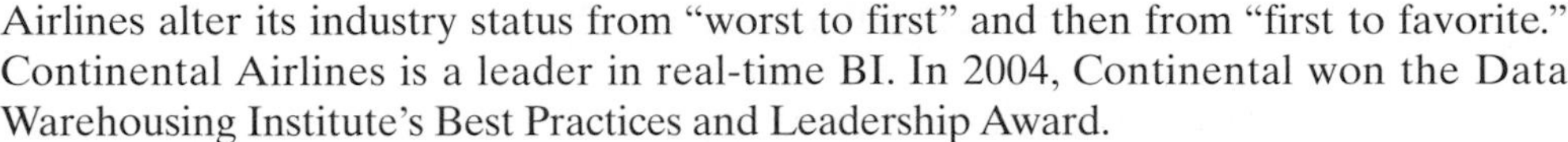

Airlines alter its industry status from "worst to first" and then from "first to favorite." Continental Airlines is a leader in real-time BI. In 2004, Continental won the Data Warehousing Institute's Best Practices and Leadership Award.

BIG PROBLEMS

Continental Airlines was founded in 1934, with a single-engine Lockheed aircraft in the Southwestern U.S. As of 2006, Continental (Houston) is the fifth largest airline in the United States and the seventh largest in the world. Continental has the broadest global route network of any U.S. airline, with more than 2,300 daily departures to more than 227 destinations.

Back in 1994, Continental was in deep financial trouble. It had filed for Chapter 11 bankruptcy protection twice and was heading for its third, and probably final, bankruptcy. Ticket sales were hurting because performance on factors that are important to customers was dismal, including a low percentage of on-time departures, frequent baggage arrival problems, and too many customers turned away due to overbooking.

SOLUTION

The revival of Continental began in 1994, when Gordon Bethune became CEO and initiated the Go Forward plan, which consisted of four interrelated parts to be implemented simultaneously. Bethune targeted the need to improve customer-valued performance measures by better understanding customer needs as well as customer perceptions of the value of services that were and could be offered. Financial management practices were also targeted for a significant overhaul. As early as 1998, the airline had separate databases for marketing and operations, all hosted and managed by outside vendors. Processing queries and instigating marketing programs to its high-value customers were time-consuming and ineffective. In additional, information that the workforce needed to make quick decisions was simply not available. In 1999, Continental chose to integrate its marketing, IT, revenue, and operational data sources into a single, in-house, enterprise data warehouse (EDW). The data warehouse provided a variety of early, major benefits.

As soon as Continental returned to profitability and ranked first in the airline industry in many performance metrics, Bethune and his management team raised the bar by escalating the vision. Instead of just performing best, they wanted Continental to be their customers' favorite airline. The Go Forward plan established more actionable ways to move from first to favorite among customers. Technology became increasingly critical for supporting these new initiatives. In the early days, having access to historical, integrated information was sufficient. This produced substantial strategic value. But it became increasingly imperative for the data warehouse to provide real-time, actionable information to support enterprise-wide tactical decision making and business processes.

Luckily, the warehouse team had expected and arranged for the real-time shift. From the very beginning, the team had created an architecture to handle real-time data feeds into the warehouse, extracts of data from legacy systems into the warehouse, and tactical queries to the warehouse that required almost immediate response times. In 2001, real-time data became available from the warehouse, and the amount stored grew rapidly. Continental moves real-time data (ranging from to-the-minute to hourly) about customers, reservations, check-ins, operations, and flights from its main operational systems to the warehouse. Continental's real-time applications include the following:

- Revenue management and accounting
- Customer relationship management (CRM)

- Crew operations and payroll
- Security and fraud
- Flight operations

BENEFITS

In the first year alone, after the data warehouse project was deployed, Continental identified and eliminated over $7 million in fraud and reduced costs by $41 million. With a $30 million investment in hardware and software over six years, Continental has reached over $500 million in increased revenues and cost savings in marketing, fraud detection, demand forecasting and tracking, and improved data center management. The single, integrated, trusted view of the business (i.e., the single version of the truth) has led to better, faster decision making.

Continental is now identified as a leader in real-time BI, based on its scalable and extensible architecture, practical decisions on what data are captured in real-time, strong relationships with end users, a small and highly competent data warehouse staff, sensible weighing of strategic and tactical decision support requirements, understanding of the synergies between decision support and operations, and changed business processes that use real-time data. (For a sample output screen from the Continental system, see **teradata.com/t/page/139245/**.)

Sources: Adapted from H. Wixom, J. Hoffer, R. Anderson-Lehman, and A. Reynolds, "Real-Time Business Intelligence: Best Practices at Continental Airlines," *Information Systems Management Journal*, Winter 2006, pp. 7–18; R. Anderson-Lehman, H. Watson, B. Wixom, and J. Hoffer, "Continental Airlines Flies High with Real-Time Business Intelligence," *MIS Quarterly Executive*, Vol. 3, No. 4, December 2004, pp. 163–176 (available at **teradatauniversitynetwork.com**); H. Watson, "Real Time: The Next Generation of Decision-Support Data Management," *Business Intelligence Journal*, Vol. 10, No. 3, 2005, pp. 4–6; M. Edwards, "2003 Best Practices Awards Winners: Innovators in Business Intelligence and Data Warehousing," *Business Intelligence Journal*, Fall 2003, pp. 57–64; R. Westervelt, *Continental Airlines Builds Real-Time Data Warehouse*, August 20, 2003, **searchoracle.techtarget.com**; R. Clayton, "Enterprise Business Performance Management: Business Intelligence + Data Warehouse = Optimal Business Performance," *Teradata Magazine*, September 2005, **teradata.com/t/page/139245/**; and The Data Warehousing Institute, *2003 Best Practices Summaries: Enterprise Data Warehouse*, 2003, **tdwi.org/display.aspx?ID=6749**.

Questions for the Opening Vignette

1. Describe the benefits of implementing the Continental Go Forward strategy.
2. Explain why it is important for an airline to use a real-time data warehouse.
3. Examine the sample system output screen at **teradata.com/t/page/139245/**. Describe how it can assist the user in identifying problems and opportunities.
4. Identify the major differences between the traditional data warehouse and a real-time data warehouse, as was implemented at Continental.
5. What strategic advantage can Continental derive from the real-time system as opposed to a traditional information system?

WHAT WE CAN LEARN FROM THIS VIGNETTE

The opening vignette illustrates the strategic value of implementing a data warehouse, along with its supporting BI methods. Continental was able to move from being one of the worst-ranked airlines, in bankruptcy, to a top-notch carrier in a short time, generating significant increases in revenue and reductions in costs. The cost reductions in the first full year of deployment more than covered the six-year investment in the system. The data warehouse integrated various databases throughout the organization into a

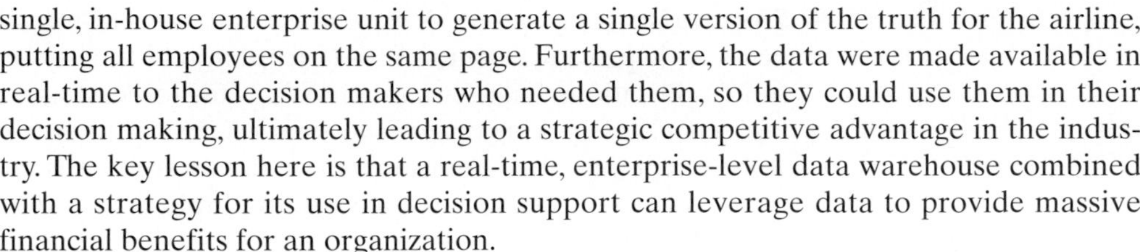

single, in-house enterprise unit to generate a single version of the truth for the airline, putting all employees on the same page. Furthermore, the data were made available in real-time to the decision makers who needed them, so they could use them in their decision making, ultimately leading to a strategic competitive advantage in the industry. The key lesson here is that a real-time, enterprise-level data warehouse combined with a strategy for its use in decision support can leverage data to provide massive financial benefits for an organization.

5.2 DATA WAREHOUSING DEFINITIONS AND CONCEPTS

Using real-time data warehousing in conjunction with decision support systems (DSS) and BI tools is an important way to conduct business processes. The opening vignette demonstrates a scenario in which a real-time data warehouse supported decision making, through analyzing large amounts of data from various sources to provide rapid results to support critical processes. With real-time data flows, Continental can view the current state of its business and identify problems, which is the first step toward solving problems analytically. In addition, customers can obtain real-time status on flights and other account information, so the system also provides a significant competitive advantage over competitors.

Decision makers require concise, dependable information about current operations, trends, and changes. Data are often fragmented in distinct operational systems, so managers often make decisions with partial information, at best. Data warehousing cuts through this obstacle by accessing, integrating, and organizing key operational data in a form that is consistent, reliable, timely, and readily available, where needed.

WHAT IS A DATA WAREHOUSE?

In simple terms, a **data warehouse (DW)** is a pool of data produced to support decision making; it is also a repository of current and historical data of potential interest to managers throughout the organization. Data are usually structured to be available in a form ready for analytical processing activities (e.g., online analytical processing [OLAP], data mining, querying, reporting, other decision support applications). A data warehouse is a subject-oriented, integrated, time-variant, nonvolatile collection of data in support of management's decision-making process.

CHARACTERISTICS OF DATA WAREHOUSING

A common way of introducing data warehousing is to refer to its fundamental characteristics (see Inmon, 2005):

- *Subject oriented.* Data are organized by detailed subject, such as sales, products, or customers, containing only information relevant for decision support. Subject orientation enables users to determine not only how their business is performing but why. A data warehouse differs from an operational database in that most operational databases have a product orientation and are tuned to handle transactions that update the database. Subject orientation provides a more comprehensive view of the organization.
- *Integrated.* Integration is closely related to subject orientation. Data warehouses must place data from different sources into a consistent format. To do so, they must deal with naming conflicts and discrepancies among units of measure. A data warehouse is presumed to be totally integrated.

- *Time variant (time series).* A warehouse maintains historical data. The data do not necessarily provide current status (except in real-time systems). They detect trends, deviations, long-term relationships for forecasting and comparisons, leading to decision making. There is a *temporal* quality to every data warehouse. Time is the one important dimension that all data warehouses must support. Data for analysis from multiple sources contain multiple time points (e.g., daily, weekly, monthly views).
- *Nonvolatile.* After data are entered into a data warehouse, users cannot change or update the data. Obsolete data are discarded, and changes are recorded as new data. This enables the data warehouse to be tuned almost exclusively for data access.

Some additional characteristics may include the following:

- *Web based.* Data warehouses are typically designed to provide an efficient computing environment for Web-based applications.
- *Relational/multidimensional.* A data warehouse uses either a relational structure or a multidimensional structure.
- *Client/server.* A data warehouse uses the client/server architecture to provide easy access for end users.
- *Real-time.* Newer data warehouses provide real-time, or active, data access and analysis capabilities (see Basu, 2003; and Bonde and Kuckuk, 2004).
- *Include metadata.* A data warehouse contains metadata (data about data) about how the data are organized and how to effectively use them.

Whereas a data warehouse is a repository of data, *data warehousing* is literally the entire process (see Watson, 2002). Data warehousing is a *discipline* that results in applications that provide decision support capability, allows ready access to business information, and creates business insight. There are three main types of data warehouses: data marts, operational data stores (ODS), and EDW. In addition to discussing these next, we also discuss metadata.

DATA MARTS

Whereas a data warehouse combines databases across an entire enterprise, a data mart is usually smaller and focuses on a particular subject or department. A **data mart** is a subset of a data warehouse, typically consisting of a single subject area (e.g., marketing, operations). A data mart can be either *dependent* or *independent*. A **dependent data mart** is a subset that is created directly from the data warehouse. It has the advantages of using a consistent data model and providing quality data. Dependent data marts support the concept of a single enterprise-wide data model, but the data warehouse must be constructed first. A dependent data mart ensures that the end user is viewing the same version of the data that are accessed by all other data warehouse users. The high cost of data warehouses limits their use to large companies. As an alternative, many firms use a lower-cost, scaled-down version of a data warehouse referred to as an *independent data mart*. An **independent data mart** is a small warehouse designed for a strategic business unit (SBU) or a department, but its source is not an EDW.

OPERATIONAL DATA STORES

An **operational data store (ODS)** provides a fairly recent form of customer information file (CIF). This type of database is often used as an interim staging area for a data warehouse. Unlike the static contents of a data warehouse, the contents of an ODS are updated through the course of business operations. An ODS is used for short-term decisions involving mission-critical applications rather than for the medium- and long-term decisions associated with an EDW. An ODS is similar to short-term memory in that it stores only very recent information. In comparison, a data warehouse is like long-term memory because it stores permanent information. An ODS consolidates data from multiple source systems and provides a near-real-time, integrated view of volatile, current data. The ETL processes (discussed later in this chapter) for an ODS are identical to those for a data warehouse. Finally, **oper marts** (see Imhoff, 2001) are created when operational data need to be analyzed multidimensionally. The data for an oper mart come from an ODS.

ENTERPRISE DATA WAREHOUSES (EDW)

An **enterprise data warehouse (EDW)** is a large-scale data warehouse that is used across the enterprise for decision support. It is the type of data warehouse that Continental developed, as described in the opening vignette. The large-scale nature provides integration of data from many sources into a standard format for effective BI and decision support applications. EDW are used to provide data for many types of DSS, including CRM, supply-chain management (SCM), business performance management (BPM), business activity monitoring (BAM), product lifecycle management (PLM), revenue management, and sometimes even knowledge management systems (KMS). For an example in practice, see MindTree Consulting's case study "Building an Enterprise Data Warehousing for a Major Pharmaceutical Company," available at **mindtree.com/clt/cs_dw_pharma.html**.

METADATA

Metadata are data about data (e.g., see Sen, 2004; and Zhao, 2005). Metadata describe the structure of and some meaning about data, thereby contributing to their effective or ineffective use. Mehra (2005) indicated that few organizations really understand metadata, and fewer understand how to design and implement a metadata strategy. Metadata are generally defined in terms of usage as *technical* or *business* metadata. *Pattern* is another way to view metadata. According to the pattern view, we can differentiate between *syntactic metadata* (i.e., data describing the syntax of data), *structural metadata* (i.e., data describing the structure of the data), and *semantic metadata* (i.e., data describing the meaning of the data in a specific domain).

We next explain traditional metadata patterns and insights into how to implement an effective metadata strategy via a holistic approach to enterprise metadata integration. The approach includes ontology and metadata registries; enterprise information integration (EII); extraction, transformation, and load (ETL); and service-oriented architectures (SOA). Effectiveness, extensibility, reusability, interoperability, efficiency and performance, evolution, entitlement, flexibility, segregation, user interface, versioning, versatility, and low maintenance cost are some of the key requirements for building a successful metadata-driven enterprise.

According to Kassam (2002), *business metadata* comprise information that increases our understanding of traditional (i.e., structured) data. The primary purpose of metadata should be to provide context to the reported data; that is, it provides enriching information that leads to the creation of knowledge. Business metadata, though difficult to provide efficiently, release more of the potential of structured data. The context need not be the same for all users. In many ways, metadata assist in the conversion of data and information into knowledge. Metadata form a foundation for a *metabusiness* architecture (see Bell, 2001). Tannenbaum (2002) described how to identify metadata requirements.

Vaduva and Vetterli (2001) provided an overview of metadata management for data warehousing. Zhao (2005) described five levels of metadata management maturity: (1) ad hoc, (2) discovered, (3) managed, (4) optimized, and (5) automated. These levels help in understanding where an organization is in terms of how and how well it uses its metadata.

The design, creation, and use of metadata—descriptive or summary data about data—and its accompanying standards may involve ethical issues. There are ethical considerations involved in the collection and ownership of the information contained in metadata, including privacy and intellectual property issues that arise in the design, collection, and dissemination stages (for more, see Brody, 2003).

Section 5.2 Review Questions

1. What is a data warehouse?
2. How is a data warehouse different from a database?
3. What is an ODS?
4. Differentiate among a data mart, an ODS, and an EDW.
5. Explain the importance of metadata.

5.3 DATA WAREHOUSING PROCESS OVERVIEW

Organizations, private and public, continuously collect data, information, and knowledge at an increasingly accelerated rate and store them in computerized systems. Maintaining and using these data and information becomes extremely complex, especially as scalability issues arise. In addition, the number of users needing to access the information continues to increase as a result of improved reliability and availability of network access, especially the Internet. Working with multiple databases, either integrated in a data warehouse or not, has become an extremely difficult task requiring considerable expertise, but it can provide immense benefits far exceeding its cost (see the opening vignette and Application Case 5.1).

Application Case 5.1

Data Warehousing Supports First American Corporation's Corporate Strategy

First American Corporation changed its corporate strategy from a traditional banking approach to one that was centered on CRM. This enabled First American to transform itself from a company that lost $60 million in 1990 to an innovative financial services leader a decade later. The successful implementation of this strategy would not have been possible without its VISION data warehouse, which stores information about customer behavior, such as products used, buying preferences, and client value positions. VISION provides:

- Identification of the top 20 percent of profitable customers
- Identification of the 40 to 50 percent of unprofitable customers
- Retention strategies

- Lower-cost distribution channels
- Strategies to expand customer relationships
- Redesigned information flows

Access to information through a data warehouse can enable both evolutionary and revolutionary change. First American Corporation achieved revolutionary change, moving itself into the "sweet 16" of financial services corporations.

Sources: Adapted from B.L. Cooper, H.J. Watson, B.H. Wixom, and D.L. Goodhue, "Data Warehousing Supports Corporate Strategy at First American Corporation," *MIS Quarterly*, Vol. 24, No. 4, 2000, pp. 547–567; and B.L. Cooper, H.J. Watson, B.H. Wixom, and D.L. Goodhue, *Data Warehousing Supports Corporate Strategy at First American Corporation*, SIM International Conference, Atlanta, August, 15–19, 1999.

Many organizations need to create data warehouses—massive data stores of time-series data for decision support. Data are imported from various external and internal resources and are cleansed and organized in a manner consistent with the organization's needs. After the data are populated in the data warehouse, data marts can be loaded for a specific area or department. Alternatively, data marts can be created first, as needed, and then integrated into an EDW. Often, though, data marts are not developed, but data are simply loaded onto PCs or left in their original state for direct manipulation using BI tools.

In Figure 5.1, we show the data warehouse concept. These are the major components of a data warehousing process:

- *Data sources*. Data are sourced from multiple independent operational "legacy" systems and possibly from external data providers (such as the U.S. Census). Data may also come from an online transaction processing (OLTP) or enterprise

FIGURE 5.1 Data Warehouse Framework and Views

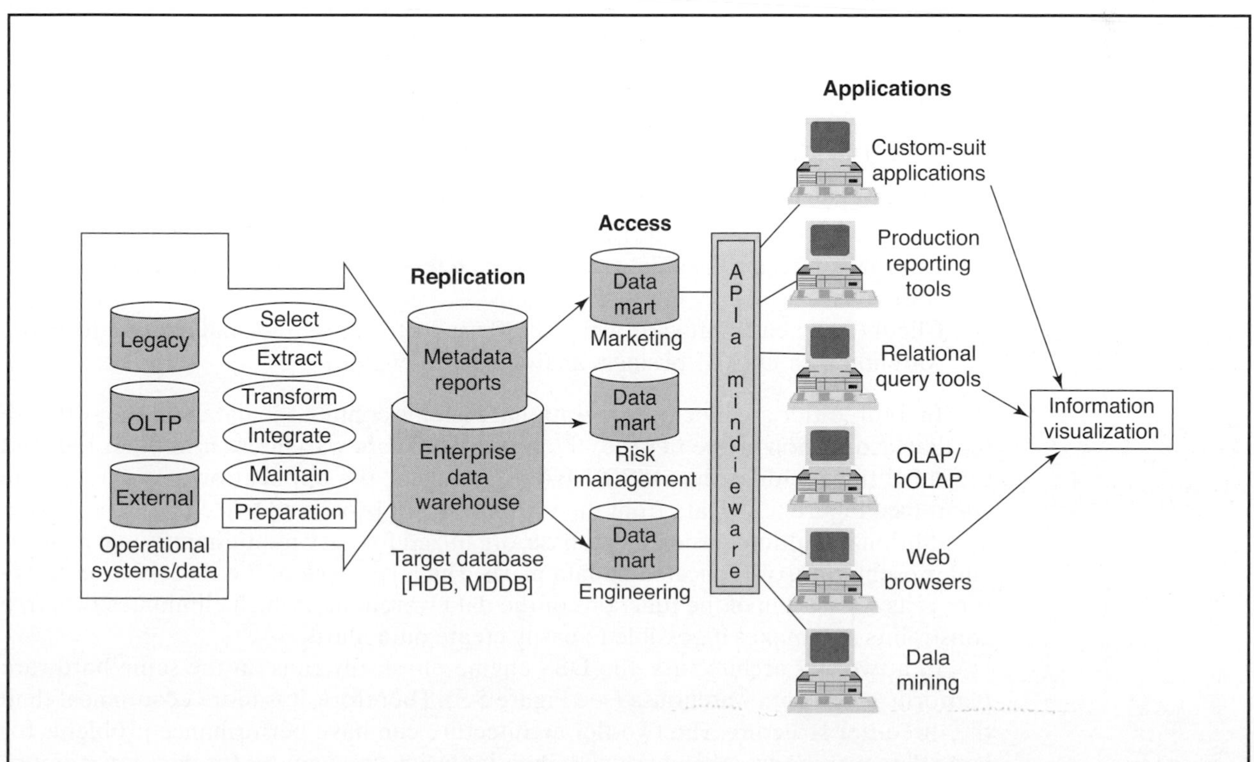

resource planning (ERP) system. Web data in the form of Web logs may also feed a data warehouse.

- *Data extraction.* Data are extracted using custom-written or commercial software called ETL.
- *Data loading.* Data are loaded into a staging area, where they are transformed and cleansed. The data are then ready to load into the data warehouse.
- *Comprehensive database.* Essentially, this is the EDW to support all decision analysis by providing relevant summarized and detailed information originating from many different sources.
- *Metadata.* Metadata are maintained so that they can be assessed by IT personnel and users. Metadata include software programs about data and rules for organizing data summaries that are easy to index and search, especially with Web tools.
- *Middleware tools.* Middleware tools enable access to the data warehouse. Power users such as analysts may write their own SQL queries. Others may employ a managed query environment, such as Business Objects, to access data. There are many front-end applications that business users can use to interact with data stored in the data repositories, including data mining, OLAP, reporting tools, and data visualization tools.

Section 5.3 Review Questions

1. Describe the data warehousing process.

2. Describe the major components of a data warehouse.

3. Identify the role of middleware tools.

5.4 DATA WAREHOUSING ARCHITECTURES

There are several basic architectures for data warehousing. Two-tier and three-tier architectures are common (see Figures 5.2 and 5.3), but sometimes there is simply one tier. Hoffer et al. (2007) distinguished among these by dividing the data warehouse into three parts:

1. The data warehouse itself, which contains the data and associated software.
2. Data acquisition (back-end) software, which extracts data from legacy systems and external sources, consolidates and summarizes them, and loads them into the data warehouse.
3. Client (front-end) software, which allows users to access and analyze data from the warehouse (a DSS/BI/business analytics [BA] engine)

In a three-tier architecture, operational systems contain the data and the software for data acquisition in one tier (i.e., the server), the data warehouse is another tier, and the third tier includes the DSS/BI/BA engine (i.e., the application server) and the client (see Figure 5.2). Data from the warehouse are processed twice and deposited in an additional multidimensional database, organized for easy multidimensional analysis and presentation, or replicated in data marts. The advantage of the three-tier architecture is its separation of the functions of the data warehouse, which eliminates resource constraints and makes it possible to easily create data marts.

In a two-tier architecture, the DSS engine physically runs on the same hardware platform as the data warehouse (see Figure 5.3). Therefore, it is more economical than the three-tier structure. The two-tier architecture can have performance problems for large data warehouses that work with data-intensive applications for decision support.

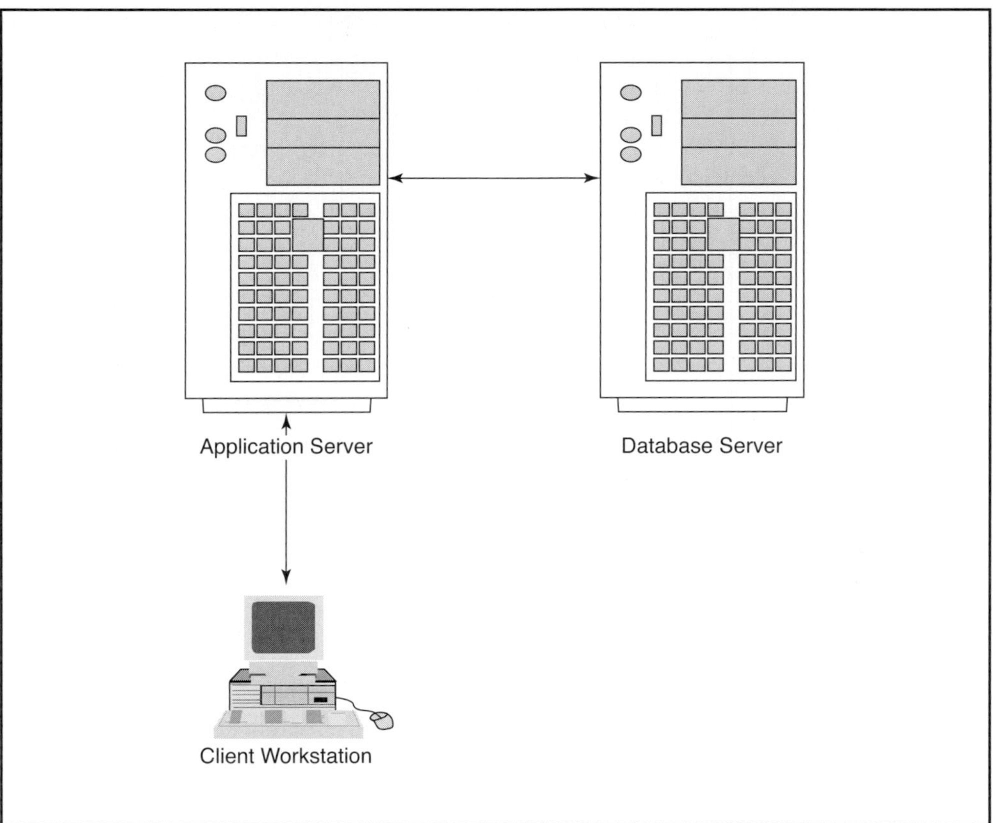

FIGURE 5.2 Architecture of a Three-Tier Data Warehouse

Much of the common wisdom assumes an absolutist approach, maintaining that one solution is better than the other, despite the organization's circumstances and unique needs. To further complicate these architectural decisions, many consultants and software vendors focus on one portion of the architecture, therefore limiting their capacity and motivation to assist an organization through the options based on its needs. But these aspects are being questioned and analyzed. For example, Ball (2005) provided decision criteria for organizations that plan to implement a BI application and have already determined their need for multidimensional data marts but need help deciding about the appropriately tiered architecture. His criteria revolve around forecasting needs for space and speed of access (see Ball, 2005, for details).

Data warehousing and the Internet are two key technologies that offer important solutions for managing corporate data. The integration of these two technologies produces Web-based data warehousing. In Figure 5.4 we show the architecture of Web-based data warehousing. The architecture is three tiered and includes the PC client, Web server, and application server. On the client side, the user needs an Internet connection and a Web browser (preferably Java enabled) through the familiar graphical user interface (GUI). The Internet/intranet/extranet is the communication medium between client and servers. On the server side, a Web server is used to manage the inflow and outflow of information between client and server. It is backed by both a data warehouse and an application server. Web-based data warehousing offers several compelling advantages, including ease of access, platform independence, and lower cost.

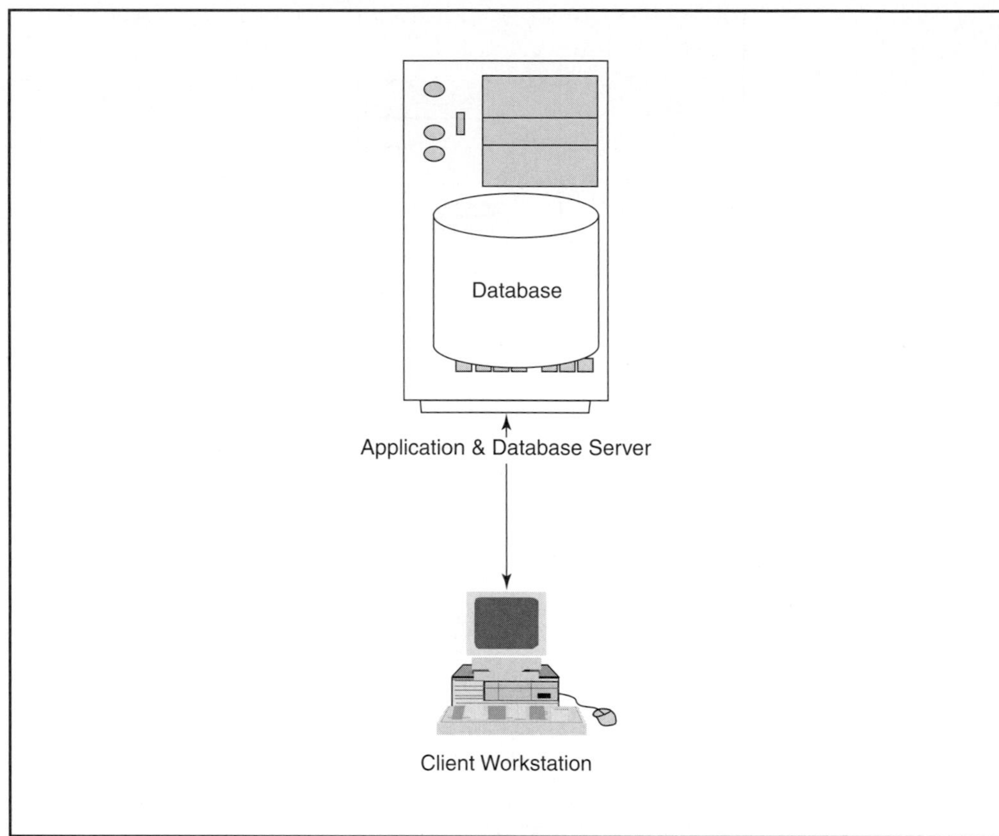

FIGURE 5.3 Architecture of a Two-Tier Data Warehouse

The Vanguard Group moved to a Web-based, three-tier architecture for its enterprise architecture to integrate all its data and provide customers with the same views of data as internal users (Dragoon, 2003). Likewise, Hilton migrated all its independent client/server systems to a three-tier data warehouse, using a Web design enterprise system. This change involved an investment of $3.8 million (excluding labor) and affected

FIGURE 5.4 Architecture of Web-Based Data Warehousing

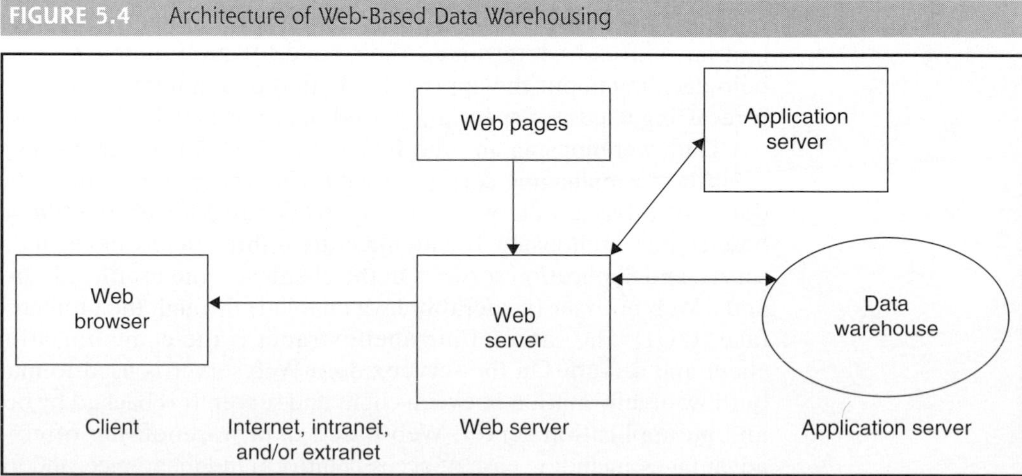

1,500 users. It increased processing efficiency (speed) by a factor of 6. When it was deployed, Hilton expected to save between $4.5 to $5 million annually. Finally, Hilton experimented with Dell's clustering (i.e., parallel computing) technology to enhance scalability and speed (see Anthes, 2003).

Web architectures for data warehousing are similar in structure to other data warehousing architectures, requiring a design choice for housing the Web data warehouse with the transaction server or as a separate server(s). Page loading speed is an important consideration in designing Web-based applications; therefore, server capacity must be carefully planned.

There are several issues to consider when deciding which architecture to use. Among them are the following:

- *Which database management system (DBMS) should be used?* Most data warehouses are built using relational database management systems (RDBMS). Oracle (Oracle Corporation, **www.oracle.com**), SQL Server (Microsoft Corporation, **microsoft.com/sql/**), and DB2 (IBM Corporation, **www.306.ibm.com/software/data/db2/**) are most commonly used. Each of these products supports both client/server and Web-based architectures.
- *Will parallel processing and/or partitioning be used?* Parallel processing enables multiple CPUs to process data warehouse query requests simultaneously and provides scalability. Data warehouse designers need to decide whether the database tables will be partitioned (i.e., split into smaller tables) for access efficiency and what the criteria will be. This is an important consideration that is necessitated by the large amounts of data contained in a typical data warehouse. Teradata (**teradata.com**) has successfully adopted this approach.
- *Will data migration tools be used to load the data warehouse?*
- *What tools will be used to support data retrieval and analysis?*

ALTERNATIVE ARCHITECTURES

The data warehouse architecture design viewpoints can be generally categorized into enterprise-wide data warehouse design and data mart design. In Figure 5.5 (a-e), we show some alternatives to the basic architectural design types, including a hub-and-spoke

FIGURE 5.5 Alternative Data Warehouse Architectures

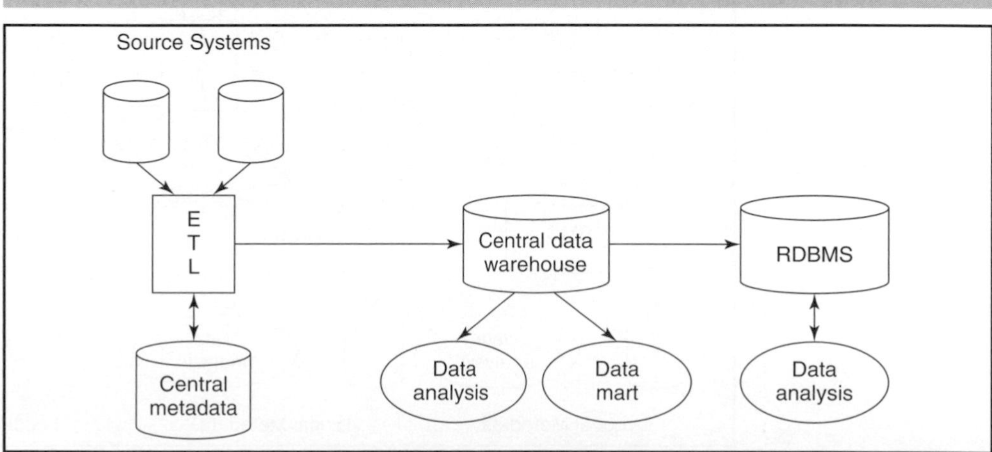

5.5a Enterprise Data Warehousing Architecture

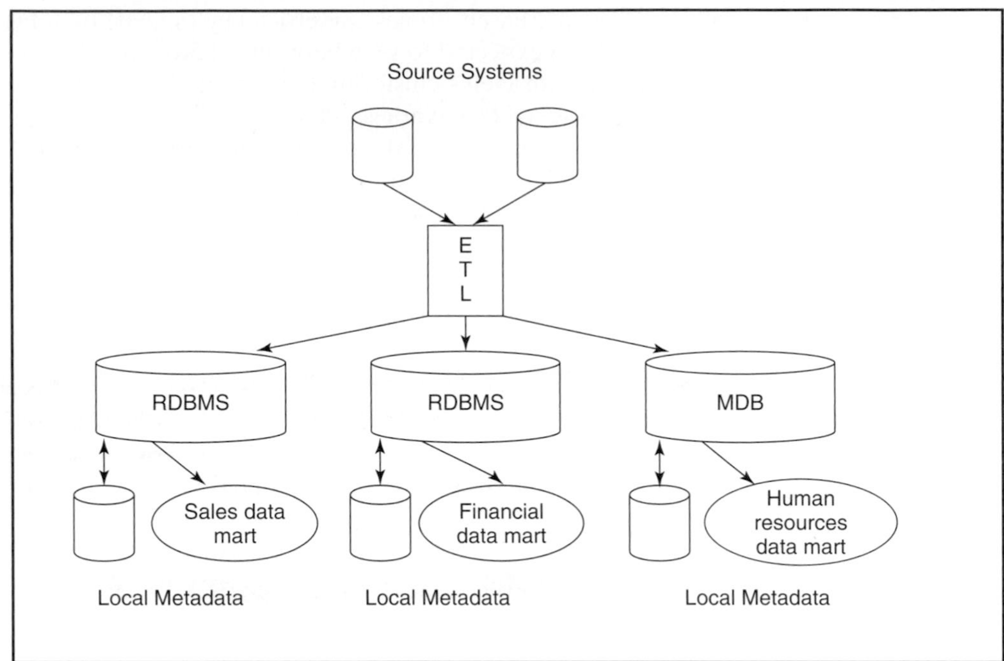

FIGURE 5.5b Data Mart Architecture

architecture, an enterprise warehouse with ODS (i.e., real-time access support), and a distributed EDW architecture. Sen and Sinha (2005) analyzed 15 different data warehousing methodologies. The sources of these methodologies are classified into three broad categories: core-technology vendors, infrastructure vendors, and information-modeling companies. See Sen and Sinha (2005) for further details.

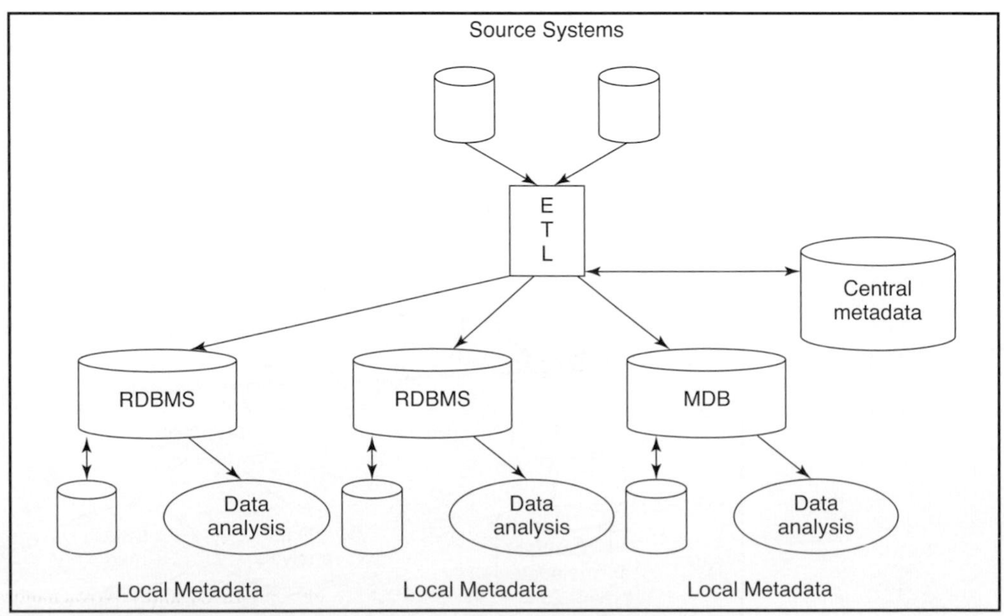

FIGURE 5.5c Hub-and-Spoke Data Mart Architecture

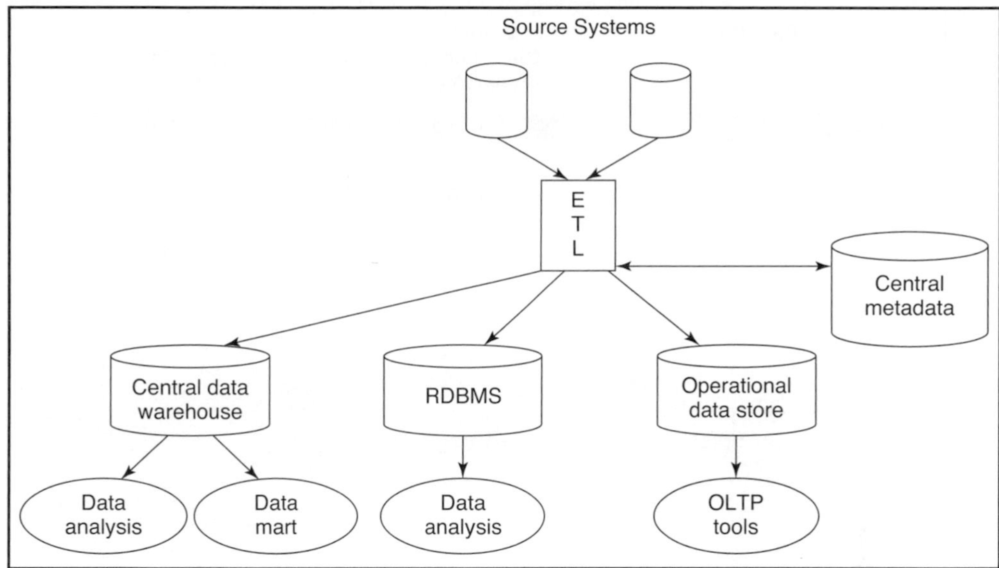

FIGURE 5.5d Enterprise Warehouse and Operational Data Store

The data warehousing literature provides additional discussions about a variety of architectures, such as independent data marts, data mart bus architecture with linked dimensional data marts, and federated data marts (see Ariyachandra and Watson, 2005, 2006a, 2006b); see Figure 5.6. In independent data marts, the marts are developed to

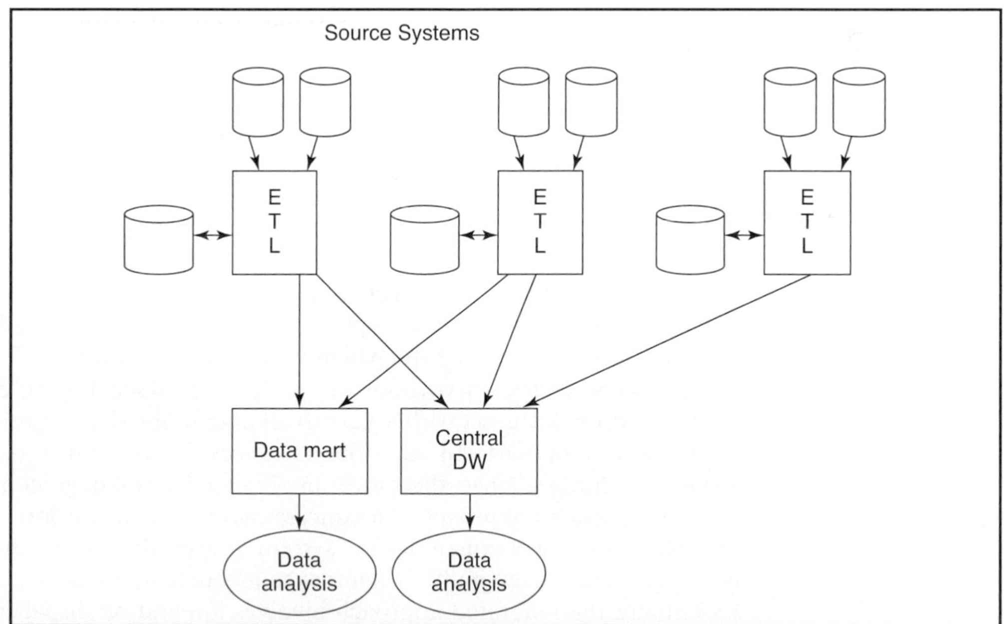

FIGURE 5.5e Distributed Data Warehouse Architecture

Source: Adapted from A. Sen and P. Sinha, "A Comparison of Data Warehousing Methodologies," *Communications of the ACM,* Vol. 48, No. 3, 2005, pp. 78–84; and T. Ariyachandra and H. Watson, "Which Data Warehouse Architecture Is Most Successful?" *Business Intelligence Journal*, Vol. 11, No. 1, First Quarter, 2006, pp. 4–6.

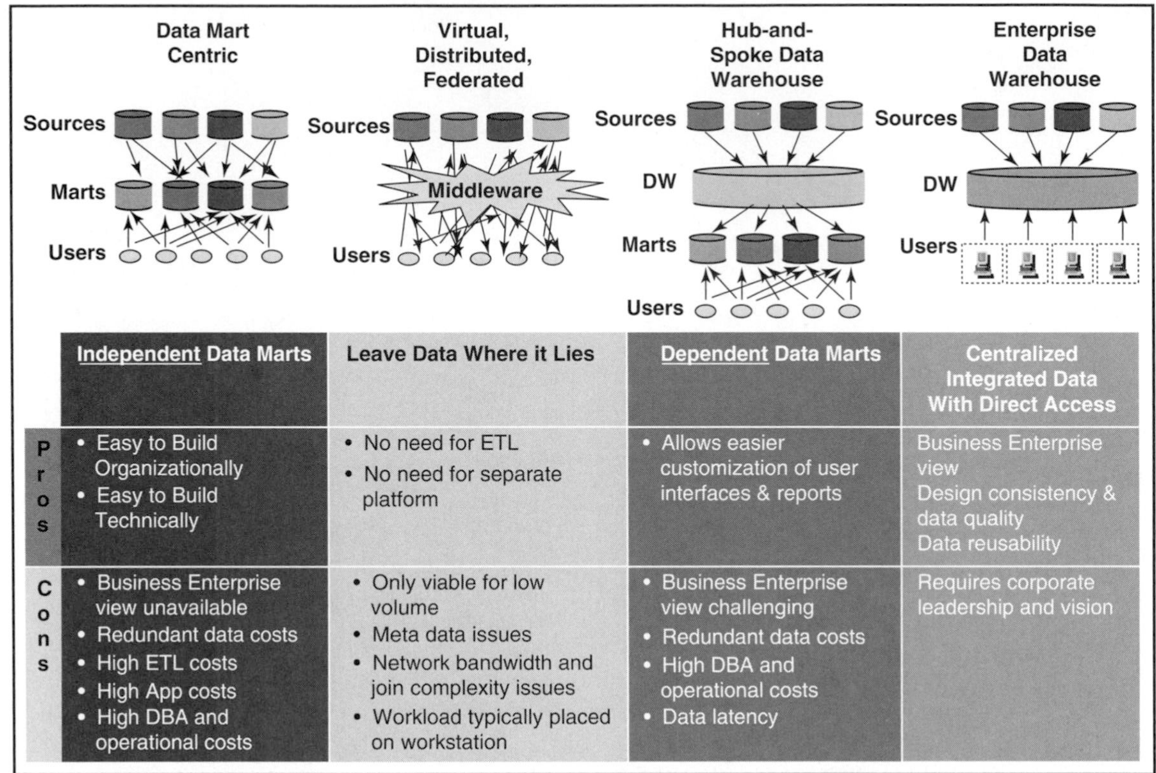

	Independent Data Marts	Leave Data Where it Lies	Dependent Data Marts	Centralized Integrated Data With Direct Access
Pros	• Easy to Build Organizationally • Easy to Build Technically	• No need for ETL • No need for separate platform	• Allows easier customization of user interfaces & reports	Business Enterprise view Design consistency & data quality Data reusability
Cons	• Business Enterprise view unavailable • Redundant data costs • High ETL costs • High App costs • High DBA and operational costs	• Only viable for low volume • Meta data issues • Network bandwidth and join complexity issues • Workload typically placed on workstation	• Business Enterprise view challenging • Redundant data costs • High DBA and operational costs • Data latency	Requires corporate leadership and vision

FIGURE 5.6 Alternative Architectures for Data Warehousing Efforts

Source: W. Eckerson, "Four Ways to Build a Data Warehouse," *What Works: Best Practices in Business Intelligence and Data Warehousing*, Vol. 15, The Data Warehousing Institute, Chatsworth, CA, June 2003, pp. 46–49. Used with permission.

operate independently of each another. Thus, they have inconsistent data definitions and different dimensions and measures, making it difficult to analyze data across the marts (i.e., it is difficult, if not impossible, to get to the "one version of the truth"). In a hub-and-spoke architecture, attention is focused on building a scalable and maintainable infrastructure; it is developed in an iterative way, subject area by subject area, and dependent data marts are developed. A centralized data warehouse is similar to the hub-and-spoke architecture except that there are no dependent data marts. The central data warehouses architecture, which is advocated mainly by Teradata Corp., advises using data warehouses without any data marts (see Figure 5.7). This centralized approach provides users with access to all data in the data warehouse instead of limiting them to data marts. In addition, it reduces the amount of data the technical team has to transfer or change, therefore simplifying data management and administration.

The *federated approach* is a concession to the natural forces that undermine the best plans for developing a perfect system. It uses all possible means to integrate analytical resources from multiple sources to meet changing needs or business conditions. Essentially, the federated approach involves integrating disparate systems. In a federated architecture, existing decision support structures are left in place, and data are accessed from those sources as needed. The federated approach is supported by middleware vendors that propose distributed query and join capabilities. These Extensible Markup Language (XML)–based tools offer users a global view of distributed data sources, including data warehouses, data marts, Web sites, documents, and operational

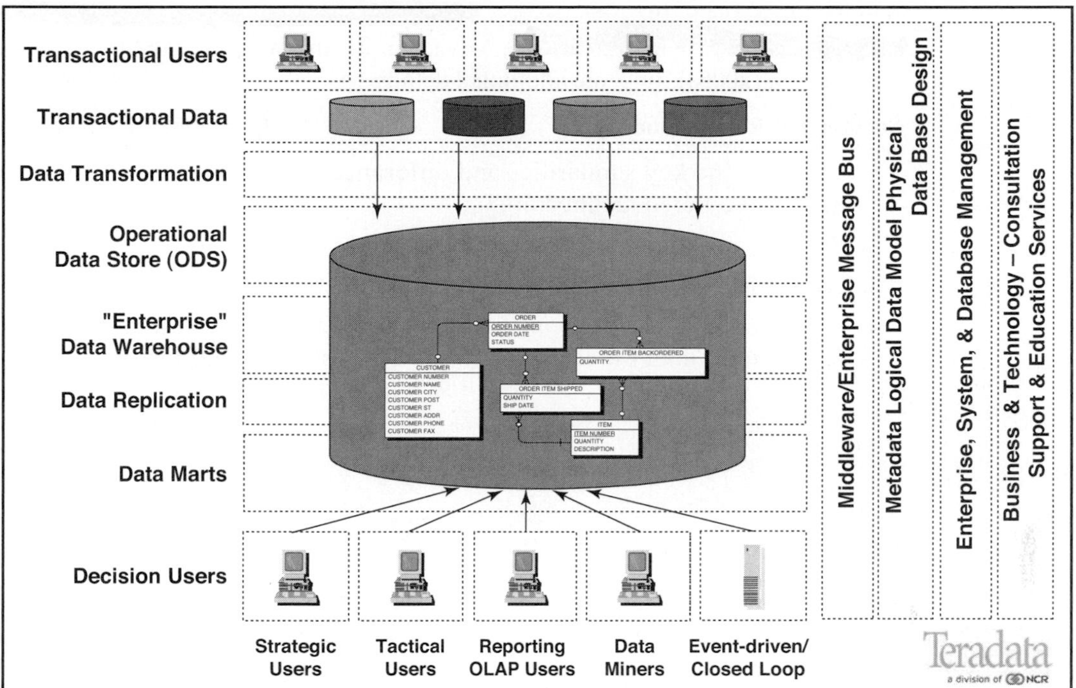

FIGURE 5.7 Teradata Corp.'s Enterprise Data Warehouse

Source: Teradata Corporation (**teradata.com**). Used with permission.

systems. When users choose query objects from this view and press the submit button, the tool automatically queries the distributed sources, joins the results, and presents them to the user. Because of performance and data quality issues, most experts agree that federated approaches work well to supplement data warehouses, not replace them (see Eckerson, 2005).

Ariyachandra and Watson (2005) identified 10 factors that potentially affect the architecture selection decision:

1. Information interdependence between organizational units
2. Upper management's information needs
3. Urgency of need for a data warehouse
4. Nature of end-user tasks
5. Constraints on resources
6. Strategic view of the data warehouse prior to implementation
7. Compatibility with existing systems
8. Perceived ability of the in-house IT staff
9. Technical issues
10. Social/political factors

These factors are similar to many success factors described in the literature for information systems projects and DSS and BI projects. Technical issues, beyond providing technology that is feasibly ready for use, is important but often not as important as behavioral issues, such as meeting upper management's information needs and user involvement in the development process (a social/political factor). Each data warehousing architecture has specific applications for which it is most (and least) effective and thus provides maximal benefits to the organization. However, overall, the data mart structure seems to be the least effective in practice (see Ariyachandra and Watson, 2006b). See Ariyachandra and Watson (2006a) for some additional details.

Section 5.4 Review Questions

1. What are the key similarities and differences between a two-tiered architecture and a three-tiered architecture?
2. How has the Web influenced data warehouse design?
3. List the alternative data warehousing architectures discussed in this section.
4. What issues should be considered when deciding which architecture to use in developing a data warehouse? List the 10 most important factors.

5.5 DATA INTEGRATION AND THE EXTRACTION, TRANSFORMATION, AND LOAD (ETL) PROCESSES

Global competitive pressures, demand for ROI, management and investor inquiry, and government regulations are forcing business managers to rethink how they integrate and manage their businesses. A decision maker typically needs access to multiple sources of data that must be integrated. Before data warehouses, data marts, and BI software, providing access to data sources was a major, laborious process. Even with modern Web-based data management tools, recognizing what data to access and providing them to the decision maker is a nontrivial task that requires database specialists. As data warehouses grow in size, the issues of integrating data grow as well.

The needs of BA continue to evolve. Mergers and acquisitions, regulatory requirements, and the introduction of new channels can drive changes in BI requirements. In addition to historical, cleansed, consolidated, and point-in-time data, business users increasingly demand access to real-time, unstructured, and/or remote data. And everything must be integrated with the contents of an existing data warehouse (see Devlin, 2003). Moreover, access via PDAs and through speech recognition and synthesis is becoming more commonplace, further complicating integration issues (see Edwards, 2003). Many integration projects involve enterprise-wide systems. Orovic (2003) provided a checklist of what works and what does not work when attempting such a project. Properly integrating data from various databases and other disparate sources is difficult. But when it is not done properly, it can lead to disaster in enterprise-wide systems such as CRM, ERP, and supply-chain projects (see Nash, 2002). Also see Dasu and Johnson (2003).

DATA INTEGRATION

Data integration comprises three major processes that, when correctly implemented, permit data to be accessed and made accessible to an array of ETL and analysis tools and data warehousing environment: data access (i.e., the ability to access and extract data from any data source), data federation (i.e., the integration of business views across multiple data stores), and change capture (based on the identification, capture, and delivery of the changes made to enterprise data sources). See Sapir (2005) for details. See Application Case 5.2 for an example of how Bank of America benefits from implementing a data warehouse that integrates data from many sources. Some vendors, such as SAS Institute, Inc., have developed strong data integration tools. The SAS enterprise data integration server includes customer data integration tools that improve data quality in the integration process. The Oracle Business Intelligence Suite assists in integrating data as well.

Application Case 5.2

Bank of America's Award-Winning Integrated Data Warehouse

In 2003, Bank of America won The Data Warehousing Institute's Best Practices and Leadership Award. Bank of America, one of the largest financial services networks in the United States, has realized significant operating savings by *integrating* its data warehouses. Its Teradata Warehouse is the platform for its integrated EDW. The data warehouse assists decision makers so they can:

- Maintain customer privacy
- Leverage customer information to develop products and identify trends
- Anticipate customer needs, leading to improved customer service and sales
- Lower costs, improve usage and performance, and respond quickly to changing business demands
- Make better and faster decisions

Sources: M. Edwards, "2003 Best Practices Awards Winners: Innovators in Business Intelligence and Data Warehousing," *Business Intelligence Journal*, Fall 2003, pp. 57–64; NCR, *Bank of America Expands Teradata Data Warehouse System*, October 6, 2005, **ncr.com/en/media_information/2005/oct/pr100605a.htm** (accessed April 2006); and Teradata, *Bank of America Expands Teradata Data Warehouse System*, October 6, 2005, **teradata.com/t/page/141826/index.html** (accessed April 2006).

A major purpose of a data warehouse is to integrate data from multiple systems. Various integration technologies enable data and metadata integration today:

- Enterprise application integration (EAI)
- Service-oriented architecture (SOA)
- Enterprise information integration (EII)
- Extraction, transformation, and load (ETL)

Enterprise application integration (EAI) provides a vehicle for pushing data from source systems into the data warehouse. It involves integrating application functionality and is focused on sharing functionality (rather than data) across systems, thereby enabling flexibility and reuse. Traditionally, EAI solutions have focused on enabling application reuse at the application programming interface (API) level. Recently, EAI is accomplished by using SOA coarse-grained services (a collection of business processes or functions) that are well defined and documented. Using Web services is a specialized way of implementing an SOA. EAI can be used to facilitate data acquisition directly into a near-real-time data warehouse or to deliver decisions to the OLTP systems. There are many different approaches to and tools for EAI implementation.

Enterprise information integration (EII) is an evolving tool space that promises real-time data integration from a variety of sources, such as relational databases, Web services, and multidimensional databases. It is a mechanism for pulling data from source systems to satisfy a request for information. EII tools use predefined metadata to populate views that make integrated data appear relational to end users. XML may be the most important aspect of EII because XML allows data to be tagged either at creation time or later. These tags can be extended and modified to accommodate almost any area of knowledge (see Kay, 2005).

Physical data integration has conventionally been the main mechanism for creating an integrated view with data warehouses and data marts. With the advent of EII tools (see Kay, 2005), new virtual data integration patterns are feasible. Manglik and Mehra (2005) discussed the benefits and constraints of new data integration patterns that can expand traditional physical methodologies to present a comprehensive view for the enterprise.

We next turn to the approach for loading data into the warehouse: ETL.

EXTRACTION, TRANSFORMATION, AND LOAD

At the heart of the technical side of the data warehousing process is **extraction, transformation, and load (ETL)**. ETL technologies, which have existed for some time, are instrumental in the process and use of data warehouses. The ETL process is an integral component in any data-centric project. IT managers are often faced with challenges because the ETL process typically consumes 70 percent of the time in a data-centric project.

The ETL process consists of *extraction* (i.e., reading data from one or more databases), *transformation* (i.e., converting the extracted data from its previous form into the form in which it needs to be so that it can be placed into a data warehouse or simply another database), and *load* (i.e., putting the data into the data warehouse). Transformation occurs by using rules or lookup tables or by combining the data with other data. The three database functions are integrated into one tool to pull data out of one or more databases and place them into another, consolidated database or a data warehouse.

ETL tools also transport data between sources and targets, document how data elements (e.g., metadata) change as they move between source and target, exchange metadata with other applications as needed, and administer all runtime processes and operations (e.g., scheduling, error management, audit logs, statistics). ETL is extremely important for data integration as well as for data warehousing. The purpose of the ETL process is to load the warehouse with integrated and cleansed data. The data used in ETL processes can come from any source: a mainframe application, an ERP application, a CRM tool, a flat file, an Excel spreadsheet, or even a message queue. In Figure 5.8, we outline the ETL process.

FIGURE 5.8 The ETL Process

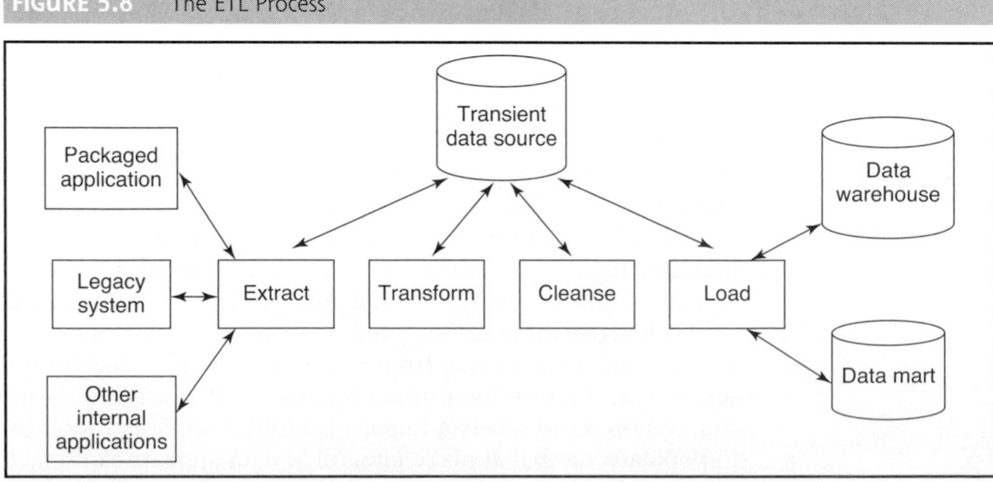

Source: Adapted from M.L. Songini, "ETL Quickstudy," *Computer World*, February 2, 2004; and T. Ariyachandra and H. Watson, "Which Data Warehouse Architecture Is Most Successful?" *Business Intelligence Journal*, Vol. 11, No. 1, First Quarter, 2006, pp. 4–6.

The process of migrating data to a data warehouse involves the extraction of data from *all* relevant sources. Data sources may consist of files extracted from OLTP databases, spreadsheets, personal databases (e.g., Microsoft Access), or external files. Typically, all the input files are written to a set of staging tables, which are designed to facilitate the load process. A data warehouse contains numerous business rules that define such things as how the data will be used, summarization rules, standardization of encoded attributes, and calculation rules. Any data quality issues pertaining to the source files need to be corrected before the data are loaded into the data warehouse. One of the benefits of a well-designed data warehouse is that these rules can be stored in a metadata repository and applied to the data warehouse centrally. This differs from an OLTP approach, which typically has data and business rules scattered throughout the system. The process of loading data into a data warehouse can be performed either through data transformation tools that provide a GUI to aid in the development and maintenance of business rules or through more traditional methods, such as developing programs or utilities to load the data warehouse, using programming languages such as PL/SQL, C++, or .NET Framework languages. This decision is not easy for organizations. Several issues affect whether an organization will purchase data transformation tools or build the transformation process itself:

- Data transformation tools are expensive.
- Data transformation tools may have a long learning curve.
- It is difficult to measure how the IT organization is doing until it has learned to use the data transformation tools.

In the long run, a transformation-tool approach should simplify the maintenance of an organization's data warehouse. Transformation tools can also be effective in detecting and scrubbing (i.e., removing any anomalies in the data). OLAP and data mining tools rely on how well the data are transformed.

As an example of effective ETL, Motorola, Inc., uses ETL to feed its data warehouses. Motorola collects information from 30 different procurement systems and sends them to its global SCM data warehouse for analysis of aggregate company spending (see Songini, 2004).

Solomon (2005) classified ETL technologies into four categories: sophisticated, enabler, simple, and rudimentary. It is generally acknowledged that tools in the sophisticated category will result in the ETL process being better documented and more accurately managed as the data warehouse project evolves.

Even though it is possible for programmers to develop software for ETL, it is simpler use an existing ETL tool. The following are some of the important criteria in selecting an ETL tool to include (see Brown, 2004):

- Ability to read from and write to an unlimited number of data source architectures
- Automatic capturing and delivery of metadata
- A history of conforming to open standards
- An easy-to-use interface for the developer and the functional user

Performing extensive ETL may be a sign of poorly managed data and a fundamental lack of a coherent data management strategy. Karacsony (2006) indicated that there is a direct correlation between the extent of redundant data and the number of ETL processes. When data are managed correctly as an enterprise asset, ETL efforts are significantly reduced, and redundant data are completely eliminated. This leads to huge savings in maintenance and greater efficiency in new development while also improving data quality. Poorly designed ETL processes are costly to maintain, change, and update. Consequently, it is crucial to make the proper choices in terms of the technology and tools to use for developing and maintaining the ETL process.

Providers of packaged ETL systems are numerous. Database vendors currently offer ETL capabilities that both enhance and compete with independent ETL tools. SAS acknowledges the importance of data quality and offers the industry's first fully integrated solution that merges ETL and data quality to transform data into strategic valuable assets. Other ETL software providers include Microsoft, Oracle, IBM, Informatica, Embarcadero, and Tibco. For additional information on ETL, see Eckerson (2003), Karaksony (2006), and Songini (2004).

Section 5.5 Review Questions

1. Describe data integration.
2. Describe the three steps of the ETL process.
3. Why is the ETL process so important for data warehousing efforts?

5.6 DATA WAREHOUSE DEVELOPMENT

A data warehousing project is a major undertaking for any organization and is more complicated than a simple, mainframe selection and implementation project because it comprises and influences many departments and many input and output interfaces, and it can be part of a CRM business strategy. A data warehouse provides several benefits that can be classified as direct and indirect. Direct benefits include the following:

- Allowing end users to perform extensive analysis in numerous ways.
- A consolidated view of corporate data (i.e., a single version of the truth).
- Better and more timely information. A data warehouse permits information processing to be relieved from costly operational systems onto low-cost servers; therefore, many more end-user information requests can be processed more quickly.
- Enhanced system performance. A data warehouse frees production processing because some operational system reporting requirements are moved to DSS.
- Simplification of data access.

Indirect benefits result from end users using these direct benefits. On the whole, these benefits enhance business knowledge, present competitive advantage, enhance customer service and satisfaction, facilitate decision making, and help in reforming business processes, and therefore they are the strongest contributions to competitive advantage. (For a discussion of how to create a competitive advantage through data warehousing, see Parzinger and Frolick, 2001.) For a detailed discussion of how organizations can obtain exceptional levels of payoffs, see Watson et al. (2002). Given the potential benefits that a data warehouse can provide and the substantial investments in time and money that such a project requires, it is critical that an organization structure its data warehouse project to maximize the chances of success. In addition, the organization must, obviously, take costs into consideration. Kelly (2001) described a return on investment (ROI) approach that considers benefits in the categories of *keepers* (i.e., money saved by improving traditional decision support functions); *gatherers* (i.e., money saved due to automated collection and dissemination of information), and *users* (i.e., money saved or gained from decisions made using the data warehouse). Costs include those related to hardware, software, network bandwidth, internal development, internal support, training, and external consulting. The net present value is calculated over the expected life of the data warehouse. Because the benefits are broken down approximately as 20 percent for keepers, 30 percent for gatherers, and 50 percent for users, Kelly indicated that users should be involved in the development process, a success factor typically mentioned as critical for systems that imply change in an organization.

Application Case 5.3 provides an example of a data warehouse that was developed and delivered intense competitive advantage for the Hokuriku (Japan) Coca-Cola Bottling Company. The system was so successful that plans are under way to expand it to encompass the more than one million Coca-Cola vending machines in Japan.

Application Case 5.3

Things Go Better with Coke's Data Warehouse

In the face of competitive pressures and consumer demand, how does a successful bottling company ensure that its vending machines are profitable? The answer for Hokuriku Coca-Cola Bottling Company (HCCBC) is a data warehouse and analytical software implemented by Teradata Corp. HCCBC built the system in response to a data warehousing system developed by its rival, Mikuni. The data warehouse collects not only historical data but also near-real-time data from each vending machine (viewed as a store) that could be transmitted via wireless connection to headquarters. The initial phase of the project was deployed in 2001. The data warehouse approach provides detailed product information, such as time and date of each sale, when a product sells out, whether someone was short-changed, and whether the machine is malfunctioning. In each case, an *alert* is triggered, and the vending machine immediately reports it to the data center over a wireless transmission system. (Note that Coca-Cola in the United States has used modems to link vending machines to distributors for over a decade.)

In 2002, HCCBC conducted a pilot test and put all its Nagano vending machines on a wireless network to gather near-real-time point of sale (POS) data from each one. The results were astounding because they accurately forecasted demand and identified problems quickly. Total sales immediately increased 10 percent. In addition, due to the more accurate machine servicing, overtime and other costs decreased 46 percent. In addition, each salesperson was able to service up to 42 percent more vending machines.

The test was so successful that planning began to expand it to encompass the entire enterprise (60,000 machines), using an *active data warehouse*. Eventually, the data warehousing solution will ideally expand across corporate boundaries into the entire Coca-Cola Bottlers network so that the more than one million vending machines in Japan will be networked, leading to immense cost savings and higher revenue.

Sources: Adapted from K.D. Schwartz, "Decisions at the Touch of a Button," *Teradata Magazine*, **teradata.com/t/page/117774/index.html** (accessed April 2006); K.D. Schwartz, "Decisions at the Touch of a Button," *DSS Resources*, March 2004, pp. 28–31, **dssresources.com/cases/coca-colajapan/index.html** (accessed April 2006); and Teradata Corp., *Coca-Cola Japan Puts the Fizz Back in Vending Machine Sales*, **teradata.com/t/page/118866/index.html** (accessed April 2006).

Clearly defining the business objective, gathering project support from management end users, setting reasonable time frames and budgets, and managing expectations are critical to a successful data warehousing project. A data warehousing strategy is a blueprint for the successful introduction of the data warehouse. The strategy should describe where the company wants to go, why it wants to go there, and what it will do when it gets there. It needs to take into consideration the organization's vision, structure, and culture. See Matney (2003) for the steps that can help in developing a flexible and efficient support strategy. When the plan and support for a data warehouse are established, the organization needs to examine data warehouse vendors. (See Table 5.1 for a sample list of vendors; also see The Data Warehousing Institute [**twdi.com**] and *DM Review* [**dmreview.com**].) Many vendors provide software demos of their data warehousing and BI product.

TABLE 5.1 Sample List of Data Warehousing Vendors

Vendor	*Product Offerings*
Computer Associates (**cai.com**)	Comprehensive set of data warehouse (DW) tools and products
DataMirror Corp. (**datamirror.com**)	DW administration, management, and performance products
Data Advantage Group, Inc. (**dataadvantagegroup.com**)	Metadata software
Dell Computer Corp. (**dell.com**)	DW servers
Embarcadero Technologies (**embarcadero.com**)	DW administration, management, and performance products
Business Objects (**businessobjects.com**)	Data cleansing software
Harte-Hanks, Inc. (**harte-hanks.com**)	Customer relationship management (CRM) products and services
Hewlett-Packard Company (**hp.com**)	DW servers
Hummingbird Ltd. (**hummingbird.com**)	DW engines and exploration warehouses
Hyperion Solutions Corp. (**hyperion.com**)	Comprehensive set of DW tools, products, and applications
IBM (**ibm.com**)	DW tools, products, and applications
Informatica Corp. (**informatica.com**)	DW administration, management, and performance products
Microsoft Corp. (**microsoft.com**)	DW tools and products
Oracle (including PeopleSoft and Siebel) (**oracle.com**)	DW, ERP and CRM tools, products, and applications
SAS Institute, Inc. (**sas.com**)	DW tools, products, and applications
Siemens (**siemens.com**)	DW servers
Sybase, Inc. (**sybase.com**)	Comprehensive set of DW tools and applications
Teradata (**teradata.com**)	DW tools, products, and applications

DATA WAREHOUSE VENDORS

McCloskey (2002) cited six guidelines that need to be considered when developing a vendor list: financial strength, ERP linkages, qualified consultants, market share, industry experience, and established partnerships. We can collect additional data from trade shows and corporate Web sites, as well as by submitting requests for specific product information. Van den Hoven (1998) differentiated three types of data warehousing products. The first type handles functions such as locating, extracting, transforming, cleansing, transporting, and loading the data into the data warehouse. The second type is a data management tool—a database engine that stores and manages the data warehouse as well as the metadata. The third type is a data access tool that provides end users with access to analyze the data in the data warehouse. This may include query generators, visualization, EIS, OLAP, and data mining capabilities.

DATA WAREHOUSE DEVELOPMENT APPROACHES

Many organizations need to create the data warehouses used for decision support. Two competing approaches are employed. The first approach is that of Bill Inmon, who is often called "the father of data warehousing." Inmon supports a top-down development approach that adapts traditional relational database tools to the development needs of an enterprise-wide data warehouse, also known as the *EDW approach*. The

TABLE 5.2 Contrasts Between the Data Mart and EDW Development Approaches

Effort	*Data Mart Approach*	*EDW Approach*
Scope	One subject area	Several subject areas
Development time	Months	Years
Development cost	$10,000 to $100,000+	$1,000,000+
Development difficulty	Low to medium	High
Data prerequisite for sharing	Common (within business area)	Common (across enterprise)
Sources	Only some operational and external systems	Many operational and external systems
Size	Megabytes to several gigabytes	Gigabytes to petabytes
Time horizon	Near-current and historical data	Historical data
Data transformations	Low to medium	High
Frequency of update	Hourly, daily, weekly	Weekly, monthly
Technology		
Hardware	Workstations and departmental servers	Enterprise servers and mainframe computers
Operating system	Windows and Linux	Unix, Z/OS, OS/390
Databases	Workgroup or standard database servers	Enterprise database servers
Usage		
Number of simultaneous users	10s	100s to 1,000s
User types	Business area analysts and managers	Enterprise analysts and senior executives
Business spotlight	Optimizing activities within the business area	Cross-functional optimization and decision making

Sources: Adapted from J. Van den Hoven, "Data Marts: Plan Big, Build Small," in *IS Management Handbook*, 8th ed., CRC Press, Boca Raton, FL, 2003; and T. Ariyachandra and H. Watson, "Which Data Warehouse Architecture Is Most Successful?" *Business Intelligence Journal*, Vol. 11, No. 1, First Quarter 2006, pp. 4–6.

second approach is that of Ralph Kimball, who proposes a bottom-up approach that employs dimensional modeling, also known as the *data mart approach*.

Knowing how these two models are alike and how they differ helps us understand the basic data warehouse concepts (e.g., see Breslin, 2004). We show some of the advantages and disadvantages of both approaches in Table 5.2. We describe these approaches in detail next.

The Inmon Model: The EDW Approach

Inmon's approach emphasizes top-down development, employing established database development methodologies and tools, such as entity-relationship diagrams (ERD), and an adjustment of the spiral development approach. The EDW approach does not preclude the creation of data marts. The EDW is the ideal in this approach because it provides a consistent and comprehensive view of the enterprise. Murtaza (1998) presented a framework for developing EDW.

The Kimball Model: The Data Mart Approach

Kimball's data mart strategy is a "plan big, build small" approach. A data mart is a subject-oriented or department-oriented data warehouse. It is a scaled-down version of a data warehouse that focuses on the requests of a specific department, such as marketing or sales. This model applies dimensional data modeling, which starts with tables. Kimball advocated a development methodology that entails a bottom-up approach, which in the case of data warehouses means building one data mart at a time.

Which Model Is Best?

There is no one-size-fits-all strategy to data warehousing. An enterprise's data warehousing strategy can evolve from a simple data mart to a complex data warehouse in response to user demands, the enterprise's business requirements, and the enterprise's maturity in managing its data resources. For many enterprises, a data mart is frequently

TABLE 5.3 Comparison of the Essential Characteristic Differences Between the Inmon and Kimball Development Approaches

Characteristic	*Inmon*	*Kimball*
Methodology and Architecture		
Overall approach	Top-down	Bottom-up
Architecture structure	Enterprise-wide (atomic) data warehouse "feeds" departmental databases	Data marts model a single business process, and enterprise consistency is achieved through a data bus and conformed dimensions
Complexity of the method	Quite complex	Fairly simple
Comparison with established development methodologies	Derived from the spiral methodology	Four-step process; a departure from relational database management system (RDBMS) methods
Discussion of physical design	Fairly thorough	Fairly light
Data Modeling		
Data orientation	Subject- or data driven	Process oriented
Tools	Traditional (entity-relationship diagrams [ERD], data flow diagrams [DFD])	Dimensional modeling; a departure from relational modeling
End-user accessibility	Low	High
Philosophy		
Primary audience	IT professionals	End users
Place in the organization	Integral part of the corporate information factory	Transformer and retainer of operational data
Objective	Deliver a sound technical solution based on proven database methods and technologies	Deliver a solution that makes it easy for end users to directly query the data and still get reasonable response times

Sources: Adapted from M. Breslin, "Data Warehousing Battle of the Giants: Comparing the Basics of Kimball and Inmon Models," *Business Intelligence Journal*, Vol. 9, No. 1, Winter 2004, pp. 6–20; and T. Ariyachandra and H. Watson, "Which Data Warehouse Architecture Is Most Successful?" *Business Intelligence Journal*, Vol. 11, No. 1, First Quarter 2006.

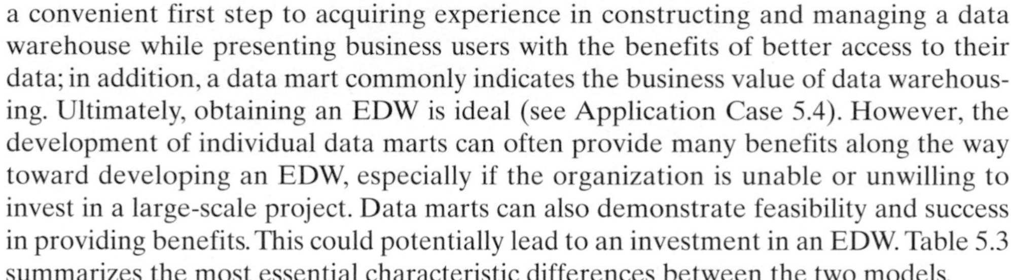
a convenient first step to acquiring experience in constructing and managing a data warehouse while presenting business users with the benefits of better access to their data; in addition, a data mart commonly indicates the business value of data warehousing. Ultimately, obtaining an EDW is ideal (see Application Case 5.4). However, the development of individual data marts can often provide many benefits along the way toward developing an EDW, especially if the organization is unable or unwilling to invest in a large-scale project. Data marts can also demonstrate feasibility and success in providing benefits. This could potentially lead to an investment in an EDW. Table 5.3 summarizes the most essential characteristic differences between the two models.

Application Case 5.4

HP Consolidates Hundreds of Data Marts into a Single EDW

In December 2005, Hewlett-Packard Co. (HP) planned to consolidate its 762 data marts around the world into a single EDW. HP took this approach both to get a superior sense of its own business and to determine how best to serve its customers. Mark Hurd, HP's president and chief executive, stated that "there was a thirst for analytic data" inside the company that had unfortunately led to the creation of many data marts. Those data silos were very expensive to design and maintain, and they did not produce the enterprise-wide view of internal and customer information that HP wanted. In mid-2006, HP started to consolidate the data in the data marts into the new data warehouse. All the disparate data marts will ultimately be eliminated.

Sources: Adapted from C. Martins, "HP to Consolidate Data Marts into Single Warehouse," *Computerworld*, December 13, 2005; C. Martins, "HP to Consolidate Data Marts into Single Warehouse," *InfoWorld*, December 13, 2005; and C. Martins, "HP to Consolidate Data Marts into One Warehouse," *ITWorld Canada*, December 14, 2005.

ADDITIONAL DATA WAREHOUSE DEVELOPMENT CONSIDERATIONS

Some organizations want to completely outsource their data warehousing efforts. They simply do not want to deal with software and hardware acquisitions, and they do not want to manage their information systems. One alternative is to use hosted data warehouses. In this scenario, another firm—ideally, one that has a lot of experience and expertise—develops and maintains the data warehouse. However, there are security and privacy concerns with this approach. See Technology Insights 5.5 for some details.

DATA WAREHOUSE STRUCTURE: THE STAR SCHEMA

A typical data warehouse structure is shown in Figure 5.1. While there are many variations on architecture, the most important one is the star schema. The data warehouse design is based on the concept of *dimensional modeling*. **Dimensional modeling** is a retrieval-based system that supports high-volume query access. The star schema is the means by which dimensional modeling is implemented. A star schema contains a central fact table surrounded by several dimension tables. The fact table contains a large number of rows that correspond to observed business or facts. A fact table contains the attributes needed to perform decision analysis, descriptive attributes used for query reporting, and foreign keys to link to dimension tables. The decision analysis attributes consist of performance measures, operational metrics, aggregated measures, and all the other metrics needed to analyze the organization's performance. In other words, the fact table primarily addresses *what* the data warehouse supports for decision analysis.

Surrounding the central fact tables (and linked via foreign keys) are *dimension tables*. The **dimension tables** contain classification and aggregation information about

TECHNOLOGY INSIGHTS 5.5

How About a Hosted Data Warehouse?

A hosted data warehouse has nearly the same, if not more, functionality as an on-site data warehouse, but it does not consume computer resources on client premises. A hosted data warehouse offers the benefits of BI minus the cost of computer upgrades, network upgrades, software licenses, in-house development, and in-house support and maintenance.

A hosted data warehouse offers the following benefits:

- Requires minimal investment in infrastructure
- Frees up capacity on in-house systems
- Frees up cash flow
- Makes powerful solutions affordable
- Enables powerful solutions that provide for growth
- Offers better quality equipment and software
- Provides faster connections
- Enables users to access data from remote locations
- Allows a company to focus on core business
- Meets storage needs for large volumes of data

Despite its benefits, a hosted data warehouse is not necessarily a good fit for every company. Large companies with revenue upwards of $500 million could lose money if they already have underused internal infrastructure and IT staff. Furthermore, companies that see the paradigm shift of outsourcing applications as loss of control of their data are not prone to use a business intelligence service provider (BISP). Finally, the most significant and common argument against implementing a hosted data warehouse is that it may be unwise to outsource sensitive applications for reasons of security and privacy.

Sources: Partly adapted from M. Thornton and M. Lampa, "Hosted Data Warehouse," *Journal of Data Warehousing*, Vol. 7, No. 2, 2002, pp. 27–34; and M. Thornton, "What About Security? The Most Common, but Unwarranted, Objection to Hosted Data Warehouses," *DM Review*, Vol. 12, No. 3, March 18, 2002, pp. 30–43.

the central fact rows. Dimension tables contain attributes that describe the data contained within the fact table; they address *how* data will be analyzed. Dimension tables have a one-to-many relationship with rows in the central fact table. Some examples of dimensions that would support a product fact table are location, time, and size. The star schema design provides extremely fast query-response time, simplicity, and ease of maintenance for read-only database structures. According to Raden (2003), setting up a star schema for real-time updating could be a straightforward approach, as long as a few rules are followed. We show a star schema example in Figure 5.9.

The **grain** (also known as granularity) of a data warehouse defines the highest level of detail that is supported. The grain indicates whether the data warehouse is highly summarized or also includes detailed transaction data. If the grain is defined too high, then the warehouse may not support detail requests to *drill down* into the data. **Drill-down** analysis is the process of probing beyond a summarized value to investigate each of the detail transactions that comprise the summary. A low level of granularity will result in more data being stored in the warehouse. Larger amounts of detail may affect the performance of queries by making the response times longer. Therefore, during the scoping of a data warehouse project, it is important to identify the right level of granularity that will be needed. See Tennant (2002) for a discussion of granularity issues in metadata.

DATA WAREHOUSING IMPLEMENTATION ISSUES

Implementing a data warehouse is generally a massive effort that must be planned and executed according to established methods. There are, however, many facets to the project lifecycle, and no single person can be an expert in each area. Here we discuss

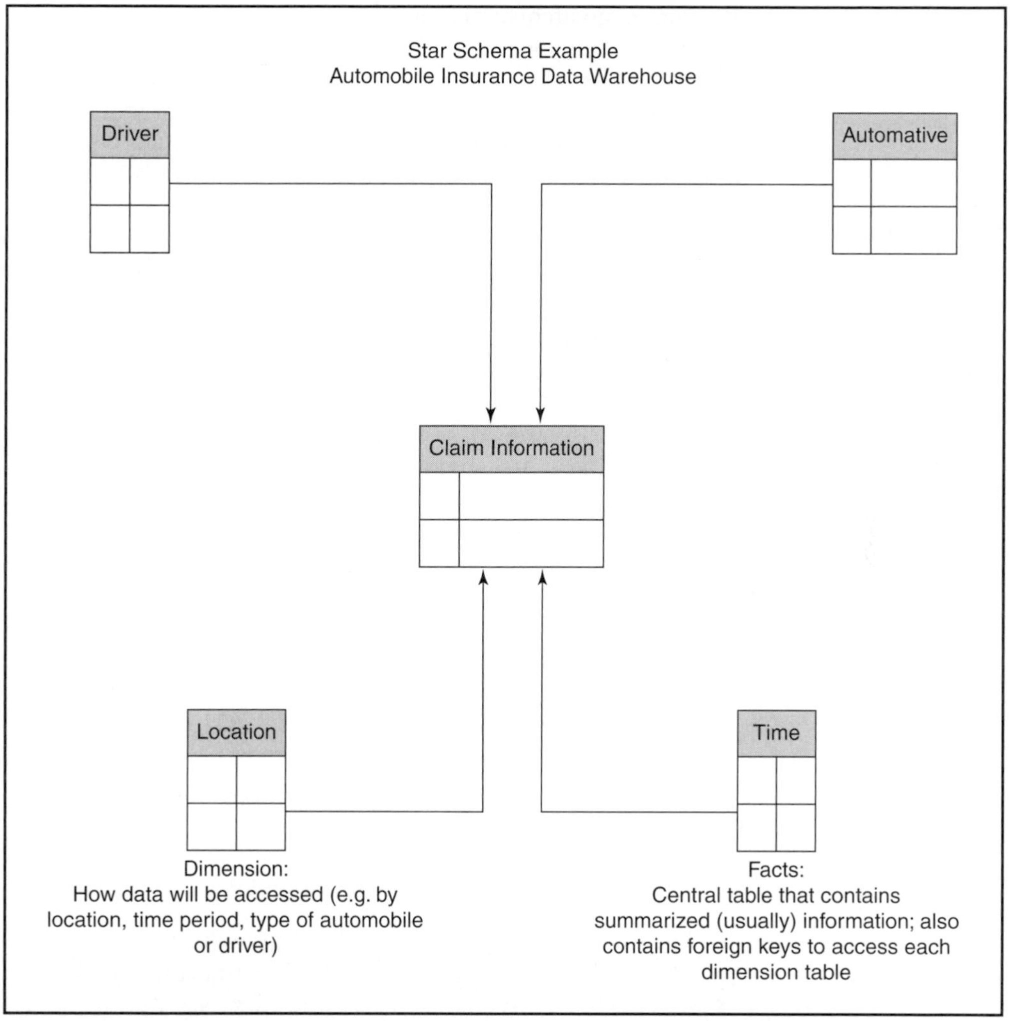

FIGURE 5.9 Star Schema

specific ideas and issues as they relate to data warehousing. Inmon (2006) provided a set of actions that a data warehouse systems programmer may use to tune a data warehouse.

Solomon (2005) provided some guidelines regarding the critical questions that must be asked, some risks that should be weighted, and some processes that can be followed to help ensure a successful data warehouse implementation. He compiled a list of 11 major tasks that could be performed in parallel:

1. Establishment of service-level agreements and data-refresh requirements
2. Identification of data sources and their governance policies
3. Data quality planning
4. Data model design
5. ETL tool selection
6. Relational database software and platform selection
7. Data transport
8. Data conversion
9. Reconciliation process

10. Purge and archive planning
11. End-user support

Following these guidelines should increase an organization's chances for success. Given the size and scope of an enterprise-level data warehouse initiative, failure to anticipate these issues greatly increases the risks of failure.

Hwang and Xu (2005) conducted a major survey of data warehousing success issues. The results established that data warehousing success is a multifaceted construct, and Hwang and Xu proposed that a data warehouse be constructed while keeping in mind the goal of improving user productivity. Extremely significant benefits of doing so include prompt information retrieval and enhanced quality information. The survey results also indicated that success hinges on factors of different dimensions.

People want to know how successful their BI and data warehousing initiatives are in comparison to those of other companies. Ariyachandra and Watson (2006a) proposed some benchmarks for BI and data warehousing success. Watson et al. (1999) researched data warehouse failures. Their results showed that people define a "failure" in different ways, and this was confirmed by Ariyachandra and Watson (2006a). The Data Warehousing Institute (**tdwi.org**) has developed a data warehousing maturity model that an enterprise can apply in order to benchmark its evolution. The model offers a fast means to gauge where the organization's data warehousing initiative is now and where it needs to go next. The maturity model consists of six stages: prenatal, infant, child, teenager, adult, and sage. Business value rises as the data warehouse progresses through each succeeding stage. The stages are identified by a number of characteristics, including scope, analytic structure, executive perceptions, types of analytics, stewardship, funding, technology platform, change management, and administration. See Eckerson (2004) for complete details.

Weir (2002) described some of the best practices for implementing a data warehouse, which include the following guidelines:

- The project must fit with corporate strategy and business objectives.
- There must be complete buy-in to the project by executives, managers, and users.
- It is important to manage user expectations about the completed project.
- The data warehouse must be built incrementally.
- Build in adaptability.
- The project must be managed by both IT and business professionals.
- Develop a business/supplier relationship.
- Only load data that have been cleansed and are of a quality understood by the organization.
- Do not overlook training requirements.
- Be politically aware.

There are many risks in data warehouse projects. Most of them are also found in other IT projects, but data warehousing risks are more serious because data warehouses are expensive, large-scale projects. Each risk should be assessed at the inception of the project. Adelman and Moss (2001) described some of these risks, including the following:

- No mission or objective
- Quality of source data unknown
- Skills not in place
- Inadequate budget
- Lack of supporting software
- Source data not understood

- Weak sponsor
- Users not computer literate
- Political problems or turf wars
- Unrealistic user expectations
- Architectural and design risks
- Scope creep and changing requirements
- Vendors out of control
- Multiple platforms
- Key people leaving the project
- Loss of the sponsor
- Too much new technology
- Having to fix an operational system
- Geographically distributed environment
- Team geography and language culture

Practitioners have unearthed a wealth of mistakes that have been made in the development of data warehouses. Watson et al. (1999) also discussed how such mistakes could lead to data warehouse failures (also see Barquin et al., 1997). Turban et al. (2006) listed failure factors that include cultural issues being ignored, inappropriate architecture, unclear business objectives, missing information, unrealistic expectations, low levels of data summarization, and low data quality.

When developing a successful data warehouse, it's important to carefully consider these issues:

- *Starting with the wrong sponsorship chain.* You need an executive sponsor who has influence over the necessary resources to support and invest in the data warehouse. You also need an executive *project driver*, someone who has earned the respect of other executives, has a healthy skepticism about technology, and is decisive but flexible. And you need an IS/IT manager to head up the project (the "you" in the project).
- *Setting expectations that you cannot meet and frustrating executives at the moment of truth.* There are two phases in every data warehousing project: Phase 1 is the selling phase, in which you internally market the project by selling the benefits to those who have access to needed resources. Phase 2 is the struggle to meet the expectations described in Phase 1. For a mere $1 to $7 million, you can, hopefully, deliver.
- *Engaging in politically naive behavior.* Do not simply state that a data warehouse will help managers make better decisions. This may imply that you feel they have been making bad decisions until now. Sell the idea that they will be able to get the information they need to help in decision making.
- *Loading the warehouse with information just because it is available.* Do not let the data warehouse become a data landfill. This would unnecessarily slow down the use of the system. There is a trend toward real-time computing and analysis. Data warehouses must be shut down to load data in a timely way.
- *Believing that data warehousing database design is the same as transactional database design.* In general, it is not. The goal of data warehousing is to access aggregates rather than a single or a few records, as in transaction-processing systems. Content is also different, as is evident in how data are organized. DBMS tend to be nonredundant, normalized, and relational, whereas data warehouses are redundant, not normalized, and multidimensional.
- *Choosing a data warehouse manager who is technology oriented rather than user oriented.* One key to data warehouse success is to understand that the users must get what they need, not advanced technology for technology's sake.

- *Focusing on traditional internal record-oriented data and ignoring the value of external data and of text, images, and, perhaps, sound and video.* Data come in many formats and must be made accessible to the right people at the right time and in the right format. They must be catalogued properly.
- *Delivering data with overlapping and confusing definitions.* Data cleansing is a critical aspect of data warehousing. It includes reconciling conflicting data definitions and formats organization-wide. Politically, this may be difficult because it involves change, typically at the executive level.
- *Believing promises of performance, capacity, and scalability.* Data warehouses generally require more capacity and speed than is originally budgeted for. Plan ahead to scale up.
- *Believing that your problems are over when the data warehouse is up and running.* DSS/BI projects tend to evolve continually. Each deployment is an iteration of the prototyping process. There will always be a need to add more and different data sets to the data warehouse, as well as additional analytic tools for existing and additional groups of decision makers. High energy and annual budgets must be planned for because success breeds success. Data warehousing is a continuous process.
- *Focusing on ad hoc data mining and periodic reporting instead of alerts.* The natural progression of information in a data warehouse is: (1) *Extract* the data from legacy systems, cleanse them, and feed them to the warehouse; (2) *support* ad hoc reporting until you learn what people want; and (3) *convert* the ad hoc reports into regularly scheduled reports.

This process of learning what people want in order to provide it seems natural, but it is not optimal or even practical. Managers are busy and need time to read reports. *Alert systems* are better than periodic reporting systems and can make a data warehouse mission critical. Alert systems monitor the data flowing into the warehouse and inform all key people who have a need to know as soon as a critical event occurs.

Sammon and Finnegan (2000) revealed the outcome of a study of four mature users of data warehousing technology. Their practices were captured in an outline of 10 organizational requisites for applying data warehousing. They think that organizations might potentially use this representation to internally evaluate the chances of the success of a data warehousing project and to recognize the parts that need attention prior to beginning implementation. A summary of their prerequisites model is as follows:

- A business-driven data warehousing initiative
- Executive sponsorship and commitment
- Funding commitment based on realistically managed expectations
- A project team
- Attention to source data quality
- A flexible enterprise data model
- Data stewardship
- A long-term plan for automated data extraction methods/tools
- Knowledge of data warehouse compatibility with existing systems
- Hardware/software proof of concept

Wixom and Watson (2001) defined a research model for data warehouse success that identified seven important implementation factors that can be categorized into three criteria (i.e., organizational issues, project issues, and technical issues):

1. Management support
2. Champion
3. Resources

4. User participation
5. Team skills
6. Source systems
7. Development technology

In many organizations, a data warehouse will be successful only if there is strong senior management support for its development and if there is a project champion. Although this would likely be true for any IT project, it is especially important for a data warehouse. The successful implementation of a data warehouse results in the establishment of an architectural framework that may allow for decision analysis throughout an organization and in some cases also provides comprehensive SCM by granting access to an organization's customers and suppliers. The implementation of Web-based data warehouses (called *Webhousing*) has facilitated ease of access to vast amounts of data, but it is difficult to determine the hard benefits associated with a data warehouse. *Hard benefits* are defined as benefits to an organization that can be expressed in monetary terms. Many organizations have limited IT resources and must prioritize projects. Management support and a strong project champion can help ensure that a data warehouse project will receive the resources necessary for successful implementation. Data warehouse resources can be a significant cost, in some cases requiring high-end processors and large increases in direct-access storage devices (DASD). Web-based data warehouses may also have special security requirements to ensure that only authorized users have access to the data.

User participation in the development of data and access modeling is a critical success factor in data warehouse development. During data modeling, expertise is required to determine what data are needed, define business rules associated with the data, and decide what aggregations and other calculations may be necessary. Access modeling is needed to determine how data are to be retrieved from a data warehouse, and it assists in the physical definition of the warehouse by helping to define which data require indexing. It may also indicate whether dependent data marts are needed to facilitate information retrieval. The team skills needed to develop and implement a data warehouse include in-depth knowledge of the database technology and development tools used. Source systems and development technology, as mentioned previously, reference the many inputs and the processes used to load and maintain a data warehouse.

MASSIVE DATA WAREHOUSES AND SCALABILITY

In addition to flexibility, a data warehouse needs to support scalability. The main issues pertaining to scalability are the amount of data in the warehouse, how quickly the warehouse is expected to grow, the number of concurrent users, and the complexity of user queries. A data warehouse must scale both horizontally and vertically. The warehouse will grow as a function of data growth and the need to expand the warehouse to support new business functionality. Data growth may be a result of the addition of current cycle data (e.g., this month's results) and/or historical data.

Hicks (2001) described huge databases and data warehouses. Wal-Mart is continually increasing the size of its massive data warehouse. Wal-Mart is believed to use a warehouse with hundreds of terabytes of data to study sales trends and track inventory and other tasks. The U.S. Department of Defense is using a 5 petabyte data warehouse and repository to hold medical records for 9 million military personnel. Because of the storage required to archive its news footage, CNN also has a petabyte-sized data warehouse.

Given that the size of data warehouses is expanding at an exponential rate, *scalability* is an important issue. Good scalability means that queries and other data-access functions will grow (ideally) linearly with the size of the warehouse. See Rosenberg (2006) for approaches to improve query performance. In practice, specialized methods have been developed to create scalable data warehouses. Scalability is difficult when managing hundreds of terabytes or more. Terabytes of data have considerable inertia, occupy a lot of physical space, and require powerful computers. Some firms use parallel processing, and others use clever indexing and search schemes to manage their data. Some spread their data across different physical data stores. As more data warehouses approach the petabyte size, better and better solutions to scalability continue to be developed.

Hall (2002) also addressed scalability issues. AT&T is an industry leader in deploying and using massive data warehouses. With its 26-terabyte data warehouse, AT&T Labs can detect fraudulent use of calling cards and investigate calls related to kidnappings and other crimes. It can also compute millions of call-in votes from TV viewers selecting the next American Idol.

For a sample of successful data warehousing implementations, see Edwards (2003). Jukic and Lang (2004) examined the trends and specific issues related to use of offshore resources in the development and support of data warehousing and BI applications. Davison (2003) indicated that IT-related offshore outsourcing had been growing at 20 to 25 percent per year. When considering offshoring data warehousing projects, careful consideration must be given to culture and security (for details, see Jukic and Lang, 2004).

Section 5.6 Review Questions

1. List the benefits of data warehouses.
2. List several criteria for selecting a data warehouse vendor and describe why they are important.
3. Does a bottom-up data warehouse development approach use an enterprise data model?
4. Describe the major similarities and differences between the Inmon and Kimball data warehouse development approaches.
5. List the different types of data warehouse architectures.

5.7 REAL-TIME DATA WAREHOUSING

Data warehousing and BI tools traditionally focus on assisting managers in making strategic and tactical decisions. Increased data volumes and accelerating update speeds are fundamentally changing the role of the data warehouse in modern business. For many businesses, making fast and consistent decisions across the enterprise requires more than a traditional data warehouse or data mart. Traditional data warehouses are not business critical. Data are commonly updated on a weekly basis, and this does not allow for responding to transactions in near-real-time.

More data, coming in faster and requiring immediate conversion into decisions, means that organizations are confronting the need for real-time data warehousing. This is because decision support has become operational, integrated BI requires closed-loop analytics, and yesterday's ODS will not support existing requirements.

In 2003, with the advent of real-time data warehousing, there was a shift toward using these technologies for operational decisions. **Real-time data warehousing (RDW)**, also known as **active data warehousing (ADW)**, is the process of loading and providing data via the data warehouse as they become available. It fairly recently evolved from the EDW concept. The active traits of an RDW/ADW supplement and expand traditional data warehouse functions into the realm of tactical decision making. People throughout the organization who interact directly with customers and suppliers will be empowered with information-based decision making at their fingertips. Even further leverage results when an ADW provides information directly to customers and suppliers. The reach and impact of information access for decision making can positively affect almost all aspects of customer service, SCM, logistics, and beyond. E-business has become a major catalyst in the demand for active data warehousing (see Armstrong, 2000). For example, online retailer Overstock.com, Inc. (**overstock.com**), connected data users to a real-time data warehouse. At Egg plc, the world's largest purely online bank, a customer data warehouse is refreshed in near-real-time. See Application Case 5.5.

Application Case 5.5

Egg Plc Fries the Competition in Near-Real-Time

Egg plc (**egg.com**) is the world's largest online bank. It provides banking, insurance, investments, and mortgages to more than 3.6 million customers, through its Internet site. In 1998, Egg selected Sun Microsystems to create a reliable, scalable, secure infrastructure to support its more than 2.5 million daily transactions. In 2001, the system was upgraded to eliminate latency problems. This new customer data warehouse (CDW) used Sun, Oracle, and SAS software products. The initial data warehouse had about 10 terabytes of data and used a 16-CPU server. The system provides near-real-time data access. It provides data warehouse and data mining services to internal users, and it provides a requisite set of customer data to the customers themselves. Hundreds of sales and marketing campaigns are constructed using near-real-time data (within several minutes). And better, the system enables faster decision making about specific customers and customer classes.

Sources: Compiled from "Egg's Customer Data Warehouse Hits the Mark," *DM Review*, Vol. 15, No. 10, October 2005, pp. 24–28; Sun Microsystems, *Egg Banks on Sun to Hit the Mark with Customers*, September 19, 2005, **sun.com/smi/Press/sunflash/ 2005-09/sunflash.20050919.1.xml** (accessed April 2006); and ZD Net UK, *Sun Case Study: Egg's Customer Data Warehouse*, **whitepapers.zdnet.co.uk/0,39025945,60159401p-39000449q,00.htm** (accessed April 2006).

As business needs evolve, so do the requirements of the data warehouse. At this basic level, a data warehouse simply reports what happened. At the next level, some analysis occurs. As the system evolves, it provides prediction capabilities, which lead to the next level of operationalization. At its highest evolution, the ADW is capable of making events happen (e.g., activities such as creating sales and marketing campaigns or identifying and exploiting opportunities). See Figure 5.10 for a graphic description of this evolutionary process.

Teradata Corp. provides the baseline requirements to support an EDW. It also provides the new traits of active data warehousing required to deliver data freshness,

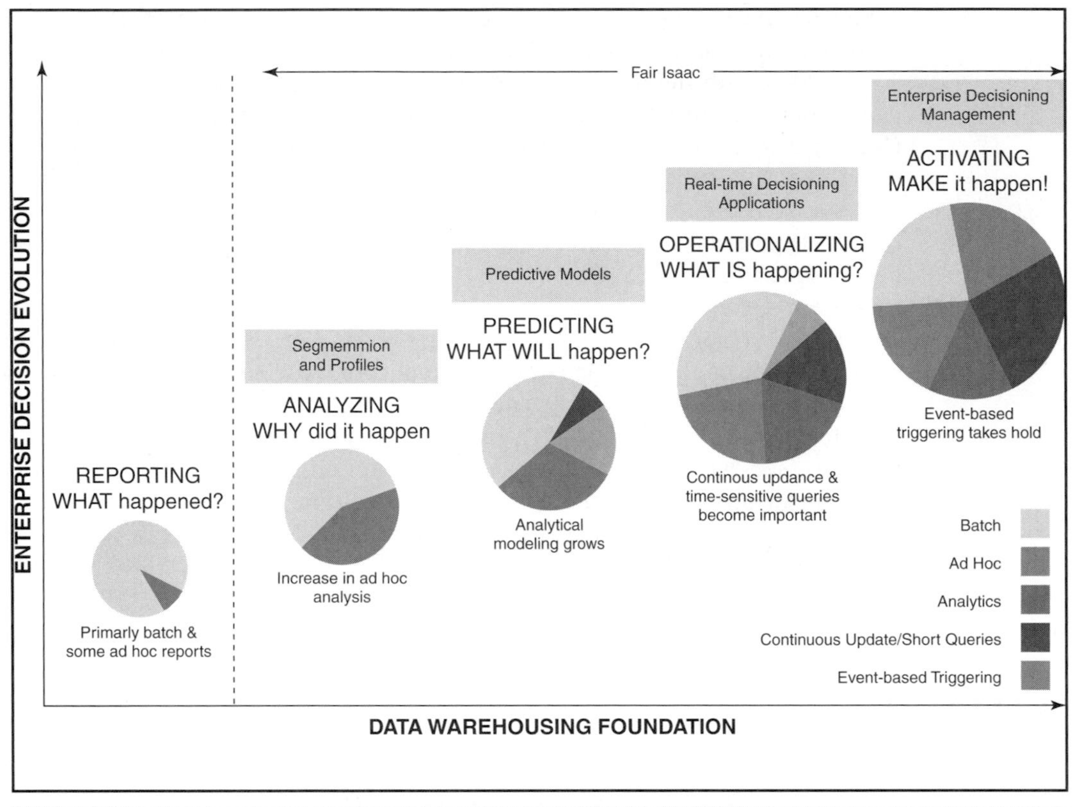

FIGURE 5.10 Enterprise Decision Evolution

Source: Courtesy of Teradata Corporation, a Division of NCR Corp. Used with permission.

performance, and availability and to enable enterprise decision management (see Figure 5.11 for an example).

An ADW offers an integrated information repository to drive strategic and tactical decision support within an organization. Real-time data warehousing upholds that instead of extracting operational data from an OLTP system in nightly batches into an ODS, data are assembled from OLTP systems as and when events happen and are moved at once into the data warehouse. This permits the instant updating of the data warehouse and the elimination of an ODS. At this point, tactical and strategic queries can be made against the RDW to use immediate as well as historical data.

According to Basu (2003), the most distinctive difference between a traditional data warehouse and an RDW is the shift in the data acquisition paradigm. Some of the business cases and enterprise requirements that led to the need for data in real-time include the following:

- A business often cannot afford to wait a whole day for its operational data to load into the data warehouse for analysis.
- Until now, data warehouses have captured snapshots of an organization's fixed states instead of incremental real-time data showing every state change and almost analogous patterns over time.
- With a traditional hub-and-spoke architecture, retaining the metadata in sync is difficult. It is also costly to develop, maintain, and secure many systems as opposed to one huge data warehouse so that data are centralized for BI/BA tools.

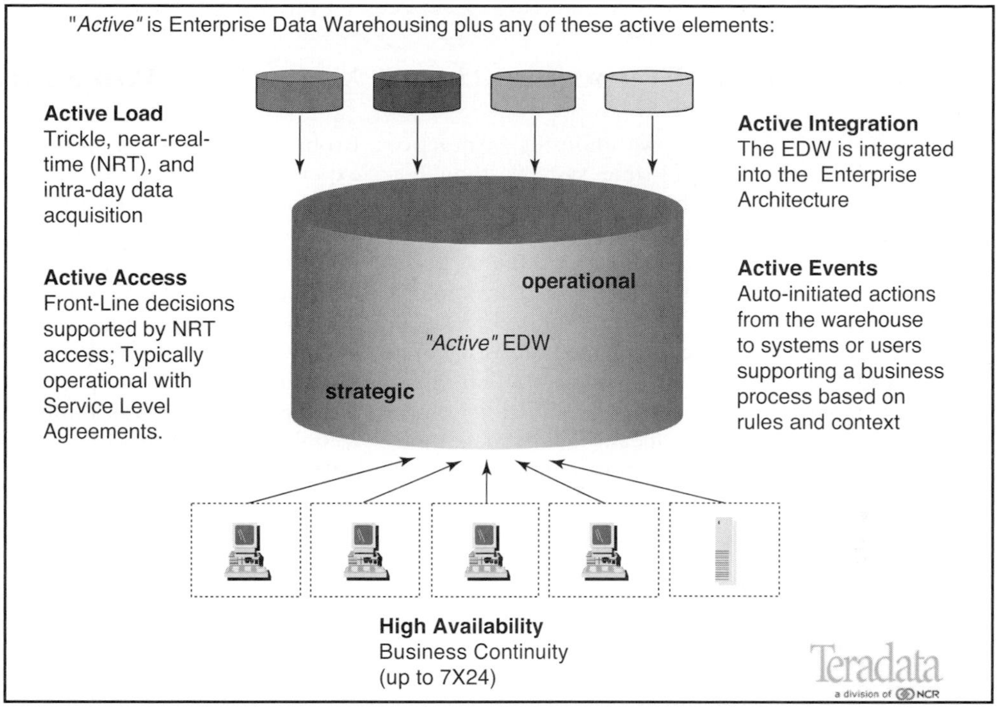

"*Active*" is Enterprise Data Warehousing plus any of these active elements:

Active Load
Trickle, near-real-time (NRT), and intra-day data acquisition

Active Access
Front-Line decisions supported by NRT access; Typically operational with Service Level Agreements.

Active Integration
The EDW is integrated into the Enterprise Architecture

Active Events
Auto-initiated actions from the warehouse to systems or users supporting a business process based on rules and context

operational
"*Active*" EDW
strategic

High Availability
Business Continuity
(up to 7X24)

Teradata
a division of NCR

FIGURE 5.11 The Teradata Active EDW

Source: Courtesy of Teradata Corporation, a Division of NCR Corp. Used with permission.

- In cases of huge nightly batch loads, the necessary ETL setup and processing power for large nightly data warehouse loading might be very high, and the processes might take too long. An EAI with real-time data collection can reduce or eliminate the nightly batch processes.

Despite the benefits of an RDW, developing one can create its own set of issues. These problems relate to architecture, data modeling, physical database design, storage and scalability, and maintainability. In addition, depending on exactly when data are accessed, even down to the microsecond, different versions of the truth may be extracted and created, which can confuse team members. For some details, refer to Basu (2003) and Terr (2004).

Real-time solutions present a remarkable set of challenges to BI activities. Although it is not ideal for all solutions, real-time data warehousing may be successful if the organization develops a sound methodology to handle project risks, incorporate proper planning, and focus on quality assurance activities. Understanding the common challenges and applying best practices can reduce the problem levels that are often a part of implementing complex data warehousing systems that incorporate BI/BA methods. Details and real implementations are discussed by Burdett and Singh (2004) and Wilk (2003). Also see Akbay (2006) and Ericson (2006).

See Technology Insights 5.7 for some details on how the real-time concept evolved. The flight management dashboard application at Continental Airlines (see the opening vignette) illustrates the power of real-time BI in accessing a data warehouse for use in face-to-face customer interaction situations. The operations staff use the real-time system to identify issues in the Continental flight network. As another example, UPS invested $600 million so it could use real-time data and processes. The investment was expected to cut 100 million delivery miles and save 14 million gallons of fuel annually by

TECHNOLOGY INSIGHTS 5.7

The Real-Time Realities of Active Data Warehousing

By 2003, the role of data warehousing in practice was growing rapidly. Real-time systems, though a novelty, were the latest buzz, along with the major complications of providing data and information instantaneously to those who need them. Many experts, including Peter Coffee, *eWeek*'s technology editor, believe that real-time systems must feed a real-time decision-making process. Stephen Brobst, CTO of the Teradata division of NCR, indicated that active data warehousing is a process of evolution in how an enterprise uses data. *Active* means that the data warehouse is also used as an operational and tactical tool. Brobst provided a five-stage model that fits Coffee's experience (2003) of how organizations "grow" in their data utilization (see Brobst et al., 2005). These stages (and the questions they purport to answer) are reporting (What happened?), analysis (Why did it happen?), prediction (What will happen?), operationalizing (What is happening?), and active warehousing (What do I want to happen?). The last stage, active warehousing, is where the greatest benefits may be obtained. Many organizations are enhancing centralized data warehouses to serve both operational and strategic decision making.

Sources: Adapted from P. Coffee, "'Active' Warehousing," *eWEEK*, Vol. 20, No. 25, June 23, 2003, p. 36; and Teradata Corp., *Active Data Warehousing*, **teradata.com/t/page/87127/index.html** (accessed April 2006).

managing its real-time package flow technologies (see Malykhina, 2003). In Table 5.4, we show a comparison of the traditional and active data warehousing environments.

Real-time data warehousing, near-real-time data warehousing, zero-latency warehousing, and active data warehousing are different names used in practice to describe the same concept. Gonzales (2005) presented different definitions for ADW. According to Gonzales, ADW is only one option that provides blended tactical and strategic data on-demand. The architecture to build an ADW is very similar to the corporate information factory architecture developed by Bill Inmon. The only difference between a corporate information factory and an ADW is the implementation of both data stores in a single environment. However, an SOA based on XML and Web services provide another option for blending tactical and strategic data on-demand.

TABLE 5.4 Comparison Between Traditional and Active Data Warehousing Environments

Traditional Data Warehouse Environment	*Active Data Warehouse Environment*
Strategic decisions only	Strategic and tactical decisions
Results sometimes hard to measure	Results measured with operations
Daily, weekly, monthly data currency acceptable; summaries often appropriate	Only comprehensive detailed data available within minutes is acceptable
Moderate user concurrency	High number (1,000 or more) of users accessing and querying the system simultaneously
Highly restrictive reporting used to confirm or check existing processes and patterns; often uses predeveloped summary tables or data marts	Flexible ad hoc reporting, as well as machine-assisted modeling (e.g., data mining) to discover new hypotheses and relationships
Power users, knowledge workers, internal users	Operational staffs, call centers, external users

Sources: Adapted from P. Coffee, "'Active' Warehousing," *eWEEK*, Vol. 20, No. 25, June 23, 2003, p. 36; and Teradata Corp., *Active Data Warehousing*, **teradata.com/t/page/87127/index.html** (accessed April 2006).

One critical issue in real-time data warehousing is that not all data should be updated continuously. This may certainly cause problems when reports are generated in real-time because one person's results may not match another person's. For example, a company using Business Objects Web Intelligence noticed a significant problem with real-time intelligence. Real-time reports are all different when produced at slightly different times (see Peterson, 2003). Also, it may not be necessary to update certain data continuously (e.g., course grades that are three or more years old).

Real-time requirements change the way we view the design of databases, data warehouses, OLAP, and data mining tools because they are literally updated concurrently while queries are active. But the substantial business value in doing so has been demonstrated, so it is crucial that organizations adopt these methods in their business processes. Careful planning is critical in such implementations.

Section 5.7 Review Questions

1. What is an RDW?
2. List the benefits of an RDW.
3. What are the major differences between a traditional data warehouse and an RDW?
4. List some of the drivers for RDW.

5.8 DATA WAREHOUSE ADMINISTRATION AND SECURITY ISSUES

Data warehouses provides a distinct competitive edge to enterprises that effectively create and use them. Due to its huge size and its intrinsic nature, a data warehouse requires especially strong monitoring in order to sustain satisfactory efficiency and productivity. The successful administration and management of a data warehouse entails skills and proficiency that go past what is required of a traditional database administrator (DBA). A **data warehouse administrator (DWA)** should be familiar with high-performance software, hardware, and networking technologies. He or she should also possess solid business insight. Because data warehouses feed BI systems and DSS that help managers with their decision-making activities, the DWA should be familiar with the decision-making processes so as to suitably design and maintain the data warehouse structure. It is particularly significant for a DWA to keep the existing requirements and capabilities of the data warehouse stable while simultaneously providing flexibility for rapid improvements. Finally, a DWA must possess excellent communications skills. See Benander et al. (2000) for a description of the key differences between a DBA and a DWA.

Security and privacy of information is a main and significant concern for a data warehouse professional. The U.S. government has passed regulations (e.g., the Gramm-Leach Bliley privacy and safeguards rules, the Health Insurance Portability and Accountability Act of 1996 [HIPAA]), instituting obligatory requirements in the management of customer information. Hence, companies must create security procedures that are effective yet flexible to conform to numerous privacy regulations. According to Elson and LeClerc (2005), effective security in a data warehouse should focus on four main areas:

1. Establishing effective corporate and security policies and procedures. An effective security policy should start at the top, with executive management, and should be communicated to all individuals within the organization.
2. Implementing logical security procedures and techniques to restrict access. This includes user authentication, access controls, and encryption technology.

TECHNOLOGY INSIGHTS 5.8

Ambeo Delivers Proven Data Access Auditing Solution

Since 1997, Ambeo (**ambeo.com**; now Embarcadero Technologies, Inc.) has deployed technology that provides performance management, data usage tracking, data privacy auditing, and monitoring to Fortune 1000 companies. These firms have some of the largest database environments in existence. Ambeo data access auditing solutions play a major role in an enterprise information security infrastructure.

The Ambeo technology is a relatively easy solution that records everything that happens in the databases, with low or zero overhead. In addition, it provides data access auditing that identifies exactly who is looking at data, when they are looking, and what they are doing with the data. This real-time monitoring helps quickly and effectively identify security breaches.

Sources: Adapted from "Ambeo Delivers Proven Data Access Auditing Solution," *Database Trends and Applications*, Vol. 19, No. 7, July 2005; and Ambeo, *Keeping Data Private (and Knowing It): Moving Beyond Conventional Safeguards to Ensure Data Privacy*, **ambeo.com/why_ambeo_white_papers.html** (accessed April 2006).

3. Limiting physical access to the data center environment.
4. Establishing an effective internal control review process with an emphasis on security and privacy.

See Technology Insights 5.8 for a description of Ambeo's important software tool that monitors security and privacy of data warehouses. Finally, keep in mind that accessing a data warehouse via a mobile device should always be performed cautiously. In this instance, data should only be accessed as read-only.

In the near term, data warehousing developments will be determined by noticeable factors (e.g., data volumes, increased intolerance for latency, the diversity and complexity of data types) and less noticeable factors (e.g., unmet end-user requirements for dashboards, balanced scorecards, master data management, information quality). Given these drivers, Agosta (2006) suggested that data warehousing trends will lean toward simplicity, value, and performance.

Section 5.8 Review Questions

1. What steps can an organization take to ensure the security and confidentiality of customer data in its data warehouse?
2. What skills should a DWA possess? Why?

5.9 RESOURCES, LINKS, AND THE TERADATA UNIVERSITY NETWORK CONNECTION

The use of this chapter and most other chapters in this book can be enhanced by the tools described in the following sections.

RESOURCES AND LINKS

We recommend looking at the following resources and links for further reading and explanations:

- The Data Warehouse Institute (**tdwi.com**)

- *DM Review* parentheses (**dmreview.com**)
- DSS Resources parentheses (**dssresources.com**)

CASES

All major MSS vendors (e.g., MicroStrategy, Microsoft, Oracle, IBM, Hyperion, Cognos, Exsys, Fair Issac, SAP, Information Builders) provide interesting customer success stories. Academic-oriented cases are available at the Harvard Business School Case Collection (**harvardbusinessonline.hbsp.harvard.edu**), Business Performance Improvement Resource (**bpir.com**), Idea Group Publishing (**idea-group.com**), Ivy League Publishing (**ivylp.com**), ICFAI Center for Management Research (**icmr.icfai.org/casestudies/icmr_case_studies.htm**), KnowledgeStorm (**knowledgestorm.com**), and other sites. For additional case resources, see Teradata University Network (**teradatauniversitynetwork.com**). For data warehousing cases, we specifically recommend the following from the Teradata University Network (**teradatauniversitynetwork.com**): *Continental Airlines Flies High with Real-Time Business Intelligence*, *Data Warehouse Governance at Blue Cross and Blue Shield of North Carolina*, *3M Moves to a Customer Focus Using a Global Data Warehouse*, *Data Warehousing Supports Corporate Strategy at First American Corporation*, *Harrah's High Payoff from Customer Information*, and *Whirlpool*. We also recommend the Data Warehousing Failures Assignment, which consists of eight short cases on data warehousing failures.

VENDORS, PRODUCTS, AND DEMOS

A comprehensive list is available at **(dmreview.com)**. Vendors are listed in Table 5.1. Also see **technologyevaluation.com**.

PERIODICALS

We recommend the following periodicals:

- *Baseline Magazine* (**baselinemag.com**)
- *Business Intelligence Journal* (**tdwi.org**)
- *CIO* (**cio.com**)
- *CIO Insight* (**cioinsight.com**)
- *Computer World* (**computerworld.com**)
- *Decision Support Systems* (**elsevier.com**)
- *DM Review* (**dmreview.com**)
- *eWEEK* (**eweek.com**)
- *InfoWeek* (**infoweek.com**)
- *InfoWorld* (**infoworld.com**)
- *InternetWeek* (**internetweek.com**)
- *Management Information Systems Quarterly (MIS Quarterly)* (**misq.org**)
- *Technology-Evaluation* online magazine (**technologyevaluation.com**)
- *Teradata Magazine* (**teradata.com**)

ADDITIONAL REFERENCES

For additional information on data warehousing, see the following.

Imhoff, C., N. Galemmo, and J.G. Geiger. (2003). *Mastering Data Warehouse Design: Relational and Dimensional Techniques*. New York: Wiley.

Marco, D., and M. Jennings. (2004). *Universal Meta Data Models*. New York: Wiley.

Wang, J. (2005). *Encyclopedia of Data Warehousing and Mining*. Hershey, PA: Idea Group Publishing.

For more on databases, the structure on which data warehouses are developed, see the following:

Watson, R. T. (2006). *Data Management*, 5th ed., New York: Wiley.

THE TERADATA UNIVERSITY NETWORK (TUN) CONNECTION

TUN (**teradatauniversitynetwork.com**) provides a wealth of information and cases on data warehousing. One of the best is the Continental Airlines case, which we require you to solve in a later exercise. Other recommended cases are mentioned earlier in this chapter. At TUN, if you click the Courses tab and select Data Warehousing, you will see links to many relevant articles, assignments, book chapters, course Web sites, PowerPoint presentations, projects, research reports, syllabi, and Web seminars. You will also find links to active data warehousing software demonstrations. Finally, you will see links to Teradata (**teradata.com**), where you can find additional information, including excellent data warehousing success stories, white papers, Web-based courses, and the online version of *Teradata Magazine*.

Chapter Highlights

- A data warehouse is a specially constructed data repository where data are organized so that they can be easily accessed by end users for several applications.
- Data marts contain data on one topic (e.g., marketing). A data mart can be a replication of a subset of data in the data warehouse. Data marts are a less expensive solution that can be replaced by or can supplement a data warehouse. Data marts can be independent of or dependent on a data warehouse.
- An ODS is a type of customer information file database that is often used as a staging area for a data warehouse.
- Data integration comprises three major processes: data access, data federation, and change capture. When these three processes are correctly implemented, data can be accessed and made accessible to an array of ETL and analysis tools and data warehousing environments.
- ETL technologies pull data from many sources, cleanse them, and load them into a data warehouse. ETL is an integral process in any data-centric project.
- Real-time or active data warehousing supplements and expands traditional data warehousing, moving into the realm of operational and tactical decision making by loading data in real-time and providing data to users for active decision making.
- The security and privacy of data and information is a critical issue for a data warehouse professional.

Key Terms

- active data warehouse (ADW)
- data integration
- data mart
- data warehouse
- data warehouse administrator (DWA)
- dependent data mart
- dimensional modeling
- dimension table
- drill-down
- enterprise application integration (EAI)
- enterprise data warehouse (EDW)
- enterprise information integration (EII)
- extraction, transformation, and load (ETL)
- grain
- independent data mart
- metadata
- oper mart
- operational data store (ODS)
- real-time data warehouse (RDW)

QUESTIONS FOR DISCUSSION

1. Compare data integration and ETL. How are they related?
2. What is a data warehouse and what are its benefits? Why is Web accessibility important with a data warehouse?
3. A data mart can replace a data warehouse or complement it. Compare and discuss these options.
4. Discuss the major drivers and benefits of data warehousing to end users.
5. List the differences and/or similarities between the roles of a database administrator and a data warehouse administrator.
6. Describe how data integration can lead to higher levels of data quality.
7. Compare the Kimball and Inmon approaches toward data warehouse development. Identify when each one is most effective.
8. Discuss security concerns involved in building a data warehouse.
9. Investigate current data warehouse development implementation through offshoring. Write a report about it. In class, debate the issue in terms of the benefits and costs, as well as social factors.

Exercises

Teradata University and Other Hands-on Exercises

1. Consider the case describing the development and application of a data warehouse for Coca-Cola Japan (a summary appears in Application Case 5.3), available at the DSS Resources Web site, **dssresources.com/cases/coca-colajapan/index.html**. Read the case and answer the nine questions for further analysis and discussion.

2. Read the Ball (2005) article and rank-order the criteria (ideally for a real organization). In a report, explain how important each criterion is and why.

3. Explain when you should implement a two- or three-tiered architecture when considering developing a data warehouse.

4. Read the full Continental Airlines case (summarized in the opening vignette) at **teradatastudentnetwork.com** and answer the questions.

5. At **teradatastudentnetwork.com**, read and answer the questions to the case "Harrah's High Payoff from Customer Information." Relate Harrah's results to how airlines and other casinos use their customer data.

6. At **teradatastudentnetwork.com**, read and answer the questions of the assignment "Data Warehousing Failures." Because eight cases are described in that assignment, the class may be divided into eight groups, with one case assigned per group. In addition, read Ariyachandra and Watson (2006a) and for each case, identify how the failure occurred as related to not focusing on one or more of the reference's success factor(s).

7. At **teradatastudentnetwork.com**, read and answer the questions with the assignment "AdVent Technology: Using the MicroStrategy Sales Analytic Model." The MicroStrategy software is accessible from the TUN site. Also, you might want to use Barbara Wixom's PowerPoint presentation about the MicroStrategy software ("Demo Slides for MicroStrategy Tutorial Script"), which is also available at the TUN site.

8. At **teradatastudentnetwork.com**, watch the Web seminars titled "Real-Time Data Warehousing: The Next Generation of Decision Support Data Management" and "Building the Real-Time Enterprise." Read the article "Teradata's Real-Time Enterprise Reference Architecture: A Blueprint for the Future of IT," also available at this site. Describe how real-time concepts and technologies work and how they can be used to extend existing data warehousing and BI architectures to support day-to-day decision making. Write a report indicating how real-time data warehousing is specifically providing competitive advantage for organizations. Describe in detail the difficulties in such implementations and operations and describe how they are being addressed in practice.

9. At **teradatastudentnetwork.com**, watch the Web seminars "Data Integration Renaissance: New Drivers and Emerging Approaches," "In Search of a Single Version of the Truth: Strategies for Consolidating Analytic Silos," and "Data Integration: Using ETL, EAI, and EII Tools to Create an Integrated Enterprise." Also read the "Data Integration" research report. Compare and contrast the presentations. What is the most important issue described in these seminars? What is the best way to handle the strategies and challenges of consolidating data marts and spreadsheets into a

unified data warehousing architecture? Perform a Web search to identify the latest developments in the field. Compare the presentation to the material in the text and the new material that you found.

10. Consider the future of data warehousing. Perform a Web search on this topic. Also, read these two articles: L. Agosta, "Data Warehousing in a Flat World: Trends for 2006," *DM Direct Newsletter*, March 31, 2006; and J.G. Geiger, "CIFe: Evolving with the Times," *DM Review*, November 2005, pp. 38–41. Compare and contrast your findings.

11. Access **teradatastudentnetwork.com**. Identify the latest articles, research reports, and cases on data warehousing. Describe recent developments in the field. Include in your report how data warehousing is used in BI and DSS.

Exercises

Team Assignments and Role-Playing Projects

1. Kathryn Avery has been a DBA with a nationwide retail chain (Big Chain) for the past six years. She has recently been asked to lead the development of Big Chain's first data warehouse. The project has the sponsorship of senior management and the CIO. The rationale for developing the data warehouse is to advance the reporting systems, particularly in sales and marketing, and, in the longer term, to improve Big Chain's CRM. Kathryn has been to a Data Warehousing Institute conference and has been doing some reading, but she is still mystified about development methodologies. She knows there are two groups—EDW (Inmon) and architected data marts (Kimball)—that have equally robust provision.

   Initially, she believed that the two methodologies were extremely dissimilar, but as she has examined them more carefully, she isn't so certain. Kathryn has a number of questions that she would like answered:

   a. What are the real differences between the methodologies?

   b. What factors are important in selecting a particular methodology?

   c. What should be her next steps in thinking about a methodology?

   Help Kathryn answer these questions. (This exercise was adapted from K. Duncan, L. Reeves, and J. Griffin, "BI Experts' Perspective," *Business Intelligence Journal*, Vol. 8, No. 4, Fall 2003, pp. 14–19.)

2. Jeet Kumar is the administrator of data warehousing at a big regional bank. He was appointed five years ago to implement a data warehouse to the support the bank's CRM business strategy. Using the data warehouse, the bank has been successful in integrating customer information, understanding customer profitability, attracting customers, enhancing customer relationships, and retaining customers.

   Over the years, the bank's data warehouse has moved closer to real-time by moving to more frequent refreshes of the data warehouse. Now, the bank wants to implement customer self-service and call center applications that require even fresher data than is currently available in the warehouse.

   Jeet wants some support in considering the possibilities for presenting fresher data. One alternative is to entirely commit to implementing real-time data warehousing. His ETL vendor is prepared to assist him make this change. Nevertheless, Jeet has been informed about EAI and EII technologies and wonders how they might fit into his plans.

   In particular, he has the following questions:

   a. What exactly are EAI and EII technologies?

   b. How are EAI and EII related to ETL?

   c. How are EAI and EII related to real-time data warehousing?

   d. Are EAI and EII required, complementary, or alternatives to real-time data warehousing?

   Help Jeet answer these questions. (This exercise was adapted from S. Brobst, E. Levy, and C. Muzilla, "Enterprise Application Integration and Enterprise Information Integration," *Business Intelligence Journal*, Vol. 10, No. 2, Spring 2005, pp. 27–32.)

3. Interview administrators in your college or executives in your organization to determine how data warehousing could assist them in their work. Write up a proposal describing your findings. Include cost estimates and benefits in your report.

4. Go through the list of data warehousing risks described in this chapter and find two examples of each in practice.

5. Access **teradata.com** and read the white papers "Measuring Data Warehouse ROI" and "Realizing ROI: Projecting and Harvesting the Business Value of an Enterprise Data Warehouse." Also, watch the

Web-based course "The ROI Factor: How Leading Practitioners Deal with the Tough Issue of Measuring DW ROI." Describe the most important issues described in them. Compare these issues to the success factors described in Ariyachandra and Watson (2006a).

6. Read the article K. Liddell Avery and Hugh J. Watson, "Training Data Warehouse End-users," *Business Intelligence Journal*, Vol. 9, No. 4, Fall 2004, pp. 40–51 (which is available at **teradatastudentnetwork.com**). Consider the different classes of end users, describe their difficulties, and describe the benefits of appropriate training for each group. Have each member of the group take on one of the roles and have a discussion about how an appropriate type of data warehousing training would be good for each of you.

Exercises

Internet Exercises

1. Search the Internet to find information about data warehousing. Identify some newsgroups that have an interest in this concept. Explore ABI/INFORM in your library, e-library, and Google for recent articles on the topic. Begin with **tdwi.com**, **technologyevaluation.com**, and the major vendors: **teradata.com**, **sas.com**, **oracle.com**, and **ncr.com**. Also check **cio.com**, **dmreview.com**, **dssresources.com**, and **db2mag.com**.
2. Survey some ETL tools and vendors. Start with **fairisaac.com** and **egain.com**. Also consult **dmreview.com**.
3. Contact some data warehouse vendors and obtain information about their products. Give special attention to vendors that provide tools for multiple purposes, such as Cognos, Software A&G, SAS Institute, and Oracle. Free online demos are available from some of these vendors. Download a demo or two and try them. Write a report describing your experience.
4. Explore **teradata.com** for developments and success stories about data warehousing. Write a report about what you have discovered.
5. Explore **teradata.com** for white papers and Web-based courses on data warehousing. Read the former and watch the latter. (Divide up the class up so that all the sources are covered.) Write up what you have discovered in a report.
6. Find recent cases of successful data warehousing applications. Go to data warehouse vendors' sites and look for cases or success stories. Select one and write a brief summary to present to your class.

End of Chapter Application Case

Real-Time Data Warehousing at Overstock.com

In spring 1999, Dr. Patrick M. Byrne recognized the potential in liquidating excess inventory through the Internet. Six months later and with no outside funding, he launched the Overstock.com Web site. Overstock.com, Inc., is an online closeout retailer that offers discount, brand-name merchandise for sale over the Internet. The company offers its customers an opportunity to shop for bargains conveniently, while offering its suppliers an alternative inventory liquidation distribution channel. Founded on the principles of value investing and fair dealing, Overstock.com has quickly become the online leader in a market valued at $60 billion in the United States. The numbers of products Overstock.com offers has grown from fewer than 100 in 1999 to more than 14,000 non-BMV (non–book, music, and video) products and approximately 650,000 BMV products as of June 2005. Overstock.com delivers the best name-brand values to consumers.

In April 2005, Overstock.com selected Teradata to provide it with an EDW with analytic applications, including CRM, data mining, BA, the Teradata e-business suite, logical data models, and consulting. This EDW integrated the firm's data into a single repository for a holistic view of the business. The Teradata EDW provides parallel database technology, a suite of data access and management utilities, and a portfolio of analytical tools that provide detailed business insight and foster interactions with a high degree of relevance to customer needs.

In August 2005, Overstock.com began to connect users to a real-time data warehouse. It used transactional data management tools from GoldenGate Software, Inc., to pull information directly from its business systems into the data warehouse. Overstock.com also adopted Teradata's Web-based framework of services for application integration to replace a process that used traditional ETL tools to build reports directly from Overstock's back-end systems. Now, the data warehouse receives Web site clickstream data in real-time, financial and product-sales data every 15 minutes, and other information hourly. "When we launch campaigns, we can look within five minutes and see they are producing lift or revenue that would not normally have happened," said Jack Garcella, the Salt Lake City–based e-tailer's vice president of data warehousing analytics and reporting. With several terabytes of data stored in the EDW and millions of transactions taking place each day, Overstock.com needed to ensure that the data warehouse was continuously updated. It selected Sunopsis Data Conductor, a powerful ETL product, to allow for automatically and efficiently working with large volumes of data from source systems.

Sources: Adapted from K. Ferrell, "Mission Possible: An Ambitious Data Warehouse Implementation—and Great Results—Are All in a Day's Work for Overstock.com," *Teradata Magazine*, Vol. 6, No. 1, March 2006,; J. Garzella, "Overstock.com Meets High-Volume, High-Performance Real-Time Data Transformation Needs with Sunopsis," *DM Review*, January 2006; C. Babcock, "Overstock.com Moves Reports to Data Warehouse," *InformationWeek*, August 3, 2005; *History*, Overstock.com *Investor Relations*, **shareholder.com** (accessed April 2006); **Shareholder.com** Investor Relations, Overstock.com, *Inc. Selects Teradata for Enterprise Data Warehouse, Customer Analytics and Single View of the Business*, **shareholder.com** (accessed April 2006); and Teradata.com, Overstock.com, *Inc. Selects Teradata for Enterprise Data Warehouse, Customer Analytics and Single View of the Business*, April 20, 2005, **teradata.com/t/go.aspx/index.html?id=133353** (accessed April 2006).

QUESTIONS FOR THE CASE

1. Describe how Overstock.com ran its campaigns before the Teradata system was developed.
2. How has the real-time data warehouse helped Overstock. com improve the performance of the business?
3. Go to the Web sites of the vendors mentioned in the case and examine the current data warehousing features and capabilities of each. Describe in detail how Overstock.com could potentially use each one.

References

Adelman, S., and L. Moss. (2001, Winter). "Data Warehouse Risks." *Journal of Data Warehousing*, Vol. 6, No. 1.

Agosta, L. (2006, January). "The Data Strategy Adviser: The Year Ahead—Data Warehousing Trends 2006." *DM Review*, Vol. 16, No. 1.

Akbay, S. (2006, Quarter 1). "Data Warehousing in Real Time." *Business Intelligence Journal*, Vol. 11, No. 1.

Anthes, G.H. (2003, June 30). "Hilton Checks into New Suite." *Computerworld*, Vol. 37, No. 26.

Ariyachandra, T., and H. Watson. (2005). "Key Factors in Selecting a Data Warehouse Architecture." *Business Intelligence Journal*, Vol. 10, No. 2.

Ariyachandra, T., and H. Watson. (2006a, January). "Benchmarks for BI and Data Warehousing Success." *DM Review*, Vol. 16, No. 1.

Ariyachandra, T., and H. Watson. (2006b, Quarter 1). "Which Data Warehouse Architecture Is Most Successful?" *Business Intelligence Journal*, Vol. 11, No. 1.

Armstrong, R. (2000, Quarter 3). "E-nalysis for the E-business," *Teradata Magazine Online*, **teradata.com**.

Ball, S.K. (2005, November 14). *Do You Need a Data Warehouse Layer in Your Business Intelligence Architecture?* **datawarehouse.ittoolbox.com/documents/industry-articles/do-you-need-a-data-warehouse-layer-in-your-business-intelligence-architecture-2729** (accessed April 2006).

Barquin, R., A. Paller, and H. Edelstein. (1997). "Ten Mistakes to Avoid for Data Warehousing Managers." In R. Barquin and H. Edelstein (eds.). *Building, Using, and Managing the Data Warehouse*. Upper Saddle River, NJ: Prentice Hall.

Basu, R. (2003, November). "Challenges of Real-Time Data Warehousing." *DM Review*.

Bell, L.D. (2001, Spring). "MetaBusiness Meta Data for the Masses: Administering Knowledge Sharing for Your Data Warehouse." *Journal of Data Warehousing*, Vol. 6, No. 2.

Benander, A., B. Benander, A. Fadlalla, and G. James. (2000, Winter). "Data Warehouse Administration and Management," *Information Systems Management*, Vol. 17, No. 1.

Bonde, A., and M. Kuckuk. (2004, April). "Real World Business Intelligence: The Implementation Perspective." *DM Review*, Vol. 14, No. 4.

Breslin, M. (2004, Winter). "Data Warehousing Battle of the Giants: Comparing the Basics of Kimball and Inmon Models." *Business Intelligence Journal*, Vol. 9, No. 1.

Brobst, S., E. Levy, and C. Muzilla. (2005, Spring). "Enterprise Application Integration and Enterprise Information Integration." *Business Intelligence Journal*, Vol. 10, No. 2.

Brody, R. (2003, Summer). "Information Ethics in the Design and Use of Metadata." *IEEE Technology and Society Magazine*, Vol. 22, No. 2.

Brown, M. (2004, May 9–12). "8 Characteristics of a Successful Data Warehouse." *Proceedings of the Twenty-Ninth Annual SAS Users Group International Conference (SUGI 29).* Montreal.

Burdett, J., and S. Singh. (2004). "Challenges and Lessons Learned from Real-Time Data Warehousing." *Business Intelligence Journal*, Vol. 9, No. 4.

Coffee, P. (2003, June 23). "'Active' Warehousing." *eWEEK*, Vol. 20, No. 25.

Dasu, T., and T. Johnson. (2003). *Exploratory Data Mining and Data Cleaning*. New York: Wiley.

Davison, D. (2003, November 14). "Top 10 Risks of Offshore Outsourcing." META Group Research Report, now Gartner, Inc., Stamford, CT.

Devlin, B. (2003, Quarter 2). "Solving the Data Warehouse Puzzle." *DB2 Magazine*.

Dragoon, A. (2003, July 1). "All for One View." *CIO*.

Eckerson, W. (2003, Fall). "The Evolution of ETL." *Business Intelligence Journal*, Vol. 8, No. 4.

Eckerson, W. (2004, November) "Gauge Your Warehouse Maturity." *DM Review*, Vol. 14, No. 11.

Eckerson, W. (2005, April 1). "Data Warehouse Builders Advocate for Different Architectures." *Application Development Trends*.

Edwards, M. (2003, Fall). "2003 Best Practices Awards Winners: Innovators in Business Intelligence and Data Warehousing." *Business Intelligence Journal*, Vol. 8, No.4.

Elson, R., and R. LeClerc. (2005). "Security and Privacy Concerns in the Data Warehouse Environment." *Business Intelligence Journal*, Vol. 10, No. 3.

Ericson, J. (2006, March). "Real-Time Realities." *BI Review*.

Gonzales, M. (2005, Quarter 1). "Active Data Warehouses Are Just One Approach for Combining Strategic and Technical Data." *DB2 Magazine*.

Hall, M. (2002, April 15). "Seeding for Data Growth." *Computerworld*, Vol. 36, No. 16.

Hicks, M. (2001, November 26). "Getting Pricing Just Right." *eWEEK*, Vol. 18, No. 46.

Hoffer, J.A., M.B. Prescott, and F.R. McFadden. (2007). *Modern Database Management*, 8th ed. Upper Saddle River, NJ: Prentice Hall.

Hwang, M., and H. Xu. (2005, Fall). "A Survey of Data Warehousing Success Issues." *Business Intelligence Journal*, Vol. 10, No. 4.

Imhoff, C. (2001, May). "Power Up Your Enterprise Portal." *E-Business Advise*.

Inmon, W.H. (2005). *Building the Data Warehouse*, 4th ed. New York: Wiley.

Inmon, W.H. (2006, January). "Information Management: How Do You Tune a Data Warehouse?" *DM Review*, Vol. 16, No. 1.

Jukic, N., and C. Lang. (2004, Summer). "Using Offshore Resources to Develop and Support Data Warehousing Applications." *Business Intelligence Journal*, Vol. 9, No. 3.

Karacsony, K. (2006, January). "ETL Is a Symptom of the Problem, not the Solution." *DM Review*, Vol. 16, No. 1.

Kassam, S. (2002, April 16). "Freedom of Information." *Intelligent Enterprise*, Vol. 5, No. 7.

Kay, R. (2005, September 19). "EII." *Computerworld*. Vol. 39, No. 38.

Kelly, C. (2001, June 14). "Calculating Data Warehousing ROI." *SearchSQLServer.com Tips*.

Malykhina, E. (2003, January 3). "The Real-Time Imperative." *InformationWeek*, Issue 1020.

Manglik, A., and V. Mehra. (2005, Winter). "Extending Enterprise BI Capabilities: New Patterns for Data Integration." *Business Intelligence Journal*, Vol. 10, No. 1.

Matney, D. (2003, Spring). "End-User Support Strategy." *Business Intelligence Journal*, Vol. 8, No. 2.

McCloskey, D.W. (2002). *Choosing Vendors and Products to Maximize Data Warehousing Success*. Auerbach Publications, **auerbach-publications.com**.

Mehra, V. (2005, Summer). "Building a Metadata-Driven Enterprise: A Holistic Approach." *Business Intelligence Journal*, Vol. 10, No. 3.

Murtaza, A. (1998, Fall). "A Framework for Developing Enterprise Data Warehouses." *Information Systems Management*, Vol. 15, No. 4.

Nash, K.S. (2002, July). "Chemical Reaction." *Baseline*.

Orovic, V. (2003, June). "To Do & Not to Do." *eAI Journal*.

Parzinger, M.J., and M.N. Frolick. (2001, July). "Creating Competitive Advantage Through Data Warehousing." *Information Strategy*, Vol. 17, No. 4.

Peterson, T. (2003, April 21). "Getting Real About Real Time." *ComputerWorld*, Vol. 37, No. 16.

Raden, N. (2003, June 30). "Real Time: Get Real, Part II." *Intelligent Enterprise*.

Rosenberg, A. (2006, Quarter 1). "Improving Query Performance in Data Warehouses." *Business Intelligence Journal*, Vol. 11, No. 1.

Sammon, D., and P. Finnegan. (2000, Fall). "The Ten Commandments of Data Warehousing." *Database for Advances in Information Systems*, Vol. 31, No. 4.

Sapir, D. (2005, May). "Data Integration: A Tutorial." *DM Review*, Vol. 15, No. 5.

Sen, A. (2004, April). "Metadata Management: Past, Present and Future." *Decision Support Systems*, Vol. 37, No. 1.

Sen, A., and P. Sinha (2005). "A Comparison of Data Warehousing Methodologies." *Communications of the ACM*, Vol. 48, No. 3.

Solomon, M. (2005, Winter)."Ensuring a Successful Data Warehouse Initiative." *Information Systems Management Journal*.

Songini, M.L. (2004, February 2). "ETL Quickstudy." *Computerworld*, Vol. 38, No. 5.

Tannenbaum, A. (2002, Spring). "Identifying Meta Data Requirements." *Journal of Data Warehousing*, Vol. 7, No. 2.

Tennant, R. (2002, May 15). "The Importance of Being Granular." *Library Journal*, Vol. 127, No. 9.

Terr, S. (2004, February). "Real-Time Data Warehousing: Hardware and Software." *DM Review*, Vol. 14, No. 2.

Turban, E., D. Leidner, E. McLean, and J. Wetherbe. (2006). *Information Technology for Management*, 5th ed. New York: Wiley.

Vaduva, A., and T. Vetterli. (2001, September). "Metadata Management for Data Warehousing: An Overview." *International Journal of Cooperative Information Systems*, Vol. 10, No. 3.

Van den Hoven, J. (1998). "Data Marts: Plan Big, Build Small." *Information Systems Management*, Vol. 15, No. 1.

Watson, H.J. (2002). "Recent Developments in Data Warehousing." *Communications of the ACM*, Vol. 8, No. 1.

Watson, H., J. Gerard, L. Gonzalez, M. Haywood, and D. Fenton. (1999), "Data Warehouse Failures: Case Studies and Findings." *Journal of Data Warehousing*, Vol. 4, No. 1.

Watson, H.J., D.L. Goodhue, and B.H. Wixom. (2002). "The Benefits of Data Warehousing: Why Some Organizations Realize Exceptional Payoffs." *Information & Management*, Vol. 39.

Weir, R. (2002, Winter). "Best Practices for Implementing a Data Warehouse." *Journal of Data Warehousing*, Vol. 7, No. 1.

Wilk, L. (2003, Spring). "Data Warehousing and Real-Time Computing." *Business Intelligence Journal*, Vol. 8, No. 2.

Wixom, B., and H. Watson. (2001, March). "An Empirical Investigation of the Factors Affecting Data Warehousing Success." *MIS Quarterly*, Vol. 25, No. 1.

Zhao, X. (2005, October 7). "Meta Data Management Maturity Model," *DM Direct Newsletter*.

Business Analytics and Data Visualization

Learning Objectives

- Describe business analytics (BA) and its importance to organizations
- List and briefly describe the major BA methods and tools
- Describe how online analytical processing (OLAP), data visualization, and multidimensionality can improve decision making
- Describe advanced analysis methods
- Describe geographical information systems (GIS) and their support to decision making
- Describe real-time BA
- Describe how business intelligence (BI) supports competitive intelligence
- Describe automated decision support (ADS) systems and their benefits
- Explain how the Web relates to BA
- Describe Web intelligence and Web analytics and their importance to organizations
- Describe implementation issues related to BA and success factors for BA

Many organizations have amassed vast amounts of data that employees can use to unlock valuable relationships to enable the organization to compete successfully. Some organizations do this extremely well, using analytical tools, but others are quite ineffective. Enabling decision analysis through access to all relevant data and information is known as *business analytics (BA)*. BA includes OLAP, multidimensionality, data visualization, GIS, data mining, and advanced analytical techniques. The input data analyzed using BA can be found in a data warehouse, can be operational data, or can be in Web files. Conducting the analysis is not simple and may fail if not properly conducted. This chapter describes these issues in the following sections:

6.1 Opening Vignette: Lexmark International Improves Operations with Business Intelligence

6.2 The Business Analytics (BA) Field: An Overview

6.3 Online Analytical Processing (OLAP)

6.4 Reports and Queries

6.5 Multidimensionality

6.1 OPENING VIGNETTE: LEXMARK INTERNATIONAL IMPROVES OPERATIONS WITH BUSINESS INTELLIGENCE

Lexmark International (**lexmark.com**) is a global manufacturer of printing products and solutions, with about 12,000 employees and more than 50 sales offices worldwide. Thousands of retail partners sell Lexmark's products in more than 160 countries.

PROBLEM

Being in an extremely competitive business, Lexmark needs detailed, accurate, and timely information for decision support and strategy implementation. This is especially important when it comes to data flow between Lexmark and its retail partners. The most important information is about sales volumes everywhere and inventory levels. The old system was slow, inefficient, and riddled with errors. Problems occurred both with flows from the partners and with data delivery. In delivering the data, results were often copied from spreadsheets and pasted into reports, typically taking four days or longer to produce answers to common business questions. Sales representatives out in the field had to dial into the intranet. After a connection was established, analysts and sales representatives had to write Structured Query Language (SQL) queries and navigate the mainframe to generate reports for management, some of which were based on inaccurate, week-old data.

SOLUTION

Lexmark implemented a BI solution from MicroStrategy. The application is a BI adaptation for retailing, known today as Retail BI System. The system enables buyers, financial analysts, marketing analysts, regional managers, merchandisers, and field sales representatives to analyze sales and inventory data from their desktop or mobile devices. The system, which is fed by IBM's data warehouse, provides users with the ability to track sales performance and inventory levels of every Lexmark product at thousands of retail stores worldwide. A large number of reporting and analysis tools are included in the software, including extensive reports, more than 50 statistical models, and visualization techniques (described later in this chapter). Using the system, Lexmark's user community can answer queries such as these instantly and easily:

- What are my weekly sales and inventory levels in each of a specific customer's stores throughout the country?
- Who were my top retailers for a given product last week, last month, or this weekend versus last weekend?
- Looking at a given store that reports electronic data interchange (EDI) sales and inventory data to Lexmark, what are the inventory levels of a certain top-selling product?

RESULTS

Lexmark reported that decision makers now receive timely, accurate, and detailed information. The new system helped to identify sales opportunities, increased partner loyalty, eliminated inventory problems, and increased profitability. For example, when the company identifies that a specific retail location is about to sell out of a certain printer, an automatic *alert* is sent to the store manager and, within hours, a replenishment order is placed, avoiding a stockout. Overall, 100,000 potentially lost sales were recovered. Retail stores like Lexmark because of this service, which makes Lexmark a preferred vendor.

Almost all Lexmark employees are using the system. Novice workers are able to use the information to improve how they do their job. Managers can better understand business trends and make appropriate strategic decisions. They have a better understanding of consumer demand by country and store, so they can better decide, for example, on pricing and promotions. Also, customer and partner services have been greatly improved.

Sources: Compiled from MicroStrategy, *Success Story: Lexmark*, 2006, **microstrategy.com/Customers/Successes/lexmark.asp** (accessed February 2006); and L. Valentine, "Lexmark CIO Croswell P. Chambers: Supporting a Changing Business Environment," *CIO Today*, July 21, 2004, **cio-today.com/story.xhtml?story_id=25966** (accessed March 2006).

Questions for the Opening Vignette

1. Identify the challenges Lexmark faced regarding information flow.
2. How were information flows provided before and after implementation of the system?
3. Identify decisions supported by the new system.
4. How can the new system improve customer service?
5. Go to **microstrategy.com**. Examine the capabilities of Retail BI System. Prepare a list of the capabilities.
6. Go to **sas.com** and find the Retail Intelligence product; take the interactive tour. Compare it to MicroStrategy's product. Also, compare it to Oracle Retail (see **oracle.com/applications/retail.html**).

WHAT WE CAN LEARN FROM THIS VIGNETTE

The Lexmark case indicates the need for collecting and analyzing information, which may be in thousands of locations, and doing so in a timely manner. Also, information needs to be distributed quickly. This can be accomplished by:

- Creating a data warehouse that integrates and standardizes data from the many sources and locations
- Using software that enables easy querying of the data from any place, any time
- Using software to prepare and distribute reports
- Using BI software to conduct various analyses on the data to discover opportunities or problems as well as to find solutions and trends
- Using BI software to alert managers and others
- Finding the status of sales and inventories quickly and accurately (i.e., using **status reports**)

These capabilities are typical to the activities conducted using BI analytics software, and they are the subject of this chapter. We refer to them as *business analytics*.

6.2 THE BUSINESS ANALYTICS (BA) FIELD: AN OVERVIEW

As described in Chapters 1 and 5, **business intelligence (BI)** involves acquiring data and information (and perhaps knowledge) from a wide variety of sources, organizing them in a data warehouse, and using them for decision making. BA provides the models and the analysis procedures to BI. It also involves tracking data and then analyzing them for competitive advantage. For details, see Eckersen (2003). Let's look at how BA work.

THE ESSENTIALS OF BA

Analytics is the science of analysis. Generally, it refers to analysis of data. There are many ways to conduct such an analysis. Indeed, there are many methods and hundreds of software tools to conduct the analysis.

Business analytics (BA) is a broad category of applications and techniques for gathering, storing, analyzing, and providing access to data to help enterprise users make better business and strategic decisions. BA is also known as *analytical processing*, *BI tools, BI applications*, and just *BI*. (Note: For a glossary of these and other related terms, see Devlin, 2006.) BI is becoming a major tool for most medium and large corporations. Pizza Hut, for example, has significantly boosted its sales revenue by using BI tools (see Langnau, 2003). Based on 20 years' worth of data on consumers, Pizza Hut knows what kind of pizzas customers order, what kind of coupons they usually use, and how much customers spend in a given time period. Marketing managers can run this information through a BI analysis that forecasts, for example, the probability of a customer's next order. The company then uses this information to determine marketing strategies to influence the customer to buy more pizzas without spending more on that marketing strategy than it has to. The process of BI usually, but not necessarily, involves the use, or even the construction, of a data warehouse.

An analytic application is a step upward in sophistication from merely providing analytic techniques or tools. It allows for activities such as:

- Automating the thinking and, in most cases, a portion of the decision making of a human being
- Typically using complex quantitative techniques, such as multivariate regression analysis, data mining, artificial intelligence, or nonlinear programming

Example

An analytic application used for credit scoring for a loan applicant might:

- Calculate a credit-worthiness score
- Automatically accept or deny the loan application
- Select the loan limit
- Select which credit card product (interest rate, payment terms, etc.) to issue to this applicant or which other type of loan to approve

Using BA software, the user can make queries, request ad hoc reports, or conduct analyses. For example, analysis can be carried out by performing multilayer queries. Because all the databases are linked, you can search for what products are overstocked in a particular store. You can then determine which of those products commonly sell with popular items, based on previous sales. After planning a promotion to move the excess stock along with the popular products (e.g., bundling them together), you can dig deeper into the data to see where this promotion would be most popular (and most profitable). The results of your request can be reports, predictions, alerts, and/or graphical presentations. These can be disseminated to decision makers. For an example of an application at Ben & Jerry's, see Application Case 6.1.

Application Case 6.1

Ben & Jerry's Excels with BA

At the Ben & Jerry's (**benjerry.com**) factory in Waterbury, Vermont, huge pipes pump out more than 200,000 pints of ice cream each day. Throughout the day, refrigerated tractor-trailers pull up, pick up the pints, and deliver them to depots. From there, the ice cream is shipped out to more than 60,000 grocery stores in the United States and in 14 other countries. There, the ice cream is placed on freezer shelves for sale.

At the company's headquarters, the life of each pint of ice cream—from ingredients to sale—is tracked. After a pint is stamped and sent out, Ben & Jerry's stores its tracking number in an Oracle data warehouse and later analyzes the data. Using BA software, the sales team can check to see if Chocolate Chip Cookie Dough is gaining ground on Cherry Garcia for the coveted number-one sales position. The marketing department checks to see whether company promotions and advertising are leading to increased sales. The finance people use the tracking numbers in their analyses to show the profit generated from each type of ice cream. Since the company started using the software, the accounting department has sharply reduced the amount of time it takes to close the monthly books. And probably most important to a company focused on customer loyalty, the consumer affairs staff match up each pint with the hundreds of calls and e-mails received each week, checking to see if there were any complaints.

Sources: Compiled from J. Schlosser. "Looking for Intelligence in Ice-Cream" *Fortune*, March 17, 2003; and Ben & Jerry's Homemade Inc./Information Systems, **essaypage.com/cgi-bin/query?mss=essaypage&stq=10 &q=Ben%20and%20Jerry%27s** (accessed July 2006).

More advanced applications of BA include activities such as financial modeling, budgeting, resource allocation, and competitive intelligence. Advanced BA systems include components such as decision models, business performance analysis, metrics, data profiling, reengineering tools, and much more. (For details, see **dmreview.com**.) Finally BA can be conducted in real-time (see Bonde and Kuckuk, 2004, and Microsoft's IT BI, at **microsoft.com/sql/solutions/bi/overview.mspx**).

THE TOOLS AND TECHNIQUES OF BA

BA employs large numbers of analytic tools and techniques. We can divide them into three major categories, as shown in Figure 6.1.

As shown in the figure, the first category is *information and knowledge discovery*. Some of its activities are discussed in this chapter. Data, text, and Web mining are described in Chapter 7. The second category is *decision support and intelligent systems*, which are described in Chapter 3, here, and in Chapters 11–13. The final category, *visualization*, is discussed here.

Vendors classify BA tools in several different ways. We present two of them next.

MicroStrategy's Classification of BA Tools: The Five Styles of BI

MicroStrategy divides its products into five categories (referred to as *styles*; see details at MicroStrategy, 2006). These are the five styles:

1. *Enterprise reporting.* Enterprise reporting products are used to generate highly formatted static reports destined for broad distribution to many people. They are pixel-perfect report formats for operational reporting and dashboards.

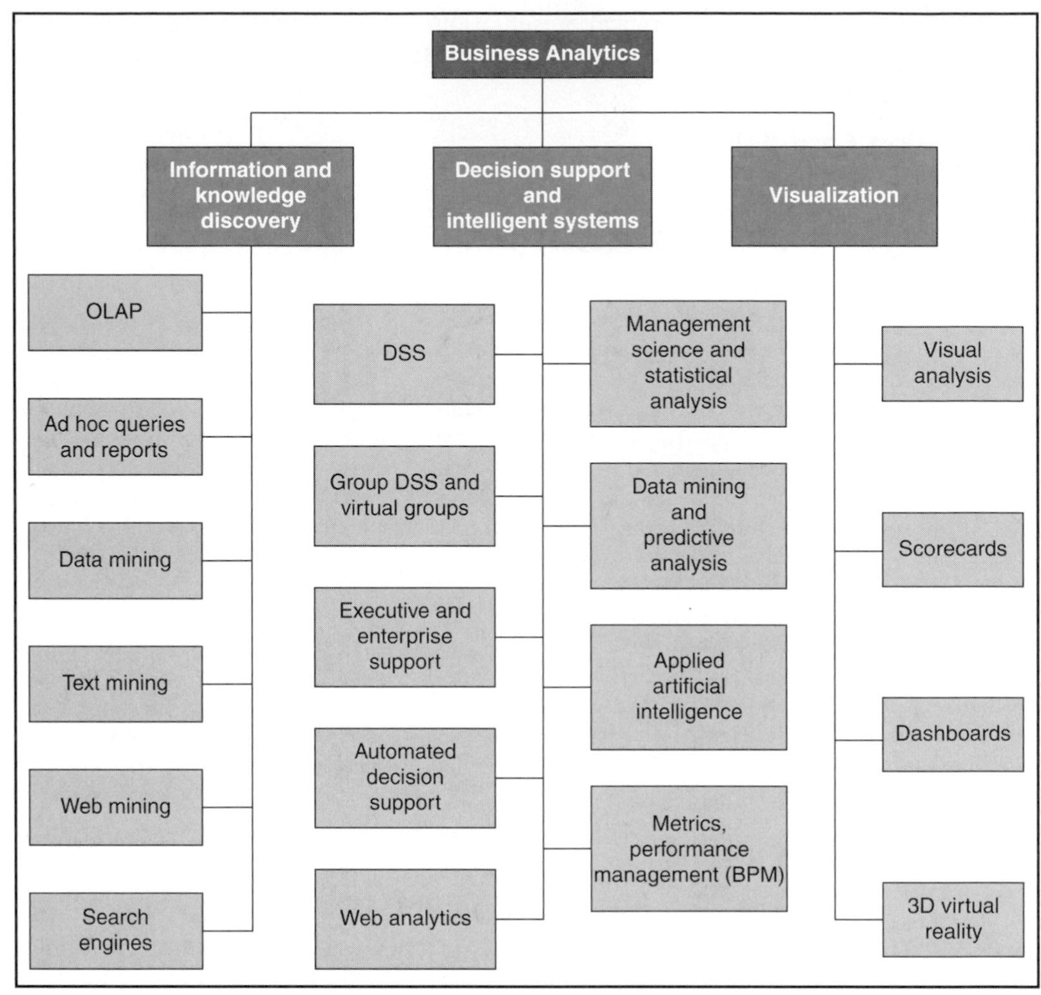

FIGURE 6.1 Categories of Business Analytics

2. *Cube analysis*. Cube-based BI tools are used to provide simple OLAP multidimensional slice-and-dice analytical capabilities to business managers in a limited-range environment.
3. *Ad hoc querying and analysis*. Relational OLAP tools are used to allow power users to query a database for any answer, slice-and-dice the entire database, and drill down to the lowest level of transactional information. This investigative querying is targeted to information explorers and power users.
4. *Statistical analysis and data mining*. Statistical, mathematical, and data mining tools are used to perform predictive analysis or to discover the cause-and-effect correlation between two metrics. Financial analyses and forecasts are also performed.
5. *Report delivery and alerting*. Report distribution engines are used proactively to send full reports or alerts to large user populations (internal and external), based on subscriptions, schedules, or threshold events in the databases.

MicroStrategy's prime product (currently MicroStrategy 8) is constructed along this classification (see Figure 6.2). Notice that the architecture allows for a single and unified plug-and-play structure, so users can find all the necessary tools integrated in one place.

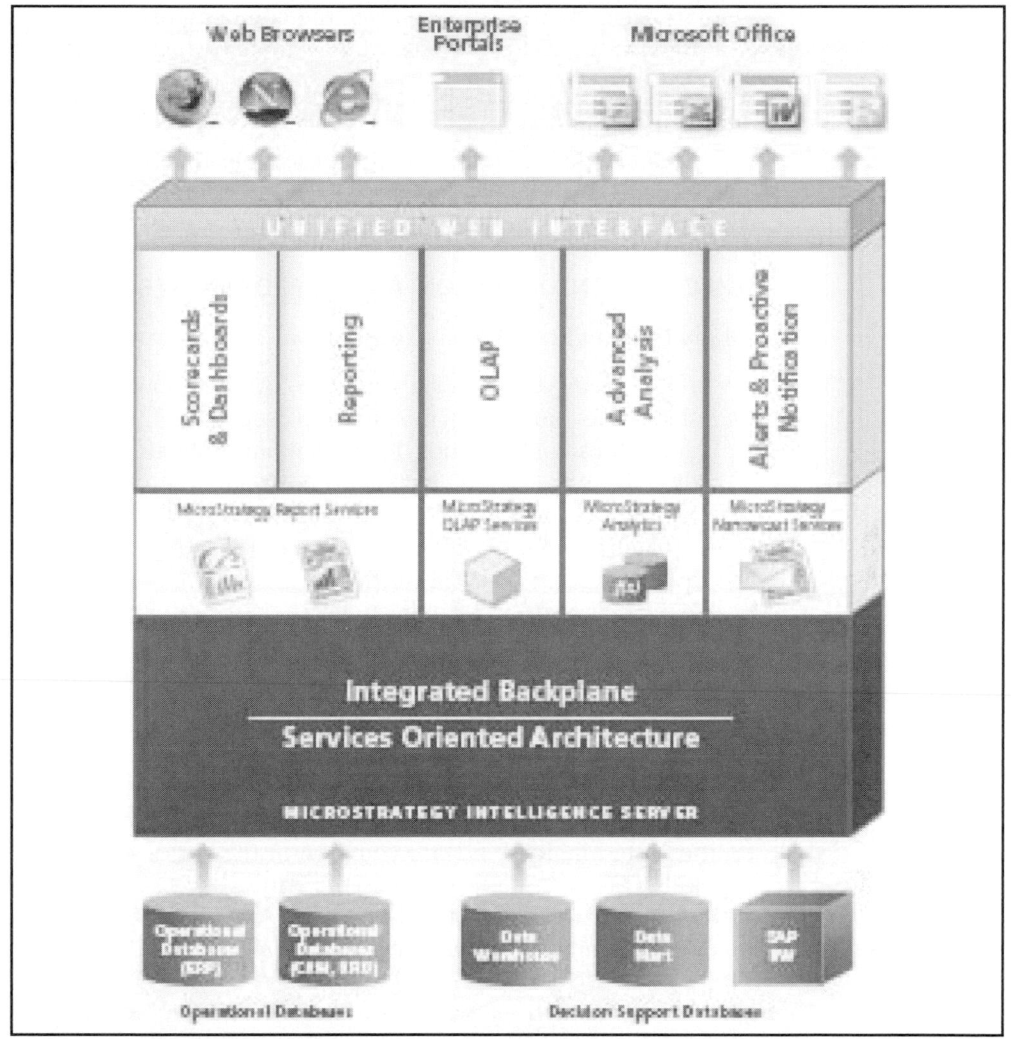

FIGURE 6.2 MicroStrategy 8 Architecture

Source: **microstrategy.com/Software/index.asp**

Other BI vendors offer similar classifications for their products. A notable exception is SAP AG.

SAP's Classification of Strategic Enterprise Management: Operational, Managerial, and Strategic

SAP AG (**sap.com**) is the world's largest vendor of enterprise software products, such as enterprise resource planning (ERP) tools. The company develops its products according to three levels of support:

1. *Operational.* ERP (SAP R/3) mainly supports transaction processing on the *operational level.*
2. *Managerial.* At the *managerial level,* middle managers can use SAP R/3 to access all reports, arranged by functional areas (e.g., marketing, finance). Managers can make queries and drill down.

3. *Strategic*. At the *strategic level*, the company offers products under the title SAP SEM (Strategic Enterprise Management), which includes BA (SAP SEM/BA).

For further descriptions of the SAP levels, see Thompson and Jakovljevic (2005), Meier et al. (2005), and **sap.com**.

We have divided this chapter into sections that are similar to MicroStrategy's classification. Before we present the details, we examine some of the popular activities of BA, most of which are inherited from *executive information system (EIS)* capabilities.

EXECUTIVE INFORMATION AND SUPPORT SYSTEMS

Many BI activities evolved from two tools:

- *Executive information systems (EIS)*. An EIS is a computer-based system that serves the information needs of top executives. It provides rapid access to timely and relevant information, to aid in monitoring an organization's performance by directly accessing management reports and to improve managerial growth and learning. An EIS is very user friendly, is supported by graphics, and provides the capabilities of *exception reporting* (i.e., reporting only the results that deviate from a set standard) and **drill-down** (i.e., investigating information in increasing detail). An EIS is also easily connected with online information services and e-mail.
- *Executive support systems (ESS)*. An ESS is a comprehensive support system that goes beyond EIS to include analysis support, communications, office automation, and intelligence support.

EIS and ESS vary in their capabilities and benefits. Capabilities common to many EIS/ESS are summarized in Table 6.1.

Details of some of these capabilities are provided in Online File W6.1. The capabilities listed in Table 6.1 are common in the various BA tools presented in the next sections. One of these capabilities, the critical success factor (CSF), is measured by key performance indicators (KPI) and is presented in Chapter 9. Many BA tools appear under the name *online analytical processing (OLAP)*, which we describe next.

TABLE 6.1 Capabilities of EIS/ESS

Capability	*Description*
Drill-down	The ability to go to additional details at one or several levels. It can be done through a series of menus or by direct queries (using intelligent agents and natural language processing).
Critical success factors (CSF)	The factors most critical for the success of business. These can be organizational, industry, departmental, etc.
Key performance indicators (KPI)	The specific measures of each CSF.
Status reports	The latest data available on KPI or some other metric, ideally in real-time.
Trend analysis	Short-, medium-, and long-term trend of KPI or metrics, projected using forecasting methods.
Ad hoc analysis	Analysis made at any time and with any desired factors and relationships.
Exception reporting	Using reports that highlight deviations larger than certain thresholds. Reports may include only deviations.
Slicing and dicing	Rearranging data so that they can be viewed from different perspectives.

Section 6.2 Review Questions

1. Define BA and explain its strategic value.
2. Relate BA to data warehousing.
3. List and describe the three categories of tools shown in Figure 6.1.
4. List MicroStrategy's five styles of BI.
5. Describe SAP's BI tool categorization.
6. Define *EIS* and *ESS*.
7. List the major capabilities of EIS/ESS (refer to Table 6.1).

6.3 ONLINE ANALYTICAL PROCESSING (OLAP)

The term **online analytical processing (OLAP)** refers to a variety of activities usually performed by end users in online systems. There is no universal agreement on what activities are considered OLAP. Usually OLAP includes such activities as generating and answering queries, requesting ad hoc reports and graphs and executing them, conducting traditional or modern statistical analyses, and building visual presentations. Many people also think of multidimensional analysis and presentations, EIS/ESS, and data mining as OLAP. Essentially, OLAP products provide modeling, analysis, and visualization capabilities to large data sets, either to database management systems (DBMS) or, more often, data warehouse systems, and they also provide a multidimensional conceptual view of the data.

OLAP VERSUS OLTP

For many years, IT concentrated on building mission-critical systems that mainly supported corporate *transaction processing*. Such systems must be virtually fault tolerant and provide efficient execution and rapid response. An effective solution was provided by *online transaction processing (OLTP)*, which centers on routine and repetitive activities, using a distributed *relational database* environment. The latest developments in this area are the use of ERP and supply-chain management (SCM) software for transaction processing tasks, customer relationship management (CRM) applications, and integration with Web-based technologies and intranets. Many tools were created for developing OLTP applications; the Informix Dynamic Server (see **www-306.ibm.com/software/data/informix/ids**) is an example of one such effective tool.

Access to data is often needed by *both* OLTP and management support system (MSS) applications. Unfortunately, trying to serve both types of requests may be problematic (see Gray and Watson, 1998). Therefore, some companies elect to separate information systems into OLTP types and OLAP types.

OLTP concentrates on processing repetitive transactions in large quantities and conducting simple manipulations. OLAP involves examining many data items (frequently many thousands or even millions) in *complex relationships*. In addition to answering users' queries, OLAP may analyze these relationships and look for patterns, trends, and exceptions. In other words, OLAP is a direct decision support method.

A typical OLAP query might access a multigigabyte or terabyte, multi-year sales database in order to find all product sales in each region for each product type. After reviewing the results, an analyst might further refine the query to find sales volume for each sales channel within a region or within certain product classifications. As a last step, the analyst might want to perform year-to-year or quarter-to-quarter comparisons for each sales channel. This whole process must be carried out *online*, with rapid response time so that the analysis process is undisturbed.

OLAP also differs from OLTP (and also from data mining) in that users can ask specific, open-ended questions. Users, typically analysts, *drive* OLAP, whereas data mining looks for relationships, with only some direction from the analyst. OLAP is generally facilitated by working with the data warehouse (or with data marts or a multidimensional database) and with a set of OLAP tools. These tools can be query tools, spreadsheets, data mining tools, data visualization tools, and the like. For a list of OLAP tools, see Alexander (2003), **baseline.com**, and periodic reviews in the software sections of *PCWeek*, *DM Review*, *Intelligent Enterprise*, and *Software Review*. The major vendors of these tools include BusinessObjects, Computer Associates, Cognos Inc., Geas, Hyperion Software Corp., Informatica Corp., Information Builders, IBM, Intersolve, Microsoft, MicroStrategy Corp., Oracle, SAS Institute, Inc., SPSS, and Temtec.

TYPES OF OLAP

The major types of OLAP are:

- *Multidimensional OLAP (MOLAP).* When OLAP is implemented via a specialized multidimensional database (or data store), it is called **multidimensional OLAP (MOLAP)** because it summarizes transactions into multidimensional views (see Section 6.6) ahead of time. Data are organized into a *cube structure* that the user can rotate; this is particularly suited for financial summaries. With MOLAP, queries are fast because the consolidation has already been done.
- *Relational OLAP (ROLAP).* When an OLAP database is implemented on top of an existing relational database, it is called **relational OLAP (ROLAP)**. Relational OLAP tools extract data from relational databases. Using complex SQL statements against relational tables, ROLAP is also able to create multidimensional views on-the-fly. ROLAP tends to be used on data that has a large number of attributes, where it cannot be easily placed into a cube structure. For example, customer data with numerous descriptive fields, rather than financial data, are typically ROLAP candidates.
- *Database OLAP and Web OLAP (DOLAP and WOLAP). Database OLAP* refers to a relational database management system (RDBMS) that is designed to host OLAP structures and perform OLAP calculations. *Web OLAP* refers to OLAP data that is accessible from a Web browser.
- *Desktop OLAP.* Desktop OLAP involves low-priced, simple OLAP tools that perform local multidimensional analysis and presentation of data downloaded to client machines from relational or multidimensional databases. Web versions often move the desktop processing to an intermediate server, which increases the scalability; however, the functionality remains, at best, comparable to that of the desktop version.

EXAMPLES OF SUCCESSFUL OLAP APPLICATIONS

ING Antai Insurance Co. (Taiwan) uses IBM's OLAP Server to analyze large amounts of data to detect fraudulent claims and speed up the processing of claims. Now, it takes only a couple of days to analyze data that previously took several weeks. As the tools and hardware improve, claims can be analyzed faster—even instantaneously. The cost of processing claims has been greatly reduced. Another example is TCF Bank, which uses OLAP to provide information directly to those who need it. The bank now understands its customer base more accurately so that it can better target its marketing efforts.

According to Cognos.com (2002), Allied Building Products Corp. has grown its building materials distribution company by increasing market share and customers.

Allied implemented Cognos Finance, a BI solution from Cognos, in under 90 days. As a result, Allied was able to standardize data company-wide and automate processing to deliver a single, coordinated view of financial performance. Cognos Finance allows Allied to reduce manual labor in producing reports and at the same time provides access to budgets, forecasts, and actuals across all its branch operations. This has enabled an integrated view of information and accelerated accurate financial reporting.

Table 6.2 provides additional examples of OLAP applications in a variety of organizations.

TABLE 6.2 Representative OLAP Applications

Company	*Description*
British Petroleum Exploration and Production (**bp.com**)	BP uses a large-scale, worldwide planning system, now in its second-generation OLAP-based incarnation, which replaced a slower, more complex spreadsheet-based implementation.
Bromford Iron & Steel Co. Ltd. (**bromfordsteels.co.uk**)	This is a rare example of an OLAP application being used to analyze detailed production data for a small steel manufacturer, to improve efficiency, reduce energy consumption, refine product strategy, and improve financial performance.
Blue Rhino (**bluerhino.com**)	Even smaller companies with minimal in-house IT resources can take full advantage of flexible OLAP applications across the whole organization.
Time Warner (**timewarner.com**)	Time Warner supports users on three continents with a strategic market planning and analysis system that uses an OLAP database server.
The World Bank (**worldbank.org**)	The World Bank uses OLAP tools to perform complex statistical analyses on a mass of worldwide econometric data.
British Airways (**ba.com**)	British Airways has reduced its processing costs and gotten better analysis capabilities by using OLAP databases in conjunction with a new general ledger.
Deluxe Corp. (**deluxe.com**)	Planning and analysis applications have saved $10 million and provided more accurate forecasting capabilities for the world's number-one check printer.
Dun & Bradstreet (**dnb.com**)	OLAP technology provides a vital link between the result of analysis of customers' corporate data and the underlying detailed information, an essential ingredient of selling business information.
GlaxoSmithKline (**gsk.com**)	OLAP databases are used for international financial reporting from a mainframe consolidation system.
Subaru of America (**subaru.com**)	An OLAP tool has helped to more effectively allocate inventory to franchised dealers in order to minimize inventory holdings while maximizing sales and customer service.
Sun Microsystems (**sun.com**)	Practicing what it preaches about network-centric computing, Sun has used a networked OLAP tool to implement a new business planning application that is entirely Web based and uses intelligent agents to create business intelligence.
Ford Motor Co. (**ford.com**)	To answer queries from 5,500 dealerships, hundreds of car rental businesses, and more, Ford has equipped the employees in more than 300 call centers with access to BI-developed information.

Sources: Compiled from The OLAP Report **olapreport.com** (accessed January 2006) and from several BI vendor Web sites.

OLAP TOOLS AND VENDORS

Using SQL and other conventional data access and analysis tools is helpful, but it is not sufficient for OLAP. In OLAP, a special class of tools is used, including BA front ends, data-access front ends, database front ends, and visual information access systems. Also, OLAP methods go well beyond spreadsheets in power and results; they are intended to *empower* users. For details, see Perry and Post (2007).

Characteristics of OLAP Tools

OLAP tools have characteristics that distinguish them from MIS tools that are designed to support traditional OLTP reporting applications. E.F. Codd et al. (1993) succinctly defined the characteristics of OLAP tools in the 12 rules summarized in Table 6.3. The 12 rules are used for the standardization of multidimensional data modeling, and they define four types of processing that are performed by analysts in an organization:

1. *Categorical analysis* is a static analysis based on historical data. It relies on the premise that past performance is an indicator of the future. This is the primary analysis supported by OLTP transaction-based databases.
2. *Exegetical analysis* is also based on historical data, and it adds the capability of drill-down analysis. *Drill-down analysis* is the ability to query further into data to determine the detail data that were used to determine a derived value.
3. *Contemplative analysis* allows a user to change a single value to determine its impact.
4. *Formulaic analysis* permits changes to multiple variables.

Representative OLAP Tools

Vendors in the BI arena are maneuvering to empower end users with the ability to customize analytic applications to meet evolving business needs. These include, for example, Spotfire's DecisionSite analytics platform (**spotfire.com**), Business Objects'

TABLE 6.3 OLAP Product Evaluation Rules: Codd's 12 Rules for OLAP

1. Multidimensional conceptual view for formulating queries
2. Transparency to the user
3. Easy accessibility: batch and online access
4. Consistent reporting performance
5. Client/server architecture: the use of distributed resources
6. Generic dimensionality
7. Dynamic sparse matrix handling
8. Multiuser support rather than support for only a single user
9. Unrestricted cross-dimensional operations
10. Intuitive data manipulation
11. Flexible reporting
12. Unlimited dimensions and aggregation level

Sources: Adapted from E.F. Codd, S.B. Codd, and C.T. Salley, *Providing OLAP to User-Analysts: An IT Mandate,* **dev.hyperion.com/resource_library/white_papers/providing_olap_to_user_analysts.pdf** (accessed February 2006); and M. Meier, W. Sigzig, and P. Mertens, *Enterprise Management with SAP SEM/Business Analytics,* 2nd ed., Springer, Berlin, 2005.

Enterprise BI Suite (**businessobjects.com**), and QlikTech's QlikView (**qliktech.com**). For details, see Havenstein (2003b).

Temtec Executive Viewer provides all the major OLAP features, including multidimensional views of data, dimension expansion and collapse, dynamic column selection, automatic calculations (sums, etc.), automatic charting and graphing, physical maps to display data (see Section 6.7), and instantaneous *drill-down* and *roll-up*.

An example of OLAP output—the result of a Cognos Impromptu query—is shown in Figure 6.3.

For more on OLAP, see Paris Technologies (**olap.com**) and Havenstein (2003a). For another real-world application of OLAP, see Application Case 6.2.

One of the major benefits of OLAP for end users (as reported by **temtec.com**) has been the elimination of the need for manually (or semi-manually) writing reports and abstracting data. The major activities of OLAP are reporting, querying, and analysis, which are described in more detail in the following sections.

Section 6.3 Review Questions

1. Define *OLAP* and compare it to OLTP.
2. Describe the major characteristics and benefits of OLAP.
3. Describe the types of OLAP.
4. List and briefly describe the major OLAP tools.

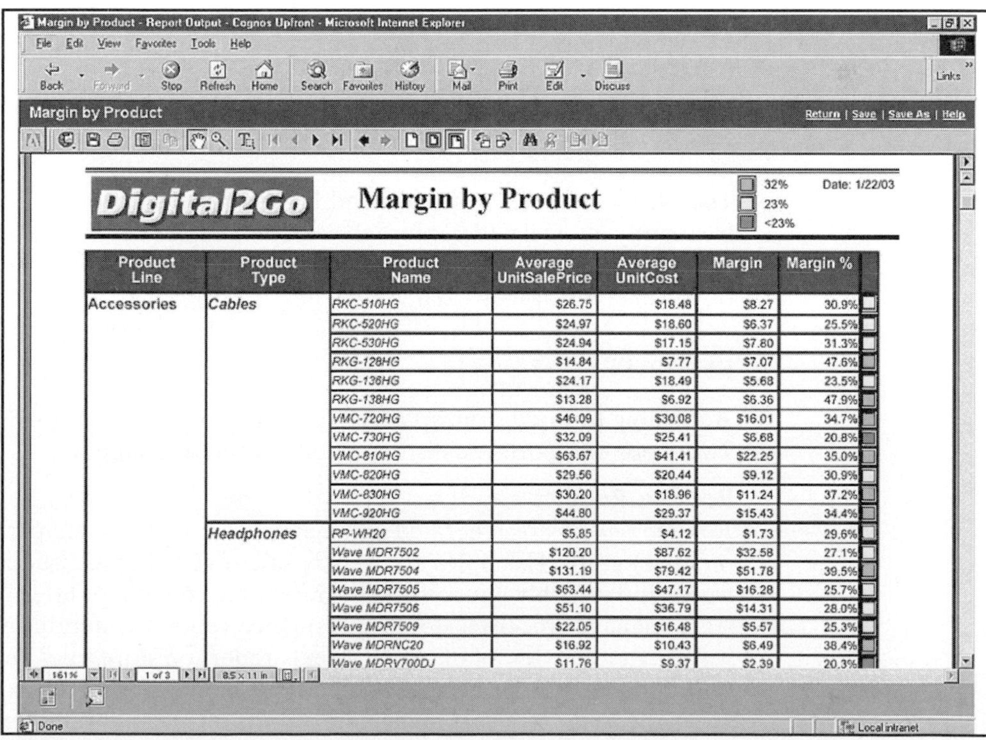

Digital2Go **Margin by Product** 32% 23% <23% Date: 1/22/03

Product Line	Product Type	Product Name	Average UnitSalePrice	Average UnitCost	Margin	Margin %
Accessories	*Cables*	*RKC-510HG*	$26.75	$18.48	$8.27	30.9%
		RKC-520HG	$24.97	$18.60	$6.37	25.5%
		RKC-530HG	$24.94	$17.15	$7.80	31.3%
		RKG-128HG	$14.84	$7.77	$7.07	47.6%
		RKG-136HG	$24.17	$18.49	$5.68	23.5%
		RKG-138HG	$13.28	$6.92	$6.36	47.9%
		VMC-720HG	$46.09	$30.08	$16.01	34.7%
		VMC-730HG	$32.09	$25.41	$6.68	20.8%
		VMC-810HG	$63.67	$41.41	$22.25	35.0%
		VMC-820HG	$29.56	$20.44	$9.12	30.9%
		VMC-830HG	$30.20	$18.96	$11.24	37.2%
		VMC-920HG	$44.80	$29.37	$15.43	34.4%
	Headphones	*RP-WH20*	$5.85	$4.12	$1.73	29.6%
		Wave MDR7502	$120.20	$87.62	$32.58	27.1%
		Wave MDR7504	$131.19	$79.42	$51.78	39.5%
		Wave MDR7505	$63.44	$47.17	$16.28	25.7%
		Wave MDR7506	$51.10	$36.79	$14.31	28.0%
		Wave MDR7509	$22.05	$16.48	$5.57	25.3%
		Wave MDRNC20	$16.92	$10.43	$6.49	38.4%
		Wave MDRV700DJ	$11.76	$9.37	$2.39	20.3%

FIGURE 6.3 Cognos Impromptu Sample Output

Source: Courtesy of Cognos, Inc.

Application Case 6.2

TCF Financial Corp.: Conducting OLAP, Reporting, and Data Mining

One of the largest regional banks in the Midwestern United States, TCF Bank (**tcfbank.com**) has more than 400 branches in six states and serves customers from all income groups. TCF Bank also operates the fourth-largest supermarket branch-banking system in the United States. TCF focuses on being a convenient one-stop shop for customers; it is one of the few banks in the United States that is open 12 hours per day, 7 days per week, including holidays.

Users in the bank's major groups (i.e., retail banking, consumer loans, mortgage banking, and brokerage) found that the IT reports were not meeting their decision support needs. Instead, they had had to develop custom processes to download files from operational raw data and then load the data into spreadsheets for further analysis. The time required to create a standard graph report was up to a month. It took up to six weeks to generate a customer marketing list.

TCF's information management department needed to come up with a better process to enable users to gain customer insight in order to uncover opportunities and effectively offer new services to customers. TCF therefore adopted Informatica Corp.'s PowerCenter and Power Analyzer in mid-2002. PowerAnalyzer's report-creating wizard, metrics-based reporting, and analysis-path drill-down features were important factors in the adoption decision because of their ease-of-use functions. A number of key indicator starter reports for user dashboards were also developed. In a week, 550 loan officers and executives were using these and other reports on a daily basis.

With the new OLAP system, which includes a cross-sell application, TCF is able to identify classes of customers to approach with specific matching services and products. This is especially critical in identifying the needs of new customers. In addition, reports are generated and OLAP is provided for easy further analysis.

Sources: Adapted from T. Ledman, "TCF Bank," *What Works: Best Practices in Business Intelligence and Data Warehousing*, Vol. 15, The Data Warehousing Institute, Chatsworth, CA, June 2003, p. 10; breaking news at **securityindustry.com**, June 20, 2005; and **informatica.com** (accessed February 2006).

6.4 REPORTS AND QUERIES

The oldest activities of OLAP and BI are using reports and using queries. These are frequently interrelated because the result of a query is often a report, and a report may call for a query. OLAP enables users to easily craft their own reports/views and analyze trends and performance daily.

REPORTS

According to Codd's rules, OLAP reporting must be uniform, flexible, and adjustable. Two types of reports are distinguished: routine and ad hoc.

Routine Reports

Routine reports are generated automatically and distributed periodically to subscribers on mailing lists. Examples are weekly sales figures, units produced each day and each week, and monthly hours worked. Here is an example of how a report is used in BI: A store manager receives store performance reports generated weekly by the BI software. After a review of one such weekly report on store sales, the manager notices that sales for computer peripherals have dropped off significantly from previous weeks. She clicks on her report and immediately drills down to another enterprise report, which shows her that the three best-selling hard drives are surprisingly underperforming. Now the manager needs to investigate why. Further drill-down by individual day may reveal that bad weather caused the problem.

Reports can be generated directly from operational data (e.g., ERP, point-of-sales [POS] systems) and/or from a data warehouse.

Ad Hoc (or On-Demand) Reports

Ad hoc reports are created for a specific user whenever needed. These reports can be similar to routine reports, but for different time intervals or for only a subset of the data. An example would be to provide a list of all customers who purchased a company's products for more than $5,000 each during January 2006.

Multilingual Support

Several vendors offer report translation to several languages (e.g., Microsoft to 12 languages). This support includes all interface help (e.g., menu bars, character sets, currency conversion and formats, business attributes).

Examples of Vendors' Products for Reporting

All BI software vendors offer report creation, access, and maintenance capabilities. Examples and demos of reports are available at most BI vendors' Web sites. Typical examples are:

- *Business Objects' Crystal Reports* is a tool kit that helps in rapidly creating flexible, feature-rich reports and integrates them into Web and Windows applications.
- *MicroStrategy* provides monitoring and report-creation tools for production and operational reports, such as invoices and statements, profit-and-loss reports, and performance reports. Personalized reports, as well as multilingual support (12 languages), are available. The reports are print perfect and pixel perfect (for quality graphs and charts).
- *Cognos 8 Business Intelligence* reporting includes a complete list of self-serve report types, adaptable to any data source. It also provides multilingual support.
- *Hyperion* provides a full spectrum of management reporting capabilities that combine both operational and financial information. You can customize high-volume, pixel-perfect reports for publishing to tens of thousands of consumers over the Web with superior throughput. A specialized financial reporting module with predefined formatting and built-in financial intelligence lets you quickly assemble and publish production-quality report books for management control and regulatory filings. And for ad hoc querying and reporting, business users can create their own interactive reports for monitoring their performance and spotting trends. Hyperion also provides interactive reporting.
- *Microsoft* has included in its Report Builder a user-friendly feature that allows report creation or modification without the need to write SQL queries (see Swoyer, 2005).

Representative Types of Reports

BI software can be used to produce dozens of reports in all functional areas. For representative examples, see Table 6.4.

Scorecards and Dashboards

Scorecards and dashboards are considered extended reporting tools because they provide tabular and graphical views of various reports, including comparisons to metrics. These are presented in Chapter 9. Similarly, data visualization (see Section 6.7) include visual presentation of reports.

TABLE 6.4 Representative OLAP-Produced Reports

Area	*Description*
Finance/accounting	Accounts receivable and payable reporting and analysis, balance sheet reporting and analysis, cash flow analysis, financial budgeting and forecasting, profit-and-loss/income statement analysis, risk management
Human resources	Benefits administration reporting, career path reporting and analysis, compliance reporting, compensation reporting and analysis, employee expense reporting, head-count trend analysis, time and labor management reporting
Sales forecasting and marketing	Channel analysis, competitor analysis, sales force performance reporting, sales pipeline reporting and analysis
Customer relationship management	Campaign analysis; customer acquisition, retention, and attrition analysis; customer cross-sell analysis; customer profitability analysis; customer scorecards; customer segmentation analysis; customer service analysis; loyalty analysis
Product sales	Category performance analysis/category management, discounts and promotions analysis, fraud analysis and loss prevention, inventory analysis, merchandising analysis, product scorecards
Operation and supply-chain management	Call center analysis, manufacturing scheduling and production planning, network optimization, order fulfillment analysis, quality control, regulatory management, strategic sourcing analysis and vendor scorecards, supply-and-demand planning
Web site analysis	E-commerce analysis, Web navigation analysis, Web traffic analysis, Web visitor analysis

Report Delivery and Alerting

All major vendors of BI software offer *report delivery and alerting* to proactively distribute a large number of reports and alerts to a potentially very large number of users (both internal and external to the enterprise). For example, software products can centrally distribute e-mails to a large user population, with enclosures, and on a scheduled basis. In addition, some vendors offer additional features, such as the following offered by MicroStrategy:

- *Report distribution through any touchpoint.* A company can use e-mail, printers, file servers, and portals using HTML, Excel, RTF, PDF, and ZIP containers to carry the report content.
- *Self-subscription as well as administrator-based distribution.* A company can mix centrally mandated report distributions with individually driven information needs.
- *Delivery on-demand, on-schedule, or on-event.* A company can trigger report distribution through whatever means are most appropriate to the user.
- *Automatic content personalization.* A company can make a report more relevant and secure for all users. Personalized reports save time for users by showing them only data and information they request.

For details, see MicroStrategy (2006).

REPORTS AND QUERIES

Ad Hoc Queries

Any query that cannot be determined prior to the moment the query is issued is considered an **ad hoc query**. The user may decide to place such a query after she gets a report. Ad hoc queries allow users to request from the computer information that is not available in periodic reports, as well as to generate new queries or modify old ones, with significant flexibility in terms of content, layout, and calculations. These answers are needed to expedite or facilitate decision making. The system must be intelligent enough to understand what the user wants. Simple ad hoc query systems are often based on menus. More intelligent systems use SQL and query-by-example approaches. The most intelligent systems are based on natural language understanding, and some can communicate with users using voice recognition. Queries can be done on static data or on dynamic (i.e., real-time) data. (Later in this chapter, we will discuss the use of Web tools to facilitate queries.) Finally, BusinessObjects provides an Intelligent Questions tool that guides users to ask the right questions.

SQL for Querying

Structured Query Language (SQL) is a standard data language for data access and manipulation in relational DBMS. It is an English-like language that consists of several layers of increasing complexity and capability. SQL is used for online access to databases, DBMS operations from programs, and database administration functions. It is also used for data access and manipulation functions in some leading DBMS software products (e.g., Oracle 9i and 10i, IBM's DB2, Microsoft SQL Server 2005). For details, see Perry and Post (2007).

Because SQL is nonprocedural and fairly user friendly, many end users can use it to create their own queries and database operations. SQL can be used for programs written in any standard programming language; thus, it facilitates software integration. Queries can also be conducted in natural languages (see Chapter 13).

Querying systems are frequently combined with reporting systems. For an example of such a combination in a video rental store, see Amato-McCoy (2003).

ANALYSIS OF REPORTS' RESULTS

In many cases, the data provided by reports require further investigation. Such investigation needs to be done fairly quickly—sometimes immediately after data are viewed—and it must be done by the end users at a low cost. For this reason, vendors provide reporting tools that enable further investigation. For example, a quick drill-down may provide an explanation for lost sales, or a trend analysis may set up an alert. Many tools are provided with OLAP products. Such an analysis can be facilitated with multidimensionality, discussed next.

Section 6.4 Review Questions

1. Define *routine report* and *ad hoc report.*
2. List the major categories of reports (according to MicroStrategy).
3. What kind of reports are included in the major vendors' kits?
4. Explain why scorecards and dashboards are viewed as a special category of reporting.
5. Define *report delivery* and *alerting*.
6. Define *ad hoc query*. How can an ad hoc query be generated?

6.5 MULTIDIMENSIONALITY

Raw and summary data can be organized in different ways for analysis and presentation. An efficient way to do this is called **multidimensionality**. The major advantage of multidimensionality is that it enables data to be organized the way individual managers, rather than system analysts, like to see them. Different presentations of the same data can be arranged easily and quickly.

MULTIDIMENSIONAL PRESENTATION

Spreadsheet tables have two dimensions. Information with three or more dimensions can be presented by using a set of two-dimensional tables or one fairly complex table. In decision support, an attempt is made to simplify information presentation and allow the user to easily and quickly change the structure of tables to make them more meaningful (e.g., by flipping columns and rows, aggregating several rows and columns-rollup, disaggregating a set of rows or columns).

Three factors are considered in multidimensionality: *dimensions, measures*, and *time*. Here are some examples:

- *Dimensions*. Some examples of dimensions are products, salespeople, market segments, business units, geographic locations, distribution channels, countries, and industries.
- *Measures*. Some examples of measures are money, sales volume, head count, inventory, and actual versus forecasted profit.
- *Time*. Some examples of time are daily, weekly, monthly, quarterly, and yearly.

A **multidimensional database** is a database in which the data are organized specifically to support easy and quick multidimensional analysis. The data are transported from the data warehouse. Creating and maintaining such a database adds cost that must be compared to the added benefits.

Here is an example of how multidimensionality works: A manager wants to know the sales of a product (by units or dollars) in a certain geographic area, by a specific salesperson, during a specified month. The answer to such a question can be provided regardless of the database structure much faster by the user herself if the data are organized in multidimensional databases or if the query or related software products are designed for multidimensionality. In either case, users can navigate through the many dimensions and levels of data via tables or graphs and are able to make quick interpretations, such as uncovering significant deviations or important trends.

MULTIDIMENSIONAL DATA CUBES AND THEIR ANALYSIS

A **data cube** is used to represent data along some measure of interest. Although called a "cube," it can be two-dimensional, three-dimensional, or higher-dimensional. Each dimension represents some attribute in the database, and the cells in the data cube represent measures of interest.

Example

A database contains transaction information relating company sales of products (*p*) to a customer (c) at different store (s) locations. The data cube formed from this database is a three-dimensional representation, with each cell (i.e., *p*, c, s) of the cube representing a combination of values for *product*, *customer*, and *store location*. A sample data cube for this combination is shown in Figure 6.4. The contents of each cell is the count of the number of times that specific combination of values occurs together in the database. Cells that appear blank have a value of zero. The cube can be used to retrieve information within the database about, for example, which store should be given a certain product to sell in order to make the greatest profit.

Data cubes provide an opportunity to retrieve decision support information in an efficient way. *Cube analysis* lets people perform queries by flipping through a series of

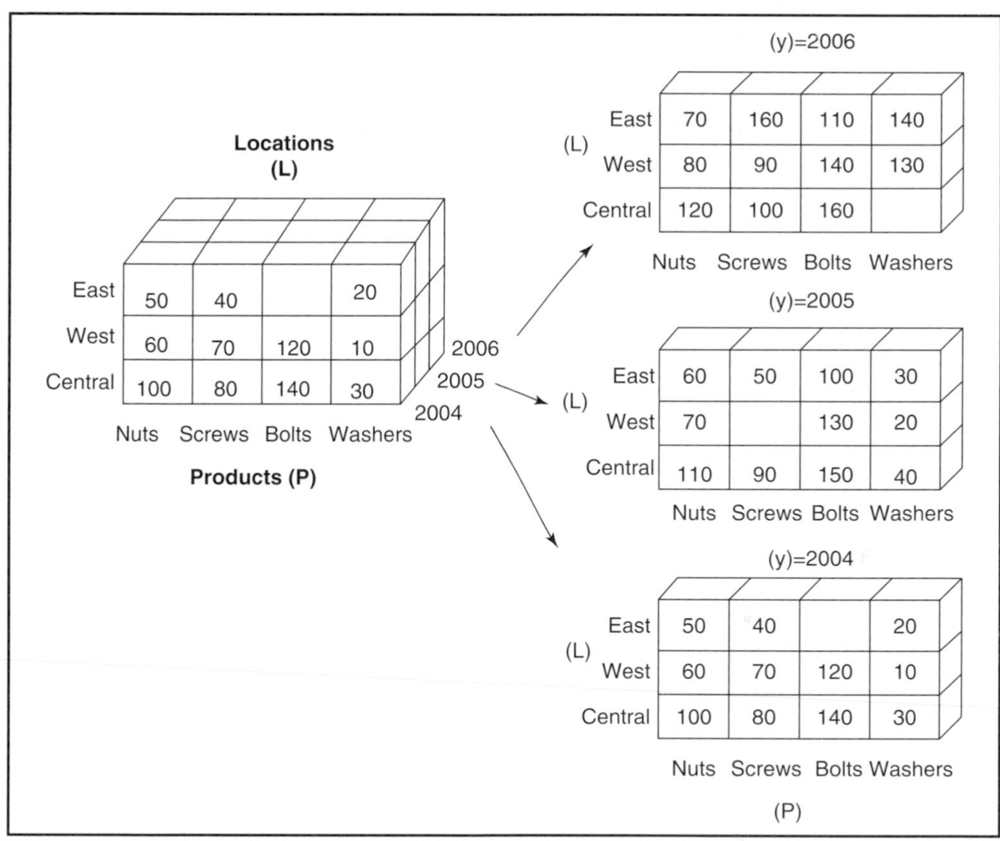

FIGURE 6.4 Cube Analysis and Views

report views, using the OLAP software features page-by, pivot, sort, filter, and drill-up/drill-down, which allow users to slice-and-dice a cube of data or analyze a cube by using simple mouse clicks. The term **cube** refers to a subset of highly interrelated data that is organized to allow users to combine any attributes in a cube (e.g., stores, products, customers, suppliers) with any metrics in the cube (e.g., sales, profit, units, age) to create various two-dimensional views, or *slices*, that can be displayed on a computer screen (see Figure 6.5).

For information on how cube analysis is done, see vendors' sites and products such as MicroStrategy's Intelligent Cubes (MicroStrategy, 2005).

Multidimensionality is available in different degrees of sophistication. Thus there are several types of commercial software (at different price levels) from which multidimensional systems can be constructed.

Multidimensional Tools and Vendors

Tools with multidimensional capabilities often work in conjunction with database query systems and other OLAP tools. For example, Seagate Software's part of Seagate Technology LLC, **seagate.com**) Crystal Reports builds reports that extract and analyze data from relational databases. Crystal Analysis Professional builds reports that extract and analyze multidimensional data from OLAP systems (e.g., Hyperion's Essbase) as well as from mainstream databases with built-in OLAP technology (e.g., Microsoft SQL Server 2000, IBM DB2). See Hoffer et al. (2005). Other tools include

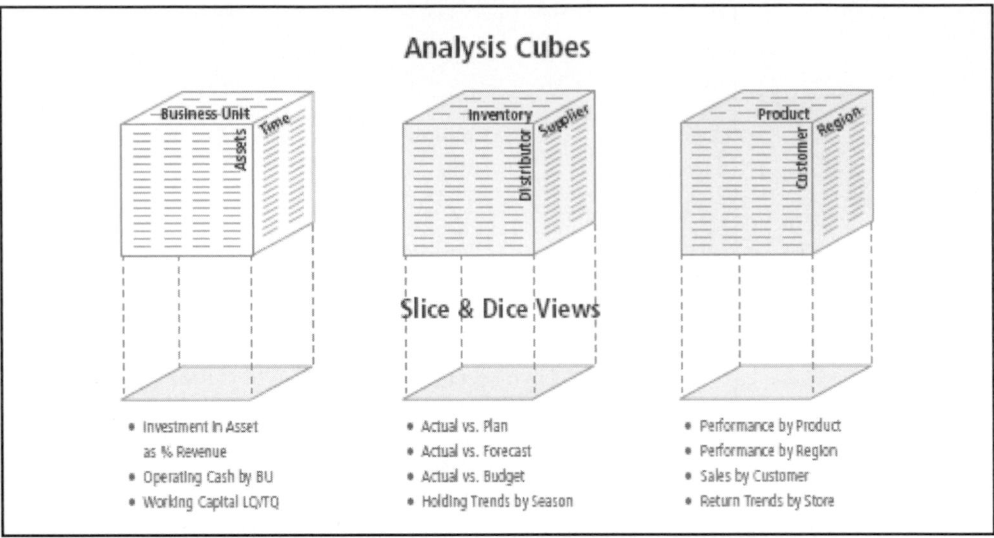

FIGURE 6.5 Slice-and-Dice Cubes

Source: Microstrategy, "The Five Styles of Business Intelligence," 2003, Figure 21, p.35.

PowerPlay (**cognos.com**), InterNetivity Databeacon (**databeacon.com**), and Business Objects (**businessobjects.com**).

IBM's Cube Views automates the creation of OLAP metadata at the database level so that metadata can be shared among applications that access the database. Cube Views aggregates data into multidimensional charts, allowing users to access the data from different perspectives, and it returns answers to queries as XML-based Web services. Cube Views is supported by many BI vendors, including Hyperion, Cognos, Inc., MicroStrategy, Inc., Informatica Corp., InterNetivity, and BusinessObjects. See Callaghan (2003b) for details.

For examples of BI software that readily handles multidimensionality, see Callaghan (2003b) and the "Annual Product Review" issue of *DM Review* every July (**dmreview.com**).

LIMITATIONS OF DIMENSIONALITY

Multidimensionality has some limitations, according to a Gartner Group research report (cited by Gray and Watson, 1998):

- The multidimensional database can take up significantly more computer storage room than a summarized relational database.
- Multidimensional products cost significantly more than standard relational products.
- Database loading consumes significant system resources and time, depending on data volume and the number of dimensions.
- Interfaces and maintenance are more complex in multidimensional databases than in relational databases.

These limitations become less of a problem as time passes due to improved technology.

Section 6.5 Review Questions

1. Define *multidimensionality* and describe its benefits.
2. Define *multidimensional database* and describe the limitations of these databases.
3. Define *cube* and *data cube*.
4. What is meant by *slice-and-dice*?
5. List the limitations of multidimensionality.

6.6 ADVANCED BUSINESS ANALYTICS

While OLAP concentrates on reporting and queries, other analytics have been developed to analyze data and information in more sophisticated ways. As a matter of fact, today, companies worldwide use hundreds of mathematical, financial, statistical, and other models for solving problems, exploring opportunities, improving productivity, and gaining strategic advantage.

An example of the power of BA can be seen in the case of KeySpan, a distributor of natural gas in the Northeastern U.S. KeySpan's business customers, the "marketers" that sell gas to end users, can log in to the KeySpan extranet, view gas usage projections, and make informed decisions about how much gas should be brought through the pipelines on any given day. KeySpan uses MicroStrategy technology to analyze such factors as historical data and weather conditions to project how much gas should be distributed. Four times a day, MicroStrategy Narrowcast Server compares the actual flow of gas to the projection made earlier in the day and then sends an exception report via e-mail or pager to the marketer and the gas operations department controlling the valves. The alerts notify marketers when they have under- or overprojected gas usage so that they can make appropriate adjustments.

In the following sections we present only a few representative examples of advanced BA. (For more examples, see customer success stories at **sas.com** and **spss.com**.) Users can perform sophisticated statistical and mathematical analyses such as hypothesis testing, multiple regression and correlation, churn predictions, and customer scoring models. Such investigation cannot be done with basic OLAP and require special tools, including data mining and predictive analysis.

DATA MINING AND PREDICTIVE ANALYSIS

A major step in managerial decision making is forecasting or estimating the results of different alternative courses of action. To do so, we can use one or more methods. The simplest methods involve only two variables, such as *sales* over *time* or *price* over *time*. Indeed, many statistical formulas are available to conduct such analyses (e.g., regression and correlation, trend analysis). The formulas for such methods appear as Excel or MicroStrategy functions.

However, in many cases, a prediction is more complex, involving more than two variables. For such cases, we can use more complex statistical methods, such as multiple regression analysis, or special forecasting and prediction methods. Two such methods are described next: data mining and predictive analysis.

Data Mining

Data mining tools automatically extract hidden, predictive information from databases. They also search for the patterns in large transaction databases. These tools are usually driven by complex statistical formulas. The easiest way to distinguish data mining from the various forms of OLAP is that OLAP can only answer questions you are certain to ask, whereas data mining answers questions you don't necessarily know you should ask. The details of data mining are provided in Chapters 7 and 8.

Predictive Analysis

Predictive analysis tools help determine the probable future outcome for an event or the likelihood of a situation occurring. They also identify relationships and patterns. An example is provided in Application Case 6.3.

Application Case 6.3

Predictive Analysis Can Help You Avoid Traffic Jams

Predictive analysis can now be used to predict traffic congestion levels hours or even days in advance, with almost 90 percent accuracy. Inrix (**inrix.com**) is a startup company that provides such predictions for $20 to $120 per year. The predictive analysis is done with a mass of data obtained from government sources, including:

- Real-time traffic flow and incident information collected by gadgets installed on highways (tool-tag readers, cameras, radar units, and magnetic sensors embedded in the pavement)
- Speed and location data collected by global positioning system (GPS) units of vehicles owned by participating trucking and delivery companies
- Two years of historical traffic flow data
- Weather forecasts and conditions
- Other events (e.g., road construction schedules, school calendars, sports, concerts, other scheduled special events)

Inrix's proprietary predictive algorithms combine these data to create a snapshot of current traffic flows and expected congestion and road conditions over the next hours and days. Obviously, each city requires its own unique model and database (0.2 to 2 terabytes per city). In 2006, Inrix offered this prediction in 30. The service is combined with digital maps (see **teleatlas.com**, the provider of information to GIS companies such as MapQuest). Also, Inrix partners with cell phone operators, traditional satellite broadcasters, and in-car navigation services. In the Seattle area, where Inrix is located, the company delivers traffic information via smart phones and electronic boards on sections of highways, using color codes for signals. The phones also display estimated time for the roads to be either clear or become jammed.

The Inrix system suggests automated decisions such as the following:

- Best route for a delivery van
- Ideal time to go to or leave work (for those on a flex schedule)
- How to reroute a trip to avoid an accident

The following are some of the technologies in use for sensing and controlling traffic:

- Magnetic loop detectors in the road surface (in 32 percent of U.S. cities)
- Closed-circuit TV cameras monitoring traffic conditions (in 29 percent of U.S. cities)
- Information about traffic conditions provided by radio and on the Internet in real-time (in 19 percent of U.S. cities)
- Freeway access ramps controlled by the traffic lights (in 9 percent of U.S. cities)

Sources: Compiled from E. Jonietz, "Traffic Avoidance," *Technology Review*, December 2005/January 2006; and J. Barke, "Traffic Taming," *Technology Review*, October 3, 2005.

According to Fogarty (2004), predictive analysis uses sophisticated algorithms designed to sift through a data warehouse and identify patterns of behavior that suggest, for example, which offers your customers might respond to in the future or which customers you might be in danger of losing. For instance, when sifting through a bank's data warehouse, predictive analysis might recognize that customers who cancel an automatic bill payment or automatic deposit often move to another bank within a certain period of time.

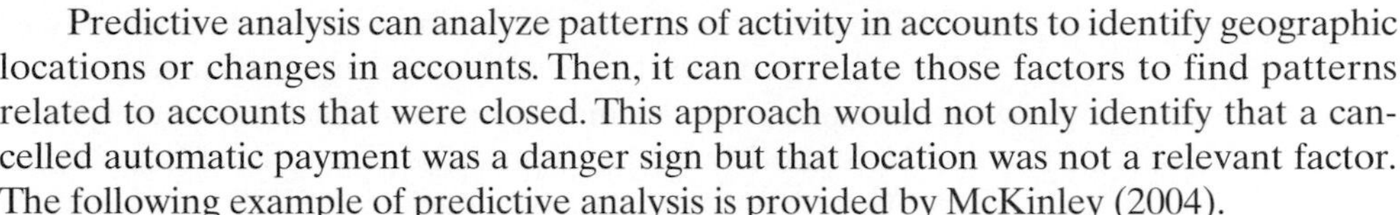

Predictive analysis can analyze patterns of activity in accounts to identify geographic locations or changes in accounts. Then, it can correlate those factors to find patterns related to accounts that were closed. This approach would not only identify that a cancelled automatic payment was a danger sign but that location was not a relevant factor. The following example of predictive analysis is provided by McKinley (2004).

Example: Recognizing What Customers Want Even Before They Enter a Restaurant

HyperActive Technologies (**hyperactivetechnologies.com**) has developed a system by which cameras mounted on the roof of a fast food restaurant track vehicles pulling into the parking lot (or drive-through). Other cameras track the progress of customers moving through the ordering queue. Using predictive analysis, the system predicts what customers might order. In addition, a database includes historical car-ordering data, such as 20 percent of cars entering the lot will usually order at least one cheeseburger at lunch time. Based on the camera's input and the database, the system predicts what customers will order 1.5 to 5 minutes before they actually order. This gives the cooks a chance to prepare the food, minimizing customers' waiting time. Also, the food does not have a chance to get cold (reheating takes time, expense, and makes the food less tasty).

Predictive analysis is used to automatically analyze large amounts of data with different variables; it includes clustering, decision trees, market-basket analysis, regression modeling, neural nets, genetic algorithms, text mining, hypothesis testing, decision analytics, and more.

The core element of predictive analytics is the *predictor*, a variable that can be measured for an individual or entity to predict future behavior. For example, a credit card company could consider age, income, credit history, and other demographics as predictors in determining an applicant's risk factor. For more on predictive analysis, see Zaman (2005).

Example: Aligning BI with ERP and SCM, Using Advanced Analytics

The second generation of ERP and SCM products is characterized by the addition of decision support/BI tools. An example is SAP analytics (see Online File W6.1).

REPRESENTATIVE VENDORS' TOOLS FOR ADVANCED ANALYTICS

The following list shows specific BI analytics products offered by major vendors in the field.

- *MicroStrategy* provides more than 400 statistical, mathematical, and financial functions for creating reports and analyzing their results. These include tools such as drill-anywhere, data segmentation, data grouping, and optimization.
- *Hyperion's System 9 BI+* includes the Essbase Analytics module for quickly performing sophisticated analyses that enable managers to interpret complex data. Special modules are dedicated to the finance side, enterprise analysis, customer behavior patterns, cost reduction, compliance, and corporate performance.
- *Cognos 8 Business Intelligence* analytics include customizable time-series analysis and trends, deep competitive analysis, drill-down, forecasting, and optimization. Cognos also offers business event management.
- *Microsoft* offers advanced analytics in its Microsoft Dynamics GP 9.0.
- *Fair Isaac* offers intelligent tools for conducting risk analysis, fraud detection, profitability analysis, and intelligent querying.
- *ILOG* offers a sophisticated optimization suite. With optimization, as discussed in Chapter 4, it is possible to maximize resource utilization, uncover options for problem solving, and conduct cost–benefit analyses.

- *SAS* is a leader in predictive analytics and data mining (e.g., SAS Enterprise Miner). It provides financial, forecasting, and statistical tools for problem solving. A special area is risk management and assessment, using credit scoring models.
- *SPSS* is another leader in predictive analysis and data mining. Known for years for its sophisticated statistical packages, SPSS today is more for predictive analysis.
- *Oracle* provides several tools for predictive analysis, data mining, and other advanced analytics tools.
- Other vendors include Insightful Corp., StatSoft, Inc., Knowledge eXtraction ENgines, Unica, Angoss Software, and IBM.

Section 6.6 Review Questions

1. Why are advanced analytics tools necessary for businesses?
2. List some tools of advanced BA.
3. Define *data mining*.
4. Define *predictive analysis* and describe its capabilities.
5. List some tools of predictive analysis.

6.7 DATA VISUALIZATION

Visual technologies can condense 1,000 numbers in one picture and make decision support applications more attractive and understandable to users. **Data visualization** refers to technologies that support visualization and sometimes interpretation of data and information at several points along the data processing chain (see Fayyad et al., 2002). It includes digital images, GIS, graphical user interfaces, graphs, virtual reality, dimensional presentations, videos, and animation. Visual tools can help identify relationships such as trends.

The ability to quickly identify important trends in corporate and market data can provide competitive advantage. When we visually recognize trends, we can check their magnitude by using predictive models that provide significant business advantages in applications that drive content, transactions, or processes. Confident action, based on superior methods of visual data analysis, helps companies improve income and avoid costly mistakes (see Hallett, 2001). For example, Consonus (**consonus.com**) designs, builds, and operates data centers, IT networks, and Web-enabled application delivery systems. Consonus uses the Hewlett-Packard OpenView Management Suite to help manage these data centers. OpenView also helps manage Web systems and provides users with an understanding of how customers view their sites' performance and availability. See McCarthy and McCarthy (2002) for details.

Data visualization also enables BA, using Web-based tools. Rather than having to wait for reports or compare sterile columns of numbers, a manager can use a browser interface in real-time to look at vital organizational performance data. By using visual analysis technologies, managers, engineers, and other professionals may spot problems that have gone undetected by standard analysis methods for years.

Data visualization is easier to implement when the necessary data are in a data warehouse or, better yet, in a multidimensional special database or server. An example is Harrah's Entertainment (see the Harrah's case at **teradatauniversitynetwork.com**), which installed Compudigm International's (**compudigm.com**) visualization technology at its Las Vegas headquarters and other casinos. A visualization environment presents data in a form that allows decision makers to see depth and worth in real-time and affect performance. Decision makers at Harrah's can now view the flow of traffic across the casino floor in real-time. They can identify which slot machines are popular with the customers and which are most profitable, by the minute. They can install more of the better ones when needed. The data visualization software also enables managers to determine casino layout on-the-fly. They can visually examine their CRM rewards program. Compudigm initially developed this product for the gaming industry but has since extended its technology into financial services and telecommunications.

VISUALIZATION SPREADSHEETS

As described in Chapters 3 and 4, spreadsheets are the major end-user tools for programming decision support applications. Microsoft Excel offers dozens of mathematical, statistical, report generation, querying (e.g., what-if analysis, goal-seeking), and other BI tools.

Excel has been widely adopted as an easy-to-use and powerful tool for free-form data manipulation. Excel has evolved beyond a simple data calculation tool to the point where it is now used as a sophisticated and flexible tool for collecting, analyzing, and summarizing data from multiple sources. People use Excel, for example, to track travel expenses, devise budgets and forecasts, and create reports. Some users are adept enough to create advanced pivot tables and macros that rival the work of IT programmers. According to Brath and Peters (2006), the power of Excel can be leveraged with visualization in many different ways, including enhancing effectiveness, focusing communications, helping make anomalies pop out, facilitating comprehension, and empowering collaboration. Brath and Peters provided the following two examples:

Example: Risk Management

Figure 6.6 shows the power of visualization. The spreadsheets on the left represent 2 pages from a risk report that has approximately 100 pages of risk scenarios and their resultant impacts (center image, generated using standard Excel charts). The same report presented as an animated and interactive visualization (right side of figure) consolidates all 100 pages of the information into a single screen.

Example: Understanding MSS Models

When building spreadsheets that have many formulas, it can be a challenge to try to understand the impact of a change and explore various what-if scenarios. Consider the credit-modeling

FIGURE 6.6 Visual Spreadsheet of Risk Analysis

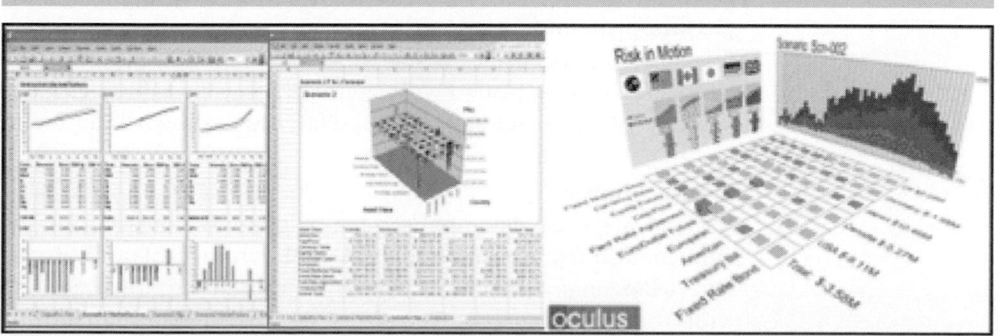

Source: R. Brath and M. Peters, "Visualizing Spreadsheets: Add Exponential Value to Excel for Monitoring, Analysis and Modeling," *DM Direct Newsletter*, January 6, 2006.

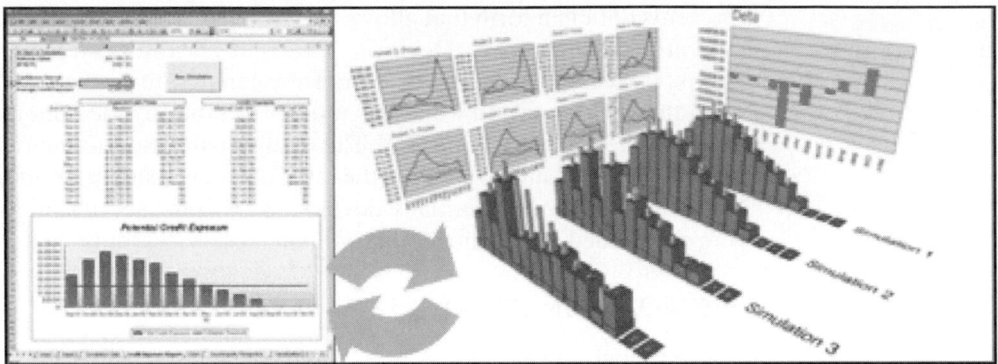

FIGURE 6.7 Visual Spreadsheet of Credit Modeling

Source: R. Brath and M. Peters, "Visualizing Spreadsheets: Add Exponential Value to Excel for Monitoring, Analysis and Modeling," *DM Direct Newsletter*, January 6, 2006.

application shown in Figure 6.7. The spreadsheet at left provides a snapshot of a potential transaction. The visualization on the right is updated each time the user creates another potential transaction and adds it as another row (on the floor) and another pair of charts (on the wall). The viewer can then pick and compare any pair of transactions (shown on the back wall) to better understand the trade-offs and determine which scenario is best.

Several other examples of visualizing spreadsheets and their benefits are provided by Brath and Peters (2006).

NEW DIRECTIONS IN DATA VISUALIZATION

Since the late 1990s, data visualization has moved both into mainstream computing, where it is integrated with decision support tools and applications, and into intelligent visualization, which includes data (information) interpretation. For interesting areas and trends, see Online File W6.3.

Major OLAP vendors provide three-dimensional visualization tools with their decision support tools. For example, Forest Tree 6.0 is a Web-enabled development tool that has a three-dimensional visualization version that enables users to visualize and easily manage multiple dimensions of data in a single view. New visual tools are continually being developed to analyze Web site performance. ADVIZOR Solutions (**advizorsolutions.com**) is one such tool.

Dashboards and Scorecards

Visualization has been proven to be extremely important for busy executives. The EIS of the 1990s were loaded with charts, graphs, and tables. These evolved to management cockpit products (see **sap.com**) and later to dashboards and scorecards (see Chapter 9).

Visual Analysis

Today, enterprise data analysis can be done by nontechnical users who glean valuable information from business data. VizQL (from Tableau Software) is a visual database query language that powers Hyperion's Visual Explorer. Several other companies provide tools for visual analysis (e.g., Analytica [**lumina.com**], Endeca [**endeca.com**]). Visual analysis can be done interactively (e.g., see **navteq.com**). One area of visual analysis is described next.

Financial Data Visualization

One of the common applications of BI data visualization is in the area of finance. To prevent systems from automatically identifying meaningless patterns in data, chief financial officers (CFOs) want to make sure that the processing power of a computer is always tempered with the insight of a human being. One way to do this is through data visualization. Andrew W. Lo, director of the Laboratory for Financial Engineering at Massachusetts Institute of Technology's Sloan School of Management, developed a program in which a CFO can use a mouse to "fly" over a three-dimensional landscape representing the *risk*, *return*, and *liquidity* of a company's assets. With practice, the CFO can begin to zero in on the choicest spot on the three-dimensional landscape: the one where the balance of risk, return, and liquidity is most beneficial.

CFOs have increasingly been using three-dimensional visualization in cyberspace, but many still spend the bulk of their time on routine matters, such as generating reports for the Securities and Exchange Commission, using traditional tools. However, this situation is changing, as described in Application Case 6.4.

Application Case 6.4

Financial Data Visualization at Merrill Lynch

SmartMoney.com's Web-based Maps gives Merrill Lynch analysts an easy-to-examine visual representation of financial information and customized three-dimensional pictures of the ever-changing financial markets. For financial services providers such as Merrill Lynch, visualization is becoming ubiquitous in many applications; in addition, developers are extending visualization use to serve increasingly diverse audiences. From the financial services industry to highly technical quality engineering companies that create testing tools to service providers using powerful network monitoring tools, visualization is becoming an on-demand, value-added tool. Future uses are on the drawing boards, as research scientists discover applications for tomorrow's business.

The financial services industry is a robust adopter, with an increasingly sophisticated market and a high level of competition. To respond to some of this data complexity, Merrill Lynch uses maps for its internal, proprietary data products to access real-time updates on stocks and mutual funds.

Merrill Lynch brokers can track client holdings individually or in aggregate, giving the brokers investment snapshots of their own portfolios and their clients' portfolios. The mapping technology can present data (e.g., through colors) with volume, value, and hierarchy, and it allows users to click on and call up specific data sets from the map. Users can build dynamic, interactive, three-dimensional trees from hierarchical company financial reports, share them with users via the Internet, and integrate them into existing applications.

Sources: Compiled from J. McCarthy, "Envisioning Enterprise Data," *InfoWorld*, November 18, 2002; and H. Goldberg, "Unleashing the Power of Data," *DBZ Magazine*, Quarter 2, 2004.

VENDORS AND PRODUCTS

Visualization software packages offer users capabilities for self-guided exploration and visual analysis of large amounts of data. For example, see the ILOG Visualization Suite (**ilog.com**). Some examples of OLAP systems that offer excellent visualization include **eBizinsights** V(isual Insights) and nVizn (SPSS, Inc.). Cognos Visualizer uses traffic-light displays in tables and graphs. Numeric results are displayed in red, yellow, and green to indicate their status. SPSS's nVizn is a Java-based developer's tool kit for creating visualization applications. Visualization technologies can be integrated to create different information presentations, especially with virtual reality (VR) methods (see Online File W6.4). Executive Viewer (from Temtec) also uses the idea of traffic lights in its display of data, and it integrates data into a multidimensional framework (see Exercise 1 under "Team Assignments and Role-Playing Projects," at the end of this chapter).

Section 6.7 Review Questions

1. Define *data visualization* and list its major advantages.
2. Describe spreadsheet visualization.
3. Describe financial data visualization.

6.8 GEOGRAPHIC INFORMATION SYSTEMS (GIS)

A **geographical information system (GIS)** is a computer-based system for capturing, storing, modeling, retrieving, checking, integrating, manipulating, analyzing, and displaying geographically referenced data by using digitized maps. For more on digitized maps, see **gpsy.com/maps**. The most distinguishing characteristic of GIS is that every record or digital object has an identified geographic location. By integrating maps with spatially oriented (i.e., geographic location) databases (called *geocoding*) and other databases, users can generate information for planning, problem solving, and decision making, thereby increasing their productivity and the quality of their decisions. Areas as diverse as retailing, banking, transportation, agriculture, natural resource management, public administration, NASA, the military, emergency preparedness, and urban planning have all successfully used GIS since the beginning of the 1970s (see Ursery, 2004). For typical sources of geographic data, see Saarenvirta (2004).

GIS APPLICATIONS

As GIS tools become increasingly sophisticated and affordable, they help more companies and governments understand precisely where their trucks, workers, and resources are; where they need to go to service a customer; and the best way to get from here to there. The areas of targeted marketing are growing rapidly, and organizations can easily segment a population by using GIS. For example, the Credit Union of Texas (**cuoftexas.org**) uses a GIS to help decide where to place billboards and ATMs and to help identify the areas most responsive to direct mailing. The typical response rate for this credit union is from 5 to 10 percent, much better than the traditional average of 1 to 2 percent. Customers also enjoy receiving less mail from the credit union because they receive only targeted mailings. See Franklin (2002) and Ursery (2004) for details.

Example

The state of Louisiana is using WebFOCUS from Information Builders (**informationbuilders.com/products/webfocus/index.html**) to identify individuals who traffic in food stamps. It also uses GIS in its police departments to find geographic patterns in crimes as well as to deploy officers. It also uses GIS in physical asset management. For details, see Schwartz (2005).

For many companies, the intelligent organization of data within a GIS can provide a framework to support the processes of decision making and designing alternative strategies. Some examples of successful GIS applications are summarized in Table 6.5. Leading companies incorporate GIS into their BI systems. GIS *ideally* incorporate census data (see **census.gov**) as a source of demographic data for effective decision making. For many organizations, GIS and related spatial analyses are a top priority. For

TABLE 6.5 GIS Applications

Organization	*GIS Application*
Pepsi Cola, Inc., Super Value, Acordia, Inc.	Use GIS in site selection for new Taco Bell and Pizza Hut restaurants. Combine demographic data and traffic patterns.
CIGNA (health insurance)	Uses GIS to answer questions such as How many CIGNA-affiliated physicians are available within an 8-mile radius of a business?
Western Auto (a subsidiary of Sears)	Integrates data with GIS to create a detailed demographic profile of a store's neighborhood to determine the best product mix to offer at the store.
Sears, Roebuck & Co./Kmart	Uses GIS to support planning of truck routes.
Health maintenance organizations	Track cancer rates and rates of other diseases to determine expansion strategy and allocation of expensive equipment in their facilities.
Wood Personnel Services (employment agencies)	Maps neighborhoods where temporary workers live to locate marketing and recruiting cities.
Wilkening & Co. (consulting services)	Designs optimal sales territories and routes for its clients, reducing travel costs by 15 percent.
CellularOne Corporation	Maps its entire cellular network to identify clusters of call disconnects and to dispatch technicians accordingly.
Sun Microsystems	Manages leased property in dozens of places worldwide.
Consolidated Rail Corporation	Monitors the condition of 20,000 miles of railroad track and thousands of parcels of adjoining land.
Federal Emergency Management Agency	Assesses damage due to hurricanes, floods, and other natural disasters by relating videotapes of the damage to digitized maps of properties.
Toyota and other automobile manufacturers	Combine GIS and GPS as a navigation tool to direct drivers to destinations via the best routes.

example, Sears invested several million dollars in GIS technology for logistics, leading to a savings of $52 million per year (see Gonzales, 2003).

Many banks use GIS to support activities such as:

- Determining branch and ATM locations
- Analyzing customer demographics (e.g., residence, age, income level) for each of a bank's products
- Analyzing volume and traffic patterns of business activities
- Analyzing the geographic area served by each branch
- Determining the market potential for banking activities
- Evaluating strengths and weaknesses against those of the competition
- Evaluating branch performance

Banks also use GIS as geographic spreadsheets that allow managers to model business activities and perform what-if analyses (e.g., What if we close a branch or merge branches? What if a competitor opens a branch?). Each map consolidates pages of analyses.

GIS AND DECISION MAKING

GIS provide a large amount of extremely useful information that can be analyzed and used in decision making. The graphical format of a GIS makes it easy for managers to visualize the data. For example, as Janet M. Hamilton, market research administrator for Dow Elanco, a $2 billion maker of agricultural chemicals based in Indianapolis, explained, "I can put 80-page spreadsheets with thousands of rows into a single map. It would take a couple of weeks to comprehend all the information from the spreadsheet, but in a map, the story can be told in seconds" (Hamilton, 1996, p. 21).

There are countless applications of GIS to improve decision making in the public and private sectors (see Saarenvirta, 2004), including the dispatch of emergency vehicles, transit management, facility site selection, drought risk management, and wildlife management. GIS are extremely popular in local governments, where they are used not only for mapping but for many other decision-making applications (see Ursery, 2004). States, cities, and counties are using GIS applications related to property assessment, mapping, flood control, and more.

Saarenvirta (2004) explored the value of GIS and its relationship to BI. He described spatial analysis in areas such as customer mapping, thematic mapping, trade area analysis, and retail location.

GIS COMBINED WITH GPS

The U.S. Department of Defense has invested some $21 billion in the satellite system that feeds **global positioning systems (GPS)**. GPS devices are wireless and use satellites to enable users to detect the position on earth of items the devices are attached to (e.g., cars, people), with reasonable precision (see **trimble.com/gps**). GPS in conjunction with GIS are making major inroads in BI applications. Commercial and government uses are endless because detection devices are relatively inexpensive. See Application Case 6.5 for examples of how these technologies are being used.

Application Case 6.5

GIS and GPS Track Where You Are and Help You with What You Do

The following are some examples of how GIS in conjunction with GPS help firms differentiate their products and delivery services and improve performance:

- UltraEx, a West Coast company that specializes in same-day delivery of items such as emergency blood supplies and computer parts, equips all its vehicles with @Road's GPS receivers and wireless modems. In addition to giving dispatchers a big-picture view of the entire fleet, @Road helps UltraEx keep clients happy by letting them track the location and speed of their shipments on the Web in real-time. This service shows customers a map of the last place the satellite detected the delivery vehicle and how fast it was traveling. Drivers use AT&T's Mobile Data Service to communicate with dispatchers, and drivers who own their vehicles are unable to falsify mileage sheets because @Road reports exact mileage for each vehicle.
- New York City pioneered CompStat, which uses GIS to map criminal activity and police deployment by date, time, and location. By making precinct commanders accountable for their own policing strategies, it has been a major factor in reducing the city's violent crime rate by nearly 70 percent in the past decade.
- Some police departments, neighborhood activists, and concerned citizens in many cities are using GIS to fight crime. Geographical information about neighborhoods is integrated with crime reports to analyze crime patterns. By identifying trends and providing information to citizens, police are better able to set up surveillance activities, and citizens can modify behaviors, leading to lower crime in these areas.
- CSX Transportation, Inc., has equipped 3,700 locomotives with GPS. The Union Pacific Railroad has installed satellite-based monitoring devices on thousands of its freight cars for car tracking. By combining

GIS with GPS, a freight company can identify the position of a railroad car or truck to within 330 feet at any time. For example, it can identify locomotives that have left their route and the specific cars that have been left behind or sent with the wrong locomotive. A further benefit is the ability to minimize accidents.

- At the University of Georgia's National Environmentally Sound Production Agriculture Laboratory, scientists developed a farm tractor that is controlled by a gyroscope and GPS. Bad weather and visibility issues are not a problem anymore because the tractor knows where to go. Scientists have developed devices that enable the system to detect small obstacles, using a robotic vision system and artificial intelligence methods to interpret what the robot sees.
- In location commerce (l-commerce), advertising is targeted to an individual whose location is known (via a GPS and GIS combination). Similarly, emergency medical systems identify the location of a car accident in seconds, and the attached GIS helps in directing ambulances to the scene. For other interesting applications, see Turban et al. (2006).

Sources: Adapted from A. Dragoon, "Putting IT on the Map," *CIO*, May 15, 2003, and L. Rosencrance, "Railroads Hot for Satellite Monitoring," *Computerworld*, April, 2000.

GIS AND THE INTERNET/INTRANETS

Most major GIS software vendors provide Web access, such as embedded browsers, or a Web/Internet/intranet server that hooks directly to their software. Thus, users can access dynamic maps and data via the Internet or a corporate intranet. GIS Web services are proliferating. These geographical systems form an information-rich global infrastructure that adds a new dimension to the GIS field by integrating multiple and disparate application services. GIS Web services are revolutionizing how companies use and interact with geospatial information. For example, GIS can help the manager of a retail operation determine whether to open a store located on a major city intersection, within a 15-minute drive of a freeway exit ramp, surrounded by middle-class neighborhoods of professional families (see Gonzales, 2003). Big Horn Computer Services (Buffalo, NY) used a Web-adapted GIS to develop a custom application for a national television network that wanted its affiliate stations to be able to access an intranet containing demographic information about their viewers. Using a Web browser, employees at each station can now thematically view shaded maps to analyze their markets.

A number of firms are deploying GIS on the Internet for internal use or for use by their customers. For example, Visa Plus, which operates a network of ATMs, has developed a GIS application that lets Internet users call up a map to locate any of the company's 300,000 ATMs worldwide. Store locators are available from many vendors (e.g., **borders.com**). Such a locator will give you the address of the nearest store, with a map of how to get there. As vendors deploy GIS Web server software, more applications will be developed. Maps, GIS data, and information about GIS are available on the Web through a number of vendors and public agencies. Government sources (via the Internet and CD-ROM) provide some data, and vendors provide diversified commercial data as well. Some of this information is free (see CD-ROMs from MapInfo and downloadable material from **esri.com** and **data.geocomm.com**). Related to this is the inclusion of spatial data in data warehouses for later use with Web technology.

Some examples of important GIS software are ArcView and ArcInfo (ESRI), AGISMap (AGIS), GeoMedia (Intergraph), and MapInfo Professional (MapInfo). ArcInfo's (**esri.com/arcinfo8/**) data model provides tools to model complex spatial systems with no programming. Culpepper (2002) described how the CommunityViz (**communityviz.com**) software integrates city-planning simulation and modeling functionality into ESRI's ArcView GIS software. The user can set up and run different scenarios, based on user-specified variables and constraints, to determine relationships among municipal projects and social, environmental, or economic indicators. Users can test entire sets of policies.

Section 6.8 Review Questions

1. Define *GIS* and describe its benefits.
2. How can banks use GIS?
3. Describe GIS/GPS applications.
4. Why is the combination of GIS and GPS so useful?
5. How is GIS related to the Web/Internet?

6.9 REAL-TIME BUSINESS INTELLIGENCE, AUTOMATED DECISION SUPPORT (ADS), AND COMPETITIVE INTELLIGENCE

Three emerging technologies are closely related to BA: real-time BI, automated decision support (ADS) systems, and competitive intelligence.

REAL-TIME BI

Business users are increasingly demanding access to real-time, unstructured, or remote data, integrated with the contents of a data warehouse (see Devlin, 2003). For example, the buses in Houston, Texas, have been more reliable and efficient since they were equipped with instantaneous data-gathering devices, giving the traffic controllers the ability to access information and modify traffic light intervals (see "Houston Buses Due for 'Intellectual Overhaul,'" 2003). In many cases, real-time data updates and access are critical for an organization's success or even survival. For example, according to Baer (2002), the city of Richmond, British Columbia, uses real-time data collection and analysis. Richmond is on a coastal island and has an average elevation of only 3 feet above sea level. It is important for city officials to know instantly whether its network of flood-control pumps is operating, how well it is working, and whether there are any problems. Clearly, this is also important in other parts of the world, such as New Orleans and The Netherlands.

Data warehousing and BI tools traditionally focused on assisting managers in making strategic and tactical decisions by using *historical data*. In 2003, with the advent of real-time data warehousing, a shift began toward using these technologies for operational decisions. This "active" use of data warehouses is just beginning to change the focus of these tools (see Coffee, 2003), and IBM, Oracle, Microsoft, and many other IT vendors are moving to such active uses. Hewlett-Packard moved toward an adaptive enterprise strategy for delivering on-demand computing (see Follett, 2003; and "Infrastructure and Management Solutions," 2003).

The trend toward BI software producing real-time data updates for real-time analysis and real-time decision making is growing rapidly (see "The 2003 CIO Insight Business Intelligence Research Study," 2003; Coffee, 2003; Patel, 2005; Raden, 2003a, 2003b; and White, 2004). Part of this push involves getting the right information to operational and tactical personnel—who generally deal with the short-term aspects of running an organization—so that they can use new BA tools and up-to-the-minute results to make decisions.

Today, many customers demand current data. Therefore, more and more IT managers are facing the question of how to conduct business analysis in real-time. More and more real-time data warehousing/analytics projects are under development and being deployed. The demand for real-time applications continues to grow. The proliferation of ADS and business rules management, for example, creates pressure to implement more automated business processes that can best be implemented in a real-time data warehouse environment. When processes that require instantaneous updates are needed for answering analytical questions, a real-time response is necessary. Therefore, response times for queries, OLAP, and data mining must be close to zero (see Raden, 2003a).

To achieve real-time business analysis, real-time data warehouses need to be updated very frequently, not just weekly or monthly. In 2003, daily updating became popular; the time interval continues to shrink. In addition to real-time queries, BA applications are being deployed. These applications can instantaneously identify, for example, customer buying patterns based on store displays, and recommend immediate changes for placement or the display itself. Other applications include call-center support, fraud detection, revenue management, transportation, and many financial-related transactions.

Real-time requirements change the way we view the design of databases, data warehouses, OLAP, and data mining tools because they are updated while queries are active. On the other hand, the substantial business value in doing this has been demonstrated, so it is crucial that organizations consider adopting these methods in their business processes.

Examples of Web-based, real-time BI software include Web Intelligence (Business Objects), Supply Chain Analytics and BI Series 8 (Cognos), Live business (Data Mirror), DB2 Intelligent Miner Scoring (IMS; IBM), Analytics Delivery Platform (Informatica), PowerCenter Standard and Advanced versions (Informatica), Databeacon (Databeacon, Inc.), LiveSheet for Excel (KnowNow), NetIQ Corp., WebTrends, Supply Chain Intelligence Suite (SAS), and SonicMQ (Sonic Software). For reviews, see Havenstein (2003b) and Lindquist (2003).

Concerns About Real-Time Systems

Despite the many uses for real-time systems, an important issue in real-time computing is that not all data should be updated continuously. This may certainly cause problems when reports are generated in real-time because one person's results may not match another person's. For example, a company using WebIntelligence (from Business Objects) noticed a significant problem with real-time intelligence. Real-time reports are all different when produced at slightly different times (see Peterson, 2003). Also, it may not be necessary to update certain data continuously.

Real-time data are necessary in many cases for the creation of ADS systems.

AUTOMATED DECISION SUPPORT (ADS)

In Chapter 1 we defined **automated decision support (ADS)** systems as rule-based systems that provide solutions to repetitive managerial problems. ADS systems are also known as **enterprise decision management (EDM)** systems. ADS systems are closely related to BI and BA in the following ways:

- Some BA models are used to create and/or operate the business rules.
- The business rules can be used to trigger the automatic decisions that can be a part of BI applications. This is especially true in performance monitoring and analysis systems in which the results of what is monitored are analyzed and some action is triggered by the ADS.

Before we examine how ADS systems are implemented, let's look at business rules.

Business Rules

Automating the decision-making process is usually achieved by encapsulating business user expertise in a set of *business rules* that are embedded in a rule-driven workflow (or other action-oriented) engine. These business rules can be part of expert systems (see Chapters 12) or other intelligent systems. As BA is called for (e.g., by a performance monitoring system), a signal is passed to the rule engine for evaluation against associated business rules. These rules determine what action needs to be taken, based on the results of the evaluation.

White (2004) described four types of business rules. These rules are usually found in real-time BI and are associated with business performance management (BPM), as described in Chapter 9. The four types of rules are analysis rules, context rules, exception rules, and action rules. *Analysis rules* are used to calculate performance metrics from detailed business transaction data, and *context rules* enable performance metrics to be tied to business goals and forecasts. Some basic BPM automation can be achieved by applying *exception rules* to metrics and sending an alert to a business user when a metric exceeds a threshold defined in the exception rule. Decision making can be further improved by including in the alert the Web address of a guided analysis workflow that identifies other analyses and reports that can be run to further investigate the issue.

Full right-time automated actions can be achieved by defining the manual decision-making process that business users go through as a series of *action rules* in a workflow. These action workflows can then be implemented in a rules engine to automate the decision-making process. An ADS can be built using rules.

Characteristics and Benefits of ADS

ADS are most suitable for decisions that must be made frequently and/or rapidly, using information that is available electronically. The knowledge and decision criteria, as well as the business rules that express them, must be highly structured, and the problem situation must be well understood. High-quality data and/or knowledge about the problem domain must be available. Approval of a loan and granting of a credit line to a customer are typical examples.

Using ADS can produce precise, agile decision making because ADS afford the following capabilities:

- Rapidly builds rules-based applications to automate or guide decision makers, and deploys the applications into almost any operating environment.
- Injects predictive analytics into rules-based applications, increasing their potency and value.
- Provides decisioning services to legacy systems, expanding their capabilities while minimizing technical risk.
- Combines business rules, predictive models, and optimization strategies flexibly into state-of-the-art decision-management applications.
- Accelerates the uptake of learning from decision criteria into strategy design, execution, and refinement.

ADS Applications

Davenport and Harris (2005) provided numerous examples of successful ADS systems in a variety of industries. Some typical examples are:

- *Product or service configuration.* Customers are allowed to customize a product (or service) such as a PC. The ADS then configures the most appropriate final product (service) and its cost (considering profitability to the manufacturer).

- *Yield (price) optimization.* Airlines have extensively used automated decision-making applications to set prices based on seat availability and hour or day of purchase, also known as *revenue management*, or *yield management*. Other manufacturing, logistics, and transportation companies use these applications to improve operating efficiency. A method known as *price optimization*, or *smart pricing* (see Fleischmann et al., 2004), is being used experimentally with variable pricing (e.g., rental housing). For examples in mortgage pricing, see Barrett and Carr (2005).
- *Routing or segmentation decisions.* Significant productivity improvements have been made by companies that design automated filters for sorting cases and transactions. Examples include the insurance industry, where clear-cut claims are handled as "priority," and emergency rooms, which manage a variety and volume of patients.
- *Corporate and regulatory compliance.* Routine policy decisions are time-consuming and technical; however, rules must be current and need to be applied consistently. For example, in the home mortgage industry, lenders must categorize and process loans that conform to government regulations as well as the requirements of the lenders. If this is completed efficiently, the cost savings is marked.
- *Fraud detection.* The Internal Revenue Service and the U.S. Securities and Exchange Commission use automated screening to identify fraud. Banking and other lending companies must improve their systems because of the Sarbanes-Oxley Act and other legislation. For examples, see Barrett and Carr (2005).
- *Dynamic forecasting.* Increased automated demand forecasting by manufacturers allows companies to align customer forecasts (i.e., inventory levels) with their own manufacturing and sales plans (see Chapter 10).
- *Operational control.* Some ADS systems are programmed to sense changes in the physical environment and respond based on rules or algorithms (e.g., temperatures affecting power supply needs, traffic lights at intersections based on real-time traffic volume recorded by cameras).

Implementing ADS

Software companies provide the following components to ADS:

- *Rule engines.* Companies such as Exsys (**exsys.com**), ILOG (**ilog.com**) see BRMS, Fair Isaac (**fairisaac.com**) see Blaze Advisor for risk analysis and Falcon for fraud analysis, ARulesXL (**arulesxl.com**), and Pegasystems (**pega.com**) provide processing of business rules (see Chapter 12 for rule-based systems).
- *Mathematical and statistical algorithms.* Companies such as SAS and SPSS provide formulas for finding optimal solutions (e.g., price, inventory level), conducting trend analyses, and so on. (See Section 6.6.) For example, SAS provides pricing and product optimization (e.g., see **sas.com/success/autozone.html**).
- *Industry-specific packages.* Dozens of companies provide software packages for specific industries (e.g., LendingTree for consumer financing and mortgages, CSC Continuum for insurance).
- *Enterprise systems.* Companies such as SAP and Oracle offer applications that automate, join, and direct information flows and transaction processing in complex organizations that use automated decision technology for particular functions (e.g., SCM).
- *Workflow applications.* After a rule engine makes a decision, the workflow system moves information-intensive business processes through the required steps. Key vendors of such systems include Documentum and FileNet Corp.

COMPETITIVE INTELLIGENCE

Information about one's competitors can mean the difference between winning and losing a battle in business. Many companies continuously monitor the activities of their competitors to acquire *competitive intelligence*. Such information gathering drives business performance by increasing market knowledge, improving knowledge management, and raising the quality of strategic planning. For example, consider the following uses of computer-based competitive intelligence, cited by Comcowich (2002):

- A sporting goods company found an activist group planning a demonstration and boycott months in advance, enabling the company to implement a counter strategy.
- Within days of launch, a software firm found dissatisfaction with specific product features, enabling the technicians to write a patch that fixed the problem within days instead of the months normally required to obtain customer feedback and implement software fixes.
- A packaging company was able to determine the location, size, and production capacity for a new plant being built by a competitor. The otherwise well-protected information was found by an automated monitoring service in building permit documents in the Web site of the town where the new plant was being built.
- A telecommunications company uncovered a competitor's legislative strategy, enabling the company to gain an upper hand in a state-by-state lobbying battle. (Remarkably, the strategy was posted on the competitor's own Web site.)
- The creative team embarking on development of a new video game used the Internet to identify cutting-edge product attributes that game players prefer. The intensive research uncovered three key "gotta haves" that had not been identified in focus groups and had not been included in the original design specification.

Competitive intelligence can be facilitated with technologies such as optical character recognition, radio frequency identification (RFID), intelligent agents, and especially the Internet. The Internet is becoming a company's most important tool in supporting competitive intelligence. The visibility of information that a competitor places on the Internet and the power of Web-based tools to interrogate Web sites for information about prices, products, services, and marketing approaches have generated increased corporate interest in these intelligence-gathering activities. For example, online niche bookseller Fatbrain (now part of **barnesandnoble.com**) used "e-spionage" firm Rivalwatch.com to keep track of competitors in Fatbrain's specialist professional and educational book market. By tracking prices at rival firms such as Amazon.com, Fatbrain could offer competitive prices without giving away profit margins when it did not need to.

Pawar and Sharda (1997) proposed a framework in which the Internet capabilities are shown to provide information for strategic decisions. According to the framework, the external information required and the methods of acquiring information can be supported by Internet tools for communication, searching, browsing, and information retrieval. Pawar and Sharda emphasized the search capability of the various tools of the Internet. By using these tools, an organization can implement specific search strategies, as illustrated in Online File W6.5.

However, it's not enough just to gather information about a competitor. Analyzing and interpreting the information is as important as collecting it. For these tasks, we can use BI tools ranging from *intelligent agents* (i.e., software tools that allow the automation of tasks that require intelligence; see Chapters 14) to *data mining* (i.e., searching in large databases for relationships among bits of data, using specialized logic tools; see Chapter 7). For example, J.P. Morgan Chase (New York) uses data mining to track several sources of information. The company's goal is to determine the possible impact of the information on the bank, the customers, and the industry.

Another, more sinister, aspect of competitive intelligence is *industrial espionage*. Corporate spies, who actually do exist in some industries, look for confidential marketing plans, cost analyses, proposed products/services, and strategic plans. Industrial espionage is considered to be unethical and usually illegal. One type of industrial espionage is the theft of portable computers at airports, hotels, and conferences. Many of the thieves are interested in the information stored in the computers, not the computers themselves. Protecting against such activities is an important part of maintaining competitive advantage.

Baseline magazine dedicated its December 15, 2005, issue to security threats, including competitor attacks (e.g., Gage, 2005). However, according to the Society of Competitive Intelligence Professionals (**scip.org**), competitive intelligence does not include espionage. *Espionage* is the use of illegal means to gather information. *Competitive intelligence*, on the other hand, uses legal and ethical means to gather and analyze information. Many companies assist in competitive intelligence (e.g., **fuld.com**). For comprehensive resources on BI, see **b-eye-network.com**.

Section 6.9 Review Questions

1. Define *real-time BI.*
2. List the benefits of real-time BI.
3. What technologies are needed to provide real-time BI?
4. List some concerns about real-time systems.
5. Define *ADS system* and describe the benefits of ADS.
6. Describe yield management.
7. List the major categories of ADS.
8. Describe competitive intelligence.
9. How can the Internet facilitate competitive intelligence?

6.10 BUSINESS ANALYTICS AND THE WEB: WEB INTELLIGENCE AND WEB ANALYTICS

BI activities—from data acquisition, through warehousing, BA, and mining—are mostly performed using Web tools. Users with browsers can log on to a system, make inquiries, get reports, and so on, in real-time. This is done through intranets for corporate insiders and for outsiders via the Internet or extranets.

USING THE WEB IN BA

Most BA applications are related to the Web. For example, software vendors provide Web tools that connect a data warehouse with e-commerce ordering and cataloging systems. One example is RETSbond, a product of HotScripts (**hotscripts.com**). Hitachi's e-commerce tool suite combines e-commerce activities such as catalog management, payment applications, mass customization, and order management with data warehouses (or data marts) and ERP systems.

Data warehousing and analytics and decision support vendors are integrating their products with Web technologies and e-commerce, and they are also creating new ones for the same purpose. Examples are Web Intelligence from Business Objects and

Hyperion's Appsource "wired for OLAP" product, which integrates OLAP with Web tools. IBM's Decision Edge is another tool that offers OLAP capabilities on an intranet from anywhere in the corporation, using browsers, search engines, and other Web technologies. BA can also be facilitated by using products such as Oracle's Financial Analyzer and Sales Analyzer, as well as Hummingbird BI/Web and BI/Broker.

WEB ANALYTICS

Web analytics is the application of BA activities to Web-based processes, including e-commerce. This term is used to describe the application of BA to Web sites. The tools and methods are highly visual in nature. Schlegel (2003) described the basics of Web analytics and provided a proposed architecture for *clickstream analysis* (i.e., an implementation of Web analytics). For a comprehensive description, see Peterson (2005). For an overview of Web site analysis, methods, and products, see Rapoza (2004).

Clickstream Analyses

Clickstream analysis refers to the analysis of data that occur inside the Web environment; the data, known as **clickstream data**, provide a trail of the user's activities and show the user's browsing patterns: which sites are visited, which pages are accessed, how long is spent at the site, and so on. By analyzing and interpreting these data, a firm can, for example, find the effectiveness of promotions and determine which products and ads attract the most attention.

As clickstream operations increase, the amount of data to process grows exponentially, and scalability issues become critical for Web analytics. Werner and Abramson (2001) described a method (based on sorting and aggregation) to process 1 billion records per day for a Web data warehouse. See also Ruber (2003) for information about Web clickstream analysis.

According to Edelstein (2001), performing clickstream analysis requires the following:

- Raw clickstream data must be obtained from multiple servers.
- Individual customer data are usually buried in a mass of other data about pages served, hosts, referring pages, and browser types.
- A single page request can generate multiple entries in server logs.
- Creating a session of page views based on a sequence of log records involves lots of data cleansing to eliminate superfluous data.
- Identifying the sessions in a data stream is complex. It requires cookies or other session identification numbers in URLs.
- Proxy servers (i.e., where customer requests do not come from the home server) confuse the identity of a session and why it ended.
- Data preparation can consume 80 percent of a project's resources.

VENDOR SUPPORT FOR WEB ANALYTICS

Most vendors provide extensive Web support for their BI products. The following are some illustrative examples:

- *BusinessObjects* provides a Web-enabled, full client solution to querying and analysis called Web Intelligence. It allows business users to easily track and manage information stored in multiple data sources within and beyond the enterprise in an integrated manner from a desktop computer.
- *Cognos* provides a complete Web services architecture in its Cognos 8 product. This enables easier software development.

- *Informatica* has focused closely on using the Web to enable organizations to track business performance. Using the Power Center 8 BI platform, organizations gather business performance metrics via voice systems, the Web, and wireless transmissions. The Informatica Analytics Delivery Platform is an Internet-based system that provides real-time business performance results.
- The *WebTrends* BI tool focuses on real-time analysis of Web traffic and online transactions. For example, WebTrends enables organizations to track consumer purchasing trends, revenue, and the effectiveness of ad campaigns or sales promotions through millions of site visits daily. Site59.com, Inc., a travel site that specializes in last-minute getaway packages, discovered through WebTrends live analyses that visitors could not easily find all the available travel packages on the site. The analysis indicated how to streamline and improve the design. Since then, Site59.com has experienced an increase in the number of visitors and the proportion of those who make online purchases (see Pallatto, 2002).
- *Google* offers its *Google Analytics* to small organizations for free. It is software for clickstream analysis of Web logs.
- *ADVISOR Solutions* offers an interactive library of charts that supports business display needs, integrated analytics (e.g., Visual Discovery, predictive analytics), on-demand real-time analysis of multiple data sources, and point-and-click self-service using Visual Discovery. For further details, see **advizorsolutions.com/solutions.htm**.
- *Angoss* KnowledgeStudio is another example of a Web mining/analytic tool. See Figure 6.8 for a sample screenshot.

The usability of clickstream analysis is demonstrated in Application Case 6.6.

Application Case 6.6

Web Analytics Improves Performance for Online Merchants

E-commerce sales are growing rapidly, fueled by growth in new product categories and retailer mastery of digital marketing, Web analytics, and multichannel marketing.

Online merchants anxious to improve the return of their Web site investment must learn their visitors' activities in real-time. This goes well beyond performing standard clickstream analysis and collecting the transaction reports with separate tools.

It is critical to understand customers' online behavior to determine how and what to advertise and market to them. Understanding and properly using the operating metrics of an e-commerce site can make or break a business. For example, special product promotions can be put online in a matter of days, versus the months required for expensive catalog revisions and nationwide mailings.

Web analytics can boost the bottom line. For example, Yun-Hui Chong, Internet director for Newport News (**newport-news.com**), says that the data her company collects on the activities of its about 2 million monthly Web visitors enables the company to assess the return on investment (ROI) of all its online marketing campaigns. Based on that, the company optimizes banners and the presentation of merchandise. It also uses the information to do clickstream analysis in order to understand how customers are reacting to changes in the site. It has become particularly important to identify customers who abandon the site or browse only certain categories. The firm sends those customers very customized e-mail promotions about their preferred categories. Since the company began doing so, there have been significant increases in e-mail conversion and revenue per e-mail sent. Targeting browsers and abandoners via e-mail on three product categories experiencing the worst conversion rates resulted in a better than sixfold increase in revenue per e-mail sent, while the cost per order dropped some 83 percent. Web analytics clearly pays off!

Sources: Compiled from P. Ruber, "Analytics Improve Merchandising," *Internetworld*, June 2003, and V. Rhodes, "SAS Improves Evaluation of Campaign Segments for Newport News," *DM Review Magazine*, March, 2002.

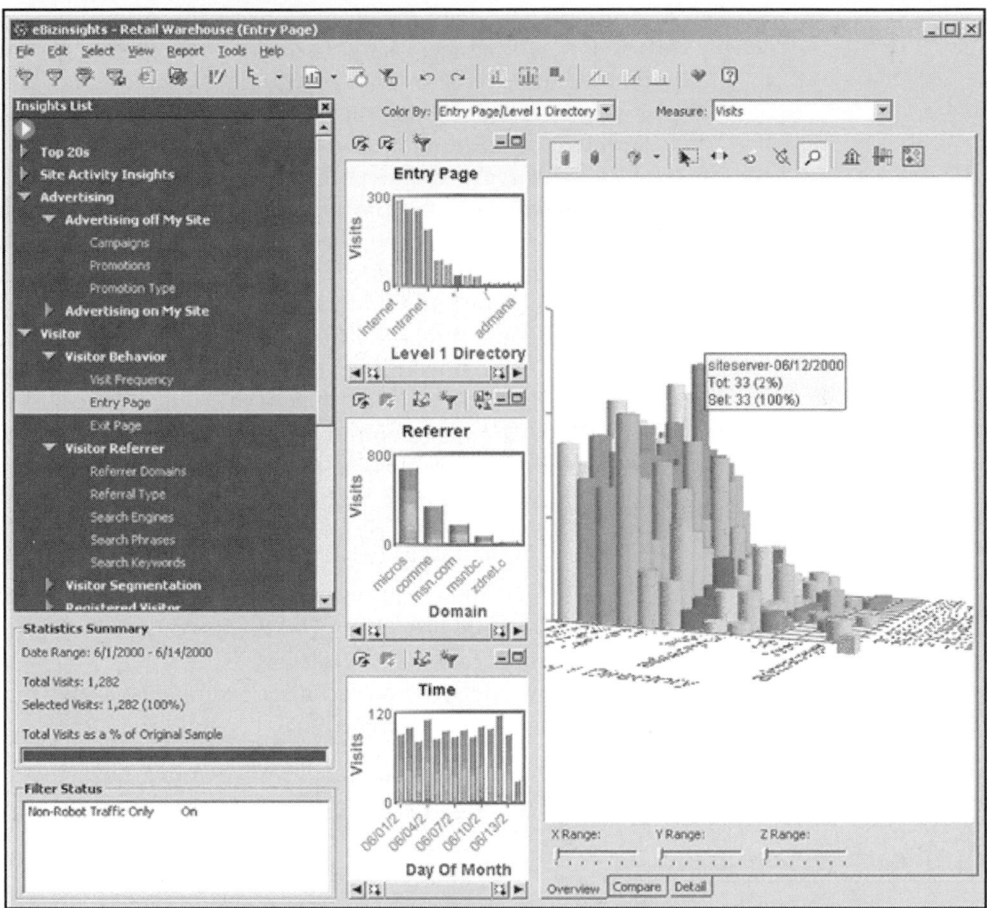

FIGURE 6.8 Screen Shot from the eBizInsights Visual Portal Analysis of Web Performance

Source: Courtesy of Visual Insights.

Section 6.10 Review Questions

1. Describe the use of the Web to enhance BI activities.
2. Define *Web analytics*.
3. Describe applications of Web analytics.
4. Define *clickstream analysis*.
5. How are clickstream data used?

6.11 USAGE, BENEFITS, AND SUCCESS OF BUSINESS ANALYTICS

The use of BA is spreading rapidly, and most medium to large companies use it successfully. Next, we look at some usage and implementation issues.

USAGE OF BA

Almost all managers and executives can use some BA systems, but some find the tools too complicated to use. Sometimes managers are not trained properly. Distributing analytics tools throughout a company is a major challenge; most businesses want a greater percentage of the enterprise to leverage analytics, but most of the challenges related to technology adoption involve culture, people, and processes (see Bonde and Kuckuk, 2004). A critical issue is to align BA applications to the business needs. If the system does not provide useful information, it is considered useless. See Technology Insights 6.7 for details of a study on how executives use BI and BA tools. Additional data and success lessons can be found in Thompson (2004).

SUCCESS AND USABILITY OF BA

According to an IDC report from fall 2002, organizations that have successfully implemented and used analytic applications have realized returns ranging from 17 percent to more than 2000 percent, with a median ROI of 122 percent (see Morris et al., 2002). Even so, more than half of all BI projects fail. As with data warehousing, BI activities should be regarded not simply as another set of IT projects but as a constantly evolving strategy, vision, and architecture that continuously seeks to align an organization's operations and direction with its strategic business goals. For a success story, see Online File W6.6.

BI tools have been used to identify white-collar theft in organizations. They can be used to identify inflated invoices, embezzlement, customer impersonation, and similar offenses. According to Dorrington (2003), the estimate of total fraud in the United Kingdom is almost US$30 billion. Fraud committed by employees causes median losses of $60,000, and fraud committed by managers or executives causes median losses of $250,000. When managers and employees conspire, the median loss rises to $500,000.

TECHNOLOGY INSIGHTS 6.7

Are BI Systems Making Firms Smarter?

More than 570 IT executives responded to *CIO Insight*'s Business Intelligence Research Study. *CIO Insight* discovered some interesting facts about the 2003 state of BI and BA (which is still current):

- Most notably, the use of BI technologies is relatively high, and it is growing.
- Larger companies are usually more likely than smaller companies to use BI.
- In 2002, successful companies spent almost 50 percent more on BI technology than unsuccessful companies. BI seems to be necessary (but not sufficient) for success.
- The government uses virtually every commercially available BA tool at a significantly higher rate than any other sector of the economy.
- The technologies used to collect, aggregate, analyze, and report on competitive intelligence, along with the percentage response in parentheses, are reporting tools (82.1 percent), automated data/information feeds (79 percent), intranets/portals (70.4 percent), data warehousing (69.8 percent), content management (63 percent), data visualization software (41.4 percent), specialty search engines (41.4 percent), workflow software (41.4 percent), and harvesting (e.g., intelligent agents) (38.9 percent).
- Just 49 percent of the less successful companies are happy with their competitive intelligence efforts.
- Some 88 percent of companies have confidence in the accuracy of the customer information they gather using BI tools.
- Dissatisfaction with BI usually derives from difficulty in distributing the results.
- CIOs want to move firms to being real-time enterprises that use BI.

Source: Compiled from "The 2003 CIO Insight Business Intelligence Research Study: Are Your BI Systems Making You Smarter?" *CIO Insight*, May 23, 2003, and *CIOs Rate SAS Tops for Increasing ROI, Delivering Business Value and Reliability*, February 9, 2004, **sas.com/news/preleases/020904/news1.html** (accessed February 2006).

If all internal data systems are integrated with a data warehouse for fraud analysis, internal data can be compared to external fraud-related data so that patterns and anomalies become more readily identifiable. Suspicious activities can be isolated, measured, and tracked.

Williams-Sonoma Corp. saves millions with targeted marketing and multichannel branding by using the SAS data mining software, Enterprise Miner, along with a suite of CRM applications from SAS. The new marketing system models and explores customer data from more than 30 million households to help the retailer create a personalized, cohesive shopping experience across multiple channels and multiple brands. See Bolen (2003) for details. Callaghan (2003a) described how SPSS Predictive Web Analytics and SAS Web can be used to predict customer Web behavior and develop customer segmentation models (clusters) that lead to better business performance. Retailers frequently use BI tools, shown in Application Case 6.8.

Application Case 6.8

Retailers Make Steady BI Progress

Most brick-and-mortar retailers lag behind other industries in their use of BI. Notable exceptions include Wal-Mart Stores, Inc., and Sears. Other retailers continue to make impressive strides. The following are a few examples:

- Hudson's Bay Co. turned 333 in May 2003. Despite its age, Hudson's Bay upgraded its information systems to give executives, store managers, and key suppliers methods to analyze reams of sales and customer data. The challenge the firm faces is to determine how to transform the data into useful information. The firm uses two data warehouses and BI tools from Teradata to track sales and make decisions about product inventory and sales.
- At Harry Rosen, Inc., a chain of 17 men's clothing stores, executives use Cognos, Inc.'s, data analysis tools, integrated into a merchandising system. More than a dozen sales and inventory reports for analyzing sales help the firm identify sales trends, manage inventory, and improve gross profit margins.
- Reno-Depot, a Canadian home improvement and renovation retailer with more than 20 stores, uses customer traffic information, POS sales data, and so on to develop, forecast, and build optimal labor scheduling. The software performs an analysis of existing labor situations, dynamically creating shifts with workers' assignments.
- Coldwater Creek creates reports by integrating data produced on disparate applications by using data warehousing and Microsoft SQL Server 2000. Reporting preparation time has been reduced significantly.
- Using BI and analysis tools from BusinessObjects, TruServ Corp. (the parent company of True Value Hardware and Taylor Rental) reduced its "red zone" inventory (i.e., products that have not sold in one-half year) by $50 million over two years by analyzing product stockpiles. The system has also identified products sitting in the company's 14 distribution centers that might sell better in other parts of the country.

Other retailers are looking for similar ways to obtain a competitive edge. Putting the right products in the right place at the right time at the right price is one goal of retailers. Doing it right determines who succeeds and who fails.

Traditional retailers are learning from online retailers about how to perform analytic investigations of customer performance. For example, J. Crew Group and Nordstrom, Inc., use DigiMine to analyze online sales. Nordstrom had a situation in which online shoppers were searching for navel rings just like the one that a model wore in an advertisement. Nordstrom was able to quickly obtain the rings for both its stores and online customers, even though it had not carried the product beforehand.

An increased number of retailers are resorting to automated price-setting programs.

Sources: Compiled from R. Whiting, "Business-Intelligence Buy-in," *InformationWeek*, May 12, 2003, Hammacher Schlemmer & Company, Inc., **stores.com** (accessed April 2006); and "A Breath of Fresh Air: Coldwater Creek Freshens Up Its Reporting." *Retail Technology Quarterly*, July 2005.

New forms of BI continue to emerge. Performance management systems (PMS), also known as corporate performance management (CPM; see Chapter 9), are one of the new forms. These are BI tools that provide scorecards and other relevant information that decision makers can use to determine their level of success in reaching their goals.

Why BI/BA Projects Fail

Organizations must understand and address many critical challenges for achieving BI success. According to Atre (2003), there are 10 major reasons BI projects fail:

1. Failure to recognize BI projects as cross-organizational business initiatives and to understand that, as such, they differ from typical standalone solutions
2. Unengaged or weak business sponsors
3. Unavailable or unwilling business representatives from the functional areas
4. Lack of skilled (or available) staff, or suboptimal staff utilization
5. No software release concept (i.e., no iterative development method)
6. No work breakdown structure (i.e., no methodology)
7. No business analysis or standardization activities
8. No appreciation of the negative impact of "dirty data" on business profitability
9. No understanding of the necessity for and the use of metadata
10. Too much reliance on disparate methods and tools

SYSTEM DEVELOPMENT AND THE NEED FOR INTEGRATION

Developing an effective BI decision support application can be fairly complex; for a methodology and a guide, see Moss and Atre (2004). Integration, whether of applications, data sources, or even development environment, is a major CSF for BI. For this reason, most BI vendors (notably Oracle, BusinessObjects, MicroStrategy, IBM, and Microsoft) offer highly integrated collections of applications, including connection to ERP and CRM. Ho et al. (2004) provided an example of integrating OLAP that uses data warehouses and neural networks (see Chapter 8). In the example, the output of OLAP in a logistics workflow system was analyzed by the neural network. Most BI vendors provide for application integration (see Callaghan, 2005), usually Web enabled (see **businessobjects.com**).

Section 6.11 Review Questions

1. List the major benefits of BA.

2. List three factors regarding the implementation of BI.

3. Identify some BI tools.

4. List five reasons why BI projects fail.

Chapter Highlights

- BA involve many methods that can be organized in different ways. These methods can be classified as information discovery, decision support, and CPM tools. BA is usually conducted on the data in the data warehouse.
- Another classification of BA includes reports, queries, advanced analytics, multidimensionality, and scorecards and dashboards.
- OLAP is a set of tools for timely data analysis. It is extremely important in MSS/BI applications.
- EIS/ESS are the predecessors of BI and BA. Their major features are drill-down, KPI, status reports, trend analysis, CSF, and slice-and-dice.
- OLAP is the umbrella term for the BI tools developed in the 1990s. These include mostly reporting, querying, simple statistical analysis, and visualization. The major types of OLAP are MOLAP and ROLAP.
- Reports can be routine or on-demand (ad hoc). There are dozens of types of reports in different functional areas.

- Data multidimensionality enables people to view data quickly in different dimensions, even if the data are located in different files and databases. It is the core of OLAP.
- Advanced reports include alerting and dashboards. They can be queried quickly and easily.
- Ad hoc queries can be made in intelligent ways, using intelligent systems. A major query tool is SQL.
- Data cubes allow quick generation of queries and reports by end users.
- Advanced BA includes predictive analysis and data mining.
- BI is moving toward real-time capabilities.
- Data visualization is an important BI capability.
- Predictive analysis uses different algorithms to forecast results and relationships among variables as well as to identify data patterns.
- Spreadsheet visualization enables instant views of complex data in a single picture.
- GIS present geographical reference data as digital maps. They can support decision making in many applications that relate to locations.
- GIS can be integrated with GPS to create many applications, especially those related to transportation and l-commerce.
- Many business decisions need to be done in real-time (or very close to it). Supporting such decisions with BA requires a real-time data warehouse and special BA features.
- ADS uses business rules, which are generally executed with intelligent systems, to support large numbers of repetitive decisions, such as pricing optimization and product configuration.
- Competitive intelligence can be conducted over the Internet by using BA tools.
- A considerable number of BA applications are conducted on the Web.
- Web intelligence (or Web analytics) refers to analysis of Web data (known as clickstream data). Such analyses are useful in market research and competitive intelligence.
- Almost all medium to large companies use some type of BA, with or without a data warehouse, for significant cost savings.
- To ensure success of BI and BA projects, it is important to identify success factors (e.g., user participation) and cultivate these factors.

Key Terms

- ad hoc query
- analytics
- automated decision support (ADS)
- business analytics (BA)
- business intelligence (BI)
- clickstream analysis
- clickstream data
- cube
- data cube
- data visualization
- drill-down
- enterprise decision management (EDM)
- geographical information systems (GIS)
- global positioning systems (GPS)
- multidimensional database
- multidimensional OLAP (MOLAP)
- multidimensionality
- online analytical processing (OLAP)
- predictive analysis
- relational OLAP (ROLAP)
- status report
- Structured Query Language (SQL)
- Web analytics

QUESTIONS FOR DISCUSSION

1. Relate data warehousing to OLAP and data visualization.
2. Compare OLTP to OLAP.
3. Explain the relationship between OLAP and data mining.
4. Describe multidimensionality and explain its potential benefits for MSS.
5. Discuss the strategic benefits of BA.
6. Describe the concepts underlying Web intelligence and Web analytics.
7. Why do vendors that offer ERP tools (e.g., SAP, Oracle) offer BA tools as well?
8. Compare data mining and predictive analysis and discuss why some think that they are similar while others think the opposite.
9. Will BI replace the business analyst? Discuss. (Hint: See McKnight, 2005.)
10. Will ADS tools replace the business analyst?
11. Discuss the benefits of GIS as visualization support to decision making.

12. Differentiate predictive analysis from data mining. What do they have in common?
13. Relate competitive analysis to BI.
14. Discuss how ADS can support frontline employees (e.g., those who provide customer service).
15. Why is real-time BA becoming critical?
16. Relate advanced analytics to ERP and SCM.
17. Discuss the relationship between visualization and Excel.

Exercises

Teradata University and Other Hands-on Exercises

1. Visit **teradatastudentnetwork.com**. Describe recent developments in the field.
   a. Find the Web seminar on information visualization. Answer the following questions:
      i. What are the capabilities of Tableau Software's products?
      ii. Compare the two presentations and cite similarities and differences between them.
   b. Find the assignment "AdVent Technology" and use MicroStrategy's sales analytical model. Answer the three questions. Ask your instructor for directions.
   c. Find the tutorial on dimensional modeling from **freedatawarehouse.com**. Prepare a summary of the five most important points in the tutorial.
2. Investigate the integration of data warehouses and GIS. Start with **mapinfo.com**.
3. Take a test drive of demos of BA from BrightStor, Computer Associates, Temtec, Hyperion, and Cognos. Prepare a report about these products.
4. Consider the problem facing the city of London. Since February 17, 2003, the city has instituted an entrance fee for automobiles and trucks in the central city district. About 1,000 cameras digitally photograph the license plate of every vehicle passing by. Computers read the plate numbers and match them against records in a database of cars for which the fee has been paid for that day. If a match is not found, the car owner receives a citation by mail. The citations range from about US$128 to US$192, depending on when they are paid. Examine the issues pertaining to how this is done, the mistakes that are made, and the size of the databases involved, including that of the images from the license plates. Also examine how well the system is working by investigating press reports. Finally, relate the exercise to OLAP, BA, and OLAP. (This exercise was inspired by R. Hutton, "London on $8 a Day!" *Car and Driver*, August 2003, pp. 130–131, **caranddriver. com/article.asp?section_id=4&article_id=6859**)
5. Conduct an investigation of clickstream analysis. Compare Google Analytics with Web Trend and other products.
6. Read "Business Analytics" in *Baseline*, May 23, 2005, at **baselinemag.com**. Examine the success stories. Why do you think BI is one of the top projects of 2005?
7. Go to **businessintelligence.ittoolbox.com**. Identify all types of BA software. Join a discussion group about topics discussed in this chapter. Prepare a report about your findings.

Exercises

Team Assignments and Role-Playing

1. Visit **temtec.com** and go to the Executive Viewer overview.
   a. Take the guided tour. Interact with each feature. Write a report about your experience.
   b. Take the live test and create five queries and views. Write a report.
   c. Test the software with your own data.
2. Data visualization is offered by all major BI vendors, as well as by other companies, such as ILOG (**ilog.com**) and crystalxcelsius (**xcelsius.com**). Each student should be assigned a vendor to find the products and their capabilities. (For lists of vendors, see **tdwi.org** and **dmreview.com**.) Each group should summarize the products and their capabilities.
3. Interview administrators in your college or executives in your organization to determine how data warehousing, data mining, OLAP, and visualization

BI tools could assist them in their work. Write up a proposal describing your findings. Include cost estimates and benefits in your report.

4. Go to **dmreview.com/resources/demos.cfm**. Examine the list of demos and identify software that has analytical capabilities. Each group should prepare a report on at least five companies.
5. Go to **sas.com** and look for success stories related to BI. Find five that include SAS videos and prepare a summary of each in a class presentation.
6. Prepare a report on vendors in Web analytics. Each group should present the capabilities of two companies, such as Digital River, WebSideStory, Omniture, ClickTracks, and NetIQ.
7. Use **google.com** to find combined GIS/GPS applications. Also, look at vendor sites for GIS/GPS application success stories. (For GPS vendors, look at **biz.yahoo.com** and **google.com**). Each group should make a presentation of five applications and their benefits.

Exercises

Internet Exercises

1. America Online, stock brokerages, and many portals (e.g., **money.cnn.com**, **bloomberg.com**) provide a free personalized service that shows the status of investors' desired or actual list of stocks, including profits (losses) and prices (with a 15-minute delay or even in real-time). How is such individualized information retrieved so quickly? Why must such data be updated so quickly?
2. Find recent cases of successful BA applications. Try BI vendors and look for cases or success stories (e.g., **sap.com**, **businessobjects.com**, **microstrategy.com**). What do you find in common among the various success stories? How do they differ?
3. Go to BI Web sites (e.g., MicroStrategy, Oracle, Hyperion, Microsoft, SAP, SAS, SPSS, Cognos, Temtec, Business Objects) and look at the BA tools offered. Compare the major tools and list their capabilities.
4. Go to **olapreport.com** and read about OLAP relationships to Codd's 12 rules. Prepare a report.
5. Go to **ilog.com/products/optimization** and identify the BA products (Backup Recovery and Media Services, BRMS). Prepare a list of their capabilities.
6. Go to **fairisaac.com** and find products for fraud detection and risk analysis. Prepare a report about your findings.
7. Go to **spss.com** and find the demo on predictive analysis. Write a summary of the usability and benefits.
8. Go to **baselinemag.com** and find a list of more than 100 BI products. Identify 10 for BA.
9. Go to **sas.com** and find its BA-related products. Prepare a list of their capabilities.
10. Go to **microsoft.com/office/dataanalyzer/evaluation/tour**. Take the four-part tour. Summarize the major capabilities of Data Analyzer in a report.
11. Go to **ibm.com** and find all of the company's BI products and services (see the BI demo). Prepare a report about your findings.
12. Go to **navteq.com**. Review the company's products and applications. Prepare a report on five applications.

End of Chapter Application Case

State Governments Share Geospatial Information

GeoStor (**geostor.arkansas.gov**) is a public GIS system operated by the state of Arkansas. It includes mapping, charting, surveying of land and real estate, and other public data about Arkansas. It is an enterprise system that has its own data warehouse (Oracle Applications Server 10g) and a special device (Oracle MapViewer) for visualizing geospatial data. A major use of the system is to help businesses make decisions about where to locate (or relocate) facilities in Arkansas. For example, according to the Arkansas Geographical Information System (reported by Wiseth, 2004), an industrial prospect with a strict list of criteria—distance to transportation, including rail and road, and availability of water, electric, and gas utilities—was in the process of evaluating a site in Arkansas as a new location for its business. It used the data available through GeoStor to pull together labor information, education resources, health care resources, and numerous other details, providing a complete package of information within the 24-hour time limit the prospect required. The result was a new business in Osceola, Arkansas—and 500 new jobs in that community.

GeoStor was developed in Arkansas but is now being installed in several other states in the United States. It supports many daily activities involved in running a state: everything from improving education to providing critical, up-to-date location information for responding to emergencies and natural disasters. For example, GeoStor is being used to identify the locations of all education resources in Arkansas and to map that information against school performance metrics so that policymakers at the Arkansas Department of Education can visualize how educational resources are performing today and plan the future of education in Arkansas.

BENEFITS OF THE SYSTEM

GeoStor supports policy and decision making, as well as saving money for the state (over $2 million in the first 18 months). The savings resulted from reducing the search time per document from 23.5 hours to 1.5 hours. One of the key reasons time was reduced so significantly is because working with geospatial data in traditional systems is time and labor intensive. For example, the typical GIS is map or file based: Users download an entire file of a particular area or section of a map and then work to extract just what they need; conversely, users might have to knit together a multitude of files that comprise the area of interest. GeoStor, on the other hand, allows users to get just the area they need. Perhaps more important than cost savings and improved efficiency, however, are quality-of-life issues. Because the system provides a single source of truth to various agencies and supports interoperability of all client applications that need to make use of it, the information in the GeoStor data warehouse can be kept absolutely current—a fact that may even translate into saved lives. When there is a disaster, for example, it's important that all state infrastructure entities be up-to-date; whether a bridge exists, for example, can mean the difference between life and death for emergency personnel.

Finally, as described earlier, the GeoStor system provides competitive advantage to the state of Arkansas over other states. It can also provide competitive advantage to firms using the system to make location decisions.

Sources: Compiled from K. Wiseth, "The Expanding Role of Location," *Oracle Magazine*, January/February 2004, and **geostor.arkansas.gov** (accessed February 2006). For additional information about the topic, see **opengis.org** and **otn.oracle.com/products/spatial**. To download Oracle MapViewer 10g Preview for free, go to **otn.oracle.com/software/htdocs/devlic.html?/software/ products/spatial/htdocs/winsoft.html**.

QUESTIONS FOR THE CASE

1. Why is a data warehouse needed in the GeoStor system?
2. List the major benefits of GeoStor to Arkansas and to private-sector users.
3. Check Oracle's MapViewer and comment about its data visualization capabilities.
4. The state of Arkansas was the first to have such a system, so it has a competitive edge in attracting new business to the state. Explain why. Can this advantage be sustained when other states will use a similar system in the future?
5. Can any GIS data be combined with GPS data? For what uses?

References

"The 2003 CIO Insight Business Intelligence Research Study: Are Your BI Systems Making You Smarter?" (2003, May 23). *CIO Insight*, Vol. xx, No. 26, pp. xx–xx.

Alexander, S. (2003, February 24). "Web Site Adds Inventory Control and Forecasting." *Computer World*, Vol. xx, No. xx, pp. xx–xx.

cognos.com/news/releases/2002/1119_3.html.

Amato-McCoy, D.M. (2003, May). "Movie Gallery Mines Data to Monitor Associate Activities." *Stores*, Vol. xx, No. xx, pp. xx–xx.

Atre, S. (2003, June 30). "The Top 10 Critical Challenges for BI Success." *Computer World*, Vol. xx, No. xx, special advertising supplement.

Baer, T. (2002, April). "Analyzing Data at Real Time." *Application Development Trends*, Vol. xx, No. xx, pp. xx–xx.

Barrett, L., and D.F. Carr. (2005, September). "Proud Sponsor of the American Dream." *Baseline*.

Bolen, A. (2003, Quarter 2). *SAS Cooks Up Success at Williams-Sonoma*, **sas.com/success/williamssonoma.html**.

Bonde, A., and M. Kuckuk. (2004, April). "Real-World Business Intelligence: The Implementation Perspective," *DM Review*.

Brath, R., and M. Peters. (2006, January). "Visualization Spreadsheets." *DM Direct*.

Callaghan, D. (2005, February 7). "BI Vendors Stress Need for Integration." *eWEEK*.

Callaghan, D. (2003a, May 26). "SPSS, SAS Take Predictive Paths." *eWEEK*.

Callaghan, D. (2003b, June 2). "IBM Builds Bridge for DB2." *eWEEK*.

Codd, E.F., S.B. Codd, and C.T. Salley. (1993, July). "Beyond Decision Support." *Computerworld*.

Coffee, P. (2003, June 23). "'Active' Warehousing." *eWEEK*.

Cognos.com, (2002, November 19). "Allied Building Products Corporation Monitors Corporate Performance with Cognos Finance." **cognos.com/news/releases/2002/1119_3.html** (accessed October 2006).

Comcowich, W.J. (2002, October 22). *Integrated Internet Monitoring Solutions for CI*, **imakenews.com/scip2/e_article000101312.cfm** (accessed February 2006).

Culpepper, R.B. (2002, October). "Quick-Take Reviews: CommunityViz 1.3." *GeoWorld*.

Davenport, T.H., and J.G. Harris. (2005, Summer). "Automated Decision Making Comes of Age." *MIT Sloan Management Review*.

Devlin, B. (2003, May 14). "Solving the Data Warehouse Puzzle." *DB2 Magazine*, available at **datawarehouse.ittoolbox.com/documents/industry-articles/solving-the-data-warehouse-puzzle-1583** (accessed March 2006).

Dorrington, P. (2003, Quarter 2). *Innovative, Industrious and Nefarious Fraudsters!* **sas.com/news/sascom/2003q2/feature_fraudsters.html**.

Eckersen, W. (2003). *Smart Companies in the 21st Century*. Seattle, WA: The Data Warehousing Institute.

Edelstein, H.A. (2001, March 12). "Pan for Gold in the Clickstream." *InformationWeek*.

Fayyad, U., G. Grinstein, and A. Wierse (eds). (2002). *Information Visualization in Data Mining and Knowledge Discovery*. San Francisco: Morgan Kaufman.

Fleischmann, M., J.M. Hall, and D.F. Pyke. (2004, Winter). "Smart Pricing." *MIT Sloan Management Review*.

Fogarty, K. (2004, December 1). "Primer: Predictive Analytics." *Baseline*, **baselinemag.com/article2/0,1397,1744175,00.asp**.

Follett, J.H. (2003, June 23). "HP Gives Partners an Open View of Adaptive Enterprises." *CRN*.

Franklin, D. (2002, November). "Any Way You Slice It." *Credit Union Management*.

Gage, D. (2005, December 13). "Forget Hackers; Watch Out for Competitors," *Baseline*, **baselinemag.com/article2/0,1397,1901400,00.asp** (accessed March 2006).

Gonzales, M.L. (2003, February 1). "The New GIS Landscape." *Intelligent Enterprise*.

Gray, P., and H.J. Watson. (1998). *Decision Support in the Data Warehouse*. Upper Saddle River, NJ: Prentice Hall.

Hallett, P. (2001, June). "Web-Based Visualization." *DM Review*.

Hamilton, J. M. (1996, March 15). "A Mappable Feast." *CIO Magazine*.

Havenstein, H. (2003a, April 28). "Real-Time Smarts." *InfoWorld*.

Havenstein, H. (2003b, May 26). "BAM Bolsters Data Visibility." *InfoWorld*.

Ho, G.T.S., H.C.W. Lau, W.H. Ip, and A. Ning. (2004, July). "An Intelligent Information Infrastructure to Support the Streamlining of Integrated Logistics Workflow." *Expert Systems*.

Hoffer, J.A., M.B. Prescott, and F.R. McFadden. (2005). *Modern Database Management*, 7th ed. Upper Saddle River, NJ: Prentice Hall.

"Houston Buses Due for 'Intellectual Overhaul.'" (2003, June). *OR/MS Today*, p. 19, **lionhrtpub.com/orms/news/realworld/rw603buses.html** (access no longer available online).

Infrastructure and Management Solutions for the Adaptive Enterprise. (2003). **hp.com/products1/promos/adaptive_enterprise/pdfs/vision_for_ae.pdf** (accessed February 2006).

Langnau, L. (2003, November). *Business Intelligence and Ethics: Can They Work Together? Controls & Systems Editorial—Industry Overview*, **mhmonline.com/nID/1180/iID/20865/MHM/viewStory.asp** (accessed August 2006).

Lindquist, C. (2003, May 15). "Real Timing." *CIO*.

McCarthy, J., and M. McCarthy. (2002). *Software for Your Head: Core Protocols for Creating and Maintaining Shared Vision*. Boston: Addison-Wesley.

McKinley, E. (2004, November). "We're Not Asking, We Know You Want Fries with That Predictive Technology." *Stores*.

McKnight, W. (2005, February). "Building Business Intelligence: Will Business Intelligence Replace the Business Analyst?" *DM Review*, **dmreview.com/article_sub.cfm?articleId=1018117** (accessed March 2006).

Meier, M., W. Sigzig, and P. Mertens. (2005). *Enterprise Management with SAP SEM/Business Analytics*, 2nd ed. Berlin: Springer.

MicroStrategy. (2006). *The 5 Styles of Business Intelligence*, **microstrategy.com/Solutions/5Styles/enterprise_reporting.asp**.

MicroStrategy. (2005). *Applications of Industrial-Strength Business Intelligence*, **microstrategy.com/Solutions/AppsBook.asp** (accessed August 2006).

Morris, H., S. Graham, P. Andersen, K. Moser, R. Blumstein, D. Vesset, N. Martinez, and M. Carr. (2002,

October). "The Financial Impact of Business Analytics." *IDC*.

Moss, L.T., and S. Atre. (2003). *Business Intelligence Roadmap*. Indianapolis: Addison-Wesley.

Pallatto, J. (2002, February). "Business Tools Get Smart." *InternetWorld*.

Patel, J. (2005, May). "Seven Simple Rules for Successful Real-Time Business Intelligence." *DM Review*.

Pawar, S.P., and R. Sharda. (1997). "Obtaining Business Intelligence on the Internet." *Long Range Planning*, Vol. 30, No. 1.

Perry, J.J., and G.V. Post. (2007). *Introduction to Oracle 10G*. Upper Saddle River, NJ: Prentice Hall.

Peterson, E. (2005, August). *Web Analytics Demystified*. Sebastopol, CA: O'Reilly Media.

Peterson, T. (2003, April 21). "Getting Real About Real Time." *Computerworld*.

Raden, N. (2003a, June 17). "Real Time: Get Real, Part I." *Intelligent Enterprise*.

Raden, N. (2003b, June 30). "Real Time: Get Real, Part II." *Intelligent Enterprise*, Vol. xx, No. xx, pp. xx–xx.

Rapoza, J. (2004, June 7). "Site Analysis Gets Expert Treatment." *eWEEK*.

Ruber, P. (2003, June). "Analytics Improve Merchandising." *InternetWorld*.

Saarenvirta, G. (2004, Winter). "The Untapped Value of GIS," *Business Intelligence Journal*.

Schlegel, K. (2003, June). "Web Analytics Essentials." *InternetWorld*.

Schwartz, M. (2005, Fall). "Louisiana Bottles Food Stamp Fraud." *Business Intelligence Journal*.

Swoyer, S. (2005, Summer). "BI Case Study: Summit Partners." *Business Intelligence Journal*.

Thompson, O. (2004, October 9). *Business Intelligence Success, Lessons Learned*., **technologyevaluation.com**.

Thompson, O., and P.J. Jakovljevic. (2005, June). *Business Intelligence Status Report* (seven-part comprehensive report including real-time and on-demand capabilities), **technologyevaluation.com**.

Turban, E., et al. (2006). *E-Commerce: A Managerial Perspective*. Upper Saddle River, NJ: Prentice Hall.

Ursery, S. (2004, February). "GIS More Prevalent in Big Cities," *The American City and County*.

Werner, V., and C. Abramson. (2001, Summer). "Managing Clickstream Data." *Journal of Data Warehousing*, Vol. 6, No. 3.

White, C. (2004, September). "Now Is the Right Time for Real-Time BI." *DM Review*.

Wiseth, K. (2004, January 14). "The Expanding Role of Location." *Oracle Magazine*. **oracle.com/technology/oramag/oracle/04-jan/o14geostore_feature.html** (accessed February 2006).

Zaman, M. (2005, November 8). "Predictive Analytics; the Future of Business Intelligence." *Technology Evaluation Centers*.

CHAPTER 7 Data, Text, and Web Mining

Learning Objectives

- Describe data mining and list its objectives and benefits
- Understand different purposes and applications of data mining
- Understand different methods of data mining, especially clustering and decision tree models
- Build expertise in the use of some data mining software
- Learn the process of data mining projects
- Understand data mining pitfalls and myths
- Describe text mining and its objectives and benefits
- Appreciate the use of text mining in business applications
- Describe Web mining and its objectives and benefits

Data mining refers to developing business intelligence from data that an organization collects, organizes, and processes. Data mining techniques are being used by organizations to gain a better understanding of their customers and their own operations. In this chapter, we study some of the major data mining techniques such as decision trees and cluster analysis, their applications, and the processes of data mining.

7.1 OPENING VIGNETTE: HIGHMARK, INC., EMPLOYS DATA MINING TO MANAGE INSURANCE COSTS

Highmark, Inc., based in Pittsburgh, has a long tradition of providing access to affordable, quality health care to its members and communities. Highmark was formed in 1996 by the merger of two Pennsylvania licensees of the Blue Cross and Blue Shield Association: Pennsylvania Blue Shield (now Highmark Blue Shield) and a Blue Cross plan in western Pennsylvania (now Highmark Blue Cross Blue Shield). Highmark is currently one of the largest health insurers in the United States.

DATA IN MANAGED CARE ORGANIZATIONS

The amount of data floating around in managed care organizations such as Highmark is vast. These data, often considered to be occupying storage space and thought of as a menace to be dealt with, provide some interesting new uses. Data mining companies provide useful tools for analyzing patient data and unraveling mysteries that could lead to better managed care at lower costs—a mission that most managed care companies are trying to achieve.

Each day managed care companies receive millions of data items about their customers, and each piece of information updates the case history of each member. Companies have become aware of the usefulness of the data at their disposal and use data reporting tools and other analytic software to extract patient clusters that are more costly than average to treat. Earlier efforts at using computer technology in order to extract patient information were limited in establishing a connection between two diseases. For example, the software could scan through the data and report that diabetics or people suffering from coronary heart diseases were the most expensive to treat. However, the earlier software and reporting tools were inefficient in finding why these patients were getting sick or why some patients were more affected by certain diseases than others. Data mining tools can solve some of the problems by analyzing the information produced and generating succinct relationships and correlations.

Employing data mining is costly as well as complex. It also depends on the efficiency of data an organization possesses. Organizations primarily need to invest in data warehousing to manage voluminous data. Data warehousing needs continuous monitoring and maintenance, which entails more investment. Most organizations are not integrated to a considerable extent; they still use multiple servers and warehouses. The presence of multiple warehouses makes the integration of the information difficult because the format of data in the different warehouses is frequently different. Organizations also stress the importance of consistency in the data gathering effort; however, they are focused on gathering data that are relevant to their operations. Internal management struggles can also hamper the use of data mining applications.

Managed care organizations are inundated with data, and some of the companies do not want to add to the complexity by adding data mining applications. They may want to scan data for various reasons but are unable to decide why and how to analyze their data. Things are becoming brighter for patients as well as companies, however, because health insurance regulations are clearing the way for efficient data and structuring analysis.

THE NEED FOR DATA MINING

Market pressures are driving managed care organizations to take data mining seriously. Customers and competitors are getting focused, which leads to more customized products. This customization brings us to the originating point of why and where medical costs are occurring. Many organizations have started to use predictive software to predict who is likely to fall sick and who will be expensive to treat in the future. A look into the future has enabled organizations to filter out their costly patients and lower their Medicare costs by using preventive measures. Another important application of predictive studies is the management of premiums. An employer group that has a large number of employees falling in a higher cost bracket would see its rates increase.

Predictive modeling might be able to predict which patients are likely to get sick in the future. A predictive modeling application might rate a diabetic patient as a high risk of increased medical costs. However, data mining used at Highmark will draw a relationship between a diabetic patient and other parameters. For example, a patient with a specific cardiac condition might be at high risk of contracting diabetes; this relationship is drawn because the cardiac medication could lead the patient to developing diabetes later. Highmark officials testify to this fact by saying that they would not have monitored the patient for the cardiac medication and might not have drawn a relationship between the cardiac medication and diabetes. Medical research has been successful in codifying many of the complexities associated with patient conditions. Data mining has laid the foundation for intervention programs.

Sources: Condensed from G. Gillespie, "Data Mining: Solving Care, Cost Capers," *Health Data Management*, November 2004, **findarticles.com/p/articles/mi_km2925/is_200411/ai_n8622737** (accessed April 2006); and *Highmark Enhances Patient Care, Keeps Medical Costs Down with SAS*, **sas.com/success/highmark.html** (accessed April 2006).

Questions for the Opening Vignette

1. Why are companies such as Highmark using data mining applications?
2. Why were managed care organizations initially hesitant to use data mining applications?
3. What are the potential threats that could arise due to data mining applications?
4. What complexities arise when data mining is used in health care organizations?
5. Assume that you are an employer and that your managed care organization raises your rate based on the results of data mining and predictive modeling software. Would you accept the organization's software predictions?

WHAT WE CAN LEARN FROM THIS VIGNETTE

The health care industry is a prime candidate for data mining. The amount of data generated by the health care industry is voluminous, but only a small fraction of it is being mined to develop deeper understanding of interrelationships in health care issues. In this chapter, you will see other health care applications of data mining, along with applications in many other industries. These applications create legal and ethical questions that companies must address.

7.2 DATA MINING CONCEPTS AND APPLICATIONS

In a recent article in *Harvard Business Review*, Davenport (2006) argued that the latest strategic weapon for companies is analytical decision making. He gave examples of companies such as Amazon.com, Capital One, Marriott International, and others that have used analytics to better understand their customers and optimize their extended supply chains to maximize their returns on investment, while providing the best customer service. This level of success is highly dependent on a company understanding its customers, vendors, supply chain, and so on, very well. A large component of this understanding comes from analyzing the data that a company collects. The cost of storing and processing data has decreased dramatically in the recent past and, as a result, the amount of data stored in electronic form has grown at an explosive rate. With the creation of large databases came the possibility of analyzing the data stored in them. The term *data mining* was originally used to describe the process through which previously undiscovered patterns in data were identified. This definition has since been stretched beyond those limits to include most forms of data analysis. As a consequence, the *data mining* label is often used to add sales value to almost any type of data analysis tool.

Although the term *data mining* is relatively new, the ideas behind it are not. Many of the techniques used in data mining have their roots in traditional statistical analysis and artificial intelligence work from the 1980s. Why, then, has it suddenly gained the attention of the business world? Cavoukian (1998) quotes six factors from an IBM report behind this sudden rise in popularity:

1. General recognition of the untapped value in large databases
2. Consolidation of database records, tending toward a single customer view
3. Consolidation of databases, including the concept of an information warehouse
4. Reduction in the cost of data storage and processing, providing for the ability to collect and accumulate data
5. Intense competition for a customer's attention in an increasingly saturated marketplace
6. Movement toward the de-massification (conversion of information resources into nonphysical form) of business practices

Disciplines such as astronomy and nuclear physics accumulate large quantities of data on a routine basis. Data on the Internet are increasing in volume and complexity. Large volumes of genomic data are being accumulated all over the world. Medical and pharmaceutical researchers use data mining applications to identify successful therapies for illnesses and to discover new and improved drugs.

On the commercial side, perhaps the most common use of data mining has been in the finance, retail, and health care sectors. Data mining is used to reduce fraudulent behavior, especially in insurance claims and credit card use (Chan et al., 1999); to identify customer buying patterns (Hoffman, 1999); to reclaim profitable customers (Hoffman, 1998); to identify trading rules from historical data; and to aid in market basket analysis. Data mining is already widely used to better target clients, and with the development of e-commerce, this can only become more important with time.

DEFINITIONS, CHARACTERISTICS, AND BENEFITS

Data mining is a term used to describe knowledge discovery in databases. **Data mining** is a process that uses statistical, mathematical, artificial intelligence, and machine-learning techniques to extract and identify useful information and subsequent knowledge from large databases. Formerly, the term was used to describe the process through which undiscovered patterns in data were identified. However, over time, the original definition has been modified to include most types of (automated) data analysis. Data mining is the process of finding mathematical patterns from usually large sets of data. These patterns can be rules, affinities, correlations, trends, or prediction models (see Nemati and Barko, 2001).

Data mining lies at the interface of computer science and statistics, using advances in both disciplines to make progress in extracting information from large databases. It is an emerging field that has attracted much attention in a very short time. Glymour et al. (1997) discussed statistical themes and lessons directly relevant to data mining, as well as some opportunities for synergy between the computational and statistical communities for further advances in data analysis.

Data mining includes tasks such as knowledge extraction, data archaeology, data exploration, data pattern processing, data dredging, and information harvesting. All these activities are conducted automatically and allow quick discovery even by nonprogrammers (see Application Case 7.1). The following are the major characteristics and objectives of data mining:

- Data are often buried deep within very large databases, which sometimes contain data from several years. In many cases, the data are cleansed and consolidated in a data warehouse.
- The data mining environment is usually a client/server architecture or a Web-based architecture.
- Sophisticated new tools, including advanced visualization tools, help to remove the information ore buried in corporate files or archival public records. Finding it involves massaging and synchronizing the data to get the right results. Cutting-edge data miners are also exploring the usefulness of soft data (i.e., unstructured text stored in such places as Lotus Notes databases, text files on the Internet, or enterprise-wide intranets).
- The miner is often an end user, empowered by data drills and other power query tools to ask ad hoc questions and obtain answers quickly, with little or no programming skill.
- Striking it rich often involves finding an unexpected result and requires end users to think creatively.
- Data mining tools are readily combined with spreadsheets and other software development tools. Thus, the mined data can be analyzed and processed quickly and easily.
- Because of the large amounts of data and massive search efforts, it is sometimes necessary to use parallel processing for data mining.

Application Case 7.1

Data Help Foretell Customer Needs

Soothsayers at First Health Group Corp. (FHG Corp.) are busy finding out what questions and concerns their customers could have about their health plans. Executives can foretell what health plan members need by using data mining applications that delve into their databases. FHG Corp. built rules based on a data mining engine to understand and document the telephone calls that their customers make to predict what type of question or concern someone is likely to have.

FHG Corp. employs data mining technology to collect information from its core information systems and present it to customer service people through a proprietary customer relationship management (CRM) application. The data mining application creates a list of calls to be made by the customer service associates every morning.

Rules are based on the types of questions members ask about benefits, claims, and other services. These rules are then run against the latest information in the databases. The rules engine scans through the data on various criteria and builds files. Then customer service staff use the files to contact members on various issues related to health claims and future health care needs.

Some of the benefits of this system include reduced claims turnaround time and a 65 to 70 percent decrease in the number of pending claims.

Sources: B. Briggs, "Data Helps Foretell Customer Needs," *Health Data Management*, Vol. 12, No. 2, February 2004, and *Health Data Management*, **Keepmedia.com,** February 2, 2004.

A company that effectively leverages data mining tools and technologies can acquire and maintain a strategic competitive advantage. Data mining offers organizations an indispensable decision-enhancing environment to exploit new opportunities by transforming data into a strategic weapon. See Nemati and Barko (2001).

HOW DATA MINING WORKS

According to Dunham (2003), intelligent data mining discovers information within data warehouses that queries and reports cannot effectively reveal. Data mining tools find patterns in data and may even infer rules from them. Three methods are used to identify patterns in data (see Nemati and Barko, 2001):

- Simple models (e.g., SQL-based queries, online analytical processing [OLAP], human judgment)
- Intermediate models (e.g., regression, decision trees, clustering)
- Complex models (e.g., neural networks, other rule induction)

These patterns and rules can be used to guide decision making and forecast the effects of decisions. Data mining can speed analysis by focusing attention on the most important variables. The dramatic drop in the cost–performance ratio of computer systems has enabled many organizations to start applying the complex algorithms of data mining techniques. Data mining algorithms traditionally fall into four broad categories: classification, clustering, association, and sequence discovery. Other data analysis tools, such as regression and time-series analysis, also find their way into practice, as does visualization.

Classification

Classification, or supervised induction, is perhaps the most common of all data mining activities. The objective of classification is to analyze the historical data stored in a database and automatically generate a model that can predict future behavior. This induced model consists of generalizations over the records of a training data set, which help distinguish redefined classes. The hope is that the model can then be used to predict the classes of other unclassified records.

Common tools used for classification are neural networks, decision trees, and if-then-else rules that need not have a tree structure. Neural networks (see Chapter 8 and Online Tutorial T4: Statistica Sample Software Application Project) involve the development of mathematical structures that have the capability to learn. They tend to be most effective where the number of variables involved is very large and the relationships between them is complex and imprecise. A neural network can easily be implemented in a parallel environment, with each node of the network doing its calculations on a different processor. Neural networks have disadvantages as well as advantages. For example, it is usually very difficult to provide a good rationale for the predictions made by a neural network. Also, neural networks tend to need considerable training. Unfortunately, the time needed for training tends to increase as the volume of the data increases, and in general, neural networks cannot be trained on very large databases. These and other factors have limited the acceptability of neural networks.

Decision trees classify data into a finite number of classes, based on the values of the input variables. Decision trees are comprised of essentially a hierarchy of if-then statements and are thus significantly faster than neural networks. They are most appropriate for categorical and interval data because incorporating continuous variables into a decision tree framework can be difficult. A related classification tool is rule induction; unlike in a decision tree, with rule induction, the if-then statements used need not be hierarchical.

Clustering

Clustering partitions a database into segments whose members share similar qualities. Some of the ideas used for classification, such as neural networks, pertain in part to situations involving clustering. However, unlike in classification, in clustering, the clusters are unknown when the algorithm starts. Consequently, before the results of clustering techniques are put to use, it might be necessary for an expert to interpret, and potentially modify, the suggested clusters. After reasonable clusters have been identified, they can be used to classify new data. Not surprisingly, clustering techniques include optimization; the goal is to create groups so that the members within each group have maximum similarity and the members across groups have minimum similarity.

Association

Associations establish relationships about items that occur together in a given record. Data gathering has been drastically simplified as a result of scanners, and determining associations among items that sell together can be of substantial benefit to retailers. This is often called *market basket analysis* because one of the primary applications of this technique is the analysis of sales transactions.

Sequence Discovery

Sequence discovery is the identification of associations over time. When appropriate information is available (e.g., the identity of a customer in a retail shop), a temporal analysis can be conducted to identify behavior over time. Some sequence discovery techniques keep track of elapsed time between associated events and the frequency of occurring sequences. This provides a considerable amount of information that could be used to increase sales or to detect fraud.

Visualization

The insights to be gained from visualizing data cannot be overemphasized. This holds true for most data analysis techniques but is especially true with data mining. Given the sheer volume of data in the databases being considered, visualization in general is a difficult endeavor. However, it can be used in conjunction with data mining to gain a clearer understanding of many underlying relationships.

Regression

Regression is a well-known statistical technique that is used to map data to a prediction value. Linear and nonlinear regression techniques are used. Regression is a form of estimation. It often involves identifying metrics and evaluating an item (e.g., a customer) along the metrics by assigning scores. Sales predictions may be accomplished as well.

Forecasting

Forecasting is another form of estimation. It estimates future values based on patterns within large sets of data (e.g., demand forecasting). There is an attempt to use statistical time-series methods to predict future sales (for more information see Online Tutorial T2).

TABLE 7.1 Data Mining Functions, Algorithms, and Application Examples

Data Mining Function	*Algorithm*	*Application Examples*
Association	Statistics, set theory	Market basket analysis
Classification	Decision trees, neural networks, control, risk assessment, rules	Target marketing, quality
Clustering	Neural networks, statistics, optimization, discriminate analysis	Market segmentation
Sequence discovery	Statistics, set theory	Market basket analysis over time, customer life cycle analysis
Modeling	Linear and nonlinear regression, curve fitting, neural networks	Sales forecasting, interest rate, prediction, inventory control
Drill-down and aggregate view of data	Visualization, using many different approaches	Virtually all the preceding applications

Source: Adapted from J.P. Bigus, *Data Mining with Neural Networks*, McGraw-Hill, New York, 1996.

Data Mining Functions Summary

In Table 7.1, we show the data mining functions described so far, along with representative algorithms and application examples. Also see Groth (1998).

Firms often effectively use their data mining systems to perform market segmentation with cluster analysis. Cluster analysis is a means of identifying classes of items so that items in a cluster have more in common with each other than with items in other clusters. It can be used in segmenting customers and directing appropriate marketing products to the segments at the right time in the right format at the right price. Tillett (2000) described how another bank effectively mines customer data via cluster analysis, using Web-based tools. Application Case 7.2 describes how cluster analysis was combined with other data mining techniques to verify the causes of accidents.

Application Case 7.2

Motor Vehicle Accidents and Driver Distractions

Driver distraction is at center stage in highway safety. A study published in 1996 by the National Highway Traffic Safety Administration (NHTSA) concluded that roughly 25- to 30 percent of the injuries caused by car crashes were due to driver distraction. In 1999, according to the Fatality Analysis Reporting System (FARS) developed by the National Centre for Statistics and Analysis (NCSA), 11 percent of fatal crashes (i.e., 4,462 fatalities) were due to driver inattention.

A study was conducted to extract the patterns of distraction factors and traffic crashes. Data mining was the main tool used to draw the correlation of data from the crash information provided by FARS. Three data mining techniques—Kohonen networks, decision trees, and neural networks to find different combinations of distraction factors that explain the high accident rates—were used in the research. Kohonen networks detected clusters and revealed patterns of input variables in the collection of data. Decision trees explored and classified the effect of each incident on successive events; decision trees suggested the relationship between inattentive drivers and physical/mental conditions. Data mining techniques were applied to the data sets to correlate inattention and other driver-related factors in traffic crashes. Finally, a neural network model was trained and tested to observe the effectiveness of the model. Clementine from SPSS was used to mine the data derived from the FARS database in three models.

The system identified 1,255 drivers who were involved in accidents in which inattention was one of the leading driver factors that led to a crash. Rear and head collisions and angle collisions, among other various output variables, were predicted with 78 and 77 percent accuracy.

Sources: W. S. Tseng, H. Nguyen, J. Liebowitz, and W. Agresti, "Distractions and Motor Vehicle Accidents: Data Mining Application on Fatality Analysis Reporting System (FARS) Data Files, "*Industrial Management & Data Systems.*, Vol. 105, No. 9, January 2005, pp. 1188–1205; and J. Liebowitz, "New Trends in Intelligent Systems," Presentation made at University of Granada, **docto-si.ugr.es/seminario/presentaciones/jay.ppt** (accessed August 2006).

Data mining can be either *hypothesis driven* or *discovery driven*. **Hypothesis-driven data mining** begins with a proposition by the user, who then seeks to validate the truthfulness of the proposition. For example, a marketing manager may begin with the proposition, "Are DVD player sales related to sales of television sets?" Application Case 7.2 illustrates how data mining techniques covered in this chapter and Chapter 8 can be used to verify assumptions. **Discovery-driven data mining** finds patterns, associations, and relationships among data. It can uncover facts that an organization had not previously known or even contemplated. Application Case 7.3 describes a process for converting such data into actionable information.

Application Case 7.3

Data Mining to Identify Customer Behavior

Understanding customer behavior is important in adjusting business strategies, increasing revenues, and identifying new opportunities. Many organizations have a massive amount and impressive variety of data and information resources that promise to reveal much more about customer behavior than was previously thought possible. Many firms have reached a point of rich data and poor utilization. For most retail environments, three sources of customer data are most critical to data mining efforts aimed at better understanding behavior:

- Demographic data
- Transaction data
- Online interaction data

Clickstream analytics can be used to identify who did and did not buy a product, why, and when.

The process of data mining in retail has three steps:

1. *Web analytics*. Gather Web site statistics that track customers' online behavior: hits, pages, sales volume, and so on. This helps in adjusting a Web site to meet customer needs.
2. *Customer analytics*. Customer analytics adds depth to understanding customer interactions. Firms gather data from multiple sources, including Web site interactions, transaction data from offline purchases, and demographic data. This is critical in CRM and revenue management because a better understanding allows an organization to cluster customers into groupings.
3. *Optimization*. Optimization promises great payoff. Subtle patterns can be detected and used to optimize customer interactions. This is the goal of CRM and revenue management.

Consider J.Crew, a major online and catalog retailer of men's and women's apparel, shoes, and accessories. J.Crew has had immense success with optimization analytics. The company previously used a cumbersome manual procedure to recommend similar and complementary styles to online purchasers. In fall 2002, J.Crew deployed optimization analytics. The analytic engine recommendations, which are done automatically, generate twice as many sales as the older, manual system.

Sources: Adapted from U. Fayyad, "Optimizing Customer Insight," *Intelligent Enterprise*, Vol. 6 No. 8, May 1, 2003, pp. 23–26, 33; and U. Fayyad, *Optimize Customer Interactions—and Profits—with Advanced Data Mining Techniques*, **watts-associates.com/docs/articles/digiMine.pdf** (accessed April 2006).

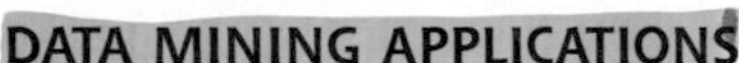

DATA MINING APPLICATIONS

Data mining can be very helpful, as shown by the following representative examples. The intent of most of these examples is to identify a business opportunity and create a sustainable competitive advantage:

- *Marketing*. Predicting which customers will respond to Internet banners or buy a particular product and segmenting customer demographics.
- *Banking*. Forecasting levels of bad loans and fraudulent credit card usage, credit card spending by new customers, and which kinds of customers will best respond to new loan offers or other products and services.
- *Retailing and sales*. Predicting sales and determining correct inventory levels and distribution schedules among outlets.
- *Manufacturing and production*. Predicting when to expect machinery failures and finding key factors that control the optimization of manufacturing capacity.
- *Brokerage and securities trading*. Predicting when bond prices will change, forecasting the range of stock fluctuation for particular issues and the overall market, and determining when to trade stocks.
- *Insurance*. Forecasting claim amounts and medical coverage costs, classifying the most important elements that affect medical coverage, and predicting which customers will buy new policies with special features.
- *Computer hardware and software*. Predicting disk drive failure, forecasting how long it will take to create new chips, and predicting potential security violations.
- *Government and defense*. Forecasting the cost of moving military equipment, testing strategies for military engagements, and predicting resource consumption.
- *Airlines*. Capturing data not only on where customers are flying but also the ultimate destination of passengers who change carriers mid-itinerary. With this information, airlines can identify popular locations they are not currently serving in order to add routes and capture lost business.
- *Health care*. Correlating demographics of patients with critical illnesses. Using data mining, doctors can develop better insights on symptoms and how to provide proper treatments. See Application Case 7.4 for an emerging use of data mining technologies.
- *Broadcasting*. Predicting what programs are best shown during prime time and how to maximize returns by knowing where to insert advertisements.
- *Police*. Tracking crime patterns, locations, criminal behavior, and attributes to help solve criminal cases.
- *Homeland security*. Used extensively in the homeland security initiatives. See Application Case 7.5 for a recent example of use of data mining to track funding of terrorists' activities.

Application Case 7.4

Customizing Medicine

Research has come a long way in customizing health care. Practitioners in medical treatments are trying to find the best way to customize treatment (e.g., choosing the best-suited chemotherapy treatment for a cancer patient with a specific genetic marker). To better customize treatment, Mayo Clinic and IBM are applying pattern recognition and data mining to patient records.

Data are gathered from different sources in Mayo's hospitals, including digitized patient files, lab results, x-rays, and electrocardiograms. Custom algorithms are applied on the data to identify patterns based on age, medical history, genetics, and other factors. The analysis relates how the patients would respond to various treatments and how to personalize their care. This also helps researchers in developing therapies. Pattern-recognition tools are used to find relationships among proteins, genetic coding, and responses to specific treatments. Data mining technologies are extremely useful in uncovering correlations and discoveries that would have previously been ignored.

Moving to electronic medical records brings with it the persistent problem of data trust. Only key individuals should be permitted access to patient information, and data mining needs to be applied only to aggregate data. At Mayo Clinic, patients can decide whether their medical data should be used for analysis. Mayo has named its data mining project Data Trust to remind the employees working with the project that the success of the project depends on patient data privacy, security, and confidentiality.

Sources: M.K. McGee, "Mayo Builds Toward Customized Medicine," *InformationWeek*, August 9, 2004, p. 24; and *Mayo Clinic, IBM Aim to Drive Medical Breakthroughs*, **mayoclinic.org/spotlight/mayoibmcollaboration.html** (accessed April 2006).

Application Case 7.5

A Mine on Terrorist Funding

The terrorist attack on the Word Trade Center on September 11, 2001, underlined the importance of open source intelligence. The USA Patriot Act and the creation of the U.S. Department of Homeland Security (DHS) heralded the potential application of information technology and data mining techniques to detect money laundering and other forms of terrorist financing. Law enforcement agencies have been focusing on money laundering activities via normal transactions through banks and other financial service organizations. International trade pricing has come to the fore since the terrorist attacks as the focus of law enforcement agencies.

International trade has been used by launderers to move money silently out of a country without attracting government attention. Overvaluing imports and undervaluing exports are strategies to achieve this transfer. The modus operandi in overvaluing could be as follows: The domestic importer and foreign exporter could form a nexus and overvalue imports, thereby transferring money from the home country, resulting in crimes related to customs fraud, income tax evasion, and money laundering. The foreign exporter could be a member of a terrorist organization.

The data mining techniques focus on analysis of data on import and export transactions from the U.S. Department of Commerce and other bodies related to commerce. Import prices that exceed the upper quartile import prices and export prices that are lower than the lower quartile export prices are tracked. The focus is on abnormal transfer prices between corporations that may result in shifting taxable income and taxes out of the United States. An observed price deviation may be related to income tax avoidance/evasion, money laundering, or terrorist financing. The observed price deviation may also be due to an error in the U.S. trade database.

The total estimated money moved out of the U.S. for 2001 was $156.22 billion. Data mining will result in efficient evaluation of data, which in turn will aid in the crusade against terrorism. The application of information technology and data mining techniques to financial transactions can contribute to increasing the quality of intelligence information.

Sources: J.S. Zdanowic, "Detecting Money Laundering and Terrorist Financing via Data Mining," *Communications of the ACM*, Vol. 47, No. 5, May 2004, p. 53; and R.J. Bolton, "Statistical Fraud Detection: A Review," *Statistical Science*, Vol. 17, No. 3, January 2002, p. 235.

Palshikar (2001) provided several examples of effective data mining in practice. See Application Case 7.8, later in this chapter, for information about data mining and analysis efforts at the DHS. Census data can be combined with other market data when segmenting customers (see Grimes, 2001).

A less typical application of data mining was used to improve the performance of National Basketball Association (NBA) teams in the United States. The NBA developed Advanced Scout, a PC-based data mining application that coaching staff use to discover interesting patterns in basketball game data. The process of pattern

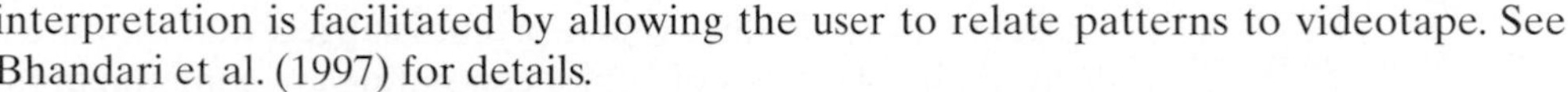

interpretation is facilitated by allowing the user to relate patterns to videotape. See Bhandari et al. (1997) for details.

When organizations are plagued by fraud, especially in financial transactions, as in e-commerce, they turn to specialized data mining tools to detect patterns in the data. Generally, these methods use neural networks in addition to clustering and statistical methods. SAS Anti-Money Laundering is one example of software that can do this. See customer success of Unity Trust Bank at **sas.com/news/sascom/2003q3/feature_launderer.html.**

A team of Norwegian biologists have developed intelligent methods to search and mine the Web for genetic studies that contain information relevant to their endeavors. Methods such as these become increasingly important for scientific researchers as well as businesses because the amount of information generated and stored doubles every three years (see Pallatto, 2002). See Copeland (2001) for how this Web mining is accomplished.

Section 7.2 Review Questions

1. Define *data mining*.
2. What factors have increased the popularity of data mining recently?
3. Identify at least five applications of data mining.
4. What are some major characteristics of data mining?
5. What are some of the main categories of data mining technologies? Define at least three of them.

7.3 DATA MINING TECHNIQUES AND TOOLS

There are many methods for performing data mining. Data mining software may use one or more of these techniques. Data mining tools and techniques can be classified based on the structure of the data and the algorithms used. These are the main ones:

- *Statistical methods*. These include linear and nonlinear regression, point estimation, Bayes's theorem (i.e., probability distribution), correlations, and cluster analysis.
- *Decision trees*. **Decision trees** are used in classification and clustering methods. They break down problems into increasingly discrete subsets by working from generalizations to increasingly more specific information. A decision tree can be defined as a root followed by internal nodes. Each node (including the root) is labeled with a question. The arcs associated with each node cover all possible responses. Each response represents a probable outcome (see Dunham, 2003).
- *Case-based reasoning*. The case-based reasoning approach uses historical cases to recognize patterns. For example, customers of Cognitive Systems, Inc., use such an approach for help desk applications. One customer has a 50,000-query case library. New cases can be quickly matched against the 50,000 samples in the library, and answers are automatically provided to queries, with more than 90 percent accuracy. For more on case-based reasoning, see Chapter 13.
- *Neural computing*. Neural networks use many connected nodes (which operate in a manner similar to how the neurons of the human brain function). This approach examines a massive amount of historical data for patterns. Thus, we can go through large databases and, for example, identify potential customers for a new

product or companies whose profiles suggest that they are heading for bankruptcy. Applications of neural computing are common in financial services (see Fadlalla and Lin, 2001) and manufacturing. A comprehensive description of neural networks is provided in Chapter 8.

- *Intelligent agents*. One of the most promising approaches for retrieving information from databases, especially external ones, is the use of intelligent agents. With the availability of a vast and growing amount of information through the Internet, finding the right information is becoming increasingly difficult. Web-based data mining applications are typically enabled by intelligent software agents. This topic is discussed in Chapter 14.
- *Genetic algorithms*. Genetic algorithms work on the principle of expansion of possible outcomes. Given a fixed number of possible outcomes, genetic algorithms seek to define new and better solutions. Genetic algorithms are used for clustering and association rules.
- *Other tools*. Several other tools can be used for data mining, including rule induction and data visualization. The best source for information on new tool development is vendor Web sites.

When dealing with customer behavioral data, which can encompass 100 dimensions or more, algorithms are capable of dealing effectively with high-dimensional data. These algorithms must also work with business constraints and rules. Simple statistics do not work. Knowledge of the business constraints, of the relationships between products, and of the various behavioral segments of customers is a must. The following sections introduce algorithms for two common problems addressed by data mining: classification and clustering.

CLASSIFICATION

Classification, as the name implies, involves identifying patterns of data to belong to a certain category. These tasks may include credit approval (i.e., good or bad credit risk), store location (e.g., good, moderate, bad), target marketing (e.g., likely customer, no hope), fraud detection (i.e., yes, no), and telecommunication (e.g., likely to churn to another phone company, yes/no). These methods involve seeding a set of data with a known set of classes and mapping all other items (e.g., customers) into those sets. Classification can be based on previously known classes or totally unknown classes. When the classes are not known for any data, *cluster analysis* is used.

A more common application of classification is to develop a model that learns from previously known classes of data patterns and then is able to classify new data into the classes. The inputs into the model then are a training set of patterns, each with one class label. The model assigns a class label to each pattern, based on the combination of characteristics. After a model has been trained, it can be used to predict classes of new patterns where the class label is unknown. The basic process of building these models is to train an algorithm, using sample data whose classes are known. Then the algorithm's performance is tested by giving it a set of data in which the actual class is known but the model is asked to predict the class. The algorithms can then be compared on the basis of a number of factors:

- *Predictive accuracy*, which refers to the ability of the model to correctly predict the class label of new or previously unseen data. To compute this accuracy, a known class of test samples is matched against the class predicted by the model. Accuracy can then be computed as Accuracy rate = Percentage of test set samples correctly classified by the model. Of course, depending on the problem, we may

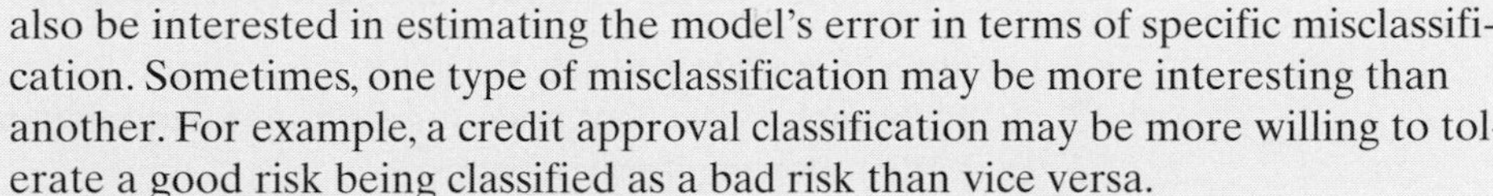

also be interested in estimating the model's error in terms of specific misclassification. Sometimes, one type of misclassification may be more interesting than another. For example, a credit approval classification may be more willing to tolerate a good risk being classified as a bad risk than vice versa.

- *Speed*, which refers to the computation costs involved in generating and using the model.
- *Robustness*, which is the capability of the model to make correct predictions, given noisy data or data with missing values.
- *Scalability*, which refers to the ability to construct the model efficiently, given a large amount of data.
- *Interpretability*, which refers to the level of understanding and insight provided by the model.

There are many classification techniques in use today, including the following:

- Decision tree classification
- Statistical analysis
- Neural networks
- Bayesian classifiers
- Genetic algorithms
- Rough set approach

A complete description of all these classification techniques is beyond the scope of this book. Neural networks are covered in Chapter 8. Next, we focus on the class of algorithms called decision trees.

Decision Trees

To describe a decision tree, we need to discuss some simple terminology. First, the data patterns include many input variables that may have an impact on the classifications of those patterns. These input variables are usually called *attributes*. For example, if we were to build a model to classify loan risks on the basis of just two characteristics—income and a credit rating—these would be the attributes. The resulting output would be the class label. Second, a tree consists of branches and nodes. A branch represents the outcome of a test to classify a pattern on the basis of a test, using an attribute. A leaf node at the end represents the final class choice for a pattern. An intermediate node represents a test on an attribute.

The basic idea of a decision tree is that it recursively divides a training set until each division consists entirely or primarily of examples from one class. Each non-leaf node of the tree contains a *split point*, which is a test on one or more attributes and determines how the data are to be divided further. Decision tree algorithms, in general, build an initial tree from the training data such that each leaf node is pure, and they then prune the tree to increase its accuracy on test data.

In the growth phase, the tree is built by recursively dividing the data until each division is either pure (i.e., contains members of the same class) or relatively small. The basic idea is to ask questions whose answers would provide the most information, similar to what we may do when playing the "Twenty Questions" game.

The split used to partition the data depends on the type of the attribute used in the split. For a continuous attribute A, splits are of the form value(A) $<$ x, where x is a value of A. For example, the split based on income could be "Income $<$ 50000." For a categorical attribute A, splits are of the form value(A) belongs to X, where X is a subset of A. As an example, the split could be on the basis of gender: "Gender is Male."

The very general algorithm for building a decision tree is as follows:

1. Create a root node and select a splitting attribute.
2. Add a branch to the root node for each split candidate value and label.
3. Take the following iterative steps:
   a. Classify data by applying the split value.
   b. If a stopping point is reached, then create leaf node and label it. Otherwise, build another subtree.

Many different algorithms have been proposed for creating decision trees. The algorithms differ primarily in terms of the choice of splitting attributes, the order of splitting attributes, the number of splits, the tree structure, the stopping criteria, and the pruning of the tree. Some of the most well-known algorithms are ID3, C4.5, C5 from machine learning, Classification and Regression Trees (CART) from statistics, and Chi-squared Automatic Interaction Detector (CHAID) from pattern recognition.

While building a decision tree, the goal at each node is to determine the split point that best divides the training records belonging to that leaf. To evaluate the goodness of the split, some splitting indices have been proposed. Two of the most common ones are the Gini index and information gain. The Gini index is used in CART and SPRINT (Scalable PaRalleizable Induction of Decision Trees) algorithms. Versions of information gain are used in ID3, C4.5, and its new versions. We describe Gini index next to illustrate what happens in building a decision tree.

The Gini Index The **Gini index** has been used in economics to measure the diversity of a population. The same concept can be used to determine the purity of a specific class as a result of a decision to branch along a particular attribute or variable. The best split is the one that increases the purity of the sets resulting from a proposed split. For example, consider a simple problem of building a decision tree for the data in Table 7.2. This table includes three columns to relate income and credit rating to a loan risk assessment. If we could build a classifier based on the historical data provided in Table 7.2, we could use it to assess loan risks for other applicants in the future. (Of course, we know that the real-life application would probably involve more than these two factors, but we want to keep it simple to be able to learn the details of the algorithm.) The second column of Table 7.2 gives income, the third column gives the credit rating, and the fourth column lists the corresponding loan risk.

Let us first define the Gini index. It is calculated as:

$$\text{Gini}(S) = 1 - \Sigma p_j^2$$

where:

S is a data set that contains examples from n classes
p_j is a relative frequency of class j in S

TABLE 7.2 Sample Patterns for Training a Decision Tree to Predict Loan Risk

Pattern #	*Income*	*Credit Rating*	*Loan Risk*
0	23	High	High
1	17	Low	High
2	43	Low	High
3	68	High	Low
4	32	Moderate	Low
5	20	High	High

For example, if there are two classes, High and Low, and data set S with p High elements and n Low elements, we use the following:

$$p_{high} = p/(p + n) \qquad p_{low} = n/(n + p)$$

$$\text{Gini}(S) = 1 - p_{high}^{\ 2} - p_{low}^{\ 2}$$

If data set S is split into S_1 and S_2, the splitting index is defined as follows:

$$\text{Gini}_{SPLIT}(S) = (p_1 + n_1)/(p + n) \times \text{Gini}(S_1) + (p_2 + n_2)/(p + n) \times \text{Gini}(S_2)$$

where p_1, n_1 (p_2, n_2) denote p_1 High elements and n_1 Low elements in the data set S_1 (S_2). In this definition, the best split point is the one with the lowest value of the Gini_{SPLIT} index.

To illustrate the use of the Gini index in developing a decision tree, consider the data in Table 7.2. We need to decide which attribute to consider first for branching. There are many special implementations to help make this decision, but we can simply start with the only numeric attribute we have in the data: income. That is, we can try to segment the data so that the choice of income can help us determine whether a loan risk is high or low. We can reorder the data in Table 7.2 to see the following summary on the basis of the Income attribute:

Income	*Pattern #*	*Loan Risk*
17	1	High
20	5	High
23	0	High
32	4	Low
43	2	High
68	3	Low

Thus, the possible values of a split point for the Income attribute are Income $\leq$ 17, Income $\leq$ 20, Income $\leq$ 23, Income $\leq$ 32, Income $\leq$ 43, and Income $\leq$ 68. We can now compute the Gini index for each of these levels of splits.

Consider the choice of dividing the data at Income $\leq$ 17. We have the following choices of classifications:

Pattern Count	*High*	*Low*
Income $\leq$ 17	1	0
Income $>$ 17	3	2

Let us compute the Gini index for Income $\leq$ 17 and Income $>$ 17. First,

$$G(\text{Income} \leq 17) = 1 - (\text{Proportion of records with High risk})^2 - (\text{Proportion of records with Low risk})^2$$

That is,

$$G(\text{Income} \leq 17) = 1 - (1^2 + 0^2) = 0$$

Similarly,

$$G(\text{Income} > 17) = 1 - ((3/5)^2 + (2/5)^2) = 1 - (13/25) = 12/25$$

The Gini index for the split choice is computed as follows:

$$G_{SPLIT} = (\text{Proportion of records at Income} \leq 17) \times G(\text{Income} \leq 17) + (\text{Proportion of records at Income} > 17) \times G(\text{Income} > 17)$$

$$G_{SPLIT} = (1/6) \times 0 + (5/6) \times (12/25) = 2/5$$

Now consider the choice Income ≤ 20:

Pattern Count	*High*	*Low*
Income ≤ 20	2	0
Income > 20	2	2

The Gini index for this split is computed as follows:

$$G(\text{Income} \leq 20) = 1 - (1^2 + 0^2) = 0$$

$$G(\text{Income} > 20) = 1 - ((1/2)^2 + (1/2)^2) = 1/2$$

$$G_{SPLIT} = (2/6) \times 0 + (4/6) \times (1/2) = 1/3$$

Similarly, consider Income split at 23:

Pattern Count	*High*	*Low*
Income ≤ 23	3	0
Income > 23	1	2

The Gini index for this split is computed as follows:

$$G(\text{Income} \leq 23) = 1 - (1^2 + 0^2) = 0$$

$$G(\text{Income} > 23) = 1 - ((1/3)^2 + (2/3)^2) = 1 - (1/9) - (4/9) = 4/9$$

$$G_{SPLIT} = (3/6) \times 0 + (3/6) \times (4/9) = 2/9$$

Finally, consider Income split at 32:

Pattern Count	*High*	*Low*
Income ≤ 32	3	1
Income > 32	1	1

The Gini index for this split is computed as follows:

$$G(\text{Income} \leq 32) = 1 - ((3/4)^2 + (1/4)^2) = 1 - (10/16) = 6/16 = 3/8$$

$$G(\text{Income} > 32) = 1 - ((1/2)^2 + (1/2)^2) = 1/2$$

$$G_{SPLIT} = (4/6) \times (3/8) + (2/6) \times (1/2) = (1/8) + (1/6) = 14/48 = 7/24$$

The lowest value of G_{SPLIT} is for Income ≤ 23. So we take the two nearest values and average them. Thus, we have a split point at Income = (23 + 32) / 2 = 27.5.

Attribute lists are divided at the split point. That is, we expect to have a rule that says:

If Income ≤ 27.5
Then . . .
Else If Income > 27.5
Then . . .

Now we examine the patterns to fill the Then part of the rule. Let's see if we can get all the records of a particular category together.

The following is the attribute list for Income ≤ 27.5:

Income	***Pattern #***	***Loan Risk***
17	1	High
20	5	High
23	0	High

Examining these same records for Credit Rating also reveals the following:

Credit Rating	***Pattern #***	***Loan Risk***
Moderate	0	High
Low	1	High
Moderate	5	High

Thus, it appears that a rule can be formulated: If Income ≤ 27.5, then Loan Risk = High, regardless of the level of Credit Rating.

Now let us examine the other branch of this decision tree by checking the attribute lists for Income > 27.5. The following tables suggest that Income > 27.5 is not a definitive indicator of Loan Risk:

Income	***Pattern #***	***Loan Risk***
32	4	Low
43	2	High
68	3	Low

Credit Rating	***Pattern #***	***Loan Risk***
Low	2	High
Moderate	3	Low
High	4	Low

Now we develop a subtree by examining the Credit Rating attribute.

Credit Rating is a categorical variable. The rules for developing a decision branch for a categorical variable such as gender are slightly different from those for a continuous, real valued attribute such as income. Recall that the Gini index is defined as:

$$\text{Gini(two proportions)} = 1 - p^2_{\text{one\_proportion}} - p^2_{\text{the other\_proportion}}$$

In the case of a categorical variable, this means, for example, that one proportion is the set of records of Credit Rating = {Low}. The other proportion then means Credit Rating = not {Low}. In our case, this also means: Credit Rating ∈ {Moderate, High}. Thus, we have to compute proportions of each category and its complement. In general, then, we have to evaluate the splitting index for each of the 2^N combinations, where N is the cardinality of the categorical attribute:

Pattern Count	***High***	***Low***
Credit Rating = {Low}	1	0
Credit Rating = {Moderate}	0	1
Credit Rating = {High}	0	1

First, we compute the Gini index for each category:

$$G(\text{Credit Rating} = \{\text{Low}\}) = 1 - 1^2 - 0^2 = 0$$

$$G(\text{Credit Rating} = \{\text{Moderate}\}) = 1 - 0^2 = 1^2 = 0$$

$$G(\text{Credit Rating} = \{\text{High}\}) = 1 - 0^2 - 1^2 = 0$$

This is not a surprise because there is only one record of each type. Next, we compute the Gini index for the complement categories:

$$G(\text{Credit Rating} \in \{\text{Low, Moderate}\}) = 1 - (1/2)^2 - (1/2)^2 = 1/2$$

$$G(\text{Credit Rating} \in \{\text{Low, High}\}) = 1/2$$

$$G(\text{Credit Rating} \in \{\text{Moderate, High}\}) = 1 - 0^2 - 1^2 = 0$$

Finally, we can compute the Gini index values for the possible branches. For a branch choice of Credit Rating = Low and Credit Rating = {Moderate, High}, we would have:

$$G_{SPLIT} = (\text{Proportion of records with Credit Rating} = \text{Low}) \times G(\text{Credit Rating} \in \{\text{Low}\}) + (\text{Proportion of records with Credit Rating} = \text{not Low}) \times G(\text{Credit Rating} = \text{not}\{\text{Low}\})$$

Or, we might have:

$$G_{SPLIT} = (\text{Proportion of records with Credit Rating} = \text{Low}) \times G(\text{Credit Rating} \in \{\text{Low}\}) +$$

$$(\text{Proportion of records with Credit Rating} = \text{Moderate, High}) \times G(\text{Credit Rating} = \text{Moderate, High})$$

That is:

$$G_{SPLIT}(\text{Credit Rating} = \{\text{Low}\}) = (1/3) \times 0 + (2/3) \times 0 = 0$$

The rest of the Gini indices for other choices of split can then be computed as follows:

$$G_{SPLIT}(\text{Credit Rating} = \{\text{Moderate}\}) = (1/3) \times 0 + (2/3) \times (1/2) = 1/3$$

$$G_{SPLIT}(\text{Credit Rating} = \{\text{High}\}) = (1/3) \times 0 + (2/3) \times (1/2) = 1/3$$

$$G_{SPLIT}(\text{Credit Rating} \in \{\text{Low, Moderate}\}) = (2/3) \times (1/2) + (1/3) \times 0 = 1/3$$

$$G_{SPLIT}(\text{Credit Rating} \in \{\text{Low, High}\}) = (2/3) \times (1/2) + (1/3) \times 0 = 1/3$$

$$G_{SPLIT}(\text{Credit Rating} \in \{\text{Moderate, High}\}) = (2/3) \times 0 + (1/3) \times 0 = 0$$

The lowest value of the Gini index for the split is zero at Credit Rating = Low and Credit Rating ∈ {Moderate, High}, thus this is our split point, and these are the next-level branches. The decision tree we have built is shown in Figure 7.1.

Information Gain The Gini index is only one of the many methods of creating a decision tree. Perhaps the most widely known decision tree approach involves the ID3 algorithm (see Quinlan, 1986) and its variants. The basic idea of the ID3 algorithm is to use a concept called *entropy* in place of the Gini index. **Entropy** measures the extent of uncertainty or randomness in a data set. If all the data in a subset belong to just one class, there is no uncertainty or randomness in that data set; the entropy is zero. The objective of this approach is to build subtrees so that the entropy of each final subset is zero.

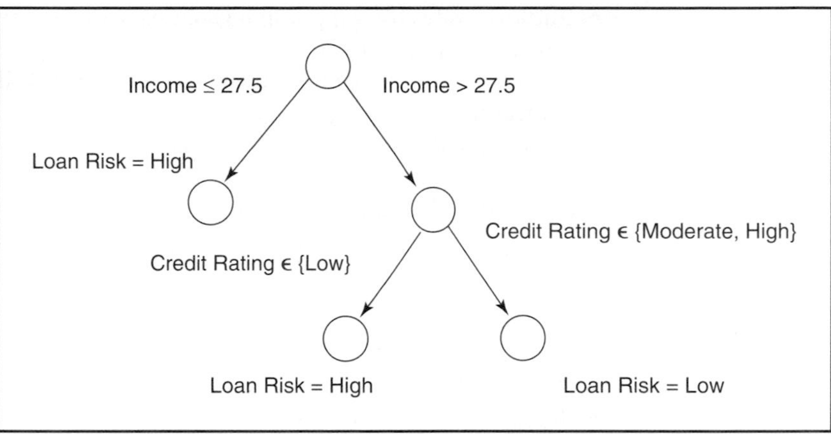

FIGURE 7.1 Decision Tree Using Gini Index for Split Criteria

As is the case with the CART/SPRINT algorithms that use the Gini index, the entropy of each candidate subset is computed, and then an information gain measure is computed to determine which way to partition. The basic ideas are the same; the specific details of the algorithms, of course, vary. Quinlan (1986) described the basic ID3 algorithm. Quinlan's company offers newer versions of ID3 called C4.5 and See5. The section "Data Mining Software," later in this chapter, describes many related offerings.

CLUSTER ANALYSIS FOR DATA MINING

Cluster analysis is a very important set of methods for classifying items into common groupings called *clusters*. The methods are common in biology, medicine, genetics, social sciences, anthropology, archaeology, astronomy, character recognition, and even management information system (MIS) development. As data mining has increased in popularity, the methods have been applied to business, especially to marketing. Cluster analysis has been used extensively for fraud detection, both credit card and e-commerce fraud, and market segmentation of customers in CRM systems. More applications in business continue to be developed as the strength of cluster analysis is understood and used.

Cluster analysis is an exploratory data analysis tool for solving classification problems. The object is to sort cases (e.g., people, things, events) into groups, or clusters, so that the degree of association is strong between members of the same cluster and weak between members of different clusters. Each cluster describes the class to which its members belong. An obvious one-dimensional example of cluster analysis is to establish score ranges into which to assign class grades for a college class. This is similar to the cluster analysis problem that the U.S. Treasury faced when establishing new tax brackets in the 1980s. A fictional example of clustering occurs in J.K. Rowling's *Harry Potter* books. The Sorting Hat determines to which House (e.g., dormitory) to assign first-year students at the Hogwarts School. Another example involves determining how to seat guests at a wedding. As far as data mining goes, the importance of cluster analysis is that it may reveal associations and structures in data that were not previously apparent but are sensible and useful once found.

Cluster analysis results may be used to:

- Help identify a classification scheme (e.g., types of customers)
- Suggest statistical models to describe populations

- Indicate rules for assigning new cases to classes for identification, targeting, and diagnostic purposes
- Provide measures of definition, size, and change in what were previously broad concepts
- Find typical cases to represent classes

CLUSTER ANALYSIS METHODS

Cluster analysis may be based on one or more of the following general methods:

- Statistical (including both hierarchical and nonhierarchical) methods
- Optimal methods
- Neural networks
- Fuzzy logic
- Genetic algorithms

Each of these methods generally works with one of two general method classes:

- *Divisive.* With divisive classes, all items start in one cluster and are broken apart.
- *Agglomerative.* With agglomerative classes, all items start in individual clusters, and the clusters are joined together.

Most cluster analysis methods involve the use of a distance between pairs of items. That is, there is a measure of similarity between every pair of items to be clustered. Often, they are based on true distances that are measured, but this need not be so, as is typically the case in information system (IS) development. Weighted averages may be used to establish these distances. For example, in an IS development project, individual modules of the system may be related by the similarity between their inputs, outputs, processes, and the specific data used. These factors are then aggregated, pairwise by item, into a single distance measure.

CLUSTERING EXAMPLE

Consider the similarity (distance) matrix that represents the similarities among eight items shown in Table 7.3. Items 4 and 5 have a lot in common, as do items 1 and 3 and items 3 and 10; 1 and 10 are moderately related, and 1 and 5 have little in common. To evaluate a solution, we add the pairwise values of all the items in each cluster. If we

TABLE 7.3 Similarity (Distance) Matrix

The values below the diagonal equal the values above; that is, the distance from 1 to 2 is the same as from 2 to 1. Diagonal values do not exist.

Item	1	2	3	4	5	6	7	8
1	–	3	9	2	1	6	4	5
2		–	4	5	6	2	3	8
3			–	5	7	10	4	2
4				–	10	2	8	1
5					–	4	9	3
6						–	3	3
7							–	5
8								–

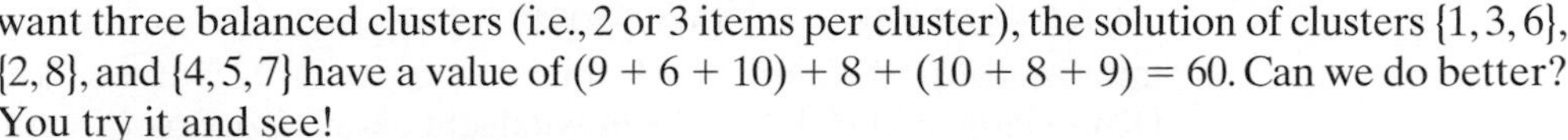

want three balanced clusters (i.e., 2 or 3 items per cluster), the solution of clusters {1, 3, 6}, {2, 8}, and {4, 5, 7} have a value of (9 + 6 + 10) + 8 + (10 + 8 + 9) = 60. Can we do better? You try it and see!

Now that we have a data set, we need to address some critical issues:

- How many clusters are to be found (i.e., when do we stop)?
- Should all the clusters have approximately the same number of items?
- How do we handle dimensional scaling when different measures are used in establishing the distance value?
- Can distance really be measured?

HIERARCHICAL CLUSTERING METHOD AND EXAMPLE

As an example of hierarchical clustering, we start with a set of items, each within its own cluster. We determine the maximum number of clusters we want to have. The basic method is as follows:

1. Decide which data to record from the items (i.e., measures of similarity).
2. Calculate the distances between all initial clusters. Store the results in a distance matrix.
3. Search through the distance matrix and find the two most similar clusters.
4. Fuse those two clusters together to produce a cluster that has at least two items.
5. Calculate the distances between this new cluster and all the other clusters (some of which may contain one item).
6. Repeat steps 3 to 5 until you have reached the prespecified maximum number of clusters.

Note that some methods go all the way to a single cluster of all items. To identify the solution you want, you need to identify when you have obtained the desired number of clusters, and then you stop.

For example, we can apply the hierarchical method to the matrix from the preceding section, with a goal of three balanced clusters. The initial solution is:

$$\{1, 2, 3, 4, 5, 6, 7, 8\} \text{ at a value of } 134.$$

Although this is an excellent value, we want three clusters. We therefore first combine items 4 and 5 (value = 10) to get:

$$\{4, 5\}\ \{1, 2, 3, 6, 7, 8\} \text{ at } 10 + 71 = 81$$

This is pretty good. We next combine items 3 and 6 (value = 10) to get:

$$\{3, 6\}\ \{4, 5\}\ \{1, 2, 7, 8\} \text{ at } 10 + 10 + 28 = 48.$$

Next, we combine item 7 into the cluster with items 4 and 5 to get:

$$\{3, 6\}\ \{4, 5, 7\}\ \{1, 2, 8\} \text{ at } = 53.$$

We stop because we have three clusters as balanced as can be with these data (i.e., two groups of three items, one group of two items).

Although it is not balanced, the cluster solution {1, 3, 4}, {3, 5, 6}, and {5} has a value of 72, which is better than the solutions described earlier.

DATA MINING SOFTWARE

Data mining software features more complicated algorithms for neural networking, clustering, segmentation, and classifications that are generally more sophisticated than

OLAP methods (see Finlay, 2001). Many software vendors provide powerful data mining tools. Examples of these vendors are Angoss Knowledge Engineering (KnowledgeSTUDIO and KnowledgeSeeker), Cognos (a variety of tools), Teradata, SPSS (Clementine and others), IBM (DB2 Intelligent Miner Scoring [IMS]), Megaputer Intelligence, Inc. (PolyAnalyst), and SAS (a variety of tools). Another powerful tool is STATISTICA Data Miner from StatSoft, which is available for limited-time use to students and instructors using this book. Angoss KnowledgeSeeker induces rules from data. These rules can be used in expert systems. IBM's DB2 IMS provides real-time relational data mining analyses and scoring. It uses Predictive Model Markup Language (PMML) from the data mining group. This software brings the data mining process one step closer to automation. PolyAnalyst includes both intelligent data mining and text mining methods. Many companies (most of the ones just mentioned) are moving to offering consulting services by using their own products rather than just selling software.

Buck (2000) organized the classes of data mining tools and techniques as they relate to information and business intelligence (BI) technologies. Her taxonomy is:

- Mathematical and statistical analysis packages
- Personalization tools for Web-based marketing
- Analytics built into marketing platforms
- Advanced CRM tools
- Analytics added to other vertical industry-specific platforms
- Analytics added to database tools (e.g., OLAP)
- Standalone data mining tools

WEKA is an open source collection of machine learning algorithms for data mining tasks, and it includes neural network capabilities. WEKA can be downloaded from **cs.waikato.ac.nz/~ml/weka.** Some software firms make their data mining and OLAP tools available to university scholars for free or at greatly discounted prices. Check individual vendors' Web sites for information about this. Table 7.4 lists a few of the major products and their Web sites.

TABLE 7.4 Selected Data Mining Software

Product Name	*URL*
Clementine	**spss.com/clementine/**
Delta Master	**bissantz.de**
iData Analyzer	**infoacumen.com**
Fair Isaac Business Science	**fairisaac.com/edm**
GhostMiner	**fqs.pl/ghostminer**
IBM DB2 Data Warehouse Edition	**ibm.com/software/data/db2/dwe**
KnowledgeMiner	**knowledgeminer.net**
Oracle Data Mining (ODM)	**otn.oracle.com/products/bi/9idmining.html**
PolyAnalyst	**megaputer.com/products/pa/index.php3**
Salford Systems Data Mining Suite	**salfordsystems.com**
SAS Enterprise Miner	**sas.com/technologies/bi/analytics/index.html**
STATISTICA	**statsoft.com/products/dataminer.htm**
Teradata Warehouse Miner	**ncr.com/products/software/teradata_mining.htm**
XLMiner	**xlminer.net**

Cluster Analysis Software

Aside from data mining methods in which cluster analysis methods are embedded, there are several specialized packages for cluster analysis. These include ClustanGraphics (Clustan), DecisionWORKS Suite (Advanced Software Applications), SPSS (SPSS), and PolyAnalyst Cluster Engine (Megaputer). In addition, free cluster analysis code is available from many academic sites. Do a Web search to find them.

Section 7.3 Review Questions

1. Identify at least three of the main methods of data mining.
2. Give examples of situations in which classification would be an appropriate data mining technique.
3. List at least two classification techniques.
4. What are some of the criteria for comparing and selecting the best classification technique?
5. Briefly describe the general algorithm used in decision trees.
6. Define *Gini index*. What does it measure?
7. Give examples of situations in which cluster analysis would be an appropriate data mining technique.
8. What is the major difference between cluster analysis and classification?
9. What are some of the methods for cluster analysis?
10. What is the measure of similarity in a cluster analysis setting?

7.4 DATA MINING PROJECT PROCESSES

Similarly to other major initiatives in an organization, data mining projects have to follow a project management process. Data mining practitioners and researchers have proposed several different approaches to managing this process. The basic processes they all propose are relatively similar. We briefly review some of the proposed models.

One such model, Cross-Industry Standard Process for Data Mining (CRISP-DM), was proposed in the mid-1990s by a European consortium of companies to serve as a nonproprietary standard process model for data mining. Figure 7.2 illustrates this proposed process, which includes a sequence of steps (which are not purely sequential) for data mining projects. Much iterative work takes place, especially in the first few steps of developing a better understanding of the business needs and the available data. It is not uncommon for a data mining project to take as much as 60 percent of the estimated time in developing data and business understanding and then preparing the data for actual modeling steps. Almost always, the process of modeling leads to a need for further data preparation.

Another process that has been proposed for data mining projects is based on the popular Six Sigma methodology. Six Sigma is a well-structured, data-driven methodology for eliminating defects, waste, and quality control problems of all kinds in manufacturing, service delivery, management, and other business activities. This model has recently become very popular due to its successful implementations in various U.S. industries, and it appears to be gaining favor worldwide. In the context of data mining, the five steps of the Define, Measure, Analyze, Improve, and Control (DMAIC) model are given in Figure 7.3. The basic idea of these steps is to have an early idea of what to

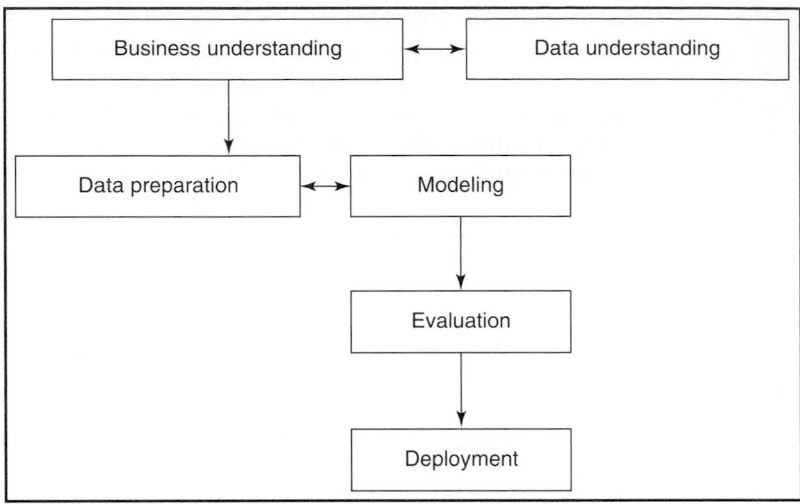

FIGURE 7.2 Data Mining Process Recommended by CRISP-DM

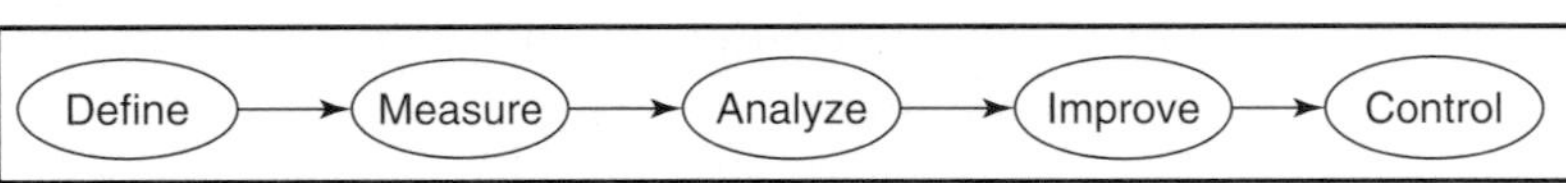

FIGURE 7.3 Six Sigma–Based Data Mining Process

expect, apply measurement at each step, and develop feedback mechanisms. Six Sigma processes have been used in manufacturing industries worldwide for quality improvement and process controls. Proponents of the Six Sigma process for data mining argue that the same type of efficiency can be achieved in data mining projects.

Finally, the SAS Institute, a provider of data mining technologies and services, has proposed a framework that is somewhat similar to Six Sigma. It is called Sample, Explore, Modify, Model, Assess (SEMMA). Figure 7.4 illustrates this proposed process. The focus of SEMMA is on the technical activities of a data mining project.

As pointed out by StatSoft, "all of these models are concerned with the process of how to integrate data mining methodology into an organization, how to "convert data into information," how to involve important stakeholders, and how to disseminate the information in a form that can easily be converted by stake-holders into resources for strategic decision making." (statsoft.com 2006). So the underlying goal of the different processes is very similar.

Some practitioners commonly use the term *knowledge discovery in databases* as a synonym for data mining. Fayyad et al. (1996) defined **knowledge discovery in databases (KDD)** as a process of using data mining methods to find useful information and patterns in the data, as opposed to data mining, which involves using algorithms to identify patterns in data derived through the KDD process. KDD is a comprehensive process that encompasses data mining. The input to the KDD process consists of organizational data. The enterprise data warehouse enables KDD to be implemented efficiently because it provides a single source for data to be mined. Dunham (2003) summarized the KDD process as consisting of the following steps:

FIGURE 7.4 SEMMA Process of Data Mining

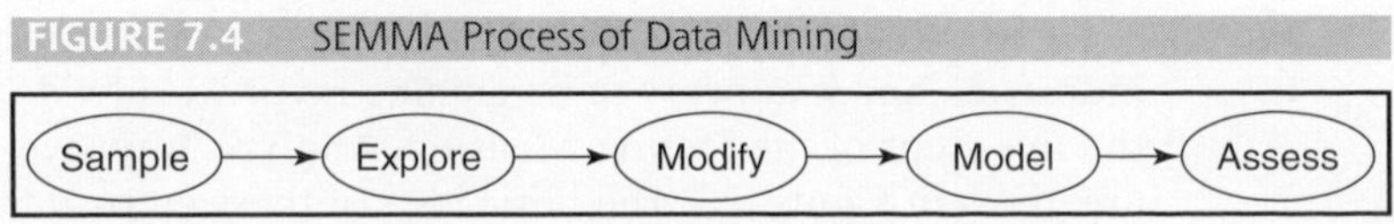

TECHNOLOGY INSIGHTS 7.6

Data Mining Myths

Data mining is a powerful analytical tool that enables business executives to advance from describing historical customer behavior to predicting the future. It finds patterns that unlock the mysteries of customer behavior. The results of data mining can be used to increase revenue, reduce expenses, identify fraud, and identify business opportunities, offering new competitive advantage. There are a number of myths about data mining, including the following:

Myth	Reality
Data mining provides instant, crystal-ball predictions.	Data mining is a multistep process that requires deliberate, proactive design and use.
Data mining is not yet viable for business applications.	The current state-of-the-art is ready to go for almost any business.
Data mining requires a separate, dedicated database.	Because of advances in database technology, a dedicated database is not required, even though it may be desirable.
Only those with advanced degrees can do data mining.	Newer Web-based tools enable managers of all educational levels to do data mining.
Data mining is only for large firms that have lots of customer data.	If the data accurately reflect the business or its customers, a company can use data mining.

Data mining visionaries have gained enormous competitive advantage by understanding that these myths are just that: myths.

Sources: Adapted from A. Zaima, "The Five Myths of Data Mining," *What Works: Best Practices in Business Intelligence and Data Warehousing*, Vol. 15, The Data Warehousing Institute, Chatsworth, CA, June 2003, pp. 42–43 and D. Kuonen, "Data Mining And Statistics: What Is The Connection?" *TDAN.com,* October 2004. **tdan.com/i030fe01.htm** (accessed October 2006).

TECHNOLOGY INSIGHTS 7.7

Data Mining Blunders

The following 10 data mining mistakes are often made in practice, and you should try to avoid them:

1. Selecting the wrong problem for data mining.
2. Ignoring what your sponsor thinks data mining is and what it really can and cannot do.
3. Leaving insufficient time for data preparation. It takes more effort than is generally understood.
4. Looking only at aggregated results and not at individual records. IBM's DB2 IMS can highlight individual records of interest.
5. Being sloppy about keeping track of the mining procedure and results.
6. Ignoring suspicious findings and quickly moving on.
7. Running mining algorithms repeatedly and blindly. It is important to think hard enough about the next stage of data analysis. Data mining is a very hands-on activity.
8. Believing everything you are told about data.
9. Believing everything you are told about your own data mining analysis.
10. Measuring your results differently from the way your sponsor measures them.

Sources: Adapted from D. Skalak, "Data Mining Blunders Exposed!" *DB2 Magazine*, Vol.6, No. 2, Second Quarter 2001, pp. 10–13; and R. Shultz, *Live from NCDM: Tales of Database Buffoonery*, December 7, 2004, **directmag.com/news/ncdm-12-07-04/index.html** (accessed April 2006).

1. *Selection*. This step involves identification of the data that will be considered within the data mining process.
2. *Preprocessing*. Erroneous and missing data must be dealt with; this involves correction and/or use of predicted values.
3. *Transformation*. The data must be converted into a single common format for processing; this may involve encoding data or reducing the number of variables with which to deal.
4. *Data mining*. Algorithms are applied to the transformed data in order to produce output.
5. *Interpretation/evaluation*. To be useful, the results must be presented in a manner that is meaningful to the user.

As you can see from the presentation of these various process models, data mining is iterative because data miners learn from experimentation. Actually, the whole process of discovery is iterative. Thomas A. Edison quipped that he failed to invent the light bulb 100 times before he succeeded. So, just like the famous inventor's work process, data mining is a process of discovery. It is an experimental process that requires sound experimental design.

A number of misconceptions have developed about data mining. We describe them in Technology Insights 7.6. Many of them reflect the way that data mining is used in practice. For example, data mining methods are typically used mainly by IT staff, managers, and consultants/analysts because it is too difficult for nontechnical personnel to interpret results. But this is changing as the tools become easier to use. See Technology Insights 7.7 for specific errors that data miners typically make in practice because they often do not understand the process but do understand the expected results.

Since the terrorist attacks on September 11, 2001, there have been numerous advances in the utilization of data mining methods by law-enforcement agencies to track terrorism and crime in general. However, this has raised many ethical, legal, and privacy issues. Indeed, it has also become a big political issue. In developing data mining applications, we cannot ignore these aspects. See Application Case 7.8 for details and an example.

Application Case 7.8

DHS Data Mining Spinoffs and Advances in Law Enforcement

In late 2002, John Poindexter, former head of the National Security Council, caused a flap with his proposal for a new Information Awareness Office within the Pentagon. Critics blasted Poindexter's plans for data mining numerous credit, banking, and retail purchase records of U.S. citizens in the name of detecting possible terrorist patterns of behavior.

In reality, agencies such as the National Reconnaissance Office (NRO) and the National Security Agency (NSA) have been doing this for years, and in mid-2003, the Northern Command did so as well. In fact, data mining tools used by national intelligence agencies were already being used by domestic law enforcement agencies in the United States. The tools transferred data from the U.S. Space Command to Northern Command, and from there to the DHS, showing both the common technology base for all environments and the possible civil liberties concerns inherent in such technology transfers. Better intelligence coordination with state and local police forces while observing respect for civil liberties is an important issue.

The NRO and NSA use large-scale commercial database tools and specialized pattern-recognition tools. Defense contractors are responsible for integrating tools together in software suites that are useful to intelligence agencies. Many were working with the DHS's constituent agencies before DHS formed at the end of 2002. They deploy the tools for domestic drug enforcement and counterterrorism duties through the channels of the Northern Command and DHS.

For example, Northrop-Grumman's Web-enabled Temporal Analysis System (WebTAS) was developed in conjunction with the Air Force Research Labs and used during the Iraq campaign. It is available to regional police intelligence coalitions through the DHS. WebTAS displays maps and shows links corresponding to relationships among targets. Clicking a link calls up related databases that can tell an analyst, for example, all the calls that the target has made in the past few days. To pick up patterns that might be buried in the noise of too much information, an embedded behavioral-correlation engine predicts possible trends for developing situations and flags circumstances that identify problems for gathering further intelligence.

New cooperation among DHS investigators, especially in mining data, is producing major breakthroughs in nonterrorist cases, including the deaths of 19 illegal aliens found stuffed into a trailer in Victoria, Texas, on May 14, 2003. Detected via data mining techniques, money transfers and phone calls made by victims and more than 50 witnesses who survived the incident led authorities to a legal U.S. resident, whom they believe led a smuggling ring that took aliens across the Mexican border to U.S. cities for a substantial fee. Coconspirators around the United States were also identified. After the suspect fled the country, she was lured by a sting operation to Honduras, where she was arrested and extradited to the United States.

Sources: Adapted from L. Wirbel, "Data Mining Comes Down to Earth," *Electronic Engineering Times*, No. 1270, May 19, 2003, pp. 18, 22; and M. Hosenball, "Crime Breakthrough," *Newsweek*, Vol. 141, No. 26, June 20, 2003, p. 9.

Section 7.4 Review Questions

1. Briefly describe the CRISP-DM model of the data mining process.
2. What are the steps of data mining, according to the Six Sigma method?
3. What steps are recommended by the SAS Institute's SEMMA model of the data mining process?
4. Define *KDD*.
5. Identify some of the myths of data mining.
6. What are some of the common errors made in data mining projects?

7.5 TEXT MINING

Text mining is the application of data mining to unstructured or less structured text files. Data mining takes advantage of the infrastructure of stored data to extract additional useful information. For example, by applying data mining to a customer database, an analyst might discover that everyone who buys product A also buys products B and C six months later. Text mining operates with less structured information. Documents rarely have a strong internal infrastructure, and when they do, it is frequently focused on document format rather than document content. Text mining helps organizations:

- Find the "hidden" content of documents, including additional useful relationships.
- Relate documents across previous unnoticed divisions (e.g., discover that customers in two different product divisions have the same characteristics).
- Group documents by common themes (e.g., all the customers of an insurance firm who have similar complaints and cancel their policies).

Text mining is not the same thing as a search engine on the Web. In a search, we are trying to find what others have prepared. With text mining, we want to discover new patterns, nuggets of knowledge that may not be obvious or known.

Essentially, text mining entails the generation of meaningful numeric indices from the unstructured text and then processing those indices, using the various data mining algorithms introduced in previous sections of this chapter. By creating these numeric indices, we can summarize documents in terms of key concepts, cluster documents on the basis of similarity, visualize relationships between documents, and so on. Indeed, organizations are now recognizing that a major source of competitive advantage is the unstructured knowledge contained in an organization's knowledge store in the form of documents, memos, e-mails, policies and procedures, minutes of meetings, and so on. All this textual information needs to be codified and extracted so that predictive data mining tools can help the organization generate real value from this repository.

Some business players use *text mining* as a generic term to imply all types of text processing. But at least three specialties have emerged in this domain: information retrieval, information extraction, and information summarization. First, *information retrieval* in the context of text mining refers to querying text, finding text, and presenting textual information. In addition, either natural language processing or computational linguistics is used to analyze and process text. This is usually referred to as *information extraction*. For example, programs have been developed to automatically read thousands of resumes and extract the key information, such as names, addresses, and skills. There are also programs that provide automatic summary of documents. A very good demonstration of this capability can be seen at **newsinessence.com.** According to the Web site, the NewsinEssence system collects documents from a number of news sites, creates clusters based on topics, and summarizes each cluster. Systems such as NewsinEssence are good examples of information extraction and illustrate just a glimpse of the power of natural language processing.

- Qualitative analysis of documents to detect deception (see Cao et al., 2003). The documents are decomposed into numeric indices, and then various data mining techniques, such as neural networks, are used to learn and detect lies in the documents.

Perhaps one of the biggest application areas for text mining in general and information extraction in particular is biological sciences. Data being collected and compiled include textual information. This has led to a lot of activity in applying text mining techniques to the biological domain. See Witte (2006) for examples. Homeland security is another area where this type of growth in applications is evident. In the next section, we discuss some examples in which Web mining and text mining are combined. Application Case 7.9 describes an application of text mining in the airline industry.

Application Case 7.9

Flying Through Text

Text mining has proved to be a valuable tool in extracting organizational knowledge from reports in digitized form. Analysts are using text mining software to focus on key problem areas through pattern identification. For example, companies in the airline industry can apply text mining to incident reports to increase the quality of organizational knowledge. They can study mechanical, organizational, and behavioral problems a timely manner through the use of text mining.

Airlines operate with a thorough and systematic analysis of operations. An incident report is prepared whenever an event occurs that might lead to a problem. Key issues can be identified from the masses of incident reports, using text mining. The huge databases that airlines maintain have limited human interpretation, and the terminology appears different to a computer than to a human..

For example, data from Aer Lingus **(aerlingus.com)** over the period January 1998 through December 2003 were used to find patterns and correlations, leading to further analysis and model development. Aer Lingus used Megaputer's PolyAnalyst **(megaputer.com)** data and text mining software. Its goal was to visualize a process that investigators could regularly use to identify patterns and associations in types of incidents, locations, times, and other incident details. The most frequently occurring terms were initially identified. PolyAnalyst carries a lexicon of terms that is not complete but that provides a valuable starting point for text analysis. It can generate a list of key terms (or their semantic equivalents) occurring in the data. A report called a *frequent-terms report* is created, which contains the terms identified, with their frequency. The objective is to identify interesting clusters. A narrative summary carries a set of terms that divide the narrative descriptions into meaningful groups. For example, the key term *spillage* can be associated with four other key terms: *food, fuel, chemical*, and *toilet*. From the key terms, in terms of spillage, *food* is semantically related to *coffee, tea*, and *drink*. Thus, *food* becomes the category node, and the different food products reported as spilled are matched to food.

Text mining of airline incident reports can identify incidents that might lead to trouble. Text mining can be used with a large set of incident data reports to validate predetermined theories and to cull new patterns of knowledge.

Sources: J. Froelich, S. Ananyan, and D.L Olson, "Business Intelligence Through Text Mining," *Business Intelligence Journal*, Vol.10, No. 1, Winter 2005, p. 43–50; and *Gain Full Value from Text Responses*, **spss.com/textanalysis_surveys/** (accessed April 2006).

HOW TO MINE TEXT

Ellingsworth and Sullivan (2003) described the process of text mining. They also described how the Fireman's Fund Insurance Company uses text mining to help predict expected claims and understand why outcomes deviate from predictions. Text mining is used to extract entities and objects for frequency analysis, identify files that have certain attributes for further statistical analysis, and create entirely new data features for predictive modeling. The first of these three methods was used in dealing with the court cases involving Firestone tires on Ford SUVs. In Online File W7.1, we describe details of an effective pharmaceutical text mining application.

Term extraction is the most basic form of text mining. Like all other text mining techniques, it maps information from unstructured data into a structured format. The simplest data structure in text mining is the feature vector, or weighted list of words. The most important words in a text are listed, along with a measure of their relative importance. Text is reduced to a list of terms and weights. The entire semantics of the text may not be present, but the key concepts are identified. To do this, text mining involves these steps:

1. *Eliminate commonly used words (the, and, other)*. These are commonly called *stop-words*.
2. *Replace words with their stems or roots (e.g., eliminate plurals and various conjugations and declensions)*. In this step, the terms *phoned*, *phoning*, and *phones* would be mapped to *phone*. These are called *stemming algorithms*.
3. *Consider synonyms and phrases*. Words that are synonyms need to be combined in some fashion. For example, *student* and *pupil* may need to be grouped together. It is also important to consider phrases. As pointed out by StatSoft, *Microsoft Windows* refers to the computer operating system, but individually, the word *Windows* might be more relevant to a house project (statsoft.com 2006).
4. *Calculate the weights of the remaining terms*. The most common method is to calculate the frequency with which the word appears. There are two common measures: the term frequency, or *tf factor*, measures the actual number of times a word appears in a document, and the inverse document frequency, or *idf factor*, indicates the number of times the word appears in all documents in a set. The reasoning is that a large *tf* factor increases the weight, whereas a large *idf* factor decreases it

because terms that occur frequently in all documents would be common words to the industry and not be considered important.

For example, suppose that analysis of a paragraph leads to the observation that there are some 20 terms with 28 occurrences when we factor out common words. Here is a list of terms that appear more than once, along with their relative frequencies (*tf* factors) out of a total of 28:

Term	*Term Factor*
data	.0714
structure	.0714
term	.0714
text	.0714
text mining	.1429
weight	.0714

When you consider all the important words in the paragraph, they comprise one-half of its total importance and could be used to identify its semantics. Clearly, the paragraph is about text mining (weight = 0.1429) and involves text and data with structure and weight.

There are many components of a text mining system, including the following:

- A system for handling documents in various forms (e.g., plain text, word processor formats, PDF) from many different sources (e.g., files, Web forms, e-mails).
- Components used to process these documents and create data files that can then be mined. These include "sentence splitters, parts of speech, taggers, . . . , full parsers, . . . summarizers," and so on (Witte, 2006, p. 134–138).
- Data mining tools such as cluster algorithms, classifier algorithms, and so on.

There are two general, open source frameworks available for the first two tasks. One popular framework is called General Architecture for Text Engineering (GATE), and it is available from the University of Sheffield, UK, at **gate.ac.uk.** Another platform, supported by IBM, is called Unstructured Information Management Architecture (UIMA), and it is available at research.ibm.com/UIMA/. In addition to these tools, many data mining vendors offer text mining capabilities in their software suites. Because this area is still under major research and development, the capabilities of the software change rapidly. Here is a list of some popular text mining tools and vendors:

- SAS Text Miner (**sas.com**)
- IBM Intelligent Miner for Text (**ibm.com**)
- SPSSLexiquest (**spss.com**)
- Insightful Miner for Text (**insightful.com**)
- Megaputer Intelligence TextAnalyst (**megaputer.com**)
- StatSoft Data Miner (**statsoft.com**)

Online Tutorial T3 provides step-by-step instructions for a complete text mining project using StatSoft's Text Miner and the Data Miner facilities. Online Tutorial T3 shows how to analyze the documents. The specific example relates to analyzing car reviews prepared by many different individuals. This type of "opinion mining" is another common text mining application.

Given that perhaps 80 percent of all the nonnumeric data we collect and store is in text format, it is natural that text mining is emerging as a major growth area. Although we do not have full natural language processing capabilities yet, much progress has been made in this area in the past few years. It is one area where significant potential for the next generation of useful applications exists.

Section 7.5 Review Questions

1. What is text mining?
2. What are some of the text processing specialties related to text mining?
3. Give examples of automated information extraction applications.
4. Identify some current and potential applications of text mining.
5. What are some of the basic steps in performing text mining?
6. Identify the basic components of any text mining system.

7.6 WEB MINING

The Web is perhaps the world's biggest data/text repository, and the amount of information on the Web is growing every day. There is interesting information on the Web in whose home page is linked to which other pages, how many people have hyperlinks to a specific Web page on their own sites, and how a particular site is organized. In addition, each visitor to a Web site, each search on a search engine, each click on a link, and each transaction on an e-commerce site leads to the creation of additional data. Analysis of this information can help us make better use of Web sites and also helps us provide a better relationship and value to the visitors of our own Web sites.

Web mining can be defined as the discovery and analysis of interesting and useful information from the Web, about the Web, and usually through Web-based tools. The term *Web mining* was first used by Etzioni (1996); today, many conferences, journals, and books focus on Web data mining. It represents one of the continually evolving areas of technology and business practices. Figure 7.5 presents three different areas of Web mining: Web content, Web structure, and Web usage mining.

Web content mining refers to the extraction of useful information from Web pages. The documents may be extracted in some machine-readable format so that automated

FIGURE 7.5 Types of Web Mining

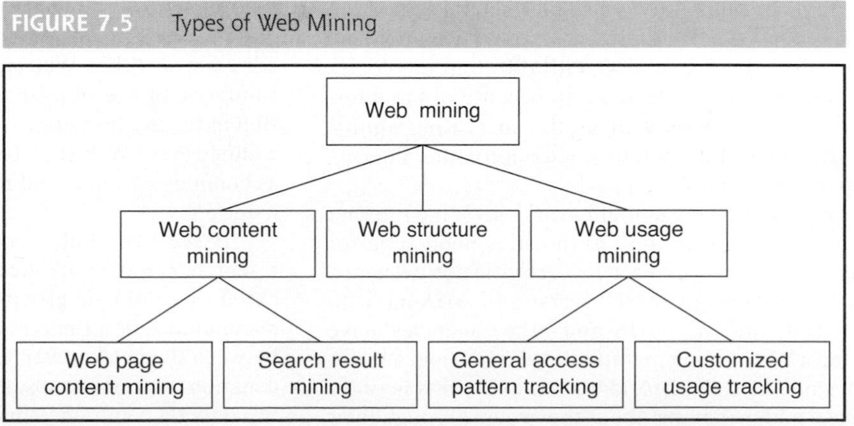

Source: Adapted from P. Galeas, *Web Mining*, **galeas.de/webmining.htm** (accessed April 2006).

techniques can generate some information about the Web pages. Web crawlers are used to read through the content of a Web site automatically. The automated information may include document characteristics similar to what is used in text mining, but may include additional concepts, such as document hierarchy. Web content mining may also be used to enhance the results produced by search engines. For example, Turetken and Sharda (2004) described a visualization system that takes the results of a search from a search engine such as Google, reads the top 100 documents, clusters those documents by processing them using IBM's Intelligent Text Miner, and then presents the results in a fisheye-view–based graphical format.

Web structure mining refers to developing useful information from the links included in Web documents. This information can be useful in determining the popularity of a document, a cornerstone of the page-rank algorithm that is central to search engines such as Google. Just as links going to a document can indicate the popularity of the document, links within the document can indicate the depth of coverage of a topic. Kleinberg (1998) identified a mechanism to find "hubs" and "authorities" through hyperlink analysis. *Hubs* are pages that point to many authorities in the field. On the other hand, *authority pages* are those that are linked by many hubs. A good understanding of the structure of a Web site is helpful in determining which pages should be added to a collection of Web sites. A significant duplication of Web links on a page might suggest that you do not need to link to two different sites, for example. Analysis of links is very important in understanding interrelationships. Sometimes, it can even lead to developing a better understanding of a specific Web community, clan, or clique. Zhou et al. (2005) described a major project in which they used both Web content mining and Web structure mining to better understand how U.S. extremist groups are connected (see Application Case 7.10).

Application Case 7.10

Caught in a Web

We normally search for answers to our problems outside our environment. Often, however, the trouble can stem from within. In taking action against global terrorism, internal domestic extremist groups go unnoticed. However, domestic extremists with different ideologies pose a significant threat to security because of the information they possess as well as the increasing ability, through the use of Internet, to reach out to other international extremist groups.

Keeping tabs on the content available on the Internet is difficult. Researchers and authorities need superior tools to analyze and monitor the activities of extremist groups. Researchers at the University of Arizona, with support from the U.S. DHS and other agencies, have developed a Web mining methodology to find and analyze Web sites operated by these domestic extremists in order to increase understanding about the groups through their usage of the Internet. Extremist groups use the Internet to communicate, access private messages, and raise money online. The research methodology initially gathers a superior-quality collection of relevant extremist and terrorist Web sites. Hyperlink analysis is performed, which leads to other extremists and terrorist Web sites. The interconnectedness with other Web sites is crucial in estimating the similarity of the objectives of various groups. The next step in the methodology is content analysis, which further codifies these Web sites, based on various attributes, such as communications, fund raising, and ideology sharing, to name a few.

Based on link analysis and content analysis, researchers have narrowed down to 97 Web sites of U.S. extremists and hate groups. Oftentimes the links between communities don't necessarily represent any cooperation between them. However, finding numerous links between common interest groups helps in clustering the communities under a common banner. A major purpose of extremists and hate groups is to bring to light their definitions of existence and purposes. Further research using data mining to automate the process has a global aim, trying to establish links between international hate and extremist groups and domestic U.S. groups.

Sources: Y. Zhou, E. Reid, J. Qin, H. Chen, and G. Lai, "U.S. Domestic Extremist Groups on the Web: Link and Content Analysis," *IEEE Intelligent Systems*, Vol. 20, No. 5, September/October 2005, pp. 44–51, **ai.arizona.edu/go/intranet/papers/Colorprint.pd**f (accessed April 2006); and P.B. Gerstenfeld, D.R. Grant, and C.-P. Chiang, "Hate Online: A Content Analysis of Extremist Internet Sites," *Analyses of Social Issues and Public Policy*, Vol. 3, No. 1, December 2003, pp. 29–44.

Web usage mining refers to extracting useful information from the data being generated through Web page visits, transactions, and so on. Srivastava et al. (2002) state that at least three types of data are generated through Web page visits:

- Automatically generated data stored in server *access* logs, *referrer* logs, *agent* logs, and client-side *cookies*
- User profiles
- Metadata such as page attributes, content attributes, and usage data

Analyzing the information collected by Web servers can help us understand user behavior. This is usually called *clickstream analysis*. By using the data mining techniques covered earlier in this chapter, a company might be able to discern interesting patterns from the clickstreams. For example, it might learn that 60 percent of the visitors who searched for "hotels in Maui" had earlier searched for "air fares to Maui." This information could be useful in deciding where to place online advertisements. Clickstream analysis might also be useful for knowing *when* visitors access a site. For example, if you knew that 70 percent of the software downloads from your site occurred between 7 and 11 p.m. Eastern time, you could plan for better customer support and network bandwidth during those hours. Srivastava (2006) listed the following examples of uses for Web mining:

- Determine the lifetime value of clients
- Design cross-marketing strategies across products
- Evaluate promotional campaigns
- Target electronic ads and coupons at user groups, based on their access patterns
- Predict user behavior based on previously learned rules and users' profiles
- Present dynamic information to users based on their interests and profiles

Amazon.com provides a good example of how Web usage history usage can be leveraged dynamically. A registered user who revisits Amazon.com is greeted by name. This is a simple task that involves recognizing the user by reading a cookie (i.e., a small text file written by a Web site on the visitor's computer). Amazon.com also presents the user with a choice of products in a personalized store, based on previous purchases and an association analysis of similar users. It also makes special "Gold Box" offers that are good for a short amount of time. All these recommendations involve a detailed analysis of the visitor as well as the user's peer group, using clustering, sequence pattern discovery, association, and other mining techniques. Figure 7.6 illustrates this personalization at Amazon.com.

Software for analysis of Web usage is widely available. In addition, most major data mining products include the ability to analyze the data generated through a Web site's clickstream logs. Table 7.5 includes a partial listing of software products that are directly aimed at analysis of Web log data. More products in this category can be found online at **kdnuggets.com/software/web-mining.html** and other similar sites.

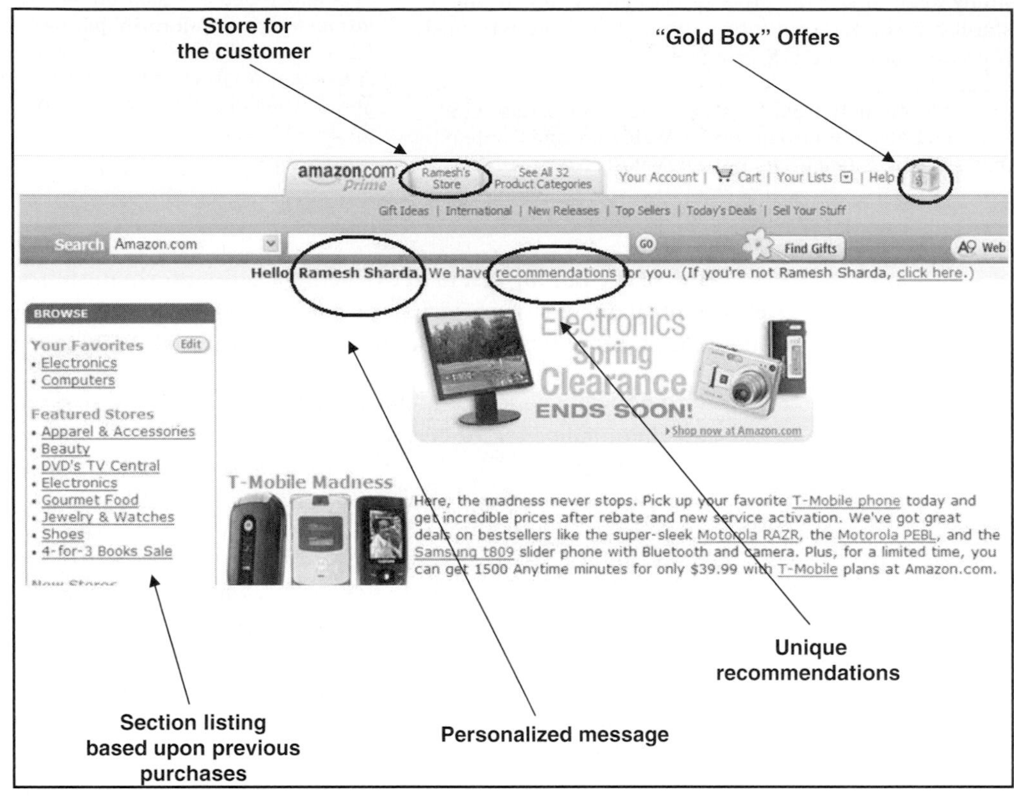

FIGURE 7.6 Example of Customization Using Web Usage Mining

TABLE 7.5 A Sample of Web Usage Mining Software

Product Name	*URL*	*Description*
Angoss Knowledge WebMiner	**angoss.com**	Combines ANGOSS KnowledgeSTUDIO and clickstream analysis
ClickTracks	**clicktracks.com**	Visitor patterns can be shown on Web site
LiveStats from DeepMetrix	**deepmetrix.com**	Real-time log analysis, live demo on site
Megaputer WebAnalyst	**http://megaputer.com/products/wm.php3**	Data and text mining capabilities
MicroStrategy Web Traffic Analysis Module	**microstrategy.com/Solutions/Applications/WTAM**	Traffic highlights, content analysis, and Web visitor analysis reports
SAS Web Analytics	**sas.com/solutions/webanalytics/**	Analyzes Web site traffic
SPSS Web Mining for Clementine	**spss.com/web_mining_for_clementine**	Extraction of Web events
WebTrends	**webtrends.com**	Data mining of Web traffic information.
XML Miner	**scientio.com**	A system and class library for mining data and text expressed in XML, using fuzzy logic expert system rules

Section 7.6 Review Questions

1. Define *Web mining*.
2. Identify the three main areas of Web mining.
3. What uses are made of Web structure mining?
4. What types of information do Web servers collect when you visit a Web page and engage in an interactive activity?
5. List five examples of observations a Web mining analyst may be able to make by Web usage data.
6. Identify applications developed by major e-commerce sites that may be based on Web usage mining.

Chapter Highlights

- Data mining is the discovery of knowledge in databases. It is often done on data in data warehouses.
- Companies use data mining to better understand their customers and optimize their operations.
- Data mining applications are in virtually every area of business and government, including health care, finance, marketing, and homeland security.
- Four broad categories of algorithms are used in data mining: classification, clustering, association, and sequence discovery.
- Classification methods learn from previous examples containing inputs and the resulting class, and they are able to classify future patterns.
- Clustering partitions pattern records into segments or clusters. Each segment's members share similar qualities.
- Data mining can be hypothesis driven or discovery drive. Hypothesis-driven data mining begins with a proposition by the user. Discovery-driven data mining is a more open-ended expedition.
- A number of different algorithms are commonly used for classification. Commercial implementations include ID3, C4.5, C5, CART, and SPRINT.
- Using decision trees involves building a tree to partition the data by branching along different attributes so that the leaf node has all patterns of one class.
- Using the Gini index and using information gain (entropy) are two ways to determine branching choices in a decision tree.
- The Gini index measures the purity of a sample. If everything in a sample belongs to one class, the Gini index value is zero.
- Cluster algorithms are used where the data records do not have pre-defined class identifiers. That is, we do not know as to what class a particular record belongs.
- Cluster algorithms compute measures of similarity in order to group similar patterns more closely.
- Similarly to other initiatives, a data mining project must follow a project management process.
- KDD is a process of using data mining to discover patterns in data.
- Text mining is the application of data mining to text files. Given that a great deal of information is in text form, text mining is growing fast.
- Text mining is closely related to information extraction, natural language processing, and document summarization.
- Text mining entails creating numeric indices from unstructured text and then applying data mining algorithms to these indices.
- Web mining can be defined as the discovery and analysis of interesting and useful information from the Web, about the Web, and usually using Web-based tools.
- Web mining can be viewed as consisting of three areas: Web content mining, Web structure mining, and Web usage mining.
- Web content mining refers to the automatic extraction of useful information from Web pages. It may be used to enhance search results produced by search engines.
- Web structure mining refers to generating interesting information from the links included in Web pages. This is used in Google's page rand algorithm to order the display of pages, for example.
- Web structure mining can also be used to identify the members of a specific community and perhaps even the roles of the members in the community.

- Web usage mining refers to developing useful information through analysis of Web server logs, user profiles, and transaction information.
- Web usage mining can assist in better CRM, personalization, site navigation modifications, and improved business models.
- Data, text, and Web mining are emerging as critical components of the next generation of IT tools to enabling organizations to compete successfully.

Key Terms

- association
- classification
- clustering
- data mining
- decision tree
- discovery-driven data mining
- entropy
- Gini index
- hypothesis-driven data mining
- knowledge discovery in databases (KDD)
- sequence discovery
- text mining
- Web content mining
- Web mining
- Web structure mining
- Web usage mining

Questions for Discussion

1. Explain the relationship between OLAP and data mining.
2. Discuss what an organization should consider before making a decision to purchase data mining software.
3. Distinguish data mining from other analytic tools.
4. Define *data mining* and list its major technologies.
5. Differentiate data mining, text mining, and Web mining.
6. Distinguish between KDD and data mining. Explain how the Web is affecting BI/business analytics methods and technologies.
7. Discuss what an organization should consider before making a decision to purchase data mining software.
8. Distinguish data mining from other analytic tools.
9. Explain the process of text mining.
10. Describe why visualization is so important in BI.
11. In what situations might classification and clustering software be used together?
12. Discuss why text mining is not the same thing as natural language processing.

Exercises

Teradata University and Other Hands-on Exercises

1. Visit **teradatastudentnetwork.com**. Identify cases about data mining. Describe recent developments in the field.
2. Go to **teradatastudentnetwork.com** or the URL given by your instructor. Locate Web seminars related to data mining. In particular, locate a seminar given by C. Imhoff and T. Zouqes. Watch the Web seminar. Then answer the following questions:
   a. What are some of the interesting applications of data mining?
   b. What types of payoffs and costs can organizations expect from data mining initiatives?
3. For this exercise, your goal is to build a model to identify inputs or predictors that differentiate risky customers from others (based on patterns pertaining to previous customers) and then use those inputs to predict the new risky customers. This sample case is typical for this domain.

   The sample data to be used in this exercise are in Online File W8.2, in the file CreditRisk.xls. The data set has 425 cases and 15 variables pertaining to past and current customers who borrowed from a bank for various reasons. The data set contains various information related to the customers, financial standing, reason for the loan, employment, demographic information, and the outcome or dependent variable for credit standing, classifying each case as good or bad, based on the institution's past experience. Take 400 of the cases as training cases and set aside the other 25 for testing. Then build a decision tree model to learn the characteristics of the problem. Test its performance on the other 25 cases. Report on your model's learning and testing performance. Prepare a report that identifies the decision tree model and, training parameters, as well as the resulting performance on the test set. Use any decision tree software.

(This exercise is courtesy of StatSoft, Inc., based on a German data set from **ftp://ftp.ics.uci.edu/pub/machine-learning-databases/statlog/german** renamed CreditRisk and altered.)

Exercises

Team Assignments and Role-Playing

1. Examine how new data-capture devices such as radio frequency identification (RFID) tags help organizations accurately identify and segment their customers for activities such as targeted marketing. Many of these applications involve data mining. Scan the literature and the Web and then propose five potential new data mining applications of RFID technology. What issues could arise if a country's laws required such devices to be embedded in everyone's body for a national identification system?

2. Interview administrators in your college or executives in your organization to determine how data warehousing, data mining, OLAP, and visualization BI/DSS tools could assist them in their work. Write a proposal describing your findings. Include cost estimates and benefits in your report.

3. There is a very good repository of data that have been used to test the performance of many machine learning algorithms. This repository can be accessed at **ics.uci.edu/~mlearn/MLRepository.html.** Some of the data sets are meant to test the limits of current machine learning algorithms and compare their performance with new approaches to learning. However, some of the smaller data sets can be useful for exploring the functionality of any data mining software or the software that is available as companion software with this book, such as STATISTICA DataMiner. Download at least one data set from this repository (e.g., Credit Screening Databases, Housing Database). Then apply decision tree or clustering methods, as appropriate. Prepare a report on your results. (Some of these exercises may even be proposed as semester-long projects for term papers, for example.)

4. Consider the following data set, which includes three attributes and a classification for admission decisions into an MBA program:

GMAT	GPA	Quantitative GMAT Score (percentile)	Decision
650	2.75	35	No
580	3.50	70	No
600	3.50	75	Yes
450	2.95	80	No
700	3.25	90	Yes
590	3.50	80	Yes
400	3.85	45	No
640	3.50	75	Yes
540	3.00	60	?
690	2.85	80	?
490	4.00	65	?

   a. Using the data shown here as examples, develop your own manual expert rules for decision making.

   b. Build a decision tree by using SPRINT (i.e., the Gini index). You can build it using manual calculations or a spreadsheet to perform the basic calculations.

   c. Use an automated decision tree software program to build a tree for the same data.

Exercises

Internet Exercises

1. Go to **cs.ualberta.ca/~aixplore/**, which is a project called AI Exploratorium. Click the Decision Tree link. Read the narrative on basketball game statistics. Examine the data and then build a decision tree. Report your impressions of the accuracy of this decision tree. Also, explore effects of different algorithms.

2. Survey some data mining tools and vendors. Start with **fairisaac.com** and **egain.com.** Also consult **dmreview.com** and identify some data mining products and service providers that are not mentioned in this chapter.

3. Find recent cases of successful data mining applications. Try data mining vendors and look for cases or success stories. Prepare a report summarizing five new case studies.
4. Go to Web sites (especially those of SAS, SPSS, Cognos, Teradata, StatSoft, and Fair Isaac) and look at success stories for BI (OLAP and data mining) tools. What do you find in common among the various success stories? How do they differ?
5. Go to **statsoft.com.** Select Downloads and download at least three white papers of applications. Which of these applications may have used the data/text/Web mining techniques discussed in this chapter?
6. Go to **sas.com.** Select Downloads and download at least three white papers of applications. Which of these applications may have used the data/text/Web mining techniques discussed in this chapter?
7. Go to **spss.com.** Select Downloads and download at least three white papers of applications. Which of these applications may have used the data/text/Web mining techniques discussed in this chapter?
8. Go to **teradata.com.** Select Downloads and download at least three white papers of applications. Which of these applications may have used the data/text/Web mining techniques discussed in this chapter?
9. Go to **fairisaac.com.** Select Downloads and download at least three white papers of applications. Which of these applications may have used the data/text/Web mining techniques discussed in this chapter?
10. Go to **salfordsystems.com.** Select Downloads and download at least three white papers of applications. Which of these applications may have used the data/text/Web mining techniques discussed in this chapter?
11. Go to **rulequest.com.** Select Downloads and download at least three white papers of applications. Which of these applications may have used the data/text/Web mining techniques discussed in this chapter?
12. Go to **kdnuggets.com.** Explore the sections on applications as well as software. Find names of at least three additional packages for data mining and text mining.

End of Chapter Application Case

Hewlett-Packard and Text Mining

Hewlett-Packard Company (HP), founded in 1939 by William R. Hewlett and David Packard, is headquartered in Palo Alto, California. The company provides products, technologies, solutions, and services to individuals, small- and medium-sized businesses, and large enterprises on a global basis. HP also offers management software solutions that enable enterprise customers to manage their IT infrastructure, operations, applications, IT services, and business processes, as well as carrier-grade platforms for various applications. Some of HP's popular product categories are commercial and consumer personal computers, workstations, handheld computing devices, inkjet printers, laser printers, digital entertainment systems, calculators and related accessories, software and services, digital photography and entertainment, graphics, imaging and printer supplies for printer hardware, printing supplies, scanning devices, and network infrastructure products, including Ethernet switch products. Retailers form the distribution channel of the company. The company also sells through distribution partners, original equipment manufacturers, and systems integrators.

TEXT MINING

Customers of HP communicate with the company through millions of e-mails. Structured data analysis is effective in finding out parameters such as from whom, when, where, and how the messages originated. A wealth of information would be available if mining techniques could find out why these e-mails were sent. One of the common interaction points between the customer and the company is the call center. HP is impressed by the business insights that could be culled from communications, such as word documents, e-mails, and other sources. The combination of the structured and unstructured data can create a tremendous potential for companies to find valuable business insights.

SYSTEM

The standard tools that HP previously used could not report useful information from customer-related communications. Now, HP used SAS Institute's Text Miner to uncover analytical insights from customer-related data in call center applications and then standardized those insights. HP implemented Text Miner to combine structured data and text data to produce a hybrid structured/unstructured data set that is stored in a Microsoft SQL Server database with an Analysis Services OLAP engine. The system, today, encompasses 300,000 text documents and is roughly 50 gigabytes in size, covering an 18-month period and three call centers.

HP implemented Executive Viewer, a Web-based tool developed by Temtec (**temtec.com**) that enables HP to augment the OLAP cubes with predictive modeling, loyalty scores, and customer differentiations created by SAS Enterprise Miner.

PROCESS

Various concepts, such as products used, call frequency, and common customer issues are used to aggregate text data; the result is consolidated into probabilistic text clusters. This consolidated cluster is then combined with the structured data from third-party providers. HP can now combine and analyze structured data such as revenue with customer desires, attitudes, and needs.

Text analysis is challenging due to dimensionality and data dispersal. Different customer databases contain different structured information that could be integrated without much difficulty. The challenge lies in combining the structured data with unstructured data from text. SAS Text Miner uses a technique called *singular value decomposition*. Text mining software includes a pre-built dictionary of words and synonym lists; it is an overwhelming task for the organization to customize the text information generated in its business environments. Text data are available at various sources that are outside the realms of traditional data warehousing. Some of the largest challenges that SAS Text Miner faces are customer activity at the HP Web site as well as finding insights into the businesses of HP's customers.

In addition to the major application of text mining, SAS Text Miner could be used proactively on customer Web sites to generate insights into the customer needs that HP could satisfy. The tool could also be used to analyze multiple suppliers/vendors with various numbers and descriptions in text.

RESULTS

SAS Text Miner was successfully able to develop standard data definitions and product classification models with more than 80 percent accuracy. The system is now being used to support HP in contributing to the top line through improved cross-selling, targeted marketing, customer retention, and better anticipation of customer needs. The information generated from structured/unstructured data now supports multiple business users in various departments.

Sources: M. Hammond, "BI Case Study: What's in a Word? For Hewlett-Packard, It's Customer Insight." *Business Intelligence Journal*, Vol. 9, No. 3, Summer 2004, p. 48–51; and B. Beal, "Text Mining: A Golden Opportunity for HP," *SearchCRM.com*, June 6, 2005, **searchdatamanagement.techtarget.com/originalContent/0,289142,sid91_gci1136611,00.html** (accessed April 2006).

QUESTIONS FOR THE CASE

1. What is the practical application of text mining?
2. How do you think text mining techniques could be used in other businesses?
3. What were HP's challenges in text mining? How were they overcome?
4. In what other areas, in your opinion, can HP use text mining?

References

Bhandari, I., E. Colet, J. Parker, Z. Pines, R. Pratap, and K. Ramanujam. (1997). "Advanced Scout: Data Mining and Knowledge Discovery in NBA Data." Data Mining and Knowledge Discovery, Vol. 1,. No. 1, pp. 121–125

Buck, N. (December 2000/January 2001). "Eureka! Knowledge Discovery." *Software Magazine*.

Cao, J., J.M. Crews, M. Lin, J.K. Burgoon, and J.F. Nunamaker, Jr. (2003, June 2–3). "Designing Agent99 Trainer: A Learner-Centered, Web-Based Training System for Deception Detection." *Proceedings of the First NSF/NIJ Symposium on Intelligence and Security Informatics (ISI 2003)*, Tucson, AZ, pp. 358–365.

Cavoukian, A (1998). Data Mining: Staking A Claim on Your Privacy, Report by Information and Privacy Commissioner, Ontario, Canada. **ipc.on.ca/index.asp?navid=468fid1=342** (accessed August 2006).

Chan, P.K., W. Phan, A. Prodromidis, and S. Stolfo. (1999, November/December). "Distributed Data Mining in Credit Card Fraud Detection," *IEEE Intelligent Systems*.

Copeland, L. (2001, October 22). "Developers Approach Extreme Programming with Caution." *Computerworld*.

Davenport, T.H. (2006, January). "Competing on Analytics." *Harvard Business Review*.

Dunham, M. (2003). *Data Mining: Introductory and Advanced Topics*. Upper Saddle River, NJ: Prentice Hall.

Ellingsworth, M., and D. Sullivan. (2003, July). "Text Mining Improves Business Intelligence and Predictive Modeling in Insurance." *DM Review*.

Etzioni, O. (1996). "The World Wide Web: Quagmire or Gold Mine." *Communications of the ACM*, Vol. 39, No. 11.

Fadlalla, A., and C-H. Lin. (2001, August). "An Analysis of the Applications of Neural Networks in Finance." *Interfaces*,

Fayyad, U., G. Piatetsky-Shapiro, and P. Smyth. (1996). "From Knowledge Discovery in Databases." *AI Magazine*, Vol. 17, No. 3.

Finlay, D. (2001, April 15). "Real-Time Intelligence Scores Over OLAP," *Software Development Times*.

Grimes, S. (2001, June 13). "Mining a Demographic Mother Lode." *Intelligent Enterprise*.

Glymour, C., D. Madigan, D. Pregibon, and P. Smyth. (1997). "Statistical Themes and Lessons for Data Mining." *Data Mining and Knowledge Discovery*, Vol. 1, No. 1.

Groth, R. (1998). *Data Mining: A Hands-on Approach for Business Professionals*. Upper Saddle River, NJ: Prentice Hall.

Hoffman, T. (1999, April 19). "Insurers Mine for Age-Appropriate Offering." *Computer World*.

Hoffman, T. (1998, December 7). "Banks Turn to IT to Reclaim Most Profitable Customers." *Computer World*.

Kleinberg, K.M. (1998, January 25–27). "Authoritative Sources in Hyperlinked Environment," *Proceedings of the Ninth Annual ACM-SIAM Symposium on Discrete Algorithms*, San Francisco.

Morris, S.A., and K.W. Boyack. (2005, July 24–28). "Visualizing 60 Years of Anthrax Research." *Proceedings of the10th International Conference of the International Society for Scientometrics and Informetrics*, Stockholm, Sweden.

Nemati, H.R., and C.D. Barko. (2001, Winter). "Issues in Organizational Data Mining: A Survey of Current Practices." *Journal of Data Warehousing*, Vol. 6, No. 1.

Pallatto, J. (2002, February). "Business Tools Get Smart." *Internet World*.

Palshikar, G.K. (2001, April 16). "Matching Patterns." *Intelligent Enterprise*.

Quinlan, J.R. (1986, March). "Induction of Decision Trees." *Machine Learning*.

Statsoft.com. (2006). "Data Mining Techniques." **statsoft.com/textbook/stdatmin.html** (accessed August 2006).

Srivastava J., P. Desikan and V. Kumar (2002, November 1–3), "Web Mining: Accomplishments and Future Directions," *Proceedings of the US National Science Foundation Workshop on Next-Generation Data Mining* (NGDM), National Science Foundation, 2002, Baltimore, MD. **csee.umbc.edu/~kolari1/Mining/papers/srivastava.pdf** (accessed August 2006).

Zhou, Y., E. Reid, J. Qin, H. Chen, and G. Lai. (2005, September/October). "U.S. Domestic Extremist Groups on the Web: Link and Content Analysis." *IEEE Intelligent Systems*.

CHAPTER 8 Neural Networks for Data Mining

Learning Objectives

- Understand the concept and different types of artificial neural networks (ANN)
- Learn the advantages and limitations of ANN
- Understand how backpropagation neural networks learn
- Understand the complete process of using neural networks
- Appreciate the wide variety of applications of neural networks

Neural networks have emerged as advanced data mining tools in cases where other techniques may not produce satisfactory predictive models. As the term implies, neural networks have a biologically inspired modeling capability, but are essentially statistical modeling tools. In this chapter, we study the basics of neural network modeling, some specific applications, and the process of implementing a neural network project.

8.1 OPENING VIGNETTE: USING NEURAL NETWORKS TO PREDICT BEER FLAVORS WITH CHEMICAL ANALYSIS

Coors Brewers Ltd., based in Burton-upon-Trent, Britain's brewing capital, is proud of having the United Kingdom's top beer brands, a 20 percent share of the market, years of experience, and of the best people in the business. Popular brands include Carling (the country's best-selling lager), Grolsch, Coors Fine Light Beer, Sol, and Korenwolf.

PROBLEM

Today's customer is confronted with variety of options regarding what he or she drinks. A drinker's choice depends on various factors, such as mood, venue, and occasion. The goal of Coors is to ensure that the customer chooses a Coors brand every time.

According to Coors, creativity is the key to being successful in the long term. To be the customer's choice brand, Coors needs to be creative and anticipative about the customer's ever-changing moods. An important issue with beers is the flavor; each beer has a distinctive flavor. These flavors are mostly determined through panel tests. However, such tests take time. If Coors could understand the beer flavor based solely on its chemical composition, it would open up new avenues to create beer that would suit customer expectations.

The relationship between chemical analysis and beer flavor is not clearly understood yet. Substantial data exists about its chemical composition and sensory analysis. Coors needed a mechanism to link those two together. Neural networks were applied to create the link between chemical composition and sensory analysis.

SOLUTION

Over the years, Coors Brewers Ltd. has accumulated a significant amount of data related to the final product analysis, which has been supplemented by sensory data provided by the trained in-house testing panel. Some of the analytical inputs and sensory outputs are shown here:

Analytical Data: Inputs	*Sensory Data: Outputs*
Alcohol	Alcohol
Color	Estery
Calculated bitterness	Malty
Ethyl acetate	Grainy
Iso butyl acetate	Burnt
Ethyl butyrate	Hoppy
Iso amyl acetate	Toffee
Ethyl hexanoate	Sweet

A single neural network, restricted to a single quality and flavor, was first used to model the relationship between the analytical and sensory data. The neural network was based on a package solution supplied by NeuroDimension, Inc. (**nd.com**). The neural network consisted of a multilayer perceptron (MLP) architecture with two hidden layers. Data were normalized within the network, thereby enabling comparison between the results for the various sensory outputs. The neural network was trained (to learn the relationship between the inputs and outputs) through the presentation of many combinations of relevant input/output combinations. When there was no observed improvement in the network error in the last 100 epochs, training was automatically terminated. Training was carried out 50 times to ensure that a considerable mean network error could be calculated for comparison purposes. Prior to each training run, a different training and cross-validation data set was presented by randomizing the source data records, thereby removing any bias.

This technique produced poor results, due to two major factors. First, concentrating on a single product's quality meant that the variation in the data was pretty low. The neural network could not extract useful relationships from the data. Second, it was probable that only one subset of the provided inputs would have an impact on the selected beer flavor. Performance of the neural network was affected by "noise" created by inputs that had no impact on flavor.

A more diverse product range was included in the training range to address the first factor. It was more challenging to identify the most important analytical inputs. This challenge was addressed by using a software switch that enabled the neural network to be trained on all possible combinations of inputs. The switch was not used to disable a significant input; if the significant input were disabled, we could expect the network error to increase. If the disabled input was insignificant, then the network error would either remain unchanged or be reduced due to the removal of noise. This approach is called an *exhaustive search* because all possible combinations are evaluated. The technique, although conceptually simple, was computationally impractical with the numerous inputs; the number of possible combinations was 16.7 million per flavor.

A more efficient method of searching for the relevant inputs was required. A genetic algorithm (see Chapter 13) was the solution to the problem. A genetic algorithm was able to manipulate the different input switches in response to the error term from the neural network. The objective of the genetic algorithm was to minimize the network error term. When this minimum was reached, the switch settings would identify the analytical inputs that were most likely to predict the flavor.

RESULTS

After determining what inputs were relevant, it was possible to identify which flavors could be predicted more skillfully. The network was trained using the relevant inputs previously identified multiple times. Before each training run, the network data were randomized to ensure that a different training and cross-validation data set was used. Network error was recorded after each training run. The testing set used for assessing the performance of the trained network contained approximately 80 records out of the sample data. The neural network accurately predicted a few flavors by using the chemical inputs. For example, "burnt" flavor was predicted with a correlation coefficient of 0.87.

Today, a limited number of flavors are being predicted by using the analytical data. Sensory response is extremely complex, with many potential interactions and hugely variable sensitivity thresholds. Standard instrumental analysis tends to be of gross parameters, and for practical and economical reasons, many flavor-active compounds are simply not measured. The relationship of flavor and analysis can be effectively modeled only if a large number of flavor-contributory analytes are considered. What is more, in addition to the obvious flavor-active materials, mouth-feel and physical contributors should also be considered in the overall sensory profile.

With further development of the input parameters, the accuracy of the neural network models will improve.

Sources: C.I. Wilson and L. Threapleton, "Application of Artificial Intelligence for Predicting Beer Flavours from Chemical Analysis," *Proceedings of the 29th European Brewery Congress*, Dublin, May 17–22, 2003, **neurosolutions.com/resources/apps/beer.html** (accessed April 2006); R. Nischwitz, M. Goldsmith, M. Lees, P. Rogers, and L. MacLeod, "Developing Functional Malt Specifications for Improved Brewing Performance," *The Regional Institute Ltd.*, **regional.org.au/au/abts/1999/nischwitz.htm** (accessed April 2006); and **coorsbrewers.com** (accessed April 2006).

Questions for the Opening Vignette

1. Why is beer flavor important to the profitability of Coors?
2. What is the objective of the neural network used at Coors?
3. Why were the results of the Coors neural network initially poor, and what was done to improve the results?

4. What benefits might Coors derive if this project is successful?
5. What modifications would you provide to improve the results of beer flavor prediction?

WHAT WE CAN LEARN FROM THIS VIGNETTE

As you will see in this chapter, applications of neural networks abound in many areas, from standard business problems of assessing creditworthiness of individuals to manufacturing, security, and health applications. This vignette illustrates an innovative application in a setting where human expertise may be considered the only way to assess quality. The vignette shows that the imagination of an analyst is the only limitation to exploring applications of data mining techniques in general and neural networks in particular. We also learn that in many real-life applications, we have to combine more than one advanced technique in order to create a useful application. In this particular situation, neural networks were combined with genetic algorithms (see Chapter 13), but other combinations are possible as well.

8.2 BASIC CONCEPTS OF NEURAL NETWORKS

Neural networks represent a brain metaphor for information processing. These models are biologically inspired rather than an exact replica of how the brain actually functions. Neural networks have been shown to be very promising systems in many forecasting applications and business classification applications due to their ability to "learn" from the data, their nonparametric nature (i.e., no rigid assumptions), and their ability to generalize. **Neural computing** refers to a pattern recognition methodology for machine learning. The resulting model from neural computing is often called an **artificial neural network (ANN)** or a *neural network*. Neural networks have been used in many business applications for pattern recognition, forecasting, prediction, and classification. Neural network computing is a key component of any data mining (see Chapter 7) tool kit. Applications of neural networks abound in finance, marketing, manufacturing, operations, information systems, and so on. Therefore, we devote this chapter to developing a better understanding of neural network models, methods, and applications.

The human brain possesses bewildering capabilities for information processing and problem solving that modern computers cannot compete with in many aspects. It has been postulated that a model or a system that is enlightened and supported by the results from brain research, with a structure similar to that of biological neural networks, could exhibit similar intelligent functionality. Based on this bottom-up postulation, ANN (also known as connectionist models, parallel distributed processing models, neuromorphic systems, or simply neural networks) have been developed as biologically inspired and plausible models for various tasks.

Biological neural networks are composed of many massively interconnected primitive biological neurons. Each neuron possesses *axons* and *dendrites*, finger-like projections that enable the neuron to communicate with its neighboring *neurons* by transmitting and receiving electrical and chemical signals. More or less resembling the structure of their counterparts, ANN are composed of interconnected, simple processing elements called *artificial neurons*. In processing information, the processing elements in an ANN operate concurrently and collectively in a similar fashion to biological neurons. ANN possess some desirable traits similar to those of biological neural networks, such as the capabilities of learning, self-organization, and fault tolerance.

Coming along a winding journey, ANN have been investigated by researchers for more than half a century. The formal study of ANN began with the pioneering work of McCulloch and Pitts in 1943. Stimulated by results of biological experiments and observations, McCulloch and Pitts (1943) introduced a simple model of a binary artificial neuron that captures some functions of a living neuron. Considering information processing machines as a means for modeling the brain, McCulloch and Pitts built their neural networks model using a large number of interconnected binary artificial neurons. Led by a school of researchers, neural network research was quite popular in the late 1950s and early 1960s. After a thorough analysis of an early neural network model (called the **perceptron**, which used no hidden layer) as well as a pessimistic evaluation of the research potential by Minsky and Papert in 1969, the interest in neural networks diminished.

During the past two decades, there has been an exciting resurgence in the studies of ANN due to the introduction of new network topologies, new activation functions, and new learning algorithms, as well as progress in neuroscience and cognitive science. On the one hand, advances in theory and methodology have overcome many obstacles that hindered neural network research a few decades ago. Evidenced by the appealing results of numerous studies, neural networks are gaining acceptance and popularity. On the other hand, as complex problems solvers, ANN have been applied to solve numerous problems in a variety of application settings. The desirable features in neural information processing make neural networks attractive for solving complex problems. The initial success in neural network applications has inspired renewed interest from industry and business.

BIOLOGICAL AND ARTIFICIAL NEURAL NETWORKS

The human brain is composed of special cells called **neurons**. These cells do not die when a human is injured (all other cells reproduce to replace themselves and then die). This phenomenon may explain why we retain information. Information storage spans sets of neurons. The estimated number of neurons in a human brain is 50 to 150 billion, of which there are more than 100 different kinds. Neurons are partitioned into groups called *networks*. Each network contains several thousand highly interconnected neurons. Thus, the brain can be viewed as a collection of neural networks.

The ability to learn and react to changes in our environment requires intelligence. The brain and the central nervous system control thinking and intelligent behavior. People who suffer brain damage have difficulty learning and reacting to changing environments. Even so, undamaged parts of the brain can often compensate with new learning.

A portion of a network composed of two cells is shown in Figure 8.1. The cell itself includes a **nucleus** (the central processing portion of the neuron). To the left of cell 1, the **dendrites** provide input signals to the cell. To the right, the **axon** sends output signals to cell 2 via the axon terminals. These axon terminals merge with the dendrites of cell 2. Signals can be transmitted unchanged, or they can be altered by synapses. A **synapse** is able to increase or decrease the strength of the connection from neuron to neuron and cause excitation or inhibition of a subsequent neuron. This is where information is stored.

An ANN model emulates a biological neural network. Neural computing actually uses a very limited set of concepts from biological neural systems (see Technology Insights 8.1). It is more of an analogy to the human brain than an accurate model of it. Neural concepts are usually implemented as software simulations of the massively parallel processes that involve processing elements (also called *artificial neurons*, or *neurodes*)

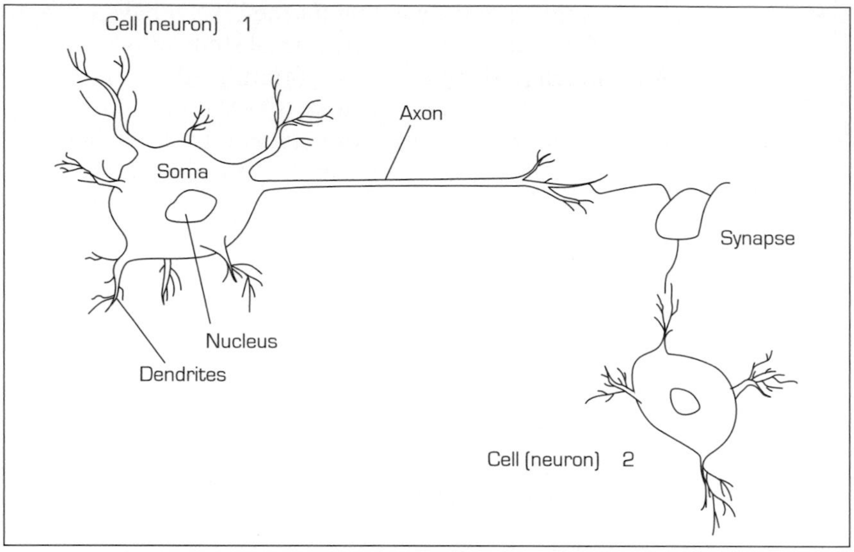

FIGURE 8.1 Portion of a Network: Two Interconnected Biological Cells

interconnected in a network architecture. The artificial neuron receives inputs analogous to the electrochemical impulses the dendrites of biological neurons receive from other neurons. The output of the artificial neuron corresponds to signals sent out from a biological neuron over its axon. These artificial signals can be changed by weights in a manner similar to the physical changes that occur in the synapses (see Figure 8.2).

Several ANN paradigms have been proposed for applications in a variety of problem domains. For example, see Application Case 8.2. Perhaps the easiest way to differentiate between the various models is on the basis of how these models structurally emulate the human brain, the way in which the neural model processes information and how the neural models learn to perform their designated tasks.

As they are biologically inspired, the main processing elements of a neural network are individual neurons, analogous to the brain's neurons. These artificial neurons

FIGURE 8.2 Processing Information in an Artificial Neuron

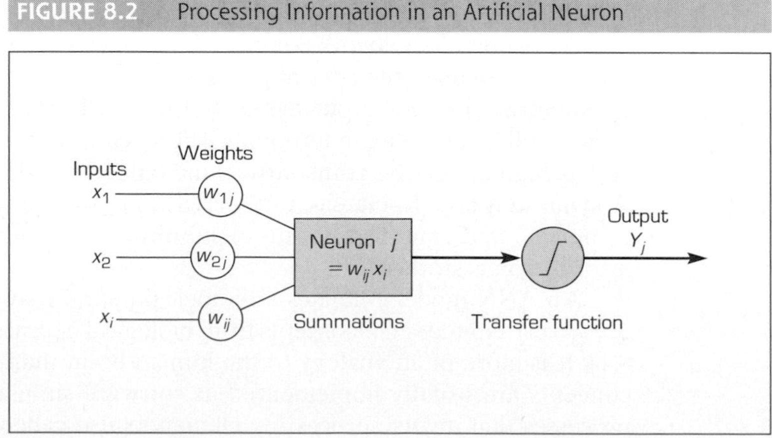

TECHNOLOGY INSIGHTS 8.1

The Relationship Between Biological and Artificial Neural Networks

The following list shows some of the relationships between biological and artificial networks:

Biological	Artificial
Soma	Node
Dendrites	Input
Axon	Output
Synapse	Weight
Slow speed	Fast speed
Many neurons (10^9)	Few neurons (a dozen to hundreds of thousands)

Zahedi (1993) talked about a dual role for ANN. We borrow concepts from the biological world to improve the design of computers. ANN technology is used for complex information processing and machine intelligence. On the other hand, neural networks can also be used as simple biological models to test hypotheses about "real" biological neuronal information processing. Of course, in the context of data mining, we are interested in the use of neural networks for machine learning and information processing.

Sources: L. Medsker and J. Liebowitz, *Design and Development of Expert Systems and Neural Networks*, Macmillan, New York, 1994, p. 163; and F. Zahedi, *Intelligent Systems for Business: Expert Systems with Neural Networks*, Wadsworth, Belmont, CA, 1993.

receive the sum "information" from other neurons or external input stimuli, perform a transformation on the inputs, and then pass on the transformed information to other neurons or external outputs. This is similar to how it is presently thought that the human brain works. Passing information from neuron to neuron can be thought of as a way to activate, or trigger a response from certain neurons based on the information or stimulus received.

Thus, how information is processed by a neural network is inherently a function of its structure. Neural networks can have one or more layers of neurons. These neurons can be highly or fully interconnected, or only certain layers can be connected together. Connections between neurons have an associated weight. In essence, the "knowledge" possessed by the network is encapsulated in these interconnection weights. Each neuron calculates a weighted sum of the incoming neuron values, transforms this input, and passes on its neural value as the input to subsequent neurons. Typically, although not always, this input/output transformation process at the individual neuron level is done in a nonlinear fashion.

Application Case 8.2

Neural Networks Help Reduce Telecommunications Fraud

The Forum of International Irregular Network Access (FIINA) estimates that telecommunications fraud results in a loss of US$55 billion per year worldwide. South Africa's largest telecom operator was losing over US$37 million per year to fraud. Subscription fraud—in which a customer either provides fraudulent details or gives valid details and then disappears—was the company's biggest cause of revenue leakage. By the time the telecom provider is alerted about the fraud, the fraudster has already moved to other target victims. Other types of fraud include phone card manipulation, which involves tampering and cloning of phone cards. In clip-on fraud, a fraudster clips on to customers' telephone lines and then sell calls to overseas destinations for a fraction of normal rates.

Minotaur, developed by Neural Technologies (**neuralt .com**), was implemented to prevent fraud. Minotaur uses a hybrid mixture of intelligent systems and traditional computing techniques to provide customer subscription and real-time call monitoring fraud detection. It processes data from numerous fields, such as event data records (e.g., switch/CDR, SS#7, IPDRs, PIN/authentication) and customer data (e.g., billing and payment, point of sale, provisioning), using a multistream analysis capacity. Frauds are detected on several levels, such as on an individual basis using specific knowledge about the subscriber's usage, and on a global basis, using generic knowledge about subscriber usage and known fraud patterns. The neural capability of Minotaur means it learns from experience, making use of adaptive feedback to keep up-to-date with changing fraud patterns. A combination of call/network data and subscriber information is profiled and then processed, using intelligent neural, rule-based, and case-based techniques. Probable frauds are identified, collected into cases, and tracked to completion by means of a powerful and flexible workflow-based operational process.

In the first three months of installation of this neural network–based software:

- The average fraud loss per case was reduced by 40 percent.
- The detection time was reduced by 83 percent.
- The average time taken to analyze suspected fraud cases was reduced by 75 percent.
- The average detection hit rate was improved by 74 percent.

The combination of neural, rule-based, and case-based technologies provides a fraud detection rate superior to that of conventional systems. Furthermore, the multistream analysis capability makes it extremely accurate.

Sources: Combating Fraud: How a Leading Telecom Company Solved a Growing Problem, **neuralt.com/iqs/dlsfa.list/ dlcpti.7/downloads.html**; A. Shukla, *Neural Technologies and Sevis Partner to Eliminate Fraudulent Calls in Fixed and Mobile Networks*, February 3, 2006, **news.tmcnet.com/news/-neural-sevis-fraud-mobile/2006/02/03/1340423.htm** (accessed April 2006); P.A. Estévez, M.H. Claudio, and C.A. Perez, *Prevention in Telecommunications Using Fuzzy Rules and Neural Networks*, **cec.uchile.cl/~pestevez/RI0.pdf** (accessed April 2006); and *Members and Associate Members Success Stories*, **gsm.org/about/membership/success/nt.shtml** (accessed April 2006).

ELEMENTS OF ANN

A neural network is composed of processing elements organized in different ways to form the network's structure. The basic processing unit is the neuron. A number of neurons are organized into a network. There are many ways to organize neurons; they are referred to as **topologies**. One popular approach, known as the feedforward-backpropagation paradigm (or simply **backpropagation**), allows all neurons to link the output in one layer to the input of the next layer, but it does not allow any feedback linkage (Haykin, 1999). This is the most commonly used paradigm.

Processing Elements

The **processing elements (PE)** of an ANN are artificial neurons. Each of the neurons receives inputs, processes them, and delivers a single output, as shown in Figure 8.2. The input can be raw input data or the output of other processing elements. The output can be the final result (e.g., 1 means yes, 0 means no), or it can be inputs to other neurons.

Network Structure

Each ANN is composed of a collection of neurons, grouped in layers. A typical structure is shown in Figure 8.3. Note the three layers: *input*, *intermediate* (called the *hidden layer*), and *output*. A **hidden layer** is a layer of neurons that takes input from the previous layer and converts those inputs into outputs for further processing. Several hidden layers can be placed between the input and output layers, although it is quite common to use only one hidden layer. In that case, the hidden layer simply converts inputs into a nonlinear combination and passes the transformed inputs to the output layer. The most common interpretation of the hidden layer is as a feature extraction mechanism. That is, the hidden layer converts the original inputs in the problem into some higher-level combinations of such inputs.

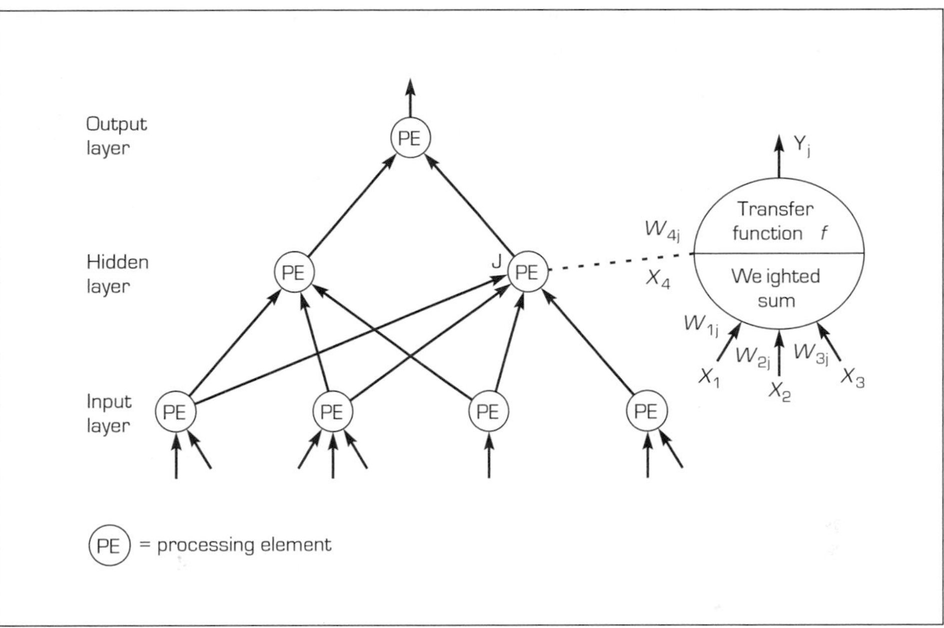

FIGURE 8.3 Neural Network with One Hidden Layer

Like a biological network, an ANN can be organized in several different ways (i.e., topologies or architectures); that is, the neurons can be interconnected in different ways. Therefore, ANN appear in many configurations called *architectures*. When information is processed, many of the processing elements perform their computations at the same time. This **parallel processing** resembles the way the brain works, and it differs from the serial processing of conventional computing.

Network Information Processing

Once the structure of a neural network is determined, information can be processed. We now present the major concepts related to the processing.

Inputs Each input corresponds to a single attribute. For example, if the problem is to decide on approval or disapproval of a loan, some attributes could be the applicant's income level, age, and home ownership. The numeric value, or representation, of an attribute is the input to the network. Several types of data, such as text, pictures, and voice, can be used as inputs. Preprocessing may be needed to convert the data to meaningful inputs from symbolic data or to scale the data.

Outputs The outputs of a network contain the solution to a problem. For example, in the case of a loan application, the outputs can be yes or no. The ANN assigns numeric values to the outputs, such as 1 for yes and 0 for no. The purpose of the network is to compute the values of the output. Often, postprocessing of the outputs is required because some networks use two outputs: one for yes and another for no. It is common to have to round the outputs to the nearest 0 or 1.

Connection Weights **Connection weights** are the key elements in an ANN. They express the relative strength (or mathematical value) of the input data or the many connections that transfer data from layer to layer. In other words, weights express the relative importance of each input to a processing element and, ultimately, the outputs.

Weights are crucial in that they store learned patterns of information. It is through repeated adjustments of weights that a network learns.

Summation Function The **summation function** computes the weighted sums of all the input elements entering each processing element. A summation function multiplies each input value by its weight and totals the values for a weighted sum Y. The formula for n inputs in one processing element (see Figure 8.4a) is:

$$Y = \sum_{i=1}^{n} X_i W_i$$

For the jth neuron of several processing neurons in a layer (see Figure 8.4b), the formula is:

$$Yj = \sum_{i=1}^{n} X_i W_{ij}$$

Transformation (Transfer) Function The summation function computes the internal stimulation, or activation level, of the neuron. Based on this level, the neuron may or

FIGURE 8.4 Summation Function for a Single Neuron (a) and Several Neurons (b)

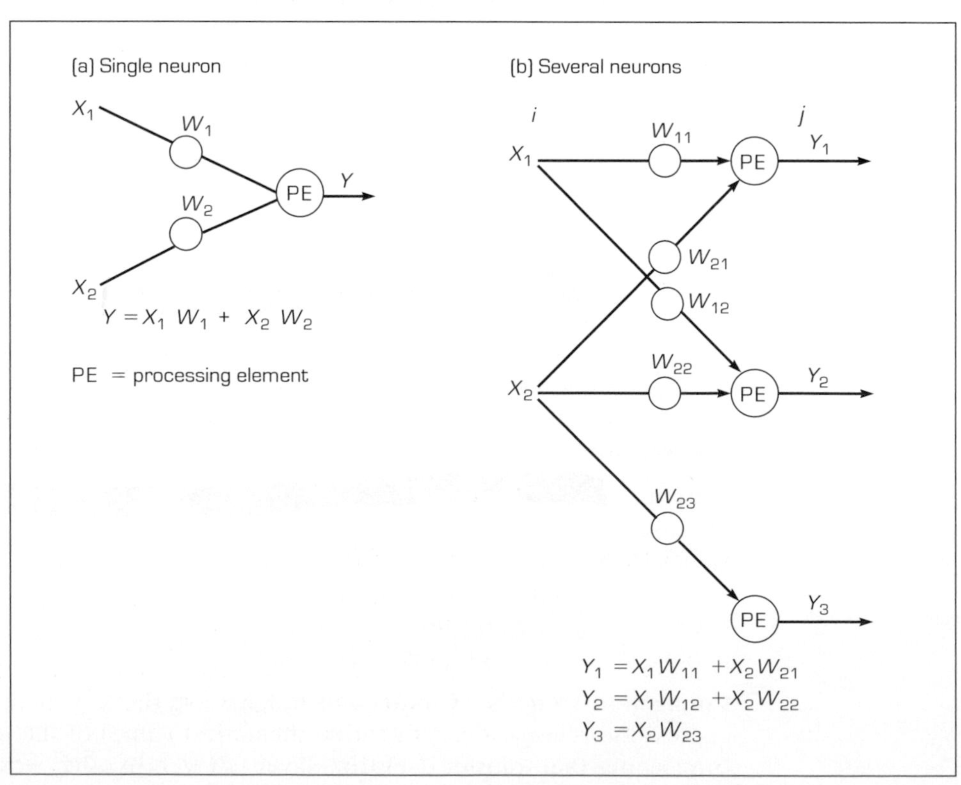

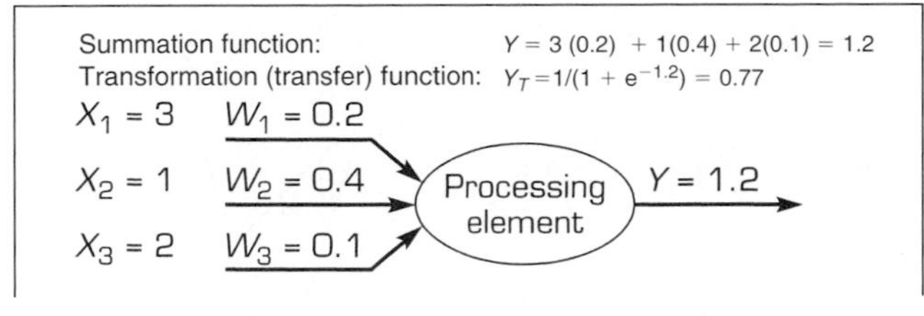

FIGURE 8.5 Example of ANN Functions

may not produce an output. The relationship between the internal activation level and the output can be linear or nonlinear. The relationship is expressed by one of several types of *transformation (transfer) functions*. The **transformation (transfer) function** combines (i.e., adds up) the inputs coming into a neuron from other neurons/sources and then produces an output based on the choice of the transfer function. Selection of the specific function affects the network's operation. The **sigmoid (logical activation) function** (or sigmoid *transfer function*) is an S-shaped transfer function in the range of 0 to 1, and it is a popular as well as useful nonlinear transfer function:

$$Y_T = 1/(1 + e^{-Y})$$

where Y_T is the transformed (i.e., normalized) value of Y (see Figure 8.5).

The transformation modifies the output levels to reasonable values (typically between 0 and 1). This transformation is performed before the output reaches the next level. Without such a transformation, the value of the output becomes very large, especially when there are several layers of neurons. Sometimes, instead of a transformation function, a *threshold value* is used. A **threshold value** is a hurdle value for the output of a neuron to trigger the next level of neurons. If an output value is smaller than the threshold value, it will not be passed to the next level of neurons. For example, any value of 0.5 or less becomes 0, and any value above 0.5 becomes 1. A transformation can occur at the output of each processing element, or it can be performed only at the final output nodes.

Hidden Layers

Complex practical applications require one or more hidden layers between the input and output neurons and a correspondingly large number of weights. Many commercial ANN include three and sometimes up to five layers, with each containing 10 to 1,000 processing elements. Some experimental ANN use millions of processing elements. Because each layer increases the training effort exponentially and also increases the computation required, the use of more than three hidden layers is rare in most commercial systems.

NEURAL NETWORK ARCHITECTURES

There are several effective neural network models and algorithms (see Haykin, 1999). Some of the most common are *backpropagation* (or *feedforward*), *associative memory*, and the *recurrent network*. The backpropagation architecture is shown in Figure 8.3. The other two architectures are shown in Figures 8.6 and 8.7.

Ultimately, the operation of the entire neural network model is driven by the task it is designed to address. For instance, neural network models have been used as classi-

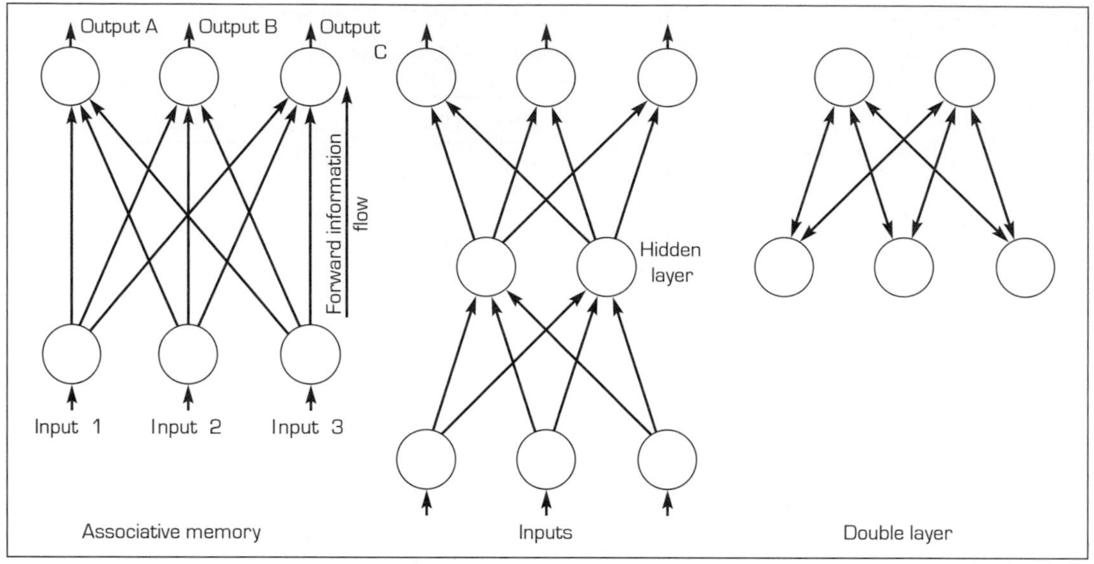

FIGURE 8.6 Neural Network Structures: Feedforward Flow

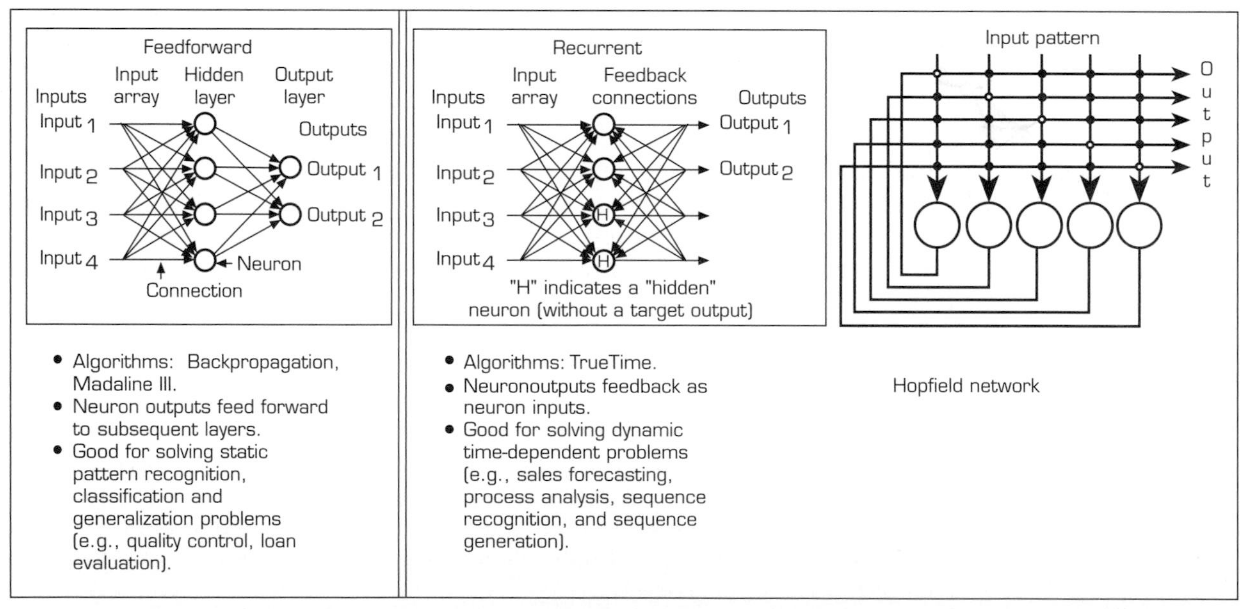

FIGURE 8.7 Recurrent Structure Compared with Feedforward Source

Source: Based on *PC AI*, May/June 1992, p. 35.

fiers, as forecasting tools, and as general optimizers. As shown later in this chapter, neural network classifiers are typically multilayer models in which information is passed from one layer to the next, with the ultimate goal of mapping an input to the network to a specific category, as identified by an output of the network. A neural model used as an optimizer, on the other hand, can be a single layer of neurons, highly interconnected, and can compute neuron values iteratively until the model converges to a stable state. This stable state would then represent an optimal solution to the problem under analysis.

Finally, how a network is trained to perform its desired task is another identifying model characteristic. Neural network learning can occur in either a supervised or unsupervised mode. In supervised learning, a sample training set is used to "teach" the network about its problem domain. This training set of exemplar cases (input and the desired output[s]) is iteratively presented to the neural network. Output of the network in its present form is calculated and compared to the desired output. The **learning algorithm** is the training procedure that an ANN uses. The learning algorithm being used determines how the neural interconnection weights are corrected due to differences in the actual and desired output for a member of the training set. Updating of the network's interconnection weights continues until the stopping criteria of the training algorithm are met (e.g., all cases must be correctly classified within a certain tolerance level).

Alternatively, in unsupervised learning, there are no target answers that the network tries to learn. Instead, the neural network learns a pattern through repeated exposure. Thus, this kind of learning can be envisioned as the neural network appropriately self-organizing or clustering its neurons related to the specific desired task.

Multilayer, feedforward neural networks are a class of models that show promise in classification and forecasting problems. As the name implies, these models structurally consist of multiple layers of neurons. Information is passed through the network in one direction, from the input layers of the network, through one or more hidden layers, toward the output layer of neurons. Neurons of each layer are connected only to the neurons of the subsequent layer.

Section 8.2 Review Questions

1. What is an ANN?
2. Explain the following terms: *neuron*, *axon*, and *synapse*.
3. How do weights function in an ANN?
4. What is the role of the summation function?
5. What is the role of the transformation function?

8.3 LEARNING IN ANN

An important consideration in an ANN is the use of an appropriate learning algorithm (or *training algorithm*). Learning algorithms specify the process by which a neural network learns the underlying relationship between input and outputs, or just among the inputs. There are hundreds of them. Learning algorithms in ANN can also be classified as supervised learning and unsupervised learning (see Figure 8.8).

Supervised learning uses a set of inputs for which the appropriate (i.e., desired) outputs are known. For example, a historical set of loan applications with the success or failure of the individual to repay the loan has a set of input parameters and presumed known outputs. In one type, the difference between the desired and actual outputs is used to calculate corrections to the weights of the neural network. A variation of this

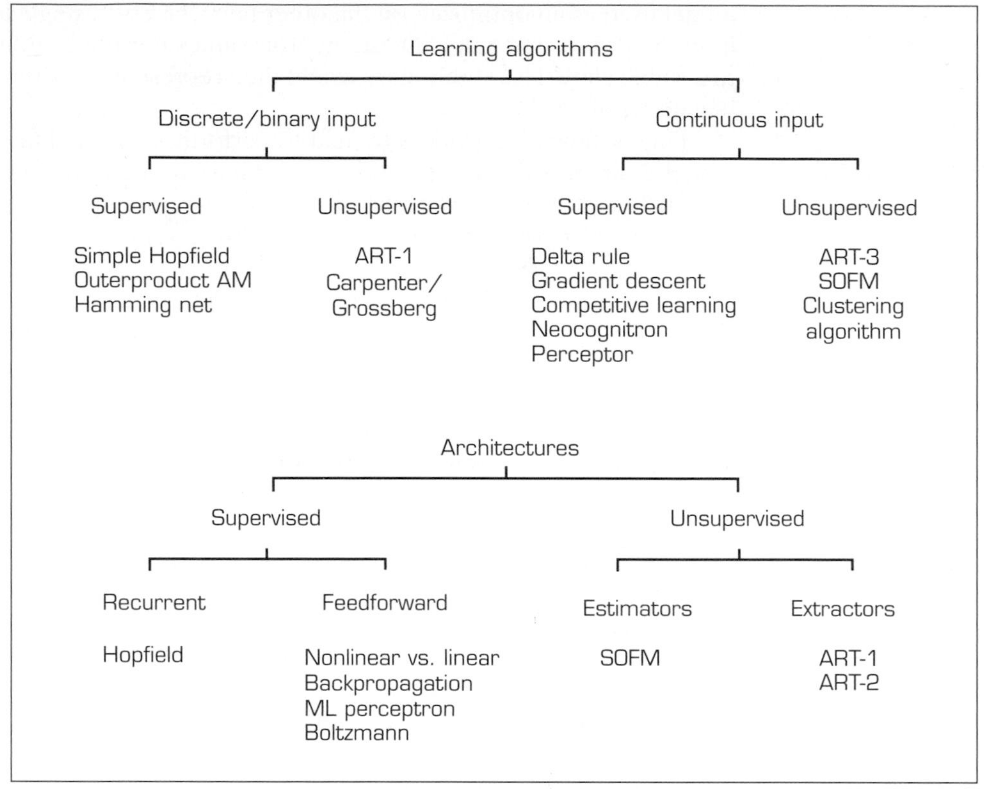

FIGURE 8.8 Taxonomy of ANN Architectures and Learning Algorithms

Source: Based on L. Medsker and J. Liebowitz, *Design and Development of Expert Systems and Neural Computing,* Macmillan, New York, 1994, p. 166.

approach simply acknowledges for each input trial whether the output is correct as the network adjusts weights in an attempt to achieve correct results. Examples of this type of learning are backpropagation and the Hopfield network (Hopfield, 1982). Application Case 8.3 illustrates an application of supervised learning at Microsoft for improving the response rate to target mailings to potential customers.

Application Case 8.3

Neural Networks Help Deliver Microsoft's Mail to the Intended Audience

Microsoft, the world leader in computer software, based in Redmond, Washington, uses BrainMaker neural network software from California Scientific (**calsci.com**) to maximize returns on direct mail. Every year, Microsoft sends about 40 million pieces of direct mail to 8.5 million registered customers, aimed at encouraging people to upgrade their software or to buy other related products. Generally, the first mailing includes everyone in the database. The key is to direct the second mailing to only those who are most likely to respond.

Several variables were fed into the BrainMaker neural network to get productive results. The first step was to identify the variables that were relevant and to eliminate the variables that did not cause any effect. The following were some of the significant variables:

- Recency, calculated in number of days, which measures the last time something was bought and registered. It is likely that the more recently a customer has bought something, the better the chance that he or she is going to buy more.
- First date to file, which is the date an individual made his or her first purchase. This is a measure of loyalty. Chances are high that a customer will buy again if he or she has been a loyal customer.
- The number of products bought and registered.
- The value of the products bought and registered, calculated at the standard reselling price.
- The number of days between the time the product came out and when it was purchased; research has shown that people who tend to buy things as soon as they are available are the key individuals to be reached.

Several other personal characteristics were also added and scored with yes/no responses.

Before training, the information obtained from the customer responses was fed into a format the network could use, and yes/no responses were transformed to numeric data. Minimums and maximums were set on certain variables.

Initially, the network was trained with 25 variables. The data were taken from seven or eight campaigns to make it varied and represent all aspects of the business, including the Mac and Windows sides, from high and low price-point products.

Before Microsoft began using BrainMaker, an average mailing would get a response rate of 4.9 percent. By using BrainMaker, the response rate has increased to 8.2 percent. The neural network was tested on data from 20 different campaigns with known results not used during training. The results showed repeated and consistent savings. An average mailing resulted in a 35 percent cost savings for Microsoft.

Sources: California Scientific, "Maximize Returns on Direct Mail with BrainMaker Neural Networks Software," **calsci.com/DirectMail.html**; and G. Piatesky-Shapiro, *ISR:Microsoft success Using Neural Network for Direct Marketing,* **Kdnuggets.com/news/94/n9.txt** (accessed March 2006).

In **unsupervised learning**, only input stimuli are shown to the network. The network is **self-organizing**; that is, it organizes itself internally so that each hidden processing element responds strategically to a different set of input stimuli (or groups of stimuli). No knowledge is supplied about which classifications (i.e., outputs) are correct, and those that the network derives may or may not be meaningful to the network developer (this is useful for cluster analysis). However, by setting model parameters, we can control the number of categories into which a network classifies the inputs. Regardless, a human must examine the final categories to assign meaning and determine the usefulness of the results. Examples of this type of learning are **adaptive resonance theory (ART)** (i.e., a neural network architecture that is aimed at being brain-like in unsupervised mode) and **Kohonen self-organizing feature maps** (i.e., neural network models for machine learning).

As mentioned earlier, many different and distinct neural network paradigms have been proposed for various decision-making domains. A neural model that has been shown appropriate for classification problems (e.g., bankruptcy prediction) is the feedforward MLP. Multilayered networks have continuously valued neurons (i.e., processing elements), are trained in a supervised manner, and consist of one or more layers of nodes (i.e., hidden nodes) between the input and output nodes. A typical feedforward neural network is shown in Figure 8.3. Input nodes represent where information is presented to the network, output nodes provide the "decision" of the neural network, and the hidden nodes via the interconnection weights contain the proper mapping of inputs to outputs (i.e., decisions).

The backpropagation learning algorithm is the standard way of implementing supervised training of feedforward neural networks. It is an iterative gradient-descent technique designed to minimize an error function between the actual output of the network and its desired output, as specified in the training set of data. Adjustment of the interconnection weights, which contain the mapping function per se, starts at the output node where the error measure is initially calculated and is then propagated back through the layers of the network, toward the input layer. More details are included in the following section.

THE GENERAL ANN LEARNING PROCESS

In supervised learning, the learning process is inductive; that is, connection weights are derived from existing cases. The usual process of learning involves three tasks (see Figure 8.9):

1. Compute temporary outputs.
2. Compare outputs with desired targets.
3. Adjust the weights and repeat the process.

When existing outputs are available for comparison, the learning process starts by setting the connection weights, either via rules or randomly. The difference between the actual output (Y or Y_T) and the desired output (Z) for a given set of inputs is an error called *delta* (in calculus, the Greek symbol delta, Δ, means "difference").

The objective is to minimize the delta (i.e., reduce it to 0 if possible), which is done by adjusting the network's weights. The key is to change the weights in the right direction, making changes that reduce the delta (i.e., error). We will show how this is done later.

Information processing with an ANN consists of an attempt to recognize patterns of activities (i.e., **pattern recognition**). During the learning stages, the interconnection weights change in response to training data presented to the system.

Different ANN compute delta in different ways, depending on the learning algorithm being used. There are hundreds of learning algorithms for various situations and configurations, some of which are discussed later in this chapter.

HOW A NETWORK LEARNS

Consider a single neuron that learns the inclusive OR operation—a classic problem in symbolic logic. There are two input elements, X_1 and X_2. If either or both of them have a positive value, the result is also positive. This can be shown as follows:

FIGURE 8.9 Learning Process of an ANN

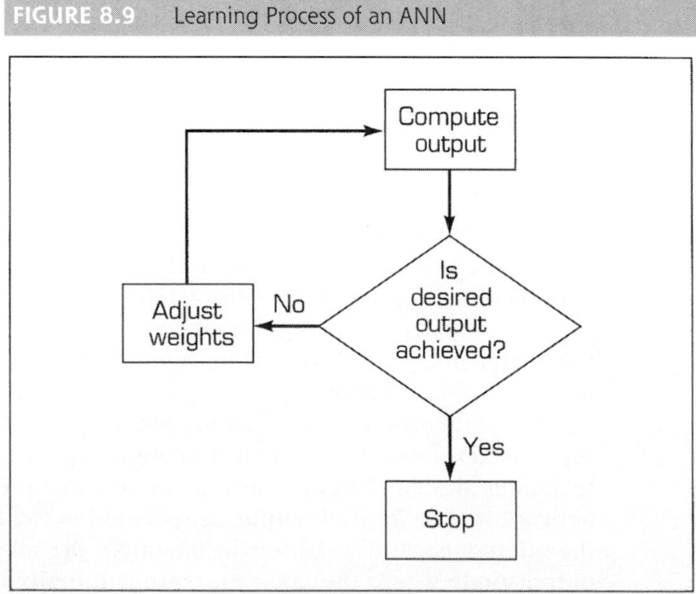

	Inputs		
Case	X_1	X_2	*Desired Results*
1	0	0	0
2	0	1	1 (positive)
3	1	0	1 (positive)
4	1	1	1 (positive)

The neuron must be trained to recognize the input patterns and classify them to give the corresponding outputs. The procedure is to present to the neuron the sequence of the four input patterns so that the weights are adjusted after each iteration (using feedback of the error found by comparing the estimate to the desired result). This step is repeated until the weights converge to a uniform set of values that allow the neuron to classify each of the four inputs correctly. The results shown in Table 8.1 were produced in Excel. In this simple example, a threshold function is used to evaluate the summation of input values. After calculating outputs, a measure of the error (i.e., delta) between the output and the desired values is used to update the weights, subsequently reinforcing the correct results. At any step in the process for a neuron j we have:

$$\text{delta} = Z_j - Y_j$$

where Z and Y are the desired and actual outputs, respectively. Then, the updated weights are:

$$W_i(\text{final}) = W_i(\text{initial}) + \text{alpha} \times \text{delta} \times X_i$$

where alpha is a parameter that controls how fast the learning takes place. This is called a **learning rate**. The choice of the learning rate parameter can have an impact on how fast (and how correctly) a neural network learns. A high value for the learning rate can

TABLE 8.1 Example of Supervised Learning[a]

				Initial				Final	
Step	X_1	X_2	Z	W_1	W_2	Y	*Delta*	W_1	W_2
1	0	0	0	0.1	0.3	0	0.0	0.1	0.3
	0	1	1	0.1	0.3	0	1.0	0.1	0.5
	1	0	1	0.1	0.5	0	1.0	0.3	0.5
	1	1	1	0.3	0.5	1	0.0	0.3	0.5
2	0	0	0	0.3	0.5	0	0.0	0.3	0.5
	0	1	1	0.3	0.5	0	0.0	0.3	0.7
	1	0	1	0.3	0.7	0	1.0	0.5	0.7
	1	1	1	0.5	0.7	1	0.0	0.5	0.7
3	0	0	0	0.5	0.7	0	0.0	0.5	0.7
	0	1	1	0.5	0.7	1	0.0	0.5	0.7
	1	0	1	0.5	0.7	0	1.0	0.7	0.7
	1	1	1	0.7	0.7	1	0.0	0.7	0.7
4	0	0	0	0.7	0.7	0	0.0	0.7	0.7
	0	1	1	0.7	0.7	1	0.0	0.7	0.7
	1	0	1	0.7	0.7	1	0.0	0.7	0.7
	1	1	1	0.7	0.7	1	0.0	0.7	0.7

[a]Parameters: alpha = 0.2; threshold = 0.5, output is zero if the sum ($W_1*X_1+W_2*X_2$) is not greater than 0.5.

lead to too much correction in the weight values, resulting in going back and forth among possible weights values and never reaching the optimal, which may lie somewhere in between the endpoints. Too low a learning rate may slow down the learning process. In practice, a neural network analyst may try using many different choices of learning rates to achieve optimal learning.

Most implementations of the learning process also include a counterbalancing parameter called *momentum* to provide a balance to the learning rate. Essentially, whereas learning rate is aimed at correcting for the error, **momentum** is aimed at slowing down the learning. Many of the software programs available for neural networks today can automatically select these parameters for the user or let the user experiment with many different combinations of such parameters.

As shown in Table 8.1, each calculation uses one of the X_1 and X_2 pairs and the corresponding value for the OR operation, along with the initial values W_1 and W_2 of the neuron's weights. Initially, the weights are assigned random values, and the learning rate, alpha, is set low. Delta is used to derive the final weights, which then become the initial weights in the next iteration (i.e., row).

The initial values of weights for each input are transformed using the equation shown earlier to assign the values that are used with the next input (i.e., row). The threshold value (0.5) sets the output Y to 1 in the next row if the weighted sum of inputs is greater than 0.5; otherwise, Y is set to 0. In the first step, two of the four outputs are incorrect (delta = 1), and a consistent set of weights has not been found. In subsequent steps, the learning algorithm improves the results, until it finally produces a set of weights that give the correct results ($W_1 = W_2 = 0.7$ in step 4 of Table 8.1). Once determined, a neuron with these weight values can quickly perform the OR operation.

In developing an ANN, an attempt is made to fit the problem characteristic to one of the known learning algorithms. There are software programs for all the different algorithms, such as backpropagation, which we describe next. Many variants of this algorithm exist, but the core concepts of them all are similar.

BACKPROPAGATION

Backpropagation (short for *back-error propagation*) is the most widely used supervised learning algorithm in neural computing (Principe et al., 2000). It is very easy to implement. A backpropagation network includes one or more hidden layers. This type of network is considered feedforward because there are no interconnections between the output of a processing element and the input of a node in the same layer or in a preceding layer. Externally provided correct patterns are compared with the neural network's output during (supervised) training, and feedback is used to adjust the weights until the network has categorized all the training patterns as correctly as possible (the error tolerance is set in advance).

Starting with the output layer, errors between the actual and desired outputs are used to correct the weights for the connections to the previous layer (see Figure 8.10). For any output neuron j, the error (delta) = $(Z_j - Y_j)\ (df/dx)$, where Z and Y are the desired and actual outputs, respectively. Using the sigmoid function, $f = [1 + \exp(-x)]^{-1}$, where x is proportional to the sum of the weighted inputs to the neuron, is an effective way to compute the output of a neuron in practice. With this function, the derivative of the sigmoid function $df/dx = f(1 - f)$ and the error is a simple function of the desired and actual outputs. The factor $f(1 - f)$ is the *logistic function*, which serves to keep the error correction well bounded. The weights of each input to the jth neuron are then changed in proportion to this calculated error. A more complicated expression can be derived to work backward in a similar way from the output neurons through the hidden

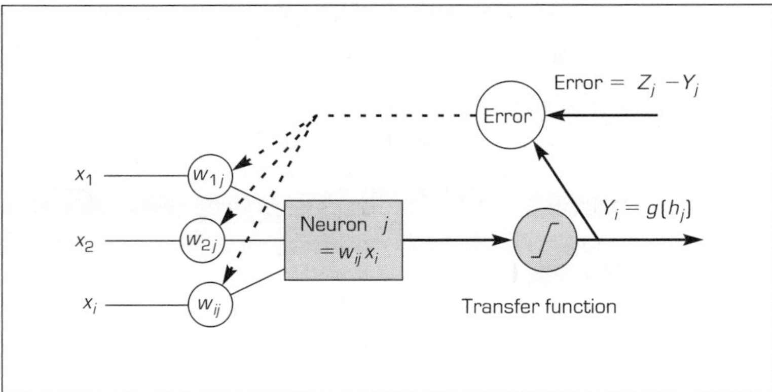

FIGURE 8.10 Backpropagation of Errors for a Single Neuron

layers to calculate the corrections to the associated weights of the inner neurons. This complicated method is an iterative approach to solving a nonlinear optimization problem that is very similar in meaning to the one characterizing multiple-linear regression.

The learning algorithm includes the following procedures:

1. Initialize weights with random values and set other parameters.
2. Read in the input vector and the desired output.
3. Compute the actual output via the calculations, working forward through the layers.
4. Compute the error.
5. Change the weights by working backward from the output layer through the hidden layers.

This procedure is repeated for the entire set of input vectors until the desired output and the actual output agree within some predetermined tolerance. Given the calculation requirements for one iteration, a large network can take a very long time to train; therefore, in one variation, a set of cases are run forward and an aggregated error is fed backward to speed up learning. Sometimes, depending on the initial random weights and network parameters, the network does not converge to a satisfactory performance level. When this is the case, new random weights must be generated, and the network parameters, or even its structure, may have to be modified before another attempt is made. Current research is aimed at developing algorithms and using parallel computers to improve this process. For example, genetic algorithms (described in Chapters 12 and 13) can be used to guide the selection of the network structure, as mentioned in the opening vignette.

Section 8.3 Review Questions

1. Briefly describe backpropagation.

2. What is the purpose of a threshold value in a learning algorithm?

3. What is the purpose of a learning rate?

4. How does error between actual and predicted outcomes affect the value of weights in neural networks?

8.4 DEVELOPING NEURAL NETWORK–BASED SYSTEMS

Although the development process of ANN is similar to the structured design methodologies of traditional computer-based information systems, some phases are unique or have some unique aspects. In the process described here, we assume that the preliminary steps of system development, such as determining information requirements, conducting a feasibility analysis, and gaining a champion in top management for the project, have been completed successfully. Such steps are generic to any information system.

As shown in Figure 8.11, the development process for an ANN application includes nine steps. In step 1, the data to be used for training and testing the network are collected. Important considerations are that the particular problem is amenable to neural network solution and that adequate data exist and can be obtained. In step 2, training data must be identified, and a plan must be made for testing the performance of the network.

In steps 3 and 4, a network architecture and a learning method are selected. The availability of a particular development tool or the capabilities of the development personnel may determine the type of neural network to be constructed. Also, certain problem types have demonstrated high success rates with certain configurations (e.g., multilayer feedforward neural networks for bankruptcy prediction, as described in the next section). Important considerations are the exact number of neurons and the number of layers. Some packages use genetic algorithms to select the network design.

There are parameters for tuning the network to the desired learning-performance level. Part of the process in step 5 is the initialization of the network weights and parameters, followed by the modification of the parameters as training-performance feedback is received. Often, the initial values are important in determining the efficiency and length of training. Some methods change the parameters during training to enhance performance.

Step 6 transforms the application data into the type and format required by the neural network. This may require writing software to preprocess the data or performing these operations directly in an ANN package. Data storage and manipulation techniques and processes must be designed for conveniently and efficiently retraining the neural network, when needed. The application data representation and ordering often influence the efficiency and possibly the accuracy of the results.

In steps 7 and 8, training and testing are conducted iteratively by presenting input and desired or known output data to the network. The network computes the outputs and adjusts the weights until the computed outputs are within an acceptable tolerance of the known outputs for the input cases. The desired outputs and their relationships to input data are derived from historical data (i.e., a portion of the data collected in step 1).

In step 9, a stable set of weights is obtained. Now the network can reproduce the desired outputs, given inputs such as those in the training set. The network is ready for use as a standalone system or as part of another software system where new input data will be presented to it and its output will be a recommended decision.

In the following sections, we examine these steps in more detail.

DATA COLLECTION AND PREPARATION

The first two steps in the ANN development process involve collecting data and separating them into a training set and a testing set. The training cases are used to adjust the weights, and the testing cases are used for network validation. The data used for training

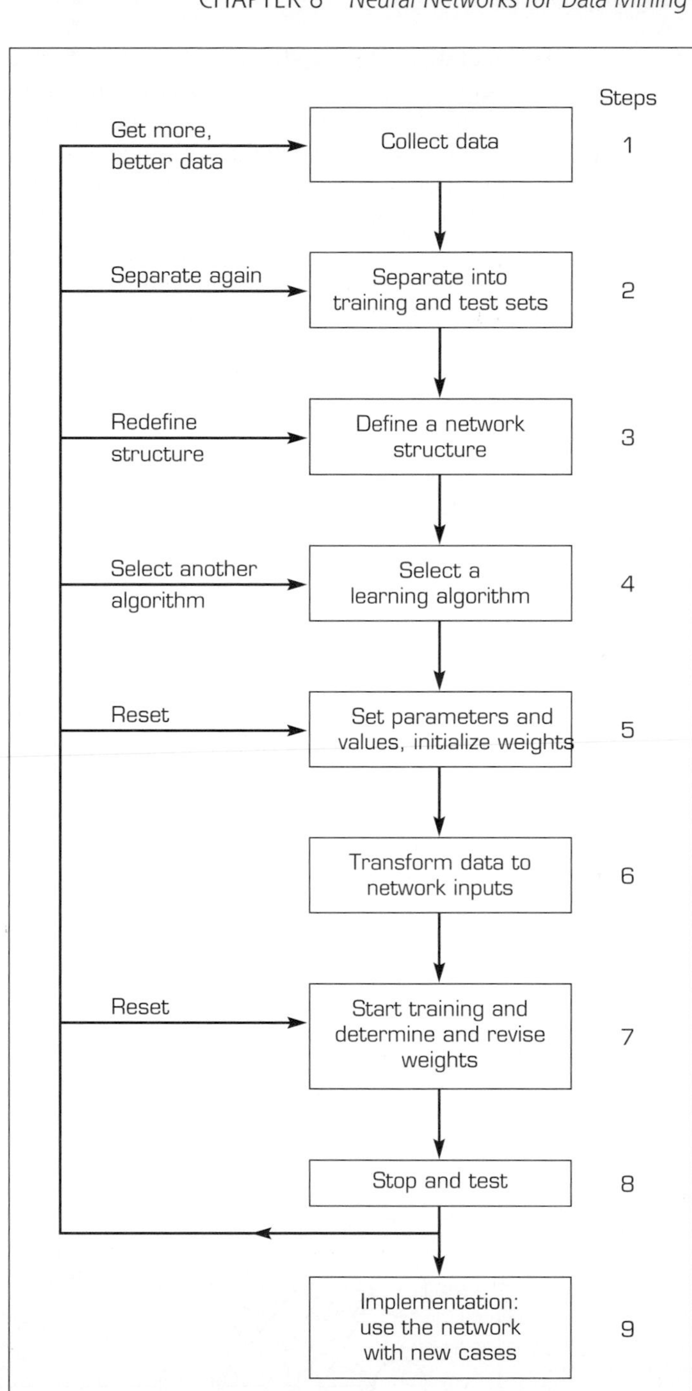

FIGURE 8.11 Flow Diagram of the Development Process of an ANN

and testing must include all the attributes that are useful for solving the problem. The system can only learn as much as the data can tell. Therefore, collection and preparation of data is the most critical step in building a good system.

In general, the more data used, the better. Larger data sets increase processing time during training but improve the accuracy of the training and often lead to faster convergence to a good set of weights. For a moderately sized data set, typically 80 percent of the data are randomly selected for training and 20 percent are selected for testing; for small data sets, typically all the data are used for training and testing; and for large data sets, a sufficiently large sample is taken and treated like a moderately sized data set.

For example, say a bank wants to build a neural network–based system in order to use clients' financial data to determine whether they may go bankrupt. The bank needs to first identify what financial data may be used as inputs and how to obtain them. Five attributes may be useful inputs: (1) working capital/total assets, (2) retained earnings/total assets, (3) earnings before interest and taxes/total assets, (4) market value of equity/total debt, and (5) sales/total sales. The output is a binary variable: bankruptcy or not.

SELECTION OF NETWORK STRUCTURE

After the training and testing data sets are identified, the next step is to design the structure of the neural networks. This includes the selection of a topology and determination of (1) input nodes, (2) output nodes, (3) number of hidden layers, and (4) number of hidden nodes. The multilayer feedforward topology is often used in business applications, although other network models are beginning to find some business use as well.

The design of input nodes must be based on the attributes of the data set. In the example of predicting bankruptcy, for example, the bank might choose a three-layer structure that includes one input layer, one output layer, and one hidden layer. The input layer contains five nodes, each of which is a variable, and the output layer contains a node with 0 for bankrupt and 1 for safe. Determining the number of hidden nodes is tricky. A few heuristics have been proposed, but none of them is unquestionably the best. A typical approach is to choose the average number of input and output nodes. In the previous case, the hidden node may be set to (5 + 1)/2 = 3. Figure 8.12 shows a possible structure for the bankruptcy-prediction problem.

FIGURE 8.12 Architecture of the Bankruptcy Prediction Neural Network

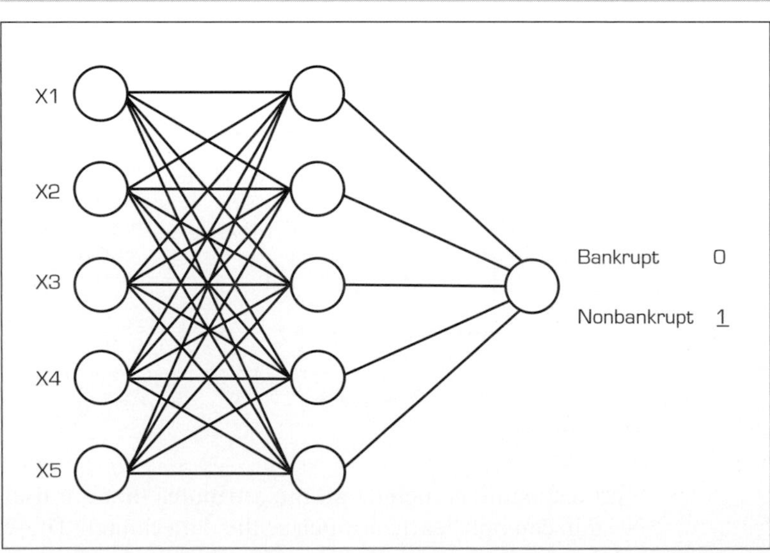

LEARNING ALGORITHM SELECTION

After the network structure is chosen, we need to find a learning algorithm to identify a set of connection weights that best cover the training data and have the best predictive accuracy. For the feedforward topology we chose for the bankruptcy-prediction problem, a typical approach is to use the backpropagation algorithm. Because many commercial packages are available on the market, there is no need to implement the learning algorithm by ourselves. Instead, we can choose a suitable commercial package to analyze the data. Technology Insights 8.4 summarizes information on different types of neural network software packages that are available.

NETWORK TRAINING

Training of ANN is an iterative process that starts from a random set of weights and gradually enhances the fitness of the network model and the known data set. The iteration continues until the error sum is converged to below a preset acceptable level. In the

TECHNOLOGY INSIGHTS 8.4

ANN Software

There are many tools for developing neural networks (see this book's Web site and the periodic resource lists in *PC AI*, **pcai.com**). Some of these tools function like expert system shells. They provide a set of standard architectures, learning algorithms, and parameters, along with the ability to manipulate the data. Some development tools can support up to several dozen network paradigms and learning algorithms.

Neural network implementations are also available in most of the comprehensive data mining tools, such as the SAS Enterprise Miner, Clementine, and STATISTICA Data Miner. WEKA is an open source collection of machine learning algorithms for data mining tasks, and it includes neural network capabilities. WEKA can be downloaded from **cs.waikato.ac.nz/~ml/weka**. STATISTICA is available on trial basis to adopters of this book.

Many specialized neural network tools enable the building and deployment of a neural network model in practice. Any listing of such tools would be incomplete. Online resources such as Wikipedia (**en.wikipedia.org/wiki/Artificial_neural_network**), the Google or Yahoo software directory, and vendor listings on **pcai.com** are good places to locate the latest information on neural network software vendors. Some of the vendors that have been around for a while and have reported industrial applications of their neural network software include California Scientific (BrainMaker), NeuralWare, NeuroDimension Inc., Ward Systems Group (Neuroshell), and Megaputer. Again, the list can never be complete.

Some ANN development tools are spreadsheet add-ins. Most can read spreadsheet, database, and text files. Some are freeware or shareware. Some ANN systems have been developed in Java to run directly on the Web and are accessible through a Web browser interface. Other ANN products are designed to interface with expert systems as hybrid development products.

Developers may instead prefer to use more general programming languages, such as C++, or a spreadsheet to program the model and perform the calculations. A variation on this is to use a library of ANN routines. For example, hav.Software (**hav.com**) provides a library of C++ classes for implementing standalone or embedded feedforward, simple recurrent, and random-order recurrent neural networks. Computational software such as MATLAB also includes neural network–specific libraries.

How are neural networks implemented in practice? After the analyst/developer has conducted enough tests to ascertain that a neural network can do a good job for the application, the network needs to be implemented in the existing systems. A number of neural network shells can generate code, in C++, Java, or Visual Basic, that can be embedded in another system that can access source data or is called directly by a graphical user interface for deployment, independently of the development system. Or, after training an ANN in a development tool, given the weights, network structure, and transfer function, one can easily develop one's own implementation in a third-generation programming language such as C++. Most of the ANN development packages as well as data mining tools can generate such code. The code can then be embedded in a standalone application or in a Web server application.

backpropagation algorithm, two parameters, *learning rate* and *momentum*, can be adjusted to control the speed of reaching a solution. These determine the ratio of the difference between the calculated value and the actual value of the training cases. Some software packages may have their own parameters in their learning heuristics to speed up the learning process. It is important to read carefully when using this type of software.

Some data conversion may be necessary in the training process. This includes (1) changing the data format to meet the requirements of the software, (2) normalizing the data scale to make the data more comparable, and (3) removing problematic data. When the training data set is ready, it is loaded into the package, and the learning procedure is executed. Depending on the number of nodes and the size of the training data set, reaching a solution may take from a few thousand to millions of iterations.

TESTING

Recall that in step 2 of the development process shown in Figure 8.11, the available data are divided into training and testing data sets. When the training has been completed, it is necessary to test the network. Testing (step 8) examines the performance of the derived network model by measuring its ability to classify the testing data correctly. **Black-box testing** (i.e., comparing test results to historical results) is the primary approach for verifying that inputs produce the appropriate outputs. Error terms can be used to compare results against known benchmark methods.

The network is generally not expected to perform perfectly (zero error is difficult, if not impossible, to attain), and only a certain level of accuracy is really required. For example, if 1 means nonbankrupt and 0 means bankrupt, then any output between 0.1 and 1 might indicate a certain likelihood of nonbankrupty. The neural network application is usually an alternative to another method that can be used as a benchmark against which to compare accuracy. For example, a statistical technique such as multiple regression or another quantitative method may be known to classify inputs correctly 50 percent of the time.

The neural network implementation often improves on this. For example, Liang (1992) reported that ANN performance was superior to the performance of multiple discriminant analysis and rule induction. Ainscough and Aronson (1999) investigated the application of neural network models in predicting retail sales, given a set of several inputs (e.g., regular price, various promotions). They compared their results to those of multiple regression and improved the adjusted R^2 (correlation coefficient) from .5 to .7. If the neural network is replacing manual operations, performance levels and speed of human processing can be the standard for deciding whether the testing phase is successful.

The test plan should include routine cases as well as potentially problematic situations. If the testing reveals large deviations, the training set must be reexamined, and the training process may have to be repeated (some "bad" data may have to be omitted from the input set).

Note that we cannot equate neural network results exactly with those found using statistical methods. For example, in stepwise linear regression, input variables are sometimes determined to be insignificant, but because of the nature of neural computing, a neural network uses them to attain higher levels of accuracy. When they are omitted from a neural network model, its performance typically suffers.

IMPLEMENTATION OF AN ANN

Implementation of an ANN (step 9) often requires interfaces with other computer-based information systems and user training. Ongoing monitoring and feedback to the developers are recommended for system improvements and long-term success. It is also important to gain the confidence of users and management early in the deployment to ensure that the system is accepted and used properly.

Section 8.4 Review Questions

1. List the nine steps in conducting a neural network project.
2. What are some of the design parameters for developing a neural network?
3. Describe different types of neural network software available today.
4. How are neural networks implemented in practice when the training/testing is complete?
5. What parameters may need to be adjusted in the neural network training process?

8.5 A SAMPLE NEURAL NETWORK PROJECT

We next describe a typical application of neural networks to predict bankruptcy of companies using the same data and a similar experimental design as used by Wilson and Sharda (1994). For comparative purposes, the performance of neural networks is contrasted with logistic regression.

The Altman (1968) study has been used as the standard of comparison for many bankruptcy classification studies using discriminant analysis and logistic regression; follow-up studies have identified several other attributes to improve prediction performance. We use the same financial ratios as in Altman's study, realizing that more sophisticated inputs to the neural network model should only enhance its performance. These ratios are as follows:

X_1: Working capital/total assets
X_2: Retained earnings/total assets
X_3: Earnings before interest and taxes/total assets
X_4: Market value of equity/total debt
X_5: Sales/total assets

Step 1 consists of collecting relevant data. The sample of firms for which these ratios was obtained from *Moody's Industrial Manuals*. It consisted of firms that either were in operation or went bankrupt between 1975 and 1982. The sample consists of a total of 129 firms, 65 of which went bankrupt during the period and 64 nonbankrupt firms matched on industry and year. Data used for the bankrupt firms are from the last financial statements issued before the firms declared bankruptcy. Thus, the prediction of bankruptcy is to be made about 1 year in advance.

Step 2 requires us to break the data set into a training set and a testing set. Because the determination of the split may affect experimental findings, a resampling procedure can be used to create many different pairs of training and testing sets, which also ensures that there is no overlap in the composition of the matched training and testing sets. For example, a training set of 20 patterns can be created by randomly setting 20 records from the collected set. A set of 20 other patterns/records can be created as a test set.

In addition, the results of this (and any other) study could be affected by the proportion of nonbankrupt firms to bankrupt firms in both the training and testing sets; that is, the population of all firms contains a certain proportion of firms on the verge of bankruptcy. This base rate may have an impact on a prediction technique's performance in two ways. First, a technique may not work well when the firms of interest (i.e., those that are bankrupt) constitute a very small percentage of the population (i.e., a low base rate). This would be due to a technique's inability to identify the features necessary for classification. Second, there are differences in base rates between training samples and testing samples. If a classification model is built using a training sample with a certain base rate, does the model still work when the base rate in the test population is different? This issue is important for one more reason: If a classification model based on a certain base rate works across other proportions, it may be possible to build a model using a higher proportion of cases of interest than actually occur in the population.

To study the effects of this proportion on the predictive performance of the two techniques, we create three proportions (or base rates) for the testing set composition while holding the composition of the training set fixed at a 50/50 base rate. The first factor level (or base rate) can be a 50/50 proportion of bankrupt to nonbankrupt cases, the second level could be an 80/20 proportion (80 percent nonbankrupt, 20 percent bankrupt), and the third level could be an approximate 90/10 proportion. We do not really know the actual proportion of firms going bankrupt; the 80/20 and 90/10 cases should be close.

Within each of the three different testing set compositions, 20 different training–testing set pairs could be generated via Monte Carlo resampling from the original 129 firms. Thus, a total of 60 distinct training and testing data set pairs were generated from the original data. In each case, the training set and test set pairs contained unique firms (i.e., no overlap was allowed). This restriction provides a stronger test of a technique's performance. To summarize, neural networks and logistic regression models are developed using training sets of equal proportions of firms to determine the classification function but are evaluated with test sets containing 50/50, 80/20, and 90/ 10 base rates. (The data set used here is available from this book's Web site.)

Steps 3 through 6 relate to getting ready for a neural network experiment. We can use any neural network software package that implements the aforementioned backpropagation training algorithm to construct and test trained neural network models. We would have to decide on the size of the neural network, including the number of hidden layers and the number of neurons in the hidden layer. For example, one possible structure to use here is 5 input neurons (1 for each financial ratio), 10 hidden neurons, and 2 output neurons (1 indicating a bankrupt firm and the other indicating a nonbankrupt firm). (Figure 8.13 illustrates this network configuration.) Neural output values range from 0 to 1. Output node BR indicates a firm to be classified as likely to go bankrupt, and the node NBR, not so.

A user of a neural network has two difficult decisions to make in the training process (step 6): At what point has the neural network appropriately learned the relationships, and what is the threshold of error with regard to determining correct classifications of the test set? Typically, these issues are addressed by using training tolerances and testing tolerances that state the acceptable levels of variance for considering classifications as "correct."

Step 7 refers to the actual neural network training. In training the networks in this example, a heuristic backpropagation algorithm was used to ensure convergence (i.e., all firms in the training set classified correctly). The training set is presented to the neural network software repeatedly until the software has sufficiently learned the relationship between the attributes of the cases and whether the firm is distressed. Then, to accurately assess the prediction efficacy of the network, the holdout sample (i.e., test set) is presented to the network, and the number of correct classifications are noted (step 8).

In determining correct classifications, a testing threshold of 0.49 was used. Thus, the output node with a value over 0.5 was used to assess whether the network provided

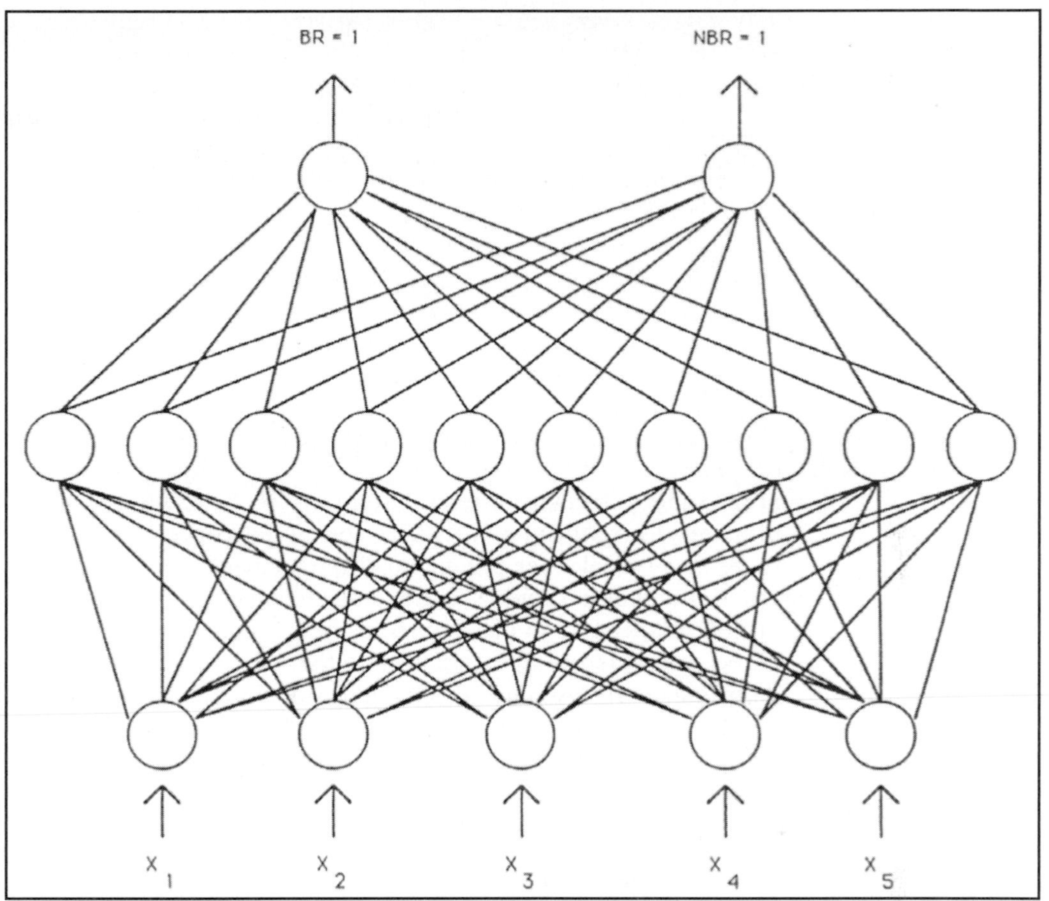

FIGURE 8.13 A Typical Neural Network Model for Bankruptcy Prediction

a correct classification. Cases in which both output neurons provided output levels either less than 0.5 or greater than 0.5 were automatically treated as misclassifications.

To compare the performance of the neural network against using classical statistical techniques, a logistic regression approach was implemented via SYSTAT, a statistical software package. Table 8.2 represents the average percentage of correct classifications provided by the two different techniques when evaluated by the 20 holdout samples for each of the three different test set base rates. When the testing sets contained an equal number of the two cases, neural networks correctly classified 97.5 percent of the holdout cases, whereas logistic regression was correct 93.25 percent of the time. Similarly, when the testing sets contained 20,070 bankrupt firms, neural networks classified at a 95.6 percent correct rate, whereas logistic regression correctly classified at a 92.2 percent rate.

A nonparametric test, the Wilcoxon test for paired observations, was undertaken to assess whether the correct classification percentages for the two techniques were significantly different. Those instances where statistically significant differences were found are indicated in Table 8.2 by footnotes. In general, neural networks performed significantly better than logistic regression.

Table 8.2 also illustrates the correct percentages of bankrupt firm predictions and nonbankrupt firm predictions. In the prediction of bankrupt cases, neural networks predicted significantly better than logistic regression for test sets of equal proportion,

TABLE 8.2 Performance Comparison of Neural Networks and Logistic Regression

	Test Proportions					
	50/50		*80/20*		*90/10*	
Criteria	*NN*	*LR*	*NN*	*LR*	*NN*	*LR*
Overall percentage of correct classification	97.5[a]	93.25	95.6[a]	92.2	95.68[b]	90.23
Bankrupt firm classification success rate	97.0[a]	91.90	92.0	92.0	92.5	95.0 ($p = .282$)
Nonbankrupt firm classification success rate	98.0[a]	95.5	96.5[a]	92.25	96.0[b]	89.75

[a]$p < .01$.
[b]$p < .05$.

at the same percentage when the ratio was 80/20, and a little worse (although not significantly) for 90/10 test sets. The neural networks clearly outperform the logistic regression model in the prediction of the nonbankrupt firms.

A number of studies in the recent past have investigated the performance of neural networks in predicting business failure. Typically, these studies have compared neural network performance to that of traditional statistical techniques such as discriminant analysis and logistic regression. In addition, some studies have compared neural networks to other artificial intelligence techniques, such as inductive learning methods (e.g., ID3). The purpose of this section is only to illustrate how a neural network project can be completed, not necessarily to argue that the neural networks do better in this problem domain.

Section 8.5 Review Questions

1. What parameters can be used to predict failure of a firm?
2. How were data divided between training and test sets for this experiment?
3. Explain what is meant by *resampling* in this context? How was resampling used for this problem?
4. What were the network parameters for this neural network experiment?
5. How was an output converted to mean bankrupt or nonbankrupt?
6. How did the neural network model compare with a logistic regression model in this experiment?

8.6 OTHER NEURAL NETWORK PARADIGMS

MLP-based neural networks described in this chapter thus far are just one specific type of neural networks. Literally hundreds of different neural networks have been proposed. Many are variants of the MLP model that you have already seen; they just differ in their implementations of input representation, learning process, output processing, and so on. But there are many types of neural networks that are quite different from the MLP model. Some of these are introduced later in this chapter. Others include radial basis function networks, probabilistic neural networks, generalized regression neural networks, and support vector machines. Many online resources describe details of these types of neural networks. A good resource introduced in Chapter 7 is the e-book StatSoft (**statsoft.com/textbook/stathome.html**). The next subsection introduces some of the classic varieties of neural networks.

HOPFIELD NETWORKS

A neural network model of interest is the Hopfield network (Hopfield, 1982). John Hopfield showed in a series of papers in the 1980s how highly interconnected networks or nonlinear neurons can be extremely effective in computing. These networks provided a rapid computed solution for problems stated in terms of desired optima, often subject to constraints.

A general Hopfield network is a single large layer of neurons with total interconnectivity—that is, each neuron is connected to every other neuron. In addition, the output of each neuron may depend on its previous values. One use of Hopfield networks has been in solving constrained optimization problems, such as the classic traveling salesman problem (TSP). In this type of application, each neuron represents the desirability of a city n being visited in position m of a TSP tour. Interconnection weights are specified, representing the constraints of feasible solution to the TSP (e.g., forcing a city to appear in a tour only once). An energy function is specified, which represents the objective of the model solution process (e.g., minimize total distance in the TSP tour) and is used in determining when to stop the neural network evolution to a final state. The network starts with random neuron values and, using the stated interconnection weights, the neuron values are updated over time. Gradually, the neuron values stabilize, evolving into a final state (as driven by the global energy function) that represents a solution to the problem. At this point in the network evolution, the value of neuron (n,m) represents whether city n should be in location m of the TSP tour. While Hopfield and Tank (1985) and others claimed great success in solving the TSP, further research has shown those claims to be somewhat premature. Nonetheless, this novel approach to a classic problem offers promise for optimization problems, especially when technology allows for taking advantage of the inherent parallelism of neural networks.

Hopfield networks are distinct from feedforward networks because the neurons are highly interconnected, weights between neurons tend to be fixed, and there is no training per se. The complexity and challenge in using a Hopfield network for optimization problems is in the correct specification of the interconnection weights and the identification of the proper global energy function to drive the network evolution process.

SELF-ORGANIZING NETWORKS

Kohonen's network, also known as a self-organizing network is another neural network model. Such networks learn in an unsupervised mode. The biological basis of these models is the conjecture that some organization takes place in the human brain when an external stimulus is provided. Kohonen's algorithm forms "feature maps," where neighborhoods of neurons are constructed. These neighborhoods are organized such that topologically close neurons are sensitive to similar inputs into the model. Self-organizing maps, or self-organizing feature maps, can sometimes be used to develop some early insight into the data. For example, self-organizing maps could learn to identify clusters of data so that an analyst could build more refined models for each subset/cluster. In cases in which the analyst does not have a good idea of the number of classes or output or actual output class for any given pattern, the self-organizing maps can work well.

Section 8.6 Review Questions

1. List some of the different types of neural networks.
2. What is one key difference between an MLP network and a Kohonen network?
3. What is another name for a Kohonen network?
4. Briefly describe a Hopfield network.

8.7 APPLICATIONS OF ANN

ANN have been applied in many domains. A survey of their applications in finance can be found in Fadlalla and Lin (2001). There have been several tests of neural networks in financial markets. Collard (1990) stated that his neural network model for commodity training would have resulted in significant profits over other trading strategies. Kamijo and Tanigawa (1990) used a neural network to chart Tokyo Stock Exchange data. They found that the results of the model would beat a "buy and hold" strategy. Finally, a neural model for predicting percentage change in the S&P 500 five days ahead, using a variety of economic indicators, was developed (Fishman et al., 1991). The authors claim that the model has provided more accurate prediction than alleged experts in the field using the same indicators.

Neural networks have been successfully trained to determine whether loan applications should be approved (Gallant, 1988). It has also been shown that neural networks can predict mortgage applicant solvency better than mortgage writers (Collins et al., 1988). Predicting rating of corporate bonds and attempting to predict their profitability is another area where neural networks have been successfully applied (see Dutta and Shakhar, 1988; and Surkan and Singleton, 1990). Neural networks outperformed regression analysis and other mathematical modeling tools in predicting bond rating and profitability. The main conclusion reached was that neural networks provided a more general framework for connecting financial information of a firm to the respective bond rating.

Fraud prevention is another area of neural network application in business. Chase Manhattan Bank successfully used neural networks in dealing with credit card fraud (Rochester, 1990), with the neural network models outperforming traditional regression approaches. Also, neural networks have been used in the validation of bank signatures (see Francett, 1989; and Mighell, 1989). These networks identified forgeries significantly better than any human expert.

Another significant area of statistical application of neural networks is in time-series forecasting. Several studies have attempted to use neural networks for time-series prediction. Examples include Fozzard et al. (1989), Tang et al. (1991), and Hill et al. (1994). The general conclusion is that neural networks appear to do at least as well as the Box-Jenkins forecasting technique.

Because neural networks have been a subject of intense study since late 1980s, there have been many applications of as well as experiments with applications. You can do simple Web searches to find recent examples in addition to the ones listed in this chapter. Other recent reports include live intrusion tracking (see Thaler, 2002), Web content filtering (Lee et al., 2002), exchange rate prediction (Davis et al., 2001), and hospital bed allocation (Walczak et al., 2002). Newer applications are emerging in health care and medicine. See Application Case 8.5, for example.

Application Case 8.5

Neural Networks for Breast Cancer Diagnosis

ANN have proven to be a useful tool in pattern recognition and classification tasks in diverse areas, including clinical medicine. Despite the wide applicability of ANN, the large amount of data required for training makes using them an unsuitable classification technique when the available data are scarce. Magnetic resonance spectroscopy (MRS) plays a pivotal role in the investigation of cell biochemistry and provides a reliable method for detection of metabolic changes in breast tissue. The scarcity of data and the complexity of interpretation of relevant physiological information impose extra demands that prohibit the applicability of most statistical and machine learning techniques developed. Knowledge-based artificial neural networks (KBANN) help to prevail over such difficulties and complexities. A KBANN combines knowledge from a domain, in the form of simple rules, with connectionist learning. This combination trains the network through the use of small sets of data (as is typical of medical diagnosis tasks). The primary structure is based on the dependencies of a set of known domain rules, and it is necessary to refine those rules through training.

The KBANN process consists of two algorithms. One is the Rules-to-Network algorithm, in which the main task is the translation process between a knowledge base containing information about a domain theory and the initial structure of a neural network. This algorithm maps the structure of an approximately correct domain theory, with all the rules and their dependencies, into a neural network structure. The defined network is then trained using the backpropagation learning algorithm.

Feedback mechanisms, which inhibit or stimulate the growth of normal cells, control the division and replacement of cells in normal tissues. In the case of tumors, that process is incapable of controlling the production of new cells, and the division is done without any regard to the need for replacement, disturbing the structure of normal tissue. Changes observed in phospholipid metabolite concentrations, which are associated with differences in cell proliferation in malignant tissues, have served as the basic inputs for the identification of relevant features present in malignant or cancerous tissues but not in normal tissues. The abnormal levels of certain phospholipid characteristics are considered indicators of tumors. These include several parameters, such as PDE, PME, Pi, PCr, γATP, αATP, and βATP. KBANN produced an accurate tumor classification of 87 percent from a set of 26, with an average pattern error of 0.0500 and a standard deviation of 0.0179.

Sources: M. Sordo, H. Buxton, and D. Watson, "A Hybrid Approach to Breast Cancer Diagnosis," in *Practical Applications of Computational Intelligence Techniques*, Vol. 16, in L. Jain and P. DeWilde (eds.), Kluwer, Norwell, MA, 2001, **acl.icnet.uk/PUBLICATIONS/sordo/chapter2001.pdf** (accessed March 2006).

In general, ANN are suitable for problems whose inputs are both categorical and numeric, and where the relationships between inputs and outputs are not linear or the input data are not normally distributed. In such cases, classical statistical methods may not be reliable enough. Because ANN do not make any assumptions about the data distribution, their power is less affected than traditional statistical methods when data are not properly distributed. Finally, there are cases in which the neural networks simply provide one more way of building a predictive model for the situation at hand. Given the ease of experimentation using the available software tools, it is certainly worth exploring the power of neural networks in any data modeling situation.

Section 8.7 Review Questions

1. List some applications of neural networks in accounting/finance.
2. What are some engineering applications of neural networks?
3. How have neural networks been used in the health care field?
4. What are some applications of neural networks in information security?
5. Conduct a Web search to identify homeland security applications of neural networks.

8.8 A NEURAL NETWORK SOFTWARE DEMONSTRATION

Online Tutorial T4 provides a software demonstration of using neural networks. That section is used, with permission, from STATISTICA Software Tutorial. Students and professors using this book are eligible to receive a six-month license to use STATISTICA software for completion of the exercises in Chapters 7 and 8. Request for this copy of the software is to be made by the instructor by completing the coupon available in Online File W8.5. Note that similar software projects can also be completed by using tools identified in Technology Insights 8.4.

Chapter Highlights

- Neural computing involves a set of methods that emulate the way the human brain works. The basic processing unit is a neuron. Multiple neurons are grouped into layers and linked together.
- In a neural network, the knowledge is stored in the weight associated with each connection between two neurons.
- Backpropagation is the most popular paradigm in business applications of neural networks. Most business applications are handled using this algorithm.
- A backpropagation-based neural network consists of an input layer, an output layer, and a certain number of hidden layers (usually one). The nodes in one layer are fully connected to the nodes in the next layer. Learning is done through a trial-and-error process of adjusting the connection weights.
- Each node at the input layer typically represents a single attribute that may affect the prediction.
- Neural network learning can occur in supervised or unsupervised mode.
- In supervised learning mode, the training patterns include a correct answer/classification/forecast.
- In unsupervised learning mode, there are no known answers. Thus, unsupervised learning is used for clustering or exploratory data analysis.
- The usual process of learning in a neural network involves three steps: (1) compute temporary outputs based on inputs and random weights, (2) compute outputs with desired targets, and (3) adjust the weights and repeat the process.
- The delta rule is commonly used to adjust the weights. It includes a learning rate and a momentum parameter.
- Developing neural network–based systems requires a step-by-step process. It includes data preparation and preprocessing, training and testing, and conversion of the trained model into a production system.
- Neural network software is available to allow easy experimentation with many models. Neural network modules are included in all major data mining software tools. Specific neural network packages are also available. Some neural network tools are available as spreadsheet add-ins.
- After a trained network has been created, it is usually implemented in end-user systems through programming languages such as C++, Java, and Visual Basic. Most neural network tools can generate codes for the trained network in these languages.
- Many neural network models beyond backpropagation exist, including radial basis functions, support vector machines, Hopfield networks, and Kohonen's self-organizing maps.
- Neural network applications abound in almost all business disciplines as well as in virtually all other functional areas.
- Business applications of neural networks included finance, firm failure prediction, time series forecasting, and so on.
- New applications of neural networks are emerging in health care, security, and so on.

Key Terms

- adaptive resonance theory (ART)
- artificial neural network (ANN)
- axon
- backpropagation
- black-box testing
- connection weight
- dendrite
- hidden layer
- Kohonen self-organizing feature map
- learning algorithm
- learning rate

- momentum
- neural computing
- neural network
- neuron
- nucleus
- parallel processing
- pattern recognition
- perceptron
- processing element (PE)
- self-organizing
- sigmoid (logical activation) function
- summation function
- supervised learning
- synapse
- threshold value
- topology
- transformation (transfer) function
- unsupervised learning

Questions for Discussion

1. Compare artificial and biological neural networks. What aspects of biological networks are not mimicked by artificial ones? What aspects are similar?
2. The performance of ANN relies heavily on the summation and transformation functions. Explain the combined effects of the summation and transformation functions and how they differ from statistical regression analysis.
3. ANN can be used for both supervised and unsupervised learning. Explain how they learn in a supervised mode and in an unsupervised mode.
4. Explain the difference between a training set and a testing set. Why do we need to differentiate them? Can the same set be used for both purposes? Why or why not?
5. Say that a neural network has been constructed to predict the creditworthiness of applicants. There are two output nodes: one for yes (1 = yes, 0 = no) and one for no (1 = no, 0 = yes). An applicant receives a score of 0.83 for the "yes" output node and a 0.44 for the "no" output node. Discuss what may have happened and whether the applicant is a good credit risk.
6. Everyone would like to make a great deal of money on the stock market. Only a few are very successful. Why is using an ANN a promising approach? What can it do that other decision support technologies cannot do? How could it fail?

Exercises

Teradata University and Other Hands-on Exercises

1. Go to Teradata Student Network Web site (at **teradatastudentnetwork.com**) or the URL given by your instructor. Locate Web seminars related to data mining and neural networks. Specifically, view the seminar given by Professor Hugh Watson at the SPIRIT2005 conference at Oklahoma State University. Then answer the following questions:
   a. Which real-time application at Continental Airlines may have used a neural network?
   b. What inputs and outputs can be used in building a neural network application?
   c. Given that Continental's data mining applications are real-time, how might Continental implement a neural network in practice?
   d. What other neural network applications would you propose for the airline industry?
2. Go to Teradata Student Network Web site (at **teradatastudentnetwork.com**) or the URL given by your instructor. Locate the Harrah's case. Read the case and answer the following questions:
   a. Which of the Harrah's data applications are most likely implemented using neural networks?
   b. What other applications could Harrah's develop using the data it is collecting from its customers?
   c. What are some concerns you might have as a customer at this casino?
3. This exercise relates to the sample project in this chapter. Bankruptcy prediction problem can be viewed as a problem of classification. The data set you will be using for this problem includes five ratios that have been computed from the financial statements of real-world firms. These five ratios have been used in studies involving bankruptcy prediction. The first sample includes data on firms that went bankrupt and firms that didn't. This will be your training sample for the neural network. The second sample of 10 firms also consists of some bankrupt firms and some nonbankrupt firms. Your goal is to train a neural network, using the first 20 data, and then test its performance on the other

10 data. (Try to analyze the new cases yourself manually before you run the neural network and see how well you do.) The following tables show the training sample and test data you should use for this exercise:

Training Sample

Firm	WC/TA	RE/TA	EBIT/TA	MVE/TD	S/TA	BR/NB
1	0.165	0.1192	0.2035	0.813	1.6702	1
2	0.1415	0.3868	0.0681	0.5755	1.0579	1
3	0.5804	0.3331	0.081	1.1964	1.3572	1
4	0.2304	0.296	0.1225	0.4102	3.0809	1
5	0.3684	0.3913	0.0524	0.1658	1.1533	1
6	0.1527	0.3344	0.0783	0.7736	1.5046	1
7	0.1126	0.3071	0.0839	1.3429	1.5736	1
8	0.0141	0.2366	0.0905	0.5863	1.4651	1
9	0.222	0.1797	0.1526	0.3459	1.7237	1
10	0.2776	0.2567	0.1642	0.2968	1.8904	1
11	0.2689	0.1729	0.0287	0.1224	0.9277	0
12	0.2039	−0.0476	0.1263	0.8965	1.0457	0
13	0.5056	−0.1951	0.2026	0.538	1.9514	0
14	0.1759	0.1343	0.0946	0.1955	1.9218	0
15	0.3579	0.1515	0.0812	0.1991	1.4582	0
16	0.2845	0.2038	0.0171	0.3357	1.3258	0
17	0.1209	0.2823	−0.0113	0.3157	2.3219	0
18	0.1254	0.1956	0.0079	0.2073	1.489	0
19	0.1777	0.0891	0.0695	0.1924	1.6871	0
20	0.2409	0.166	0.0746	0.2516	1.8524	0

Test Data

Firm	WC/TA	RE/TA	EBIT/TA	MVE/TD	S/TA	BR/NB
A	0.1759	0.1343	0.0946	0.1955	1.9218	?
B	0.3732	0.3483	−0.0013	0.3483	1.8223	?
C	0.1725	0.3238	0.104	0.8847	0.5576	?
D	0.163	0.3555	0.011	0.373	2.8307	?
E	0.1904	0.2011	0.1329	0.558	1.6623	?
F	0.1123	0.2288	0.01	0.1884	2.7186	?
G	0.0732	0.3526	0.0587	0.2349	1.7432	?
H	0.2653	0.2683	0.0235	0.5118	1.835	?
I	0.107	0.0787	0.0433	0.1083	1.2051	?
J	0.2921	0.239	0.0673	0.3402	0.9277	?

Describe the results of the neural network prediction, including software, architecture, and training information. Submit the trained network file(s) so that your instructor can load and test your network.

4. For this exercise, your goal is to build a model to identify inputs or predictors that differentiate risky customers from others (based on patterns pertaining to previous customers) and then use those inputs to predict the

new risky customers. This sample case is typical for this domain.

The sample data to be used in this exercise are in Online File W8.2, CreditRisk.xls. The data set has 425 cases and 15 variables pertaining to past and current customers who borrowed from a bank for various reasons. The data set contains various information related to the customers, financial standing, reason to loan, employment, demographic information, and so on, and finally the outcome or dependent variable for credit standing, classifying each case as good or bad, based on the institution's past experience.

You should take 400 of the cases as training cases and use the other 25 for testing. Then build a neural network model to learn the characteristics of the problem and test its performance on the other 25 cases. Report on your model's learning and testing performance. Prepare a report that identifies the neural network architecture, training parameters, and resulting performance on the test set.

(This exercise is courtesy of StatSoft, Inc., based on a German data set from **ftp://ftp.ics.uci.edu/pub/machine-learning-databases/statlog/german** renamed CreditRisk and altered.)

5. Forecasting box-office receipts for a particular motion picture is an interesting challenge. Despite the difficulty associated with the unpredictable nature of the problem domain, several researchers have tried to predict the total box-office receipt of motion pictures after a movie's initial theatrical release. In this problem, you explore forecasting the financial performance of a movie at the box office before its theatrical release by converting the forecasting problem into a classification problem. That is, rather than forecasting the point estimate of box-office receipts, you classify a movie based on its box-office receipts in one of nine categories, ranging from flop to blockbuster, taking into account a number of factors decided by feedback received from the industry experts and previous studies. The following is the list of the variables:

Attributes	**Values- range**	**Type**
MPAA rating	5 possible rating categories: G, PG, PG-13, R, NR	Binary (0,1)
Competition	3 pseudo-variables: high, medium, low competition	Binary (0,1)
Star value	3 variables of degree of star value: A+/A (high), B (medium), C (insignificant)	Binary (0,1)
Content category (genre)	10 categories: sci-fi, historic epic drama, modern drama, politically related, thriller, horror, comedy, cartoon, action, documentary	Binary (0,1)
Technical effects	3 binary independent variables: high, medium, low technical effects ratings	Binary (0,1)
Sequel	1 variable to specify whether a movie is a sequel	Binary (0,1)
Number of screens	Continuous variable	Positive integer

Each categorical-independent variable (except the genre variable) is converted into a 1-of-*N* binary representation. For example, the 5 MPAA ratings are represented as five 0–1 variables. In the process of value assignment, all such pseudo-representations of a categorical variable are given the value of 0, except the one that holds true for the current case, which is given the value of 1. For a movie of rating PG, the second input variable is at level 1, the others (1 and 3–5) are at level 0.

The variable of interest here is box-office gross revenues. A movie based on its box-office receipts is classified in one of nine categories, ranging from a flop to a blockbuster. The dependent variable can be converted into nine classes, using the following breakpoints:

Class Number	**Range (in millions)**
1	<1 (flop)
2	>1 and <10
3	>10 and <20
4	>20 and <40
5	>40 and <65
6	>65 and <100
7	>100 and <150
8	>150 and <200
9	>200 (blockbuster)

Download the training set data from Online File W8.3, movietrain.xls, which has 184 records and is in Microsoft Excel format. Use the data description here to understand the domain and the problem you are trying to solve. Pick and choose your independent variables; develop at least three classification models (e.g., decision tree, logistic regression, neural networks). Compare the accuracy results (using 10-fold cross validation and percentage split techniques), use confusion matrices, and comment on the outcome. Test the models developed on the test set (see Online File W8.4, movietest.xls, 29 records) and analyze the results with different models and come up with the best classification model, supporting it with your results.

Exercises

Team Assignments and Role-Playing

1. Consider the following set of data that relates daily electricity usage as a function of outside high temperature (for the day):

Temperature, X	Kilowatts, Y
46.8	12,530
52.1	10,800
55.1	10,180
59.2	9,730
61.9	9,750
66.2	10,230
69.9	11,160
76.8	13,910
79.7	15,110
79.3	15,690
80.2	17,020
83.3	17,880

   a. Plot the raw data. What pattern do you see? What do you think is really affecting electricity usage?
   b. Solve this problem with linear regression $Y = a + bX$ (in a spreadsheet). How well does this work? Plot your results. What is wrong? Calculate the sum-of-the-squares error and R^2.
   c. Solve this problem by using nonlinear regression. We recommend a quadratic function, $Y = a + b_1X + b_2X^2$. How well does this work? Plot your results. Is anything wrong? Calculate the sum-of-the-squares error and R^2.
   d. Break up the problem into three sections (look at the plot) and solve it using three linear regression models—one for each section. How well does this work? Plot your results. Calculate the sum-of-the-squares error and R^2. Is this modeling approach appropriate? Why or why not?
   e. Build a neural network to solve the original problem. (You may have to scale the X and Y values to be between 0 and 1.) Train it (on the entire set of data) and solve the problem (i.e., make predictions for each of the original data items). How well does this work? Plot your results. Calculate the sum-of-the-squares error and R^2.
   f. Which method works best and why?

2. Build a real-world neural network. Using demo software downloaded from the Web (e.g., Braincel, at **promland.com**, or another site), identify real-world data (e.g., start searching on the Web at **ics.uci.edu/~mlearn/MLRepository.html** or use data from an organization with which someone in your group has a contact) and build a neural network to make predictions. Topics might include sales forecasts, predicting success in an academic program (e.g., predict GPA from high school rating and SAT scores; being careful to look out for "bad" data, such as GPAs of 0.0), or housing prices; or survey the class for weight, gender, and height and try to predict height based on the other two factors. (Hint: Use U.S. census data, on this book's Web site or at **census.gov**, by state, to identify a relationship between education level and income.) How good are your predictions? Compare the results to predictions generated using standard statistical methods (regression). Which method is better? How could your system be embedded in a DSS for real decision making?

3. For each of the following applications, would it be better to use a neural network or an expert system? Explain your answers, including possible exceptions or special conditions.
   a. Diagnosis of a well-established but complex disease
   b. **Price-lookup** subsystem for a high-volume merchandise seller
   c. Automated voice-inquiry processing system
   d. Training of new employees
   e. Handwriting recognition

4. Consider the following data set, which includes three attributes and a classification for admission decisions into an MBA program:

GMAT	GPA	Quantitative GMAT	Decision
650	2.75	35	NO
580	3.50	70	NO
600	3.50	75	YES
450	2.95	80	NO
700	3.25	90	YES
590	3.50	80	YES
400	3.85	45	NO
640	3.50	75	YES
540	3.00	60	?
690	2.85	80	?
490	4.00	65	?

   a. Using the data given here as examples, develop your own manual expert rules for decision making.

b. Build a decision tree using SPRINT (Gini index). You can build it by using manual calculations or use a spreadsheet to perform the basic calculations.

c. Build another decision tree, using the entropy and information gain (ID3) approach. You can use a spreadsheet calculator for this exercise.

d. Although the data set here is extremely small, try to build a little neural network for it.

e. Use automated decision tree software (e.g., See5; download a trial version from **rulequest.com**) to build a tree for these data.

f. Report the predictions on the last three observations from each of the five classification approaches.

g. Comment on the similarity and differences of the approaches. What did you learn from this exercise?

5. You have worked on neural networks and other data mining techniques. Give examples of where each of these has been used. Based on your knowledge, how would you differentiate among these techniques? Assume that a few years from now, you come across a situation in which neural network or other data mining techniques could be used to build an interesting application for your organization. You have an intern working with you to do the grunt work. How will you decide whether the application is appropriate for a neural network or for another data mining model? Based on your homework assignments, what specific software guidance can you provide to get your intern to be productive for you quickly? Your answer for this question might mention the specific software, describe how to go about setting up the model/neural network, and validate the application.

Exercises

Internet Exercises

1. Explore the Web sites of several neural network vendors, such as California Scientific Software (**calsci.com**), NeuralWare (**neuralware.com**), and Ward Systems Group (**wardsystems.com**), and review some of their products. Download at least two demos and install, run, and compare them.

2. There is a very good repository of data that has been used to test the performance of neural network and other machine learning algorithms. This repository can be accessed at **ics.uci.edu/~mlearn/MLRepository.html**. Some of the data sets are really meant to test the limits of current machine learning algorithms and compare their performance against new approaches to learning. However, some of the smaller data sets can be useful for exploring the functionality of the software you might download in Internet Exercise 1 or the software that is available as companion software with this book, such as STATISTICA Data Miner. Download at least one data set from the UCI repository (e.g., Credit Screening Databases, Housing Database). Then apply neural networks as well as decision tree methods, as appropriate. Prepare a report on your results. (Some of these exercises could also be completed in a group or may even be proposed as semester-long projects for term papers and so on.)

3. Go to **calsci.com** and read about various business applications. Prepare a report that summarizes the applications.

4. Go to **nd.com**. Read about the company's applications in investment and trading. Prepare a report about them.

5. Go to **nd.com**. Download the trial version of Neurosolutions for Excel and experiment with it, using one of the data sets from the exercises in this chapter. Prepare a report about your experience with the tool.

6. Go to **neoxi.com**. Identify at least two software tools that have not been mentioned in this chapter. Visit Web sites of those tools and prepare a brief report on the capabilities of those tools.

7. Go to **neuroshell.com**. Look at Gee Whiz examples. Comment on the feasibility of achieving the results claimed by the developers of this neural network model.

8. Go to **easynn.com**. Download the trial version of the software. After the installation of the software, find the sample file called Houseprices.tvq. Retrain the neural network and test the model by supplying some data. Prepare a report about your experience with this software.

9. Visit **statsoft.com**. Go to Downloads and download at least three white papers of applications. Which of these applications may have used neural networks?

10. Go to **neuralware.com**. Prepare a report about the products the company offers.

End of Chapter Case

Sovereign Credit Ratings Using Neural Networks

Companies such as Standard & Poor's Corporation, Moody's Investors Service, and Fitch Ratings provide alphabetical indicators of credit risk. Over a long period of time, these ratings have been in use to assess companies and financial institutions. However, issuing sovereign ratings is relatively new but has seen rapid expansion in recent years. The number of rated sovereigns grew from 17 in 1989 to 63 in 1998. Sovereign credit ratings are receiving a lot of global importance, as both a measure of credit risk for a country and of the firms that operate within the country. The Bank for International Settlements (**bis.org**) has been at the forefront in using credit ratings prominently in determining capital adequacy.

Multiple factors are used in performing credit risk analysis for sovereign country ratings. These include financial ratios; the economic, political, and regulatory environment; and industry trends. In the context of quantitative models, using financial, economic, and business data to arrive at a credit rating is a challenging process due to the complex and nonlinear interactions between different variables. However, this risk assessment process lacks a well-defined theory, which makes it difficult to apply conventional mathematical or rule-based techniques, although there are numerous quantitative approaches.

ANN are suited for modeling the determinants of ratings because they do not require prior specification of theoretical models. Their particular strength in classifying outcomes lends itself to producing a calibrated rating scale. ANN provide an alternative to the econometric approaches in that there are no assumptions with respect to the underlying properties and relationships within the data. ANN score above all other models in deriving meaning from complicated or imprecise data. A successful ANN implementation will generate a system of relationships that has been learned from observing past examples, and it can generalize and apply these lessons to new examples.

Bennell et al. (2006) compared ANN implementations to the standard credit risk analysis approach of probit. The sample set included 1,383 annual (end-of-calendar-year) observations of long-term foreign-currency sovereign credit ratings, assigned by 11 international credit rating agencies to 70 sovereign borrowers during the period from 1989 to 1999. The input variables were chosen to be consistent with the factors stressed in both the theoretical and empirical literature as determining the capacity and willingness of sovereign borrowers to service external debt. Some of the economic indicators that were chosen as explanatory variables are as follows:

Input Variable	**Description**
External debt/export	Total external debt relative to exports for the previous year
Fiscal balance	Average annual central government deficit (−) or surplus (+) relative to GDP for the previous three years (percentage)
External balance	Average annual current account balance relative to GDP for the previous three years (percentage)
Rate of inflation	Average annual consumer price inflation rate for the previous three years (percentage)
GDP per capita	GDP for the previous year (U.S. dollars)
GDP growth	Average annual real GDP growth on a year-over-year basis for the previous four years (percentage)
Development indicator	International Monetary Fund country classification for the current year (1 = industrial, 0 = not industrial)

Source: Adapted from J. Bennell, D. Crabbe, S. Thomas, and O. Gwilym, "Modelling Sovereign Credit Ratings: Neural Networks Versus Ordered Probit," *Expert Systems with Applications*, April 2006, pp. 415–425.

In addition to the macroeconomic variables specified here, two sets of indicator variables were included to capture effects on sovereign ratings in a given year: sovereign rating assigned by other rating agencies and the sovereign's location in a specific geographic region.

The data were split into three distinct groups: training (in sample), testing (out of sample), and cross-validation. A target split of the data of 65 percent, 20 percent, and 15 percent was set for training, testing, and cross-validation, respectively. However, the partitioning of the data was constrained by the 16 replication of ratings by different agencies. Multilayer feedforward networks, each with one hidden layer, were implemented. The number of neurons in the hidden layer was optimized by sequentially adding additional neurons until no further improvement in out-of-sample classification was achieved.

The authors used different learning rates and momentum values, ranging from 0.7 to 1. The training was performed for different number of cycles (called *epochs*): 1,000, 2,000, 3,000, 4,000, and 5,000. By comparing the mean absolute error across different trials, the authors selected a generalized feedforward (GFF) network as the best-performing network.

Multiple criteria are important in assessing the performance of neural networks. It is important to distinguish between within-sample modeling accuracy and out-of-sample predictive accuracy. Further informative criteria are included as well: percentage correctly classified within two and three rating notches, maximum deviation from correct rating, and mean absolute error. The neural network models were tested a number of times, and the authors reported the average performances as well as the best performance on each performance criterion.

The rating agencies collectively assign foreign currency sovereign ratings by assessing factors consistent with those stressed by the theory as vital to determine sovereign capacity and willingness to service external debt. In the case of the classification and regression models, the best model was obtained from training for 5,000 epochs. Keeping in mind the percentage of ratings accurately classified, the classification-based neural network model performs its best at 42.4 percent correct, with an average performance of 40.4 percent, followed by the regression-based neural network model, with 33.9 percent and 34.6 percent for best and average performance, respectively. Correctly classified ratings within one notch were achieved in 67.3 percent and 73.5 percent of cases and an average performance of 63.6 percent and 68.9 percent cases for the classification and regression models, respectively. Within three notches, the regression-based neural network model accurately classifies on average 96.7 percent of ratings, with the other two models approaching the 90 percent accuracy mark.

In comparing the two neural network models, the regression model achieves a lower percentage of correctly classified ratings than the classification model, but it tends to deviate much less if a rating is not precisely correct.

The findings indicate that ANN for fitting credit ratings for corporations as practiced by the major rating agencies (e.g., Moody's, S&P) can be successfully applied to sovereign ratings. An analyst's role and partly subjective process of assigning a credit rating cannot be eliminated by neural networks. However, it appears that ANN could inform and support the analyst in the decision-making process.

Sources: J. Bennell, D. Crabbe, S. Thomas, and O. Gwilym, "Modelling Sovereign Credit Ratings: Neural Networks versus Ordered Probit," *Expert Systems with Applications*, April 2006, pp. 415–425; and S. Hoti and M. McAleer, *Country Risk Ratings: An International Comparison*, **e.u-tokyo.ac.jp/cirje/research/papers/mcaleer/mcaleer4.pdf** (accessed March 2006).

QUESTIONS FOR THE CASE

1. What are sovereign ratings? Why are sovereign ratings important?
2. What role do rating agencies play?
3. What is the role of neural networks in sovereign ratings? Do you think we should entirely rely on neural network prediction?
4. What would you conclude from the outcomes of neural network–based rating prediction experiments?
5. You are a credit analyst at Standard & Poor's. You have been asked to rate India's sovereign credit. What factors would you consider in arriving at a credit rating, and how would you use neural networks in arriving at a result? Explain.

References

Ainscough, T.L., and J.E. Aronson. (1999). "A Neural Networks Approach for the Analysis of Scanner Data." *Journal of Retailing and Consumer Services*, Vol. 6.

Altman, E.I. (1968). "Financial Ratios, Discriminant Analysis and the Prediction of Corporate Bankruptcy." *Journal of Finance*, Vol. 23.

Bennell, J., D. Crabbe, S. Thomas, and O. Gwilym. (2006, April). "Modelling Sovereign Credit Ratings: Neural Networks versus Ordered Probit," *Expert Systems with Applications*.

Collard, J.E. (1990). "Commodity Trading with a Neural Net." *Neural Network News*, Vol. 2, No. 10.

Collins, E., S. Ghosh, C.L. and Scofield. (1988). "An Application of a Multiple Neural Network Learning System to Emulation of Mortgage Underwriting Judgments," *IEEE International Conference on Neural Networks*.

Davis, J.T., A. Episcopos, and S. Wettimuny. (2001). "Predicting Direction Shifts on Canadian–U.S. Exchange Rates with Artificial Neural Networks," *International Journal of Intelligent Systems in Accounting, Finance and Management*, Vol. 10, No. 2.

Dutta, S., and S. Shakhar. (1988, July 24–27). "Bond-Rating: A Non-Conservative Application of Neural

Networks" *Proceedings of the IEEE International Conference on Neural Networks*, San Diego.

Fadlalla, A., and C. Lin. (2001). "An Analysis of the Applications of Neural Networks in Finance." *Interfaces*, Vol. 31, No. 4.

Fishman, M., D. Barr, and W. Loick. (1991, April). "Using Neural Networks in Market Analysis," *Technical Analysis of Stocks and Commodities*.

Fozzard, R., G. Bradshaw, and L. Ceci. (1989). "A Connectionist Expert System for Solar Flare Forecasting," in D.S. Touretsky (ed.), *Advances in Neural Information Processing Systems* Vol.1. San Mateo, CA: Kaufman Publishing.

Francett, B. (1989, January). "Neural Nets Arrive." *Computer Decisions*.

Gallant, S. (1988, February). "Connectionist Expert Systems," *Communications of the ACM*, Vol. 31, No. 2.

Haykin, S.S. (1999). *Neural Networks: A Comprehensive Foundation*, 2nd ed. Upper Saddle River, NJ: Prentice Hall.

Hill, T., T. Marquez, M. O'Connor, and M. Remus. (1994). "Neural Network Models for Forecasting and Decision Making," *International Journal of Forecasting*, Vol. 10.

Hopfield, J. (1982, April). "Neural Networks and Physical Systems with Emergent Collective Computational Abilities." *Proceedings of National Academy of Science*, Vol. 79, No. 8.

Hopfield, J.J., and D.W. Tank. (1985). "Neural Computation of Decisions in Optimization Problems," *Biological Cybernetics*, Vol. 52.

Kamijo, K., and T. Tanigawa. (1990, June 7–11). "Stock Price Pattern Recognition: A Recurrent Neural Network Approach," *International Joint Conference on Neural Networks*, San Diego.

Lee, P.Y., S.C. Hui, and A.C.M. Fong. (2002, September/October). "Neural Networks for Web Content Filtering." *IEEE Intelligent Systems*.

Liang, T.P. (1992). "A Composite Approach to Automated Knowledge Acquisition." *Management Science*, Vol. 38, No. 1.

McCulloch, W.S., and W.H. Pitts. (1943). "A Logical Calculus of the Ideas Imminent in Nervous Activity." *Bulletin of Mathematical Biophysics*, Vol. 5.

Mighell, D. (1989). "Back-Propagation and Its Application to Handwritten Signature Verification," in D. S. Touretsky (ed.), *Advances in Neural Information Processing Systems*. San Mateo, CA: Kaufman.

Minsky, M., and S. Papert. (1969). *Perceptrons*. Cambridge, MA: MIT Press.

Principe, J.C., N.R. Euliano, and W.C. Lefebvre. (2000). *Neural and Adaptive Systems: Fundamentals Through Simulations*. New York: Wiley.

Rochester, J. (ed.). (1990, February). "New Business Uses for Neurocomputing." *I/S Analyzer*.

Surkan, A., and J. Singleton. (1990). "Neural Networks for Bond Rating Improved by Multiple Hidden Layers." *Proceedings of the IEEE International Conference on Neural Networks*, Vol. 2.

Tang, Z., C. de Almieda, and P. Fishwick. (1991). "Time-Series Forecasting Using Neural Networks vs. Box-Jenkins Methodology." *Simulation*, Vol. 57, No. 5.

Thaler, S.L. (2002, January/February). "AI for Network Protection: LITMUS:—Live Intrusion Tracking via Multiple Unsupervised STANNOs." *PC AI*.

Walczak, S., W.E. Pofahi, and R.J. Scorpio. (2002). "A Decision Support Tool for Allocating Hospital Bed Resources and Determining Required Acuity of Care." *Decision Support* Systems, Vol. 34, No. 4.

Wilson, R., and R. Sharda. (1994). "Bankruptcy Prediction Using Neural Networks." *Decision Support Systems*, Vol. 11.

Zahedi, F. (1993). *Intelligent Systems for Business: Expert Systems with Neural Networks*. Belmont, CA: Wadsworth.

Business Performance Management

Learning Objectives

- Understand the all-encompassing nature of business performance management (BPM)
- Understand the closed-loop processes linking strategy to execution
- Describe some of the best practices in planning and management reporting
- Describe the difference between performance management and measurement
- Understand the role of methodologies in BPM
- Describe the basic elements of the balanced scorecard and Six Sigma methodologies
- Describe the differences between scorecards and dashboards
- Understand some of the basics of dashboard design
- Understand the potential uses of business activity monitoring (BAM)

Business performance management (BPM) represents the next phase in the evolution of decision support systems (DSS), enterprise information systems (EIS), and business intelligence (BI). It has been at least 25 years in the making. Like decision support, BPM is more than a technology. It is an integrated set of processes, methodologies, metrics, and applications designed to drive the overall financial and operational performance of an enterprise. It helps enterprises translate their strategies and objectives into plans, monitor performance against those plans, analyze variations between actual results and planned results, and adjust their objectives and actions in response to this analysis.

This chapter examines the processes, methodologies, metrics, and systems underlying BPM. Because BPM is distinguished from DSS and BI by its focus on strategy and objectives, the chapter begins with an exploration of the notions of enterprise strategy and execution and the gap that often exists between them. The specific sections are:

9.1 Opening Vignette: Cisco and the Virtual Close

9.2 Business Performance Management (BPM) Overview

9.3 Strategize: Where Do We Want to Go?

9.4 Plan: How Do We Get There?

9.5 Monitor: How Are We Doing?

9.1 OPENING VIGNETTE: CISCO AND THE VIRTUAL CLOSE

Cisco Systems bills itself as the "worldwide leader in networking for the Internet." It provides networking solutions—hardware, software, and services—that connect the computing devices and networks that comprise the Internet and most of the corporate, education, and government networks around the globe. Cisco was founded in 1984. For most of its history, it has been financially successful. For example, in 2005, Cisco reported revenues of just over $25 billion. The company's market capitalization (i.e., the value of its outstanding stock shares) is over $100 billion, which makes Cisco one of the largest computer companies in the world.

PROBLEM

Besides being a pioneer and market leader in the computer industry, Cisco is also a pioneer in management and financial reporting. During the Internet and dot-com boom, Cisco's revenues grew at an annual compound rate greater than 60 percent. Much of the growth was fueled by the acquisition of smaller companies. The chief financial officer, Larry Carter, was worried that Cisco's financial reporting system could not keep pace with the rapid growth. To solve the problem, he decided to institute a process called the "virtual close," which would provide the capability to determine the financial state of the company with an hour's notice and to disseminate the information instantly through the company's intranet. To accomplish this, Cisco would have to post all of its financial transactions (e.g., inventory, payables, billing) in near real-time. At that time, it was taking Cisco two weeks to close its financial books. Today, it still takes many companies two or more weeks to accomplish the task. By 1999, Cisco's financial department had succeeded in instituting the new process.

Cisco's new process was heralded by the press and market analysts. The system worked well for a couple years, until the dot-com bust in 2001. In that year, when the telecommunications companies started to fail, demand for Cisco's products declined dramatically. Cisco was suddenly overstocked with inventory. By the third quarter of that year, the company reported losses of almost $3 billion. Its stock went from approximately $80 per share to around $8 per share. What went wrong with the virtual close? The system was supposed to provide Cisco with the capability to react rapidly to changing market conditions. One explanation provided by CEO John Chambers was that the virtual close allowed the company to track financials and other operational information on a daily basis, but it didn't allow Cisco to predict the future, especially macroeconomic trends. Whatever the explanation, Cisco was unable to avoid the dramatic economic downturns that started at the beginning of 2001, even though it had in place a state-of-the-art measuring and monitoring system.

SOLUTION

Unlike many other companies, Cisco was able to weather what Chambers labeled "a hundred-year storm." It took a combination of analysis, strategic thinking, and tactical execution. It wasn't the measurement system that was at fault. In fact, some analysts suggested that the damage to Cisco would have been greater if the virtual close hadn't been in place. Based on their analysis, Cisco's senior management reasoned that the telecommunications market was shrinking but that it wouldn't disappear. It was simply a cyclical downturn, not a permanent change. There was no need to switch products or to dramatically change Cisco's business model. Instead, the company needed to dramatically improve its profitability at lower revenue levels by reducing operating costs and improving productivity. It did this through a series of steps. Cisco drastically reduced its inventory and took a $2.5 billion inventory write-down. Next, it cut costs by reducing headcount by 20,000 employees. Finally, the company reduced the number of models for each product group and started using internal product development rather than relying on product acquisitions to bolster its product offerings.

Of course, it's easy to improve profitability by slashing costs. But that can work for only a short period of time. Eventually, a company has to figure out ways to grow its business if it wants to survive in the long run. Fortunately, Cisco also adjusted its growth strategy at the same time it was addressing costs and productivity. It believed that it could leverage its business and technical expertise to enter new markets. By 2003, Cisco had entered six new product areas, including optical networks, wireless local area networks (LANs), network security, IP telephony, storage networking, and consumer/home networking. Chambers expressed his belief that each of these new areas had the potential to create $1 billion in revenues.

RESULTS

In 2005, Cisco's revenues were over $25 billion, with a net income close to $6 billion. This represented a 12 percent increase in sales over the year before. The company's growth continues to be fueled by acquisitions, such as the purchase in 2003 of the home and small business networking company Linksys, as well as its internal investments in new product areas. As Cisco predicted, the new product areas have turned into billion-dollar opportunities. For example, Cisco's network security and IP telephony offerings now generate about $1 billion each in sales per year.

Cisco is leading the transition to intelligent network environments. Its success has resulted from continuously planning three to five years ahead of important market transitions. As Chambers said, "Historically, the transitions we've been a part of have been technological; they've been relatively orderly and predictable. Now, however, we're seeing a wider-reaching, more dramatic transition. So our ability to predict successfully where the market will go is even more critical and offers much greater potential import for the company."

Sources: Compiled from A. Hartman, *Ruthless Execution*, Prentice Hall, Upper Saddle River, NJ, 2004; G. Moore, *Dealing with Darwin*, Penguin, New York, 2005; and *Corporate Overview*, **newsroom.cisco.com/dlls/company_overview.html** (accessed April 2006).

Questions for the Opening Vignette

1. What is the virtual close system?
2. What explanation did John Chambers, Cisco CEO, give for the company's downturn in 2001?
3. What was Cisco's strategic response to its financial downturn in 2001?

WHAT WE CAN LEARN FROM THIS VIGNETTE

Cisco's virtual close enabled the company to monitor key indicators of operational or tactical importance. What it didn't do was provide the company with the means to model certain critical strategic assumptions, such as market growth or the lack of growth. As Cisco learned, effective business performance requires an organization to model and monitor not only its tactics but also its strategies and the assumptions on which those strategies are built.

9.2 BUSINESS PERFORMANCE MANAGEMENT (BPM) OVERVIEW

As Cisco's experience exemplifies, it is difficult for a business or an enterprise to align its strategies, plans, analytical systems, and actions in such a way that they ensure successful performance. It is this alignment that performance management, as opposed to performance measurement, addresses.

BPM DEFINED

In the business and trade literature, performance management has a number of names, including BPM, corporate performance management (CPM), enterprise performance management (EPM), and strategic enterprise management (SEM). Although different terms are used, they all mean essentially the same thing. For example, SEM is a term that SAP (**sap.com**) uses, and it has been defined as "the management techniques, metrics and related tools (such as computer software) designed to assist companies in making high-level strategic decisions" (Wikipedia.org, 2006). Similarly, the market analyst firm Gartner (**gartner.com**) has defined CPM as an "umbrella term covering the processes, methodologies, metrics and technologies for enterprises to measure, monitor, and manage business performance" (Buytendijk, 2004). Finally, the BPM Standards Group (2005) (**bpmstandardsgroup.org**) has defined **business performance management (BPM)** as "a framework for organizing, automating, and analyzing business methodologies, metrics, processes, and systems to drive the overall performance of the enterprise. It helps organizations translate a unified set of objectives into plans, monitor execution, and deliver critical insight to improve financial and operational performance." In this chapter, the term *BPM* is used rather than the other terms because it is the term used by the standards group.

BPM AND BI COMPARED

BPM is an outgrowth of BI and incorporates many of its technologies, applications, and techniques. Some critics of BPM wonder why BI can't deliver the insight needed to improve overall business performance. From a theoretical viewpoint, it can. From a practical standpoint, it hasn't. For example, many companies have focused their BI initiatives on departmental issues rather than enterprise-wide problems. Table 9.1 details some of the ways in which enterprises have traditionally used BI versus the way in which BI needs to be deployed to support BPM.

BPM is not new. Every organization of a certain size has processes in place (e.g., budgets, detailed plans, execution, measurement) that feed back to the overall plan. What the concept of BPM adds to what organizations have been doing for years is the integration of these processes, methodologies, metrics, and systems. BPM is an enterprise-wide strategy that seeks to prevent organizations from optimizing local business at the expense of overall corporate performance. It is not a "one-off" project but rather an ongoing process—part of the daily work of managers.

TABLE 9.1 Differences Between Traditional BI and BI for BPM

Factor	*Traditional BI*	*BI for BPM*
Scale	Departmental	Enterprise-wide
Focus	Historical	Timely
Decisions	Strategic and tactical	Strategic, tactical, and operational
Users	Analysts	Everyone
Orientation	Reactive	Proactive
Process	Open-ended	Closed-loop
Measures	Metrics	Key performance indicators
Views	Generic	Personalized
Visuals	Tables/charts	Dashboards/scorecards
Collaboration	Informal	Built-in
Interaction	Pull (ad hoc queries)	Push (alerts)
Analysis	Trends	Exceptions
Data	Numeric only	Numeric, text, etc.

Source: W. Eckerson, *Best Practices in Business Performance Management: Business and Technical Strategies*, March 2004, **tdwi.org/display.aspx?id=6972** (accessed October 2006).

SUMMARY OF BPM PROCESSES

BPM encompasses a closed-loop set of processes that link strategy to execution in order to optimize business performance (see Figure 9.1). The loop implies that optimum performance is achieved by setting goals and objectives (i.e., strategize), establishing initiatives and plans to achieve those goals (i.e., plan), monitoring actual performance against

FIGURE 9.1 BPM Closed-Loop Processes

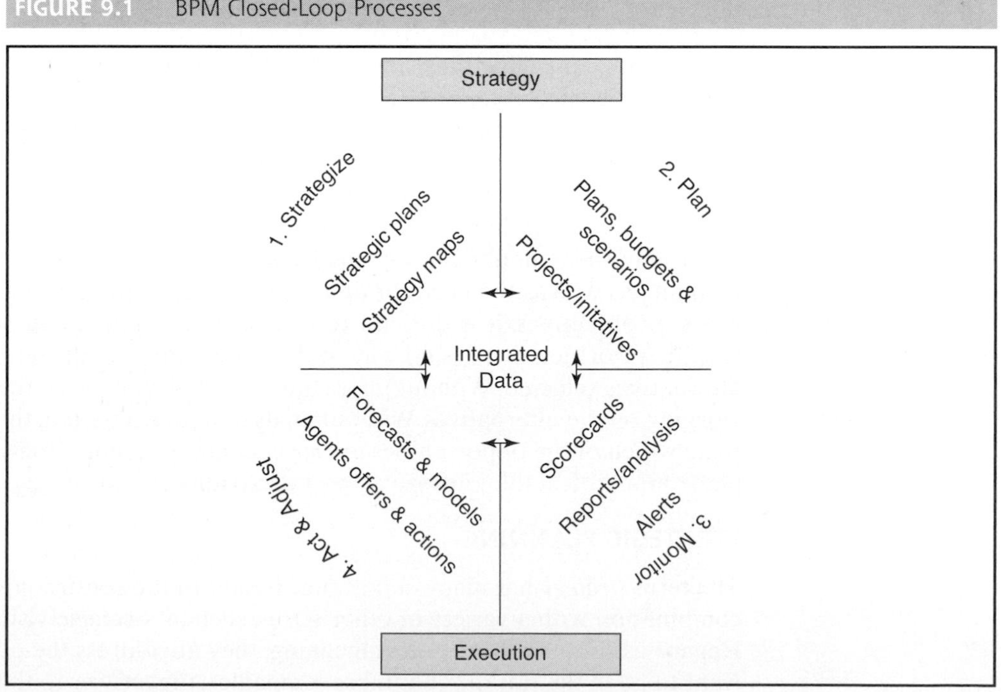

Source: W. Eckerson. *Performance Dashboard*, Wiley. Hoboken, NJ, 2006.

the goals and objectives (i.e., monitor), and taking corrective action (i.e., act and adjust). In Sections 9.3 through 9.6, each of these major processes is examined in detail.

Section 9.2 Review Questions

1. Define *BPM*.
2. Summarize the ways in which BI for BPM differs from traditional BI.
3. List the major BPM processes.

9.3 STRATEGIZE: WHERE DO WE WANT TO GO?

During the dot-com era, many managers and business pundits were convinced that strategy was superfluous. In their minds, the complexity and pace of change in the business environment would make any strategy obsolete within a short period of time. In the words of one of these pundits (Tarlow and Tarlow, 2002),

> Much of the standard business literature still relies on the idea that we need to define our goals, set priorities, develop our strategies, manage our outcomes, the words of one of these pundits (Tarlow and Tarlow, 2002), and evaluate our impacts. I can assure you that if you operate this way, someone has already beaten you to the finish line. You cannot plan fast enough. We need behaviors that are far more bold and attuned to the unique nature of our time.

As Michael Porter (2001) noted in his McKinsey Award–winning *Harvard Business Review* article "Strategy and the Internet," many companies followed this sort of advice. During this period, "both dot-coms and established companies violated nearly every precept of good strategy"—chasing customers indiscriminately, pursuing indirect revenues, offering every conceivable product or service rather than focusing on profits, concentrating on delivering value, and making competitive trade-offs. The results of following this advice are now well known. In March 2000, there were 378 publicly traded Internet companies. Their market cap was $1.5 trillion. Yet, they had combined annual sales of only $40 billion, and 87 percent never showed a quarterly profit. By the summer of 2001, their market cap had dropped 75 percent, they had laid off 31,000 employees and 130 had closed their doors. The new economy was over almost before it began.

Today, the pendulum has swung back. Companies recognize the value of strategic planning as well as the need for operational or execution excellence. Without specific goals or objectives, it is difficult to evaluate alternative courses of action. Without specific priorities, there is no way to determine how to allocate resources among the alternatives selected. Without plans, there is no way to guide the actions among those working on the alternatives. Without analysis and evaluation, there is no way to determine which of the opportunities are succeeding or failing. Goals, objectives, priorities, plans, and critical thinking are all part of a well-defined strategy.

STRATEGIC PLANNING

The term *strategy* has many definitions. To add to the confusion, it is also often used in combination with a variety of other terms, such as strategic vision and strategic focus. Regardless of the differences in meaning, they all address the question "Where do we want to go in the future?" For most companies, the answer to this question is provided

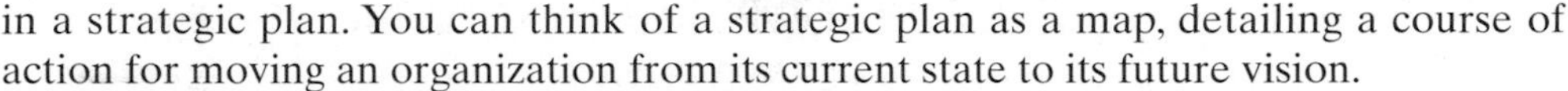

in a strategic plan. You can think of a strategic plan as a map, detailing a course of action for moving an organization from its current state to its future vision.

Typically, strategic plans start at the top and begin with an enterprise-wide view. From there, strategic plans are created for the company's business units or functional units. The following tasks are quite common to the strategic planning process, regardless of the level at which the planning is done—enterprise-wide, business unit, or functional unit (Wade and Recardo, 2001):

1. *Conduct a current situation analysis.* This analysis reviews the company's current situation ("Where are we?") and establishes a baseline, as well as key trends, for financial performance and operational performance.
2. *Determine the planning horizon.* Traditionally, organizations produce plans on a yearly basis, with the planning horizon running three to five years. In large part, the time horizon is determined by the volatility and predictability of the market, product life cycles, the size of the organization, the rate of technological innovation, and the capital intensity of the industry. The more volatile, the less predictable, the shorter the life cycles, the smaller the organization, the faster the rate of innovation, and the less the capital intensity, the shorter the planning horizon.
3. *Conduct an environment scan.* An environment scan is a standard strengths, weaknesses, opportunities, and threats (SWOT) assessment of the company. It identifies and prioritizes the key customer, market, competitor, government, demographic, stakeholder, and industry factors potentially or actually affecting the company.
4. *Identify critical success factors.* **Critical success factors (CSF)** delineate those things that an organization must excel at to be successful in its market space. For a product-focused company, product quality and product innovation are examples of CSF. For a low-cost provider such as Wal-Mart, distribution capabilities are a CSF.
5. *Complete a gap analysis.* Like the environment scan, a gap analysis is used to identify and prioritize the internal strengths and weaknesses in an organization's processes, structures, and technologies and applications. The gaps reflect what the strategy actually requires and what the organization actually provides.
6. *Create a strategic vision.* An organization's **strategic vision** provides a picture or mental image of what the organization should look like in the future—the shift in its products and markets. Generally, the vision is couched in terms of its strategy focus and identifies the as-is state and the desired state.
7. *Develop a business strategy.* The challenge in this step is to produce a strategy that is based on the data and information from the previous steps and is consistent with the strategic vision. Common sense tells us that the strategy needs to exploit the organization's strengths, take advantage of its opportunities, address weaknesses, and respond to threats. The company needs to ensure that the strategy is internally consistent, that the organizational culture is aligned with the strategy, and that there are sufficient resources and capital to implement the strategy.
8. *Identify strategic objectives and goals.* A strategic plan that fails to provide clear directions for the operational and financial planning process is incomplete. Before an operational or financial plan can be established, strategic objectives must be established and refined into well-defined goals or targets. A **strategic objective** is a broad statement or general course of action that prescribes targeted directions for an organization. Before a strategic objective can be linked to an operational plan or a financial plan, it should be converted into a well-defined goal or target. A **strategic goal** is a quantification of an objective for a designated period of time. For example, if an organization has an objective of improving return on assets (ROA) or increasing overall profitability, these objectives need to be turned into quanti-

fied targets (e.g., an increase of ROA from 10 percent to 15 percent or an increase in profit margin from 5 percent to 7 percent) before the organization can begin to detail the operational plans needed to achieve these targets. In the same vein, when Cisco declared that it was going to expand its product offerings in six advanced technology product areas, this objective needed to be transformed into a well-defined target, such as growing each advanced technology product area to a $1 billion per year run rate, before the company could make product investment and acquisition decisions. Strategic goals and targets guide operational execution and allow progress to be tracked against overall objectives.

THE STRATEGY GAP

It's one thing to create a long-term strategy and another to execute it. An often-quoted *Fortune* magazine study from 1999 found that 70 percent of CEO failures were the result of poor execution rather than poor strategies (Charan and Colvin, 1999). Niven (2005) pinpointed four sources for the gap between strategy and execution:

1. *Vision.* A line in the movie *Cool Hand Luke*, "What we have here is a failure to communicate," applies to strategic vision. In many organizations, only a very small percentage (around 5 percent) of the employees understand the organization's strategy. Without this knowledge, it is difficult, if not impossible, for employees to make decisions and act in accordance with the strategic plan.
2. *People.* Linking pay to performance is important for successful execution. However, incentive plans are often linked to short-term financial results, not to the strategic plan or even the strategic initiatives articulated in the operational plan. Maximizing short-term gains leads to less than rational decision making.
3. *Management.* Management often spends time on the periphery of issues rather than concentrating on the core elements. Hours can be spent debating line items on a budget, with little attention given to the strategy, the linkage of the financial plan to the strategy, or the assumptions underlying the linkage.
4. *Resources.* In recent times, critics (e.g., the Beyond Budgeting Round Table [**bbrt.org**]) have called into question the necessity of budgets and the budgeting process. Unless strategic initiatives are properly funded and resourced, their failure is virtually assured.

Section 9.3 Review Questions

1. Why does a company need a well-formulated strategy?

2. What are the basic tasks in the strategic planning process?

9.4 PLAN: HOW DO WE GET THERE?

When operational managers know and understand the *what* (i.e., the organizational objectives and goals), they will be able to come up with the *how* (i.e., detailed operational and financial plans). Operational and financial plans answer two questions. What tactics and initiatives will be pursued to meet the performance targets established by the strategic plan? What are the expected financial results of executing the tactics?

OPERATIONAL PLANNING

An **operational plan** translates an organization's strategic objectives and goals into a set of well-defined tactics and initiatives, resource requirements, and expected results for some future time period, usually but not always a year. In essence, an operational plan is like a project plan that is designed to ensure that an organization's strategy is realized. Most operational plans encompass a portfolio of tactics and initiatives. The key to successful operational planning is integration. Strategy drives tactics, and tactics drive results. Basically, the tactics and initiatives defined in an operational plan need to be directly linked to key objectives and targets in the strategic plan. If there is no linkage between an individual tactic and one or more strategic objectives or targets, management should question whether the tactic and its associated initiatives are really needed at all. The BPM methodologies discussed in Section 9.8 are designed to ensure that these linkages exist.

Operational planning can be either tactic-centric or budget-centric (see Axson, 2003). In a *tactic-centric* plan, tactics are established to meet the objectives and targets established in the strategic plan. Conversely, in a *budget-centric* plan, a financial plan or budget is established that sums to the targeted financial values. Best practice organizations use tactic-centric operational planning. This means that they begin the operational planning process by defining the alternative tactics and initiatives that can be used to reach a particular target. For example, if a business is targeting a 10 percent growth in profit margin (i.e., the ratio of the difference between revenue and expenses divided by revenue), the business will first determine whether it plans to increase the margin by increasing revenues, by reducing expenses, or some combination of both. If it focuses on revenues, then the question will become whether it plans to enter new markets or increase sales to existing markets, whether it plans to enhance existing products or introduce new products, or some combination of these. The alternate scenarios and associated initiatives have to be weighed in terms of their overall risk, resource requirements, and financial viability. Online File W9.1 discusses the steps used in making decisions among the various scenarios.

FINANCIAL PLANNING AND BUDGETING

In most organizations, resources tend to be scarce. If they weren't, organizations could simply throw people and money at their opportunities and problems and overwhelm the competition. Given the scarcity of resources, an organization needs to put its money and people where its strategies and linked tactics are. An organization's strategic objectives and key metrics should serve as top-down drivers for the allocation of an organization's tangible and intangible assets. While continuing operations clearly need support, key resources should be assigned to the most important strategic programs and priorities. Most organizations use their budgets and compensation programs to allocate resources. By implication, both of these need to be carefully aligned with the organization's strategic objectives and tactics in order to achieve strategic success.

The best way for an organization to achieve this alignment is to base its financial plan on its operational plan or, more directly, to allocate and budget its resources against specific tactics and initiatives. For example, if one of the tactics is to develop a new sales channel, budgeted revenues and costs need to be assigned to the channel rather than simply having costs assigned to particular functional units, such as marketing and R&D. Without this type of tactical resource planning, there is no way to measure the success of those tactics and hence the strategy. This type of linkage helps organizations avoid the problem of "random" budget cuts that inadvertently affect associated strategies. Tactic-based budgeting ensures that the link between particular budget-line items and particular tactics or initiatives is well established and well known.

The financial planning and budgeting process has a logical structure that typically starts with those tactics that generate some form of revenue or income. In organizations that sell goods or services, the ability to generate revenue is based on either the ability to directly produce goods and services or acquire the right amount of goods and services to sell. After a revenue figure has been established, the associated costs of delivering that level of revenue can be generated. Quite often, this entails input from several departments or tactics. This means the process has to be collaborative and that dependencies between functions need to be clearly communicated and understood. In addition to the collaborative input, the organization also needs to add various overhead costs, as well as the costs of the capital required. This information, once consolidated, shows the cost by tactic as well as the cash and funding requirements to put the plan into operation.

Section 9.4 Review Questions

1. What is the goal of operational planning?
2. What is tactic-centric planning? What is budget-centric planning?
3. What is the primary goal of a financial plan?

9.5 MONITOR: HOW ARE WE DOING?

When the operational plan and financial plans are under way, it is imperative that the performance of the organization be monitored. A comprehensive framework for monitoring performance should address two key issues: what to monitor and how to monitor. Because it is impossible to look at everything, an organization needs to focus on monitoring specific issues. After the organization has identified the indicators or measures to look at, it needs to develop a strategy for monitoring those factors and responding effectively.

In Sections 9.7 and 9.8, we examine in detail how to determine what should be measured by a BPM system. For the moment, we simply note that the "what" is usually defined by the CSF and the goals or targets established in the strategic planning process. For example, if an instrument manufacturer has a specified strategic objective of increasing the overall profit margin of its current product lines by 5 percent annually over the next three years, the organization needs to monitor the profit margin throughout the year to see whether it is trending toward the targeted annual rate of 5 percent. In the same vein, if this company plans to introduce a new product every quarter for the next two years, the organization needs to track new product introduction over the designated time period.

DIAGNOSTIC CONTROL SYSTEMS

Most companies use what is known as a *diagnostic control system* to monitor organizational performance and correct deviations from present performance standards. This is true even for those organizations that do not have formal BPM processes or systems. A **diagnostic control system** is a cybernetic system, meaning that it has inputs, a process for transforming the inputs into outputs, a standard or benchmark against which to compare the outputs, and a feedback channel to allow information on variances between the outputs and the standard to be communicated and acted upon. Virtually

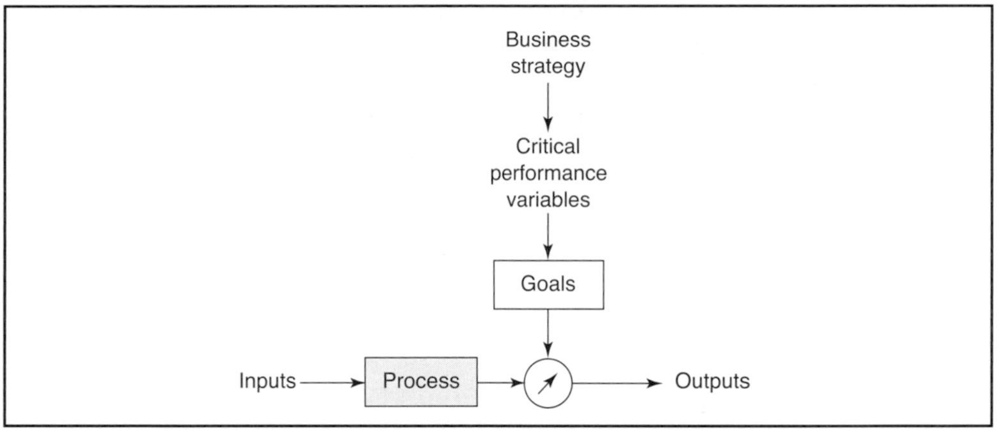

Business strategy → Critical performance variables → Goals → Inputs → Process → Outputs

FIGURE 9.2 Diagnostic Control System

Source: R. Simons, *Performance Measurement and Control Systems for Implementing Strategy*, Prentice Hall, Upper Saddle River, NJ, 2002.

any information system can be used as a diagnostic control system if it is possible to (1) set a goal in advance, (2) measure outputs, (3) compute or calculate absolute or relative performance variances, and (4) use the variance information as feedback to alter inputs and/or processes to bring performance back in line with present goals and standards. The key elements of a diagnostic control system are depicted in Figure 9.2. Balanced scorecards, performance dashboards, project monitoring systems, human resources systems, and financial reporting systems are all examples of systems that can be used diagnostically.

An effective diagnostic control system encourages *management by exception*. Instead of constantly monitoring a variety of internal processes and target values and comparing actual results with planned results, managers receive regularly schedule exception reports. Measures that are aligned with expectations receive little attention. If, on the other hand, a significant variation is identified, then—and only then—managers need to invest time and attention to investigate the cause of the deviation and initiate appropriate remedial action.

PITFALLS OF VARIANCE ANALYSIS

In many organizations, the vast majority of the exception analysis focuses on negative variances when functional groups or departments fail to meet their targets. Rarely are positive variances reviewed for potential opportunities, and rarely does the analysis focus on assumptions underlying the variance patterns. Consider, for a moment, the two paths depicted in Figure 9.3. In this figure, the dashed line from A to B represents planned or targeted results over a specified period of time. Recognizing that there will be minor deviations from the plan, we might expect the actual results to deviate slightly from the targeted results. When the deviation is larger than expected, this is typically viewed as an operational error that needs to be corrected. At this point, managers usually direct their employees to do whatever it takes to get the plan back on track. If revenues are below plan, they are chided to sell harder. If costs are above plan, they are told to stop spending.

However, what happens if our strategic assumptions—not the operations—are wrong? What if the organization needs to change strategic directions toward point C

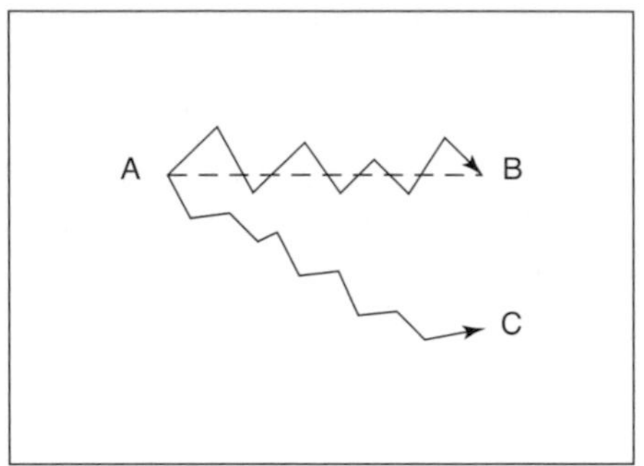

FIGURE 9.3 Operational Variance or Strategic Issue?

rather than continuing with the original plan? As Application Case 9.1 exemplifies, the results of proceeding on the basis of fallacious assumptions can be disastrous. The only way to make this sort of determination is to monitor more than actual versus targeted performance. Whatever diagnostic control system is being used needs to track underlying assumptions, cause-and-effect relationships, and the overall validity of the intended strategy. Consider, for instance, a growth strategy that is focused on the introduction of a new product. This sort of strategy is usually based on certain assumptions about market demand or the availability of parts from particular suppliers. As the strategy unfolds, management needs to monitor not only the revenues and costs associated with the new product but also variations in the market demand or availability of parts or any other key assumptions.

Application Case 9.1

Discovery-Driven Planning: The Case of Euro Disney

Remember FedEx's Zapmail product? What about Polaroid's instant movie venture? You probably don't remember either one of them because they were resounding failures. Any new venture—new products, markets, partnerships, and the like—has a high chance of failure, but many such failures could be prevented with the right approach to planning, measurement, and performance management.

There is a difference between planning for a conventional line of business and planning for a new venture. Conventional planning operates on the premise that a business can extrapolate future results from a well-understood, predictable platform of past experience. In platform-based planning, deviations from plan are bad, signaling that management needs to get the business back on course. New ventures require a business to envision what is unknown, uncertain, and not yet obvious to the competition. New ventures are undertaken with a high ratio of assumption to solid knowledge. Because assumptions associated with a new venture usually turn out to be wrong, deviations from plan are to be expected rather than regretted. In these cases, if platform-based planning is used, the results can be quite disastrous because assumptions are treated as facts rather than estimates that need to be questioned and tested.

EXPERIENCE OF EURO DISNEY

The Walt Disney Company is well known for its theme parks. Its success in this market has not been confined to the United States. Tokyo Disneyland has been a financial and public relations success from its opening in 1983. Euro Disney (now called Disneyland Paris) is another story. Within two years of opening, it had reached its target of 11 million admissions. However, this was only accomplished by dropping ticket prices drastically. Average spending per visit was far below plan. The result was a $1 billion loss.

While there were many factors underlying the loss, one of the major problems is that Disney had built its strategic and operational plans on the assumption that visitors to Euro Disney would behave essentially the same as visitors to the company's other theme parks. Basically, it treated Euro Disney as an ongoing business rather than a new venture. In particular, it assumed that the European visitors would willingly pay a high entrance price ($40, at the time), that they would stay an average of four days in one of the park's hotels, that they would eat regularly throughout the day, and that they would buy a similar mix of souvenirs to what visitors at the company's other parks buy. As it turned out, they stayed away from the park because of the high entrance fee, they stayed only an average of two days because there were many fewer rides at Euro Disney than at the other parks (at the time, 15 versus 45), they often left the park to eat because the restaurants were designed to handle a continuous stream of visitors rather than large European crowds that were accustomed to eating lunch at noon, and they bought fewer souvenirs, especially the higher-margin items.

DISCOVERY-DRIVEN PLANNING

Like Disney, other companies have paid a similar price for using platform-based planning built on implicit assumptions that later turned out to be faulty. To avoid these errors, McGrath and MacMillan (1995, 2000) suggested that companies use discovery-driven planning. *Discovery-driven planning* offers a systematic way to uncover problematic assumptions that otherwise remain unnoticed and unchallenged. It is called *discovery-driven* because plans evolve as new data are uncovered and new potentials are discovered. Discovery-driven planning rests on four interrelated steps:

1. *Reverse-income statement.* Instead of using forecasted revenues to plan costs and profits, the company specifies its profitability goals and derives the required revenues and allowed costs that will generate the desired profitability.
2. *Pro forma operations specs.* The second step is to lay out all the activities required to produce, sell, service, and deliver the product or service to the customer. Together, these activities represent the allowable costs.
3. *Assumption checklist.* Virtually every industry or market has external and internal standards and benchmarks that can be used to produce a checklist of performance metrics that can be tracked and evolved as the venture unfolds. Examples include things like asset-to-sales ratios, inventory turns, profit margins, and sales calls per day.
4. *Milestone planning.* Every plan lays out particular milestones. With each milestone, particular assumptions from the checklist need to be tested. The results of those tests are used to make decisions about continued resource investments.

Sources: Compiled from R. McGrath and I. MacMillan. "Discovery-Driven Planning," *Harvard Business Review*, July–August 1995; R. McGrath and I. MacMillan. *The Entrepreneurial Mindset*, Harvard Business School Press, Boston, 2000; and P. Schoemaker, *Profiting from Uncertainty*, The Free Press, New York, 2002.

Section 9.5 Review Questions

1. What are the key elements of a diagnostic control system?

2. What is *management by exception*?

3. What is one of the major pitfalls of variance analysis, from a managerial perspective?

4. What types of planning problems are addressed by discovery-driven planning?

5. What are the major steps in discovery-driven planning?

9.6 ACT AND ADJUST: WHAT DO WE NEED TO DO DIFFERENTLY?

Organizations spend an enormous amount of money and time developing plans, collecting data, and generating management reports. The Hackett Group (**thehackettgroup.com**) has spent a substantial amount of time benchmarking the planning and reporting habits of more than 2,000 organizations, including a number of the largest companies in the United States. The structure of its studies is detailed in Technology Insights 9.2. According to

Hackett Group's benchmarks, the average billion-dollar company devotes 23,000 and 25,000 person–days each year to planning and management reporting. These same firms take close to 5 months to create their strategic plans, 4 months to devise a tactical plan, 5 days to close their financial books at the end of an accounting period, 11 days after month end to produce management reports, and 15 days after month end to produce revised forecasts. Part of the problem is that the average company is infatuated with details, developing financial plans for an average of 370 line items (i.e., budget accounts) and inundating managers with an average of 140 distinct performance metrics. The overall result is that professional staff members spend half their time collecting and validating data and little time analyzing the data.

PAUCITY OF ANALYSIS

The overall impact of the planning and reporting practices of the average company is that management has little time to review results from a strategic perspective, decide what should be done differently, and act on the revised plans. As a research report by Neely and Bourne (2000) put it:

> The whole process of measuring performance is completely wasted unless action is taken on performance data that are collected. Far too often, and in far too many organizations, management fails to do this. They produce the charts. They produce the reports, but then they fail to analyze the data and decide what they are going to do differently inside the organization to make sure that next month's figures are better than this month's figures. It is almost as if managers today have become so obsessed with measuring performance that they no longer have time to act on the performance data once they have been gathered.

Research figures indicate that top management spends about 3 hours a month discussing strategy and 80 percent of their time on issues that account for less than 20 percent of the company's long-term value. Even organizations that spend time reviewing results frequently dwell on operational details and budget line items rather than strategic objectives and linked initiatives. Again, as The Hackett Group benchmarks indicate, most of the review is focused on financial rather than operational metrics (65 percent), lagging indicators rather than leading indicators (75 percent), and internal measures rather than external measures (80 percent). The problem is that internal measures of financial performance for prior time periods offer little evidence of what should be done in the future.

Because the average company spends such an inordinate amount of time creating its strategic and operational plans, the last thing it wants to do is revisit those plans except on an annual basis. In contrast, best practice companies revisit and adjust their strategic plans and forecasts frequently throughout the year and reassign resources based on these adjusted plans and forecasts. Indeed, best practice companies use "rolling forecasts" to make these adjustments, a process that is discussed in Online File W9.2. Again, they are able to make these adjustments because they focus on a small set of key performance indicators that are tied to their strategic objectives rather than a large collection of metrics and line items that number in the hundreds. Imagine for a moment, that you are part of the management team for a large manufacturing company. How hard is it for the management team to plan and forecast demand for a single product? How about multiple products? How about 100 line items (e.g., manufacturing costs, distribution costs) for those products, not just sales revenue? It is an impossible

TECHNOLOGY INSIGHTS 9.2

Benchmarking Best Practices for BPM

Since 1991, The Hackett Group, part of the consulting firm Answerthink (**answerthink.com**), has been benchmarking the planning and management reporting practices of client organizations. For each client, the result of a benchmarking study is a comprehensive comparison of the client's processes relative to the average organization and to world-class organizations. Today, The Hackett Group's benchmarking database includes results from more than 2,400 clients. The clients include 97 percent of the Dow Jones Industrials, 81 percent of the *Fortune 100*, and 88 percent of the Dow Jones Global Titans Index.

The benchmarking process measures both the *efficiency* and *effectiveness* of an organization's planning and management reporting practices. Efficiency is measured by examining an organization's cost and productivity (e.g., headcount, days to close the books, transaction costs), and effectiveness is measured by looking at its quality and value (e.g., days sales outstanding, percentage of accounts payable errors). World-class organizations are those whose efficiency and effectiveness are in the top 25 percent.

The Hackett Group's benchmarking process divides planning and management reporting into four subprocesses: strategic planning, operational and financial planning, reporting, and forecasting. Each subprocess is evaluated in terms of five dimensions of efficiency and effectiveness:

1. *Strategic alignment*. Focuses on the linkage of the process to the objectives and strategies of the organization.
2. *Partnering*. Assesses the level of collaboration among different constituencies both inside and outside the organization.
3. *Process*. Measures cycle time, cost, and quality.
4. *Technology*. Measures the degree to which technology has been leveraged effectively across the planning and reporting process.
5. *People and organizations*. Addresses a broad range of factors, such as staffing levels, skills, experience, organizational structure, leadership, education, training, roles and responsibilities, and compensation.

Overall, a benchmark provides an organization with a comprehensive view of its performance that enables the organization's management to clearly identify the opportunities for improvement and to ensure the appropriate balance between efficiency and effectiveness. The guiding principle of a best practice program is first to eliminate all unnecessary work, to then standardize and simplify all work that remains, and only then to seek to apply technology to achieve superior performance. The assumption is that there is no reason to simplify or automate activities that should not exist.

Over the past couple years, The Hackett Group's benchmarking results indicate that:

- World-class companies are significantly more efficient than their peers at managing costs. Much of the reduction is the outcome of swapping labor for technology, process optimization, and outsourcing.
- World-class companies focus on operational excellence and experience significantly reduced rates of voluntary employee turnover, which is due in part to allocating more staff to addressing employee life cycle issues.
- World-class companies have hybrid sourcing strategies that combine shared services and outsourcing. Both of these practices are used to drive down costs.
- World-class companies provide management with the tools and training to leverage corporate information and to guide strategic planning, budgeting, and forecasting.
- World-class companies closely align strategic and tactical plans, enabling functional areas (e.g., marketing) to contribute more effectively to overall business goals. These functional areas are more effective at aligning operation areas with strategic business goals and provide greater value to their companies.

Recent results also indicate that the gap between average and world-class companies is growing. Detailed results from The Hackett Group benchmarking study for planning and management reporting can be found in Hoblitzell (2003) and Axson (2003) and at **thehackettgroup.com**.

Sources: Compiled from T. Hoblitzell, *Best Practices in Planning and Budgeting*, 2003, **answerthink.com/pdf/pdf_services/04_intelligence/whitepapers/wp_bpm_planbudget.pdf** (accessed March 2006); D. Axson, *Best Practices in Planning and Management Reporting*, Wiley, Hoboken, NJ, 2003; and **thehackettgroup.com**.

task to accomplish with any degree of accuracy and certainty. This is why best practice companies spend their time ensuring that their strategic plans are tightly integrated with their operational plans and monitoring processes (something that occurs in only 25 percent of all companies, according to The Hackett Group).

Section 9.6 Review Questions

1. What do The Hackett Group benchmarks measure?
2. Based on The Hackett Group benchmark results, in what ways do world-class companies differ from average companies?
3. According to The Hackett Group, how much time and resources does the average company spend on planning and management reporting?
4. What is one of the major reasons companies spend so little time analyzing the management data they collect?

9.7 PERFORMANCE MEASUREMENT

Underlying BPM is a performance measurement system. According to Simons (2002), **performance measurement systems**:

> Assist managers in tracking the implementations of business strategy by comparing actual results against strategic goals and objectives. A performance measurement system typically comprises systematic methods of setting business goals together with periodic feedback reports that indicate progress against goals.

All measurement is about comparisons. Raw numbers are rarely of little value. If you were told that a salesperson completed 50 percent of the deals he or she was working on within a month, that would have little meaning. Now, suppose you were told that the same salesperson had a monthly close rate of 30 percent last year. Obviously, the trend is good. What if you were also told that the average close rate for all salespeople at the company was 80 percent. Obviously, that particular salesperson needs to pick up the pace. As Simons's definition suggests, in performance measurement, the key comparisons revolve around strategies, goals, and objectives.

PROBLEMS WITH EXISTING PERFORMANCE MEASUREMENT SYSTEMS

If you were to survey most companies today, you would have a hard time finding a company that doesn't use a performance measurement system. The most popular system in use is some variant of Kaplan and Norton's (1996) balanced scorecard (BSC). For example, The Hackett Group benchmarks (Hackett Group, 2004) indicated that 96 percent of all companies had implemented or were planning to implement a BSC. Of course, among these companies, there seems to be some confusion about what constitutes "balance." The BSC Collaborative (**bscol.com**) has established a set of criteria for certifying BSC applications (i.e., software systems providing BSC capabilities). In their words (BSC Collaborative, 2000, p. 2):

> Central to the BSC methodology is a holistic vision of a measurement system tied to the strategic direction of the organization. It is based on a four-perspective

> view of the world, with financial measures supported by customer, internal, and learning and growth metrics. By measuring and managing the business using this holistic set of metrics, an organization can ensure rapid and effective implementation of strategy and facilitate organizational alignment and communication.

Yet, among the companies in The Hackett Group benchmark study, the overwhelming majority of the measures are financial or operational in nature (better than 80 percent). What these companies really have is a "scorecard"—a set of reports, charts, and specialized displays that enable them to compare actual results with planned results for a miscellaneous collection of measures.

Calendar-driven financial reports are a major component of most performance measurement systems. This is no surprise. First, most of these systems are under the purview of the finance department. Second, most executives place little faith in anything except financial or operational numbers. Research studies indicate that executives value a variety of different types of information (e.g., financial, operational, market, customer), but they think that outside the financial or operational arenas, most of the data are suspect, and they are unwilling to bet their jobs on the quality of that information (Schiemann and Lingle, 1999).

The drawbacks of using financial data as the core of a performance measurement system are well known. Among the limitations most frequently cited are:

- Financial measures are usually reported by organizational structures (e.g., research and development expenses) and not by the processes that produced them.
- Financial measures are lagging indicators, telling us what happened, not why it happened or what is likely to happen in the future.
- Financial measures (e.g., administrative overhead) are often the product of allocations that are not related to the underlying processes that generated them.
- Financial measures are focused on the short term and provide little information about the longer term.

Financial myopia is not the only problem plaguing many of the performance measurement systems in operation today. Measurement overload and measurement obliquity are also major problems confronting the current crop of systems.

It is not uncommon to find companies proudly announcing that they are tracking 200 or more measures at the corporate level. It's hard to imagine trying to drive a car with 200 dials on the dashboard. Yet we seem to have little trouble driving companies with 200 dials on the corporate dashboard, even though we know that humans have major difficulty keeping track of more than a handful of issues and that anything else is simply shoved to the side. This sort of overload is exacerbated by the fact that companies rarely retire the measures they collect. If some new data or request for data comes along, it is simply added to the list. If the number of measures is 200 today, it will be 201 tomorrow, and 202 the day after that. Even though plans change and opportunities and problems come and go with increasing frequency, little effort is made to determine whether the list of measures we are tracking is still applicable to the current situation.

For many of the measures being tracked, management lacks direct control. Michael Hammer (2003) called this the *principle of obliquity*. On the one hand, measures such as earnings per share (EPS), return on equity (ROE), profitability, market share, and customer satisfaction need to be monitored. On the other hand, these measures can only be pursued in an oblique fashion. What can be controlled are the actions of individual workers or employees. Unfortunately, the impact of any individual action on a corporate strategy or business unit strategy is negligible. What is required to tie the critical with the controllable is a strategic business model or methodology that starts at the top and links corporate goals and objectives all the way down to the bottom-level initiatives being carried out by individual performers.

EFFECTIVE PERFORMANCE MEASUREMENT

A number of books provides recipes for determining whether a collection of performance measures is good or bad. Among the basic ingredients of a good collection are the following:

- Measures should focus on key factors.
- Measures should be a mix of past, present, and future.
- Measures should balance the needs of shareholders, employees, partners, suppliers, and other stakeholders.
- Measures should start at the top and flow down to the bottom.
- Measures need to have targets that are based on research and reality rather than be arbitrary.

Online File W9.3 provides a more detailed methodology and set of templates for making the determination.

While all the characteristics just listed are important, the real key to an effective performance measurement system is to have a good strategy. Measures need to be derived from the corporate and business unit strategies and from an analysis of the key business processes required to achieve those strategies. Of course, this is easier said than done. If it were simple, most organizations would already have effective performance measurement systems in place, but they don't.

Application Case 9.3, which describes the Web-based key performance indicator (KPI) portal at International Truck and Engine Corporation, offers insights into the steps one company took to implement its performance measurement system. It also provides a list of the factors that are critical to the success of a performance measurement system.

Application Case 9.3

International Truck and Engine Corporation

International Truck and Engine Corporation is an operating company of Navistar International Corporation. The company produces commercial trucks, school buses, and a variety of diesel engines for trucks, vans, and sport utility vehicles. The company has approximately 15,000 employees and operates manufacturing facilities in North America and Mexico.

KPI PORTAL

In the past, International's managers used a hodgepodge of paper-based operational reports to monitor and manage their operational performance. A couple years ago, the company rolled out a KPI Web-based portal in an effort to help 500 of its managers and executives track and manage the organization's performance across 130 KPI.

The KPI portal provides executives and business group managers with personalized views of key business drivers. In this way, they can get to the root cause of a problem in hours or days rather than weeks or months.

The KPI portal project was initiated by International's vice president and controller. His goal was to accelerate the company's monthly financial closing cycle, a process that had been taking up to two weeks at the end of each month. More timely data would offer International's managers a better view of the company's profitability and the factors affecting profitability. He said that the focus was on capturing and disseminating key business metrics more frequently than the traditional monthly reports to the frontline managers making decisions affecting overall company business strategies, plans, and forecasts.

DETERMINING REQUIREMENTS

As a first step, International surveyed its financial managers to determine the information and metrics needed to manage operations and speed the financial close. A team of eight internal staff and contractors was established to gather and analyze the information. The survey identified 133 distinct KPI. To ensure the continued relevance of the portal, the team conducts the survey annually to determine which measures should be added, continued, or dropped. In addition, the team delved into the collection of KPI to determine the detailed data underlying the top-level metrics. A Detail button was added to the display to allow end users to view the underlying details.

ROLLING OUT THE SYSTEM

Rather than rolling out the system one department or function at a time, the team decided to deliver KPI one source at a time. It began with the Truck group's income statement and unit count data. In this case, the required data were already in the company's data warehouse. Subsequent measures required the team to load the data from various source systems into the data warehouse.

The portal is updated daily from 32 source systems into the data warehouse, which rests on an Informix database. Summary data are fed from the data warehouse into a Hyperion Solutions data mart (see Technical Insights 9.5, later in this chapter). End users access the data mart through the Web. The KPI portal provides end users with charts for all the metrics as well as reports and other relevant documents. Users can customize the portal to show only those metrics that are of interest to them. Users also have the ability to drill down or across the information in order to access the underlying detail.

Overall usage was critical to the success of the program. To address this issue, the team made sure that the Web-based interface was intuitive to use and provided users with training about the nature and origin of the underlying data. To help build trust in the system, the team reconciled the data and information in the new system with the data in existing systems. Over time, the managers and executives began to recognize the value of the portal and became convinced that the portal provided a single version of the truth.

SUCCESS FACTORS

The KPI system has been successful. The key factors responsible for its success include the following:

- A highly committed executive sponsor
- Adequate funding
- An incremental development and release schedule
- A thorough Web-based requirements assessment
- A knowledgeable and talented team
- A core of subject matter experts
- An existing data warehouse
- A pilot to demonstrate the value and validity of the product
- Trust in the data
- Communication to explain the benefits, functionality, and rollout of the new system

---

Sources: Compiled from W. Eckerson, "BI Case Study: International Truck and Engine Corporation," *Business Intelligence Journal*, Winter 2004; and W. Eckerson, *Performance Dashboards*, Wiley, Hoboken, NJ, 2006.

Section 9.7 Review Questions

1. What is a performance measurement system?
2. What are some of the drawbacks of relying solely on financial metrics for measuring performance?
3. What is the principle of obliquity?
4. What are some of the characteristics of a "good" collection of performance measures?
5. What steps did International Truck and Engine use to create the measures for its system? What factors were critical to its success?

9.8 BPM METHODOLOGIES

There is more to performance measurement than simply keeping score. An effective performance measurement system should help do the following:

- Align top-level strategic objectives and bottom-level initiatives.
- Identify opportunities and problems in a timely fashion.
- Determine priorities and allocate resources based on those priorities.
- Change measurements when the underlying processes and strategies change.
- Delineate responsibilities, understand actual performance relative to responsibilities, and reward and recognize accomplishments.
- Take action to improve processes and procedures when the data warrant it.
- Plan and forecast in a more reliable and timely fashion.

A holistic or systematic performance measurement framework is required to accomplish these aims, as well as others. Over the past 40 or more years, various systems have been proposed. Some of them, such as activity-based costing or management, are financially focused. Others, such as total quality management (TQM), are process oriented. In the discussion that follows, we examine two widely used approaches that support the basic processes underlying BPM: BSC (see **bscol.com**) and Six Sigma (see **mu.motorola.com**).

BALANCED SCORECARD (BSC)

Probably the best-known and most widely used performance management system is the BSC. Kaplan and Norton first articulated this methodology in their *Harvard Business Review* article "The Balanced Scorecard: Measures That Drive Performance," which appeared in 1992. A few years later, in 1996, these same authors produced a ground-breaking book—*The Balanced Scorecard: Translating Strategy into Action*—that documented how companies were using the BSC to not only supplement their financial measures with nonfinancial measures but also to communicate and implement their strategies. Over the past few years, BSC has become a generic term (much like Coke or Xerox) that is used to represent virtually every type of scorecarding application and implementation, regardless of whether it is balanced or strategic. In response to this bastardization of the term, Kaplan and Norton released a new book in 2000, *The Strategy-Focused Organization: How Balanced Scorecard Companies Thrive in the New Business Environment*. This book was designed to reemphasize the strategic nature of the BSC methodology. This was followed a few years later, in 2004, by *Strategy Maps: Converting Intangible Assets into Tangible Outcomes*, which describes a detailed process for linking strategic objectives to operational tactics and initiatives.

The Meaning of Balance

From a high-level viewpoint, **balanced scorecard (BSC)** is both a performance measurement and management methodology that helps translate an organization's financial, customer, internal process, and learning and growth objectives and targets into a set of actionable initiatives. As a measurement methodology, BSC is designed to overcome the limitations of systems that are financially focused. It does this by translating an organization's vision and strategy into a set of interrelated financial and nonfinancial objectives, measures, targets, and initiatives. The relationships among the financial and nonfinancial objectives are depicted in Figure 9.4. The nonfinancial objectives fall into one of three perspectives:

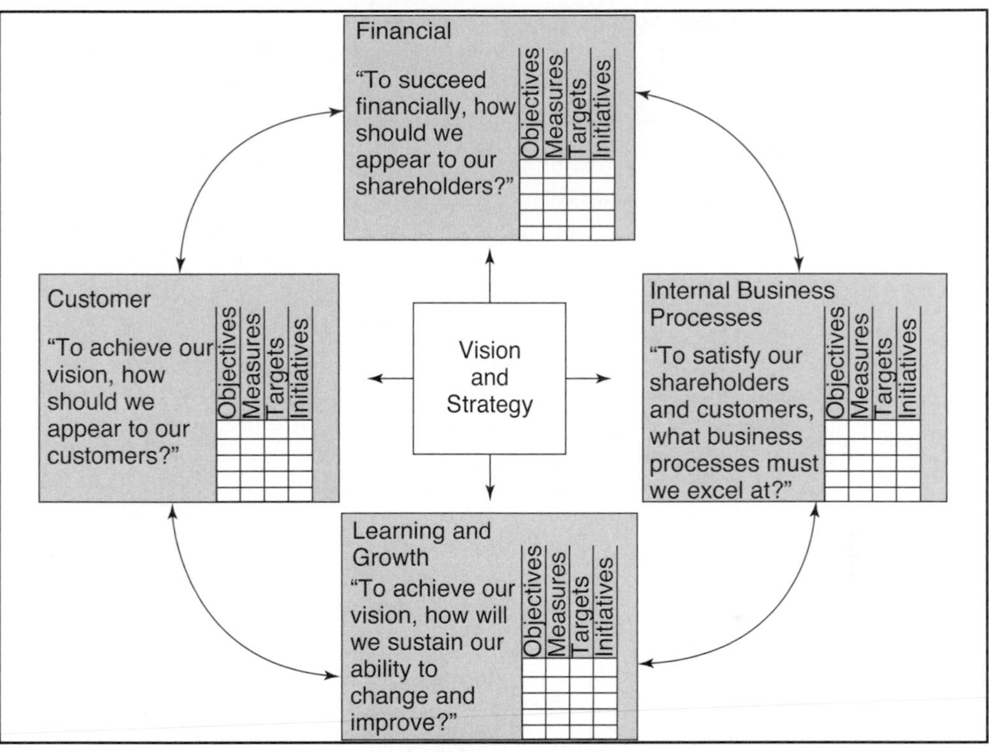

FIGURE 9.4 Balanced Scorecard Perspectives

Source: Balanced Scoreboard Institute. **balancedscorecard.org/basics/bscl.html** (accessed April 2006)

- *Customer.* These objectives define how the organization should appear to its customers if it is to accomplish its vision.
- *Internal business process.* These objectives specify the processes the organization must excel at in order to satisfy its shareholders and customers.
- *Learning and growth.* These objectives indicate how an organization can improve its ability to change and improve in order to achieve its vision.

In BSC, the term *balance* arises because the combined set of measures are supposed to encompass indicators that are:

- Financial and nonfinancial
- Leading and lagging
- Internal and external
- Quantitative and qualitative
- Short term and long term

Aligning Strategies and Actions

As a strategic management methodology, BSC enables an organization to align its actions with its overall strategies. BSC accomplishes this task through a series of interrelated steps. The specific steps that are involved vary from one book to the next. In our case, the process can be captured in five steps:

1. Identify strategic objectives for each of the perspectives (about 15 to 25 in all).
2. Associate measures with each of the strategic objectives; a mix of quantitative and qualitative should be used.

3. Assign targets to the measures.
4. List strategic initiatives to accomplish each of the objectives (i.e., responsibilities).
5. Link the various strategic objectives through a cause-and-effect diagram called a *strategy map*.

As an example of the process, consider the strategy map shown in Figure 9.5. A **strategy map** delineates the relationships among the key organizational objectives for all four BSC perspectives. In this instance, the map specifies the relationships among seven objectives that cover four different perspectives. Like other strategy maps, this one begins at the top with a financial objective (i.e., exceed growth in key segments). This objective is driven by a customer objective (i.e., build strong customer relationships). In turn, the customer objective is the result of an internal (i.e., process) objective (i.e., identify/capture new business opportunities). The map continues down to the bottom of the hierarchy, where the learning objectives are found (e.g., develop key skills).

FIGURE 9.5 Sample Strategy Map

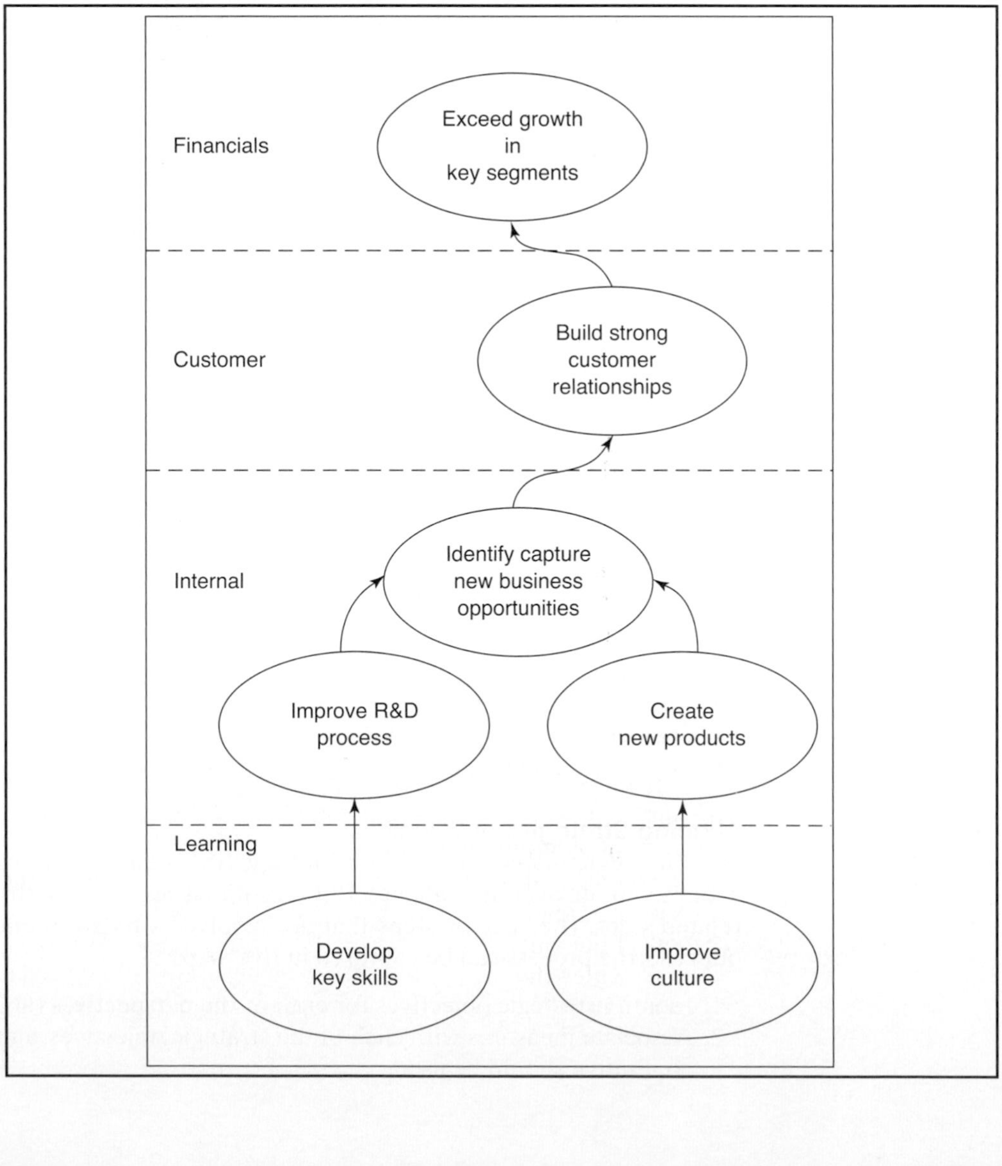

TABLE 9.2 Specifying Objectives, Measures, Targets, and Initiatives

Objective	*Measure*	*Target*	*Initiative*
What the strategy is trying to achieve	How success or failure against objectives is monitored	Level of performance or rate of improvement needed	Key action programs required to achieve target
Build strong customer relationships	Customer satisfaction	Customer service index	Implement customer feedback database

Each objective that appears in a strategy map has an associated measure, target, and initiative. For example, the objective "build strong customers relationships" might be measured by customer satisfaction. For this measure, we might be targeting a 15 percent improvement over last year's figure in our customer service index. One of the ways of accomplishing this improvement is by implementing the customer feedback database. The various components of this example are shown in Table 9.2.

Overall, strategy maps like the one in Figure 9.5 represent a hypothetical model of a segment of the business. When specific names (of people or teams) are assigned to the various initiatives, the model serves to align the bottom-level actions of the organization with the top-level strategic objectives. When actual results are compared with targeted results, a determination can be made about whether the strategy that the hypothesis represents should be called into question or whether the actions of those responsible for various parts of the hypothesis need to be adjusted.

BSC Certification

The BSC Collaborative offers software vendors the opportunity to have their applications certified against a well-defined set of criteria. To qualify, an application must support the key elements discussed in the preceding section. That is, the application must offer an end user the ability to view (1) strategic objectives from the four perspectives; (2) the measures, targets, and initiatives associated with each objective; and (3) the cause-and-effect relationships among the objectives. The BSC Collaborative has also established a new Extensible Markup Language (XML) schema that defines an underlying data structure for all the data objects in a BSC application. Use of this standard will facilitate the integration of BSC information with other applications and across enterprises.

SIX SIGMA

Since its inception in the mid-1980s, Six Sigma has enjoyed widespread adoption by companies throughout the world. For the most part, it has not been used as a performance management methodology. Instead, most companies use it as a process improvement methodology that enables them to scrutinize their processes, pinpoint problems, and apply remedies. In recent years, some companies, such as Motorola, have recognized the value of using Six Sigma for strategic purposes. In these instances, Six Sigma provides the means to measure and monitor key processes related to a company's profitability and to accelerate improvement in overall business performance. Because of its focus on business processes, Six Sigma also provides a straightforward way to address performance problems after they are identified or detected.

Six Sigma Defined

The history of Six Sigma dates to the late 1970s, although many of its ideas can be traced to earlier quality initiatives (see Isixsigma, 2006). The term *Six Sigma* was coined by Bill Smith, an engineer at Motorola. In fact, Six Sigma is a federally registered trademark of Motorola. In the late 1970s and early to mid-1980s, Motorola was driven to Six Sigma by internal and external pressures. Externally, it was being beaten in the market place by competitors who were able to produce higher-quality products at a lower price. Internally, when a Japanese firm took over a U.S. Motorola factory that manufactured Quasar television and was able to produce TV sets with 1/20 the number of defects produced under regular operating procedures, Motorola executives had to admit that their quality was not good. In response to these pressures, Motorola's CEO, Bob Galvin, led the company down a quality path called Six Sigma. Since that time, hundreds of companies around the world, including General Electric, Allied Signal, DuPont, Ford, Merrill Lynch, and Toshiba, have used Six Sigma to generate billions of dollars of top-line growth and bottom-line earnings improvement.

In Six Sigma, a business is viewed as a collection of processes. A *business process* is a set of activities that transform a set of inputs, including suppliers, assets, resources (e.g., capital, material, people), and information into a set of outputs (i.e., goods or services) for another person or process. Table 9.3 lists some categories of business processes that can affect overall corporate performance.

Sigma, σ, is a letter in the Greek alphabet that statisticians use to measure the variability in a process. In the quality arena, *variability* is synonymous with the number of defects. Generally, companies have accepted a great deal of variability in their business processes. In numeric terms, the norm has been 6,200 to 67,000 defects per million opportunities (DPMO). For instance, if an insurance company handles 1 million claims, then under normal operating procedures, 6,200 to 67,000 of those claims would be defective (e.g., mishandled, have errors in the forms). This level of variability represents a 3- to 4-sigma level of performance. To achieve a Six Sigma level of performance,

TABLE 9.3 Categories of Business Processes
Accounting and measurements
Administrative and facility management
Audits and improvements
Business planning and execution
Business policies and procedures
Global marketing and sales
Information management and analysis
Leadership and profitability
Learning and innovation
Maintenance and collaboration
Parterships and alliances
Production and service
Purchasing and supply-chain management
Recruitment and development
Research and development

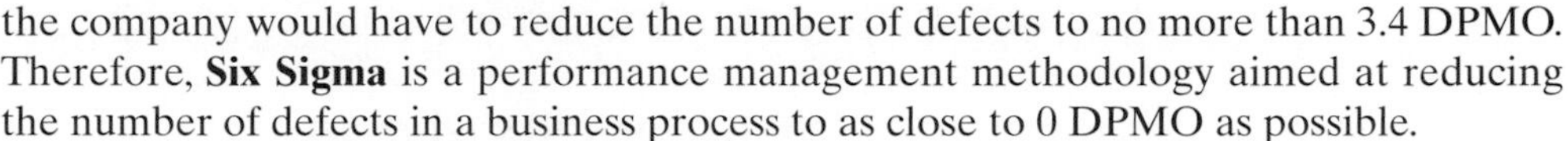

the company would have to reduce the number of defects to no more than 3.4 DPMO. Therefore, **Six Sigma** is a performance management methodology aimed at reducing the number of defects in a business process to as close to 0 DPMO as possible.

The DMAIC Performance Model

Six Sigma rests on a simple performance improvement model known as DMAIC. Like BPM, **DMAIC** is a closed-loop business improvement model, and it encompasses the steps of defining, measuring, analyzing, improving, and controlling a process. The steps can be described as follows:

1. *Define*. Define the goals, objectives, and boundaries of the improvement activity. At the top level, the goals are the strategic objectives of the company. At lower levels—department or project levels—the goals are focused on specific operational processes.
2. *Measure*. Measure the existing system. Establish quantitative measures that will yield statistically valid data. The data can be used to monitor progress toward the goals defined in the previous step.
3. *Analyze*. Analyze the system to identify ways to eliminate the gap between the current performance of the system or process and the desired goal.
4. *Improve*. Initiate actions to eliminate the gap by finding ways to do things better, cheaper, or faster. Use project management and other planning tools to implementing the new approach.
5. *Control*. Institutionalize the improved system by modifying compensation and incentive systems, policies, procedures, manufacturing resource planning (MRP), budgets, operation instructions, or other management systems.

For new processes, the model that is used is called *DMADV* (define, measure, analyze, design, and verify). Traditionally, DMAIC and DMADV have been used primarily with operational issues. However, nothing precludes the application of these methodologies to strategic issues such as company profitability.

Limitations of Six Sigma

Six Sigma experts and pundits are quick to praise the methodology and point to companies such as General Electric as proof of its value. What they usually fail to point out is that many organizations have tried the methodology and failed. For example, in a November 2004 survey of 276 senior executives conducted by Celerant Consulting (**celerantconsulting.com**), 43 percent of the respondents noted that the performance improvement initiatives undertaken by their companies over the past three years had failed to achieve their objectives (see Eagle, 2005). According to the survey, the least successful of the initiatives was Six Sigma. All other initiatives—including business process optimization, outsourcing, and lean manufacturing—achieved better results. The primary reason for the failure was the lack of integration among the various Six Sigma projects across the enterprise. Another reason was that the companies failed to institute the roles required to support the methodology (see Online File W9.4 for a discussion of these roles). The overall impact was that the effects of the various Six Sigma projects within an enterprise were localized, having little overall impact on either the top line or bottom line of the company.

In an effort to overcome these and other limitations, some companies, such as Motorola and Duke University Hospital, have combined their Six Sigma initiatives with the BSC initiatives. In this way, their quality initiatives are directly tied to their strategic objectives and targets. In the same vein, Gupta (2004) developed a hybrid methodology called Six Sigma Business Scorecard that directly ties the process

TECHNOLOGY INSIGHTS 9.4

BSC Meets Six Sigma

BSC and Six Sigma are both widely adopted performance management tools and methodologies. Yet most companies that have adopted both treat them as separate initiatives. However, according to Stan Elbaum, senior vice president of research at Aberdeen Group in Boston, these are complementary programs. The true benefits of each can't be achieved unless the two are integrated. The BSC approach enables companies to quickly and accurately identify critical performance weaknesses and uncover opportunities for improvement and growth. What BSC has a hard time doing is showing how to fix the performance problems. On the other hand, Six Sigma projects often flounder because project teams "bounce all over the organization looking for performance weaknesses or focusing attention on areas where improvements will yield only marginal returns" (Leahy, 2005, p. 48). Taken together, however, BSC and Six Sigma enable a company to dig down to the underlying causes of a performance shortfall.

A recent survey (Docherty, 2005) of companies that had adopted BSC or Six Sigma programs revealed that nearly half the programs had failed to break even in the first three years of adoption, but those that made them work had achieved substantial financial benefit. The companies with the biggest net returns were those that had found a way to integrate the two. The integration was achieved by doing the following:

- *Translating their strategy into quantifiable objectives.* This was done by mapping the strategy and using a scorecard to monitor the associated metrics.
- *Cascading objectives through the organization.* They broke enterprise-wide goals into lower-level operational objectives by applying the causal reasoning underlying Six Sigma.
- *Setting targets based on the voice of the customer.* They used BSC and Six Sigma together to ensure that operational targets would directly impact customer expectations.
- *Implementing strategic projects using Six Sigma.* They used Six Sigma to drive improvements in product and process quality.
- *Executing processes in a consistent fashion to deliver business results.* They viewed the organization from a process perspective. Six Sigma was used to control process variation, and process measures were included in their BSC.

While the integration of the two methodologies can yield substantial benefits, an organization faces substantial challenges in taking this approach. From an organizational perspective, the company must ensure the following:

- That the actions of individuals throughout the organization are aligned with the measures that flow from the organizational objectives.
- That the prevailing management culture is aligned with the fact-based approach of BSC and Six Sigma rather than resorting to a "fix-it-now" approach.
- That the information technology (IT) infrastructure supports the integration of BSC and Six Sigma.

To achieve this latter requirement, the IT infrastructure must do the following:

- Allow executives to create and share strategy in chunks or segments that make sense at the operational level.
- Allow initiatives to be linked to strategic objectives and KPI.
- Provide project and program management capabilities so that project teams can drive initiatives to their completion.
- Enable processes to be measured and automated in real-time.
- Support the complete strategic planning and execution loop.

The first and second of these requirements are supported by BSC. The next two requirements are provided by Six Sigma tools and methodologies. The last of these requirements is provided by a complete BPM system.

Companies that have successfully combined the two methodologies say that they can't understand why an organization would want to do one without the other. However, they also advise that it takes about a year to provide the necessary workforce training and to overcome existing cultural and organizational barriers.

Sources: Compiled from P. Docherty, *From Six Sigma to Strategy Execution*, 2005, **i-solutionsglobal.com/secure/FromSixSigmaToStrateg_AAC8C.pdf** (accessed March 2006); and T. Leahy, "The One-Two Performance Punch." *Business Finance*, February 2005, **businessfinancemag.com/magazine/archives/article.html?articleID=14364** (accessed March 2006).

improvement aspects of Six Sigma to the financial perspective of the BSC. The benefits and structure of this combination are discussed in Technology Insights 9.4.

Section 9.8 Review Questions

1. What are the characteristics of an effective performance measurement system?
2. What are the four perspectives in BSC?
3. What does the term *balanced* refer to in BSC?
4. What steps are used in creating a BSC?
5. What is a strategy map?
6. What does Six Sigma refer to?
7. What are the basic processes in the DMAIC model?
8. How can BSC and Six Sigma be integrated? What are some of the barriers to integrating the two?

9.9 BPM ARCHITECTURE AND APPLICATIONS

There is no single technology or application that constitutes BPM. Instead, BPM is supported by a variety of technologies and applications. In the absence of a definitive list or collection, the BPM Standards Group (**bpmstandardsgroup.org**) has proposed a BPM technology architecture (see Figure 9.6) that highlights the enabling technologies and some of the key applications needed to support the closed-loop BPM processes that link strategy to execution. As Figure 9.6 indicates, the proposed architecture is multitiered and consists of a user interface layer, a database layer, and a source data layer. While there is no single technology or application that provides complete coverage for all the tiers and components summarized in Figure 9.6, several BPM software vendors provide comprehensive suites of applications that cover broad aspects of the proposed architecture. In the following sections, we discuss this architecture. We also review some of the application suites provided by the BPM vendors.

BPM ARCHITECTURE

The term **system architecture** refers to both the logical and physical design of a system. The logical design details the functional elements of a system and their interactions. The physical design specifies how the logical design is actually implemented and deployed across a specific set of technologies, such as desktop computers, servers, databases, communication protocols, and the like. The BPM architecture proposed by the BPM Standards Group is a logical architecture that can be physically deployed in a variety of ways.

You can think of a BPM system and its architecture as a vehicle (see Coveney et al., 2003). One of the major functions of a vehicle is to transport passengers from their current position to a desired destination somewhere down the road. A vehicle is an integration of individual components, each of which is important but relatively useless if they are not all integrated as a complete package. Provided that the driver knows how to operate the vehicle and where to go, there are three major components in the vehicle that contribute to the success of a trip: the chassis, onto which everything is bolted; the engine, which moves the vehicle forward; and the controls used to steer and regulate the vehicle. The design and integration of these components as a whole is

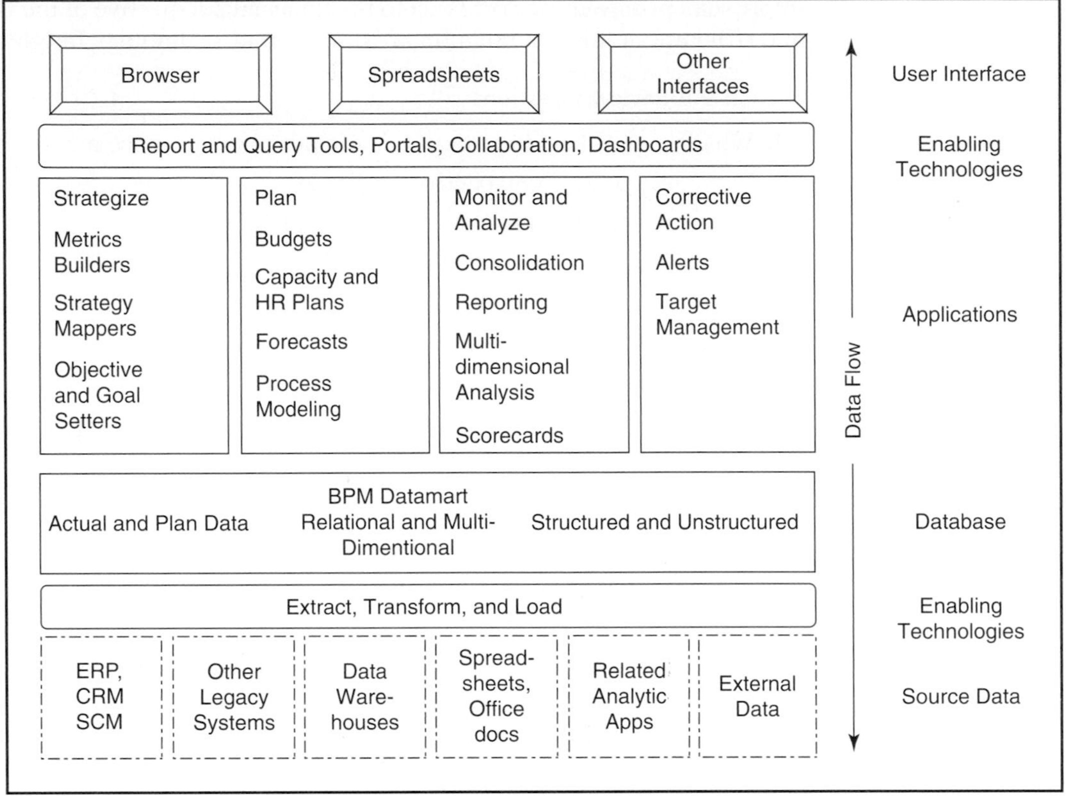

FIGURE 9.6 BPM Architecture

Source: BPM Standards Group, *Business Performance Management: Industry Framework Document*, September 2005. **bpmstandardgroup.org/documents/BPMIndustryFrameworkV5.0090905.pdf** (accessed March 2006).

critical to the drivability of the vehicle and determines how effectively the passengers reach their destination.

In the same vein, a BPM system is an integration of individual components, each of which is vital by itself but is almost useless if not integrated with other components. A BPM system needs three components in order to contribute to the successful implementation of strategy:

- *Database tier.* The database tier is the chassis of a BPM system. It contains a definition of the organization, covering the past, present, and future, and it is expressed in terms of structures and business rules. It also contains information, or links to information, in the form of plans and results. It is on this data model that the other components of a BPM system operate.
- *Application tier.* The application tier is analogous to a car's engine. This tier powers the BPM processes by transforming user interaction and source data into budgets, plans, forecasts, reports, and analyses.
- *Client or user interface tier.* The user interface or client tier is used to steer and regulate the implementation of strategy through communication, collaboration, and guidance of user interaction. It also monitors the success, direction, and progress of strategic initiatives, and it provides warnings of real and potential problems and opportunities.

The final ingredient is source data, which fuel the BPM system. In a BPM system, source data can come from a variety of internal systems and applications, such as enterprise resource planning (ERP) systems and data warehouses, as well as from external sources, such as market research firms.

The architecture of a BPM system can dramatically affect what that system can do, how well it will scale as more users come online, and the amount of effort it will require to maintain. The components of a solution can be the best in the world, but unless they actually fit and complement each other well, the resulting system is substantially less than the sum of its parts.

Database Tier

In the BPM architecture, the database tier provides both the metadata and data on which the BPM applications rest. The metadata includes field definitions, hierarchical structures, measurement definitions, account attributions, currency conversion methods, and the like. Much of the data in the database tier is structured or quantitative in nature and is stored in relational tables or multidimensional cubes. However, the database tier also houses other structured and unstructured data artifacts that are important elements of the various BPM processes. Included are things like strategy documents, tactical plans, assumptions, comments, and top-down targets.

The database tier in a BPM system can be designed in a number of ways. Some of the designs that are currently in use include:

- *Transactional data stores.* In this design, the database tier does not hold data, but rather the applications directly access the underlying transactional data sources—such as the general ledger. Although this design provides up-to-the-minute information, it is likely to result in poor performance because the BPM applications will have to continually access and transform the data from the various data sources. The data in these sources are likely to be stored in relational databases that are optimized for transaction processing, not query or analytical processing. In addition, there is no guarantee that the metadata and data within the various sources are consistent. For example, there is no guarantee that "sales revenue" means the same thing across the various sources or that the data for sales revenue are the same across all the sources.
- *Application data marts.* In this design, there are separate data marts for the various BPM applications. The data marts are fed with source data from the underlying operational or transactional systems. Typically, this is accomplished with an extraction, transformation, and load (ETL) tool that is designed to extract, transform, and load data from one system to another. This design is relatively quick to implement and typically performs well. A number of the BI vendors that provide some of the underpinnings for BPM systems use data marts of this sort. One disadvantage of this design is that it can become difficult to administer and integrate as the number of applications and data marts grows. As with transactional stores, it is also difficult to deliver one version of the truth across all the applications (e.g., similar measures can have different definitions and values from one data mart to the next).
- *Centralized data warehouse.* In this design, one centralized database holds the vast majority of the data for all the BPM applications. This design is favored by ERP vendors (i.e., SAP and Oracle) and is used by some BPM vendors. While this design ensures one version of the truth, it can be expensive to implement (especially if it is started from scratch) and maintain. Again, the centralized data warehouse is fed from various transactional and operational data sources.

Most BPM systems use either data marts or a data warehouse. The data in a data mart or data warehouse are usually stored in a multidimensional or online analytical processing

(OLAP) database. *Multidimensional* describes the way in which numeric information can be categorized, viewed, and analyzed. A multidimensional database consists of a series of dimensions (e.g., measures or accounts, time, location, product, and version). The members of a dimension are hierarchically organized. For example, the members of a time dimension can be hierarchically organized as years, quarters, months, weeks, and days. The value of a measure within the database is described by the values of its dimension members (e.g., actual sales revenue for the eastern region in Quarter 1).

In a multidimensional database, data are stored in cubes that combine the various business dimensions. The advantage of a multidimensional database over a relational database is that it performs extremely well in complex data analysis, and it is also relatively easy to set up and maintain. A multidimensional database also enables end users to slice-and-dice the data (i.e., look at the information for a particular combination of dimension members), drill up or down the hierarchy (e.g., look at sales revenues for the year and then the quarter), and pivot the data (e.g., look at sales revenue by product and then by location). The disadvantages of multidimensional databases are that they are number based and need additional technologies to handle information in text and date form, which is essential for BPM solutions. They also lack standards, meaning that many applications featuring multidimensional databases are proprietary. At best, the organization has to learn a new technology in order to maintain or extend the application. At worst, it means the organization is forever at the mercy of the database vendor in providing updates and new functionality to allow the organization to retain a competitive advantage with its IT infrastructure.

Most of the data in BPM data marts or data warehouses does not originate in them. Instead, the data are fed from a wide variety of sources. As Figure 9.7 in Technology Insights 9.5 indicates, the sources can include large-scale supply-chain and operational systems (e.g., ERP, SCM, or CPM applications), other legacy applications (e.g., general ledgers), other data marts or data warehouses, spreadsheets and other office applications, related analytical applications (e.g., the forecasting system feeding the budgeting system), and external data (e.g., market survey data). In BPM, ETL tools are usually used to move data to and from the BPM data marts or data warehouses. IBM's Websphere Data Stage and Microsoft's Biztalk are examples of ETL tools.

BPM Applications

In BPM, a wide variety of applications are needed to cover the closed-loop processes running from strategic planning to operational planning and budgeting to monitoring to adjustment and action. Despite the breadth of the processes, the industry analyst group Gartner contends that the majority of the processes can be handled by the following applications (see Rayner et al., 2005a):

1. *Budgeting, planning, and forecasting.* These applications support the development of all aspects of budgets, plans, and forecasts. They encompass short-term financially focused budgets, longer-term plans, and high-level strategic plans. These applications should deliver workflow capabilities to manage budget/plan creation, submission, and approval, and they provide the facility to dynamically create forecasts and scenarios. They should also support the development of an enterprise-wide planning model that links operational plans to financial budgets. In addition, they must be capable of sharing data with domain-specific applications, such as supply-chain planning.
2. *Profitability modeling and optimization.* These applications include activity-based costing (ABC) applications that determine and allocate costs at a highly granular

level and activity-based management applications that provide capabilities to enable users to model the impact on profitability of different cost and resource allocation strategies. Some applications have moved beyond the traditional ABC focus to enable revenue to be allocated in addition to costs for model packaging, bundling, pricing, and channel strategies.

3. *Scorecard applications.* Scorecards are a generic BI capability that can also link performance indicators to a strategy map with a hierarchical cause-and-effect relationship among the KPI. Scorecards are often used in conjunction with a particular methodology, such as BSC or Six Sigma.
4. *Financial consolidation.* This type of application enables organizations to reconcile, consolidate, summarize, and aggregate financial data based on different accounting standards and federal regulations. These applications are a fundamental part of CPM because they create the audited, enterprise-level view of financial information that must be shared with other CPM applications to analyze variance from targets.
5. *Statutory and financial reporting.* BPM applications require specialized reporting tools that can format output as structured financial statements. They may also need to support specific generally accepted accounting principles (GAAP) presentation rules, such as U.S. GAAP or international financial reporting standards. They also include visualization techniques that are specifically designed to support the analysis of variance from budgets or targets, such as hyperbolic trees.

BPM User Interface

The user interface is the bridge between the BPM applications and the end user. The particular interface that is provided depends on the specific application being accessed, as well as the role of the user, the user's objectives, and the user's expertise. For example, a manager who is a casual user and interested in reviewing results will likely need and use a different interface than an operational manager who is a frequent user and is interested in investigating various tactical or budget scenarios.

Over the past few years, the Web browser has become the primary tool for accessing information in a BPM system. Web-based systems are extremely efficient when it comes to broad deployment across the enterprise. There is no need to load or maintain software on a user machine. An end user simply needs a Web address and a browser to access an application. The Web allows changes to be made to the BPM system continuously, without requiring an arduous rollout process. Any changes made to a Web-based system are instantly communicated to all users, without the need to send files, templates, or anything else. The Web also provides access to a variety of data—text, formatted numbers, images, video, sound, documents, and the like. This means that it can be used with a wide variety of applications.

For some users and some applications, a Web browser is not enough. This is especially true for planning and forecasting applications, where a rich user interface is needed to support the analytical and computation needs of the user. In these cases, spreadsheets have become a popular alternative. In this instance, the spreadsheet program, such as Excel, serves as a window to the application and the back-end BPM database. The application data appear directly in the cells of the spreadsheet. The end user can take advantage of the spreadsheet's calculation, reporting, and charting capabilities. In many cases, this also allows the end user to work offline after disconnecting from the application and the supporting database and to submit changes to the application after reconnecting.

One thing that all BPM interfaces should provide is guidance to the end user. Because there are so many data and some of the processes are so complex, an end user can be easily buried by data overload and easily confused while trying to navigate through a system. This is one of the reasons that BI capabilities such as color-coded exceptions, exception alerts, sorted lists, and the like are so valuable. Without these types of user interface components, an end user could spend hours sifting through the data, trying to find significant variances and trends. These sorts of capabilities are provided by BPM scorecards and dashboards (see Section 9.10)

COMMERCIAL BPM SUITES

According to estimates by Gartner, the commercial software market for BPM suites was approximately $500 million in 2003, and it is forecasted to be around $1 billion by 2009 (Rayner et al., 2005b). In contrast, the research firm International Data Corporation (IDC) estimated that the BPM applications market was $1.2 billion in 2003 and expected the market to grow to $2.1 billion in 2008 (Whiting, 2005). The market consists of those software companies offering suites with at least three of the core BPM applications (i.e., budgeting, planning, and forecasting; profitability modeling and optimization; scorecarding; financial consolidation; and statutory and financial reporting). Because the compound annual growth rate (CAGR) of the market is around 10 percent, the number of new entrants in the market has grown over the past year. At the same time, there have been a number of acquisitions by BPM software companies seeking to expand their BPM application offerings.

As they do with a number of the software markets that they follow, Gartner has established a *magic quadrant* for the vendors of CPM suites (see Rayner et al., 2005b). The quadrant positions companies in terms of their ability to execute (as a company) and the completeness of their visions. The combination of the two dimensions results in four categories of companies. The software vendors within each of the categories are shown in Table 9.4.

TABLE 9.4 BPM Suites Magic Quadrant

	Vision	
Execution	***Limited***	***Strong***
Strong	Challengers: SAP	Leaders: Hyperion Solutions, Cognos
Limited	Niche: Oracle/PeopleSoft EPM, Lawson Software, Applix, Systems Union, Coda, Clarity Systems, CorVu	Visionaries: Oracle CPM, Business Objects, SAS Institute, OutlookSoft, Cartesis, Longview Solutions, ALG Software

Source: N. Rayner et al., "Magic Quadrant for CPM Suites, 2005." *Gartner RAS Core Research Note G00131208*, October 2005.

Based on Gartner's rankings, the clear leaders in the BPM suite market are Hyperion Solutions and Cognos. The discussion in Technology Insights 9.5 provides a detailed look at one of the market-leading BPM suites: Hyperion System 9.

TECHNOLOGY INSIGHTS 9.5

The Structure and Benefits of a Commercial BPM Suite

Hyperion uses the term *BPM* to describe its performance management offerings. Its BPM suite is called Hyperion System 9. Hyperion System 9 combines Hyperion's BI platform with its suite of financial application. It has been designed and constructed using a modern, n-tier, service-oriented architecture (SOA). As shown in Figure 9.7, the SOA architecture is similar to the architectural framework provided by the BPM Standards Group.

SYSTEM ARCHITECTURE

Conceptually, Hyperion System 9 consists of four tiers:

1. *Client*. For end users, System 9 provides a rich, zero-footprint user environment delivered via dynamic HTML (DHTML). It provides business users with a single point of access to all their BPM content that can be personalized to the individual user's need. It also offers Smart View, a Microsoft Office add-in that allows business users to work directly in the Office environment (i.e., Excel, Word, PowerPoint, Outlook) while interacting live with their Hyperion BPM content.
2. *Web*. The Hyperion System 9 Web tier uses Java 2 Enterprise Edition (J2EE) Web application servers, such as BEA WebLogic and IBM WebSphere, and it consists of a collection of Web applications constructed as Java servlets and JSP pages. These purpose-oriented Web applications incorporate logic specific to the type of BPM functionality to be delivered and provide highly scalable capabilities.
3. *Services*. The services that deliver specialized BPM functionality are purpose-built to provide the content for analytic, reporting, application, and data access capabilities of Hyperion System 9. These functionalities include the Financial Reporting service for producing financial-oriented report data; the Production reporting service for delivering pixel-perfect operational report content; the Data Access Service used by the Interactive Reporting

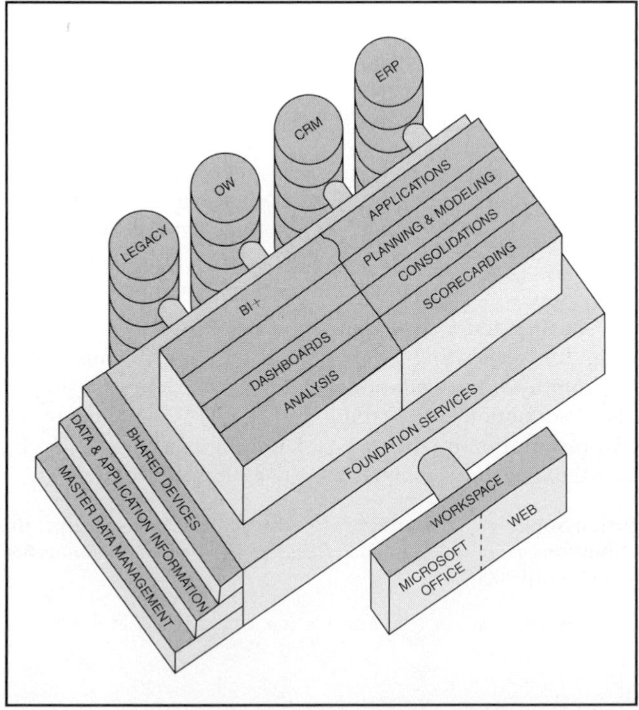

FIGURE 9.7 Hyperion Solutions's BPM Architecture

Source: **hyperion.com/products/.**

(continued)

TECHNOLOGY INSIGHTS 9.5 (continued)

module for access to relational databases; the Interactive Reporting service for managing the dashboards, queries, pivots, charts, and management reports; and the sophisticated Web Analysis service for navigating multidimensional OLAP data.

3. *Data*. Hyperion System 9 unifies reporting, queries, and analysis, and it seeds financial applications across a wide range of data sources. Hyperion System 9 supports access to a wide variety of relational, legacy, and multidimensional sources. Hyperion System 9 applications leverage the appropriate database technology to deliver the requisite business functionality required by the application. For example, Hyperion Planning exploits a multidimensional data structure to store its data in order to optimize the write-back and business rules capabilities required by planning users, whereas metadata and annotations are stored in a relational database.

HYPERION SYSTEM 9 APPLICATIONS

Hyperion System 9 supports a wide variety of financial and BI reporting applications. Among the BPM financial applications provided by the suite are financial modeling (i.e., Strategic Finance); Web-based financial planning, budgeting, and forecasting (i.e., Planning); headcount, salary, and compensation planning (i.e., Workforce Planning); and Web-based financial systems software for delivering global collection reporting and analysis (i.e., Financial Management). In addition to this array of financial functionality, Hyperion System 9 also provides a range of BI reporting applications, including: Interactive Reporting for user-directed query and analysis; Financial Reporting for generating book-quality financial reports that comply with regulations and external requirements; Production Reporting for generating high-volume, presentation-quality formatted reports; Compliance Management Dashboard for combining internal control information with financial data to provide an assessment of potential risk exposures; and Enterprise Metrics, which is a centralized metrics library and engine that reduces the time and expense of creating, measuring, and reporting KPI.

TOTAL COST OF OWNERSHIP (TCO)

As companies strive to better manage their expense line, IT is looking to lower the TCO of all managed systems. Hyperion System 9 delivers on this objective in the following ways:

- Hyperion System 9 is a unified approach to BPM, incorporating functional breadth in both BI tools and financial applications—all in one product set. With one system to license and one vendor to partner with, a company can address all its BPM needs, driving lower TCO.
- Hyperion System 9 is built using SOA principles and modern technologies, such as DHTML, CSS, XML, JavaScript, and J2EE. It embraces the rich Internet application paradigm by leveraging AJAX techniques, offers an unparalleled user experience, and conforms to the demanding standards set by today's IT organizations.
- Hyperion System 9 can start small and grow with a company's analytical requirements or be rapidly scaled enterprise-wide. Hyperion's "start anywhere" philosophy allows companies to prioritize their needs, install only the services necessary, and then deploy solutions as required, and its multi-tiered architecture allows for very advanced deployments.
- Hyperion System 9 is easy to use, manage, and maintain. Because of its common look and feel, users need to be trained only once, and they can quickly come up to speed as new applications become available. Central points of administration ease the burden on IT.

Sources: Compiled from Hyperion Solutions, "A Strategy for Performance Management," *Business Intelligence Journal*, Summer 2004; and Hyperion Solutions, *Hyperion System 9: Business Performance Management Architecture*, **hyperion.com/products/** (accessed April 2006).

Section 9.9 Review Questions

1. What is a system architecture?
2. What are the three key elements of a BPM system architecture?
3. What does a BPM database provide?
4. What are some alternative designs for a BPM database?
5. What are the major categories of BPM applications?
6. What are some of the types of BPM user interfaces?
7. What are the basic categories in Gartner's magic quadrant? Who are some of the vendors in the various categories?
8. What are some of the BPM applications that Hyperion Solutions supports?

9.10 PERFORMANCE DASHBOARDS

Scorecards and dashboards are common components of most, if not all, performance management systems, performance measurement systems, and BPM suites. Dashboards and scorecards both provide visual displays of important information that is consolidated and arranged on a single screen so that information can be digested at a single glance and easily explored. A typical dashboard is shown in Figure 9.8. This

FIGURE 9.8 Sample Performance Dashboard

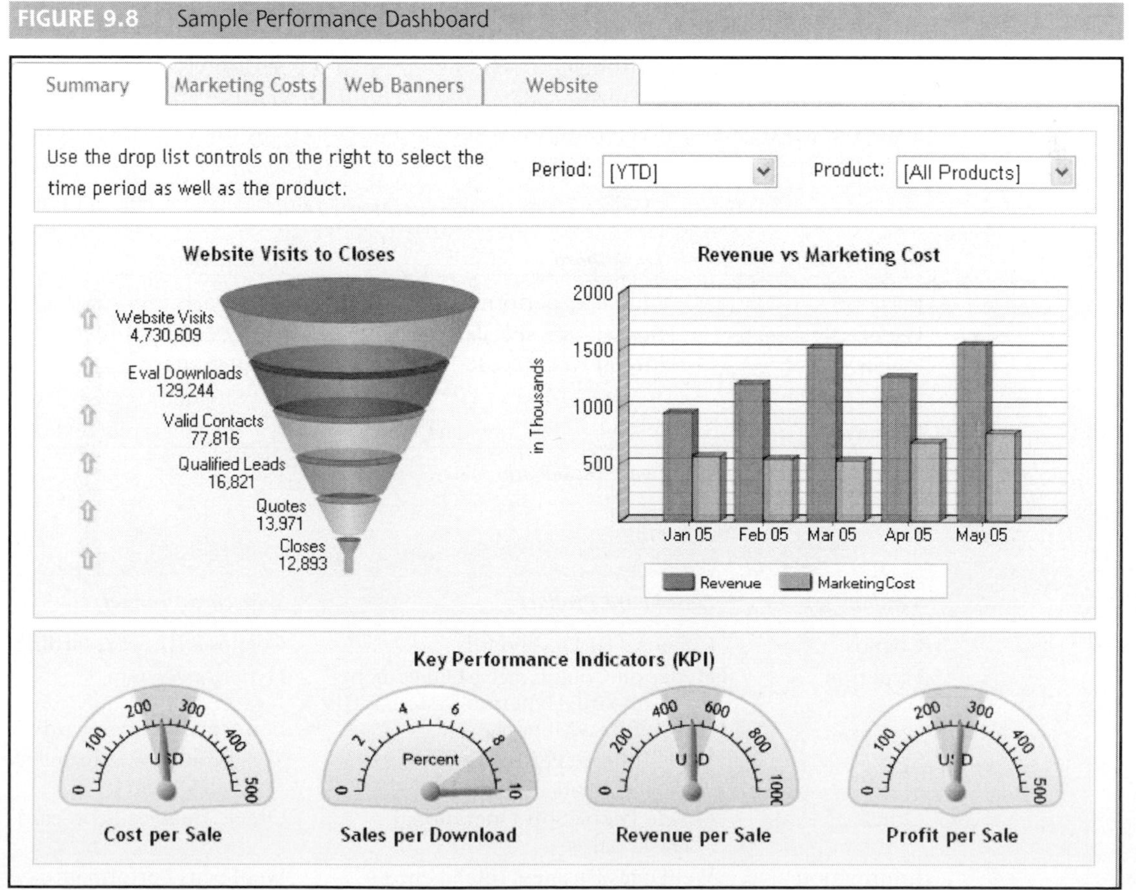

Source: Dundas Software, **demos1.dundas.com/DundasGauge/MarketingDashboard/WebSite.aspx.**

particular dashboard displays a number of KPI and pipeline data for a software company that produces specialized charting and visual display components for software developers and sells them directly on the Web. From the dashboard, it is easy to see, for instance, that the KPI are all good (i.e., they are all in the green, although they appear in gray in this book), that for all stages of the pipeline the figures are trending upward (i.e., they are all green arrows pointing upward, although the arrows are gray in this book), and that the growth in revenues is outpacing the increase in marketing costs. This particular dashboard enables end users to see whether there are any differences by time period or product (the dropdowns on the upper right) and to further analyze marketing costs and the Web pipeline (by selecting different tabs on the top).

DASHBOARDS VERSUS SCORECARDS

Although dashboards and scorecards share much in common, there are differences between the two. Some of the differences are summarized in Table 9.5. The key difference is that **performance dashboards** are visual displays used to monitor operational performance, while **performance scorecards** are visual displays used to chart progress against strategic and tactical goals and targets.

In the trade journals, the two terms are often used interchangeably, although many CPM and BI vendors offer separate scorecard and dashboard solutions and applications. Table 9.6 provides a list of some of these commercial offerings.

With most commercial offerings, the term *scorecard* is virtually synonymous with the concept of a BSC. In fact, most of the BPM scorecard products have been certified by the BSC Collaborative, which means they all have relatively similar display characteristics. For example, they all provide a semblance of a strategy map.

Eckerson, a leading authority on BI in general and performance dashboards in particular, suggested that one term—*performance dashboards*—fits all. In his vernacular, a performance dashboard is "a multilayered application built on a business intelligence

TABLE 9.5 Differences Between Performance Dashboards and Scorecards

Characteristic	*Dashboard*	*Scorecard*
Purpose	Measures performance	Charts progress
Users	Supervisors, specialists	Executives, managers, staff
Updates	"Right-time" feeds	Periodic snapshots
Data	Events	Summaries
Display	Visual graphs, raw data	Visual graphs, text comments

Source: W. Eckerson, *Performance Dashboards*, Wiley, Hoboken, NJ, 2006.

TABLE 9.6 Commercial Dashboard and Scorecard Software Products

Vendor	*Dashboard Product*	*Scorecard Product*
Cognos	Cognos 8 BI Dashboards	Cognos 8 BI Scorecarding
Hyperion	Hyperion Compliance Management Dashboard, Hyperion System 9 BI+ Enterprise Metrics	Hyperion System 9 Performance Scorecard
SAS	SAS Strategic Performance Management	SAS Strategic Performance Management
Oracle	Oracle PeopleSoft Operational Dashboards	Oracle Balance Scorecard
Information Builders	WebFocus Business Intelligence Dashboard	WebFocus Performance Management Framework

and data integration infrastructure that enables organizations to measure, monitor, and manage business performance more effectively" (Eckerson, 2006). Under his scheme, distinctions can be made among three types of performance dashboards:

1. *Operational dashboards.* Used by frontline workers and supervisors to monitor key operational data that are lightly summarized and updated frequently throughout the day.
2. *Tactical dashboards.* Used by managers and analysts to track on a daily or weekly basis detailed and summarized data generated from departmental processes and projects. The emergency room system discussed in Application Case 9.6 exemplifies this type of dashboard.
3. *Strategic dashboards.* Used by executives, managers, and staff to monitor on a monthly or quarterly basis detailed and summarized data pertaining to the execution of strategic objectives.

Application Case 9.6

Dashboards for Doctors

One of the driving forces behind the acceptance of performance dashboards is the desire to put BI functionality into the hands of users other than business analysts or power users. A case in point is the Emergency Medicine and Analysis Report System (EMARS) developed for physicians that is used by Emergency Medical Associates (EMA), a not-for-profit, physician-owned medical group that manages emergency rooms for 16 hospitals in New York and New Jersey. As Jonathan Rothman, director of data management at EMA stated, "The dashboard is really the best [solution] for the emergency department (ED). The speedometers are great for quick analysis of data, because once you understand the metric, and once you understand from the end user what their targets and thresholds are, then all they essentially have to do is look at metrics and then look for something red."

IMPETUS

EMA was looking for a more intuitive way for physicians to access the information stored in EMA's Oracle data warehouse. Prior to the introduction of the dashboard system, the only way for physicians to gain access to the warehouse data was through a legacy patient tracking and electronic medical records system. The legacy system, which was called the Emergency Department Information Manager (EDIM), was built on Visual FoxPro and provided a number of predefined clinical templates and predefined reports. Despite these built-in capabilities, the system was difficult to use and hard to extend.

To overcome the limitations of the EDIM system, EMA turned to Business Objects's Application Foundation Dashboard Manager, an analytical tool kit that enables application developers to create rich analytical dashboards with minimal effort. Application Foundation enables developers to present top-level metrics in dashboard form, and it enables developers to tie top-level metrics to the underlying operational detail. In this way, end users can drill down to the detail for any top-level metrics exhibiting patterns of interest.

METRICS OF INTEREST

What kinds of metrics are of interest to ED physicians and administrators? Not medical information per se. Instead, ED physicians and administrators want data that help them monitor the health of the department itself. Total revenue, total expenses, number of patient visits, and overall ED admission percentages are some of the metrics available from the EMARS dashboards. Essentially, the dashboards give physicians and other personnel a statistical view of the "wellness" of the emergency room, in both financial and service terms.

There are two types of dashboards in EMARS: those associated with billing and collecting and those associated with emergency department services. The billing and collecting dashboards are pretty straightforward, providing information on revenues and expenses. These are the sorts of metrics found on the dashboards of many organizations. In contrast, the service metrics are pretty specific to emergency room operations. Take, for example, a performance metric called "left without being seen" (LWOB). In hospital lingo, this means that the patient came to the emergency room, waited, and finally left the facility, possibly to seek help elsewhere. Having information of this sort helps EMA become more successful. If a particular emergency room has an LWOB that exceeds some predetermined threshold, it implies that service is slow and changes need to be made. The same holds true with other service metrics. Some of the other metrics tracked by EMARS include total pediatric visits, total patient admissions, and percentage of patients who left against medical advice (AMA).

In addition to these high-level service metrics, EMARS also provides more granular information. An example is the time that elapses between when a patient is first registered and when he or she is actually seen by a physician. Other examples are turnaround time for admitted patients and turnaround time for discharged patients.

Many of the service metrics have national benchmarks. This has enabled EMA to predefine thresholds for many of them. When a threshold is exceeded, an e-mail alert is sent to interested physicians and administrators. The alert pinpoints not only the exception but also the types of analysis that might help the recipient understand why the exception occurred.

From an IT perspective, one of the drawbacks of the dashboards is that the underlying Oracle data warehouse has to be fed from a variety of external sources by an ETL tool. One of the key sources is actually Crystal Reports repositories. (Crystal Reports is owned by Business Objects.) In the future, the IT department would like to bypass this step and simply post the Crystal Reports directly to the dashboard. Business Objects has indicated that it plans to provide this capability in the future.

Sources: Compiled from D. Bartholomew, "Gauging Success with Dashboards, What You See Is Only Part of What You Get," *CFO IT*, August 2005, **cfo.com/article.cfm/4077408/c_3242196** (accessed March 2006); and S. Swoyer, "Dashboards for Doctors," *BI Intelligence Journal*, Fall 2004.

DASHBOARD DESIGN

Dashboards pack of lot of information into a single screen. "The fundamental challenge of dashboard design is to display all the required information on a single screen, clearly and without distraction, in a manner that can be assimilated quickly" (Few, 2005). Online File W9.5 details part of this challenge. For the most part, dashboards display quantitative measures of what's going on. To speed assimilation of the numbers, the numbers need to be placed in context. This can be done by comparing the numbers of interest to other baseline or target numbers, by indicating whether the numbers are good or bad, by denoting whether a trend is better or worse, and by using specialized display widgets or components to set the comparative and evaluative context.

One way to place numbers in context is through comparison. By itself, a number has little meaning. If someone tells you that a company's sales revenue was $20 million for the past quarter, it is hard to determine what that means in terms of the company's performance. However, if someone tells you that the company budgeted $25 million for the quarter or that last year it made $30 million for the same quarter, this puts the numbers in a different light. Given these comparisons, you could probably surmise that the company's performance is not where the company wants it to be. Some of the common comparisons that are typically made in a BPM system include comparisons against past values, forecasted values, targeted values, benchmark or average values, multiple instances of the same measure, and the values of other measures (e.g., revenues vs. costs). In Figure 9.8, the various KPI are set in context by comparing them with targeted values, the revenue figure is set in context by comparing it with marketing costs, and the figures for the various stages of the sales pipeline are set in context by comparing one stage with another.

Even with comparative measures, it is important to specifically point out whether a particular number is good or bad and whether it is trending in the right direction. Without these sorts of evaluative designations, it can be time-consuming to determine the status of a particular number or result. Typically, either specialized visual objects (e.g., traffic lights) or visual attributes (e.g., color coding) are used to set the evaluative context. Again, for the dashboard in Figure 9.8, color coding is used with the gauges to designate whether the KPI are good or bad, and green up arrows are used with the various stages of the sales pipeline to indicate whether the results for those stages are trending up or down and whether up or down is good or bad. While they are not used in this particular example, additional colors—red and orange, for instance—could be used to represent other evaluate states on the various gauges.

WHAT TO LOOK FOR IN A DASHBOARD

Although there are differences between performance dashboards and standard performance scorecards, these two systems share some of the same characteristics. First, they both fit within the larger BPM or performance measure system. This means that their underlying architecture is the BI or performance management architecture of the larger system. Second, all well-designed dashboards and scorecards possess the following characteristics:

- They use visual components (e.g., charts, performance bars, sparklines, gauges, meters, stoplights) to highlight, at a glance, the data and exceptions that require action.
- They are transparent to the user, meaning that they require minimal training and are extremely easy to use.
- They combine data from a variety of systems into a single, summarized, unified view of the business.
- They enable drill-down or drill-through to underlying data sources or reports, providing more detail about the underlying comparative and evaluative context.
- They present a dynamic, real-world view with timely data refreshes, enabling the end user to stay up-to-date with any recent changes in the business.
- They require little, if any, customized coding to implement, deploy, and maintain.

Section 9.10 Review Questions

1. What are the major differences between a scorecard and a dashboard?
2. What is an operational dashboard? What is a tactical dashboard? What is a strategic dashboard?
3. What type of dashboard—operational, tactical, or strategic—was the EMARS system? Why was this type useful for physicians and administrators in an emergency room?
4. What criteria are important in selecting the particular display widgets to use with particular metrics on a dashboard?
5. What are the characteristics of a well-designed dashboard?

9.11 BUSINESS ACTIVITY MONITORING (BAM)

Business activity monitoring (BAM) is a term coined by Gartner. The term reflects their interest and the interests of others in the strategic concepts of the zero-latency enterprise and straight-through processing (reported by McKie, 2003; and Systar, 2002). In this context, *latency* refers to the gap between when data are collected and when they are available for decision making. A *zero-latency organization* is one in which data are immediately available, enabling an enterprise to be proactive rather than reactive. *Straight-through processing* refers to processing in which inefficient steps (such as manual entry) have been eliminated.

BAM systems consist of real-time systems that alert managers to potential opportunities, impending problems, and threats, and then empower them to react through models and collaboration. IT can collect data from a variety of internal and external sources in real-time, analyze them to detect unexpected patterns that indicate an emerging situation, and then deliver the results to those responsible for reacting. This technically agile aspect of the *real-time enterprise* is often labeled *BAM* (see Keating, 2003).

The major users of BAM include line-of-business executives, department managers, business operations staff, and CFOs. Typically, BAM is used to monitor the activities of a specific facility, such as a factory or a call center, or a specific business process. Application Case 9.7, which describes the Albuquerque city government's use of BAM, illustrates the single-minded, process-oriented nature of BAM.

Application Case 9.7

City of Albuquerque Goes Real-Time

In a 2003 survey conducted by Ventana Research, 1,300 business and IT managers were asked to name the top three goals for monitoring their business. The main reasons given were to manage or reduce costs (29 percent), improve efficiency of the organization (29 percent), increase focus on revenue priorities (19 percent), align individual actions to priorities (15 percent), and respond to competitors (5 percent). Not unexpectedly, efficiency won out over effectiveness.

Efficiency is the main reason the Albuquerque city government instituted a BAM system. The city government relies on NoticeCast from Cognos, a prominent BPM and BI software vendor, to proactively push e-mail notices of important events in near real-time to city employees, residents, and vendors. NoticeCast has the capability to monitor three basic categories of events:

- *Notification events.* The system notifies users whenever a report, an OLAP cube, or a query is updated.
- *Performance events.* The system notifies users whenever an actual or projected threshold is crossed.
- *Operational events.* The system notifies users whenever a specific transaction occurs in day-to-day operations.

NoticeCast also allows end users to create their own events, provides flexible delivery of alerts to wired and wireless devices, and integrates with Cognos's BI and BPM suites.

In the Albuquerque system, NoticeCast sits outside the city's firewall on an extranet, and it monitors events by periodically querying Oracle database tables that are populated periodically and often automatically by other municipal information system. The types of events the system monitors include the following (Anthes, 2003):

- Every morning, NoticeCast sends an e-mail to each vendor that was issued an electronic payment during the night, directing the vendor to a Web site on the extranet where it can get a remittance report.
- Every evening, NoticeCast sends an e-mail to each Albuquerque resident for whom a water bill was produced. The e-mail contains all the pertinent billing information and directs the resident to a Web site where he or she can pay the bill online.
- Once a day, the system sends e-mail to certain city employees, letting them know of all online payments made to the city during the past 24 hours.
- Whenever a candidate files a contribution report, NoticeCast sends e-mail to city employees responsible for tracking campaign law compliance.

The BAM system helps the city monitor events faster and more thoroughly than before. It also enables them to perform a number of activities, such as online billing, that were difficult or too expensive in the past. In the future, the city plans to deploy the system inside its firewall, on its intranet.

Sources: Compiled from G. Anthes, "Eyes Everywhere: Business Activity Monitoring Offers a Constant Watch on Business Processes," *Computerworld*, November 2003, **computerworld.com/printthis/2003/0,4814,86895,00.html** (accessed March 2006); and **cognos.com**.

BAM depends on a wide range of technologies working in concert. The following are of particular importance (McKie, 2003):

- *ETL technology* to gather data from multiple sources that may be relevant to a cross-application activity visualized by
- *Process modeling technology* that defines the scope of relevant activities and identifies the individual process steps in those activities that are subject to

- *Rules engines* that define and apply the rules that enable significant events within those activities to be recognized and responded to using
- *Messaging servers* that package and communicate or propagate the response to these events in a variety of formats in order to act as a provider to
- *E-mail in-boxes, portals, dashboards,* and *Web services* that consume these responses to expose them to decision makers who can act on them or systems that can process them further (perhaps to trigger another event or whole workflow)

BENEFITS OF BAM

BAM helps not just in recognizing and responding to events but also in enabling managers to resolve event occurrences quickly and review their impacts to make more timely and informed decisions (see McKie, 2003). Essentially, the two most important benefits are real-time data access in a usable format and access to tools to collaborate and model the problem, leading to a quick solution. Faster and presumably better decisions will therefore be made.

A business activity has to be intelligently automated in order to be monitored. The monitoring must be intelligent, and the results must be easy to access, visualize, or act on to derive value. Activity modeling is the first step in creating a successful BAM system. It involves finding activities worth monitoring, defining their steps and events, and tying those events to performance metrics to be monitored (see McKie, 2003). Analyzing activities leads to improved processes.

BAM ISSUES

BAM systems suffer from many of the shortcomings of all other EIS. Often, executives fail to consider the readiness of technology or of the business processes they want to monitor. This was one reason for the failure of the McDonald's enterprise system (see Application Case 17.2). Enterprise systems require a senior management champion and proper involvement and training of users. Integration issues can plague a BAM effort. Data must be extracted from many different sources and provided to many users.

Change management issues are paramount. As with most EIS, adopting the model and method requires not only technology but also a change in business processes (i.e., change management). In the case of BAM, delays built into information flows to allow lower-level managers to respond to them are eliminated. This has caused problems in EIS, and higher-level managers must learn to leave some problems in the hands of those responsible, at least for a time, to allow them the opportunity to respond. Executives must not undermine the authority of their employees.

As with any EIS, effective BAM requires working closely with the business units to identify the key indicators (CSF) and analytical techniques that provide reliable early warnings of impending issues (i.e., alerts). Also, as for any other EIS, a good way to start with real-time BAM is to focus on a well-defined business problem with a demonstrable return (see Keating, 2003).

BAM has the capacity to more quickly get the right information to the people who need it. Simultaneously, the information is reported higher in management. Executives must let the responsible managers on the frontlines deal with their problems and issues in a timely manner before reacting (see the next section). The key to success is to provide those closest to the situation with the information they need for decision making and at the same time help higher levels of management to more effectively monitor the effects of the decisions (see Keating, 2003).

BAM VENDORS

The BAM software market is in the early stages of development. Like any other emerging software market, it is experiencing definition and growing pains. A couple years ago, there were a number of pure-play BAM software vendors. Today, it is difficult to find a software vendor that designates itself as strictly a BAM vendor. Synthean and Quantive are both pure-play exceptions. Some of the early pure-play companies such as SeeRun are no longer around or, like Elity, have been acquired. Many, however, have focused on special verticals (e.g., FirstRain) or have re-focused on particular aspects of performance management (e.g., Celequest's shift to operational performance management and operational dashboards). Finally, a number of software companies offer BAM components or functionality as part of their larger performance management or BI suites. Cognos, Tibco, Savvion, and Mentisys are some of the vendors that support BAM in their larger offerings. For a detailed, but slightly dated, list of BAM vendors, see **computerworld.com/softwaretopics/software/story/0,10801,86894,00**.

Section 9.11 Review Questions

1. Define *BAM*.
2. Describe the BAM system used by the city government of Albuquerque.
3. What are the key technical elements of a BAM system?
4. What are some of the key issues that arise in implementing BAM?

Chapter Highlights

- BPM is an umbrella term covering the business methodologies, metrics, processes, and systems used to drive the overall performance of an enterprise.
- BPM is an outgrowth of BI, and it incorporates many of its technologies, applications, and techniques.
- BPM encompasses a closed-loop set of processes that link strategy to execution in order to optimize business performance.
- The key processes in BPM are strategize, plan, monitor, act, and adjust.
- Today, companies recognize the value of strategic planning as well as the need for operational and execution excellence.
- Strategy answers the question "Where do we want to go in the future?"
- The gap between strategy and execution is found in the broad areas of vision, people, management, and resources.
- Operational and tactical plans address the question "How do we get to the future?"
- The tactics and initiatives defined in an operational plan need to be directly linked to key objectives and targets in the strategic plan.
- An organization's strategic objectives and key metrics should serve as top-down drivers for the allocation of the organization's tangible and intangible assets.
- Monitoring addresses the question of "How are we doing?"
- BSC, performance dashboards, project monitoring systems, human resources systems, and financial reporting systems are all examples of diagnostic control systems.
- Most monitoring focuses on negative variances and pays little attention to underlying assumptions or strategies.
- There is a difference between planning for a conventional line of business and planning for a new venture.
- According to benchmark studies, the average billion-dollar company devotes thousands of person–days each year to planning and management reporting.
- Research figures indicate that top management spends about three hours a month discussing strategy and 80 percent of their time on issues that account for less than 20 percent of the company's long-term value.
- In best practice companies, forecasting is a decision support process that is used to refine strategic thinking, revise plans, and adjust resource allocation in response to changing events.

- Performance measurement systems assist managers in tracking the implementation of business strategy by comparing actual results against strategic goals and objectives.
- The drawbacks of using financial data as the core of a performance measurement system are well known.
- Performance measures need to be derived from the corporate and business unit strategies and from an analysis of the key business processes required to achieve those strategies.
- Probably the best-known and most widely used performance management system is the BSC.
- Central to the BSC methodology is a holistic vision of a measurement system tied to the strategic direction of the organization.
- As a measurement methodology, BSC is designed to overcome the limitations of systems that are financially focused.
- As a strategic management methodology, BSC enables an organization to align its actions with its overall strategies.
- Most companies use Six Sigma as a process improvement methodology that enables them to scrutinize their processes, pinpoint problems, and apply remedies.
- Six Sigma is a performance management methodology aimed at reducing the number of defects in a business process to as close to zero DPMO as possible.
- Six Sigma uses DMAIC, a closed-loop business improvement model that involves the steps of defining, measuring, analyzing, improving, and controlling a process.
- Substantial performance benefits can be gained by integrating BSC and Six Sigma.
- The standard BPM architecture is multitiered and consists of a user interface layer, a database layer, and a source data layer.
- The major BPM applications include budgeting, planning, and forecasting; profitability analysis and optimization; scorecarding; financial consolidation; and statutory and financial reporting.
- Scorecards and dashboards are common components of most, if not all, performance management systems, and BPM suites.
- Although scorecards and dashboards both provide visual displays of performance, there are significant differences between them.
- The fundamental challenge of dashboard design is to display all the required information on a single screen, clearly and without distraction, in a manner that can be assimilated quickly.
- BAM is used to monitor the real-time activities and events of a specific facility, such as a factory or a call center, or a specific business process.
- BAM helps not just in recognizing and responding to events but also in enabling managers to resolve event occurrences quickly and review their impacts to make more timely and informed decisions.

Key Terms

- balanced scorecard (BSC)
- business activity monitoring (BAM)
- business performance management (BPM)
- critical success factor (CSF)
- diagnostic control system
- DMAIC
- operational plan
- performance dashboard
- performance measurement system
- performance scorecard
- Six Sigma
- strategic goal
- strategic objective
- strategic vision
- strategy map
- system architecture

QUESTIONS FOR DISCUSSION

1. SAP uses the term strategic enterprise management (SEM), Cognos uses the term corporate performance management (CPM), and Hyperion uses the term business performance management (BPM). Are they referring to the same basic ideas? Provide evidence to support your answer.
2. BPM encompasses four basic processes: strategize, plan, monitor, act, and adjust. Select one of these processes and discuss the types of software tools and applications that are available to support it.
3. Select a public company of interest. Using the company's 2006 annual report, create five strategic financial objectives for 2007. For each objective, specify a strategic goal or target. The goals should be consistent with the company's 2006 financial performance.

4. In recent years, the Beyond Budgeting Round Table (BBRT; **bbrt.org**) has called into question traditional budgeting practices. A number of articles on the Web discuss the BBRT's position. In the BBRT's view, what is wrong with today's budgeting practices? What does the BBRT recommend as a substitute?
5. Describe how a BSC fits the description of a diagnostic control system.
6. Distinguish performance management and performance measurement.
7. The Performance Prism established by Andrew Neely and others at Cranfield University provides an alternative performance measurement and management framework. Using materials from the Web, discuss the major tenets of the framework. Compare the framework to BSC and Six Sigma.
8. Create a measure for some strategic objective of interest (you can use one of the objectives formulated in Discussion Question 3). For the selected measure, complete the measurement template found in Table W9.3.1 in the online file for this chapter.
9. Create a strategy for some hypothetical company, using the four perspectives of the BSC. Express the strategy as a series of strategic objectives. Produce a strategy map depicting the linkages among the objectives.
10. Compare and contrast the DMAIC model with the closed-loop processes of BPM.
11. Gartner's BPM magic quadrant lists the major software vendors that provide BPM suites. Compare and contrast two of the offerings (other than the Hyperion Solutions suite).
12. A number of companies provide both scorecard and dashboard products. Compare and contrast the scorecard and dashboard offerings from one company.
13. Using the criteria established in Table 9.2, compare BAM with traditional BI and BI for BPM. Based on this comparison, which type of BI is BAM closer to?

Exercises

Teradata University and Other Hands-on Exercises

1. Go to **TeradataStudentNetwork.com** and search for "performance management" by typing this phrase in the Search box. After the search results have been rendered, select the Web seminar "Facilitating High-Performance Business." This seminar describes Harrah's use of Cognos's performance management and BI capabilities. Based on this discussion, answer the following questions:
   a. What pressures are driving the rise of CPM?
   b. What is the strategic value of CPM?
   c. What are the core elements of CPM?
   d. What three application areas are key to CPM?
   e. What were the strategic issues (pain points) driving changes in Harrah's analytical and performance management capabilities?
   f. Briefly describe Harrah's closed-loop marketing system.
   g. What technologies are used in Harrah's marketing system?
   h. How does Harrah's closed-loop analysis compare to the closed loop for BPM?
   i. What KPI are of primary interest to Harrah's?
   j. What lessons did Harrah's learn in implementing and using its system?
2. Go to **TeradataStudentNetwork.com**. Select the demos under the Resources tab. View the "Supply Chain Intelligence (SCI)" demo. Briefly summarize the scenario being demonstrated. Describe the BAM capabilities provided by Teradata's SCI and predictive analytics.
3. There are several articles describing the pitfalls associated with dashboard design. One of these is "Dashboard Design: Why Design Is Important," by Richard Brath and Micheal Peters. Download (**dmreview.com/article_sub.cfm?articleId=1011285**) and read this article. Then go to **dundas.com**. Dundas provides components for developing custom scorecard applications. Under the "Product" menu, select the .NET "gauges" components. Next, go to the gauge demos. Run the Executive Digital Dashboard demo. Browse through the various tabs and answer the following questions:
   a. What sorts of information are provided by the executive dashboard? Briefly describe the status of the company represented by this demo.
   b. Using concepts from the article by Brath and Peters, provide a critique of the demo dashboard design. In what ways could the design be improved?

4. Develop a prototype dashboard to display the financial results of a public company. The prototype can be either paper based or Excel based. Use data from the 2006 annual plans of two public companies to illustrate the features of your dashboard.

Exercises

Team Assignments and Role-Playing

1. As a team, select a particular vendor from the BPM magic quadrant (excluding Hyperion). For each vendor, summarize the BPM offerings, the architecture, and the applications provided. Virtually every vendor provides case studies describing its customers' BPM and BI implementations. Select three such case studies. For each, summarize the problem the customer was trying to address, the applications or solutions implemented, and the benefits the customer received from the system.

2. Computerworld provides a fairly complete listing of BAM vendors (see **computerworld.com/ software-topics/software/story/0,10801,86894,00**). Have each group select a particular vendor from the list. For each vendor, summarize the BAM offerings, the architecture, and the BAM applications provided. Virtually every vendor provides case studies describing its customers' BAM implementations. Select three such case studies. For each, summarize the problem the customer was trying to address, the applications or solutions implemented, and the benefits the customer received from the system.

Exercises

Internet Exercises

1. A survey conducted by Economist Intelligence Unit and reported in S. Taub, "Closing the Strategy-to-Performance Gap," *CFO Magazine*, February 22, 2005 (**cfo.com/article.cfm/3686974?f=related**), explores the relationship between strategy development and execution. Based on the survey, which is more important for performance management—strategy development or execution? What reasons do respondents give for poor execution? In what ways do respondents think they can improve performance?

2. In their article "Discover-Driven Planning," McGrath and MacMillian proposed a method for planning for new ventures in the face of uncertain assumptions. A recent article by Sunil Sharma, "Discovery Driven Planning," applied the method to a small, fictitious company (for consistency **marketremarks.com/narad.php? ContentId=10**). The article also provides access to the spreadsheet used with the example. Using the spreadsheet, develop a dashboard that the fictitious company could use to track its plans.

3. An article by Tom Hoblitzell, "Best Practices in Planning and Budgeting," summarizes many of the findings from The Hackett Group benchmarking study. Download the article from **answerthink. com/pdf/pdf_services/04_intelligence/whitepapers/w p_bpm_planbudget.pdf**. Write a report summarizing the major findings from the study.

4. The BCS Collaborative (**bscol.com**) provides a list of vendors that offer certified BSC products (**bscol .com/bsc_online/technology/**). Compare and contrast two of the products.

5. Tektronix recently won a CMO Best Practices Award for its marketing dashboard. The system is described at BtoBOnline.com, (**btobonline.com/article.cms? articleId=23849**. Briefly describe the system. What are some of the metrics that the system tracks? What benefits did Tektronix reap from the system?

6. Hyperion Solutions provides a whitepaper titled "Business Performance Management," at (**hyperion.com/downloads/wp_bpm_0603.pdf**), that describes the Hyperion Management Model. Download the paper. Describe the Hyperion Management Model. Compare it to the closed-loop BPM processes described in this chapter.

7. A recent article titled "Is BPM Performing? Surveys Highlight the Market's Needs," by Meg Waters (see **bpmmag.net/magazine/article.html?articleID= 14437**), discusses the results from two separate BPM surveys designed to answer the general question "How well are the BPM vendors delivering?" Describe the surveys. Provide a summary of the survey results discussed in the article.

End of Chapter Application Case

Vigilant Information Systems at Western Digital

Western Digital (WD) is a $3 billion global designer and manufacturer of high-performance hard drives for desktop PCs, corporate networks, enterprise storage, and home entertainment applications. The company is headquartered in Lake Forest, California, and it has manufacturing facilities in Malaysia and Thailand and distribution centers in Europe. The company employs about 18,000 people worldwide.

For the past decade, competition in the hard drive industry has been fierce. Like many other industries, this industry faces constantly changing customer requirements, price pressures due to global competition, short product life cycles, and high demand for product quality and reliability. As a result, the industry has shrunk from 11 manufacturers to 3 to 5, depending on the product line. During this period, WD has excelled, and it is now the third-largest-volume producer.

NEED FOR NEW INFORMATION DELIVERY

As part of their survival strategy, WD management expressed a need for a new mode of information delivery. They wanted the ability to react more quickly. They also wanted integrated information so they could manage enterprise-wide in a "follow the sun" manner, passing information across the time zones as the workday closes in one and opens in another. The solution to these needs is WD's Vigilant Information System (VIS).

The word *vigilant* means being ever watchful. VIS "integrates data and distills information and business intelligence from various sources to detect changes, initiate alerts, assist with diagnosing and analyzing problems, and supports communication for quick action." Unlike traditional information systems, VIS is proactive rather than passive. As changes are made in the data, the data are reanalyzed. If the data meet certain prespecified conditions, the system alerts the user.

VIS ARCHITECTURE

WD's VIS has a multitiered architecture. At the bottom of the system are raw data from various transaction sources. These data flow into a number of functional applications (e.g., ERP, point-of-sale, manufacturing). On top of this tier is the BI tier, which analyzes the data to determine whether they meet certain prespecified conditions. The data that satisfy these conditions initiate alerts that are sent to the dashboard tier at the top.

Three capabilities form the foundation of WD's VIS: the ERP system, which was implemented in 1997 and provides up-to-date data on enterprise operations; the data warehouse, which was implemented in 1999 and provides integrated data from 12 disparate legacy systems; and Quality Information System (QIS), which was initiated in 1999 and provides insight into overall manufacturing quality. Even though these systems form the foundation of VIS and have been in effect for some time, they failed to provide managers with the view of operations that they needed. In particular, a number of legacy systems still remained non-integrated, the data refresh rate of the systems was inadequate, and the systems lacked adequate analytical capabilities.

Management felt that VIS, in combination with real-time management dashboards, could provide the visibility they wanted, as long as certain policy changes were instituted. First, they had to translate strategic enterprise goals into a set of aligned, measurable, time-based operational objectives for each department. Next, they had to monitor KPI in real-time, both horizontally across the organization and vertically within the business units. Finally, they had to foster cross-team collaborative decision making across teams, departments, enterprises, and geographies.

DASHBOARDS

Two types of real-time dashboards were developed: one for factory data and one for corporate information, including demand planning, distribution, and sales. The factory dashboards—aimed at yield, material, production output, station monitoring, and quality—were built from scratch. Each of the five factory dashboards displayed various KPI and metrics, allowed drill-down to underlying detail, and issued alerts. In contrast, the corporate dashboards—aimed at billings and returns, backlogs, outlook, finished goods inventory, and the like—were built using Cognos's BI suite. The suite provided the same capabilities as the factory dashboards, as well as a number of other specialized analytical features.

In addition to providing needed visibility to WD's operational systems, the combination of VIS and dashboards also supported WD's OODA decision methodology. OODA stands for the integrated processes of *observing* (i.e., seeing change signals), *orienting* (i.e., interpreting the signals), *deciding* (i.e., formulating an appropriate response), and *acting* (i.e., executing the selected response). From WD's perspective, companies that can execute OODA loops faster have a competitive advantage.

BUSINESS IMPACT

By 2004, more than 200 managers and professionals at all levels of WD were using the dashboards. The payoffs from the system and the dashboards have come in two forms:

- *Cost savings*. The system and dashboards provided a better view of inventory turns and other carrying costs. The result was a net savings of $3 million. The system also reduced the costs of producing customized management reports. The cost savings here is estimated at $900,000 per year. Finally, the system has reduced information overload and, in turn, the amount of time spent in meetings. In this case, the savings are estimated at $350,000 per year.
- *Strategic advantages*. The system and dashboards speed the delivery of data and information to executives and managers at all levels. This means that problems and opportunities can be addressed more rapidly, that strategic decisions can be made more quickly, and that the processes in the OODA loop can be executed more swiftly.

LESSONS LEARNED

WD's experiences provides a number of lessons for implementing and using VIS and performance dashboards. Some of the most important lessons include the following:

- Design the real-time management dashboards to be the nerve center for managing the enterprise.
- Plan and schedule the coordination among teams to use the dashboards to manage enterprise-wide.
- Build a learning loop around each OODA loop to foster group learning because the faster the loop, the more important the learning reviews and the more frequent they need to be.
- Match the latency of each OODA loop to the organization's needs and capabilities to become truly vigilant.
- Provide the building blocks for the "sense and respond" real-time enterprise through VIS and real-time management dashboards.
- Justify VIS on a strategic basis rather than a cost or return-on-investment basis.
- Make implementation of an enterprise-wide VIS a management initiative because it requires active collaborative engagement from top management to instill the needed organizational transformation.

Sources: Compiled from R. Houghton, O.A. El Sawy, P. Gray, C. Donegan, and A. Joshi, "Vigilant Information Systems for Managing Enterprises in Dynamic Supply Chains: Real-time Dashboards at Western Digital," *MIS Quarterly*, March 2004; and **westerndigital.com** (accessed October 2006).

QUESTIONS FOR THE CASE

1. What is VIS?
2. In what ways is the architecture of VIS similar to or different from the architecture of BPM?
3. What are the similarities and differences between the closed-loop processes of BPM and the processes in the OODA decision cycle?
4. Using Eckerson's dashboard types, describe the types of dashboards provided in the WD system.
5. What are the basic benefits provided by WD's VIS and dashboards?
6. What sorts of advice can you provide to a company that is getting ready to create its own VIS and dashboards?

References

Axson, D. (2003). *Best Practices in Planning and Management Reporting*. Hoboken, NJ: Wiley.

BPM Standards Group. (2005, September). *Business Performance Management: Industry Framework Document*, **bpmstandardsgroup.org/documents/BPMIndustryFramework-V5.0090905.pdf** (accessed March 2006).

BSC Collaborative. (2000). *Functional Standards*, **bscol.com/pdf/bsc99-standards.pdf** (accessed March 2006).

Buytendijk, F., et al. (2004, January). "Drivers and Challenges of Corporate Performance Management." *Gartner Research Report R-22-0730*.

Charan, R., and G. Colvin. (1999, July). "Why CEOs Fail." *Fortune*.

Coveney, M., et al. (2003). *The Strategy Gap*. Hoboken, NJ: Wiley.

Eagle, J. (2005, March). *Cross-Industry Study by Economist Intelligence Unit Finds More Companies May Undertake Six Sigma This Year*, **sixsigmazone.com/press-releases/cross-industry-study-by-economist-intelligence-unit** (accessed March 2006).

Eckerson, W. (2006). *Performance Dashboards*. Hoboken, NJ: Wiley.

Few, S. (2005, Winter). "Dashboard Design: Beyond Meters, Gauges, and Traffic Lights." *Business Intelligence Journal*.

Gupta, P. (2004). *Six Sigma Business Scorecard*. New York: McGraw-Hill.

Hackett Group. (2004, August). *Gap Between World-Class and Median Continues to Widen According to 2004 Performance Research from The Hackett Group*. **answerthink.com/04_news/01_press/pr_2004/pr_08102004_01.html** (accessed March 2006).

Hammer, M. (2003). *Agenda: What Every Business Must Do to Dominate the Decade*. Pittsburgh, PA: Three Rivers Press.

Hoblitzell, T. (2003). *Best Practices in Planning and Budgeting*, **answerthink.com/pdf/pdf_services/04_intelligence/whitepapers/wp_bpm_planbudget.pdf** (accessed March 2006).

Isixsigma. (2006). *The History of Six Sigma*, 2006, **isixsigma.com/library/content/c020815a.asp** (accessed March 2006).

Kaplan, R., and D. Norton. (1992, January–February). "The Balanced Scorecard—Measures That Drive Performance." *Harvard Business Review*, pp. 71–79.

Kaplan, R., and D. Norton. (1996). *The Balanced Scorecard: Translating Strategy into Action*. Boston: Harvard University Press.

Kaplan, R., and D. Norton. (2000). *The Strategy-Focused Organization: How Balanced Scorecard Companies Thrive in the New Business Environment*. Boston: Harvard Business School Press.

Kaplan, R., and D. Norton. (2004). *Strategy Maps: Converting Intangible Assets into Tangible Outcomes*. Boston: Harvard Business School Press.

Keating, W. (2003, March). "Fast Tracking," *Optimize*, **optimizemag.com/article/showArticle.jhtml?articleId=17700874** (accessed March 2006).

McGrath, R., and I. MacMillan. (1995, July–August). "Discovery-Driven Planning." *Harvard Business Review*.

McKie, S. (2003, July 18). "The Big BAM." *Intelligent Enterprise*, **intelligententerprise.com/030718/612feat3_1.jhtml; jsessionid=KSXCENUTF1TDYQS-NDLOSKH0CJUNN2JVN** (accessed October 2006).

A. Neely, A., and M. Bourne. (2000, December). "Why Measurement Initiatives Fail." *Measuring Business Excellence*, Vol. 4, No. 1.

Niven, P. (2005). *Balanced Scorecard Diagnostics*. Hoboken, NJ: Wiley.

Porter, M.E. (2001, March). "Strategy and the Internet." *Harvard Business Review*.

Rayner, N., et al. (2005a, October). "Corporate Performance Management Applications Explained." *Gartner RAS Core Research Note G00130282*.

Rayner, N., et al. (2005b, October). "Magic Quadrant for CPM Suites, 2005." *Gartner Research Note G00131208*.

Schiemann, W., and Lingle, J. (1999). *BULLSEYE! Hitting Your Strategic Targets Through High-Impact Measurement*. New York: The Free Press.

Simons, R. (2002). *Performance Measurement and Control Systems for Implementing Strategy*. Upper Saddle River, NJ: Prentice Hall.

Systar. (2002, April). *Business Activity Monitoring*, **systar.com/docs/solutions_bam_wp.pdf** (accessed April 2006).

Tarlow, M., and Tarlow, P. (2002). *Digital Aboriginal*. New York: Warner.

Wade, D., and R. Recardo. (2001). *Corporate Performance Management*. Boston: Butterworth-Heinemann.

Whiting, R. (2005, April). "A Closer Look at Performance." *InformationWeek*, **informationweek.com/story/showArticle.jhtml?articleID=160901247** (accessed April 2006).

Wikipedia.org. (2006, January). *Strategic Enterprise Management*, **en.wikipedia.org/wiki/Strategic_enterprise_management** (accessed April 2006).

PART

IV

Collaboration, Communication, Group Support Systems, and Knowledge Management

Learning Objectives for Part IV

- Understand the concepts and process of groupwork
- Describe how IT-based collaboration and communication support groupwork in general and decision making in particular
- Understand the fundamental principles and capabilities of groupware and group support systems (GSS)
- Describe the fundamental principles and capabilities of knowledge management (KM)
- Describe tools of KM and how they relate to decision support
- Relate KM, collaboration, and communication to each other

Millions of people and thousands of organizations worldwide use the decision support and business intelligence (BI) concepts and tools described in Chapters 1 through 9 to successfully support their decision making. However, individual decision makers do not work in a vacuum. Typically, groups (or teams) of people work and make decisions together. Very effective computerized methods have evolved to support the complex situations and different settings of work groups. Part IV describes collaborative computing in several situations and settings, supporting people in one room and supporting people in different locations (see Chapter 10). The principles of KM are the subject of Chapter 11. Also of interest in this part of the book is coverage of the emerging use of enterprise information systems in frontline decision making (see Chapter 17, an online chapter).

Group decision support systems (GDSS) were the first specialized form of collaborative decision making supported by computers. Today, many group support system (GSS) technologies can facilitate electronic meetings, including virtual meetings. Many organizations now routinely use GSS, even in asynchronous modes (i.e., different times and different places), usually over the Web, for either direct or indirect support of decision making. Similarly, KM can be considered a form of enterprise-wide collaborative computing that makes any needed knowledge of an organization available in a meaningful form to anyone, anyplace, and anytime. The Web is the platform that enables collaborative support systems, including sharing of data, information, and knowledge.

Collaborative Computer-Supported Technologies and Group Support Systems

Learning Objectives

- Understand the basic concepts and processes of groupwork, communication, and collaboration
- Describe how computer systems facilitate communication and collaboration in an enterprise
- Explain the concepts and importance of the time/place framework
- Explain the underlying principles and capabilities of groupware, such as group support systems (GSS)
- Understand the concepts of process gain, process loss, task gain, and task loss and explain how GSS introduces, increases, or decreases each of them
- Describe indirect support for decision making, especially in synchronous environments
- Become familiar with the GSS products of the major vendors, including Lotus, Microsoft, WebEx, and Groove
- Understand the concept of GDSS and describe how to structure an electronic meeting in a decision room
- Describe the three settings of GDSS
- Describe specifically how a GDSS uses parallelism and anonymity and how they lead to process/task gains and losses
- Understand how the Web enables collaborative computing and group support of virtual meetings
- Describe the role of emerging technologies in supporting collaboration
- Define *creativity* and how it can be facilitated by computers

People work together, and groups make most of the complex decisions in organizations. The increase in organizational decision-making complexity increases the need for meetings and groupwork. Supporting groupwork where team members may be in different locations and working at different times emphasizes the important aspects of communications, computer technologies, and work methodologies. Group support is a critical aspect of decision support systems (DSS). Effective computer-supported systems have evolved to increase gains and decrease losses in task performance and processes. In addition, creativity is an important element of decision making that collaborative computing can enhance. The sections of this chapter are as follows:

10.1 Opening Vignette: Collaborative Design at Boeing-Rocketdyne
10.2 Making Decisions in Groups: Characteristics, Process, Benefits, and Dysfunctions
10.3 Supporting Groupwork with Computerized Systems
10.4 Tools for Indirect Support of Decision Making
10.5 Integrated Groupware Suites
10.6 Direct Computerized Support for Decision Making: From Group Decision Support Systems (GDSS) to Group Support Systems (GSS)
10.7 Products and Tools for GDSS/GSS and Successful Implementation
10.8 Emerging Collaboration Support Tools: From VoIP to Wikis
10.9 Collaborative Efforts in Planning, Design, and Project Management
10.10 Creativity, Idea Generation, and Computerized Support

10.1 OPENING VIGNETTE: COLLABORATIVE DESIGN AT BOEING-ROCKETDYNE

PROBLEM

Boeing-Rocketdyne, a major U.S. manufacturer of rocket engines, faced a bold challenge: Drive the cost of rocket engines down 95 percent, be able to get the engine to market 10 times faster than it had been able to do in the past for space shuttle main engines, and increase the useful life of a rocket engine by a factor of three. Obviously, this required a radically new design, significant creativity, and unusual innovation. None of the technical senior managers at Boeing thought this was possible. Only a daring program manager was willing to try to respond to the challenge.

SOLUTION

The company created an eight-person team including experts from business partner organizations. Most members were in different locations, up to 1,000 miles away. Most members spent only 15 percent of their time on the joint design in the team, and they spent 85 percent of their time on their regular jobs. Thus, they constituted a virtual team because it was impractical to bring them to face-to-face meetings more than twice in the 10 months of the life of the project (once to start the project and be trained in the collaborative tools and once to celebrate the successful completion of the project). The team had 89 virtual meetings (2 or 3 meetings per week for the 41 weeks the project lasted). These meetings were supported by specially designed collaborative technology. Such support was necessary due to the need for an unusual solution from a virtual team whose members came from different organizations, with different experiences, in many disciplines, and who had never worked closely together.

Collaborative Technology Used

Custom software known as the *Internet Notebook* was developed in response to the wishes of the team. Team members could access the software securely from anywhere.

They could create, comment on, reference-link, search, and sort entries, which could consist of sketches, snapshots, hotlinks to desktop applications, text, or templates. They could also use an *electronic whiteboard* that allowed multiple team members near-instantaneous access to the same entry. In addition, a coordination protocol was used to facilitate the collaboration process.

A second software product, called *Project Vault*, allowed secured common file storage and transfer of these files on an as-needed basis. Thus, all members shared exactly the same data all the time.

The software tools were modified over the 10-month project period to allow flexibility. The protocol was also modified. For example, face-to-face meetings among two or more members, which were forbidden in the beginning, were later allowed, provided that their content was posted online for group sharing.

The major tools used to support the lengthy virtual meetings were teleconferencing and videoconferencing. Members in their offices used powerful desktop analysis software to analyze designs during the meeting, so results could be discussed in real-time (e.g., immediate feedback about proposed design ideas was provided in seconds). This allowed all those with the relevant skills and tools to participate in real-time virtual meetings. Hundreds of ideas were generated, leading to 20 conceptually distinct designs that were quickly evaluated using *electronic brainstorming*. The ability to analyze solutions from the desktop during the meetings greatly sped up the design process. All this encouraged knowledge sharing. Thus, decisions were made quickly and creatively, and frequent integration with all team members was easy and encouraged, leading to spontaneous and better decisions. The system allowed shared understanding of problems, possible solutions, analysis methods, constraints, and so on, as well as rapid creation (and discarding) of highly content-specific information. In addition to technology, it was necessary to formulate interorganizational strategy and structure a conducive work environment.

RESULTS

The team successfully designed a product made of 6 parts instead of the normal 1,200, at a cost of $0.5 million (versus $14 million) and a quality level of 9 sigma (instead of the normal 2–6 sigma, reducing defects to 1 projected failure in 10 billion). The team did all this in 10 months instead of 6 years, with production cost of $47,000 (instead of $4.5 million) and with more than a 5 percent reduction in total engineering hours. All these achievements are really amazing.

Sources: Compiled from A. Majchrzak; R. Carman, and V. Lott, "Radical Innovation Without Collocation: A Case Study at Boeing-Rocketdyne," *MIS Quarterly*, June 2001; and R. Carman, V. Lott, A. Malhotra, and A. Majchrzak, "Virtual Cross-Supply Chain Concept Development Collaborative Teams: Spurring Radical Innovations at Boeing-Rocketdyne," *Society for Information Management,* 2000, **simnet.org/Content/NavigationMenu/Resources/Library/Paper_Award_Winners/Download_Page2res/20001stPl.pdf** (accessed February 2006).

Questions for the Opening Vignette

1. Why was a group needed and why were the members in different locations?
2. Why did the project take so long? Why were so many meetings needed?
3. What computer support was provided? What type of software was used?
4. Comment on idea generation in this process.
5. Comment on sharing and collaboration in this process.

WHAT WE CAN LEARN FROM THIS VIGNETTE

The opening vignette illustrates how a temporary team that is properly supported by collaborative technologies and procedures can achieve incredible results. The team was virtual, meaning it met electronically, using telephone, videoconferencing, a document-sharing device, and other computer-based tools, some of which were customized for specific tasks. It shows the ability to make better and faster complex decisions with the support of computerized systems.

10.2 MAKING DECISIONS IN GROUPS: CHARACTERISTICS, PROCESS, BENEFITS, AND DYSFUNCTIONS

Managers and staff continuously make decisions, design and manufacture products, develop policies and strategies, design software, and so on. When people work in groups, they perform *groupwork*. **Groupwork** refers to work done by two or more people together.

CHARACTERISTICS OF GROUPWORK

The following are some of the functions and characteristics of groupwork:

- A group performs a task (sometimes decision making, sometimes not).
- Group members may be located in different places.
- Group members may work at different times.
- Group members may work for the same organization or for different organizations.
- A group can be permanent or temporary.
- A group can be at one managerial level or can span several levels.
- There can be synergy (leading to process and task gains) or conflict in groupwork.
- There can be gains and/or losses in productivity from groupwork.
- The task may have to be accomplished very quickly.
- It may be impossible or too expensive for all the team members to meet in one place, especially when the group is called for emergency purposes.
- Some of the needed data, information, or knowledge may be located in many sources, some of which may be external to the organization.
- The expertise of non-team members may be needed.
- Groups perform many tasks; however, groups of managers and analysts frequently concentrate on decision making.
- The decisions made by a group are easier to implement if supported by all (or at least most) members.

THE GROUP DECISION-MAKING PROCESS

Even in hierarchical organizations, decision making is usually a shared process. A group may be involved in a decision or in a decision-related task, such as creating a short list of acceptable alternatives or choosing criteria for evaluating alternatives and prioritizing them. The following activities and processes characterize *meetings*:

- The decision situation is important, so it is advisable to make it in a group in a meeting.
- A meeting is a joint activity engaged in by a group of people typically of equal or nearly equal status.

- The outcome of a meeting depends partly on the knowledge, opinions, and judgments of its participants and the support they give to the outcome.
- The outcome of a meeting depends on the composition of the group and on the decision making *process* the group uses.
- Differences in opinions are settled either by the ranking person present or, often, through negotiation or arbitration.
- The members of a group can be in one place, meeting face-to-face, or they can be a **virtual team**, in which case they are in different places while in a meeting.
- The process of group decision making can create benefits as well as dysfunctions.

THE BENEFITS AND LIMITATIONS OF GROUPWORK

Some people endure meetings as a necessity; others hate them. Groupwork may have both potential benefits and potential drawbacks.

Process gains are the benefits of working in groups. The unfortunate dysfunctions that may occur when people work in groups are called **process losses**. Examples of both are listed in Technology Insights 10.1.

TECHNOLOGY INSIGHTS 10.1

Benefits of Working in Groups and Dysfunctions of the Group Process

Benefits of Working in Groups (Process Gains)	Dysfunctions of the Group Process (Process Losses)
• It provides learning. Groups are better than individuals at understanding problems. • People readily take ownership of problems and their solutions. They take responsibility. • Group members have their egos embedded in the decision, so they are committed to the solution. • Groups are better than individuals at catching errors. • A group has more *information* (i.e., knowledge) than any one member. Group members can combine their knowledge to create new knowledge. More and more creative alternatives for problem solving can be generated, and better solutions can be derived (e.g., through *stimulation*). • A group may produce *synergy* during problem solving. The effectiveness and/or quality of groupwork can be greater than the sum of what is produced by independent individuals. • Working in a group may stimulate the creativity of the participants and the process.	• Social pressures of conformity may result in **groupthink** (i.e., people begin to think alike and do not tolerate new ideas; they yield to *conformance pressure*). • It is a time-consuming, slow process (i.e., only one member can speak at a time). • There can be lack of coordination of the meeting and poor meeting planning. • Inappropriate influences (e.g., domination of time, topic, or opinion by one or few individuals; fear of contributing because of the possibility of *flaming*). • There can be a tendency for group members to either dominate the agenda or rely on others to do most of the work (free-riding). • Some members may be afraid to speak up. • There can be a tendency to produce compromised solutions of poor quality.

(continued)

TECHNOLOGY INSIGHTS 10.1 (continued)

Benefits of Working in Groups (Process Gains)	Dysfunctions of the Group Process (Process Losses)
• A group may have better and more precise communication working together. • Risk propensity is balanced. Groups moderate high-risk takers and encourage conservatives.	• There is often nonproductive time (e.g., socializing, preparing, waiting for latecomers—*air-time fragmentation*). • There can be a tendency to repeat what was already said (because of failure to remember or process). • There is a high cost of meeting (e.g., travel, participation). • There can be incomplete or inappropriate use of information. • There can be too much information (i.e., information overload). • There can be incomplete or incorrect task analysis. • There can be inappropriate or incomplete representation in the group. • There can be attention blocking. • There can be concentration blocking.

IMPROVING THE MEETING PROCESS

Meetings can be very effective if the participants recognize what can go wrong there and try to improve the process of conducting a meeting.

Researchers have developed methods for improving the processes of groupwork; that is, increasing some of the benefits of meetings and eliminating or reducing some of the losses (see Duke Corporate Education, 2005). Some of these methods are known as *group dynamics*. Two representative methods are the **nominal group technique (NGT)**, which is a simple brainstorming process for non-electronic meetings, and the **Delphi method**, which is a qualitative forecasting methodology that uses anonymous questionnaires. These questionnaires are effective for technological forecasting and for forecasting involving sensitive issues. These methods were initially manual approaches to supporting groupwork. See Lindstone and Turroff (1975) for details. Also see Online File W10.1 for a description of seven things that do and do not work in meetings. Technography.com provides information, surveys, and tips about how to run more effective meetings.

The limited success of manual methods such as NGT and the Delphi method led to attempts to use information technology to support group meetings. (Today, both NGT and Delphi are supported by computers in some organizations.)

Section 10.2 Review Questions

1. Define *groupwork*.
2. List five characteristics of groupwork.
3. Describe the process of a group meeting for decision making.
4. Describe five potential gains of group meetings.
5. Describe five potential losses of group meetings.

10.3 SUPPORTING GROUPWORK WITH COMPUTERIZED SYSTEMS

When people work in teams, especially when the members are in different locations and may be working at different times, they need to communicate, collaborate, and access a diverse set of information sources in multiple formats. This makes meetings, especially virtual ones, complex, with a great chance for process losses. It is important to follow a certain process for conducting meetings. Computerized support may help, as was used at Boeing-Rocketdyne in the opening vignette. Other reasons for support are cost savings, expedited decision speed, the need to support virtual teams, the need for external experts (e.g., the Boeing-Rocketdyne case), and improving the decision-making process.

Almost all organizations, small and large, are using some computer-based communication and collaboration methods and tools to support people working in teams or groups. For example, Johnson Controls has cut production costs by $20 million with a collaboration portal that integrates supplier applications (see Hall, 2002). Lockheed Martin won a $19 billion contract on the basis of its collaboration capabilities (see Konicki, 2001). In Boeing-Rocketdyne's case, considerable support was provided to the temporary, virtual design group.

AN OVERVIEW OF GROUP SUPPORT SYSTEMS (GSS)

For groups to collaborate effectively, appropriate communication methods and technologies are needed. The Internet and its derivatives (i.e., intranets and extranets) are the infrastructures on which much communication for collaboration occurs. The Web supports intra- and interorganizational collaborative decision making through collaboration tools and access to data, information, and knowledge from inside and outside the organization.

Intraorganizational networked decision support can be effectively supported by an *intranet*. People within an organization can work with Internet tools and procedures through enterprise information portals (see Chapter 17, an online chapter). Specific applications can include important internal documents and procedures, corporate address lists, e-mail, tool access, and software distribution.

An *extranet* links people in different organizations. For example, several automobile manufacturers have involved their suppliers and dealers in extranets to help them to deal with inventories and customer complaints (see **covisint.com**). Other extranets are used to link teams together to design products when several different suppliers must collaborate on design and manufacturing techniques.

There are many Web-based collaborative configurations and tools, as described in the opening vignette. Other examples are Autodesk's Architectural Studio and CoCreate's OneSpace, which allow several designers to work together simultaneously. Most major auto manufacturers are moving toward using such tools to substantially reduce the cost and time of bringing new car models to market (see Application Case 10.2).

Computers have been used for several decades to facilitate groupwork and group decision making. Lately, collaborative tools have received even greater attention due to their increased capabilities and ability to save money (e.g., on travel cost) as well as their ability to expedite decision making. Such computerized tools are called *groupware*.

GROUPWARE

Many computerized tools have been developed to provide group support. These tools are called **groupware** because their primary objective is to support groupwork. Groupware tools can support decision making *directly* or *indirectly*, and they are

Application Case 10.2

How General Motors Is Collaborating Online

PROBLEM

Designing a car is a complex and lengthy process. Take, for example, just a small part of the process at General Motors (GM). Each model created needs to go through a frontal crash test. GM builds prototypes that cost about $1 million each and tests how they react to a frontal crash. GM crashes these cars, makes improvements, and then crashes them again. Even as late as the 1990s, GM crashed as many as 70 prototype versions of each new model.

The information regarding a new design collected from these crashes and other tests has to be shared among approximately 11,000 designers and engineers in hundreds of divisions and departments at 16 GM design labs, located all over the world. In addition, GM must communicate and collaborate with the design engineers of the more than 1,000 key suppliers. All this communication and collaboration slowed the design process and increased costs. It took over four years to get a new model to market, and the new car often looked stale on arrival because public tastes had changed during the course of development.

SOLUTION

GM, like its competitors, has been transforming itself into an e-business. This gradual transformation has been going on since the mid-1990s, when Internet bandwidth increased sufficiently. GM's first task was to examine more than 7,000 existing legacy IT systems and reduce that number to about 3,000 and make them Web-enabled. GM's new electronic commerce (EC) system is centered on a computer-aided design (CAD) program from EDS (**eds.com**). This system, known as Unigraphics, allows 3D design documents to be shared online by both the designers (internal and external) and engineers, all of whom are connected by the EDS software. In addition, collaborative and Web conferencing software tools, including Microsoft's NetMeeting and EDS's eVis, were added to enhance teamwork. In 2003, the company moved to eVis 4.0, which allows all the suppliers, from large companies to mom-and-pop operations, to communicate with GM. These tools have radically changed the vehicle-review process.

To understand how GM now collaborates with a supplier, let's take as an example a needed cost reduction in a new seat frame made by Johnson Controls. GM electronically sends its specifications for the seat to the vendor's product data system. Johnson Controls's collaboration system (eMatrix) is integrated with EDS's Unigraphics. This collaboration enables joint searching, designing, tooling, and testing of the seat frame in real-time, expediting the process and cutting costs by more than 10 percent. Finally, use of math-based modeling and a real-time, Web-based review process enable GM to electronically "crash" some of the cars during the design phases rather than doing it physically after each design change. GM supports this collaboration with its Advanced Design studio and Virtual Realty lab.

RESULTS

It now takes less than 18 months to bring a new car to market, and the design cost is now much lower than it used to be. For example, during the design phases, 60 cars are now "crashed" electronically, and only 10 prototype cars are crashed physically. The change has produced enormous savings. In addition, the shorter cycle time enables GM to bring out more new car models more quickly, providing the company with a competitive edge.

These changes have translated into profit. Despite the economic slowdown, GM's revenues increased more than 6 percent in 2002, and its earnings in the second quarter of 2002 doubled those of the same period in 2001. By 2004, assembly-line defects dropped by 25 percent, cutting inventory costs by 20 percent.

Sources: Compiled from M. Sullivan, "GM Moves Into the Passing Lane," *Forbes* (*Best of the Web supplement*), October 7, 2002; G. Rifkin, "GM's Internet Overhaul," *MIT Technology Review,* October 2002; and S. Ulfelder, "GM Gears Up with Collaboration Based on Web Services," *NetworkWorldFusion,* May 6, 2003, **nwfusion.com/research/2003/0526gm.html?page=1** (accessed March 2006).

described in the remainder of this chapter. For example, generating creative solutions to problems is a direct support. Some e-mail programs, chat rooms, instant messaging (IM), and teleconferencing provide indirect support.

Groupware provides a mechanism for team members to share opinions, data, information, knowledge, and other resources. Different computing technologies support groupwork in different ways, depending on the purpose of the group, the task, and the time/place category in which the work occurs.

TIME/PLACE FRAMEWORK

The effectiveness of a collaborative computing technology depends on the location of the group members and on the time that shared information is sent and received. DeSanctis and Gallupe (1987) proposed a framework for classifying IT communication support technologies. In this framework, communication is divided into four cells, which are shown together with representative computerized support technologies in Figure 10.1. The four cells are organized along the two dimensions *time* and *place*.

When information is sent and received almost simultaneously, the communication is **synchronous (real-time)**. Telephones, IM, and face-to-face meetings are examples of synchronous communication. **Asynchronous** communication occurs when the receiver gets the information at a different time than it was sent, such as in e-mail. The senders and the receivers can be in the same room or in different places.

As shown in Figure 10.1, time and place combination can be viewed as a four-cell matrix or framework. The four cells of the framework are as follows:

- *Same time/same place.* Participants meet face-to-face in one place at the same time, as in a traditional meeting or decision room. This is still an important way to meet, even when Web-based support is used, because it is sometimes critical for participants to leave the office to eliminate distractions.
- *Same time/different place.* Participants are in different places, but they communicate at the same time (e.g., with videoconferencing).
- *Different time/same place.* People work in shifts. One shift leaves information for the next shift.
- *Different time/different place (any time, any place).* Participants are in different places, and they also send and receive information at different times. This occurs when team members are traveling, have conflicting schedules, or work in different time zones.

FIGURE 10.1 Time/Place Communication Framework and Some Collaborative Computer-Supported Technologies

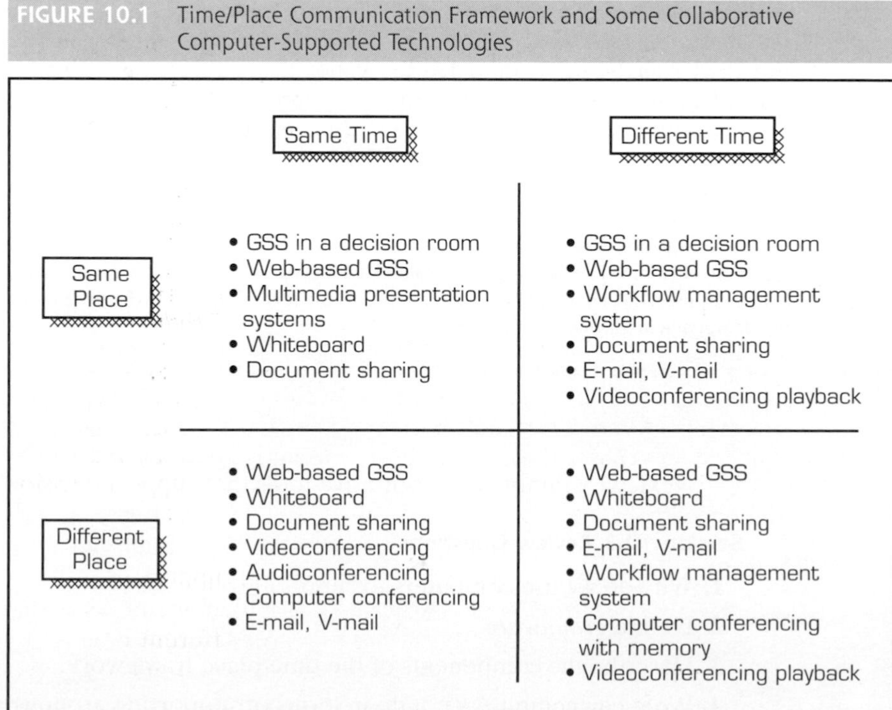

Groups and groupwork (also known as *teams* and *teamwork*) in organizations are proliferating. Consequently, groupware continues to evolve to support effective groupwork, mostly for communication and collaboration.

WHAT COMPUTERS CAN AND CANNOT DO

Modern Web-based information technologies provide an inexpensive, fast, capable, and reliable means of supporting communications. But computers cannot support all communication areas. (See Technology Insights 10.3 for some unsupported aspects of communication.) Networked computer systems, such as the Internet, intranets, extranets, and proprietary private networks, are the enabling platforms that support communication.

TECHNOLOGY INSIGHTS 10.3

Unsupported Aspects of Communication

Communication can be problematic in general because computerized communication methods do not transmit most of our nonverbal cues, which are important in establishing the richer meaning of a message by adding context. A large part of what we mean (perhaps exceeding 50 percent) is conveyed via nonverbal cues. Facial expressions, body language, voice tone, expression, inflection, touching, and distance are but a few. (For example, it is possible to fairly accurately determine who will win a U.S. presidential election by measuring the average rate of each candidate's eye blinking. The one who blinks the least has won every election from the Kennedy–Nixon contest in 1960 through 2000. Jay Aronson used this method in analyzing the third debate of the 2000 U.S. presidential election to predict the winner correctly.) Cross-cultural aspects and language subtleties are not easily transmitted through computer-mediated communication channels.

Emoticons were a first attempt to include nonverbal cues in text-based e-mail. For example, in the emoticon system, the characters :) are a happy face called a "smiley," and writing your message in all capital letters means you are SHOUTING! These have been updated into icons in IM software.

Some aspects of communication, such as the frequency of touching and the interpersonal distance between participants, are difficult to capture through technology. However, video technology can show facial expressions and some body language. Researchers are attempting to develop collaborative systems that capture more of this imprecise nature of human communication that makes the meaning of the message received more precise. They are also developing output devices (e.g., robot faces that can reflect mood) to do the same. Other devices are being developed to interpret facial cues, voice changes, and body movement.

Sources: D. Ferber, "The Man Who Mistook His Girlfriend for a Robot," *Popular Science*, September 2003, **popsci.com/popsci/science/ c0c80b4511b84010vgnvcm1000004eecbccdrcrd.html** (accessed August 2006); and D. Rosenbergm and J.A.A. Sillince, "Verbal and Nonverbal Communication in Computer Mediated Settings," *International Journal of Artificial Intelligence in Education*, 2000, Vol. 11.

Next, we examine representative tools that support decision making indirectly.

Section 10.3 Review Questions

1. Why do we use computers to support groupwork?
2. Define *groupware*.
3. Describe the components of the time/place framework.
4. What can computers not do in terms of supporting groupwork?

10.4 TOOLS FOR INDIRECT SUPPORT OF DECISION MAKING

A large number of tools and methodologies are available to facilitate e-collaboration, communication, and decision support. The following sections present the major tools that support decision making indirectly.

GROUPWARE TOOLS

Groupware products provide a way for groups to share resources and opinions. Groupware implies the use of networks to connect people, even if they are in the same room. Many groupware products are available on the Internet or an intranet to enhance the collaboration of a large number of people worldwide (e.g., see Henrie, 2004). Also, groupware tools are available in Microsoft Windows and Office 2007.

Groupware products and features that support collaboration and conferencing are listed in Table 10.1.

Synchronous Versus Asynchronous Products

Notice that the features in Table 10.1 may be *synchronous*, meaning that communication and collaboration are done in real-time, or *asynchronous*, meaning that communication and collaboration are done by the participants at different times. Web conferencing and IM as well as Voice over IP (VoIP) are associated with synchronous mode. Associated with asynchronous modes are e-mail, wikilogs, and *online workspaces*, where participants can collaborate, for example, on joint designs or projects, but work at different times. Vignette, Inc. (**vignette.com**), and Groove Networks (**groove.net**) allow users to set up online workspaces for sharing and storing documents. According to Henrie (2004), many of the tools offered by vendors are converging. This is occurring thanks to new technologies such as VoIP.

Groupware products are either standalone products that support one task (such as e-mail) or integrated kits that include several tools. In general, groupware technology products are fairly inexpensive and can easily be incorporated into existing information systems.

Virtual Meeting Systems

The advancement of Web-based systems opens the door for improved, electronically supported **virtual meetings**, where members are in different locations and even in different countries. For example, online meetings and presentation tools are provided by **webex.com** and **gotomeeting.com.**

The events of September 11 and the economic slowdown of 2001 through 2003 helped to make virtual meetings more popular (e.g., see Bray, 2004; and Powell et al., 2004). It is difficult for companies to ignore reported cost savings, such as the $4 million per month that IBM reported it saved just from cutting travel-related meeting expenses (Callaghan, 2002). In addition, improvements in supporting technology, reductions in the price of the technology, and the acceptance of virtual meetings as a respected way of doing business are fueling their growth.

Virtual meetings are supported by a variety of groupware tools, as discussed in the remainder of this section. We begin our discussion with the support provided by real-time support tools.

REAL-TIME COLLABORATION TOOLS

The Internet, intranets, and extranets offer tremendous potential for real-time and synchronous interaction for people working in groups. *Real-time collaboration (RTC)* tools

TABLE 10.1 Groupware Products and Features

General (can be either synchronous or asynchronous)
• Built-in e-mail, messaging system
• Browser interface
• Joint Web-page creation
• Sharing of active hyperlinks
• File sharing (graphics, video, audio, or other)
• Built-in search functions (by topic or keyword)
• Workflow tools
• Use of corporate portals for communication, collaboration, and search
• Shared screens
• Electronic decision rooms
• Peer-to-peer networks
Synchronous (same-time)
• Instant messaging (IM)
• Videoconferencing, multimedia conferencing
• Audio conferencing
• Shared whiteboard, smart whiteboard
• Instant video
• Brainstorming
• Polling (voting), and other decision support (consensus builder, scheduler)
Asynchronous (different times)
• Workspaces
• Threaded discussions
• Users can receive/send e-mail, SMS
• Users can receive activity notification alerts, via e-mail or SMS
• Users can collapse/expand discussion threads
• Users can sort messages (by date, author, or read/unread)
• Auto responder
• Chat session logs
• Bulletin boards, discussion groups
• Use of blogs, wikis, and wikilogs
• Collaborative planning and/or design tools
• Use of bulletin boards

help companies bridge time and space to make decisions and collaborate on projects. RTC tools support synchronous communication of graphical and text-based information. These tools are also being used in distance training, product demonstrations, customer support, e-commerce, and sales applications.

RTC tools can be purchased as standalone tools or used on a subscription basis (as offered by several vendors). One such vendor is WebEx (described later in this chapter).

Electronic Teleconferencing

Teleconferencing is the use of electronic communication to allow two or more people at different locations to have a simultaneous conference. It is the simplest infrastructure for supporting a virtual meeting. Several types of teleconferencing are possible.

The oldest and simplest is a *telephone conference call*, wherein several people talk to each other from three or more locations. The biggest disadvantage of this method is that it does not allow for face-to-face communication. Also, participants in one location cannot see graphs, charts, and pictures at other locations. Although the latter disadvantage can be overcome by using faxes, this is a time-consuming, expensive, and frequently poor-quality process. One solution is *video teleconferencing*, in which participants can see each other as well as documents.

Video Teleconferencing In **video teleconferencing (videoconferencing)**, participants in one location can see participants at other locations. Dynamic pictures of the participants can appear on a large screen and/or on a desktop computer. Originally, videoconferencing was the transmission of live, compressed TV sessions between two or more points. Today, videoconferencing is a digital technology capable of linking various types of computers across networks. When conferences are digitized and transmitted over networks, they become computer applications.

With videoconferencing, participants can share data, voice, pictures, graphics, and animation. Data can also be sent along with voice and video. Such **data conferencing** makes it possible to work on documents and to exchange computer files during videoconferences. This allows several geographically dispersed groups to work on the same project and to communicate by video simultaneously.

Videoconferencing offers various benefits. For example, it improves employee productivity, cuts travel costs, conserves the time and energy of key employees, and increases the speed of business processes (e.g., product development, contract negotiation, customer service). It also improves the efficiency and frequency of communications and saves an electronic record of a meeting, enabling specific parts of a meeting to be reconstructed for future purposes. It can also be used to improve customer service (see Application Case 10.4). Videoconferencing also makes it possible to hold classes at different locations. Finally, videoconferencing can be used to conduct meetings with business partners as well as to interview candidates for employment.

Web Conferencing *Web conferencing* is conducted on the Internet for as few as two and for as many as thousands of people. It allows users to simultaneously view something on their computer screens, such as a sales presentation in Microsoft PowerPoint or a product drawing; interaction takes place via messaging or a simultaneous phone teleconference. Web conferencing is much less expensive than videoconferencing because it runs over the Internet. An example of an application of Web conferencing is banks in Alaska that use video kiosks in sparsely populated areas instead of building branches that would be underutilized. A video kiosk operates on a bank's intranet and provides videoconferencing equipment for face-to-face interactions. A variety of other communication tools, such as online polls, whiteboards, and question-and-answer boards may also be used. Such innovations can be used to educate staff members about a new product line or technology, to amplify a meeting with investors, or to walk a prospective client though an introductory presentation. People can use Web conferencing to view presentations, seminars, and lectures and to collaborate on documents.

Web conferencing is becoming very popular. Almost all Web conferencing products provide whiteboarding and polling features and allow users to give presentations and demos and share applications. Popular Web conferencing products are Centra EMeeting, Genesys Meeting Center, PlaceWare, Go To Meeting, and WebEx Meeting Center.

Application Case 10.4

Videoconferencing Is Ready for Prime Time

Videoconferencing technology can cut travel expenses and increase a company's productivity. Dan Denardo, manager of global videoconferencing at Dow Chemical Company, says that videoconferencing vastly improves customer service and helps Dow deliver products to the market faster. "We know it can decrease cycle time, since we can hold more meetings in the same amount of time," Denardo says. Dow has about 160 video cameras at its headquarters in Midland, Michigan, and it has achieved an estimated annual travel cost savings of more than $7 million. At Dow, the technology is advancing from in-house conference rooms to customer sites. "It is fairly cheap hardware, the customers really like it and it sets us apart," Denardo commented.

Quantum Corporation (**quantum.com**), a large storage vendor, saves about $500,000 per month in travel expenses, lost-time avoidance, and productivity increase, according to Albert Villarde, a network analyst. Quantum has more than 20 video-equipped conference rooms around the globe. The primary business advantage of this is the speed-up in information sharing.

Estimates vary, but Pat Conway, product marketing manager at videoconferencing vendor VTEL Corporation, estimates that videoconferencing could reduce a firm's travel budget by about 15 percent. The most significant savings come from the increased speed of information delivery because more frequent, impromptu meetings occur.

Technology varies from PC desktop video to standalone conference rooms. Most companies use DSL, cable television Internet connections, or ISDN lines because of their higher bandwidth. Videoconferencing is an economical way to cut travel costs and boost productivity. Since September 11, 2001, these technologies have become critical because air travel is not as convenient as it previously was.

Lately, Dow implemented an IP-based communication system network that includes individual conference rooms with collaborative tools.

Sources: Compiled from L. Wood, "Videoconferencing Shows It's Ready for Prime Time," *InternetWeek*, July 12, 1999, p. 26; and SPL Integrated Solutions, "The Dow Chemical Company, Implementing IP Global Communication Network." **splis.com/VideoConferencingSolutions/ dow_ams.html** (no longer available online).

Interactive Whiteboards

Whiteboards are a type of groupware. Computer-based whiteboards work like real-world whiteboards with markers and erasers, except for one big difference: Instead of one person standing in front of a meeting room drawing on the whiteboard, all participants can join in. Throughout a meeting, each user can view and draw on a single document that is "pasted" onto the electronic whiteboard on a computer screen. Users can save digital whiteboarding sessions for future use. Some whiteboarding products let users insert graphics files that the group can annotate. For further information, see Online File W10.2.

Screen Sharing

In collaborative work, team members are frequently in different locations. By using **screen sharing** software, group members can work on the same document, which is shown on the PC screen of each participant. For example, two authors can work on a single manuscript. One may suggest a correction and execute it so that the other author can view the change. Collaborators can work together on the same spreadsheet or on the resultant graphics. Changes can be made by using the keyboard or by touching the screen. This capability can expedite the design of products, the preparation of reports and bids, and the resolution of conflicts.

Groove Networks (**groove.net**) offers a special screen-sharing capability. Its product enables the joint creation and editing of documents on a PC. (See the discussion of Groove later in this chapter.)

Instant Video

The spread of IM and Internet telephony has naturally led to the idea of linking people via both voice and audio. Called *instant video*, the idea is a kind of video chat room. Instant video allows users to chat in real-time and see the person(s) with whom they are meeting. A simple way to do this is to add video cameras to the participants' computers. A more sophisticated and better-quality approach is to integrate an existing online videoconferencing service with IM software, creating a service that offers the online equivalent of a videophone.

This idea is still in the early stages. One instant video pioneer is CUworld (**cuworld.com**). Here is how its CUworld software works: Users gets free CUworld software that can compress and decompress video signals sent over an online connection. To start a conference, a user sends a request to an online buddy via IM. The CUworld software goes to the directory of the IM service to determine the Internet addresses of the users' connections, and, using the Web addresses, the computers of the video participants are linked directly via the Internet. A videoconference can then begin.

Instant video sounds like a good product, but no one knows for sure how commercially viable it will be.

SUPPORT OF ASYNCHRONOUS COMMUNICATION

Asynchronous communication is supported mainly by e-mail and short message service (SMS) wireless messages. In the past few years, we have seen an increase in other tools that are not subject to spam. The two major tools, blogs and wikis, are discussed in Section 10.8. Other tools not discussed here are online bulletin (discussion) groups, auto responders, and workflow and interactive portals (see Chapter 17, an online chapter).

A major new asynchronous tool is the online workspace (see Henrie, 2004).

Online Workspaces

Online (electronic) workspaces are online screens that allow people to share documents, files, project plans, calendars, and so on in the same online place, though not necessarily at the same time. An online workspace is an extension of screen sharing, which was developed mainly for synchronous collaboration. An example is Intraspect from Vignette Corp., which allows users to set up workspaces for sharing and storing documents and other unstructured data. Another example is Microsoft's SharePoint, which allows employees to create Web sites, invite co-workers to join discussions, and post documents. Groove Networks sells an online workspace especially suited to users who are frequently outside a company's firewalls. Finally, CollabNet, Inc., offers an online workspace specifically to support collaboration of software developers.

Section 10.4 Review Questions

1. List the major groupware tools and divide them into synchronous and asynchronous types.
2. Describe the various types of electronic teleconferencing, including Web-based conferencing.
3. Describe whiteboards and screen sharing.
4. Describe instant video.
5. Describe the online workspace.

10.5 INTEGRATED GROUPWARE SUITES

Because groupware technologies are computer based and have the objective of supporting groupwork, it makes sense to integrate them among themselves and/or with other computer-based technologies. A *software suite* is created when several products are integrated into one system. Integrating several technologies can save time and money for users. For example, Polycom, Inc. (**polycom.com**), in an alliance with software developer Lotus, developed an integrated desktop videoteleconferencing product that uses Lotus Notes. Using this integrated system, publisher *Reader's Digest* has built several applications that have videoconferencing capabilities. *Groupware suites* provide seamless integration.

Groupware typically contains capabilities for at least one of the following: **electronic brainstorming** (i.e., brainstorming supported by computers), electronic conferencing or meetings, scheduling of meetings, calendaring, planning, conflict resolution, model building, videoconferencing, electronic document sharing (e.g., screen sharing, whiteboards, liveboards), voting, and organizational memory. Some groupware—such as Lotus Notes/Domino (**lotus.com**), Microsoft NetMeeting (**microsoft.com**), Groove (**groove.net**), WebEx (**webex.com**), and GroupSystems OnLine (**groupsystems.com**)—supports a fairly comprehensive range of activities. These products are known as *suites* and are described next.

LOTUS NOTES/DOMINO AND LOTUSPHERE

Lotus Notes/Domino (**ibm.com/software/lotus**) was the first widely used groupware (see Langley, 2004). Lotus Notes/Domino enables collaboration by letting users access and create shared information through specially programmed Notes documents. Notes provides online collaboration capabilities through Web conferencing on demand, work group e-mail, distributed databases, bulletin whiteboards, text editing, (electronic) document management, workflow capabilities, consensus building, voting, ranking, and various application-development tools, all integrated into one environment with a graphical menu-based user interface. Notes fosters a virtual corporation and creates interorganizational alliances. Notes broadens personal information management (PIM) data to supported mobile or wireless devices, including PDAs, pagers, and mobile phones, and makes available online access to critical business information using mobile devices. It also supports a variety of Web browsers on Linux as well as Microsoft Windows, while providing security features to help protect business-critical information. The software integrates presence awareness and IM to assist in collaboration with colleagues without launching a separate application and gives mobile workers the convenience of working while disconnected from the network.

Although increased competition is cutting into its market share, there are millions of Notes users in thousands of organizations. Many applications have been programmed directly in Lotus Notes (e.g., Learning Space, a courseware package that supports distance learning). Lotusphere is IBM's conferencing software with its Workplace platform, which is integrated with Domino. Workplace Builder allows nontechnical business users to create applications based on templates. For companies that have fewer than 1,000 employees, IBM offers Lotus Domino Express. For examples, see success stories at IBM (2006).

MICROSOFT NETMEETING AND LIVE MEETING

Microsoft NetMeeting is a real-time collaboration package that includes whiteboarding (i.e., support of relatively free-form graphics to which all participants can contribute simultaneously), application sharing (of any Microsoft Windows application document), remote desktop sharing, file transfer, text chat, data conferencing, and desktop audio- and videoconferencing. This application sharing is a vast improvement over what was called *whiteboarding* in the early 1990s. The NetMeeting client is included in the Windows operating system. See Application Case 10.5 for an example of a successful use of NetMeeting. Also see the "NetMeeting in Action" stories at **microsoft.com**. Live Meeting is a hosted Web conferencing tool (see *eWEEK* Reviews, 2005, for software evaluation).

Application Case 10.5

NetMeeting Provides a Real-Time Advantage

Jack O'Donnell is CEO of O'Donnell & Partners, a corporate interior contracting firm in Manhattan with branch offices in Chicago, London, and Milan. Until recently, O'Donnell felt the need to be on-site when any project was in its crucial stages. "Phone calls weren't enough, nor was e-mail—especially when you're dealing with a team of architects, designers, and contractors who speak different languages and all have their own professional jargon," he says. "Add to that the need for working on plans, sketches, and blueprints together at meetings, and my partners and I found we were spending most of our time at airports."

Microsoft NetMeeting provides collaborative computing support for groupwork, including application sharing through its Remote Desktop Sharing feature. It also provides real-time video. Now O'Donnell and his team members meet online. "Everyone can prepare a presentation that shows and doesn't just tell the progress of their part of the project," says O'Donnell. "We can work on files together, as if we were sitting across from each other at a conference table. And we can see each other's expressions, so it feels more like a real meeting."

O'Donnell estimates that Web conferencing saved his company at least a $0.5 million in travel costs in 1999. And that did not include the benefit of having fewer people out sick with whatever virus they picked up on their last plane trip. By 2000, the company started using VoIP to enhance collaboration using NetMeeting.

Sources: Compiled from M. Delio, "Power Meetings in Cyberspace," *Knowledge Management*, Vol. 2, No. 12, December 1999, pp. 77–78; and B. Stamler, "Making Face-to-Face Time Possible on the PC," *New York Times on the Web*, October 25, 2000. **partners.nytimes.com/library/tech/00/10/biztech/technology/25stam.html** (accessed August 2006).

Microsoft also offers a hosted Web conferencing product for Web conferencing called Live Meeting.

GROOVE NETWORKS

Groove Virtual Office is a product from Groove (**groove.net**; a Microsoft's company). It is an end-user application for secure discussions, file sharing, projects, and meetings. The software supports seamless shared project documents, allows work between project team members inside and outside an organization, and enables communication about project status and such, live virtual meetings, allocation and tracking of action items and tasks, and access to the latest project information (online or offline).

Used alone or with Groove Enterprise Servers and Hosted Services, Groove Workspace enables spontaneous, online–offline collaboration that reduces project costs and speeds time-to-market for products and services. The Groove Outliner tool is an open-ended brainstorming tool that allows shared space members to build structured hierarchical lists of videos and concepts. Groove's Sketchpad enhances collaboration on drawings and designs. The Groove peer-collaboration platform works across corporate firewalls and requires no special configuration or IT administration.

A very functional demo version (with no videoconferencing, however) is available for download. Although it takes a while to structure a first meeting and download all files to users, it is definitely an inexpensive, useful peer-to-peer package. A screenshot of a Groove Outliner session is shown in Figure 10.2.

WEBEX MEETING CENTER AND PLACEWARE CONFERENCE CENTER

WebEx Meeting Center (**webex.com**) is pay-per-use groupware. It provides a low-cost, simplified way to hold electronic meetings over the Web. WebEx contains all the features you need to run a meeting. WebEx Meeting Center integrates data, voice, and video within a standard Web browser for real-time meetings over the Internet from any desktop, laptop, or wireless handheld device. WebEx delivers active and interactive presentations, allows real-time collaboration with remote co-workers and partners, enhances demonstration of products and services, and assists in document management by allowing viewing, annotation, and editing of documents in real-time. Spontaneous Q&A sessions can be held, and closer relationships are built through interactive meetings with customers and partners from an individual's desktop. WebEx contains all the tools needed to share documents or opinions. WebEx Meeting Center is a fully hosted solution, enabling the initiation of online meetings that require no IT staff involvement, and it has very low startup costs. The WebEx MediaTone Network also provides fast communication for videoconferencing. For an interesting case with a

FIGURE 10.2 Example of Electronic Brainstorming in the Groove Workspace

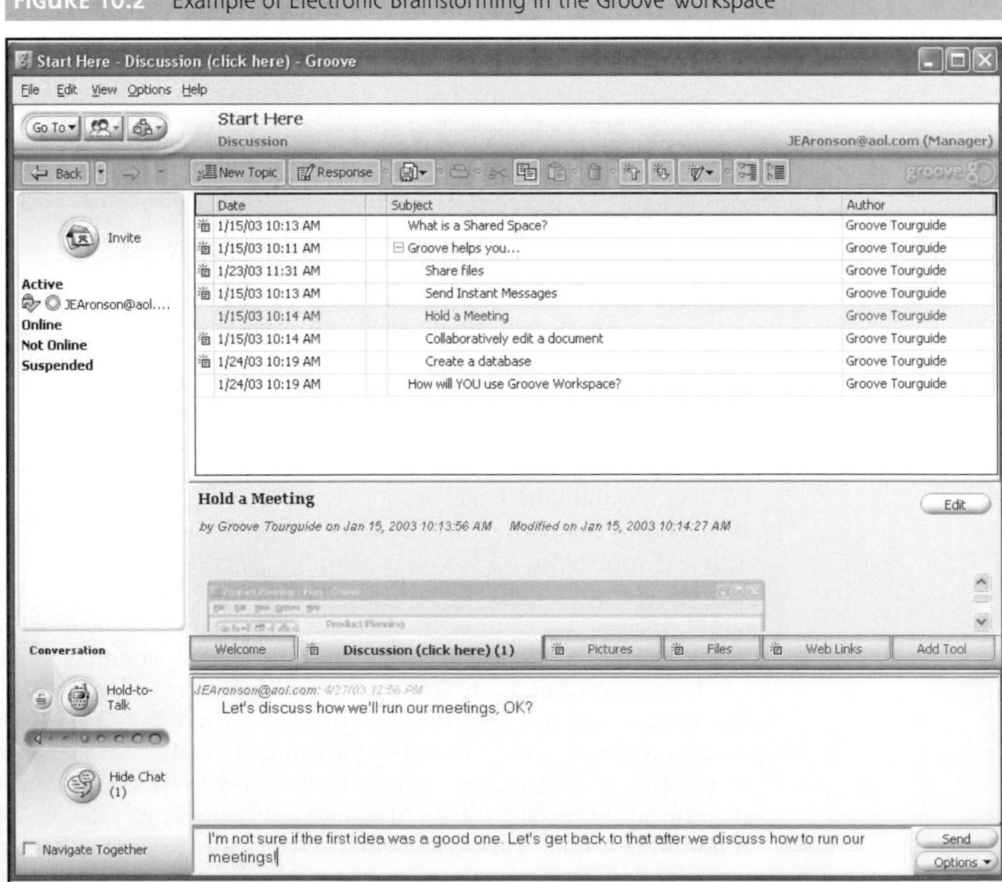

savings of $6 million, see Smith (2004). Finally, MeetMeNow is designed specifically for the support of data with integrated audio.

The PlaceWare Conference Center (main.placeware.com/services/pw_conference_ctr.cfm), now a subsidiary of Microsoft, provides Live Meeting and is capable of supporting multiple presenters and concurrent meetings with up to 2,500 participants per session. It is used to conduct product launches, sales demonstrations, training sessions, and more. Live Meeting is easily integrated with existing productivity tools (e.g., sessions can be scheduled quickly through a Microsoft Outlook calendar). The collaborative experience is enhanced through added features such as live polling, audience feedback, and mood indicators. PlaceWare also offers a virtual classroom, a distance-learning environment for training and seminars (**main.placeware.com/services/virtual_corp_training_orgs.cfm**).

GROUPSYSTEMS AND OTHER VENDORS

GroupSystems (**groupsystems.com**) MeetingRoom was one of the first comprehensive same time/same place electronic meeting packages. GroupSystems OnLine offers similar capabilities, and it runs in asynchronous mode (anytime/anyplace) over the Web (MeetingRoom runs over a local area network [LAN]). GroupSystems products are used in many academic studies to establish needed tools and teach how they should operate. We discuss these systems in Section 10.8.

Another specialized product is eRoom (now owned by EMC/Documentum at **software.emc.com**). This is a comprehensive Web-based suite of tools that can support a variety of collaboration scenarios. Yet another product is Team Expert Choice (EC11), which is an add-on product for Expert Choice (**expertchoice.com**). It has limited decision support capabilities, mainly supporting one-room meetings. Finally, the Zimbra Collaboration Suite is available at **zimbra.com**.

CONCLUSIONS ABOUT GROUPWARE SUITES

Successful **enterprise-wide collaboration systems** such as Lotus Notes/Domino can be expensive to develop and operate. To obtain the full benefits of such groupware, a well-trained, full-time support staff is required to develop applications and operate the system. On the other hand, Groove is relatively inexpensive and provides easy-to-use and easy-to-set-up collaboration for an organization.

Industry reports estimate that all forms of groupware (e.g., audioconferencing, videoconferencing, data conferencing, Web-based conferencing) have become a more established part of the corporate decision-making process. The total collaboration software market is growing rapidly. This growth is driven by time and money savings due to reduced travel and by organizational decentralization and globalization.

Electronic meeting services such as WebEx Meeting Center (**webex.com**), PlaceWare Conference Center (**main.placeware.com/services/pw_conference_ctr.cfm**), and Verizon Conferencing (**e-meetings.mci.com**) enable anyone to hold a meeting for a fee per rental.

Section 10.5 Review Questions

1. Define *integrated collaboration suite*.
2. Describe Lotus/Domino and its major capabilities.
3. Describe Microsoft's collaboration products.
4. What is unique about Groove?
5. Describe the process of renting a place for a virtual meeting, using companies such as WebEx.

10.6 DIRECT COMPUTERIZED SUPPORT FOR DECISION MAKING: FROM GROUP DECISION SUPPORT SYSTEMS TO GROUP SUPPORT SYSTEMS

Decisions are made at many meetings, some of which are called in order to make one specific decision. For example, the federal government meets periodically to decide on the short-term interest rate. Directors may be elected at shareholder meetings, organizations allocate budgets in meetings, a company decides on which candidate to hire, and so on. Some of these decisions are lengthy, as in the Boeing-Rocketdyne case. Others can be controversial, as in resource allocation by a city government. Process gains and dysfunctions can be very large in such meetings, and, therefore, computerized improvements have been attempted by researchers from different disciplines (see Duke Corporate Education, 2005; and Powell et al., 2004). These appeared under different names, such as *GDSS, computer-supported collaborative work (CSCW)*, and *electronic meeting systems (EMS)*, and they are the subject of this section.

GROUP DECISION SUPPORT SYSTEMS (GDSS)

During the 1980s, researchers realized that computerized support to managerial decision making needed to be expanded to groups because major organizational decisions are made by groups such as executive committees, special task forces, and departments. The result was the creation of *group decision support systems* (see Powell et al., 2004).

A **group decision support system (GDSS)** is an interactive computer-based system that facilitates the solution of semistructured and unstructured problems by a group of decision makers. The goal of GDSS is to improve the productivity of decision-making meetings, either by speeding up the decision-making process, by improving the quality of the resulting decisions, or both.

The following are the major characteristics of a GDSS:

- Its goal is to support the *process* of group decision makers by providing automation of subprocesses, using information technology tools.
- It is a specially designed information system, not merely a configuration of already-existing system components. It can be designed to address one type of problem or a variety of group-level organizational decisions.
- It encourages generation of ideas, resolution of conflicts, and freedom of expression. It contains built-in mechanisms that discourage development of negative group behaviors, such as destructive conflict miscommunication and groupthink.

The first generation of GDSS was designed to support face-to-face meetings in a *decision room*. Today, support is provided mostly over the Web to virtual groups (e.g., the Boeing-Rocketdyne case in the opening vignette). The group can meet at the same time or at different times by using e-mail, sending documents, and reading transaction logs. GDSS is especially useful when controversial decisions have to be made (e.g., resource allocation, determining which individuals to lay off). GDSS applications require a facilitator when done in one room or a coordinator or leader when done using virtual meetings.

GDSS can improve the decision-making process in various ways. For one, GDSS generally provides structure to the planning process, which keeps the group on track, although some applications permit the group to use unstructured techniques and methods for idea generation. In addition, GDSS offer rapid and easy access to external and stored information needed for decision making. GDSS also support parallel processing of information and idea generation by participants and allow asynchronous computer discussion. They make possible larger meetings that would otherwise be unmanageable; having a larger group means that more complete information, knowledge, and skills will be represented in the meeting. Finally, voting can be anonymous, with instant results, and all information that passes through the system can be recorded for future analysis (producing *organizational memory*).

GDSS initially was confined to face-to-face meetings. To provide the necessary technology, a special facility (i.e., room) was created. Also, the groups usually had a clearly defined, narrow task, such as allocation of scarce resources or prioritization of goals in a long-range plan.

Over time, it became clear that the support teams need is broader than that provided by GDSS. For example, as indicated in the opening vignette, the task is not a single decision but rather a broad challenge that includes several goals and many decisions, some of which are unknown at the initiation of the project. Furthermore, it became clear that what is really needed is support for virtual teams, both in different place/same time (as in Boeing-Rocketdyne's case) and different place/different time situations. Also, it became clear that teams need indirect support in most decision-making cases (e.g., help in searching information or collaboration) rather than direct support for the decision making. While GDSS expanded to virtual team support, it was unable to meet all the other needs. Thus, a broader term, GSS, was created. We use the terms interchangeably in this book.

GROUP SUPPORT SYSTEMS

A **group support system (GSS)** is any combination of hardware and software that enhances groupwork either in direct or indirect support of decision making. *GSS* is a generic term that includes all forms of collaborative computing. GSS evolved after information technology researchers recognized that technology could be developed to support the many activities normally occurring at face-to-face meetings (e.g., idea generation, consensus building, anonymous ranking).

A complete GSS is still considered a specially designed information system (e.g., the Boeing-Rocketdyne case), but since the mid-1990s, many of the special capabilities of GSS have been embedded in standard productivity tools. For example, Microsoft NetMeeting Client is part of Windows. Most GSS are easy to use because they have a Windows graphical user interface (GUI) or a Web browser interface. Most GSS are fairly general and provide support for activities such as idea generation, conflict resolution, and voting. Also, many commercial products have been developed to support only one or two aspects of teamwork (e.g., videoconferencing, idea generation, screen sharing, wikis).

An **electronic meeting system (EMS)** is a form of GSS that supports anytime/anyplace meetings. Group tasks include, but are not limited to, communication, planning of a meeting, idea generation, problem solving, issue discussion, negotiation, conflict resolution, and collaborative group activities, such as document preparation and sharing. EMS may include desktop videoconferencing, whereas in the past, GSS did not. However, there is a blurring between these two concepts, so today they should be considered synonymous.

GSS settings range from a group meeting at a single location for solving a specific problem to virtual meetings conducted in multiple locations and held via telecommunication channels for the purpose of considering a variety of problems (e.g., see the Boeing-Rocketdyne case in the opening vignette). Using effective new collaboration methods and tools that continue to evolve, GSS can operate effectively in asynchronous mode.

GSS can be considered in terms of the common group activities that can benefit from computer-based support: *information retrieval*, including access of data values from an existing database and retrieval of information from other group members; *information sharing*, the display of data for the whole group on a common screen or at group members' workstations for viewing; and *information use*, the application of software technology (e.g., modeling packages, specific application programs), procedures, and group problem-solving techniques for reaching a group decision (e.g., see Technology Insights 10.6). In addition, creativity in problem solving (discussed in Section 10.10) can be enhanced via GSS.

TECHNOLOGY INSIGHTS 10.6

Modeling in Group Decision Making: EC11 for Groups

Based on the analytic hierarchy process (AHP) decision-making methodology implemented as Expert Choice (see Chapter 4), EC11 for Groups helps group members define objectives, goals, criteria, and alternatives and then organize them into a hierarchical structure. Using PCs, participants compare and prioritize the relative importance of the decision variables. EC11 for Groups then synthesizes the group's judgments to arrive at a conclusion and allows individuals to examine how changing the weighting of their criteria affects the outcome.

EC11 for groups imitates the way people naturally make decisions: gathering information, structuring the decision, weighing the variables and alternatives, and reaching a conclusion. It supports the decision process. The group structures an AHP decision hierarchy for the problem as members perceive it; members provide the judgments, and members make the decision. A decision portal provides team members with models they can use to evaluate objectives and alternatives from their desktops.

Source: Partly adapted from Expert Choice Inc., **expertchoice.com** (accessed March 2006); and *Expert Choice Unveils Latest Enterprise Portfolio Analysis Solutions*, July 12, 2004, **dssresources.com/news/80.php** (accessed April 2006).

How GDSS (or GSS) Improves Groupwork

The goal of GSS is to provide support to meeting participants to improve the productivity and effectiveness of meetings by streamlining and speeding up the decision-making process (i.e., efficiency) or by improving the quality of the results (i.e., effectiveness). GSS attempts to increase process and task gains and decrease process and task losses. Overall, GSS has been successful in doing just that (see Holt, 2002); however, some process and task gains may decrease, and some process and task losses may increase. Improvement is achieved by providing support to group members for the generation and exchange of ideas, opinions, and preferences. Specific features such as **parallelism** (i.e., the ability of participants in a group to work simultaneously on a task, such as brainstorming or voting) and anonymity produce this improvement. The following are some specific GDSS support activities:

- GDSS supports parallel processing of information and idea generation (parallelism).
- GDSS enables the participation of larger groups with more complete information, knowledge, and skills.
- GDSS permits the group to use structured or unstructured techniques and methods.
- GDSS offers rapid, easy access to external information.
- GDSS allows parallel computer discussions.

- GDSS helps participants frame the big picture.
- Anonymity allows shy people to contribute to the meeting (i.e., get up and do what needs to be done).
- Anonymity helps prevent aggressive individuals from driving a meeting.
- GDSS provides for multiple ways to participate in instant, anonymous voting.
- GDSS provides structure for the planning process to keep the group on track.
- GDSS enables several users to interact simultaneously (i.e., conferencing).
- GDSS records all information presented at a meeting (i.e., organizational memory).

(For GSS success stories, see vendors' Web sites. In many of these cases, collaborative computing led to dramatic speed-ups in process and cost savings, as shown in the opening vignette.)

Note that the electronic generation of a large number of ideas does not necessarily mean that electronic brainstorming is better than verbal brainstorming. As a matter of fact, Dennis and Reinicke (2004) proved that the opposite may be true. More research is needed.

FACILITIES FOR GDSS

There are three options for deploying GDSS/GSS technology: (1) in a special-purpose decision room, (2) using a multiple-use facility, and (3) as Internet or intranet-based groupware, with clients running wherever the group members are.

Decision Rooms

The earliest GDSS were installed in expensive, customized, special-purpose facilities called **decision rooms** (or electronic meeting rooms) with PCs and large public screens at the front of each room. The original idea was that only executives and high-level managers would use the facility. The software in a special-purpose electronic meeting room usually runs over a LAN, and these rooms are fairly plush in their furnishings. Electronic meeting rooms can be constructed in different shapes and sizes. A common design includes a room equipped with 12 to 30 networked PCs, usually recessed into the desktop (for better participant viewing). A server PC is attached to a large-screen projection system and connected to the network to display the work at individual workstations and aggregated information from the facilitator's workstation. Adjacent to the decision room are sometimes breakout rooms equipped with PCs connected to the server, where small subgroups can consult. The output from the subgroups can also be displayed on the large public screen.

Some organizations (e.g., universities, large companies, government agencies) still use electronic decision rooms, and these rooms support same time/same place meetings. One Ohio school district even built a portable facility in a bus (the driver's seat turns around to become the facilitator's seat). However, there is still a need and a desire for groups to meet face-to-face. A facility like this can conveniently provide videoconferencing for communication with outsiders or team members who cannot attend the meeting, can provide other groupware, and may also function as a fairly expensive computer lab. Decision rooms have been found especially useful when the decision topic is controversial (e.g., resource allocation or long-range planning) and the decision support can provide excellent results. For an example, see Application Case 10.7 and customer success stories at **groupsystems.com.**

Application Case 10.7

Eastman Chemical Boosts Creative Processes and Saves $500,000 with Groupware

PROBLEM

Eastman Chemical Co. (**eastman.com**) wanted to use creative problem-solving sessions to process ideas. Team members would present problems in a face-to-face meeting using flip charts and sticky notes to come up with better solutions, but organizing and studying the notes took far too long. The company needed more ideas and better methods to meet customers' needs. Traditional methods were not effective. The process was extremely unproductive and time-consuming.

SOLUTION

Eastman Chemical chose GroupSystems to support its problem-solving process meetings. Here's how the meetings work now. First, participants define the problem and frame it. Then participants brainstorm ideas to develop potential solutions to the problem, trying for "outside-the-box" thinking using creativity techniques. Recently, some 400 ideas were generated by nine people in a two-hour session through parallelism. After categorizing similar items, the team establishes common decision criteria to choose the top three ideas, using the Alternative Analysis tool. Results are then copied into an Excel spreadsheet to develop an action plan.

Eastman ran 100 research and development managers through collaborative sessions to determine top strategies. They defined 8 opportunities, with an action plan for the top 3—after generating 2,200 ideas!

RESULTS

Henry Gonzales, manager of the polymer technology core competency group at Eastman, stated, "We found that with GroupSystems, we had more unusual ideas, a richer pool to choose from, and we got to the point a lot faster. I did a study and calculated that the software saved 50 percent of people's time, and projected a cost savings of over $500,000 for the 12 people during a year's time." Consequently, Eastman Chemical bought a second site license and upgraded to another facility so that more people could use the groupware.

Sources: Adapted from *Eastman Chemical—Creativity and Team Center*, **groupsystems.com/resource-center/customersandcases/CorporateCaseStudies/Eastman-Case-Study** (accessed August 2006); and **eastman.com** (accessed February 2006).

Multiuse Facilities

A *multiuse facility* can also be constructed for GSS. This is sometimes a general-purpose computer lab or computer classroom that is also a less elegant but equally useful GDSS or GSS room. For example, at the Terry College of Business of The University of Georgia, Sanford Hall has a 48-seat lab/computer classroom with GroupSystems MeetingRoom installed. This room "triples" as a distance-learning classroom because it contains the latest academic videoconferencing software and hardware. Because a decision room is rarely used 100 percent of the time for groupwork, making such a room a multiuse room is an effective way to lower or share costs.

Internet/Intranet-Based Systems

Since the late 1990s, the most common approach to GSS facilities has been to use *Web-based* or *intranet-based groupware* that allows group members to work from any location at any time (e.g., Lotus Notes, Groove, WebEx, PlaceWare, GroupSystems, NetMeeting). This groupware often includes audioconferencing and videoconferencing. The availability of relatively inexpensive groupware (for purchase or for rent) combined with the power and low cost of capable PCs, makes this type of system very attractive. Some groupware vendors, notably Groove, run in peer-to-peer mode, where each person works on a copy of the entire conference so that only differences among the files need to be transmitted. This capability makes this approach even more attractive.

Which GSS Facility to Use?

For the first and second options, a trained facilitator is necessary to coordinate and facilitate the meetings. The group leader works with the facilitator to structure the meeting. The success of a GSS session depends largely on the quality, activities, and support of the facilitator. For the third option, a coordinator is needed, but the required facilitating skills are much lower.

The high cost of constructing a facility and finding an experienced facilitator, and the need to have participants connect from other locations at any time, have reduced the need for the first two approaches. Therefore, the third option is most frequently used today. However, time deadlines are generally needed for each phase of an anytime/anyplace meeting. (The deadlines are set to allow for time zones and travel.) A problem for non-face-to-face meetings is that participants want to see the people with whom they are working. Some systems have access to still pictures, and others use

TABLE 10.2 Collaborative Computing/GSS and Web Impacts

Collaborative Computing/GSS	*Web Impacts*	*Impacts on the Web*
Collaboration	• Provides a consistent, friendly graphical user interface (GUI) for client units • Provides convenient, fast access to team members • Provides improved collaboration tools • Enables access to data/information/knowledge on servers • Enables document sharing • Enables anytime/anywhere collaboration • Enables collaboration between companies, customers, and vendors	• Enables improvements in management, hardware, software, and infrastructure, due mainly to collaboration in (Web-based) CASE and other systems analysis and design tools • Enables improvements in site design and development methods • Allows simultaneous Web surfing (e.g., Groove)
Communication	• Provides improved, fast communication among group members and links to data/information/knowledge sources • Makes audio- and videoconferencing a reality, especially for individuals not using a local area network (LAN)	Same as above
Decision room	• Provides a consistent, friendly GUI for clients • Supports communication • Provides access to Web-based tools • Enables room design teams to collaborate to provide dramatic improvements in facilities	Same as above
Mixed-mode facility	Same as above	Same as above
Colocated team facility (members in different locations)	• Provides fast connections to enable real-time collaboration	Same as above

videoconferencing to enhance some meeting aspects by showing the faces of the participants and sometimes their body language.

In Table 10.2, we provide a list of collaborative computing/GSS and Web impacts. Next, we describe some of the features and structure of a comprehensive GSS, using GroupSystems as an example.

Section 10.6 Review Questions

1. Define *GDSS* and list the limitations of the initial GDSS software.
2. Define *GSS* and list its benefits.
3. Define *EMS*.
4. List process gain improvements made by GSS.
5. Define *decision room*.
6. Describe a GSS multiuse facility.
7. Describe Web-based GSS.
8. Why is the third option for a GDSS facility the most popular?

10.7 PRODUCTS AND TOOLS FOR GDSS/GSS AND SUCCESSFUL IMPLEMENTATION

Products and tools designed specifically to support meetings that deal with decision support may appear in groupware products or in special suites, such as that of GroupSystems. GroupSystems offers two products: MeetingRoom (for face-to-face meetings) and OnLine (for supporting virtual teams). Before we describe the products, let's take a look at how to get ready to use them.

ORGANIZING A GSS SESSION

Face-to-face, same time/same place electronic meetings generally follow a common progression. First, the group leader meets with the facilitator to plan the meeting (this is critically important), select the software tools, and develop an agenda. Second, the participants meet in the decision room, and the leader poses a question or problem to the group. Third, the participants type their ideas or comments (i.e., brainstorm), and the results are displayed publicly. Because the participants can see on their own monitors what others are typing, they can provide comments or generate new ideas. Fourth, the facilitator, using idea organization software, searches for common themes, topics, and ideas and organizes them into rough categories (i.e., key ideas) with appropriate comments; new research is attempting to automate this part of the electronic meeting. The results are publicly displayed. Fifth, the leader starts a discussion, either verbal or electronic. The participants next prioritize the ideas. Sixth, the top 5 or 10 topics are sent to idea-generation software following a discussion. The process (idea generation, idea organization, prioritization) can be repeated, or a final vote can be taken.

The major activities of a typical GDSS session are listed in Technology Insights 10.8. For examples of GSS use in practice, see **groupsystems.com**.

It is important to remind participants of where they are in the group meeting process and to keep them focused on long-term tasks. Other issues include security (to protect valuable information from theft), universal access (i.e., from home or other sites), folder invitations and information (i.e., participants must be invited to participate in meeting segments), information about the participants (i.e., on virtual business

TECHNOLOGY INSIGHTS 10.8

The Standard GSS Process

Here are the major steps in the GSS process:

Idea generation. This exploratory step looks at the problem and attempts to develop creative ideas about its important features (or alternative solutions in a problem-solving session). The ideas can have anything to do with the problem; they can be potential solutions, criteria, or mitigating factors. An electronic brainstorming tool is appropriate; its output is a list of ideas. Typical time for this step is 30 to 45 minutes.

Idea organization. An idea-organizing tool groups the many ideas generated (possibly hundreds) into a list of key issues. The output of this stage is a list of a few key ideas (about 1 for every 20 original ideas) with the supporting details. Typical time for this step is 45 to 90 minutes.

Prioritization. At this stage, the key ideas are prioritized. A voting tool can be appropriate (see Online File W10.3); its output is a prioritized list of ideas and details. Typical time for this step is 10 to 20 minutes.

Additional idea generation. New ideas are generated based on the prioritization of the key ideas. A brainstorming tool that provides structure, such as a topic commentator tool, is appropriate here. The ideas generated are typically focused on solutions. This stage's output may consist of up to 20 ideas for each of the original key ideas.

This process continues in iterations until a final idea is selected as a solution to the problem that prompted the meeting or a few solutions are identified to be investigated in more depth. Some meetings are oriented toward decision making. Others are exploratory in nature and are focused on generating ideas to pursue in follow-up meetings or individual work. Often, a GDSS meeting takes longer than an unsupported meeting, but participants are generally more thorough in their brainstorming and analysis, and they feel that they have made a better decision by using the system.

cards), indication of who is on the system (to alleviate feelings of loneliness), and facilitator controls (i.e., to start and stop sessions, to restrict access to activities).

Planning the session is one of the most critical issues. Facilitators must provide incentives and develop investment in the outcome, communicate often and explicitly, assign roles and tasks with accountability, and be explicit in goal and activity communication. To illustrate this process, let's look at GroupSystems and its products.

GROUPSYSTEMS PRODUCTS: MEETINGROOM AND ONLINE

GroupSystems MeetingRoom and OnLine are comprehensive groupware products that support a wide variety of group processes and are designed specifically to support group decision-making processes. MeetingRoom is the LAN version, designed for one-room meetings, and OnLine is the Web-enabled version, for participants in different locations. The two products provide the same set of capabilities. We refer to this software simply as *GroupSystems*. An overview of the tools and their relationship to the major GSS activities is shown in Figure 10.3. Agenda is the control panel for scheduling and running GroupSystems activities; it is the meeting manager.

The tools in GroupSystems are divided into standard tools and advanced tools, and they are listed in Online File W10.4.

GSS SUCCESS FACTORS

The success of a GSS depends mostly on its results. A system succeeds if it cuts costs (especially travel costs), supports participants in making better decisions, and/or increases productivity substantially. In order to succeed, a GSS needs many of the usual information system success factors: organizational commitment, an executive

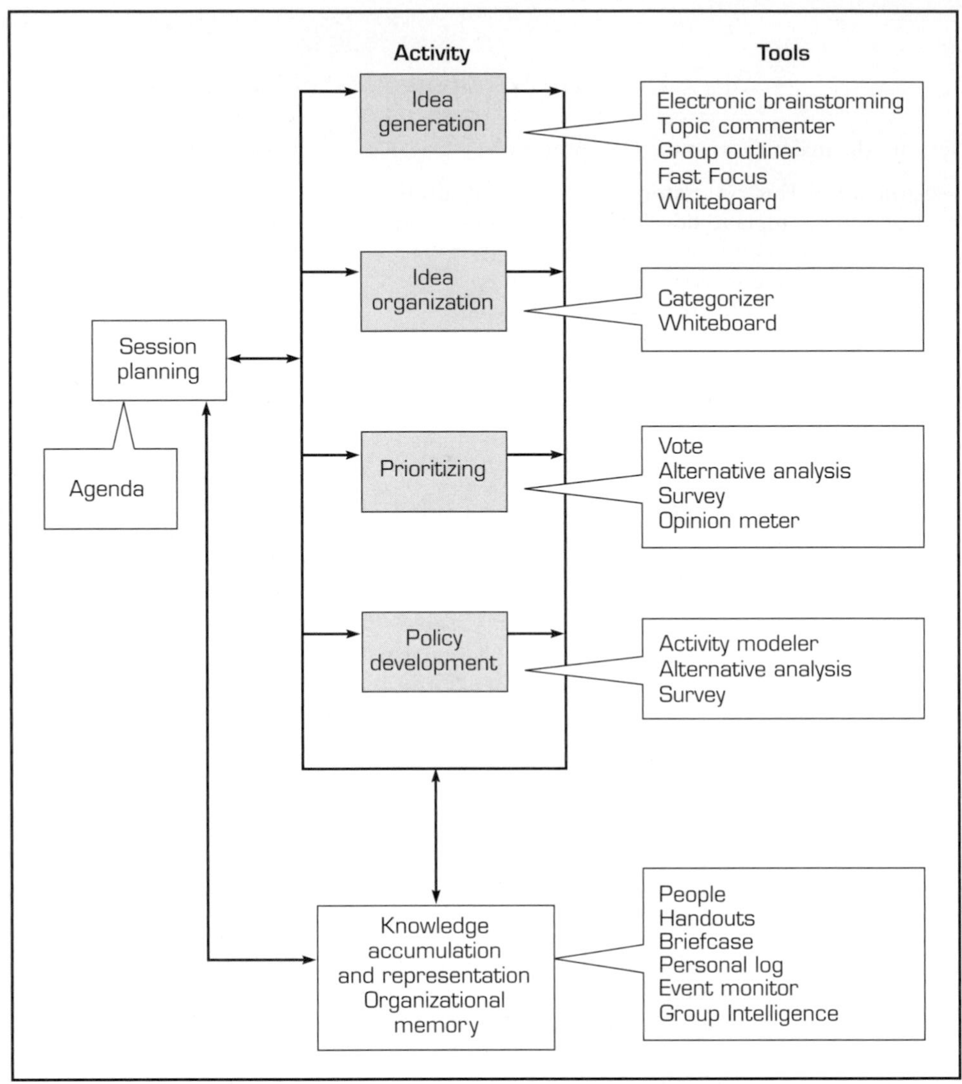

FIGURE 10.3 Structure of GroupSystems for Windows

sponsor, an operating sponsor, user involvement and training, a user-seductive interface, and so on. If the organizational culture does not readily support face-to-face collaboration, then it must be changed to do so before a GSS is introduced. Otherwise, the system will not be used, and it will be deemed a failure. This is also a critical issue in knowledge management (see Chapter 11), which involves collaboration at the enterprise level. Having a dedicated, well-trained, personable facilitator is also critical. The GSS must have the correct tools to support the organization's groupwork and must include parallelism and anonymity to provide process and task gains. Good planning is also a key to running successful meetings, including electronic meetings. If anything, bad planning might make a group believe that the GSS is to blame for its poor performance. Finally, GSS must demonstrate cost savings, either through a more effective and efficient meeting process or through reduced travel costs. Tangible results are necessary, but not sufficient; a collaborative culture is necessary.

Crafting a Collaborative Culture

Collaboration is about people; however, a collaboration tool will not change their attitudes. Technology provides support to the solution. It is also important to motivate the users to really use the new system. The managers must create a work environment that supports collaboration. According to Agrew (2000), this involves three simple steps:

1. *Know what you want.* Get team members to articulate their definition of success (or performance). This is part of the team-building process. For example, at Boeing-Rocketdyne, the team created a formal contract indicating goals and how the team would function.
2. *Determine resource constraints.* These include everything from the geographic distribution of team members to reporting relationships to motivations. Each constraint limits the possible tools the team can use.
3. *Determine what technologies can be used to overcome resource constraints.* It is important to keep in mind business needs rather than fun, new, or convenient technologies. For example, videoconferencing and detailed product and code design work require high-bandwidth connections.

When all this is determined, it is necessary to set up group sessions with good facilitation to guide and train the participants in the tools used. For more on cultural aspects and international perspectives, see de Vreede and Ackermann (2005).

IMPLEMENTATION ISSUES FOR ONLINE COLLABORATION

This chapter has presented numerous online collaboration issues of different sorts. In addition, a few implementation issues must be addressed when planning online collaboration. First, to connect business partners, an organization needs an effective collaborative environment. Such an environment is provided by groupware suites such as Lotus Notes/Domino or Cybozu Share360 (**cybozu.com**). Another issue is the need to connect collaborative tools with file management products on an organization's intranet. Two products that offer such connection capabilities are the WiredRed server and client (**wiredred.com**) and the eRoom server (**software.emc.com**).

Another important issue in collaboration is automatic language translation. This is required for global teams in which not all the participants speak the same language. For discussion on this, see Chapter 13 and Transclick.com.

In addition, to create a truly collaborative environment, protocols are needed for easy integration of different applications and to standardize communication. One such protocol, which is relatively new, is WebDAV (Web Distributed Authoring and Versioning protocol; see **webdav.org**).

An example of a tool that facilitates collaboration administration is Vignette Collaboration 7.0. For administrators, the tool supports clustering and eases administration of user access policies through improved mapping to corporate directories. The tool also enables the display, storage, and search of any Unicode-supported language. Also available is integration with Microsoft's Live Communications Server for presence awareness and IM.

Finally, note that online collaboration is not a panacea for all occasions or all situations. Many times, a face-to-face meeting is a must. People sometimes need the facial cues and the physical closeness that no computer system can currently provide. (A technology called *pervasive computing* attempts to remove some of these limitations by interpreting facial cues.)

Section 10.7 Review Questions

1. List the steps of organizing a GDSS session.
2. List GroupSystems's major products.
3. List some success factors of GDSS/GSS.
4. How can a company create a collaborative culture?
5. List three implementation issues of GDSS/GSS.

10.8 EMERGING COLLABORATION TOOLS: FROM VOIP TO WIKIS

A large number of new collaborative tools have appeared on the market in the past few years. Representative examples are presented here.

VOICE OVER IP

Voice over IP (VoIP) refers to communication systems that transmit voice calls over Internet Protocol (IP)-based networks. Corporations are moving their phone systems to Internet standards to cut costs and boost efficiency. VoIP is also known as **Internet telephony**. Free Internet telephony software is available from **pc-telephone.com**. Most browsers provide for VoIP capabilities. The browsers enable you to receive telephone calls initiated on the Internet (with a microphone and special VoIP software, which may be provided with the sender's browser). VoIP is helping educational institutions, as discussed in Technology Insights 10.9.

TECHNOLOGY INSIGHTS 10.9

VoIP Systems Help Increase Productivity and Enhance Learning Experiences at the State University of New York (SUNY)

The Cortland campus of SUNY was one of two winners recognized at the EDUCAUSE 2003 annual conference. The award honors innovative programs or practices that improve network infrastructure and architecture, integration, and quality of service on a campus or within an educational system and that positively affect a campus community or significant subcommunity.

The Cisco IP Communications system replaced a traditional private branch exchange (PBX)–based voice network and a shared 10-megabit-per-second Ethernet data network. The new converged network includes 700 Cisco IP phones that work with 3,000 existing analog phones connected via Cisco VG-248 IP gateways.

Daniel Sidebottom, director or Administrative Computing Services at SUNY, stated that the return-on-investment (ROI) analysis for the IP communications system anticipated a return on the technology investment in less than one year.

The new system helps university faculty, staff, and students communicate more effectively and provides applications to enhance the academic experience. For example, university faculty and students are able to use streaming video, file sharing, and other high-bandwidth applications, adding considerable value to the curricula as well as driving operational effectiveness. The combined voice and data network features a single call center system to support the admissions and financial aid offices to better serve students, parents, and others who need information and assistance. The solution delivers streamlined voice, data communications, and video to the entire campus and strengthens SUNY Cortland's mission to provide students with the opportunity to develop and use technology in their studies.

Sources: Compiled from T. Spangler, "Cisco to Replace VoIP Tools," *Baseline*, October 1, 2005; and J.A. Pirani, *Implementing an IP-Based Voice, Data and Video an SUNY Cortland*, 2005, **educause.edu/LibraryDetailPage/666?ID=ECS0503** (accessed March 2006).

The Benefits of VoIP

According to a Siemens Communication (**communications.USA.Siemens.com**) special advertisement, the following are the benefits of VoIP communications:

For the business:

- Allows chief information officers to explore different deployment options for company's communications needs
- Lowers total cost of ownership through voice/data convergence
- Lowers operational costs through use of integrated applications
- Reduces hardware requirements on the server side for certain applications (e.g., VoIP)
- Provides a holistic approach to security, enhanced by encryption and identity management
- Helps streamline workflows by empowering companies to communications-enable different business processes
- Enables optimized conferencing tools to replace business travel

For the user:

- Eliminates unwanted interruptions and unproductive actions by intelligently filtering communications
- Provides access to real-time presence information, which helps decisions get made faster
- Initiates ad hoc conferencing/collaboration sessions without the need to prearrange separate audio- or videoconferencing bridges
- Enables participation in conferencing sessions quickly and easily via a variety of mobile devices

COLLABORATIVE WORKFLOW

Collaborative workflow refers to software products that address project-oriented and collaborative types of processes. They are administered centrally yet are capable of being accessed and used by workers from different departments and even from different physical locations. The goal of collaborative workflow tools is to empower knowledge workers. The focus of an enterprise solution for collaborative workflow is on allowing workers to communicate, negotiate, and collaborate within an integrated environment. Some leading vendors of collaborative workflow applications are Lotus, EpicData, FileNet, and Action Technologies.

WIKIS

A **wiki** is a piece of server software available in a Web site that allows users to freely create and edit Web page content, using any Web browser. A wiki supports hyperlinks and has a simple text syntax for creating new pages and cross-links between internal pages on-the-fly. It is especially suited for collaborative writing.

Wikis are unusual among group communication mechanisms in that they allow the organization of contributions to be edited in addition to the content itself. (The term *wiki* means "quick" or "to hasten" in the Hawaiian language; e.g., "Wiki Wiki" is the name of the shuttle bus in Honolulu International Airport.) The term *wiki* also refers to the collaborative software that facilitates the operation of a wiki Web site.

A wiki enables documents to be written collectively in a very simple markup, using a Web browser. A single page in a wiki is referred to as a "wiki page," and the entire body of pages, which are usually highly interconnected via hyperlinks, is "the wiki"; in effect, it is a very simple, easier-to-use database. For further details, see **en.wikipedia.org/wiki/Wiki** and **wiki.org.**

Wikis come in many shapes and formats, one of which is a wikilog.

Wikilog

A wikilog (or wikiblog) is an extension of a blog, which is usually created by an individual (or maybe a small group) and may have a discussion board. A **wikilog** is essentially a blog that allows everyone to participate as a peer (a combination of wikis and blogs, also known as a *bliki*). Anyone may add, delete, or change content. It is like a loose-leaf notebook with a pencil and eraser left in a public place. Anyone can read it, scrawl notes, tear out a page, and so on. Creating a wikilog is a collaborative process. Any information being collected in a wiki can be changed or deleted by anyone (though many wikis preserve previous copies of posted contributions in the background). Unlike protected Web pages, articles added to a wiki are at the editorial mercy of the wiki's other participants. For further details, see **usemod.com/cgi-bin/mb.pl?WikiLog.**

Commercial Aspects of Wikis and Their Derivatives

Because wikis are a relatively new technology, it is difficult to assess their commercial potential. However, the research firm Gartner Group predicts that wikis will become mainstream collaboration tools in at least 50 percent of companies by 2009 (see WikiThat.com, 2005). In addition to being used for collaboration, wikis can replace e-mail because wikis are open source, spam-free communication tools. The benefits of the technology are demonstrated in the DrKW application case at the end of this chapter. A major vendor of wiki commercialization is Socialtext (**socialtext.com**).

COLLABORATION HUBS

One of the most popular forms of B2B e-commerce is the **collaboration hub**, which is used by the members of a supply chain to help improve effectiveness between manufacturing companies, their suppliers, and contract producers by reducing inventory, improving flexibility, and increasing supply-chain transparency through the Internet. For details, see Turban et al. (2006).

COLLABORATIVE NETWORKS

Traditionally, collaboration took place among supply-chain members, frequently those that were close to each other (e.g., a manufacturer and its distributor, a distributor and a retailer). Even if more partners were involved, the focus was on the optimization of information and product flow between existing nodes in the traditional supply chain. Advanced approaches, such as collaborative planning, forecasting, and replenishment (CPFR; see Section 10.9), do not change this basic structure.

Traditional collaboration results in a vertically integrated supply chain. However, Web technologies can fundamentally change the shape of the supply chain, the number of players in it, and their individual roles. In a *collaborative network*, partners at any point in the network can interact with each other, bypassing traditional partners. Interaction may occur among several manufacturers or distributors, as well as with new players, such as software agents that act as aggregators, business-to-business (B2B) exchanges, or logistics providers. For discussion and examples, see Turban et al. (2006) and **logility.com**

CORPORATE (ENTERPRISE) PORTALS

A **corporate (enterprise) portal** is a gateway to a corporate Web site that enables communication, collaboration, and access to company information. A corporate portal is a personalized, single point of access through a Web browser to critical business information located inside and outside an organization. In contrast with commercial portals such as Yahoo! and MSN, which are gateways to general information on the Internet, corporate portals provide a single point of access to information and applications available on the Internet, intranets, and extranets of a specific organization. Several types of corporate portals facilitate communication and collaboration. For details, see Chapter 17 (an online chapter).

Section 10.8 Review Questions

1. Describe VoIP and its advantages.
2. Define *collaborative workflow*.
3. Define *wiki* and *wikilog*.
4. Define *collaborative hub*.
5. Define *corporate (enterprise) portal*.

10.9 COLLABORATIVE EFFORTS IN DESIGN, PLANNING, AND PROJECT MANAGEMENT

Three major collaborative efforts are in the areas of joint design, collaborative planning, and project management.

COLLABORATIVE DESIGN AND PRODUCT DEVELOPMENT

The opening vignette in this chapter illustrates the potential benefits of computer-supported design and new product development.

Collaborative product development involves the use of product design and development techniques across multiple companies to improve product launch success and reduce cost and time to market. During product development, engineering and design drawings can be shared over a secure network among the contract firm, testing facility, marketing firm, and downstream manufacturing and service companies. Other techniques include sharing specifications, test results, design changes, and using online prototyping to obtain customer feedback. Development costs can be reduced by tightly integrating and streamlining communication channels.

Example: Reduction of Product Development Time: Caterpillar, Inc.

Caterpillar, Inc. (**caterpillar.com**), is a multinational heavy-machinery manufacturer. In the traditional mode of operation, cycle time along the supply chain was long because the process involved paper-document transfers among managers, salespeople, and technical staff. To solve the problem, Caterpillar connected its engineering and manufacturing divisions with its active suppliers, distributors, overseas factories, and customers through an extranet-based global collaboration system. By means of the collaboration system, a request for a customized tractor component, for example, can be transmitted from a customer to a Caterpillar dealer and on to designers and suppliers, all in a very short time. Customers can use the extranet to retrieve and modify detailed order information while the vehicle is still on the assembly line. Remote collaboration capabilities between the customer and product developers have decreased cycle time delays caused by rework time. Suppliers are also connected to the system, so they can deliver materials or parts directly to Caterpillar's repair shops or directly to the customer, if appropriate. The system is also used for expediting maintenance and repairs.

For comprehensive coverage of collaborative virtual design environments, see Manninen (2004). For an example of how General Motors collaborates on designing its new models using its Advanced Design Studio to support collaboration of its design engineers with design engineers of more than 1,000 key suppliers, refer to Application Case 10.2.

COLLABORATIVE PLANNING ALONG THE SUPPLY CHAIN

Collaborative planning is designed to synchronize production and distribution plans and product flows, optimize resource utilization over an expanded capacity base, increase customer responsiveness, and reduce inventories. In *collaborative planning*, business partners—manufacturers, suppliers, distribution partners, and others—create the initial demand (or sales) forecasts, provide changes as necessary, and share information (e.g., actual sales, their own forecasts). Thus, all parties work according to a unified schedule aligned to a common view and all have access to order and forecast performance that is globally visible through electronic links. Schedule, order, and product changes trigger immediate adjustments to all parties' schedules. There is an industry project in this area known as CPFR.

The CPFR Project

Collaborative planning, forecasting, and replenishment (CPFR) is an industry-wide project in which suppliers and retailers collaborate in planning and demand forecasting in order to ensure that members of the supply chain will have the right amount of raw materials and finished goods when they need them. When implementing a CPRF project, the collaborators agree on a standard process, shown in Figure 10.4. The process ends with an order forecast. CPFR provides a standard framework for collaborative planning. Retailers and vendors determine the "rules of engagement," such as how often and at what level information will be provided. Typically, they share greater

FIGURE 10.4 The CPFR Process

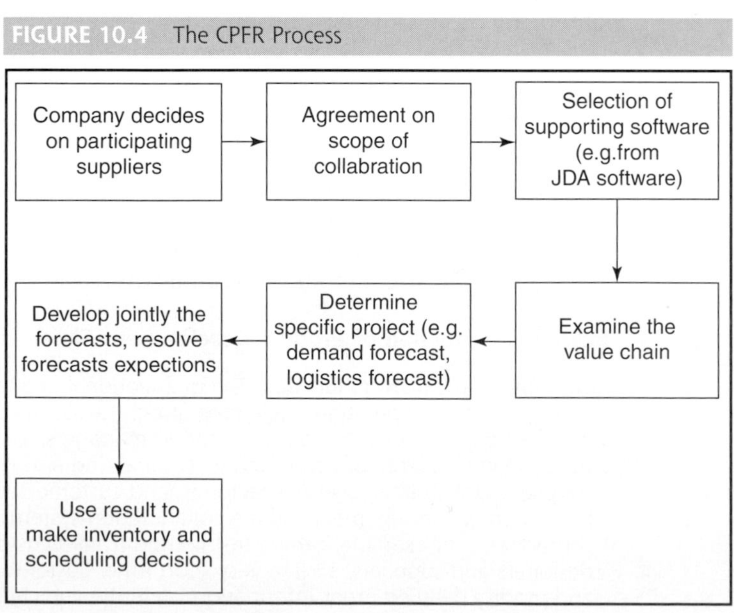

amounts of more detailed information, such as promotion schedules and item point-of-sale history, and use store-level expectations as the basis for all forecasts.

The idea of CPFR is to improve demand forecasting for all the partners in the supply chain and then communicate forecasts, using information-sharing applications (already developed by technology companies such as Manugistics, Oracle, and i2). For the retailer, collaborative forecasting means fewer out-of-stocks and resultant lost sales and less stored inventory. For the manufacturer, collaborative forecasting means fewer expedited shipments, optimal inventory levels, and optimally sized production runs.

Besides working together to develop production plans and forecasts for stock replenishment, suppliers and retailers also coordinate the related logistics activities (such as shipment or warehousing), using a common language standard and new information methodologies.

A 2002 survey (see Bradley, 2002) found that 67 percent of 43 large food, beverage, and consumer products companies were researching, piloting, or implementing CPFR. About half of the respondents who were looking at CPFR said they planned to go ahead with their initiatives. However, CPFR is not the answer for all trading partners or all types of stock-keeping units (SKUs). According to Tim Paydos, a vice president of marketing at Syncra Systems, CPFR has generated the highest payback with either highly promoted or seasonal goods, whose inventories historically have often been misaligned with demand. "If I'm going to make the investment in CPFR," noted Paydos, "I want to do it with the products with the greatest return" (Bradley, 2002).

The CPFR strategy has been driven by Wal-Mart and various benchmarking partners. After a successful pilot between Wal-Mart and Warner-Lambert involving Listerine products, a Voluntary Interindustry Commerce Standards (VICS) subcommittee was established to develop the proposed CPFR standard for the participating retailing industries (i.e., Wal-Mart's suppliers).

Ace Hardware Corp. and Sears have had interesting applications of CPFR as discussed in Application Case 10.10.

CPFR can be used with a company-centric B2B, sell-side, or buy-side marketplaces. For more on the benefits of CPFR, see **vics.org/committees/cpfr**.

Vendor-Managed Inventory

With **vendor-managed inventory (VMI)**, retailers make their suppliers responsible for determining when to order and how much to order. The retailer provides the supplier with real-time information (e.g., point-of-sale data), inventory levels, and a threshold below which orders are to be replenished. The reorder quantities also are predetermined and usually recommended by the supplier. By using this approach, the retailer is no longer burdened with inventory management, demand forecasting becomes easier, the supplier can see the potential need for an item before the item is ordered, there are no purchase orders, inventories are kept low, and stockouts occur infrequently. This method was initiated by Wal-Mart in the 1980s and was supported by an electronic data interchange (EDI). Today, it can be supported by CFPR and special software. VMI software solutions are provided by Sockeye Solutions, Cactus Communications, and JDA Software. For details, see Bury (2004).

For other innovative collaborative solutions to supply-chain problems, see **logility.com**.

PROJECT MANAGEMENT

Developing large-scale projects requires collaboration of a large number of units and individuals inside and outside an organization. Effective and efficient communication and collaboration is a must. Here is an example of how one company is doing it effectively:

Application Case 10.10

CPFR Initiatives at Ace Hardware and Sears

Ace Hardware Corp. (**acehardware.com**), based in Oak Brook, Illinois, is a chain of 5,100 independently owned stores that sell everything from 10-penny nails to toasters. In 1999, Ace implemented a CPFR process, using its buy-side private exchange, to achieve more intelligent relationships with its suppliers. This platform creates and executes a single, shared demand forecast, allowing Ace to increase revenue while reducing costs.

Ace began using CPFR with a single supplier, Henkel Consumer Adhesives, a manufacturer of duct tape, adhesives, and other do-it-yourself home and office products. During the first year of implementation, the two companies improved forecast accuracy by 10 percent, lowered distribution costs by 28 percent, lowered freight costs by 18 percent, increased annual sales by 9 percent, and increased employee productivity by more than 20 percent.

Since then, Ace has implemented CPFR initiatives with several dozen suppliers, including Black & Decker, Rust-Oleum, Master Lock, and Sherwin-Williams. More accurate forecasts and seasonal profiles ensure that products are available when consumers want to buy them. Improved service levels, increased sales, and decreased supply-chain costs have combined to make Ace Hardware more competitive.

To improve efficiency and effectiveness of inventory management with its major suppliers, Sears (**sears.com**) is using CPFR software from GNX (**gnx.com**). The system enables total supply-chain visibility. The first experiment was with all major tire vendors (e.g., Michelin, Goodyear, Sumitomo). Using this software, all partners collaborated weekly about optimal replenishment and inventory plans to minimize stock, maximize customer service level, and optimize transport. Each week's actual and forecast sales information were refreshed for more than 500 SKUs related to tires. The initial results of the pilot project were so successful that Sears is implementing the program with all its strategic partners.

Sources: Compiled from D. Buss, "CPFR Initiative Allows Ace to Boost Revenue While Cutting Costs," *Stores*, September 2002; and H.L. Richardson, "The Ins & Outs of VMI," *Logistics Today*, Vol. 45, No. 3, 2004.

Example: Pfizer's Computer-Aided Document Management and Collaborative System

The process of bringing a new drug to market may take 6 to 10 years, and fewer than 10 percent of drugs actually make it. Food and Drug Administration (FDA) approval, which is the final step, takes 18 to 24 months. The U.S. government is putting pressure on drug manufacturers to collaborate with the FDA to cut this step to 12 months. To do so, Pfizer developed a special system called Electronic Submission Navigator (ESUB) that has the following capabilities:

- Provides a global view of the status of a trial or application process.
- Enhances Pfizer's competitive advantage by linking drug researchers around the world; ESUB has attracted business partners, including other drug manufacturers seeking to forge strategic alliances with Pfizer to help market and distribute their drugs.
- Enables Pfizer to penetrate world markets much more quickly by filing concurrent submissions in different countries.
- Gives the company the ability to deliver five new drugs every 12 months—the fastest rate in the industry.
- Allows portable review with a full-featured system, which is important because the FDA frequently uses outside consultants.

For details, see M. Blodgett, "Prescription Strength," *CIO*, February 1, 2000, and **pfizer.com** (accessed April 2006).

For an example of project management at Safeway, see Online File W10.5.

Section 10.9 Review Questions

1. Define *CPFR* and describe its process.
2. Define *VMI.*
3. Describe the benefits of collaboration to project management.

10.10 CREATIVITY, IDEA GENERATION, AND COMPUTERIZED SUPPORT

A major task in the decision-making/problem-solving process is generation of alternative courses of actions. Knowledge and experience can help in this task, but we frequently need new and innovative ideas. These can be achieved via creativity and idea generation.

CREATIVITY

Creativity is the human trait that leads to the production of acts, items, and instances of novelty and the achievement of creative products. *Creativity* is complex. Personality-related creativity traits include inventiveness, independence, individuality, enthusiasm, and flexibility, and these traits have been assessed through the widely-used Torrance Tests of Creative Thinking (TTCT; e.g., Cramond, 1995). However, researchers have established that creativity can be learned and improved and is not as strongly dependent on individual traits as originally thought. Innovative companies recognize that creativity may not necessarily be the result of having traits (i.e., being a genius) as much as the result of being in an idea-nurturing work environment (e.g., see Gatignon et al., 2002).

After a problem is formulated, potential criteria and alternatives must be identified. Creative ideas generally lead to better solutions. In brainstorming, there are some specific creativity measures: the quantitative (number of ideas) and qualitative (quality of ideas) components. Both can be positively affected by the use of software that concentrates on idea generation and evaluation of creative solutions to problems.

When creativity is unleashed, it can dramatically enhance productivity and profitability in the long run. Creativity is important in problem solving (see Handzic and Cule, 2002), and thus it is critical to develop computerized support systems for it.

Creativity and innovation can be stimulated also by a number of environmental factors. An environment that meets the "serious play" criterion is part of the process. Stimulation by other creative people in the environment can push a group forward. How? Some stimulation can come directly from exciting ideas developed as a consequence of association (i.e., synergy) among creative people (e.g., during brainstorming). This can be done, for example, by presenting a person with a string of related (even distantly related) concepts. Some stimulation may even come from friction among employees. Some research suggests that some dissatisfaction and discomfort is a must to spark innovation. A manager should not hire people like himself or herself because their differences cause stimulation; for example, in brainstorming, they broaden the viewpoints (see Sutton, 2001). These differences were capitalized at Boeing-Rocketdyne in using a GSS, as Malhotra et al. (2001) described, "Innovation, most often, comes from the collaboration of individuals from a cross-section of disciplines, inside and outside of an organization."

A number of association methods have been proposed and empirically proven to be effective in stimulating creativity. And viewing ideas in a different frame (e.g., outside the box, from different angles) can stimulate creativity (see von Oech, 2002; and Creative Think, at **creativethink.com**). Next, we discuss creativity and innovation in the context of idea generation and electronic brainstorming.

IDEA GENERATION THROUGH ELECTRONIC BRAINSTORMING

Idea generation methods and techniques have been adopted to enhance the creativity of both individuals and groups. **Idea generation** software (e.g., *electronic brainstorming*) helps to stimulate the free flow of turbulent creative thinking: ideas, words, pictures, and concepts set loose with fearless enthusiasm, based on the principle of synergy (i.e., association). Some packages are designed to enhance the creative thought process of the human mind and can be used to create new product ideas, marketing strategies, promotional campaigns, names, titles, slogans, or stories, or they can be used just for brainstorming.

Bombarding the user with many ideas is a key feature of idea-generating GDSS software. This is critical because it helps the user move away from an analytic mode and into a creative mode. Psychological research indicates that people tend to anchor their thoughts early on, using their first ideas as springboards for other ideas. Therefore, subsequent ideas may not be significantly new but simply minor variations of the original idea. Because brainstorming software is free of human subjectivity, it can help broaden the thinking platform and encourage truly unique ideas to emerge.

By definition, idea generation in GDSS is a collaborative effort. One person's idea triggers another's ideas, which trigger even more ideas (in *idea chains* developed by association). With collaborative computing-support tools (e.g., GDSS), the individuals do all the thinking, and the software system encourages them to proceed. The technology is an anonymous, safe way to encourage participants to voice opinions that they might be reluctant to express in a more conventional setting. By building on each other's ideas, people can obtain creative insights they did not have before, based on associations with existing ideas and with their memories. There is a percolation effect as ideas work their way through the process. Associations trigger memories that can activate creativity. The exchange of information (i.e., learning) can lead to increases in output and creativity (see Rees and Koehler, 1999). There are many relatively inexpensive idea-generation packages on the market. Under the right electronic brainstorming conditions, more ideas and ideas that are more creative overall can be generated. A number of different conditions have been explored.

Generally, if the right approach is used in electronic brainstorming, more ideas and more creative ideas are generated. But a word of caution is in order: Sometimes a group may experience a process gain in the number of ideas and the number of creative ideas but also experience a process loss resulting from information overload or lack of group well-being and member support (see Dennis and Reinicke, 2004). The results of each idea-generation session can be stored in the organizational memory so that results can be carried over from one meeting to another to enhance the creativity of more people.

What if an individual needs to brainstorm alone? There are methods for enhancing individual brainstorming. Satzinger et al. (1999) developed a simulated brainstorming package to help individuals trigger more creative responses when brainstorming alone. They compared the impact of a simulator that randomly generates ideas to an individual decision maker with an individual decision maker not using a simulator in brainstorming. The participants using the simulator generated more ideas and more creative ideas than the others.

Loosely related to brainstorming, *cognitive maps* (e.g., Banxia's Decision Explorer) can help an individual or a group understand a messy problem, develop a common frame, and enhance creativity. A cognitive map shows how concepts relate to each other, thus helping users organize their thoughts and ideas. In this way, they can visualize the problem they are trying to solve (**banxia.com**).

CREATIVITY-ENHANCING SOFTWARE

Although electronic brainstorming enhances creativity, it is primarily human beings who produce the results. In the next two subsections, we describe software and methods (other than brainstorming) that enhance human creativity by actually performing some of the creative tasks of a human being. Some of these systems actually exhibit creative behavior.

Computer Programs That Exhibit Creative Behavior

For several decades, people have attempted to write computer programs that exhibit intelligent behavior. A major characteristic of intelligent behavior is creativity. Can computers be creative?

Intelligent agents (i.e., smartbots) can function as facilitators in GDSS. Chen et al. (1995) described an experiment in which an intelligent agent assisted in idea convergence. The agent's performance was comparable to that of a human facilitator in identifying important meeting concepts, but it was inferior in generating precise and relevant concepts. However, the agent was able to complete its task faster than its human counterparts. This concept is in its infancy but has potential for supporting Web-based GDSS, where the facilitator cannot be available on a 24/7 basis.

Rasmus (1995) described three creativity tools. The first one is called Copycat, a program that seeks analogies in patterns of letters. Identifying patterns is the essence of intelligence. Copycat, consisting of several intelligent agents, can find analogies to strings of letters (e.g., find an analogy for transforming *aabc* to *aabd*). This ability can be generalized to other problems that require conceptual understanding and the manipulation of objects. The capability of the program to anticipate the meaning of the transformation and find analogous fits provides evidence that computers can mimic a human being's ability to create analogies. The second system, Tabletop, is also capable of finding analogies. A third system, AARON, is a sophisticated art drawing program that has resulted from 15 years of research. Its developer, Harold Cohen, created a comprehensive knowledge base to support AARON. Similar computer programs have been developed to write poems and music and create works in other media. The increased knowledge base, processing speed, and storage now available enable such programs to create artwork of good quality.

Electronic Idea Generation for Problem Solving

Goldfire (from Invention Machine Corp., **invention-machine.com**) is an intelligent partner that accelerates technical innovation. Goldfire's semantic processing technology reads, understands, and extracts key concepts from company databases, intranets, and the Internet. The software reads content, creates a problem solution tree (i.e., knowledge index), and delivers an abstract listing of the technical content in relevant documents. Goldfire uses scientific and engineering knowledge as the foundation for its semantic algorithms to accelerate new product and process design innovations.

Goldfire is based on the theory of inventive problem solving (TRIZ—a Russian acronym). TRIZ was first developed by Genrich Altshuller and his colleagues in Russia in 1946 (Altshuller Institute for TRIZ Studies, 2006). More than 2 million patents were examined, classified by level of inventiveness, and analyzed to look for the following innovation principles:

- Problems and solutions are repeated across industries and sciences.
- Patterns of technical evolution are repeated across industries and sciences.
- Innovations may successfully use scientific effects outside the field where they were developed.

The TRIZ creative process is described on the Web sites of *The TRIZ Journal* (**triz-journal.com**) and Ideation International (**ideationtriz.com**).

Software That Facilitates Human Creativity

Several software packages can help stimulate creativity. Some have very specific functions, and others use word associations or questions to prompt users to take new, unexplored directions in their thought patterns. This activity can help users break cyclic thinking patterns, get past mental blocks, or overcome procrastination. Such software can use several different approaches to release the user's flow of ideas. Creative WhackPack is an example of this type of software.

Creative Think (**creativethink.com**) provides the Creative WhackPack, a deck of 64 cards that "whack" you out of habitual thought patterns and let you look at your problem in a new way. The cards ("a physical package") are designed to stimulate the imagination. Fortunately, all 64 illustrated cards are up and running on the Web site (as software); you can click the Give Me Another Creative Whack button to select one at random.

Section 10.10 Review Questions

1. Define *creativity*.
2. Relate creativity to collaboration and problem solving.
3. List software categories of creativity enhancement.
4. Describe software programs that exhibit intelligent behavior.

Chapter Highlights

- People collaborate in their work (called groupwork). Groupware (i.e., collaborative computing software) supports groupwork.
- Group members may be in the same organization or may span organizations; they may be in the same location or in different locations; they may work at the same time or at different times.
- The time/place framework is a convenient way to describe the communication and collaboration patterns of groupwork. Different technologies can support different time/place settings.
- Working in groups may result in many benefits, including improved decision making.
- Meetings have some limitations and dysfunctions. Computerized support can help.
- When people work in teams, especially when the members are in different locations and may be working at different times, they need to communicate, collaborate, and access a diverse set of information sources in multiple formats.
- Communication can be synchronous (i.e., same time), or asynchronous (i.e., sent and received in different times).
- Groupware refers to software products that provide collaborative support to groups (including conducting meetings).
- Groupware can support decision making/problem solving directly or can provide indirect support by improving communication between team members.
- Collaborative computing is known by a number of terms, including groupware, GSS, GDSS, and CSCW.
- Groups and groupwork (i.e., teams and teamwork) in organizations are proliferating. Consequently, groupware continues to evolve to support effective groupwork.
- The Internet (Web), intranets, and extranets support decision making through collaboration tools and access to data, information, and knowledge.
- An extranet links a work group from several different organizations. A common situation is to use the extranet and groupware in managing a supply chain involving several collaborative organizations.
- People may work together and communicate and collaborate at the same time or at different times and in the same place or in different places.
- Groupware for direct support such as GDSS typically contains capabilities for electronic brainstorming, electronic conferencing or meeting, group scheduling, calendaring, planning, conflict resolution, model building, videoconferencing, electronic document sharing, stakeholder identification, topic commentator, voting, policy formulation, and enterprise analysis.
- Groupware can support anytime/anyplace groupwork.
- A GSS is any combination of hardware and software that facilitates meetings. Its predecessor is known as GDSS, which provided direct support to decision meetings, usually in a face-to-face setting.
- GDSS attempts to increase process and task gains and reduce process and task losses of groupwork.
- Parallelism and anonymity provide several GDSS gains.

- GDSS may be assessed in terms of the common group activities of information retrieval, information sharing, and information use.
- GDSS can be deployed in an electronic decision room environment, in a multipurpose computer lab, or over the Web.
- Web-based groupware is the norm for anytime/any-place collaboration.
- GDSS for same time/same place meetings generally follow these steps: (1) planning, (2) question posing, (3) brainstorming, (4) idea organization, (5) discussion and idea prioritization, and (6) more idea generation.
- Internet telephony, or VoIP, is an efficient communications media with many applications that facilitate collaboration.
- Creativity is a complex concept that is used to generate alternative courses of actions in decision making.
- Creativity can be learned and fostered with good managerial techniques and a supportive environment.
- Idea generation (i.e., electronic brainstorming) allows participants to generate and share ideas simultaneously and anonymously.
- Human creativity can be supported with idea generation (i.e., electronic brainstorming) systems.
- Creativity software programs use association and "thinking outside the box" to trigger new concepts.

Key Terms

- asynchronous
- collaboration hub
- collaborative planning, forecasting, and replenishment (CPFR)
- corporate (enterprise) portal
- data conferencing
- decision room
- Delphi method
- electronic brainstorming
- electronic meeting system (EMS)
- enterprise-wide collaboration system
- group decision support system (GDSS)
- group support system (GSS)
- groupthink
- groupware
- groupwork
- idea generation
- Internet telephony
- nominal group technique (NGT)
- online (electronic) workspace
- parallelism
- process gain
- process loss
- screen sharing
- synchronous (real-time)
- teleconferencing
- vendor-managed inventory (VMI)
- video teleconferencing (videoconferencing)
- virtual meeting
- virtual team
- Voice over IP (VoIP)
- wiki
- wikilog

Questions for Discussion

1. How does groupware attain its primary objective?
2. What is nonverbal communication? Explain why it is important in human-to-human interaction. What methods are currently being used to incorporate nonverbal communication into collaborative computing?
3. Explain why it is useful to describe groupwork in terms of the time/place framework.
4. Describe the kinds of support that groupware can provide to decision makers.
5. Explain why most groupware is deployed today over the Web.
6. Compare GDSS and noncomputerized group decision making.
7. Explain why meetings can be so inefficient. Given this, explain how effective meetings can be run.
8. Discuss the details of process gains (i.e., benefits) of groupwork.
9. Discuss the details of process losses (i.e., dysfunctions) of groupwork.
10. Explain how GDSS can increase some of the benefits of collaboration and decision making in groups and eliminate or reduce some of the losses.
11. The original term for group support system (GSS) was group decision support system (GDSS). Why was the word *decision* dropped? Does this make sense? Why or why not?
12. Discuss how parallelism and anonymity can produce improvements in group processes.
13. Describe the three technologies through which GSS is deployed. What are the advantages and disadvantages of each?

14. Explain in detail what creativity is and how it relates to decision support.
15. Explain how GSS can support creativity.
16. Explain how idea generation (i.e., electronic brainstorming) works.
17. Can computers be creative? Why or why not? Discuss.
18. Discuss the benefits of CPFR to retailers and suppliers.
19. Discuss the improvements to supply-chain management that result from using CPFR and VMI.
20. Explain the potential benefits of wikis to a director of marketing.
21. Discuss the benefits of VoIP as a facilitator of communication.
22. Discuss the benefits of collaborative design.
23. Discuss the benefits of CPFR and relate it to decision support.

Exercises

Teradata University and Other Hands-on Exercises

1. Make a list of all the communications methods (both work and personal) you use during your day. Which are the most effective? Which are the least effective? What kind of work or activity does each communications method enable?
2. Investigate the impact of turning off every communication system in a firm (i.e., telephone, fax, television, radio, all comter systems). How effective and efficient would the following types of firms be: airline, bank, insurance company, travel agency, department store, grocery store? What would happen? Do customers expect 100 percent uptime? (When was the last time a major airline's reservation system was down?) How long would it be before each type of firm would not be functioning at all? Investigate what organizations are doing to prevent this situation from occurring.
3. Read Application Case 10.10 ("CPFR Initiatives at Ace Hardware and Sears") and answer the following questions:
   a. What motivated Ace to try CPFR?
   b. Describe how Ace deployed its CPFR system.
   c. Can you guess the common characteristics of the suppliers Ace used first?
   d. Why did Sears start using CPFR with tires?
   e. What are the benefits of CPFR to Sears and to its suppliers?
4. Investigate how researchers are trying to develop collaborative computer systems that portray or display nonverbal communication factors.
5. For each of the following software packages, check the trade literature and the Web for details and explain how computerized collaborative support system capabilities are included: Groove, GroupSystems OnLine, NetMeeting, and WebEx.
6. From your own experience or from the vendor's information, list all the major capabilities of Lotus Notes and explain how they can be used to support decision making.
7. Compare Simon's four-phase decision-making model (see Chapters 1 and 3) to the steps in using GDSS.

Exercises

Team Assignments and Role-Playing

1. Access **groove.net.** Download the demo software to each group member's computer and use it to brainstorm and vote on a specific problem or issue. When brainstorming, think broadly. Did you feel comfortable with the software? Why or why not?
2. Access the Web site of a for-lease Web-based groupware service (e.g., Meetmenow at WebEx). Describe what features it offers and how they could help the members of a group work together. If the site offers a free trial, have your group try it out and report your experience to the class.
3. Some GDSS researchers are concerned with the cross-cultural effects of computer system use. This is especially important in GDSS where opinions are usually entered and synthesized by meeting participants at different places around the globe. Examine the literature and write a report on the major issues of how GDSS provides either process gains or processes losses in a multicultural electronic meeting setting.
4. Access a demo version of a GSS (e.g., Groove, WebEx, NetMeeting) on the Web. Use the system for a meeting of your group to solve another group assignment for any of your courses (check with your instructor). Explain why you did or did not feel comfortable with the software.

5. Prepare a study of all the major Web conferencing software—Centra EMeeting, Genesys Meeting Center, GoToMeeting.com, WebEx Meeting Center, Microsoft Live Meeting, and Oracle.
6. Go to **ifip-dss.org** and find recent material on GSS. At this site, also look at the June 2006 conference proceedings on creativity and innovation in decision support. Prepare a report on your findings.
7. A major claim in favor of wikis is that they can replace e-mail, eliminating its disadvantages (e.g., spam). Go to **socialtext.com** and review such claims. Find other supporters of switching to wikis. Then find counter arguments and conduct a debate on the topic.
8. Go to **ibm.com/software** and find information on the Workplace family of products. Identify all the products that facilitate collaboration and list their major capabilities. Make sure to check Lotusphere and Lotus Domino Express.

Exercises

Internet Exercises

1. Search the Internet to identify sites that describe methods for improving meetings. Investigate ways that meetings can be made more effective and efficient.
2. Go to **groupsystems.com** and identify its current GSS products. List the major capabilities of those products.
3. Go to the Expert Choice, Inc., Web site (**expertchoice.com**) and find information about the company's group support products and capabilities. Team Expert Choice is related to the concept of the AHP described in Chapter 4. Evaluate this product in terms of decision support. Do you think that keypad use provides process gains or process losses? How and why? Also prepare a list of the product analytical capabilities. Examine the free trial. How can it support groupwork?
4. Identify five real-world GSS success stories at vendor Web sites (using at least three different vendors). Describe them. How did GSS software and methods contribute to the successes? What common features do they share? What different features do individual successes have?
5. Go to **creativethink.com** with a problem in mind that you are trying to solve (e.g., selecting a graduate school or a job). Click the Give Me Another Whack button to enhance your thinking. Try a few whacks to see if they can help you. Do they?
6. For one of the creativity software packages described in the text, go to the company's Web site, download and try out a demo, and describe your experience in a report. Include what you liked and didn't like and what you found useful and didn't find useful.
7. Go to **groove.net**, **collabnet.com**, and other companies that provide workspace products. Summarize the capabilities of each product.
8. Go to **logility.com**. Review collaborative products that optimize supply chains.
9. Go to **software.emc.com/products/software_az/eroom_enterprise.htm?hlnav=T** and find the product's capabilities. Write a report.

End of Chapter Application Case

Dresdner Kleinwort Wasserstein Uses Wiki for Collaboration

Dresdner Kleinwort Wasserstein (DrKW) is the international investment banking arm of Dresdner Bank. Based in Europe, DrKW provides a range of capital markets and advisory services, and it employs approximately 6,000 people worldwide.

Because of the large number employees, their geographic distribution, and the diversity of cultures, it became necessary to provide a range of collaborative tools, from blogs and wikis to IM, chat and audio/videoconferencing in order to allow people to move between modes, depending on which was most appropriate at the time. DrKW installed a primitive open source wiki in 1997. The company reviewed Socialtext products in March 2004 and ran a small pilot on the hosted service in July

2004. Based on the pilot, DrKW decided to upgrade to Socialtext Enterprise, which was installed in the third quarter of 2004.

DrKW chose Socialtext because the company was willing to work with DrKW on better authentication, permissioning, and sharing of information and communication among silos as well as the vendor, and it understood the necessity for information to flow across multiple forms of communications. Because DrKW is highly regulated, everything must be recordable, archivable, searchable, and retrievable.

USAGE AND BENEFITS

The Information Strategy team was the first group to use Socialtext on a hosted service. Because its work needed structure, skills were geographically dispersed, and publication and collaboration at an individual level gained many capabilities through the Socialtext workspace. The team uses it as a communications tool, a collective discussion tool, and as a storehouse for documents and information.

The user-centered design (UCD) team incorporates usability into external-facing applications used across all business lines. The wiki allows all team members to upload information more easily, which encourages collaboration and transparency by making the sharing of e-mail conversations and other ideas uncomplicated. UCD also uses the wiki to help explain what user-centered design is and why it is important to a wider DrKW community as well as to share presentations, documents, and reports.

One of the most important roles of the wiki is to track project development so that the team and management know what progress is being made, regardless of individual geographical locations and to raise the team's awareness about what each person is doing, the status of each project, and what actions should follow.

In 2004, the Equity Delta1 equity financing team was one of the largest users of the wiki. This unit deals with loans, equity swaps, and so on. It began using the wiki workspace to eliminate the cumbersome number of e-mails, to view the development of business plans, and to store commonly used information. The team also creates an open forum where anyone can post views, comments, and questions on given subjects, publish and share white papers and bulletins, coordinate sales and marketing activities, and organize important team tasks.

The E-Capital London Team develops back-end applications for the Digital Markets business line and supports a number of legacy systems. It uses Socialtext to share and develop new system specifications and product overviews and to help with documentation. The wiki provides an instantly editable collaboration platform that simplifies the publication process. The version history function is useful for product specs, where it is important to retain a complete audit trail.

Socialtext also enables individuals to edit the intranet quickly and easily. For example, it is helping build an internal glossary that defines company jargon through employees doing similar jobs. The Wikipedia-style usage cuts down the training time and costs of new hires because it helps them understand internal and external jargon more quickly and easily. It also simplifies the roles of people writing in other locations and languages. Eventually, the wiki will be used for informal training, which will encourage its use.

Sources: SocialText, Dresdner Kleinwort Wasserstein (DrKW), 2004, **socialtext.com/customers/customerdrkw/** (accessed February 2006); and "E-mail Is So Five Minutes Ago," *BusinessWeek Online*, November, 28, 2005, **businessweek.com/magazine/content/05_48/b3961120.htm** (accessed August 2006).

QUESTIONS FOR THE CASE

1. What capabilities of a wiki are not available in e-mail?
2. Describe the applications of wikis in finance and operations.
3. How does DrKW's wiki increase employee productivity?
4. How does DrKW's wiki help with foreign languages and training?

References

Agrew, M. (2000, July 10). "Collaboration on the Desktop." *InformationWeek*.

Altshuller Institute for TRIZ Studies. (2006). **aitriz.org** (accessed August 2006).

Bradley, P. (2002, April). "CPFR Gaining Converts." *Logistics*.

Bray, R. (2004). "Virtual Meetings: The New Business Travel: Business Travel Briefing." *Financial Times.*

Bury, S. (2004). "Vendor-Managed Inventory." *Purchasing B2B*, Vol. 46, No. 3.

Callaghan, D. (2002, June 26). "IBM: E-Meetings Save $ Million a Month." *eWEEK*.

Chen, H., et al. (1995). *Intelligent Meeting Facilitation Agents: An Experiment on GroupSystems*. Tucson: University of Arizona, **ai.bpa.arizona.edu/papers/tool95/tool95.html** (accessed August 2006).

Cramond, B. (1995). "The Torrance Tests of Creative Thinking: From Design Through Establishment of Predictive Validity." In R.F. Subotnik and K.D. Arnold (eds.). *Beyond Terman: Contemporary Studies of*

Giftedness and Talent. Norwood, NJ: Ablex Publishing Co., pp. 229–254.

de Vreede, G., and F. Ackermann. (2005, July). "International Perspectives in Group Decision and Negotiation Research." *Group Decision and Negotiation*.

Dennis, A.R., and B.A. Reinicke (2004, March). "Beta vs. VHS and the Acceptance of Electronic Brainstorming Technology." *MIS Quarterly*.

DeSanctis, G., and R.B. Gallupe. (1987). "A Foundation for the Study of Group Decision Support Systems." *Management Science*, Vol. 33, No. 5.

Duke Corporate Education. (2005). Building Effective Teams. Chicago: Dearborn Trade Publications.

eWEEK Reviews. (2005, April 25). "Microsoft Live Meeting 2005." *eWEEK*, **eweek.com/article2/0,1895,1788786,00.asp** (accessed August 2006).

Gatignon, H., M.L. Tushman, W. Smith, and P. Anderson. (2002, September). "A Structural Approach to Assessing Innovation: Construct Development of Innovation Locus, Type and Characteristics." *Management Science*, Vol. 48, No. 9.

Hall, M. (2002, July 1). "Decision Support Systems." *Computerworld*, Vol. 36, No. 27.

Handzic, M., and M. Cule. (2002, July 4–7). "Creative Decision Making: Review, Analysis and Recommendations." *Proceedings of DSIage2002*, Cork, Ireland.

Henrie, K.S. (2004, July). "All Together Now." *CIO Insight*.

Holt, K. (2002, August 5). "Nice Concept: Two Days' Work in a Day," *Meeting News*, Vol. 26, No. 11.

IBM. (2006). *Case Studies*, **ibm.com/software/success/cssdb.nsf/customerindexVW?OpenView&Start=91&Count=30&RestrictToCategory=default**_C (accessed April 2006).

Konicki, S. (2001, November 12). "Collaboration Is the Cornerstone of $19B Defense Contract." *InformationWeek*.

Langley, N. (2004, March 23). "Notes Users Can Spread Their Skills." *ComputerWeekly*.

Lindstone, H., and M. Turroff. (1975). *The Delphi Method: Technology and Applications*. Reading, MA: Addison-Wesley.

Malhotra, A., A. Majchrzak, R. Carman, and V. Lott. (2001, June). "Radical Innovation Without Collocation: A Case Study at Boeing-Rocketdyne." *MIS Quarterly*, Vol. 25, No. 2.

Manninen, M. (2004). *Rich Interaction Model for Game and Virtual Environment Design*. Academic Dissertation, Department of Information Processing Science, University of Oulu, **herkules.oulu.fi/isbn9514272544/isbn9514272544.pdf** (accessed April 2006).

Powell, A., G. Piccoli, and B. Ives. (2004, Winter). "Virtual Teams: A Review of Current Literature and Directions for Future Research." *Data Base*.

Rasmus, D.W. (1995). "Creativity and Tools." *PC AI*, Pt. 1: May/June; Pt. 2: July/August; Pt. 3: September/October.

Rees, J., and G. Koehler. (1999). "Brainstorming, Negotiating and Learning in Group Decision Support Systems: An Evolutionary Approach." *Proceedings of the Thirty-Second Annual Hawaii International Conference on System Sciences HICSS-32*. Los Alamitos, CA: IEEE Computer Society.

Satzinger, J.W., M.J. Garfield, and M. Nagasundaram. (1999, Spring). "The Creative Process: The Effects of Group Memory on Individual Idea Generation." *Journal of Management Information Systems*, Vol. 15, No. 4.

Smith, C. (2004, March 26). *Emerson Saves $6 Million with WebEx Web Conferencing Services*, **webex.com/pr/pr287.html** (accessed August 2006).

Sutton, R.I. (2001, October). "The Creativity Dilemma." *CIO Insight*.

Turban, E., et al. (2006). *Electronic Commerce 2006*. Upper Saddle River, NJ: Prentice Hall.

von Oech, R. (2002). *Expect the Unexpected or You Won't Find It: A Creativity Tool Based on the Ancient Wisdom of Heraclitus*. San Francisco: Berrett-Koehler.

WikiThat.com. (2005, January 18). *BusinessWeek Highlights Wiki Use (Again)*, **wikithat.com/wiki_that/2005/11/index.html** (accessed April 2006).

CHAPTER 11

Knowledge Management

Learning Objectives

- Define *knowledge* and describe the different types of knowledge
- Describe the characteristics of knowledge management
- Describe organizational learning and its relationship to knowledge management
- Describe the knowledge management cycle
- Describe the technologies that can be used in a knowledge management system (KMS)
- Describe different approaches to knowledge management
- Describe the activities of the chief knowledge officer and others involved in knowledge management
- Describe the role of knowledge management in organizational activities
- Describe ways of evaluating intellectual capital in an organization
- Describe how KMS are implemented
- Describe the roles of technology, people, and management in knowledge management
- Describe the benefits and drawbacks of knowledge management initiatives
- Describe how knowledge management can revolutionize the way an organization functions

In this chapter, we describe the characteristics and concepts of knowledge management. In addition, we explain how firms use information technology (IT) to implement KMS and how these systems are transforming modern organizations. Knowledge management, while conceptually ancient, is a relatively new form of collaborative computing. The goal of knowledge management is to capture, store, maintain, and deliver useful knowledge in a meaningful form to anyone who needs it, anyplace and anytime, within an organization. Knowledge management is collaboration at the organization level. Knowledge management has the potential to revolutionize the way we collaborate and use computing, as discussed in the following sections:

11.1 Opening Vignette: Siemens Knows What It Knows Through Knowledge Management

11.2 Introduction to Knowledge Management

11.3 Organizational Learning and Transformation

11.4 Knowledge Management Activities

11.5 Approaches to Knowledge Management

11.1 OPENING VIGNETTE: SIEMENS KNOWS WHAT IT KNOWS THROUGH KNOWLEDGE MANAGEMENT

PROBLEM

Siemens AG, a $73 billion electronics and electrical-engineering conglomerate, produces everything from light bulbs to x-ray machines, from power-generation equipment to high-speed trains. During its 156-year history, Siemens has become one of the world's largest and most successful corporations. Siemens is well known for the technical brilliance of its engineers, but much of their knowledge used to be locked and unavailable to other employees. Facing the pressure to maximize the benefits of corporate membership of each business unit, Siemens AG needed to learn how to leverage the knowledge and expertise of its 460,000 employees worldwide.

SOLUTION

The roots of knowledge management at Siemens go back to 1996, when a number of people in the corporation who had an interest in knowledge management (KM) formed a *community of interest*. They researched the subject, learned what was being done by other companies, and determined how KM could benefit Siemens. Without suggestion or encouragement from senior executives, mid-level employees in Siemens business units began creating repositories, communities of practice, and informal techniques of sharing knowledge. By 1999, the central board of Siemens AG confirmed the importance of KM to the entire company by creating an organizational unit that would be responsible for the worldwide deployment of knowledge management.

Siemens's movement toward KM has presented several challenges to the company, the most notable of which are technological and cultural. At the heart of Siemens's technical solution to knowledge management is a Web site called ShareNet, which combines elements of a database repository, a chat room, and a search engine. Online entry forms allow employees to store information they think might be useful to colleagues. Other Siemens employees are able to search the repository or browse by topic and then contact the authors for more information, using one of the available communication channels. In addition, the system lets employees post alerts when they have an urgent questions. Although knowledge management implementation at Siemens involved establishing a network to collect, categorize, and share information using databases and intranets, Siemens realized that IT was only the tool that enabled knowledge management. Randall Sellers, director of knowledge management for the Americas Region of Siemens, stated, "In my opinion, the technology or IT role is a small one. I think it's 20 percent IT and 80 percent change management—dealing with cultural change and human interfaces."

Siemens used a three-pronged effort to convince employees that it is important to participate in the exchange of ideas and experiences and to share what they know. The challenge is managing the people who manage the knowledge. You have to make it easy for them to share, or they won't. Siemens has assigned 100 internal evangelists around the world to be responsible for training, answering questions, and monitoring the system. Siemens's top management has shown its full support for the KM projects. And the company is providing incentives to overcome employees' resistance to change. When employees post documents to the system or use the knowledge, Siemens rewards them with "shares" (similar to frequent-flyer miles). An employee's accumulation of shares can be exchanged for things such as consumer electronics or discounted trips to other countries. However, the real incentive of the system is much more basic. Commission-driven salespeople have already learned that the knowledge and expertise of their colleagues available through ShareNet can be indispensable in winning lucrative contracts. Employees in marketing, service, research and development, and other departments are also willing to participate and contribute when they realize that the system provides them with useful information in a convenient way.

ShareNet has undergone tremendous growth, which has resulted in several challenges for Siemens. The company strives to maintain a balance between global and local knowledge initiatives as well as between KM efforts that support the entire company and those that help individual business units. Furthermore, Siemens works to prevent ShareNet from becoming so overloaded with knowledge that it becomes useless. A group is assigned to monitor the system and remove trivial and irrelevant content.

RESULTS

ShareNet has evolved into a state-of-the-art Web-based knowledge management system (KMS) that stores and catalogs volumes of valuable knowledge, makes it available to every employee, and enhances global collaboration. Numerous companies, including Intel, Philips Electronics, and Volkswagen, studied ShareNet before setting up their own KMS. Teleos, an independent knowledge management research company, has acknowledged Siemens as one of the most admired knowledge enterprises worldwide for five years in a row.

Siemens has realized a variety of quantifiable benefits afforded by knowledge management. For example, in April 1999, the company developed a portion of Share Net to support the Information & Communications Networks Group, at the cost of $7.8 million. Within two years, the tool helped to generate $122 million in additional sales.

Ultimately, knowledge management may be one of the major tools that will help Siemens prove that large, diversified conglomerates can work and that being big might even be an advantage in the information age.

Sources: Adapted from G.S. Vasilash, "447,000 Heads Are Better Than One," *Automotive Design & Production*, June 2002; "Business: Electronic Glue," *The Economist*, June 2, 2001; S. Williams, "The Intranet Content Management Strategy Conference," *Management Services*, September 2001; M. Santosus, "How Siemens Keeps KM Blooming," *In the Know at CIO.com*, February 2003, **cio.com/research/knowledge/edit/k021003_bloom.html** (accessed April 2006); and K.A. Zimmermann, "Happy Together: Knowledge Management and Collaboration Work Hand-in-Hand to Satisfy the Thirst for Information," *KMWorld*, May 2003.

Questions for the Opening Vignette

1. How did the Siemens KMS evolve?
2. How does Siemens view knowledge (i.e., intellectual) assets?
3. What does leveraging expertise mean? How did Siemens do this? Explain how this relates to Siemens's high return on investment.

4. Describe the benefits of the Siemens ShareNet KMS.
5. Explain the meaning of culture transformation as it occurred at Siemens. Include in your answer how the various constituencies bought into the system.
6. Explain how Internet and Web technologies enabled the Siemens KMS.

WHAT WE CAN LEARN FROM THIS VIGNETTE

Knowledge is an important asset, and the more it can be shared within a company, the better. However, even large companies have difficulties sharing knowledge because knowledge exists in many places in the organization, is stored in different formats, and is owned by many.

Starting in an informal way and then formalizing it and creating communities of users, Siemens created a knowledge collection that it shares across its many units worldwide. How to conduct such a project is the subject of this chapter.

11.2 INTRODUCTION TO KNOWLEDGE MANAGEMENT

Knowledge management is a broad discipline that is defined and explained in the following section.

KNOWLEDGE MANAGEMENT CONCEPTS AND DEFINITIONS

The opening vignette illustrates the importance and value of identifying an organization's knowledge and sharing it throughout the organization. In a major initiative, Siemens AG developed ShareNet and other KMS to leverage its *intellectual assets* (also called *intellectual capital*): the valuable knowledge of its employees. Siemens transformed its culture as the KMS was deployed, leading to significantly lower operating costs and more collaboration throughout the global enterprise. Although these assets are difficult to measure, organizations recognize the value of their intellectual assets. Fierce global competition drives companies to better use their intellectual assets by transforming themselves into organizations that foster the development and sharing of knowledge.

With roots in organizational learning and innovation, the idea of KM is not new (see Ponzi, 2004; and Schwartz, 2006). However, the application of IT tools to facilitate the creation, storage, transfer, and application of previously uncodifiable organizational knowledge is a new and major initiative in organizations. Successful managers have long used intellectual assets and recognized their value. But these efforts were not systematic, nor did they ensure that knowledge gained was shared and dispersed appropriately for maximum organizational benefit. *Knowledge management* is a process that helps organizations identify, select, organize, disseminate, and transfer important information and expertise that are part of the organization's memory and that typically reside within the organization in an unstructured manner. **Knowledge management (KM)** is the systematic and active management of ideas, information, and knowledge residing in an organization's employees. The structuring of knowledge enables effective and efficient problem solving, dynamic learning, strategic planning, and decision making. KM initiatives focus on identifying knowledge, explicating it in such a way that it can be shared in a formal manner, and leveraging its value through reuse. The IT that makes KM available throughout an organization is referred to as a KMS (see Holsapple, 2003a, 2003b; Park and Kim, 2006; Sedighi, 2006; and Zhang and Zhao, 2006.)

Through a supportive organizational climate and modern IT, an organization can bring its entire organizational memory and knowledge to bear on any problem, anywhere in the world, and at any time (see Bock et al., 2005). For organizational success, knowledge, as a form of capital, must be exchangeable among persons, and it must be able to grow. Knowledge about how problems are solved can be captured so that KM can promote organizational learning, leading to further knowledge creation.

KNOWLEDGE

Knowledge is very distinct from data and information in the IT context (see Figure 11.1). Whereas data are facts, measurements, and statistics, *information* is organized or processed data that is timely (i.e., inferences from the data are drawn within the time frame of applicability) and accurate (i.e., with regard to the original data) (see Hoffer et al. 2002; and Kankanhalli et al., 2005). **Knowledge** is information that is contextual, relevant, and actionable. For example, a map that gives detailed driving directions from one location to another could be considered data. An up-to-the-minute traffic bulletin along the freeway that indicates a traffic slowdown due to construction several miles ahead could be considered information. Awareness of an alternative, back-roads route could be considered knowledge. In this case, the map is considered data because it does not contain current relevant information that affects the driving time and conditions from one location to the other. However, having the current conditions as information is useful only if you have knowledge that enables you to avert the construction zone. The implication is that knowledge has strong experiential and reflective elements that distinguish it from information in a given context.

Having knowledge implies that it can be exercised to solve a problem, whereas having information does not carry the same connotation. An ability to act is an integral part of being knowledgeable. For example, two people in the same context with the same information may not have the same ability to use the information to the same degree of success. Hence, there is a difference in the human capability to add value. The differences in ability may be due to different experiences, different training, different perspectives, and other factors. While data, information, and knowledge may all be viewed as assets of an organization, knowledge provides a higher level of meaning about data and information. It conveys meaning and hence tends to be much more valuable, yet more ephemeral.

FIGURE 11.1 Data, Information, and Knowledge

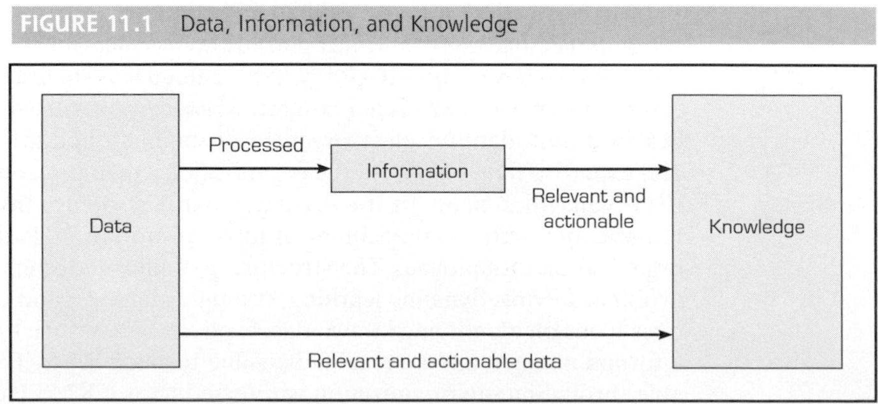

Unlike other assets, knowledge has the following characteristics (see Gray, 1999):

- *Extraordinary leverage and increasing returns.* Knowledge is not subject to diminishing returns. When it is used, it is not consumed. Its consumers can add to it, thus increasing its value.
- *Fragmentation, leakage, and the need to refresh.* As knowledge grows, it branches and fragments. Knowledge is dynamic; it is information in action. Thus, an organization must continually refresh its knowledge base to maintain it as a source of competitive advantage.
- *Uncertain value.* It is difficult to estimate the impact of an investment in knowledge. There are too many intangible aspects.
- *Uncertain value of sharing.* It is difficult to estimate the value of sharing knowledge, or even who will benefit most.

Over the past few decades, the industrialized economy has been going through a transformation from being based on natural resources to being based on intellectual assets (see Alavi, 2000; and Tseng and Goo, 2005). The **knowledge-based economy** is a reality (see Godin, 2006). Rapid changes in the business environment cannot be handled in traditional ways. Firms are much larger today than they used to be, and in some areas, turnover is extremely high, fueling the need for better tools for collaboration, communication, and knowledge sharing. Firms *must* develop strategies to sustain competitive advantage by leveraging their intellectual assets for optimal performance (e.g., in the National Basketball Association; see Berman et al., 2002). Competing in the globalized economy and markets requires quick response to customer needs and problems. To provide service, managing knowledge is critical for consulting firms spread out over wide geographical areas and for virtual organizations.

There is a vast amount of literature about what *knowledge* and *knowing* mean in epistemology (i.e., the study of the nature of knowledge), the social sciences, philosophy, and psychology. Although there is no single definition of what knowledge and KM specifically mean, the business perspective on them is fairly pragmatic. Information as a resource is not always valuable (i.e., information overload can distract from what is important); knowledge as a resource is valuable because it focuses attention back toward what is important (see Carlucci and Schiuma, 2006; and Hoffer et al., 2002). Knowledge implies an implicit understanding and experience that can discriminate between its use and misuse. Over time, information accumulates and decays, whereas knowledge evolves. Knowledge is dynamic in nature. This implies, though, that today's knowledge may well become tomorrow's ignorance if an individual or organization fails to update knowledge as environmental conditions change. For more on the potential drawbacks of managing and reusing knowledge, see Section 11.9.

The term **intellectual capital**, often used as a synonym for *knowledge*, implies that there is a financial value to knowledge. Not all intellectual capital can be classified as knowledge. Brand and customer are aspects of intellectual capital, but in today's marketplace, the most significant and valuable aspect of intellectual capital is indeed knowledge in all its forms (see Ariely, 2006). Although intellectual capital is difficult to measure, some industries have tried. For example, in 2000, the value of the intellectual capital of the property-casualty insurance industry was estimated to be between $270 billion to $330 billion (see Mooney, 2000).

Knowledge evolves over time with experience, which puts connections among new situations and events in context. Given the breadth of the types and applications of knowledge, we adopt the simple and elegant definition that *knowledge* is information in action.

EXPLICIT AND TACIT KNOWLEDGE

Polanyi (1958) first conceptualized the difference between an organization's explicit and tacit knowledge. **Explicit knowledge** deals with more objective, rational, and technical knowledge (e.g., data, policies, procedures, software, documents). **Tacit knowledge** is usually in the domain of subjective, cognitive, and experiential learning; it is highly personal and difficult to formalize.

Explicit knowledge comprises the policies, procedural guides, white papers, reports, designs, products, strategies, goals, mission, and core competencies of an enterprise and its IT infrastructure. It is the knowledge that has been codified (i.e., documented) in a form that can be distributed to others or transformed into a process or strategy without requiring interpersonal interaction. For example, a description of how to process a job application would be documented in a firm's human resources policy manual. Explicit knowledge has also been called **leaky knowledge** because of the ease with which it can leave an individual, a document, or an organization due to the fact that it can be readily and accurately documented (see Alavi, 2000).

Tacit knowledge is the cumulative store of the experiences, mental maps, insights, acumen, expertise, know-how, trade secrets, skill sets, understanding, and learning that an organization has, as well as the organizational culture that has embedded in it the past and present experiences of the organization's people, processes, and values. Tacit knowledge, also referred to as *embedded knowledge* (see Tuggle and Goldfinger, 2004), is usually either localized within the brain of an individual or embedded in the group interactions within a department or a branch office. Tacit knowledge typically involves expertise or high skill levels.

Sometimes tacit knowledge could easily be documented but has remained tacit simply because the individual housing the knowledge does not recognize its potential value to other individuals. Other times, tacit knowledge is unstructured, without tangible form, and therefore difficult to codify. It is difficult to put some tacit knowledge into words. For example, an explanation of how to ride a bicycle would be difficult to document explicitly and thus is tacit. Successful transfer or sharing of tacit knowledge usually takes place through associations, internships, apprenticeship, conversations, other means of social and interpersonal interactions, or even simulations (see Robin, 2000). Nonaka and Takeuchi (1995) claimed that intangibles such as insights, intuitions, hunches, gut feelings, values, images, metaphors, and analogies are the often-overlooked assets of organizations. Harvesting these intangible assets can be critical to a firm's bottom line and its ability to meet its goals. Tacit knowledge sharing requires a certain context or situation in order to be facilitated because it is less commonly shared under normal circumstances (see Shariq and Vendelø, 2006).

Historically, management of information systems (MIS) departments have focused on capturing, storing, managing, and reporting explicit knowledge. Organizations now recognize the need to integrate both types of knowledge in formal information systems. For centuries, the mentor–apprentice relationship, because of its experiential nature, has been a slow but reliable means of transferring tacit knowledge from individual to individual. When people leave an organization, they take their knowledge with them. One critical goal of knowledge management is to retain the valuable know-how that can so easily and quickly leave an organization. **Knowledge management systems (KMSs)** refer to the use of modern IT (e.g., the Internet, intranets, extranets, Lotus Notes, Software filters, Agents, Data Warehouses) to systematize, enhance, and expedite intra- and inter-firm KM (see Alavi and Leidner, 1999).

KMS are intended to help an organization cope with turnover, rapid change, and downsizing by making the expertise of the organization's human capital widely accessible.

They are being built in part because of the increasing pressure to maintain a well-informed, productive workforce. Moreover, they are built to help large organizations provide a consistent level of customer service, as illustrated in Application Case 11.1. For more on the basics of knowledge and the economy, see Ahlawat and Ahlawat (2006), Holsapple (2003a, 2003b), and Teece (2003).

Application Case 11.1

Cingular Calls on Knowledge

How do you make sure that each of your customer service agents at 22 call centers nationwide can answer virtually any question asked by one of your 22 million clients? That was the challenge faced by Cingular Wireless (**cingular.com**), a major mobile communications provider based in Atlanta.

Cingular Wireless turned to KM to accomplish this massive task. Cingular benchmarked KM solutions of technology-oriented companies, such as Dell and Microsoft. Steve Mullins, vice president of customer experience for Cingular Wireless, and Monica Browning, Cingular's director of knowledge management, met with several KM software vendors to learn how their tools operate. "We thought about how [the knowledge management software] would integrate with what we envisioned the future desktop to look like," said Mullins. "This system would be the foundation for what we use throughout all of our departments."

Following a review of KM solutions used by other companies, Cingular chose eService Suite by ServiceWare (**serviceware.co.jp**).

ServiceWare's decision integrity department helped Cingular put together a basis for proving the software's return on investment (ROI).

To ensure successful implementation of the system, Cingular embarked on a campaign to obtain the support of everyone involved, from senior executives to each call center agent who would use the system. A pilot program was initiated in technical support departments at three call centers.

To help manage the organizational changes that accompany a shift to knowledge management, Cingular enlisted the help of leading consulting firms Cap Gemini Ernst & Young and Innovative Management Solutions.

A major issue in developing the KMS involved capturing knowledge and storing it in the system. Cingular accomplished this by combining the efforts of its employees and an external authoring group from Innovative Management Solutions. Cingular divided the process into phases. This made it possible to populate the knowledge base with technical support information, common topics, information on rate plans, and so on. Browning estimated that it took about four months for the knowledge repository to be ready for the first group of users.

The Cingular KMS uses complex (artificial intelligence–based) algorithms to process natural language queries and provide customer service agents with lists of the most likely answers to their questions. The software also determines the relevance of possible answers by ranking them partly on exact text and phrase matching. In addition, the system can match synonyms and assign additional weight to certain expressions. The system attempts to provide even more focused solutions by retrieving answers from the pool of knowledge that is relevant to a particular user and his or her profile.

Understanding that knowledge must grow and evolve, Cingular encourages users to contribute their expertise to the system. The software can automatically record a sequence of steps that an agent took to find a correct solution to a certain problem and give the agent an option to provide additional feedback.

Cingular realized that ensuring validity and integrity of the knowledge stored and distributed by the KMS is one of the key factors of the system's success. To that end, the company has a knowledge management team that is responsible for monitoring, maintaining, and expanding the system. The team consists of about 25 full-time employees based in Cingular's Atlanta headquarters. The knowledge management team works closely with various departments of the company and subject-matter experts to ensure that the knowledge base has the right answers in a user-friendly format at the right time. In addition, the team reviews contributions to the knowledge base made by the agents and makes appropriate changes or additions to the knowledge base.

Cingular's clients are often the ultimate beneficiaries of the company's knowledge. That is why Cingular plans to bring its knowledge closer to its customers by extending the KMS online and to retail stores. Customers will be able to access instructions on using wireless services and features, handsets, and other devices that Cingular carries, as well as troubleshooting tips.

Sources: Adapted from J. O'Herron, "Building the Bases of Knowledge," *Call Center Magazine*, January 2003; and *Cingular Wireless Benefits Knowledge Management Web Site*, 2005, **mergeagency.com/case_study.php?id=23** (accessed April 2006).

Section 11.2 Review Questions

1. Define *knowledge management* and describe its purposes.
2. Distinguish between knowledge and data.
3. Describe the knowledge-based economy.
4. Define *tacit knowledge* and *explicit knowledge*.
5. Define *KMS* and describe the capabilities of KMS.

11.3 ORGANIZATIONAL LEARNING AND TRANSFORMATION

Knowledge management is rooted in the concepts of organizational learning and organizational memory. When members of an organization collaborate and communicate ideas, teach, and learn, knowledge is transformed and transferred from individual to individual (see Bennet and Bennet, 2003; and Jasimuddin et al., 2006).

THE LEARNING ORGANIZATION

The term **learning organization** refers to an organization's capability of learning from its past experience. Before a company can improve, it must first learn. Learning involves an interaction between experience and competence. In communities of practice, these are tightly related. Communities of practice provide not only a context for newcomers to learn but also a context for new insights to be transformed into knowledge (see Wenger, 2002). We discuss communities of practice later in this chapter.

To build a learning organization, three critical issues must be tackled: (1) meaning (determining a vision of what the learning organization is to be), (2) management (determining how the firm is to work), and (3) measurement (assessing the rate and level of learning). A learning organization as one that performs five main activities well: solving problems systematically, experimenting creatively, learning from past experience, learning from the best practices of others, and transferring knowledge quickly and efficiently throughout the organization (see Vat, 2006). For example, Best Buy deliberately and successfully structured its KM efforts around creating a learning organization where it captured best practices (see Brown and Duguid, 2002).

ORGANIZATIONAL MEMORY

A learning organization must have an **organizational memory** and a means to save, represent, and share its organizational knowledge. Estimates vary, but it is generally believed that only 10 to 20 percent of business data are actually used. Organizations "remember" the past in their policies and procedures. Individuals ideally tap into this memory for both explicit and tacit knowledge when faced with issues or problems to be solved. Human intelligence draws from the organizational memory and adds value by creating new knowledge. A KMS can capture the new knowledge and make it available in its enhanced form. See Nevo and Wand (2005) and Jennex and Olfman (2003).

ORGANIZATIONAL LEARNING

Organizational learning is the development of new knowledge and insights that have the potential to influence an organization's behavior. It occurs when associations, cognitive systems, and memories are shared by members of an organization (see Schulz, 2001). Learning skills include the following (see Garvin, 2000):

- Openness to new perspectives
- Awareness of personal biases
- Exposure to unfiltered data
- A sense of humility

Establishing a corporate memory is critical for success (see Hinds and Aronson, 2002). IT plays a critical role in organizational learning, and management must place emphasis on this area to foster it (see Ali et al., 2006; Craig, 2005; Davenport and Sena, 2003; and O'Leary, 2003).

Because organizations are becoming more virtual in nature, they must develop methods for effective organizational learning. Modern collaborative technologies can help in KM initiatives. Organizational learning and memory depend less on technology than on people issues, as we describe next.

ORGANIZATIONAL CULTURE

An organization's ability to learn, develop memory, and share knowledge is dependent on its culture. Culture is a pattern of shared basic assumptions (see Kayworth and Leidner, 2003; and Schein 1999). Over time, organizations learn what works and what doesn't work. As the lessons become second nature, they become part of the **organizational culture**. New employees learn the culture from their mentors, along with know-how.

The impact of corporate culture on an organization is difficult to measure. However, strong culture generally produces strong, measurable bottom-line results: net income, return on invested capital, and yearly increases in stock price (see Hibbard, 1998). For example, Buckman Laboratories, a pharmaceutical firm, measures culture impact by sales of new products. Buckman undertook to change its organizational culture by making knowledge sharing part of the company's core values. After instituting a knowledge-sharing initiative, sales of products less than five years old rose to 33 percent of total sales, up from 22 percent (see Hibbard, 1998; also see Martin, 2000). Sharing initiatives and proper motivation are critical for the success of knowledge management. This is especially tricky in the public sector. On the other hand, an organizational culture that does not foster sharing can severely cripple a KM effort (see Alavi et al., 2005/2006; Hinds and Aronson, 2002; Jones et al., 2006; and Riege, 2005).

Encouraging employees to use a KMS, both for contributing knowledge and for seeking knowledge, can be difficult. Riege (2005) reviewed past studies and identified a number of possible reasons that people do not like to share knowledge:

- General lack of time to share knowledge and time to identify colleagues in need of specific knowledge
- Apprehension or fear that sharing may reduce or jeopardize people's job security
- Low awareness and realization of the value and benefit of the knowledge others possess
- Dominance in sharing explicit over tacit knowledge, such as know-how and experience that requires hands-on learning, observation, dialogue, and interactive problem solving
- Use of a strong hierarchy, position-based status, and formal power
- Insufficient capture, evaluation, feedback, communication, and tolerance of past mistakes that would enhance individual and organizational learning effects
- Differences in experience levels
- Lack of contact time and interaction between knowledge sources and recipients

- Poor verbal/written communication and interpersonal skills
- Age differences
- Gender differences
- Lack of a social network
- Differences in education levels
- Ownership of intellectual property due to fear of not receiving just recognition and accreditation from managers and colleagues
- Lack of trust in people because they may misuse knowledge or take unjust credit for it
- Lack of trust in the accuracy and credibility of knowledge due to the source
- Differences in national culture or ethnic backgrounds and values and beliefs associated with it

Sometimes a technology project fails because the technology does not match the organization's culture. (This is a much deeper issue than having a poor fit between the technology and the task and hand; see McCarthy et al., 2001.) This is especially true for KMS because they rely so heavily on individuals contributing their knowledge. Most KMS that fail in practice do so because of organizational culture issues (see Zyngier, 2006).

Section 11.3 Review Questions

1. Define *learning organization* and identify the characteristics of learning organizations.
2. Define *organizational memory*.
3. Describe *organizational learning*.
4. Define *organizational culture* and relate it to knowledge management.

11.4 KNOWLEDGE MANAGEMENT ACTIVITIES

Several major activities take place in knowledge management projects. They are described next.

KNOWLEDGE MANAGEMENT INITIATIVES AND ACTIVITIES

Given the changing dynamics of the global marketplace and the increasingly intense competition, there is a need for organizations to leverage intellectual resources in order to reduce the loss of intellectual capital due to people leaving the company, as well as to reduce costs by decreasing the number of times the company has to repeatedly solve the same problem. IDC estimated that the cost for an organization of 1,000 knowledge workers to find existing knowledge they need, to waste time searching for nonexistent knowledge, and to re-create knowledge that is available but could not be located can be more than $6 million per year (see Weiss et al., 2004). In addition, knowledge has been recognized as the single most important source for generating value in the modern company (see Weir, 2004). For instance, companies can use business intelligence (BI) to reveal opportunities and then create revenue-generating programs to exploit them. In some highly skilled professions, such as medicine, retaining and using knowledge of best practices is critical in life-and-death situations (see Lamont, 2003a). It is precisely these types of difficulties that have led to the systematic attempt to manage knowledge (see Compton 2001; and Holsapple 2003a, 2003b). Between early 2001 and early 2003, U.S. firms laid off 3.6 million workers (not including retirements). Nineteen percent of baby boomers in executive, administrative, or managerial positions are expected to retire by 2008. When people leave an organization, their knowledge assets leave with them; as Taylor (2001) said, "Intellectual capital has legs."

A KPMG Peat Marwick survey of European firms in 1998 found that almost half of the companies reported having suffered a significant setback due to losing key staff. Similarly, a Cranfield University survey conducted in the same year found that the majority of responding firms believed that much of the knowledge they needed existed inside the organization but that finding and leveraging it were ongoing challenges.

Most KM initiatives have one of three aims: (1) to make knowledge visible, mainly through maps, yellow pages, and hypertext; (2) to develop a knowledge-intensive culture; or (3) to build a knowledge infrastructure. These aims are not mutually exclusive, and, indeed, firms may attempt all three as part of a knowledge management initiative.

Several activities or processes surround the management of knowledge. These include the creation of knowledge, the sharing of knowledge, and the seeking and use of knowledge. Various terms have been used to describe these processes. More important than any particular label assigned to a knowledge activity is having an understanding of how knowledge flows through an organization (see Wenger et al., 2002).

KNOWLEDGE CREATION

Knowledge creation is the generation of new insights, ideas, or routines. Nonaka (1994) described knowledge creation as an interplay between tacit and explicit knowledge and as a growing spiral as knowledge moves among the individual, group, and organizational levels. There are four modes of knowledge creation: socialization, externalization, internalization, and combination. The socialization mode refers to the conversion of tacit knowledge to new tacit knowledge through social interactions and shared experience among organization members (e.g., mentoring). The combination mode refers to the creation of new explicit knowledge by merging, categorizing, reclassifying, and synthesizing existing explicit knowledge (e.g., statistical analyses of market data). The other two modes involve interactions and conversion between tacit and explicit knowledge. Externalization refers to converting tacit knowledge to new explicit knowledge (e.g., producing a written document describing the procedures used in solving a particular client's problem). Internalization refers to the creation of new tacit knowledge from explicit knowledge (e.g., obtaining a novel insight through reading a document). For further information, see Wickramasinghe (2006).

KNOWLEDGE SHARING

Knowledge sharing is the willful explication of one person's ideas, insights, solutions, experiences (i.e., knowledge) to another individual either via an intermediary, such as a computer-based system, or directly. However, in many organizations, information and knowledge are not considered organizational resources to be shared but individual competitive weapons to be kept private. Organizational members may share personal knowledge with a certain trepidation; they perceive that they are of less value if their knowledge is part of the organizational public domain. Research in organizational learning and knowledge management suggests that some facilitating conditions include trust, interest, and shared language (see Hanssen-Bauer and Snow, 1996); the fostering access to knowledgeable members (see Brown and Duguid, 1991); and a culture marked by autonomy, redundancy, requisite variety, intention, and fluctuation (see King, 2006).

KNOWLEDGE SEEKING

Knowledge seeking, also referred to as *knowledge sourcing* (see Gray and Meisters, 2003), is the search for and use of internal organizational knowledge. Lack of time or lack of reward may hinder the sharing of knowledge, and the same is true of knowledge seeking. Individuals may sometimes prefer to not reuse knowledge if they feel that their own performance review is based on the originality or creativity of their ideas. Such was the case for marketing employees in a global consumer goods organization described in Alavi et al. (2003).

Individuals may engage in knowledge creation, sharing, and seeking with or without the use of IT tools. For example, storytelling (described in Chapter 2 as a decision-making technique) is an ancient approach to transmitting and gathering knowledge. Nuances of how a story is told cue the gatherer as to importance and detail. Storytelling may be considered a form of verbal best practices. See Gamble and Blackwell (2002) and Reamy (2002) for details on how storytelling is used in knowledge management.

We next describe several common approaches to knowledge management.

Section 11.4 Review Questions

1. Why do companies need knowledge management initiatives?
2. Describe the process of knowledge creation.
3. What are the characteristics of knowledge sharing?
4. Define *knowledge seeking* (or *sourcing*).

11.5 APPROACHES TO KNOWLEDGE MANAGEMENT

There are two fundamental approaches to knowledge management: the process approach and the practice approach (see Table 11.1). We next describe these two approaches as well as hybrid approaches.

THE PROCESS APPROACH TO KNOWLEDGE MANAGEMENT

The **process approach** to knowledge management attempts to codify organizational knowledge through formalized controls, processes, and technologies (see Hansen et al., 1999). Organizations that adopt the process approach may implement explicit policies governing how knowledge is to be collected, stored, and disseminated throughout the organization. The process approach frequently involves the use of IT, such as intranets, data warehousing, knowledge repositories, decision support tools, and groupware (see Ruggles, 1998) to enhance the quality and speed of knowledge creation and distribution in the organization. The main criticisms of the process approach are that it fails to capture much of the tacit knowledge embedded in firms and it forces individuals into fixed patterns of thinking (see Kiaraka and Manning, 2005). This approach is favored by firms that sell relatively standardized products that fill common needs. Most of the valuable knowledge in these firms is fairly explicit because of the standardized nature of the products and services. For example, a kazoo manufacturer has minimal product

TABLE 11.1 The Process and Practice Approaches to Knowledge Management

	Process Approach	***Practice Approach***
Type of knowledge supported	Explicit knowledge—codified in rules, tools, and processes	Mostly tacit knowledge—unarticulated knowledge not easily captured or codified
Means of transmission	Formal controls, procedures, and standard operating procedures, with heavy emphasis on information technologies to support knowledge creation, codification, and transfer of knowledge	Informal social groups that engage in storytelling and improvisation
Benefits	Provides structure to harness generated ideas and knowledge Achieves scale in knowledge reuse Provides spark for fresh ideas and responsiveness to changing environment	Provides an environment to generate and transfer high-value tacit knowledge
Disadvantages	Fails to tap into tacit knowledge. May limit innovation and forces participants into fixed patterns of thinking	Can result in inefficiency Abundance of ideas with no structure to implement them.
Role of information technology (IT)	Requires heavy investment in IT to connect people with reusable codified knowledge	Requires moderate investment in IT to facilitate conversations and transfer of tacit knowledge

Source: Compiled from M. Alavi, T. Kayworth, and D. Leidner, *An Empirical Investigation of the Impact of Organizational Culture on KM Initiatives* (forthcoming Journal of Management Information Systems, 2006).

changes or service needs over the years, and yet there is steady demand and a need to produce the item. In these cases, the knowledge is typically static in nature.

Even large firms that use tacit knowledge, such as Cap Gemini Ernst & Young, have invested heavily to ensure that the process approach works efficiently. The 250 people at Cap Gemini Ernst & Young's Center for Business Knowledge manage an electronic repository and help consultants find and use information. Specialists write reports and analyses that many teams can use. Each of Cap Gemini Ernst & Young's more than 40 practice areas has a staff member who helps codify and store documents. The resulting area databases are linked through a network (see Hansen et al., 1999). Naturally, people-to-documents is not the only way consultants in firms such as Cap Gemini Ernst & Young and Accenture share knowledge; they talk with one another as well. But they do place a high degree of emphasis on the codification strategy (see Hansen et al., 1999).

THE PRACTICE APPROACH TO KNOWLEDGE MANAGEMENT

In contrast to the process approach, the **practice approach** to knowledge management assumes that a great deal of organizational knowledge is tacit in nature and that formal controls, processes, and technologies are not suitable for transmitting this type of understanding. Rather than build formal systems to manage knowledge, the focus of this approach is to build the social environments or communities of practice necessary to facilitate the sharing of tacit understanding (see Hansen et al., 1999; Leidner et al.,

2006; and Wenger and Snyder, 2000). These communities are informal social groups that meet regularly to share ideas, insights, and best practices. This approach is typically adopted by companies that provide highly customized solutions to unique problems. For these firms, knowledge is shared mostly through person-to-person contact. Collaborative computing methods (e.g., group support systems [GSS], e-mail) help people communicate. The valuable knowledge for these firms is tacit in nature, which is difficult to express, capture, and manage. In this case, the environment and the nature of the problems being encountered are extremely dynamic. Because tacit knowledge is difficult to extract, store, and manage, the explicit knowledge that points to how to find the appropriate tacit knowledge (i.e., people contacts, consulting reports) is made available to an appropriate set of individuals who might need it. Consulting firms generally fall into this category. Firms adopting the codification strategy implicitly adopt the network storage model in their initial KMS (see Alavi, 2000).

The challenge for firms that adopt the personalization strategy, and hence the network storage model, is to develop methods to make the valuable tacit knowledge explicit, capture it, and contribute it to and transfer it from a knowledge repository in a KMS. Several major consulting firms are developing methods to do so. They store pointers to experts within the KMS, but they also store the tips, procedures, and best practices, as well as the context in which they work. To make their personalization strategies work, firms such as Bain invest heavily in building networks of people and communications technology, such as telephone, e-mail, and videoconferencing. They also commonly have face-to-face meetings (see Hansen et al., 1999).

In reality, a knowledge management initiative can, and usually does, involve both approaches. Process and practice are not mutually exclusive. Alavi et al. (2003) described the case of an organization that began its KM effort with a large repository but evolved the KM initiative into a community-of-practice approach that existed side-by-side with the repository. In fact, community members would pass information from the community forum to the organizational repository when they felt that the knowledge was valuable outside their community. Application Case 11.2 illustrates how Texaco successfully manages its knowledge by using the practice approach.

Application Case 11.2

Texaco Drills for Knowledge

Texaco (**texaco.com**), a company that pumps over a million barrels of oil a day, has discovered a new source of power: the collective knowledge and expertise of its 18,000 employees in 150 countries around the world. Texaco believes that connecting people who have questions with people who have answers gives it the power to work faster and more efficiently.

At Texaco, managing knowledge is a critical business challenge. John Old, Texaco's knowledge guru, approaches this challenge with a strategy that leverages human connections. Old has stated that knowledge, by its nature, is contextual; thus, systems that simply allow people to record what they know are ineffective. He strongly believes that a successful KM solution must recognize the importance of human connections.

Texaco uses technology to help people build personal relationships and share knowledge. One of the systems at work at Texaco is PeopleNet, a search engine for employees on the company's intranet. Employees who have questions can use PeopleNet to review profiles of their colleagues who might have the right answers. Texaco discovered that having biographies and pictures of its employees online makes it possible to establish credibility and trust between people who have not met each other. And it is trust that makes effective knowledge transfer possible.

Another tool that Texaco uses to connect its employees is a software system called Knowledge Mail from Tacit Knowledge Systems. This software analyzes e-mail sent and received by employees to help them make good contacts with colleagues who work on the same issues.

John Old has spoken of several important lessons that Texaco has learned while managing knowledge. He pointed out that people are more eager to share knowledge when they are united by a clear, specific, and measurable business purpose. Knowledge sharing becomes even more successful when they trust each other and see direct benefits that can be derived from the knowledge exchange. In addition, it is important to give people enough time to reflect on what they know and what they need to learn.

Texaco's approach to KM has provided many positive results. The knowledge management efforts help Texaco's employees successfully resolve numerous issues, ranging from adjusting oil well pumps to deciding whether to enter into new lines of business.

Sources: Compiled from F. Warner, "He Drills for Knowledge," *Fast Company*, September 2001; and D. Drucker, "Theory Doesn't Equal Practice," *Internetweek.com*, January 29, 2001, **internetweek.cmp.com/newslead01/lead012901.htm** (accessed April 2006).

HYBRID APPROACHES TO KNOWLEDGE MANAGEMENT

Many organizations use a hybrid of the process and practice approaches. Early in the development process, when it may not be clear how to extract tacit knowledge from its sources, the practice approach is used so that a repository stores only explicit knowledge that is relatively easy to document. The tacit knowledge initially stored in the repository is contact information about experts and their areas of expertise. Such information is listed so that people in the organization can find sources of expertise (e.g., the process approach). From this start, best practices can eventually be captured and managed so that the knowledge repository will contain an increasing amount of tacit knowledge over time. Eventually, a true process approach may be attained. But if the environment changes rapidly, only some of the best practices will prove useful. Regardless of the type of KMS developed, a storage location for the knowledge (i.e., a knowledge repository) of some kind is needed.

The J.D. Edwards intranet-based Knowledge Garden helps its consultants share best practices (i.e., practice approach) and find subject experts (i.e., process approach) who can help them solve problems faster and more consistently. The application codifies the company's knowledge base, using Site Server taxonomies, and delivers personalized updates automatically based on user needs (see Microsoft Corp., 2000).

Hansen et al. (1999) indicated that firms that attempted to straddle the two strategies (i.e., to use about half of each) in their knowledge management efforts have generally failed. Management consulting firms run into serious trouble when they straddle the strategies. When firms use either strategy exclusively, they also run into trouble. The most successful efforts involve about an 80 percent/20 percent split in the strategies. With the practice approach, there is a need to provide some codified knowledge in a repository so that people can access it on an as-needed basis. With the process approach, it is necessary to provide access to knowledge contributors because additional advice and explanations might prove useful or even necessary.

On the other hand, certain highly-skilled, research-oriented industries exhibit traits that require nearly equal efforts with both approaches. For example, Koenig (2001) argued that the pharmaceutical firms in which he has worked indeed require about a 50/50 split. We suspect that industries that require both a lot of engineering effort (i.e., how to create products) and heavy-duty research effort (where a large percentage of research is unusable) would fit the 50/50 hybrid category. Ultimately, any knowledge that is stored in a knowledge repository must be reevaluated; otherwise, the repository will become a knowledge landfill.

For many examples of these strategies in practice, see Gamble and Blackwell (2002) and Martin (2000).

BEST PRACTICES

Best practices are the activities and methods that the most effective organizations use to operate and manage various functions. Chevron, for example, recognizes four levels of best practices (see O'Dell et al., 1998):

1. A good idea that is not yet proven but makes intuitive sense.
2. A good practice, an implemented technique, a methodology, a procedure, or a process that has improved business results.
3. A local best practice, a best approach for all or a large part of the organization based on analysis of hard data. In other words, the scope within the organization of the best practice is identified: Can it be used in a single department or geographical region, or can it be used across the organization or anywhere in between?
4. An industry best practice, similar to the third level but using hard data from industry.

Historically, the first knowledge repositories simply listed best practices and made them available within the firm. Now that knowledge repositories are electronic and Web accessible, they can have wide-ranging impact on the use of knowledge throughout a firm. For example, Raytheon has successfully used best practices to merge three distinct corporate cultures. See O'Dell and Grayson (2003) and O'Dell et al. (2003) for more on best practices.

KNOWLEDGE REPOSITORIES

A **knowledge repository** is neither a database nor a knowledge base in the strictest sense of the terms. Rather, a knowledge repository stores knowledge that is often text based and has very different characteristics. It is also referred to as *organizational knowledge base*. Do not confuse a knowledge repository with the knowledge base of an expert system. They are *very* different mechanisms: A knowledge base of an expert system contains knowledge for solving a specific problem. An organizational knowledge base contains all the organizational knowledge.

Capturing and storing knowledge is the goal for a knowledge repository. The structure of the repository is highly dependent on the types of knowledge it stores. The repository can range from simply a list of frequently asked (and obscure) questions and solutions, to a listing of individuals with their expertise and contact information, to detailed best practices for a large organization.

Developing a Knowledge Repository

Most knowledge repositories are developed using several different storage mechanisms, depending on the types and amount of knowledge to be maintained and used. Each has strengths and weaknesses when used for different purposes within a KMS. Developing a knowledge repository is not an easy task. The most important aspects and difficult issues are making the contribution of knowledge relatively easy for the contributor and determining a good method for cataloging the knowledge. "One of the biggest hurdles in putting a formalized knowledge management structure to collaborative systems is making the structure as seamless as possible," said to Terry Jordan, vice president of marketing for Hyperwave (**hyperwave.com**). "You really have to make the process painless, or you lose all of the knowledge that you are trying to capture because people don't want to have to go through an enormous number of steps" (Zimmermann, 2003b). The users should not be involved in running the storage and retrieval mechanisms of the knowledge repository. Typical development approaches include developing a large-scale Internet-based system or purchasing a formal electronic document management system or a knowledge management suite. The structure

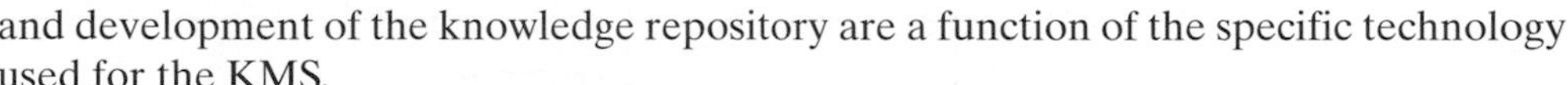

and development of the knowledge repository are a function of the specific technology used for the KMS.

Measuring the success of a knowledge repository system is a tricky affair; is the repository is only as good as the information stored in it and the willingness of the target users to use it. Also, it is critical that the value of the repository be measured or estimated and that it continually be reestimated because the value is sure to fluctuate when knowledge reuse occurs and newer information is collected (see Qian and Bock, 2005).

Section 11.5 Review Questions

1. Define the process approach to knowledge management.
2. Describe the practice approach to knowledge management.
3. Why is a hybrid approach to KM desirable?
4. Describe best practices as they relate to knowledge management.
5. Define *knowledge repository* and describe how to create a knowledge repository.

11.6 INFORMATION TECHNOLOGY (IT) IN KNOWLEDGE MANAGEMENT

The two primary functions of IT in knowledge management are retrieval and communication. IT also extends the reach and range of knowledge use and enhances the speed of knowledge transfer. Networks facilitate collaboration in KM.

THE KMS CYCLE

A functioning KMS follows six steps in a cycle (see Figure 11.2). The reason for the cycle is that knowledge is dynamically refined over time. The knowledge in a good KMS is never finished because the environment changes over time, and the knowledge must be updated to reflect the changes. The cycle works as follows:

1. *Create knowledge.* Knowledge is created as people determine new ways of doing things or develop know-how. Sometimes external knowledge is brought in. Some of these new ways may become best practices.
2. *Capture knowledge.* New knowledge must be identified as valuable and be represented in a reasonable way.
3. *Refine knowledge.* New knowledge must be placed in context so that it is actionable. This is where human insights (i.e., tacit qualities) must be captured along with explicit facts.
4. *Store knowledge.* Useful knowledge must be stored in a reasonable format in a knowledge repository so that others in the organization can access it.
5. *Manage knowledge.* Like a library, a repository must be kept current. It must be reviewed to verify that it is relevant and accurate.
6. *Disseminate knowledge.* Knowledge must be made available in a useful format to anyone in the organization who needs it, anywhere and anytime.

As knowledge is disseminated, individuals develop, create, and identify new knowledge or update old knowledge, which they replenish in the system (see Allard, 2003; and Gaines, 2003).

Knowledge is a resource that is not consumed when used, although it can age. (For example, driving a car in 1900 was different from driving one now, but many of the basic principles still apply.) Knowledge must be updated. Thus, the amount of knowledge grows over time.

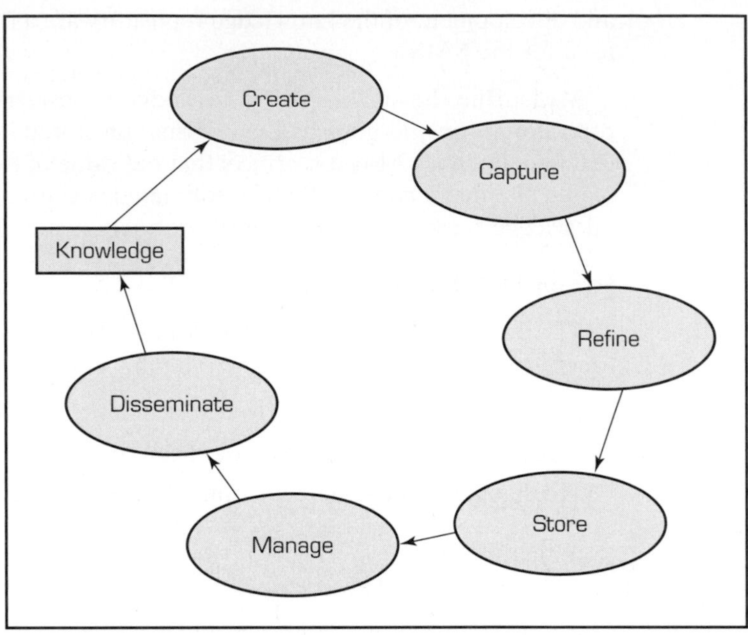

FIGURE 11.2 The Knowledge Management Cycle

COMPONENTS OF KMS

Knowledge management is more a methodology applied to business practices than a technology or a product. Nevertheless, IT is crucial to the success of every KMS. IT enables knowledge management by providing the enterprise architecture on which it is built. KMS are developed using three sets of technologies: communication, collaboration, and storage and retrieval.

Communication technologies allow users to access needed knowledge and to communicate with each other—especially with experts. E-mail, the Internet, corporate intranets, and other Web-based tools provide communication capabilities. Even fax machines and telephones are used for communication, especially when the practice approach to knowledge management is adopted.

Collaboration technologies provide the means to perform groupwork. Groups can work together on common documents at the same time (i.e., synchronous) or at different times (i.e., asynchronous); they can work in the same place or in different places. Collaboration technologies are especially important for members of a community of practice working on knowledge contributions. Other collaborative computing capabilities, such as electronic brainstorming, enhance groupwork, especially for knowledge contribution. Additional forms of groupwork involve experts working with individuals trying to apply their knowledge; this requires collaboration at a fairly high level. Other collaborative computing systems allow an organization to create a virtual space so that individuals can work online anywhere and at any time (see Van de Van, 2005)

Storage and retrieval technologies originally meant using a database management system (DBMS) to store and manage knowledge. This worked reasonably well in the early days for storing and managing most explicit knowledge—and even explicit knowledge about tacit knowledge. However, capturing, storing, and managing tacit knowledge usually requires a different set of tools. Electronic document management systems and

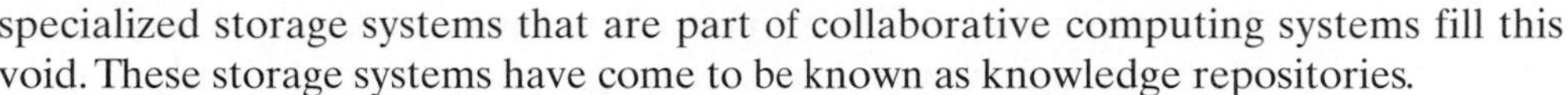

specialized storage systems that are part of collaborative computing systems fill this void. These storage systems have come to be known as knowledge repositories.

We describe the relationship between these knowledge management technologies and the Web in Table 11.2.

TECHNOLOGIES THAT SUPPORT KNOWLEDGE MANAGEMENT

Several technologies have contributed to significant advances in knowledge management tools. Artificial intelligence, intelligent agents, knowledge discovery in databases, and Extensible Markup Language (XML) are examples of technologies that enable advanced functionality of modern KMS and form the basis for future innovations in the knowledge management field. See Gray and Tehrani (2003), Malafsky (2003), and O'Leary (2003) for descriptions of how many of these technologies are used in KMS.

Artificial Intelligence

In the definition of knowledge management, *artificial intelligence (AI)* is rarely mentioned. However, practically speaking, AI methods and tools are embedded in a number of KMS, either by vendors or by system developers. AI methods can assist in identifying

TABLE 11.2 Knowledge Management Technologies and Web Impacts

Knowledge Management	*Web Impacts*	*Impacts on the Web*
Communication	Consistent, friendly graphical user interface (GUI) for client units Improved communication tools Convenient, fast access to knowledge and knowledgeable individuals Direct access to knowledge on servers	Knowledge captured and shared is used in improving communication, communication management, and communication technologies.
Collaboration	Improved collaboration tools Enables anywhere/anytime collaboration Enables collaboration between companies, customers, and vendors Enables document sharing Improved, fast collaboration and links to knowledge sources Makes audio- and videoconferencing a reality, especially for individuals not using a local area network	Knowledge captured and shared is used in improving collaboration, collaboration management, and collaboration technologies (i.e., GSS).
Storage and retrieval	Consistent, friendly GUI for clients Servers provide for efficient and effective storage and retrieval of knowledge	Knowledge captured and shared is utilized in improving data storage and retrieval systems, database management/knowledge repository management, and database and knowledge repository technologies.

expertise, eliciting knowledge automatically and semi-automatically, interfacing through natural language processing, and intelligently searching through intelligent agents. AI methods—notably expert systems, neural networks, fuzzy logic, and intelligent agents—are used in KMS to do the following:

- Assist in and enhance searching knowledge (e.g., intelligent agents in Web searches)
- Help establish knowledge profiles of individuals and groups
- Help determine the relative importance of knowledge when it is contributed to and accessed from the knowledge repository
- Scan e-mail, documents, and databases to perform knowledge discovery, determine meaningful relationships, glean knowledge, or induce rules for expert systems
- Identify patterns in data (usually through neural networks)
- Forecast future results by using existing knowledge
- Provide advice directly from knowledge by using neural networks or expert systems
- Provide a natural language or voice command–driven user interface for a KMS

Intelligent Agents

Intelligent agents are software systems that learn how users work and provide assistance in their daily tasks. There are other kinds of intelligent agents as well (see Chapter 14). Intelligent agents can help in KMS in a number of ways. Typically, they are used to elicit and identify knowledge. The following are some examples:

- IBM (**ibm.com**) offers an intelligent data mining family, including Intelligent Decision Server (IDS), for finding and analyzing massive amounts of enterprise data.
- Gentia (Planning Sciences International, **gentia.com**) uses intelligent agents to facilitate data mining with Web access and data warehouse facilities.

Combining intelligent agents with enterprise knowledge portals is a powerful technique that can deliver to users exactly what they need to perform their tasks. The intelligent agent learns what the user prefers to see and how the user organizes it. Then the intelligent agent takes over to provide that information at the desktop, just as a good administrative assistant would.

Knowledge Discovery in Databases

Knowledge discovery in databases (KDD) is a process used to search for and extract useful information from volumes of documents and data. It includes tasks such as knowledge extraction, data archaeology, data exploration, data pattern processing, data dredging, and information harvesting. All these activities are conducted automatically and allow quick discovery, even by nonprogrammers. Data and document mining is ideal for eliciting knowledge from databases, documents, e-mail, and so on. Data are often buried deep within very large databases, data warehouses, text documents, or knowledge repositories, all of which may contain data, information, and knowledge gathered over many years. (For more on data mining, see Chapter 7.)

AI methods are useful data mining tools that include automated knowledge elicitation from other sources. Intelligent data mining discovers information within databases, data warehouses, and knowledge repositories that queries and reports cannot effectively reveal. Data mining tools find patterns in data and may even (automatically) infer rules from them. Patterns and rules can be used to guide decision making and forecast the effects of decisions. KDD can also be used to identify the meaning of data or text, using knowledge management tools that scan documents and e-mail to build an expertise profile of a firm's employees. *Data mining* can speed up analysis by providing needed knowledge.

Extending the role of data mining and knowledge discovery techniques for knowledge externalization, Bolloju et al. (2002) proposed a framework for integrating knowledge management into enterprise environments for next-generation decision support systems (DSS). Their framework, shown in Figure 11.3, includes model marts and model warehouses. **Model marts** and **model warehouses** for models are analogous to data marts and data warehouses for data (refer to Chapter 7). They act as repositories of knowledge created by using knowledge-discovery techniques on past decision instances stored in data marts and data warehouses. The model marts and model warehouses capture operational and historical decision models, similar to the data in data marts and data warehouses. For example, a model mart can store decision rules corresponding to problem solving knowledge of different decision makers in a particular domain, such as loan approvals in a banking environment.

This integrated framework accommodates different types of knowledge transformations. Systems built around this framework are expected to enhance the quality of support provided to decision makers; support knowledge management functions such as acquisition, creation, exploitation, and accumulation; facilitate discovery of trends and patterns in the accumulated knowledge; and provide means for building up organizational memory.

Extensible Markup Language (XML)

Extensible Markup Language (XML) enables standardized representations of data structures so that data can be processed appropriately by heterogeneous systems without case-by-case programming. This method suits e-commerce applications and supply-chain management (SCM) systems that operate across enterprise boundaries. XML can not only automate processes and reduce paperwork, it can also unite business partners and supply chains for better collaboration and knowledge transfer. XML-based messages can

FIGURE 11.3 Framework for Integrating Decision Support and Knowledge Management Systems

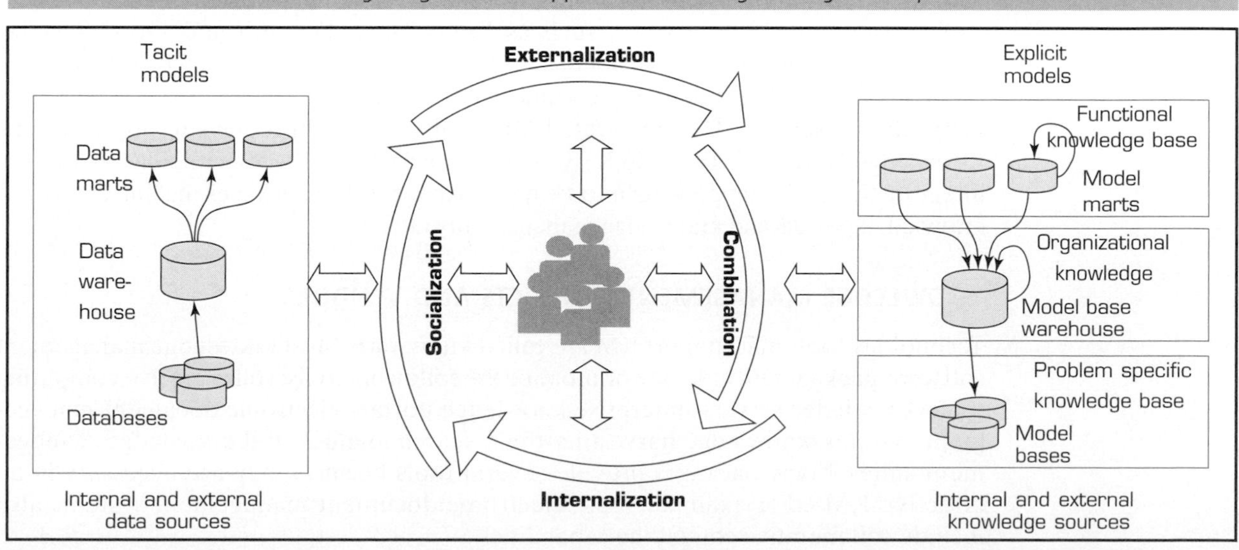

Source: N. Bolloju, M. Khalita, and E. Turban, "Integrating Knowledge Management into Enterprise Environments for the Next Generation of Decision Support," *Decision Support Systems*, Vol. 33, June 2002.

be taken from back-end repositories and fed out through the portal interface and back again. A portal that uses XML allows the company to communicate better with its customers, linking them in a virtual demand chain where changes in customer requirements are immediately reflected in production plans. Wide adoption of XML can pretty much solve the problem of integrating data from disparate sources. Due to its potential to tremendously simplify systems integration, XML may become the universal language that all portal vendors embrace (see Ruber, 2001).

Vendors are moving quickly to integrate the advantages offered by XML standards. For example, Interwoven's content management software, Teamsite, now fully supports XML, enabling organizations to provide content available in any format across the enterprise. Sequoia Software's XML Portal Server (XPS) and Hummingbird's Enterprise Portal Suite also support the XML standard for data exchange.

Section 11.6 Review Questions

1. Describe the KMS cycle.
2. List and describe the components of KMS.
3. Describe how AI and intelligent agents support knowledge management.
4. Relate XML to knowledge management and to knowledge portals.

11.7 KNOWLEDGE MANAGEMENT SYSTEMS IMPLEMENTATION

The challenge with KMS is to identify and integrate the three essential components—communication technologies, collaboration technologies, and storage and retrieval technologies—to meet the knowledge management needs of an organization. The earliest KMS were developed with networked technology (i.e., intranets), collaborative computing tools (i.e., groupware), and databases (for the knowledge repository). They were constructed from a variety of off-the-shelf IT components. Many organizations, especially large management consulting firms such as Accenture and J.D. Edwards, developed their knowledge architecture with a set of tools that provided the three technology types. Collaborative computing suites such as Lotus Notes/Domino and GroupSystems OnLine provide many KMS capabilities. Other systems were developed by integrating a set of tools from a single or multiple vendors. For example, J.D. Edwards (an Oracle company) used a set of loosely integrated Microsoft tools and products to implement its Knowledge Garden KMS, as did KPMG. In the early 2000s, KMS technology evolved to integrate the three components into a single package. These packages include enterprise knowledge portals and knowledge management suites

KNOWLEDGE MANAGEMENT PRODUCTS AND VENDORS

Technology tools that support KM are called **knowware**. Most knowledge management software packages include one or more of the following tools: collaborative computing tools, knowledge servers, enterprise knowledge portals, electronic document management systems, knowledge harvesting tools, search engines, and knowledge management suites. Many packages provide several tools because they are necessary in an effective KMS. For example, most electronic document management systems also include collaborative computing capabilities.

KMS can be purchased in whole or in part from one of numerous software development companies and enterprise information system (EIS) vendors, they can be

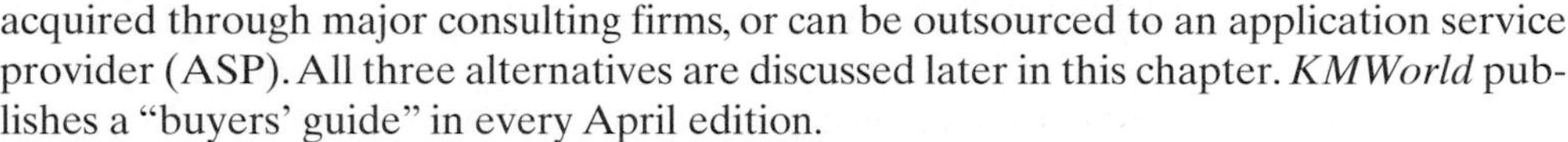

acquired through major consulting firms, or can be outsourced to an application service provider (ASP). All three alternatives are discussed later in this chapter. *KMWorld* publishes a "buyers' guide" in every April edition.

Software Development Companies and EIS Vendors

Software development companies and EIS vendors offer numerous knowledge management packages, from individual tools to comprehensive knowledge management suites. The variety of knowware that is readily available on the market allows companies to find tools that meet their unique KM needs. We next review some software packages and their vendors in each of the seven knowware categories identified earlier.

Collaborative Computing Tools Collaboration tools, or groupware, were the first tools used to enhance tacit knowledge transfer within an organization. One of the earliest collaborative computing systems, GroupSystems, provides many of the tools that support groupwork, including tools for electronic brainstorming and idea categorization. Lotus Notes/Domino provides an enterprisewide collaborative environment. Other collaboration tools include MeetingPlace (Latitude), QuickPlace (Lotus Development Corp.), eRoom (eRoom Technology Inc.), Groove Networks (**groove.net**), and Microsoft Office Live Meeting (Microsoft) For details, see Chapter 10.

Knowledge Servers A knowledge server contains the main knowledge management software, including the knowledge repository, and provides access to other knowledge, information, and data. Examples of knowledge servers include the Hummingbird Knowledge Server, the Intraspect Software Knowledge Server, the Hyperwave Information Server, the Sequoia Software XML Portal Server, and Autonomy's Intelligent Data Operating Layer (IDOL) Server. Autonomy's IDOL Server connects people to content, content to content, and people to people through modules that enable organizations to integrate various personalization, collaboration, and retrieval features. The server provides a knowledge repository—a central location for searching and accessing information from many sources, such as the Internet, corporate intranets, databases, and file systems—thereby enabling the efficient distribution of time-sensitive information. The server seamlessly extends and integrates with the company's e-business suite, allowing rapid deployment applications that span the enterprise and can even leverage AI-assisted technology to harvest knowledge assets.

Enterprise Knowledge Portals **Enterprise knowledge portals (EKP)** are the doorways into many KMS. They have evolved from the concepts underlying EIS, GSS, Web browsers, and DBMS. Using EKP is an ideal way to configure a KMS. Most EKP combine data integration, reporting mechanisms, and collaboration, while a server handles document and knowledge management. An enterprise information portal is a virtual place on a network of online users. The portal aggregates each user's total information needs: data and documents, e-mail, Web links and queries, dynamic feeds from the network, and shared calendars and task lists.

When enterprise information portals first entered the market, they did not contain knowledge management features. Now most do; hence they are now called EKP. Leading portal vendors include Autonomy, Corechange, DataChannel, Dataware, Epicentric, Glyphica, Intraspect, Hummingbird, InXight, KnowledgeTrack, IBM/Lotus, Knowmadic, OpenText, Plumtree, Portera, Sequoia Software, Verity, and Viador. Database vendors such as Microsoft, Oracle, and Sybase also sell knowledge portals.

The KnowledgeTrack Knowledge Center offers integrated business-to-business (B2B) functions and can scale from dot-coms to large enterprises. Knowledge Center can be built into the enterprise architecture instead of simply sitting on top, the way most intranet portals do. The Knowledge Center integrates with external data sources, including enterprise resource planning (ERP), online analytical processing (OLAP), and customer relationship management (CRM) systems. IT also supports communities of practice and enables them for large-project management, allowing information to be shared among all the extended enterprise value chains. (See Chapter 17, an online chapter.)

Hyperwave's Hyperwave Information Portal (HIP) aggregates information from disparate sources and features dynamic link management, which verifies the quality of the link and hides links to unauthorized content. HIP manages connections between information sources and makes structured and unstructured corporate information searchable via a standard browser.

In Application Case 11.3, we describe how Smith Lyons, a Canadian law firm, developed a successful EKP. See Levinson (2002) for an example of how a university used a portal to connect students, faculty, staff, alumni, and businesses to share services, research, and applications. For more on portals, see Baalen et al. (2005), Firestone (2003), Roberts-Witt (2000), Zhang (2006), Zimmermann (2002).

Application Case 11.3

Portal Opens the Door to Legal Knowledge

Richard Van Dyk, CIO of Smith Lyons (**smithlyons.com**), a Toronto-based international law firm, knew exactly what kind of system he was looking for to manage the firm's documents and knowledge. He had spent a year defining his requirements and had composed a complex flowchart on his whiteboard. Smith Lyons wanted to take thousands of pieces of information, give people different views into that information, and have a high level of link management. Van Dyk considered document management tools to be too inflexible for the way lawyers practice law. "We needed a flexible environment that we could massage and manipulate and that would allow people to continue working as they have," said Van Dyk.

"Lawyers are basically document generators," he said. "Due to time constraints, they spend more time collecting documents than organizing them." Because the firm's 550 attorneys and support specialists each had a distinct working methodology, often reflecting the requirements of a specific area of practice, Van Dyk knew they would resent having a rigid system they could not easily personalize.

The profusion of document management, knowledge management, and portal systems makes finding the right product difficult. Each has strengths and weaknesses. Organizations coming from a document-centric perspective, like Smith Lyons, need to organize and manage content at the back end while developing highly customized individual user interfaces at the front end.

The solution that best met Van Dyk's criteria was the Hyperwave Information Portal from Hyperwave Information Management (**hyperwave.com**). "What I liked about Hyperwave's portal environment was that as soon as we installed it, we had a framework to begin knowledge mapping—tagging and indexing documents by subject and key words and phrases—and for building the database structures in our repositories," said Van Dyk. The firm had definite ideas on how to structure templates and specific pieces of information that are unique to a legal practice. These issues included myriad legal forms and documents generated by the proprietary software applications used for different practice areas.

Once the portal was set up, developers at Smith Lyons began to customize the views for each desktop PC by creating wizards that connect users to their own secure information areas and to intranet pages containing company activity information. In addition, the company is developing an extranet on which lawyers will be able to post status reports to clients and deliver confidential documents and contracts.

"That flexibility in building our DM portal allows our lawyers and specialists to be incredibly specific in their searches," said Van Dyk. Lawyers can also share their accumulated knowledge more easily with colleagues in the same practice areas by referencing legal citations, court decisions, and winning strategies that have worked in the past.

Sources: Compiled from P. Ruber, "Finding the Right Balance: A Canadian Law Firm Interrogated Its Requirements before Selecting a Portal Solution," *Knowledge Management*, September 2000; and *Smith Lyons Chooses Hyperwave as Its Portal to Legal Knowledge*, June 9, 2000, **hyperwave.com/e/news/pr16.html** (accessed April 2006).

Electronic Document Management (EDM) **Electronic document management (EDM)** systems use the document in electronic form as the collaborative focus of work. EDM systems allow users to access needed documents, generally via a Web browser over a corporate intranet. EDM systems enable organizations to better manage documents and workflow for smoother operations. They also allow collaboration on document creation and revision.

Many KMS use an EDM system as the knowledge repository. There is a natural fit in terms of the purpose and benefits of the two. Pfizer uses a large-scale document management system to handle the equivalent of truckloads of paper documents of drug approval applications passed between Pfizer and the Food & Drug Administration (FDA), its regulating agency. This EDM system dramatically cut the time required for FDA submission and review, making Pfizer more competitive in getting new and effective drugs to market (Blodgett, 2000).

Systems such as DocuShare (Xerox Corporation) and Lotus Notes (Lotus Development Corporation) allow direct collaboration on a common document. Some other EDM systems include EDMS (Documentum, Inc.), Enterprise Work Management (Eastman Software, Inc.), FYI (Identitech), The Discovery Suite (FileNet Corp.), Livelink (Open Text Corp.), PageKeeper Pro (Caere Corp.), Pagis Pro (ScanSoft, Inc.), Xpedio (IntraNet Solutions), and CaseCentral.com (Document Repository, Inc.).

A new approach to EDM, called **content management systems (CMSs)**, is changing the way documents and their content are managed. A CMS produces dynamic versions of documents and automatically maintains the "current" set for use at the enterprise level. With the explosion of Web-based materials, organizations need a mechanism to provide content that is consistent and accurate across the enterprise. EDM systems, EKP, and other CMS fill that need. The goal is to provide large numbers of knowledge workers with access to large amounts of unstructured text (see Sullivan, 2001). An IDC survey of attendees at the KMWorld 2001 Conference and Exposition indicated that 63 percent of all respondents had or planned to implement CMS, while 59 percent rated CMS as very to critically important (see Feldman, 2002). Also see Bankes (2003) and Lamont (2003b).

A subset of CMS is business rules management. New software tools and systems, such as Ilog JRules and Blaze Advisor, have been developed to handle these smaller chunks of content.

Knowledge Harvesting Tools Tools for capturing knowledge unobtrusively are helpful because they allow a knowledge contributor to be minimally (or not at all) involved in the knowledge-harvesting efforts. Embedding this type of tool in a KMS is an ideal approach to knowledge capture. Tacit Knowledge Systems's Knowledge-mail is an expertise-location software package that analyzes users' outgoing e-mail to parse subject expertise. It maintains a directory of expertise and offers ways to contact experts while maintaining privacy controls for them. Autonomy's ActiveKnowledge performs a similar analysis on e-mail and other standard document types. Intraspect Software's Knowledge Server monitors an organization's group memory; captures the context of its use, such as who used it, when, for what, how it was combined with other information, and what people said about it; and then makes the information available for sharing and reuse. KnowledgeX by KnowledgeX, Inc., and a number of other products provide similar functionality.

Search Engines Search engines perform one of the essential functions of knowledge management—locating and retrieving necessary documents from vast collections accumulated in corporate repositories. Companies such as Google, Verity, and Inktomi offer a wide selection of search engines capable of indexing and cataloging files in various formats as well as of retrieving and prioritizing relevant documents in response to user queries.

Knowledge Management Suites Knowledge management suites are complete knowledge management solutions out-of-the-box. They integrate the communications, collaboration, and storage technologies into a single convenient package. A knowledge management suite must access internal databases and other external knowledge sources, so some integration is required to make the software truly functional. IBM/Lotus offers an extensive range of knowledge management products, including the Domino platform, QuickPlace and Sametime, Discovery Server and Learning Space, and the WebSphere portal. See Application Case 11.4 to learn how Commerce Bank implemented a KMS based on the IBM/Lotus platform. Several vendors also provide fairly comprehensive sets of tools for knowledge management initiatives, including Dataware Knowledge Management Suite and KnowledgeX by KnowledgeX, Inc. Autonomy Knowledge Management Suite offers document categorization and workflow integration. Microsoft provides central components of knowledge management solutions and is working on developing an encompassing knowledge management framework. Some EIS vendors, such as SAP, PeopleSoft, and Oracle, are developing knowledge management–related technologies as a platform for business applications. Siebel Systems is repositioning itself as a business-to-employee knowledge management platform. Using a knowledge management suite is a powerful approach to developing a KMS because it has one user interface and one data repository, and it is from one vendor.

Application Case 11.4

Knowledge Management: You Can Bank on It at Commerce Bank

Commerce Bank is a $15.4 billion financial institution that is quickly growing to become a dominant player in the financial services market of Philadelphia and Southern New Jersey. During its 30 years of existence, it has developed a network of 214 branches and made ambitious plans for continuous growth. Commerce Bank calls itself "America's Most Convenient Bank." It lives up to that name by maintaining a strong banking network and by empowering each branch to make business decisions in an effort to better meet the needs of its customers.

While undergoing explosive growth, Commerce Bank encouraged its associates to learn all about its customers and the right ways to service them. However, the company realized that its most important asset, knowledge, was locked away in the file cabinets and in the heads of its associates. To support this initiative, Commerce Bank needed to tap into that knowledge and find a way to train employees consistently and conveniently across the entire branch network.

The first step for new employees is Commerce University, a boot camp where they are instilled with the fundamentals of customer service. But the program covers only a few of the range of issues that an associate might encounter.

The need for knowledge management at Commerce Bank was apparent. Jack Allison, vice president of systems development, said, "We had folks in administration that could spend 70 percent of their time answering calls and clarifying answers for branches. At times, we could wait weeks or months for the right answer to certain questions. Knowing that training may not give answers for every scenario, we needed to give associates a tool that could help them find any answer to any topic at any time. We have so many regulations and products; we needed a way to give our employees all the knowledge to process these."

Commerce bank envisioned a solution—a workflow-based KMS that could provide instant answers to questions for the bank's employees and online customers. To make this vision a reality, Commerce chose to develop a system based on IBM's Lotus Notes, which the bank has been using since 1995. Using IBM's Domino server, the Lotus Notes client, and an application development tool

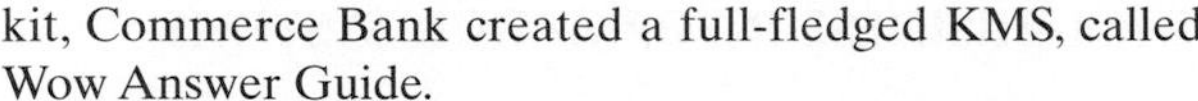

kit, Commerce Bank created a full-fledged KMS, called Wow Answer Guide.

Introduced in 2000, Wow Answer Guide provides a central repository of knowledge about all bank transactions, it helps employees learn a process and respond to customer inquirie, and stores information electronically. In addition, the system allows employees to register for the bank's continuing education courses.

The complete Wow Answer Guide contains more than 400 applications, and Commerce plans to add even more, such as a CRM system. The flexibility of the platform simplifies the application-development process and allows the addition of new features and the expansion of functionality with minimal investments of time and effort.

"[The Wow Answer Guide] is especially good for the green associate or veteran who is still learning how to process a new product," said Allison. "We don't want our associates on a scavenger hunt to get the correct information."

Commerce Bank realized that knowledge management would be beneficial not only to the bank's employees but also to its clients. "We wanted to put information in our customers' hands so they could conduct [online] transactions with confidence," said Allison. In the summer of 2000, Commerce Bank deployed a new version of Wow Answer Guide that empowered the bank's online customers.

Knowledge management at Commerce Bank proved to be an effective investment. According to Allison, the application has saved the bank $20,000 per week, or approximately $1 million a year. In fact, the bank achieved an ROI within a month of launching Wow Answer Guide.

By drawing on the power of the Domino platform, Commerce Bank created workflow-based applications that streamline internal knowledge sharing and route data and information to the appropriate employees within the organization. This dramatically reduces the completion time for approval-intensive transactions, improves the bank's capacity, and minimizes labor costs.

Sources: Adapted from D. Amato-McCoy, "Commerce Bank Manages Knowledge Profitably," *Bank Systems & Technology*, January 2003; and *Knowledge Infusion Helps Commerce Bank Experience Big Pay Off with Talent Management Initiative*, October 19, 2005, **onlypunjab.com/money/fullstory-insight-money+finance-newsID-9368.html** (accessed April 2006).

Knowledge Management Consulting Firms

All the major consulting firms (e.g., Accenture, Cap Gemini Ernst & Young) have massive internal knowledge management initiatives. Usually, these become products after they succeed internally and provide assistance in establishing KMS and measuring their effectiveness. Consulting firms also provide some direct, out-of-the-box proprietary systems for vertical markets. Most of the major management consulting firms define their knowledge management offerings as services. For more on consulting firm activities and products, see McDonald and Shand (2000).

Knowledge Management ASPs

ASPs have evolved as a form of KMS outsourcing on the Web. There are many ASPs for e-commerce on the market. For example, Communispace is a high-level ASP collaboration system that focuses on connecting people to people (not just people to documents) to achieve specific objectives, regardless of geographic, time, and organizational barriers. As a hosted ASP solution, Communispace is easy to rapidly deploy within organizations. Unlike conventional KMS that organize data and documents or chat rooms, where people simply swap information, Communispace contains a rich assortment of interactions, activities, and tools that connect people to the colleagues who can best help them make decisions, solve problems, and learn quickly. Communispace is designed to build trust online; it attempts to make a community self-conscious about taking responsibility for its actions and knowledge. Its climate component helps participants measure and understand how people are feeling about the community. Its Virtual Café gives dispersed employees a way to meet and learn about each other through pictures and profiles.

A recent trend among ASPs is to offer a complete KM solution, including a knowledge management suite and the consulting to set it up, as Communispace does.

INTEGRATION OF KMS WITH OTHER BUSINESS INFORMATION SYSTEMS

Because a KMS is an enterprise system, it must be integrated with other enterprise and information systems in an organization. Obviously, when it is designed and developed, it cannot be perceived as an add-on application. It must be truly integrated into other systems. Through the structure of the organizational culture (which is changed, if necessary), a KMS and its activities can be directly integrated into a firm's business processes. For example, a group involved in customer support can capture its knowledge to provide help on customers' difficult problems. In this case, help-desk software would be one type of package to integrate into a KMS, especially into the knowledge repository.

Because a KMS can be developed on a knowledge platform/server consisting of communication, collaboration, and storage technologies, and because most firms already have many such tools and technologies in place, it is often possible to develop a KMS in the organization's existing tools (e.g., Lotus Notes/Domino). Or an EKP can provide universal access and an interface into all of an individual's relevant corporate information and knowledge. In this case, the KMS effort would provide the linkage for everyone into the entire EIS.

Integration of KMS with DSS/BI Systems

KMS typically do not involve running models to solve problems. This is typically done in DSS/BI systems. However, because a KMS provides help in solving problems by applying knowledge, part of the solution may involve running models. A KMS can integrate into a set of models and data, and it can activate them if a specific problem calls for it. Also, the know-how and best practice application of models can be stored in a KMS.

Integration of KMS with AI

KM has a natural relationship with AI methods and software, although knowledge management, strictly speaking, is not an artificial intelligence method. There are a number of ways KM and AI can integrate. For example, if the knowledge stored in a KMS is to be represented and used as a sequence of if-then-else rules, an expert system becomes part of the KMS (see Rasmus, 2000). An expert system could also assist a user in identifying how to apply a chunk of knowledge in the KMS. Natural language processing assists the computer in understanding what a user is searching for. Artificial neural networks help to understand text to determine the applicability of a specific chunk of knowledge as it applies to a particular problem. They are also used to enhance search engines. The most common integration of AI and KM is in identifying and classifying expertise by examining e-mail messages and documents. These include AI-based tools, such as ActiveNet and Knowledge-mail from Tacit Software, Inc. (**tacit.com**), and Categorizer from Inxight Software (**inxight.com**).

Much work is being done in the field of AI relating to knowledge engineering; tacit-to-explicit knowledge transfer; and knowledge identification, understanding, and dissemination. Companies are attempting to realign these technologies and the resultant products with knowledge management. The AI technologies most often integrated with KM are intelligent agents, expert systems, neural networks, and fuzzy logic. Several specific methods and tools are described earlier in this chapter.

Integration of KMS with Databases and Information Systems

Because a KMS uses a knowledge repository, sometimes constructed out of a database system or an EDM system, it can automatically integrate to this part of the firm's information system. As data and information updates are made, the KMS can use them. As described earlier in this chapter, KMS also attempt to glean knowledge from documents and databases through AI methods, in a process known as KDD. This knowledge is then represented textually within the knowledge repository described earlier.

Integration of KMS with CRM Systems

CRM systems help users in dealing with customers (see Chapter 17, an online chapter). One aspect is the help-desk notion described earlier. But CRM goes much deeper than that. It can develop usable profiles of customers and predict their needs so that an organization can increase sales and better serve its clients. A KMS can certainly provide tacit knowledge to people who use CRM directly in working with customers.

Integration with SCM Systems

The supply chain is often considered to be the logistics end of a business. If products do not move through the organization and go out the door, the firm will fail. It is therefore important to optimize the supply chain and manage it properly. A new set of software called *SCM systems* attempts to do so (see Chapter 17, an online chapter). SCM can benefit from integration with KMS because there are many issues and problems in the supply chain that require the company to combine tacit and explicit knowledge. Accessing such knowledge directly improves supply-chain performance.

Integration of KMS with Corporate Intranets and Extranets

Communication and collaboration tools and technologies are necessary for KMS to function. A KMS is not simply integrated with the technology of intranets and extranets; it is typically developed on them as the communications platform. Extranets are specifically designed to enhance the collaboration of a firm with its suppliers and sometimes with customers. If a firm can integrate its KMS into its intranets and extranets, not only will knowledge flow more freely, both from a contributor and to a user (either directly or through a knowledge repository), but the firm can also capture knowledge directly, with little user involvement, and can deliver it when the system thinks that a user needs knowledge.

Section 11.7 Review Questions

1. Define *knowware*.
2. Describe the major categories of knowledge management tools.
3. Define *EKP*.
4. Define *EDM* and relate it to knowledge management and to CMS.
5. Describe tools for knowledge harvesting.
6. List the major systems that are frequently integrated with KMS.

11.8 ROLES OF PEOPLE IN KNOWLEDGE MANAGEMENT

Managing a KMS requires great effort. As with any other IT, getting it started, implemented, and deployed requires a champion's effort. Many issues of management, people, and culture must be considered to make a KMS a success. In this section, we address those issues. Managing the knowledge repository typically requires a full-time staff (similar to a reference library staff). This staff examines, structures, filters, catalogs, and stores knowledge so that it is meaningful and can be accessed by the people who need it.

The staff assists individuals in searching for knowledge and performs environmental scanning: If they identify specific knowledge that an employee or a client might need, they send it directly to whoever needs it, thus adding value to the organization. (This is standard procedure for Accenture knowledge management personnel.) Finally, the knowledge repository staff may create communities of practice (see the End of Chapter Application Case) to gather individuals with common knowledge areas to identify, filter, extract, and contribute knowledge to a knowledge repository.

Most of the issues concerning the success, implementation, and effective use of a KMS are people issues. And because a KMS is an enterprisewide effort, many people are involved. They include the chief knowledge officer (CKO), the CEO, the other officers and managers of the organization, members and leaders of communities of practice, KMS developers, and KMS staff. Each person or group has an important role in either the development, management, or use of a KMS. By far, the CKO has the most visible role in a KMS effort, but the system cannot succeed unless the roles of all the players are established and understood. And the team must consist of the right people, possessing the appropriate level of experience, to take on the various roles (see Riege, 2005).

THE CHIEF KNOWLEDGE OFFICER

Knowledge management projects that involve establishing a knowledge environment conducive to the transfer, creation, or use of knowledge attempt to build cultural receptivity. These attempts are centered on changing the behavior of the firm to embrace the use of knowledge management. Behavior-centric projects require a high degree of support and participation from the senior management of the organization to facilitate their implementation. Most firms developing KMS have created a knowledge management officer, a **chief knowledge officer (CKO)**, at the senior level. The objectives of the CKO's role are to maximize the firm's knowledge assets, design and implement KM strategies, effectively exchange knowledge assets internally and externally, and promote system use. The CKO is responsible for developing processes that facilitate knowledge transfer (see Adams, 2001).

According to Duffy (1998), a CKO must do the following:

- Set knowledge management strategic priorities
- Establish a knowledge repository of best practices
- Gain a commitment from senior executives to support a learning environment
- Teach information seekers how to ask better and smarter questions
- Establish a process for managing intellectual assets
- Obtain customer satisfaction information in near real-time
- Globalize knowledge management

The CKO is responsible for defining the area of knowledge within the firm that will be the focal point, based on the mission and objectives of the firm (see Davis, 1998). The CKO is responsible for standardizing the enterprisewide vocabulary and controlling the knowledge directory. This is critical in areas that must share knowledge across departments, to ensure uniformity. The CKO must get a handle on the company's repositories of research, resources, and expertise, including where they are stored and who manages and accesses them (e.g., perform a knowledge audit). Then the CKO must encourage pollination among disparate workgroups with complementary resources (see McKeen and Staples, 2003).

The CKO is responsible for creating an infrastructure and cultural environment for knowledge sharing. He or she must assign or identify (and encourage/motivate) the *knowledge champions* within the business units. The CKO's job is to manage the

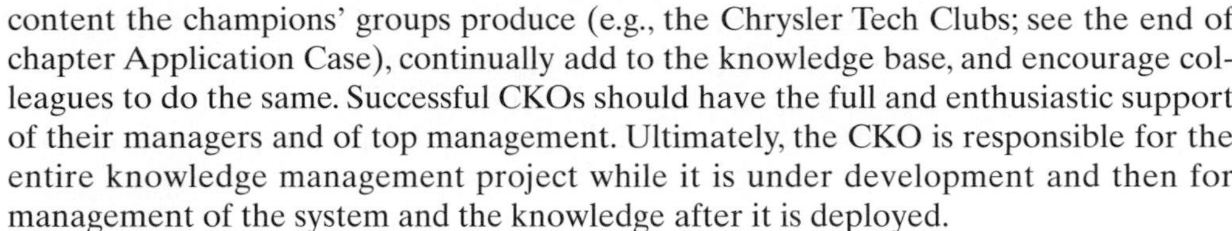

content the champions' groups produce (e.g., the Chrysler Tech Clubs; see the end of chapter Application Case), continually add to the knowledge base, and encourage colleagues to do the same. Successful CKOs should have the full and enthusiastic support of their managers and of top management. Ultimately, the CKO is responsible for the entire knowledge management project while it is under development and then for management of the system and the knowledge after it is deployed.

A CKO needs a range of skills to make knowledge management initiatives succeed. These attributes are indispensable, according to CKOs and consultants (see Flash, 2001a):

- Interpersonal communication skills to convince employees to adopt cultural changes
- Leadership skills to convey the knowledge management vision and passion for it
- Business acumen to relate knowledge management efforts to efficiency and profitability
- Strategic thinking skills to relate knowledge management efforts to larger goals
- Collaboration skills to work with various departments and persuade them to work together
- The ability to institute effective educational programs
- An understanding of IT and its role in advancing knowledge management

THE CEO, OFFICERS, AND MANAGERS OF THE ORGANIZATION

Briefly, the CEO is responsible for championing a knowledge management effort. He or she must ensure that a competent and capable CKO is found and that the CKO can obtain all the resources (including access to people with knowledge sources) needed to make the project a success. The CEO must also gain organization-wide support for contributions to and use of the KMS. The CEO must also prepare the organization for the cultural changes that are about to occur. Support is the critical responsibility of the CEO. The CEO is the primary change agent of the organization (see Flash, 2001b).

The officers generally must make available to the CKO the resources needed to get the job done. The chief financial officer (CFO) must ensure that the financial resources are available. The chief operating officer (COO) must ensure that people begin to embed knowledge management practices into their daily work processes. There is a special relationship between the CKO and chief information officer (CIO). Usually, the CIO is responsible for the IT vision of the organization and for the IT architecture, including databases and other potential knowledge sources. The CIO must cooperate with the CKO in making these resources available. KMS are expensive propositions, and it is wise to use existing systems if they are available and capable.

Managers must also support the knowledge management effort and provide access to sources of knowledge. In many KMS, managers are an integral part of the communities of practice.

COMMUNITIES OF PRACTICE

The success of many KMS has been attributed to the active involvement of the people who contribute to and benefit from using the knowledge. Consequently, communities of practice have appeared within organizations that are serious about their knowledge management efforts. A **community of practice (COP)** is a group of people in an organization with a common professional interest. Ideally, all the KMS users should each be in at least one COP. Properly creating and nurturing COP is one key to KMS success (see Liedtka, 2002; and Wenger, 2002).

COP are where the organizational culture shift really happens when developing and deploying KMS. A supportive culture must be developed for a KMS to succeed (see Wenger, 2002; and Wenger et al., 2002). In Application Case 11.5, we describe how Xerox Corp. successfully generated improved practices and cost savings through COP.

Application Case 11.5

Online Knowledge Sharing at Xerox

In the early 1990s, Xerox Corporation had a nationwide database that contained information that could be used to fix its copiers, fax machines, and high-speed printers. However, the information was not readily available to the 25,000 service and field employees and engineers who repaired the machines at customer sites. Satisfaction with customer service was low.

The engineers at Xerox's Palo Alto Research Center (PARC) spent six months observing repair personnel, watching how they worked, noting what their frustrations were, and identifying what kind of information they needed. They determined that the repair personnel needed to share their knowledge with their peers. PARC engineers developed Eureka, an online knowledge-sharing system created to assist the service people with time-consuming and complicated repair problems.

Ray Everett, program manager for Eureka, described the powerful impact the program has had on service, "You went from not knowing how to fix something to being able to get the answer instantly. Even better, you could share any solutions you found with your peers around the globe within a day, as opposed to the several weeks it used to take."

Since its inception in 1996, Eureka has been implemented in 71 countries. It has helped solve 350,000 problems and has saved \$3 to \$4 million in parts and labor every year. The system is available to all of Xerox's service engineers via notebook computers and is accessed through the Internet. Product fixes (50,000 of them), documentation updates, and product-update bulletins are delivered over the Web. Individual service employees and engineers can enter into the system possible new solutions to problems. A solution appears in Eureka, giving credit to the author and noting the service employee's country of origin. An alert about a new solution is sent to validators who test the solution; if it works consistently, it is sent to all engineers via Eureka updates.

Since 2004, Eureka has been designed to work over wireless Internet connections. Eureka is a constantly evolving and growing system that connects and shares the collective knowledge of Xerox's service force.

One of Eureka's guiding principles is, "We should never create the same solution twice. If a solution already exists, it should be used rather than recreating a new solution. In addition, we should focus on continuously improving existing solutions." Eureka! It works!

Sources: Compiled from S. Barth, "Knowledge as a Function of X," *Knowledge Management*, February 2000; and S.L. Roberts-Witt, "The @HP Way," *Portals Magazine*, November 2002.

In a sense, a COP owns the knowledge that it contributes because it manages the knowledge on its way into the system and must approve modifications to it. The COP is responsible for the accuracy and timeliness of the knowledge it contributes and for identifying its potential use. A number of researchers have investigated how successful COPs form and function. In Table 11.3, we illustrate the many ways that COP add value to an organization through KM efforts. Basically, COP make organizations run smoothly because they enable knowledge flow. Informed people make better decisions. People who are involved are happier at work.

Wenger et al. (2002) recommended seven design principles for successful COP. Each of these facilitates knowledge creation and use. We describe them in Technology Insights 11.6.

Storck and Hill (2002) investigated one of the earliest COP at Xerox. When established at Xerox, the COP was a new organizational form. The word *community* captured the sense of responsible, independent action that characterized the group, which continued to function within the standard boundaries of the large organization.

TABLE 11.3 How Communities of Practice Add Value to an Organization

Name of Added Value	*Attributes That Create Value*
Creation of higher-quality knowledge	• Diversity in membership and less emphasis on hierarchical status reduce the likelihood of groupthink. • Limited requirements for formal reporting allow people to perform riskier brainstorming. • A reflection process at the end of a meeting consolidates learning.
Fewer surprises and plan revisions	• Broad participation diffuses knowledge across business units. • Openness of interaction format results in effective conflict resolution.
Greater capacity in dealing with unstructured problems	• Work occurs under a set of superordinate goals, not task goals. • The sponsoring organization accepts a self-evolving community role. • Knowledge leaders can emerge based on issues instead of by assignment to a team or roles within a team.
More effective knowledge sharing among business and corporate staff units	• Voluntary participation implies higher motivation, leading to faster, deeper learning internalization. • Trust increases due to indeterminate life span and long-term relationships.
Improved likelihood of implementing joint goals	• The community yields greater external validity because it exists externally to the formal organizational structure. • The community has more influence than an individual, given the organizational level of the community members.
More effective individual development and learning	• Group learning is more effective than individual learning. • The community's development process embodies learning opportunities through practice.

Source: Adapted from Table 5.2, "Strategic Community: Adding Value to the Organization," in E.L. Lesser, M.A. Fontaine, and J.A. Slusher (eds.), *Knowledge and Communities*, Butterworth-Heinemann, Woburn, MA, 2000, p. 77.

Management sponsored the community but did not mandate it. Community members were volunteers. We list and describe the six key principles that support COP at Xerox in Table 11.4. Brailsford (2001) described how Hallmark Cards built its COP and made similar discoveries to those at Xerox. For more on COP, see Barth (2000a), Brown and Duguid (2002), Lesser and Prusak (2002), McDermott (2002), Smith and McKeen (2003), Storck and Hill (2002), and Wenger (2002). For a successful application case, see Online File W11.1.

KMS DEVELOPERS

KMS developers are the team members who actually develop the system. They work for the CKO. Some are organizational experts who develop strategies to promote and manage the organizational culture shift. Others are involved in system software and hardware

TECHNOLOGY INSIGHTS 11.6

Seven Principles for Designing Successful COP

Here are seven ways to encourage vibrant COP in an organization:

1. *Design for evolution.* COP are organic, and many organizational factors influence their direction. Plan carefully. One does not so much manage a community as shepherd it.
2. *Open a dialog between inside and outside.* Good community design requires an understanding of the community's potential to develop and steward knowledge, but it often takes an outside perspective to help members see possibilities. The COP should not close in on itself.
3. *Invite different levels of participation.* There are typically three main levels of community participation. The first is a small core of people who actively participate in discussions. As the COP matures, this group evolves into the leadership. The next level is the active group. These members attend meetings regularly and participate occasionally in the community forums but not as regularly or as intensely as the core group. A large portion of the COP is peripheral and rarely participates. Do not exclude these people. They often use the knowledge generated. The key to good community participation, and a healthy degree of movement between levels, is to design community activities that allow participants at all levels to feel like full members.
4. *Develop public and private spaces.* The heart of a community is the web of relationships among community members, and private space is necessary to get the relationships to grow.
5. *Focus on value.* Because participation is generally voluntary, a COP must provide value. Communities must create events, activities, and relationships that help their potential value emerge and enable them to discover new ways to harvest it rather than determine expected value in advance.
6. *Combine familiarity and excitement.* Vibrant communities supply divergent thinking and activity. Routine activities provide stability for relationship building.
7. *Create a rhythm for the community.* There is a tempo associated with the members' interactions. This rhythm is the strongest indicator of its life and potential. The COP should contain a balance between large- and small-group sessions and between idea-sharing forums and tool-building projects. The rhythm will evolve with the community, but it is important to find the right one at each stage.

Sources: Compiled from E. Wenger, R. McDermott, and W.M. Snyder, *Cultivating Communities of Practice*, Harvard Business School Press, Boston, 2002; and E. Wenger, R. McDermott, and W.M. Snyder. "It Takes a Community," *CIO*, May 15, 2002.

selection, programming, testing, deployment, and maintenance. Still others are initially involved in training users. Eventually, the training function moves to the KMS staff.

KMS STAFF

Enterprisewide KMS require a full-time staff to catalog and manage the knowledge. This staff is either located at the firm's headquarters or dispersed in knowledge centers throughout the organization. Most large consulting firms have more than one knowledge center.

Earlier in this chapter we described the function of the staff as being similar to that of reference librarians. However, KMS staff actually do much more. Some members are functional area experts who are now cataloging and approving knowledge contributions and pushing the knowledge out to clients and employees whom they believe can use the knowledge. These functional experts may also work in a liaison role with the functional areas of the COP. Others work with users to train them on the system or help them with their searches. Still others work on improving the system's performance by identifying better methods with which to manage knowledge. For example, Cap Gemini Ernst & Young has 250 people managing the knowledge repository and assisting

TABLE 11.4 The Six Key Principles Supporting Communities of Practice at Xerox

Community Characteristic	*Actions*
Interaction format	Consists of meetings, collaborative computing, interaction structure, e-mail, etc.
Organizational culture	Leverages common training, experience, and vocabulary. Facilitates working around constraints.
Mutual interest	Builds commitment and promotes continuous improvement of processes.
Individual and collective learning	Recognizes and rewards knowledge contribution and use, leverages knowledge, and provides a culture of knowledge sharing.
Knowledge sharing	Embeds knowledge sharing into work practices. Reinforces with immediate feedback the value of knowledge sharing.
Community processes and norms	Builds trust and identity. Minimizes linkage to the formal control structure. Motivates the community to establish its own governance processes.

Source: Adapted from J. Storck and P.A. Hill, "Knowledge Diffusion Through Strategic Communities," *Sloan Management Review*, Vol. 41, No. 2, Winter 2000.

people in finding knowledge at its Center for Business Knowledge. Some staff members disseminate knowledge, and others are liaisons with the 40 practice areas. They codify and store documents in their areas of expertise (see Hansen et al., 1999).

Section 11.8 Review Questions

1. Describe the role of the CKO.
2. What other managers are involved with knowledge management?
3. Describe COP and relate them to knowledge management.
4. What is the importance of COP in organizations?

11.9 ENSURING THE SUCCESS OF KNOWLEDGE MANAGEMENT EFFORTS

While there are many cases of knowledge management success, there are also many cases of failure. Let's look at the reasons.

SUCCESS STORIES OF KNOWLEDGE MANAGEMENT

Organizations can gain several benefits from implementing a knowledge management strategy. Tactically, they can accomplish some or all of the following: reduce loss of intellectual capital due to people leaving the company; reduce costs by decreasing the number of times the company must repeatedly solve the same problem and by achieving economies of scale in obtaining information from external providers; reduce redundancy of knowledge-based activities; increase productivity by making knowledge available more quickly and easily; and increase employee satisfaction by enabling greater personal development and empowerment. The best reason of all may be a strategic need to gain a competitive advantage in the marketplace. Many factors are necessary for knowledge management to succeed. For example, Gold et al. (2001) described how a knowledge infrastructure consisting of technology, structure, and culture, along with a knowledge process architecture of acquisition, conversion, application, and protection, are essential "preconditions" for effective knowledge management. The situation in an organization must be right in order for a KM effort to succeed. See Application Case 11.7 for an example of a knowledge management success in law enforcement. See O'Dell et al. (2003), Smith and McKeen (2003), and Firestone and McElroy (2005) for more KM successes.

Application Case 11.7

The British Broadcasting Corporation Knowledge Management Success

The British Broadcasting Corporation (BBC) runs on knowledge. When Euan Semple became chief knowledge manager at the BBC, he recognized this, and he recognized that the BBC was all about knowledge. Instead of developing a large-scale, expensive KMS, Semple opted to focus on a network-based, conversationally oriented system that matched the way the BBC functions: as a *social network*. Semple basically focused on the social network and how he could best make it connect smoothly and effectively. His first tool was the Talk.Gateway bulletin board. By late 2005, 8,000 users (out of 25,000 employees) were performing some 450,000 page views per month. Using Talk.Gateway, people ask questions and get answers. Knowledge moves around rapidly, and Talk.Gateway also generates knowledge. Executives watch it to identify the first signs of problems. In one case, the BBC's director general, Greg Dyke, resigned because of errors in the reporting of the death of an Iraqi arms expert. There was a flood of activity on the bulletin board when this happened.

The next project was Connect, a people finder. People entered their expertise and interests so others could find them. When someone needed to translate a document into Dutch, more than 25 names popped up (zeker!). And, through Connect, COP can and do form. There are more than 200 of these interest groups that span the BBC's organizational charts, breaking down silos and spreading knowledge. A blogging server went online next; some of the blogs are by individuals, and others are by interest groups. Wikis have come online as well.

All these systems represent a significant shift from conventional information management and afford the possibility of speedy, effective communication between dispersed individuals and groups in modern, complex organizations. These social networking tools enable new, modern forms of collaboration. High-tech and large budgets aren't necessary to attain knowledge management success. What is necessary is for the KMS and the organization's culture to have a good fit. At the BBC, it meant connecting people together through effective social networking tools.

Sources: Adapted from D. Weinberger, "The BBC's Low-Tech Knowledge Management," *KMWorld*, September 2005; E. Semple, "Social Networking at the BBC," *Online Information 2005 Conference*, December 1, 2005. **infotodayblog.com/2005/12/social-networking-at-bbc.shtml** (accessed August 2006); "The Knowledge: Euan Semple," *Inside Knowledge*, (**ikmagazine.com**), Vol. 8, No. 9, June 16, 2005, **ikmagazine.com/xq/asp/sid.8958E0B9-338C-457E-93BC-E245E4E779E9/articleid.1A6CE759-39C4-45CA-8C44-389FC031C967/qx/display.htm** (accessed August 2006); and **bbc.co.uk**.

USEFUL APPLICATIONS OF KMS

While there is increasingly strong interest in KMS (see, e.g., **en.wikipedia.org/wiki/Knowledge_Management**), there are very few standalone KMS applications. In many cases, as described earlier, KMS are integrated with other enterprise systems or are modules attached to ERP, BI, or CRM. Furthermore, very few companies maintain separate organizational knowledge bases. They keep knowledge in a data warehouse or in knowledge bases of specific applications.

A relatively new standalone application is known as an *expert location system*.

Finding Experts Electronically and Using Expert Location Systems

Companies know that IT can be used to find experts. People who need help can post their problem on a corporate intranet (see Chapter 10) and ask for help. Similarly, companies can ask for advice on how to exploit an opportunity. IBM frequently uses this method. Sometimes it obtains hundreds of useful ideas within a few days. It is a kind of brainstorming. The problem with this approach is that it may take days to get answers, if answers are even provided, and the answers may not be from the top experts. Therefore, companies employ expert location systems. **Expert location systems** are interactive computerized systems that help employees find and connect with colleagues who have the expertise required for specific problems—whether they are across the country or across the room—in order to solve specific, critical business problems in seconds. Such software is made by companies such as AskMe and Tacit Knowledge Systems, Inc. These systems work by exploring knowledge bases for either an answer to the problem (if it exists there) or to locate qualified experts. The process includes the following steps:

1. An employee submits a question into the expert location system.
2. The software searches its database to see if an answer to the question already exists. If it does, the information (e.g., research reports, spreadsheets) is returned to the employee. If an answer does not exist, the software searches documents and archived communications for an "expert."
3. When a qualified candidate is located, the system asks if he or she is able to answer a question from a colleague. If so, the expert submits a response. If the candidate is unable (perhaps he or she is in a meeting or otherwise indisposed), the person can elect to pass on the question. The question is then routed to the next appropriate candidate until one responds.
4. After the response is sent, it is reviewed for accuracy and sent back to the person who entered the query. At the same time, it is added to the knowledge database. This way, if the question comes up again, it will not be necessary to seek real-time assistance.

Application Case 11.8 demonstrates how an expert location system works for the U.S. government.

Application Case 11.8

How the U.S. Department of Commerce Uses an Expert Location System

The U.S. Commercial Service Division at the Department of Commerce (DOC) conducts approximately 200,000 counseling sessions a year, involving close to $40 billion in trade. The division employs many specialists who frequently need to do research or call on experts to answer questions posed by U.S. corporations.

For example, in May 2004, a U.S.-based software company called Brad Anderson, a DOC specialist, for advice. The software company wanted to close a deal with a customer in Poland, but the buyer wanted to charge the U.S. company a 20 percent withholding tax, a tax it attributed to Poland's recent admission into the European Union (EU). Was the tax legitimate?

To find out, Anderson turned to the DOC Insider, an expertise location system (from AskMe). After typing in his question, Anderson first found some documents that were related to his query, but they did not explain the EU tax code completely. Anderson next asked the system to search the 1,700-strong Commercial Service for a live expert, and, within seconds, he was given a list of 80 people in the DOC who might be able to help him. Of those, he chose the 6 people he felt were most qualified and then forwarded his query.

Before the DOC Insider was in place, Anderson says, it would have taken him about three days to find an answer to the question. "You have to make many phone calls and deal with time zones," he said. Thanks to the expert location system, however, he had three responses within minutes and a complete answer within an hour, and the sale went through the following morning. Anderson estimated that he now uses the system for roughly 40 percent of the work he does.

The DOC Insider is an invaluable tool. Anderson said that the tool is vital enough to provide it to other units at the agency. In the first nine months the system was in place, it saved more than 1,000 labor-hours.

Sources: Compiled from D. D'Agostino, "Expertise Management: Who Knows About This?" *CIO Insight*, July 1, 2004; and P. Fox, *Using IT to Tap Experts' Know-How*, March 15, 2004. **computerworld.com/softwaretopics/software/apps/story/0,10801,91174,00.html** (accessed April 2006).

KNOWLEDGE MANAGEMENT VALUATION

In general, companies take either an asset-based approach to knowledge management valuation or an approach that links knowledge to its applications and business benefits (see Skyrme and Amidon, 1998). The former approach starts by identifying intellectual assets and then focuses management's attention on increasing their value. The second uses variants of a balanced scorecard, where financial measures are balanced against customer, process, and innovation measures. Among the best-developed measurement methods in use are the balanced scorecard approach (see Kestelyn, 2002; and Zimmermann, 2003a), Skandia's Navigator, Stern Stewart's economic value added (EVA), M'Pherson's inclusive valuation methodology, the return on management ratio, and Levin's knowledge-capital measure. Lunt (2001) described how Duke Children's Hospital, Hilton, and Borden improved performance across their enterprises through the balanced scorecard approach, leading to better customer service. See Skyrme and Amidon (1998) for details on how these measures work in practice.

Another method of measuring the value of knowledge is to estimate its price if it were offered for sale. Most firms are reluctant to sell knowledge unless they are expressly in the business of doing so. Generally, a firm's knowledge is an asset that has competitive value, and if it leaves the organization, the firm loses its competitive advantage. However, the knowledge and access to the knowledge can be priced at a value, making it worth a firm's while to sell. For example, American Airlines's Decision Technologies Corp. grew from a small internal analysis team in the 1970s. Initially, the team was created to solve problems and provide decision support only to American Airlines. As it grew, it became an independent corporation within AMR Corp., and it began to provide consulting systems to other airlines, including American's competitors. The major consulting firms are in the business of selling expertise. Therefore, their knowledge management efforts, which began as internal systems, evolved into quite valuable systems that their clients use on a regular basis. Clearly, the same knowledge can be sold repeatedly.

Success indicators with respect to knowledge management are similar to those for assessing the effectiveness of other business-change projects. They include growth in the resources attached to the project, growth in the volume of knowledge content and usage, the likelihood that the project will survive without the support of a particular individual or individuals, and some evidence of financial return either for the knowledge management activity itself or for the entire organization.

Financial Metrics for Knowledge Management Valuation

Even though traditional accounting measures are incomplete for measuring knowledge management, they are often used as a quick justification for a knowledge management initiative. ROI is reported to range from 20:1 for chemical firms to 4:1 for

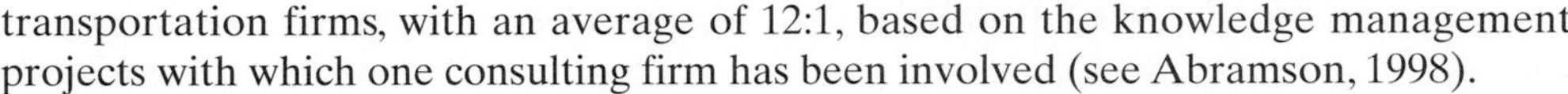

transportation firms, with an average of 12:1, based on the knowledge management projects with which one consulting firm has been involved (see Abramson, 1998).

In order to measure the impact of knowledge management, experts recommend focusing knowledge management projects on specific business problems that can be easily quantified. When the problems are solved, the value and benefits of the system become apparent (see MacSweeney, 2002).

At Royal Dutch/Shell, the ROI was explicitly documented: The company had invested $6 million in a KMS in 1999, and within two years, it obtained $235 million in reduced costs and new revenues (see King, 2001). Hewlett-Packard offers another example of documented financial returns. Within six months of launching its @HP company-wide portal in October 2000, Hewlett-Packard realized a $50 million return on its initial investment of $20 million. This was largely due to a reduction in volume of calls to internal call centers and to the new paperless processes (see Roberts-Witt, 2002).

The financial benefit might be perceptual, rather than absolute, but it need not be documented in order for a KMS to be considered a success.

Nonfinancial Metrics for Knowledge Management Valuation

Traditional methods of financial measurement may fall short when measuring the value of a KMS, because they do not consider intellectual capital an asset. Therefore, it is necessary to develop procedures for valuing the intangible assets of an organization as well as to incorporate models of intellectual capital that in some way quantify innovation and the development and implementation of core competencies.

When evaluating intangibles, there are a number of new ways to view capital. In the past, only customer goodwill was valued as an asset. Now the following are included as well:

- *External relationship capital.* This is a measure of how an organization links with its partners, suppliers, customers, and regulators.
- *Structural capital.* This type of capital is based on systems and work processes that leverage competitiveness, such as information systems.
- *Human capital.* People have individual capabilities, knowledge, skills, and so on.
- *Social capital.* This is the quality and value of relationships with the larger society.
- *Environmental capital.* This is the value of relationships with the environment.

For example, a knowledge management initiative that Partners HealthCare System, Inc., undertook has not resulted in quantifiable financial benefits, but it has greatly increased the company's social capital. The KMS that Partners implemented for physicians reduced the number of serious medication errors by 55 percent at some of Boston's most prestigious teaching hospitals. Calculating ROI for such a system is an extremely difficult proposition, which is why only a small fraction of hospitals use similar systems. While Partners is unable to determine how the system affects its bottom line, it is willing to justify the costs based on the system's benefits to the society (see Melymuka, 2002). For more on knowledge management valuation, see Kankanhalli and Tan (2005), Chen (2005), Conway (2003), Hanley and Malafsky (2003), Smith and McKeen (2003), Stone and Warsone (2003), and Zimmermann (2003a).

CAUSES OF KNOWLEDGE MANAGEMENT FAILURE

No system is infallible. There are many cases of KMS failing. Estimates of knowledge management failure rates range from 50 percent to 70 percent, where a failure is interpreted to mean that *all* the major objectives were not met by the effort (Ambrosio,

2000). Failures typically happen when the knowledge management effort mainly relies on technology and does not address whether the proposed system will meet the needs and objectives of the organization and its individuals (see Swan et al., 2000; also see the opening vignette, Barth, 2000b; Berkman, 2001; Malhotra, 2003; McDermott, 2002; Roberts-Witt, 2000; and Sviokla, 2001). Other issues include lack of commitment (this occurred at a large Washington, DC, constituent lobbying organization) and the failure to provide reasonable incentive for people to use the system (as occurred at Pillsbury Co.; see Barth, 2000b). Application Case 11.9 illustrates how Accenture's KMS failed. The disasters of September 11, 2001, might have been avoided or lessened; therefore, in the United States, the Department of Homeland Security is making a massive effort to integrate its sources of knowledge (see Matthews 2002; see also the Chapter 5 opening vignette). Soo et al. (2002) pointed out several knowledge traps that can lead to failure. We describe these in Technology Insights 11.10. Barth (2000b) described several important knowledge management initiatives that failed miserably. Finally, Roberts-Witt (2002) outlined how enterprises implementing portals can and do fail.

Application Case 11.9

When KMS Fail, They Can Fail in a Big Way

Accenture was a pioneer in organization-wide knowledge management efforts. Even though Accenture devoted significant resources to its global KMS, it simply failed at being effective in capturing and disseminating knowledge throughout the organization. Since the early 1990s, Accenture has spent over $500 million on IT and employees to support its global knowledge management strategy. And it continues to support it. In a study of its efforts, researchers discovered that it just was not working as well as it could have. One major problem was cultural. Accenture did not take into consideration local or regional challenges at a reasonable level. For example, the firm was totally unsuccessful in getting its East Asian consultants to contribute to the system because managers never demonstrated appreciation for these efforts. Accenture also apparently did not handle cross-cultural challenges well. Finally, because this was a global effort, the needs of local offices were totally subsumed.

Some of this can be explained by a recent research study. In an examination of five well-documented knowledge management failures, it was discovered that knowledge management failure factors fall into four categories: technology, culture, content, and project management. Clearly, Accenture had culture-based problems.

Other famous knowledge management failures include those of Ford and Firestone. When the tires started blowing out on the Ford Explorer, it cost of the company $1.25 billion. In this case, the knowledge was available; it was just not integrated in a way that allowed stakeholders to access and analyze it. International police agencies historically have not effectively shared knowledge; therefore, terrorist activities, such as those that led to the events of September 11, 2001, continue. Today, despite the fact that much can be learned from failures, it is difficult to extract information about them from most organizations.

Sources: Partly adapted from Y. Park and D.Y. Choi, "The Shortcomings of a Standardized Global Knowledge Management System: The Case Study of Accenture," *Academy of Management Executive*, Vol. 19, No. 2, May 2005, pp. 81–85; and S. Patton, "Putting the Pieces Together," *Darwin*, February 2002.

FACTORS THAT LEAD TO KNOWLEDGE MANAGEMENT SUCCESS

To increase the probability of success of knowledge management projects, companies must assess whether there is a strategic need for knowledge management in the first place. The next step is to determine whether the current process of dealing with organizational knowledge is adequate and whether the organization's culture is ready for procedural changes. Only when these issues are resolved should the company consider technology infrastructure and decide whether a new system is needed. When the right technological solution is chosen, it becomes necessary to properly introduce it to the

TECHNOLOGY INSIGHTS 11.10

Knowledge Management Traps

A recent study of the knowledge management practices of six firms identified several knowledge traps into which even the best firms fell. These can help show the way to avoid failure in knowledge management efforts. The following lessons were learned:

- Formal databases must be treated as strategic tools rather than mere storage facilities. Sometimes database systems are perceived as too complicated to use, so they are underused. Strategic information is overlooked because it is too difficult to get to. The organization must make it possible to get to the information and to really capture and codify knowledge.
- Managing formal database systems per se does not equate to knowledge management. Databases are important for capturing information, but a strong, informal network is necessary for good access. Also, databases are only one component of a KMS. When textual data are stored, we really consider this a knowledge repository, not a database.
- Informal networking is an important source of knowledge, but overreliance on it can be detrimental. Even though informal channels often contain critical information, there is an inherent risk that informal interactions may be too dependent on chance. Lack of structure can lead to knowledge loss.
- To reduce the susceptibility of informal networking to randomness, it should be made more structured.
- Senior management may not know the true state of their firm's KMS. There is a distinct difference between the perceptions of senior managers and junior managers in their views of the effectiveness of their KMS. This is mainly because the senior managers do not actively use the system, while junior managers do. The attitudes of senior managers may not be the best measure of the success of a KMS.
- You can't teach an old dog new tricks. Generally, older managers do not absorb new training well.
- Unless carefully managed, knowledge is a dark power. It is difficult to determine how to generate knowledge that is truly useful for an organization. Organizational factors may hinder the capture and free distribution of knowledge. Trust is critical.
- Creativity in problem solving is the main driver of new knowledge creation and innovation. But creativity must be supported by appropriate mechanisms. Resources must be provided to help employees be creative. Often, lack of time hinders individuals. They may be expected to contribute and use knowledge in a KMS, while not diminishing any other aspect of their jobs.

Sources: Adapted from C. Soo, T. Devinney, D. Midgley, and A. Dering, "Knowledge Management: Philosophy, Processes, and Pitfalls, *California Management Review*, Summer 2002, Vol. 44, No. 4, pp. 129–150; and Y. Malhotra, "Why Knowledge Management Systems Fail: Enablers and Constraints of Knowledge Management in Human Enterprises," in M.E.D. Koenig and T.K. Srikantaiah (eds.), *Knowledge Management Lessons Learned: What Works and What Doesn't*, Information Today Inc., Medford, NJ, 2004, pp. 87–112, **brint.org/WhyKMSFail.htm** (accessed April 2006).

entire organization and gain the participation of every employee (see Kaplan, 2002). It is important not to rely too heavily on technology to succeed (see the opening vignette and Jacob and Ebrahimpur, 2001). Typically, a knowledge management effort is only about 10 to 20 percent technology. The rest of the effort is organizational.

Major factors that lead to knowledge management project success (adapted from Davenport et al., 1998) include the following:

- A link to a firm's economic value, to demonstrate financial viability and maintain executive sponsorship.
- A technical and organizational infrastructure on which to build.
- A standard, flexible knowledge structure to match the way the organization performs work and uses knowledge. Usually, the organizational culture must change to effectively create a knowledge-sharing environment.
- A knowledge-friendly culture that leads directly to user support.

- A clear purpose and language, to encourage users to buy into the system. Sometimes simple, useful knowledge applications need to be implemented first.
- A change in motivational practices, to create a culture of sharing.
- Multiple channels for knowledge transfer—because individuals have different ways of working and expressing themselves. The multiple channels should reinforce one another. Knowledge transfer should be easily accomplished and as unobtrusive as possible.
- A level of process orientation to make a knowledge management effort worthwhile. In other words, new, improved work methods can be developed.
- Nontrivial motivational methods, such as rewards and recognition, to encourage users to contribute and use knowledge.
- Senior management support. This is critical to initiate a project, provide resources, help identify important knowledge on which the success of the organization relies, and market the project.

Effective knowledge sharing and learning require cultural change within the organization, new managerial practices, senior management commitment, and technological support. The organizational culture must shift to a culture of sharing. This should be handled through strong leadership at the top and by providing knowledge management tools that truly make people's jobs better. As far as encouraging system use and knowledge sharing goes, people must be properly motivated to contribute knowledge. The mechanism for doing so should be part of their jobs, and their salaries should reflect this. People must also be motivated to use the knowledge in the KMS. Again, this should be part of their jobs and their reward structures.

As more companies develop knowledge management capabilities, some of the ground rules are becoming apparent. Success depends on a clear strategic logic for knowledge sharing, the choice of appropriate infrastructure (technical or nontechnical), and an implementation approach that addresses the typical barriers: motivation to share knowledge, resources to capture and synthesize organizational learning, and ability to navigate the knowledge network to find the right people and data.

POTENTIAL DRAWBACKS OF KMS

Although managing knowledge has many positive outcomes, as discussed in examples throughout this chapter, it would be short-sighted to not consider the potential negative outcomes associated with reusing knowledge. Henfridsson and Söderholm (2000) analyzed the situation that Mrs. Fields Gifts faced. Mrs. Fields grew remarkably fast and successfully during the early 1980s. A key aspect of the company's strategy was to provide expertise directly from the headquarters to every store. As the number of stores increased, the only feasible way to achieve direct control was through the use of information systems designed to mimic the decision making of the real Debbi Fields. Systems placed in each store would input data (e.g., temperature, day of the week, date); the system would process them and output instructions telling the store manager, say, how many cookies of each type to bake each hour. In essence, the software provided each store manager with explicit directions for planning each day's production, sales, and labor scheduling, along with inventory control and ordering. Because of the well-functioning computer systems, which in principle were systems designed to make the company's tacit knowledge available to all stores, Mrs. Fields was able to successfully function with few managerial levels. However, Mrs. Fields was very slow to respond as the market began to change and consumers became more health conscious. By embedding so much knowledge into systems that were incapable of adaptation, the organization tied itself to a certain way of doing things and failed to engage in knowledge creation (i.e., failed to pick up the signals in the environment that might have suggested a change in strategy or product focus). By the early 1990s, the company had fallen into bankruptcy. The situation at Mrs. Fields illustrates that while organizations may achieve significant short-term gains through KMS, they must not neglect the creative process of new knowledge creation, lest they find themselves applying yesterday's solutions to tomorrow's problems.

CLOSING REMARKS ON KNOWLEDGE MANAGEMENT

For millennia, we have known about the effective use of knowledge and how to store and reuse it. Intelligent organizations recognize that knowledge is an intellectual asset, perhaps the only one that grows over time, and, when harnessed effectively, can sustain competition and innovation. Organizations can use IT to perform true knowledge management. Leveraging an entire organization's intellectual resources can have tremendous financial impact.

With knowledge management, the definition is clear, the concepts are clear, the methodology is clear, the challenges are clear and surmountable, the benefits are clear and can be substantial, and the tools and technology—though incomplete and somewhat expensive—are viable. Key issues are organizational culture, executive sponsorship, and measurement of success. Technological issues are minimal compared to these. Knowledge management is not just another expensive management fad. Knowledge management is a new paradigm for how we work.

Section 11.9 Review Questions

1. Describe the need for measuring the success of KMS.
2. What are the issues in knowledge management valuation?
3. List some financial (tangible) metrics of knowledge management.
4. List some intangible (nonfinancial) metrics of knowledge management.
5. List failure factors associated with knowledge management.
6. List success factors associated with knowledge management.
7. What are the potential drawbacks of KMS?
8. Describe expert location systems.

Chapter Highlights

- Knowledge is different from information and data. Knowledge is information that is contextual, relevant, and actionable. It is dynamic in nature.
- Tacit (i.e., unstructured, sticky) knowledge is usually in the domain of subjective, cognitive, and experiential learning; explicit (i.e., structured, leaky) knowledge deals with more objective, rational, and technical knowledge, and it is highly personal and difficult to formalize.
- A learning organization has an organizational memory and a means to save, represent, and share it.
- Organizational learning is the development of new knowledge and insights that have the potential to influence behavior.
- The ability of an organization to learn, develop memory, and share knowledge is dependent on its culture. Culture is a pattern of shared basic assumptions.
- Knowledge management is a process that helps organizations identify, select, organize, disseminate, and transfer important information and expertise that typically reside within the organization in an unstructured manner.
- The fastest, most effective and powerful way to manage knowledge assets is through the systematic transfer of best practices.
- Knowledge management requires a major transformation in organizational culture to create a desire to share (i.e., give and receive) knowledge and a

commitment to knowledge management at all levels of the firm.

- The knowledge management model involves the following cyclical steps: create, capture, refine, store, manage, and disseminate knowledge.
- The CKO is primarily responsible for changing the behavior of the firm to embrace the use of knowledge management and then managing the development operation of a KMS.
- A COP provides pressure to break down the cultural barriers that hinder knowledge management efforts.
- Knowledge management is an effective way for an organization to leverage its intellectual assets.
- It is difficult to measure the success of a KMS. Traditional methods of financial measurement fall short because they do not consider intellectual capital an asset.
- Two knowledge management approaches are the process approach and the practice approach.
- The two strategies used for knowledge management initiatives are the personalization strategy and the codification strategy.
- The two storage models used for knowledge management projects are the repository storage model and the network storage model.
- Standard knowledge management initiatives involve the creation of knowledge bases, active process management, knowledge centers, collaborative technologies, and knowledge webs.
- A KMS is generally developed using three sets of technologies: communication, collaboration, and storage.
- A variety of technologies can make up a KMS, including the Internet, intranets, data warehousing, decision support tools, and groupware. Intranets are the primary vehicles for displaying and distributing knowledge in organizations.
- Knowledge management is not just another expensive management fad. It is a new paradigm for the way we work.

Key Terms

- best practices
- chief knowledge officer (CKO)
- community of practice (COP)
- content management system (CMS)
- electronic document management (EDM)
- enterprise knowledge portal (EKP)
- expert location system
- explicit knowledge
- intellectual capital
- knowledge
- knowledge-based economy
- knowledge discovery in databases (KDD)
- knowledge management
- knowledge management system (KMS)
- knowledge repository
- knowware
- leaky knowledge
- learning organization
- model mart
- model warehouse
- organizational culture
- organizational learning
- organizational memory
- practice approach
- process approach
- tacit knowledge

QUESTIONS FOR DISCUSSION

1. Why is the term *knowledge* so difficult to define?
2. Describe and relate the different characteristics of knowledge to one another.
3. Explain why it is important to capture and manage knowledge.
4. Compare and contrast tacit knowledge and explicit knowledge.
5. Explain why organizational culture must sometimes change before knowledge management is introduced.
6. How does knowledge management attain its primary objective?
7. How can employees be motivated to contribute to and use KMS?
8. What is the role of a knowledge repository in knowledge management?
9. Explain the importance of communication and collaboration technologies to the processes of knowledge management.
10. Explain why firms adopt knowledge management initiatives.
11. Explain how the wrong organizational culture can reduce the effectiveness of knowledge management.
12. Explain the role of the CKO in developing a KMS. What major responsibilities does he or she have?
13. What is meant by a culture of knowledge sharing?
14. Discuss the factors related to knowledge management success.

15. Why is it so difficult to evaluate the impacts of knowledge management?
16. Explain how the Internet and related technologies (e.g., Web browsers, intranets) enable knowledge management.
17. List three top technologies most frequently used for implementing KMS and explain their importance.
18. Explain the roles of a community of practice.
19. Describe an EKP and explain its significance.

Exercises

Teradata University and Other Hands-on Exercises

1. Make a list of all the knowledge management methods you use during your day (work and personal). Which are the most effective? Which are the least effective? What kinds of work or activities does each knowledge management method enable?
2. Investigate the literature for information on the position of CKO. Find out what percentage of firms with knowledge management initiatives have CKOs and what their responsibilities are.
3. Investigate the literature for new measures of success (metrics) for knowledge management and intellectual capital. Write a report on your findings.
4. Describe how each of the key elements of a knowledge management infrastructure can contribute to its success.
5. Based on your own experience or on the vendor's information, list the major capabilities of a particular knowledge management product and explain how it can be used in practice.
6. Describe how to ride a bicycle, drive a car, or make a peanut butter and jelly sandwich. Now have someone else try to do it based solely on your explanation. How can you best convert this knowledge from tacit to explicit (or can't you)?
7. Examine the top five reasons that firms initiate KMS and investigate why they are important in a modern enterprise.
8. Read the article by E. Berkman titled "Don't Lose Your Mind Share," available at **cio.com/archive/100100/mindshare.html**. Describe the major problems that Hill and Knowlton faced in February 1999 and what Ted Graham did to solve them.
9. Read *How the Irish Saved Civilization* by Thomas Cahill (New York: Anchor, 1996) and describe how Ireland became a knowledge repository for Western Europe just before the fall of the Roman Empire. Explain in detail why this was important for Western civilization and history.
10. Examine your university, college, or company and describe the roles that the faculty, administration, support staff, and students have in the creation, storage, and dissemination of knowledge. Explain how the process works. Explain how technology is currently used and how it could potentially be used.

Exercises

Team Assignments and Role-Playing

1. Compare and contrast the capabilities and features of electronic document management with those of collaborative computing and of KMS. Each team should represent one type of system.
2. Search the Internet for knowledge management products and systems and create categories for them. Assign one vendor to each team. Describe the categories you created and justify them.
3. Consider a decision-making project in industry for this course or from another class or from work. Examine some typical decisions in the project. How would you extract the knowledge you need? Can you use that knowledge in practice? Why or why not?
4. Read the article by A. Genusa titled "Rx for Learning," available at **cio.com/archive/020101/ tufts. html**, which describes Tufts University Medical School's experience with knowledge management. Determine how these concepts and such a system could be implemented and used at your college or university. Explain how each aspect would work, or if it would not work, explain why it would not.

Exercises

Internet Exercises

1. How does knowledge management support decision making? Identify products or systems on the Web that help organizations accomplish knowledge management. Start with **brint.com** and **knowledgemanagement.com**. Try one out and report your findings to the class.

2. Try the KPMG Knowledge Management Framework Assessment Exercise at **kmsurvey.londonweb.net** and assess how well your university (or company) is doing with knowledge management. Are the results accurate? Why or why not?

3. Search the Internet to identify sites that deal with knowledge management. Start with **google.com**, **kmworld.com**, **kmmag.com**, and **km-forum.org**. How many did you find? Categorize the sites based on whether they are academic, consulting firms, vendors, and so on. Sample one of each and describe the main focus of the site.

4. Identify five real-world knowledge management success stories by searching vendor Web sites (use at least three different vendors). Describe them. How did KMS and methods contribute to their success? What features do they share? What different features do individual successes have?

5. Search the Internet for vendors of knowledge management suites, EKP, and out-of-the-box knowledge management solutions. Identify the major features of each product (use three from each) and compare and contrast their capabilities.

6. Access Microsoft Web site and investigate the current capabilities of its knowledge management initiative.

End of Chapter Application Case

DaimlerChrysler EBOKs with Knowledge Management

In 1980, Chrysler Corporation (**daimlerchrysler.com**) came back from near bankruptcy with innovative designs and a view of a shared culture in design, development, and manufacturing. The company began new ways of looking at its business, its suppliers, and its workers. After the acquisition of American Motors Corporation (AMC) in 1987, executives developed and deployed advanced, dedicated platform design and production methods that showed enormous potential. Jack Thompson, the technology center development director, worked closely with Chairman Lee Iacocca on the development of a modern new engineering and design facility. Thompson designed the center around knowledge-sharing and productivity principles: open air, natural light, and escalators (because people don't talk on elevators/lifts).

In 1994, the tech center opened, providing a home for a transformed engineering culture. Two years later, the corporate headquarters was moved next to the tech center so executives could be nearby. By 2000, more than 11,000 people were working at the Auburn Hills, Michigan, center. In November 1998, Daimler-Benz became the majority owner of Chrysler Corporation, renaming the company DaimlerChrysler. Chrysler's fast, efficient, and innovative nature, as a result of the extremely successful platform approach to design and engineering, led to the buy-in—the largest merger in manufacturing history.

Platform production at DaimlerChrysler has teams of engineers focused on a single type of car platform (e.g., small car, minivan), working on new models as a system from concept to production. Cars are designed by a single team, considering customer needs and preferences, as opposed to the standard practice of organizing the new designs by organizational functions (i.e., silos). Platform teams of employees work and learn together, focused on the product, with a payoff in market responsiveness, reduced cost, and increased quality. The Chrysler LH, the first model developed with the platform approach, took 39 months to produce; typically, the time to market exceeds 50 months. Since then, major automobile manufacturers have greatly reduced these times.

While the benefits were clear, Chrysler executives noticed that unexplained errors were popping up in the new platforms (e.g., leaving a moisture barrier out of car doors). There was an organizational memory problem: Mentoring and peer support became limited. Informal and formal professional collaboration had stopped. The same mistakes were being made, corrected, and repeated. People were not learning about new developments in their core areas. The typical collaboration found among groups doing similar work was sharply reduced, so problems and solutions were not being documented or shared.

Collaboration and communication needed to be reestablished within groups with common training, interests, and responsibilities (e.g., design, engineering, body, engine, manufacturing). The goal was to reestablish these links while becoming more competitive with even faster product-cycle times. Chrysler needed to institutionalize knowledge sharing and collaboration. In 1996, Chrysler Corporation made knowledge management a vital condition for design and engineering, leading to dramatic improvements in productivity.

First, engineers mapped out where the knowledge was within the organization (by doing a *knowledge audit*; see Rapport, 2001). There were many categories, or "buckets of knowledge," ranging from product databases to CAD/CAM systems to manufacturing, procurement, and supply vehicle test data. Within each category, details were identified and codified. Sharing knowledge meant integrating these knowledge buckets while resolving cultural issues that impeded sharing across platform boundaries. Chrysler created informal cross-platform tech clubs, functionally organized communities of practice to reunite designers and engineers with peers from other platform groups. Each community codified its knowledge and provided mentoring and apprenticing opportunities for learning.

The Engineering Book of Knowledge (EBOK) is Chrysler's intranet, supporting a knowledge repository of process best practices and technical know-how to be shared and maintained. It was initially developed by two engineering managers, and it continues through encouraged employee participation in grassroots (i.e., supported at the lower levels of the organization) tech clubs. EBOK is written in GrapeVine (GrapeVine Technologies), running as a Lotus Notes application, and it is accessed with the Netscape browser and NewsEdge.

Knowledge is explored and entered into the EBOK through an iterative team approach: the tech clubs. Best practices are identified, refined, confirmed, and finally entered into the EBOK in a secure, interactive electronic repository. When an author proposes a best practice, users in the tech club responsible for that area of knowledge react by commenting on the knowledge through a discussion list. One manager, the book owner, is ultimately responsible for approving new entries and changes to the book. The book owner joins the conversation. The author can respond to the comments by either building a better case or going along with the discussion. Ultimately, the tech club decides, and the book owner enters the new knowledge. The book owner is the individual who is ultimately responsible for the accuracy of the book and therefore approves entries to, modifications to, and deletions from the book.

The EBOK is DaimlerChrysler's official design review process. The EBOK even contains best-practices information about DaimlerChrysler's competitors. Daimler Chrysler has determined that EBOK is both a best practices tool (i.e., the codification strategy with a repository storage model) and a collaboration tool (i.e., the personalization strategy with a network storage model). DaimlerChrysler officials recognize that because the environment changes and new methods are being continually developed, the EBOK will never be fully complete. The EBOK is a living book. It leverages technology knowledge.

The EBOK is central to DaimlerChrysler's new way of working. The plan is to have more than 5,000 users with access to 3,800 chapters, of which just over half were completed by early 1999. Through the EBOK, DaimlerChrysler reconciled its platform problems and developed a technical memory while tracking competitive information, quality information, and outside standards. Even though there is no central budget for books of knowledge and associated processes, DaimlerChrysler is deploying knowledge in other departments, such as manufacturing, finance, and sales and marketing.

In a first for an automotive company in Germany, DaimlerChrysler is combining all employee-related e-business activities under the umbrella of DC eLife. In the framework of this business-to-employee (B2E) offensive, all employees will have the opportunity to extend and improve their IT skills.

"With DC eLife, our employees get the opportunity to use e-business extensively for themselves and for the company," said Günther Fleig, DaimlerChrysler board member for human resources. "Furthermore, quicker access to information helps boost the efficiency of knowledge management. By means of DC eLife, we are not only guaranteeing the attractiveness of our company but also the professional opportunities of our employees."

Sources: Adapted from W. Karlenzig, "Chrysler's New Know-Mobiles," *Knowledge Management*, May 1999, pp. 58–66; M. Rapport, "Unfolding Knowledge," *Knowledge Management Magazine*, July 2001; and *DaimlerChrysler Launches Employee e-Business Offensive with DC eLife*, July 11, 2001. **autointell.com/News-2001/July-2001/July-2001-2/July-11-01-p5.htm**, (accessed April 2006).

QUESTIONS FOR THE CASE

1. Platform design at DaimlerChrysler led directly to a reduction in the time to market and in costs for new vehicles. Explain how it caused new problems.
2. What is meant by a COP? How did DaimlerChrysler leverage the knowledge within such a community?
3. Describe DaimlerChrysler's EBOK. Explain how it is updated by adding new knowledge of practice.
4. The correct function for all knowledge management tools is to leverage technology in the service to human thinking. Explain this statement.
5. How successful was the knowledge management initiative at DaimlerChrysler?
6. Consider how a book of knowledge could affect another organization, ideally one with which you are affiliated (e.g., your university, job, part-time job, family business). Describe the potential impacts and list the benefits. Would there be any organizational culture issues to deal with? Why or why not?

References

Abramson, G. (1998, June 15). "Measuring Up." *CIO*.

Adams, K.C. (2001, October 24). "Peak Performance." *Intelligent Enterprise*.

Ahlawat, S.S., and S. Ahlawat. (2006, March). "Competing in the Global Knowledge Economy: Implications for Business Education." *Journal of American Academy of Business*, Vol. 8, No. 1.

Alavi, M. (2000). "Managing Organizational Knowledge." Chapter 2 in W.R. Zmud, (ed.). *Framing the Domains of IT Management: Projecting the Future*. Cincinnati, OH: Pinnaflex Educational Resources.

Alavi, M., and D. Leidner. (1999, February). "Knowledge Management Systems: A Descriptive Study of Key Issues, Challenges, and Benefits." *Communications of the AIS*.

Alavi, M., T. Kayworth, and D. Leidner. (2003). *An Empirical Investigation of the Impact of Organizational Culture on KM Initiatives* (working paper). Waco, TX: Baylor University.

Alavi, M., T. Kayworth, and D. Leidner (2005/2006). "An Empirical Examination of the Influence of Organizational Culture on Knowledge Management Practice." *Journal of Management Information Systems*, Vol. 22, No. 3.

Ali, I., L. Warne, and C. Pascoe. (2006). "Learning in Organizations." In D.G. Schwartz, (ed.). *Encyclopedia of Knowledge Management*. Hershey, PA: Idea Group Reference.

Allard, S. (2003). "Knowledge Creation." Chapter 18 in C.W. Holsapple (ed.). *Handbook of Knowledge Management: Knowledge Matters*, Vol. 1. Heidelberg: Springer-Verlag.

Ambrosio, J. (2000, July 3). "Knowledge Management Mistakes." *Computerworld,* Vol. 34, No. 27.

Ariely, G. (2006). "Intellectual Capital and Knowledge Management." In D.G. Schwartz, (ed.). *Encyclopedia of Knowledge Management*. Hershey, PA: Idea Group Reference.

Baalen, P.V., J. Bloemhof-Ruwaard, and E. V. Heck. (2005, June). "Knowledge Sharing in an Emerging Network of Practice: The Role of Knowledge Portal," *European Management Journal*, Vol. 23, No, 3.

Bankes, A. (2003, April). "Taking on the Challenge of ECM." *KMWorld*, Special Supplement.

Barth, S. (2000a, February). "Knowledge as a Function of X." *Knowledge Management*.

Barth, S., (2000b, October). "KM Horror Stories." *Knowledge Management*.

Bennet, D., and A. Bennet. (2003). "The Rise of the Knowledge Organization." Chapter 1 in C.W. Holsapple (ed.). *Handbook of Knowledge Management: Knowledge Matters*, Vol. 1. Heidelberg: Springer-Verlag.

Berkman, E. (2001, April 1). "When Bad Things Happen to Good Ideas." *Darwin*.

Berman, S.L., J. Down, and C.W.L. Hill. (2002). "Tacit Knowledge as a Source of Competitive Advantage in the National Basketball Association." *Academy of Management Journal*, Vol. 45, No. 1.

Blodgett, M. (2000, February 1). "Prescription Strength." *CIO*.

Bock, G.-W., R. Zmud, Y. Kim, and J. Lee. (2005). "Behavioural Intention Formation in Knowledge Sharing: Examining the Roles of Extrinsic Motivators, Social Psychological Forces and Organizational Climate." *MIS Quarterly Journal*, Vol. 29, No. 1.

Bolloju, N., M. Khalifa, and E. Turban. (2002, June). "Integrating Knowledge Management into Enterprise Environments for the Next Generation of Decision Support." *Decision Support Systems*, Vol. 33.

Brailsford, T.W. (2001, September/October). "Building a Knowledge Community at Hallmark Cards." *Research Technology Management*, Vol. 44, No. 5.

Brown, J.S., and P. Duguid. (1991). "Organizational Learning and Communities-of-Practice: Toward a Unified View of Working, Learning, and Innovation." *Organization Science*, Vol. 2, No. 1.

Brown, J.S., and P. Duguid. (2002). "Organizational Learning and Communities of Practice: Toward a Unified View of Working, Learning, and Innovation." Chapter 7 in E.L. Lesser, M.A. Fontaine, and J.A. Slusher. (eds.). *Knowledge and Communities*. Woburn, MA: Butterworth-Heinemann.

Carlucci, D., and G. Schiuma. (2006, January-March). "Knowledge Asset Value Spiral: Linking Knowledge Assets to Company's Performance" *Knowledge and Process Management*, Vol. 13, No. 1.

Chen, A.N.K. (2005, June). "Assessing Value in Organizational Knowledge Creation: Consideration for Knowledge Workers" *MIS Quarterly*, Vol. 29, No. 2.

Compton, J. (2001, July). "Climbing Out of the Abyss." *Knowledge Management*.

Conway, S. (2003). "Valuing Knowledge Management Behaviors: Linking KM Behaviors to Strategic Performance Measures." Chapter 24 in C.W. Holsapple (ed.). *Handbook of Knowledge Management: Knowledge Matters*, Vol. 1. Heidelberg: Springer-Verlag.

Craig, C.R. (2005). "Purchasing Social Responsibility and Firm Performance: The Kee Mediating Roles of Organizational Learning and Supplier Performance." *International Journal of Physical Distribution & Logistics Management*, Vol. 35, No. 3.

Davenport, T., D.W. DeLong, and M.C. Beers. (1998, Winter). "Successful Knowledge Management Projects." *Sloan Management Review*, Vol. 39, No. 2.

Davenport, D., and M. Sena. (2003). "Technologies for Knowledge Derivation." Chapter 40 in C.W. Holsapple (ed.). *Handbook of Knowledge Management: Knowledge Directions*, Vol. 2. Heidelberg: Springer-Verlag.

Davis, M. (1998, Fall). "Knowledge Management." *Information Strategy: The Executive's Journal*.

Duffy, D. (1998, November). "Knowledge Champions." *CIO*.

Feldman, S. (2002, June). "What Technologies Are KM Professionals Buying?" *KMWorld*.

Firestone, J. (2003, April). "Portal Progress and Knowledge Management: eKnowledge Portal." *KMWorld*.

Firestone, J.M., and M.W. McElroy. (April 2005). "Doing Knowledge Management." *The Learning Journal*, Vol. 12, No. 2.

Flash, C. (2001a, May). "Who Is the CKO?" *Knowledge Management*.

Flash, C. (2001b, August). "Personal Chemistry." *Knowledge Management*.

Gaines, B. (2003). "Organizational Knowledge Acquisition." Chapter 16 in C.W. Holsapple (ed.). *Handbook of Knowledge Management: Knowledge Matters*, Vol. 1. Heidelberg: Springer-Verlag.

Gamble, P., and J. Blackwell. (2002). *Knowledge Management: A State-of-the-Art Guide*. London: Kogan Page.

Garvin, D.A. (2000). *Learning in Action*. Boston: Harvard Business School Press.

Godin, B. (2006). "Knowledge-Based Economy: Conceptual Framework or Buzzword." *The Journal of Technology Transfer*, Vol. 31, No. 1.

Gold, A.H., A. Malhotra, and A.H. Segars. (2001, Summer). "Knowledge Management: An Organizational Capabilities Perspective." *Journal of Management Information Systems*, Vol. 18, No. 1.

Gray, P. (1999). "Tutorial on Knowledge Management." *Proceedings of the Americas Conference of the Association for Information Systems*, Milwaukee.

Gray, P., and D. Meisters. (2003). *Knowledge Sourcing Effectiveness* (working paper). Pittsburgh: University of Pittsburgh.

Gray, P., and S. Tehrani. (2003). "Technologies for Knowledge Distribution." Chapter 38 in C.W. Holsapple (ed.). *Handbook of Knowledge Management: Knowledge Directions*, Vol. 2. Heidelberg: Springer-Verlag.

Hanley, S., and G. Malafsky. (2003). "A Guide for Measuring the Value of Knowledge Management Investments." Chapter 49 in C.W. Holsapple (ed.). *Handbook of Knowledge Management: Knowledge Directions*, Vol. 2. Heidelberg: Springer-Verlag.

Hansen, M., et al. (1999, March/April). "What's Your Strategy for Managing Knowledge?" *Harvard Business Review*, Vol. 77, No. 2.

Hanssen-Bauer, J., and C.C. Snow. (1996, July/August). "Responding to Hypercompetition: The Structure and Process of a Regional Learning Network." *Organization Science*.

Henfridsson, O., and A. Söderholm. (2000). "Barriers to Learning: On Organizational Defenses and Vicious Circles in Technological Adoption." *Accounting, Management and Information Technologies*, Vol. 10, No. 1, pp. 33–51.

Hibbard, J. (1998, September 21). "Cultural Breakthrough." *InformationWeek*.

Hinds, R.S., and J.E. Aronson. (2002, August). "Developing the Requisite Organizational, Attitudinal, and Behavioral Conditions for Effective Knowledge Management." *Proceedings of the Americas Conference for Information Systems*, Dallas.

Hoffer, J., M. Prescott, and F. McFadden. (2002). *Modern Database Management*, 6th ed. Upper Saddle River, NJ: Prentice Hall.

Holsapple, C.W. (ed.). (2003a). *Handbook of Knowledge Management: Knowledge Matters*, Vol. 1. Heidelberg: Springer-Verlag.

Holsapple, C.W. (ed.). (2003b). *Handbook of Knowledge Management: Knowledge Directions*, Vol. 2. Heidelberg: Springer-Verlag.

Jacob, M., and G. Ebrahimpur. (2001). "Experience vs. Expertise: The Role of Implicit Understandings of Knowledge in Determining the Nature of Knowledge Transfer in Two Companies." *Journal of Intellectual Capital*, Vol. 2, No. 1.

Jasimuddin, S.M., N.A.D. Connell, and J.H. Klein. (2006). "Understanding Organizational Memory." In D.G. Schwartz, (ed.) *Encyclopedia of Knowledge Management*. Hershey, PA: Idea Group Reference.

Jennex, M., and L. Olfman. (2003). "Organizational Memory and Its Management." Chapter 11 in C.W. Holsapple (ed.). *Handbook of Knowledge Management: Knowledge Matters*, Vol. 1. Heidelberg: Springer-Verlag.

Jones M.C., M. Cline, S. Ryan. (2006, January). "Exploring Knowledge Sharing in ERP Implementation: An Organizational Culture Framework." *Decision Support Systems*, Vol. 41, No. 2.

Kankanhalli, A., and B.C.Y. Tan. (2005). "Knowledge Management Metrics: A Review and Directions for Future Research." *International Journal of Knowledge Management*, Vol. 1, No. 2.

Kankanhalli, A., B.C.Y. Tan, and K.K.Wei. (2005, March). "Contributing Knowledge to Electronic Knowledge Repositories: An Empirical Investigation." *MIS Quarterly*, Vol. 29, No. 1.

Kaplan S. (2002, July 15). "KM the Right Way." *CIO*.

Kayworth, T., and D. Leidner. (2003). "Organizational Culture as a Knowledge Resource." Chapter 12 in C.W. Holsapple (ed.). *Handbook of Knowledge Management: Knowledge Matters*, Vol. 1. Heidelberg: Springer-Verlag.

Kestelyn, J. (2002, July 28). "Microsoft's New Methodology Will Further Validate Balanced Scorecards." *Intelligent Enterprise*.

Kiaraka, R.N., and K. Manning. (2005). "Managing Organizations through a Process-Based Perspective: Its Challenges and Rewards." *Knowledge and Process Management*, Vol. 12, No. 4.

King, J. (2001, July/August). "Shell Strikes Knowledge Gold." *Computerworld*.

King, W.R. (2006). "Knowledge Sharing." In D.G. Schwartz (ed.). *Encyclopedia of Knowledge Management*. Hershey, PA: Idea Group Reference.

Koenig, M. (2001, September). "Codification vs. Personalization." *KMWorld*.

Lamont, J. (2003a, April). "Prognosis Good for KM in Patient Treatment and Diagnostics." *KMWorld*.

Lamont, J. (2003b, May). "Dynamic Taxonomies: Keeping Up with Changing Content." *KMWorld*.

Leidner, D., M. Alavi, and T. Kayworth. (2006). "The Role of Culture in Knowledge Management: A Case Study of Two Global Firms." *International Journal of e-Collaboration*, Vol. 2, No. 1.

Lesser, E., and L. Prusak. (2002). "Communities of Practice, Social Capital and Organizational Knowledge." Chapter 8 in E.L. Lesser, M.A. Fontaine, and J.A. Slusher (eds.). *Knowledge and Communities*. Woburn, MA: Butterworth-Heinemann.

Lesser, E.L., M.A. Fontaine, and J.A. Slusher (eds.). (2000). *Knowledge and Communities*. Woburn, MA: Butterworth-Heinemann.

Levinson, M. (2002, April 15). "The Art of the Shmooze." *CIO*.

Liedtka, J. (2002). "Linking Competitive Advantage with Communities of Practice." Chapter 9 in E.L. Lesser, M.A. Fontaine, and J.A. Slusher. (eds.). *Knowledge and Communities*. Woburn, MA: Butterworth-Heinemann.

Lunt, P. (2001, July). "Know the Score." *Customer Support Management*.

MacSweeney, G. (2002, June). "The Knowledge Management Payback." *Insurance & Technology*.

Malafsky, G. (2003). "Technology for Acquiring and Sharing Knowledge Assets." Chapter 36 in C.W. Holsapple (ed.). *Handbook of Knowledge Management: Knowledge Directions*, Vol. 2. Heidelberg: Springer-Verlag.

Malhotra, Y. (2003). "Why Knowledge Management Systems Fail: Enablers and Constraints of Knowledge Management in Human Enterprises." Chapter 30 in C.W. Holsapple (ed.). *Handbook of Knowledge Management: Knowledge Matters*, Vol. 1. Heidelberg: Springer-Verlag.

Martin, B. (2000). "Knowledge Management Within the Context of Management: An Evolving Relationship." *Singapore Management Review*, Vol. 22, No. 2.

Matthews, W. (2002, April 25). "Knowledge Management's Worst Nightmare." *Federal Computer Week*.

McCarthy, R.V., K. Mazouz, and J.E. Aronson. (2001, August). "Measuring the Validity of Task-Technology Fit for Knowledge Management Systems." *Proceedings of the America's Conference on Information Systems (AMCIS 2001)*, Boston.

McDermott, R. (2002). "Why Information Technology Inspired but Cannot Deliver Knowledge Management." Chapter 2 in E.L. Lesser, M.A. Fontaine, and J.A. Slusher. (eds.). *Knowledge and Communities*. Woburn, MA: Butterworth-Heinemann.

McDonald, M., and D. Shand. (2000, March). "Request for Proposal: A Guide to KM Professional Services." *Knowledge Management*.

McKeen, J., and S. Staples. (2003). "Knowledge Managers: Who Are They and What Do They Do?" Chapter 2 in C.W. Holsapple (ed.). *Handbook of Knowledge Management: Knowledge Matters*, Vol. 1. Heidelberg: Springer-Verlag.

Melymuka, K. (2002, July 22). "Taking Projects to the Extreme." *Computerworld,* Vol. 36, No. 30.

Microsoft Corp. (2000). "Microsoft Windows Media Adopted by J.D. Edwards & Co. As Corporate Communication Solution," *Microsoft.com*, February 14, 2000. **microsoft.com/Presspass/press/2000/feb00/jdedwardspr.mspx** (accessed August 2006).

Mooney, S.F. (2000, December 18–25). "P-C 'Knowledge Capital' Can Be Measured." *National Underwriter*, Vol. 104, Nos. 51–52.

Nevo, D., and Y. Wand. (2005). "Organizational Memory Information Systems: A Transactive Memory Approach." *Decision Support Systems*, Vol. 39, No. 4.

Nonaka, I. (1994). "A Dynamic Theory of Organizational Knowledge Creation." *Organization Science*, Vol. 5, pp. 14–37.

Nonaka, I., and H. Takeuchi. (1995). *The Knowledge-Creating Company: How Japanese Companies Create the Dynamics of Innovation*. New York: Oxford University Press.

O'Dell, C., and C.J. Grayson. (2003). "Identifying and Transferring Internal Best Practices." Chapter 31 in

C.W. Holsapple (ed.). *Handbook of Knowledge Management: Knowledge Matters*, Vol. 1. Heidelberg: Springer-Verlag.

O'Dell, C., C.J. Grayson, Jr., and N. Essaides. (1998). *If Only We Knew What We Know: The Transfer of Internal Knowledge and Best Practice*. New York: The Free Press.

O'Dell, C., F. Hasanali, C. Hubert, K. Lopez, P. Odem, and C. Raybourn. (2003). "Successful KM Implementations: A Study of Best Practice Organizations." Chapter 51 in C.W. Holsapple (ed.). *Handbook of Knowledge Management: Knowledge Directions*, Vol. 2. Heidelberg: Springer-Verlag.

O'Leary, D. (2003). "Technologies for Knowledge Storage and Assimilation." Chapter 34 in C.W. Holsapple (ed.). *Handbook of Knowledge Management: Knowledge Directions*, Vol. 2, Heidelberg: Springer-Verlag.

Park, Y.T., and S. Kim. (2006, May/June). "Knowledge Management Systems for Fourth Generation R&D: KNOWVATION." *Technovation*, Vol. 26, Nos. 5, 6.

Polanyi, M. (1958). *Personal Knowledge*. Chicago: University of Chicago Press.

Ponzi, L.J. (2004). "Knowledge Management: Birth of a Discipline." In M.E.D. Koenig and T.K. Srikantaiah (eds.). *Knowledge Management Lessons Learned: What Works and What Doesn't*. Medford, NJ: Information Today.

Qian, Z., and G.W. Bock. (2005). "An Empirical Study on Measuring the Success of Knowledge Repository Systems." *System Sciences*.

Rapport, M. (2001, July). "Unfolding Knowledge." *Knowledge Management*.

Rasmus, D.W. (2000, March/April). "Knowledge Management: More Than AI but Less Without It." *PC AI*, Vol. 14, No. 2.

Reamy, T. (2002, July/August). "Imparting Knowledge Through Storytelling." *KMWorld*, Vol. 11, No. 7.

Riege, A. (2005). "Three Dozen Knowledge-Sharing Barriers Managers Must Consider." *Journal of Knowledge Management*, Vol. 9, No. 3.

Roberts-Witt, S.L. (2000, October). "Portal Pitfalls." *Knowledge Management*.

Roberts-Witt, S.L. (2002, November). "The @HP Way." *Portals Magazine*.

Robin, M. (2000, March). "Learning by Doing." *Knowledge Management*.

Ruber, P. (2001, January 11). "Build a Dynamic Business Portal with XML." *Knowledge Management*.

Ruggles, R. (1998). "The State of the Notion: Knowledge Management in Practice." *California Management Review*, Vol. 40, No. 3.

Schein, E. (1999). *The Corporate Culture Survival Guide*. San Francisco: Jossey-Bass.

Schulz, M. (2001, August). "The Uncertain Relevance of Newness: Organizational Learning and Knowledge Flows." *Academy of Management Journal*, Vol. 44, No. 4.

Schwartz, D.G. (ed.). (2006). *Encyclopedia of Knowledge Management*, Hershey, PA: Idea Group Reference.

Sedighi A. (2006, January/February). "An Indispensable Guide to Knowledge Management Systems." *IEEE Software*, Vol. 23, No. 1.

Shariq, S.G., and M.T. Vendelø. (2006). "Tacit Knowledge Sharing." In D. G. Schwartz, (ed.), *Encyclopedia of Knowledge Management*. Hershey, PA: Idea Group Reference.

Smith, H., and J. McKeen. (2003). "Creating and Facilitating Communities of Practice." Chapter 20 in C. W. Holsapple (ed.). *Handbook of Knowledge Management: Knowledge Matters*, Vol. 1. Heidelberg: Springer-Verlag.

Skyrme, D.J., and D.M. Amidon. (1998, January/February). "New Measures of Success." *Journal of Business Strategy*, Vol. 19, No. 1.

Soo, C., T. Devinney, D. Midgley, and A. Dering. (2002, Summer). "Knowledge Management: Philosophy, Processes, and Pitfalls." *California Management Review*, Vol. 44, No. 4.

Stone, D., and S. Warsone. (2003). "Does Accounting Account for Knowledge?" Chapter 13 in C.W. Holsapple (ed.). *Handbook of Knowledge Management: Knowledge Matters*, Vol. 1. Heidelberg: Springer-Verlag.

Storck, J., and P.A. Hill. (2002). "Knowledge Diffusion Through Strategic Communities." Chapter 5 in E.L. Lesser, M.A. Fontaine, and J.A. Slusher. (eds.). *Knowledge and Communities*. Woburn, MA: Butterworth-Heinemann.

Sullivan, D. (2001, August 31). "5 Principles of Intelligent Content Management." *Intelligent Enterprise*.

Sviokla, J.J. (2001, February 15). "Knowledge Pays." *CIO*.

Swan, J., M.. Robertson, and S. Newell. (2000, January). "Knowledge Management—When Will People Management Enter the Debate?" *Proceedings, 33rd HICSS*, Vol. 3. Los Alamitos, CA: IEEE Computer Society Press.

Taylor, C. (2001, March 12). "Intellectual Capital." *Knowledge Management*, Vol. 35, No. 11.

Teece, D. (2003). "Knowledge and Competence as Strategic Assets." Chapter 7 in C.W. Holsapple (ed.). *Handbook of Knowledge Management: Knowledge Matters*, Vol. 1. Heidelberg: Springer-Verlag.

Tseng, C., and J. Goo. (2005). "Intellectual Capital and Corporate Value in an Emerging Economy: Empirical Study of Taiwanese Manufacturers." *R&D Management*, Vol. 35, No.2.

Tuggle, F.D., and W.E. Goldfinger (2004). "A Methodology for Mining Embedded Knowledge from Process Maps," *Human Systems Management*, Vol. 23, No. 1.

Van de Van, A.H. (2005, June). "Running in Packs to Develop Knowledge-Intensive Technologies." *MIS Quarterly*, Vol. 29, No. 2.

Vat, K.H. (2006, April–June). "Developing a Learning Organization Model for Problem-Based Learning: The Emergent Lesson of Education from the IT Trenches." *Journal of Cases on Information Technology*, Vol. 8, No. 2.

Weir, J. (2004). "Bringing Structure to the Unstructured." *KMWorld*.

Weiss, L.M., M.M. Capozzi, and L. Prusak. (2004). "Learning from the Internet Giants." *MIT Sloan Management Review*, Vol. 45, No. 4.

Wenger, E. (2002). *Communities of Practice: Learning, Meaning, and Identity*. New York: Cambridge University Press.

Wenger, E., R. McDermott, and W.M. Snyder. (2002). *Cultivating Communities of Practice*. Boston: Harvard Business School Press.

Wenger, E.C., and W.M. Snyder. (2000, January/February). "Communities of Practice: The Organizational Frontier." *Harvard Business Review*, pp. 139–145.

Wickramasinghe, N. (2006). "Knowledge Creation." In D. G. Schwartz, (ed.). *Encyclopedia of Knowledge Management*. Hershey, PA: Idea Group Reference.

Zhang, D.S., and J.L. Zhao. (2006, January–March). "Knowledge Management in Organizations." *Journal of Database Management*, Vol. 17, No. 1.

Zhang, W. (2006). "Wonders Knowledge Portal." *Communications of the Association for Information Systems*, Vol. 17, No. 1.

Zimmermann, K.A. (2002, June). "Portals Help Insurers and Their Customers." *KMWorld*.

Zimmermann, K.A. (2003a, April). "Can You Measure Return on Knowledge?" *KMWorld*.

Zimmermann, K.A. (2003b, May). "Happy Together: Knowledge Management and Collaboration Work Hand-in-Hand to Satisfy the Thirst for Information." *KMWorld*.

Zyngier, S. (2006). "Knowledge Management Governance." In D.G. Schwartz (ed.). *Encyclopedia of Knowledge Management*. Hershey, PA: Idea Group Reference.

PART

V

Intelligent Systems

Learning Objectives for Part V

- Understand the foundations, definitions, and capabilities of artificial intelligence and knowledge-based systems
- Understand the process and tools for developing knowledge-based intelligent systems
- Understand how artificial neural networks (ANN) are used to develop intelligent decision support systems (DSS)
- Understand how genetic algorithms are used to develop intelligent systems
- Understand how fuzzy logic can be used to develop intelligent systems
- Understand state-of-the art applications of intelligent agents and recommendation systems on the Internet

In this part, we focus on using artificial intelligent techniques to develop intelligent systems for decision support. These systems include rule-based expert systems (ES) and second-generation advanced intelligent systems that use ANN, genetic algorithms, case-based reasoning, and intelligent agent techniques. In this part, we first present an overview of artificial intelligence and rule-based ES in Chapter 12. Chapter 13 describes advanced technologies that are commonly used in the commercial world, including case-based reasoning, genetic algorithms, fuzzy logic applications, natural language processing, and voice technologies. Chapter 14 describes the most cutting-edge decision support technologies on the Internet, with a focus on intelligent agents and recommendation systems that have gained much attention recently. Also relevant to the content in this section is the description of the process of knowledge acquisition, representation, inference mechanisms, knowledge validation, and uncertainty processing (see Chapter 18, an online chapter).

CHAPTER 12 Artificial Intelligence and Expert Systems

Learning Objectives

- Understand the concept and evolution of artificial intelligence
- Understand the importance of knowledge in decision support
- Describe the concept and evolution of rule-based expert systems (ES)
- Understand the architecture of rule-based ES
- Explain the benefits and limitations of rule-based systems for decision support
- Identify proper applications of ES
- Learn about tools and technologies for developing rule-based DSS

In addition to the use of data and mathematical models, some managerial decisions are qualitative in nature and need judgmental knowledge that resides in human experts. Thus, it is necessary to incorporate such knowledge in developing decision support systems (DSS). A system that integrates knowledge from experts is called a *knowledge-based decision support system (KBDSS)* or an *intelligent decision support system (IDSS)*. A KBDSS can enhance the capabilities of decision support not only by supplying a tool that directly supports a decision maker but also by enhancing various computerized DSS. The foundation for building such systems is the techniques and tools that have been developed in the area of artificial intelligence—rule-based ES being the primary one. This chapter introduces the essentials of both artificial intelligence and ES, in the following sections:

12.1 OPENING VIGNETTE: CIGNA USES BUSINESS RULES TO SUPPORT TREATMENT REQUEST APPROVAL

CIGNA, founded in 1865, is a major health insurance company. Through more than 120 years of growth, the company has become a major player in the business. It is particularly sensitive to the introduction of new information technology and has been very successful in using information technology to support its operation in the United States and other countries, such as China, Brazil, and Argentina. In 2005, CIGNA received the top award for "Best Technology Introduced by a Health Plan Organization for Employee/Consumer Choice."

PROBLEM

CIGNA Behavioral Health covers 16 million Americans in all 50 states and internationally and supports a professional network of more than 50,000 professionals. It needed a system to approve requests submitted by therapists for additional patient care quickly and automatically. CIGNA Behavioral Health's business processes for making approval determinations were scattered throughout many different software applications. Certain rules sometimes conflicted with each other, and knowledge was often lost due to employee turnover. In addition, the rules were hard-coded in complex if-then statements. As a result, accessing and changing the rules was a slow, cumbersome, and expensive process.

SOLUTION

In order to reduce the knowledge loss due to employee turnover and increase the consistency and efficiency of rule maintenance, CIGNA Behavioral Health decided to adopt rule-based intelligent systems that can automate certain decision-making events. The tools CIGNA chose were HaleyAuthority knowledge management software and HaleyRules inference engine to build a Web-based benefit management system called Provider eCare Online. With the eCare system, therapists submit requests for authorization of benefits over the Internet and receive automatic approval. HaleyAuthority is a software tool that allows an expert to describe knowledge in plain English. The software converts that description into business rules, which can be incorporated into a rule base for further inference. CIGNA Behavioral Health compiled the experience and expertise of behavioral health clinicians and then used HaleyAuthority to convert that knowledge into a series of straightforward, easily modifiable business rules. HaleyRules, integrated with the company's Java-based Web site, applies the approval policies in HaleyAuthority to therapist requests.

RESULTS

One benefit of the project is that more than 30 percent of all requests for authorization of benefits are now approved automatically through eCare, enabling CIGNA Behavioral Health to handle more requests with its existing staff. By expressing business processes in English using HaleyAuthority, eCare specialists can implement changes in hours instead of weeks. The adoption of knowledge-based systems has successfully helped CIGNA enhance operational efficiency and reduce costs. The tools of HaleyAuthority and HaleyRules, in combination, provide a convenient platform for the implementation of such intelligent systems.

Sources: Compiled from Haley Case Brief, *CIGNA Creates eCare Treatment Request Approval System with Haley Systems' Technology*, February, 2006; and **cigna.com** (accessed October 2006).

Questions for the Opening Vignette

1. Describe CIGNA's motivation for developing the eCare system.
2. Explain the role of the intelligent systems and their potential benefits in the case.
3. What major difficulties could be anticipated in the process of developing the system?
4. How are the systems in this case different from traditional DSS described in previous chapters?

WHAT WE CAN LEARN FROM THIS VIGNETTE

Many repetitive activities in business can be automated to achieve higher accuracy at lower costs. Taking advantage of rule-based technology can substantially enhance the performance of process-oriented business activities.

12.2 CONCEPTS AND DEFINITIONS OF ARTIFICIAL INTELLIGENCE

The opening vignette illustrates that in some decision situations, the support offered by data and model management alone may not be sufficient. At CIGNA, additional support was provided by rule-based expert systems (ES) to substitute for human expertise by supplying the necessary knowledge. However, several other intelligent technologies can be used to support decision situations that require expertise. All these technologies use qualitative *knowledge* rather than mathematical models to provide the needed supports; they are referred to as **knowledge-based systems (KBS)**. The major technology underlying these applications is *artificial intelligence*.

ARTIFICIAL INTELLIGENCE (AI) DEFINITIONS

Artificial intelligence (AI) is an area of computer science. The term encompasses many definitions, and most experts agree that AI is concerned with two basic ideas. First, it involves studying the thought processes of humans (to understand what intelligence is); second, it deals with representing and duplicating those processes via machines (e.g., computers, robots).

One well-publicized, classic definition of AI is "behavior by a machine that, if performed by a human being, would be called intelligent." Rich and Knight (1991) provided a thought-provoking definition: "Artificial intelligence is the study of how to make computers do things at which, at the moment, people are better."

A well-known application of artificial intelligence is the chess program called *Deep Blue*, developed by a research team in IBM (see Application Case 12.1). The system beat the world champion Garry Kasparov in a game that usually only highly intelligent people can win.

Application Case 12.1

Intelligent Systems Beat Chess Grand Master

Games are a classic application domain for intelligent systems. An extremely successful system is the computer chess program developed by IBM. In 1997, Deep Blue, a computer system armed with artificial intelligence, beat 34-year-old Russian World Chess Champaign Garry Kasparov in a six-game match. This was the first time a computer demonstrated its intelligence in an area that requires human intelligence. The system ran on an IBM RS/6000 SP machine that was capable of examining 200 million moves per second—or 50 billion positions—in the three minutes allocated for a single move in a chess game.

A six-person design team led by Chung-Jen Tan designed a hybrid heuristic and brute-force search model to assess the values of different moves. Although the victory of this computer does not imply that computer intelligence will prevail, it does indicate the potential of artificial intelligence, particularly in the area of intelligent decision support. Computers armed with intelligent reasoning capabilities can help managers minimize risks and maximize performance.

In February 2003, another human–computer match between Garry Kasparov and Deep Junior, a three-time computer chess champion programmed by Air Ban and Shay Bushinsky in Israel, ended in a 3–3 tie. This further confirmed that the knowledge captured in the computer chess program could be as powerful as that of the best human player. In 2004, a computer–computer match between Deep Junior and Fritz ended in a draw. Fritz is an intelligent system, designed by German scientists, that can execute 350,000 operations per second.

These successful chess programs indicate the power of artificial intelligence techniques and the powerful potential of having computer systems to support decision making in the future.

Sources: IBM, *Deep Blue Wins*, May 1997. **researchweb.watson.ibm.com/deepblue** (accessed March 2006); and U.S. Chess Online, *Kasparov Ties Championship Match with Deep Junior*, February 8, 2003, **uschess.org/news/press/uspr0307.html** (accessed March 2006).

To understand what artificial intelligence is, let's first look at the abilities that are considered signs of intelligence:

- Learning or understanding from experience
- Making sense out of ambiguous or contradictory messages
- Responding quickly and successfully to a new situation (i.e., different responses, flexibility)
- Using reasoning in solving problems and directing conduct effectively
- Dealing with perplexing situations
- Understanding and inferring in ordinary, rational ways
- Applying knowledge to manipulate the environment
- Thinking and reasoning
- Recognizing the relative importance of different elements in a situation

Alan Turing designed an interesting test to determine whether a computer exhibits intelligent behavior; it is called the **Turing test**. According to this test, a computer can be considered smart only when a human interviewer cannot identify the computer while conversing with both an unseen human being and an unseen computer.

In the next section, we discuss the major characteristics of artificial intelligence.

CHARACTERISTICS OF ARTIFICIAL INTELLIGENCE

Although AI's ultimate goal is to build machines that mimic human intelligence, the capabilities of current commercial AI products are far from exhibiting any significant success in the abilities just listed. Nevertheless, AI programs are continuously improving, and they increase productivity and quality by automating several tasks that require some human intelligence. Artificial intelligence techniques usually have the features described in the following sections.

Symbolic Processing

Symbolic processing is an essential characteristic of artificial intelligence, as reflected in the following definition: **Artificial intelligence (AI)** is the branch of computer science that deals primarily with symbolic, nonalgorithmic methods of problem solving. This definition focuses on two characteristics:

- *Numeric versus symbolic*. Computers were originally designed specifically to process numbers (i.e., numeric processing). However, people tend to think symbolically; our intelligence is based in part on our mental ability to manipulate *symbols* rather than just numbers. Although symbolic processing is at the core of AI, this does not mean that AI does not involve math; rather, the emphasis in AI is on the manipulation of symbols.

- *Algorithmic versus heuristic.* An *algorithm* is a step-by-step procedure that has well-defined starting and ending points and is guaranteed to find a solution to a specific problem. Most computer architectures readily lend themselves to this step-by-step approach. Many human reasoning processes tend to be nonalgorithmic; in other words, our mental activities consist of more than just following logical, step-by-step procedures. Rather, human thinking relies more on rules learned from previous experience and gut feelings.

Heuristics

Heuristics are intuitive knowledge, or rules of thumb, learned from experience. AI deals with ways of representing knowledge using symbols with heuristics methods for processing information. By using heuristics, we do not have to rethink completely what to do every time we encounter a similar problem. For example, when a salesperson plans to visit clients in different cities, a popular heuristic is to visit the next nearest one (i.e., the nearest neighbor heuristic). Many AI methods use some kind of heuristics to reduce the complexity of problem solving.

Inferencing

As an alternative to heuristics, artificial intelligence also includes reasoning capabilities that can build higher-level knowledge from existing heuristics. This reasoning consists of inferencing from facts and rules, using heuristics or other search approaches.

Machine Learning

Learning is an important capability for human beings. Artificial intelligent systems do not have the learning capabilities humans have, but they do have some sort of mechanical learning capabilities, called *machine learning*, that allow the systems to adjust their behavior and react to changes in the outside environment. Many machine-learning methods, including inductive learning, artificial neural networks (ANN), and genetic algorithms, exist for developing intelligent systems.

Section 12.2 Review Questions

1. What is artificial intelligence?
2. What are the major capabilities of artificial intelligence?
3. What are the major characteristics of artificial intelligence?
4. What are heuristics? Give an example.

12.3 THE ARTIFICIAL INTELLIGENCE FIELD

The field of AI is quite broad. In this section, we introduce its evolution, compare artificial intelligence with natural intelligence, and overview a few major applications.

EVOLUTION OF ARTIFICIAL INTELLIGENCE

The evolution of artificial intelligence includes five major stages. Figure 12.1 shows the evolution from 1960 until now.

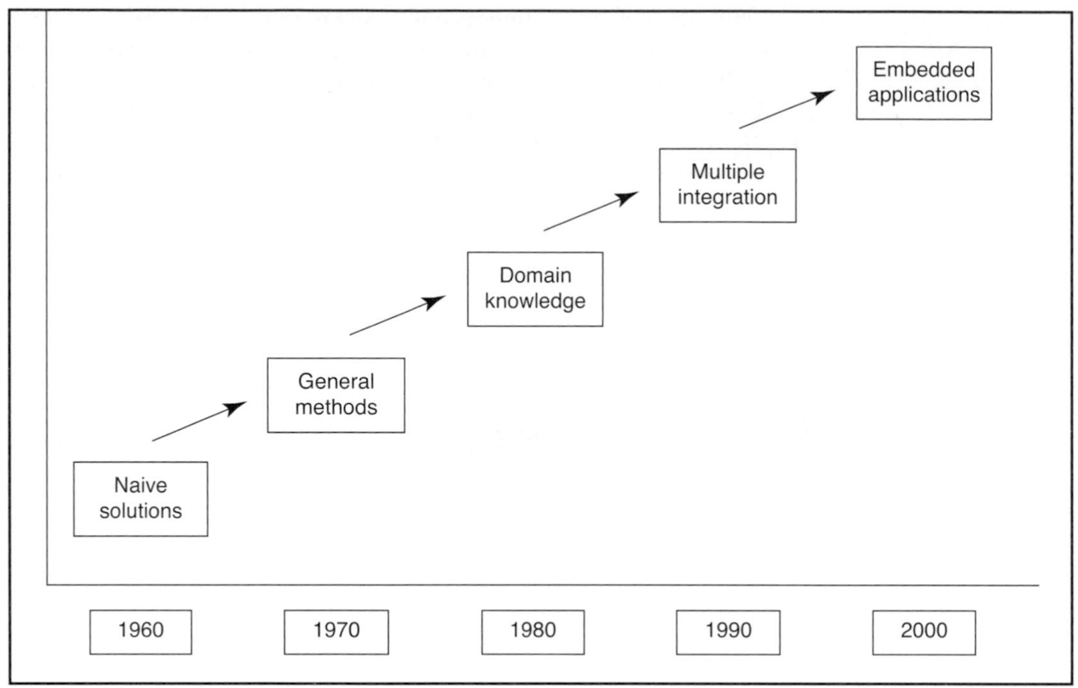

FIGURE 12.1 Five Stages of AI Evolution

A major event that triggered the wave of artificial intelligence is the Dartmouth Meeting. A group of computer scientists gathered at Dartmouth College to discuss the great potential of computer applications in 1956. They were confident that, given the enormous computing power, computers would be able to solve many complex problems and outperform human beings in many areas. At that time, scientists had little understanding of the complexity of human intelligence and were overly optimistic about what computers could achieve. Many solutions created at that time were primitive, and hence the stage is called the *naïve solutions stage*.

After several years of trial and error, scientists started focusing on developing more effective problem-solving methods, such as knowledge representation schemes, reasoning strategies, and effective search heuristics. Because the feature of this stage is the development of general-purpose methods, it is called the *general methods stage*.

After building enough general-purpose methods, people started applying them to real-world applications. The application at this stage is different from the first one in that people already knew that how to solve commonsense problems is difficult to program into a computer. Therefore, most applications were targeted at a narrowly defined domain with specialized knowledge. This kind of systems is called an *expert system* or a *knowledge-based system*. Acquisition of expert knowledge plays a key role in development of such systems. We call this the *domain knowledge stage*.

After 1990, more advanced problem-solving methods were developed, and there was a strong need to integrate multiple techniques and solve problems in multiple domains. Hybrid systems, such as integrations of rule-based and case-based systems and integrations of ANN and genetic algorithms become necessary. We call this the *multiple integration stage*.

Since 2000, the trend has been to embed various intelligent components in popular applications. Intelligent systems and robotics continue to spread into everyday use,

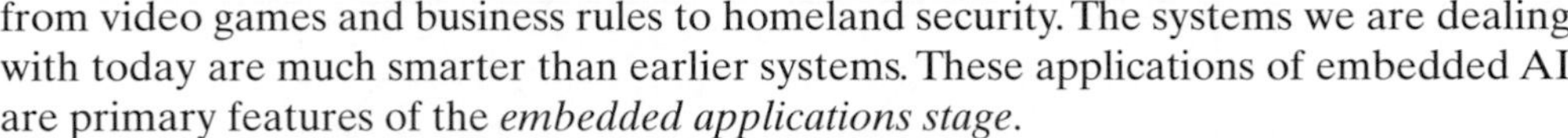

from video games and business rules to homeland security. The systems we are dealing with today are much smarter than earlier systems. These applications of embedded AI are primary features of the *embedded applications stage*.

The use of artificial intelligence in DSS has advantages and limitations. See Technology Insights 12.2 for a comparison between artificial and natural intelligence.

APPLICATIONS OF ARTIFICIAL INTELLIGENCE

Artificial intelligence is a collection of concepts and ideas that are related to the development of an intelligent system. These concepts and ideas may be developed in different areas and be applied to different domains. In order to understand the scope of AI, therefore, we need to see a group of areas that may be called the AI family. Figure 12.2 shows the major branches of AI studies that are built on the foundation technologies in computer science, philosophy, electrical engineering, management science, psychology, and linguistics. They are briefly described next.

TECHNOLOGY INSIGHTS 12.2

Artificial Intelligence Versus Natural Intelligence

The potential value of artificial intelligence can be better understood by contrasting it with natural, or human, intelligence. AI has several important advantages:

- AI is more permanent. Natural intelligence is perishable from a commercial standpoint, in that workers can change their place of employment or forget information. However, AI is permanent as long as the computer systems and programs remain unchanged.
- AI offers ease of duplication and dissemination. Transferring a body of knowledge from one person to another usually requires a lengthy process of apprenticeship; even so, expertise can seldom be duplicated completely. However, when knowledge is embedded in a computer system, it can easily be transferred from that computer to any other computer on the Internet or on an intranet.
- AI can be less expensive than natural intelligence. There are many circumstances in which buying computer services costs less than having corresponding human power carry out the same tasks. This is especially true when knowledge is disseminated over the Web.
- AI, being a computer technology, is consistent and thorough. Natural intelligence is erratic because people are erratic; they do not always perform consistently.
- AI can be documented. Decisions made by a computer can be easily documented by tracing the activities of the system. Natural intelligence is difficult to document. For example, a person may reach a conclusion but at some later date may be unable to re-create the reasoning process that led to that conclusion or to even recall the assumptions that were part of the decision.
- AI can execute certain tasks much faster than a human can.
- AI can perform certain tasks better than many or even most people.

Natural intelligence does have some advantages over AI, such as the following:

- Natural intelligence is *creative*, whereas AI is rather *uninspired*. The ability to acquire knowledge is inherent in human beings, but with AI, tailored knowledge must be built into a carefully constructed system.
- Natural intelligence enables people to benefit from and use *sensory experience* directly, whereas most AI systems must work with symbolic input and representations.

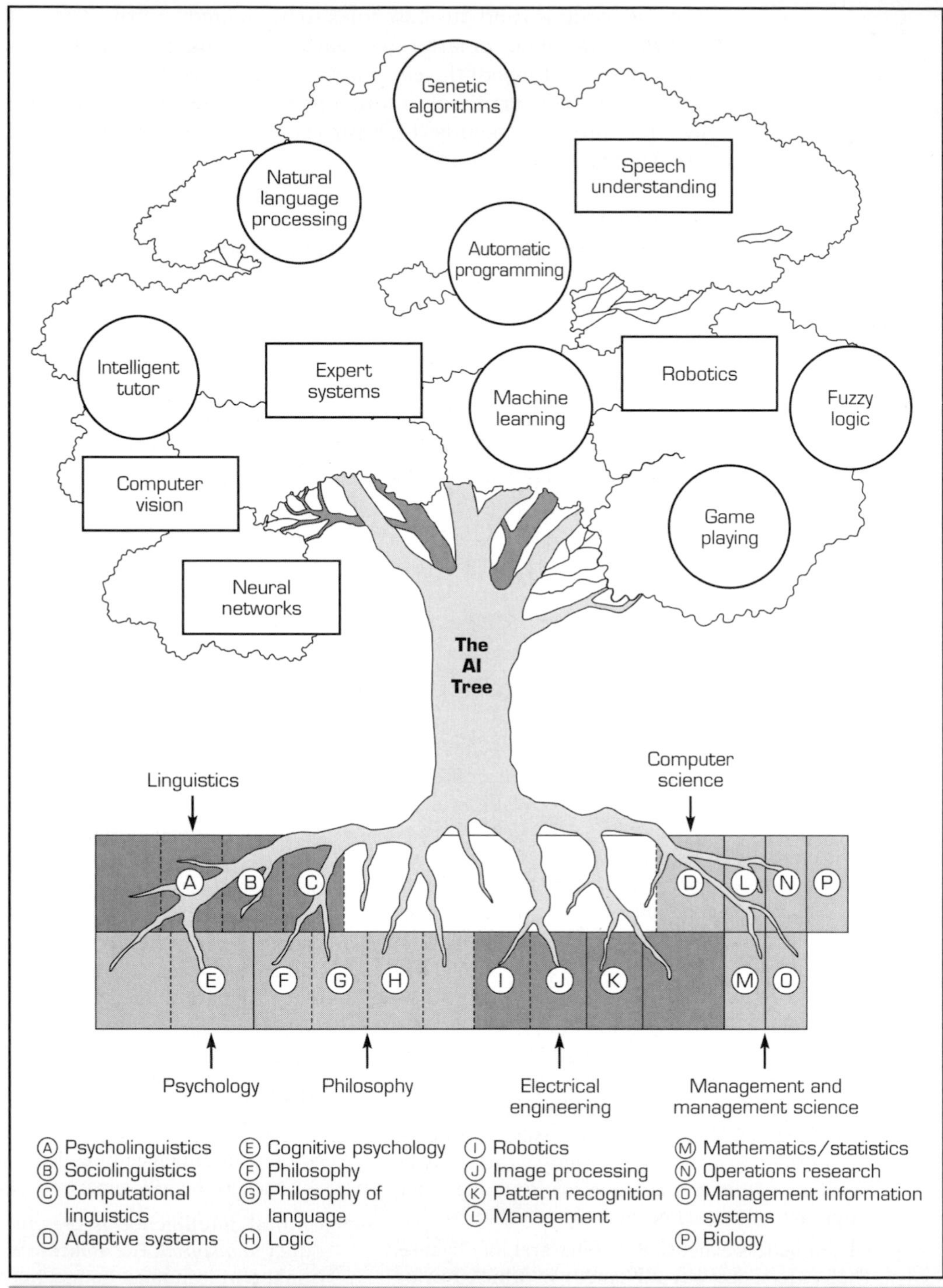

FIGURE 12.2 The Disciplines and Applications of AI

Expert Systems

The term *expert system* was derived from the term *knowledge-based expert system*. An **expert system (ES)** is a system that uses human knowledge captured in a computer to solve problems that ordinarily require human expertise. Later sections of this chapter provide details.

Natural Language Processing

Natural language processing (NLP) technology gives computer users the ability to communicate with a computer in their native language (see Technology Insights 12.3). This technology allows for a conversational type of interface, in contrast to using a programming language that consists of computer jargon, syntax, and commands. It includes two subfields:

- Natural language understanding investigates methods of enabling computers to comprehend instructions given in ordinary English so that the computers can understand people more easily.
- Natural language generation strives to have computers produce ordinary English language so that people can understand the computers more easily.

Limited success in this area is typified by current systems that can recognize and interpret written sentences. More information on this is available in Chapter 13.

Speech (Voice) Understanding

Speech (voice) understanding is the recognition and understanding of spoken language by a computer. Applications of this technology have become more and more popular. For instance, many companies have adopted this technology in their call centers (see

TECHNOLOGY INSIGHTS 12.3

Natural Language Processing (NLP)

The goal of NLP is to capture the meaning of sentences, which involves finding a representation for the sentences that can be connected to more general knowledge about the world. NLP usually includes the following stages:

- *Stage 1: The conversion stage.* The first stage of NLP is to convert the spoken utterance into a string of words. This process is extremely complex and requires a great deal of knowledge about the real world. The current technology can handle words in certain limited domains. We can think of this stage as producing a few alternative interpretations of the speech signal, one of which is likely to be correct.
- *Stage 2: Syntax analysis.* The second stage of NLP is syntax analysis that determines the structure of the sentence, usually in terms of phrases, such as noun phrases, verb phrases, and prepositional phrases. These nested phrases serve as the base for all subsequent processing. Syntactic analysis is probably the best-developed area in computational linguistics but, nevertheless, there is no universally reliable "grammar of English" that one can use to parse sentences as well as educated human beings.
- *Stage 3: Semantic analysis.* The third stage of NLP takes the given sentence structure and begins to attach meaning to the sentence—that is, it translates the syntactic structure into some form of logical representation of the meaning, but without knowing the context.
- *Stage 4: The pragmatic stage.* This stage involves disambiguating the various possible senses of words, possible syntactic structures, and so on. In addition, it tries to identify the antecedents of pronouns and the referents of descriptive phrases. This is the least developed area so far in NLP.

NLP has been used in some intelligent software, such as the HaleyAuthority business rules management system (BRMS). HaleyAuthority allows its users to directly capture and organize business logic, policies, regulations, and other related knowledge in plain English. This makes the implementation of business rules much easier.

Sources: E. Matais, "Enhancing Information Systems Management with Natural Language Processing Techniques," *Data and Knowledge Management*, June 2002; and description of Haley products at **haley.com** (accessed October 2006).

Application Case 12.4). An interesting application is Literacy Innovation that Speech Technology ENables (LISTEN), developed at Carnegie Mellon University, which provides a pleasant and automated environment to improve literacy by listening to children read aloud (**cs.cmu.edu/~listen**). More information is available in Chapter 13.

Application Case 12.4

Automatic Speech Recognition in Call Centers

More and more companies are using automated speech recognition technology for interacting with customers. This is particularly popular in call centers. In the United States alone, more than 50,000 call centers spend more than $90 billion dealing with customers' requests. With human operators costing around $1 per minute to maintain, speech recognition offers companies an opportunity to lower their overheads.

Charles Schwab, a U.S. discount stockbroker, introduced the first speech system for retail broking in 1996. That year, the number of new accounts with the company increased by 41 percent, and the call centers took 97 million calls. An automated attendant in this system can understand 15,000 names of individual equities and funds, takes up to 100,000 calls per day, and is 93 percent accurate in identifying queries the first time they are made. Costs have been cut to $1 per call, down from $4 to $5 per call.

Hotel chain Wyndham International has used speech automation technology to develop intelligent agents to provide conversational skills to handle advanced customer service calls at Wyndham's call center.

In 2004, U.S. companies spent $480 million on speech-enabled self-service technology (SESST). By 2008, 1 billion speech-enabled service centers are expected to be in operation, replacing functions currently taking place in call centers in India and some other nations. A call serviced through speech automation would cost approximately 15 to 25 percent of the cost of a call handled by an agent in India. The voice technology may lead to a change the operation outsourcing trend.

Sources: Adapted from "Just Talk to Me," *The Economist Technology Quarterly*, December 8, 2001; and P. Gooptu, *Threat to Call Centers: Voice Automation!* November 23, 2004, **rediff.com/money/2004/nov/23bpo.htm** (accessed March 2006).

Robotics and Sensory Systems

Sensory systems, such as vision systems, tactile systems, and signal-processing systems, when combined with AI, define a broad category of systems generally called *robots*. A **robot** is an electromechanical device that can be programmed to perform manual tasks. The Robotics Institute of America formally defines a robot as "a reprogrammable multifunctional manipulator designed to move materials, parts, tools, or specialized devices through variable programmed motions for the performance of a variety of tasks" (Currie, 1999).

An "intelligent" robot has some kind of sensory apparatus, such as a camera, that collects information about the robot's operation and its environment. The intelligent part of the robot allows it to interpret the collected information and to respond and adapt to changes in its environment rather than just follow instructions. A recent report described the humanoid HRP-2 robots, named *Promets*, developed by the National Institute of Advanced Industrial Science and Technology in Japan. These robots are designed to respond to verbal instructions to perform certain tasks, such as moving chairs or turning on a TV, and they are capable of capturing three-dimensional images of objects and locating them through an infrared sensor (see Yamaguchi, 2006). A recent Reuters report indicates that Toyota intends to sell service robots by 2010 (Reuters, 2005).

Computer Vision and Scene Recognition

Visual recognition is the addition of some form of computer intelligence and decision making to digitized visual information received from a machine sensor, such as a camera. The combined information is then used to perform or control such operations as robotic movement, conveyor speed, and production-line quality.

The basic objective of computer vision is to interpret scenarios rather than generate pictures. Interpreting scenarios is defined in different ways, depending on the application. For example, in interpreting pictures taken by a satellite, it may be sufficient to roughly identify regions of crop damage. On the other hand, robot vision systems can be designed to precisely identify assembly components to correctly affix them to the item being assembled.

Intelligent Computer-Aided Instruction

Intelligent computer-aided instruction (ICAI) refers to machines that can tutor humans. To a certain extent, such a machine can be viewed as an ES. However, the major objective of an ES is to render advice, whereas the purpose of an ICAI is to teach.

Computer-assisted instruction, which has been in use for many years, brings the power of a computer to bear on the educational process. Now AI methods are being applied to the development of ICAI systems in an attempt to create computerized tutors that shape their teaching techniques to fit the learning patterns of individual students. These are known as **intelligent tutoring systems (ITS)**, many of which have been implemented on the Web. An application can be found in Online File W12.2 (see also Lopez et al., 2003).

Automatic Programming

Writing computer programs has always been a tedious and error-prone task. Automatic programming allows computer programs to be automatically generated, usually based on specifications that are higher level and easier for humans to specify than ordinary programming languages. Automatic programming occurs when AI techniques are embedded in compilers.

Neural Computing

A **neural (computing) network** is a set of mathematical models that simulate the way a human brain functions. Such models have been implemented in flexible, easy-to-use PC-based neural network packages such as BrainMaker (**calsci.com**) and NeuroShell (**wardsystems.com**). The applications of neural networks in business are abundant. For examples, Fadlalla and Lin (2001) provided a number of financial applications of neural networks. We discussed neural computing in depth in Chapter 8.

Game Playing

Game playing is one of the first areas that AI researchers studied. It is a perfect area for investigating new strategies and heuristics because the results are easy to measure. The success of Deep Blue (described in Application Case 12.1) is a good example of successful game playing development.

Language Translation

Automated translation uses computer programs to translate words and sentences from one language to another without much interpretation by humans. For example, you can use Babel Fish Translation, available at **world.altavista.com,** to try more than 20 different combinations of language translation.

Fuzzy Logic

Fuzzy logic is a technique for processing linguistic terms. It extends the notions of logic beyond simple true/false statements to allow for partial (or even continuous) truths. Inexact knowledge and imprecise reasoning are important aspects of expertise in applying commonsense to decision-making situations. In fuzzy logic, the value of true or false is replaced by the degree of set membership. For example, in the traditional Boolean logic, a person's credit record is either good or bad. In fuzzy logic, the credit record may be assessed as both good and bad, but with different degrees. See Chapter 13 and Nguyen and Walker (1999) for more details.

Genetic Algorithms

Genetic algorithms are intelligent methods that use computers to simulate the process of natural evolution to find patterns from a set of data. For a specific problem, the solution is represented as a "chromosome," which generally contains a sequence of 0s and 1s, indicating values of decision variables. A genetic method starts with a randomly generated population of solutions and randomly combines portions of chromosomes to form new solutions with multiple generations of duplication and an occasional mutation. The evolution continues until a satisfactory solution is reached. See Goldberg (1994) for an excellent classic introduction. Ghanea-Hercock and Ghanea-Hercock (2003) discussed Java implementation, and Chapter 13 provides more descriptions of genetic algorithms.

Intelligent Agents

Intelligent agents (IA) are small programs that reside on computers to conduct certain tasks automatically. An intelligent agent runs in the background, monitors the environment, and reacts to certain trigger conditions. A good example is a virus detection program. It resides on your computer, scans all incoming data, and removes found viruses automatically. Intelligent agents are applied in personal digital assistants (PDAs), e-mail and news filtering and distribution, appointment handling, and Web applets for e-commerce and information gathering. See Application Case 12.5 for an example and Chapter 14 for more details.

Application Case 12.5

Agents for Travel Planning at USC

Planning business trips is a tedious task that includes selecting a flight, reserving a hotel, and possibly reserving a car. When a schedule is set, many other decisions must be made, based on past experiences, such as whether driving to the airport or taking a taxi. The time and effort required to make more informed decisions usually outweighs the cost. Schedules can change, prices can decrease after purchasing a ticket, flight delays can result in missed connections, and hotel rooms and rental cars can be given away because of late arrivals. All these contingencies add stress for the traveler.

To address these issues, the University of Southern California developed an integrated travel planning and monitoring system, called Travel Assistant. The system provides the user with the information necessary to make an informed travel plan. It uses information agents to provide information for planning and monitoring agents to trace any changes in the original plan. An information agent takes a particular information request, navigates to the appropriate Web site, extracts information from the Web site, and then returns the information as an XML document for processing.

Monitoring agents are built on top of the information agents and keep track of the status of the schedule. If any information (e.g., cancellation or delay of the flight) that might cause schedule changes is found, the agents send a message to the user. These agents perform their tasks at regular intervals. Major messages sent by these agents include messages about flight delays, messages about flight cancellations, faxes to a hotel, messages about reductions in airfares, and messages about availability of earlier flights.

An intelligent agent project that supports travel and tourism planning was also conducted at RMIT University in Australia. That system supports mobile applications on PDAs and other devices.

Sources: Adapted from C. Knoblock. "Agents for Gathering, Integrating, and Monitoring Information for Travel Planning," *IEEE Intelligent Systems*, Vol. 17, NO. 6., 2003; and L. Mathies, L. Padgham, and B.Q. Vo, "Agent Based Travel and Tourism Planning," *Proceedings of the Autonomous Agents and Multiagent Systems Conference*, Utrecht University, the Netherlands, July 25–29, 2005.

Section 12.3 Review Questions

1. What are the major advantages of artificial intelligence over natural intelligence?
2. What are the major disadvantages of artificial intelligence compared to natural intelligence?
3. What are the major characteristics of artificial intelligence?
4. Describe an application of artificial intelligence.
5. What technology can help move call centers that have been outsourced to other countries back to the United States?
6. Define *NLP* and describe an application of NLP.
7. Define *speech recognition* and discuss one application of the technology.
8. Define *intelligent agent* and describe one application of intelligent agents.

12.4 BASIC CONCEPTS OF EXPERT SYSTEMS (ES)

ES are computer-based information systems that use expert knowledge to attain high-level decision performance in a narrow problem domain. MYCIN, developed at Stanford University in the early 1980s for medical diagnosis, is the most well-known ES. ES has also been used in taxation, credit analysis, equipment maintenance, and fault diagnosis. ES has been popular in large- and medium-sized organizations as a major tool for improving productivity and quality (see Nedovic and Devedzic, 2002; and Nurminen et al., 2003).

The basic concepts of ES include how to determine who experts are, the definition of *expertise*, how expertise can be transferred from a person to a computer, and how the system works. We describe these concepts in the following sections.

EXPERTS

An **expert** is a person who has the special knowledge, judgment, experience, and methods to give advice and solve problems, along with the ability to apply these talents. It is an expert's job to provide knowledge about how he or she performs a task that a KBS will perform. An expert knows which facts are important and understands the meaning of the relationships among facts. In diagnosing a problem with an automobile's electrical system, for example, an expert mechanic knows that fan belts can break and cause the battery to discharge.

There is no standard definition of *expert*, but decision performance and the level of knowledge a person has are typical criterion we use to determine whether a particular person is an expert. Typically, experts must be able to solve a problem and achieve a performance level that is significantly better than the average. In addition, experts are relative. An expert at a time or in a region may not be an expert in another time or region. For example, an attorney in New York may not be a legal expert in Beijing, China. A medical student may be an expert compared to the general public but is not an expert in surgery. Experts have expertise that can solve problems and explain certain phenomena in the problem domain. Typically, human experts are capable of doing the following:

- Recognizing and formulating a problem
- Solving a problem quickly and correctly
- Explaining a solution
- Learning from experience
- Restructuring knowledge
- Breaking rules, if necessary
- Determining relevance
- Degrading gracefully (i.e., being aware of one's limitations)

EXPERTISE

Expertise is the extensive, task-specific knowledge that experts possess. The level of expertise determines the performance of a decision. Expertise is often acquired through training, reading, and experience in practice. It includes explicit knowledge, such as theories learned from a textbook or in a classroom, and implicit knowledge, gained from experience. The following is a list of possible knowledge types:

- Theories about the problem domain
- Rules and procedures regarding the general problem domain
- Heuristics about what to do in a given problem situation
- Global strategies for solving these types of problems
- Metaknowledge (i.e., knowledge about knowledge)
- Facts about the problem area

These types of knowledge enable experts to make better and faster decision than non-experts when solving complex problems.

Expertise often includes these characteristics:

- Expertise is usually associated with a high degree of intelligence, but it is not always associated with the smartest person.
- Expertise is usually associated with a vast quantity of knowledge.
- Expertise is based on learning from past successes and mistakes.
- Expertise is based on knowledge that is well-stored, organized, and quickly retrievable from an expert who has excellent recall of patterns from previous experiences.

FEATURES OF ES

ES must have the following features:

- *Expertise.* As described in the previous section, experts differ in their levels of expertise. An ES must possess expertise that enables it to make expert-level decisions. The system must exhibit expert performance and adequate robustness.

- *Symbolic reasoning.* The basic rationale of artificial intelligence is to use symbolic reasoning rather than mathematical calculation. This is also true for ES. That is, knowledge must be represented symbolically, and the primary reasoning mechanism must be symbolic. Typical symbolic reasoning mechanisms include backward chaining and forward chaining, which are described later in this chapter.
- *Deep knowledge.* Deep knowledge concerns the level of expertise in a knowledge base. The knowledge base must contain complex knowledge not easily found among non-experts.
- *Self-knowledge.* ES must be able to examine their own reasoning and provide proper explanations as to why a particular conclusion was reached. Most experts have very strong learning capabilities to update their knowledge constantly. ES also need to be able to learn from their successes and failures as well as from other knowledge sources.

The development of ES is divided into two generations. Most first-generation ES use if-then rules to represent and store their knowledge. Second-generation ES are more flexible in adopting multiple knowledge representation and reasoning methods. They may integrate neural networks with rule-based inference to pursue higher decision performance. A scenario of using ES is shown in Technology Insights 12.6.

Table 12.1 provides a comparison between conventional systems and ES.

WHY WE NEED ES

There are several reasons for a company to adopt ES. First, experts in the company may retire or leave. ES are an excellent tool for preserving professional knowledge crucial to a company's competitiveness. Second, certain knowledge needs to be

TECHNOLOGY INSIGHTS 12.6

Sample Sessions of a Rule-Based ES

A rule-based ES contains rules in its knowledge base. The rules are used to generate questions for the user. The user's responses allow the system to provide recommendations. Suppose that you have an ES that recommends notebook computers based on a customer's needs. The following is a possible consultation session:

1. What is your primary task to be performed on the notebook computer?
   - ☐ Word processing
   - ☐ Communications
   - ☐ Multimedia applications

   Answer: 1 (click the first check box)
2. Where are you going to use the notebook most often?
   - ☐ In the office
   - ☐ While traveling

   Answer: 2 (click the second check box)
3. What is your budget range?
   - ☐ Below $1K
   - ☐ Between $1K and $2K
   - ☐ Above $2K

   Answer: 2 (click the third check box)

System recommendation: You should consider buying a Dell Latitude X1

Reasons: It is light (2.5 pounds) and more suitable for your word processing and travel needs; it is also priced at US $1,950, which fits your budget.

TABLE 12.1 Comparison of Conventional Systems and Expert Systems

Conventional Systems	*Expert Systems*
Information and its processing are usually combined in one sequential program.	The knowledge base is clearly separated from the processing (inference) mechanism (i.e., knowledge rules are separated from the control).
The program does not make mistakes (programmers or users do).	The program may make mistakes.
Conventional systems do not (usually) explain why input data are needed or how conclusions are drawn.	Explanation is a part of most ES.
Conventional systems require all input data. They may not function properly with missing data unless planned for.	ES do not require all initial facts. ES can typically arrive at reasonable conclusions with missing facts.
Changes in the program are tedious (except in DSS).	Changes in the rules are easy to make.
The system operates only when it is completed.	The system can operate with only a few rules (as the first prototype).
Execution is done on a step-by-step (algorithmic) basis.	Execution is done by using heuristics and logic.
Large databases can be effectively manipulated.	Large knowledge bases can be effectively manipulated.
Conventional systems represent and use data.	ES represent and use knowledge.
Efficiency is usually a major goal. Effectiveness is important only for DSS.	Effectiveness is the major goal.
Conventional systems easily deal with quantitative data.	ES easily deal with qualitative data.
Conventional systems use numeric data representations.	ES use symbolic and numeric knowledge representations.
Conventional systems capture, magnify, and distribute access to numeric data or information.	ES capture, magnify, and distribute access to judgment and knowledge.

documented or examined. An ES is an excellent tool for documenting professional knowledge for examination or improvement. Third, education and training is an important but difficult task. An ES is a good tool for training new employees and disseminating knowledge in an organization. Finally, experts are often rare and expensive. ES allow knowledge to be transferred more easily at a lower cost. ES can also be useful tools for knowledge storage and transfer in organizations.

Of course, ES are not real experts. They have advantages and shortcomings. Table 12.2 shows a comparison between human experts and ES.

Section 12.4 Review Questions

1. What is an ES?
2. Explain why we need ES.
3. What are the major features of ES?
4. What is expertise? Provide an example of expertise.
5. Define *deep knowledge* and give an example of it.

TABLE 12.2 Differences Between Human Experts and Expert Systems

Features	*Human Experts*	*Expert Systems*
Mortality	Yes	No
Knowledge transfer	Difficult	Easy
Knowledge documentation	Difficult	Easy
Decision consistency	Low	High
Unit usage cost	High	Low
Creativity	High	Low
Adaptability	High	Medium
Knowledge scope	Broad	Narrow
Knowledge type	Commonsense and technical	Technical
Knowledge content	Experience	Rules and symbolic models

12.5 APPLICATIONS OF EXPERT SYSTEMS

ES have been applied in many business and technological areas to support decision making. Application Case 12.7 shows a few real-world applications of ES. (Also see Online Files W12.1 and W12.4.)

Application Case 12.7

Sample Applications of ES

ES can have many applications. Below are a few examples.

CUSTOMER SUPPORT AT LOGITECH

Logitech is one of the largest vendors of mouse devices and Web cameras in the world. Because the company offers many different models of these tools, customer support is a major challenge. To take advantage of the Internet and technologies in intelligent systems, Logitech deploys an interactive knowledge portal to provide Web-based self-help customer support to its QuickCam customer in North America. The noHold Knowledge Platform emulates the way a human would interact with a customer, allows the user to ask questions or describe problems in natural language, and carries on an intelligent conversation with the user until it has enough information to provide an accurate answer.

CHINA'S FREIGHT TRAIN SYSTEM

An ES was developed in China to allocate freight cars and determine what and how much to load on each car. The ES is integrated with the existing management information system (MIS), and the system is distributed to many users.

ELECTRICITY MARKET FORECASTER

EnvaPower developed an electricity market forecasting system, called MarketMonitor, that uses artificial intelligence techniques to gather, synthesize, and analyze a large number of factors that may affect the consumption of electricity.

RULE-BASED ENGINE FOR MOBILE GAMES

In reaction to the rapid growth in mobile devices and entertainment needs, a group of researchers in the United Kingdom is creating a rule-based AI engine that can support the development of games on mobile devices. The system allows downloadable games to have AI components so that they can become more intelligent.

SEI INVESTMENT'S FINANCIAL DIAGNOSIS SYSTEM

SEI Investment uses business rules management technologies to create an enabling platform for delivering "financial wellness" solutions to its client. The system includes rules for regulatory and application checks, transaction management governance, and automation of transactions without human interruption.

Sources: "Logitech Deploys Online Customer Support," *Expert Systems*, November 2001; G. Geng, B. Zhang, J. Zhu, and C.H. Zhong, "Applying AI to Railway Freight Loading." *Expert Systems with Applications*, January 1999; *Expert Systems*, May 2002, Vol. 19, No. 2; and L. Hall, A. Gordon, R. James, and L. Newell, "A Lightweight Rule-Based AI Engine for Mobile Games," *ACM SIG International Conference on Advances in Computer Entertainment Technologies*, 2004.

Table 12.3 shows some representative ES and their application domains.

CLASSICAL SUCCESSFUL ES

Early ES applications, such as DENDRAL for molecular structure identification and MYCIN for medical diagnosis, were primarily in the science domain. XCON for configuration of the VAX computer system at Digital Equipment Corp. (a major producer of minicomputers around 1990 that was later taken over by Compaq) was a successful example in business.

DENDRAL

The DENDRAL project was initiated by Edward Feigenbaum in 1965. It used a set of knowledge- or rule-based reasoning commands to deduce the likely molecular structure of organic chemical compounds from known chemical analyses and mass spectrometry data. DENDRAL proved to be fundamentally important in demonstrating how rule-based reasoning could be developed into powerful knowledge engineering tools and led to the development of other rule-based reasoning programs at the Stanford Artificial Intelligence Laboratory (SAIL). The most important of those programs was MYCIN.

MYCIN

MYCIN is a rule-based ES that diagnoses bacterial infections of the blood. It was developed by a group of researchers at Stanford University in 1970s. By asking questions and backward chaining through a rule base of about 500 rules, MYCIN can recognize approximately 100 causes of bacterial infections, which allows the system to recommend effective drug prescriptions. In a controlled test, its performance was rated to be equal that of human specialists. The reasoning and uncertainty processing methods used in MYCIN are pioneers in the area and have generated long-term impact in ES development.

TABLE 12.3 Sample Applications of Expert Systems

Expert System	*Organization*	*Application Domain*
Classical Applications		
MYCIN	Stanford University	Medical diagnosis
XCON	DEC	System configuration
Expert Tax	Coopers & Lybrand	Tax planning
Loan Probe	Peat Marwick	Loan evaluation
La-Courtier	Cognitive Systems	Financial planning
LMOS	Pacific Bell	Network management
PROSPECTOR	Stanford Research Institute	Discovery of new mineral deposits
New Applications		
Fish-Expert	North China	Disease diagnosis in fish
HelpDeskIQ	BMC Remedy	Help desk management
Authorete	Haley	Business rule automation
eCare	CIGNA	Insurance claims
SONAR	NSAD	Stock market monitoring

XCON

XCON is a rule-based system developed at Digital Equipment Corp. This **rule-based system** uses rules to help determine the optimal system configuration that fits customer requirements. The system could handle a customer request within 1 minute, which typically took the sales team 20 to 30 minutes. With the ES, the service accuracy increased to 98 percent, from a manual approach with accuracy of 65 percent, which saves millions of dollars every year.

NEWER APPLICATIONS OF ES

More recent applications of ES include risk management, pension fund advising, business rule automation, automated market surveillance, and homeland security.

Credit Analysis Systems

ES are developed to support the needs of commercial lending institutions. They can help analyze the credit record of a customer and assess a proper credit line. Rules in the knowledge base can also help assess the risk and risk-management policies. These kinds of systems are used in over one-third of the top 100 commercial banks in the United States and Canada.

Pension Fund Advisors

Nestlé Foods Corporation has developed an ES that provides information on an employee's pension fund status. The system maintains an up-to-date knowledge base to give participants advice concerning the impact of regulation changes and conformance with new standards. A system offered on the Internet at the Pingtung Teacher's College in Southern Taiwan has functions that allow participants to plan their retirement through what-if analysis that calculates their pension benefits under different scenarios.

Automated Help Desks

BMC Remedy (**remedy.com**) offers HelpDeskIQ, a rule-based help desk solution for small businesses. This browser-based tool enables small businesses to deal with customer requests more efficiently. Incoming e-mails automatically pass into HelpDeskIQ's business rule engine. The messages are sent to the proper technician, based on defined priority and status. The solution assists help desk technicians in resolving problems and tracking issues more effectively. For other examples of uses of ES with automated help desks, see Online File W12.3.

Homeland Security Systems

PortBlue Corp. (**portblue.com/pub/solutions-homeland-security**) has developed an ES for homeland security. It is designed for assessing terrorist threats and provides (1) an assessment of vulnerability to terrorist attack, (2) indicators of terrorist surveillance activity, and (3) guidance for managing interactions with potential terrorists.

The U.S. Internal Revenue Service uses intelligent systems to detect irregular international financial information and to block possible money laundering and terrorist financing.

Market Surveillance Systems

The National Association of Security Dealers (NASD) has developed an intelligent surveillance system called Securities Observation, New Analysis, and Regulations (SONAR) that uses data mining, rule-based inference, knowledge-based data representation, and NLP to monitor the stock markets and futures markets for suspicious patterns. The system generates 50 to 60 alerts per day for review by several groups of regulatory analysts and investigators ("Automatic Market Surveillance," 2004).

Business Process Reengineering Systems

Reengineering involves the exploitation of information technology to improve business processes. KBS are used in analyzing the workflow for business process reengineering. For example, Gensym's System Performance Analysis Using Real-Time Knowledge-based Simulation (SPARKS) can help model the formal and informal knowledge, skills, and competencies that must be embedded in a reengineered system. SPARKS has three components: process flow model, resource model, and work volumes and descriptions.

AREAS FOR ES APPLICATIONS

As indicated in the preceding examples, ES have been applied commercially in a number of areas, including the following:

- *Finance.* Finance ES include insurance evaluation, credit analysis, tax planning, fraud prevention, financial report analysis, financial planning, and performance evaluation.
- *Data processing.* Data processing ES include system planning, equipment selection, equipment maintenance, vendor evaluation, and network management.
- *Marketing.* Marketing ES include customer relationship management, market analysis, product planning, and market planning.
- *Human resources.* Examples of human resources ES are human resources planning, performance evaluation, staff scheduling, pension management, and legal advising.
- *Manufacturing.* Manufacturing ES include production planning, quality management, product design, plant site selection, and equipment maintenance and repair.
- *Homeland security.* Homeland security ES include terrorist threat assessment and terrorist finance detection.
- *Business process automation.* ES have been developed for help desk automation, call center management, and regulation enforcement.
- *Health care management.* ES have been developed for bioinformatics and other health care management issues

Now that you are familiar with a variety of different ES applications, it is time to look at the internal structure of an ES and how the goals of the ES are achieved.

Section 12.5 Review Questions

1. What problem domain is MYCIN designed for solving?
2. Find two applications of ES in finance and describe their benefits.
3. Find two applications of ES in marketing and describe their benefits.
4. Find two applications of ES in homeland security and describe their benefits.

12.6 STRUCTURE OF EXPERT SYSTEMS

ES can be viewed as having two environments: the development environment and the consultation environment (see Figure 12.3). An ES builder uses the **development environment** to build the components and put knowledge into the knowledge base. A non-expert uses the **consultation environment** to obtain expert knowledge and advice. These environments can be separated when a system is complete.

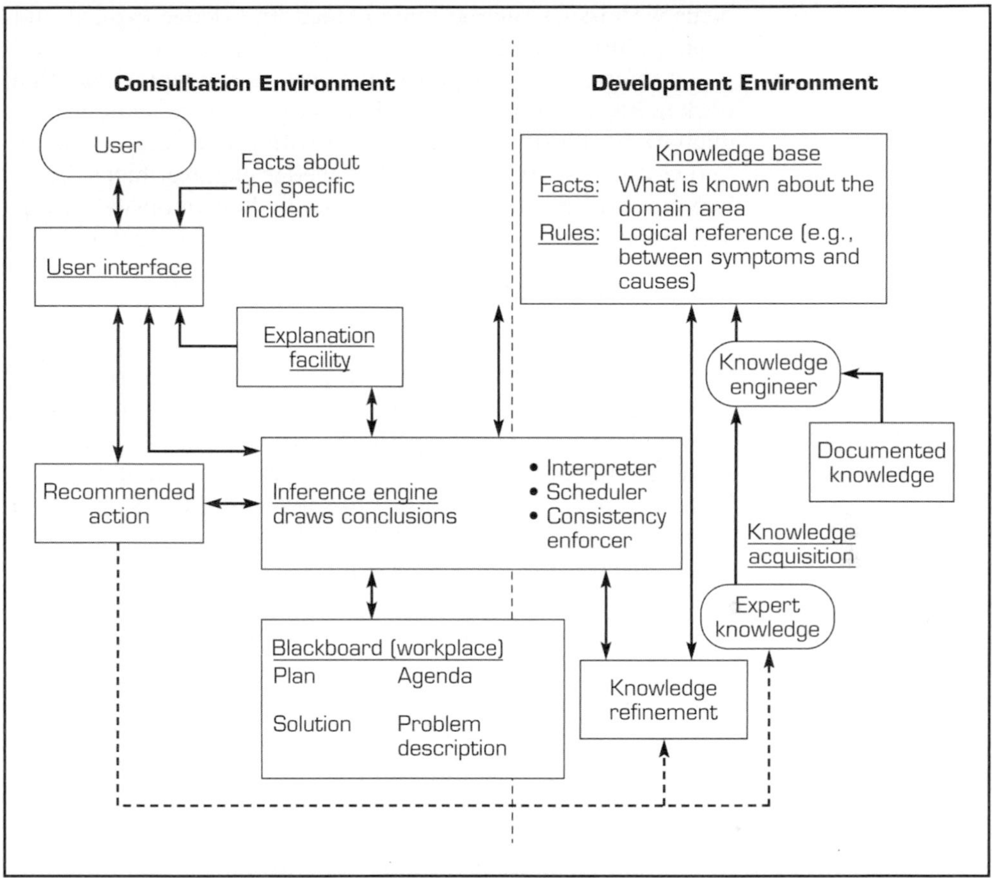

FIGURE 12.3 Structure of an Expert System

The three major components that appear in virtually every ES are the *knowledge base*, *inference engine*, and *user interface*. In general, though, an ES that interacts with the user can contain the following additional components:

- Knowledge acquisition subsystem
- Blackboard (workplace)
- Explanation subsystem (justifier)
- Knowledge refining system

Currently, most ES do not contain the knowledge refinement component. A brief description of each of these components follows.

KNOWLEDGE ACQUISITION SUBSYSTEM

Knowledge acquisition is the accumulation, transfer, and transformation of problem-solving expertise from experts or documented knowledge sources to a computer program for constructing or expanding the knowledge base. Potential sources of knowledge include human experts, textbooks, multimedia documents, databases (public and private), special research reports, and information available on the Web.

Currently, most organizations have collected a large volume of data, but the organization and management of organizational knowledge is limited. Knowledge acquisition deals with issues such as making tacit knowledge explicit and integrating knowledge from multiple sources.

Acquiring knowledge from experts is a complex task that often creates a bottleneck in ES construction. In building large systems, a knowledge engineer or knowledge elicitation expert needs to interact with one or more human experts in building the knowledge base. Typically, the knowledge engineer helps the expert structure the problem area by interpreting and integrating human answers to questions, drawing analogies, posing counterexamples, and bringing conceptual difficulties to light.

KNOWLEDGE BASE

The **knowledge base** is the foundation of an ES. It contains the relevant knowledge necessary for understanding, formulating, and solving problems. A typical knowledge base may include two basic elements: (1) facts such as the problem situation and the theory of the problem area, and (2) special heuristics or rules that direct the use of knowledge to solve specific problems in a particular domain. (In addition, the inference engine can include general-purpose problem-solving and decision-making rules.) The heuristics express the informal judgmental knowledge in an application area. Knowledge, not mere facts, is the primary raw material of ES.

It is important to differentiate the knowledge base of an ES and the knowledge base of an organization. The knowledge stored in the knowledge base of an ES is often represented in a special format and can be used to solve a particular problem. The organizational knowledge base, however, contains various kinds of knowledge in different formats and may be stored in different places. The knowledge base of an ES is only a small subset of an organization's knowledge base.

INFERENCE ENGINE

The "brain" of an ES is the **inference engine**, also known as the control structure or the rule interpreter (in rule-based ES). This component is essentially a computer program that provides a methodology for reasoning about information in the knowledge base and on the blackboard and for formulating conclusions. The inference engine provides directions about how to use the system's knowledge by developing the agenda that organizes and controls the steps taken to solve problems whenever consultation takes place. It is further discussed in Section 12.7.

USER INTERFACE

An ES contains a language processor for friendly, problem-oriented communication between the user and the computer, known as the **user interface**. This communication can best be carried out in a natural language. Due to technological constraints, most existing systems use the question-and-answer approach to interact with the user. Sometimes it is supplemented by menus, electronic forms, and graphics.

BLACKBOARD (WORKPLACE)

The **blackboard** is an area of working memory set aside as a database for the description of a current problem, as specified by the input data; it is also used for recording intermediate hypotheses and decisions. Three types of decisions can be recorded on the blackboard: a *plan* (i.e., how to attack the problem), an *agenda* (i.e., potential actions awaiting execution), and a *solution* (i.e., candidate hypotheses and alternative courses of action that the system has generated thus far).

Consider an example. When your car fails, you can enter the symptoms of the failure into a computer for storage in the blackboard. As the result of an intermediate

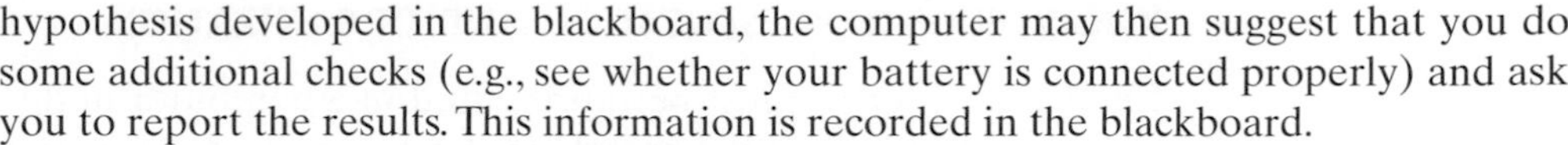

hypothesis developed in the blackboard, the computer may then suggest that you do some additional checks (e.g., see whether your battery is connected properly) and ask you to report the results. This information is recorded in the blackboard.

EXPLANATION SUBSYSTEM (JUSTIFIER)

The ability to trace responsibility for conclusions to their sources is crucial both in the transfer of expertise and in problem solving. The **explanation subsystem** can trace such responsibility and explain the ES behavior by interactively answering questions such as these:

- Why was a certain question asked by the ES?
- How was a certain conclusion reached?
- Why was a certain alternative rejected?
- What is the plan to reach the solution? For example, what remains to be established before a final diagnosis can be determined?

In simple ES, the explanation shows the rules that were used to derive the specific recommendations.

KNOWLEDGE-REFINING SYSTEM

Human experts have a **knowledge-refining system**; that is, they can analyze their own knowledge and its use, learn from it, and improve on it for future consultations. Similarly, such evaluation is necessary in computerized learning so that a program can analyze the reasons for its success or failure. This could lead to improvements that result in a more accurate knowledge base and more effective reasoning.

The critical component for knowledge refinement is the machine-learning component that allows the system to adjust its activities based on evaluation of past performance. Such a component is not yet mature in commercial ES at the moment but is being developed in experimental ES at several universities and research institutions.

Section 12.6 Review Questions

1. Describe the ES development environment and contrast it with the consultation environment.
2. List and define the major components of an ES.
3. What are the major activities performed in the ES blackboard (workplace)?
4. What are the major roles of the explanation subsystem?
5. Describe the difference between a knowledge base of an ES and an organizational knowledge base.

12.7 HOW EXPERT SYSTEMS WORK: INFERENCE MECHANISMS

Among the components in Figure 12.3, the knowledge base and inference engine are the most critical modules for an ES to function properly. Knowledge must be represented and organized properly in the knowledge base. The inference engine can then use the knowledge to infer new conclusions from existing facts and rules. In this section, we introduce the knowledge base structure and the inference engine of rule-based systems.

KNOWLEDGE REPRESENTATION AND ORGANIZATION

Expert knowledge must be represented in a computer-understandable format and organized properly in the knowledge base of an ES. There are many different ways of representing human knowledge, including production rules, semantic networks, and logic statements; detailed descriptions of these are provided in Chapter 17, an online chapter. In rule-based systems, knowledge in the knowledge base is represented in if-then rules that combine the condition and the conclusion for handling a specific situation. The IF part indicates the condition for the rule to be activated, and the THEN part shows the action or conclusion if all IF conditions are satisfied.

Let's again consider the example of selecting a notebook computer. Several rules can be defined for choosing between a Toshiba Satellite A100 and a Dell Latitude X1:

Rule 1:
IF the primary task = word processing
AND primary usage = travel
THEN weight requirement = light

Rule 2:
IF the primary task = word processing
AND primary usage = office
THEN weight requirement = don't care

Rule 3:
IF budget <=2,000
AND budget >1,000
AND weight requirement = light
THEN NB model = Dell Latitude X1

Rule 4:
IF budget < 1,000
AND weight requirement = don't care
THEN NB model = Toshiba Satellite A100

The advantage of using production rules is that this method is easy to understand, and new rules can easily be added to the knowledge base without affecting existing rules. Uncertainty associated with each rule can be added to enhance its accuracy. *Uncertainty processing* is a topic that is discussed in Chapter 13.

A major task of ES development is to acquire knowledge from human experts and then convert it into production rules that an inference engine can handle. The inference engine chooses applicable rules from the knowledge base, integrates them, and then reasons to find the conclusion.

THE INFERENCE PROCESS

In complex decisions, expert knowledge often cannot be represented in single rules. Instead, rules may be chained together dynamically to cover numerous conditions. The process of chaining multiple rules together based on available data is called *inference*. The component that conducts inference in an ES is called the *inference engine*. Two popular approaches for inferencing are forward chaining and backward chaining. More reasoning strategies, such as case-based reasoning and advanced techniques, are discussed in Chapters 13 and 14.

Forward Chaining

Forward chaining looks for the IF part of a rule first. When all IF conditions are met, the rule is chosen for deriving the conclusion. If the conclusion derived from the first state is not final, then it is used as a new fact to match with the IF condition of other rules to find a more useful conclusion. This process continues until a final conclusion is reached.

Think again about the notebook selection rule base described in this section. In this example, forward chaining would check two IF conditions associated with Rules 1 and 2: whether the primary task is word processing and whether the primary usage is in office or travel. If the task is word processing and usage is travel, then Rule 1 applies, and the weight requirement is set to light. Because the weight requirement is not the final goal, the inference engine further searches the knowledge base and finds that one IF condition of Rule 3 matches the conclusion from Rule 1. Because Rule 3 has more IF conditions to be checked, the inference engine triggers Rule 3 and checks whether the price condition is satisfied. If the price condition is also satisfied, then Rule 3 is activated, and the system recommends Dell Latitude X1 to the user. The sequence of activating rules in the rule base is Rule 1 → Rule 2 → Rules 3 or 4 (depending on the result in the previous step). Table 12.4 shows consultation sessions using different inference strategies.

Backward Chaining

Backward chaining is the reverse of forward chaining. It starts from the conclusion and hypothesizes that the conclusion is true. The inference engine then identifies the IF conditions necessary for making the conclusion true and locates facts to test whether

TABLE 12.4 Consultation Sessions Using Different Inference Strategies

Forward Chaining	*Backward Chaining*
What is your primary task to be performed on the notebook computer? ☐ Word processing ☐ Communications ☐ Multimedia applications Answer: 1 (click the first check box)	What is your budget range? ☐ Below $1K ☐ Between $1K and $2K ☐ Above $4K Answer: 2 (click the third check box)
Where are you going to use the notebook most often? ☐ In the office ☐ While traveling Answer: 2 (click the second check box)	What is your primary task to be performed on the notebook computer? ☐ Word processing ☐ Communications ☐ Multimedia applications Answer: 1 (click the first check box)
What is your budget range? ☐ Below $1K ☐ Between $1K and $2K ☐ Above $4K Answer: 2 (click the third check box)	Where are you going to use the notebook most often? ☐ In the office ☐ While traveling Answer: 2 (click the second check box)
System recommendation: You should consider buying a Dell Latitude X1.	System recommendation: You should consider buying a Dell Latitude X1.
Reasons: It is light and more suitable for your word processing and travel needs, and it also fits your budget.	Reasons: It is light and more suitable for your word processing and travel needs, and it also fits your budget.

the IF conditions are true. If all IF conditions are true, then the rule is chosen, and the conclusion is reached. If some conditions are false, then the rule is discarded, and the next rule is used as the second hypothesis. If there are not adequate facts to prove that all IF conditions are true or false, the inference engine continues to look for rules whose conclusion would match the undecided IF condition to move a step further for checking the conditions. This chaining process continues until a set of rules is found to reach a conclusion or to prove unable to reach a conclusion.

Using the notebook selection example, the inference process of backward chaining starts from Rule 3. The inference engine assumes the Dell Latitude X1 to be a product for recommendation and checks the IF conditions of weight requirement and budget. Because weight requirement is the conclusion of Rules 1 and 2, the engine chains these two rules with Rule 3. The new IF conditions become primary task and primary usage. The sequence of activating rules in this case is Rule 3 → Rule 1 → Rule 2. Table 12.4 shows the sessions with the user.

DEVELOPMENT PROCESS OF ES

ES development is a process for eliciting knowledge from experts and then storing the knowledge in the knowledge base. Because human experts may be unwilling or unable to articulate their knowledge, knowledge acquisition is a critical and tough task.

A typical process for developing ES includes knowledge acquisition, knowledge representation, selection of development tools, system prototyping, evaluation, and improvement. Because the inference engine is common to different systems, ES shells are useful tools that can implement a rule-based system in a very short time. An *ES shell* is an ES without the knowledge in the knowledge base. The system runs when the knowledge is stored in the knowledge base. ES shells are discussed in detail in Section 12.9.

Section 12.7 Review Questions

1. Write down two production rules that can represent the knowledge of repairing your car.
2. Describe how ES perform inference.
3. Describe the reasoning procedures of forward chaining and backward chaining.

12.8 PROBLEM AREAS SUITABLE FOR EXPERT SYSTEMS

ES can be classified in several ways. One way is by the general problem areas they address. For example, *diagnosis* can be defined as "inferring system malfunctions from observations." Diagnosis is a generic activity performed in medicine, organizational studies, computer operations, and so on. The generic categories of ES are listed in Table 12.5. Some ES belong to two or more of these categories. A brief description of each category follows:

- *Interpretation systems* infer situation descriptions from observations. This category includes surveillance, speech understanding, image analysis, signal interpretation, and many kinds of intelligence analyses. An interpretation system explains observed data by assigning them symbolic meanings that describe the situation.
- *Prediction systems* include weather forecasting; demographic predictions; economic forecasting; traffic predictions; crop estimates; and military, marketing, and financial forecasting.

TABLE 12.5 Generic Categories of Expert Systems

Category	*Problem Addressed*
Interpretation	Inferring situation descriptions from observations
Prediction	Inferring likely consequences of given situations
Diagnosis	Inferring system malfunctions from observations
Design	Configuring objects under constraints
Planning	Developing plans to achieve goals
Monitoring	Comparing observations to plans and flagging exceptions
Debugging	Prescribing remedies for malfunctions
Repair	Executing a plan to administer a prescribed remedy
Instruction	Diagnosing, debugging, and correcting student performance
Control	Interpreting, predicting, repairing, and monitoring system behaviors

- *Diagnostic systems* include medical, electronic, mechanical, and software diagnoses. Diagnostic systems typically relate observed behavioral irregularities to underlying causes.
- *Design systems* develop configurations of objects that satisfy the constraints of the design problem. Such problems include circuit layout, building design, and plant layout. Design systems construct descriptions of objects in various relationships with one another and verify that these configurations conform to stated constraints.
- *Planning systems* specialize in planning problems, such as automatic programming. They also deal with short- and long-term planning in areas such as project management, routing, communications, product development, military applications, and financial planning.
- *Monitoring systems* compare observations of system behavior with standards that seem crucial for successful goal attainment. These crucial features correspond to potential flaws in the plan. There are many computer-aided monitoring systems for topics ranging from air traffic control to fiscal management tasks.
- *Debugging systems* rely on planning, design, and prediction capabilities for creating specifications or recommendations to correct a diagnosed problem.
- *Repair systems* develop and execute plans to administer a remedy for certain diagnosed problems. Such systems incorporate debugging, planning, and execution capabilities.
- *Instruction systems* incorporate diagnosis and debugging subsystems that specifically address the student's needs. Typically, these systems begin by constructing a hypothetical description of the student's knowledge that interprets her or his behavior. They then diagnose weaknesses in the student's knowledge and identify appropriate remedies to overcome the deficiencies. Finally, they plan a tutorial interaction intended to deliver remedial knowledge to the student.
- *Control systems* adaptively govern the overall behavior of a system. To do this, a control system must repeatedly interpret the current situation, predict the future, diagnose the causes of anticipated problems, formulate a remedial plan, and monitor its execution to ensure success.

Not all the tasks usually found in each of these categories are suitable for ES. However, thousands of decisions do fit into these categories.

Section 12.8 Review Questions

1. Describe a sample ES application for prediction.
2. Describe a sample ES application for diagnosis.
3. Describe a sample ES application for the rest of the generic ES categories.

12.9 DEVELOPMENT OF EXPERT SYSTEMS

The development of ES is a tedious process and typically includes defining the nature and scope of the problem, identifying proper experts, acquiring knowledge, selecting the building tools, coding the system, and evaluating the system.

DEFINING THE NATURE AND SCOPE OF THE PROBLEM

The first step in developing an ES is to identify the nature of the problem and define a proper scope. Some domains may not be appropriate for the application of ES. For example, a problem that can be solved by using mathematical optimization algorithms is often inappropriate for ES. In general, rule-based ES are appropriate when the nature of the problem is qualitative, knowledge is explicit, and experts are available to solve the problem effectively and provide their knowledge.

Another important factor is to define a feasible scope. The current technology is still very limited and is capable of solving relatively simple problems. Therefore, the scope of the problem should be specific and reasonably narrow. For example, it may be possible to develop an ES for detecting abnormal trading behavior and possible money laundering, but it not be possible to use an ES to determine whether a particular transaction is criminal.

IDENTIFYING PROPER EXPERTS

After the nature and scope of the problem have been clearly defined, the next step is to find proper experts who have the knowledge and are willing to assist in developing the knowledge base. No ES can be designed without the strong support of knowledgeable and supportive experts. A project may identify one expert or a group of experts. A proper expert should have a thorough understanding of problem-solving knowledge, the role of ES and decision support technology, and good communication skills.

ACQUIRING KNOWLEDGE

After identifying helpful experts, it is necessary to start acquiring decision knowledge from the expert. The process of eliciting knowledge is called **knowledge engineering**. The person who is interacting with experts to document the knowledge is called a **knowledge engineer**.

Knowledge acquisition is a time-consuming and risky process. Experts may be unwilling to provide their knowledge for various reasons. First, their knowledge may be proprietary and valuable. Experts may not be willing to share their knowledge without a reasonable payoff. Second, even though an expert is willing to share, certain knowledge is tacit, and the expert may not have the skill to clearly dictate the decision rules and considerations. Third, experts may be too busy to have enough time to communicate with the knowledge engineer. Fourth, certain knowledge may be confusing or contradictory in nature. Finally, the knowledge engineer may misunderstand the expert and inaccurately document knowledge.

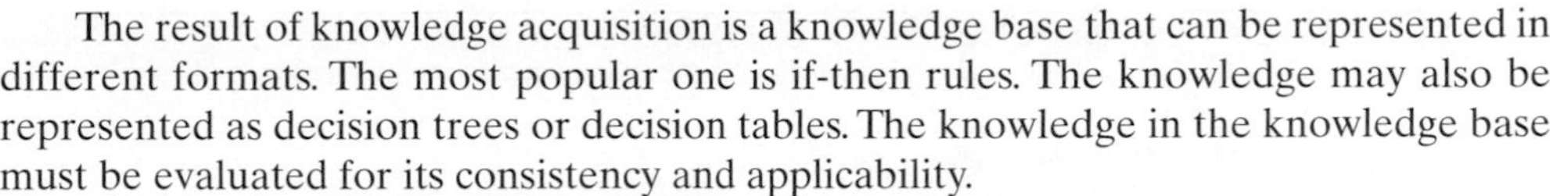

The result of knowledge acquisition is a knowledge base that can be represented in different formats. The most popular one is if-then rules. The knowledge may also be represented as decision trees or decision tables. The knowledge in the knowledge base must be evaluated for its consistency and applicability.

SELECTING THE BUILDING TOOLS

After the knowledge base is built, the next step is to choose a proper tool for implementing the system. There are three different kinds of development tools, as described in the following sections.

General-Purpose Development Environment

The first tool is general-purpose computer languages, such as C++, Prolog, and LISP. Most computer programming languages support the if-then statement. Therefore, it is possible to use C++ to develop an ES for a particular problem domain (e.g., disease diagnosis). Because these programming languages do not have the built-in inference capabilities, using them in this way is often very costly and time-consuming. Prolog and LISP are two early languages for developing intelligent systems. It is easier to use them than to use C++, but they are still specifically designed for professional programmers and are not very friendly. For recent Web-based applications, Java and computer languages that support Web services (such as the Microsoft .NET platform) are also useful.

ES Shells

The second type of development tools, called the ES shell, is specifically designed for ES development. An **expert system (ES) shell** already has built-in inference capabilities and user interface, but the knowledge base is empty. System development is therefore a process of feeding the knowledge base with proper rules elicited from the expert.

A popular ES shell is the CORVID system developed by Exsys (**exsys.com**). The system is an object-oriented development platform that is composed of three types of operations: variables, logic blocks, and command blocks. *Variables* define the major factors considered in problem solving. *Logic blocks* are the decision rules acquired from experts. *Command blocks* determine how the system interacts with the user, including the order of execution and user interfaces. Figure 12.4 shows a screenshot of a logic block that shows the decision rules. More products are available from business rules management vendors, such as Haley (**haley.com**), ILOG (**ilog.com**), and LPA's VisiRule (**lpa.co.uk/vsr.htm**), which is based on a general-purpose tool called Micro-Prolog. Figure 12.5 shows a sample screen from VisiRule.

Tailored Turn-Key Solutions

The third tool is tailored to a specific domain and can be adapted to a similar application very quickly. Basically, a tailored turn-key tool contains specific features often required for developing applications in a particular domain. This tool must adjust or modify the base system by tailoring the user interface or a relatively small portion of the system to meet the unique needs of an organization. For example, both Haley and ILOG offer various tailor-made solutions for insurance, medical, scheduling, and homeland security applications.

Choosing an ES Development Tool

Choosing among these tools for ES development depends on a few criteria. First, you need to consider the cost benefits. The tool is more expensive if a tailored turn-key solution is chosen. However, you need to consider the total cost, not just the cost of the tool. Second, you need to consider the technical functionality and flexibility of the tool.

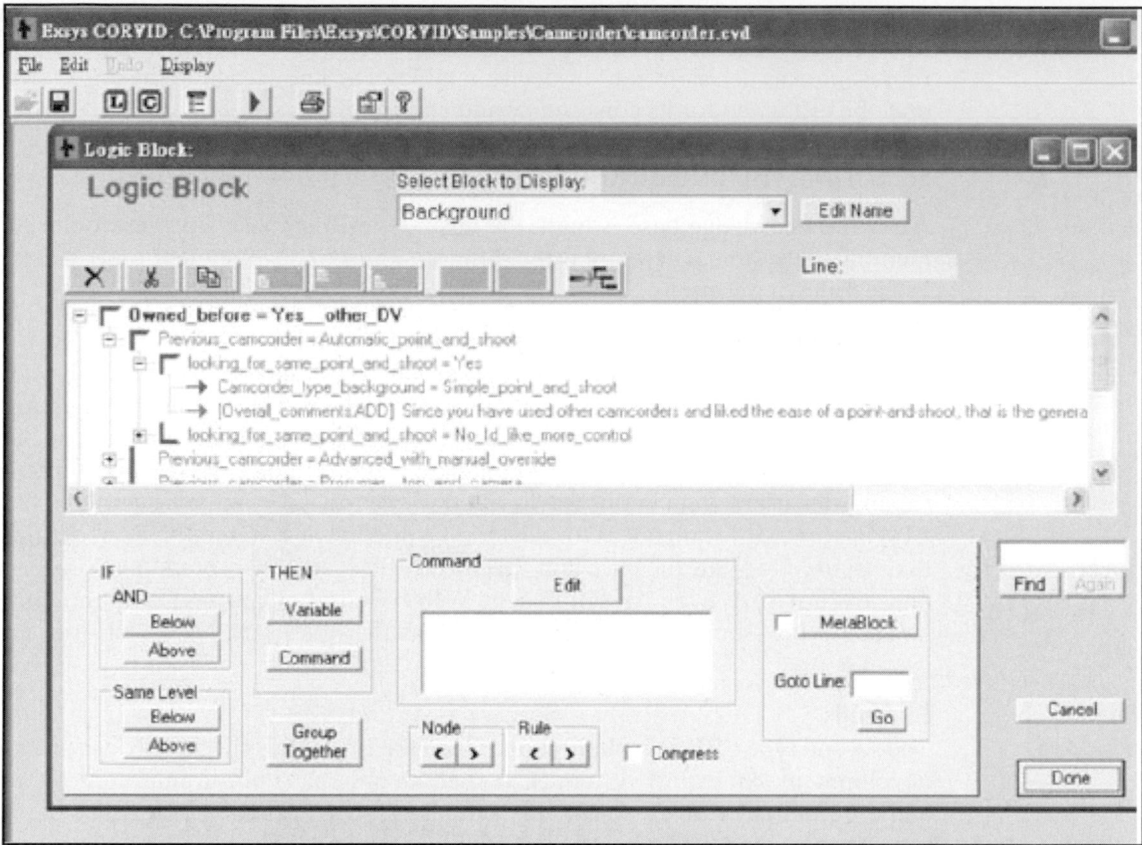

FIGURE 12.4 A Sample Screen of CORVID Rules

That is, you need to determine whether the tool provides the function you need and how easily it allows the development team to make necessary changes. Third, you need to consider the tool's compatibility with the existing information infrastructure in the organization. Most organizations have many existing applications already, and the tool must be compatible with those applications and needs to be able to be integrated as part of the whole information infrastructure. Finally, you need to consider the reliability of and support from the vendor. The vendor's experiences in similar domains and training programs are critical to the success of an ES project.

CODING THE SYSTEM

After choosing a proper tool, the development team can focus on coding the knowledge based on the syntactic requirement of the tool. The major concern at this stage is whether the coding process is efficient and properly managed to avoid errors. Skilled programmers are helpful and important.

EVALUATING THE SYSTEM

After an ES system is built, it must be evaluated. There are two kinds of evaluation: verification and validation. *Verification* ensures that the resulting knowledge base contains knowledge exactly the same as that acquired from the expert. In other words, verification ensures that no error occurred at the coding stage. *Validation* ensures that the

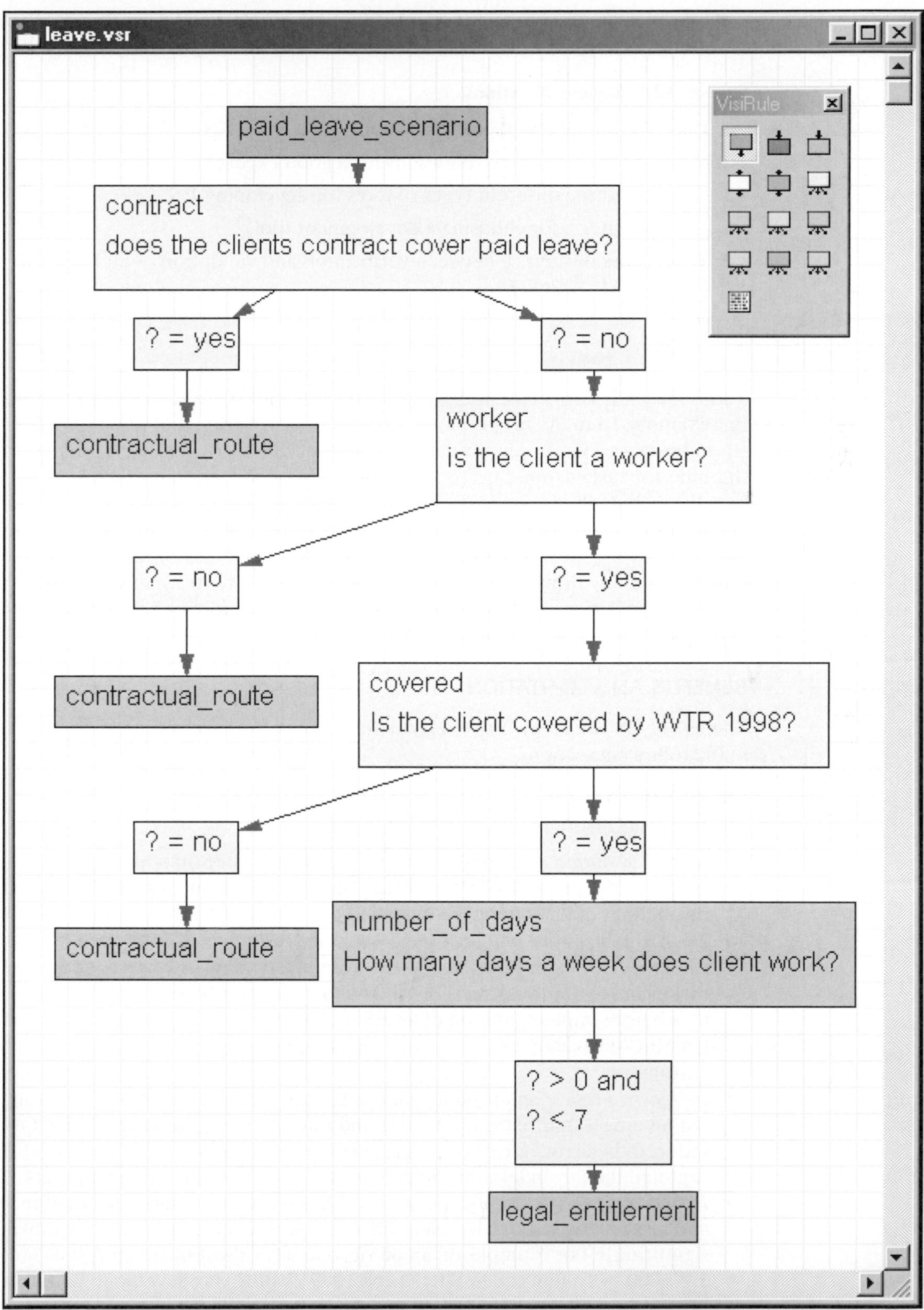

FIGURE 12.5 A Sample Screen of LPA's VisiRule. *Source:* ipa.com

system can solve the problem correctly. In other words, validation checks whether the knowledge acquired from the expert can indeed solve the problem effectively.

Section 12.9 Review Questions

1. Describe the major steps in developing rule-based ES.
2. What are the necessary conditions for a good expert?
3. Compare three different types of tools for developing ES.
4. List the criteria for choosing a development tool.
5. What is the difference between verification and validation of an ES?

12.10 BENEFITS, LIMITATIONS, AND SUCCESS FACTORS OF EXPERT SYSTEMS

Thousands of ES are in use today in almost every industry and in every functional area. For example, Eom (1996) prepared a comprehensive survey of about 440 operational ES in business. His survey revealed that many ES have a profound impact, shrinking the time for tasks from days to hours, minutes, or seconds, and that nonquantifiable benefits include improved customer satisfaction, improved quality of products and services, and accurate and consistent decision making. ES in finance and in engineering applications are described in Nedovic and Devedzic (2002) and Nurminen, et al. (2003). For many firms, ES have become indispensable tools for effective management, but the application of ES may also have limitations. In this section, we outline the major benefits and limitations of this technology.

BENEFITS AND LIMITATIONS OF ES

The use of ES can create benefits and at the same time incur limitations, as explained in the following sections.

Benefits of ES

The following are some of the benefits of ES:

- *Increased output and productivity.* ES can work faster than humans can. For example, the classic XCON enabled Digital Equipment Corp. to increase the throughput of its popular VAX minicomputers configuration orders fourfold.
- *Decreased decision-making time.* Using the recommendations of an ES, a human can make decisions much faster. For example, American Express authorities make charge approval decisions in less than 5 seconds, compared to about 3 minutes before implementation of an ES. This property is important in supporting frontline decision makers who must make quick decisions while interacting with customers.
- *Increased process and product quality.* ES can increase quality by providing consistent advice and reducing the size and rate of errors. For example, XCON reduced the error rate of configuring computer orders from 35 percent to 2 percent and then even less, thus improving the quality of the minicomputers.
- *Reduced downtime.* Many operational ES are used for diagnosing malfunctions and prescribing repairs. By using ES, it is possible to reduce machine downtime significantly. For example, on an oil rig, one day of lost time can cost as much as $250,000. A system called DRILLING ADVISOR was developed to detect malfunctions in oil rigs. This system saved a considerable amount of money for the company by significantly reducing downtime.

- *Capture of scarce expertise.* The scarcity of expertise becomes evident in situations in which there are not enough experts for a task, the expert is about to retire or leave the job, or expertise is required over a broad geographic area. In the opening vignette, for example, more than 30 percent of all requests for authorization of benefits are approved automatically through eCare, enabling CIGNA Behavioral Health to handle more requests with its existing staff.
- *Flexibility.* ES can offer flexibility in both the service and manufacturing industries.
- *Easier equipment operation.* An ES makes complex equipment easier to operate. For example, Steamer is an early ES intended to train inexperienced workers to operate complex ship engines. Another example is an ES developed for Shell Oil Company to train people to use complex computer program routines.
- *Elimination of the need for expensive equipment.* Often, a human must rely on expensive instruments for monitoring and control. ES can perform the same tasks with lower-cost instruments because of their ability to investigate the information provided by instruments more thoroughly and quickly.
- *Operation in hazardous environments.* Many tasks require humans to operate in hazardous environments. An ES can allow humans to avoid such environments. They can enable workers to avoid hot, humid, or toxic environments, such as a nuclear power plant that has malfunctioned. This feature is extremely important in military conflicts.
- *Accessibility to knowledge and help desks.* ES make knowledge accessible, thus freeing experts from routine work. People can query systems and receive useful advice. One area of applicability is the support of help desks, such as the HelpDeskIQ system offered by BMC Remedy.
- *Ability to work with incomplete or uncertain information.* In contrast to conventional computer systems, ES can, like human experts, work with incomplete, imprecise, and uncertain data, information, or knowledge. The user can respond with "don't know" or "not sure" to one or more of the system's questions during a consultation, and the ES can produce an answer, although it may not be a certain one.
- *Provision of training.* ES can provide training. Novices who work with ES become more and more experienced. The explanation facility can also serve as a teaching device, and so can notes and explanations that can be inserted into the knowledge base.
- *Enhancement of problem solving and decision making.* ES enhance problem solving by allowing the integration of top experts' judgment into the analysis. For example, an ES called Statistical Navigator was developed to help novices use complex statistical computer packages.
- *Improved decision-making processes.* ES provide rapid feedback on decision consequences, facilitate communication among decision makers on a team, and allow rapid response to unforeseen changes in the environment, thus providing a better understanding of the decision-making situation.
- *Improved decision quality.* ES are reliable. They do not become tired or bored, call in sick, or go on strike, and they do not talk back to the boss. ES also consistently pay attention to all details and do not overlook relevant information and potential solutions, thereby making fewer errors. In addition, ES provide the same recommendations to repeated problems.
- *Ability to solve complex problems.* One day, ES may explain complex problems whose solution is beyond human ability. Some ES are already able to solve problems in which the required scope of knowledge exceeds that of any one individual. This allows decision makers to gain control over complicated situations and improve the operation of complex systems.

- *Knowledge transfer to remote locations.* One of the greatest potential benefits of ES is its ease of transfer across international boundaries. An example of such a transfer is an eye care ES for diagnosis and recommended treatment, developed at Rutgers University in conjunction with the World Health Organization. The program has been implemented in Egypt and Algeria, where serious eye diseases are prevalent but eye specialists are rare. The PC program is rule based and can be operated by a nurse, a physician's assistant, or a general practitioner. The Web is used extensively to disseminate information to users in remote locations. The U.S. government, for example, places advisory systems about safety and other topics on its Web sites.
- *Enhancement of other information systems.* ES can often be found providing intelligent capabilities to other information systems. Many of these benefits lead to improved decision making, improved products and customer service, and a sustainable strategic advantage. Some may even enhance an organization's image.

Problems and Limitations of ES

Available ES methodologies may not be straightforward and effective, even for many applications in the generic categories. The following problems have slowed down the commercial spread of ES:

- Knowledge is not always readily available.
- It can be difficult to extract expertise from humans.
- The approach of each expert to a situation assessment may be different, yet correct.
- It is difficult, even for a highly-skilled expert, to abstract good situational assessments when under time pressure.
- Users of ES have natural cognitive limits.
- ES work well only within a narrow domain of knowledge.
- Most experts have no independent means of checking whether their conclusions are reasonable.
- The vocabulary, or jargon, that experts use to express facts and relations is often limited and not understood by others.
- Help is often required from knowledge engineers who are rare and expensive, and this could make ES construction costly.
- Lack of trust on the part of end users may be a barrier to ES use.
- Knowledge transfer is subject to a host of perceptual and judgmental biases.
- ES may not be able to arrive at conclusions in some cases. For example, the initial fully-developed XCON could not fulfill about two percent of the orders presented to it. Human experts must step in to resolve these problems.
- ES, like human experts, sometimes produce incorrect recommendations.

The Web is the major facilitator of ES that overcomes several of these limitations. The ability to disseminate ES to the masses makes them more cost-effective. Consequently, more money can be spent on better systems.

Gill (1995) discovered that only about one-third of all commercial ES studied survived over a 5-year period. The short-lived nature of so many systems was generally not attributable to failure to meet technical performance or economic objectives. Instead, managerial issues—such as lack of system acceptance by users, inability to retain developers, problems in transitioning from development to maintenance, and shifts in organizational priorities—appeared to be the most significant factors resulting in long-term ES disuse. Proper management of ES development and deployment can resolve most of these issues in practice.

These limitations clearly indicate that some ES fall short of generally intelligent human behavior. Although there is no recent follow-up research, the rapid progress of

information technology can reduce the possibility of failure, and several of these limitations will diminish or disappear with technological improvements over time.

ES SUCCESS FACTORS

Several researchers have investigated the reasons ES succeed and fail in practice. As with many MIS, many studies have shown that the level of managerial and user involvement directly affects the success level of MIS, specifically ES. However, these factors alone are not sufficient to guarantee success, and the following issues should also be considered:

- The level of knowledge must be sufficiently high.
- Expertise must be available from at least one cooperative expert.
- The problem to be solved must be mostly qualitative (fuzzy) and not purely quantitative (otherwise, a numeric approach should be used).
- The problem must be sufficiently narrow in scope.
- ES shell characteristics are important. The shell must be of high quality and naturally store and manipulate the knowledge.
- The user interface must be friendly for novice users.
- The problem must be important and difficult enough to warrant development of an ES (but it need not be a core function).
- Knowledgeable system developers with good people skills are needed.
- The impact of ES as a source of end-user job improvement must be considered.
- The impact should be favorable. End-user attitudes and expectations must be considered.
- Management support must be cultivated.
- End-user training programs are necessary.
- The organizational environment should favor adoption of new technology.
- The application must be well-defined and structured, and it should be justified by strategic impact.

Managers attempting to introduce ES technology should establish end-user training programs, thus demonstrating its potential as a business tool. As part of the managerial support effort, the organizational environment should favor new technology adoption.

Section 12.10 Review Questions

1. Describe the major benefits of using ES.
2. Describe some of the limitations of ES.
3. Describe the success factors of ES.

12.11 EXPERT SYSTEMS ON THE WEB

The relationship between ES and the Internet and intranets can be divided into two categories. The first is the use of ES on the Web. In this case, the Web supports ES (and other AI) applications. The second is the support ES (and other AI methods) give to the Web.

One of the early reasons for ES development was its potential to provide knowledge and advice to large numbers of users. Because the Web enables knowledge to be disseminated to many people, the cost per user becomes small, making ES very attractive.

However, according to Eriksson (1996), attaining this goal has proven to be very difficult. Because advisory systems are used infrequently, they need a large number of users to justify their construction. As a result, very few ES disseminate knowledge to many users.

The widespread availability and use of the Internet and intranets provide the opportunity to disseminate expertise and knowledge to mass audiences. By implementing ES (and other intelligent systems) as knowledge servers, it becomes economically feasible and profitable to publish expertise on the Web. ES running on servers can support a large group of users who communicate with the system over the Web. In this way, user interfaces based on Web protocols and the use of browsers provide access to the knowledge servers. This implementation approach is described in Eriksson (1996). If you go to the Web site of Exsys (**exsys.com**), you can try the Banner with Brains, which integrates ES capabilities into a Web banner (see Application Case 12.9). Another example is a rule-based system for intelligent online dialogue, developed by German scholars (see Application Case 12.10). Gensym (**gensym.com**) offers a real-time supporting tool called G2 and has been applied to many mission-critical domains, such as chemical, oil, gas, and process manufacturing.

Application Case 12.9

Banner with Brains: Web-Based ES for Restaurant Selection

Selecting a restaurant for dating or business in a foreign city has never been easier, thanks to the availability of services over the Web and support from expert systems. At **exsys.com**, you can try a demo system that integrates an ES with a banner. All interactions occur through the banner.

The ES is familiar with restaurants in Albuquerque. When you need to find a restaurant, the system asks about the occasion and the type of food you desire. The preference data is then fed to a spreadsheet of information on the various restaurants. The system creates a probabilistic ranking of the restaurants that meet your needs. It then weighs various factors, based on the specified occasion, and displays up to five restaurants. It also explains why it recommends these restaurants. This kind of application will become increasingly popular in the future.

Sources: Exsys, *CORVID Restaurant Selection Knowledge Automation Expert System*, **exsys.com/Demos/Restaurant/restaurant_demo.html** (accessed March 2006); and G. Adomavicius and A. Tuzhilin, "Toward the Next Generation of Recommender Systems: A Survey of the State-of-the-Art and Possible Extensions," *IEEE Transactions on Knowledge and Data Engineering*, June 2005, Vol. 17, No. 6.

Application Case 12.10

Rule-Based System for Online Student Consultation

A group of German scientists took advantage of the convenience of the Internet to offer a Web-based online consultation system for intelligent dialogue in assisting and conducting interviews. Traditionally, interviews are conducted face-to-face or over the telephone. The new system is used by a university to interview applicants and assess their chances of being admitted and by companies to screen job applicants. The system consists of a rule-based knowledge base that can dynamically adjust the questions to ask, based on user responses to previous questions. The system can also be used to support social workers in interacting with their clients online.

Sources: S. Mertens, M. Rosu, and Y. Erdani., "An Intelligent Dialogue for Online Rule-Based Expert Systems, *9th International Conference on Intelligent User Interface*, January 13–16, 2004; and **expertise2go.com** (accessed March 2006).

ES can be transferred over the Web not only to human users but also to other computerized systems, including DSS, robotics, and databases. Other ES Web support possibilities include system construction. Here, collaboration between builders, experts, and knowledge engineers can be facilitated by Internet-based groupware. This can reduce the cost of building ES. Knowledge acquisition costs can be reduced, for example, in cases in which there are several experts or in which the expert is in a different location from the knowledge engineer. Knowledge maintenance can also facilitate the use of the Internet, which is also helpful to users.

Finally, the Web can greatly support the spread of multimedia-based ES. Such systems, called *intellimedia systems*, support the integration of extensive multimedia applications and ES. Such systems can be very helpful for remote users, such as those in the tourism industry (see Stabb et al., 2002) and in remote equipment failure diagnosis.

The other aspect of the ES–Internet relationship is the support that ES and other AI technologies can provide to the Internet and intranets. The major contributions of AI to the Internet and intranets are summarized in Table 12.6.

Information about the relationships among ES, intelligent agents, and other AI and the Internet is readily available on the Internet. For example, the Web sites of *PC AI* magazine (**pcai.com**) and the American Association for Artificial Intelligence (**aaai.org**) provide good sets of hyperlinks to related Web sites. University of Maryland, Baltimore County (**agents.umbc.edu**) provides a good collection of resources on intelligent agents. In the future, more applications on the Internet will be available,

TABLE 12.6 AI/ES and Web Impacts

Aspects	*Impacts from the Web*	*Impacts on the Web*
Knowledge acquisition	Experts in different areas can collaborate over the Internet. Knowledge acquisition can be done at different times to fit the schedules of different experts. Knowledge acquired from different experts can be share on the Internet to stimulate discussion for enhancement.	Knowledge of Web operations and activities can be acquired and managed for sharing and use.
Expert systems development	Collaborative design of expert systems by a geographically distributed team becomes possible. Outsourcing of the design effort becomes feasible. ES evaluation can be done remotely. The Web provides a unified multimedia user interface for easy system integration. Web services provide an improved platform for designing ES.	ES can be designed to support Web activities, automatic services, and better performance.
Expert systems consultation	Users in remote areas can use the system to solve problems. Expertise can easily be disseminated to a large body of users.	Application of ES are available for Web browsing and monitoring.

TECHNOLOGY INSIGHTS 12.11

Automated and Real-Time Decision Systems

A technology called *automated decision systems (ADS)* is taking off, and it embodies the best attributes of artificial intelligence and ES. ADS are rule based like ES; and like DSS, they often involve statistical or algorithmic analysis of data. They typically make decisions in real-time after weighing all the data and rules for a particular customer or case. Sometimes they also carry genes from another ancestor, business process management, or workflow, leading some observers to classify them as "smart business process management" systems.

The most salient characteristic of these systems is that they actually make a decision, such as what price to charge a particular customer, whether to grant a loan or an insurance policy, which delivery truck to reroute, or what drug to prescribe to a diabetic patient. In many cases, their decisions are made without any human intervention at all; in others—sometimes for legal or ethical reasons—they work alongside a human expert such as a doctor. For the most part, these systems are used for decisions that must be made frequently and very rapidly, using information available online. The decision domains are relatively highly structured, with well-understood decision factors.

"Real-time" can be looked at from both business and technology perspectives. From the business perspective, *real-time* signifies that the users need to have rapid responses to customer requests. From the technology perspective, *real-time* signifies that the system needs to have enough power to respond quickly to a user request. Real-time ES are also used widely for environmental protection and chemical processes.

For example, RTXPS is a **real-time expert system** environment designed for online dynamic decision support, mission-critical command, and control and communication tasks such as (1) emergency management for technological and environmental hazards, including early warning for events such as floods, toxic or oil spills, tsunamis, land slides, and so on; and (2) complex control and assessment tasks, including coordination of first response, recovery, restoration, and cleanup operations (see **ess.co.at/RTXPS/**).

Sources: C. White, "Intelligent Business Strategies: Near Real-Time and Automated Decision Making," *DM Review Magazine*, October 2002; and T. Davenport, "Decision Evolution," *CIO Magazine*, October 2004.

particularly those that provide automated decision making and real-time decision support (see Technology Insights 12.11).

Section 12.11 Review Questions

1. What are the benefits of deploying an ES on the Web?
2. How can an ES help a decision maker use the Web to find relevant information?
3. Visit **exsys.com** and run two of the demo systems. What comments do you have about them?

Chapter Highlights

- Artificial intelligence is a discipline that investigates how to build computer systems to perform tasks that can be characterized as intelligent.
- The major characteristics of AI are symbolic processing, the use of heuristics instead of algorithms, and the application of inference techniques.
- AI has several major advantages over people: It is permanent, it can be easily duplicated and disseminated, it can be less expensive than human intelligence, it is consistent and thorough, and it can be documented.
- Natural (human) intelligence has advantages over AI: It is creative, it uses sensory experiences directly, and it reasons from a wide context of experiences.
- Knowledge rather than data or information is the major focus of AI.

- Major areas of AI include ES, NLP, speech understanding, intelligent robotics, computer vision, fuzzy logic, intelligent agents, ICAI, automatic programming, neural computing, game playing, and language translation.
- ES is the most applied AI technology. ES attempt to imitate the work of experts. They capture human expertise and apply to problem solving.
- For an ES to be effective, it must be applied to a narrow domain, and the knowledge must include qualitative factors.
- NLP investigates techniques that allow users to communicate with computers in a natural language. It includes text-based and voice-based natural language user interfaces.
- An intelligent robot is a computer-based program or machine that can respond to changes in its environment. Most of today's robots do not have full capabilities as human beings have, but they are improving rapidly.
- Intelligent tutoring systems use artificial intelligence technology to help the user learn knowledge. Artificial intelligence can improve the performance of training and teaching.
- The power of an ES is derived from the specific knowledge it possesses, not from the particular knowledge representation and inference schemes it uses.
- Expertise is task-specific knowledge acquired through training, reading, and experience.
- ES technology can transfer knowledge from experts and documented sources to the computer and make it available for use by non-experts.
- The major components of an ES are the knowledge acquisition subsystem, knowledge base, inference engine, user interface, blackboard, explanation subsystem, and knowledge-refinement subsystem.
- The inference engine provides reasoning capability for an ES.
- ES inference can be done by using forward chaining or backward chaining.
- Knowledge engineers are professionals who know how to capture the knowledge from an expert and structure it in a form that can be processed by the computer-based ES.
- The development process of ES includes defining the nature and scope of the problem, identifying proper experts, acquiring knowledge, selecting the building tools, coding the system, and evaluating the system.
- ES are popular in a number of generic categories: interpretation, prediction, diagnosis, design, planning, monitoring, debugging, repair, instruction, and control.
- The ES shell is an ES development tool that has the inference engine and building blocks for the knowledge base and the user interface. Knowledge engineers can easily develop a prototype system by entering rules in the knowledge base.
- ES have many benefits. The most important are improvement in productivity or quality, preservation of scarce expertise, enhancement of other systems, ability to cope with incomplete information, and provision of training.
- Many ES failures are caused by nontechnical problems, such as lack of managerial support and poor end-user training.
- Although there are several technical limitations to the use of ES, some of them will disappear with improved technology.
- Some ES provide advice in a real-time mode.
- ES and AI provide support to the Internet and intranets.

Key Terms

- artificial intelligence (AI)
- backward chaining
- blackboard
- consultation environment
- development environment
- expert
- expert system (ES)
- expert system (ES) shell
- expertise
- explanation subsystem
- forward chaining
- fuzzy logic
- heuristics
- inference engine
- intelligent agent (IA)
- intelligent computer-aided instruction (ICAI)
- intelligent tutoring system (ITS)
- knowledge acquisition
- knowledge base
- knowledge engineer
- knowledge engineering
- knowledge-based system (KBS)
- knowledge-refining system
- natural language processing (NLP)
- neural (computing) network
- real-time expert system
- robot
- rule-based system
- speech (voice) understanding
- Turing test
- user interface
- visual recognition

Questions for Discussion

1. Compare numeric and symbolic processing techniques and give an example to illustrate their differences.
2. Do you agree with the statement that using speech communication as the user interface could increase people's willingness to use ES? Why or why not?
3. It is said that powerful computers, inference capabilities, and problem-solving heuristics are necessary but not sufficient for solving real problems. Why?
4. Explain how the Web improves the benefit–cost ratio of ES and enables systems that otherwise are not justifiable.
5. Explain the relationship between the development environment and the consultation (i.e., runtime) environment.
6. Explain the difference between forward chaining and backward chaining and describe when each one is most appropriate.
7. What kind of mistakes might ES make and why? Why is it easier to correct mistakes in ES than in conventional computer programs?
8. Review the limitations of ES discussed in this chapter. From what you know, which of these limitations are the most likely to still be limitations in the year 2100? Why?
9. An ES for stock investment is developed and licensed for US $1,000 per year. The system can help you identify the most undervalued securities on the market and the best timing for buying and selling the securities. Will you order a copy as your investment adviser? Explain why or why not.
10. Given the current status of the Web, discuss how it is changing the availability of ES and how it is being used to embed expertise in other systems.

Exercises

Teradata University and Other Hands-on Exercises

1. Go to **teradatastudentnetwork.com** and search for stories about Chinatrust Commercial Bank's (CTCB's) use of the Teradata Relationship Manager and its reported benefits. Study the functional demo of the Teradata Relationship Manager to answer the following questions:
   a. What functions in the Teradata Relationship Manager are useful for supporting the automation of business rules? In CTCB's case, identify a potential application that can be supported by rule-based ES and solicit potential business rules in the knowledge base.
   b. Access Haley and compare the Teradata Relationship Manager and Haley's Business Rule Management System. Which tool is more suitable for the application identified in the previous question?
2. We list 10 categories of ES applications in the chapter. Find 20 sample applications, 2 in each category, from the various functional areas in an organization (i.e., accounting, finance, production, marketing, and human resources).

Exercises

Team Assignments and Role-Playing

1. Find applications of artificial intelligence and ES. Identify an organization with which at least one member of your group has a good contact who has a decision-making problem that requires some expertise (but is not too complicated). Understand the nature of its business and identify the problems that are supported or can potentially be supported by rule-based systems. Some examples include selection of suppliers, selection of a new employee, job assignment, computer selection, market contact method selection, and determination of admission into graduate school.
2. Identify and interview an expert who knows the domain of your choice. Ask the expert to write down his or her knowledge. Choose an ES shell and build a prototype system to see how it works.

Exercises

Internet Exercises

1. Go to **exsys.com** to play with the restaurant selection example in its demo systems. Analyze the variables and rules contained in the example's knowledge base.

2. In 1995, there were about 2,000 Web sites related to AI. Today there are substantially more. Do a search at Google and describe how many Web sites you find. Categorize the first 20 into groups, or if you used a search engine that grouped them, what groups did you find?

3. Search the Internet using the keyword *expert systems* and describe what you find. List the first five applications in your search result and compare their differences.

4. Access the Web site of the American Association for Artificial Intelligence (**aaai.org**). Examine the workshops it has offered over the past year and list the major topics related to intelligent systems.

5. Choose a few Web sites that you found in the previous search to find a few ES development tools not listed in the book. Classify them into different categories.

End of Chapter Application Case

Business Rule Automation at Farm Bureau Financial Services

Financial service is a major area for ES because the process involves a number of complicated rules. Farm Bureau is a 60-year-old comprehensive financial services provider that offers a broad range of innovative products. With the 2003 merger of three Farm Bureau insurance companies into Farm Bureau Financial Services, the carrier's new management team believed technology would enable the organization to improve the business processes each of the entities had performed in the past. One area the carrier sought to improve was underwriting, and it turned to a rule-based system that would eliminate many of the touches previously required of underwriters.

"Farm Bureau's goal was to get the carrier's business rules out of the legacy code so the rules would be more manageable," explained Brett Clausen, vice president of the property/casualty companies for Farm Bureau. "The question we asked ourselves initially was 'How could we use this tool to achieve speed to market while at the same time underwriting more effectively and efficiently?'" Farm Bureau identified several benefits it expected to gain with rules-based underwriting. That list included reduction in workloads, better policy issuance times, improved consistency in underwriting risks, adaptable response to market regulatory changes, expense reduction, underwriters being able to focus more on exposures that create a higher liability to the company, and the ability to better manage and monitor results.

The benefit of using rule-based systems is quite clear. "Our challenge early on was a lot of our policies going through were being reviewed," Clausen said. "There was a very low percentage—about 10 percent to 12 percent—of transactions that were going through without being reviewed. We've increased that now to more than 60 percent of transactions going through without being reviewed."

With such an increase, Clausen pointed out that it was easy to see how many rules had changed in the past two years. The cautious pace allowed users to identify the business rules that were important and had an impact on business results and to eliminate some of the rules that didn't have an impact on decision making. "We wanted to be conservative and targeted 20 percent as a good pass-through rate," he said. "That would give us the ability to step back and look at what rules were firing and what rules were not firing." Audits were conducted to make sure the policies that were passing through without being looked at were quality business and also to ensure that a policy that the carrier normally would not have written didn't get through.

"We were pleased with that initial juncture, and then we started looking at the rules again," Clausen said. It wasn't hard for Farm Bureau's underwriters and customer service representatives to reexamine the rules because the results of those rules were showing up in their workload. As a result, Farm Bureau has reduced its transaction time by about 75 percent, Clausen claimed. "The amount of transactions that are coming through is phenomenal," he said. "In 2005, we had about 450,000 transactions come through our automated underwriting rules base. Roughly 250,000 of those passed without being looked at. When you look at the impact that has on the human resource perspective, getting our underwriters to focus on where we want them to focus, and our customer service representatives to focus on building relationships with our policyholders, that's a major step."

Sources: Compiled from R. Hyle, "Business Rules Streamline Underwriting for Farm Bureau Financial Services," *Tech Decisions*, February 2006; and **fbfs.com** (accessed March 2006).

QUESTIONS FOR THE CASE

1. Describe the role of business rules in Farm Bureau and why those rules are very important.
2. Describe the benefit of using the rule-based system at Farm Bureau and explain why the system can generate these benefits.
3. Evaluate potential tools for implementing such a rule-based system and list the criteria that you would use in tool selection.
4. Find a proper application outside the financial services domain (such as manufacturing or retailing) and evaluate whether the rule-based system will generate the same level of benefits as those in the Farm Bureau system and explain why.

References

"Automatic Market Surveillance." (2004, February). *Expert Systems*.

Currie, A., (1999). "The History of Robotics," **faculty.ucr.edu/~currie/roboadam.htm** (accessed September 2006).

Eom, S.B. (1996, September/October). "A Survey of Operational Expert Systems in Business (1980–1993)." *Interfaces*, Vol. 26, No. 5.

Eriksson, H. (1996, June). "Expert Systems as Knowledge Servers." *IEEE Expert*.

Fadlalla, A., and C. Lin. (2001). "An Analysis of the Applications of Neural Networks in Finance." *Interfaces*, Vol. 31, No. 4.

Ghanea-Hercock, R., and R.K. Ghanea-Hercock. (2003), *Applied Evolutionary Algorithms in Java*. New York: Springer-Verlag.

Gill, T.G. (1995, March). "Early Expert Systems: Where Are They Now?" *MIS Quarterly*, Vol. 19, No. 1.

Goldberg, D.E. (1994, March). "Genetic and Evolutionary Algorithms Come of Age." *Communications of the ACM*, Vol. 37, No. 3.

Lopez, M.A., C.H. Flores, and E.G. Garcia. (2003). "An Intelligent Tutoring System for Turban Startup Training of Electronic Power Plant Operators." *Expert Systems with Applications*, Vol. 24, No. 1.

Nedovic, L., and V. Devedzic. (2002). "Expert Systems in Finance: A Cross-Section of the Field." *Expert Systems with Applications*, Vol. 23, No. 1.

Nguyen H.T., and E.A. Walker. (1999). *A First Course in Fuzzy Logic.* Boca Raton, FL: CRC Press.

Nurminen, J., O. Karonen, and K. Hätönen. (2003). "What Makes Expert Systems Survive Over 10 Years: Empirical Evaluation of Several Engineering Applications." *Expert Systems With Applications*, Vol. 24, No. 1.

Rich, E., and K. Knight. (1991). *Artificial Intelligence*, 2nd ed. New York: McGraw-Hill.

Reuters. (2005, June 2). "Toyota Aims to Sell Service Robots by 2010?" *Rueters.com*. **robots.net/article/1517-.html** (accessed March 2006).

Stabb, S., H. Werther, F. Ricci, A. Zipf, U. Gretzel, D. Fesenmaier, C. Paris, and C. Knoblock. (2002, November/December). "Intelligent Systems for Tourism." *IEEE Intelligent Systems*, Vol. 17, No. 6.

Yamaguchi, M. (2006, January 27). "Japanese Lab Develops Robot for Errands." *The Associated Press*.

Advanced Intelligent Systems

Learning Objectives

- Understand machine-learning concepts
- Learn the concepts and applications of case-based systems
- Understand the concepts and applications of genetic algorithms
- Understand fuzzy set theories and their applications in designing intelligent systems
- Understand the concepts and applications of natural language processing (NLP)
- Learn the concepts, advantages, and limitations of voice technologies
- Learn about integrated intelligent support systems

In addition to rule-based systems, a few advanced techniques are available for designing intelligent systems that can learn by themselves. These include case-based systems, genetic algorithms, and fuzzy reasoning systems. A case-based system contains a case base that maintains unique expert experience. Genetic algorithms modify the natural-selection process to find useful knowledge. Fuzzy systems convert between symbolic reasoning and mathematical calculation to improve decision performance in certain problem domains. Related technologies involve machines' understanding of the content of text and voice. These concepts and their integration are described in this chapter. The chapter is organized into the following sections:

13.1 Opening Vignette: Improving Urban Infrastructure Management in the City of Verdun
13.2 Machine-Learning Techniques
13.3 Case-Based Reasoning (CBR)
13.4 Genetic Algorithm Fundamentals
13.5 Developing Genetic Algorithm Applications
13.6 Fuzzy Logic Fundamentals
13.7 Natural Language Processing (NLP)
13.8 Voice Technologies
13.9 Developing Integrated Advanced Systems

13.1 OPENING VIGNETTE: IMPROVING URBAN INFRASTRUCTURE MANAGEMENT IN THE CITY OF VERDUN

PROBLEM

Like many other cities, the city of Verdun (Quebec, Canada) is attempting to rehabilitate its infrastructure. The city is attempting different strategies to restore the quality of the environment, to manage its many large and complex systems of services (e.g., education, social services), and to maintain and rehabilitate its existing infrastructure. The problem is that in order to do all these things, the city needs more resources than it has—a typical problem in almost all cities.

One of the many areas that require attention in Verdun is citizens' requests and complaints, which need to be addressed by city employees in different departments, such as the Department of Public Works. In addition to actions that result from citizen complaints and reports of employees, action may result from reports of sensors and other devices that monitor city infrastructure (e.g., water level in a pumping station). In this vignette, we deal only with the area of complaints management in the Department of Public Works.

SOLUTION

An information system was constructed to handle the complaint management system for Verdun's Department of Public Works. This system presents the sequential and parallel procedures to determine the immediate action to resolve new complaints received. Each time a complaint (or an alert recorded by sensors) is received, the system follows certain steps before it resolves the problem. Those steps can be disaggregated in seven major categories, where many people and many software components intervene, such as databases, knowledge bases, model-based systems, and intelligent decision support systems (IDSS).

In the core of the IDSS is an intelligent technology called *case-based reasoning (CBR)*, a technology that uses a repository (or library) of knowledge about historical problems, situations, actions, and solutions (some good and some bad). The CBR, as discussed in Section 13.2, includes a mechanism to manage that knowledge, such as knowledge storage, retrieval, and presentation. The technology helps manage and analyze each complaint, using similar historical complaints. The system classifies each complaint and then prioritizes it automatically, using CBR. The system then routes the complaint to the proper place for resolution. Each complaint may go through up to four analyses. The analyses consider legal, financial, and other constraints.

When a complaint is routed to a department, a solution (resolution) needs to be generated. The CBR automatically proposes solutions, based on past experience (i.e., comparison of case characteristics). The CBR tries to see if a past solution will solve the new problem. The computer may present several possible solutions to a manager. This is an interactive process between the user and the CBR. Finally, the manager considers priorities against the available resources.

RESULTS

Verdun's system can find similarities between current complaints and previous complaints/calls to the Department of Public Works. Also, the system can find complaints of the same type that occur in the same area at the same time. This kind of complaint analysis helps diminish the number of interventions. Case retrieval is based first on the type similarity and then on geographical similarity. When a case has been solved, it is automatically added to the **case library**—the knowledge base of a CBR system.

Verdun's CBR-based system helped improve the delivery, performance, and coordination of municipal services. Complaints are now resolved faster and frequently with fewer resources.

Sources: Compiled from A. Quintero, D. Konare, and S. Pierre, "Decision-Aid to Improve Organizational Performance," *European Journal of Operations Research*, May 2005; and F. Burstein and H. Linger, "Supporting Post-Fordist Work Practices: A Knowledge Management Framework for Supporting Knowledge Work," *Information Technology & People*, September 2003.

Questions for the Opening Vignette

1. Explain how CBR supports, rather than replaces, managers in the Verdun system.
2. Describe the CBR process in the Verdun system.
3. What were the specific capabilities and benefits of the CBR in the Verdun system?
4. Why are historical cases a good knowledge source?
5. Can an expert system (ES) be used instead of CBR? Why or why not?

WHAT WE CAN LEARN FROM THIS VIGNETTE

Complex decision situations with many variables can be solved by using a special intelligent system—a CBR. The major property of CBR is that it uses historical cases and their solution(s). A computer attempts to match the characteristics of a new case with those of an old one(s). Then, a proven solution of an old case can be recommended for a new one. This technology is an example of machine learning because a machine (i.e., a computer) learns from historical cases. Such learning can provide necessary knowledge quickly and inexpensively so that complex decisions can be made.

13.2 MACHINE-LEARNING TECHNIQUES

Machine-learning techniques enable learning and acquisition of knowledge from historical data. They overcome deficiencies of manual knowledge acquisition (see Chapter 18, an online chapter).

MACHINE-LEARNING CONCEPTS AND DEFINITIONS

Attempts at discovering problem-solving knowledge have been made for generations, starting long before the computer age. Some examples are statistical models, such as regression and forecasting; management science models, such as those for inventory level determination and resource allocation; and financial models, such as those for make-versus-buy decisions and equipment-replacement methods. Unfortunately, such methods are often limited to processing quantifiable and well-known factors. When problems are complex and factors are both quantitative and qualitative, standard models cannot solve them; additional, deeper, richer knowledge is needed.

Many organizations use neural networks to automate complex decision making. Neural networks (see Chapter 8) can readily identify patterns from which they generate recommended courses of action. Because such networks learn from past experience to improve their own performance, they are members of a technology family called *machine learning*. **Machine learning** is a family of methods that attempt to allow machines to acquire knowledge for problem solving by showing them historical cases. It is different in several ways from the conventional knowledge-acquisition methods described in Chapter 18 (an online chapter). Knowledge acquisition from human experts often suffers from an expert's unwillingness or inability to provide accurate knowledge, whereas machine learning is an attempt to implicitly induce expert knowledge from historical decisions. In other words, instead of asking the experts to articulate their decision knowledge, the learning module of the system is able to identify patterns and rules from the historical data available in the database or organizational files.

Machine learning is considered an artificial intelligence method, even though some of its technologies do not formally exhibit intelligence. However, it is definitely useful for designing an intelligent DSS, as shown in the opening vignette.

LEARNING

Learning is a process of self-improvement and thus an important feature of intelligent behaviors. Understanding learning is a critical area of artificial intelligence because it is an investigation into the basic principles that underlie intelligence rather than an application itself. Machine learning is also essential to providing intelligent management support systems (MSS) with self-enhancement capabilities.

Human learning is a combination of many complicated cognitive processes, including induction, deduction, analogy, and other special procedures related to observing or analyzing examples. Machine-learning techniques are very similar to human learning techniques; most of them adopt similar ideas and have them implemented on computers. The following are relevant observations on how learning relates to intelligent systems:

- Learning systems demonstrate interesting learning behaviors, some of which (e.g., chess- and checkers-playing programs) actually challenge the performance of humans.
- Although artificial intelligence sometimes matches human-level learning capabilities, it is not able to learn as well as humans or in the same way that humans do (e.g., checkers-playing programs learn quite differently from humans).
- There is no claim that machine learning can be applied in a creative way, although such systems can handle cases to which they have never been exposed. Simulated creativity is an intensely studied artificial intelligence topic (see the Imagination Engines, Inc., Web site, at **imagination-engines.com**).
- Learning systems are not anchored in any formal bedrock; thus, their implications are not well understood. Many systems have been tested exhaustively, but exactly why they succeed or fail is not precisely clear.
- A common thread running through most artificial intelligence approaches to learning (distinguishing them from non–artificial intelligence approaches to learning) is the manipulation of symbols rather than numeric information.

MACHINE-LEARNING METHODS

Machine learning has two major categories: supervised learning and unsupervised learning. **Supervised learning** is a process of inducing knowledge from a set of observations whose outcomes are known. For example, say we induce a set of rules from historical loan-evaluation data. Because the decisions on these loan cases are known, we can test how the induced model performs when it is applied to these cases. **Unsupervised learning** is used to discover knowledge from a set of data whose outcomes are unknown. A typical application is to classify customers into several different lifestyles. Before the classification, we do not know how many different kinds of lifestyles are available, nor do we know which customer belongs to a particular lifestyle. Figure 13.1 shows the machine-learning methods in each category.

Following are several machine-learning methods and algorithms:

1. *Inductive learning*. This method is used in knowledge acquisition, as in rule induction. It is discussed in Chapter 18 (an online chapter).
2. *Case-based reasoning*. This approach is used in knowledge acquisition and inferencing.
3. *Neural computing*. This approach can be used for knowledge discovery, forecasting, and pattern recognition (see Chapter 8).
4. *Genetic algorithms*. These algorithms attempt to follow the evolutionary processes of biological systems in which the fittest survive and are excellent learners.
5. *Natural language processing (NLP)*. In NLP, an attempt is made to teach machines to understand the content and meaning of written or spoken words and sentences.
6. *Cluster analysis*. This approach is used to put data into several groups, based on their similarity. The groups can then be used for marketing or other purposes.
7. *Statistical methods*. Some statistical methods, such as multiple-discriminant analysis, are suitable for analyzing knowledge that is quantifiable in nature. These methods have been applied to knowledge acquisition, forecasting, and problem solving.
8. *Explanation-based learning*. The **explanation-based learning** approach combines existing theories and new cases, using the new cases to modify existing theories and using theories to explain why one instance is or is not a prototypical member of a class (see Mitchell et al., 1986).

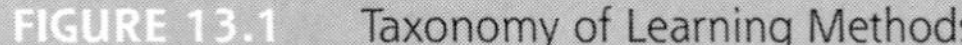

FIGURE 13.1 Taxonomy of Learning Methods

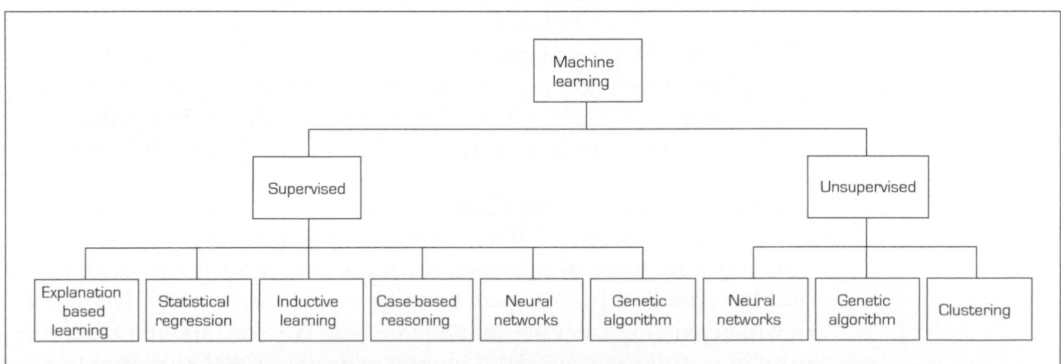

Section 13.2 Review Questions

1. Define *machine learning.*
2. What is learning?
3. What are the differences between supervised learning and unsupervised learning?
4. List several techniques for supervised learning and unsupervised learning.
5. List five machine-learning methods.

13.3 CASE-BASED REASONING (CBR)

The basic premise of machine learning is that there are data that preserve previous decision experience. These experience-based records are called *cases*. They may be used either as direct references to support similar decisions in the future or to induce rules or decision patterns. The former, called **case-based reasoning (CBR)** (also known as **analogical reasoning**), adapts solutions used to solve old problems for use in solving new problems. The latter, called **inductive learning**, allows the computer to examine historical cases and generates rules that can be chained (forward or backward) to solve new problems or for automated decision support systems. In this section, we describe the concept of CBR and its application in intelligent MSS. Inductive learning is introduced in Chapter 18 (an online chapter).

THE BASIC IDEA AND PROCESS OF CBR

CBR is based on the premise that new problems are often similar to previously encountered problems and that, therefore, past solutions may be of use in the current situation. Cases are often derived from legacy databases, thereby converting existing organizational resources into exploitable knowledge. CBR is particularly applicable to problems in which the domain is not understood well enough for a robust statistical model or system of equations to be formulated. CBR is commonly used for diagnosis (or, more generally, for classification tasks), such as determining a fault from observed attributes.

CBR has been formalized as a four-step process:

1. *Retrieve*. Given a target problem, retrieve from a library of past cases the most similar cases that are relevant to solving the current case.
2. *Reuse*. Map the solution from the previous case to the target problem. Reuse the best old solution to solve the current case.
3. *Revise*. Having mapped the previous solution to the target situation, test the new solution in the real world (or a simulation) and, if necessary, revise the case.
4. *Retain*. After the solution has been successfully adapted to the target problem, store the resulting experience as a new case in the case library.

Further details of the CBR process are provided later in this section.

The foundation of CBR is a repository (or library) of cases called a *case base* that contains a number of previous cases for decision making. For an overview, see Shiu and Pal (2004). CBR has proved to be an extremely effective approach for problems in which existing rules are inadequate (see Watson, 2002). In fact, because experience is an important ingredient in human expertise, CBR is thought to be a more psychologically plausible model of the reasoning of an expert than a rule-based model.

TABLE 13.1 Comparison of CBR and Rule-Based Systems

Criterion	*Rule-Based Reasoning*	*Case-Based Reasoning*
Knowledge unit	Rule	Case
Granularity	Fine	Coarse
Knowledge acquisition units	Rules, hierarchies	Cases, hierarchies
Explanation mechanism	Backtrack of rule firings	Precedent cases
Characteristic output	Answer and confidence measure	Answer and precedent cases
Knowledge transfer across problems	High if backtracking; low if deterministic	Low
Speed as a function of knowledge base size	Exponential if backtracking; linear if deterministic	Logarithmic if index tree is balanced
Domain requirements	Domain vocabulary Good set of inference rules Either few rules or rules apply sequentially Domain mostly obeys rules	Domain vocabulary Database of example cases Stability (a modified good solution is probably still good) Many exception to rules
Advantages	Flexible use of knowledge Potentially optimal answers	Rapid knowledge acquisition Explanation by examples
Disadvantages	Possible errors due to misfit rules and problem parameters Black-box answers	Suboptimal solutions Redundant knowledge base Computationally expensive Long development time

Source: Based on a discussion with Marc Goodman, Cognitive Systems, Inc., in 1995.

A theoretical comparison of the two is summarized in Table 13.1. According to Riesbeck and Schank (1989), the use of this approach is justified by the fact that human thinking does not use logic (or reasoning from first principles) but is basically a processing of the right information being retrieved at the right time. So the central problem is the identification of pertinent information whenever needed.

DEFINITION AND CONCEPTS OF CASES IN CBR

A case is the primary knowledge element in a CBR application. It is a combination of the problem features and proper business actions associated with each situation. These features and actions may be represented in natural language or in a specific structured format (e.g., objects).

Kolodner (1993) classified cases into three categories—ossified cases, paradigmatic cases, and stories—based on their different characteristics and the different ways of handling them. **Ossified cases** appear very often and are quite standard. They can be generalized into rules or other forms of knowledge through inductive learning. **Paradigmatic cases** contain certain unique features that cannot be generalized. They need to be stored and indexed in a case base for future reference. **Stories** are special cases that contain rich contents and special features with deep implications. Figure 13.2 shows the way the three types of cases can be handled. CBR is particularly designed for processing paradigmatic cases that cannot be properly handled by rule-based reasoning.

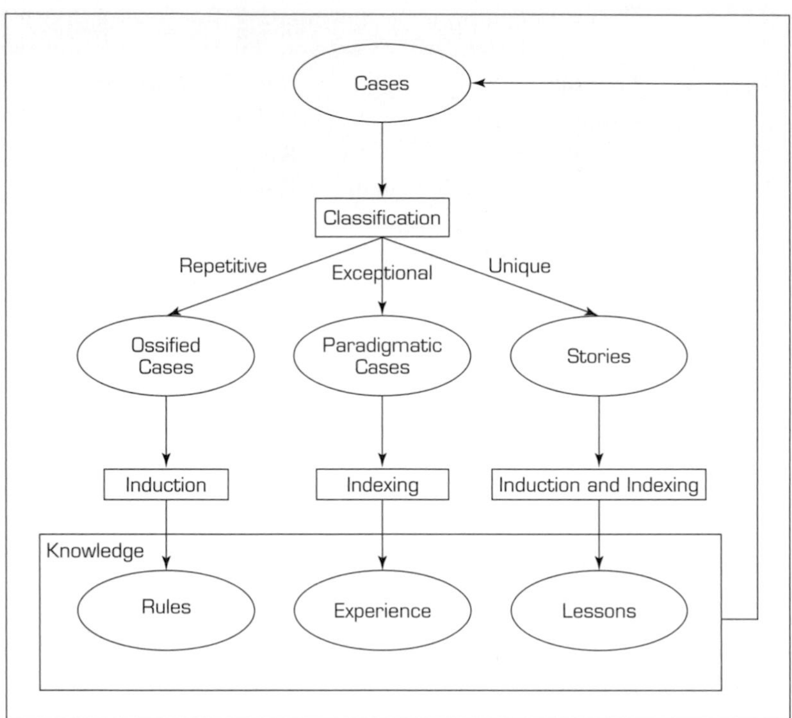

FIGURE 13.2 Deriving Knowledge from Different Types of Cases

Example: Loan Evaluation Using CBR

Let's consider a possible scenario of CBR in loan evaluation. When a new case is received, the system builds a set of features to represent it. Let's assume that the applicant is a 40-year-old married man, with a $50,000 annual income job in a midsize manufacturing company. The set of features is [age = 40, marriage = yes, salary = 50,000, employer = midsize, industry = manufacturing]. The system goes to the case base to find similar cases. Suppose the system finds the following three similar cases:

John = [age = 40, marriage = yes, salary = 50,000, employer = midsize, industry = bank]

Ted = [age = 40, marriage = yes, salary = 45,000, employer = midsize, industry = manufacturing]

Larry = [age = 40, marriage = yes, salary = 50,000, employer = small, industry = retailing]

If John and Ted performed well in paying their loans, and if Larry was unable to pay back due to company bankruptcy, then the system can recommend that the loan be approved because John and Ted, who are more similar to the new applicant (four of the five attributes are the same), were able to pay back without problems. Larry is considered less similar to the new applicant (only three of the five attributes are the same) and hence is less useful for reference.

BENEFITS AND USABILITY OF CBR

CBR makes learning much easier and the recommendation more sensible. Many applications of CBR have been implemented. For example, Shin and Han (2001) reported an application of CBR to corporate bond rating. Hastings et al. (2002) applied CBR to rangeland management. Humphreys et al. (2003) described an application of CBR to evaluate supplier environment-management performance. Park and Han (2002) applied CBR to bankruptcy prediction. Khan and Hoffmann (2003) reported the development of a case-based recommendation system without the involvement of human knowledge engineers. Finally, Pham and Setchi (2003) applied CBR to design adaptive product manuals.

The following are the advantages of using CBR:

- Knowledge acquisition is improved. It is easier to build, simpler to maintain, and less expensive to develop and support knowledge acquisition.
- System development time is faster than when using manual knowledge acquisition.
- Existing data and knowledge are leveraged.
- Complete formalized domain knowledge (as required with rules) is not required.
- Experts feel better discussing concrete cases (not general rules).
- Explanation becomes easier. Rather than showing many rules, a logical sequence can be shown.
- Acquisition of new cases is easy (i.e., can be automated).
- Learning can occur from both successes and failures.

THE PROCESS OF CBR

The process of using CBR is shown graphically in Figure 13.3. Boxes represent processes, and ovals represent knowledge structure. The major steps in the process are described in Online File W13.1.

FIGURE 13.3 The Process of Case-Based Reasoning

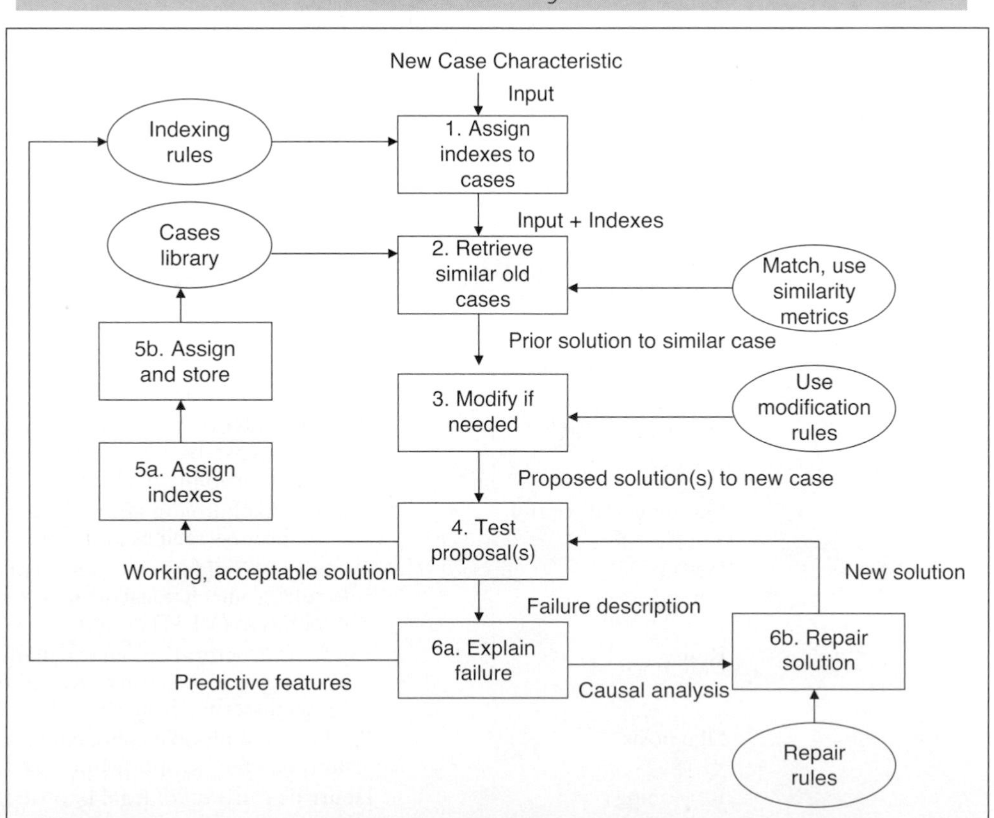

Sources: Compiled from C.K. Riesback and R.I. Schank, *Inside Case-Based Reasoning*, Lawrence Erlbaum Associates, Hillsdale, NJ, 1989, p. 32; and *AI Magazine*, Spring 1991, p. 46.

A detailed description of the reasoning process and recent applications can be found in Humphreys et al. (2003). An examination of case libraries in problem solving is available in Hernandez-Serrano and Jonassen (2003).

USES, ISSUES, AND APPLICATIONS OF CBR

CBR can be used on its own or can be combined with other reasoning paradigms. Several implementations of CBR systems combine rule-based reasoning (RBR) in order to address limitations such as accuracy in case indexing and adaptation.

Table 13.2 describes CBR applications in different fields. For a comprehensive CBR Web site, see **ai-cbr.org**, maintained by the University of Kaiserslautern in Germany. It contains applications, demos, and research material.

Designers must give careful thought to the following issues and questions regarding case-based implementation:

- What makes up a case? How can we represent case memory?
- Automatic case-adaptation rules can be very complex.
- How is memory organized? What are the indexing rules?
- The quality of the results is heavily dependent on the indexes used.
- How does memory function in relevant information retrieval?
- How can we perform efficient searching (i.e., knowledge navigation) of the cases?
- How can we organize (i.e., cluster) the cases?
- How can we design the distributed storage of cases?
- How can we adapt old solutions to new problems? Can we simply adapt the memory for efficient querying, depending on context? What are the similarity metrics and the modification rules?
- How can we factor errors out of the original cases?
- How can we learn from mistakes? That is, how can we repair and update the case base?

TABLE 13.2 Case-Based Reasoning Application Categories and Examples

Category	*Examples*
Electronic commerce	Intelligent product catalog searching, intelligent customer support, and sales support
Web and information search	Browsing advisor, retrieval of tour packages from travel catalogs, case-based information retrieval in construction, and skill profiling in electronic recruitment
Planning and control	Conflict resolution in air traffic control and planning of bioprocess recipes in the brewing industry
Design	Conceptual building design aid, conceptual design aid for electromechanical devices, and very large-scale integration (VLSI) design
Reuse	Reuse of structural design calculation documents, reuse of object-oriented software, and reuse assistant for engineering designs
Diagnosis	Prediction of blood alcohol content, online troubleshooting and customer support, and medical diagnosis
Reasoning	Heuristic retrieval of legal knowledge, reasoning in legal domains, and computer-supported conflict resolution through negotiation or mediation

- The case base may need to be expanded as the domain model evolves, yet much analysis of the domain may be postponed.
- How can we integrate CBR with other knowledge representations and inferencing mechanisms?
- Are there better pattern-matching methods than the ones we currently use?
- Are there alternative retrieval systems that match the CBR schema?

Since 1995, increasing evidence has shown positive results for the use of CBR in solving practical problems (see Lee and Kim, 2002; and Luu et al., 2003; also see Online File W13.2). Application Case 13.1 summarizes a successful application of CBR in jet engine maintenance.

Application Case 13.1

CBR Improves Jet Engine Maintenance, Reduces Costs

Snecma is the leading French manufacturer of aircraft engines, ranking fourth in the world. One of Snecma's goals is to improve engine maintenance technology to reduce the cost of ownership for its customers. The CASSIOPÉE project was designed to perform engine troubleshooting using CBR. It performs technical maintenance of the CFM 56-3 aircraft engines on all Boeing 737s.

Troubleshooting accounts for 50 percent of the average engine's downtime. The 16,000 cases studied here were culled from an eight-year history of all CFM 56-3 engines sold. Error cases were removed from the set, and the model was supplemented with technical parameters of the engines. A decision tree is used to organize the cases and drive the questioning. On average, a case is described by 40 attributes out of a total of 80 (not all are used simultaneously).

CASSIOPÉE has demonstrated the following benefits:

- Reduced downtime for the engines, avoiding delays for the airlines
- Minimized diagnosis costs
- Reduced diagnostic errors
- Development of a record and documentation of the expertise of the most skilled maintenance specialists to build a corporate memory and help transfer know-how to novices

The CASSIOPÉE system is in use in the after-sale division at CFM-International, a subsidiary of Snecma and General Electric. It is fully integrated in the end-user environment. CASSIOPÉE assists CFM engineers in offering quicker and better advice to airline maintenance crews when airplanes are at the departure gate.

Sources: Abstracted and modified from M. Lenz, *Case-Based Reasoning Technology: From Foundations to Application*, Springer-Verlag Telos, New York, 1998; and M. Manago and E. Auriol, *Integrating Induction and Case-Based Reasoning for Troubleshooting CFM-56 Aircraft Engines, XPS'95*, Fourth German Conference on Expert Systems, University of Kaiserslautern, Kaiserslautern, Germany, April 5–7, 1995.

SUCCESS FACTORS FOR CBR SYSTEMS

CBR systems exhibit some unique properties that, if properly managed and implemented, can lead to very successful systems. Klahr (1997) described the following seven principles for a successful CBR strategy:

1. *Determine specific business objectives*. Every software project should have a business focus. Call center and help desk environments have great potential for CBR methods.
2. *Understand your end users and customers*. A successful case base directly supports the end user. The case base (i.e., knowledge) must be at the level of expertise of the end users. Shortcuts should be provided for more knowledgeable end users.

3. *Design the system appropriately*. This includes understanding the problem domain and types of information the case base will provide and recognizing system and integration requirements.
4. *Plan an ongoing knowledge-management process*. The knowledge in the case base must be updated as new cases arise (i.e., to avoid gaps in the case base) or as new products or services are delivered (i.e., as new content is added).
5. *Establish achievable returns on investment (ROI) and measurable metrics*. Develop a level of acceptable ROI (e.g., 5–13 percent is being achieved in the field) and a means to measure it (e.g., 20 fewer phone calls, with a 13 percent larger customer base handled; or the ability to handle four times more questions than under the manual system).
6. *Plan and execute a customer-access strategy*. The strength of CBR is that it can be put into the hands of customers, even over the Web, thus providing service 24 hours every day (e.g., Broderbund Software's Gizmo Trapper). This empowers customers to obtain the assistance they need when they need it. It also further broadens the use of the system, which helps in identifying exceptions and updating the case base. This is a key component of success.
7. *Expand knowledge generation and access across the enterprise*. Just as knowledge is made available to customers, internal customers who are in direct contact with external customers may be able to provide helpful feedback and knowledge.

TOOLS FOR BUILDING CBR

Some of the tools available for developing CBR systems are described in Technology Insights 13.2.

TECHNOLOGY INSIGHTS 13.2

Tools for Developing CBR Systems

CBR systems are usually built with the help of special tools. Some representative tools are listed in the following table:

Vendor and Product(s)	URL
PolyAnalyst, Megaputer Intelligence, Inc.	**megaputer.com**
ARTEnterprise MindBox, Inc.	**mindbox.com**
Kaidara Advisor, Kaidara	**kaidara.com**
Spotlight, CaseBank Technologies, Inc.	**casebank.com**
Induce-It, Inductive Solutions, Inc.	**inductive.com**
eGain Service, eGain Communications	**egain.com**
Knowledge Server, Intellix	**intellix.com**
HELPDESK, 3TreeTools	**treetools.com.br**

Sources: AI-CBR, **ai-cbr.org** (accessed April 2006) and PCAI, *Intelligent Web Applications & Agents,* Vol.19 No. 2, 2005.

The Web sites of AI-CBR (**ai-cbr.org**) and the University of Kaiserslautern (**ai-cbr.org**) provide details and pointers for numerous CBR tools and applications.

Although this site is no longer being maintained, there's still plenty of basic information and leads to additional resources. There's something for everyone at this site, such as a page about applied CBR, a page offering actual case bases you can download, a searchable bibliography, and even a virtual library.

A comprehensive toolkit is available from LPA (**lpa.co.uk/cbr.htm**). It includes modules for selection of source, construction of an input query, retrieval of records, and reordering of retrieved records. It also includes source code examples and an example of a CBR application.

Section 13.3 Review Questions

1. Define *CBR*.
2. Describe the four steps of the CBR process. Briefly discuss each step.
3. List five benefits of CBR.
4. Comment on the usability of CBR.
5. List three success factors of CBR.

13.4 GENETIC ALGORITHM FUNDAMENTALS

Genetic algorithms are programs that attempt to find optimal solutions to problems when it is possible to specify the criteria that can be used to evaluate the optimal solutions. Genetic algorithms are sets of computational procedures that conceptually follow steps inspired by the biological processes of evolution. Better and better solutions evolve from previous generations, until an optimal or near-optimal solution is obtained.

Genetic algorithms (also known as *evolutionary algorithms*) demonstrate self-organization and adaptation in much the same way that the fittest biological organisms survive and reproduce. The method learns by producing offspring that are better and better, as measured by a fitness-to-survive function. Algorithms of this type have been applied to problems such as vehicle routing (see Baker and Syechew, 2003), bankruptcy prediction (see Shin and Lee, 2002), and Web searching (see Nick and Themis, 2001).

Example: The Vector Game

To illustrate how genetic algorithms work; we describe the classical Vector game (see Walbridge, 1989). This game is similar to MasterMind. As your opponent gives you clues about how good your guess is (i.e., a fitness function), you create a new solution, using knowledge of the current solutions and their quality.

Description of the Vector Game

Vector is played against an opponent who secretly writes down a string of six digits. (In a genetic algorithm, this string consists of chromosomes.) Each digit can be either 0 or 1. For example, say that the secret number is 001010. You must try to guess this number as quickly as possible. You present a number (a guess) to your opponent, and he or she tells you how many of the digits (but not which ones) you guessed are correct (i.e., the fitness function or quality of your guess). For example, the guess 110101 has no correct digits (score = 0). The guess 111101 has only one correct digit (the third one). Thus, the score (the fitness, or value, of the solution) = 1.

Random Trial and Error

There are 64 possible six-digit strings of numbers. If you pick numbers at random, you will need, on average, 32 guesses to obtain the right answer. Can you do it faster? Yes, if you can interpret the feedback provided to you by your opponent (a measure of the goodness or fitness of your guess). This is how a genetic algorithm works.

Genetic Algorithm Solution

The following are the steps in solving the genetic algorithm for the Vector game:

Step 1. Present to your opponent four strings, selected at random. (Select four arbitrarily. Through experimentation, you may find that five or six would be better.) Assume that you have selected these four:

(A) 110100; score = 1 (i.e., one digit correctly guessed)

(B) 111101; score = 1

(C) 011011; score = 4

(D) 101100; score = 3

Because none of the strings is entirely correct, continue.

Step 2. Delete (A) and (B) because of their low scores. Call (C) and (D) parents.

Step 3. "Mate" the parents by splitting each number as shown here between the second and third digits (the position of the split is randomly selected):

(C) 01:1011

(D) 10:1100

Now combine the first two digits of (C) with the last four of (D) (this is called *crossover*). The result is (E), the first offspring:

(E) 011100; score = 3

Similarly, combine the first two digits of (D) with the last four of (C). The result is (F), the second offspring:

(F) 101011; score = 4

It looks as though the offspring are not doing much better than the parents.

Step 4. Now copy the original (C) and (D).

Step 5. Mate and crossover the new parents, but use a different split. Now you have two new offspring, (G) and (H):

(C) 0110:11

(D) 1011:00

(G) 0110:00; score = 4

(H) 1011:11; score = 3

Next, repeat step 2: Select the best "couple" from all the previous solutions to reproduce. You have several options, such as (G) and (C). Select (G) and (F). Now duplicate and crossover. Here are the results:

(F) 1:01011

(G) 0:11000

(I) 111000; score = 3

(J) 001011; score = 5

You can also generate more offspring:

(F) 101:011

(G) 011:000

(K) 101000; score = 4

(L) 011011; score = 4

Now repeat the processes with (J) and (K) as parents, and duplicate the crossover:

(J) 00101:1

(K) 10100:0

(M) 001010; score = 6

This is it! You have reached the solution after 13 guesses. Not bad compared to the average of 32 for a random guess out of 64 possibilities.

Note: Using common sense and logic, this problem can be solved faster than the random average. However, this example is easy to follow; if the problem is complex, the logical solution is not as obvious.

GENETIC ALGORITHM PROCESS AND TERMINOLOGY

A genetic algorithm is an iterative procedure that represents its candidate solutions as strings of genes called **chromosomes** and measures their viability with a fitness function. The *fitness function* is a measure of the objective to be obtained (i.e., maximum or minimum). As in biological systems, candidate solutions combine to produce offspring in each algorithmic iteration, called a *generation*. The offspring themselves can become candidate solutions. From the generation of parents and children, a set of the fittest survive to become parents that produce offspring in the next generation. Offspring are produced using specific genetic operators that include reproduction, crossover, and mutation:

- *Reproduction.* Through **reproduction**, genetic algorithms produce new generations of improved solutions by selecting parents with higher fitness ratings or by giving such parents a greater probability of being contributors and by using random selection.
- *Crossover.* Many genetic algorithms use strings of binary symbols for chromosomes, as in the Vector game described earlier, to represent solutions. **Crossover** means choosing a random position in the string (e.g., after two digits) and exchanging the segments either to the right or the left of that point with those of another string partitioned similarly to produce two new offspring.
- *Mutation.* This genetic operator was not shown in the Vector game example. **Mutation** is an arbitrary change in a situation. Sometimes it is used to prevent an algorithm from getting stuck. The procedure changes a 1 to a 0 or a 0 to a 1 instead of duplicating them. This change occurs with a very low probability (say, 1 in 1,000).

HOW A GENETIC ALGORITHM WORKS

Figure 13.4 is a flow diagram of a typical genetic algorithm process. The problem to be solved must be described in a manner amenable to solution using a genetic algorithm. Typically, this means that a string of 1s and 0s can represent a solution and that an easily computed fitness function, which we assume is to be maximized, can be established. (In the general case, integers or continuous variables can be used; minimization presents no conceptual problem.) An initial set of solutions is generated, and their fitness functions are computed. The sum of the fitness functions is computed, and each solution's probability of being selected to generate a pair of offspring is equal to its fitness function divided by the sum.

A set of new offspring is generated through crossover and a small random amount of mutation. Parents are selected based on the probability distribution described previously. The next generation consists of a set of the best new offspring and parents. The process continues until a good enough solution is obtained, an optimum is guaranteed, or no improvement occurs over several generations.

A few parameters must be set for the genetic algorithm. Their values are dependent on the problem being solved and are usually determined through trial and error:

- Number of initial solutions to generate
- Number of offspring to generate
- Number of parents and offspring to keep for the next generation
- Mutation probability (very low)
- Probability distribution of crossover point occurrence (generally equally weighted)

Sometimes these parameters can be varied for better performance while the algorithm is running. For more information on the methodology, see Niettinen et al. (1999) and Grupe and Jooste (2004).

Example: The Knapsack Problem

The knapsack problem is a conceptually simple optimization problem that can be solved directly by using analytical methods. Even so, it is ideal for illustrating a genetic algorithm approach. Say that you are going on an overnight hike and have a number of items that you could take along. Each item has a weight (in pounds) and a benefit or value to you on the hike (say, in U.S. dollars), and you can take one, at most, of each item (sorry, no partial items allowed—it's all or nothing). There is a capacity limit on the weight you can carry (only one

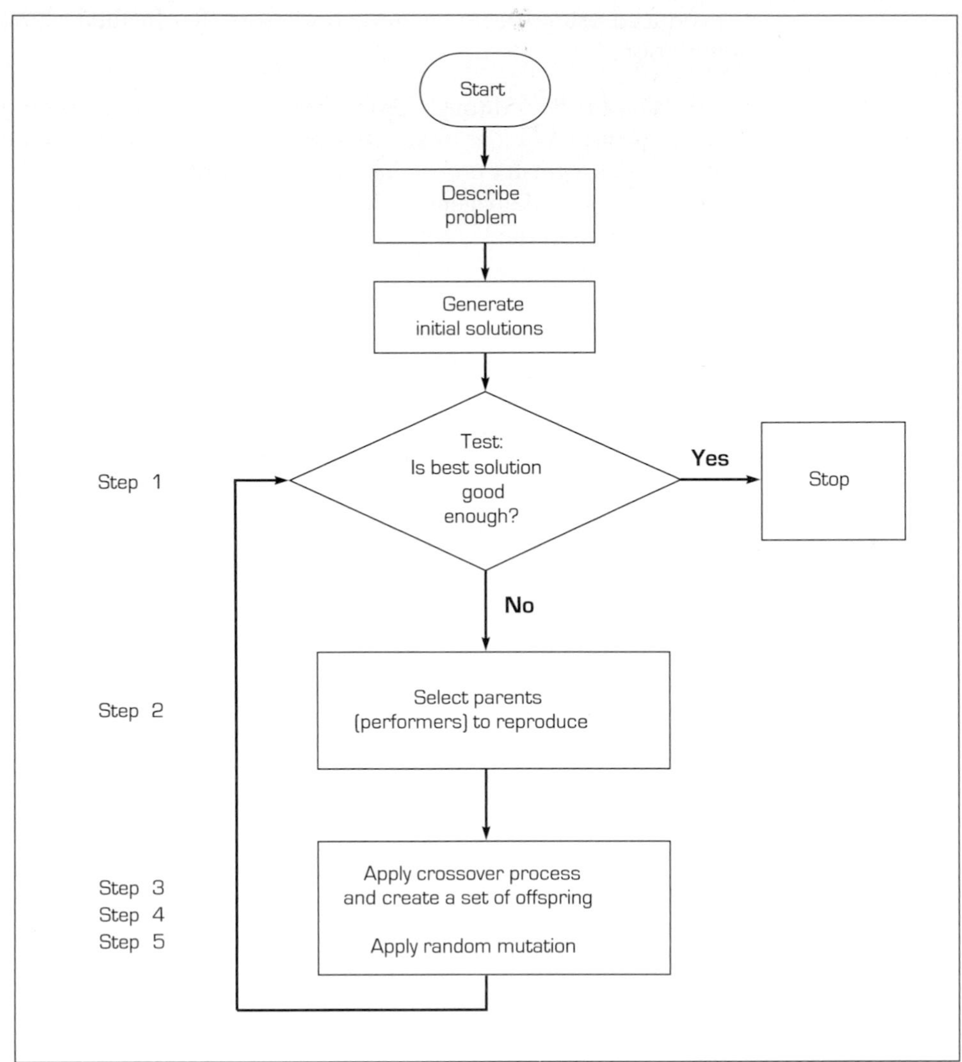

FIGURE 13.4 Flow Diagram of the Genetic Algorithm Process

constraint, but there can be several measures and capacities, including volume, time, etc.). The knapsack problem has many important applications, including determining what items to carry on a space shuttle mission. For our example, there are seven items, numbered 1 through 7, with respective benefits and weights as follows:

Item	1	2	3	4	5	6	7
Benefit	5	8	3	2	7	9	4
Weight	7	8	4	10	4	6	4

The knapsack holds a maximum of 22 pounds. The string 1010100, with a total benefit or fitness of 7 + 4 + 4 = 15, can represent a solution of items 1, 3, and 5.

We set up the problem in an Excel worksheet, where we represent a solution as a string of seven 1s and 0s and the fitness function as the total benefit, which is the sum of the gene values in a string solution multiplied by their respective benefit coefficients. The method generates a set of random solutions (i.e., initial parents), uses the objective function (i.e., total benefit) for the fitness function, and selects parents randomly to create generations of offspring through

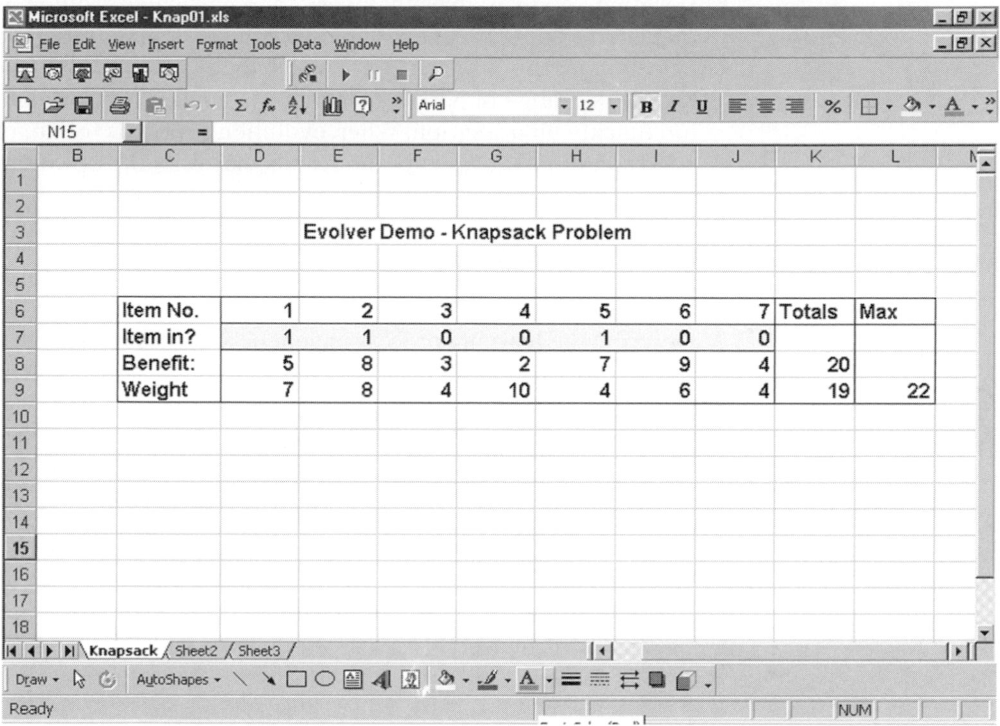

Evolver Demo - Knapsack Problem

Item No.	1	2	3	4	5	6	7	Totals	Max
Item in?	1	1	0	0	1	0	0		
Benefit:	5	8	3	2	7	9	4	20	
Weight	7	8	4	10	4	6	4	19	22

FIGURE 13.5 Evolver Solution to the Knapsack Problem Example

crossover and mutation operations. Selection is statistically based on the parents' fitness values. Higher values are more likely to be selected than lower ones. In Figure 13.5, we show the best solution found by Evolver, an easy-to-use Excel add-in genetic algorithm package (from Palisade Corp., **palisade.com**; demo available online).

Another interesting example of using a genetic algorithm is the shortest-tracks-route example provided by Grupe and Jooste (2004).

Limitations of Genetic Algorithms

According to Grupe and Jooste (2004), among the limitations of genetic algorithms are the following:

- Not all problems can be framed in the mathematical manner that genetic algorithms demand.
- Development of a genetic algorithm and interpretation of the results requires an expert who has both the programming and statistical/mathematical skills demanded by the genetic algorithm technology in use.
- It is known that in a few situations, the "genes" from a few comparatively highly fit (but not optimal) individuals may come to dominate the population, causing it to converge on a local maximum. When the population has converged, the ability of the genetic algorithm to continue to search for better solutions is effectively eliminated.
- Most genetic algorithms rely on random number generators that produce different results each time the model runs. While there is likely to be a high degree of consistency among the runs, they may vary.

- Locating good variables that work for a particular problem is difficult. Obtaining the data to populate the variables is equally demanding.
- Selecting methods by which to evolve the system requires thought and evaluation. If the range of possible solutions is small, a genetic algorithm will converge too quickly on a solution. When evolution proceeds too quickly, thereby altering good solutions too quickly, the results may miss the optimum solution.

Section 13.4 Review Questions

1. Define *genetic algorithm*.
2. Describe the learning process in genetic algorithms. Why is it similar to the biological learning process?
3. Describe the major genetic algorithm operators.

13.5 DEVELOPING GENETIC ALGORITHM APPLICATIONS

Genetic algorithms are a type of machine learning for representing and solving complex problems. They provide a set of efficient, domain-independent search heuristics for a broad spectrum of applications, including the following:

- Dynamic process control
- Induction of optimization of rules
- Discovery of new connectivity topologies (e.g., neural computing connections, i.e., neural network design)
- Simulation of biological models of behavior and evolution
- Complex design of engineering structures
- Pattern recognition
- Scheduling
- Transportation and routing
- Layout and circuit design
- Telecommunication
- Graph-based problems

A genetic algorithm interprets information that enables it to reject inferior solutions and accumulate good ones, and thus it learns about its universe. Genetic algorithms are also suitable for parallel processing.

Over the past two decades, the number of successful business applications of genetic algorithms has increased. For example, since 1993, Channel 4 television (England) has been using a genetic algorithm embedded in an ES to schedule its commercials to maximize revenues (see **attar.com**). And a team of researchers at the Electrotechnical Laboratory (ETL) in Japan has developed a hardware-implemented genetic algorithm on a central processing unit (CPU) chip that minimizes the impact of imperfect clock cycles in integrated-circuit fabrication variations. This team has demonstrated that increasing the chip yield rate from 2.9 percent to 51.1 percent clears the path toward inexpensive gigahertz clock rate CPUs for PCs (see Johnson, 1999).

Examples of genetic algorithms applied to real problems include those for assembly-line balancing (see Application Case 13.3), facility layout, machine and job shop scheduling, production planning, industrial packing and cutting, task assignment for earth-observing satellites, construction scheduling with limited resources, utility pricing, personnel planning, sawmill board-cut selection, scheduling of ship maintenance for a large fleet, solution of routing problems based on the traveling salesperson problem (see Baker and Syechew, 2003), design and improvement of water-distribution systems and similar networks, and determination of creditworthiness and aircraft design. Several other applications are listed in Grupe and Jooste (2004). These include driver scheduling for a public transportation system, job shop scheduling, vehicle routing (see Baker and Syechew 2003), and Web searching (see Nick and Themis, 2001). Genetic algorithms are often used to improve the performance of other artificial intelligence methods, such as ES or neural networks. A role genetic algorithms play in neural networks is to dynamically adjust to find the optimal network weights (see Kuo and Chen, 2004). The integration of multiple intelligent methods is discussed in Section 13.9. For a genetic algorithm environment for the Internet, see Tan et al. (2005).

Application Case 13.3

Genetic Algorithms Schedule Assembly Lines at Volvo Trucks North America

The buyer of a Volvo 770 trailer cab has dozens of choices: engine size, paint color, fabric, wood-grain finish, stereo, type of suspension, axles, bumpers, pneumatic systems, transmissions, and so on. When the cost is more than $100,000 and the time to be spent in the cab is about 2,000 hours a year, the buyer should have plenty of options. This leads to millions of configurations Volvo can use to build a truck. When a specific truck is to be built, all the tools and parts must be available, but this is difficult to schedule with so many possible combinations.

Gus N. Riley is responsible for scheduling the assembly line in Volvo's million-square-foot factory in Dublin, Virginia. He must cope with hundreds of constraints. Until 1995, Riley solved this operations research problem by eyeballing the production requirements for each week (on the average output of 550 trucks per week) and sorting color-coded punch cards, each representing one truck and its characteristics that might affect scheduling. It took four days to construct a week's schedule, and there were always bottlenecks as conditions changed on the factory floor.

In August 1996, Volvo installed OptiFlex (from i2 Technologies), which uses genetic algorithms to evolve a good schedule from a sequence of so-so schedules. Jeffrey Herrmann, a vice president at i2 Technologies, explained, "You tell it what the production at the end of a period should be and then you go have a cup of coffee." The program randomly devises 100 feasible solutions and ranks them according to cost, labor constraints, materials availability, and productivity. Then the program connects parts of good schedules to parts of other ones in an effort to find even better solutions.

The offspring of these genetic pairings are thrown into the pool, which is evaluated and ranked again. The pool is always kept at 100 by deleting poorer solutions. Running through roughly five iterations per second, OptiFlex comes up with maybe not the best possible schedule but a good one—in minutes.

Each Wednesday, Riley feeds in data to make the weekly schedule five weeks out. He eyeballs it and tinkers with it by tightening some constraints and loosening others. He catches errors in data entry. OptiFlex, running on a PC connected to the factory network, accepts corrections and quickly generates new solutions. Creating a schedule takes only one day instead of four. And reworking the schedule because of unforeseen events, such as customers changing their minds about features or broken equipment, takes only minutes.

Sources: Adapted from S.S. Rao, "Evolution at Warp Speed," *Forbes*, January 12, 1998, pp. 82–83; and "Job-Shop Scheduling at the Volvo Truck Plant," *CNN Interactive*, November 6, 1998 (no longer available online).

Because the kernel of genetic algorithms is pretty simple, it is not difficult to write computer codes to implement them. For better performance, there are software packages available on the market. A brief description is provided in Technology Insights 13.4.

Section 13.5 Review Questions

1. List major areas of genetic algorithm application.
2. Describe in detail three genetic algorithm applications.
3. Describe the capability of Evolver as an optimization tool.

TECHNOLOGY INSIGHTS 13.4

Genetic Algorithm Software

Several genetic algorithm codes are available for fee or for free (try searching the Web for research and commercial sites). In addition, a number of commercial packages offer online demos. Representative commercial packages include Microsoft Solver and XpertRule GenAsys, an ES shell with an embedded genetic algorithm (see **xpertrule.com**). Genetic algorithms are also related to artificial life scenarios, such as John Conway's Game of Life (e.g., Stephen Stuart's Java implementation at **tech.org/~stuart/life**). Also see the predictive suite from Predictive Dynamix, Inc. (**predictivedynamix.com**)

Evolver (from Palisade Corp., **palisade.com**) is an optimization add-in for Excel. It uses an innovative genetic algorithm to quickly solve complex optimization problems in finance, scheduling, manufacturing, and so on. See the example in Figure 13.6.

FIGURE 13.6 Evolver Finds an Optimal Solution by Using a Genetic Algorithm

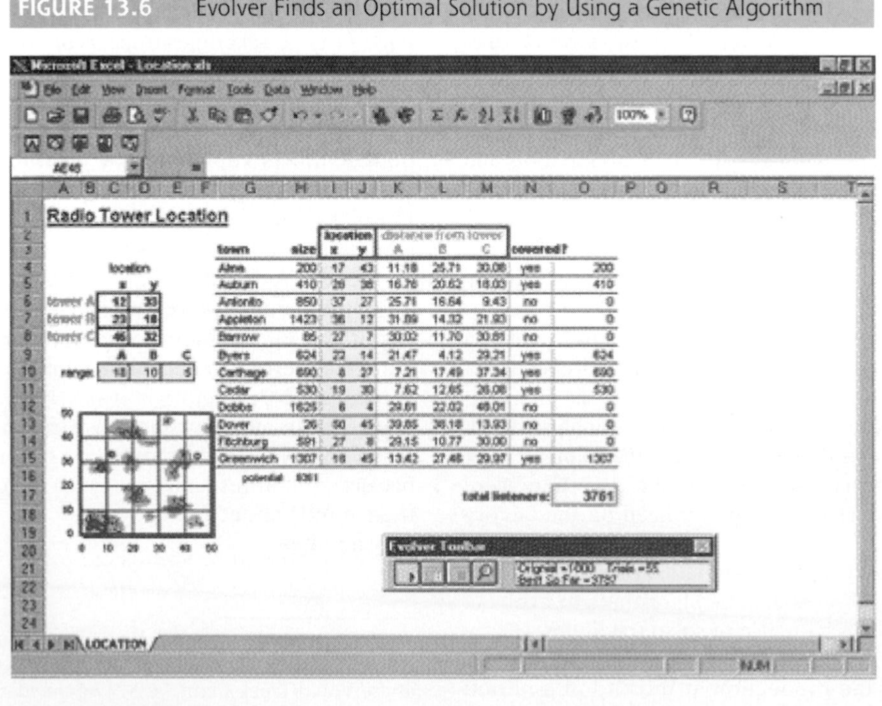

Source: Palisade.com

13.6 FUZZY LOGIC FUNDAMENTALS

Fuzzy logic deals with the kind of uncertainty and partial information that is inherently human in nature. This technique, which uses the mathematical theory of **fuzzy sets** (see Ross, 2004), simulates the process of human reasoning by allowing the computer to behave less precisely and logically than conventional computer methods require. The thinking behind this approach is that decision making is not always a matter of black and white or true or false; it often involves gray areas, or "maybes." In fact, creative decision-making processes are unstructured, playful, contentious, and rambling.

Fuzzy logic can be useful because it is an effective way to describe human perceptions of many decision-making problems in situations that are not 100 percent true or false. Many control and decision-making problems do not easily fit into the strict true/false situation required by mathematical models; or if they can be described that way, it is not the best way to do so. Introductions to fuzzy logic can be found in Dwinnell (2002) and at **en.wikipedia.org/wiki/Fuzzy_logic**.

Example: Fuzzy Set for a Tall Person

Let's look at an example of a fuzzy set that describes a tall person. If we survey people to define the minimum height a person must attain before being a man is considered tall, the answers could range from 5 to 7 feet (1 foot is about 30 cm, 1 inch is 2.54 cm). The distribution of answers might look like this:

Height	Proportion Voted For
5′10″	0.05
5′11″	0.10
6′	0.60
6′1″	0.15
6′2″	0.10

Suppose that Jack's height is 6 feet. From probability theory, we can use the cumulative probability distribution and say there is a 75 percent chance that Jack is tall.

In fuzzy logic, we say that Jack's degree of membership in the set of tall people is 0.75. The difference is that in probability terms, Jack is perceived as either tall or not tall, and we are not completely sure whether he is tall. In contrast, in fuzzy logic, we agree that Jack is more or less tall. Then we can assign a membership function to show the relationship of Jack to the set of tall people (i.e., the fuzzy logic set):

<Jack, 0.75 = Tall>

This can be expressed in a knowledge-based system as "Jack is tall" (CF = 0.75). An important difference from probability theory is that related memberships in fuzzy sets do not have to total 1. For example, the statement "Jack is short" (CF = 0.15) indicates that the combination is only 0.90. In probability theory, if the probability that Jack is tall is .75, then the probability that he is not tall (i.e., that he is short, assuming only two events) must be .25.

In contrast to certainty factors that include two values (e.g., the degrees of belief and disbelief), fuzzy sets use a spectrum of possible values called *belief functions*. We express our belief that a particular item belongs to a set through a membership function, as shown in Figure 13.7. At a height of 69 inches, a person starts to be considered tall, and at 74 inches, he or she is definitely tall. Between 69 and 74 inches, the person's membership function value varies from 0 to 1. Likewise, a person has a membership function value in the set of short people and medium-height people, depending on his or her height. The medium range spans both the short and tall ranges, so a person has a

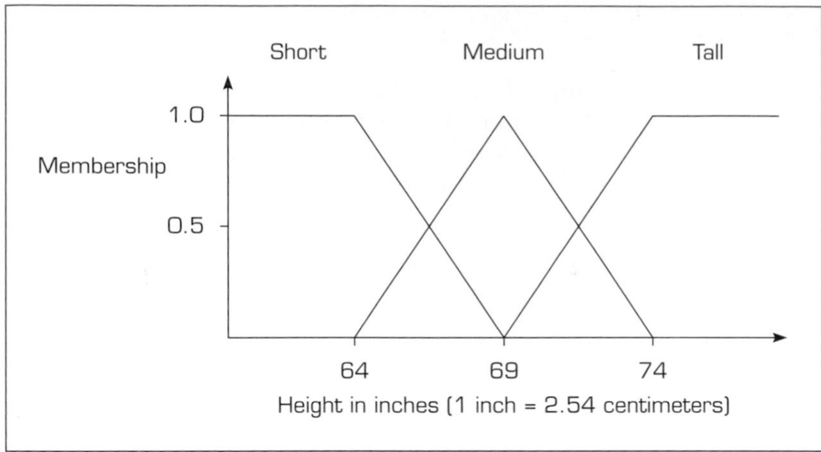

FIGURE 13.7 Membership Functions in Fuzzy Sets

belief of potentially being a member of more than one fuzzy set at a time. This is a critical strength of fuzzy sets: They lack crispness, yet they are consistent in their logic.

The application of fuzzy logic to managerial decision support has recently been gaining momentum despite the fact that it is complex to develop, requires considerable computing power, and is difficult to explain to users. However, thanks to increasing computational power and software, this situation has been changing since the 1990s.

FUZZY LOGIC APPLICATIONS

Fuzzy logic is difficult to apply when people supply the membership information. The problems range from linguistic vagueness to difficulty in supplying the definitions needed. Fuzzy logic is being used extensively in the area of consumer products, where the input is provided by sensors rather than by people. Fuzzy logic in consumer products is sometimes called *continuous logic* (after all, who wants a fuzzy camcorder?). Fuzzy logic provides smooth motion in consumer products. This is appropriate for subway control systems and for other motor controls and navigation (see Ross, 2004).

Fuzzy Logic Applications for Manufacturing and Management

Fuzzy logic applications are well known in consumer products such as air-conditioners, antilock brakes, toasters, cameras, camcorders, dishwashers, and microwaves. Fuzzy logic has also been applied to the following industrial and managerial areas:

- Selection of stocks to purchase (e.g., the Japanese Nikkei stock exchange)
- Retrieval of data (because fuzzy logic can find data quickly)
- Inspection of beverage cans for printing defects
- Matching of golf clubs to customers' swings
- Risk assessment
- Control of the amount of oxygen in cement kilns
- Accuracy and speed increases in industrial quality-control applications
- Sorting problems in multidimensional spaces
- Enhancement of models involving queuing (i.e., waiting lines)
- Managerial decision support applications

- Project selection
- Environmental control building
- Control of the motion of trains
- Paper mill automation
- Space shuttle vehicle orbiting
- Regulation of water temperature in shower heads

Fuzzy Logic Applications in Business: Examples

Many fuzzy logic applications in the area of controls and automation have been reported. We next provide three examples of fuzzy logic applications in business.

Example 1: Fuzzy Strategic Planning

Hall (1987) developed STRATASSIST, a fuzzy ES that helps small- to medium-sized firms plan strategically for a single product. During a consultation, STRATASSIST asks questions in five strategic, competitive areas that a firm should consider in evaluating its own strengths and weaknesses:

- Threat of new entries to the industry
- Threat of substitute products
- Buyer group power (i.e., consumers' power)
- Supplier group power
- Rivalry in the industry

Each question asks the user to rate the firm in each of these competitive areas. STRATASSIST feeds the answers into its fuzzy knowledge base, which consists of rules such as the following:

IF the importance of personal service in the distribution of your product is high,

THEN strategic action should be to distribute the firm's product or service through small, flexible, local units.

Hall used uncommonly rigorous experimental design procedures to test STRATASSIST's effectiveness. He asked MBA students to develop strategic plans for a fictional company. One-third of the students used STRATASSIST output in their planning, one-third used answers to the questions in the five strength/weakness areas, and one-third worked without STRATASSIST. Twelve expert judges from academia and industry rated the students' plans. The students who used STRATASSIST were judged to have formulated significantly better strategies than the others. See Dwinnell (2002) for additional applications of fuzzy logic in strategic decision making.

Example 2: Fuzziness in Real Estate

In conducting property appraisals, it is necessary to use judgment to generate estimates. Experience and intuition are essential factors. Some of the needed estimates are land value, value of buildings, building replacement costs, and the amount the building has appreciated. Then it is necessary to review sales of comparable properties, decide what is relevant, and, finally, estimate the net income. Most of such data are fuzzy. See Bagnoli and Smith (1998) for fuzzy logic applications in real estate.

Example 3: A Fuzzy Bond-Evaluation System

The value of bonds depends on such factors as company profitability, assets, and liability; market volatility; and possibly fluctuations in foreign exchange and risk. There is considerable fuzziness in factors such as foreign exchange risk. Chorafas (1994) constructed a fuzzy logic system that helps in making decisions about investing in bonds. The results indicate superior values over an average noncomputerized bond evaluation.

New applications of fuzzy logic are continually being developed because of its effectiveness. For examples, a fuzzy logic system was proposed for terrorist detection (see Cox, 2001). For other applications, see Liao (2003) and Xu and Xu (2003).

Software companies in this field include Rigel Corp. (**rigelcorp.com/flash.htm** and Inform Software Corp. (**informusa.com/fuzzy/index.htm**).

Section 13.6 Review Questions

1. Define *fuzzy logic* and describe its characteristics.
2. What are the basic premises on which the fuzzy logic approach is based?
3. What are the major advantages of fuzzy logic? What are its major limitations?
4. List some non-business applications of fuzzy logic.
5. List some business applications of fuzzy logic.

13.7 NATURAL LANGUAGE PROCESSING (NLP)

Machine-learning techniques are useful in knowledge acquisition and are used to solve complex problems that require specialized knowledge in a fast and/or economic way. To communicate with these and other software tools, it is necessary to consider two interrelated tools: natural language processing and machine translation.

TYPES OF NATURAL LANGUAGE PROCESSING

Today, when you tell a computer what to do, you usually type standard commands on the keyboard. In responding to a user, the computer outputs message symbols or other short, cryptic informational notes. Many human–computer interaction problems could be minimized or even eliminated if we could communicate with computers in our own language. We would simply type in directions, instructions, queries, or information. Better yet, we would converse with the computer using voice. The computer would be smart enough to interpret the input, regardless of its format. **Natural language processing (NLP)** refers to communicating with a computer in English or any other language you speak.

NLP is a subfield of artificial intelligence and linguistics that deals with analyzing, understanding, and generating the languages that humans prefer to use naturally in order to interface with computers in both written and spoken contexts, using natural human languages instead of computer languages.

One of the challenges inherent in NLP is teaching computers to understand the way humans learn and use language. Unfortunately, even a simple sentence may have multiple meanings, depending, for example, on which word is used as the verb because this helps determine which word is used as a noun or an adjective. In the course of human communication, the meaning of a sentence depends on both the context in which it is communicated and each person's understanding of the ambiguity in human languages.

For more information on NLP, see **en.wikipedia.org/wiki/The_Natural_Language_Processing**.

To understand a natural language inquiry, a computer must have the knowledge to analyze and then interpret the input. This may include linguistic knowledge about words, domain knowledge, commonsense knowledge, and even knowledge about the users and their goals. When the computer understands the input, it can take the desired action.

In this section, we briefly discuss two types of NLP:

1. *Natural language understanding.* This type of NLP investigates methods of allowing a computer to comprehend instructions given in ordinary English, via the keyboard or by voice (i.e., speech understanding; see Section 13.8), so that computers are able to understand people.
2. *Natural language generation.* This type of NLP strives to allow computers to produce ordinary English language, on the screen or by voice (known as voice synthesis; see Section 13.8), so people can understand computers more easily.

Some Problems That Make NLP Difficult

According to **wikipedia.org**, the following are problem areas for NLP:

- *Word boundary detection.* In spoken language, there are usually no gaps between words; where to place a word boundary often depends on what choice makes the most sense grammatically, given the context. In written form, languages such as Chinese do not signal word boundaries either.
- *Word sense disambiguation.* Many words have more than one meaning; we have to select the meaning that makes the most sense in context.
- *Syntactic ambiguity.* The grammar for natural languages is ambiguous—that is, there are often multiple possible parse trees for a given sentence. Choosing the most appropriate one usually requires semantic and contextual information.
- *Imperfect or irregular input.* Input problems can occur because of foreign or regional accents and vocal speech impediments; typing or grammatical errors; and optical character recognition (OCR) errors in text.
- *Speech acts and plans.* Sentences often don't literally mean what they say; for instance, a good answer to "Can you pass the salt?" is to pass the salt; in most contexts "Yes" is not a good answer, although "No" is better, and "I'm afraid that I can't see it" is more descriptive still.

The Current NLP Technology

The current NLP technology is still in its early stages and cannot use more than the first few basic levels of language, but its use is beginning to be widespread. Its most prolific use right now is for searching and information retrieval. A person enters a certain phrase, word, or sentence on which to search the Internet or some database, and NLP is then used to construct the best query possible. For instance, Google uses low levels of language processing to allow for more accurate searches for its patrons. The engine can, for example, automatically stem query words for singular and plural forms. Systems that go beyond this language understanding are rare. InQuery (from **inquiry.com**), another system, can parse sentences, stem words, and identify proper nouns and concepts through term co-occurrence.

Applications of NLP

NLP programs have been applied in several areas. The most important are human–computer interfaces, which include machines' abstracting and summarizing text, analyzing grammar, understanding speech (e.g., see the End of Chapter Application Case), and even composing letters. These programs also translate one natural language to another or one computer language to another, and they even translate Web pages.

By far the most dominant use of NLP is for front ends for other software packages, such as querying a database that allows the user to operate the applications programs with everyday language. A representative vendor of NLP is ISYS Search Software (**isys-search.com**).

Example: Neiman Marcus Uses Natural Language Search to Boost Online Sales

The online portion of Neiman Marcus (**neimanmarcus.com**), one of the industry leaders in luxury retail, determined that more than 50 percent of its customers had abandoned its Web site because they could not find what they were looking for. The problem was not lack of inventory. In fact, in most cases, Neiman Marcus had the product, but the search engine worked so poorly that it frequently could not find the product. To overcome this problem, Neiman Marcus implemented an iPhrase Technologies One Step natural language search engine. This allows customers to input queries in English-language sentences. The search language improves search capabilities by removing ambiguities and often suggests other products, thereby improving the sales experience and increasing sales. For details, see Scheiner (2003).

The following sections look at some other applications of NLP in more detail.

Text Mining As described in Chapter 4 and Online Tutorial 3, NLP is one of the methods used in text mining. The manner in which it works is described by Miller (2005).

Text can be mined directly to locate concepts and discover syntactic variations and synonyms that are useful in a data model. Information can be exploited to find similarities between situations, issues, and questions for accurate knowledge capture and retrieval of answers from a repository of possible solutions, resolving the problem of inconsistent vocabulary when reporting customer issues. The software enriches textual material so that it can be analyzed with standard reporting tools and statistical techniques for decision support. Using reporting tools and analytic methods, managers can identify common patterns, such as the frequency of a problem or the most effective path to problem resolution. Data can uncover product design problems and identify future customer requirements, such as required spare parts. For examples, see **kaidara.com** and **textanalysis.com**.

FAQs and Query Answering Examples of NLP used in FAQ finders and search engines:

- *Automated question answering search engines by BrainBoost.com*. These search engines do not rely on human editors to locate answers. They use artificial intelligence technology to understand a question and match it with relevant answers.
- *WordPerfect, proprietary systems, and more*. ISYS Search Software (**isys-search.com**) offers multiple query methods, including Natural Language Query, which uses NLP to rank and generate Web search results. Proprietary NLP technology uses several variables to ascertain the context of a query to enhance the relevance in results sets.
- InQuira.com. This company's software allows users to search for information by using natural language queries. Customers find not only links but specific answers to queries. This product is especially useful for searching technical data.

As described next, a major NLP application is machine translation.

MACHINE TRANSLATION

A major application of NLP is automatic translation of documents from one language to another. Such translation is important for creating Web pages for a multinational audience, for understanding large volumes of documents in foreign languages (e.g., for security reasons), for learning foreign languages, for collaboration in teams whose members speak different languages, and for conducting global e-business. Let's see how such translation works.

Translation of Content to Other Languages

In the global marketplace, content created in one language often needs to be translated to another in order to reach collaborative business partners in other countries. This is true for both paper and Internet documents. For example, in some cases, an effective Web site may need to be specifically designed and targeted to the market it is trying to reach. Language translation is especially important in countries such as China, Japan, and Korea, where relatively few people understand English well enough to use it online. The language barrier between countries and regions presents an interesting and complicated challenge (see **worldlingo.com**).

For example, travelers may not be able to read signs in other countries, or they might prefer information to be in their native, or a selected other language. A device called InfoScope (from IBM) can read signs, restaurant menus, and other text written in one language and translate it into several other languages. Currently, such translators are available only for short messages.

The primary problems with language translation and Web customization are cost and speed. It currently takes a human translator about a week to translate a medium-size Web site into just one language. For larger sites, the cost ranges from $30,000 to $500,000, depending on the complexity of the site and languages of translation.

WorldPoint (**worldpoint.com**) presents a creative solution to these translation issues with its WorldPoint Passport multilingual software tool. The WorldPoint Passport solution allows Web developers to create a Web site in one language and to deploy it in several other languages. However, automatic translation may be inaccurate. Therefore, many experts advocate manual translation with the help of a computer as a productivity booster. As time passes, though, automatic translation is improving.

According to Sullivan (2001), the best way to assess machine translation is to use the following criteria: (1) intelligibility (i.e., How well can a reader get the gist of a translated document?), (2) accuracy (i.e., How many errors occur during a translation?), and (3) speed (i.e., How many words per second are translated?).

For more on automatic language translation of Web pages, including some translation tools, see Online File W13.3.

Machine translation and other NLP applications are closely related to voice technologies, which are described next.

Section 13.7 Review Questions

1. Define *NLP* and list its major types.
2. List some NLP applications.
3. Define *machine translation*.
4. List advantages and limitations of machine translation.

13.8 VOICE TECHNOLOGIES

By its nature, a user–computer voice interface has a number of advantages over other user interfaces. Humans have used the spoken word to issue commands and convey information for thousands of years. Entering numeric or textual information via a numerical keypad is a relatively new phenomenon and is often awkward. Using computerized voice technologies is becoming very popular, and as the number of applications increase, better and less expensive technologies are entering the marketplace.

Voice technologies fall into three broad categories: voice (or speech) recognition, voice (or speech) understanding, and text-to-voice (or voice synthesis).

VOICE RECOGNITION AND UNDERSTANDING

Voice (speech) recognition is a process that allows humans to communicate with a computer by speaking to it. The term speech recognition is sometimes applied only to the first part of the communication process, in which the computer recognizes words that have been spoken, without necessarily interpreting their meanings. Speech recognition technologies allow computers equipped with a source of sound input, such as a microphone, to interpret human speech (e.g., for transcription or as an alternative method of interacting with a computer). The other part of the process, in which the meaning of speech is ascertained, is called **speech understanding**. It may be possible to understand the meaning of a spoken sentence without actually recognizing every word and vice versa. A speech recognition and understanding system usually contains an NLP system. The result is an overall system that not only recognizes voice input but also understands it (see Dettmer, 2003). For further details, see **en.wikipedia.org/wiki/Speech_recognition**.

Advantages of Voice Technologies

The ultimate goal of voice technologies is to allow a computer to understand the natural speech of any human speaker at least as well as a human listener could understand it. Speech recognition offers several advantages:

- *Ease of access.* Many more people can speak than can type. As long as communication with a computer depends on typing skills, many people may not be able to use computers effectively.
- *Speed.* Even the most competent typists can speak more quickly than they can type. It is estimated that the average person can speak twice as quickly as a proficient typist can type.
- *Manual freedom.* Obviously, communicating with a computer through typing occupies your hands. There are many situations in which computers might be useful to people whose hands are otherwise engaged, such as product assemblers, aircraft pilots, and busy executives. Speech recognition also enables people with hand-related physical disabilities to use computers.
- *Remote access.* Many computers can be accessed remotely by telephones. If a remote database included speech recognition capabilities, you could retrieve information from it by issuing oral commands into a telephone.
- *Accuracy.* People tend to make mistakes, especially in spelling, when typing. These errors could be reduced with voice input.
- *Communicating while driving.* Although communicating while driving may always be safe, voice interface does not require visual inspection or manipulation, so it enables a person to communicate with a computer while on the road.
- *Quick selection.* In applications that require a caller to select from a long list of choices, speaking is usually the easiest way of making a selection. For example, saying the name of a city to get a weather report is easier than typing the name of the city on the keypad of a telephone or other mobile device.
- *Security.* An individual's voice has a characteristic voice print, analogous to a thumbprint or written signature, which can be used to authenticate a caller before allowing access to confidential information. Thus a voice user interface is often a preferable and sometimes necessary medium for delivering self-service applications to people on the go.

- *Cost–benefit*. According to an Oracle report (2006), call centers with live call agents cost a company between $5 and $25 per call. Handling the same calls with a voice-enabled application costs between $0.25 and $0.50 per call. This same comparison can be made for voice alerts. An automated system can make outbound trigger- or time-based notification calls for little more than the cost of the phone call. Paying a human operator to make outbound calls costs at least 10 times as much.

Despite all these benefits, there are also some limitations to voice technologies.

Limitations of Speech Recognition and Understanding

The major limitation of speech understanding is its inability to recognize long sentences, or the excessive length of time needed to accomplish that understanding. The better the system is at speech recognition, the higher its cost. Also, in voice recognition systems, you cannot manipulate icons and windows, so speech may need to be combined with keyboard entry, which slows communication.

VOICE SYNTHESIS

The technology by which computers convert text to voice (i.e., speak) is known as **voice synthesis**. Voice synthesis, also known as *text-to-speech*, is the artificial production of human speech. The synthesis of voice by a computer differs from the simple playback of a prerecorded voice by either analog or digital means. As the term synthesis implies, sounds that make up words and phrases are electronically constructed from basic sound components and can be made to form any desired voice pattern.

A text-to-speech system is composed of two parts: a front end and a back end. Broadly, the front end takes input in the form of text and outputs a symbolic linguistic representation. The back end takes the symbolic linguistic representation as input and outputs the synthesized speech waveform (i.e., actual sound).

The current quality of synthesized voice is very good, but the technology remains somewhat expensive. Anticipated lower cost and improved performance of synthetic voice should encourage more widespread commercial voice applications, especially those on the Web. Opportunities for its use will encompass almost all applications that can provide automated responses to users, such as inquiries by employees pertaining to payroll and benefits. A number of banks already offer voice services to their customers, informing them about their balances, which checks have been cashed, and so on. Many credit card companies provide similar services, telling customers about current account balances, recent charges, and payments received.

VOICE TECHNOLOGY APPLICATIONS

Voice technology applications appear under several categories. The major ones are:

- *Call center*. A call center is a location where a group of employees answer customer service lines for a business and either provide answers or direct the caller further.
- *Contact of customer care center*. This is a kind of call center that covers not only telephone calls from customers but also e-mail, chat, and other Web-based queries.
- *Computer/telephone integration (CTI)*. CTI is the integration of computers with telephones, often to create sophisticated automated call centers.

- *Interactive voice response (IVR).* This is a type of automated service that relies on speech recognition, speech concatenation, or both to create a dialog between a computer and a person.
- *Voice portal.* A voice portal is a Web site with an audio interface that can be accessed through a telephone call for getting information from the Internet, including in real-time.
- *Voice over IP (VoIP).* VoIP is a technology that uses Internet protocol, instead of speech recognition, as the conduit for a telephone-like voice conversation. This technology permits inexpensive overseas calls via the Internet.

Some examples of real-world applications of voice technologies are listed in Table 13.3. Of these, VoIP is discussed in Chapter 10, and voice portals are discussed next.

Voice Portals

Voice portals are Web sites, usually portals, with audio interfaces. This means that they can be accessed by using a standard telephone or a mobile phone. AOLbyPhone is an example of a service that allows users to retrieve e-mail, news, and other Internet content via telephone. It uses both speech recognition and text-to-speech technologies. Companies such as Tellme.com (**tellme.com**) and BeVocal (**bevocal.com**) offer access to the Internet from telephones and tools to build voice portals. Voice portals are especially popular for enterprise toll-free numbers that provide self-service to customers with information available in Internet databases (e.g., finding flight status at **delta.com**).

An example of a voice portal is travel information received by dialing 511. This system was developed by Tellme.com, initially for the state of Utah during the 2002 Winter Olympic games, and is now offered in many states. In this system, a computer answers travelers' queries, saving money for the government and time for the travelers (no busy lines, no telephone or Internet connection cost). A 411 service (directory assistance) is also widely available on voice portals. A variation is the service provided by AT&T, as described in the following example:

Example: Visual Text to Speech from AT&T

A traveler gets stuck in traffic on the way to the airport. She calls the airport on her mobile phone and hears "All agents are busy. You are important to us; please stay on the line." With Visual Text to Speech technology from AT&T, she can click on "talk to agent" on her Internet-enabled smartphone. The smiling face of a virtual agent appears on the phone screen. The traveler tells the agent her problem and asks to reschedule her flight. A voice confirmation is provided in seconds, and action is taken within a short time.

In addition to retrieving information, some sites provide true interaction. iPing (**iping.com**) is a reminder and notification service that allows users to enter information via the Web and receive reminder calls. In addition, iPing can call a group of people to notify them of a meeting or conference call. Voice portals are becoming very popular as both communication and collaboration tools.

Section 13.8 Review Questions

1. Define *voice recognition*.
2. Define *voice understanding*.
3. Define *voice synthesis*.
4. List the advantages of voice technologies.
5. List the limitations of voice technologies.
6. Describe voice portals.

TABLE 13.3 Examples of Voice Technology Applications

Companies	*Applications*
Scandinavian Airlines and other airlines	Answering inquiries about reservations, schedules, lost baggage, etc.*
Citibank and other banks	Informing credit card holders about balances and credits, providing bank account balances and other information to customers*
Delta Dental Plan (CA)	Verifying coverage information*
FedEx	Requesting pickups, ordering supplies†
Illinois Bell and other telephone companies	Giving information about services,* receiving orders†
Domino's Pizza	Enabling stores to order supplies, providing price information*,†
General Electric, Rockwell International, Austin Rover, Westpoint Pepperell, Eastman Kodak	Allowing inspectors to report results of quality assurance tests†
Cara Donna Provisions	Allowing receivers of shipments to report weights and inventory levels of various meats and cheeses†
Weidner Insurance, AT&T	Conducting market research and telemarketing†
U.S. Department of Energy, Idaho National Engineering Laboratory, Honeywell	Notifying people of emergencies detected by sensors*
New Jersey Department of Education	Notifying parents when students are absent and about cancellation of classes*
Kaiser-Permanente Health Foundation	Calling patients to remind them of appointments, summarizing and reporting results*
Automobile manufacturers	Activating radios, heaters, and so on by voice†
Taxoma Medical Center	Logging in and out by voice to the payroll department†
St. Elizabeth's Hospital	Prompting doctors in the emergency room to conduct all necessary tests, reporting of results by doctors*,†
Hospital Corporation of America	Sending and receiving patient data by voice, searching for doctors, preparing schedules and medical records*,†

*Output device.
†Input device

13.9 DEVELOPING INTEGRATED ADVANCED SYSTEMS

Neural computing, ES, CBR, genetic algorithms, and fuzzy logic are effective tools for efficiently dealing with complex problems. Each of these methods handles uncertainty and ambiguity differently, and these technologies can often be blended to use the best features of each to achieve impressive results. For example, a combination of neural computing and fuzzy logic can result in synergy that improves speed, fault tolerance, and adaptability.

There are many real-world applications of integrated intelligent systems. These include the system described in the opening vignette, which combines CBR with intelligent agents and ES; the United Technologies Carrier product-reliability system, which integrates a rule-based system and a neural network (see Deng and Tsacle, 2000); a construction price estimation tool that integrates an ES and a neural network (see Li and Love, 1999); a forecasting tool that integrates genetic algorithms and fuzzy logic (see Li and Kwan, 2003); and a prediction and optimization system for a ceramic casting process that integrates neural networks and fuzzy logic (see Kuo and Chen, 2004). Additional discussion and examples are provided in Chapter 16. The sections that follow show a few examples of integration of multiple intelligent technologies.

FUZZY NEURAL NETWORKS

Fuzzy neural networks combine fuzzy logic with artificial neural networks (ANN). The integration can occur either way. The input and output variables can be processed by the fuzzy logic before entering the neural networks for learning. This step is called **fuzzification**. The neural network uses the fuzzified input and output to derive a model. The model is then converted back to the original input and output scales. This step is called **defuzzification**. The output of the defuzzified fuzzy system can further become the input to another intelligent system. This kind of integration can also be applied to fuzzy decision trees and fuzzy ES. Combining fuzzy logic with rule induction produces fuzzy rules (see Dubois et al., 2003). The following is an example of combining fuzzy logic with ANN:

Example: International Stock Selection

An international investment company uses a combination of fuzzy logic and ANN called FuzzyNet to forecast the expected returns from stocks, cash, bonds, and other assets to determine the optimal allocation of assets. Because the company invests in global markets, it is first necessary to determine the creditworthiness of various countries, based on past and estimated performances of key socioeconomic ratios. The system then selects specific stocks, based on company, industry, and economic data. The final stock portfolio must be adjusted according to the forecast of foreign exchange rates, interest rates, and so forth, which are handled by a currency exposure analysis. The integrated network architecture of the system, shown in Figure 13.8, includes the following technologies:

- *Expert system*. The system provides the necessary knowledge for both country and stock selection (i.e., rule-based system).
- *Neural network*. The neural network conducts forecasting based on the data included in the database.
- *Fuzzy logic*. The fuzzy logic component supports the assessment of factors for which there are no reliable data. For example, the credibility of rules in the rule base is given only as a probability. Therefore, the conclusion of the rule can be expressed either as a probability or as a fuzzy membership degree.

The rule base feeds into FuzzyNet (see Figure 13.9) along with data from the database. FuzzyNet is composed of three modules: a membership function generator (MFG), a fuzzy information processor (FIP), and a backpropagation neural network (BPN). The modules are interconnected, and each performs a different task in the decision process.

GENETIC ALGORITHMS AND NEURAL NETWORKS

The genetic learning method can perform rule discovery in large databases, with the rules fed into a conventional ES or some other intelligent system. A typical way to integrate genetic algorithms with neural network models is to use a genetic algorithm to search for potential weights associated with network connections. A good genetic learning method can significantly reduce the time and effort needed to find the optimal neural network model. Kim and Han (2003) developed a hybrid system to conduct activity-based costing. Wang (2003) presented a hybrid intelligent method for modeling an electrical discharge machining (EDM) process. Integrating rules and CBR is also a good way of improving rule-based systems.

By using several advanced technologies, it is possible to handle a broader range of information and solve more complex problems (see Application Case 13.7). This concept is valid not only in cutting-edge technologies but also in any integration of decision models.

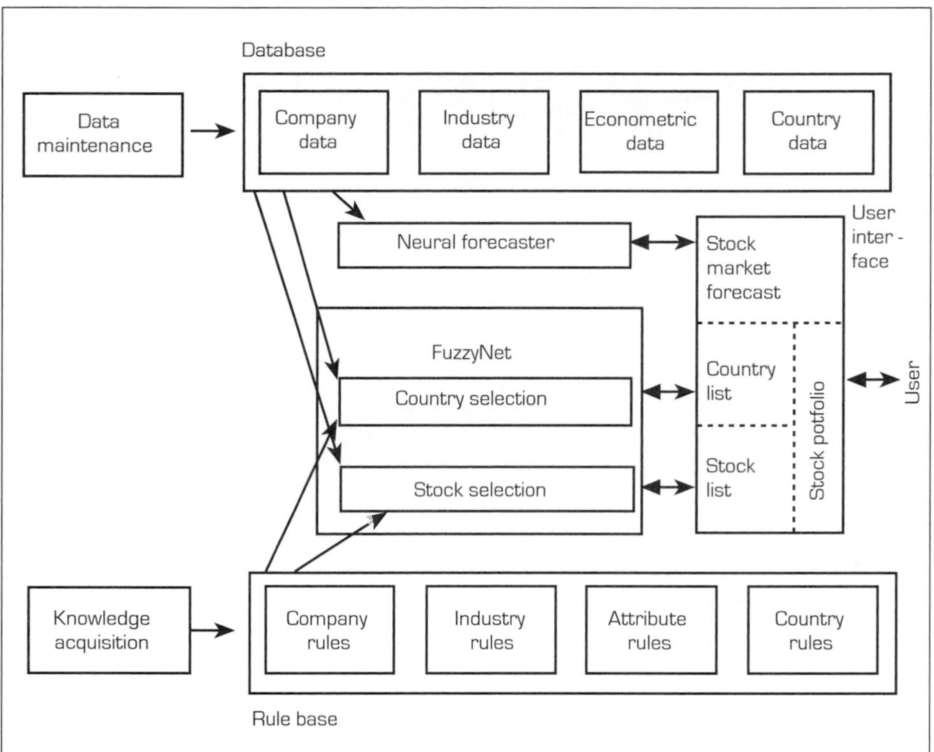

FIGURE 13.8 FuzzyNet Architecture

Source: F. Wong et al., "Neural Networks, Genetic Algorithms, and Fuzzy Logic for Forecasting," *Proceedings, International Conference on Advanced Trading Technologies*, New York, July 1992, p.48. Adapted, with permission, from *Financial Analysts Journal*, January/February 1992. Copyright 1992. Association for Investment Management and Research, Charlottesville, VA. All rights reserved.

Application Case 13.7

Hybrid ES and Fuzzy Logic System Dispatches Trains

The Carajás line is one of the busiest railway routes and leading carriers of iron ore in the world. The 892-kilometer-long single-track line connects São Luís harbor with the Carajás iron ore mine in the state of Pará in the Amazon (Brazil). The line has become even busier because a unique real-time knowledge-based system is increasing its productivity and reducing its operating costs, without compromising safety.

Train dispatchers try to keep the trains running safely all day and all night while attempting to maximize the amount of iron ore transported per day, economize on fuel consumption, and minimize train delays. For over 10 years, paper and pencil were used to solve this difficult task.

An innovative, rule-based ES that uses fuzzy logic has transformed the culture of the train operations. Operational rules are directly used in the ES. Fuzzy logic techniques analyze train movements and help the operators make the best possible decisions (e.g., priorities of trains). The module that generates the initial train-movement plans has helped increase the volume of iron ore transported by about 15 percent while saving about 1.6 liters of fuel per 1,000 metric tons of ore transported. With system improvements, further gains are expected.

Sources: Modified from P. Vieira and F. Gomide, "Computer-Aided Train Dispatch," *IEEE Spectrum*, July 1996, Vol. 33, No. 7, pp. 51–53; and R. Santos, J.A. Meech, and L. Ramos, "Thickener Operations at Carajás Using a Fuzzy Logic Controller," *Proceedings of the 6th International Fuzzy Systems Association World Congress, IFSA-95*, Sao Paulo, Brazil, July 1995.

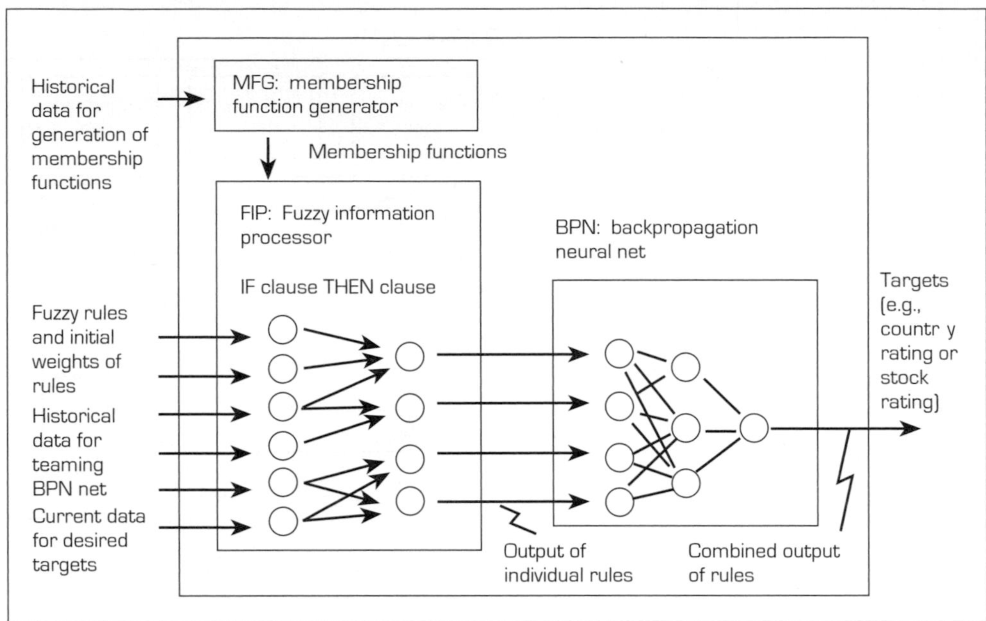

FIGURE 13.9 Information Flow in FuzzyNet

Source: Adapted, with permission, from *Financial Analysts Journal*, January/February 1992. Copyright 1992, Association for Investment Management and Research, Charlottesville, VA. All rights reserved.

Section 13.9 Review Questions

1. What is a fuzzy neural network? Give an example of an application of a fuzzy neural network.
2. Describe how genetic algorithms can be integrated with other intelligent methods and give a sample application.

Chapter Highlights

- Machine learning is a family of methods that allow machines to acquire knowledge for problem solving by showing them historical cases.
- Machine-learning methods can be classified into supervised and unsupervised learning. Supervised learning methods derive knowledge from cases whose outcomes are known, and unsupervised learning methods derive knowledge from cases whose outcomes are unknown.
- Popular machine-learning methods include inductive learning, CBR, neural networks, genetic algorithms, cluster analysis, and fuzzy logic.
- CBR is based on experience with similar situations.
- In CBR, the attributes of an existing case are compared with critical attributes derived from cases stored in a case library.
- Cases in CBR include ossified cases, paradigmatic cases, and stories. Different types of cases must be handled differently to maximize the effect of learning.
- CBR has advantages over rule-based reasoning in that it can capture expert knowledge, better explain decisions, and build up incremental learning capabilities.
- Genetic algorithms are learning methods that emulate the natural evolution process. They include three basic operations: reproduction, crossover, and mutation.
- Reproduction is a process that creates the next-generation population based on the performance of different cases in the current population.
- Crossover is a process that allows elements in different cases to be exchanged to search for a better solution.
- Mutation is a process that changes an element in a case to search for a better solution.

- Fuzzy logic deals with the kind of uncertainty that is inherently human in nature. It allows numeric data to be converted into linguistic terms, such as *young* or *good*, for symbolic processing.
- Fuzzy logic can be combined with other techniques, such as rule induction and neural networks, to achieve better performance.
- Fuzzy logic–based systems involve two steps. The first, called *fuzzification*, converts numerical data into fuzzy terms. The second, called *defuzzification*, converts the fuzzy description back to the original scale.
- NLP facilitates human–computer interaction by enabling a computer to understand human rather than computer language.
- NLP involves natural language understanding (i.e., comprehending instructions in ordinary language) and natural language generation (i.e., producing easy-to-understand text or speech from computerized output).
- NLP is no match to human language processing, but it is getting increasingly better and less expensive.
- NLP has many applications, mostly in querying databases, text mining, and machine translation.
- Automatic translation between human languages can save considerable time and money, and it is improving with time.
- Voice technologies include speech recognition, speech understanding, and text-to-voice.
- Voice portals allow audio interface with the Internet.

Key Terms

- analogical reasoning
- case library
- case-based reasoning (CBR)
- chromosome
- crossover
- defuzzification
- explanation-based learning
- fuzzification
- fuzzy logic
- fuzzy set
- genetic algorithm
- inductive learning
- machine learning
- mutation
- natural language processing (NLP)
- ossified case
- paradigmatic case
- reproduction
- speech understanding
- story
- supervised learning
- unsupervised learning
- voice portal
- voice (speech) recognition
- voice synthesis

QUESTIONS FOR DISCUSSION

1. Machine learning is a discipline that investigates how computers can learn from existing data. Scholars disagree about whether machines can really learn. Some insist that computers do not learn and are only taught by humans. Do you agree? Please comment.
2. CBR produces new decisions based on past cases. Advocates claim that the process can capture the experiences of experts and alleviate problems of knowledge acquisition from human experts in rule-based systems. Do you agree? Why or why not?
3. How can an investor use genetic algorithms to make a fortune on the stock market? Can a genetic algorithm–based system perform better than a neural network–based system? Why or why not?
4. Describe three advantages of fuzzy reasoning and provide an example to support each. If you disagree that any of these cases are actually advantages of fuzzy reasoning explain why.
5. Discuss the advantages and disadvantages of integrating multiple methods for developing complex intelligent systems. Describe all the possible integrations between CBR, ANN, genetic algorithms, fuzzy logic, and rule-based systems and assess their feasibility.
6. Discuss the logic of combining NLP with voice technologies.
7. What kind of intelligence is needed in NLP?
8. Discuss the benefits and limitations of machine translation.
9. Many companies push their customers to use text and/or voice automated call centers. Why? Are there any benefits to the customers?
10. Discuss the relationship between NLP, queries, and computer searches.

Exercises

Teradata University and Other Hands-on Exercises

1. Access **home.earthlink.net/~dwaha/research/case-based-reasoning.html**. Examine the latest CBR research and demo software. How is CBR different from rule-based concepts? Try some reasoning software, compare that method to rule-based inferencing, and write about your experience in a report.

2. Identify a newsgroup that is interested in NLP. Post a question regarding recent successful applications of NLP and see what feedback you get. What are the latest concerns and questions?

3. Express the following statements in terms of fuzzy sets:
   a. The chance for rain today is 80 percent. (Rain? No rain?)
   b. Mr. Smith is 60 years old (young?).
   c. The salary of the president of the United States is $250,000 per year. (Low? High? Very high?)
   d. The latest survey of economists indicates that they believe that the recession will bottom out in April (20%), in May (30%), or in June (22%).

4. You are trying to identify a specific number in the set 1–16. You can ask questions such as, "Is this number in the set 1–8?" The answer can be only yes or no. In either case, you continue to ask more questions until you identify the number.
   a. How many questions are needed in the worst and the best possible cases to identify such a number?
   b. Is this problem suitable for parallel processing? Why or why not?

5. Relate the problem in Exercise 4 to a solution using a genetic algorithm.

6. Compare the effectiveness of genetic algorithms against standard methods for problem solving, as described in the literature. How effective are genetic algorithms?

7. Solve the knapsack problem from Section 13.5 manually, and then solve it using Evolver. Try another code (find one on the Web). Finally, develop your own genetic algorithm code in Visual Basic, C++, or Java.

8. Download a free copy of VR Commander from **vrcommander.com**. Test the main features and prepare a short report that describes them.

9. Many companies induce employees and customers to use self-service functions such as updating their own addresses or finding the balance in their banking accounts. Explain how the technologies described in this chapter can facilitate this type of self-service.

Exercises

Team Assignments and Role-Playing

1. Identify a real-world application problem that is suitable for CBR and develop a plan for developing an intelligent system that integrates case-based and rule-based approaches.

2. Examine the marketplace for consumer products that incorporate fuzzy logic. (Remember that sometimes this feature is called *continuous logic*.) Try some of the products out if they are available in your area. Determine the advantages and disadvantages (if any) of these products over their nonfuzzy counterparts.

3. Survey your class by having everyone write down a height representing tall, medium, and short for men and for women. Tally the results and determine what is meant by tall, medium, and short in a fuzzy way. Create the membership functions in these sets and examine the results.

4. Join an artificial intelligence discussion group at **groups.yahoo.com/group/pcai/join**. Trace postings on the topics of this chapter during the past two years. Prepare a report about your findings.

5. Go to **solver.com/gabasics.htm** and **palisade.com/evolver/**. Compare Solver and Evolver in terms of using genetic algorithms to solve problems.

6. Investigate the status of text-to-speech technology (e.g., **naturalreaders.com**) and speech-to-text technology (Avoke STX, from **bbn.com**), as well as the combination of both (**naturalvoices.att.com** and **ivoice.com**). Write a report about your findings.

7. Research the area of knowledge acquisition using NLP and voice technologies. Give a presentation about your findings.

Exercises

Internet Exercises

1. Search the Web for genetic algorithm–based games and simulations. Be sure to try out J.J. Merelo's MasterMind (**kal-el.ugr.es/mastermind.html**) and M.S. Miller's Manna Mouse (**caplet.com/MannaMouse.html**). Write a report on your findings.
2. Access *PC AI* magazine's Web site, which provides a free sample of one issue. Search for vendors of fuzzy logic, genetic algorithms, neural networks, and hybrid intelligent systems used in business. Examine definitions and vendors. What is new in these areas?
3. CBR has been used lately for data mining. Explore the Web to find vendors and research literature about this topic.
4. Examine genetic algorithm vendor Web sites and investigate the business applications of their products. What kinds of applications are most prevalent?
5. Examine fuzzy logic vendor Web sites and identify the kinds of problems to which fuzzy logic is currently being applied. Find a demo version of a system and try it out. Report your findings to the class.
6. Access the Web and e-journal in your library to find at least three reports on the use of integrated intelligent methods for intelligent decision support. Evaluate whether the applications are feasible in the real world.
7. Go to **lpa.co.uk/cbr.htm** and find information about LPA's intelligent products. Write a one-page summary. Also, find information at the LPA Web site about products for the other systems described in this chapter. View the demos. Write a short report about your findings.
8. Go to **voiceingov.org/blog** and **fluencyvoice.com** and select three applications in each of the voice technologies. Write a summary about your findings.
9. Go to **lec.com** and **languageweaver.com** and review all their machine translation products. Write a report about your findings.
10. Go to **palisade.com** and examine the capabilities of Evolver. Write a summary about your findings.
11. Go to **ivoice.com** and describe the capabilities of iVoice's products.

End of Chapter Application Case

Barclays Uses Voice Technology to Excel

Barclays is one of the largest financial services groups in the United Kingdom. It is also a leading provider of coordinated global services to multinational corporations and financial institutions worldwide. Barclays has been involved in banking for over 300 years and operates in more than 60 countries, with more than 76,200 employees.

BUSINESS CHALLENGE

Barclays aims to make financial services available to its employees at preferential rates as part of their employee benefits package. For Barclays, these were the key drivers:

- To reward employees with preferential offers on Barclays products and services
- To promote familiarity with products so that staff can be more effective when discussing Barclays products, services, and benefits with customers
- To generate product advocacy among staff
- To facilitate a testing ground for new products

The challenge was to effectively communicate to nearly all employees. However, employees found it very difficult to keep up with new products and changes, they were never sure what was on offer, and they did not know where to find information. The product range is also available to staff pensioners; because they are outside the business, these issues were especially difficult for them. Employees and staff pensioners sometimes missed out on favorable pricing. Barclays needed a way to boost employee satisfaction, address competitive leakage, and build product advocacy in sales to customers.

SOLUTION

Barclays decided that a "one-number" service that could inform callers and direct them to product specialists would be the most effective solution. Barclays implemented a voice technology application (from Fluency Voice Technology; **fluencyvoice.com**) in its customer contact center.

Fluency provided a packaged, speech-enabled call-routing application that was customized for Barclays. This system delivers recorded information about Barclays products and listens for the callers' choices, which can be spoken at any point in the application. Callers are then routed via the hosted contact center infrastructure to product teams at Barclays.

The application can be easily updated with new products and changes to ensure that it remains current. The service allows access to different menus that logically group products, and callers can speak over the application at any point if they know what they want, making the system simple and intuitive to use.

IMPACTS

The Barclays system delivered the following key business benefits:

- Employees and staff pensioners had immediate access to portfolio products at preferential rates.
- Competitive leakage was reduced because staff and pensioners were more informed and less likely to use alternative providers.
- Employee satisfaction was improved, as measured by consistently favorable feedback.
- Barclays realized the business benefit of product advocacy and brand reinforcement in customer sales, and employees were more confident about products and felt happier to advise customers on their associated benefits.
- The application attained quick sponsorship from employees of Barclays because it was simple to use and informative, and it connected them quickly with the appropriate skill centers for the products.

OUTCOMES

The one-number service at Barclays includes identification and verification of callers within the application and a speech portal that delivers summary information. Without a doubt, the confidence in the bank's products has had a positive impact on productivity and employee satisfaction. The new one-number service has helped employees stay up to date, more confident about products, and more contented advising customers. The service has been used to help pilot new products in the employee and staff pensioner community. Valuable feedback from this process helps refine products for the external market.

Sources: Compiled from Hewitt, Bacon, and Woodrow Ltd., *Flex Comes of Age*, 2004, **hewittassociates.com/Intl/NA/en-US/AboutHewitt/Newsroom/PressReleaseDetail.aspx?cid=1824.com** (accessed August 2006); and *One Voice for 75,000 Barclay's Staff*, October 21, 2004, **fluencyvoice.com/news_and_events/press_room/press_releases/OneVoicefor75000BarclaysStaff.php** (accessed April 2006).

QUESTIONS FOR THE CASE

1. Go to **fluencyvoice.com** and investigate the capabilities of speech. Write a report about your findings.
2. What does it mean that "callers can speak over the application at any point"?
3. Relate the case to the three configurations of voice technologies described in this chapter.
4. How does the Barclays system enable call routing?

References

Bagnoli, C., and H.C. Smith. (1998). "The Theory of Fuzzy Logic and Its Application to Real Estate Valuation." *Journal of Real Estate Research*, Vol. 16, No. 2.

Baker, B.M., and M.A. Syechew. (2003). "A Genetic Algorithm for the Vehicle Routing Problem." *Computers and Operations Research*, Vol. 30.

Chorafas, D. N. (1994). *Chaos Theory in the Financial Markets*. Chicago: Probus Publishing.

Cox, E. (2001). "Building Intelligent Business Applications with Semantic Nets and Business Rules." *PC AI*, Vol. 15, No. 1.

Deng, P.S., and E.G. Tsacle. (2000). "Coupling Genetic Algorithm and Rule-Based Systems for Complex Decisions." *Expert Systems with Applications*, Vol. 19, No. 3.

Dettmer, R. (2003, June). "It's Good to Talk [Speech Technology for On-Line Services Access]." *IEE Review*.

Dubois, D., E. Hüllermeier, and H. Prade. (2003). "On the Representation of Fuzzy Rules in Terms of Crisp Rules." *Information Sciences*, Vol. 151.

Dwinnell, W. (2002, March/April). "Putting Fuzzy Logic to Work: An Intro to Fuzzy Logic." *PC AI*.

Grupe, F. H., R. Urwiler, and N. K. Ramarapu. (1998). "The Application of Case-Based Reasoning to the Software Development Process." *Information and Software Technology*, Vol. 40, No. 9.

Grupe, F.H., and S. Jooste. (2004, March). "Genetic Algorithms: A Business Perspective." *Information Management and Computer Security*.

Hall, N. (1987). "A Fuzzy Decision Support System for Strategic Planning." In E. Sanchez and L. Zadeh (eds.). *Approximate Reasoning in Intelligent Systems, Decision, and Control*. Oxford, UK: Pergamon Press.

Hastings, J., K. Branting, and J. Lockwood. (2002). "CARMA: A Case-Based Rangeland Management Adviser." *AI Magazine*.

Hernandez-Serrano, J., and D.H. Jonassen. (2003). "The Effect of Case Libraries on Problem Solving." *Journal of Computer-Assisted Learning*, Vol. 19, No. 1.

Humphreys, P., R.T. McIvor, and F.T.S Chan. (2003). "Using Case-Based Reasoning to Evaluate Supplier Environmental Management Performance." *Expert Systems with Applications*, Vol. 25.

Johnson, R.C. (1999, August 16). "Genetic Algorithms Adapt Fast ICs to Fab Variations." *Electronic Engineering Times*, No. 1074.

Khan, A.S., and A. Hoffmann. (2003). "Building a Case-Based Recommendation Systems without a Knowledge Engineer." *Artificial Intelligence in Medicine*, Vol. 27, No. 2.

Kim, K., and I. Han. (2003). "Application of a Hybrid Algorithm and Neural Network Approach in Activity-Based Costing." *Expert Systems with Applications*, Vol. 24, No. 1.

Klahr, P. (1997, January/February). "Getting Down to Cases." *PC AI*.

Kolonder, J. (1993). *Case-Based Reasoning*. Mountain View, CA: Morgan Kaufmann.

Kuo, R.J., and C.A. Chen. (2004). "A Decision Support System for Order Selection in Electronic Commerce Based on Fuzzy Neural Network Supported by Real-Coded Genetic Algorithm." *Expert Systems with Applications*.

Lee, J.K., and J.K. Kim. (2002). "A Case-Based Reasoning Approach for Building a Decision Model." *Expert Systems*, Vol. 19, No. 3.

Li, H., and P.E.D. Love. (1999, March). "Combining Rule-Based Expert Systems and Artificial Neural Networks for Mark-up Estimation." *Construction Management and Economics*, Vol. 17, No. 2.

Li, J., and R.S.K. Kwan (2003). "A Fuzzy Genetic Algorithm for Driver Scheduling." *European Journal of Operational Research*, Vol. 147.

Liao, T.W. (2003). "Classification of Welding Flaw Types with Fuzzy Expert Systems." *Expert Systems with Applications*, Vol. 25, No. 1.

Luu, D.T., S.T. Ng, and S.E. Chen. (2003). "A Case-Based Procurement Advisory System for Construction." *Advances in Engineering Software*, Vol. 34, No. 7.

Marling, C., et al. (2002, Spring). "Case-Based Reasoning Integrations." AI Magazine, pp. 69–86.

Miller, T. W. (2005). *Data and Text Mining: A Business Applications Approach*. Upper Saddle River, NJ: Prentice Hall.

Mitchell, T.M., R.M. Keller, and S.T. Kedar-Cabelli. (1986). "Explanation-Based Generalization: A Unifying View." *Machine Learning*, No. 1.

Nick, Z., and P. Themis. (2001). "Web Search Using a Genetic Algorithm." *IEEE Internet Computing*, Vol. 5, No. 2.

Niettinen, K., et al. (1999). *Recent Advances in Genetic Algorithms*. New York: Wiley.

Oracle. (2006). *New to Voice Technology*, **oracle.com/technology/tech/wireless/beginner/voice.html?_template5/ocom/t** (accessed March 2006).

Park, C., and I. Han. (2002). "A Case-Based Reasoning with the Feature Weights Derived by Analytic Hierarchy Process for Bankruptcy Prediction." *Expert Systems with Applications*, Vol. 23, No. 3.

Pham, D.T., and R.M. Setchi. (2003). "Case-Based Generation of Adaptive Product Manuals." *Journal of Engineering Manufacturing*, Vol. 217, No. 3.

Riesbeck, C.K., and R.L. Schank. (1989). *Inside Case-Based Reasoning*. Hillsdale, NJ: Erlbaum Associates.

Ross, T.J. (2004). *Fuzzy Logic with Engineering Applications*, 2nd ed., New York: Wiley.

Scheiner, M. (2003, July). "Neiman Marcus Uses Natural Language Search to Boost Online Sales." *Customer Relationship Management*.

Shin, K., and I. Han. (2001). "A Case-Based Approach Using Inductive Indexing for Corporate Bond Rating." *Decision Support Systems*, Vol. 42.

Shin, K., and Y. Lee. (2002). "A Genetic Algorithm Application in Bankruptcy Prediction Modeling." *Expert Systems with Applications*, Vol. 23, No. 3.

Shiu, S., and S.K. Pal. (2004, March). *Foundations of Soft Case-Based Reasoning*. New York: Wiley Interscience.

Sullivan, D. (2001, August 31). "5 Principles of Intelligent Content Management." *Intelligent Enterprise*.

Tan, K.C., M.L. Wong, and W. Peng. (April 2005). "A P2P Genetic Environment for the Internet." *Communication of the ACM*.

Walbridge, C.T. (1989, June). "Genetic Algorithms: What Computers Can Learn from Darwin." *Technology Review*.

Wang, Y. (2003). "Using Genetic Algorithm Models to Solve Course Scheduling Problems." *Expert Systems with Applications*, Vol. 25, No. 1.

Watson, I. (2002). *Applying Knowledge Management: Techniques for Building Corporate Memories*. San Francisco: Morgan Kauffman.

Xu, J. X., and X. Xu. (2003, January 1). "A New Fuzzy Logic Learning Control Scheme for Repetitive Trajectory Tracking Problems," *Fuzzy Sets and Systems*.

Intelligent Systems over the Internet

Learning Objectives

- Understand the cutting-edge intelligent systems that run over the Internet
- Understand the concept and power of intelligent agents
- Learn various applications of intelligent agents
- Learn the concept of representing semantic knowledge over the Internet
- Learn the concept of recommendation systems over the Internet
- Understand methods for designing recommendation systems

Second-generation intelligent systems are armed with powerful learning algorithms, as described in Chapter 13. Since the mid-1990s, the dramatic increase of Internet users has driven the application of intelligent systems to a new platform, the World Wide Web (or, simply, the Web). In this chapter, we focus on important new technologies that have been implemented on the Web, including intelligent agents, recommendation systems, and the semantic Web. This chapter is organized as follows:

14.1 Opening Vignette: Netflix Gains High Customer Satisfaction from DVD Recommendation
14.2 Web-Based Intelligent Systems
14.3 Intelligent Agents: An Overview
14.4 Characteristics of Intelligent Agents
14.5 Why Use Intelligent Agents?
14.6 Classification and Types of Intelligent Agents
14.7 Internet-Based Software Agents
14.8 Decision Support Systems Agents and Multiagents
14.9 The Semantic Web: Representing Knowledge for Intelligent Agents
14.10 Web-Based Recommendation Systems
14.11 Managerial Issues of Intelligent Agents

14.1 OPENING VIGNETTE: NETFLIX GAINS HIGH CUSTOMER SATISFACTION FROM DVD RECOMMENDATION

Netflix (**netflix.com**) is an online DVD rental company based in Los Gatos, California. Today, the company has more than 1,200 employees and more than 4 million subscribers. It offers more than 55,000 titles and more than 42 million DVDs. A typical neighborhood movie store generally has fewer than 3,000 titles, and it has multiple copies available only for a fraction of these titles. Netflix distributes 1 million DVDs each day.

PROBLEM

In the early days, Netflix ran a business model of renting DVDs by mail. Including shipping, a single rental cost more than $4, and you paid late fees if you didn't get the disc back within a week. Netflix tried lowering prices and extending the rental period to two weeks, but in its first year of operations, only 250,000 discs were rented, and few customers returned for a second trial. "It wasn't working. People weren't coming back," Netflix CEO Reed Hastings recalled. In a late-night brainstorming session in 1999, Hastings and his lieutenants hit on the idea of a subscription model, and they launched it that September. Customers could rent as many movies as they could watch for $20 a month, as long as they had no more than three DVDs out at a time.

One problem with the rapid increase in DVD rental was that there were so many titles, customers often had difficulty sorting out the ones they liked. In most cases, they picked up the popular ones, which increased the need to maintain more and more copies of the same title, and some unpopular titles were not selling well, even though they matched certain customers' preferences very well. For Netflix, finding the right titles for customers and managing the right level of inventory became critical.

SOLUTION

Netflix reacted successfully to its problem by taking advantage of a recommendation engine called CineMatch, a combination of 29,000 unique lines of code and a database of 180 million film ratings. This recommendation engine allowed Netflix to become the leader in the area. Both Blockbuster and Walmart.com are emulating its model. With the recommendation system, Netflix doesn't just deliver DVDs, it tells subscribers which ones they'll probably like. Netflix turned to using the recommender based on the assumption that movie viewers all watch the same narrow range of big-budget films only because they don't know any better.

CineMatch doesn't focus on the mass market; it caters to individuals. Netflix encourages subscribers to rate the movies they've viewed, and CineMatch recommends titles similar to those well liked—regardless of a film's popularity at the box office. With Netflix, the recommendations are included in the cost of a subscription, and CineMatch acts a lot like a geeky clerk at a small movie store: He sets aside titles he knows you'll like and tells you to return them whenever. Netflix subscribers can also invite one another to become "friends" and make movie recommendations, peek at one another's rental lists, and see how other subscribers have rated other movies. All these personalized functions make the online rental store very customer friendly.

BENEFITS

As a result of implementing its CineMatch system, Netflix has seen very fast growth in sales and membership. The benefits of the recommendation system include the following:

- *Increased customer satisfaction and loyalty.* "The movies we recommend generate more satisfaction than the ones [customers] choose from the new releases page," said Neil Hunt, Netflix's chief product officer. As a result, between 70 and 80 percent of Netflix rentals come from the company's back catalog of 38,000 films rather than recent releases. Hunt said that the system "increases customer loyalty to the site."
- *Broadened title coverage.* A average renter expands his or her tastes. Seventy percent of the movies Netflix customers rent are recommended to them on the site; 80 percent of rental activity comes from 2,000 titles. This decreases demand for popular new releases, which is good for Netflix, whose revenue-sharing agreements require larger payouts for such films.

  Take, for example, *Control Room*, a documentary about Arab television outlet Al Jazeera. Netflix has a 12 percent share of the movie rental market, and you would expect its share of the rentals for *Control Room* to be in the same range. But Netflix accounted for 34 percent of the title's rental activity in the United States the week it was released on DVD. The difference, according to Hunt, is primarily due to Netflix's recommendation tools.
- *Better understanding of customer preference.* Mr. Hunt said Netflix's recommendation system collects more than 2 million ratings forms from subscribers daily to add to its huge database of users' likes and dislikes. This valuable information helps the company to make much more accurate predictions of customer interests.
- *Fast membership growth.* "The most reliable prediction for how much a customer will like a movie is what they thought of other movies," Mr. Hunt said. The company credits the system's ability to make automated yet accurate recommendations as a major factor in its growth from 600,000 subscribers in 2002 to nearly 4 million in 2006.

CineMatch has become the core competence of the company. Netflix's future relies heavily on CineMatch making accurate recommendations and subscribers accepting them.

Sources: Compiled from L.J. Flynn, "Like This? You'll Hate That. (Not All Web Recommendations Are Welcome)," *The New York Times*, January 23, 2006; C. Null, *How Netflix Is Fixing Hollywood by Finding a Market for Niche Titles*, July 1, 2003, **money.cnn.com/magazines/business2/business2_archive/2003/07/01/345263/index.htm** (accessed April 2006); and J.M. O'Brien, *The Netflix Effect: Still Waiting for Video-on-Demand*, December 2002, **wired.com/wired/archive/10.12/netflix.html** (accessed April 2006).

Questions for the Opening Vignette

1. Describe why Netflix adopted the movie recommendation system and what problems the company may have if it did not do so.
2. List the benefits of the CineMatch system. Are there any other benefits that you can foresee that are not described in the vignette?
3. Describe how CineMatch makes recommendations. Review the techniques that you have learned in previous chapters and choose one that you think can be used to implement a similar one for online movie recommendations.
4. Do you like getting recommendations when you visit a physical movie store such as Blockbuster? How about recommendations from an online rental store, such as Netflix? Why do you like or dislike getting recommendations at these stores?

WHAT WE CAN LEARN FROM THIS VIGNETTE

The opening vignette illustrates an application of a movie recommendation system, CineMatch. Such programs are often implemented as *intelligent agents*, software programs that can perform certain tasks automatically according to the rules and inference mechanisms given by the designer. In the remaining sections, we discuss concepts and applications of intelligent agents and recommendation systems in various domains.

14.2 WEB-BASED INTELLIGENT SYSTEMS

Since the introduction of the Internet and the Web, intelligent systems have become armed with a Web-based architecture and friendly user interface. Given the explosion of information on the Web, autonomous agents and recommendation systems will become very popular. In fact, many Internet services are already using them to provide better services. For example, a retailing store may use an agent to answer frequently asked questions (FAQs) or reply to e-mails automatically. An auction Web site might use these software agents to monitor the auctioning process. In this section, we introduce the concept and applications of Web-based intelligent systems, and then we provide more detailed descriptions of intelligent agents and Web-based recommendation systems in the rest of the chapter.

A major feature of Web-based intelligent systems is that they use the Web as a platform to deliver services; their user interfaces are Web enabled. Moreover, they are able to communicate with each other through a Web-based protocol. For example, when a Web-based system is used to reply to a customer's e-mail message, it must be able to retrieve keywords from the e-mail, determine the theme of the e-mail, and choose a proper answer from its knowledge base for replying. Figure 14.1 shows an example of how a Web-based system works. The user enters the request in the box and clicks the Find It button. The system interprets the query and converts it into a set of machine-understandable codes for execution. The system then outputs the findings at the bottom of the page. The Web-based user interface is a friendly channel through which a user interacts with the system. The kernel of the system (including the knowledge base and the interpreting and reasoning mechanisms) is hidden behind the Web. Most users do not notice their existence.

Web-based intelligent systems can be used for many purposes and take different forms. Small systems that perform very specific tasks are often called *agents*. A popular example that we use everyday is a virus protection agent, such as PC Cillin or similar products. These agents automatically identify files that are contaminated with viruses in order to protect computers. An agent may also be a complicated system that contains sophisticated knowledge in its knowledge base (e.g., a system that analyzes the profile of a customer) or a system that is composed of many separate agents.

The example shown in Figure 14.1 is a very simple search agent for finding information. In real-world applications, intelligent systems can be much more complicated and may have many different categories. For example, a Web-based intelligent system for travel planning may include both information and monitoring agents (see Mathieson et al., 2005). An *information agent* takes a particular information request and navigates to the appropriate page on a Web site, locates the required information, and returns it as an Extensible Markup Language (XML) document for processing by another agent. *Monitoring agents* are built on top of the information agent to keep track of previously returned results, such as price or schedule changes in travel

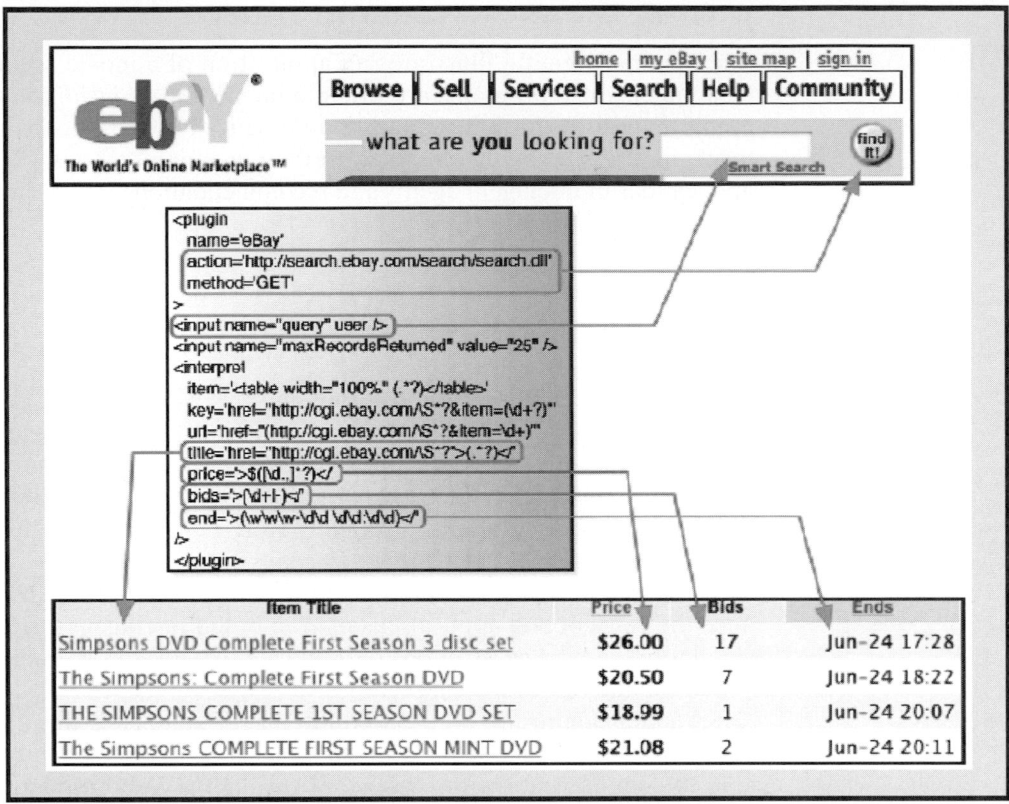

FIGURE 14.1 A Simplified Mechanism for Product Searching in a Web-Based Intelligent System

Source: Adapted from Menczer, et al., 2002.

planning. They need to know the current state before performing the job. To track price changes, for example, the agent must know about previous prices.

A special type of information agents is called *recommender* or *recommendation agents*, such as the CineMatch system described in the opening vignette. They are gaining attention because customized and personalized services are critical to maintaining good customer relationships. Online bookstores, such as Amazon.com and bn.com, use them to recommend books to clients; online movie rental companies use them to recommend new movies to clients. A recommender system opens a whole new arena for the application of Web-based intelligent systems (see Montaner et al., 2003).

The development of good Web-based intelligent applications needs to incorporate more semantic information. The semantic Web is being developed to allow semantic information to be included and represented. In later sections of the chapter, we introduce concepts and applications of intelligent agents, the semantic Web, and recommendation systems.

Section 14.2 Review Questions

1. Describe Web-based intelligent systems and their unique features.
2. Explain the functions of a search agent and give an example of one.
3. Explain the function of a monitoring agent and give an example of one.

14.3 INTELLIGENT AGENTS: AN OVERVIEW

An **intelligent agent (IA)** is a computer program that helps a user with routine computer tasks. It performs a specific task, based on predetermined rules and knowledge stored in a knowledge base. IA are powerful tools for overcoming the most critical limitation of the Internet—information overflow—and make e-commerce a viable organizational tool. In the following sections, we provide definitions and discuss the capabilities of such agents.

INTELLIGENT AGENTS: DEFINITIONS

The term *agent* is derived from the concept of agency, referring to employing someone to act on your behalf. A human agent represents a person and interacts with others to accomplish a predefined task.

The concept of agents goes surprisingly far back. More than 50 years ago, Vannevar Bush envisioned a machine called a memex. He imagined the memex assisting humans through huge fields of data and information. In the 1950s, John McCarthy developed Advice Taker, a software robot that would navigate the networks of information that would develop in time (see McCarthy, 1958). Advice Taker's similarity to today's agents is amazing. Given a task by a human user, the robot takes the necessary steps or asks for advice from the user when it gets stuck. The futuristic prototypes of intelligent personal agents, such as Apple's Phil and Microsoft's Bob, perform complicated tasks for their users, following the functions laid out by McCarthy in Advice Taker. The modern approach to intelligent agents moved to mobile and multiple agents in the mid-1980s, under research topics such as distributed artificial intelligence (see Bond and Gasser, 1988) and agency theory.

During the development process, several names have been used to describe intelligent agents, including *software agents* (see Brenner et al., 1998), *wizards*, *software daemons*, and *softbots* (for "intelligent software robots"). These terms sometimes refer to different types of agents or agents with different intelligence levels. Throughout this chapter and this book, we use the terms *intelligent agent* and *software agent* interchangeably. One of the most common examples of learning agents is the software assistant found in many commercial software programs (e.g., Microsoft Office applications). These agents offer hints to the user, based on patterns the program detects in the user's activities. Some of the newer Internet search engines boast intelligent agents that can learn from previous requests the user has made.

Daemon was a popular term for an agent in early stages of development. Daemons are small computer programs that run in the background and take action by alerting the user of certain situations in which prespecified conditions are met. An example is the X Window program xbiff. This program continually monitors a user's incoming e-mail and indicates via an icon whether the user has any unread messages. Virus detection agents and incoming e-mail agents are similar examples. Recently, the term **bot**, an abbreviation for *robot*, has become a common substitute for the term *agent*. Bots have been given specific prefixes, according to their use. Typical bots are *chatterbots*, *docbots*, *hotbots*, *jobbots*, *knowbots*, *mailbots*, *musicbots*, *shopbots*, *spiderbots*, *spambots*, and *sexbots* (of course—it had to be).

Intelligent agent can be defined in a number of ways, and each definition seems to explicate the definer's perspective. Here are some examples:

- According to IBM (**ibm.com**), *intelligent agents* are software entities that carry out some set of operations on behalf of a user or another program, with some degree of independence or autonomy, and in so doing, employ some knowledge or representation of the user's goals or desires (Knapik and Johnson, 1998).

- Maes (1995, p. 108) said that *autonomous agents* are computational systems that inhabit some complex dynamic environment, sense and act autonomously in that environment, and by doing so realize a set of goals or tasks for which they are designed.
- According to Wooldridge (2002), *intelligent agents* continuously perform three functions: perception of dynamic conditions in the environment, action to affect conditions in the environment, and reasoning to interpret perceptions, solve problems, draw inferences, and determine actions.
- According to Hess et al. (2002), an intelligent agent is a software implementation of a task in a specified domain, on behalf or in lieu of an individual or another agent. The implementation contains homeostatic goal(s), persistence, and reactivity to the degree that the implementation (1) will persist long enough to carry out the goal(s), and (2) will reach sufficiently within its domain to allow the goal(s) to be met and to know that fact.
- Wooldridge (2002) said that an *agent* is a computer system that is situated in some environment and that is capable of autonomous action in that environment in order to meet its design objectives.
- Franklin and Graesser (1996) defined *autonomous agent* as a system situated within and part of an environment that senses the environment and acts on it, over time, in pursuit of its own agenda, so as to effect what it senses in the future.
- On the Internet, said Gilbert (1998), an *intelligent agent* is a program that gathers information or performs some other service without a human's immediate presence and on some regular schedule.

These definitions from different perspectives point out the characteristics and capabilities of agents, which are described later.

INTELLIGENCE LEVELS

Intelligence is a key feature that differentiates agents from intelligent agents. Wooldridge (2002) and Stenmark (1999) suggested the following features of intelligent agents:

- *Reactivity.* Intelligent agents are able to perceive their environment and respond in a timely fashion to changes that occur in it in order to satisfy their design objectives.
- *Proactiveness.* Intelligent agents are able to exhibit goal-directed behavior by taking the initiative in order to satisfy their design objectives.
- *Social ability.* Intelligent agents are capable of interacting with other agents (and possibly humans) in order to satisfy their design objectives.
- *Autonomy.* Intelligent agents must have control over their own actions and be able to work and launch actions independently of the user or other actors.

In classic literature, Lee et al. (1997) identified four different levels of intelligence:

- *Level 0 (the lowest).* Agents at this level retrieve documents for a user under straight orders. Popular Web browsers fall into this category. The user must specify the URLs where the documents are. These agents help in navigating the Web.

- *Level 1.* Agents at this level provide a user-initiated searching facility for finding relevant Web pages. Internet search agents such as Google and AltaVista are examples. Information about pages, titles, and word frequency is stored and indexed. When the user provides keywords, the search engine matches them against the indexed information. These agents are referred to as *search engines*.
- *Level 2.* Agents at this level maintain users' profiles. They monitor Internet information and notify the users whenever relevant information is found. An example of such agents is WebWatcher, a tour guide agent for the Web developed at Carnegie Mellon University (**cs.cmu.edu/afs/cs/project/theo-6/web-agent/www/project-home.html**). Agents at this level are frequently referred to as *semi-intelligent* or *software agents*.
- *Level 3.* Agents at this level have a learning and deductive component to help a user who cannot formalize a query or specify a target for a search. DiffAgent (from Carnegie Mellon University) and Letizia (from MIT) are examples of such agents. Agents at this level are referred to as *learning* or *truly intelligent agents*.

COMPONENTS OF AN AGENT

Intelligent agents are computer programs that contain the following components:

- *Owner.* The owner is the user name, parent process name, or master agent name. Intelligent agents can have several owners. Either humans or the process itself can spawn agents (e.g., a stock broker or the brokerage process using IAs) to monitor prices, and other intelligent agents can spawn their own supporting agents.
- *Author.* The author is the development owner, service, or master agent name. Intelligent agents can be created by people or processes and then supplied as templates for users to personalize.
- *Account.* An intelligent agent must have an anchor to an owner's account and an electronic address for billing purposes or as a pointer to its origin.
- *Goal.* A clear statement of successful agent task completion is necessary, as are metrics for determining a task's point of completion and the value of the results. Measures of success can include simple completion of a transaction within the boundaries of the stated goal or a more complex measure.
- *Subject description.* The subject description details the goal's attributes. These attributes provide the boundaries of the agent, task, possible resources to call on, and class of need (e.g., stock purchase price, airline ticket price).
- *Creation and duration.* The creation and duration are the request and response dates requested.
- *Background.* Supporting information is needed.
- *Intelligent subsystem.* An intelligent subsystem, such as a rule-based expert system (ES) or a neural computing system, provides several of the characteristics described here.

Section 14.3 Review Questions

1. Define *IA*.
2. Describe the different intelligence levels of software agents.
3. Describe the major components of an agent.
4. Describe major features of intelligent agents.

14.4 CHARACTERISTICS OF INTELLIGENT AGENTS

In most cases, an agent is designed to accomplish a single task. A single task could be searching the Internet to find where and when certain items are auctioned, or it might be filtering e-mail. Although more advanced agents are capable of doing multiple tasks, it is likely that many future agent systems will really be *multiagents*, collections of different agents, each handling a simple task (Wooldridge 2002). Although there is no single commonly accepted definition for the term *intelligent agent*, several traits and abilities that many people think of when they discuss intelligent agents can be considered their major characteristics. The following sections describe these traits and abilities.

AUTONOMY OR EMPOWERMENT

An agent is autonomous; that is, it is capable of acting on its own or of being empowered. An agent must be able to make some decisions on its own as a result of being goal-oriented, collaborative, and flexible. It must be able to alter its course of behavior when it meets an obstacle and find ways around the impediment. Maes (1995) pointed out that regular computers respond only to direct manipulation, but with the advent of agents, users are able to give open-ended commands to their electronic agents in order to get work done. For example, an agent should be able to accept high-level requests and decide on its own where and how to carry out each request. In the process, the agent should be able to ask clarification questions and modify requests instead of blindly obeying commands.

Autonomy implies that an agent takes initiative and exercises control over its own actions by having the following characteristics:

- *Goal oriented.* The agent should accept high-level requests indicating what a human wants, and it should be responsible for deciding how and where to satisfy the requests. Hess et al. (2000) referred to these goals as homeostatic goal(s).
- *Collaborative.* The agent should not blindly obey commands but be able to modify requests, ask clarification questions, or even refuse to satisfy certain requests.
- *Flexible.* Actions are not scripted; an agent should be able to dynamically choose which actions to invoke, and in what sequence, in response to the state of its external environment.
- *Self-starting.* Unlike standard programs directly invoked by a user, an agent should sense changes in its environment and decide when to act.

The autonomy capability is also based on an agent's intelligence, mobility, and interactivity attributes, which are described later.

COMMUNICATION (INTERACTIVITY)

Many agents are designed to interact with other agents, humans, or software programs. This is a critical ability in view of the narrow repertoire of any given agent. Instead of making a single agent conduct several tasks, additional agents can be created to handle undelegated tasks; thus, there is a need for communication. Agents communicate by following certain communication languages and standards, such as ACL and KQML (see Bradshaw, 1997; and Jennings et al., 1998).

AUTOMATING REPETITIVE TASKS

An agent is designed to perform narrowly defined tasks, which it can do over and over without getting bored or sick or going on strike.

REACTIVITY

Agents perceive their environment—which may be the physical world, a user via a graphical user interface, a collection of other agents, the Internet, or perhaps all of these combined—and respond in a timely fashion to changes that occur in it. This means agents can recognize changes in their environment.

PROACTIVENESS (OR PERSISTENCE)

Agents do not simply act in response to their environment. They are able to exhibit goal-directed behavior by taking initiative.

TEMPORAL CONTINUITY

An agent should be a continuously running process, not a one-shot deal that terminates after completing a series of commands. The program can also be temporarily inactive, waiting for something to occur.

PERSONALITY

For an agent to be effective, it must be believable and be able to interact with human users.

OPERATING IN THE BACKGROUND: MOBILITY

An agent must be able to work out of sight, within the realm of cyberspace or other computer systems, without the constant attention of its user (or "master"). Some developers use the terms *remote execution* and *mobile agents* in referring to this attribute.

In the Internet environment, an agent may need mobility to work on different machines (called a *mobile agent*). A mobile agent can transport itself across different system architectures and platforms, and it is far more flexible than agents that cannot. Many e-commerce agents are mobile.

INTELLIGENCE AND LEARNING

Currently, the majority of agents are not truly intelligent because they cannot learn; only some agents can learn. For an intelligent agent, learning goes beyond mere rule-based reasoning (see Chapter 12) because the agent is expected to learn and behave autonomously. Although many in the artificial intelligence community argue that few people want agents that learn by "spying" on their users, the ability to learn often begins with the ability to observe users and predict their behavior.

Agents may be confused with objects and ES. A summary of their differences is provided in Technology Insights 14.1.

Section 14.4 Review Questions

1. Describe what *the autonomy* of *IA* means.
2. List the major characteristics of IA.
3. Define *mobile agent* and describe the difference between mobile agents and multiagents.

TECHNOLOGY INSIGHTS 14.1

Intelligent Agents, Objects, and ES

Objects and agents have some similarity in that they are both designed for independent operation. They are also different in some ways. *Objects* are defined as computational entities that encapsulate some state, are able to perform actions or methods on this state, and communicate through message passing. The major difference between objects and agents is that agents have clear intentions and goals. In other words, after receiving a message, an object in a computer program has to receive and react. An agent, however, may choose not to if the request is not consistent with its goal. The distinction has been nicely summarized in the slogan "Objects do it for free; agents do it because they want to."

To summarize, the differences between objects and agents include the following:

- Agents embody a stronger notion of autonomy than objects; in particular, they decide for themselves whether to perform an action on request from another agent.
- Agents are capable of flexible (e.g., reactive, proactive, social) behavior, and the standard model of objects has nothing to say about these types of behavior.
- A multiagent system is inherently multithreaded, in that each agent is assumed to have at least one thread of control.

Agents are often considered a realization of small ES over the Internet. Although they also have similarities in that both intend to incorporate domain knowledge to automate decision making, agents and ES are different in the following aspects:

- Classic ES are not coupled to any environment in which they act; rather, they act through a user as a middleman. Agents can actively search information from the environment in which they reside.
- ES are not generally capable of reactive and proactive behavior.
- ES are not generally equipped with social ability in the sense of cooperation, coordination, and negotiation.

Sources: Compiled from M. Wooldridge, *An Introduction to MultiAgent Systems*, Wiley, New York, 2002; and P. Ciancarini, *Agent-Oriented Software Engineering,* Springer, New York, 2001.

14.5 WHY USE INTELLIGENT AGENTS?

Alvin Toffler, in *Future Shock* (1970) warned of an impending flood—not of water but of information. He predicted that people would become so inundated with data that they would become paralyzed and unable to choose between options. His prediction is becoming a reality.

Information overload is one of the unintended by-products of the information age. Managers and other decision makers cannot be expected to read every document that crosses their desks, every relevant datum available in databases, every article in the magazines and journals to which they subscribe, or even all the e-mail that hits their computer mailboxes. The Gartner Group believes that:

- The amount of data collected by large enterprises doubles every year.
- Knowledge workers can analyze only about 5 percent of this data.
- Most of knowledge workers' efforts are spent in trying to discover important patterns in the data (60 percent or more), a much smaller percentage is spent determining what these patterns mean (20 percent or more), and very little time (10 percent or less) is spent actually doing something about the patterns.
- Information overload reduces our decision-making capabilities by 50 percent.

The real crisis started to develop with the emergence of the Internet. The Internet contains a collection of information-generating and -replicating machines. Thousands of new systems and even more new users bring new sources of data onto the Web every minute. It can be an overwhelming experience to log on for the first time because so many resources are immediately available. Experienced users look for ways to filter the data so that they can make sense out of the streams of information found online. Search engines and directories help with the winnowing process, but even they bring up volumes of data, much of which is only loosely tied to the immediate concerns of the decision maker. In addition, search engines rarely discriminate between copies of the same information offered through different sources, so replication adds to the pile of useless information. Despite all this, managers are expected to take into account key business information and make good decisions.

A major value of intelligent agents is that they are able to assist in searching through all the data. They save time by making decisions about what is relevant to the user. With these agents at work, a competent user's decision-making ability is enhanced with information rather than paralyzed by too much input. Agents are artificial intelligence's answer to a need created by computers (e.g., Nwana and Ndumu, 1999).

Information access and navigation are today's major applications of intelligent agents, but there are several other reasons this technology is expected to grow rapidly. For example, intelligent agents can improve computer network management and security, support e-commerce, empower employees, and increase productivity and quality (see Papazoglou, 2001; and Vlahavas et al., 2002). The advantage of agents can be even greater when a wireless computing environment is involved. Agents can handle many routine activities that need to be done quickly. The cost of non-agent-based wireless systems for information discovery is very high.

The reasons for the success of agents are as follows:

- *Decision support.* There is a need for increased support for tasks performed by knowledge workers, especially in decision making. Timely and knowledgeable decisions made by these professionals greatly increase their effectiveness and the success of their businesses in the marketplace.
- *Frontline decision support.* In a call center, there is a need to empower employees interacting with customers at the frontline. Such empowerment can be achieved by using intelligent agents.
- *Repetitive office activities.* There is a pressing need to automate tasks performed by administrative and clerical personnel in functions such as sales or customer support to reduce labor costs and increase office productivity.
- *Mundane personal activity.* In a fast-paced society, time-strapped people need new ways to minimize the time spent on routine personal tasks such as booking airline tickets so that they can devote more time to professional activities.
- *Search and retrieval.* It is not possible to directly manipulate a distributed database system in an e-commerce setting with millions of data objects. Users rely on agents for the tasks of searching, costing, and other comparisons. These agents perform the tedious, time-consuming, repetitive tasks of searching databases, retrieving and filtering information, and delivering information to users.
- *Domain experts.* It is advisable to model costly expertise and make it widely available. Examples of expert software agents could be models of real-world agents, such as translators, lawyers, diplomats, union negotiators, stockbrokers, and even members of the clergy.

An agent can perform a number of management-oriented tasks, including the following: advise, alert, broadcast, browse, critique, distribute, enlist, empower, explain, filter, guide, identify, match, monitor, navigate, negotiate, organize, present, query, remind, report, retrieve, schedule, search, secure, solicit, sort, store, suggest, summarize, teach, translate, and watch.

In short, software agents can improve an end user's productivity by performing a variety of tasks. The most important of these are gathering information, filtering it, and using it for decision support.

Section 14.5 Review Questions

1. List the major benefits of IA.
2. Describe why information overload is a by-product of the information age.
3. List the reasons for the success of intelligent agents.
4. Give an example of repetitive office work for which intelligent agents can help automate the process.

14.6 CLASSIFICATION AND TYPES OF INTELLIGENT AGENTS

Agents can be classified in different ways. Some popular ones include classification by application types and classification by characteristics. Other classifications are based on control structure, computational environment, and programming language.

CLASSIFICATION BY APPLICATION TYPE

Franklin and Graesser (1996) used a taxonomic tree to classify autonomous agents (see Figure 14.2). Relevant to managerial decision making is the category of *computational* agents, *software* agents, and *task-specific* agents. They can be further differentiated by the nature of applications, as specified below.

FIGURE 14.2 Classification of Intelligent Agents

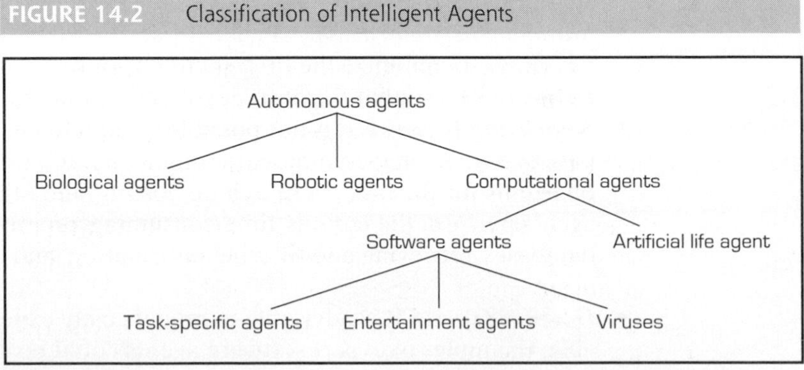

Source: S. Franklin and A. Graesser, Institute for Intelligent Systems, University of Memphis, TN.

Organizational and Personal Agents

Organizational agents execute tasks on behalf of a business process or computer application. **Personal agents** perform tasks on behalf of individual users. For example, corporate use of agent monitoring software is becoming a key component in the drive to cut support costs and increase computer productivity. Intelligent agents can search through e-mail messages for certain keywords. Depending on what keywords are contained in a message, the agent automatically sends out answers based on FAQ files. A company can use such an agent to help customers obtain answers to their questions quickly (e.g., **egain.com** and **brightware.com**).

Another example of an organizational intelligent agent is an automatic e-mail sorting system. When a new message comes in, it is automatically routed to the right file and folder.

Personal agents are very powerful. They allow users to go directly to the information they want on the Internet, saving time for busy people.

Private and Public Agents

A **private (or personal) agent** works for only one user who creates it. **Public agents** are created by a designer for the use of anybody who has access to the application, network, or database.

Software Agents and Intelligent Agents

According to Lee et al. (1997), truly intelligent agents (Level 3 of intelligence) must be able to learn and exhibit autonomy. However, most Internet and e-commerce agents do not exhibit these characteristics yet. Therefore, they are often called *software agents* (Level 2 of intelligence). The second generation of Internet and e-commerce being developed today includes some learning capabilities (see **media.mit.edu/research/ResearchPubWeb.pl?ID=23**).

Another classification by Wooldridge (2002) included the following different applications:

- Agents for workflow and business process management
- Agents for distributed sensing
- Agents for retrieval and management
- Agents for e-commerce
- Agents for human–computer interaction
- Agents for virtual environments
- Agents for social simulation

CLASSIFICATION BY CHARACTERISTICS

Of the various characteristics of agents, three are of special importance: *agency*, *intelligence*, and *mobility*.

Agency is the degree of autonomy and authority vested in an agent and can be measured, at least qualitatively, by the nature of the interaction between the agent and other entities in the system. At a minimum, an agent must run asynchronously. The degree of agency is enhanced if an agent represents a user in some way. An advanced agent can interact with other entities, such as data, applications, or services. Even more advanced agents collaborate and negotiate with other agents.

Intelligence is the degree of reasoning and learned behavior; it is an agent's ability to accept the user's statement of goals and carry out the tasks delegated to it. At a minimum, there can be some statements of preferences, perhaps in the form of rules, with an inference engine or some other reasoning mechanism to act on these preferences.

Higher levels of intelligence include a user model or some other form of understanding and reasoning about what a user wants done and planning the means to achieve this goal. Farther out on the intelligence scale are systems that learn and adapt to their environment, both in terms of the user's objectives and in terms of the resources available to the agent. Such a system, like a human assistant, might discover new relationships, connections, or concepts independently of the human user and exploit them in anticipating and satisfying user needs.

Mobility is the degree to which agents themselves travel through a network. Some agents may be static, either residing on the client machine (e.g., to manage a user interface) or initiated at the server. Mobile scripts can be composed on one machine and shipped to another for execution in a suitably secure environment; in this case, the program travels before execution, so no state data need be attached. Finally, agents can be mobile with state, transporting from machine to machine in the middle of execution and carrying accumulated state data with them. Such agents can be viewed as mobile objects, which travel to agencies, where they can present their credentials and obtain access to services and data managed by the agencies. Agencies can also serve as brokers or matchmakers, bringing together agents with similar interests and compatible goals and providing a meeting point at which they can interact safely.

Mobile agents can move from one Internet site to another and send data to and retrieve data from the user, who can focus on other work in the meantime. This can be very helpful to a user. For example, if users want to continuously monitor an electronic auction that takes a few days (e.g., at **onsale.com**), they would essentially have to be online continuously for days. Software applications that automatically watch auctions and stocks are readily available. For example, a mobile agent travels from site to site, looking for information on a certain stock, as instructed by the user. If the stock price hits a certain level, or if there is news about the stock, the agent alerts the user. What is unique about a mobile agent is that it is a software application that moves on its own to different computers to execute (see Murch and Johnson, 1999).

Nonmobile agents can be defined by two dimensions (see Figure 14.3a), and mobile agents are defined in a three-dimensional space (see Figure 14.3b). For example, in Figure 14.3a, we see that ES, which are not agents, may fall below the threshold

FIGURE 14.3 Intelligent Agents' Scope in Two Dimensions (a) and in Three Dimension (b)

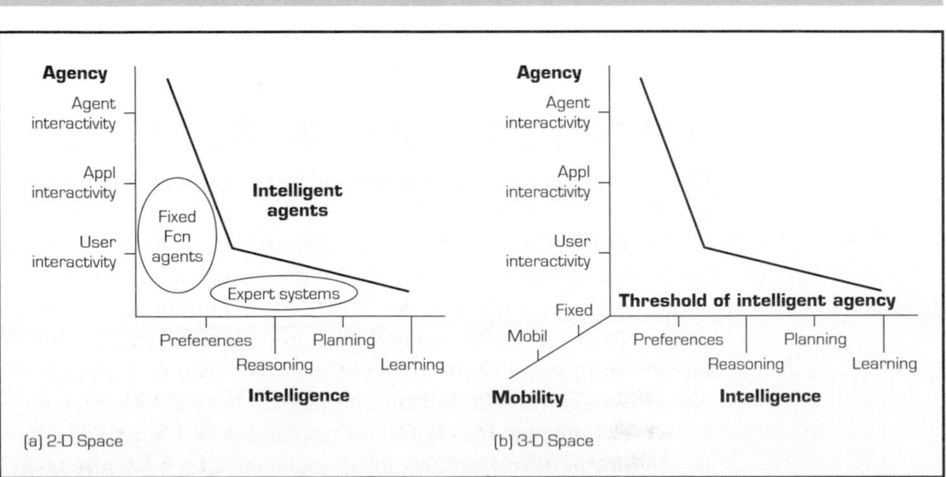

Sources: Based on IBM, Intelligent Agent Strategy, 1995; and D. Gilbert and P. Janca, *IBM Intelligent Agents*, IBM Corp., February 1997 (no longer available online).

line and so are regular software agents. True intelligent agents are listed above the threshold line.

OTHER CLASSIFICATIONS

King (1995) classified agents into interfaces, tutors, scheduling assistants, search agents, report agents, presentation agents, navigation agents, and role-playing agents. Murch and Johnson (1999) used the following categories: personal use, network management, information and Internet access, mobility management, e-commerce, user interface, application development, and military applications. Gilbert and Janca (1997) classified Internet agents into nine categories, based on their areas of application; they are presented in the next section.

Section 14.6 Review Questions

1. List and describe the types of agents.
2. Define *organizational agent* and give an example of one.
3. Define *personal agent* and give an example of one.
4. Describe the differences between software agents and intelligent agents.

14.7 INTERNET-BASED SOFTWARE AGENTS

The use of network- and Internet-based software agents is growing rapidly. New and improved applications seem to appear almost every week (see **agents.umbc.edu**).

According to an IBM white paper (see Gilbert and Janca, 1997), nine major application areas relate to Internet agents:

1. Assisting in workflow and administrative management
2. Collaborating with other agents and people
3. Supporting e-commerce
4. Supporting desktop applications
5. Assisting in information access and management, including searching and FAQs
6. Processing e-mail and messages
7. Controlling and managing network access
8. Managing systems and networks
9. Creating user interfaces, including navigation (browsing)

Many examples of agents in each of these nine categories are available in Gilbert and Janca (1997) and Wooldridge (2002). The following sections describe examples of applications in the network- and Internet-related areas.

E-MAIL AGENTS (MAILBOTS)

E-mail agents, also called mailbots, assist the user with e-mail. For example, Maxims is a classic system that monitors what the user does routinely with e-mail and memorizes the user's situation–action pairs (see Maes, 1994). These pairs are stored in a memory of examples. The situations are described in terms of a set of features, including the names of those who send messages to and receive messages from the user. When a new situation occurs, the agent analyzes the features of the situation and suggests an action to the user (e.g., read, delete, forward, archive). The process is similar to case-based reasoning. The Maxims agent communicates with Eudora, a Windows-based e-mail software system.

An e-mail agent measures the confidence (or fit) of a suggested action to a situation. If the confidence is high, the agent executes the suggestion with the approval of the user. Otherwise, the agent waits for instructions on what to do. The agent's performance improves with time as the memory of examples increases.

According to Murch and Johnson (1999), e-mail agents can do the following:

- Control any unwanted, unsolicited e-mail (e.g., recent spam control and e-mail filtering agents)
- Alert users by voice if a certain designated message arrives
- Automatically forward messages to designated destinations
- Consolidate mail from several sources, the way the user wants it
- Search the Internet for certain sources and deliver them to the user by e-mail
- Distinguish business-related e-mail from private or personal mail
- Automatically answer mail and respond according to conditions (e.g., "I am on vacation until. . . . My agent will automatically make an appointment for you.")
- Perform regular administrative tasks involving desktop e-mail (e.g., backing up files, archiving, indexing)

WEB BROWSING ASSISTING AGENTS

Some agents can facilitate browsing by offering the user a tour of the Internet. Such an agent, known as a *tour guide*, works while the user browses. For example, WebWatcher helps in finding pages related to the current page, adding hyperlinks to meet the user's search goal, and giving advice on the basis of user preference (see **cs.cmu.edu/afs/cs.cmu.edu/project/theo-6/web-agent/www/project-home.html**).

FAQ AGENTS

FAQ agents guide people to the answers to questions that are frequently asked. People tend to ask the same or similar questions; in response, newsgroups, support staffs, and vendors have developed files of FAQs and the most appropriate answer to each. The problem is that people use natural language to ask questions, thus asking the same question in several different ways. A FAQ agent addresses this problem by indexing large numbers of FAQ files and providing an interface at which people can pose their questions in a natural language. The agent uses the text of a question to locate the answer. Because of the limited number of FAQs and the semi-structuredness of the questions, the reliability of FAQ agents is very high.

A recent report indicated that a U.K. furniture retailer, MFI, arms its Web site with an automated virtual kitchen assistant named Claire that allows customers to ask for help in plain English (see Scheraga, 2005). If you type in the question "Do you have wooden kitchen with plain glass?" when the kitchen assistant screen is in action, it replies with the result shown in Figure 14.4.

INTELLIGENT SEARCH (OR INDEXING) AGENTS

Web information seeking and retrieval are becoming increasingly important and suitable for software agents (see Detlor and Glacomin, 2002). *Web robots*, *spiders*, *wanderers*, and similar names describe agents that traverse the Web and perform tasks such as information retrieval and discovery, validation of links or Hypertext Markup

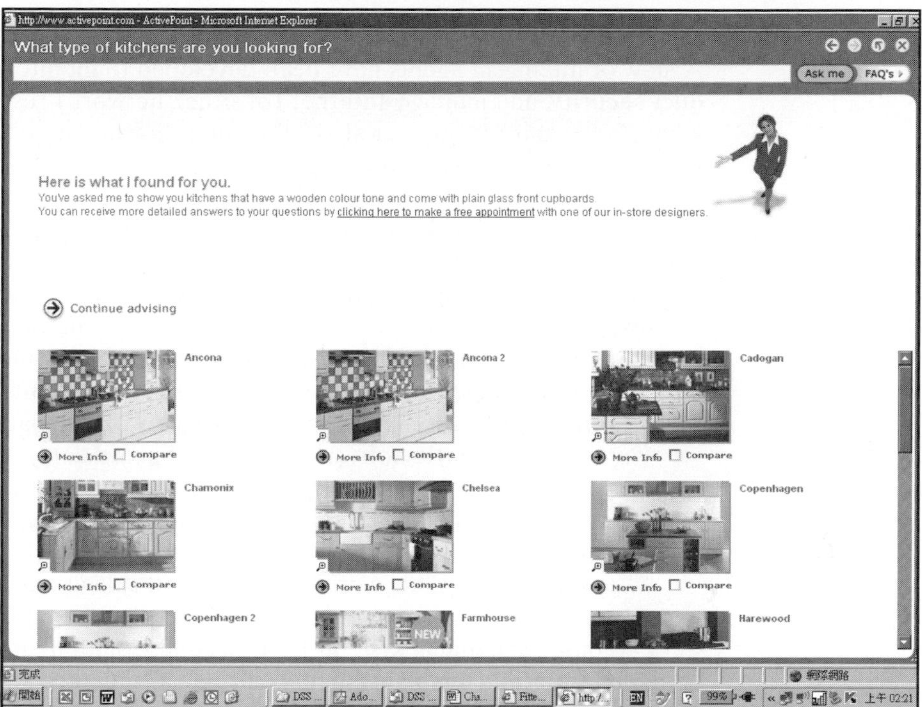

FIGURE 14.4 Sample Answer from a FAQ Agent on the Web

Source: MFI (**mfi.co.uk**).

Language (HTML), and generation of statistics. These **search engines** (or *indexing agents*) are very popular, and thousands are available, many of which are very specialized (see **searchengineguide.com**). Some examples are InfoSeek, Lycos, Excite, and Hotbot. To achieve better results, metasearch engines combine several search engines and other methods of searching. **Metasearch engines** (e.g., Spider, Savvy Search, Metacrawler, All-in-One, Web Compass) integrate the findings of the various search engines to answer queries posted by a user.

Indexing agents carry out massive autonomous searches of the Web. First, they scan millions of documents and store an index of keywords and words from document titles and texts. The user can then query the agent by asking it to find documents that contain certain keywords. Indexing agents were developed for knowledge sharing and acquisition in large databases and documents.

INTERNET SOFTBOTS FOR FINDING INFORMATION

The previously described search agents suggest locations on the Web to the user. Such suggestions are based on a weak model of what the user wants and what information is available at the suggested location. An *Internet softbot* attempts to determine what the user wants and understand the contents of information services. (For pioneering work at the University of Washington, see Etzioni and Weld, 1994.) Early softbot agents were able to work only with structured information, such as stock quotes, weather maps, and the FedEx package-tracking service. Therefore, early agents relied on a simple model of the information service for the precise semantics associated with information provided by the service, increasing the reliability of the search. Recently, Internet softbots such as **google.com** and **hotjobs.yahoo.com** have become more powerful.

NETWORK MANAGEMENT AND MONITORING

A slew of intelligent agents have been developed to monitor, diagnose problems, conduct security, and manage Internet (or other network) resources (e.g., Bhutani and Khan, 2003; and Vlahavas et al., 2002). The following are examples of agents for network management and monitoring:

- *Patrol Application Management.* This family of products uses intelligent agents to perform tasks such as monitoring and managing applications, databases, middleware, and underlying network resources. It also automates administrative action by pinpointing and correcting potential problems before they affect user productivity. AgentWorks (Legent Corp., **legendcorp.com**), which also has the capability to work with other intelligent agents, and Optivity Planning (Nortel Networks, Inc., **nortel.com**) are similar software for network management.
- *WatchGuard* (Seattle Software Labs, **watchguard.com**). WatchGuard is an intelligent Internet and intranet firewall that includes a built-in intelligent agent that is designed to simplify the configuration, management, and security of networks. The intelligence of the system provides automatic alerts to system administrators whenever questionable configurations or outside attacks are detected.
- *AlertView (Intel Corp.).* AlertView uses agents to monitor network resources, databases, and e-mail systems for threshold violations. It has about 100 predefined threshold templates to make programming these responses easier.
- *InterAp (California Software).* InterAp is a suite of Internet applications for Windows that uses agent technology to search the Web and automate file transfer.
- *News Hound. The Denver Post's* News Hound (**denverpost.com/newshound**) is a watcher agent that enables information to automatically come back to you based on your query. News Hound allows you to create a mini Nexis eclipse or a mini Dialog alert.

E-COMMERCE AGENTS

Intelligent agents are playing an increasingly important role in e-commerce (see Lee et al., 2002; Liang and Huang, 2000; Murch and Johnson, 1999; and Wooldridge, 2002). Hundreds of commercial agents perform several major e-commerce activities on the Web. The six classes of e-commerce agents parallel a customer's six steps in purchasing decision making; they are shown in Figure 14.5. Note that the process is cyclic and that the steps may overlap each other.

The classification in Figure 14.5 can help in identifying where agent technologies can be of assistance (e.g., see the CASBA system in Kraft et al., 2000). The characteristics of agents described earlier make them well suited for mediating consumer behaviors involving information filtering and retrieval, personalized evaluations, complex coordination, and time-based interactions. The following are some details and examples:

- *Need identification.* Agents can assist a buyer with need identification by providing product information and stimuli. For example, Amazon.com provides its customers with an agent that continuously monitors a set of data (e.g., the arrival of new books) and notifies customers when a book in their area of interest arrives. Similar agents watch for stocks to go below or above a certain level, sending out e-mails when that level is reached. Expedia.com notifies customers about low-priced airline tickets for a desired destination whenever they become available.

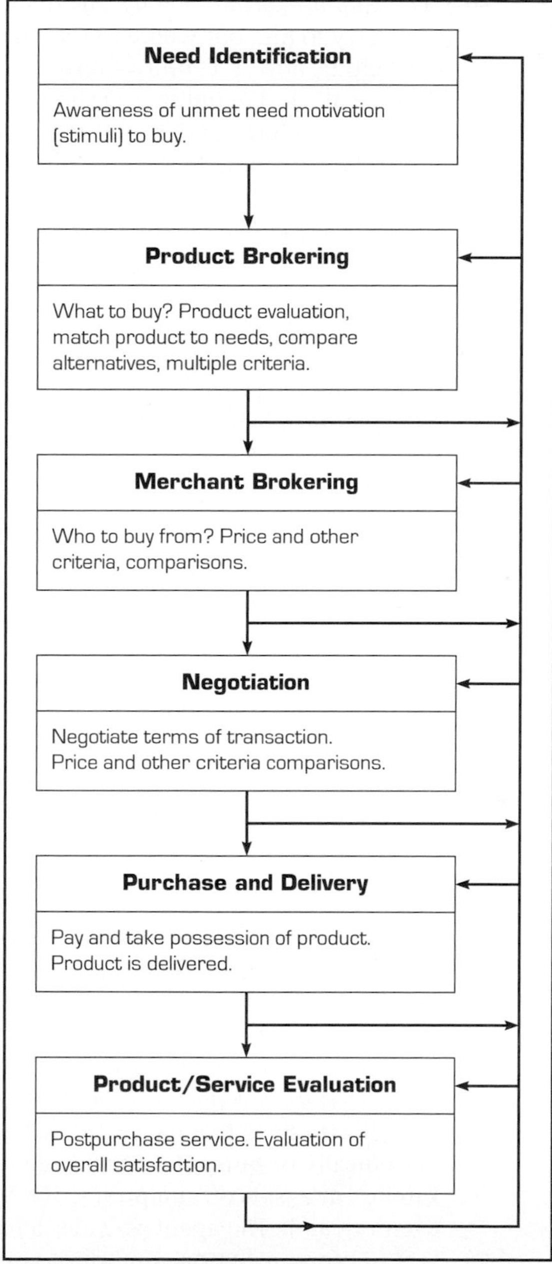

FIGURE 14.5 The Purchasing Decision-Making Process

- *Product brokering.* After a need is established, customers search for a product (or service) that will satisfy this need. Several agents are available to assist customers with this task. The pioneering agent in this category was Firefly developed at the MIT's Media Laboratory. It had a privacy-proven mechanism for analyzing customer profiles for e-commerce. The product was very successful and purchased by Microsoft to become a foundation of Microsoft passport. As another example, based on people's likes (rankings), Netflix recommends DVDs to its customers (see the opening vignette). The Web page of MFI also offers a virtual kitchen assistant to help customers find products.

- *Merchant brokering.* When a customer knows what product he or she wants, it is necessary to find out where to find the best buy. BargainFinder (Anderson Consulting, now Accenture Consulting) was the pioneering agent in this category. This agent, used in online CD shopping, queried the price of a specific CD at a number of online vendors and returned a list of prices. Web sites such as **bestwebbuys.com** help the user search more than a dozen online stores to find the lowest prices of books or CDs. As another example, agents are used in job Web sites for matching recruiters and applicants.
- *Negotiation.* In some markets, price negotiation is common. The benefit of dynamically negotiating a price is that a deal has a better chance of becoming reality. One type of negotiating agent is used in electronic auctions that last several hours or days (e.g., **ebay.com**). An agent can save a bidder's valuable time by monitoring the process and informing the bidder based on certain criteria. For example, auctionBot (which was built at the University of Michigan but was retired in 2001) allowed users to create auction agents by specifying a number of parameters that vary, depending on the type of auction selected. Then it was up to the agent to manage the auction until a final price was met or the deadline for the offer was reached. Another agent bargained with the customer on behalf of the seller. The buyer could negotiate with the agent to reach a more acceptable price (e.g., Liang and Doong, 2000). Agents can negotiate in pairs, or one agent can negotiate for a buyer with several sellers' agents. In such a case, the contact is made with each seller's agent individually, but the buyer's agent can conduct comparisons (Yan et al., 2000).
- *Purchase and delivery.* Agents are used extensively during actual e-commerce purchases, including arranging payment and delivery with the customer. For example, if you make a mistake while filling in an electronic order form, an agent points it out immediately. In buying stocks, for example, the agent tells you when a stock you want to buy on margin is not marginable or when you do not have sufficient funds.
- *Product service and evaluation*. Agents can be used to facilitate after-sale service. For example, the automatic answering agents for e-mail mentioned earlier are usually productive in answering customer queries. Agents can monitor usage and notify you that it is time to take your car in for periodic maintenance. Agents that facilitate feedback from customers are also useful.
- *Other e-commerce agents*. A large number of agents support many e-commerce activities, ranging from advertisement to payment support. See the lists provided periodically by **botspot.com** and **agents.umbc.edu** (see the Agents 101 tutorial). Intelligent agents offer a productive way to find and manage products, news, and even research. The agent provides a free service that delivers personalized content to users. mySimon.com tries to imitate human navigational behavior on the Web. Simon shops in real-time so you can find a product at the right place and at the best price.
- *Fraud-detection agents*. Fraud is a big problem in e-commerce because buyers cannot see the products or the sellers. Several vendors offer agent-based fraud-detection systems.
- *Learning agents.* Several learning agents are used in e-commerce. For example, Learn Sesame (Open Sesame) uses learning theory in monitoring customers' interactions and preferences. An agent then delivers customized advertisements. Netperceptions Corp. uses a similar approach to personalize content and to create customer loyalty programs. Finally, Plangent (Toshiba) performs tasks that rely on a knowledge base of auctions.

- *B2B information sharing.* An intelligent agent was reported to support information sharing in B2B e-marketplaces. Lyer et al. (2005) proposed an architecture to help information exchange through agent collaborations.

An application of agents in targeted marketing is described in Application Case 14.2.

Application Case 14.2

Fujitsu (Japan) Uses Agents for Targeted Advertising

With the increasing popularity of e-commerce, a large body of customer information can be readily acquired online. An important application is the customer's preference ratings for the products that a company offers. The resulting ratings can be applied to a direct marketing campaign for automatic product recommendations.

Since 1996, Fujitsu has been using an agent-based technology called Interactive Marketing Interface (iMi) that allows advertisers to interact directly with targeted customers, providing valuable services and information. The system enhances customers' Internet experience.

The iMi service gives advertisers the ability to interact directly with specific segments of the consumer market through the use of software agents, while ensuring that consumers remain anonymous to advertisers. Consumers submit a profile to iMi, indicating personal characteristics, such as product categories of interest, hobbies, travel habits, and the maximum number of e-mail messages per week they want to receive from the iMi service. In turn, customers electronically receive product announcements, advertisements, and marketing surveys from advertisers, based on their personal profile information. By answering marketing surveys or acknowledging the receipt of advertisements, consumers earn iMi points redeemable for gift certificates and telephone cards.

The iMi system demonstrates practical commercial applications of agent technology and closely maps the concept of mobile, active agents.

Sources: Compiled from K.W. Cheung, J.T. Kwok, M.H. Law, and K.C. Tsu, "Mining Customer Product Ratings for Personalized Marketing," *Decision Support Systems*, 2002, Vol. 35, No. 2, pp. 231–243; and J. Tardo and L. Valenta, "Mobile Agent Security and Telescript," *Proceedings of IEEE COMPCON '96*, February 1996.

OTHER AGENTS

Other applications of agents include, but are not limited to, the following areas:

- *User interfaces.* As user populations grow and diversify, computer interfaces need to learn user habits and preferences and adapt to individuals. Intelligent agents can help with both these problems. Intelligent agent technology allows systems to monitor the user's actions, develop models of user abilities, and automatically help out when problems arise (see Conway and Koehler, 2000).
- *Learning and tutoring.* Agents can be built in an e-learning or intelligent tutoring systems (ITS) to facilitate students. A recent study indicated that a speech-driven anthropomorphic agent embedded in the interface of an ITS could enhance students' learning experience (see Moundridou and Virvou, 2002).
- *Supply-chain management.* Several companies have developed agents that support different activities along the supply chain. An example of such an application is TacTex-03, an agent designed to participate in the Trading Agent Competition Supply Chain Management Scenario (TAC SCM). As specified by this scenario, TacTex-03 acts as a simulated computer manufacturer in charge of buying components such as chips and motherboards, manufacturing different types of computers, and selling them to customers (see Pardoe and Stone, 2004). More information is available in Villa (2002).

- *Workflow and administrative management.* Administrative management includes both workflow management and areas such as computer–telephone integration, where processes are defined and then automated. In these areas, users do not only need to make processes more efficient, they also need to reduce the cost of human agents. Intelligent agents can be used to ascertain and then automate user wishes or business processes. An example is FlowMark (IBM Corp.), which provides an environment for direct manipulation of graphical objects that define and capture the activity steps of any business process (e.g., handling a claim, approving a line of credit, registering a patent). An activity can be automated (i.e., carried out by the execution of a program) or performed by a person. The user defines the process by drawing connectors between the activities and specifying the rules for when each is to be carried out. Agents are also useful in enhancing workflow management in small and medium enterprises (see Montaldo et al., 2003).
- *Web mining.* The information discovered and extracted from Web sites must be generalized based on users' experience. Intelligent agents can learn about their users' interests (see Chau et al., 2003; Etzioni, 1996; and Menczer, 2003).
- *Monitoring and alerting.* An interesting example of a monitoring and alerting agent is NewsAlert, developed by King and Jones (1995). NewsAlert ensures that the data that reaches a manager's desktop is of paramount importance. Liu et al. (2000) implemented a similar agent in the pulp and paper industry in Finland. Their agent monitors a few dozen Web sites and provides the user with news on specific topics, prices, and any other needed information. The information is delivered as an electronic newsletter customized for the user. Agents can also help monitor the auction process (Lee et al., 2003).
- *Collaboration.* Because an agent typically represents an individual user's interests, collaboration is a natural area for agent-to-agent interaction and communication (e.g., Karacapilidis et al., 2003). IBM, for example, is exploring multiagent interaction through several research efforts. Agents operate in the background to automatically perform routine tasks for the user, such as filing documents, sending e-mail, looking for particular topics, or archiving older documents. These agents can be created by designers as part of an application for automating routine tasks such as progress tracking or serving as reminders of overdue items. They can also be used for performing more powerful functions, such as manipulating field values and bringing in data from other applications.
- *Mobile commerce.* Agents play a critical role in mobile commerce. For example, Matskin and Tveit (2001) described the application of mobile commerce agents in WAP-based services. Recommendation systems can also be applied in mobile advertising (see Yuan and Tsao, 2003).
- *System agents.* System agents run as integrated parts of operating systems or network protocol devices. They help in managing complex distributed computing environments by doing hardware inventory, interpreting network events, managing backup and storage devices, and performing virus detection. These agents do not primarily work with end-user information.
- *Recommender agents.* Recommender agents are usually collaborative; they need many profiles to be available before they can make accurate recommendations.
- *Profiling agents.* Profiling agents are used to build dynamic sites with information and recommendations tailored to match each visitor's individual taste and need. The main purpose of a profiling agent is to build customer loyalty and profitable one-to-one relationships.

Application Case 14.3 describes a sample application of intelligent agents at the call center of the hotel chain Wyndham Hotels & Resorts.

Application Case 14.3

Wyndham Uses Intelligent Agents in Its Call Center

Wyndham Hotels & Resorts (**wyndham.com**) is a hotel chain based in Dallas. It owns, leases, manages, and franchises hotels and resorts in the United States, Canada, Mexico, the Caribbean, and Europe, offering more than 36,000 rooms globally. More than 2 million prospective customers contact Wyndham's call center annually, making it one of the hotel's most critical services.

In order to enhance customer service, Wyndham deployed intelligent agent technology from Voxify (**voxify.com**) to serve its customers. This automated agent uses speech technology to greet guests, help locate hotels, book reservations, and update guests' loyalty program information. The software agent is most suitable for rapidly confirming reservations, whereas the live agents are best for helping a guest with an unusual question. Callers are given the option to reach a human agent if they don't like the computer agent. The intelligent agents were expected to be able to handle 25 to 40 percent of the company's service calls.

Sources: News, *Expert Systems*, February 2005, Vol. 22, No. 1, p. 41; and **wyndham.com** (accessed in April 2006).

Section 14.7 Review Questions

1. Describe the function of a FAQ agent and give an example of one.
2. Describe how agents that compare prices work.
3. List and describe the six steps in electronic shopping.
4. For each step identified in Question 3, describe two potential agent applications.
5. Describe a sample of a workflow agent.
6. Identify two applications of intelligent agents in mobile commerce.

14.8 DECISION SUPPORT SYSTEMS AGENTS AND MULTIAGENTS

Multiple agents can collaborate to achieve certain goals. One of the potential uses of multiple agents is to support decision making; these agents are called *decision support system (DSS) agents*. In the following sections, we describe DSS agents and the multiagent system.

DSS AGENTS

Some of the agents described earlier in this chapter can be classified as problem-solving, or DSS, agents. A framework classifies DSS agents into five types: data monitoring, data gathering, modeling, domain managing, and preference learning (see Hess et al., 2000). Furthermore, the framework maps the five types of agents against the three major components of DSS (data, modeling, user interface). This framework is shown in Figure 14.6, and it can be used as a guide in agent development and research.

Table 14.1 uses a manufacturing firm DSS to illustrate these categories by their major characteristics and three reference points.

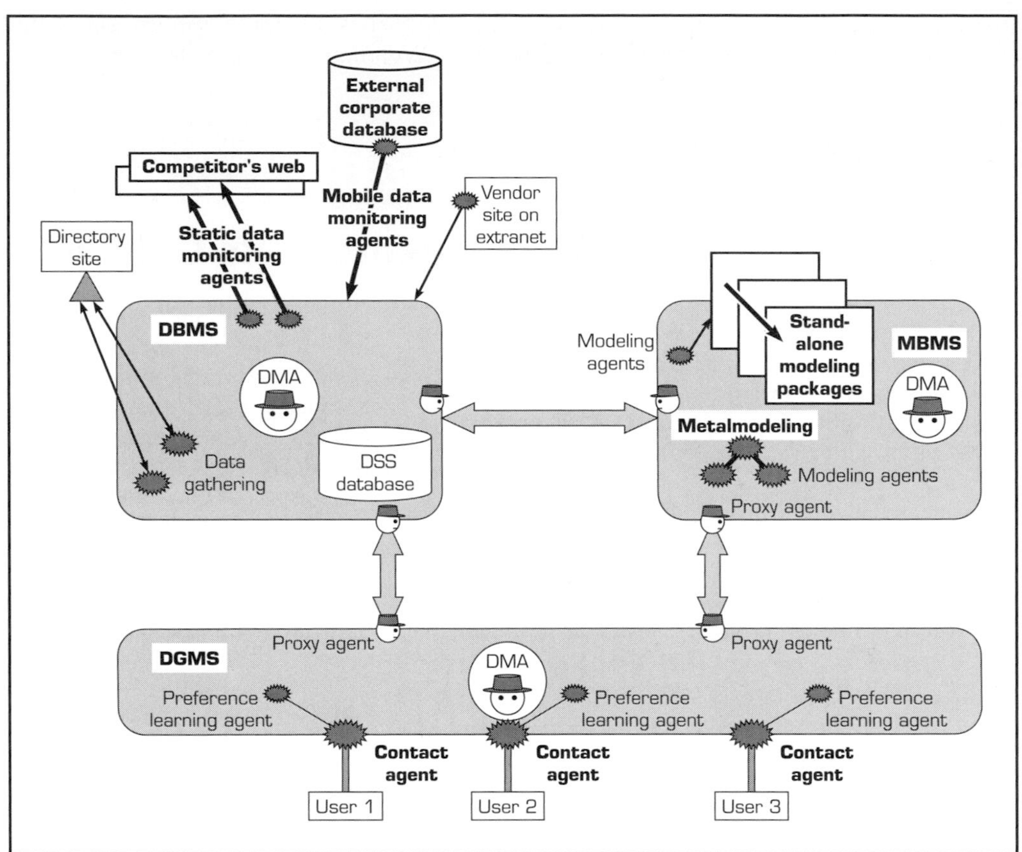

FIGURE 14.6 The Agent-Enhanced General DSS Framework

MULTIAGENTS

Multiagent systems are computer-based environments that contain multiple software agents to perform certain tasks. The theoretical basis for multiple agents started with research in a field called **distributed artificial intelligence (DAI)**, which basically represents the intelligent part of distributed problem solving. DAI is the study of distributed but centrally designed artificial intelligence systems and involves the design of a multiple-agent distributed system with a problem to solve or a task to accomplish. The issue is how to perform in an effective and efficient manner.

The DAI approach decomposes the task into subtasks, each of which is addressed by an agent. Therefore, in distributed problem solving, it is assumed that there is a single body that is able, at design time, to influence the preferences of all the agents in the system directly. The infrastructure of DAI can be constructed with an architecture known as a *blackboard* (see Avouris and Gasser, 1992).

The major difference between DAI and multiagent systems is that in multiagent systems, there is no single designer who stands behind all the agents. Each of the agents can be working toward different goals, even contradictory goals, and sometimes in parallel. Either competition or cooperation is possible among the agents (see Decker et al., 1999). In a DAI system, an agent acting in a particular way is good for the system as a whole, which is not necessarily the case in a multiagent system. However, by using incentives, it is possible to influence the agents in a multiagent system. For example, Chau et al. (2003) used a multiagent approach to Web mining. O'Hare and O'Grady (2003) proposed a

TABLE 14.1 Examples of Agents Used in the Extension of the Holsapple and Whinston Manufacturing Firm DSS

	Essential Agent Characteristics			*Reference Point*		
Autonomous Agent	***Homeostatic Goal***	***Persistence***	***Reactivity***	***Employer/ Client***	***Task***	***Domain***
Data monitoring	Report when any price change crosses given threshold values	Stay at supplier's site "forever" or as long as the vendor supplies parts	Capable of detecting vendor price changes	User	Monitor the current rates of the three types of resources and report on them	Vendor site on an extranet
Data gathering	Report discovery of potential suppliers of manufactured parts at reasonable prices	Lifetime of the DSS	Capable of examining directory sites and understanding language used there	User	Look for alternate vendors of specific part; if found, send message back with name and location of source	Travel to directory
Modeling	Maintain "optimal" price and resource policies; report significant dollar consequences	Lifetime of the DSS	Capable of receiving inputs from the domain manager agent (DMA) and passing results back to the DMA	DMA	When notified by the DMA, formulate a a linear programming model, solve it using Excel's Solver, and report the solution to the to the DMA	Model base management system (MBMS) of DSS
Domain managing (e.g., in the DBMS)	Monitor location and tasks of both local and remote agents functioning on behalf of domain activities; respond to all messages	Lifetime of the DSS	Capable of communicating with agents (even at a distance) and keeping track of their whereabouts	User	Monitor all other agents (both local and remote) acting on behalf of the domain; trigger appropriate actions on hearing from them	Database management system (DBMS) of DSS (similar agents exist in the MBMS and dialog generation and management system [DGMS])
Preference learning	Learn a specific user's preferences, based on the actual history of user/DSS interactions	"Lifetime" of a user of the DSS, even across different sessions	Capable of observing user actions and storing them	User	Record whether a specific user takes the modeling agent's advice or proceeds on his or her own	DGMS of DSS

Source: C.W. Holsapple and A.B. Whinston, *Decision Support Systems: A Knowledge-Based Approach*, West Publishing, St. Paul, MN, 1996.

multiagent system for intelligent content delivery. This should lead to better communication so that agents can solve a problem cooperatively in a distributed open system.

The agent environment is called a *multiagent processing environment (MAPE)*. Figure 14.7 shows an example of a multiagent system architecture, called Genie, in which the identification agent identifies proper user, the calendar agent schedules events, and the Web agent interacts with the user through Web-based user interfaces (see Riekki et al., 2003).

In a multiagent system, for example, a customer may want to place a long-distance call. When this information is known, agents representing the carriers submit bids simultaneously. The bids are collected, and the best bid wins. In a complex system, the customer's agent may take the process one step further by showing all bidders the offers, allowing them to re-bid or negotiate. This process is currently accomplished manually by increasing the number of companies that place projects and subassemblies up for bids in B2B e-commerce (see Turban et al., 2006).

A complex solution is decomposed into subproblems, each of which is assigned to an agent that works on the problem independently of others and is supported by a knowledge base. Knowledge processing agents that use deductive and inductive methods as well as computations acquire and interpret information. The data are refined, interpreted, and sent to the coordinator, who transfers to the user interface whatever is relevant to a specific user's inquiry or need. Multimedia agents can organize the presentation to fit individual executives. If no existing knowledge is available to answer an inquiry, knowledge creating and collecting agents of various types are triggered.

Section 14.8 Review Questions

1. Define *DSS agent* and give an example of one.
2. Define *multiagent system.*
3. Define *distributed artificial intelligence (DAI).*
4. Describe the difference between DAI and multiagent systems.

FIGURE 14.7 Genie of the Net: A Sample Multiagent System

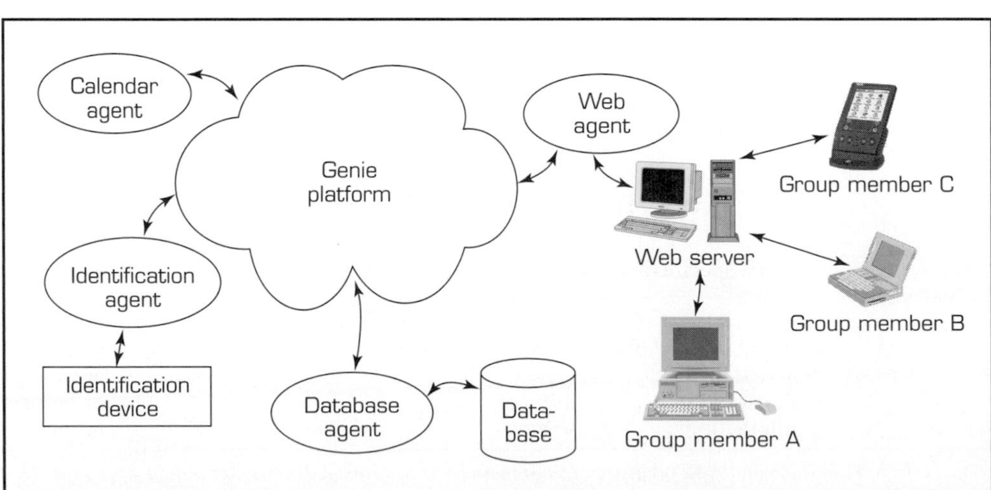

Source: Adapted from J. Riekki, J. Huhtinen, P. Ala-Siuru, P. Alahuhta, J. Kaartinen, and J. Röning, "Genie of the Net: An Agent Platform for Managing Services on Behalf of the User." *Computer Communications*, 2003, Vol. 26, pp. 1188–1198.

14.9 THE SEMANTIC WEB: REPRESENTING KNOWLEDGE FOR INTELLIGENT AGENTS

Intelligent agents need to be able to communicate in a flexible way. A key issue faced when developing intelligent agents on the Internet is that most information on the Web is not designed for other software programs to use. Traditionally, knowledge over the Web is represented in a format called *HTML*. It is designed for humans and is based on the concept that information consists of pages of text and graphics that contain links. HTML is powerful in controlling the appearance of a Web page.

Unfortunately, HTML does not present the content in a way that other software can easily understand and use. Furthermore, some data may be hidden in the database, which makes it very difficult for a software agent to acquire. For example, if a travel agent needs to find a flight from New York to Tokyo on Wednesday afternoon, it would not be able to do so on an HTML-based Web page because the Web page does not contain information that allows the agent to locate the flight schedule (unless the agent has the permission to use a query language to access the database). It is also difficult for a software agent to find a product item from a Web page that contains many products. Software agents do not care about the appearance, only the contents.

The semantic Web is a solution to this problem. It provides a content presentation and organization standard so that the content can be shared safely among different software applications. With mutually understandable semantic constructs, knowledge on the Web is easier for computer agents to access, understand, and share.

DEFINITION OF *Semantic Web*

The *semantic Web* is part of an effort to incorporate meanings and relationships among concepts into Web information. As described by Berners-Lee et al. (2001), the semantic Web is "an extension of the current Web, in which information is given well-defined meanings, better enabling computers and people to work in cooperation." The semantic Web is meant to enable an environment in which independent, Internet-connected information systems can exchange knowledge and action specifications, resulting in the execution of an activity acceptable to all systems involved.

In practice, the semantic Web is a collaborative effort led by World Wide Web Consortium (W3C), with participation from a large number of researchers and industrial partners. W3C defines the **semantic Web** as "the representation of data on the World Wide Web. It is based on the Resource Description Framework (RDF), which integrates a variety of applications using XML for syntax and Uniform Resource Identifiers (URIs) for naming" (**w3c.org**). It is built on two existing technologies: XML and Web services. The concepts of RDF, XML, and URL are described later in this section.

XML AND WEB SERVICES

Web services are an XML-based technology that has gained much support from most major software companies, such as IBM, Microsoft, and Sun Microsystems. Web services are central to the envisioned semantic Web. Technology Insights 14.4 shows a sample XML representation of the concept "birds."

More and more businesses are using XML in their systems. A typical example is the Galileo system, which connects more than 42,000 travel agency locations to 37 car rental companies, 47,000 hotels, and 350 tour operators. Without this technology, the operation of such a complicated heterogeneous system would not be possible (see Staab, 2003). Amazon.com has also taken advantage of this technology to create an

TECHNOLOGY INSIGHTS 14.4

A Sample XML Format

XML is an extension to HTML that represents meaning of concepts through user-defined tags. It is the foundation of both Web services and the semantic Web. In an HTML document, typical information includes definitions such as "title" and "fonts." These are called *tags*. XML allows more of these tags to be defined to include semantic information. For instance, we can define a tag called "product" or "account receivable" to reveal that the data content is a product or an account receivable. The following is a sample representation of the concept "birds" in XML:

```
<?XML VERSION = "1.0">
<BIRDS>
ANIMALS THAT FLY:
<BIRD>
<NAME>TWEETY</NAME?>
<COLOR>BLUE</COLOR>
<LOCATION>MIKE'SHOME</LOCATION>
<EATS>BIRDSEEDS</EATS>
</BIRD>
</BIRDS>
```

This representation contains certain attributes of birds that may be used by other applications.

XML version of its database for partners to integrate its service. The concept of Web services is quite simple: Web services define standards for connection, communication, description, and discovery among Web-based modules.

Figure 14.8 shows the major building blocks of Web services. As you can see, Web services include four layers (see Huhns, 2002):

- *Transport layer.* This layer, the foundation of the Web services stack, is responsible for data transmission. It is built on the existing data transport foundation (including HTTP, SMTP, and FTP mechanisms).

FIGURE 14.8 Architecture of Web Services

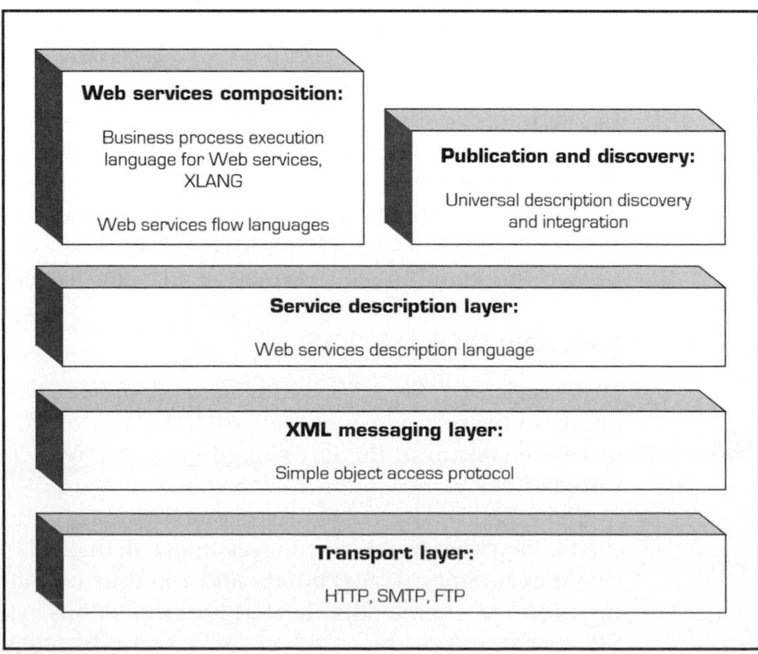

- *XML messaging layer.* The kernel at this layer is XML. Simple Object Access Protocol (SOAP) provides the protocol that systems need to communicate with each other when they need to request services, such as finding a product or flight schedule. SOAP comprises three parts: an envelope to describe the content of a message, a set of encoding rules, and a mechanism for providing remote procedure calls and responses (see Myerson, 2002).
- *Service description layer*. In order for a Web service to be known to other services, a description language is necessary. Web Services Description Language (WSDL) allows services to be described in a machine-readable form, where the names of functions, their required parameters, and their results can be specified. WSDL divides a service description into two parts: service implementation and service interface. A service interface must be created before WSDL can be implemented (see Myerson, 2002).
- *Publication and integration layer.* The top layer publishes available services for application. Universal Description, Discovery, and Integration (UDDI) gives users and businesses a "yellow page" of services so that they can easily find needed services. See **uddi.org** for details.

THE LAYER CAKE OF THE SEMANTIC WEB

The semantic Web extends the layers defined in Web services to further enhance the organization of knowledge and the interoperability of different agents. In order to present knowledge in an interchangeable way, an ontology definition becomes critical. Key components of the semantic Web technology include the following (see Preece and Decker, 2002):

- A unifying data model, such as RDF. See **w3.org/rdf**.
- Language with defined semantics, built on RDF, such as DAML + OIL (DARPA Agent Markup Language plus Ontology Inference Layer). See **daml.org** for details.
- Ontologies of standardized terminology for marking up Web resources, used by semantically rich service-level descriptions and support tools that assist in the generation and processing of semantic markup.

Berners-Lee et al. (2001) presented a "layer cake" of the semantic Web at a 2000 XML conference. This layer cake, as shown in Figure 14.9, includes the major elements of the semantic Web. The foundation consists of the basic machine-readable form of data representation in Unicode and uniform resource identifiers (URIs). XML is then used to render the data. On top of XML are RDF and a four-layer architecture to support information exchange among agents: ontology, logic, proof, and trust.

Uniform Resource Identifiers

URIs are similar to URLs (uniform resource locators) in the Internet, but they are more general. Whereas a URL points to a particular Web site, a URI points to any available Web resources. Therefore, all URLs are also URIs, but not vice versa. Resources can further be broadened to include objects not available on the Internet. Figure 14.10 shows an example of the semantic Web.

The Resource Description Framework (RDF)

The Resource Description Framework (RDF) is designed to relate one URI to another. It provides a data model that supports fast integration of data sources by

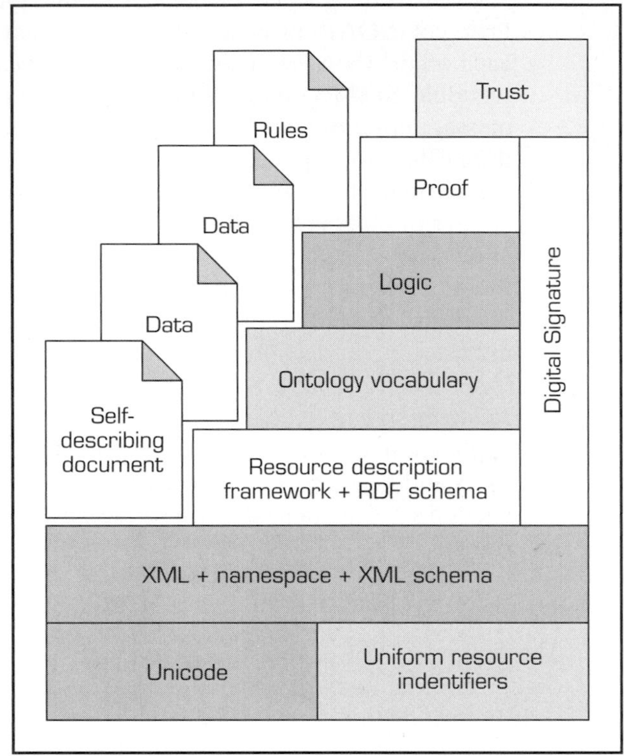

FIGURE 14.9 "Layer Cake" of the Semantic Web by Tim Berners-Lee

Source: Adapted from J. Hendler, "Agents and the Semantic Web." *IEEE Intelligent Systems*, 2001, Vol. 16, No. 2, pp. 30–37.

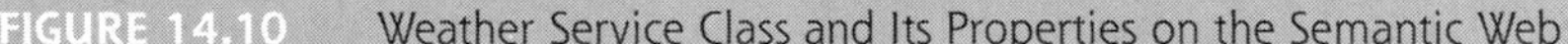
FIGURE 14.10 Weather Service Class and Its Properties on the Semantic Web

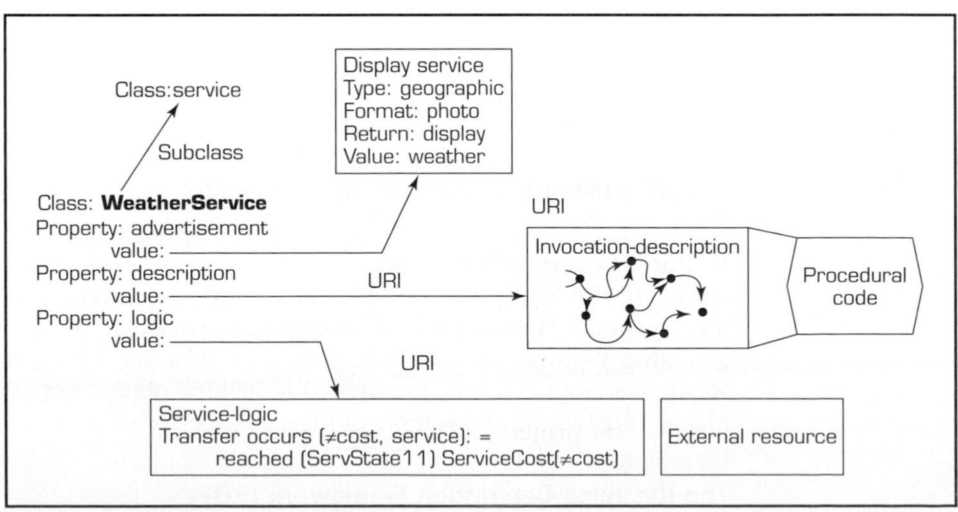

Source: Adapted from J. Hendler, "Agents and the Semantic Web." *IEEE Intelligent Systems*, 2001, Vol. 16, No. 2, pp. 30–37.

bridging semantic differences. It is a sort of statement about resources and their relationships. An RDF might express the relationship that Mary is John's sister or a new auction bid is higher than the current highest bid. Therefore, RDF is often used to represent metadata about other Web resources such as XML files and may be called *resource metadata*. More detail can be found in Decker et al. (2000) and McBride (2002).

Ontology

Ontology is defined in the *Oxford English Dictionary* as "the science or study of being." In artificial intelligence, we usually attribute the notion of ontology to the specification of a conceptualization—that is, defined terms and relationships among them. Or, simply put, ontology is a set of terms related to a knowledge domain, including the vocabulary, the semantic interconnections, and some simple rules of inference and logic for some particular topics. For example, the ontology of cooking and cookbooks may include ingredients, procedures for processing the ingredients, and the differences in various cooking styles. For the semantic Web, ontology is a collection of related RDF statements that together specify a variety of relationships among data elements and ways of making logical inferences among them.

Logic

Service logic states the rules governing the use of ontological statements. For example, if a transaction rule requires that a certain amount of money be transferred after a service invocation is reached (e.g., ServState11), the rule may be represented as follows (also see Figure 14.10):

```
TransferOccurs(#cost, Service):=
  Reached(ServState11), ServiceCost(#cost).
```

Proof and Trust

Proof and trust are high-level functions in the semantic Web. When agents must negotiate to perform certain functions, they need to check complex logic, exchange proofs, and build trust before collaboration. For example, when a bidding agent is submitting a high bid, the auction agent needs proof that the bidding agent is legitimate before its offer is accepted. The advantages and limitations of using the semantic Webs are outlined in Technology Insights 14.5.

APPLICATION OF SEMANTIC WEB SERVICES

A combination of the semantic Web and Web services is called **semantic Web services**. One of the first applications of semantic Web services is MusicBrainz (**musicbrainz.org**), which provides a large database of music metadata for sharing (see Swartz, 2002). By 2002, it already had more than 300,000 tracks. In fact, the idea of MusicBrainz can be traced back to the Internet Compact Disc Database (CDDB) project started in 1996. After CDDB was acquired by a content delivery company and no longer open for free use, several projects were created to replace it. One of them, the CDIndex, later became MusicBrainz.

The major function of MusicBrainz is to provide semantic information over the Web for other systems to use. When you purchase a new CD and insert it into your computer, your audio player is likely to come up with a generic name (such as *Audio*

TECHNOLOGY INSIGHTS 14.5

Advantages and Limitations of the Semantic Web

Using the semantic Web to design intelligent agents has the following advantages:

- *Easy to understand.* The semantic Web demonstrates objects and their relationships as graphic templates for easy understanding.
- *Easy resource integration.* It is easier to integrate systems and modules designed in the semantic Web. This also makes system analysis and maintenance easier.
- *Saving development time and costs.* The semantic Web allows incremental ontology creation, which can make a system usable more rapidly. The ability to use other resources more easily can save development time and costs.
- *Automatic update of content.* Because agents can easily locate specific knowledge on the semantic Web, they can have functions to update or import contents automatically. This adds a level of intelligence to the software agents.
- *Easy resource reuse.* The ontology-based annotations can turn briefings into reusable resources
- *Enhanced search mechanism.* Ontology-based searching could filter some seemingly appropriate but unwanted results and add some seemingly different but actually same results.
- *Virtual community.* Some enterprises with common interests can be tightly connected on the semantic Web and form a virtual enterprise due to the mutually benefited preferences defined in terms of ontology.

The limitations of the semantic Web include the following:

- *Limited representation power.* The graphical representation may be oversimplified. For example, using an arrow to represent a relation between two instances is unable to show more complicated multiple-party relations.
- *Lack of supporting tools.* The semantic Web needs to set up more tools for searching content and building references to preexisting instances.
- *Incomplete ontology.* The ontology may not be correctly defined. In some cases, the outcome may be severe. It is still difficult to proof the completeness or correctness of a defined ontology.
- *Inaccurate content.* When agents deal with parts of the semantic Web that contain information that is inconsistent, incorrect, or lacks reliable sources, they may be contaminated or lead to wrong decisions.
- *Security concerns.* Because the semantic Web allows agents from different systems to communicate and share information, security and related issues are key concerns. This is always a problem for an open system.

CD23), complete with *track 1*, *track 2*, and so on. If you were using MusicBrainz, the audio player would attempt to connect to the MusicBrainz server to see if that CD's metadata are available. If it were, your CD player would have renamed the CD and the tracks. If the metadata were not available and you had filled the names for your own use, MusicBrainz would ask you whether you want to share the information. If you did, the information would be sent to MusicBrainz to share with other users. MusicBrainz provided the metadata in RDF. Figure 14.11 shows a graphical representation of MusicBrainz RDF data.

Because MusicBrainz's data format is open and in the RDF format, it can be repurposed for numerous applications. For example, file-sharing systems (e.g., Napster, Freenet, Audio Galaxy) can use the metadata to provide more information about the MP3s that are available for download or to make it easier to search for a song. Artists can provide links so that appreciative fans can donate money if they like the music.

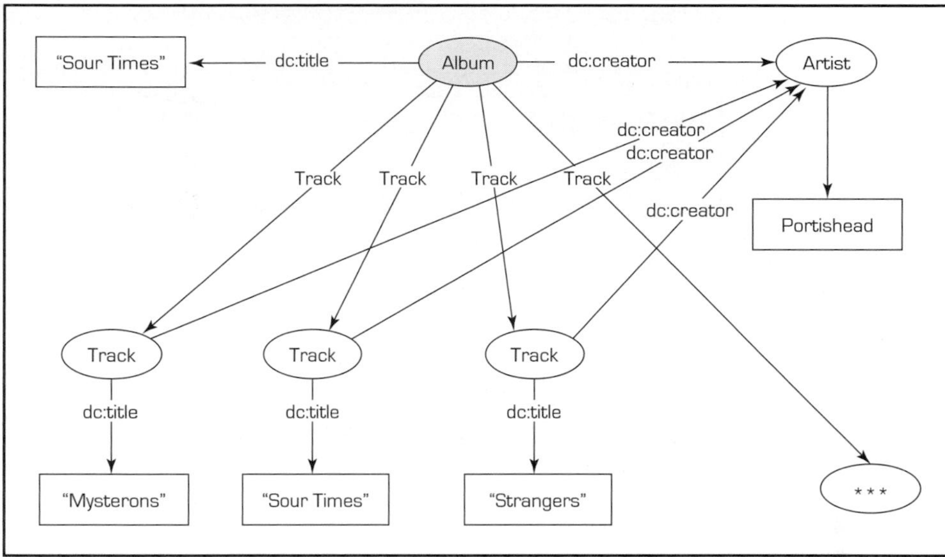

FIGURE 14.11 Graphical Representation of MusicBrainz Data

Source: Adapted from A. Swartz, "MusicBrainz: A Semantic Web Service." *IEEE Intelligent Systems*, 2002, Vol. 17, No. 1, pp. 76–77.

Section 14.9 Review Questions

1. Describe the semantic Web and explain the differences between the semantic Web and XML.
2. Define *XML* and give an example of it.
3. What are the building blocks of Web services?
4. What are the elements in the layer cake of Web services?
5. What are the advantages of using Web services?
6. What are the limitations of using Web services?
7. Describe a potential application of Web services.

14.10 WEB-BASED RECOMMENDATION SYSTEMS

A major application of intelligent systems in e-commerce is to recommend products to customers. A typical example is the book recommendation agent adopted by online bookstores (see Application Case 14.6). The DVD recommendation at Netflix, as described in the opening vignette, is another example. The "people who bought this book also bought" area in Figure 14.12 is the output of the recommendation agent at Barnes & Noble.

The major motivation for using recommendation agents is that personalization is a major trend in marketing and customer services. Each person must be treated

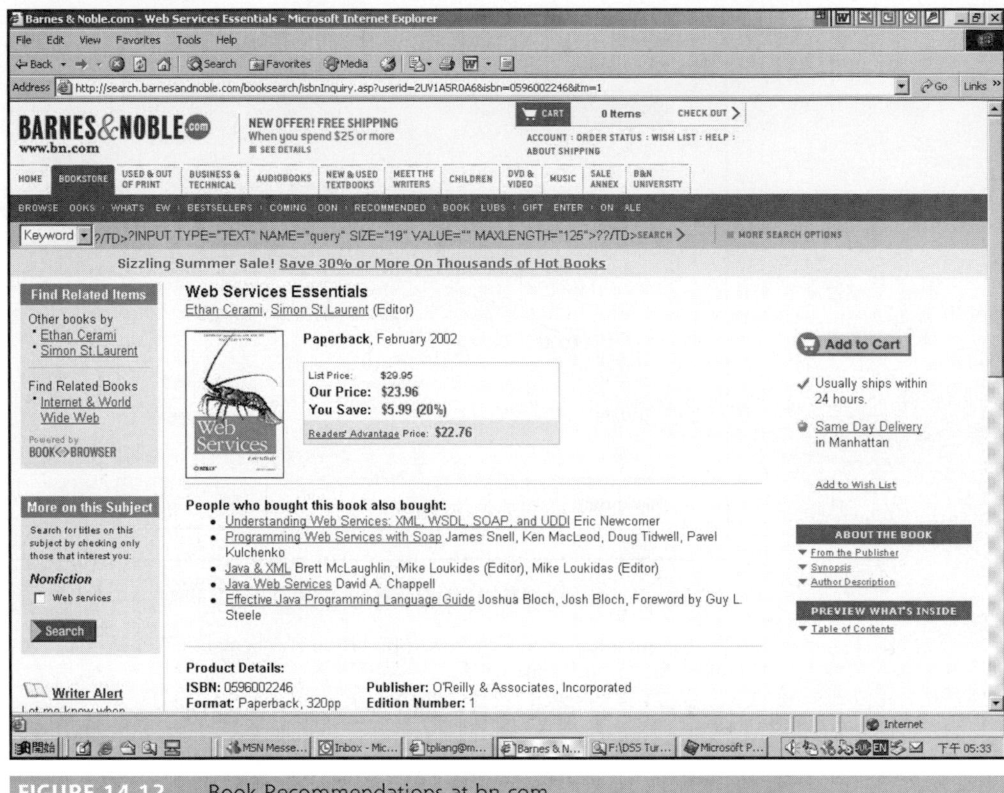

FIGURE 14.12 Book Recommendations at bn.com

as a unique customer so that products/services can be offered according to the customer's unique interests. In order to support such a marketing effort, it is essential to collect and analyze contextual information that relates to users' interests and information needs. For example, after you have visited an online bookstore, such as Amazon.com, the store keeps track of what you have viewed and purchased and uses those data as a basis for recommending new items for your consideration. Intelligent systems that provide this service are called **recommendation systems (agents)** or *recommender systems* (or *agents*). A recommendation system is an intelligent system that can identify customers' interests from existing usage data and make suggestions accordingly to enhance customer loyalty and achieve higher conversion/retention rates.

Application Case 14.6

Amazon.com Uses Collaborative Filtering to Recommend Products

Online bookstore Amazon.com has more than 29 million customers and several million catalog items. In order to enhance its marketing and customer services, Amazon.com extensively uses recommendation algorithms to personalize its Web service for each customer's unique shopping needs. Although the early version of BookMatcher was not good, the recent version works pretty well. Clicking the "Your Recommendations" link leads customers to an area where they can filter their recommendations by product line and subject area, rate the recommended products, rate their previous purchases, and see why items are recommended. Amazon.com also has an interesting function, called *shopping cart recommendation*, that offer customers product suggestions based on the items in their shopping carts.

The recommendation algorithm is a modified version of collaborative filtering, called *item-to-item collaborative filtering*, which scales to massive data sets to accommodate enormous numbers of users and product offerings and produces real-time recommendations to customers. The major difference is that, instead of matching similar customers together, the algorithm matches each of a user's purchased and rated items to similar items and subsequently recommends those similar items to the user.

MECHANISM FOR GENERATING RECOMMENDATIONS

The key concept of the Amazon.com algorithm is to process item similarity offline in order to improve computing efficiency. Rather than matching the user to similar customers, the Amazon algorithm matches each of the user's purchased and rated items to similar items, and then it combines those similar items into a recommendation list.

To determine the most similar match for a given item, the algorithm calculates the similarity between a single product and all related products to build a similar-items table by finding similar items that customers tend to purchase together. The degree of correlation between different items is constructed. Based on the similar-items table and the particular items ordered by a customer, the system is able to identify items similar to each product that the user purchased or rated. Finally, the system compiles those items into a recommendation list, which includes the most correlated or popular items as recommendations to the user.

Sources: G. Linden, B. Smith, and J. York, "Amazon.com Recommendations: Item-to-Item Collaborative Filtering," *IEEE Intelligent Systems*, 2003, pp. 76–80; and **amazon.com** (accessed April 2006).

TAXONOMY OF RECOMMENDATION MECHANISMS

The foundation of a recommendation system is the user profile. Most functions of the system are designed around the user profile. In a relatively short time period, many recommendation methods have been developed. In a comprehensive survey, Montaner et al. (2003) divided the functions into two major categories: *profile generation and maintenance* and *profile exploitation and recommendation*. A recommendation system needs to build and maintain a user profile and then extract useful information from the user profile for making recommendations. Each category includes several dimensions, as shown in Table 14.2.

Profile Generation and Maintenance

A recommendation system needs to generate and maintain a user profile in order to know the user. Unfortunately, the user often does not want to spend time indicating his or her interests to create the profile. Moreover, users' interests may change over time, making the profiles difficult to maintain. The following aspects are important for generating and maintaining the profile:

- *User profile representation.* Several approaches have been taken to represent user profiles, such as a history of purchase, Web navigation, e-mails, or the demographic features (e.g., gender, age, occupation) of the user.

TABLE 14.2 Dimensions in Recommendation Functions

Profile Generation and Maintenance	*Profile Exploitation and Recommendation*
User profile representation	Information filtering method
Initial profile generation	Item profile matching technique
Profile learning technique	User profile matching technique
Relevance feedback	Profile adaptation technique

Source: M. Montaner, B. Lopez, and J.L de la Rosa, "A Taxonomy of Recommender Agents on the Internet," *Artificial Intelligence Review*, 2003, Vol. 19, pp. 285–330.

- *Initial profile generation.* When the structure of the profile is determined, an initial set of user profile data must be created. The initial user profiles may be created manually or automatically from existing data or predefined stereotypes.
- *Profile learning technique.* User profile data must be processed to find useful patterns for recommendations. The most typical approaches for profile learning are clustering and classifiers. *Clustering* techniques allow users to be clustered into many similar clusters. Recommendations can be made based on their similarity. *Classifiers* use information about an item and the user profile as inputs and have the output category represent how strongly to recommend an item to a user. The discovery of association rules by inductive learning is a good example of classifiers.
- *Relevance feedback.* Human interests change as time passes. Therefore, a recommendation system needs to collect relevant feedback information. The feedback may be explicit or implicit. The *explicit* approach asks the user to explicitly evaluate items to indicate his or her preference (such as ranking items after browsing). The *implicit* approach has an embedded module in the system to infer user preferences by monitoring certain evidences, such as the browsed Web pages, browsing time, or keystroke sequences.
- *Profile adaptation technique.* Because a user's interests may change over time, the information gathered from relevance feedback must be analyzed to modify the user profile. The adaptation includes adding new information and gradually forgetting old information. A typical forgetting approach is to define a time window for analysis. Data moving out of the window will be forgotten.

Profile Exploitation and Recommendation

A recommendation system relies on the available information (e.g., items reviewed or purchased, user profile) to make decisions. Three main tasks are important for performing the job:

- *Information filtering method.* Information filtering means identifying useful items from a large number of candidates. Three methods are popular: demographic filtering, collaborative filtering, and content-based filtering. **Demographic filtering** uses the user's demographic data to determine what items might be appropriate for recommendation. **Content-based filtering** recommends items for the user based on the description of previously evaluated items and information available from the content (e.g., keywords). **Collaborative filtering** matches people with others who have similar interests and makes recommendations accordingly. Hybrid approaches that use more than one method are also available. Content-based and collaborative filtering are described in more detail later in this chapter.
- *Item profile matching.* Content-based filtering systems use direct comparison between the user profile and new items. Thus, user profile item matching is necessary. Several methods exist. Popular ones include keyword matching and nearest-neighbor algorithms.
- *User profile matching.* Collaborative filtering needs to find similar users before making a recommendation. In general, the process of computing includes three steps: find similar users, create a neighborhood, and compute a prediction based on the selected neighbors. Clustering and classification techniques are useful in this step.

COLLABORATIVE FILTERING

Collaborative filtering uses the concept of market segmentation (i.e., dividing customers into groups of peers that have similar needs) in predicting user preference.

In essence, it compares the profile (e.g., purchase histories, browsing behavior) of the current user to profiles of users in the rest of the population to identify users in the database who may be similar to the current user. Interests found from similar users are used to infer the interest of the particular user, and recommendations are made accordingly. The *Los Angeles Times, London Times*, CRAYON, and Tango have used such collaborative recommendation systems to provide customized online newspapers (see Goldberg et al., 1992). Figure 14.13 shows the architecture of a collaborative recommender system.

Data collected in a collaborative filtering system typically comprises a two-dimensional user–product matrix where the rows feature the users and the columns feature the products (e.g., books, movies). User preference on each of the products is represented by the value in the cell in the matrix. Unfortunately, this sort of data organization often leads to severe scaling and performance problems when data sets become very large (e.g., when millions of users and products are represented in the user–product matrix). Besides, because most users refuse to provide product evaluations or tend to purchase only a small number of items in the product catalog, the user–product matrix tends to be very spare and becomes inefficient when being applied on a large scale. These problems may be resolved partially by using dimensionality-reduction techniques such as clustering and principal component analysis. However, it is not possible to achieve a reduction in the data size without a trade-off in recommendation quality.

Similarity between customers can be measured in a number of ways. *Similarity index* is a measurement that is frequently used for assessing similarity between individuals. Commonly used similarity metrics include Jaccard's coefficient, distance measure, and the Pearson product–moment correlation coefficient. After user similarity is

FIGURE 14.13 An Architecture of Collaborative and Usage-Based Web Recommender

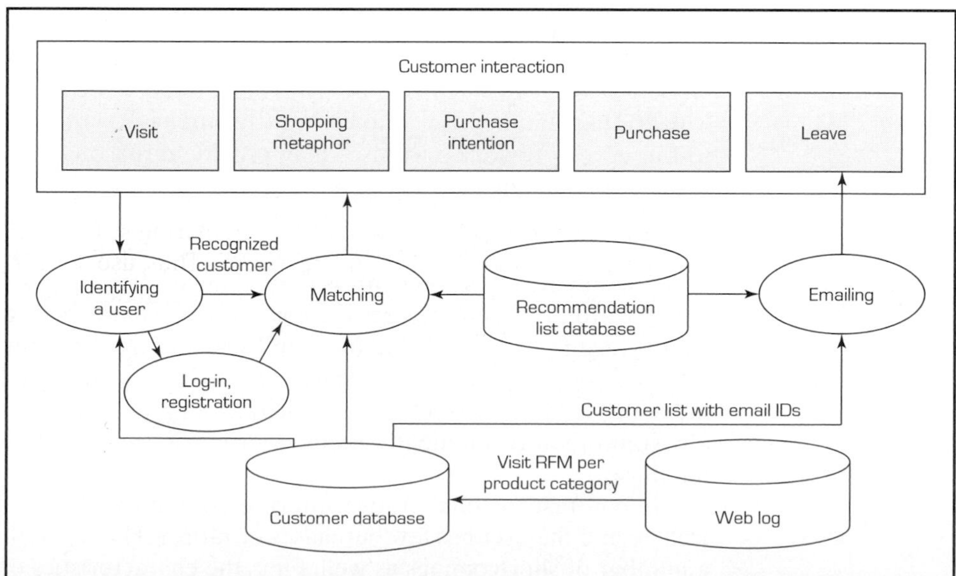

Source: S. H. Ha, "Helping Online Customers Decide Through Web Personalization," *IEEE Intelligent Systems*, 2002, Vol. 17, No. 6, pp. 34–43.

computed, clustering models are applied in order to group customers into peer groups. Cluster analysis is the most useful statistical tool for aggregating discrete units (e.g., consumers) into groups (i.e., segments) based on customers' similarities (see Iacobucci et al., 2000). Cluster analysis tools typically begin with a set of segments, each of which contains a randomly sampled user. The algorithm then matches the rest of the users against those already assigned into the segments while simultaneously tracking emerging communities of interests and weeding out unpopular segments. The process is repeated until every user in the database is assigned to one of the segments in the model.

In general, a collaborative filtering system generates recommendation by predicting a person's preferences as weighted sums of other people's preference in his or her subset, with the weights being proportional to the strength of correlation between two individuals.

It should be noted that this approach is subject to several limitations. Because the algorithm works by grouping customers into subsets, poor recommendations may be given to users whose tastes are unusual compared to the rest of the population. The system also fails to provide users with reasons for a recommendation. In addition, because the algorithm can only be used when the database contains the preference data for a particular item, it cannot generate recommendations for a new product that nobody has used or rated. For example, most collaborative filtering algorithms cannot advise a user on whether a new book is good.

CONTENT-BASED FILTERING

Unlike collaborative filtering, content-based filtering does not consider similarity between users in making recommendations. Rather, recommendations are offered solely on the basis of similarities among products or information packets. In predicting user preference, content-based filtering uses attributes associated with an object (e.g., keywords in a document) and their matches with known user rankings on previously purchased items. It seeks to identify idiosyncratic features of the items the user had bought and recommend to the user items with similar features. For instance, most classes of products can be segregated into a set of distinct categories (e.g., music can be classified by artists or types, such as pop, jazz, and classical). A person who has purchased classical music by Beethoven is more likely to be interested in classical music by Mozart than another user who has mostly purchased jazz. Hence, a list of items related to the user's previous purchases may provide a reasonable recommendation to meet the user's shopping needs.

The content-based filtering algorithm typically starts by analyzing the morphology of the texts or product descriptions of various documents/products to identify their idiosyncratic features and express their characteristics as a string of keywords or associated words. It then compares the content (i.e., characteristics) of various items in the catalog against a user profile built up by analyzing the content of items the user has rated or bought in the past. Usually, some formulas that give higher weights to certain indexing words or attributes are applied to compute the similarity of the products. The algorithm then recommends goods in order of their similarity to the user's previous purchase.

In contrast to collaborative filtering, content-based filtering scales and performs well even if the user has few purchases or ratings. However, this algorithm suffers from a number of shortcomings as well. First, the characteristics of certain classes of goods (e.g., food, drawings) cannot be comprehensively or wholesomely captured by a few discriminating words. Hence, recommendations generated by such an algorithm tend to neglect aesthetic aspects of the product, such as layout, images, diagrams, and other important qualities (e.g., loading time for Web offerings). Also, the user may miss novel information because recommendations involve only a search for items similar to the user's previous purchases. An example of content-based filtering used at EuroVacations.com is illustrated in Application Case 14.7.

Application Case 14.7

Content-Based Filtering at EuroVacations.com

Recommendation systems are increasingly being used by travel and tourism Web sites to help travelers make more informed decisions for their vacations in less time. EuroVacations.com (**eurovactions.com**), one of the most successful travel counseling Web sites, uses TripleHop Technologies TripMatcher to provide customized recommendations on destinations and travel products, according to the site visitors' stated or implied preferences.

The software, called Destination Wizard on EuroVacations.com, primarily takes a content-based approach in generating recommendations. Users are asked to indicate their needs and constraints (e.g., activities interests, budget, duration) by selecting the options available under a list of questions. The system then compares the user inputs with the attributes of a list of available travel products and destinations in the database.

To reduce user effort, the system simultaneously builds an attribute-based behavioral profile of the user as he or she interacts with the system each time he or she visits the Web site, and from this, implicit information about the users' interests can be extracted. The system then predicts the user's preference by combining statistics on his or her past queries and a weighted average of importance of different attributes assigned by similar users. Hence, users need to answer only a limited number of questions to obtain personalized recommendations targeted to their interests. The system presents the output to users in order of relevance. By exploiting content-based recommendation technology, it is possible for EuroVacations.com to achieve a higher browser-to-buyer conversion rate.

Sources: TripleHop Recommendation Engine Makes Tailored Service Available to More than 30 Million Leisure Travelers Through EuroVacations.com Software Facilitates Decision Process, **eyefortravel.com/index.asp?news=15008** (accessed in April 2006); and **eurovacations.com** (accessed April 2006).

MOBILE APPLICATIONS OF RECOMMENDATION AGENTS

Recommendation agents can operate across different device platforms. For instance, Web recommendations can help a mobile user find relevant Web pages in fewer steps by dynamically suggesting Web pages that the user is likely to access in the near future. Zhou et al. (2006) proposed an approach that combines sequential pattern mining, pattern-tree construction, and recommendation rule generations to help Web access. Figure 14.14 shows the framework of this creative application.

Section 14.10 Review Questions

1. Define *recommendation agent* and describe the role of these agents in e-commerce.
2. Briefly illustrate the mechanism for product recommendations.
3. Describe why a recommendation system needs a user profile and how a user profile can be built and maintained.
4. Describe content-based filtering and collaborative filtering. Compare their advantages and limitations.

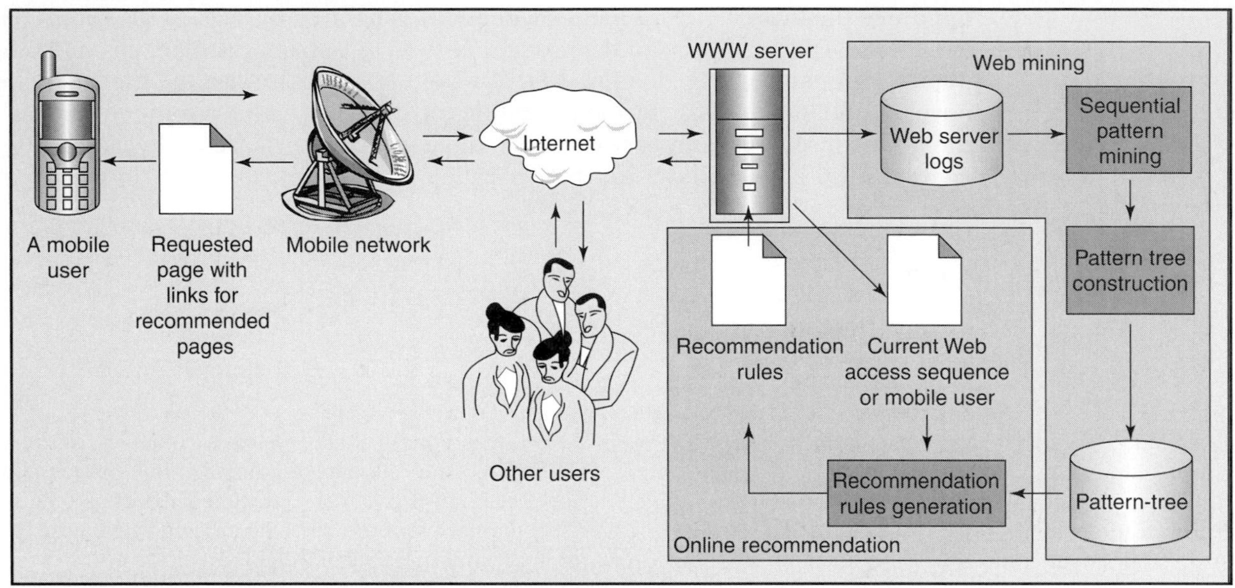

FIGURE 14.14 Architecture of a Mobile Web Recommendation System

Source: B. Zhou, S. C. Hui, and K. Chang, "Enhancing Mobile Web Access Using Intelligent Recommendations," *IEEE Intelligent Systems*, January-February 2006.

14.11 MANAGERIAL ISSUES OF INTELLIGENT AGENTS

Intelligent agents provide an innovative way to process routine tasks automatically. Because they are given certain degrees of autonomy and authorization, some managerial issues are important. This is especially true for mobile agents (see Schoder and Eymann, 2000). The following sections describe some of the important managerial issues related to intelligent agents.

COST JUSTIFICATION

With technology rapidly changing and with intelligent agents still evolving, it may be hard to justify spending a lot of money on something that may be obsolete tomorrow. Simple software agents such as wizards found in software products are fairly easy to justify because they are usually included as built-in features of the software products (e.g., in Excel).

Standalone agents that perform complex tasks, on the other hand, can be quite expensive. Most of the costs of these agents is derived from the tremendous amount of research and development that goes into creating them. In addition, they may be custom programs that require extensive programming time. Justifying agents is like justifying other DSS. The benefits are often intangible, and the results are hard to quantify, but if you do not invest in the technology, your competitor will, and you may be left behind.

SECURITY

Agents are a form of technology with many unknown ramifications. With the great concerns about the security of systems, does it make sense that a company would knowingly send out agents that could come back laden with a virus or hiding a Trojan horse? Will other companies even allow unfamiliar agents to visit their systems?

Firewalls and other available security software and hardware make it possible to forbid entry to an unknown agent, but it is difficult to stop imposters.

PRIVACY

There have been cases in which agents have intruded on people's privacy. For example, Microsoft has built cookies into some of its packages that capture information about new owners and Web users. This information is delivered back (if the user does not object) to Microsoft by its agents when the user logs on to the Internet.

INDUSTRIAL INTELLIGENCE AND ETHICS

Legitimate industrial intelligence gathering is usually expensive and time-consuming. Illegitimate business practices, such as cyber-spying, can be all the more tempting because they are hard to detect, and there are no clear-cut rules or laws governing many of these activities. If a competitor is not satisfied with just getting information about a firm, it can also arm its agents with assault capabilities. Given the borderless nature of the Internet, the risk that an unethical firm will compete unfairly by stealing another's costly research and development becomes even more frightening. What is to keep seemingly friendly programs from doing untold damage? Perhaps it will become possible to build an intelligent agent that can discriminate friendly or neutral agents from belligerent outside agents and take appropriate defensive action.

OTHER ETHICAL ISSUES

Agents represent a significant new way of interacting with the world. Just as a unique etiquette (i.e., netiquette) has evolved on the Internet, there will need to be new definitions of acceptable and unacceptable uses for agents. Who will establish the definitions and the ethical philosophy for how agents are to be used?

New technology is accompanied by new opportunities for those who have access to it. Who will have access to agents? Will all companies have agents? Will those with early access to agents be able to build insurmountable barriers to competition? Will agents displace people from jobs in research and strategic planning?

AGENT LEARNING

The theory behind intelligent agents is that the more you use them, the more they learn and, therefore, the more effective they are. Agents can learn from one of three sources. The first is defined rules established in the programming of the agent. The second is the user interface; in other words, the agent learns the Internet activities and the preferences of the user. The third source is exterior databases or a knowledge base. The managerial issue is one of justifying the cost (i.e., determining which method is most cost-effective) and making sure the agent learns what you want it to learn.

AGENT ACCURACY

Along with agent learning comes agent accuracy. Assuming that the agent develops the ability to learn, the next issue facing managers is the accuracy of the data submitted to and returned by the agent. The inherent desire is to blindly accept recommendations from an agent that has cost so much in both time and money. But is this wise? Managers must be comfortable with the source from which an agent draws data. There must be some control over the quality of this information, or the agent's results will not be believable. Even worse is the possibility that strategic decisions will be made using incorrect information.

HEIGHTENED EXPECTATIONS

With any new technology or product come high expectations. This is especially true of intelligent agents. The concept of having an agent carry out tasks in only a few minutes that would normally take hours or days to accomplish sounds wonderful. But the reality today is that agents are not yet a cure-all in the expanding world of information. Because the development of intelligent agents is far from complete, their cost-effectiveness may be small. This is likely to result in disappointment and rejection by people who are not prepared for what they get. Managers pushing for the use of intelligent agents must communicate with all those involved to ensure that expectations are realistic.

SYSTEM ACCEPTANCE

As with the introduction of any new technology, the addition of intelligent agents to an existing system can sometimes create problems. Systems have different architectures and operating systems. This, along with the presence of a whole host of different software packages that maintain databases, can reduce the effectiveness of agents or even make them nonfunctional. Methods are being developed to provide standards for inter-agent and agent-to-system interoperability.

SYSTEM TECHNOLOGY

As intelligent agents become more powerful, the systems required to run them also must be more powerful. Many companies have computer systems that are only a few years old but are obsolete. Managers must ensure that before investing in agent technology, their system can provide the resources required by the agents. In addition, agent technology is rapidly expanding, so system technology flexibility is a must.

Section 14.11 Review Questions

1. List and describe major managerial issues related to the use of IA.
2. Describe major concerns in cost justification of intelligent systems.
3. Describe major privacy concerns in using intelligent systems.

Chapter Highlights

- Although there are several definitions of IA, basically, they are computer software that execute tasks with some degree of autonomy.
- Intelligent agents can save time and are consistent. Some agents have a considerable amount of autonomy. Others have very little.
- Major characteristics of IA are autonomy, background operation, communication capabilities, and reactivity. Some are mobile (i.e., they can perform tasks in different locations, mainly on the Web). Other agents work in one place (e.g., a server or a workstation).
- The major purpose of IA is to deal with information overload. Agents can also improve productivity, quality, and speed.
- Agents can be classified into three major applications types: Internet, e-commerce, and others.
- Multiagent systems can be used to perform tasks more complex than those performed by single agents, but they have not yet matured.
- Intelligent agents play a major role in data mining, helping to find unnoticeable relationships and quickly providing answers to queries.

- The semantic Web is a new form of representing knowledge on the Web. It enables intelligent agents to exchange knowledge, based on a standard protocol.
- Web services are based on the XML format to represent information that can be shared by different application programs.
- Product recommendation is a very important application of intelligent systems. It analyzes user profiles and makes recommendations based on predicted user interests.
- Recommendation mechanisms can be collaborative, content based, and demographic filtering. Each of these methods has advantages and limitations.
- Applications of intelligent agents must also take managerial issues into consideration, including security, privacy, and other issues.

Key Terms

- agency
- bot
- collaborative filtering
- content-based filtering
- demographic filtering
- distributed artificial intelligence (DAI)
- intelligence
- intelligent agent (IA)
- metasearch engine
- mobile agent
- mobility
- multiagent system
- organizational agent
- personal agent
- private agent
- public agent
- recommendation system (agent)
- search engine
- semantic Web
- semantic Web services
- Web services

Questions for Discussion

1. Relate the Internet to today's information overload problem and discuss how IA can be used to alleviate the problem.
2. Spam control programs have become popular due to the rapid increase of junk mail on the Internet. Discuss how spam control can be done by intelligent agents and whether there are other tasks that are suitable for the application of e-mail agents.
3. Distinguish between a search engine and a metasearch engine. What roles can intelligent agents play in improving search performance?
4. What is the difference between a browsing agent and a search (indexing) agent? What are the situations in which each is more appropriate for decision support?
5. Personalogic and similar agents attempt to learn about people's preferences. Explain how such information can be used in marketing and advertising.
6. What role can IA play in e-commerce? List 10 possible applications of intelligent agents in e-commerce.
7. Some news Web sites allow the user to indicate preferences by selecting the categories of interest and then offering news reports that fit the reader's interests. Explain the pros and cons of this service and similar agents in reducing information overload.
8. Distinguish between DAI and multiagents. What are the advantages and limitations of multiagent systems?
9. Why is negotiation so important in e-commerce? List potential applications of intelligent agents in the negotiation process and the advantage of using IA in negotiation.
10. Review the four levels of IA intelligence. Provide a sample application of intelligent agents at each of these levels.
11. Why is the semantic Web useful for developing a friendlier environment for intelligent agents? What is the difference between the semantic Web and semantic networks and other mechanisms for representing information over the Internet?
12. What is the basic architecture of Web services?
13. Recommendation systems are gaining more popularity in e-commerce. Discuss the pros and cons of using the recommendation mechanism in an electronic shop. Do you like the recommendation mechanism of **amazon.com**? Why or why not?
14. In a recent article, O'Reilly proposed the future Web as Web 2.0. Visit **oreillynet.com** to find the article "What is Web 2.0?" and related articles, and discuss the role intelligent agents can play in the new platform.

Exercises

Teradata University and Other Hands-on Exercises

1. Go to **teradatastudentnetwork.com** and find materials describing the application of intelligent agents and product recommendation. Prepare a report on the role of these technologies in decision support.
2. Go to **teradatastudentnetwork.com** and find materials related to Web services and the semantic Web. Prepare a report on the role of these technologies in decision support.
3. How are IA actually constructed? Investigate the literature and write a report. Visit **robocup.org** and examine the annual RoboCup competition. Explain how IA can be used there.
4. What mundane tasks in your life would you like an intelligent agent to perform for you? List them (you may want to include some tasks that people are handling for you) and describe how an IA could help. Compare your results to those of other class members.
5. Find a software tool for developing intelligent agents, download a demo version, and develop a simple prototype that can automatically alert you when you browse a Web page that contains predefined keywords.

Exercises

Team Assignments and Role-Playing

1. Find an article that reports on the application of intelligent agents to movie recommendations and design a collaborative filtering mechanism for user profile generation and maintenance. What features must be included in the user profile? What mechanism can be used to match the user profile and item features?
2. Find an article that reports on the application of intelligent agents to music recommendation and design a content-based filtering mechanism for such a purpose.
3. Investigate the use of intelligent agents in e-commerce. You can begin with **botspot.com**, and you can find recent work by searching **media.mit.edu** to find the projects under the software agents group, and other Web sites. Prepare a report on recent development after 2000.
4. Prepare a report about the use of collaborative filtering and content-based filtering approaches in online music stores and online electronic retailers. Describe how these methods fit different types of stores.
5. Visit **w3.org** and other Web sites related to the development of the semantic Web. Summarize the rationale for its development and what tools are available for developing semantic Web–based intelligent systems.

Exercises

Internet Exercises

1. Go to **compare.net** and ask the agent to price a specific CD for you. Do you think you can get the CD cheaper at a local store?
2. RINGO (**jolomo.net/ringo.html**) is based on social information filtering. Visit the Web site and explain social information filtering and its possible use to obtain suggestions for music and movies that you might like.
3. Go to **autonomy.com**. Examine the various products and business solutions Autonomy provides. Identify where intelligent systems and agents might be used. Examine their business solutions for customer relationship management, e-commerce, and business intelligence.
4. Post several queries to **google.com** and to **ask.com**. Compare the top 10 answers from each. What are major differences between the two sites? Prepare a report to explain the differences.
5. Find Web sites that describe Web services 2.0 and compare the difference between Web services and Web services 2.0.
6. Use either **google.com** or **ask.com** to find material on recommendation systems and prepare a report on recent applications.

7. Visit **amazon.com** and **bn.com**, search for the same five or six books at each site, and compare the books the two sites then recommend for you. Prepare a report on how their recommendations fit your preferences.
8. Search the Internet to find companies that offer software tools for developing intelligent agents. Compare the major functions and limitations of these tools.

End of Chapter Application Case

Spartan Uses Intelligent Systems to Find the Right Person and Reduce Turnover

Spartan Stores is a retailing chain that owns and operates 85 supermarkets and drugstores in Michigan and Ohio under the D&W Fresh Markets, Family Fare Supermarkets, Glen's Markets, and The Pharm banners. The company also supplies 40,000 private-label and national brand products to more than 350 independent grocery stores.

Problem

Spartan's management recognized that one of the most critical factors in support of its brand position as the Neighborhood Market was in the quality and consistency in the people it hires. Spread across two large states and without centralized hiring standards, the 100+ store managers were hiring with criteria that may not have been consistent across the retail organization. They spent an inordinate amount of time screening candidates, and often not enough attention was given to the crucial qualities of the applicants.

A supermarket manager's day is unbelievably long and stressful as it is. Industry staff turnover is high, over 100 percent. It costs, on average, $3,000 to replace an employee. Spartan's director of human resources, Linda Esparza, put it this way: "We just want to operate our stores better. Customer service is what we're going to use to differentiate ourselves." Some national chains were moving into the market, and Spartan was in a good position to distinguish itself as the neighborly alternative. "It's not the sheer applicant numbers we're looking for," said Esparza. "It's more the efficiency of finding people who are the right cultural fit."

Front-end positions in a supermarket—cashiers, department managers, and baggers—tend to be most critical in terms of a customer service strategy. These are the people who are in direct contact with the customers, who remember their names, who go out of their way to help, and who make them feel welcome. They are also the key element in building customer loyalty, so how to hire the right person for these positions is vital to the success of the business.

Solution

Spartan decided to take advantage of the latest in automated hiring systems. After surveying some solutions available on the market, Spartan adopted Unicru's Hiring Management System. Unicru integrated Spartan's prescreening criteria into its automated application process. It also installed a psychological screening test designed to find the most dependable, friendly, and helpful employees. The system can analyze the profile of an applicant to assess the match between the characteristics of the applicant and the requirements of the position. It plays the role of recommending proper candidates from a huge pool of applicants and can save a substantial amount of time and money. Spartan's system provides Web-based assessments for friendly use. All applicants are asked to use the system. Those recommended by the system are further interviewed and hired. Those assessed to be inappropriate are told that no position fits them. A hiring manger can receive a screened job application within 30 seconds to 4 minutes after an application is complete, along with suggested interview questions targeted to the candidate. In some cases, managers are automatically paged in order to meet a strong candidate before he or she leaves the store.

Benefits

Despite a deep economic recession and increased competition from huge chains such as Wal-Mart, Spartan survived its first quarter (2002) of net loss in its history. By taking smart and swift actions in its operational efficiency, the company quickly returned to profitability in the spring and summer of the same year. Major benefits of deploying the automated hiring system include the following:

- *Reduced turnover rate.* The turnover rate is down from over 100 percent to 59 percent. While this may be partially attributed to the economic recession, hiring more dependable people more consistently has had a large effect.
- *Increased operational efficiency.* The system provides information about the efficiency of its hiring. Now the

human resources manager can look in detail at each store, each region, or the entire enterprise and spot immediate needs as well as long-term trends of human resources needs.

- *Higher functional integration.* The system can use the collected application data to evaluate Work Opportunity Tax Credit (WOTC) eligibility for the company. In just 19 stores, Spartan was able to apply for enough WOTC tax credit so that the system could pay for itself.

Overall, the Spartan system uses intelligent technology to help store managers use less time to achieve higher accuracy in picking the right employee fit. Similar applications can be found in companies such as the Brooks Group in Greensboro, North Carolina, and Finish Line, Inc., a leading athletic retailer based in Indianapolis.

Sources: Adapted from K. Maher, "Web-Based Tools Help Find the Right Persons for the Job," *Wall Street Journal*, November 26, 2002; "Intelligent Employment Agent" *Expert Systems*, 2001, Vol. 18, No. 3, p. 161; and *Spartan Stores: An Opportunity for HR to Impact Profitability*, **unicru.com/Code/Forms/DownloadContent.aspx?Su=48335df0ab5f&Cu=b016a8798c1a&Ct=cs** (accessed September 2006).

QUESTIONS FOR THE CASE

1. Describe the nature of the hiring decisions at Spartan and reasons that an intelligent system is suitable in this case.
2. List the benefits of the system at Spartan. Are there any other benefits that you can foresee that are not described here?
3. What kind of knowledge structure seems to be appropriate for the development and operation of the intelligent hiring system? Review the techniques that you have learned in previous chapters and explain why you picked a particular technique and think it is appropriate.
4. How do you feel about being picked or rejected by a system instead of interviewing with a human manager? What issues can you foresee in the system at Spartan?
5. Can the applicant recommendation system be implemented as a Web service? What are the pros and cons for implementing it as a Web service as compared with implementing it as a traditional rule-based system?

References

Avouris, M., and L. Gasser. (1992). *Distributed Artificial Intelligence: Theory and Praxis.* Boston: Kluwer Academic.

Berners-Lee, T., J. Hendler, and O. Lassila. (2001, May). "The Semantic Web." *Scientific American*, Vol. 284, No. 5.

Bond, A.H., and L. Gasser (eds.). (1988). *Readings in Distributed AI.* San Mateo, CA: Morgan Kaufman.

Bradshaw, J. (ed.). (1997). *Software Agents.* Menlo Park, CA: AAAI Press/MIT Press.

Brenner, W., et al. (1998). *Intelligent Software Agents.* New York: Spring-Verlag.

Bhutani, K., and B. Khan. (2003). "Optimal Distribution of a Hierarchy of Network Management Agents." *Information Sciences*, Vol. 149, No. 4.

Chau, M., D. Zeng, H. Chen, M. Huang, and D. Hendriawan. (2003). "Design and Evaluation of a Multi-Agent Collaborative Web Mining System." *Decision Support Systems*, Vol. 35, No. 1.

Conway, D.G., and G.J. Koehler. (2000, January). "Interface Agents: Caveat Mercater in E-Commerce." *Decision Support Systems*.

Decker, K., M. Fisher, M. Luck, and M. Tennenholtz. (1999, March). "Continuing Research in Multi-Agent System." *Knowledge Engineering Review.*

Decker, S., P. Mitra, and S. Melnik. (2000, November/December). "Framework for the Semantic Web: An RDF Tutorial." *IEEE Internet Computing*, Vol. 4, No. 6.

Detlor, B., and M. Glacomin. (2002). "Web Information Seeking and Retrieval in Digital Library Contexts: Towards an Intelligent Agent Solution." *Online Information Review*, Vol. 26, No. 6.

Etzioni, O. (1996, November). "The WWW: Quagmire or Gold Mine." *Communications of the ACM*, Vol. 39, No. 11.

Etzioni, O., and D.S. Weld. (1994, July). "A Softbot-Based Interface to the Internet." *Communications of the ACM*, Vol. 37, No. 7.

Franklin, S., and A. Graesser. (1996, August 12–13). "Is It an Agent, or Just a Program? A Taxonomy for Autonomous Agents." *Proceedings of the Third International Workshop on Agent Theories, Architecture and Languages, Budapest, Hungary.* Berlin: Springer-Verlag.

Gilbert, D. (1998, May). "Intelligent Agents: The Right Information at the Right Time," *IBM Report.*

Gilbert, D., and P. Janca. (1997, February). *IBM Intelligent Agents*, IBM Corp. (no longer available online).

Goldberg, D., D. Nichols, B. Oki, and D. Terry. (1992) "Using Collaborative Filtering to Weave an

Information Tapestry," *Communications of the ACM*, Vol. 35, No.2.

Hess, T.J., L.P. Rees, and T.R. Rakes. (2000, July). "Using Autonomous Software Agents to Create the Next Generation DSS." *Decision Sciences*.

Huhns, M.N. (2002). "Agents as Web Services." *IEEE Internet Computing*, Vol. 6, No. 4.

Iacobucci, D., P. Arabie, and A. Bodapati. (2000). "Recommendation Agents on the Internet." *Journal of Interactive Marketing*, Vol. 14, No. 3.

Jennings, N.R., et al. (eds.). (1998). *Agent Technology: Foundation, Applications, and Markets.* New York: Springer-Verlag.

Karacapilidis, N., G. Vouros, and J. Darzentas. (2003). "Applying Intelligent Agent Technology in a Collaborative Work Environment." *International Transactions in Operational Research*, Vol. 10, No. 1.

King, D., and K. Jones. (1995, January 3–6). "Competitive Intelligence, Software Robots and the Internet: The NewsAlert Prototype." *Proceedings of the Twenty-Eighth Hawaii International Conference on Systems Sciences HICSS-28, Wailea, HI.* Los Alamitos, CA: IEEE Computer Society Press.

King, J.A. (1995, February). "Intelligent Agents: Bringing Good Things to Life." *AI Expert*, Vol. 10, No. 2.

Knapik, M., and J. Johnson. (1998). *Developing Intelligent Agents for Distributed Systems.* New York: McGraw-Hill, 1998.

Kraft, A., M. Vetter, and S. Pitsch. (2000, January 3–6). "Agent-Driven Online Business in Virtual Communities." *Proceedings of the Thirty-Third Hawaii International Conference on Systems Sciences HICSS-33, Wailea, HI.* Los Alamitos, CA: IEEE Computer Society Press.

Lee, J.W., D.W. Cheung, B. Kao, and J. Law. (1997, January). "Intelligent Agents for Matching Information Providers and Consumers on the Web." *Proceedings of the Thirtieth Hawaii International Conference on Systems Sciences HICSS-30, Wailea, HI.* Los Alamitos, CA: IEEE Computer Society Press.

Lee, K.Y., J.S. Yoon, and G.S. Jo. (2003). "MOCAAS: Auction Agent System Using a Collaborative Mobile Agent in E-Commerce." *Expert Systems with Applications*, Vol. 24, No. 2.

Lee, W.P., C.H. Liu, and C.C. Lu. (2002). "Intelligent Agent–Based Systems for Personalized Recommendations in Internet Commerce." *Expert Systems with Applications*, Vol. 22, No. 4.

Liang, T.P., and J.S. Huang. (2000). "A Framework for Applying Intelligent Agents to Support E-Commerce." *Decision Support Systems*, Vol. 28, pp. 305–317, pp. 23–44.

Liang, T.P., and H.S. Doong. (2000, Spring). "Effect of Bargaining Agents in E-Commerce." *International Journal of E-Commerce*, Vol. 4, No. 3.

Liu, S., A. Akademi, E. Turban, and M. Lee. (2000, May). "Software Agents for Environmental Scanning in Electronic Commerce." *Information Systems Frontiers*.

Lyer, L., R. Singh, and A.F. Salam. (2005, Summer). "Intelligent Agents to Support Information Sharing in B2B e-Marketplaces." *Information Systems Management*.

Maes, P. (1994, July). "Agents That Reduce Work and Information Overload." *Communications of the ACM*, Vol. 37, No. 7.

Maes, P. (1995). "Artificial Life Meets Entertainment: Life-Like Autonomous Agents." *Communications of the ACM*, Vol. 38, No. 11.

Mathieson, I., L. Padgham, and B.Q. Vo. (2005, July 25–29). *Agent Based Travel and Tourism Planning.* AMAS'05, Utrecht, the Netherlands.

Matskin, M., and A. Tveit. (2001). "Mobile Commerce Agents in WAP-Based Services." *Journal of Database Management*, Vol. 12, No. 3.

McBride, B. (2002). "Jena: A Semantic Web Toolkit." *IEEE Internet Computing*, Vol. 6, No. 6.

McCarthy, J. (1958). "Programs with Common Sense." *The Teddington Conference on the Mechanization of Thought Processes*.

Menczer, F. (2003). "Complementing Search Engines with Online Web Mining Agents." *Decision Support Systems*, Vol. 35, No. 2.

Montaldo, E., R. Sacile, and A. Boccalatte. (2003). "Enhancing Workflow Management in the Manufacturing Information System of a Small–Medium Enterprise: An Agent-Based Approach." *Information System Frontiers*, Vol. 5, No. 2.

Montaner, M., B. Lopez, and J.L. de la Rosa. (2003). "A Taxonomy of Recommender Agents on the Internet." *Artificial Intelligence Review*, Vol. 19.

Moundridou, M., and M. Virvou. (2002). "Evaluating the Persona Effect of an Interface Agent in a Tutoring System." *Journal of Computer-Assisted Learning*, Vol. 18, No. 3.

Murch, R., and T. Johnson. (1999). *Intelligent Software Agent.* Upper Saddle River, NJ: Prentice Hall.

Myerson, J. (2002, June 1). *Advancing the Web Services Stack*, **www-128.ibm.com/developerworks/webservices/library/ws-wsa** (accessed April 2006).

Nwana, H.S., and D.T. Ndumu. (1999). "A Perspective on Software Agent Research." *Knowledge Engineering Review*, No. 2.

O'Hare, G.M.P., and M.J. O'Grady. (2003). "Gulliver's Genie: A Multi-Agent System for Ubiquitous and Intelligent Information Content Delivery." *Computer Communications*, Vol. 26, No. 11.

Papazoglou, M.P. (2001). "Agent-Oriented Technology in Support of e-Business." *Communications of the ACM*, Vol. 44, No. 4.

Pardoe, D., and P. Stone (Winter 2004), "TacTex-03: A Supply Chain Management Agent." *SIGecom Exchanges: Special Issue on Trading Agent Design and Analysis*, Vol. 4, No. 3.

Preece, S.A., and S. Decker. (2002). "Intelligent Web Services." *IEEE Intelligent Systems*, Vol. 16, No. 1.

Riekki, J., J. Huhtinen, P. Ala-Siuru, P. Alahuhta, J. Kaartinen, and J. Röning. (2003). "Genie of the Net: An Agent Platform for Managing Services on Behalf of the User." *Computer Communications*, Vol. 26.

Scheraga, D. (2005, July). "Kitchen Comfort: An Automated Agent Enables the UK's MFI to Serve Online Customers in Plain English," *Retail Technology Quarterly*.

Schoder, D., and T. Eymann. (2000). "The Real Challenges of Mobile Agents." *Communications of the ACM*, Vol. 43, No. 6.

Staab, S. (2003). "Web Services: Been There, Done That?" *IEEE Intelligent Systems*, Vol. 17, No. 1.

Stenmark, D. (1999). *Evaluation of Information Agents for the Web*. Department of Information Technology, IT University of Gothenburg, **w3.informatik.gu.se/~dixi/agent/agent.htm** (no longer available online).

Swartz, A. (2002). "MusicBrainz: A Semantic Web Service." *IEEE Intelligent Systems*, Vol. 17, No. 1.

Toffler, A. (1970). *Future Shock.* New York: Bantam Books.

Turban, E., et al. (2006). *E-Commerce: A Managerial Perspective*, 4th ed. Upper Saddle River, NJ: Prentice Hall.

Villa, A. (2002). "Emerging Trends in Large-Scale Supply Chain Management." *International Journal of Production Research*, Vol. 40, No. 15.

Vlahavas, I., N. Bassiliades, I. Sakellariou, M. Molina, and S. Ossowski. (2002). "ExperNet: An Intelligent Multiagent System for WAN Management." *IEEE Intelligent Systems*.

Wooldridge, M. (2002). *An Introduction to MultiAgent Systems.* New York: Wiley.

Yan, Y., J. Yen, and T. Bui. (2000, January 3–6). "A Multi-Agent Based Negotiation Support System for Distributed Transmission Cost Allocation." *Proceedings of the Thirty-Third Annual Hawaii International Conference on Systems Sciences HICSS-33, Wailea, HI.* Los Alamitos, CA: IEEE Computer Society Press.

Yuan, S.T., and Y.W. Tsao. (2003). "A Recommendation Mechanism for Contextual Mobile Advertising." *Expert Systems with Applications*, Vol. 24, No. 4.

Zhou, B., S.C. Hui, and K. Chang. (2006, January/February). "Enhancing Mobile Web Access Using Intelligent Recommendations." *IEEE Intelligent Systems.*

PART

VI

Implementing Decision Support Systems

Learning Objectives for Part VI

- ◆ Understand the process of building or acquiring a support system
- ◆ Describe the options of building versus buying systems
- ◆ Understand the selection criteria of development options
- ◆ Describe implementation issues related to MSS
- ◆ Describe integration issues related to MSS
- ◆ Describe MSS impacts and their future

The concluding part of this book is divided into two chapters. In Chapter 15, we describe the process of building or acquiring a management support system (MSS) infrastructure or a specific application. The chapter starts with the need for a system, describes the construction options available, and then explains some of the available software and vendors.

The MSS technologies described in this book can be implemented as standalone systems, and they can also be integrated with other computer-based systems and among themselves. Chapter 16 provides coverage of the major implementation issues related to such integration. Chapter 16 also describes the major impacts of MSS on individuals, organizations, and society. Chapter 16 closes with a brief discussion of the future of MSS.

CHAPTER 15 System Development and Acquisition

Learning Objectives

- Understand the basic concepts of systems development
- Discuss the major steps in developing a decision support system (DSS) and management support system (MSS) application
- Describe the major MSS applications and list their major functionalities
- List the major MSS application development options, along with their benefits and limitations
- Describe the four phases of the system development lifecycle: planning, analysis, development, and implementation (PADI)
- Understand prototyping and throwaway prototyping and why MSS are typically developed using these methods
- Discuss various MSS application outsourcing options, including the use of an application service provider (ASP) and utility computing
- Describe some major MSS software packages and MSS application suites
- Describe various methods for connecting an MSS application to back-end systems and databases
- Discuss the value and technical foundation of Web services in integrated applications
- Understand the service-oriented architecture (SOA) and its relationship to MSS
- Describe the criteria used in selecting an outsourcing vendor and package
- Describe the factors that lead to MSS success or failure
- Discuss the importance of project management and the skills a good project manager needs to have
- Understand the learning process that occurs during MSS development

So far in this book, we have presented the basic concepts, components, and tools of decision making and decision support. Now we describe how to implement a decision support system (DSS) and management support system (MSS). Unfortunately, acquiring an MSS is not as simple as obtaining productivity software such as a word processing program. MSS are frequently designed to handle complex situations, and few are available right off the shelf. Although online analytical processing (OLAP) software has facilitated decision support development, many MSS require some custom design, development, and implementation for each specific application. We present the MSS development process in the following sections:

15.1 OPENING VIGNETTE: OSRAM SYLVANIA THINKS SMALL, STRATEGIZES BIG TO DEVELOP THE HR INFONET PORTAL SYSTEM

The North American division of Osram GmbH (Germany) has US $3.7 billion in annual sales and 12,500 employees in 30 locations. Osram Sylvania manufactures and markets lighting, precision materials, and component products.

PROBLEM

The lighting industry is highly competitive. Human resources (HR) is strategic to Osram Sylvania. Finding, recruiting, and hiring specialized scientists, engineers, and hourly staff is a major challenge. Employee benefits administration was accomplished at Osram Sylvania with an expensive outsourcing solution. The recruitment problem needed a faster solution than the existing, slow, tedious paper-based system. With the existing system, employees could not do what-if comparisons or even see the cost of the programs they chose because it was voice activated. Another problem was that the system did not perform routine life status changes (e.g., adding a child to a family's benefits). These requests were handled manually. Improvement was clearly necessary. An interactive Web portal for employee self-service benefits would improve employee service.

Bringing job requisitions and benefits enrollment online was the initial goal of HR InfoNet. While the information technology (IT) requirements were relatively straightforward, there were two internal issues. The first was that only about one-third of the employees had computers. The second was that the head of the project, Roger Rudenstein, had been hired in 1995 to head up the PeopleSoft system group to maintain and extend the PeopleSoft HR system and the interface with the new payroll system. The group was so busy with the payroll conversion that it could not start the HR portal until early 1996.

SOLUTION

There was a sense from earlier projects that an intranet was the appropriate technology platform for the HR system at Osram Sylvania. This first decision, to build an intranet, was adopted. Roger championed the project from the IT side, and Geoff Hunt, Vice President of HR, and Nancy Dobrusin and Julie Thibodeau, also in the HR department, championed it from the business side. They also had ongoing support from Michelle Marshall and the corporate communications department throughout the process.

The team adopted the strategy "think small, strategize big." Resources were minimal for developing HR InfoNet. There were no dedicated staff, no funds to hire consultants, and no budget, despite the fact that this was a crucially strategic project. Roger targeted a solution that they could make workable. "Think small" meant that it was necessary to conserve both money and precious time. "Strategize big" meant that the development platform and solution architecture would have to handle future applications as well as current solutions as the portal grew in capability (i.e., it had to be scalable). It was almost a given that in-house technology was to be used. This cut down on IT staff training and licensing.

After a few suggestions from several co-workers and some evaluation of potential systems, the team adopted Lotus Notes and a Domino server. The team developed experience by doing the project. Within three months, the team had successfully deployed a portal application for posting job requisitions in LotusScript and Notes/Domino databases with agents. This validated the technology, so the team continued with the next application, allowing employees to examine and correct their benefits online. For employees without computers, the team developed kiosks that used standard browsers with special security features. Hourly employees were given network IDs and training.

The next step of the job requisition application process was to create an intranet-based workflow to allow managers to describe job openings and route them to the correct HR person, using online forms. These postings now can be submitted directly to the corporate Web site. After successfully creating the initial HR InfoNet portal, the team expanded it to include more HR benefits and compensation information.

RESULTS

In early 2000, the portal allowed employees to view their benefits, compare the costs of different programs, access information to help make their benefits decisions, change benefits enrollment, and perform many HR management duties, such as developing plans for salary reviews, management bonus programs, head count reports, and retirement packages. By then, the portal served as the focal point for the firm's job postings, requisitions, and hiring workflow, as well as the interface with HR benefits for all employees.

Employee feedback on the new HR capabilities has been extremely positive. Recruiting cycle time has improved, and HR productivity is higher. HR benefits administration is much more user friendly, and even kiosk users have embraced the system. By taking benefits administration in-house, the company saves $500,000 annually—an excellent return on the project.

Success leads to success, and the team is developing more applications within and like HR InfoNet. HR InfoNet proved the validity of the portal concept. The team is continuing to develop new applications in succession planning, performance management processes (PMP), and time and attendance. Over three years, Osram Sylvania estimates a 251 percent return on investment (ROI) and a savings of $1.5 million.

Sources: Compiled from R. Rudenstein, "A Bright Idea: HR Portal Helps Osram Sylvania See the Light," *Enterprise Systems Journal*, January 2000, pp. 24–30; and **sylvania.com** (accessed February 2006).

Questions for the Opening Vignette

1. What was the strategic business need in this case? What were the benefits of the completed HR InfoNet system? Explain.
2. Why was it important to have an IT champion, a functional business (HR) champion, and an executive champion involved in the project?
3. Who were the users of the project? What decisions did the system assist the users in making?
4. How were the users involved in the system development? How was management involved?
5. Do you feel that if the development team had "thought big"—that is, tried to design and develop a total solution over a long period of time—it would have succeeded? What could have gone wrong? Do you think the team knew this in advance?
6. What technology issues, behavioral issues, and implementation issues had to be worked through in developing the HR InfoNet system?
7. What implementation approach was adopted? Why?
8. Comment on how success breeds success in MSS development.

WHAT WE CAN LEARN FROM THIS VIGNETTE

The "think small, strategize big" prototyping approach led to a major success for the HR InfoNet portal at Osram Sylvania. Rather than trying to create a mega-enterprise portal for everyone and everything, companies often focus on first building a small, specialized portal that solves a pressing problem in a particular department or business function—a prototype. That is the way the small, motivated team of IT and business staff at Osram Sylvania approached HR InfoNet, a portal focused on human resources.

Instead of thinking big and trying to solve every problem at once, which is how traditional systems analysis works, the HR InfoNet team used a focused approach, tackling the key problem first and then moving on to another problem. This evolutionary development (i.e., iterative development) is known formally as *prototyping*. Thinking big can lead to million-dollar budgets, hiring of staff, preparation of thousands of pages of specifications, and so on. In addition, a large project is much less likely to succeed than a small project. Instead, the Osram Sylvania team strategized big by developing a plan and technology strategy to achieve some quick successes, while offering a solid foundation on which to build for the future.

In the Technology Insights W15.1.1 in Online File W15.1, we present Osram Sylvania's practical insights related to applying the philosophy of "think small, strategize big."

15.2 WHAT TYPES OF SUPPORT SYSTEMS SHOULD YOU BUILD?

There are a variety of MSS applications, ranging from small end-user productivity aids to large-scale enterprise (i.e., organizational) business intelligence (BI) systems. The approach you take in building a support system depends on what you are going to build as well as organizational resources and other factors, which are discussed throughout this chapter.

INTRODUCTION TO MSS DEVELOPMENT

The HR InfoNet system illustrates a number of important MSS/BI development and implementation issues. It was built using a development approach called *prototyping*. The development team started small and expanded the system over time. It developed the system sequentially, in modules. As each module was completed, the team refined it and deployed it to users. Then the next module was developed, refined, and added to the system, then the next, and so on. The system evolved as more and more subsystems could be feasibly developed within the budget and on time. In addition, as the team and managers learned more about business problems by working with users and managers throughout the development process, they were able to refine the way the older subsystems worked and use their new-found knowledge in developing the new modules. As the team learned more about the structure of the real system from MSS users and experts, it incorporated the new knowledge into the newer modules and either updated the older ones or scheduled them to be updated.

The large-scale HR InfoNet system was developed quickly by using a common inhouse technology platform. HR InfoNet was created by a team consisting of IT specialists and HR specialists. This was an enterprise MSS designed to be used on a recurring basis by many employees, some of whom were not computer literate. The system continues to evolve because its success has led managers and the team to see new ways to apply the ideas developed with this system to other decision-making situations.

Development of an MSS, especially a large one, is a complicated process. It involves issues ranging from technical (e.g., hardware selection, networking) to behavioral (e.g., user interfaces, training, the potential impact on individuals, groups, and the entire organization). This chapter concentrates mainly on MSS software development issues.

Because there are several types and categories of MSS, there is no single best approach to MSS development. There are many variations because of the differences in organizations, decision makers, and the MSS problem area. Some MSS are designed to support a one-time decision, others support multiple decisions. Some systems can be developed in a few days, using an OLAP package, a spreadsheet, or another tool, whereas others, like Osram Sylvania's HR InfoNet, took several months and continue to evolve over several years. We next explore issues involving MSS development.

TYPES OF SUPPORT SYSTEMS

Several types of decision support exist. Representative examples are described in the following sections.

Infrastructure

Infrastructure refers to hardware and/or software that is used for many decision support applications. For example, a portal can be used for data access, collaboration, or BI analyses. A data warehouse can be used for MSS applications, such as data mining, but it can also be used for e-commerce or regulatory compliance purposes. Thus, it is important to distinguish between dedicated MSS infrastructure that may not exist in an organization and must be constructed and existing shared infrastructure (e.g., networks, corporate databases).

The following are typical MSS-oriented infrastructures:

- Data warehouses and business intelligence systems (see Chapter 5)
- Knowledge management systems (see Chapter 11)
- Enterprise information systems (see Chapter 17, an online chapter)
- Portals (see the next section and Chapter 17, an online chapter)

Portals

A **portal** is a single Web interface that provides personalized access to information, applications, business processes, and much more. With portal technology, an organization can lower development and deployment costs and significantly increase productivity. By using a portal, a company can aggregate and integrate information within a particular working environment, application, or service, or it can use a single interface to target an individual user's needs and interests. Portals help to harmonize content, commerce, and collaboration with business goals, as described in the opening vignette. For detailed information on portals, see Chapter 17 (an online chapter).

Specific Applications

A specific application is software that is designed to help a user(s) perform a specific task or make a specific decision. Examples of MSS applications are how much material to order and when, whether to approve a loan request, and how to best allocate resources.

Tools and Tool Kits

In the early days of MSS, companies built their own MSS construction tools, which were used for multiple applications in one organization. Over time, vendors began to develop tools, some of which were unique to MSS and others of which could be used for non-MSS applications as well. Tools were constructed for one purpose only (e.g., a spreadsheet builder), or they were integrated in a tool kit (previously referred to as a *DSS generator*). For example, Lotus 1-2-3 was the first generator that combined three tools: (1) a spreadsheet, (2) database management functionality, and (3) graphics. Today, the most popular MSS end-user tool kit is Microsoft's Excel. It integrates dozens of tools and functions.

Intelligent systems are built with a variety of tools. These tools are listed in Chapter 12 through 14 and in Chapter 18 (an online chapter).

Platforms

For large or complex applications, which are usually built by IT professionals, a company can use complex (and expensive) tool kits usually referred to as *platforms* (or *suites*), such as MicroStrategy 8.

Section 15.2 Review Questions

1. Distinguish between in-house developed and vendor-built systems.
2. List the different types of supported systems.
3. Define *infrastructure* and list some MSS examples.

15.3 THE LANDSCAPE AND FRAMEWORK OF MANAGEMENT SUPPORT SYSTEMS APPLICATION DEVELOPMENT

The diversity of MSS models and applications requires a variety of development methodologies and approaches. Small applications with a few key components can be developed using HTML, Java, or another programming language. They can also be quickly implemented by using commercial packages, or they can be leased from an *application service provider (ASP)*. Larger or special MSS applications can be developed in-house or outsourced. Building medium to large applications requires extensive integration with existing information systems, such as corporate databases, intranets, enterprise resource planning (ERP), and other application programs.

Therefore, the process of building MSS may vary. However, in many cases, it follows a fairly standard form.

The development process for a typical MSS application has five major steps, which are shown in Figure 15.1. The steps in a development process are discussed in the following sections.

STEP 1: PLANNING, IDENTIFYING, AND JUSTIFYING MSS

MSS applications, like all other information systems, are usually built as *enablers* of some business process(es). Therefore, their planning must be aligned with that of the organization's overall business plan and the specific decisions or tasks they intended to support. Such processes may need to be restructured to fully reap the benefits of the supporting MSS. Also, if at all possible, the systems must be justified (e.g., through a cost–benefit analysis). Both of these activities may be complex, but they are necessary, especially for systems that require a great investment to acquire, operate, and maintain. The output of this step is a decision to go (or not) with a specific application and to decide on a timetable, budget, and assigned responsibility. This step is usually done

FIGURE 15.1 The Process of MSS Application Development

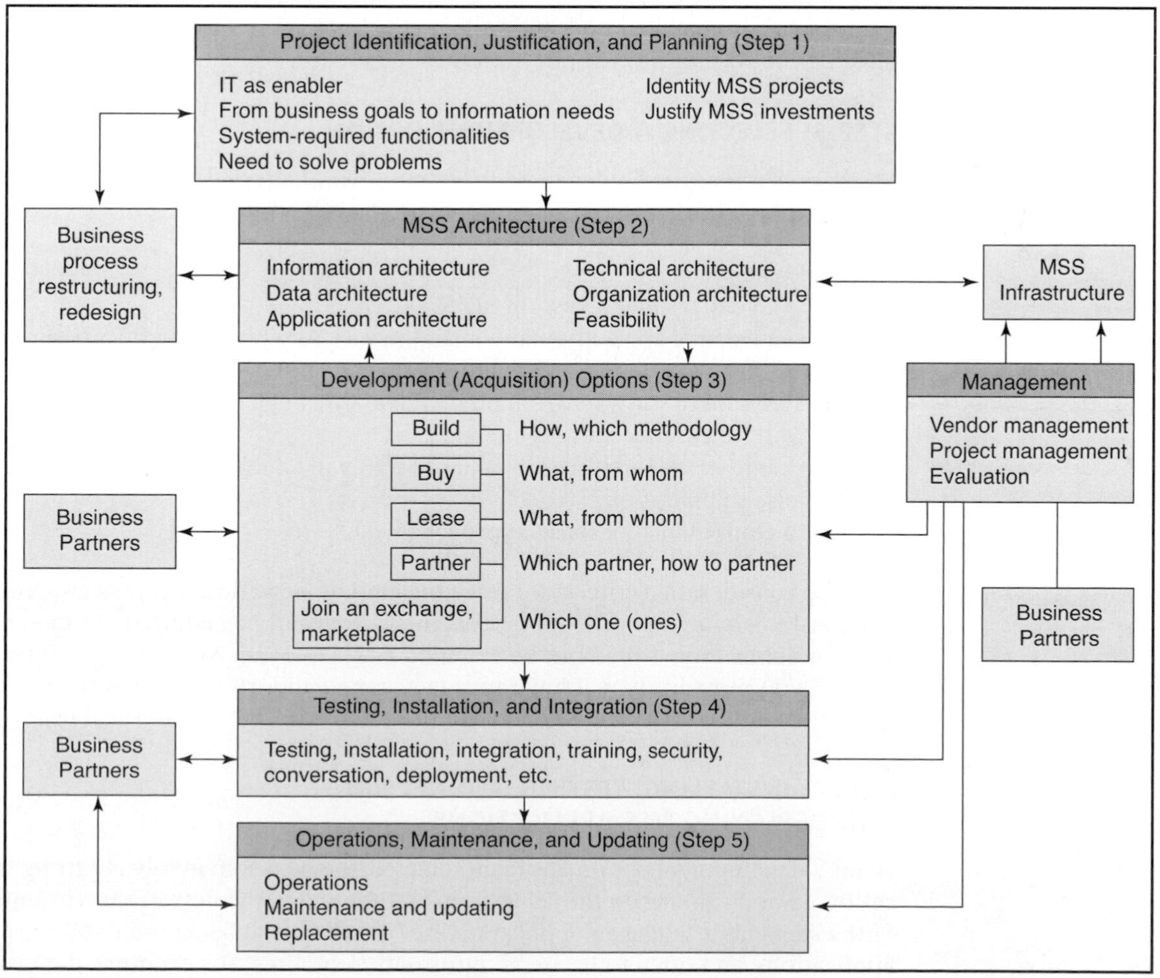

Project Identification, Justification, and Planning (Step 1)
IT as enabler
From business goals to information needs
System-required functionalities
Need to solve problems
Identity MSS projects
Justify MSS investments

Business process restructuring, redesign

MSS Architecture (Step 2)
Information architecture
Data architecture
Application architecture
Technical architecture
Organization architecture
Feasibility

MSS Infrastructure

Development (Acquisition) Options (Step 3)
Build — How, which methodology
Buy — What, from whom
Lease — What, from whom
Partner — Which partner, how to partner
Join an exchange, marketplace — Which one (ones)

Business Partners

Management
Vendor management
Project management
Evaluation

Business Partners

Testing, Installation, and Integration (Step 4)
Testing, installation, integration, training, security, conversation, deployment, etc.

Business Partners

Operations, Maintenance, and Updating (Step 5)
Operations
Maintenance and updating
Replacement

in-house (with consultants, if needed). All other steps can be done in-house, or they can be outsourced.

STEP 2: CREATING AN MSS ARCHITECTURE

An **MSS architecture** is a plan for organizing the underlying infrastructure and applications of an MSS project. The plan includes the information and data required to fulfill the business goals and vision; the application modules that will deliver and manage the information and data; the specific hardware and software on which the application modules will run, as well as the security, scalability, and reliability required by the applications; and the human resources and procedures for implementing the MSS project.

Various IT tools and methodologies can be used to support the creation of an MSS application architecture (e.g., see Kendall and Kendall, 2005). Because the creation of an architecture is an iterative process, collaborative methodologies such as joint application development (JAD) are especially useful in identifying and modifying system requirements.

The results obtained from step 2 are routed to the strategic planning level (e.g., to a steering committee). Based on the results of step 2, the application portfolio (i.e., mix of applications) or a specific project may be changed. For example, the steering committee may defer or scale down a specific project because it is too risky. When the architecture is compiled and the project gets final approval, a decision about how to develop the specific MSS application must be made.

STEP 3: SELECTING A DEVELOPMENT OPTION

MSS applications can be developed through several alternative approaches, which are discussed in detail in Section 15.4. These are the major options:

- Build the system in-house
- Have a vendor build a custom-made system
- Buy an existing application and install it, with or without modifications, by yourself or through a vendor
- Lease standard software from an ASP, lease through utility computing, or set up a software-as-a-service arrangement
- Enter into a partnership or an alliance that will enable the company to use someone else's application
- Use a combination of these approaches

The consideration criteria for selecting among the various options are presented in Section 15.6. After an option is chosen, the system can be acquired. At the end of this step, an application is ready to be installed and deployed. No matter what option you choose, you most likely will have to select some vendor(s) and/or software, and then you will need to work with and manage the vendor(s) (see Section 15.11).

STEP 4: INSTALLING, TESTING, CONNECTING, AND DEPLOYING MSS APPLICATIONS

After a development option has been selected, the next step involves getting the application up and running on the selected hardware and in the network environment. One of the steps in installing an application is connecting it to back-end databases, to other applications, and often to partners' information systems. For example, if a prospective customer orders a product from your Web site, it would be helpful if the site could determine whether the product is in stock. To do this, the ordering system would need to be connected to the inventory system. Details of the connection process are provided in Section 15.8. This step can be done in-house, or it can be outsourced.

During this step, the modules that have been installed need to be tested. A series of tests are required (see Sommerville, 2004): *unit testing* (i.e., testing the modules one at a time), *integration testing* (i.e., testing the combination of modules acting in concert), *usability testing* (i.e., testing the quality of the user's experience when interacting with your portal or Web site), and *acceptance testing* (i.e., determining whether the MSS application meets the original business objectives and vision).

When the applications pass all the tests, they can be deployed to the end users. This step involves issues such as conversion (from the old system to the new system) strategies, training, and resistance to change. These procedures are similar to those conducted for any IT application (see Whitten and Bentley, 2005).

STEP 5: OPERATIONS, MAINTENANCE, AND UPDATING

It usually takes as much time, effort, and money to operate and maintain an application as it does to build and install it in the first place. To enjoy continual usage, an application needs to be continually updated. For example, for an electronic ordering and inventory system, new products need to be added to a catalog, prices need to be changed, and new promotions need to be run. These changes and updates need to undergo the same testing procedures used during the installation process. In addition, usage patterns and performance need to be studied to determine which parts of the underlying applications should be modified or eliminated.

MANAGING THE DEVELOPMENT PROCESS

The development process can be fairly complex and must be managed properly (e.g., Xia and Lee, 2004). For medium to large applications, a project team is usually created to manage the process and the vendors. Projects can be managed with *project management* software; examples of various project management software are provided in Online File 15.2 and at **office.microsoft.com/project** and **primavera.com**. Appropriate management also includes periodic evaluations of system performance. Standard project management techniques and tools are useful for this task. Finally, implementing an MSS project may require restructuring of one or more business processes. See Kanter and Walsh (2004) for further discussion of this topic.

Section 15.3 Review Questions

1. List and briefly describe the major steps in developing an MSS application.
2. Define the various types of testing used during the MSS application development process.

15.4 DEVELOPMENT OPTIONS FOR MANAGEMENT SUPPORT SYSTEMS APPLICATIONS

There are three basic options for developing an MSS: (1) develop the MSS in-house, either from scratch or with off-the-shelf components; (2) buy a packaged MSS designed for a particular type of business; or (3) lease the MSS application from a third party. Each of these approaches has benefits and limitations, as described in the following sections.

IN-HOUSE DEVELOPMENT: INSOURCING

The first generation of MSS were constructed largely through proprietary programming and in-house development. Using this approach, programmers used generic programming languages (e.g., fourth-generation languages) as well as specifically developed programming tools, such as interactive financial planning systems (IFPS). While this first generation of MSS development built up valuable experience and achieved industrial momentum, the lack of reusability in current MSS applications and the lack of interoperability standards created a great barrier to widespread application of MSS.

Although in-house development—called *insourcing*—can be time-consuming and costly, it may create MSS applications that better fit an organization's strategy and vision and differentiate it from the competition, which may be using standard applications that can be bought or leased. However, the in-house development of MSS applications is a challenging task because most applications are novel and may involve multiple organizations. Shurville and Williams (2005) demonstrated how a combination of project management and change-management methodologies guided successful in-house development of a campus-wide information system.

Development Options for In-house Development.

Three major options exist for in-house development:

- *Building from scratch.* This option should be considered only for specialized MSS applications for which components are not available. This option is expensive and slow, but it provides the best fit to an organization's needs.
- *Building from components.* The required applications are often constructed from standard components (e.g., random-number generators, Web servers such as Microsoft's IIS). Commercially-packaged and homegrown components must integrate tightly for component-based development to meet its requirements. This is especially critical for decision support for real-time applications and for e-business. Organizations are attempting to connect their strategic MSS applications with the back office and with industry portals and even electronic communities, opening the enterprise to business partners, customers, suppliers, and new markets. The scope of component integration and code reuse is broadening, too. Component reuse may be the key to integration, especially if the components have been integrated in other applications (see Srivastava, 2004). For a methodology of evaluating component-based MSS, see Dahanayake et al. (2003).
- *Integrating applications.* The application integration option is similar to building from components, but instead of using components, this option uses entire applications. This is an especially attractive option when MSS from several business partners need to be integrated. Integration methods such as using Web services or enterprise application integration (EAI) can be used (see Bussler et al., 2005).

Insourcing is a challenging task that requires specialized IT procedures and resources. For this reason, most organizations usually rely on packaged applications or completely outsource the development and maintenance of their MSS.

METHODS USED IN IN-HOUSE DEVELOPMENT

Several methods can be used when developing MSS in-house. The major ones are discussed in the following sections.

System Development Lifecycle

The **system development lifecycle (SDLC)** is the traditional system-development method that organizations use for large MSS projects. SDLC is a structured framework that consists of sequential processes by which MSS are developed. A traditional SDLC consists of four fundamental phases—planning, analysis, design, and implementation (PADI)—which lead to a deployed system, as shown in Figure 15.2. The processes, in turn, consist of well-defined tasks. Large projects typically require all the tasks, whereas smaller MSS development projects may require only a subset of the tasks.

Other models for the SDLC may contain more or fewer than the four stages presented here. The flow of tasks, however, remains largely the same, regardless of the number of stages. In the past, developers used the *waterfall approach* to the SDLC, in which tasks in one stage were completed before the work proceeded to the next stage. Today, systems developers go back and forth among the stages, as necessary. See Satzinger et al. (2006) for a more detailed discussion of the SDLC.

Rapid Application Development

Rapid application development (RAD) methodologies adjust the SDLC so that parts of a system can be developed quickly and users can obtain some functionality as soon as possible. It is useful in developing Web-based MSS via Web programming tools. Because Web sites, especially e-commerce sites, evolve quickly and continually, RAD methods are critical for their development. The RAD methodology involves breaking a system into a series of versions that are developed sequentially. Each version has more functionality than the previous one, as they evolve into a final system. The advantage of RAD is that users gain functionality quickly; the disadvantage is that the systems with which users start to work are incomplete by design.

We now turn to the major methodology under which many MSS are developed: prototyping (see Satzinger et al., 2006).

FIGURE 15.2 The Traditional System Development Lifecycle (SDLC)

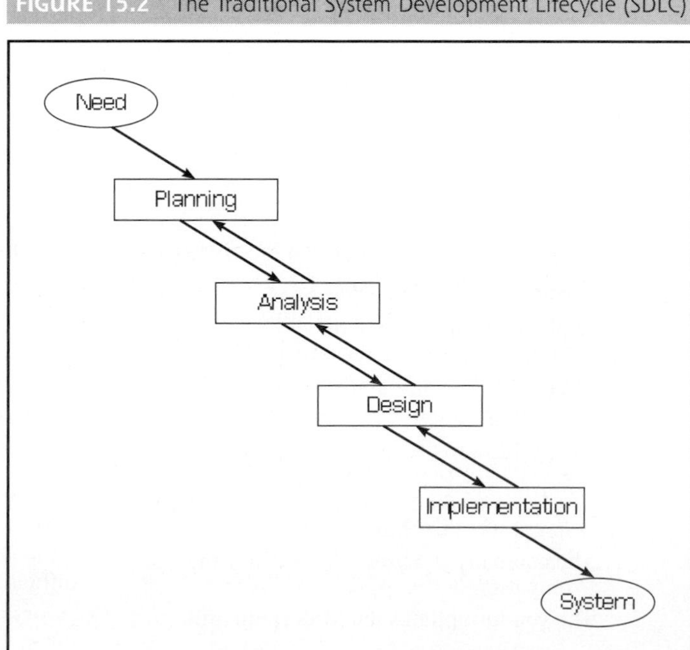

Prototyping

Prototyping involves performing the analysis, design, and implementation phases concurrently and repeatedly. Each time some work is done, it is shown to potential users. Based on their responses, an improvement is made, and the system is shown again to the user. After several iterations, no more improvements are suggested. Then the system is deployed. This method is frequently used in MSS and is discussed in Section 15.5.

Buying Applications

By definition, MSS are unstructured; however, they can support generic classes of tasks, such as resource allocation or inventory management. Therefore, a number of commercial packages provide standard features required by MSS. This option is also known as the *turnkey approach*. It involves buying a commercial MSS package, installing it, and starting it up. Buying a commercial MSS package requires much less time and money than in-house development. A particular package should not only satisfy current needs, it must also be flexible enough to handle future needs; otherwise, the package may quickly become obsolete. In addition, because one package can rarely meet all of an organization's requirements, it is sometimes necessary to acquire multiple packages. In this case, the packages need to be integrated with each other and with other software and data. Some vendors are willing to modify their packaged software to better fit with an organization's needs. Others do not allow it. The advantages and disadvantages of buying MSS software are provided in Table 15.1.

Buying a ready-made MSS package is especially attractive if the software vendor allows for modifications. However, this option may not be attractive in cases of high-obsolescence rates or high-package cost. In such cases, a company should consider leasing in what is known today as *software-as-a-service*.

Leasing Applications

Leasing an MSS package can result in substantial cost and time savings. In cases in which extensive maintenance is required or in which the cost of buying is very high, leasing is very advantageous, especially for small to medium enterprises. Leasing is also advantageous when a company wants to experiment with an MSS package before making a heavy up-front purchase investment, protect its own internal networks, quickly utilize the application, or rely on experts to establish a major project, usually with a Web site.

TABLE 15.1 Advantages and Disadvantages of Ready-Made MSS Packages

Advantages of MSS Packages	*Disadvantages of MSS Packages*
Many different types of off-the-shelf MSS packages are available.	MSS packages may not exactly meet the company's needs.
They save time and money (compared to in-house development).	MSS packages may be difficult or impossible to modify, or they may require huge business process changes.
The company need not hire programmers specifically dedicated to an MSS project.	The company may experience loss of control over improvements and new versions.
The company knows what it is getting before it invests in the MSS.	Off-the-shelf MSS applications can be difficult to integrate with existing systems.
The company is neither the first nor the only user.	Vendors may drop a product or go out of business.
The vendor updates the MSS frequently.	

Leasing can be done in several different ways:

- Lease the MSS from an *outsourcer* and then install it on the company's premises. The vendor can help with the installation and may offer to contract for the operation and maintenance of the system as well. Many conventional MSS applications are leased this way.
- Lease the MSS application from an ASP that hosts the application at its data center. An ASP is an agent or a vendor that assembles the software needed by enterprises and packages it, usually with outsourced development, operations, maintenance, and other services. Major ASPs for enterprise MSS are MicroStrategy, Oracle, Microsoft, and IBM. A variation of this option is to use utility computing, which is described in detail later in this chapter.

Software-as-a Service

Software-as-a-service(SaaS) refers to software that being rented instead of being sold. Rather than purchase a software product and pay for occasional upgrades, a company can opt for software-as-a-service, which is subscription-based and includes updates being provided during the term of the subscription. When the subscription period expires, the software is no longer valid. Web-based applications lend themselves to the software-as-a-service model because they can be easily controlled at the server level. Software-as-a-service usually costs less than store-bought software and requires users to install and boot up nothing more than a browser. The biggest obstacle to renting software is the basic inability to integrate different applications. Sharing data between a customer resource management (CRM) program and billing software, for example, is a challenge, especially if some of the applications are hosted and others are kept in-house.

A rent-versus-buy consideration is shown in Table 15.2.

These are the major factors driving the switch to software-as-a-service are (see D'Agostino, 2005):

- Reducing the risks involved in acquiring new software
- Influencing product and service quality via an ongoing relationship with vendors
- Changing usage commitments as business circumstances change

TABLE 15.2 Considerations in Renting Versus Buying Software

Consider Software as a Service if Your Company:	*Consider a Traditional License if:*
Has an expense budget that is larger than its capital budget	The application requires a great deal of customization or integration
Has limited IT support	You have a team of dedicated IT personnel
Has a distributed workforce	You have already invested significantly in internal IT operations
Has a sales- or service-oriented business model	Laws require data to remain behind your firewall
Has ever-changing computing needs and requirements	You need a fixed amount of computing resources
Needs to free IT resources to business	The application is tied to a core function of your focus on critical business operations

Sources: D. D'Agostino, "Rent or Buy," *CIO Insight*, May 2005; and L. Witner and T. Krumwiede, "Purchasing, Leasing and Developing Software," *Tax Adviser*, 2003, Vol. 34, Part 7, pp. 404–407.

- Preparing financially justifiable business cases
- More accurately predicting ongoing expenses, with IT budgets being tightened and scrutinized for better ROI and value

OUTSOURCING DEVELOPMENT OPTIONS

In developing MSS, outsourcing is a viable option because many systems need to be built quickly, and special expertise is needed. The End of Chapter Application Case illustrates how, Sterngold, a 100-year-old dental product manufacturer, took the plunge to e-commerce by trusting an application outsourcer to move its sales initiative online. MSS software delivery from ASP is another very popular option.

Outsourcing

Small- or medium-sized companies with small IT staffs and small budgets are best served by outside contractors. Outside contractors have also proven to be a good choice for large companies in certain circumstances. Use of outside contractors to provide MSS applications is called *outsourcing*. Large companies may choose outsourcing when they want to experiment with new MSS technologies without a great deal of up-front investment or a need to to rely on experts. Outsourcers can perform many tasks in MSS applications development. For example, they can plan, program, build applications, integrate, operate, and maintain. It is useful to develop good relationships with the outsourcers (see Kishore et al., 2003).

One of the most common types of MSS outsourcing is the use of ASP.

Application Service Providers (ASP)

An **application service provider (ASP)** manages MSS servers and/or a data warehouse in a centrally controlled location rather than on a customer's site. MSS applications are then accessed via the Internet or value added networks (VANs) through a standard Web browser interface. Such an arrangement provides a full range of services for the company using the ASP: MSS applications can be scaled, upgrades and maintenance can be centralized, physical security over the MSS applications and servers can be guaranteed, and the necessary critical mass of human resources can be efficiently utilized. Daylami et al. (2005) discussed the determinants of ASP adoption as an innovation.

The client businesses pay monthly fees to the ASP. In general, the fees include payment for the application software, hardware, service and support, maintenance, and upgrades. Such fees can be fixed or based on utilization. Gartner, Inc., predicted renting to be the software model of choice by 2008, with more than 50 percent of all software purchases being made on a subscription rather than license basis (reported by D'Agostino, 2005). As of 2006, however, software buying was still widespread. Leasing is growing rapidly, though, resulting in the success of new ASP vendors, such as **salesforce.com**.

Leasing MSS from an ASP is a particularly desirable option for small- to medium-sized businesses, for which in-house development and operation of IT applications can be time-consuming and expensive. Leasing from an ASP saves various expenses (such as labor costs) in the initial development stage. It also helps reduce software maintenance, upgrade, and user training costs in the long run. A company can select other software products from the same ASP to meet its changing needs and does not have to invest further in upgrading the existing one. Thus, overall business competitiveness can be strengthened through reducing the time to market and enhancing the ability to adapt to changing market conditions. Leasing from an ASP is particularly effective for MSS applications for which timing, flexibility, and agility are crucial.

Leasing from an ASP also has disadvantages. Many companies are concerned with the adequacy of protection offered by the ASP against hackers, theft of confidential information, and virus attacks. Also, leased software often does not provide the perfect fit for the desired application.

From the ASP vendor's point of view, the benefits presented by the ASP model are numerous. For one, in the long-distance carrier and Internet service providers (ISP) markets, revenues are squeezed due to heavy competition. These companies are looking to generate revenues from sources other than connectivity and transport, and ASP services offer one new outlet. An interesting institution is the ASP Industry Consortium (**aspstreet.com**), whose founding members include AT&T, Cisco, Citrix Systems, Ernst & Young, Verizon, IBM, Marimba, Sharp Electronic, Sun Microsystems, UUNET, and Verio.

A detailed list of the benefits and risks associated with ASP is provided in Table 15.3.

TABLE 15.3 Benefits and Risks of Using an ASP

Type of ASP	*Benefits*	*Potential Risks*
Business	Reduces the need to attract and retain skilled IT professionals. Enables companies to concentrate on strategic use of IT. Enables small- and medium-sized companies to use Tier 1 applications (e.g., ERP, SCM, CRM). Application scalability enables rapid growth of companies.	Leads to loss of control and high level of dependence on the ASP. The ASP may be unable to deliver quality of service; it may lack skills and experience.
Technical	Application deployment is fast and easy. Applications can be standardized to a higher degree. Enables access to a wide range of applications. Application maintenance is simplified and performed by the ASP. User support and training are simplified.	The level of customization and legacy application integration offered by the ASP may be insufficient. Bandwidth limitations may make reliability low, and slow the speed of delivery. The ASP may not be able to deal with security and confidentiality issues.
Economic	The total cost of ownership is low. Low up-front investments in hardware and software are required. Cost control is improved as a result of the subscription costs being predictable.	The ASP's pricing changes may be unpredictable for application updates and services.
Maintenance	The vendor provides maintenance for many customers. It may be possible to select another MSS application from the ASP to meet changing needs. No need to invest in upgrading the existing one.	Modification may not fit exactly the right needs. Could become the victim of pass-the-buck syndrome when calling for technical support. The ASP may not control all the processes involved in a system failure.

Sources: T. Kern and J. Kweijger, "An Exploration of the ASP Outsourcing Option," *Proceedings, 34th HICSS Conference,* Maui, Hawaii, January 3–6, 2001.

An important variation of leasing and ASP is *utility computing*, described in the next section.

Utility (On-Demand) Computing

Tapping into computing resources as easily as we plug a lamp into an electrical outlet has been a goal of many companies for years. This approach is known as **utility (on-demand) computing**. The idea is to provide unlimited computing power and storage capacity that can be used and reallocated for any application—and billed on a pay-per-use basis. Coulter (2005) explored the business values of utility computing.

Utility computing consists of a virtualized pool of self-managing MSS and other IT resources that can be continually reallocated to meet the organization's changing business and service needs. These resources can be located anywhere and managed by an organization's IT staff or a third-party service provider. Equally important, usage of these resources can be tracked and billed down to the level of an individual user or group.

As shown in Figure 15.3, the utility computing value proposition consists of three layers of tools and two types of value-added services. Each tool must be seamlessly integrated to create a comprehensive solution, but the tools are usually implemented separately. These are the three tools:

- *Policy-based service-level-management tools.* These tools coordinate, monitor, and report on the ways in which multiple infrastructure components come together to deliver a business service.
- *Policy-based resource-management tools.* These tools automate and standardize all types of IT management best practices, from initial configuration to ongoing fault management and asset tracking.
- *Virtualization tools.* These tools allow server, storage, and network resources to be deployed and managed as giant pools and seamlessly changed as needs change.

These three tools share multisourcing delivery and framework services (left side of Figure 15.3) and provide for customer access and management services (right side of Figure 15.3).

Utility computing still faces daunting obstacles. One obstacle is the immaturity of the tools. Another is the fact that each vendor prefers to push its own unique variation of the utility computing vision and standards, with different (often confusing) names

FIGURE 15.3 The Five Elements of a Successful Utility Computing Value Proposition

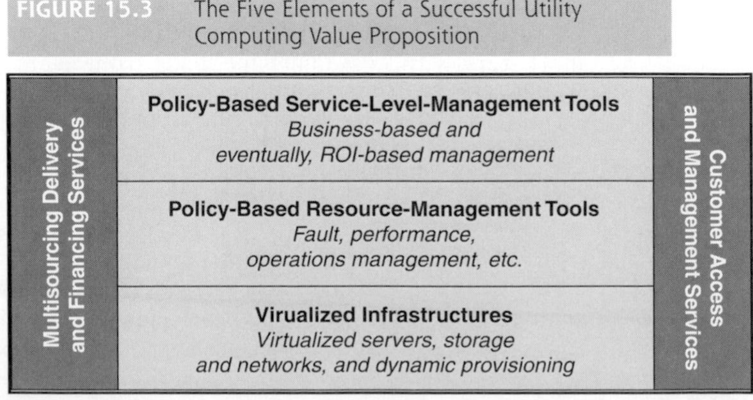

Source: T. Kucharvy, *The Five Rules for Jump-Starting the Utility-Computing Market*. Boston: Summit Strategies, Inc., January 2003, p. 5.

and terminology. However, utility computing will accelerate acceptance of ASP, which may distribute it as discussed in Application Case W15.3.1 in Online File W15.3. For current information on utility computing, see **utilitycomputing.com**.

A Hybrid Approach to MSS Development

A hybrid approach to MSS development combines the best of what a company does internally with an outsourced strategy to develop contracted partnerships. Hybrid models work best when the outsourced partner offers a high level of security, fast time to market, and service-level agreements.

Section 15.4 Review Questions

1. Define *in-house development* (i.e., *insourcing*).
2. List some of the pros and cons of using packaged MSS applications.
3. Define *outsourcing*. Is outsourcing a viable option for MSS provision?
4. Describe the major forms of MSS application leasing.
5. List some of the alternative leasing (and hosting) options.
6. What are the major factors driving a switch to software-as-a-service?
7. Define *utility computing* and describe its benefits.
8. List the major in-house development methods.

15.5 PROTOTYPING: A PRACTICAL MANAGEMENT SUPPORT SYSTEM DEVELOPMENT METHODOLOGY

Because of the semistructured or unstructured nature of problems addressed by DSS, it is quite unlikely that managers and MSS developers have a complete understanding of the decision-making situation when they start a new project. They may not understand the scope of the problem, the types of appropriate models or technologies to apply, and/or the information needs. Many MSS are therefore developed through the prototyping methodology. Prototyping is also known as *iterative design* or *evolutionary development*. (Other names are *middle-out process*, *adaptive design*, and *incremental design*.)

ADVANTAGES AND LIMITATIONS OF PROTOTYPING

The prototyping development methodology aims at building a system in a series of short steps with immediate feedback from users to ensure that development is proceeding correctly. Therefore, MSS tools must be flexible to permit changes quickly and easily.

The main advantage of prototyping is that a system can be quickly provided to users, even if it is not yet ready for institutional use. Feedback is obtained, and the system can be modified on moving to the next prototype. Further analysis may be needed as well. One disadvantage of prototyping is that changes are introduced quickly and there is no attempt to correct design decisions early on. Instead, they are repaired as the system evolves. (This concept is important in agile system development, which we discuss in Online File W15.4.) This is like what happened in the development of the Chevrolet Monza, which initially required that the engine be dropped out in order to change two of the sparkplugs during a tune-up. Customers bought the car, and eventually, in later designs, the problem was fixed by inserting panels so the plugs could be reached.

TECHNOLOGY INSIGHTS 15.1

How to Make Prototyping Work

Here are some ways to ensure success when using a prototyping approach to MSS development:

- Gain the unshakable support of the company's top business executive to obtain the proper visibility and resources for the project.
- Align new systems across several business processes, not just one. This yields a broader level of support for the project.
- Slice up a project into pieces. This allows you to manage the project better by staying on track.
- Deliver results in phases, not at the end. Early deliverables allow managers and users to see the benefits without having to wait for the big bang (especially if it doesn't do what is needed). This prototyping process encourages user input for correction and refinement.

On the other hand, if done carefully and with good design practices, prototyping is very effective (see Technology Insights 15.1). More complex plans and more functionality can be added to a system over time.

Advantages of Prototyping

The following are some of the major advantages of prototyping:

- Short development time
- Short user-reaction time (i.e., feedback from user)
- Improved user understanding of the system, its information needs, and its capabilities
- Low cost

Disadvantages and Limitations of Prototyping

When a prototyping approach is used, the gains obtained from cautiously stepping through each of the system's lifecycle stages might be lost. These gains include a thorough understanding of the information system's benefits and costs, a detailed description of the business's information needs, an easy-to-maintain information system design, a well-tested information system, and well-prepared users. However, this could be avoided by using a computer-aided systems engineering (CASE) tool to enforce consistency.

THE PROTOTYPING DEVELOPMENT PROCESS

We show the details of the prototyping methodology in Figure 15.4. The prototyping approach starts with overall MSS planning and some analysis. Users and managers, as well as an executive sponsor, must be involved.

Next, the analysis, design, and prototype implementation phases are iteratively performed until a small prototype is sufficiently developed (i.e., decided on jointly by the developers, managers, and users). Then the final implementation of this part of the system takes place. Simultaneously, further iterations occur in the loop of analysis–design–implementation–system prototype as other subsystems or capabilities are added to the deployed system until a fairly stable, comprehensive system evolves. This is how the systems in the IMERYS case in Online File W15.5 were developed.

The first major decision in prototyping involves which subproblem to build first. The user and the developer jointly identify a subproblem for which the initial MSS prototype is to be implemented. This early joint effort sets up initial working relationships between the participants and opens the lines of communication. The subproblem

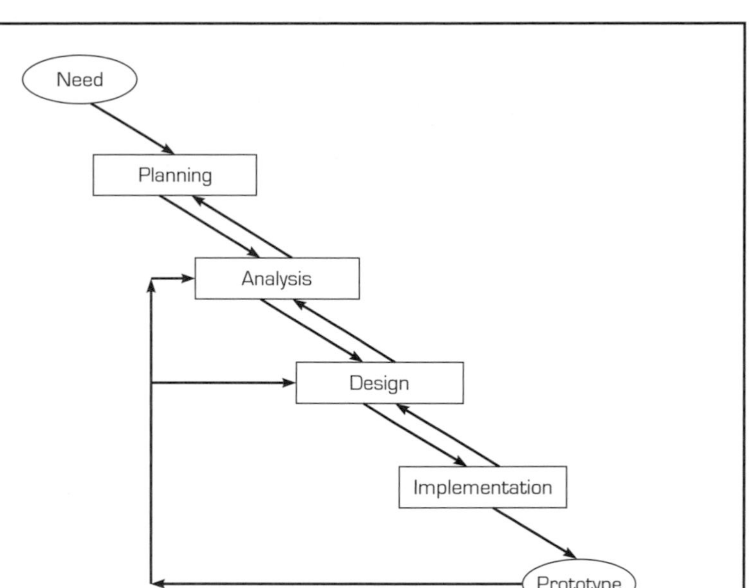

FIGURE 15.4 Prototyping Development Process: A RAD Method

should be small enough that the nature of the problem, the need for computer-based support, and the nature of this support are clear or quickly established. It should be of high-interest value to the decision maker. In the opening vignette, an employee benefits subsystem provided intense visibility for the overall system because everyone used it. For the IMERYS case in Online File W15.5, the small calcine plant and mocked-up versions of several reports played this role. This approach helps to excite managers and users about the potential of the system they want.

The Throwaway Prototyping Development Process

Throwaway prototyping is similar to both prototyping and the traditional SDLC (see Figure 15.5).

As in the SDLC, in throwaway prototyping, the analysis phase is thorough, but design prototypes are developed to assist in understanding more about the system being developed, especially when it is not clearly understood. Often, throwaway prototypes are developed as pilot tests on simpler development platforms to learn about user requirements and the final system to be deployed. For example, it is possible to work out calculation methods in Excel in order to map out the functionality of a program before committing to the formal development in a programming language. (This is a good approach when you do not fully understand what you are trying to develop.) When the pilot test is successful, the prototype is discarded, and a preliminary design is created for the real system. After that, the MSS is completed using the SDLC or prototyping approach. The design prototype helps the team work out details used in the system that is developed.

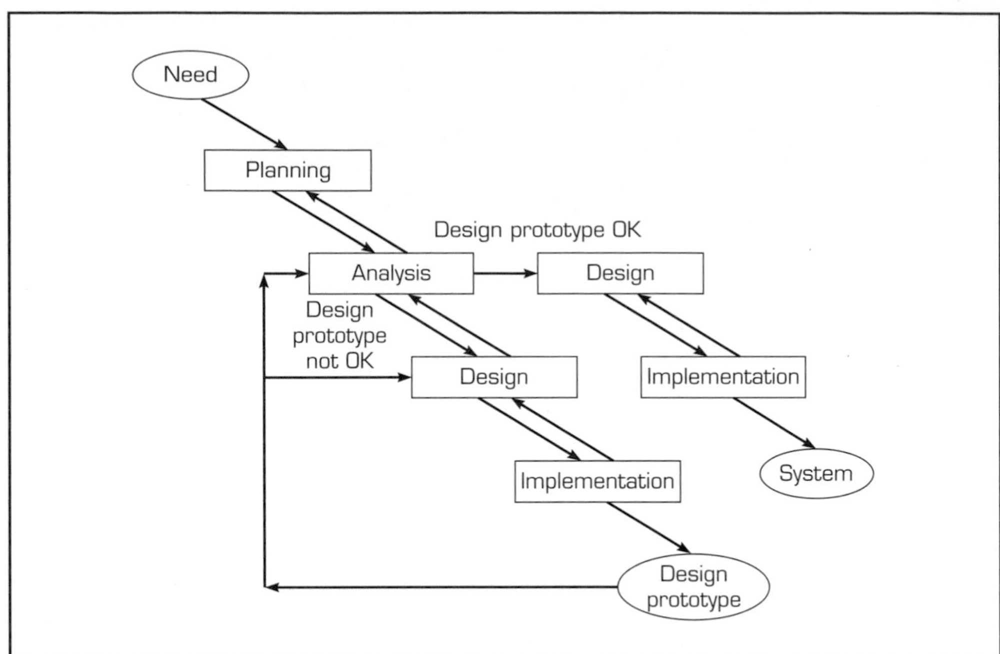

FIGURE 15.5 Throwaway Prototyping Development Process: Another RAD Method

Collaboration in Prototyping

The interaction of user, developer, and technology is extremely important in the prototyping process. Decision makers must share a common frame in order to make intelligent decisions. McCarthy and McCarthy (2002) advocated that managing a technology development group requires setting such a shared vision of a project and setting the rules for how team members work together. Malhotra et al. (2001) described how a flexible group support system (GSS) was continuously modified to support an engineering product design team.

System development teams are often scattered around the globe, sometimes working for other companies. Enhanced collaboration and teamwork are paramount. The vision is not only to build better teams by leveraging the best minds and common tools but also to potentially bring customers into development. Project management engagements are moving to a higher level of interactivity, requiring collaboration management (see Johnson, 2001). GSS can assist software developers. New CASE tools include collaborative software, such as CollabNet SourceCast (**collab.net**), and VA Software. These Web-based systems track software versions, provide online collaboration, and provide a repository (see Frye, 2002).

Evaluation in Prototyping

Evaluation is an integral part of the development process and is the control mechanism for the entire iterative design process. **Iterative design** is a systematic process for system development that is used in MSS. Iterative design involves producing a first version of MSS and then revising it and producing the second design version, and so on. The evaluation mechanism keeps the cost and effort of developing an MSS consistent with its value. A portion of the MSS is quickly constructed and then tested, improved, and enlarged in steps. At the end of the evolution, a decision is made on whether to further refine the MSS or to stop. If the prototype is okay, formal implementation of the MSS

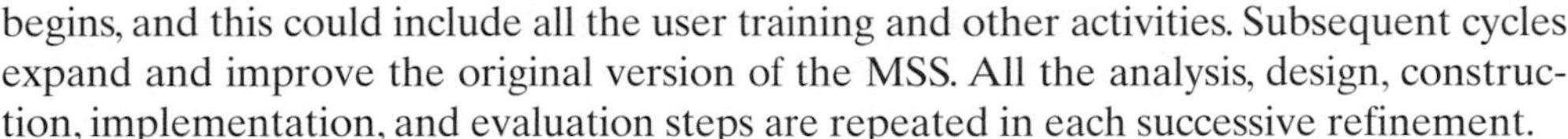

begins, and this could include all the user training and other activities. Subsequent cycles expand and improve the original version of the MSS. All the analysis, design, construction, implementation, and evaluation steps are repeated in each successive refinement.

IMPLEMENTING PROTOTYPING

Many MSS and Web sites are developed using the prototyping methodology. One reason for this is that prototyping allows the developers to get a usable (perhaps partial) system up and running relatively quickly. Because MSS and Web sites are never complete but always in a state of evolution, prototyping is an ideal methodology (see Technology Insights 15.2). Some prototyping of non-MSS is performed with the same software packages with which the MSS is developed, such as report generators and spreadsheets. A development suite is a collection of prototyping tools that enable a full range of system development activities (see Section 15.7).

SUCCESSES AND FAILURES IN PROTOTYPING

Here are some critical success factors for prototyping:

- *Users and managers should be involved in every phase and iteration.* The iterative nature of prototyping allows users to be involved in system design, which is important for MSS. This approach stems from a need for user expertise in the design and recognizes that successful implementation is more easily achieved with active involvement. Sometimes this involvement is done via the JAD method. Collaborative software (see Chapter 17, an online chapter) can be useful.
- *Learning should be explicitly integrated into the design process.* Because the users are involved in system design, both users and system developers learn about the decision making; the ill-structured, complex problem; and the technologies that can potentially be applied to the problem.
- *Prototyping should essentially bypass the formal information requirement definition in the SDLC.* Requirements evolve as experience is gained. Prototyping assumes that the requirements are only partially known at the beginning of system development, and it attempts to clarify users' needs by actively involving them in a low-cost, fast-feedback development process.
- *A key criterion associated with prototyping is the short interval between iterations.* The feedback must be fast. This criterion results from the required learning process: Accurate and timely feedback is a prerequisite to effective learning.

TECHNOLOGY INSIGHTS 15.2

How Companies Speed MSS Deployment

Here are some concepts that can move a project from impulse drive to warp drive. Many of them involve aspects of the prototyping development methodology:

- Target small, tactical applications that show quick results.
- Use software components, if possible.
- Make application deployment iterative and open to customization.
- Use commodity hardware.
- Use object technology, including tools such as Java.
- Break major projects into manageable, deliverable chunks.
- Use packaged applications whenever justifiable.
- Consider IT service providers as well as utility and grid computing.
- Use Web services, if possible.

- *The initial prototype must be low cost.* The cost of the initial prototype must fall below the minimum threshold of capital outlays requiring formal justification. The development of a prototype may be a risky decision, particularly for a DSS. However, because the benefits of an MSS are often intangible, relating to such issues as improved decision making or better understanding, a high initial investment may result in a decision not to proceed.

Prototyping Failures

Prototyping efforts in any MSS may fail. Technology Insights 15.3 provides an example.

DATA WAREHOUSE VENDORS: SUCCESS AND FAILURES

Data warehouses are developed with prototyping in practice, as are most enterprise-wide information systems. There are four common data warehousing development methodologies:

1. The NCR Data Warehousing Methodology (**ncr.com**) used by Teradata
2. The SAS Institute Rapid Data Warehousing Method (**sas.com**)
3. Microsoft Data Warehousing (**microsoft.com**)
4. The Kimball Method (**ralphkimball.com**)

TECHNOLOGY INSIGHTS 15.3

Why Data Warehouse Implementations Fail

Here are several important red flags that popped up early in real-world data warehouse implementation projects:

- No prelaunch objectives or metrics were used.
- Too many major projects were conducted simultaneously.
- The CEO set budgets and deadlines before the project team was on board. (They were not involved.)
- The budget and deadlines were not realistic.
- There was no insider presence on the data warehouse project team.
- An overburdened project manager was involved.
- The availability of source data was unconfirmed at the outset.
- No user demand for sophisticated data analysis was considered.
- No routine meetings of executive sponsors and the project manager took place.
- Business managers were not initially involved.

These early indicators predicted that the project was headed for failure. To their credit, when the prototyped pilot project failed, executives were able to quickly cut the losses and cancel the project.

Some lessons learned from this failure include the following:

- Executive sponsorship and partnership of the IT staff and end users are the most critical success factors for developing a data warehouse. If possible, a company should establish dual leadership by business and IT executives for the project or pick a project manager from the business side.
- It is important not to let the project proceed without a clear understanding of the business objectives and how they will be measured.
- An incremental pilot project should occur to determine whether it is possible to obtain the projected benefits.
- An organization should expect to make a major investment in ongoing management of the data warehouse.
- When all else fails, an organization should cut its losses and run.

Sources: Compiled from L.G. Paul, "Anatomy of a Failure," *CIO Enterprise*, November 15, 1997, pp. 55–60; and D.K. Burleson and M Ault, *Easy Oracle Data Warehousing: Practical Examples for Data Warehouse Success*, Rampant TechPress, Kittrell, NC, 2006.

O'Donnell, Arnott, and Gibson (2002) analyzed and compared these four methodologies. They found that while each is successful in its own way, some spend more effort on planning (e.g., NCR), while others do not. In most cases, when a project fails, it is due to a lack of experience on the part of the designers and implementers; in addition, the organization may have attempted to develop projects that were too large.

Section 15.5 Review Questions

1. Define *prototyping*. What are the advantages and limitation of prototyping is MSS development?
2. Describe the prototyping development process.
3. Should prototyping be used on every MSS development project? Why or why not?
4. Why is collaboration between developers and users important to the success of prototyping?

15.6 CRITERIA FOR SELECTING AN MANAGEMENT SUPPORT SYSTEMS DEVELOPMENT APPROACH

If a company decides to buy or lease an MSS application, the following representative selection criteria need to be considered:

- *Flexibility*. Commercial packages need to be modified or adapted to the specific requirements of an application. Therefore, it is important to evaluate the extent to which a package can be adapted and the willingness of the vendor to perform or support the adaptation.
- *Information requirements*. The selected package should satisfy the information requirements of the users. Information collection, storage, and retrieval capabilities and the database structure should be carefully examined.
- *User friendliness*. User friendliness is important. If the MSS application is hard for a business professional to use, it will hardly be used.
- *Hardware and software resources*. The computer type and the operating system required by the MSS package must be compatible with the existing infrastructure. The CPU and storage requirements are also important considerations.
- *Installation*. The installation effort required to implement the package should be taken into account. Some packages are complex, and their installation requires extensive consultation. The installation process may also take a considerable amount of time.
- *Maintenance services*. Because MSS application requirements could be constantly changing, continuous maintenance is required. It is important to consider how often the package needs to be upgraded and whether the vendor provides assistance for its maintenance.
- *Vendor quality and track record*. It is less risky to acquire an MSS package from a vendor that has a good reputation and track record than from one with a less-than-stellar or unknown reputation. The quality of the vendor can be indicated by its related experience in the particular application and its sales and financial records, as well as its responsiveness to clients' requests. To minimize risk, minor applications should be leased first.
- *Estimating costs*. The total costs of MSS projects are usually difficult to assess and often underestimated. In addition to the obvious costs associated with system

acquisition or development, it is also important to factor in the costs of installation, integration, customization, and maintenance.

- *Personnel.* Staffing requirements should be planned for in advance to ensure that the organization has the appropriate human resources for systems development (in the case of in-house development), implementation, operation, and maintenance. It may be difficult to recruit and retain IT personnel with appropriate knowledge and experience in certain MSS application development. Special expertise can be acquired from external consultants, but usually at a very high cost.
- *Technological evolution.* Planning ahead for technological evolution facilitates the upgrade of MSS applications and enables the organization to adopt innovations more quickly than the competition. It is therefore very important to allow for flexibility in the application design so that the chosen options do not impose major limitations on future choices. Given the rapid pace of IT evolution, it is sometimes preferable to develop MSS applications incrementally to take advantage of the latest developments in the technology.
- *Scaling.* System *scalability* refers to how big a system can grow in various dimensions to provide more service. Scalability can be measured in several ways, including the total number of users, the number of simultaneous users, and the transaction volume. These dimensions are not independent because scaling up the size of the system in one dimension can affect the other dimensions. The growth of scale is facilitated or constrained by the system architecture.
- *Sizing.* The required size and performance of an application are difficult to predict because the growth of the user population of certain MSS applications is hard to anticipate. Overloading the application decreases performance.
- *Performance.* System performance is a critical factor for business success. In addition to convenience, good performance also brings customers and competitive advantages. Performance is measured by using two main metrics: latency and throughput. *Latency* measures the time required to complete an operation, such as downloading a Web page. It is an indicator of the users' experience with the system. *Throughput* measures the number of operations completed in a given period of time. It indicates the capacity or number of users that a system can handle. Throughput and latency are interrelated. An increase in either measure leads to an increase in the other.
- *Reliability.* Reliability is an essential requirement for a successful system. System failures and downtime may lead to public embarrassment. When an MSS application fails, business is interrupted, and the company loses customers. System reliability can be enhanced through redundancy (i.e., backup systems).
- *Security.* Security is one of the most important factors for the adoption and diffusion of MSS. Data and information flow in MSS, as well as stored data, may include private and/or proprietary information. Thus, a selected package must meet strict security requirements. Systems, communication, and data security must be addressed early in the design of the applications and not after their implementation. In addition to technological solutions such as firewalls and encryption, physical and procedural security measures must also be enforced.

IN-HOUSE VERSUS OUTSOURCING MSS DEVELOPMENT

As described in Technology Insights 15.4, there are mixed opinions on the value of outsourcing MSS and other IT projects versus internal development.

For additional information on vendor selection criteria, see Satzinger et al. (2006) and Whitten and Bentley (2005).

TECHNOLOGY INSIGHTS 15.4

To Buy or To Build

Morris (2003) reported on a recent IDC study on the financial impact of business analytics (BA). IDC investigated information on costs and returns through on-site interviews with end users, IT managers, and financial executives at 43 organizations. The analytic application ranged from marketing campaign analysis to fraud detection to portfolio management, spanning a variety of industries. Overall, analytics implementations generated a mean five-year ROI of 112 percent, with a median five-year investment of just over $2 million. Returns ranged from 17 percent to over 2000 percent.

For 46 percent of the organizations, the ROI was less than 100 percent; for 34 percent, ROI was between 101 and 1,000 percent; 20 percent reported ROI of over 1000 percent. Although BA implementations are substantial investments for organizations, they can deliver substantial benefits. Such MSS applications clearly pay off. Interestingly, the median total five-year investment for organizations that developed the applications in-house was $2,088,660, with a median return of 104 percent. On the other hand, for organizations that outsourced their applications, the median total five-year investment for organizations was $1,807,656 (15% less), with a substantially higher median return of 150 percent. Of course, the decision of whether to build or buy depends on the problem being addressed, the level of skill within the organization, and the availability of packaged (i.e., ready-made) solutions, among other factors.

Sources: Adapted from H. Morris, "Build vs. Buy." *DM Review*, January 2003; and **idc.com** (accessed February 2006).

Section 15.6 Review Questions

1. List five of the major criteria to consider when deciding whether to buy or lease an MSS application.
2. Define *latency*.
3. Define *throughput*.
4. Describe in-house MSS development versus outsourcing of MSS development.

15.7 THIRD-PARTY PROVIDERS OF MANAGEMENT SUPPORT SYSTEMS SOFTWARE PACKAGES AND SUITES

If a company opts to purchase its MSS applications from a third-party vendor, two basic categories of software are available: functional packages and MSS suites.

SPECIALIZED AND FUNCTIONAL SOFTWARE PACKAGES

Specialized and functional software packages specifically for MSS construction are available from a large number of vendors. Examples are Hyperion's dashboard products (described in Chapter 9) and the Business Objects products described in Chapter 7. Other packages are described in Chapter 5 through 14 and Chapter 18 (an online chapter).

MSS SUITES

An **MSS suite** is an integrated collection of a large number of MSS tools that work together to develop applications. Suites offer builders and users flexibility, specialization, customization, and integration in supporting complete front- and back-office functionality. Over the past few years, the MSS suite marketspace has experienced a substantial amount of consolidation. Among the major products that remain on the market are MicroStrategy 8 (**microstrategy.com**), Hyperion System 9 BI+ (**hyperion.com**), BusinessObjects XI (**businessobjects.com**), Microsoft BizTalk Server 2004 (**microsoft. com**), Oracle 11i E-Business Suite (**oracle.com**), and IBM WebSphere commerce suite (**ibm.com**).

MicroStrategy 8

The MicroStrategy 8 product set is built from a single architectural foundation, delivering all five styles of BI: scorecards and dashboards, reporting, OLAP, advanced analysis, and alerts and proactive notification (see Figure 15.6).

The MicroStrategy 8 Web interface delivers a Windows-like feeling with drag-and-drop interactivity from any Web browser. The Web architecture provides a zero-footprint, using no Java or Active X controls. MicroStrategy embeds OLAP features (e.g., scorecards, dashboards) directly into enterprise reports, providing a seamless user experience that uncovers root causes without the need for programming or switching of interfaces. The suite's WYSIWYG ("what you see is what you get") report design

FIGURE 15.6 The Plug-and-Play Architecture of MicroStragegy 8

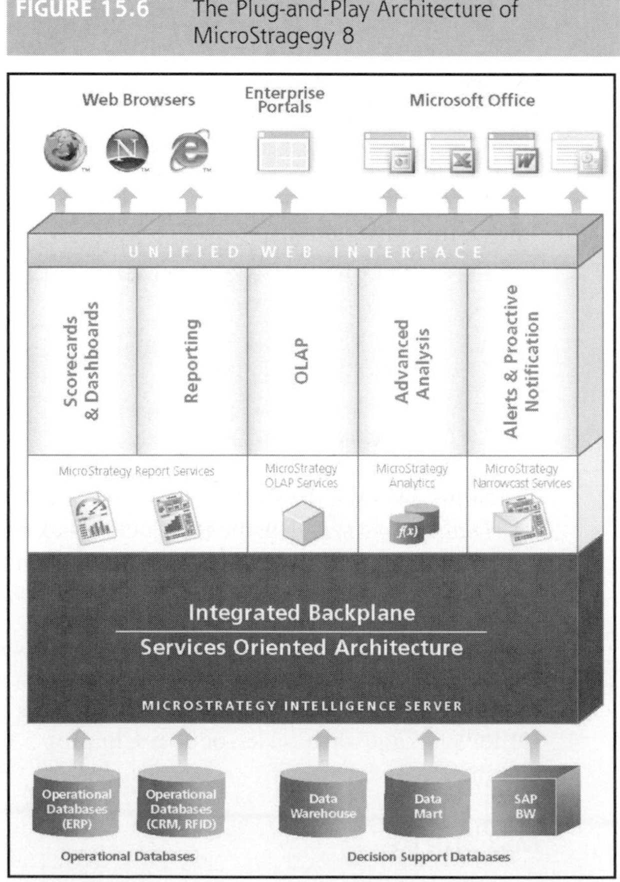

Source: MicroStrategy, *Microstrategy 8* **microstrategy.com/Download/files/news/Press/MicroStrategy8_Overview.pdf**, P. 2, Figure 1.

and editing allows end users to design and refine reports over the Web, using familiar skills similar to those used with PowerPoint or Excel. MicroStrategy 8 also supports automated report maintainability, pervasive security, and user administration.

Hyperion System 9 BI+

Hyperion System 9 BI+ is single platform that delivers comprehensive business intelligence and supports a wide range of management reporting and analysis capabilities, including the following:

- *Reporting*. The suite provides management reporting capabilities that combine both operational and financial information. Business users can create their own interactive reports for monitoring performance and spotting trends.
- *Dashboards*. Managers can create personalized dashboards to monitor key performance indicators (KPI) and be alerted to exceptions and out-of-range conditions. Enterprise metrics with cause-and-effect relationships enable executives to evaluate performances across different departments and functions.
- *Analysis*. The system provides multidimensional analytic applications, including budgeting, forecasting, profitability modeling, and scenario planning. Information can be manipulated in Microsoft Excel or analyzed in an interactive graphical environment over the Web. Users can perform free-form exploration and data mining to discover hidden patterns in complex data.

BusinessObjects XI

BusinessObjects XI is a suite of integrated BI products that provide decision support capabilities such as the following:

- *Reporting*. BusinessObjects XI allows organizations to access, format, and deliver data as meaningful information to large populations of information consumers.
- *Query and analysis*. BusinessObjects XI allows managers to interact with business information and answer ad hoc questions.
- *Performance management*. BusinessObjects XI helps managers align with strategy by tracking and analyzing key business metrics and goals via management dashboards, scorecards, and alerting.
- *Performance management applications*. BusinessObjects XI provides prepackaged metrics, reports, and industry best practices for business analysis, covering functional areas of the organization, specific industries, and compliance.
- *Data integration*. BusinessObjects XI extracts data from disparate sources, and it transforms and loads the data into data marts and warehouses.

Microsoft BizTalk Server 2004

Microsoft BizTalk Server 2004 supports the goal of creating business processes that unite separate applications into a coherent whole. This suite enables developers to connect diverse applications and then to graphically construct and modify business processes that use the services those applications provide. It includes a mechanism for specifying business rules and provides ways to manage and monitor MSS applications. BizTalk Server 2004 has a number of features for information workers, including a group of business activity services (BAS) and a business activity monitoring (BAM) framework for analyzing current business processes, supporting business process provisioning and configuration, and providing services that enable information workers to set up and manage interactions with trading partners. BizTalk Server 2004 also adds technology for creating human workflow services (HWS), making possible business processes that interact with Microsoft Outlook and other familiar clients.

An example of a business portal built using Microsoft Biz Talk Server is described in Application Case 15.5.

Application Case 15.5

Floriculture Partnership Streamlines Real-Time Ordering

The floriculture market consists of brokers who take orders from growers for plants and rootstock produced by plant-material suppliers. Until recently, the market relied on mobile salespeople to take handwritten orders from growers. The order would later be keyed into the broker's computer system and rekeyed into the suppliers' systems. From start to finish, the process required an average of 12 manual touchpoints, including tasks such as entering orders, determining inventory availability, establishing prices, and reentering data due to lost, duplicate, or inaccurate orders.

In 2002, Syngenta/S&G Flowers, a major broker, partnered with the Flower Fields Alliance (FFA), whose combined market share represents about 40 percent of the plant materials sold in the United States. They decided to build a portal that would make it easier for growers to buy plants from suppliers in the alliance. The portal was built by Advantage Factory, a Microsoft Certified (Development) Partner, using Microsoft's Commerce Server 2002, Microsoft BizTalk Server 2002, the SQL Server 2000 relational database, and the .NET development framework. It took six months to develop the portal.

Using the Microsoft tools to develop the FFA portal offered several benefits. It accelerated the development by reducing the amount of code to write and debug, thus also reducing the necessary testing cycles. It also made the connection to legacy systems easier. The ordering process of FFA has become more efficient because the software suite provides a platform for the supply-chain integration.

The portal provides growers with a single, real-time interface to the suppliers' inventory databases and the broker's order entry system. In this way, a grower can search for products across multiple suppliers and can place an order without manual assistance. The portal reduces entry errors and makes the various processes more efficient, and more importantly, it reduces by approximately 80 percent the risk that the plant materials will perish before they reach the grower. Finally, it provides information needed for pricing and inventory decisions.

After two years of using the portal, Advantage Factory upgraded it with Microsoft BizTalk Server 2004 for faster order processing, more extensible trading partner management, and enhanced monitoring capabilities. With the upgraded portal, the FFA is able to respond more quickly to partner-specific processing needs, providing a faster time to value. The group has experienced a 66 percent reduction in order processing time.

Sources: Microsoft.com, *Case Study: The Flower Fields Alliance*, July 14, 2003, **microsoft.com/resources/casestudies/casestudy.asp?casestudyid=14262** (accessed April 2006); and **sg-flowers.com** (accessed April 2006).

Oracle's MSS Products

Oracle Daily Business Intelligence (DBI) is part of the Oracle E-Business Suite. It is an integrated set of information-driven applications engineered to support managerial decision-making. Its key functions include the following:

- Dashboards with KPI, graphs, tables, and links
- KPI table with KPI comparison graphs
- Role-based design that provides insight across multiple functional areas
- Daily period-to-date summarization that provides year-to-date, quarter-to-date, month-to-date, and week-to-date summaries
- Relevant performance comparisons that measure current period-to-date results compared to the same point in time in the prior period or prior year

- A common enterprise reporting calendar
- Integration with other collaboration suites to initiate Web conferences

IBM's WebSphere Commerce Suite

IBM's WebSphere commerce suite is a comprehensive application development platform designed to support various e-commerce and decision-making tasks. See Online File W15.6 for more details about the MSS suite. For a list of other MSS suites, see **wsindex.org**.

Section 15.7 Review Questions

1. Describe the functionalities of MicroStrategy 8.
2. Describe the functions supported by Hyperion System 9 BI+.
3. Describe the basic business systems in Microsoft's BizTalk Server.
4. Describe the key MSS suites provided by Oracle.

15.8 CONNECTING TO DATABASES AND OTHER ENTERPRISE SYSTEMS

MSS applications, especially large ones, need to be connected to other systems. The major integration areas discussed in the following sections are connecting to databases and to back-end systems. For examples of connecting to other systems, see Hodge et al. (2005) and Chang (2005).

CONNECTING TO DATABASES

Virtually every MSS application requires database or data warehouse access. For example, when a customer orders a product, the product description, inventory count, and order information are likely to be retrieved from and stored in one or more databases (see Figure 15.7). An MSS application can be connected to a database in a variety of ways. Today, most of these connections are accomplished via a *multitiered application architecture* like the one shown in Figure 15.7. This architecture has four tiers:

1. A Web browser where data and information are presented to and data are collected from the end user.

FIGURE 15.7 An Example of Multitiered Application Architecture Connected to a Database

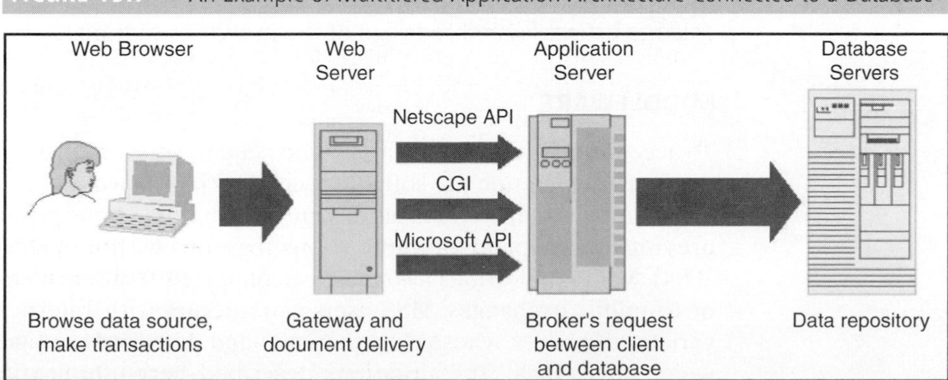

2. A Web server that delivers Web pages, collects the data sent by the end user, and passes data to and from the application server.
3. An application server that executes business rules (e.g., user authorization), formulates database queries based on the data passed by the Web server, sends the queries to the back-end database, manipulates and formats the data resulting from the database query, and sends the formatted response to the Web server.
4. A database server in which the data are stored and managed and database requests are processed.

In some cases, the data being accessed are stored in an existing (legacy) database (e.g., inventory database, order database). In these cases, it is better to tie the application server directly to the legacy database than to duplicate the data in a database established solely for the MSS application. This approach ensures that the data are up-to-date, that they are consistent across the applications accessing the data, that a minimum of storage space is used, and that there is only one database to create and maintain rather than two.

INTEGRATING MSS APPLICATIONS AND BACK-END SYSTEMS

Several technologies can be used to integrate an MSS application with a back-end database. Many of the commercial MSS suites have built-in integration capabilities. If a company wants to build its own database interface, a couple options are available. First, all the Web scripting languages (e.g., PHP, JSP, Active Server Pages [ASP]) have commands that simplify the process. Specifically, these scripting languages enable a programmer to build Web pages that can issue queries to a back-end (i.e., relational) database and process the database's response to the query. Second, a number of specialized application servers are available that simplify the task of integrating an MSS application with one or more back-end databases. Among these specialized servers, BEA Inc.'s WebLogic Server (**bea.com**) is a market leader.

In addition to connecting to back-end databases, many MSS applications also require integration with a variety of other systems—ERP, CRM, knowledge management, supply-chain management, electronic data interchange, data warehouses, and other applications, both inside and outside the company. The integration can also be handled with a class of software called *enterprise application integration (EAI)*. These products focus on the integration of large systems (see Schneider, 2004). TIBCO (**tibco.com**), webMethods (**webmethods.com**), and WebSphere InterChange Server (**ibm.com**) are examples of companies that have offerings in the EAI arena.

As described in the End of Chapter Application Case, critical to the MSS project at Sterngold was the need to integrate the ordering system with the back office (i.e., order fulfillment, inventory, accounting, payment). The integration required a study of existing processes and redesign of the processes that needed to be altered.

MIDDLEWARE

To access a data warehouse, users who need to conduct an analysis, find information, or do data visualization use software known as *middleware*.

Companies and organizations are now building enterprisewide MSS by integrating previously independent applications together with new developments (see Coffee, 2004). MSS applications also must be connected to items such as the partners' systems or to public exchanges. MSS users can interact with Internet applications through a variety of devices, whose characteristics and performance figures span an increasingly wide range. In all the situations described here, applications use communication protocols and intermediate software that resides on top of the operating systems to perform the following functions:

- Hiding distribution (i.e., the fact that an application is usually made up of many interconnected parts running in distributed locations)
- Hiding the heterogeneity of the various hardware components, operating systems, and communication protocols
- Providing uniform, standard, high-level interfaces to the application developers and integrators so that applications can be easily composed, reused, ported, and made to interoperate
- Supplying a set of common services to perform various general-purpose functions to avoid duplicating efforts and to facilitate collaboration between applications

The intermediate software layers have come to be called by the generic name *middleware*. **Middleware** essentially provides a separate program to be the interface between diverse client and server systems. Its main function is to mediate interaction between the parts of an application or between applications. (For more information, see **middleware.objectweb.org**.)

IBM is the leading provider of middleware software. It offers a number of on-demand solutions for communication, government, retail, banking, financial markets, and many other industries. IBM Middleware (**ibm.com/middleware**) helps automate systems, integrate operations, connect people, and develop software.

Section 15.8 Review Questions

1. Describe the basic elements of a multitiered application architecture.
2. List the ways in which an MSS application can be connected to back-end databases and other transaction processing systems.
3. Define *middleware* and describe its attributes.

15.9 THE RISE OF WEB SERVICES, XML, AND SERVICE-ORIENTED ARCHITECTURE

Three interrelated technologies that can greatly facilitate the development of complex MSS applications and enhance integration are Web services, XML, and the service-oriented architecture (SOA).

THE NEED FOR INTEGRATION

Except in the simplest of cases, MSS require the integration of software applications that may have been written in different programming languages and may reside on different computer hardware. Existing technologies make the integration a difficult task for a number of reasons (see Erl, 2004; and Tabor, 2002):

- *Platform-specific objects*. Existing MSS software applications may consist of a series of software *objects*. The application objects residing on different computers must have a way to communicate with one another across the enterprise.
- *Dynamic environment*. In today's rapidly changing business environment, business partners come and go, and so do software vendors and their applications. If a

software component or application is no longer available because the vendor is no longer in business or has dropped a particular product line, an existing application has to be flexible enough to substitute a new component or application for the old.

- *Security barriers*. Companies use firewalls to protect their networks against security risks. Firewalls are designed to limit the types of communications and requests that can be made from one computer to another. This makes it very difficult for one component or application residing on one computer to communicate with another component or application residing on another computer.

For these reasons, there is a need for universal standards, and this is where Web services, XML, and the SOA enter the picture (see Online File W15.7).

What is required to address these problems is a technology that can be integrated across different hardware and operating systems, that can interface with both new and legacy systems, and that minimizes network security risks. This is where Web services come into play. According to the World Wide Web Consortium (W3C; **w3.org**), a **Web service** is defined as a software system identified by a uniform resource identifier (URI), whose public interfaces and bindings are defined and described using XML (see Champion et al., 2002). Its definition can be found by other software systems. Those systems may then interact with the Web service in a manner prescribed by its definition, using XML-based messages conveyed by Internet protocols (see Online File W15.7 for details). For an example of Web services application in a large insurance company, see Application Case 15.6.

Application Case 15.6

Lincoln Financial Excels by Using Web Services

Lincoln Financial is a $5 billion provider of life insurance, retirement products, and wealth management services. The company distributes its offering through hundreds of distributors (i.e., partners), such as financial advisors, banks, and independent brokers. For its partners to become "partners of choice," the company wanted tighter integration with the distributors' Web sites. In most of the insurance industry, if consumers want to access their accounts or download a form from a broker's site, they click on a link that takes them to the insurance provider's site, where they input a separate user ID and password. Lincoln wanted to go a step further, providing content and account access within its distributors' Web sites, as well as single-sign-on for consumers. Doing this was not simple. Outlining the Lincoln content in an HTML frame wouldn't provide the partner's look and feel. A pure Web services approach was also out because most of Lincoln's partners couldn't support that kind of system (i.e., they could not process the XML messages).

For a short time, Lincoln maintained subsites for its partners that wanted them, and those sites linked to requested content. However, the maintenance of the subsites was burdensome.

The ultimate answer was a system called Service Broker. It took three developers four months to build the pilot of Service Broker, which is a Web services–based application with a front end called a *servlet*. When the servlet is installed on a partner's server, it provides a wrapper that can accept Lincoln's content and applications and still maintain the partner's look and feel.

The servlet manages many of the functions the partner would have to manage in a pure Web services application, such as authentication, digital signature, passwords, and page rendering. When the partner wants to include Lincoln content or an application, it only needs to add one line of code.

In Spring 2004, Lincoln was the only insurer that did not require customers to leave a partner's Web site to access information. This gave Lincoln a competitive advantage.

Source: Compiled from M. Brandel, "Lincoln Financial Syndicates Content with Web Services," *Computerworld*, March 15, 2004, p. A4; and **lfg.com** (accessed February 2006).

Section 15.9 Review Questions

1. List some reasons it is difficult for applications running in different environments on different computers to communicate with one another.
2. Define *Web services*.

15.10 USER-DEVELOPED MSS

PCs have diffused throughout organizations, communication with data servers (mainframes and others) has improved, and software tools have improved in capability, quality, price, and user friendliness. Consequently, users now have the necessary tools to develop their own MSS, including Web-based systems.

Broadly defined, **end-user computing** (also known as **end-user development**) is the development and use of computer-based information systems by people outside the formal information systems area. This includes users of all skill levels in all functional areas in an organization: managers, executives, staff, secretaries, and others. Web-based tools such as wikis and content management make end-user development more efficient and effective (see Application Case 15.7).

User-developed MSS has a more narrow definition than end-user computing. It includes decision makers and professionals (i.e., knowledge workers, e.g., financial analysts, tax analysts, engineers) who build or use computers to solve problems or enhance their productivity.

Application Case 15.7

End-User Development Using Wikis

In Hawaiian, "wiki wiki" means "quick." In IT speak, a *wiki* is a Web site that lets anyone quickly add or edit content. It is a Web site designed for collaboration (see Chapter 10). The concept began small, as a grassroots way to build online knowledge repositories (such as **Wikipedia.org**). But now startups such as JotSpot (**jot.com**) are out to harness the power of wikis for businesses.

JotSpot's wiki-based software lets companies create wikis for business processes. The following are some end-user developments utilized by JotSpot's customers:

- *Create an intranet.* A company can publish company information, such as news or employee guidelines (e.g., Sundia [**watermelonworks.com**]).
- *Project management.* A company can schedule project deadlines, assign tasks, and define product specifications (e.g., Roxor Games [**roxorgames.com**]).
- *Document collaboration.* Multiple users can author documents with the aid of version history and Microsoft Word integration (e.g., Symantec; [**symantec.com**], Insider Pages [**insiderpages.com**]).
- *Collaboration with virtual teams.* A company can communicate with remote contractors or clients (e.g., Wingate Studios [**wingatestudios.com**], Unimedia [**unimedia.org**]).
- *Tracking of software bugs.* It is possible to log defects and build custom queries (e.g., Al Technology [**a1technology.com**]).
- *Call center support.* A company can access case histories and increase customer support (e.g., Your Privacy Info [**yourprivacy.info**]).

Opsware (**opsware.com**), a data center automation software vendor, has used JotSpot to create in a few hours applications that might have cost $50,000 to $100,000 to develop in Java. Opsware's technical sales team uses one JotSpot wiki to manage information such as proposals and status reports associated with pilot projects for prospective customers. "It's a very rich document management system," said Jason Rosenthal, vice president of client services at Opsware. "It's so quick and easy that a new user can learn to use it in 10 to 15 minutes." The software also reduced the time it took the company to prepare for a proof of concept from 5 days to 3, Rosenthal claimed, adding that wikis will revolutionize how companies share information internally. Rosenthal said, "It's easier for new users to do what it used to take a webmaster to do."

Sources: Compiled from A. Dragoon, "End-User Development: Something Wiki This Way Comes," *CIO Magazine*, April 2005; and **jot.com** (accessed February 2006).

We next turn to the advantages and risks of user-developed MSS.

USER-DEVELOPED MSS: ADVANTAGES AND RISKS

Several important advantages explain why users want to develop their own MSS:

- Delivery time is short. There is no wait for an information systems development team to schedule and carry out development.
- The prerequisites of extensive and formal user requirements specifications are eliminated. These specifications are often incomplete or incorrect in MSS because of such issues as users' inability to specify the requirements or communication issues between analysts and users. It sometimes takes a long time to develop these specifications.
- Some MSS implementation problems are reduced.
- The cost is usually very low.

Some serious user-developed MSS risks include the following:

- User-developed MSS can be of poor quality. Lack of formal MSS design experience and the tendency of end users to ignore conventional controls, testing procedures, and documentation standards can lead to low-quality systems.
- There are three categories of potential quality risks: substandard or inappropriate tools and facilities used in MSS development; risks associated with the development process (e.g., the inability to develop workable systems or the development of systems that generate erroneous results); and data management risks (e.g., loss of data or use of stale, inappropriate, or incorrect data).
- Security risks may increase because of users' unfamiliarity with security measures.
- Lack of documentation and maintenance procedures may cause problems, especially if the developer leaves the organization.

Melymuka (2001) recommended the following steps to get users involved in MSS development:

1. Get management buy-in.
2. Understand the users' business.
3. Consider the users' priorities.
4. Assign good communicators.
5. Talk with users all along the business process.
6. Don't meet at users' offices.
7. Turn off mobile phones.
8. Focus on users' problems, not on technology.
9. Listen well; explain things back.
10. Use prototypes.

REDUCING THE RISKS OF END-USER COMPUTING

Because most personal MSS and some organizational MSS are developed by end users, it is important to manage and reduce the risks associated with user-developed MSS.

Several studies address the issue of risks and controls in end-user development. Some factors that contribute to spreadsheet errors include developer inexperience, poor design approaches, application types, problem complexity, time pressure, and the presence or absence of review procedures (see Janvrin and Morrison, 2000). Other factors, including gender, application expertise, and work group configuration, can influence spreadsheet error rates. Janvrin and Morrison (2000) proposed applying a structured design approach to developing systems in spreadsheets. This development approach reduced errors significantly in two experiments. Schultheis and Sumner (1994) determined that a number of controls are applied in practice to spreadsheet applications. Developers use more controls in high-risk spreadsheet applications. Also see Burnett et al. (2004) and Sutcliffe and Mehandjiev (2004) for quality control issues related to end-user computing.

One approach that works well in practice is to license user-developed applications. When a new end-user MSS application is to be created, the user can develop it with an organizationally approved methodology (e.g., structured design). At the inception, the basic features must be outlined in a one-page report to the MSS licensing group (MLG). A member of the MLG assists the developer by providing appropriate tools and data as well as methods to access data that reside on other systems. In this way, security is preserved. When the MSS is completed, it must be documented, and the MLG must approve its use. The documentation must be good enough so that if the developer leaves the organization, the system can be maintained by the MLG. The MSS is then approved for the individual to use. A copy of all the material is stored with the MLG, and the information about the MSS is cataloged in a knowledge base that is available to all members of the organization. This practice promotes software reuse. Employees in other departments can search for MSS related to their own work and can ask to use or expand someone else's system on an experimental basis. MSS can be licensed for individual use, several individuals' use, work group use, departmental use, organizational use, or interorganizational use. Each level up requires increasingly tight restrictions on quality and documentation to minimize the risks in MSS use.

TEAM-DEVELOPED MSS

A team-developed MSS requires a substantial effort, although the team may consist of only a few people, like the team that developed HR InfoNet in the opening vignette. Team-developed MSS need extensive planning and organization. The planning and organization depend on the specific MSS, the organization in which it will be used, and so on. Certain activities are generic and can be performed by any team.

For a complex MSS, a group of people are required to build and manage the system. The number of people in the group depends on such factors as the size of the effort and the tools used. Some companies have initiated MSS efforts with as few as 2 or 3 people; others have used as many as 12 to 15.

The organizational placement of the MSS development group varies. Some typical locations are within the information systems department, as a highly placed executive staff group, or within a functional group, such as finance, accounting, or marketing.

The process that an MSS team follows depends on the specific application. The group may be temporary, created for a specific MSS, or it may be permanent, in which case the group members are assigned to specific MSS projects.

Many of the MSS developed from the 1980s to the mid-1990s were large-scale, complex systems designed primarily to provide organizational support. Such systems are still under development for complex problems and for company-wide applications. These systems are constructed by a team composed of users, intermediaries, MSS developers, technical support experts, and information systems personnel. Because there can be several people in each category, the teams can be large, and their composition may change over time. Team development of an MSS is a complex, lengthy, costly process. Since the early 2000s, tools and suites have been improved, which means that smaller teams can now handle complex MSS development.

Section 15.10 Review Questions

1. Define *end-user computing*.
2. What are the advantages and risks of user-developed MSS?
3. List some control issues related to end-user computing.

15.11 MANAGEMENT SUPPORT SYSTEM VENDOR AND SOFTWARE SELECTION

Few organizations, especially small to medium enterprises, have the time, financial resources, or technical expertise required to develop today's complex MSS. This means that most MSS applications are built with hardware, software, hosting services, and development expertise provided by outside vendors. Thus, a major aspect of developing an MSS application revolves around the selection and management of vendors and their software offerings.

MSS DEVELOPMENT TOOL SELECTION

There are many commercially available MSS tools at a wide variety of prices. **MSS tools** are software elements (e.g., languages) that facilitate the development of MSS or MSS generators. Some of the software runs only on large mainframes, whereas other software runs only on PCs. Most of the software runs on the Internet and an intranet. Programming language surveys appear on a regular basis. For example, Kay (2000) presented a description of current programming languages, features, and a linguistic sampler. This guide may prove useful in selecting a programming language for a particular application. An organization that intends to use MSS tools must address several interdependent questions, including which tools to use, which hardware to run them on, which operating system to use, and which networks to run them on.

Hardware Selection

MSS run on hardware ranging from an individual PC (e.g., a simple Excel application) to large multiprocessor computers, such as the ones the National Oceanic and Atmospheric Administration (NOAA) uses to run national U.S. weather forecasts. Some run on networks of Unix workstations (including grid computing networks), and others use PCs as Web clients attached to a Web server. Usually, the existing hardware architecture of an organization and its availability to the users govern the choice of hardware.

Software Selection

Selecting MSS tools or suites is a complex process for the following reasons:

- At the time when selection must be made, MSS information requirements and outputs are not completely known
- There are hundreds of software packages on the market
- Software packages are updated very rapidly
- Prices change frequently
- Several people may be involved on the evaluation team
- The required capabilities of the tools may change from one application to another
- Portions of a large MSS may have to be developed with different tools

- The selection decision involves dozens of criteria against which competing packages are compared. Several criteria are intangible; others are in direct conflict with one other
- Technical, functional, end-user, and managerial issues are all considered
- Commercially available evaluations conducted by companies such as Data Pro and the buyer's guides in trade journals, such as *eWEEK* are subjective and often superficial, especially for tools that are also used for non-MSS applications
- The desirability of staying with a few vendors and the nonavailability of client/server open-system environments that allow mixing and matching of products from multiple vendors must be considered

Selecting Vendors and MSS Software Packages

Externally acquired MSS should be evaluated to ensure that they provide the organization with the following advantages:

- *On time.* The system needs to be completed and implemented on or before the scheduled target date.
- *On budget.* The system cost needs to be equal to or less than the budget.
- *Full functionality.* The system has to have all the features listed in the original specifications.

Several independent organizations and magazines conduct software package comparisons from time to time. For smaller packages, users can use "trialware" (e.g., **trialware.org**) from the Internet before making a purchase. Most vendors give users the software for a limited testing time. Also, vendors are often willing to visit a company and demonstrate their software. Martin et al. (2002) identified the following six steps in selecting a software vendor and a package:

1. Identify potential vendors.
2. Determine the evaluation criteria.
3. Evaluate vendors and packages.
4. Choose a vendor and package.
5. Negotiate a contract.
6. Establish a service-level agreement.

More details about the process of selecting a software vendor and MSS package are provided in Online File W15.8.

Section 15.11 Review Questions

1. List the major steps in selecting an MSS application vendor and package.
2. What factors make the selection of MSS software difficult?

15.12 PUTTING TOGETHER A MANAGEMENT SUPPORT SYSTEM

Integration is a difficult issue, and it is especially critical now that MSS tools have migrated to the Web and now that collaboration and communication tools are readily available to decision makers. These and other considerations must be handled as new MSS are developed and legacy systems migrate to the Web.

Development tools increase the developers' productivity and help them construct MSS that are responsive to users' needs. The philosophy of development tools is based on two simple yet very important concepts: the use of highly automated tools throughout the development process and the use of prefabricated pieces in the manufacture of a whole system whenever possible (e.g., component reuse; see Quigley, 2003). The first concept increases the productivity of the developer in the same way that an electric saw improves the productivity of a carpenter who formerly used a handsaw. The second concept increases productivity analogously to the way a prefabricated wall increases the productivity of a carpenter building a house. Fortunately, a software component is not "consumed" when it is used. It can be used again and again. As the components of an MSS are developed, care must be taken to make them fit together. This is similar to how the components of a house must fit together—the plumbing must fit inside the walls but must link the outside water supply to the sinks and tubs, and so on.

There are interfaces among MSS components and with external systems. Typically, MSS databases or data warehouses must be refreshed regularly from other source databases. There may be special tools for necessary functions such as report generation. There may be several databases and models, each of which is developed and used differently; and there may be many people involved in the development in terms of data gathering. Not only do the components have to be constructed, but the specific tools and suites for development also must be selected, installed, and managed.

The system core includes a development language or an MSS suite. Some of the necessary capabilities mentioned here are integrated into MSS suites. Others can be added as needed. These components can be used to build a new MSS or update an existing one. The construction involves the combining of software modules. Fortunately, the newer object-oriented operating systems provide a consistent, user-friendly environment for MSS development. Tools and suites that run in them can easily share results and data. Because a consistent, user-friendly interface can be developed quickly (e.g., in the Microsoft .NET Framework), component interfacing problems are generally minimal. In fact, Web browser GUI interfaces are commonly used to as front ends for legacy MSS and databases instead of a whole system being rewritten. Alternatively, legacy systems have been moved to Web servers, and Web browser front ends have been created.

MSS IMPLEMENTATION ISSUES

Several issues and trends continue to affect MSS applications. They include the following:

- Managers are more readily accepting MSS tools, techniques, and methods.
- Artificial intelligence tools and methods (e.g., expert systems, neural networks, genetic algorithms, fuzzy logic) are being embedded in MSS and in enterprise applications.
- Web technologies continue to enable new developments in MSS/BI—from data, information and knowledge access to direct communication and collaboration.
- GSS continue to proliferate through collaborative computing.
- Computer technology continues its fast-paced evolution. Capabilities are increasing dramatically, and costs are decreasing. This leads to greater capabilities being embedded in MSS.
- Enterprise resource management (ERM)/ERP systems, although extremely expensive, are proliferating. These systems often provide and incorporate MSS methods for improved decision-making.

Section 15.12 Review Questions

1. Why is integration critical to the success of MSS project development?
2. What are the issues and trends that affect the development of MSS projects?

Chapter Highlights

- Because there are so many potential MSS in different organizations, there are also different methods for developing and acquiring applications.
- Because of their cost and complexity, MSS applications need to be developed in a systematic fashion. The development of an MSS should proceed in steps. First, an MSS application portfolio is defined based on an organization's strategy. Second, the MSS architecture is created. Third, a decision is made whether to build, buy, or outsource the development. Fourth, the system is installed, tested, and deployed. Finally, the system goes into maintenance mode, with continual changes being made to ensure the system's continuing success.
- MSS applications are rarely built from scratch. Instead, an enterprise either buys a packaged MSS suite and customizes it to suit its needs or outsources the development to a third party. The selection of one option over another should be based on a systematic comparison of a detailed list of requirements that examines flexibility, information needs, user friendliness, hardware and software resources, and so on.
- Many enterprises elect to outsource the development and maintenance of their MSS applications. The most common type of MSS applications outsourcing is the use of ASP. Utility computing is an emerging option.
- The traditional SDLC is a structured approach for managing the development of information systems. The four fundamental phases of the traditional SDLC are planning, analysis, design, and implementation. Each phase of the SDLC has several small steps, each with its own techniques and deliverables.
- MSS are usually developed using the prototyping (or iterative design or evolutionary development) development methodology. Prototyping consists of rapid cycles through the fundamental phases of the SDLC, with user feedback guiding system modifications. Typically, MSS developed with prototyping continue to evolve following deployment. Iterative prototyping methodology is most common in MSS development because information requirements are not precisely known at the beginning of the process. Prototyping helps the user understand the decision-making situation as the system evolves.
- If a company decides to buy or lease an MSS application, the following selection criteria need to be considered: flexibility, information requirements, user friendliness, hardware and software resources, installation, maintenance services, vendor quality and track record, estimating costs, personnel, technological evolution, scaling, sizing, performance, reliability, and security
- An MSS is typically constructed with an MSS suite consisting of an integrated set of development tools. Selecting MSS software and hardware is difficult because it involves both quantitative and qualitative factors. There are many Web-based MSS tools and generators on the market. The appropriate ones for building a specific MSS application must be selected carefully. More complex MSS applications can be built from comprehensive MSS suites such as MicroStrategy 8, Hyperion System 9 BI**+**, BusinessObjects XI, and Oracle 11i E-Business Suite.
- MSS can be built by teams or by individuals. A team that builds an MSS must follow a structured process.
- Most end-user MSS developed with an integrated tool such as an Excel spreadsheet are used for personal support. The major benefits of end users developing their own MSS are short delivery time, users' familiarity with their needs, low cost, and ease of implementation. User-developed MSS can be of poor quality. However, appropriate controls based on system-development methods can improve quality. The two primary controls are (1) to understand the model of the problem and (2) to review the model carefully.
- Assembling an MSS can involve many components and their interfaces.

Key Terms

- application service provider (ASP)
- end-user computing (end-user development)
- iterative design
- middleware
- MSS architecture
- MSS suite
- MSS tool
- portal
- prototyping
- rapid application development (RAD)
- software-as-a-service (SaaS)
- system development lifecycle (SDLC)
- user-developed MSS
- utility (on-demand) computing
- Web services

Questions for Discussion

1. Discuss the advantages of leasing an MSS application over purchasing one.
2. What type of development approaches would be most appropriate for developing MSS? What type of development approaches would be most appropriate for developing very large systems? Why? What other factors need to be considered?
3. A large manufacturing company elects to use an MSS suite to develop its MSS application. How would the company determine whether to outsource the suite or run it in-house?
4. Why is the traditional SDLC an inappropriate methodology for developing most MSS?
5. Explain why prototyping is also known as evolutionary development. Why is it appropriate for MSS?
6. How does an iterative process secure more user input than conventional development approaches?
7. How can a user develop a better understanding of a decision-making problem by using the iterative process?
8. What are the disadvantages of letting an MSS evolve from a small prototype rather than having complete specifications for the MSS?
9. A firm decides to make its MSS more dynamic by tying its application to a back-end data warehouse. What are some of the ways in which the firm could accomplish this task?
10. Why is component reuse important? What are its advantages and disadvantages?
11. Discuss how to select MSS software. What makes this selection so difficult?
12. You have decided to use a third-party application to develop and deploy a Web-based MSS. Create a checklist for determining which third-party MSS application products will best meet your application requirements.
13. Identify the major reasons utility computing tools may become the next big thing in MSS applications development.
14. Discuss the reasons user-developed MSS can be of poor quality. What can be done to improve the situation?
15. End-user systems developers usually work for managers whose IT knowledge is limited. Discuss the types of problems this situation could lead to and suggest possible ways of dealing with these problems.

Exercises

Teradata University and Other Hands-on Exercises

1. Go to **teradatastudentnetwork.com** and take the Web-based course "What Do Business & IT Have in Common?" Learn how to create a data warehouse that meets your needs and expectations.
2. Consider throwaway prototyping. It is possible to use a spreadsheet package such as Excel to map out the functionality of a program before committing to formal development in a programming language? Do this for a problem that your instructor gives you.
3. Evaluate the following situation: Many hours and much expense were involved in developing an MSS to assist a manager in making an important decision. The prototyping approach was used, so the decision maker and the system developers worked together (and were paid). When it came time for the manager to make the decision, she queried the system, discarded the advice, and made a different decision. How could this happen? Could the system still have been beneficial to the manager? Why or why not? If so, how? Could the system still be beneficial to the organization? Why or why not? (adapted from Dennis and Wixom, 2003).

Exercises

Team Assignments and Role-Playing

1. Go to **dmreview.com/resources/demos.cfm**. Each team should concentrate on a topic assigned by the instructor. Then, team members should look for demos on this topic. Each team should view the demos and prepare a summary of 10 packages.
2. Identify and interview some end users who have developed MSS at their organizations. Ask them whether their organization has any standards for documenting and testing MSS developed by end users. If it has such policies, are they enforced? If not, what do the end users do to ensure the accuracy and maintainability of the MSS they develop?

Exercises

Internet Exercises

1. Go to **hyperion.com** and prepare a list of all the development tools available there as well as their functionalities.
2. Visit IBM's site (**ibm.com**). Find its WebSphere product. Read some of the recent customer success stories. What makes this software so popular?
3. Go to **microstrategy.com** and identify all the tasks that can be used to build MSS applications. Prepare a list of them.
4. Visit the Microsoft Web site (**microsoft.com**). Find its BizTalk product. What kind of software is this? What role could it play in an MSS application?
5. Visit Sun Microsystems (**sun.com**). What type of development platform does Sun provide for creating and deploying MSS applications? What are the capabilities and benefits of the platform?
6. Go to **businessobjects.com** and look at all the available tools for building MSS. View the demos. Prepare a list of the tools and their capabilities.
7. Select an MSS software vendor that supports integration (see, **oracle.com**, **hyperion.com**, **intersystem .com**, **icode.com**, **tibco.com**, **microsoft.com**, or **webmethods. com**). Prepare a report on how they connect MSS applications.
8. The Software Demo Lab at **dmreview.com** allows visitors to preview the latest software from industry vendors. Try some of the software demos on MSS applications. Report your findings to the class.

End of Chapter Application Case

A Fully Integrated MSS for Sterngold: An Old Dental Manufacturer Adopts New IT Tricks

Sterngold (**sterngold.com**), a century-old manufacturer of dental materials, is a subsidiary of London-based Cookson Group PLC. Sterngold is based in Attleboro, Massachusetts. It has only 90 employees but has offices in Europe and South America. The company sells more than 4,000 products both directly to between 350,000 and 400,000 dental professionals and through distributors to another 5 million dental professionals. Orders come in small quantities and, very frequently, from repeat customers, with a frequent demand for same-day shipment.

Sterngold wanted a fully integrated management support system that allows for a fast time to market, access to best-of-breed technology and people, high security, superb reliability, and the ability to focus on the company's core competency. The company also realized that moving its sales online might create easy ordering for its customers while reducing its own transaction costs and enabling customers to get their products faster—all of which would help provide competitive advantage to the company.

Sterngold decided that it had two choices to realize its new business initiatives: (1) develop an MSS application in-house, or (2) find an outsourcer to provide the MSS. Having only one IT person, the company knew that the in-house solution would require hiring additional personnel, which would temporarily create a large IT department. Therefore, Sterngold decided on the outsourcing option instead.

The question then became how to select a trusted business partner that understood the need to move quickly but carefully. After long deliberation and interviews with potential outsourcers, the company selected Surebridge, Inc., to develop and then host the e-commerce application. The selection was "blessed" by Sterngold's parent company, Cookson Group.

Surebridge followed its own proprietary eMethodology approach. First, an implementation team was created. The team evaluated Sterngold's business needs, using interviews to gather the information. Next, specific goals and a timetable were created. A major consideration was to finish the project before the industry's annual trade show so that Sterngold would be able to demonstrate to its customers the ease of ordering products using the online store.

The next step was to create an architecture. This step included a front-end ordering system (Phase I) and its integration with the back-office systems (Phase II). This was not an easy task, given that there were more than 4,000 products with information attributes residing in separate areas of the company. The relevant information was channeled into a large database. A major task was to create a search engine that would be useful to diverse groups of customers (e.g., dentists, dental labs). Each group of customers had different knowledge, requirements, and buying habits. Working hand-in-hand,

Sterngold and Surebridge completed Phase I in less than three months.

Sterngold and Surebridge faced many challenges in executing Phase II. First, expertise was needed on how financial, inventory, and order fulfillment could best be integrated with the ordering system. This required a consultant and resulted in the redesign of some business processes. For example, several internal policies were modified to support the Web initiative. Also, the company's complex pricing policy was simplified through the creation of clear rules about discounting.

The new MSS offers a number of major capabilities. Because the ordering system was integrated with the back office, manual data entry errors were reduced. Real-time inventory status is now given to customers before they place an order, and a tracking feature provides an idea of the real-time status of any order. Discounts are related to specific customers, so they know what they will pay as soon as they log in. Real-time authorization of customers' credit cards is provided when orders are placed. In addition, the company can now offer promotions to its customers without needing to send letters by mail. The site also offers the ability to track customer clickstream movements, which enables the company to personalize products and to cross-sell and up-sell products and services.

By 2005, three years after implementation of the system, Sterngold had recorded the following concrete results:

- By offering free shipping, Sterngold had encouraged more customers to order online, thus increasing the customer base (at the expense of its competitors).
- More product promotion, which is easy to do online, had resulted in additional customers and sales.
- Both the company and the customers had experienced increasing efficiencies and savings on administrative costs.
- Much of the communication via fax and postal mail had been eliminated.
- Sterngold had created a strong relationship with its technology partner. (The fact that Sterngold owns the IT infrastructure and Surebridge just operates it minimizes finger-pointing when problems arise.)

Use of an outside vendor enabled Phase I of the MSS to be finished in less than three months rather than the two to three years that would have been required had it been done in-house. This enabled Sterngold to be the first mover in its industry. The front-end Web site of the MSS is now being translated into several languages for the global market.

Sources: Compiled from G. Craig, "Old Dental Manufacturer Adopts New IT Tricks," *Outsourcing Magazine*, November–December 2003; and **sterngold.com** (accessed February 2006).

QUESTIONS FOR THE CASE

1. Sterngold used an outsourcer to build a custom-made MSS application. What questions or issues should a CIO consider when he or she faces the question of whether to buy an MSS application, build it, hire an ASP to provide it, or do without it entirely?
2. Use of an outside vendor enabled Phase I of the MSS of Sterngold to be finished in less than three months rather than the two to three years that would have been required had it been done in-house. Should fast deployment be a major consideration in the decision to build, buy, or lease an MSS application?
3. Critical to the Sterngold MSS project was the need to integrate the ordering system with the back office (i.e., order fulfillment, inventory, accounting, payment). Why is integration important to the success of MSS?
4. Sterngold created a team to implement the MSS application. Explain why the implementation of an integrated MSS requires a study of existing processes and redesign of the processes that needed alteration.

References

Burnett, M., C. Cook, and G. Rothermel. (2004, September), "End-User Software Engineering." *Communications of the ACM*, Vol. 47, No. 9, pp. 53–58.

Bussler. C., D. Fensel, and N.M. Sadeh. (2005). "Introduction to the Special Section: The Role of Semantic Web Services in Enterprise Application Integration and E-Commerce." *International Journal of Electronic Commerce*, Vol. 9, No. 2, pp. 7–10.

Champion, M., C. Ferris, E. Newcomer, and D. Orchard. (2002, November 14). *Web Services Architecture: W3C Working Draft*, **w3.org/tr/2002/wd-ws-arch-20021114** (accessed February 2006).

Chang, V. (2005). "Design of Middleware Platform to Enhance Abilities of Application Systems Integration." *Proceedings of the International Conference on Information Technology: Coding and Computing (ITCC'05)*. Washington, DC: IEEE Computer Society, pp. 461–466.

Coffee, P. (2004, February). "Data Integration Is IT's Tricks." *eWEEK*.

Coulter, T. (2005, April). "Utility Computing Reality." *Utility Computing, Line 56, Viewpoint*. **line56.com/articles/default.asp?articleid=6467** (accessed February 2006).

D'Agostino, D. (2005, May). "Rent or Buy." *CIO Insight*.

Dahanayake, A., H.G. Sol, and Z. Stojanovic. (2003, March). "Methodology Evaluation Framework for Component-Based System Development." *Journal of Database Management*.

Daylami, N., T. Ryan, L. Olfman, and C. Shayo. (2005, January 3–6). "Determinants of Application Service Provider (ASP) Adoption as an Innovation." *Proceedings of 38th Annual Hawaii International Conference on System Sciences*. Big Island, HI.

Dennis, A., and B. Wixom. (2003). *Systems Analysis and Design*, 2nd ed. New York: Wiley.

Erl, T. (2004). *Service-Oriented Architecture: A Field Guide to Integrating XML and Web Services*. Upper Saddle River, NJ: Prentice Hall PTR.

Frye, C. (2002, November). "Can IT Developers Work Together?" *Application Development Trends*.

Hodge, G., L. Hill, M.L. Zeng, J. Qin, and D. Tudhope. (2005, June 7–11). "Next Generation Knowledge Organization Systems: Integration Challenges and Strategies." *Proceedings of the 5th ACM/IEEE-CS Joint Conference on Digital Libraries*. Denver.

Janvrin, D., and J. Morrison. (2000, January). "Using a Structured Design Approach to Reduce Risks in End-User Spreadsheet Development." *Information & Management*, Vol. 37, No. 1.

Johnson, J. (2001, April/May). "Microproject Methodology Defined." *Software Magazine*.

Kanter, J., and J.J. Walsh. (2004, Summer). "Toward More Successful Project Management." *Information Strategy: The Executive Journal*.

Kay, R. (2000, July 17). "Programming Languages." *Computerworld*.

Malhotra, A., A. Majchrzak, R. Carman, and V. Lott. (2001, June). "Radical Innovation Without Collocation: A Case Study at Boeing-Rocketdyne." *MIS Quarterly*, Vol. 25, No. 2.

Martin, E.W., et al. (2002). *Managing Information Technology*, 4th ed. Upper Saddle River, NJ: Prentice Hall.

McCarthy, J., and M. McCarthy. (2002). *Software for Your Head: Core Protocols for Creating and Maintaining Shared Vision*. Boston: Addison-Wesley.

Melymuka, K. (2001, September 24). "Engaging Users." *Computerworld*.

O'Donnell, P., D. Arnott, and M. Gibson. (2002, July 4–7). "Data Warehousing Methodologies: A Comparative Analysis." *Proceedings of DSIage 2002*, Cork, Ireland.

Quigley, D.E. (2003). "Critical Business Needs Drive Software Component Reuse." *Software Development Times*.

Satzinger, J.W., R.B. Jackson, and S.D. Burd. (2006) *Systems Analysis and Design in a Changing World*, 4th ed. Boston: Course Technology.

Schneider, G.P. (2004). *Electronic Commerce: The Second Wave*, 5th ed. Boston: Course Technology.

Schultheis, R., and M. Sumner. (1994, Spring). "The Relationship of Application Risks to Application Controls: A Study of Microcomputer-Based Spreadsheet Applications." *Journal of End-User Computing*, Vol. 6, No. 2.

Shurville, S., and J. Williams. (2005, January). "Managing In-House Development of a Campus-wide Information System." *Campus-Wide Information Systems*, Vol. 22, No. 1.

Sommerville, I. (2004). *Software Engineering*, 7th ed. Boston: Addison-Wesley.

Srivastava, B. (2004, March 24–26). "A Decision-Support Framework for Component Reuse and Maintenance in Software Project Management." *Proceedings of the Eighth Euromicro Working Conference on Software Maintenance and Reengineering*. Tampere, Finland.

Sutcliffe, A., and N. Mehandjiev. (2004, September). "End-User Development." *Communications of the ACM*, Vol. 47, No. 9.

Tabor, R. (2002). *Microsoft .NET XML Web Services*. Indianapolis: Sams.

Whitten, J.L., and L.D. Bentley. (2005). *Systems Analysis and Design Methods*, 7th ed. New York: Irwin/McGraw-Hill

Xia, W., and G. Lee. (2004, May). "Grasping the Complexity of IS Development Projects." *Communications of the ACM*, Vol. 47, No. 5.

Integration, Impacts, and the Future of Management Support Systems

Learning Objectives

- Understand the need for systems integration for management support systems (MSS)
- Describe the difficulties in integrating systems
- Describe major models of MSS integration
- Describe MSS integration with enterprise systems
- Describe organizational impacts of MSS
- Learn the potential impacts of MSS on individuals
- Describe societal impacts of MSS
- List and describe major ethical and legal issues of MSS implementation
- Define *digital divide* and discuss how to close it
- Provide an overview of the future of MSS

Building or acquiring applications is necessary for MSS in decision making and problem solving. However, it is more important to introduce these systems into organizations and use them for their intended purpose. We refer to this process as *MSS implementation*. In this chapter, we introduce several related topics. First, we discuss the issue of integration of MSS technologies with one another and with other information systems. Then we discuss the organizational, personal, legal, ethical, and societal impacts of support systems that may affect their implementation. Finally, we describe the future of MSS. This chapter has the following sections:

16.1 Opening Vignette: Elite Care Supported by Intelligent Systems
16.2 Systems Integration: An Overview
16.3 Types of Management Support Systems Integration
16.4 Integration with Enterprise Systems and Knowledge Management
16.5 The Impacts of Management Support Systems: An Overview
16.6 Management Support Systems Impacts on Organizations

16.1 OPENING VIGNETTE: ELITE CARE SUPPORTED BY INTELLIGENT SYSTEMS

PROBLEM

Delivering health services to the elderly is becoming a major societal problem, especially in countries where there are relatively fewer young people to take care of more and more elderly people. The problem is already acute in Japan, and it is expected to be very serious in 10 to 15 years in several European countries as well as in China. The specific delivery depends on the health status of the individual, and it is provided in different facilities ranging from home care to nursing homes.

Managing and delivering such care involves making a large number of diversified decisions, ranging from allocation of resources to determining what treatment to provide to each patient at any given time. Elderly residents in assisted-living facilities require different levels of care. Some residents need minimal assistance, others have short-term memory problems, and yet others have more severe problems, such as Alzheimer's disease, and require more supervision and help.

SOLUTION

Elite Care (**elite-care.com**) is a family-owned business in Milwaukie, Oregon, built from the ground up to provide "high-tech, high-touch" programs. Its advisory committee, which includes, among others, representatives from the Mayo Clinic, Harvard University, the University of Michigan, the University of Wisconsin, and Sandia National Laboratory, has contributed a number of ideas that have been put into practice.

Pervasive computing and intelligent systems are being used to increase the autonomy and care level of all of Elite Care's residents, regardless of their individual needs. The entire facility is wired with a 30-mile network (wireline and wireless) of unobtrusive sensors and other devices, including the following:

- Biosensors (e.g., weight sensors) attached to each resident's bed and to chairs
- Movement sensors embedded in badges worn by the residents and staff (i.e., wearable computers)
- Panic buttons used to call for help
- Internet access accessible via touch screens in each room
- Videoconferencing using Webcams
- Climate control, lights, and other regulated appliances

The system has automatic alerts directed to the appropriate personnel. It has also applied if-then decision rules for what to do if corrective actions are not taken within certain time periods. The data collected by the monitoring devices are interpreted, frequently by intelligent systems in real time, allowing the staff to determine the following:

- *Patient location.* Staff can tell whether the resident is in an expected area of the facility.

- *Weight loss.* Weight loss can be an indicator of conditions such as impending congestive heart failure.
- *Restlessness at night.* Restlessness can indicate conditions such as insufficient pain medication.
- *Frequency of trips to the bathroom.* This can indicate medical problems such as infections.
- *Length of absence from bed.* Staff are alerted to the fact that the patient may have fallen or been incapacitated in other ways.

RESULTS

The system allows for rapid communication throughout the facility and for monitoring the location and activities of patients. This results in fewer accidents and in fast emergency care.

Close monitoring of conditions also allows for giving medicine and/or other treatments as needed rather than at a predetermined time. This enables true one-to-one care that is both more effective and less expensive.

One of the initial concerns with the monitors was that the privacy of the residents would be unnecessarily invaded. To alleviate these concerns, residents and their families are given the choice of participating or not. Most of them choose to participate because the families believe that the monitors provide better tracking and care. The monitors also increase the autonomy of the patients, because they lessen the need for staff to constantly monitor residents in person, especially those with acute care needs.

All the sensors (see **youraps.com** for information on these sensors) and intelligent systems are connected through a high-speed Ethernet network. The data produced by these sensors and systems are stored in an SQL database and can be used to alert the staff in real-time if necessary. The data are analyzed to determine patients' health status and to develop individualized care programs. The same database is also used for administrative purposes, such as monitoring staff performance in timely delivery.

A similar concept is used in Swan Village of Care in Bentley, Australia. At the present time, such projects are experimental and expensive, but someday they will be affordable to many.

Sources: Compiled from V. Stanford, "Using Pervasive Computing to Deliver Elder Care," *Pervasive Computing*, January–March 2002; **elite-care.com** (accessed April 2006); *Health Research & Innovation*, **intel.com/research/prohealth** (accessed February 2006); and **ecc.online.wa.gov.au/news**, January 14, 2003 (no longer available online).

Questions for the Opening Vignette

1. Identify the devices that support decision making at Elite Care.
2. What are the benefits of automatic monitoring over manual monitoring? Are there any limitations?
3. What were the privacy concerns at Elite Care?
4. The Elite Care system uses both wireless and wireline networks. Can decision support be improved this way? How?

WHAT WE CAN LEARN FROM THIS VIGNETTE

The opening vignette illustrates that even though MSS may be only a small part of large information systems, they are a necessary component. MSS are integrated with other information systems and even embedded in them and may have a significant impact on organizations, employees, and users of the systems. MSS may raise ethical and legal issues, such as privacy concerns. Such systems may have significant societal impacts, such as reengineering the delivery of care to the elderly and critically ill. These points and related ones are the subject of this chapter.

16.2 SYSTEMS INTEGRATION: AN OVERVIEW

Integrating information systems is widely practiced in enterprises, increasing the efficiency and/or effectiveness of the tasks supported, as shown in the opening vignette. However, such integration is not simple, as described later in this chapter. In the following sections, we look at some relevant concepts.

TYPES OF INTEGRATION

Computer-based systems can be integrated so that the constituent parts of the system function as one entity, as opposed to each being used separately, where integration is used, for example, where it is necessary to manually input outputs of some ports as inputs to other parts. Integration can be at the development level or at the application system level (known as *application integration*, our main area of interest). Integration has been considered a top issue of importance since 2000 (e.g., see Spangler, 2005). There are several types of integration: integration of data, applications, methods, and processes. Integration can also be viewed from two other characteristics: functional and physical.

Functional integration implies that different applications are provided as a single system. For example, working with e-mail, using a spreadsheet, communicating with external databases, creating graphical representations, and storing and manipulating data can all be accomplished at the same workstation. Similarly, working with a decision support system (DSS) and an expert system (ES) is done from one interface, with one menu, resulting in one output. A user can access the appropriate facilities through a single consistent interface—usually a portal and a Web browser—and can easily and quickly switch from one task to another and back again.

Physical integration refers to packaging the hardware, software, and communication features required to accomplish functional integration.

The discussion in this chapter deals primarily with functional-application integration, which can be done in two ways:

- Integration of two or more decision-support applications, creating a unified application
- Integration of one or more DSS with other information systems, such as knowledge management, databases, or a financial system

Integration can occur within a company (*internal integration*) or between systems of different companies (*external integration*).

WHY INTEGRATE?

There are several major objectives for MSS software integration:

- *Implementing MSS.* For MSS to operate, they usually need to be connected to data sources, utilities, other applications, and so on. Such connections must be accomplished effectively and efficiently.

- *Increasing the capabilities of the MSS applications.* In this case, MSS tools complement each other. Each tool performs the subtasks at which it is the best. For example, a DSS can be used to recommend an optimal resource-allocation plan, and an attached ES can provide expert advice on the minimum resources required in certain areas. In an example provided by San Pedro et al. (2005), case-based reasoning was combined with fuzzy multicriteria to forecast cyclones.
- *Enhancing the capabilities of non-MSS applications.* For example, business analytics (BA) tools can be added to enterprise resource planning (ERP) systems to provide analytical capability. Similarly, an intelligent agent can be added to a customer relationship management (CRM) system or to an electronic auction system.
- *Enabling real-time decision support.* By having tight integration, it is possible to support decision making in a real-time environment. An example is transportation systems that use wireless communication and Web services to foster data flow.
- *Enabling more powerful applications.* An example is using intelligent systems to provide real-time on-demand capabilities.
- *Facilitating system development.* Tighter integration allows faster application development and communication among system components.
- *Enhancing with intelligent tools.* Here the purpose of the integration is to enhance non-MSS software tools. For example, an ES can facilitate decision support, and artificial neural networks (ANN) can enhance the knowledge needed for an ES. ES are often used to enhance other tools or applications. For example, on a specific level, a major reason for integrating DSS and ES is the benefits that each technology provides to the other. These are organized in Table 16.1, which shows benefits by major component as well as the overall benefits.

MSS integration may also result in enhanced capabilities that are not possible otherwise. For example, Lau et al. (2004) presented an ES integrated with neural computing for enhancing airfreight decision-making models. Li (2000) described a hybrid intelligent system for developing market strategy by combining the strengths of ES, fuzzy logic, and ANN. For strategies for successful integration, see Morgenthal (2005).

LEVELS OF MSS INTEGRATION

Functional integration, discussed previously, can be considered at two different levels: across different MSS and within MSS. Integration of MSS at these levels is appropriate for systems that can be used to solve repetitive and/or sequential decision problems. MSS can also be used to facilitate integration by assisting in the transformation of the outputs of one system to inputs to another system.

Combining several MSS, each addressing a specific portion of a complex decision problem, is an example of integration across MSS. For example, a BA model for supporting marketing-campaign decisions can be combined with a production-planning supply-chain improvement model, with certain outputs of the first system as the inputs to the second system.

An integrative framework, such as the one proposed by Dutta et al. (1997), can be helpful in understanding the extended role of MSS, with an emphasis on learning to improve decisions and the decision-making process, and with a focus on the process of decision making in addition to the traditional emphasis on the final decision. Their framework also guides the design of integrated MSS that facilitate different modes of decision support.

The second level of integration refers to the integration of appropriate MSS technologies in building a specific MSS, especially to take advantage of the strengths of specific MSS technologies. For example, ANN can be used for pattern recognition as

TABLE 16.1 Summary of Integrating Expert Systems and Decision Support Systems

Type of System	*ES Contribution*	*DSS Contribution*
Database and database management systems (DBMS)	Improves construction, operation, and maintenance of DBMS Improves accessibility to large databases Improves DBMS capabilities Permits symbolic representation of data Advises on data warehouse	Provides a database to the ES Provides numeric representation of data
Models and model base management systems	Improves model management Helps in selecting models Provides judgmental elements to models Improves sensitivity analysis Generates alternative solutions Provides heuristics Simplifies the building of simulation models Makes the problem structure incrementally modifiable Speeds up trial-and-error simulation	Provides initial problem structure Provides standard model computations Provides facts (i.e., data) to models Stores specialized models constructed by experts in the model base
Interface	Enables friendlier interface Provides explanations Provides terms familiar to users Acts as a tutor Provides interactive, dynamic, visual problem-solving capability	Provides presentations to match individual cognitive and decision styles
System capabilities (synergy)	Provides intelligent advice (faster and less expensively than a human) to the DSS or its user Adds explanation capability Expands computerization of the decision-making process	Provides effectiveness in data collection Provides effective implementation Provides individualized advice to users to match their decision styles

part of the intelligence phase of the decision-making process, or for data mining, and an ES can be used to assess the recommended solution generated by a BA model. This type of integration can be either in the form of a mix of different technologies (e.g., fuzzy logic and analytic hierarchy process, ES, and ANN; see Lau et al., 2004) or in the form of supporting different phases or activities in decision making (e.g., ANN for pattern recognition in the intelligence phase and ES for the design and choice phases). Several examples of MSS integration at this level are described later in this chapter.

Embedded Systems

Over the past few years, we have seen an increasing number of systems that include embedded intelligent systems. For their evolution, see Grabowski and Sanborn (2001). In such systems, the intelligent part (e.g., an intelligent agent) is nontransparent to the user, and it may even work in real-time. The automated decision support (ADS) systems described throughout the book are of this type. For a directory of embedded intelligent systems, see **techlistings.net/xlist**.

There is an increasing trend to embed intelligent systems in large or complex information systems, as in the following examples:

- Computer telephony integration at "intelligent" call centers to select and assign a human agent for a specific customer call in real-time

- Real-time decision making built around online transaction processing (OLTP) systems, such as collaborative planning, forecasting, and replenishment in supply-chain management (SCM) and real-time scheduling DSS
- Support of strategic management planning and analysis, with built-in intelligent agents
- Intelligent DSS for process enhancements and management to support group decision-making
- An intelligent optimization system for determining item prices at large retail chains (see Chapter 1)
- Intelligent logistics support systems (Lau et al., 2004)
- A neural network combined with online analytical processing (OLAP) to facilitate resource allocation decisions (see Lau et al., 2004)

Integration and the Web

Integration is frequently performed via the Web. For the relationship between the two, see Table 16.2.

Section 16.2 Review Questions

1. List several types of integration.
2. Describe the need for MSS integration.
3. List the levels of integration.
4. Describe integration of MSS with non-MSS systems.
5. Define *embedded system*.

TABLE 16.2 The Web-Integration Connection

Topic of Integration	*Description*
Provision of infrastructure	Intranets are used for internal integration. Extranets are used for external integration.
New technologies	Web services could provide a breakthrough in facilitating difficult internal and external integration. Wireless infrastructure makes it less expensive and easier to integrate systems.
Integration methods	Use of application service provider (ASP) over the Web makes it cheaper and faster to integrate. Some integration can be done by the ASP vendor.
Improve technologies	Expensive and/or complex and inflexible technologies can be made simpler and cheaper to use (e.g., moving from electronic data interchange (EDI) to Internet/EDI).
Connecting business partners	The Web makes it cheaper, faster, and easier to connect applications and databases among several partners.
Flexibility and adoptability to change	Traditional integration tools/methods, such as middleware, are inflexible. It is necessary to modify applications to fit them. Using Web-based tools, we can integrate systems without modification and change integrated systems to adapt to changing business environment.
Opportunities and challenges	The Web enables integration of applications in different locations, faster and more easily. Connection to legacy systems is simpler.
Rich multimedia integration, Web tools, and usability	The Web enables integration of rich media applications. The support of Internet tools (e.g., hyperlinks, search engines) makes the integrated systems more usable.

16.3 TYPES OF MANAGEMENT SUPPORT SYSTEMS INTEGRATION

There are several types of MSS integration as well as several integration issues. We present only a few of them here.

MODELS OF INTEGRATING ES AND DSS[1]

Several models have been proposed for integrating ES (or other intelligent systems) and DSS. Integration of this kind appears under several names, ranging from *expert support systems* to *intelligent DSS*. The following models are described in this chapter: intelligent systems[2] attached to DSS components, ES as a separate DSS component sharing in the decision-making process, ES generating alternative solutions for DSS, and a unified approach. Integrated models are usually problem driven, so MSS integration is frequently a process of matching problems with appropriate tools that can then be integrated to provide enhanced decision support. For some early models of intelligent DSS, known as "active DSS" and "self-evolving DSS," see Online File W16.1.

Intelligent Systems Attached to DSS Components

Theoretically, intelligent systems can be integrated into any or all DSS components. The arrangement shown in an application in Figure 16.1 includes five ES (or other intelligent systems):

1. Database intelligent component.
2. Intelligent system for the model base and its management.

FIGURE 16.1 Integration of ES into All DSS Components

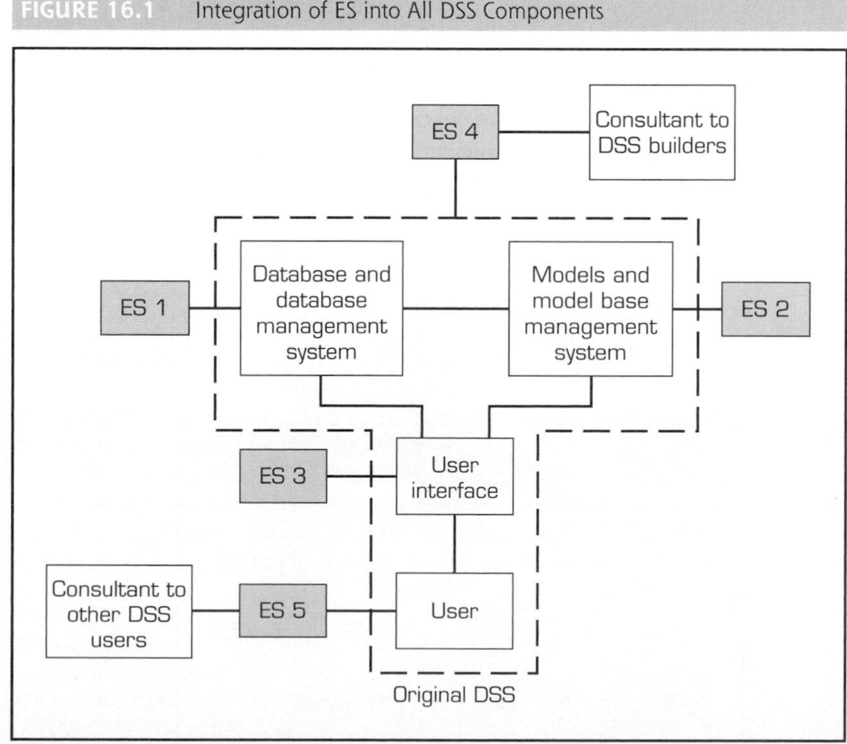

[1]The term DSS refers here to any system that supports the decision maker(s).
[2]Many of the intelligent systems are rule-based ES. Therefore, we refer to them as *ES*.

3. Intelligent system for improving the user interface.
4. Intelligent consultant to DSS builders. In addition to giving advice on constructing the various components of the DSS, this ES gives advice on how to structure a DSS, how to glue the various parts together, how to conduct a feasibility study, and how to execute the many activities involved in the construction of a DSS.
5. Intelligent consultant to users. The user of a DSS may need the advice of an expert for complex issues such as the nature of the problem, the environmental conditions, or possible implementation problems. A user may also want an ES that offers guidance on how to use the DSS and its output.

In most cases, not all five systems are considered. Often it is beneficial to attach only one or two ES (or other intelligent systems). There are many variations of this model. For example, a natural language interface could be attached to the user interface, and an intelligent inference agent could operate between the database and the model base.

An ES as a Separate Component in a DSS

An ES can be added as a separate component in a DSS. The integration is usually tight because the ES shares the interface as well as other resources. This is a common arrangement. The combined system is known as an intelligent DSS (IDSS), environmental spatial DSS (ESDSS), or expert DSS (EDSS). Such integration is also available via a communication link over the Internet or an intranet. Three possible configurations for such integration are described in the following sections. The three possibilities are illustrated in Figure 16.2.

ES Output as Input to BA The ES output is used as input to some analytical tool. For example, the ES is used during the initial phase of problem solving to determine the relative importance of a problem or to classify it. Then the problem is transferred to an analytical tool. Another example is sensory systems which collect data that are transferred to an ES for interpretation. The results, then, are transferred to a BA for analysis and recommendation.

Analysis Output as Input to ES Often, the results of computerized quantitative analysis are forwarded to an individual or a group of experts for the purpose of interpretation. Therefore, it would make sense to direct such output to an ES that can perform the same function as a human expert whenever it is less expensive or faster to do so (especially if the quality of the advice is also superior).

FIGURE 16.2 Interface Possibilities Between ES and DSS

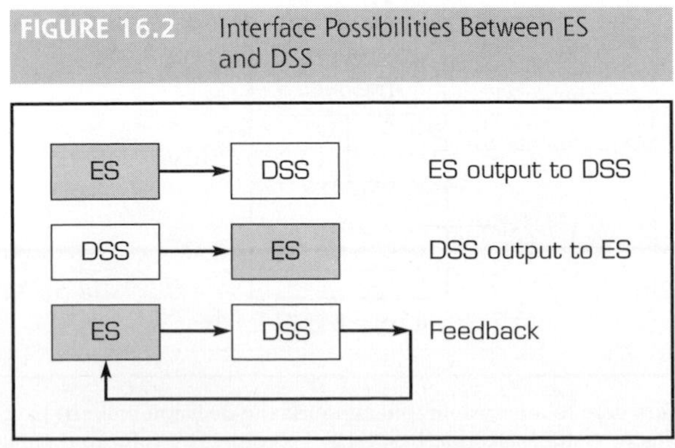

Feedback With this configuration, the output from the ES goes to an analysis, and then the output from the analysis goes back to the original ES (or vice versa).

ISSUES AND CONFIGURATIONS IN MSS INTEGRATION

MSS integration may involve issues such as those described in the following sections.

Representative Integration Factors

A framework for integrating intelligent systems in the context of design and control of modern manufacturing systems was proposed by Zaremba and Morel (2003). This framework recognizes different integrations and different intelligent systems at different stages in a product lifecycle. The authors also considered ubiquitous systems involving multisensory systems.

Many factors should be considered when integrating MSS. Some major representative problems and issues are summarized in Table 16.3; others are illustrated in Technology Insights 16.1.

Sharing in the Decision-Making Process

According to the integrated approach, an intelligent system can be used in one or more of the steps in the decision-making process. Decision making can be viewed as a multistep process consisting of such activities as specification of objectives and parameters,

TABLE 16.3 Problems and Issues of MSS Integration

Issue	*Description*
Justification	Conduct a cost–benefit and need assessment.
Feasibility	Conduct a technological, economical, organizational, and behavioral analysis. Conduct an impact study, if needed.
Architecture	Examine the best possible architecture.
Infrastructure	Determine what types of hardware, software, etc., will be involved. Determine what commercially available components to use.
Outsourcing	Decide who will do the integration and how to select and manage the vendors.
Supporting the project	Determine who is committed to the project. Also decide what support top management will give, especially if several departments are involved.
Support of business partners	Because many MSS involve connecting to business partners, especially along the supply chain, determine whether they collaborate.
Development process and tools	Depending on the architecture, infrastructure, and so on, decide on a development process and selection of tools.
Data issues	Determine how symbolic processing is handled when combined with algorithms.
Legal and privacy	Determine how secure data are in integrated systems, especially when several departments/organizations are involved. Determine whether privacy is protected.
Connectivity	Determine which options are available to assure the connectivity. Determine whether Web services are going to be used.
Web-based integration	Ensure that the integrated system will be Web-based. Determine how legacy systems, ERP, and so on are connected.
Introducing new technologies	Determine how to deal with Web services and Microsoft .NET and decide on an adoption strategy and justification.

TECHNOLOGY INSIGHTS 16.1

Integrated Fleet Management Systems Improve Performance

A large number of companies operate their own fleets of cars and trucks. Also, hundreds of companies operate fleets of cars and trucks that they lease to individuals or businesses. Managing a fleet is a critical issue, especially when gasoline prices are on the rise. Therefore, extensive software has been developed to support fleet management (known as fleet management systems [FMS]). These systems support many tasks, such as organizing dispatch, delivering freight bills, planning routes, tracking a package, and finding where a truck is at a given time. To get the functionalities required, it is necessary to integrate FMS with both internal and external systems (e.g., customers, suppliers). Also, extensive use of real-time data from wireless communication systems needs to flow to FMS. Therefore, flexible and tighter integration is needed, as are open information technology (IT) environments (e.g., Linux, XML, Web services). The latter enable easier communication between systems and faster development time, regardless of the platforms involved. This requires greater intelligence for real-time planning and strategic planning. Tools such as dashboards are used extensively in managing large FMS.

For example, say that a large shipper requires one-hour notification of delivery from a tracking company. With Web services, the shipper transmits shipment information into the system of a third-party logistics (3PL) vendor, which uses business rules to alert the proper trucking companies. Drivers with wireless data communications update the trucking company systems when they make deliveries via Web services, which then update the 3PL system and the shipper. No human being other than the driver is involved in the entire transaction. A simple example is the use of radio frequency identification (RFID) to notify people of the arrival or departure of a truck.

New technologies also offer opportunities for adding much more intelligence. For example, only the largest fleets currently have the capacity to make use of optimization systems, but with better inter-system communications, it would be possible for smaller fleets to pool their capacity for cooperative optimization. The basic technology for this cross-database optimization already exists. We know how to make systems more interconnected and more efficient. The revolutionary aspect is figuring out how to wire it all together and make it easy to use.

Sources: Compiled from J. Mele, "Fleet Management Systems: The Future Is Here," *Fleet Owner*, August, 2005; and **maddocks.ca** (accessed February 2006).

retrieval and management of data, generation of decision alternatives, prediction of the consequences of decision alternatives, evaluation of the impact of consequences, selection of an alternative, explanation and implementation of the alternative, and strategy formulation.

Some of these activities can best be supported by BA, while those that require expertise (e.g., strategy formulation, interpretation of results) are better executed with the support of intelligent systems.

Such sharing can be visualized as follows: The user works with the BA, following the activities that are amenable to analysis. Upon reaching the strategy-formulation phase or any other activity that requires expertise, the user calls on the ES, which is a completely segregated system (i.e., loose integration), although it may share a database and perhaps use some of the capabilities of the model base. This can be done on the Web by using Web services. To better understand this type of integration, assume that the ES plays the role of a human expert whom the user can call on when in need of expertise. The expert may give an answer immediately or may conduct further analysis (e.g., forecasting). For example, the analysis can be accomplished by using a forecasting model.

An example of an integrated system in the health care environment is provided by Forgionne et al. (2002). The system, illustrated in Figure 16.3, shows the integration of

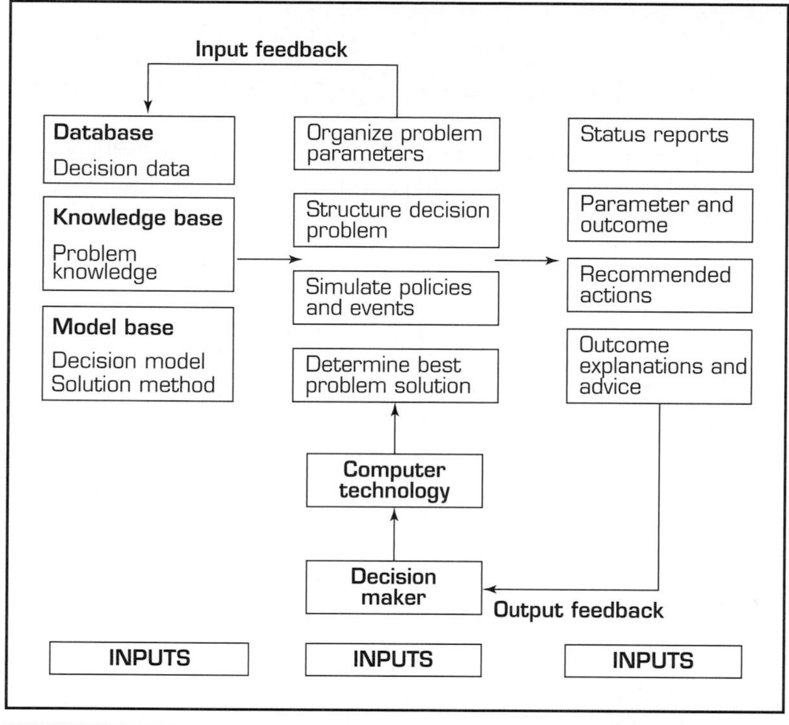

FIGURE 16.3 Global Integration

Source: G. Forgionne, M. Mora, F. Cervantes, and O. Gelman, "I-DMSS: A Conceptual Architecture for the Next Generation of Decision Making Support Systems in the Internet Age." *Proceedings of DSIage 2002, Cork, Ireland*. July 2002, Figure 2, p. 161.

knowledge and DSS models. The input includes data (for the DSS), knowledge (for an intelligent component and the decision maker), and a model base to process them. The processing capability organizes the problem and structure and then generates a proposed solution in concert with the decision maker. The proposed solution returns as a feedback to the system input. After several iterations, the system reaches stability and can generate reports, propose actions, and give explanations and advice. The output returns to the decision maker, which may change some of the problem parameters (e.g., assumptions), and the process iterates again, until stability is reached.

Feedback Loops in Integrated Systems

Feedback from processing provides additional data, knowledge, and enhanced decision models that may be useful in current as well as future decision making. Output feedback (often in the form of sensitivity analyses) is used to extend or modify the original analyses and evaluations. Similarly, data can flow from an ERP system to business intelligence (BI), and then the BI input flows to the ERP system.

Section 16.3 Review Questions

1. Describe an IDSS and name the types of DSS.
2. How can different MSS tools share in the decision-making process?
3. Relate feedback loops to integration.
4. List and describe some integration issues and factors.

16.4 INTEGRATION WITH ENTERPRISE SYSTEMS AND KNOWLEDGE MANAGEMENT

Much MSS integration today is conducted in a Web-based environment with enterprise systems, such as an ERP, knowledge management, or CRM. The objectives of such integration are to:

- Increase the functionalities of the enterprise (or other) systems by adding intelligent components or a computational engine.
- Make the enterprise systems more user friendly.
- Allow greater flexibility and ease in accessing dynamic data.
- Save money for the users by allowing them to easily integrate systems from several vendors.
- Enable easier integration of the functional systems with electronic markets and/or business partners

MSS and especially intelligent systems may be embedded in the supported systems to provide intelligent interfaces, calculating engines, and so on. They are therefore basically invisible to the user and do not appear as MSS. A most common integration is with ERP and SCM.

INTEGRATION WITH ERP AND SCM SYSTEMS

BA tools are now integrated with enterprise systems, supply chains (see **dmreview.com**, a BI portal), and ERP. ERP systems such as SAP R/3 consist of dozens of applications integrated via the ERP software. Because enterprise systems are transaction oriented, adding decision support capabilities can greatly enhance their capabilities. This is usually done by adding SCM and/or BI software (see Chapter 17, an online chapter).

Most ERP and enterprise vendors integrate some analytical capabilities into their products (e.g., see **sap.com**, **oracle.com**). According to Holsapple and Sena (2005), ERP can greatly facilitate decision making in the enterprise, as illustrated by Michel (2005).

The U.S. Navy's Supply Maintenance Aviation Reengineering Team (SMART) program is an example of integrating ERP with decision support tools (see Clarke, 2003). The SMART program allows rapid decision support for complex maintenance management activities.

One major solution to supply-chain problems is to use optimization tools that are part of SCM software. Such software is provided by i2, Manugetics, Computer Associates, Oracle, and other vendors. SCM software often includes optimization models for scheduling and resource allocation.

In another type of integration, decision support is provided to some business processes in the system. In contrast with ERP, where the SCM analytical tools support individual processes, here one segment of the chain can be the center of the system, with which either standard or custom applications are integrated.

To enhance the airfreight forwarding business, an intelligent logistics system was developed by Lau et al. (2004). The system improved container loading and transportation scheduling along the supply chain. The system also integrated an ES, neural computing, and decision support models (see the End of Chapter Application Case).

Finally, supply chains and ERP tools can benefit through integration with knowledge management systems (KMS) because knowledge is frequently required for solving problems along the supply chain.

INTEGRATION WITH KMS

MSS applications are sometimes integrated with KMS to promote knowledge sharing between individuals as well as departments and functional areas.

Integration of KMS with Other Business Information Systems

A KMS is frequently integrated with other information systems. Obviously, when it is designed and developed, it cannot be perceived as an add-on application. It must be truly integrated into other systems. Through the structure of the organizational culture, a KMS and its activities can be directly integrated into a firm's business processes. For example, a group involved in customer support can capture its knowledge in an ES in order to provide help for customers' difficult problems.

Because a KMS can be developed on a knowledge platform consisting of communication, collaboration, and storage technologies, and because many firms already have many such tools and technologies in place, it is often possible to develop a KMS with an organization's existing tools (e.g., Lotus Notes/Domino Server). Also, an enterprise knowledge portal can provide universal access and an interface into all relevant corporate information and knowledge.

Integrating DSS and Knowledge Management

While DSS and knowledge management are independent activities in many organizations, they are interrelated in many others. For a discussion of knowledge management, BI, and their integration, see Herschel and Jones (2005). For example, knowledge creation may be done by evaluating historical decisions. Alternatively, decision makers may use stored knowledge for making decisions. Bolloju et al. (2002) proposed a framework for integrating decision support and knowledge management processes, using knowledge-discovery techniques. The framework is based on the relationship shown in Figure 16.4. The decision maker is using applications fed by a data warehouse and data marts and is also using other sources of knowledge (see the right side of Figure 16.4). The DSS information and the knowledge are integrated in a system, and the knowledge can be stored in the model base.

FIGURE 16.4 Framework for Integrating DSS and KMS

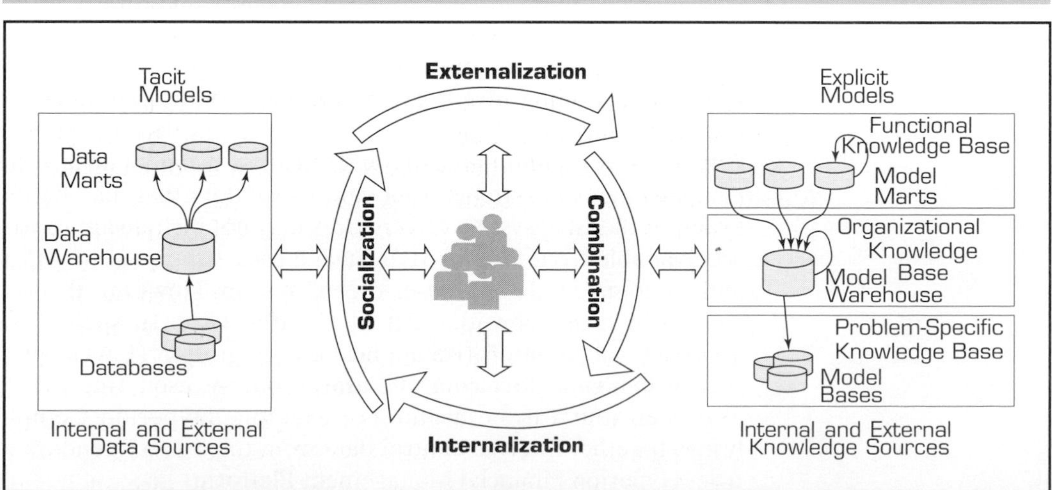

Source: N. Bolloju, et al., "Integrating Knowledge Management into Enterprise Environments for the Next Generation of Decision Support," *Decision Support Systems*, Vol. 33, No. 2, June 2002, pp. 163–176.

A study reported by Heinriches and Lim (2003) demonstrated the positive interaction obtained by integrating data mining tools to enhance the decision capability of knowledge workers who used Web-based DSS models for improving strategic performance capabilities.

Integration of Intelligent Systems and Knowledge Management

Knowledge management has a natural relationship with intelligent system methods and software. There are a number of ways in which knowledge management and intelligent systems can be integrated. For example, if the knowledge stored in a KMS is to be represented and used as a sequence of if-then-else rules, an ES becomes part of the KMS. An ES could also assist a user in identifying how to apply a chunk of knowledge in the KMS.

Much work is being done in the field of artificial intelligence related to knowledge engineering, tacit-to-explicit knowledge transfer, knowledge identification, understanding, dissemination, and so on. Companies are attempting to realign these technologies with knowledge management. The artificial intelligence technologies most often integrated with knowledge management are intelligent agents, ES, neural networks, and fuzzy logic.

Other Knowledge Management–Related Integration

The number of application integrations of MSS and knowledge management is growing. The following are some examples:

- Integration of data mining tools and business modeling for knowledge management (see Heinriches and Lim, 2003)
- An integration of intelligent data mining tools with manufacturing systems (see Lau et al., 2001)
- DSS integration with learning and training systems (see Mallach, 1994)
- Integration of BI and knowledge management (see Herschel and Jones, 2005)

INTEGRATION APPROACHES

Several approaches exist for integrating MSS applications across an enterprise. Here are four common ones:

1. *Second-generation ERP systems.* The second-generation ERP systems from SAP, Oracle, and other vendors include BI capabilities. They all provide OLAP, query tools, data mining, and more. In addition, they provide SCM tools. There are DSS tools for scheduling, inventory control, and production scheduling. One newer tool is dashboards.
2. *Enterprise application integration.* Instead of using a package from one vendor, a company can use systems from various vendors that may better fit its needs. For example, the ERP system of Vendor A may not include appropriate BI tools, which are available from Vendor B. In such a case, the company will use both A and B and try to assemble a "best-of-breed" system. However, this requires integration tools, which are considered to be *middleware*. In such cases, an integration approach called enterprise application integration (EAI)—provided by vendors such as **ibm.com**, **tibco.com**, and **oracle.com**—is used. Recently, Web services have also been found to be useful. For example, Hyperion Compliance Dashboard brings together internal control data from third-party vendors with financial data from Hyperion Financial Management Platform.
3. *Comprehensive systems.* Since 2001, there has been a trend for using all-in-one-stop systems. An example is provided in Technology Insights 16.2.

TECHNOLOGY INSIGHTS 16.2

An Oracle BI Integrated System

Oracle offers a comprehensive integrated set around which a BI system can be built. The architecture of the system is shown in Figure 16.5. Its major objective is to build intelligence into business processes for tasks such as approving loans or routing vehicles. The major components of the set parallel the concept of BI as presented in Chapter 1 and Chapter S (the special introductory section on business intelligence [BI], pp. 187–205).

FIGURE 16.5 The Oracle BI System

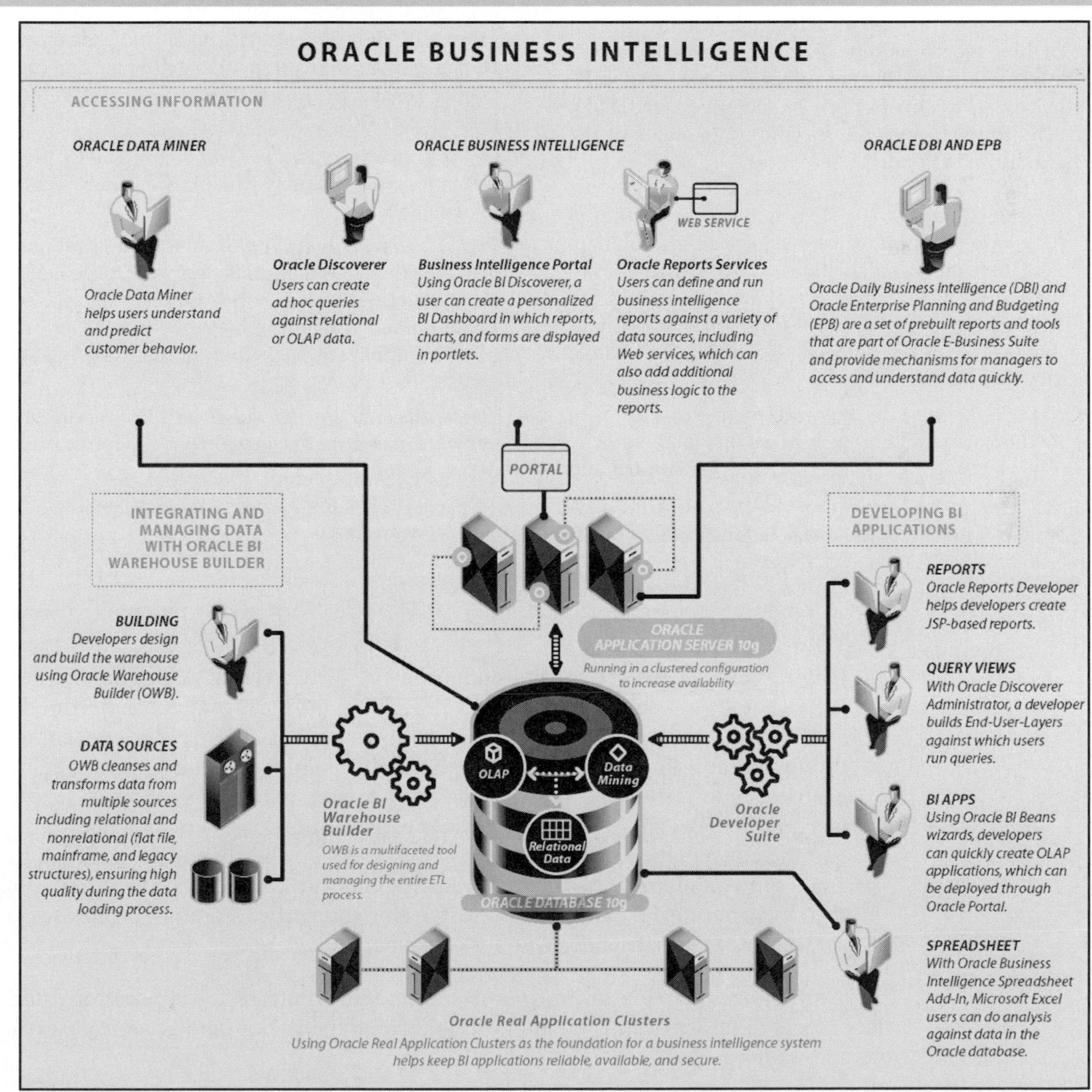

Source: A. Joch, "Eye on Information," *Oracle Magazine*, January/February 2005.

TECHNOLOGY INSIGHTS 16.2 (continued)

Oracle tools are available for data collection from multiple sources and are transferred to a data warehouse that can be built with appropriate tools such as extraction, transformation, and load (ETL) tools. The warehouse can be accessed via a BI portal that connects to Oracle's Database 10g, enabling relational data organization for the data warehouse as well as the opportunity for data mining and OLAP. Developers' tools for reports, queries, OLAP applications, and BI spreadsheets (using Excel) are also available. The integrated set enables superb multimedia presentation of analytical information. For further information about the BI system and its use by several customers, see Joch (2005).

The following are the specific components of the system shown in Figure 16.5:

- *Oracle Database 10g.* This is the core relational database platform, which includes embedded data and text-mining algorithms, statistical functions, and an OLAP engine, making it possible for enterprises to perform powerful analytics without having to move data to expensive, standalone analytical servers.
- *Oracle Business Intelligence Discoverer.* This is an ad hoc query and reporting tool that enables viewing of, reporting on, and analysis of relational and multidimensional data within the same intuitive interface.
- *Oracle Application Server 10g Portal.* This is an environment that delivers BI reports to end users in personalized Web-based formats.
- *Oracle Data Miner.* This application provides a new user interface in which data analysts can mine data, develop new insights, build predictive models, and generate model code. Developers use Oracle Data Miner's PL/SQL or Java APIs to develop advanced BI applications that automate data mining and distribute results to information consumers enterprisewide.
- *Oracle Business Intelligence Warehouse Builder.* This design tool works closely with Oracle Database 10g to manage ETL.
- *Prepackaged analytical applications.* Applications, including Oracle Balanced Scorecard, Oracle Daily Business Intelligence, and Oracle Enterprise Planning and Budgeting, work with transaction-oriented applications, including SCM and CRM applications.
- *Oracle Business Intelligence Beans.* These reusable software components jump-start BI application development.

Sources: Compiled from A. Joch, "Eye on Information." *Oracle Magazine*, January/February 2005; and *Oracle Business Intelligence Solutions*, **oracle.com/solutions/business_intelligence** (accessed April 2006).

4. *Web services*. There are several definitions of Web services. A simple one is that Web services are self-contained, self-describing business and consumer modular applications, delivered over the Internet, that users can select and combine through almost any device, from PCs to mobile phones. By using a set of shared protocols and standards, these applications permit disparate systems to talk with one another (i.e., share data and services without requiring human beings to translate the conversation). The result promises to be on-the-fly and in real-time links among the online processes of different systems and companies. These links could shrink corporate IT departments, foster new interactions among businesses, and create a more user-friendly Web for consumers.

Web services provide for inexpensive and rapid solutions for application integration, access to information, and application development. For details, see **webservices.org** and **ws-i.org**.

Section 16.4 Review Questions

1. Describe MSS integration with SCM and ERP software.
2. Describe the various modes of MSS integration with knowledge management.

3. How do vendors support MSS integration?

4. Describe the Oracle BI architecture in general terms.

16.5 THE IMPACTS OF MANAGEMENT SUPPORT SYSTEMS: AN OVERVIEW

MSS are important participants in the information, Web, and knowledge revolution. This is a cultural transformation with which most people are only now coming to terms. Unlike the slower revolutions of the past, such as the Industrial Revolution, this revolution is taking place very quickly and affecting every facet of our lives. Inherent in this rapid transformation are a host of managerial, economical, and social issues and problems. According to Gartner Group, the MSS share of the computer industry, including embedded systems and BI, is expected to grow at a 37.5 percent compound annual growth rate, and the MSS impact may be substantial (reported by Labat 2006).

Separating the impact of MSS from that of other computerized systems is a difficult task, especially because of the trend toward integrating, or even embedding, MSS with other computer-based information systems. There is very little published information about the impact of pure MSS technologies because the techniques are frequently integrated with other information systems, and their benefits are mostly intangible. Another problem is the rapid changes in MSS implementation. Thus, some of our discussion must relate to computer systems in general. We recognize, however, that MSS technologies have some unique implications, which are highlighted throughout the remainder of this chapter.

MSS can have both micro and macro implications. Such systems can affect particular individuals and jobs, and they can also affect the work structures of departments and units within an organization. They can also have significant long-term effects on total organizational structures, entire industries, communities, and society as a whole (i.e., a macro impact).

Figure 16.6 presents a framework that shows the high-level architecture of an MSS. Such a system stays in equilibrium as long as all of its parts are unchanged. If there is a major change in one of the parts or in the relevant environment, the change is likely to affect some of the other parts. The major change stimuli relevant to MSS are usually *strategy* and *technology*, especially when BI or ES are introduced.

Computer technology has already changed our world, and much more change is anticipated. In addition to the effect on individuals, there are significant societal effects. The following are some of the major areas of social impact (see Section 16.11):

- Changing role of home-bound people
- Computer crime and fraud
- Consumers
- The digital divide
- Employment levels
- Opportunities for the disabled
- Quality of life
- Work in hazardous environments

One of the major changes now occurring is the emergence of the Web and its impact on MSS (see Sikler and Gangopadhyay, 2002). Another is the relationship of decision support and knowledge management. (see Holsapple, 2003). Both are related to the organizational transformation.

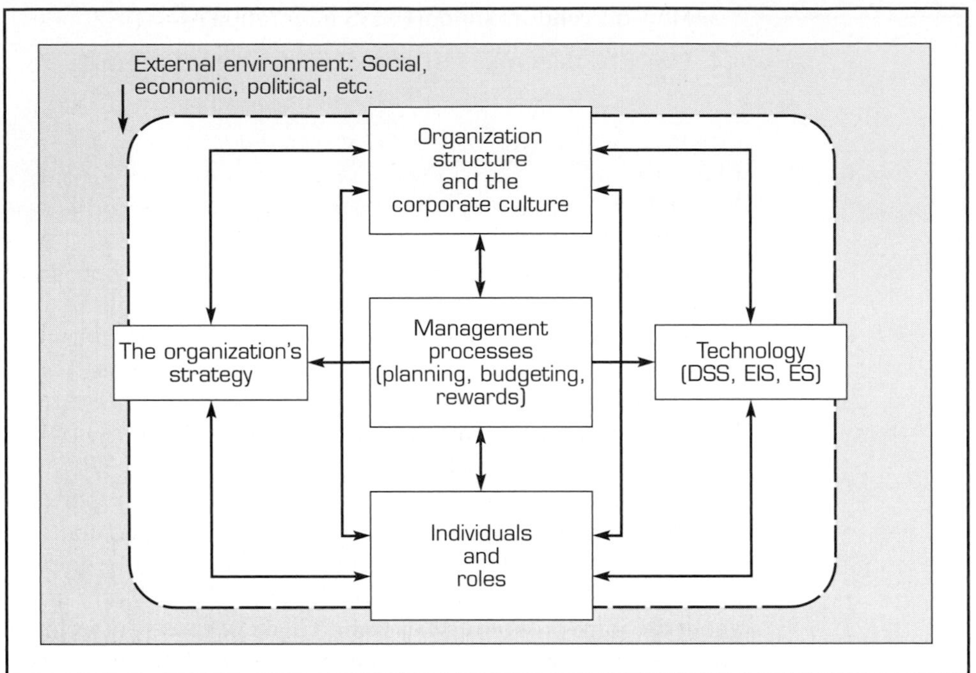

FIGURE 16.6 A Framework for Organizational and Societal Impacts of Artificial Intelligence Technology

Source: M.S. Morton, "DSS Revisited for the 1990s," Paper Presented at *DSS 1986*, Washington, DC, April 1986. Used with permission.

The impact of computers and MSS technology can be divided into three general categories: organizational, individual, and societal. In each of these, computers have had many impacts. We cannot possibly consider all of them in this chapter, so in the next section, we cover only the topics we feel are most relevant to MSS.

Section 16.5 Review Questions

1. How can MSS affect particular individuals and jobs, or the work structure of departments and units within an organization?
2. How can MSS affect organizational structures, entire industries, communities, and society as a whole?
3. What are the major stimuli for change in the MSS environment?
4. List some of the major social impacts of MSS.

16.6 MANAGEMENT SUPPORT SYSTEMS IMPACTS ON ORGANIZATIONS

Of the many organizational impacts, the following sections describe those that are closely related to MSS.

NEW ORGANIZATIONAL UNITS

One change in organizational structure is the possibility of creating a management support department, a BI department (unit), an artificial intelligence department, or a knowledge management department in which MSS play a major role. This special unit can be combined with or replace a quantitative analysis unit, or it can be a completely new entity.

Some large corporations have separate decision support units or departments. For example, many major banks have such departments in their financial services divisions. Mead Corp., for example, has a special corporate DSS applications department, although it is integrated with other enterprise activities. Many companies have small decision support or BI/data warehouse units. Several large corporations have created artificial intelligence departments. Boeing, Inc., for example, operates a large artificial intelligence department.

These types of departments are usually involved in training in addition to consulting and application development activities. A number of firms have created knowledge management departments (or units), headed by a chief knowledge officer (CKO). Others have empowered a chief technology officer over BI, intelligent systems, and e-commerce applications.

Example: Decision Support at Mead Corporation

Mead Corp. (now MeadWestco) created a DSS department in the mid-1980s that included an interactive help center, office systems, decision analysis, and financial modeling. In the 1990s, it added a new function: local area experts. These people report directly to user departments and indirectly to the director of the DSS department. They assist users in developing and maintaining DSS applications.

The system has been modified several times. A major change occurred in the late 1990s, when the DSS was integrated with enterprise systems. By 2005, all MSS units were operating from a business solution division that included ERP, MSS, DSS, e-commerce, knowledge management, collaboration, and logistics management. For details, see McNurlin and Sprague (2006).

ORGANIZATIONAL CULTURE

Organizational culture can affect the diffusion rate of technology and can be influenced by it. For example, the use of Lotus Notes changed the organizational climate of a large CPA firm by making employees more cooperative and willing to share information and use computers. In addition, virtual teams can meet anytime and anyplace. People can join a virtual team for as long as the project lasts or whenever their expertise is needed. When a project is completed, the team can disband. For changes in organizational culture due to MSS, see Watson et al. (2000).

Automated decision support (ADS) applications can empower lower-level frontline employees, giving them more autonomy. They may also reduce the size of organizations and change the organization's culture.

RESTRUCTURING BUSINESS PROCESSES AND VIRTUAL TEAMS

In many cases, it is necessary to restructure business processes before introducing new information technologies. For example, before IBM introduced e-procurement, it restructured all related business processes, including decision making, searching inventories, reordering, and shipping. When a company introduces a data warehouse and BI, the information flows and related business processes (e.g., order fulfillment) are likely to change. Such changes are often necessary for profitability or even survival. Restructuring is especially necessary when major IT projects such as ERP or BI are undertaken. Sometimes an organization-wide, major restructuring is needed, and then it is referred to as *reengineering*. Reengineering involves changes in structure, organizational culture, and processes. In a case in which an entire (or most of an) organization is involved, the process is referred to as **business process reengineering (BPR)**.

Several concepts of BPR greatly change organizational structure and mode of operation: team-based organization, mass customization, empowerment, and telecommuting. Therefore, in some cases, MSS may be used extensively as an enabler (see Turban et al., 2001). MSS also play a major role in BPR (see El Sawy, 2001). MSS allow business to be conducted in different locations, providing flexibility in manufacturing; permit quicker delivery to customers; and support rapid, paperless transactions among suppliers, manufacturers, and retailers.

ES can enable organizational changes by providing expertise to non-experts. An example is shown in Figure 16.7. The upper part of the figure shows a bank before reengineering. A customer who needed several services had to go to several departments. The bank kept multiple records and provided the customer with several monthly statements. The reengineered bank is shown in the lower part. A customer now makes contact with only one person, an account manager, who is supported by an ES. The new arrangement is less expensive, and customers save time and receive only one statement.

Related to organizational structure is the creation of virtual teams whose members are in different locations. Intelligent systems and ADS systems support these employees.

Simulation Modeling and Organizational Restructuring

It may be difficult to carry out restructuring and its planning and analysis even with a computer spreadsheet. For this reason, consultants and IT specialists are turning to an expanding class of products called *business simulation tools*. Many of these programs let users set up flowcharts to diagram the movement of resources through manufacturing or other business processes. El Sawy (2001) provided a comprehensive description of how to use simulation modeling for BPR.

THE IMPACTS OF ADS SYSTEMS

As indicated in Chapter 1 and other chapters, ADS systems, such as those for pricing, scheduling, and inventory management, are spreading rapidly, especially in industries such as airlines, retailing, transportation, and banking (see Davenport and Harris, 2005). These systems will probably have the following impacts:

- Reduction of middle management
- Empowerment of customers and business partners
- Improved customer service (e.g., faster reply to requests)
- Increased productivity of help desks and call centers

OTHER ORGANIZATIONAL IMPACTS

Several other organizational impacts can be attributed to MSS. As described throughout this book, MSS are expected to increase productivity, speed, customer satisfaction, quality, and supply-chain improvements. This results in strategic advantage. Much of this comes about in integrated systems in which a DSS or an ES is a component. For a comprehensive description of the benefits of the introduction of data warehouses and BI, see Watson et al. (2000).

The impact goes beyond one company or one supply chain, however. Entire industries are affected. The use of profitability models and optimization are reshaping retailing, real estate, banking, transportation, airlines, and car rental agencies, among other industries. For more on organizational issues, see Mora (2002).

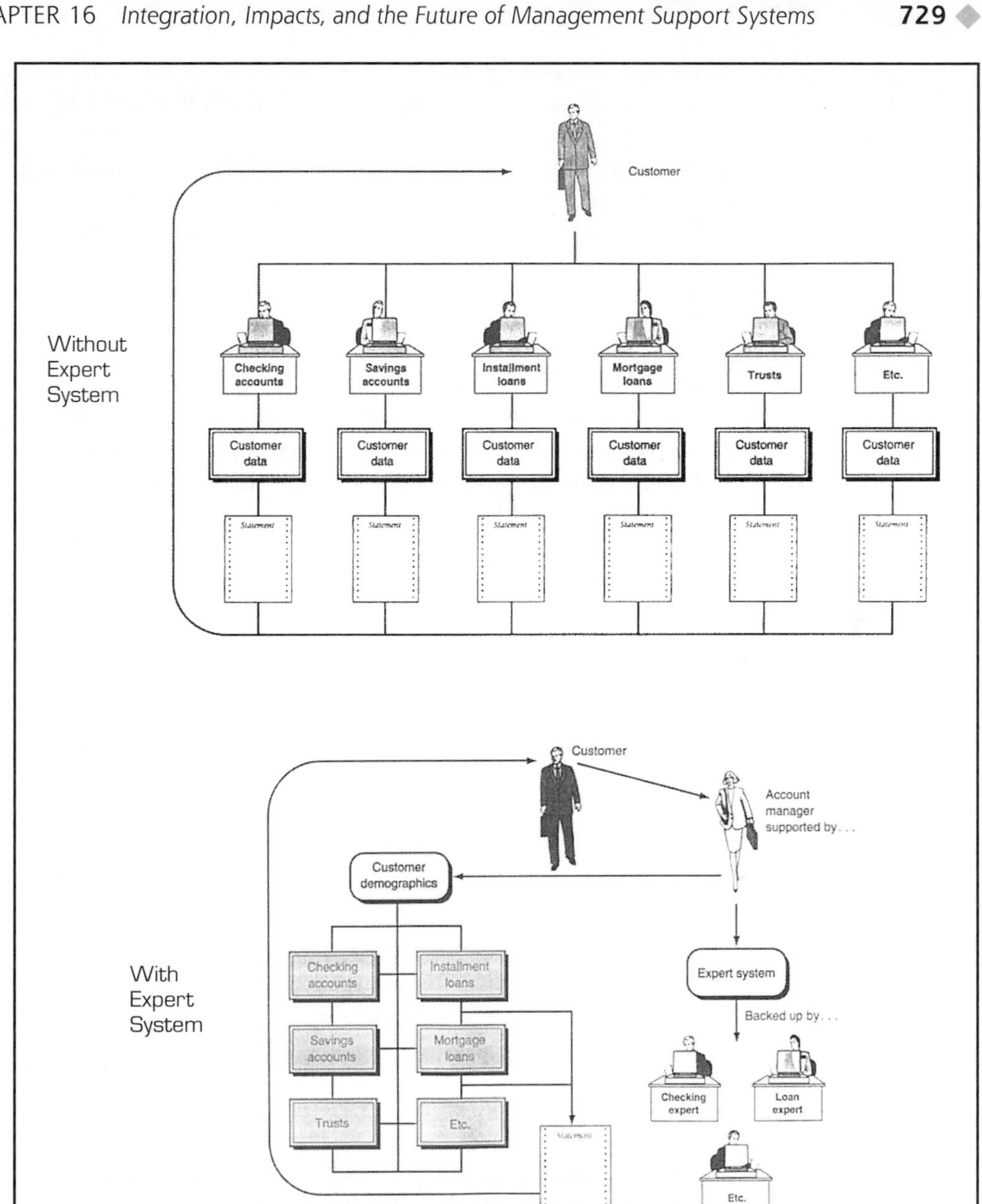

FIGURE 16.7 Restructuring a Bank with an ES

Source: E. Turban, et al., *Information Technology Management*, 3rd ed, Wiley, New York, 2001.

Section 16.6 Review Questions

1. Describe new organizational units that are created because of MSS.
2. Relate MSS to cultural organizational changes.
3. How can MSS affect restructuring of business processes?
4. Describe the impacts of ADS systems.

16.7 MANAGEMENT SUPPORT SYSTEMS IMPACTS ON INDIVIDUALS

MSS can affect individuals in various ways. What is considered to be a benefit to one individual may be a curse to another. What is an added stress today can be a relief tomorrow. Related to this is the use of computers and MSS by managers (e.g., see Elbeltagi et al., 2005). Representative areas where MSS may affect individuals, their perceptions, and behaviors are described next.

JOB SATISFACTION

Although many jobs may be substantially enriched by MSS, other jobs may become more routine and less satisfying. For example, more than 35 years ago, Argyris (1971) predicted that computer-based information systems would reduce managerial discretion in decision making and lead to managers being dissatisfied. A study by Ryker and Ravinder (1995) showed that IT has had a positive effect on four of the five core job dimensions: identity, significance, autonomy, and feedback. No significant effect was found on skill variety. In their study about ADS, Davenport and Harris (2005) found that employees using ADS systems, especially those that are empowered by the systems, were more satisfied with their jobs.

INFLEXIBILITY, DEHUMANIZATION, STRESS, AND ANXIETY

A common criticism of traditional data-processing systems is their negative effects on people's individuality. Such systems are criticized as being impersonal: They may dehumanize and depersonalize activities that have been computerized because they reduce or eliminate the human element that was present in noncomputerized systems. Some people feel a loss of identity; they feel like just another number. On the bright side, one of the major objectives of MSS is to create flexible systems and interfaces that allow individuals to share their opinions and knowledge and work together with computers. Despite all these efforts, some people are still afraid of computers, so they are stressed; others are mostly afraid of their employers watching what they do on the computer.

Job Stress and Anxiety

An increase in workload and/or responsibilities can trigger job stress. Although computerization has benefited organizations by increasing productivity, it has also created an ever-increasing and changing workload on some employees—many times brought on by downsizing and redistributing entire workloads of one employee to another. Some workers feel overwhelmed and begin to feel anxious about their jobs and their performance. These feelings of anxiety can adversely affect their productivity. Management must alleviate these feelings by redistributing the workload among workers or conducting appropriate training.

One of the negative impacts of the information age is information anxiety. This disquiet can take several forms, such as frustration with the inability to keep up with the amount of data present in our lives. The following are some other forms of information anxiety:

- Frustration with not being able to master computers as well as others.
- Frustration with the quality of information available on the Web. This information is frequently not up-to-date or is incomplete.
- Frustration due to having too many online sources of information.

- Frustration due to guilt associated with not being better informed or being informed too late (e.g., "How come everyone else knew before we did?").

COOPERATION OF EXPERTS

Human experts who are planning to give their knowledge to an organizational or to a problem-specific knowledge base may have reservations. Consider these examples of thoughts that might enter an expert's mind:

- The computer may take my knowledge and replace me
- The computer may make me less important
- Why should I tell the computer my secrets? What will I gain?
- The computer may reveal that I am not as great an expert as people think

This kind of thinking may cause the expert not to cooperate or even to give incorrect knowledge to the computer. To deal with such situations, management should motivate (and possibly compensate) the experts.

Section 16.7 Review Questions

1. How can MSS affect job satisfaction?
2. In what ways may MSS affect inflexibility, dehumanization, stress, and anxiety?
3. Describe the issue of experts' cooperation in MSS.

16.8 AUTOMATING DECISION MAKING AND THE MANAGER'S JOB

Computer-based information systems have had an impact on the jobs of managers for about five decades. However, this impact was felt mainly at the lower- and middle-managerial levels. Since 2000, MSS have been affecting almost everyone, including top managers.

The most important task of managers is making decisions. MSS technologies can change the manner in which many decisions are made and can consequently change managers' jobs. The impacts of MSS on decision-making are numerous; the most common areas are discussed next.

THE AFFECT OF MSS ON MANAGERS' ACTIVITIES AND THEIR PERFORMANCE

According to Perez-Cascante et al. (2002), an ES/DSS was found to improve the performance of both existing and new managers as well as other employees. It helped managers gain more knowledge, experience, and expertise, and it consequently enhanced the quality of their decision making.

Many managers report that computers have finally given them time to get out of the office and into the field. (BI can save an hour a day for every user.) They have also found that they can spend more time planning activities instead of putting out fires because they can be alerted to potential problems well in advance, thanks to intelligent agents, ES, and other analytical tools.

Another aspect of the managerial challenge lies in the ability of MSS to support the decision-making process in general and strategic planning and control decisions in particular. MSS could change the decision-making process and even decision-making styles. For example, information gathering for decision making is completed much more quickly when MSS are in use. Enterprise information systems are extremely useful in supporting strategic management (see Liu et al., 2002). Artificial intelligence technologies are now used to improve external environmental scanning of information. As a result, managers can change their approach to problem solving (see Huber, 2003). Research indicates that most managers tend to work on a large number of problems simultaneously, moving from one to another as they wait for more information on their current problem (see Mintzberg et al., 2002). MSS tend to reduce the time required to complete tasks in the decision-making process and eliminate some of the nonproductive waiting time by providing knowledge and information. Therefore, managers work on fewer tasks during each day but complete more of them. The reduction in startup time associated with moving from task to task could be the most important source of increased managerial productivity.

Another possible impact of MSS on the manager's job could be a change in leadership requirements. What are now generally considered good leadership qualities may be significantly altered by the use of MSS. For example, face-to-face communication is frequently replaced by e-mail, wikis, and computerized conferencing; thus, leadership qualities attributed to physical appearance could become less important.

Even if managers' jobs do not change dramatically, the methods managers use to do their jobs will. For example, an increasing number of CEOs no longer use computer intermediaries; instead, they work directly with computers and the Web. When voice recognition is of high quality, we may see a real revolution in the way managers use computers.

The following are some potential impacts of MSS on managers' jobs:

- Less expertise (experience) is required for making many decisions.
- Faster decision making is possible because of the availability of information and the automation of some phases in the decision-making process.
- Less reliance on experts and analysts is required to provide support to top executives; managers can do it by themselves with the help of intelligent systems.
- Power is being redistributed among managers. (The more information and analysis capability they possess, the more power they have.)
- Support for complex decisions makes them faster to make and of better quality.
- Information needed for high-level decision making is expedited or even self-generated.
- Automation of routine decisions or phases in the decision-making process (e.g., for frontline decision making and using ADS) may eliminate some managers.

CAN MANAGERS' JOBS BE FULLY AUTOMATED?

The generic decision-making process involves specific tasks (e.g., identifying problems, finding possible solution alternatives, forecasting consequences, evaluating alternatives). This process can be fairly lengthy, which is bothersome for a busy manager. Automation of certain tasks can save time, increase consistency, and enable better decisions to be made (see Davenport and Harris, 2005). Thus, the more tasks we automate in the process, the better. However, is it possible to completely automate the manger's job?

In general, it has been found that the job of middle managers is the most likely job to be automated. Midlevel managers make fairly routine decisions, which can be fully automated. Managers at lower levels do not spend much time on decision making.

Instead, they supervise, train, and motivate nonmanagers. Some of their routine decisions, such as scheduling, can be automated; other decisions that involve behavioral aspects cannot. However, even if we completely automate their decisional role, we could not automate their jobs. The Web provides an opportunity to automate certain tasks done by frontline employees; this empowers them, thus reducing the workload of approving managers. The job of top managers is the least routine and therefore the most difficult to automate. For further discussion, see Huber (2003).

Can Business Analysts' Jobs Be Fully Automated?

According to some experts, BI could replace business analysts. Others (e.g., McKnight 2005) disagree.

Section 16.8 Review Questions

1. List the impacts of MSS on decision making.
2. List the impacts of MSS on other managerial tasks.
3. Explain the issues related to completely automating managers' jobs.

16.9 ISSUES OF LEGALITY, PRIVACY, AND ETHICS

Several important legal, privacy, and ethical issues are related to MSS. Here we provide only representative examples and sources.

LEGAL ISSUES

The introduction of MSS, and especially of ES, may compound a host of legal issues already relevant to computer systems. For example, questions concerning liability for the actions of advice provided by intelligent machines are just beginning to be considered. The issue of computers as a form of unfair competition in business was raised in the 1990s, with the well-known dispute over the practices of airline reservation systems.

In addition to resolving disputes about the unexpected and possibly damaging results of some MSS, other complex issues may surface. For example, who is liable if an enterprise finds itself bankrupt as a result of using the advice of an MSS? Will the enterprise itself be held responsible for not testing the system adequately before entrusting it with sensitive issues? Will auditing and accounting firms share the liability for failing to apply adequate auditing tests? Will the software developers of intelligent systems be jointly liable? Consider the following specific legal issues:

- What is the value of an expert opinion in court when the expertise is encoded in a computer?
- Who is liable for wrong advice (or information) provided by an ES? For example, what happens if a physician accepts an incorrect diagnosis made by a computer and performs an act that results in the death of a patient?
- What happens if a manager enters an incorrect judgment value into an MSS and the result is damage or a disaster?
- Who owns the knowledge in a knowledge base?
- Should royalties be paid to experts who provide knowledge to an ES or a knowledge base? If so, how much should they receive?
- Can management force experts to contribute their expertise?

PRIVACY

In the opening vignette, we raised the issue of invasion of privacy when MSS is implemented.

Privacy means different things to different people. In general, **privacy** is the right to be left alone and the right to be free from unreasonable personal intrusions. Privacy has long been a legal, ethical, and social issue in many countries. The right to privacy is recognized today in every state of the United States and by the federal government, either by statute or by common law. The definition of *privacy* can be interpreted quite broadly. However, the following two rules have been followed fairly closely in past court decisions: (1) The right of privacy is not absolute. Privacy must be balanced against the needs of society. (2) The public's right to know is superior to the individual's right to privacy. These two rules show why it is difficult, in some cases, to determine and enforce privacy regulations (see Peslak, 2005). Privacy issues online have their own characteristics and policies. One area where privacy may be jeopardized is discussed next. For privacy and security issues in the data warehouse environment, see Elson and LeClerc (2005).

Collecting Information About Individuals

The complexity of collecting, sorting, filing, and accessing information manually from numerous government agencies was, in many cases, a built-in protection against misuse of private information. It was simply too expensive, cumbersome, and complex to invade a person's privacy. The Internet, in combination with large-scale databases, has created an entirely new dimension of accessing and using data. The inherent power in systems that can access vast amounts of data can be used for the good of society. For example, by matching records with the aid of a computer, it is possible to eliminate or reduce fraud, crime, government mismanagement, tax evasion, welfare cheating, family-support filching, employment of illegal aliens, and so on. However, what price must the individual pay in terms of loss of privacy so that the government can better apprehend criminals? The same is true on the corporate level. Private information about employees may aid in better decision making, but the employees' privacy may be affected. Similar issues are related to information about customers.

The Web and Information Collection

The Internet offers a number of opportunities to collect private information about individuals. Here are some of the ways it can be done:

- By reading an individual's newsgroup postings
- By looking up an individual's name and identity in an Internet directory
- By reading an individual's e-mail
- By wiretapping wireline and wireless communication lines and listening to employees
- By conducting surveillance on employees
- By asking an individual to complete Web site registration
- By recording an individual's actions as he or she navigates the Web with a browser, using cookies or spyware

The implications for online privacy are significant. The ability of law enforcement agencies to authorize installation of pen registers and trap-and-trace devices has increased. The U.S. Patriot Act also broadens the government's ability to access student information and personal financial information without any suspicion of wrongdoing by attesting that the information likely to be found is pertinent to an ongoing criminal investigation (see Electronic Privacy Information Center, 2005).

Two effective tools for collecting information about individuals are cookies and spyware (see Online File W16.2). A Microsoft component called Passport is beginning to raise some of the same concerns as cookies. Passport is an Internet instrument that lets consumers permanently enter a profile of information along with a password and use this information and password repeatedly to access services at multiple sites. Critics say that Passport creates the same opportunities as cookies to invade an individual's privacy.

The use of artificial intelligence technologies in the administration and enforcement of laws and regulations may increase public concern regarding privacy of information. These fears, generated by the perceived abilities of artificial intelligence, will have to be addressed at the outset of almost any artificial intelligence development effort.

Fortunately, individuals can take steps to improve their privacy. Tynan (2002) provides 34 tips that show how to do it (also, see PC World 2006).

Homeland Security and Individual Privacy

Using MSS technologies such as mining and interpreting the content of telephone calls, taking photos of people in certain places and identifying them, and using scanners to view your personal belongings are considered by many as an invasion of privacy. However, many people recognize the need for using MSS tools as being effective and efficient means to increase security, even though the privacy of many innocent people is compromised.

The U.S. government applies analytical technologies on a global scale in the war on terrorism. In the first year and a half after September 11, 2001, supermarket chains, home improvement stores, and other retailers voluntarily handed over massive amounts of customer records to federal law enforcement agencies, almost always in violation of their stated privacy policies. Many others responded to court orders for information, as required by law. The U.S. government has a right to gather corporate data under legislation passed after September 11, 2001. The FBI now mines enormous amounts of data, looking for activity that could indicate a terrorist plot or crime.

Privacy issues abound. Because the government is acquiring personal data to detect suspicious patterns of activity, there is the prospect of improper or illegal use of the data. Many see such gathering of data as a violation of citizens' freedoms and rights. They see the need for an oversight organization to "watch the watchers," to ensure that the Department of Homeland Security does not mindlessly acquire data. Instead, it should acquire only pertinent data and information that can be mined to identify patterns that potentially could lead to stopping terrorists' activities. This is not an easy task.

ETHICS IN DECISION MAKING AND SUPPORT

Several ethical issues are related to MSS. A comprehensive overview of ethics in problem formulation and decision making is provided by Chae et al. (2005), who suggested the model of ethical problem formulation that is shown in Figure 16.8. For generic framework of ethical issues, see Online File W16.3.

Representative ethical issues that could be of interest in MSS implementations include the following:

- Electronic surveillance
- Ethics in DSS design (see Chae et al., 2005)

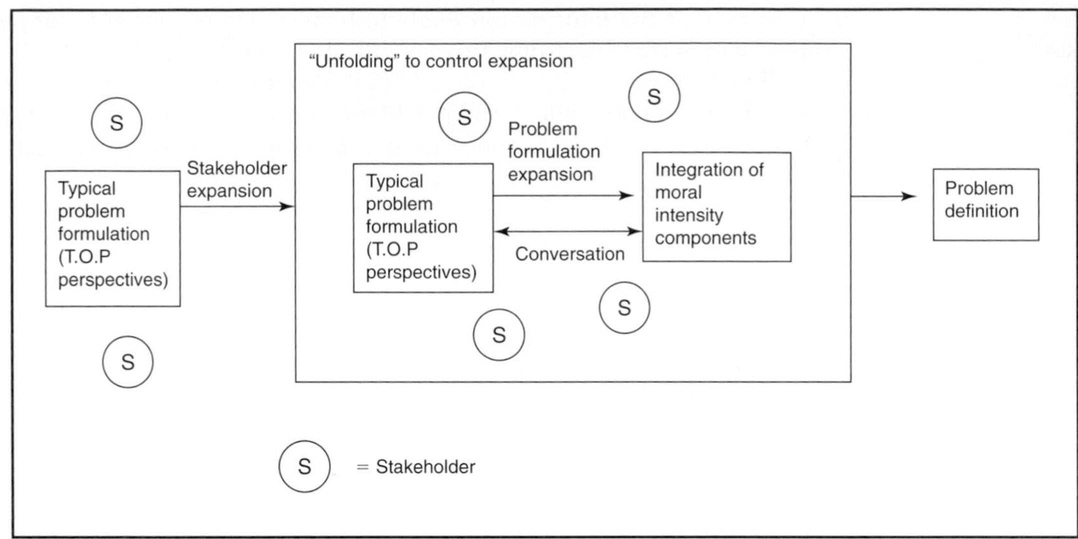

FIGURE 16.8 A Model of Ethical Problem Formulation

Source: B. Chae, D.B. Paradice, J.F. Courtney, and C.J. Cagle, "Incorporating an Ethical Perspective into Problem Formulation," *Decision Support Systems*, Vol. 40, August 2005, Figure 2.

- Software piracy
- Invasion of individuals' privacy (discussed earlier)
- Use of proprietary databases
- Use of intellectual property such as knowledge and expertise
- Exposure of employees to unsafe environments related to computers
- Computer accessibility for workers with disabilities
- Accuracy of data, information, and knowledge
- Protection of the rights of users
- Accessibility to information
- Use of corporate computers for non-work-related purposes (see Simmers, 2002, and later discussion in this chapter)
- How much decision making to delegate to computers

Personal values constitute a major factor in the issue of ethical decision making. For a comprehensive study, see Fritzsche (1995). The study of ethical issues in MSS is complex because of its multidimensionality (see Chae et al., 2005). Therefore, it makes sense to develop frameworks to describe ethics processes and systems. Mason et al. (1995) explained how technology and innovation expand the size of the domain of ethics and discuss a model for ethical reasoning that involves four fundamental focusing questions: Who is the agent? What action was actually taken or is being contemplated? What are the results or consequences of the act? Is the result fair or just for all stakeholders? They also described a hierarchy of ethical reasoning in which each ethical judgment or action is based on rules and codes of ethics, which are based on principles, which in turn are grounded in ethical theory (see Online File W16.4). For more on ethics in decision making, see Murali (2004).

Non-Work-Related Use of the Internet

Employees are tempted to use e-mail and the Web for non-work-related purposes. In some companies, this use is tremendously out of proportion with the work-related uses (see Anandarajan, 2002). The problem has several dimensions. For example, e-mail can be used to harass other employees or to pose a legal threat to a company. It can also be used to conduct illegal gambling activity (e.g., betting on results of a football game). Some employees may use corporate e-mail to advertise their own businesses. Using other corporate computing facilities for private purposes may be problematic, too. Last but not least, is the time employees waste surfing non-work-related Web sites during working hours.

Section 16.9 Review Questions

1. List some legal issues of MSS.
2. Describe privacy concerns in MSS.
3. Explain privacy concerns on the Web.
4. List ethical issues in MSS.
5. Describe an ethical framework for MSS.

16.10 INTELLIGENT AND AUTOMATED SYSTEMS AND EMPLOYMENT LEVELS

One of the major concerns of using MSS is their potential impact on employment levels.

THE IMPACT OF MSS ON EMPLOYMENT LEVELS

There is very little information on the relationship of MSS to employment levels. However, MSS and especially intelligent systems and ADS systems have the potential to significantly affect the productivity and employment of many types of employees as well to partially or even completely eliminate jobs. The material in this section summarizes the positions of some of the world's top experts with regard to the potential impact of intelligent and other computerized systems on productivity and unemployment.

Although the impact of artificial intelligence may take decades to fully materialize, there is agreement among researchers that intelligent systems are increasing the productivity of knowledge workers. Technology is getting less expensive and more capable and thus is bringing about substantial changes in jobs and job content. However, researchers disagree about the potential impact of intelligent systems on the aggregate employment level. The two extreme positions are massive unemployment and increased employment (or at least no change in the employment level). These positions have been supported by two Nobel Prize winners, Wassily Leontief (1986), who supports the massive unemployment argument, and Herbert Simon (1987), who takes the opposite position. Table 16.4 summarizes the main arguments of each side. The debate has been going on for many years. It is true that many people have lost their jobs to intelligent systems. But many new jobs and job categories have also been created.

The following is a list of newly created MSS-related jobs: biometric specialist, security expert, artificial intelligence computer lawyer, BI headhunter, BI project manager, BI hardware–architecture specialist, BI venture capitalist, BI user training specialist, MSS tool developer and vendor, industrial robotics supervisor/manager, knowledge acquisition and maintenance specialist, robotics maintenance engineer, system integrator, ANN software developer, software-agent developer and vendor, CKO, MSS integrator, knowledge maintainer, and intelligent agent builder.

The debate about how intelligent systems will affect employment raises a few other questions: Is some unemployment really socially desirable? (People could have more leisure time.) Should the government intervene more in the distribution of

TABLE 16.4 Arguments About Whether Massive Unemployment Is Coming

Massive Unemployment Will Come	*No Massive Unemployment*
• Benefit–cost advantage of computers increases with time. • Less skillful employees are needed. • Shifting displaced employees to services is getting difficult. • Many employees lost their jobs in the 1990s. • Hidden unemployment exists in many organizations. • Millions of help-desk employees will be replaced by intelligent agents. • Electronic commerce will cause millions of intermediaries and agents to lose their jobs. • Unemployment levels in certain countries are high and are increasing. • There is an upper limit to customer consumption.	• New occupations and jobs have always been created by automation. • There is much less unemployment in countries that use more automation. • Work can be expanded to accommodate everyone. • Conversion to automation is slow, and the economy can adjust. • Many tasks cannot be fully automated. • There will always be some areas where people are better than machines. • People will work less but will have more money. • E-commerce reduces the cost of many goods and services; thus their consumption will increase, resulting in more buying and more jobs.

income and in determination of the employment level? Can the "invisible hand" in the economy, which has worked so well in the past, continue to be successful in the future? Will artificial intelligence make most of us idle but wealthy? (Robots will do the work; people will enjoy life; see Teresko, 2002, and Application Case 16.7). Should the issues of income and employment be completely separated? The issue of how to handle unemployment both at the organizational and the national levels is beyond the scope of this book.

Application Case 16.7

Robots

The following are a few examples of robots at work.

ROBOT BABYSITTERS

In Japan, robots are now being used as receptionists, night guards, hospital workers, guides, pets, and more. Parents visiting the 2005 World Expo could leave their children with a robotic babysitter that recognized individual children's faces and was capable of informing parents by mobile phone in case of emergency. Also, researchers have been testing a robotic baby harp seal in nursing homes where depression and loneliness of the elderly residents is a real concern. Over time, using 30 sensors, the seal recognizes voices and hand gestures. It coos and flaps its furry white down in delight at gentle nuzzles, and it squeals in anger when handled roughly. The trials have had positive results in reducing stress and melancholy among the elderly.

LAYING FIBER-OPTIC CABLES

Cities around the world are bringing themselves into the digital era by replacing copper wires with fiber-optic cables and by installing fiber optics where there were no wires before. Because fiber-optic cables are a choice method to deliver high-speed voice and data communication, demand for them is expanding. Cities know that in order to attract and hold on to high-tech business, they must provide fiber-optic access to all commercial buildings. You may have seen this activity many times without realizing it: Workers cut up the street, creating noise, dust, and traffic problems. But the worst part of it is that the disruption to people may take weeks, or even months, just to complete one city block. Now, robots are changing it all.

One company that invented a technology to improve the situation is City Net Telecommunications (**citynetek.com**). The idea is to use the existing sewer system to lay the cables. This way, no trenches need to be dug in the streets. Pioneering work has been done in Albuquerque, Omaha, and Indianapolis. How do robots help? City Net's robots are waterproof and do not have noses, and so they are not bothered by working in the sewer. They do not complain, nor do they get sick. As a matter of fact, they work faster than humans when it comes to laying the fiber-optic cables inside the sewer system.

ROBO COP (SECURITY)

More than any other country, Japan has made extensive use of robots in industry services and homes. For example, Sohgo Security offers a 45-inch robot guard equipped with a camera and sensors that patrol shopping malls, banks, and so on. It also uses them to assist the blind and the elderly as well as to diagnose some illnesses. Also, a house-sitter robot from Sanyo Electric Co. can monitor houses.

Sources: A. Faiola, "Humanoids with Attitude: Japan Embraces a New Generation of Robots," *The Washington Post*, March 1, 2005, **washingtonpost.com/wp-dyn/articles/A25394-2005Mar10_2.html** (accessed March 2006); L. Eagle, *Stream Intelligent Networks Using Robots and Wireless Technology to Build Its Metropolitan Area Network*, July 1, 2001, **thewhir.com/features/stream.cfm** (accessed March 2006); and *Need a Housesitter? Try a Robot!* August 29, 2005, **msnbc.msn.com/id/9118256/** (accessed March 2006).

Section 16.10 Review Questions

1. List arguments as to why MSS may lead to massive unemployment.
2. List arguments as to why MSS will probably not lead to massive unemployment.
3. Describe how robots may influence employment levels.

16.11 OTHER SOCIETAL IMPACTS OF MANAGEMENT SUPPORT SYSTEMS THE DIGITAL DIVIDE

Several positive and negative social implications of MSS, and especially of artificial intelligence systems, could be far reaching (for an overview, see Papazafeiropoulou and Pouloudi, 2001). MSS have already had many direct beneficial effects on society; they are used for complicated human and social problems such as medical diagnosis, computer-assisted instruction, government program planning, environmental quality control, protection of homeland security, and law enforcement. Problems in these areas could not have been solved economically (or at all) by using other types of computer systems. Furthermore, the spread and benefits of e-commerce are greatly enhanced with the help of intelligent agents. Specific examples of potential effects of MSS are described next.

REPRESENTATIVE POSITIVE EFFECTS OF MSS

Of the many positive effects of MSS, we mention some important ones in the following sections.

Work in Hazardous Environments

ES, especially when combined with sensors and robots, can reduce or even eliminate the need for a human presence in dangerous or uncomfortable environments. For example, MSS can help in cleaning up chemical spills, and many intelligent systems are used in battlefields. A futuristic battlefield will be full of self-driving vehicles guided by global positioning systems, sensors, cameras, lasers, radar, and other computerized systems (see Olsen, 2005).

Opportunities for the Disabled and Elderly

The integration of some artificial intelligence technologies (e.g., speech recognition, vision recognition) into a computer-based information system (CBIS) could create new employment opportunities for disabled people (see **intel.com/research/prohealth/**). For example, those who cannot type could use a voice-operated keyboard, and those who cannot travel could work at home. For example, Boeing developed several ES to help disabled employees perform useful tasks. Adaptive equipment permits disabled people to do ordinary tasks by using computers. Artificial intelligence provides support for deaf, blind, and motor-disabled people. For example, Su et al. (2001) described support to deaf-blind people. For further discussion, see Turban et al. (2001).

The opening vignette illustrates the use of intelligent system in a health care facility where robots are also used (to dispense supplies and clean, for example). Finally, Hine et al. (2005) described an intelligent software systems that allows people with disabilities and their potential employers to make informed decisions about job opportunities and the impact those decisions may have on current and future benefits.

The Changing Roles of Single Parents and Home-Bound People

MSS could change the traditional workplace role of home-bound people. For example, the opportunity to work at home and the need for less travel (because of the Internet and computer teleconferencing) could help single parents with young children and even home-bound people to assume more responsible and demanding managerial positions in organizations.

Improvements in Health Care Delivery

Several early ES (e.g., MYCIN) were designed to improve the delivery of health care. Since they were first developed, we have seen an increased role for artificial intelligence technologies in supporting various tasks carried out by physicians and other health care workers. Of special interest are ES that support the diagnosis of diseases and systems involving the use of machine vision in radiology. Advancements in simulation and robotics enable surgeons to guide and perform surgeries from a distance (see Niedermair, 2005).

MSS technologies are used to support wired health care hospitals (see cases in Chapters 1 and 3) and other facilities (see the opening vignette). The digital hospital (see cases in Chapters 1 and 3) includes many intelligent systems and EDSS. Finally, physicians are using MSS models for faster and better diagnosis.

Aids for the Consumer

Several artificial intelligence products are available on the market, and many more are being developed to help ordinary people perform skilled or undesirable tasks. For example, Taxcut (**taxcut.com**) is an ES that assists in tax preparation, Willmaker (from Quicken) is an ES that helps laypeople draft simple wills, and **vinote.com** provides advice on how to select wines. Intelligent robots can clean house and mow lawns (see the lawnmower at **friendlyrobotics.com** and run the simulator). Fuzzy logic supports blur-free video cameras, has improved antilock brakes, and is used in toasters that do not burn toast. Other advances include more realistic video games and virtual reality systems. Large numbers of intelligent agents provide comparisons and evaluations for consumers (e.g., see **mysimon.com**). These and many other improvements will contribute to an improved quality of life.

Quality of Life at Home and in the Workplace

On a broad scale, MSS have implications for quality of life in general. Improved organizational efficiency may result in more leisure time. The workplace can be expanded from the traditional nine-to-five at a central location to 24 hours a day at any location. This expansion provides flexibility that can significantly improve the quality of leisure time (see **relax-guide.com**), even if the total amount of leisure time is not increased. MSS and other IT can change the workplace for the better, if designed properly (see Drucker, 2002).

Law Enforcement and Homeland Security Improvement

Computers and especially some intelligent systems excel in supporting law enforcement agencies. For example, using computer-mapping systems, police can track the location of 911 callers who use mobile phones. For an overview of DSS methods used in law enforcement, see Brown and Hagen (2003).

MSS are used in improving homeland security. Examples are explosive detection, interpretation of telephone conversation, improved teamwork (e.g., by using group decision support systems), detection of patterns in data, and so on. Robot-driven airplanes can be linked by satellite to a command center, where they are controlled by a pilot. According to ABC News on December 4, 2005, a flying robot killed a key Al-Qaida associate in Afghanistan.

POTENTIAL NEGATIVE EFFECTS

The introduction of MSS technologies may be accompanied by some negative effects. In addition to unemployment and the creation of large economic gaps among people, MSS technologies may result in other problems, some of which are common to other computer systems. The following sections describe some examples.

Computer Crime and Internet Fraud

Computer fraud and embezzlement are increasing. According to a CSI/FBI survey, financial losses resulting from security breaches were $130 million in 2006, down from $141 million in 2004. However, losses from unauthorized access to information (average loss up from $51,545 in 2004 to $303,234 in 2005) and theft of proprietary information (average loss up from $168,529 in 2004 to $355,552 in 2005 (McAlearney 2005).

With ES, there is a possibility of deliberately providing bad advice (e.g., advising employees to opt for early retirement when they should not).

On the other hand, DSS, ES, and neural computing are being used to detect and prevent computer crimes. Neural computing systems can detect stolen credit cards and mobile phones almost instantaneously when they are used illegally. Fraud on the Web is becoming a major problem (see **ftc.gov**), and intelligent systems can help. For information about fighting fraud, go to **fairisaac.com** and click on Fraud Management.

Too Much Power

Distributed MSS allow greater centralization of organizational decision making and control. This may give some individuals or government agencies too much power over other people, and this power could be used in an unethical manner (see Dejoie et al., 1995).

The Dangers of the Web

Extensive use of the Web has caused some people to neglect their families and friends, and sometimes has even led to divorce. A Web game addict in Korea died in February 2000 because he was too busy to break a nonstop playing record in order to eat. In Japan in 1999, two people died after they used the Web to purchase poison and information on how to kill themselves.

Blaming the Computer Phenomenon

Many people tend to blame computers to cover up human errors or wrongdoing. You may hear someone say, "But the ES told us to do it," to justify an action that otherwise would be unjustifiable.

Social Responsibility

Organizations need to be motivated to use MSS to improve the quality of life in general. They should design their MSS to minimize negative working conditions. This challenge should be met not only by companies that produce MSS hardware and software but also by companies that use these technologies. Properly designed systems can be implemented and used in ways that are either positive or negative (see Papazafeiropoulou and Pouloudi, 2001).

THE DIGITAL DIVIDE

Despite the factors and trends that contribute to future IT growth, we have witnessed a growing gap, since the introduction of IT technology, including MSS, between those who have and those who do not have the ability to use the technology (see Cherry et al., 2004). This gap is referred to as the **digital divide**. According to United Nations and International Telecommunication Union (ITU) reports, more than 90 percent of all Internet hosts are in developed countries (see International Telecommunication Union, 2001; and Wolfensohn, 2000), where only 15 percent of the world's population resides. In 2001, the city of New York, for example, had more Internet hosts than the whole continent of Africa. In 2006, a person in a high-income country is over 22 times more likely to be an Internet user than one in a low-income nation (eGov Monitor 2006).

The gap exists both within and between countries. Federal and state governments in the United States are attempting to close this gap within the country by encouraging training and supporting education and infrastructure. The gap among countries, however, may be widening rather than narrowing. Many governments and international organizations are trying to close the digital divide. For information on strategies for closing the divide, see Law (2004).

One device that is helping to close the gap is the smart phone that enables Internet access without the need of having a PC. Another technology is WiFi, which requires a computer but may get you free access to the Internet. Finally, note that a digital divide also exists between small businesses and large ones (see *Daily Record* staff, 2005).

Another area of the digital divide is the difficulty of accessing the Internet for disabled people. As indicated earlier, MSS provide solutions. For example, blind people can surf the Internet by using voice technologies. See "NYPL Closes Digital Divide for Blind and Visually Impaired Patrons" (2005) for information on speech synthesis.

Section 16.11 Review Questions

1. List benefits of MSS to individual people.
2. List some negative affects of MSS.
3. Define *digital divide* and relate it to MSS.

16.12 THE FUTURE OF MANAGEMENT SUPPORT SYSTEMS

Where are MSS in general and decision support and BI in particular going? Are they mature enough to be classified as mainstream IT? Are they still evolving? Are they taking new directions? Experts answer these questions differently, but most of them agree that MSS are migrating toward mainstream IT but are still evolving in certain areas (see Carlsson and Turban, 2002). Watson (2005) said that there is a continuous evolution of MSS technologies with changes in names and buzzwords but few truly new innovations. He also said that this situation will continue in the future. The following is a summary of the major expected developments:

- MSS will play a larger role in strategic management mainly due to its contribution to the area of corporate (i.e., business) performance management systems (see Chapter 9).

- As described throughout the book, MSS are certainly becoming Web-based. This can be seen not only in dissemination but also in the increasing use of the Web for MSS development and applications.
- BI is being combined with other Web-based enterprise systems, particularly CRM, ERP, and knowledge management.
- Intelligent systems, ranging from face recognition to scenario interpretations, have become major contributors in the fight against terrorism and fraud, as well as contributors to productivity and quality of life improvements.
- Web-based advisory services that provide self-diagnosis and the resulting prognoses will mushroom on the Internet. Quality control is needed to ensure quality and prevent fraud.
- More complex MSS applications are expected—so more complex problems will be solved.
- The trend toward making MSS more intelligent will continue. The major technologies that will make this happen are intelligent agents, ES, case-based reasoning, neural networks, and fuzzy logic.
- Advancements in mobile, wireless, and pervasive computing require the use of a greater and more diversified number of intelligent devices.
- MSS will be available for dissemination via application service providers (ASP). For a reasonable fee, specifically constructed centers will provide solutions to a large number of potential users. The trend toward *utility computing* (see **utilitycomputing.com**) will accelerate the use of MSS.
- Natural language-based search engines, such as **about.com** and **ask.com**, will populate the Internet, frequently specializing in certain domains. This will facilitate MSS construction by reducing costs.
- Similarly, the *semantic Web* (see **semanticweb.org**) will increase the use of MSS.
- The use of voice technologies and natural language processing will further facilitate the usage of MSS.
- Frontline decision support technologies that mostly support CRM will become an integral part of IT in most medium-sized and large organizations.
- MSS will continue to be integrated with ERP to provide better SCM, including manufacturing planning and control.
- Large numbers of experts will offer expertise on the Internet. Web sites such as **expertcentral.com**, **answers.com**, and **allexperts.com** (which allow experts to bid on requests for expertise) will become an important part of knowledge dissemination.
- More and more companies will initiate formal knowledge management programs. Some will sell the knowledge accumulated in their knowledge bases to others.
- With the greater usage of wireless technologies and the ability to access the Web with wireless devices, employees will be able to access MSS and knowledge bases anytime and from anywhere. Therefore, the usage of MSS will increase considerably. For example, handheld devices already help customers compare prices available on the Internet while they shop in physical stores.
- Intelligent agents will roam the Internet and intranets, assisting decision makers in the monitoring and interpretation of information. These agents will alert decision makers and even suggest alternative courses of action.
- Groupware technologies for remote collaboration and communication will become easier to use, more powerful, and less expensive. They will make electronic group support a viable initiative even in small organizations.

- Decision support tools for e-commerce, currently limited to recommendations of certain products and brands and to providing comparing agents, will expand to include more and better applications.
- ADS systems are spreading across and within industries, empowering and sometimes replacing employees. Systems such as those for pricing optimization will explode as they tend to serve specific industries (e.g., retailing, banking).
- Grid computing will be used for analysis of very large amounts of data.

Section 16.12 Review Questions

1. List five technological directions of MSS.
2. List some organizational developments in the future of MSS.
3. List developments related to intelligent systems.

Chapter Highlights

- Integrating MSS technology with other computer-based information systems increases the functionality of the latter.
- Functional integration differs from the physical integration required to accomplish it.
- A major area of integration is databases (and database management systems) with ES and natural language processors. The result of integration is easy access to information.
- ES can be used to improve accessibility to databases, either corporate or commercial (online).
- The second major area of integration is the use of ES to interpret results of data generated by models, particularly quantitative models.
- ES can be used to enhance knowledge management, database management, and model management.
- ES are being successfully integrated with DSS; many useful applications have resulted.
- MSS technologies are being integrated with several enterprise systems, ranging from CRM to ERP to knowledge management.
- There are several problems with respect to the integration of MSS technologies, including technical, behavioral, and managerial problems.
- MSS can affect organizations in many ways, as standalone systems or integrated among themselves or with other computer-based information systems.
- MSS could reduce the need for supervision by providing more guidelines to employees electronically.
- The impact of MSS on individuals varies; it can be positive, neutral, or negative.
- Management should motivate experts to contribute their knowledge to knowledge bases.
- Serious legal issues may develop with the introduction of intelligent systems; liability and privacy are the dominant problem areas.
- In one view, intelligent systems and other MSS will cause massive unemployment because of increased productivity, lower required skill levels, and impacts on all sectors of the economy.
- In another view, intelligent systems and other MSS will increase employment levels because automation makes products and services more affordable and so demand increases; the process of disseminating automation is slow enough to allow the economy to adjust to intelligent technologies.
- Many positive social implications can be expected from MSS. These range from providing opportunities to disabled people to leading the fight against terrorism.
- Quality of life, both at work and at home, is likely to improve as a result of MSS.
- Managers need to plan for the MSS of the future so as to be ready to make the most of them.

Key Terms

- business process reengineering (BPR)
- digital divide
- functional integration
- physical integration
- privacy

Questions for Discussion

1. Explain the following statement: "Integration of a DSS and an ES (or other intelligent system) can result in benefits during the construction (development) of the systems and during their operation." Give an example of benefits in development and benefits in operation of these systems.
2. Discuss the potential benefit of Web services to MSS integration.
3. One ES can be used to consult several DSS. What is the logic of such an arrangement? What problems may result when two or more DSS share one ES?
4. Explain how the addition of an ES capability can improve the chances of successfully implementing a DSS.
5. Review current journals and surf the Web to identify a system that you believe is an MSS integration. Analyze the system according to the integration frameworks suggested in this chapter.
6. Discuss why the Web facilitates the integration of BI and ERP.
7. Some say that MSS in general, and ES in particular, dehumanize managerial activities, and others say they do not. Discuss arguments for both points of view.
8. Discuss how enterprise systems relate to the integration issue.
9. Should managers who use ES instead of a human assistant be paid more or less for their jobs? Why?
10. The U.S. Department of Transportation in a large metropolitan area has an ES that advises an investigator about whether to open an investigation of a reported car accident. (This system, which includes 300 rules, was developed by T.J. Nagy at George Washington University.) Discuss the following questions:
    a. Should the people involved in an accident be informed that a machine is deciding the future of an investigation?
    b. What are some of the potential legal implications of this?
    c. In general, what do you think of such a system?
11. Diagnosing infections and prescribing pharmaceuticals are the weak points of many practicing physicians (according to E.H. Shortliffe, one of the developers of MYCIN). It seems, therefore, that society would be better served if MYCIN (and other ES) were used extensively, but few physicians use ES. Answer the following questions:
    a. Why do you think ES are little used by physicians?
    b. Assume that you are a hospital administrator whose physicians are salaried and report to you. What would you do to persuade them to use ES?
    c. If the potential benefits to society are so great, can society do something that will increase doctors' use of ES?
12. Discuss the potential impacts of ADS systems on various types of employees and managers.
13. Discuss the potential benefits of integrating KMS into a DSS.
14. How can intelligent systems help in closing the digital divide?

Exercises

Teradata University and Other Hands-on Exercises

1. Go to **teradatastudentnetwork.com** and read the Harrah's case. Answer Case Question 6.
2. The following is an MSS success-factors questionnaire:

   Overall Satisfaction

   - I have become dependent on MSS.
   - It seems that most people like the MSS application.
   - I have personally benefited from the existence of MSS in this organization.
   - Users enjoy working with the MSS application.
   - All in all, I think that MSS is an important system for this organization.
   - MSS is extremely useful.

   Decision-Making Satisfaction

   - The use of MSS has enabled me to make better decisions.
   - As a result of MSS, I am better able to set priorities in decision making.
   - The use of an MSS has enabled me to get timely information and make relevant decisions.
   - The use of data generated by MSS has enabled me to present arguments more convincingly.

- MSS have improved the quality of the decisions I make in this organization.
- As a result of MSS, the speed with which I analyze and reach final decisions has increased.
- MSS have led me to greater use of BA in my decision making.

Administer this questionnaire to 10 users of any DSS in your organization. Assign a 5 to strongly agree, a 4 to agree, a 3 to neutral, a 2 to disagree, and a 1 to strongly disagree. Compute the average results and rank the factors in order of their importance. Comment on the results.

3. Several hospitals are introducing or considering the introduction of an intelligent bedside assistant that provides physicians and staff with a patient's medical record database for diagnosis and prognosis. The system supplies any information required from the patient's medical records, makes diagnoses based on symptoms, and prescribes medications and other treatments. The system includes an ES as well as a DSS. The system is intended to eliminate some human error and improve patient care. You are a hospital administrator and are very excited about the benefits for the patients. However, when you called a staff meeting, the following questions were raised: What if the system malfunctions? What if there is an undetected error in the program or the rules? The system, once implemented, takes full responsibility for patient care because physicians rely on it. A loss of data or an error in the program may lead to disaster. For example, suppose there is a bug in the database program, and as a result, a critical piece of information is missing from the patient's record. A physician who relies on the system could prescribe a drug on the basis of incomplete data. The consequence of this mistake could be life threatening. Another possibility is that some of the rules in the knowledge base might not be accurate for all patients. Would you implement such a system? Why or why not?

4. One of the major complaints about the Olympic Games is that the judges are biased. We see this especially in figure skating and gymnastics. Would it be possible to use a computerized judge to do the job or at least to supplement the human judges? (Disregard the cost issue of such a system.)
   a. Is it possible to delegate such a task to a robo-judge? If your answer is no, explain in detail why not.
   b. If your answer to part (a) is yes, explain how this could be done. Specifically, what tools and techniques could be used and how?
   c. There are two possible options: supporting the judges with a computer and replacing them with a computer. Explain what could be done in each case and how; list the tools and techniques as well.

5. Perform a literature search on electronic voting, including allowing the general public to vote via the Internet (see polls at **cnn.com** and **evoting-experts.com**). Write a report describing the advantages and disadvantages of electronic voting.

Exercises

Team Assignments and Role-Playing

1. Have each team assigned to a major BI company (e.g., MicroStrategy, Business Objects, Cognus, Hyperion, SAS). Identify integrated products and prepare a list of their capabilities.

2. Meet with your group and discuss ways in which intelligent systems could be integrated into your university's advising and registration system. Are there any concrete ways in which advising and registration could be accomplished quickly and at low cost? Explain.

3. Intelligent advisory systems of all kinds are now available on the Web for a fee or for free. Experts are selling services, and corporations are selling access to their knowledge bases (e.g., **webmd.com**, **guru.com**). Each team should be assigned to one area of expertise (include training and education). Prepare a report on the legal issues that may be involved in such a venture.

4. Read Chae et al. (2005). Summarize all the ethical issues described there and then find examples in each area.

5. Divide the class into two sections: those that believe that BI will replace business analysts, and those that oppose the idea. Conduct a debate.

Exercises

Internet Exercises

1. Identify Internet resources that are related to MSS. Start your search with **dssresources.com** and **microstrategy.com**.

2. In an attempt to achieve efficiency, there is a trend toward producing ES and other intelligent systems on a chip. These chips can be embedded in other computer-based information systems. Visit the Web sites of Motorola, Intel, and other chip manufacturers and find the newest smart chips on the market.

3. Several BI, ES, and other vendors have developed tools that support the construction of integrated systems. Identify vendors that make such tools, prepare a representative list, and download and try some available demos.

4. Go to **tradeportal.com** and view its TradeMatriX Plus. Explain why it is advertised as a powerful decision support tool. Identify integration points.

5. Identify ethical issues related to managerial decision making. Search the Internet, join chat rooms, and read articles from the Internet. Prepare a report on your findings.

6. There has been considerable talk about the impact of the Internet on society. Concepts such as global village, Internet community, digital divide, Internet society, and the like are getting much attention. Search the Internet and prepare a short report on the topic. How does this concept relate to managerial decision making?

7. Search the Internet to find examples of how intelligent systems (especially ES and intelligent agents) facilitate activities such as empowerment, mass customization, and teamwork.

8. Access the Business Resource Software Web site (**brs-inc.com**). Read two case studies and information on two products. How are these products helping businesses to reengineer? Download the demo of Business Insight, install it, and try it. What does it do, and how effective do you think it could be in practice?

9. Investigate the American Bar Association's Technology Resource Center (**abanet.org/tech/ltrc/techethics.html**) and **nolo.com**. What are the major legal and societal concerns and advances addressed there? How are they being dealt with?

10. Explore several sites related to health care (e.g., **WebMD.com**, **who.int**). Find issues related to MSS and privacy. Write a report on how these sites improve health care.

11. Go to **dmreview.com** and **computerworld.com** and find five legal issues related to BI and MSS.

End of Chapter Application Case

An Intelligent Logistics Support System

Airfreight forwarding companies (e.g., ATM Transportation Limited of Hong Kong, International Movers [**intmovers.com**] of Hong Kong) rent airfreight containers from airlines, fill them with customers' goods, and ship them on the airlines' cargo planes. The amount of goods shipped by air is increasing rapidly, and so are the opportunities for the forwarding companies. Their success depends on their ability to make good decisions in terms of matching goods to be delivered with airline schedules as well as with specific boxes within the selected containers. This is called *load plan optimization*, and it requires a high level of expertise because airlines offer a variety of containers for each flight, each with different size and weight limitations. Furthermore, the forwarder needs to price its services such that it will be competitive yet make money. Making such decisions manually requires expertise, time, and timely processing of information. The situation is especially critical in countries such as Hong Kong and Singapore that are used as hubs for large amounts of air cargo.

An intelligent logistics support system (ILSS) was developed in Hong Kong. The system provides expert advice related to the airfreight forwarding business, enhancing the operations of logistics along the relevant supply-chain segments. Specifically, the system supports carriers/containers searching, load plan optimization, and cargo tracking planning. The system is composed of an integrated ES and neural network parts, as shown in Figure 16.9. The ES (with rule-based reasoning) provides domain advice and generates heuristics to support the generation of load plans. After potential outcomes are generated, a neural network engine is applied to support prediction of unexpected events (e.g., airline schedule changes). The system has been applied successfully in Hong Kong, and it has significantly reduced the planning time.

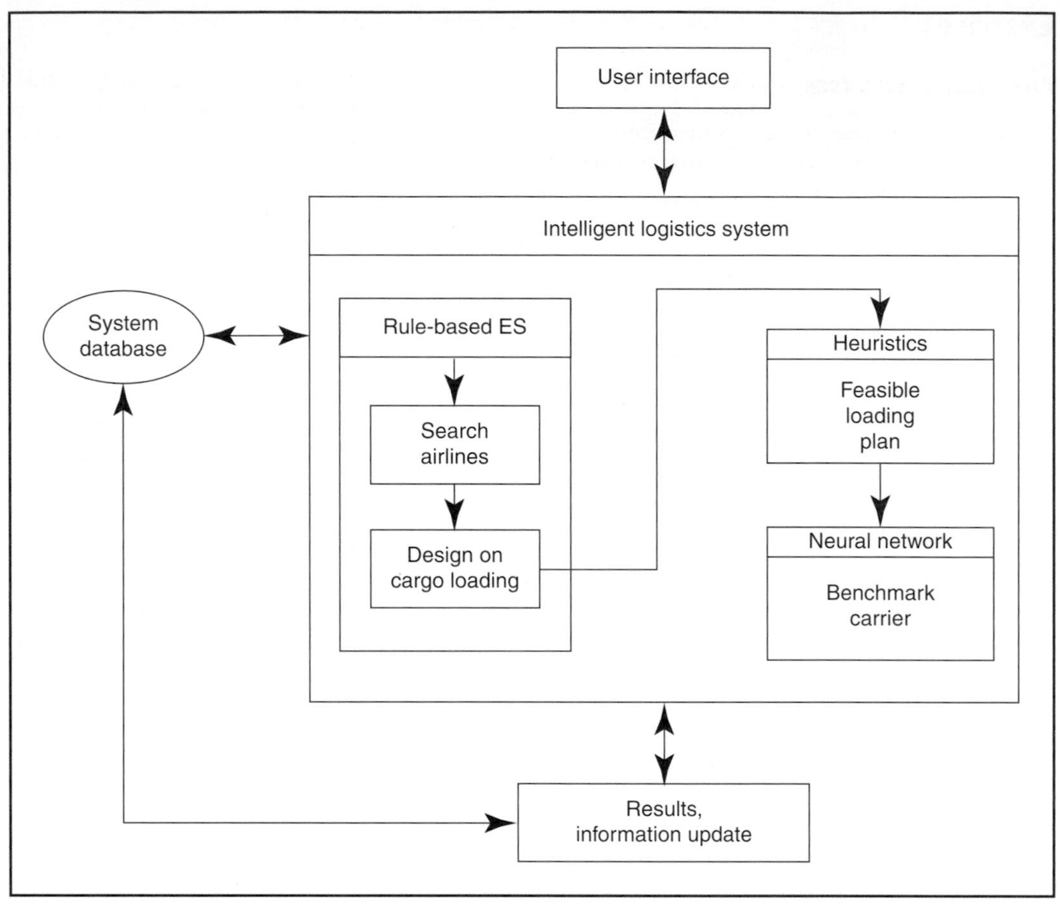

FIGURE 16.9 Intelligent Logistics Support System Architecture

Source: Lau, et al., 2004.

As can be seen in the figure, users connect with the system, which includes two integrated parts. The rule-based ES generates output that is used as input for the neural network engine, which conducts predictive analysis.

The ES supports the choice of the airline and its specific containers. Then it supports the plan of what is to be loaded in each particular container.

After the ES recommends several airlines (i.e., carriers) with the load plan, the neural computing engine benchmarks the potential carriers in order to find the most suitable one. This selection is based on attributes such as quality of service and reliability of performance.

The system was tested at ATM Transportation Limited of Hong Kong, where 90 planners are consistently busy handling huge amounts of information. The results indicate the superiority of the ILSS over humans by 30 percent. The system was also found to be cost-effective.

Sources: Compiled from H.C.W. Lau, K.L. Choy, P.K.H. Lau, W.T. Tsui, and L.C. Choy, "An Intelligent Logistics Support System for Enhancing the Airfreight Forwarding Business," *Expert Systems*, November, 2004, Vol. 21, No.5; "An Intelligent Logistics Support for Enhancing the Airfreight Forwarding Business," *Expert Systems*, November 2004; and **atmtransportation.com.hk** (accessed December 2005).

QUESTIONS FOR THE CASE

1. What kind of integration is provided by the ILSS in this case?
2. What are the benefits of this system?
3. How is decision support provided in this system?

References

Anandarajan, M. (2002, January). "Internet Abuse in the Workplace." *Communications of the ACM*.

Argyris, C. (1971, February). "Management Information Systems: The Challenge to Rationality and Emotionality." *Management Science*, Vol. 17, No. 6.

Bolloju, N. M. Khalifa, and E. Turban. (2002, June). "Integrating Knowledge Management into Enterprise

Environments for the Next Generation of Decision Support." *Decision Support Systems*, Vol. 33.

Brown, D.E., and S. Hagen. (2003, March). "Data Association Method with Applications to Law Enforcement." *Decision Support Systems*.

Carlsson C., and E. Turban (eds.). (2002, June). "The Future of DSS: Special Issue." *Decision Support Systems*.

Chae, B., D.B. Paradice, J.F. Courtney, and C.J. Cagle. (2005, August). "Incorporating an Ethical Perspective into Problem Formulation." *Decision Support Systems,* Vol. 40.

Cherry, S.M., H Goldstein, and S Cass. (2004, February). "A World Divided by Common Internet." *IEEE Spectrum*, Vol. 41, No. 2.

Clarke, K. (2003, April 9). "EDS and Navy Activate New Aviation Supply Chain Maintenance Management." *PR Newswire*.

Daily Record Staff. (2005, September 21). "Broadband Access Survey Shows Digital Divide Remains Among the Nation's Small Businesses." **findarticles.com/ p/articles/mi_qn4183/is_20050921/ai_n15362880** (accessed August 2006).

Davenport, T.H., and J.G. Harris. (2005, Summer). "Automated Decision Making Comes of Age." *MIT Sloan Management Review*.

Dejoie, R.M., et al. (1995). *Ethical Issues in Information Systems*, 2nd ed. Cincinnati: Boyd & Fraser.

Drucker, P. (2002). *Managing in the Next Society*. New York: Truman Talley Books.

Dutta, S., B. Wierenga, and A. Dalebout. (1997, June). "Designing Management Support Systems Using an Integrative Perspective." *Communications of the ACM*. Vol. 40, No. 6.

eGov Monitor. (2006). "Digital Divide Remains Wide Despite Increased Connectivity Worldwide, UNCTAD Finds." **egovmonitor.com/node/6638** (accessed August 2006).

El Sawy, O. (2001). *Redesigning Enterprise Processes for E-Business*. New York: McGraw-Hill.

Elbeltagi, I., N. McBride, and G. Hardaker. (2005, April–June). "Evaluating the Factors Affecting DSS Usage by Senior Managers in Local Authorities in Egypt." *Journal of Global Information Management*.

Electronic Privacy Information Center. (2005). *The U.S. Patriot Act*, **epic.org/privacy/terrorism/usapatriot/** (accessed March 2006).

Elson, R.J., and R. LeClerc. (2005, Summer). "Security and Privacy Concerns in the Data Warehouse Environment." *Business Intelligence Journal*.

Forgionne, G., M. Mora, F. Cervantes, and O. Gelman. (2002, July). "I-DMSS: A Conceptual Architecture for the Next Generation of Decision Making Support Systems in the Internet Age." *Proceedings of DSIage 2002*, Cork, Ireland.

Fritzsche, D. (1995, November). "Personal Values: Potential Keys to Ethical Decision Making." *Journal of Business Ethics*, Vol. 14, No. 11.

Grabowski, M., and S.D. Sanborn. (2001, Winter). "Evaluation of Embedded Intelligent Real-Time Systems." *Decision Sciences*, Vol. 32, No. 1.

Heinriches, J.H., and J.S. Lim (2003). "Integrating Web-Based Data Mining Tools with Business Models for Knowledge Management." *Decision Support Systems*, Vol. 35, No. 2.

Herschel, R.T., and N.E. Jones. (2005). "Knowledge Management and Blithe Importance of Integration." *Journal of Knowledge Management*, Vol. 9, No. 4.

Hine, M.J., P.D. Banks, D.J. Ruth, R.M. Carlson, and J.L. Troxell. (2004, September). "Empowering Persons with Disabilities with Decision Support Technology." *Communications of the ACM*.

Holsapple, C.W. (2003). "Knowledge and Its Attributes." In C.W. Holsapple (ed.). *Handbook of Knowledge Management: Knowledge Matters*, Vol. 1. Heidelberg: Springer-Verlag.

Holsapple, C.W., and Sena, M. (2005). "ERP Plans and Decision Support Benefits" *Decision Support Systems*, Vol. 38, No. 4.

Huber, G. (2003). *The Necessary Nature of Future Firms*. San Francisco: Sage.

International Telecommunication Union. (2001). "*Digital Divide: Overview*, **itu.int/ITU-D/digitaldivide/#note** (accessed March 2006).

Joch, A. (2005, January/February). "Eye on Information." *Oracle Magazine*.

Labat, A. (2006). "ESL Lives Up to Its Early Promise in Embedded Systems Design." Chip Design Magazine. **chipdesignmag.com/display.php?articleId=397** (accessed August 2006).

Lau, H.C.W., B Jiang, W.B. Lee, and K.H. Lau. (2001, September). "Development of an Intelligent Data-Mining System for a Dispersed Manufacturing Network." *Expert Systems*.

Lau, H.C.W., K.L. Choy, P.K.H. Lau, W.T. Tsui, and L.C. Choy. (2004, November). "An Intelligent Logistics Support System for Enhancing the Airfreight Forwarding Business," *Expert Systems*, Vol. 21, No.5.

Law, D. (2004). "Bridging the Digital Divide: A Review of Current Progress." *Library Management*, Vol. 25, Nos. 1 & 2.

Leontief, W. (1986). *The Future Impact of Automation on Workers*. Oxford, UK: Oxford University Press.

Li, S. (2000, January). "The Development of a Hybrid Intelligent System for Developing Marketing Strategy." *Decision Support Systems*, Vol. 27, No. 4.

Liu, S., J. Carlsson, and S. Nummila. (2002, July). "Mobile E-Services: Creating Added Value for Working Mothers." *Proceedings DSI AGE 2002*, Cork, Ireland.

Mallach, E. (1994). *Understanding Decision Support Systems and Expert Systems*. Chicago, IL: Irwin.

Mason, R.O., F.M. Mason, and M.J. Culnan. (1995). *Ethics of Information Management*. Thousand Oaks, CA: Sage.

McAlearney, S. (2005, July 18). "CSI Survey: Financial Impact of Some Security Breaches Skyrockets." SearchSecurity.com. **searchsecurity.techtarget.com/originalContent/0,289142,sid14_gci1108577,00.html** (accessed August 2006).

McKnight, W. (2005, February). "Building BI: Will BI Replace the Business Analyst." *DM Review*.

McNurlin, B.C., and R.H. Sprague, Jr. (2006). *Information Systems Management in Practice*, 7th ed. Upper Saddle River, NJ: Prentice Hall.

Michel, R. (2005, August). "In Pursuit of Peak Performance." *Manufacturing Business Technology*, **wonderware.com/about_us/msPP_supplement.pdf** (accessed February 2006).

Mintzberg, H., et al. (2002). *The Strategy Process*, 4th ed. Upper Saddle River, NJ: Prentice Hall.

Mora, M. (2002, October/December). "Management and Organizational Issues for Decision Making Support Systems." *Information Resources Management Journal*, Special Issue.

Morgenthal, J.P. (2005, October). "Strategies for Successful Integration." *Optimize*.

Murali, D. (2004, December 2). "Ethical Dilemmas in Decision Making." *BusinessLine*.

Niedermouir, H. (2005, November). "The Downloadable Surgeon." *Your Health*.

"NYPL Closes Digital Divide for Blind and Visually Impaired Patrons." (2005). *Computers in Libraries*, Vol. 25, No. 8.

Olsen, S. (2005, October 9). "Stanford Wins $2 Million in Robotic Car Race." **news.com.com/Stanford+wins+2+million+in+robotic+car+race/2100-11394_3-5892115.html** (accessed April 2006).

Papazafeiropoulou, A., and A. Pouloudi. (2001, October–December). "Social Issues in Electronic Commerce: Implications for Policy Makers." *Information Resources Management Journal*.

PC World. (2006). *Take Back Your Privacy*. **pcworld.com/downloads/collection/0,collid,1084,findid,26702,00.asp** (accessed August 2006).

Peslak, A.P. (2005, January–March). "Internet Privacy Policies." *Information Resources Management Journal*.

Perez-Cascante, L.P., M. Plaisent, L. Maguiraga, and P. Bernard. (2002, October–December). "The Impact of Expert Decision Support Systems on the Performance of New Employees." *Information Resources Management Journal*.

Ryker, R., and N. Ravinder. (1995, October). "An Empirical Examination of the Impact of Computer Information Systems on Users." *Information and Management*, Vol. 29, No. 4.

San Pedro, J., F. Burstein, and A. Sharp. (2005). "A Case-Based Fuzzy/Multicriteria Decision Support Model for Tropical Cyclone Forecasting." *European Journal of Operations Research*.

Sikler, I.U., and A. Gangopadhyay. (2002, October–December). "Design and Implementation of a Web-Based Collaborative Spatial Decision Support System: Organizational and Managerial Implications." *Information Resources Management Journal*.

Simmers, C.A. (2002, January). "Aligning Internet Usage with Business Priorities." *Communications of the ACM*.

Simon, H.A. (1987, Spring). "The Steam Engine and the Computer: What Makes Technology Revolutionary?" *EDUCOM Bulletin*, Vol. 22, No. 1, pp. 2–5.

Spangler, T. (2005, May). "Top Projects in 2005." *Baseline*.

Su, M.C., C.Y. Chen, S.Y. Su, C.H. Chou, H.F. Hsiu, and Y.C. Wang. (2001, February). "Portable Communication Aid for Deaf-Blind People." *Computing and Control Engineering Journal*.

Teresko, J. (2002, April). "Robots Revolution." *Industry Week*.

Turban, E., et al. (2001). *Information Technology for Management*, 3rd ed. New York: Wiley.

Tynan, D. (2002, June). "How to Take Back Your Privacy (34 Steps)." *PC World*.

Watson, H.J. (2005, Winter). "Sorting Out What's New in Decision Support." *Business Intelligent Journal*.

Watson, H.J., B.H. Wixom, and D.L. Goodhue. (2000, Winter). "The Effects of Technology-Enabled Business Strategy at First American Corporation." *Organization Dynamics*.

Wolfensohn, J.D. (2000). "Remarks of James D. Wolfensohn at the ECOSOC High Level Segment Policy Dialogue." *United Nations.* **un.org/esa/coordination/ecosoc/itforum/wolfensn.pdf** (no longer available online).

Zaremba, M.B., and G. Morel. (2003, February). "Integration and Control of Intelligence in Distributing Manufacturing." *Journal of Intelligent Manufacturing*.

Enterprise Systems

Learning Objectives

- Describe the concepts, definitions, and issues in enterprise information systems (EIS)
- Discuss the capabilities and characteristics of (Web-based) enterprise information portals
- Describe supply-chain management (SCM) issues and how EIS handle them
- Describe material requirements planning (MRP), enterprise resource planning (ERP), and SCM solutions
- Discuss customer relationship management (CRM) concepts and issues
- Describe the emerging EIS of product lifecycle management (PLM) and business process management (BPM)
- Describe how EIS have improved frontline decision making by providing access to real-time data

A complete version of this chapter is available onthe textbook's Web site.

Knowledge Acquisition, Representation, and Reasoning

Learning Objectives

- Understand the nature of knowledge
- Understand the knowledge-engineering process
- Learn different approaches to knowledge acquisition
- Explain the pros and cons of different knowledge acquisition approaches
- Illustrate methods for knowledge verification and validation
- Understand inference strategies in rule-based intelligent systems
- Explain uncertainties and uncertainty processing in expert systems (ES)

A complete version of this chapter is available onthe textbook's Web site.

Glossary

active data warehousing *See* real-time data warehousing.

ad hoc DSS A DSS that deals with specific problems that are usually neither anticipated nor recurring.

ad hoc query A query that cannot be determined prior to the moment the query is issued.

adaptive resonance theory (ART) An unsupervised learning method created by Stephen Grossberg. ART is a neural network architecture that is aimed at being brain-like in unsupervised mode.

agency The degree of autonomy vested in a software agent.

algorithm A step-by-step search in which improvement is made at every step until the best solution is found.

analog model An abstract, symbolic model of a system that behaves like the system but looks different.

analogical reasoning The process of determining the outcome of a problem by using analogies. It is a procedure for drawing conclusions about a problem by using past experience.

analytical models Mathematical models into which data are loaded for analysis.

analytical techniques Methods that use mathematical formulas to derive an optimal solution directly or to predict a certain result, mainly in solving structured problems.

analytics The science of analysis.

application service provider (ASP) A software vendor that offers leased software applications to organizations.

artificial intelligence (AI) The subfield of computer science concerned with symbolic reasoning and problem solving.

artificial neural network (ANN) Computer technology that attempts to build computers that operate like a human brain. The machines possess simultaneous memory storage and work with ambiguous information. Sometimes called, simply, a neural network. *See* neural computing.

association A category of data mining algorithm that establishes relationships about items that occur together in a given record.

asynchronous Occurring at different times.

automated decision support (ADS) A rule-based system that provides a solution to a repetitive managerial problem. Also known as enterprise decision management (EDM).

automated decision system (ADS) A business rules-based system that uses intelligence to recommend solutions to repetitive decisions (such as pricing).

axon An outgoing connection (i.e., terminal) from a biological neuron.

backpropagation The best-known learning algorithm in neural computing. In backpropagation, learning is done by comparing computed outputs to desired outputs of historical cases.

backward chaining A search technique (based on if-then rules) used in production systems that begins with the action clause of a rule and works backward through a chain of rules in an attempt to find a verifiable set of condition clauses.

balanced scorecard (BSC) A performance measurement and management methodology that helps translate an organization's financial, customer, internal process, and learning and growth objectives and targets into a set of actionable initiatives.

best practices In an organization, the best methods for solving problems. These are often stored in the knowledge repository of a knowledge management system.

black-box testing Testing that involves comparing test results to actual results.

blackboard An area of working memory set aside for the description of a current problem and for recording intermediate results in an expert system.

bot An intelligent software agent. Bot is an abbreviation of robot and is usually used as part of another term, such as knowbot, softbot, or shopbot.

business activity monitoring (BAM) A real-time system that alert managers to potential opportunities, impending problems, and threats and then empowers them to react through models and collaboration.

business (or system) analyst An individual whose job is to analyze business processes and the support they receive (or need) from information technology.

business analytics (BA) The application of models directly to business data. Business analytics involve using DSS tools, especially models, in assisting decision makers. It is essentially OLAP/DSS. *See* business intelligence (BI).

business intelligence (BI) A conceptual framework for decision support. It combines architecture, databases (or data warehouses), analytical tools, and applications.

business performance management (BPM) An advanced performance measurement and analysis approach that embraces planning and strategy.

business process reengineering (BPR) A methodology for introducing a fundamental change in specific business processes. BPR is usually supported by an information system.

case library The knowledge base of a case-based reasoning system.

case-based reasoning (CBR) A methodology in which knowledge and/or inferences are derived from historical cases.

certainty A condition under which it is assumed that future values are known for sure and only one result is associated with an action.

chief knowledge officer (CKO) The person in charge of a knowledge management effort in an organization.

choice phase The third phase in decision making, in which an alternative is selected.

chromosome A candidate solution for a genetic algorithm.

classification Supervised induction used to analyze the historical data stored in a database and to automatically generate a model that can predict future behavior.

clickstream analysis The analysis of data that occur in the Web environment.

clickstream data Data that provide a trail of the user's activities and show the user's browsing patterns (e.g., which sites are visited, which pages, how long).

clustering Partitioning a database into segments in which the members of a segment share similar qualities.

cognitive limits The limitations of the human mind related to processing information.

collaboration hub The central point of control for an e-market. A single collaboration hub (c-hub), representing one e-market owner, can host multiple collaboration spaces (c-spaces) in which trading partners use c-enablers to exchange data with the c-hub.

collaborative filtering A method for generating recommendations from user profile. It uses preferences of other users with similar behavior to predict the preferences of a particular user.

collaborative planning, forecasting, and replenishment (CPFR) A project in which suppliers and retailers collaborate in their planning and demand forecasting to optimize the flow of materials along the supply chain.

community of practice (COP) A group of people in an organization with a common professional interest, often self-organized, for managing knowledge in a knowledge management system.

complexity A measure of how difficult a problem is in terms of its formulation for optimization, its required optimization effort, or its stochastic nature.

connection weight The weight associated with each link in a neural network model. Neural networks learning algorithms assess connection weights.

consultation environment The part of an expert system that a non-expert uses to obtain expert knowledge and advice. It includes the workplace, inference engine, explanation facility, recommended action, and user interface.

content management system (CMS) An electronic document management system that produces dynamic versions of documents and automatically maintains the current set for use at the enterprise level.

content-based filtering A type of filtering that recommends items for a user based on the description of previously evaluated items and information available from the content (e.g., keywords)

corporate (enterprise) portal A gateway for entering a corporate Web site. A corporate portal enables communication, collaboration, and access to company information.

critical success factors (CSF) Key factors that delineate the things that an organization must excel at to be successful in its market space.

crossover The combination of parts of two superior solutions by a genetic algorithm in an attempt to produce an even better solution.

cube A subset of highly interrelated data that is organized to allow users to combine any attributes in a cube (e.g., stores, products, customers, suppliers) with any metrics in the cube (e.g., sales, profit, units, age) to create various two-dimensional views, or *slices*, that can be displayed on a computer screen.

dashboard A visual presentation of critical data for executives to view. It allows executives to see hot spots in seconds and explore the situation.

data conferencing Virtual meeting in which geographically dispersed groups work on documents together and exchange computer files during videoconferences.

data cube A two-dimensional, three-dimensional, or higher-dimensional object in which each dimension of the data represents a measure of interest.

data integration Integration that comprises three major processes: data access, data federation, and change capture. When these three processes are correctly implemented, data can be accessed and made accessible to an array of ETL, analysis tools, and data warehousing environments.

data mart A departmental data warehouse that stores only relevant data.

data mining A process that uses statistical, mathematical, artificial intelligence, and machine-learning techniques to extract and identify useful information and subsequent knowledge from large databases.

data visualization A graphical, animation, or video presentation of data and the results of data analysis.

data warehouse (DW) A physical repository where relational data are specially organized to provide enterprise-wide, cleansed data in a standardized format.

data warehouse administrator (DWA) A person responsible for the administration and management of a data warehouse.

database The organizing of files into related units that are then viewed as a single storage concept. The data in the database are generally made available to a wide range of users.

database management system (DBMS) Software for establishing, updating, and querying (e.g., managing) a database.

decision analysis Methods for determining the solution to a problem, typically when it is inappropriate to use iterative algorithms.

decision making The action of selecting among alternatives.

decision room An arrangement for a group support system in which PCs are available to some or all participants. The objective is to enhance groupwork.

decision style The manner in which a decision maker thinks and reacts to problems. It includes perceptions, cognitive responses, values, and beliefs.

decision support systems (DSS) A conceptual framework for a process of supporting managerial decision- making, usually by modeling problems and employing quantitative models for solution analysis.

decision tree A graphical presentation of a sequence of interrelated decisions to be made under assumed risk. This technique classifies specific entities into particular classes based upon the features of the entities; a root followed by internal nodes, each node (including root) is labeled with a question, and arcs associated with each node cover all possible responses.

decision variable A variable in a model that can be changed and manipulated by the decision maker. Decision variables correspond to the decisions to be made, such as quantity to produce, amounts of resources to allocate, and so on.

defuzzification The process of creating a crisp solution from a fuzzy logic solution.

Delphi method A qualitative forecasting methodology that uses anonymous questionnaires. It is effective for technological forecasting and for forecasting involving sensitive issues.

demographic filtering A type of filtering that uses the demographic data of a user to determine which items may be appropriate for recommendation.

dendrite The part of a biological neuron that provides inputs to the cell.

dependent data mart A subset that is created directly from a data warehouse.

descriptive model A model that describes things as they are.

design phase The second decision-making phase, which involves finding possible alternatives in decision making and assessing their contributions.

development environment The part of an expert system that a builder uses. It includes the knowledge base and the inference engine, and it involves knowledge acquisition and improvement of reasoning capability. The knowledge engineer and the expert are considered part of the environment.

diagnostic control system A cybernetic system that has inputs, a process for transforming the inputs into outputs, a standard or benchmark against which to compare the outputs, and a feedback channel to allow information on variances between the outputs and the standard to be communicated and acted on.

digital divide The gap between those who have and those who do not have the ability to use technology.

dimension table A table that address *how* data will be analyzed.

dimensional modeling A retrieval-based system that supports high-volume query access.

directory A catalog of all the data in a database or all the models in a model base.

discovery-driven data mining A form of data mining that finds patterns, associations, and relationships among data in order to uncover facts that were previously unknown or not even contemplated by an organization.

distributed artificial intelligence (DAI) A multiple-agent system for problem solving. DAI involves splitting a problem into multiple cooperating systems to derive a solution.

DMAIC A closed-loop business improvement model that includes these steps: defining, measuring, analyzing, improving, and controlling a process.

drill-down The investigation of information in detail (e.g., finding not only total sales but also sales by region, by product, or by salesperson). Finding the detailed sources.

DSS application A DSS program built for a specific purpose (e.g., a scheduling system for a specific company).

dynamic models Models whose input data are changed over time (e.g., a five-year profit or loss projection).

effectiveness The degree of goal attainment. Doing the right things.

efficiency The ratio of output to input. Appropriate use of resources. Doing the things right.

electronic brainstorming A computer-supported methodology of idea generation by association. This group process uses analogy and synergy.

electronic document management (EDM) A method for processing documents electronically, including capture, storage, retrieval, manipulation, and presentation.

electronic meeting systems (EMS) An information technology-based environment that supports group meetings (groupware), which may be distributed geographically and temporally.

end-user computing Development of one's own information system. Also known as end-user development.

enterprise application integration (EAI) A technology that provides a vehicle for pushing data from source systems into a data warehouse.

enterprise data warehouse (EDW) An organizational-level data warehouse developed for analytical purposes.

enterprise decision management (EDM) *See* automated decision support (ADS).

enterprise information integration (EII) An evolving tool space that promises real-time data integration from a variety of sources, such as relational databases, Web services, and multidimensional databases.

enterprise knowledge portal (EKP) An electronic doorway into a knowledge management system.

enterprisewide collaboration system A group support system that supports an entire enterprise.

entropy A metric that measures the extent of uncertainty or randomness in a data set. If all the data in a subset belong to just one class, then there is no uncertainty or randomness in that data set, and therefore the entropy is zero.

environmental scanning and analysis A process that involves conducting a search for and an analysis of information in external databases and flows of information.

expert A human being who has developed a high level of proficiency in making judgments in a specific, usually narrow, domain.

expert location system An interactive computerized system that helps employees find and connect with colleagues who have expertise required for specific problems—whether they are across the county or across the room—in order to solve specific, critical business problems in seconds.

expert system (ES) A computer system that applies reasoning methodologies to knowledge in a specific domain to render advice or recommendations, much like a human expert. An ES is a computer system that achieves a high level of performance in task areas that, for human beings, require years of special education and training.

expert system (ES) shell A computer program that facilitates relatively easy implementation of a specific expert system. Analogous to a DSS generator.

expert tool user A person who is skilled in the application of one or more types of specialized problem-solving tools.

expertise The set of capabilities that underlines the performance of human experts, including extensive domain knowledge, heuristic rules that simplify and improve approaches to problem solving, meta-knowledge and metacognition, and compiled forms of behavior that afford great economy in a skilled performance.

explanation subsystem The component of an expert system that can explain the system's reasoning and justify its conclusions.

explanation-based learning A machine-learning approach that assumes that there is enough existing theory to rationalize why one instance is or is not a prototypical member of a class.

explicit knowledge Knowledge that deals with objective, rational, and technical material (e.g., data, policies, procedures, software, documents). Also known as leaky knowledge.

extraction The process of capturing data from several sources, synthesizing them, summarizing them, determining which of them are relevant, and organizing them, resulting in their effective integration.

extraction, transformation, and load (ETL) A data warehousing process that consists of extraction (i.e., reading data from a database), transformation (i.e., converting the extracted data from its previous form into the form in which it needs to be so that it can be placed into a data warehouse or simply another database), and load (i.e., putting the data into the data warehouse).

facilitator (in a GSS) A person who plans, organizes, and electronically controls a group in a collaborative computing environment.

forecasting Predicting the future.

forward chaining A data-driven search in a rule-based system.

functional integration The provision of different support functions as a single system through a single, consistent interface.

fuzzification A process that converts an accurate number into a fuzzy description, such as converting from an exact age into categories such as young and old.

fuzzy logic A logically consistent way of reasoning that can cope with uncertain or partial information. Fuzzy logic is characteristic of human thinking and many expert systems.

fuzzy set A set theory approach in which set membership is less precise than having objects strictly in or out of the set.

genetic algorithm A software program that learns in an evolutionary manner, similar to the way biological systems evolve.

geographic information system (GIS) An information system capable of integrating, storing, editing, analyzing, sharing, and displaying geographically-referenced information.

Gini index A metric that is used in economics to measure the diversity of the population. The same concept can be used to determine the purity of a specific class as a result of a decision to branch along a particular attribute/variable.

global positioning systems (GPS) Wireless devices that use satellites to enable users to detect the position on earth of items (e.g., cars or people) the devices are attached to, with reasonable precision.

goal seeking Asking a computer what values certain variables must have in order to attain desired goals.

grain A definition of the highest level of detail that is supported in a data warehouse.

graphical user interface (GUI) An interactive, user-friendly interface in which, by using icons and similar objects, the user can control communication with a computer.

group decision support system (GDSS) An interactive computer-based system that facilitates the solution of semistructured and unstructured problems by a group of decision makers.

group support system (GSS) Information systems, specifically DSS, that support the collaborative work of groups.

groupthink In a meeting, continual reinforcement of an idea by group members.

groupware Computerized technologies and methods that aim to support the work of people working in groups.

groupwork Any work being performed by more than one person.

heuristic programming The use of heuristics in problem solving.

heuristics Informal, judgmental knowledge of an application area that constitutes the rules of good judgment in the field. Heuristics also encompasses the knowledge of how to solve problems efficiently and effectively, how to plan steps in solving a complex problem, how to improve performance, and so forth.

hidden layer The middle layer of an artificial neural network that has three or more layers.

hybrid (integrated) computer system Different but integrated computer support systems used together in one decision-making situation.

hypothesis-driven data mining A form of data mining that begins with a proposition by the user, who then seeks to validate the truthfulness of the proposition.

iconic model A scaled physical replica.

idea generation The process by which people generate ideas, usually supported by software (e.g., developing alternative solutions to a problem). Also known as brainstorming.

implementation phase The fourth decision-making phase, involving actually putting a recommended solution to work.

independent data mart A small data warehouse designed for a strategic business unit or a department.

inductive learning A machine-learning approach in which rules are inferred from facts or data.

inference engine The part of an expert system that actually performs the reasoning function.

influence diagram A diagram that shows the various types of variables in a problem (e.g., decision, independent, result) and how they are related to each other.

institutional DSS A DSS that is a permanent fixture in an organization and has continuing financial support. It deals with decisions of a recurring nature.

intellectual capital The know-how of an organization. Intellectual capital often includes the knowledge that employees possess.

intelligence A degree of reasoning and learned behavior, usually task or problem-solving oriented.

intelligence phase The initial phase of problem definition in decision making.

intelligent agent (IA) An expert or knowledge-based system embedded in computer-based information systems (or their components) to make them smarter.

intelligent computer-aided instruction (ICAI) The use of AI techniques for training or teaching with a computer.

intelligent tutoring system (ITS) Self-tutoring systems that can guide learners in how best to proceed with the learning process.

intermediary A person who uses a computer to fulfill requests made by other people (e.g., a financial analyst who uses a computer to answer questions for top management).

intermediate result variable A variable that contains the values of intermediate outcomes in mathematical models.

Internet telephony *See* Voice over IP (VoIP).

iterative design A systematic process for system development that is used in MSS. Iterative design involves producing a first version of MSS, revising it, producing a second design version, and so on.

knowledge Understanding, awareness, or familiarity acquired through education or experience; anything that has been learned, perceived, discovered, inferred, or understood; the ability to use information. In a knowledge management system, knowledge is information in action.

knowledge acquisition The extraction and formulation of knowledge derived from various sources, especially from experts.

knowledge audit The process of identifying the knowledge an organization has, who has it, and how it flows (or does not) through the enterprise.

knowledge base A collection of facts, rules, and procedures organized into schemas. A knowledge base is the assembly of all the information and knowledge about a specific field of interest.

knowledge discovery in databases (KDD) A machine-learning process that performs rule induction or a related procedure to establish knowledge from large databases.

knowledge engineer An AI specialist responsible for the technical side of developing an expert system. The knowledge engineer works closely with the domain expert to capture the expert's knowledge in a knowledge base.

knowledge engineering The engineering discipline in which knowledge is integrated into computer systems to solve complex problems that normally require a high level of human expertise.

knowledge management The active management of the expertise in an organization. It involves collecting, categorizing, and disseminating knowledge.

knowledge management system (KMS) A system that facilitates knowledge management by ensuring knowledge flow from the person(s) who knows to the person(s) who needs to know throughout the organization; knowledge evolves and grows during the process.

knowledge repository The actual storage location of knowledge in a knowledge management system. A knowledge repository is similar in nature to a database but is generally text oriented.

knowledge-based economy The modern, global economy, which is driven by what people and organizations know rather than only by capital and labor.

knowledge-based system (KBS) A typically rule-based system for providing expertise. A KBS is identical to an ES, except that the source of expertise may include documented knowledge.

knowledge-refining system A system that is capable of analyzing its own performance, learning, and improving itself for future consultations.

knowware Technology tools that support knowledge management.

Kohonen self-organizing feature map A type of neural network model for machine learning.

leaky knowledge *See* explicit knowledge.

learning algorithm The training procedure used by an artificial neural network.

learning organization An organization that is capable of learning from its past experience, implying the existence of an organizational memory and a means to save, represent, and share it through its personnel.

learning rate A parameter for learning in neural networks. It determines the portion of the existing discrepancy that must be offset.

linear programming (LP) A mathematical model for the optimal solution of resource allocation problems. All the relationships among the variables in this type of model are linear.

machine learning The process by which a computer learns from experience (e.g., using programs that can learn from historical cases).

management science (MS) The application of a scientific approach and mathematical models to the analysis and solution of managerial decision situations (e.g., problems, opportunities). Also known as operations research (OR).

management support system (MSS) A system that applies any type of decision support tool or technique to managerial decision-making.

mathematical (quantitative) model A system of symbols and expressions that represent a real situation.

mathematical programming An optimization technique for the allocation of resources, subject to constraints.

mental model The mechanisms or images through which a human mind performs sense-making in decision making.

metadata Data about data. In a data warehouse, metadata describe the contents of a data warehouse and the manner of its use.

metasearch engine A search engine that combines results from several different search engines.

middleware Software that links application modules from different computer languages and platforms.

mobile agent An intelligent software agent that moves across different system architectures and platforms or from one Internet site to another, retrieving and sending information.

mobility The degree to which agents travel through a computer network.

model base A collection of preprogrammed quantitative models (e.g., statistical, financial, optimization) organized as a single unit.

model base management system (MBMS) Software for establishing, updating, combining, and so on (e.g., managing) a DSS model base.

model building blocks Preprogrammed software elements that can be used to build computerized models. For example, a random-number generator can be employed in the construction of a simulation model.

model mart A small, generally departmental repository of knowledge created by using knowledge-discovery techniques on past decision instances. Model marts are similar to data marts. *See* model warehouse.

model warehouse A large, generally enterprisewide repository of knowledge created by using knowledge-discovery techniques on past decision instances. Model warehouses are similar to data warehouses. *See* model mart.

momentum A learning parameter in backpropagation neural networks.

MSS architecture A plan for organizing the underlying infrastructure and applications of an MSS project.

MSS suite An integrated collection of a large number of MSS tools that work together for applications development.

MSS tool A software element (e.g., a language) that facilitates the development of an MSS or an MSS generator.

multiagent system A system with multiple cooperating software agents.

multidimensional analysis (modeling) A modeling method that involves data analysis in several dimensions.

multidimensional database A database in which the data are organized specifically to support easy and quick multidimensional analysis.

multidimensional OLAP (MOLAP) OLAP implemented via a specialized multidimensional database (or data store) that summarizes transactions into multidimensional views ahead of time.

multidimensionality The ability to organize, present, and analyze data by several dimensions, such as sales by region, by product, by salesperson, and by time (four dimensions).

multiple goals Refers to a decision situation in which alternatives are evaluated with several, sometimes conflicting, goals.

mutation A genetic operator that causes a random change in a potential solution.

natural language processing (NLP) Using a natural language processor to interface with a computer-based system.

neural computing An experimental computer design aimed at building intelligent computers that operate in a manner modeled on the functioning of the human brain. *See* artificial neural networks (ANN).

neural (computing) networks An experimental computer design aimed at building intelligent computers that operate in a manner modeled on the functioning of the human brain.

neural network *See* artificial neural networks (ANN).

neuron A cell (i.e., processing element) of a biological or artificial neural network.

nominal group technique (NGT) A simple brainstorming process for nonelectronic meetings.

normative model A model that prescribes how a system should operate.

nucleus The central processing portion of a neuron.

object A person, place, or thing about which information is collected, processed, or stored.

object-oriented model base management system (OOMBMS) An MBMS constructed in an object-oriented environment.

online analytical processing (OLAP) An information system that enables the user, while at a PC, to query the system, conduct an analysis, and so on. The result is generated in seconds.

online (electronic) workspace Online screens that allow people to share documents, files, project plans, calendars, and so on in the same online place, though not necessarily at the same time.

oper mart An operational data mart. An oper mart is a small-scale data mart typically used by a single department or functional area in an organization.

operational data store (ODS) A type of database often used as an interim area for a data warehouse, especially for customer information files.

operational models Models that represent problems for the operational level of management.

operational plan A plan that translates an organization's strategic objectives and goals into a set of well-defined tactics and initiatives, resource requirements, and expected results.

optimal solution A best possible solution to a modeled problem.

optimization The process of identifying the best possible solution to a problem.

organizational agent An agent that executes tasks on behalf of a business process or computer application.

organizational culture The aggregate attitudes in an organization concerning a certain issue (e.g., technology, computers, DSS).

organizational knowledge base An organization's knowledge repository.

organizational learning The process of capturing knowledge and making it available enterprise-wide.

organizational memory That which an organization knows.

ossified case A case that has been analyzed and has no further value.

paradigmatic case A case that is unique that can be maintained to derive new knowledge for the future.

parallel processing An advanced computer processing technique that allows a computer to perform multiple processes at once, in parallel.

parallelism In a group support system, a process gain in which everyone in a group can work simultaneously (e.g., in brainstorming, voting, ranking).

parameter *See* uncontrollable variable.

pattern recognition A technique of matching an external pattern to a pattern stored in a computer's memory (i.e., the process of classifying data into predetermined categories). Pattern recognition is used in inference engines, image processing, neural computing, and speech recognition.

perceptron An early neural network structure that uses no hidden layer.

performance dashboard A visual display used to monitor operational performance.

performance measurement system A system that assists managers in tracking the implementations of business strategy by comparing actual results against strategic goals and objectives.

performance scorecard A visual display that is used to chart progress against strategic and tactical goals and targets.

personal agent An agent that performs tasks on behalf of individual users..

physical integration The seamless integration of several systems into one functioning system.

portal A gateway to Web sites. Portals can be public (e.g., Yahoo!), or private (e.g., corporate portals).

practice approach An approach toward knowledge management that focuses on building the social environments or communities of practice necessary to facilitate the sharing of tacit understanding.

predictive analysis Use of tools that help determine the probable future outcome for an event or the likelihood of a situation occurring. These tools also identify relationships and patterns.

predictive analytics A business analytical approach toward forecasting (e.g., demand, problems, opportunities) that is used instead of simply reporting data as they occur.

principle of choice The criterion for making a choice among alternatives.

privacy In general, the right to be left alone and the right to be free of unreasonable personal intrusions. Information privacy is the right to determine when, and to what extent, information about oneself can be communicated to others.

private agent An agent that works for only one person.

problem ownership The jurisdiction (authority) to solve a problem.

problem solving A process in which one starts from an initial state and proceeds to search through a problem space to identify a desired goal.

process approach An approach to knowledge management that attempts to codify organizational knowledge through formalized controls, processes, and technologies.

process gain In a group support system, improvements in the effectiveness of the activities of a meeting.

process loss In a group support system, degradation in the effectiveness of the activities of a meeting.

processing element (PE) A neuron in a neural network.

prototyping In system development, a strategy in which a scaled-down system or portion of a system is constructed in a short time, tested, and improved in several iterations.

public agent An agent that serves any user.

quantitative software package A preprogrammed (sometimes called ready-made) model or optimization system. These packages sometimes serve as building blocks for other quantitative models.

query facility The (database) mechanism that accepts requests for data, accesses them, manipulates them, and queries them.

rapid application development (RAD) A development methodology that adjusts a system development lifecycle so that parts of the system can be developed quickly, thereby enabling users to obtain some functionality as soon as possible. RAD includes methods of phased development, prototyping, and throwaway prototyping.

real-time data warehousing The process of loading and providing data via a data warehouse as they become available.

real-time expert system An expert system designed for online dynamic decision support. It has a strict limit on response time; in other words, the system always produces a response by the time it is needed.

recommendation system (agent) A computer system that can suggest new items to a user based on his or her revealed preference. It may be content based or use collaborative filtering to suggest items that match the preference of the user. An example is Amazon.com's "Other people bought this book also bought . . . " function.

relational model base management system (RMBMS) A relational approach (as in relational databases) to the design and development of a model base management system.

relational OLAP (ROLAP) The implementation of an OLAP database on top of an existing relational database.

reproduction The creation of new generations of improved solutions with the use of a genetic algorithm.

result (outcome) variable A variable that expresses the result of a decision (e.g., one concerning profit), usually one of the goals of a decision-making problem.

risk A probabilistic or stochastic decision situation.

risk analysis A decision-making method that analyzes the risk (based on assumed known probabilities) associated with different alternatives. Also known as calculated risk.

robot A machine that has the capability of performing manual functions without human intervention.

rule-based system A system in which knowledge is represented completely in terms of rules (e.g., a system based on production rules).

satisficing A process by which one seeks a solution that will satisfy a set of constraints. In contrast to optimization, which seeks the best possible solution, satisficing simply seeks a solution that will work well enough.

scenario A statement of assumptions and configurations concerning the operating environment of a particular system at a particular time.

screen sharing Software that enables group members, even in different locations, to work on the same document, which is shown on the PC screen of each participant.

search engine A program that finds and lists Web sites or pages (designated by URLs) that match some user-selected criteria.

self-organizing A neural network architecture that uses unsupervised learning.

semantic Web An extension of the current Web, in which information is given well-defined meanings, better enabling computers and people to work in cooperation.

semantic Web services An XML-based technology that allows semantic information to be represented in Web services.

sensitivity analysis A study of the effect of a change in one or more input variables on a proposed solution.

sequence discovery The identification of associations over time.

sigmoid (logical activation) function An S-shaped transfer function in the range of 0 to 1.

simulation An imitation of reality.

Six Sigma A performance management methodology aimed at reducing the number of defects in a business process to as close to zero defects per million opportunities (DPMO) as possible.

software-as-a-service (SaaS) Software that is rented instead of sold.

speech (voice) understanding Translation of the human voice into individual words and sentences that are understandable by a computer.

speech understanding An area of artificial intelligence research that attempts to allow computers to recognize words or phrases of human speech.

staff assistant An individual who acts as an assistant to a manager.

static models Models that describe a single interval of a situation.

status report A report that provides the most current information on the status of an item (e.g., orders, expenses, production quantity).

story A case with rich information and episodes. Lessons may be derived from this kind of case in a case base.

strategic goal A quantified objective that has a designated time period.

strategic models Models that represent problems for the strategic level (i.e., executive level) of management.

strategic objective A broad statement or general course of action that prescribes targeted directions for an organization.

strategic vision A picture or mental image of what the organization should look like in the future.

strategy map A visual display that delineates the relationships among the key organizational objectives for all four BSC perspectives.

Structured Query Language (SQL) A data definition and management language for relational databases. SQL front ends most relational DBMS.

suboptimization An optimization-based procedure that does not consider all the alternatives for or impacts on an organization.

summation function A mechanism to add all the inputs coming into a particular neuron.

supervised learning A method of training artificial neural networks in which sample cases are shown to the network as input, and the weights are adjusted to minimize the error in the outputs.

synapse The connection (where the weights are) between processing elements in a neural network.

synchronous (real-time) Occurring at the same time.

system architecture The logical and physical design of a system.

system development lifecycle (SDLC) A systematic process for the effective construction of large information systems.

tacit knowledge Knowledge that is usually in the domain of subjective, cognitive, and experiential learning. It is highly personal and difficult to formalize.

tactical models Models that represent problems for the tactical level (i.e., midlevel) of management.

teleconferencing The use of electronic communication that allows two or more people at different locations to have a simultaneous conference.

text mining The application of data mining to nonstructured or less structured text files. It entails the generation of meaningful numeric indices from the unstructured text and then processing those indices using various data mining algorithms.

threshold value A hurdle value for the output of a neuron to trigger the next level of neurons. If an output value is smaller than the threshold value, it will not be passed to the next level of neurons.

topology The way in which neurons are organized in a neural network.

transformation (transfer) function In a neural network, the function that sums and transforms inputs before a neuron fires. It shows the relationship between the internal activation level and the output of a neuron.

Turing test A test designed to measure the "intelligence" of a computer.

uncertainty In expert systems, a value that cannot be determined during a consultation. Many expert systems can accommodate uncertainty; that is, they allow the user to indicate whether he or she does not know the answer.

uncontrollable variable (parameter) A factor that affects the result of a decision but is not under the control of the decision maker. These variables can be internal (e.g., related to technology or to policies) or external (e.g., related to legal issues or to climate).

unsupervised learning A method of training artificial neural networks in which only input stimuli are shown to the network, which is self-organizing.

user interface The component of a computer system that allows bidirectional communication between the system and its user.

user interface management system (UIMS) The DSS component that handles all interaction between users and the system.

user-developed MSS An MSS developed by one user or by a few users in one department, including decision makers and professionals (i.e., knowledge workers, e.g., financial analysts, tax analysts, engineers) who build or use computers to solve problems or enhance their productivity.

utility (on-demand) computing Unlimited computing power and storage capacity that, like electricity, water, and telephone services, can be obtained on demand, used, and reallocated for any application and is billed on a pay-per-use basis.

vendor-managed inventory (VMI) The practice of retailers making suppliers responsible for determining when to order and how much to order.

video teleconferencing (videoconferencing) Virtual meeting in which participants in one location can see participants at other locations on a large screen or a desktop computer.

virtual meeting An online meeting whose members are in different locations, possibly even in different countries.

virtual team A team whose members are in different places while in a meeting together.

visual interactive modeling (VIM) *See* visual interactive simulation (VIS).

visual interactive simulation (VIS) A simulation approach used in the decision-making process that shows graphical animation in which systems and processes are presented dynamically to the decision maker. It enables visualization of the results of different potential actions.

visual recognition The addition of some form of computer intelligence and decision-making to digitized visual information, received from a machine sensor such as a camera.

voice (speech) recognition Translation of human voice into individual words and sentences that are understandable by a computer.

Voice over IP (VoIP) Communication systems that transmit voice calls over Internet Protocol (IP)–based networks. Also known as Internet telephony.

voice portal A Web site, usually a portal, that has an audio interface.

voice synthesis The technology by which computers convert text to voice (i.e., speak).

Web analytics The application of business analytics activities to Web-based processes, including e-commerce.

Web content mining The extraction of useful information from Web pages.

Web mining The discovery and analysis of interesting and useful information from the Web, about the Web, and usually through Web-based tools.

Web services An architecture that enables assembly of distributed applications from software services and ties them together.

Web structure mining The development of useful information from the links included in Web documents.

Web usage mining The extraction of useful information from the data being generated through Web page visits, transactions, and so on.

what-if analysis A process that involves asking a computer what the effect of changing some of the input data or parameters would be.

wiki A piece of server software available in a Web site that allows users to freely create and edit Web page content, using any Web browser.

wikilog A Web log (blog) that allows people to participate as peers; anyone can add, delete, or change content.

work system A system in which humans and/or machines perform a business process, using resources to produce products or services for internal or external customers.

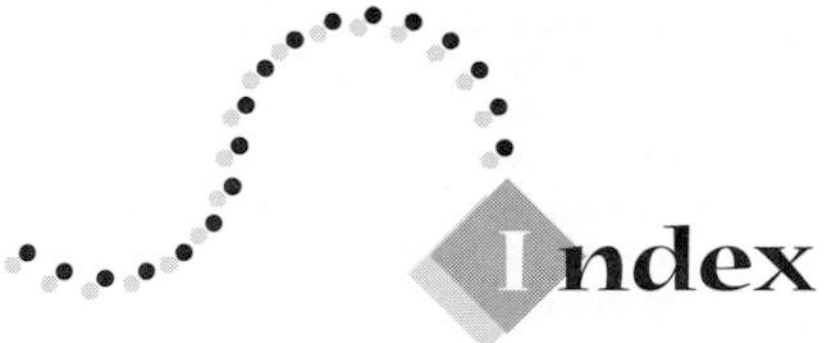

Index

Note: Page numbers followed by t or f refer to tables or figures. Those followed by A or F refer to Application Cases or Technology Insights in Focus boxes respectively.